W9-CLX-228

WAYNE PUBLIC LIBRARY   APR 1 6 2012

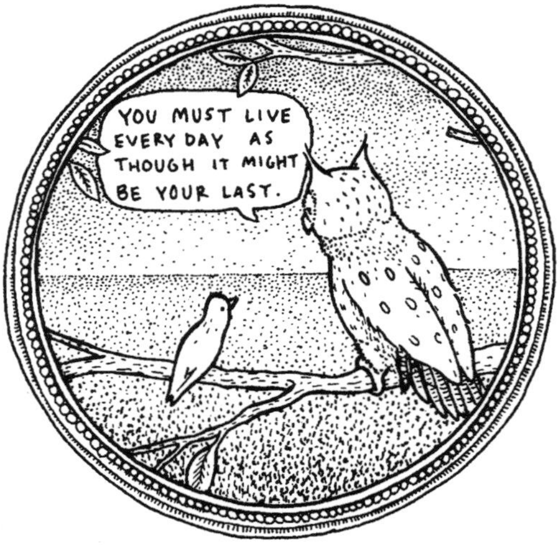
YOU MUST LIVE EVERY DAY AS THOUGH IT MIGHT BE YOUR LAST.

or Asomatognosia:
whose hand is
it anyway?

anders brekhus nilsen

Entire contents © 2011 Anders Nilsen
All rights reserved. No part of this book (except small portions for review purposes) may be reproduced
in any form without written permission from Anders Nilsen or Drawn & Quarterly.

Drawn & Quarterly
Post Office Box 48056
Montréal, Quebec
Canada H2V 4S8
www.drawnandquarterly.com

First Hardcover & Paperback Printing: August 2011
10 9 8 7 6 5 4 3 2 1
Printed in China.

Library and Archives Canada Cataloguing in Publication
Nilsen, Anders, 1973–
Big Questions / Anders Nilsen.
ISBN 978-1-77046-047-8 (paperback).—ISBN 978-1-77046-044-7 (hardcover)
1. Title.   PN6727.N56B53 2011   741.5'973   C2010-907551-X

Distributed in the USA:
Farrar, Straus and Giroux
18 West 18th ST
New York, NY 10011
Orders: 888.330.8477

Distributed in Canada by:
Raincoast Books
2440 Viking Way
Vancouver, BC V6V 1N2
Orders: 800.663.5714

Distributed in the United Kingdom by:
Publishers Group UK
8 The Arena
Mollison Avenue
Enfield, Middlesex EN3 7NL
Orders: 020.8804.0400

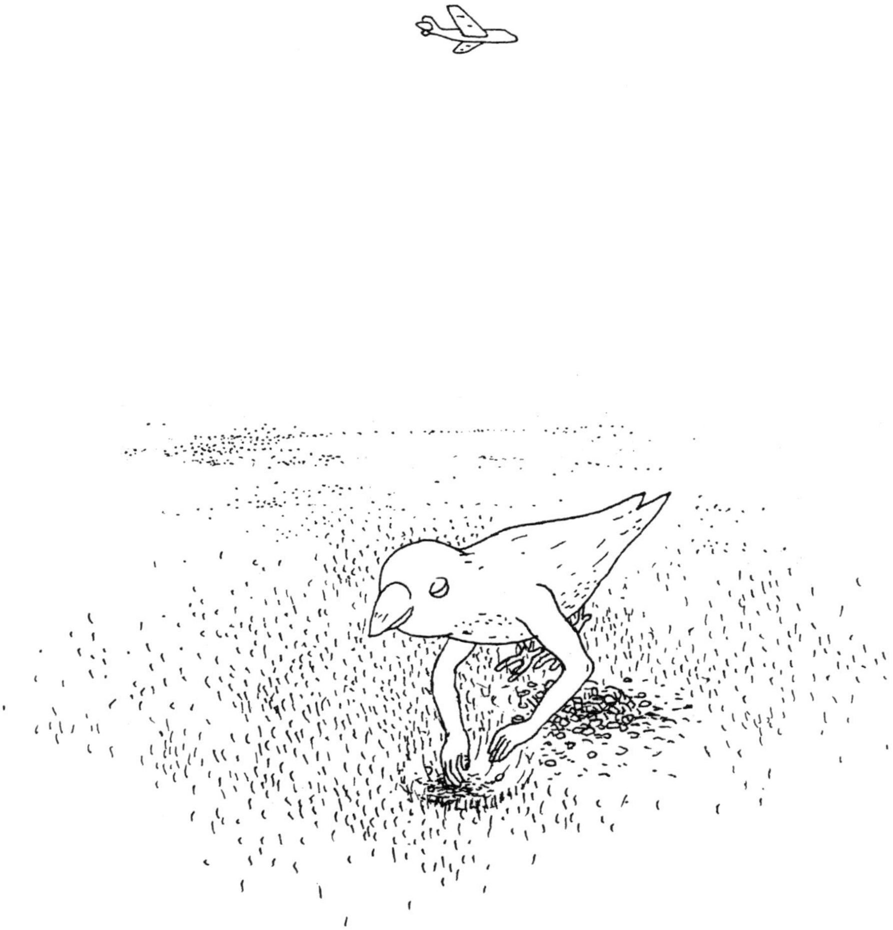

contents

seeds

SURE AM GETTING SICK OF THESE SEEDS.
I KNOW WHAT YOU MEAN.
HEY.
HI.
HEY, GUYS.
ANYTHING GOOD TODAY?
SAME OLD THING, I GUESS.
MUNCH

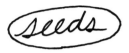

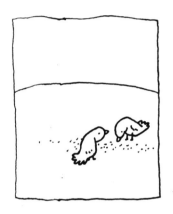

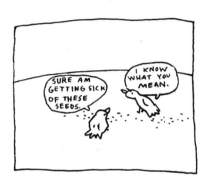

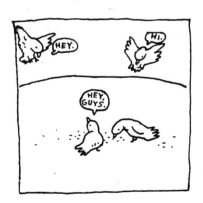

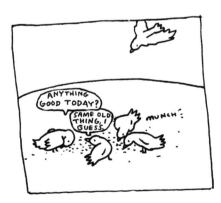

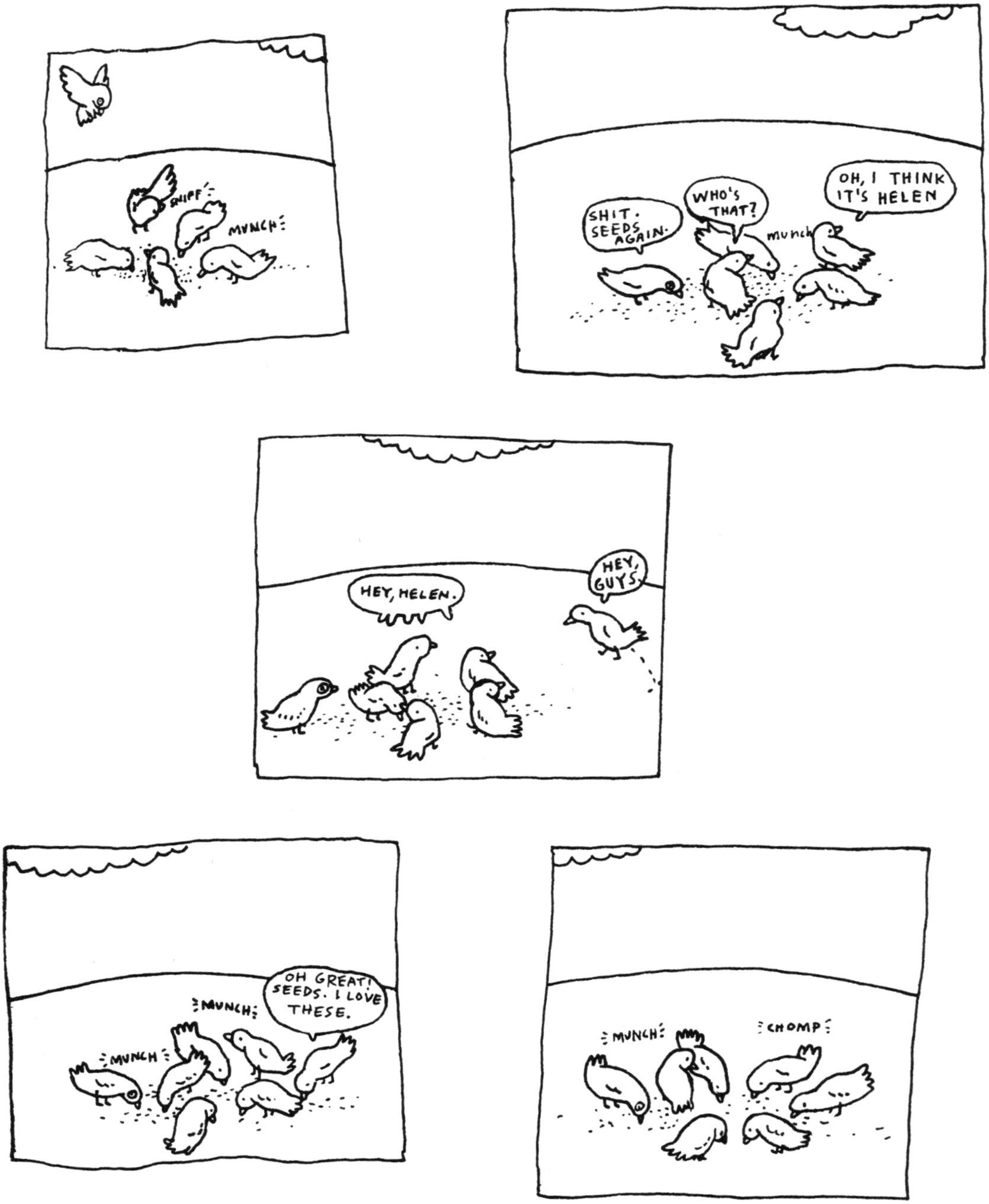
SNIFF
MUNCH
SHIT. SEEDS AGAIN.
WHO'S THAT?
munch
OH, I THINK IT'S HELEN
HEY, HELEN.
HEY, GUYS.
MUNCH
MUNCH
OH GREAT! SEEDS. I LOVE THESE.
MUNCH
CHOMP

BIG QUESTIONS

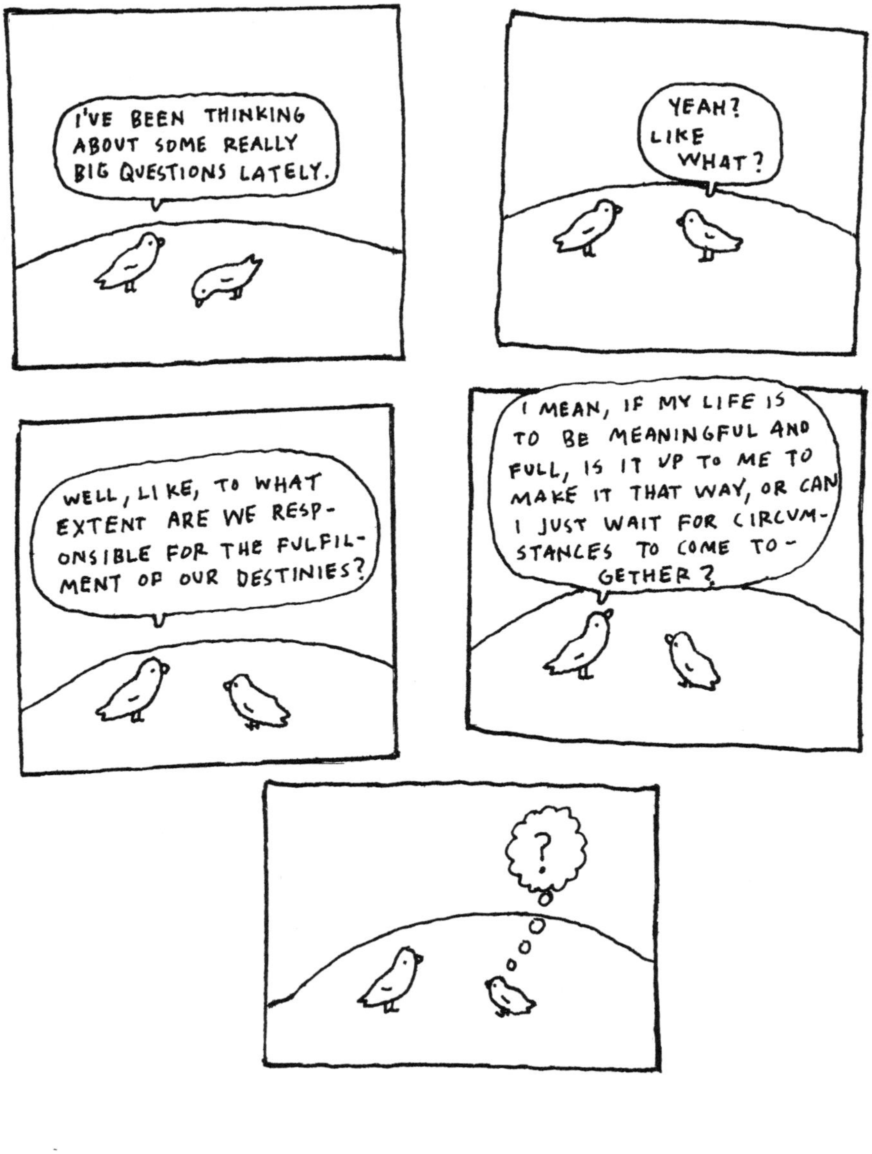
I'VE BEEN THINKING ABOUT SOME REALLY BIG QUESTIONS LATELY.
YEAH? LIKE WHAT?
WELL, LIKE, TO WHAT EXTENT ARE WE RESP-ONSIBLE FOR THE FULFIL-MENT OF OUR DESTINIES?
I MEAN, IF MY LIFE IS TO BE MEANINGFUL AND FULL, IS IT UP TO ME TO MAKE IT THAT WAY, OR CAN I JUST WAIT FOR CIRCUM-STANCES TO COME TO-GETHER?
?

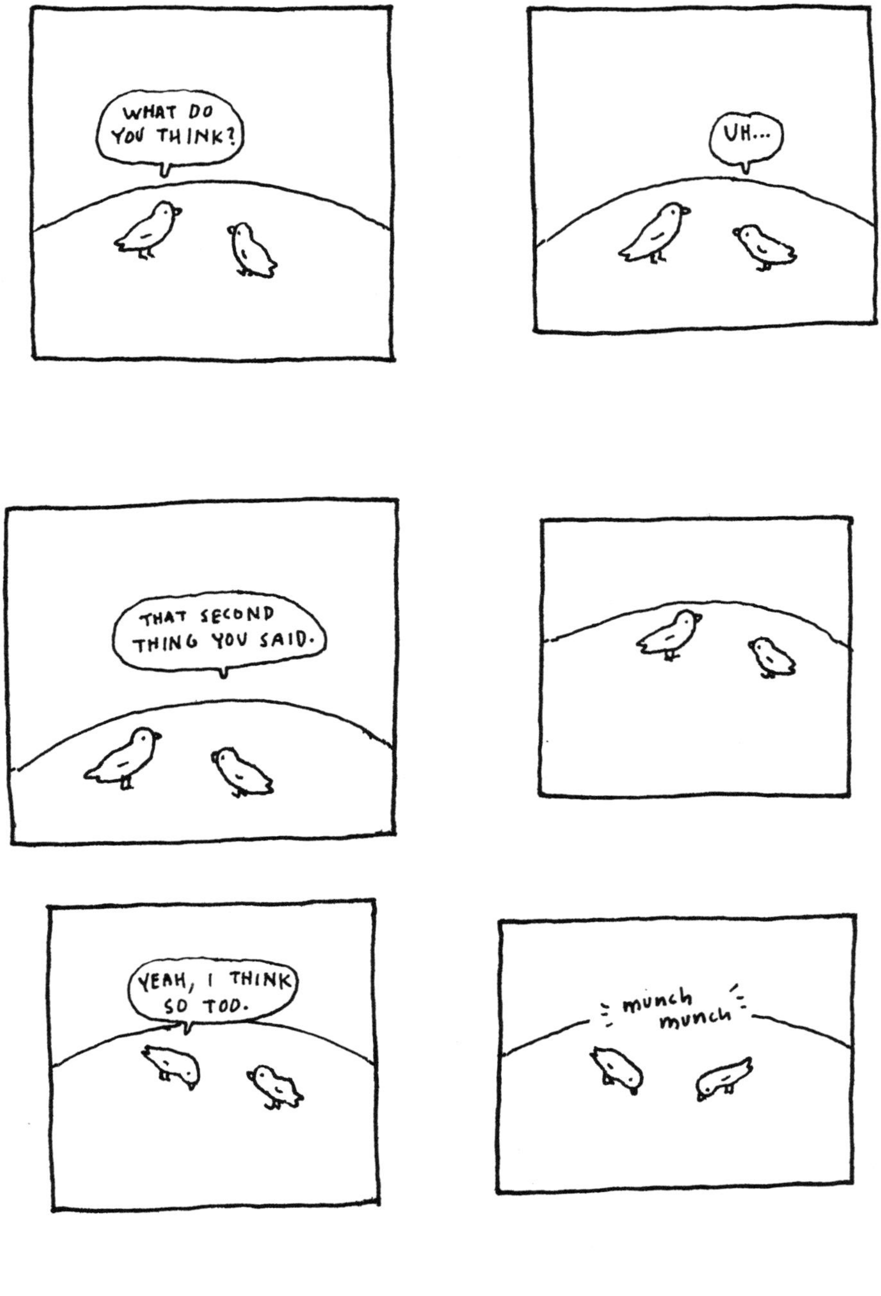
WHAT DO YOU THINK?
UH...
THAT SECOND THING YOU SAID.
YEAH, I THINK SO TOO.
munch munch

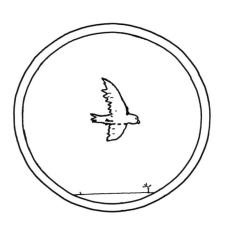

funny

TELL ME A FUNNY STORY.
I DON'T KNOW ANY FUNNY STORIES.
SURE YOU DO. YOU HAD EVERYONE IN STITCHES THE OTHER DAY AT THE PINE TREE BY THE RIVER.
YOU MEAN THAT THING ABOUT THE RED BOBCAT? THAT WASN'T A STORY. THAT REALLY HAPPENED TO ME.
IT DID?
UH-HUH.
THAT'S NOT FUNNY THEN.
YEAH, I DIDN'T THINK SO EITHER.

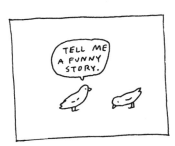

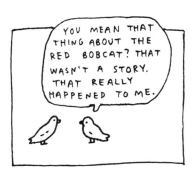

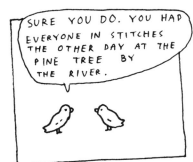

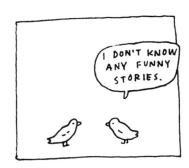

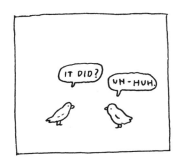

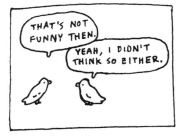

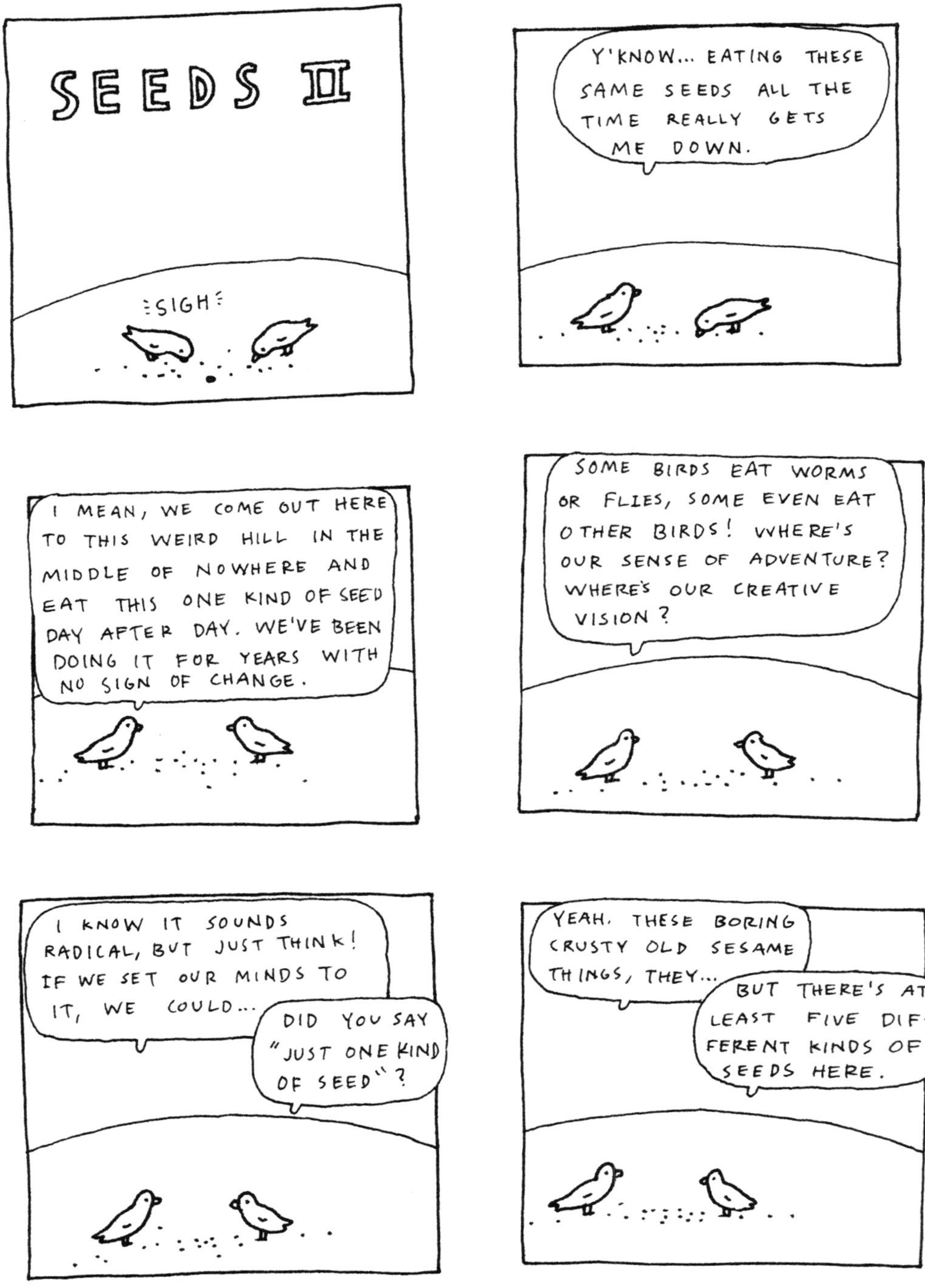
SEEDS II
SIGH
Y'KNOW... EATING THESE SAME SEEDS ALL THE TIME REALLY GETS ME DOWN.
I MEAN, WE COME OUT HERE TO THIS WEIRD HILL IN THE MIDDLE OF NOWHERE AND EAT THIS ONE KIND OF SEED DAY AFTER DAY. WE'VE BEEN DOING IT FOR YEARS WITH NO SIGN OF CHANGE.
SOME BIRDS EAT WORMS OR FLIES, SOME EVEN EAT OTHER BIRDS! WHERE'S OUR SENSE OF ADVENTURE? WHERE'S OUR CREATIVE VISION?
I KNOW IT SOUNDS RADICAL, BUT JUST THINK! IF WE SET OUR MINDS TO IT, WE COULD...
DID YOU SAY "JUST ONE KIND OF SEED"?
YEAH. THESE BORING CRUSTY OLD SESAME THINGS, THEY...
BUT THERE'S AT LEAST FIVE DIF-FERENT KINDS OF SEEDS HERE.

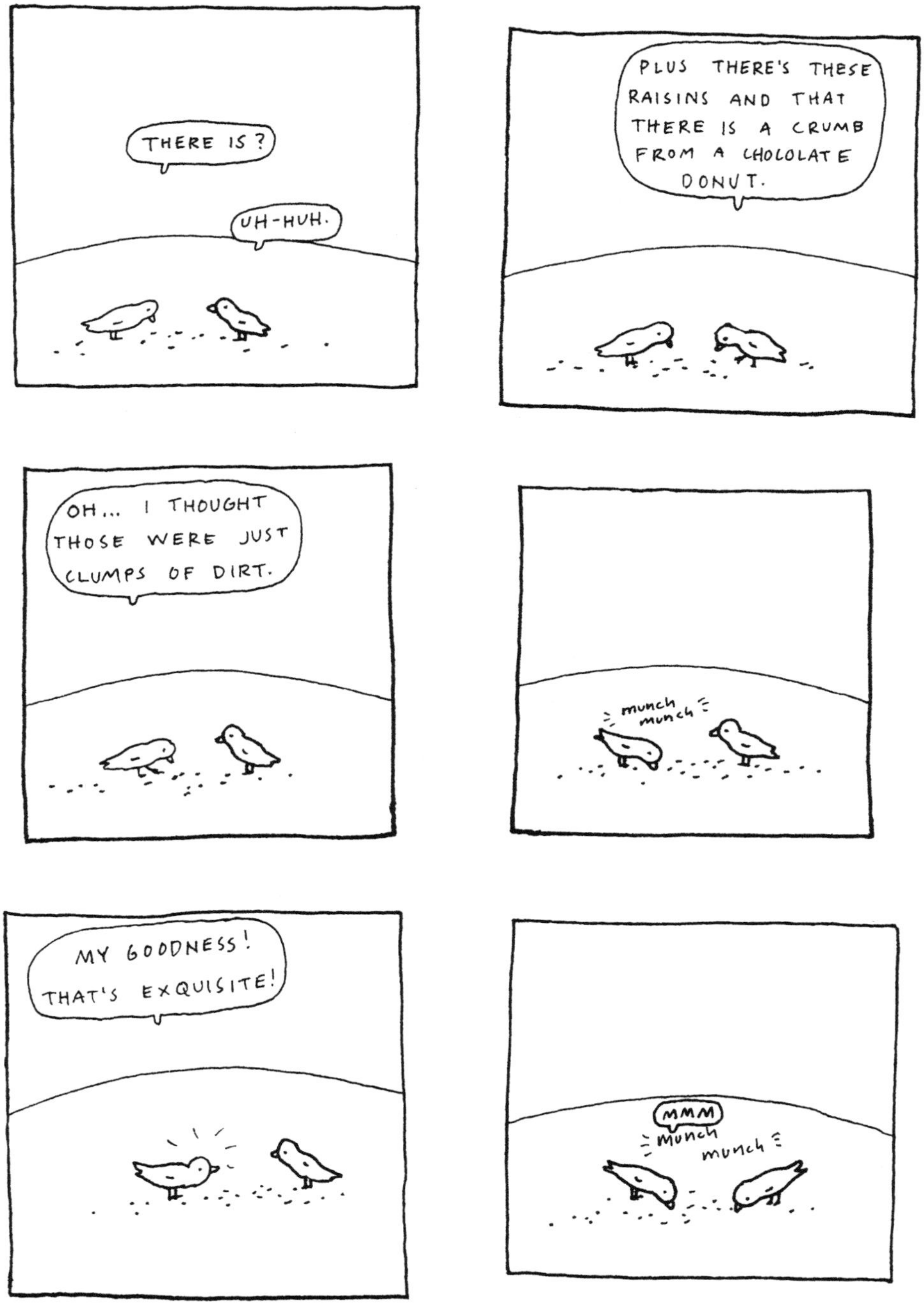
THERE IS?
UH-HUH.
PLUS THERE'S THESE RAISINS AND THAT THERE IS A CRUMB FROM A CHOCOLATE DONUT.
OH... I THOUGHT THOSE WERE JUST CLUMPS OF DIRT.
munch munch
MY GOODNESS! THAT'S EXQUISITE!
MMM
munch munch

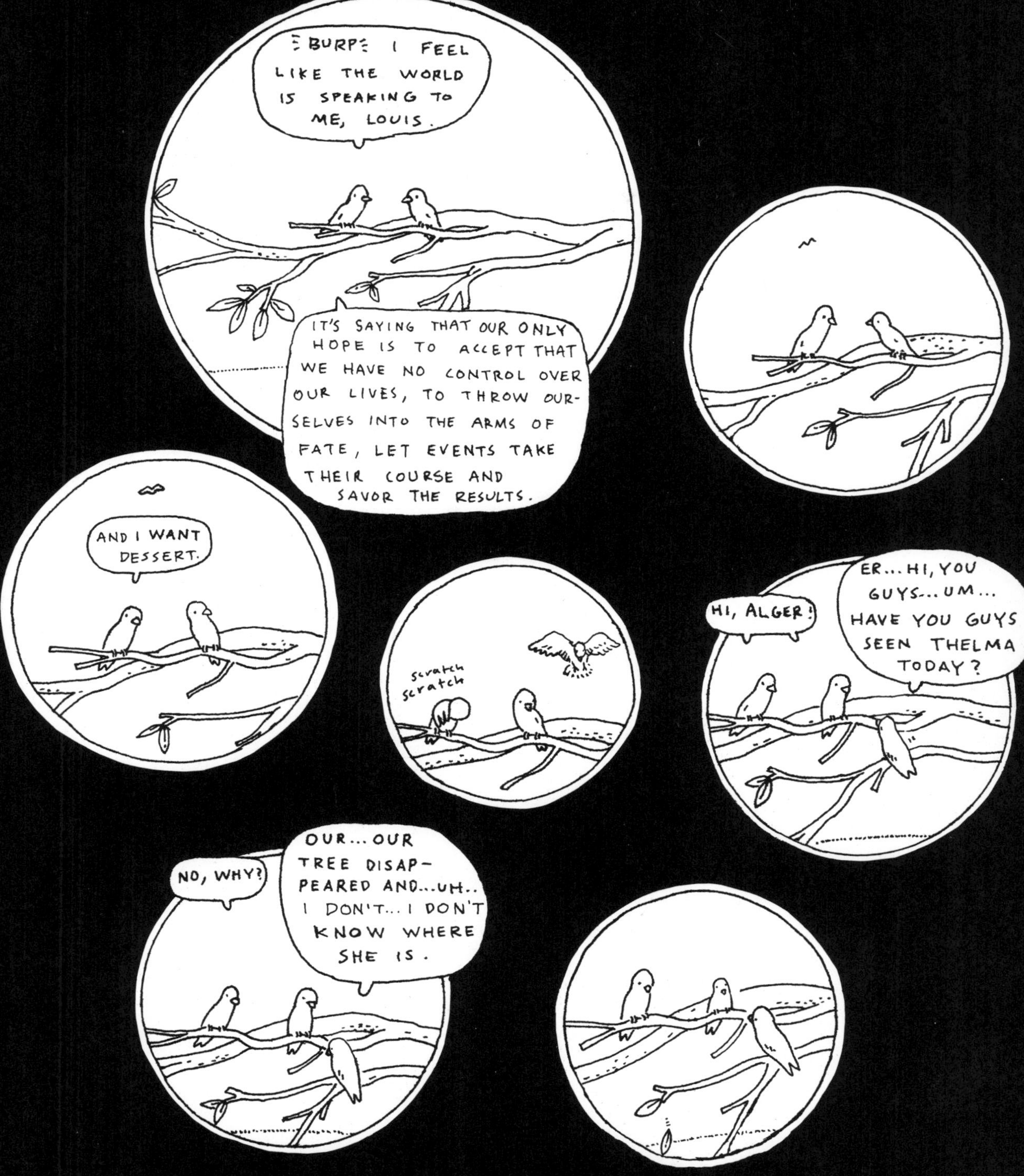

BURP I FEEL LIKE THE WORLD IS SPEAKING TO ME, LOUIS.
IT'S SAYING THAT OUR ONLY HOPE IS TO ACCEPT THAT WE HAVE NO CONTROL OVER OUR LIVES, TO THROW OURSELVES INTO THE ARMS OF FATE, LET EVENTS TAKE THEIR COURSE AND SAVOR THE RESULTS.
AND I WANT DESSERT.
scratch scratch
HI, ALGER!
ER... HI, YOU GUYS... UM... HAVE YOU GUYS SEEN THELMA TODAY?
NO, WHY?
OUR... OUR TREE DISAPPEARED AND... UH.. I DON'T... I DON'T KNOW WHERE SHE IS.

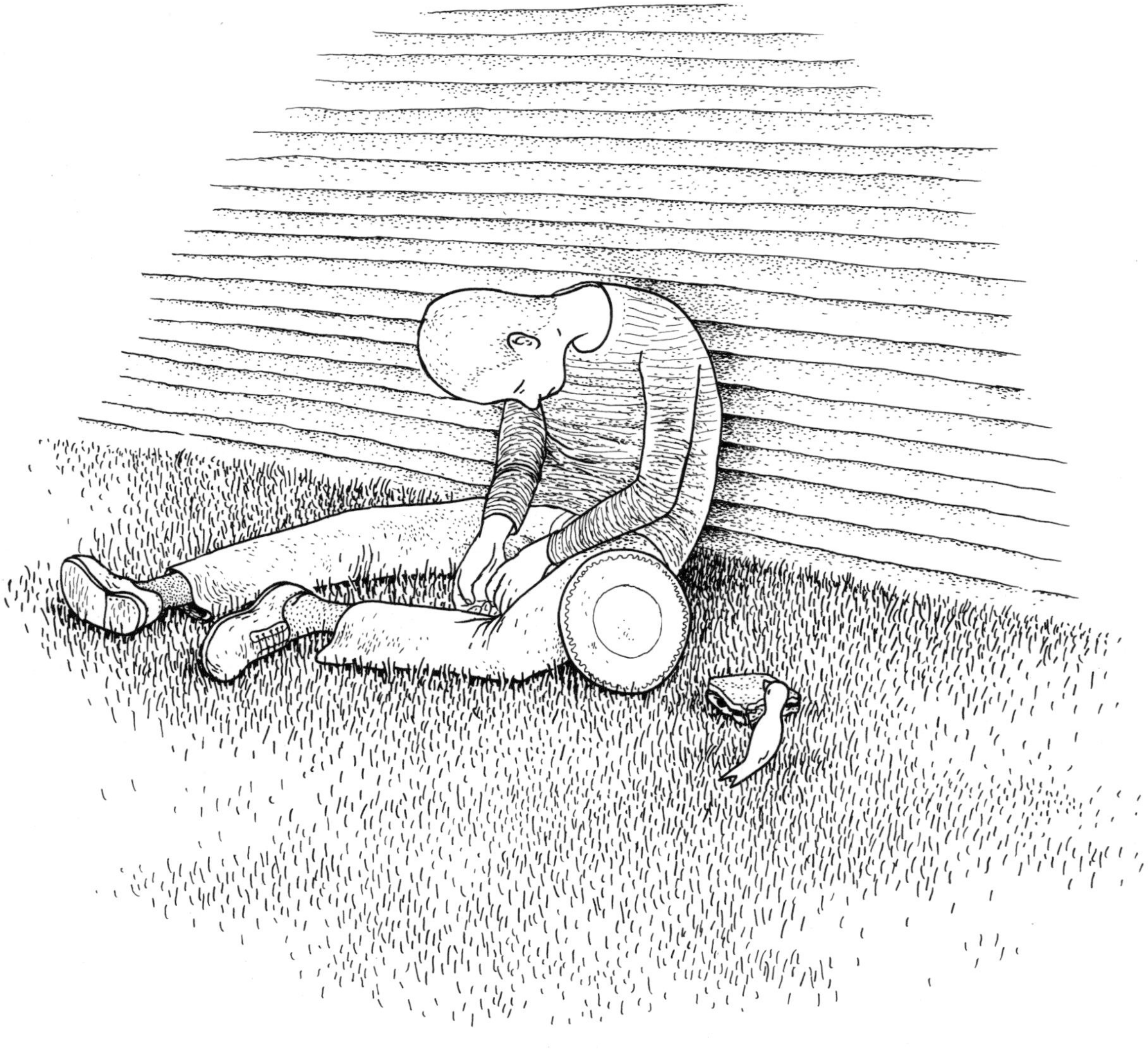

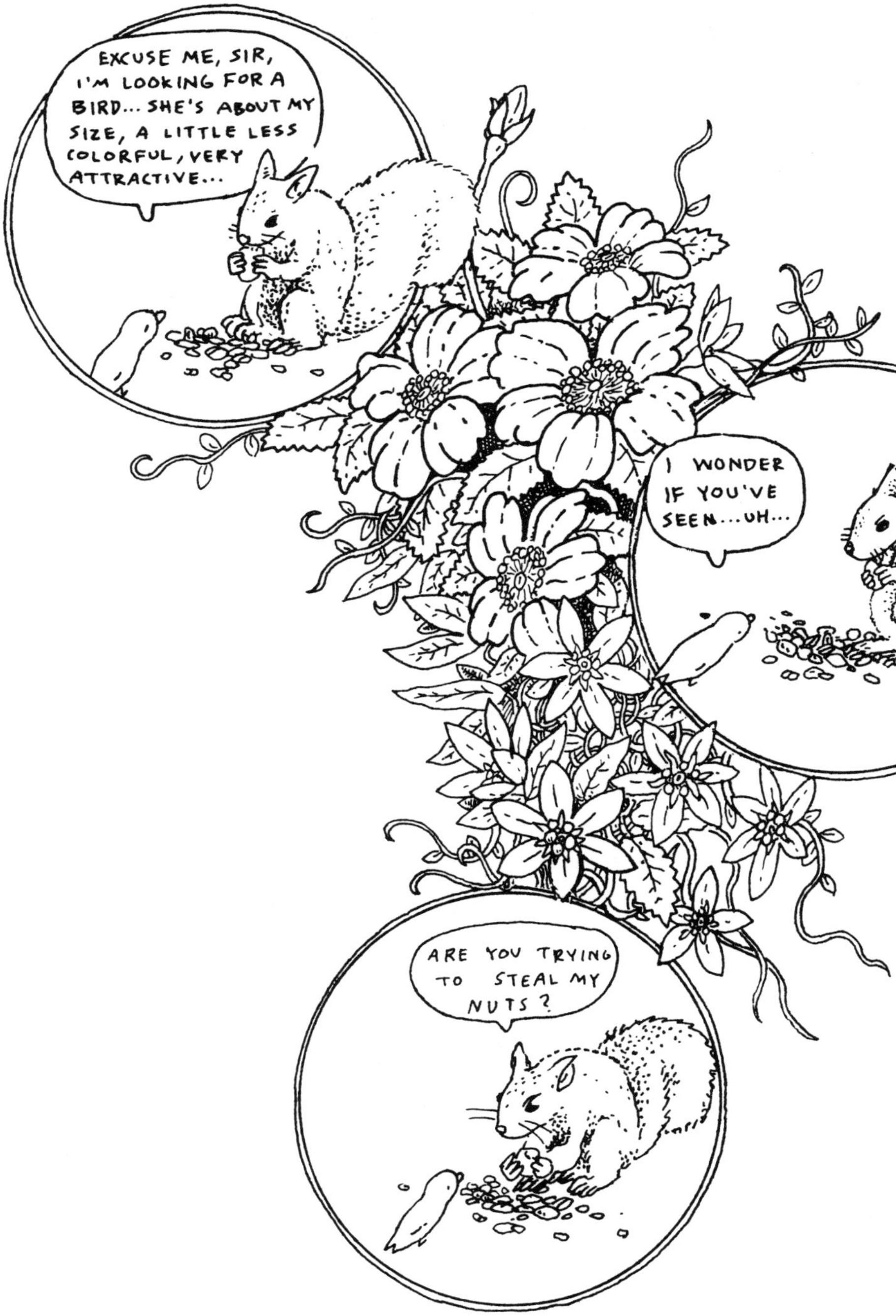
EXCUSE ME, SIR, I'M LOOKING FOR A BIRD... SHE'S ABOUT MY SIZE, A LITTLE LESS COLORFUL, VERY ATTRACTIVE...
I WONDER IF YOU'VE SEEN...UH...
ARE YOU TRYING TO STEAL MY NUTS?

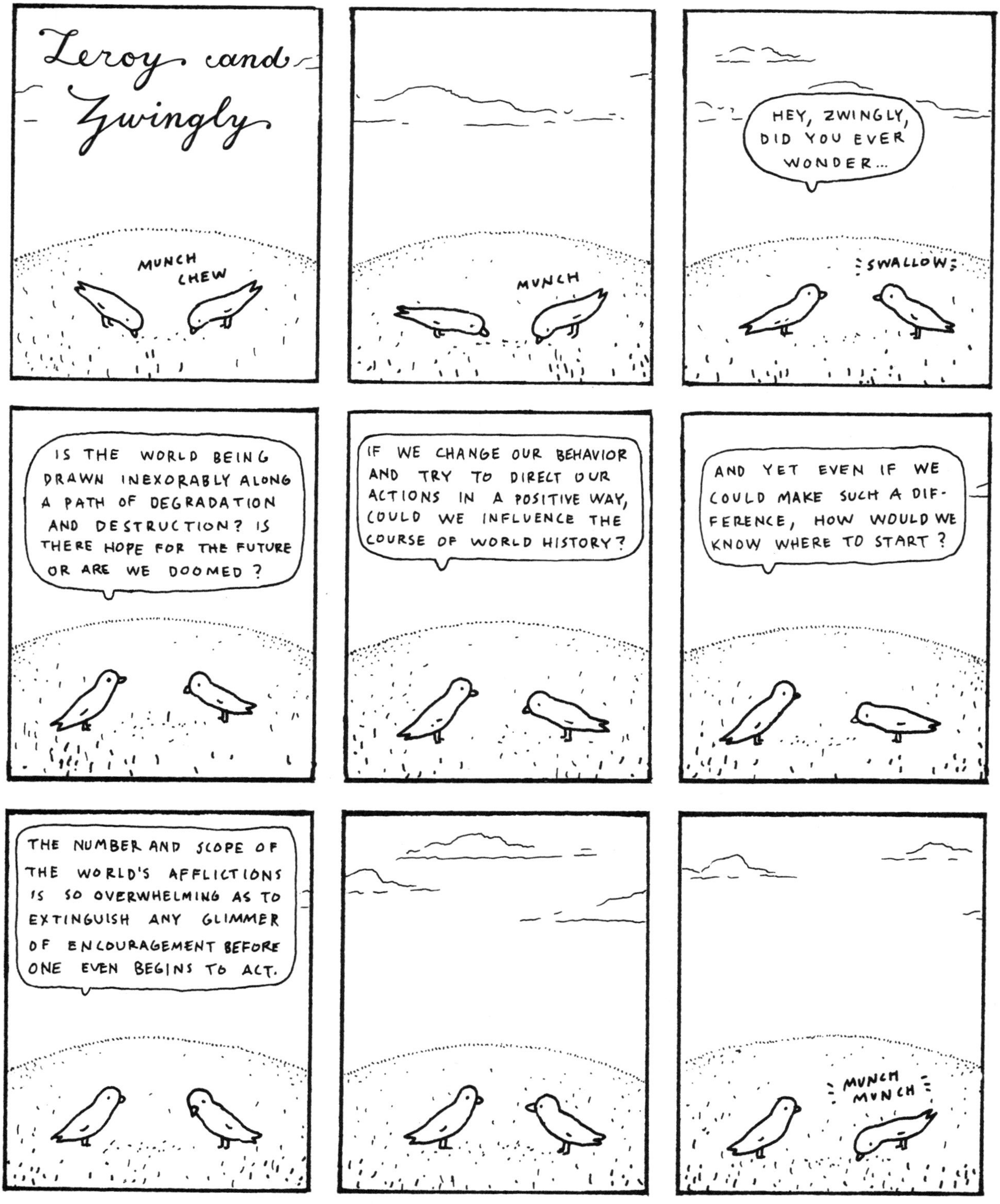
Leroy and Zwingly
MUNCH CHEW
MUNCH
HEY, ZWINGLY, DID YOU EVER WONDER...
SWALLOW
IS THE WORLD BEING DRAWN INEXORABLY ALONG A PATH OF DEGRADATION AND DESTRUCTION? IS THERE HOPE FOR THE FUTURE OR ARE WE DOOMED?
IF WE CHANGE OUR BEHAVIOR AND TRY TO DIRECT OUR ACTIONS IN A POSITIVE WAY, COULD WE INFLUENCE THE COURSE OF WORLD HISTORY?
AND YET EVEN IF WE COULD MAKE SUCH A DIF-FERENCE, HOW WOULD WE KNOW WHERE TO START?
THE NUMBER AND SCOPE OF THE WORLD'S AFFLICTIONS IS SO OVERWHELMING AS TO EXTINGUISH ANY GLIMMER OF ENCOURAGEMENT BEFORE ONE EVEN BEGINS TO ACT.
MUNCH MUNCH

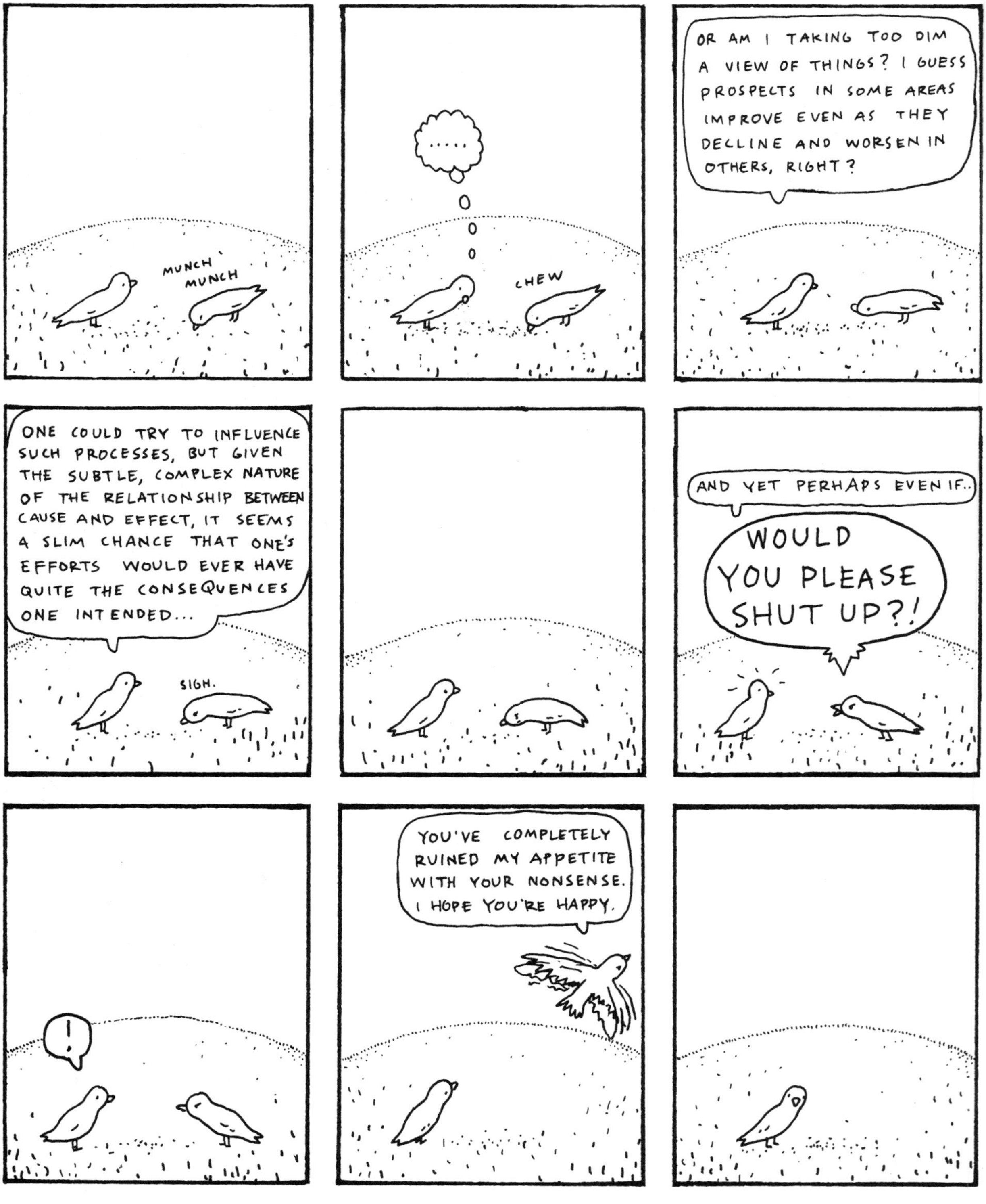
MUNCH
MUNCH
.....
CHEW
OR AM I TAKING TOO DIM A VIEW OF THINGS? I GUESS PROSPECTS IN SOME AREAS IMPROVE EVEN AS THEY DECLINE AND WORSEN IN OTHERS, RIGHT?
ONE COULD TRY TO INFLUENCE SUCH PROCESSES, BUT GIVEN THE SUBTLE, COMPLEX NATURE OF THE RELATIONSHIP BETWEEN CAUSE AND EFFECT, IT SEEMS A SLIM CHANCE THAT ONE'S EFFORTS WOULD EVER HAVE QUITE THE CONSEQUENCES ONE INTENDED...
SIGH.
AND YET PERHAPS EVEN IF..
WOULD YOU PLEASE SHUT UP?!
!
YOU'VE COMPLETELY RUINED MY APPETITE WITH YOUR NONSENSE. I HOPE YOU'RE HAPPY.

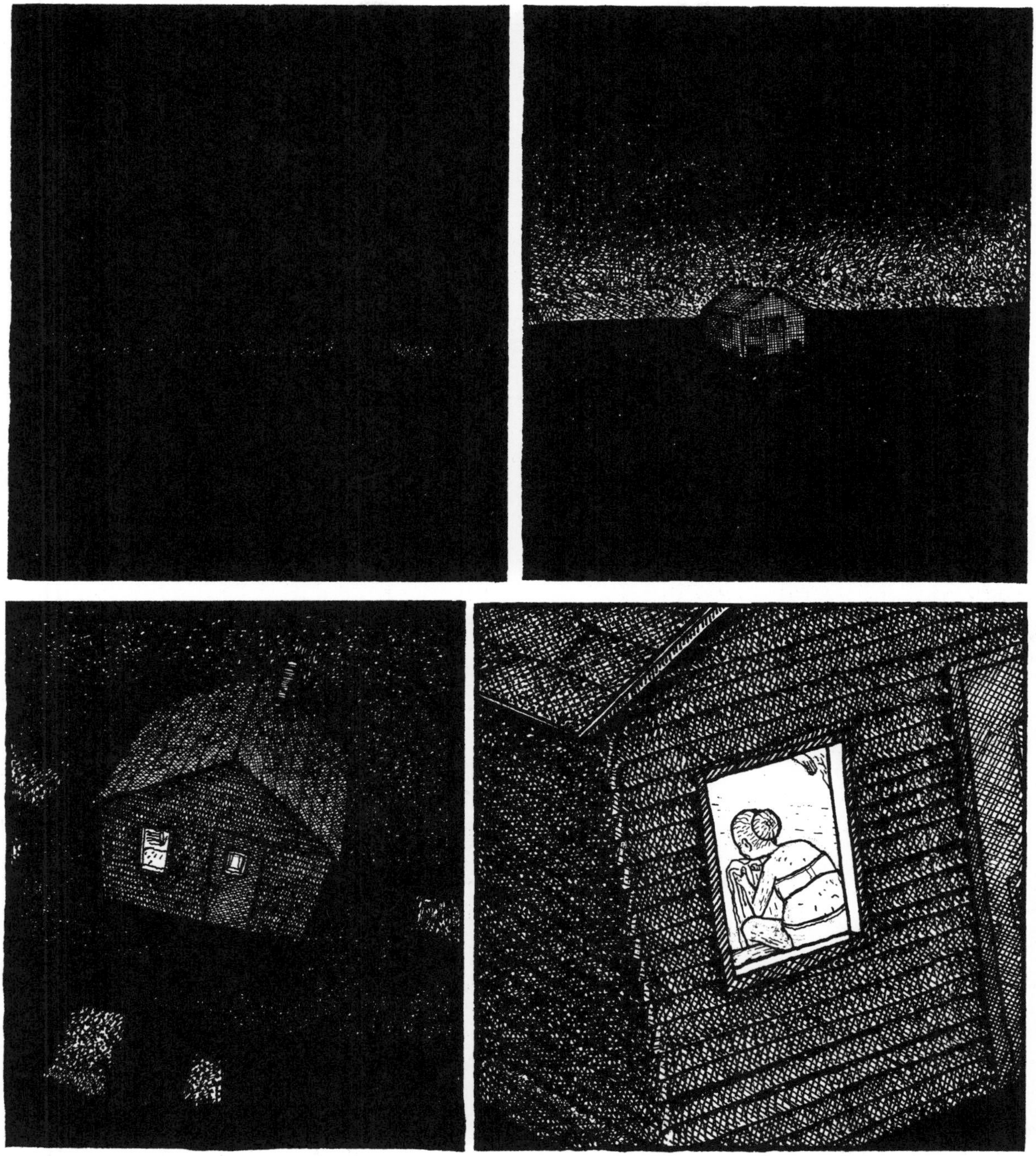

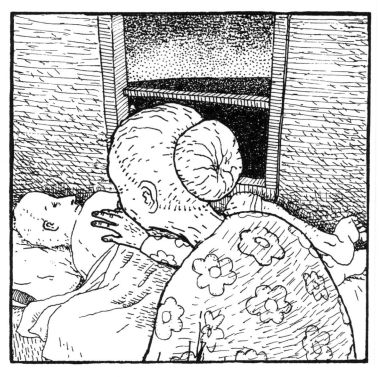

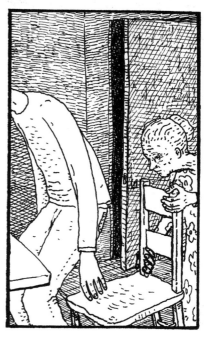

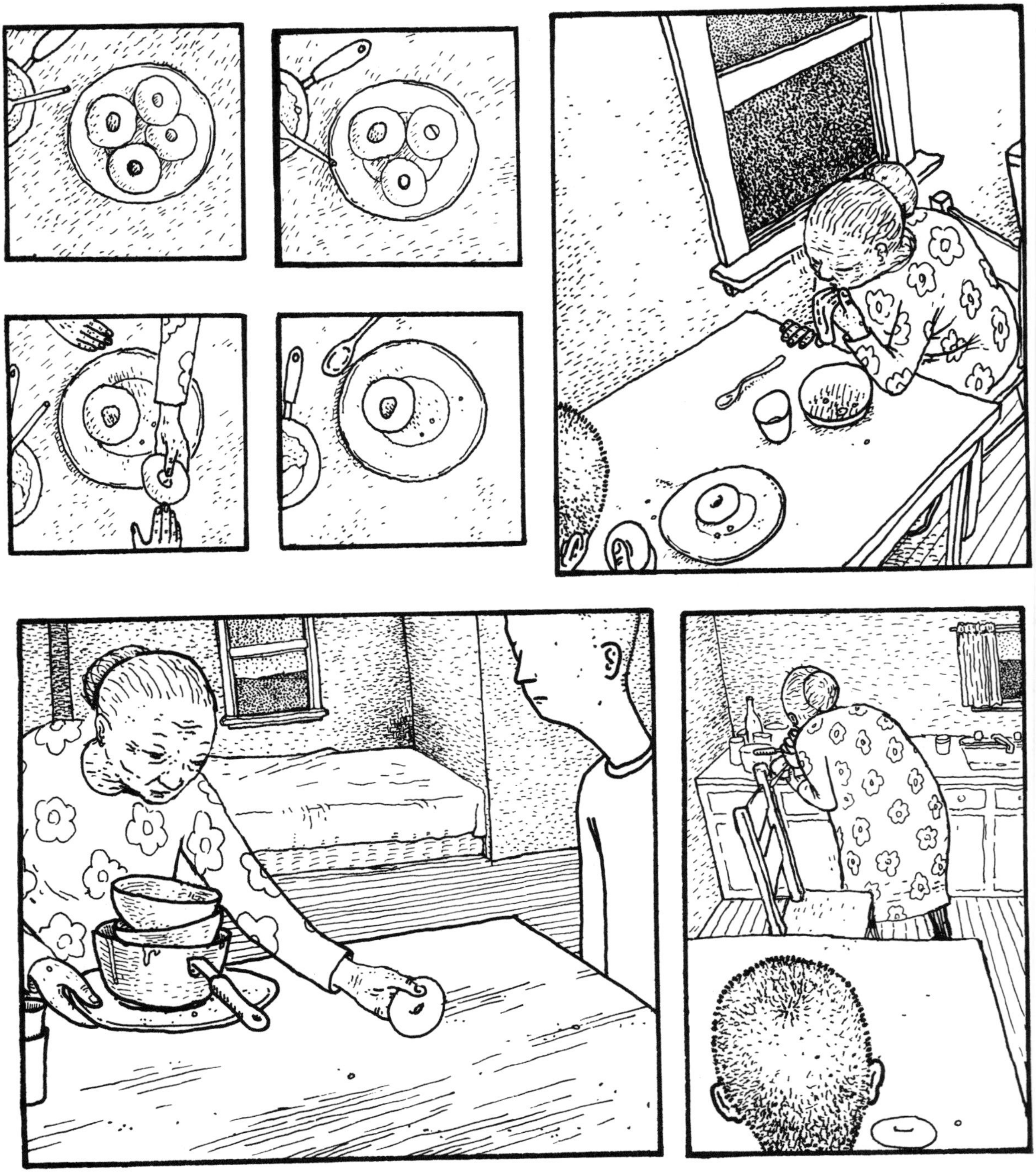

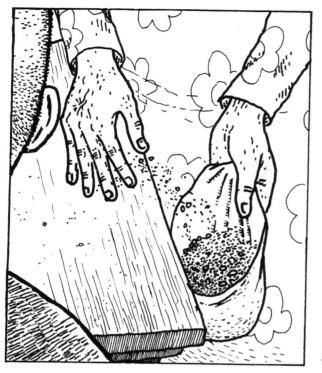

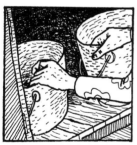

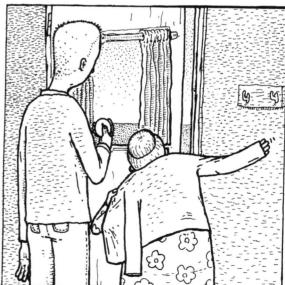
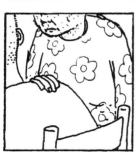

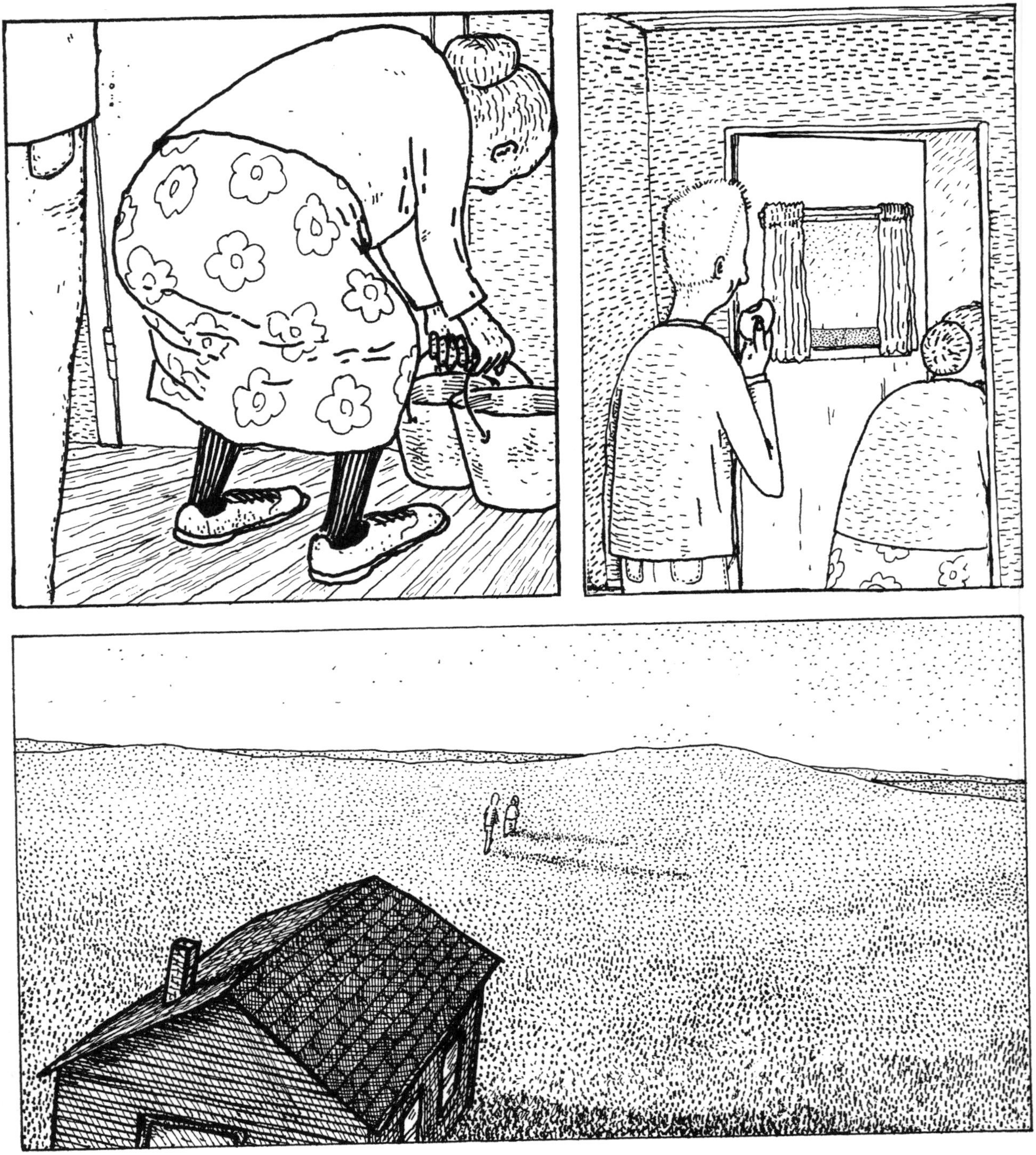

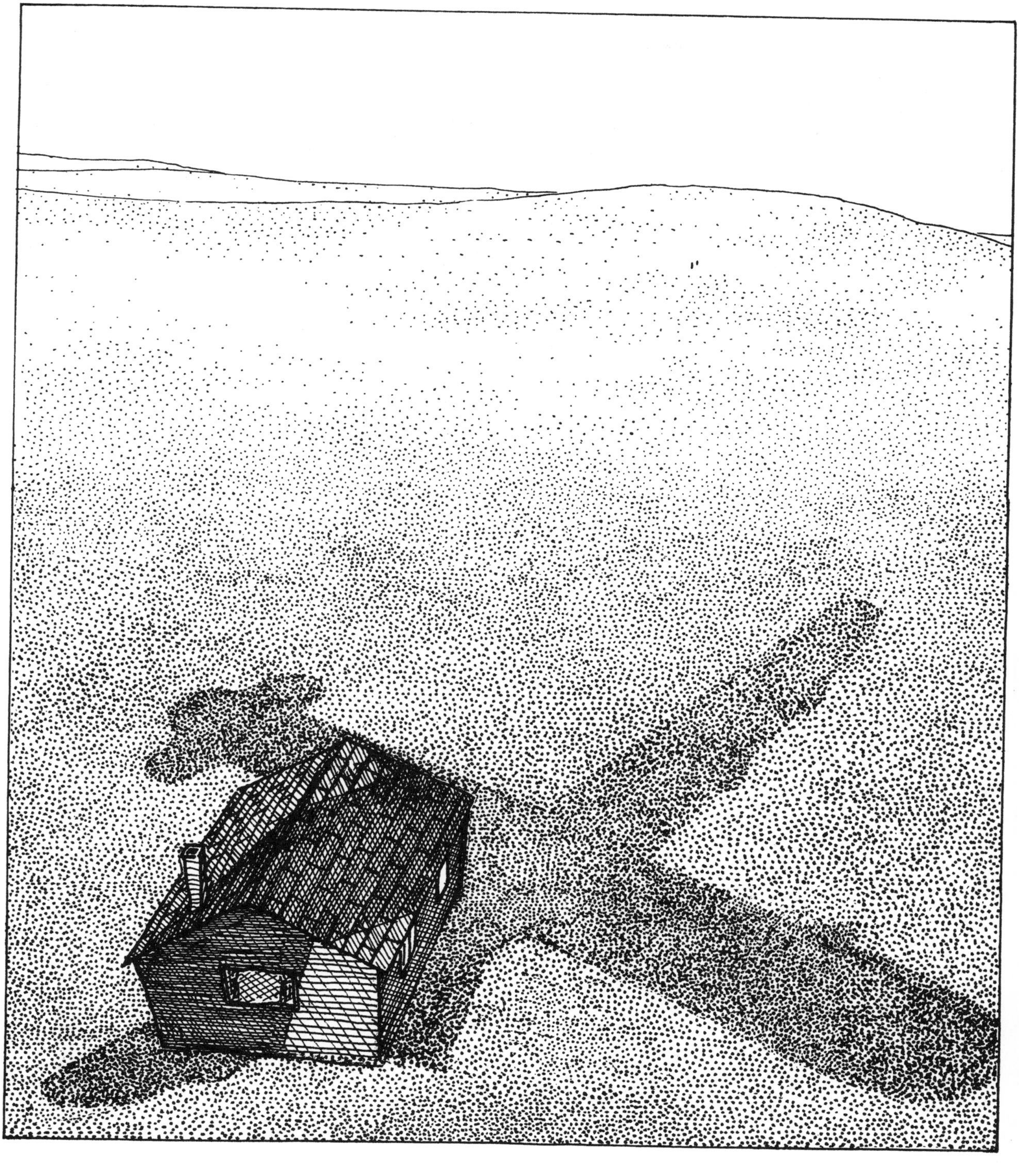

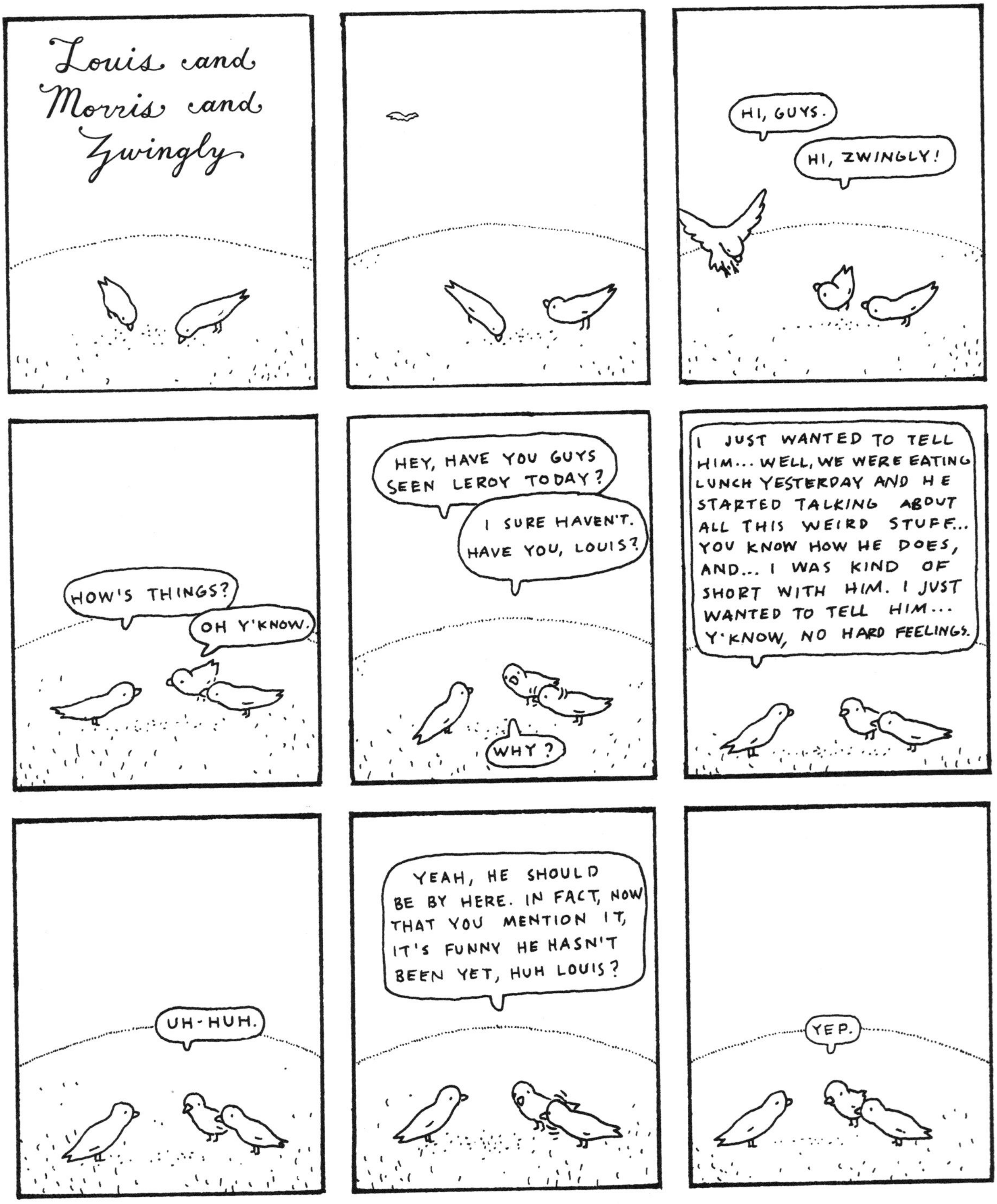
Louis and Morris and Zwingly
HI, GUYS.
HI, ZWINGLY!
HOW'S THINGS?
OH Y'KNOW.
HEY, HAVE YOU GUYS SEEN LEROY TODAY?
I SURE HAVEN'T. HAVE YOU, LOUIS?
WHY?
I JUST WANTED TO TELL HIM... WELL, WE WERE EATING LUNCH YESTERDAY AND HE STARTED TALKING ABOUT ALL THIS WEIRD STUFF... YOU KNOW HOW HE DOES, AND... I WAS KIND OF SHORT WITH HIM. I JUST WANTED TO TELL HIM... Y'KNOW, NO HARD FEELINGS.
UH-HUH.
YEAH, HE SHOULD BE BY HERE. IN FACT, NOW THAT YOU MENTION IT, IT'S FUNNY HE HASN'T BEEN YET, HUH LOUIS?
YEP.

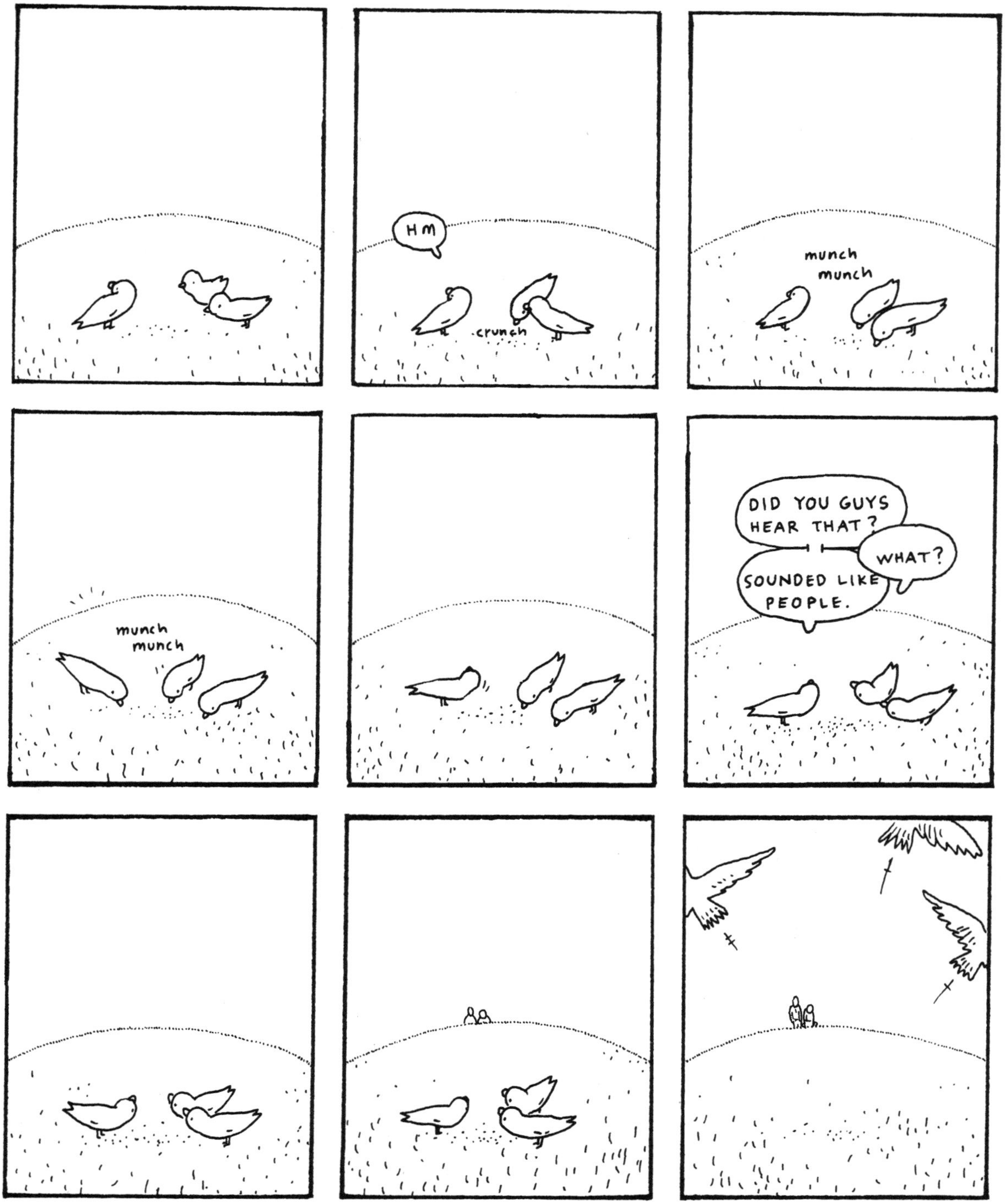
HM
crunch
munch
munch
munch
munch
DID YOU GUYS HEAR THAT?
WHAT?
SOUNDED LIKE PEOPLE.

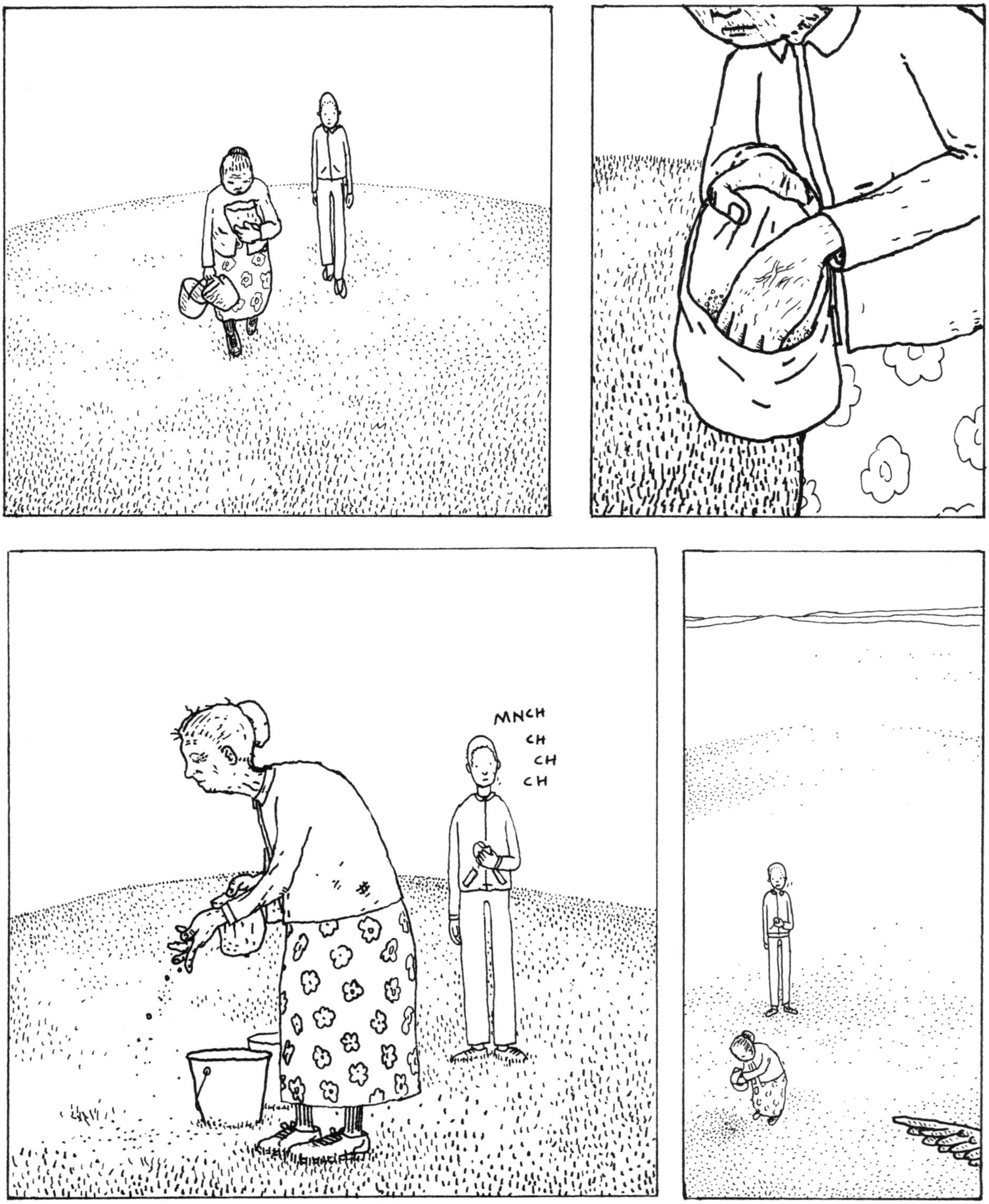
MNCH
CH
CH
CH

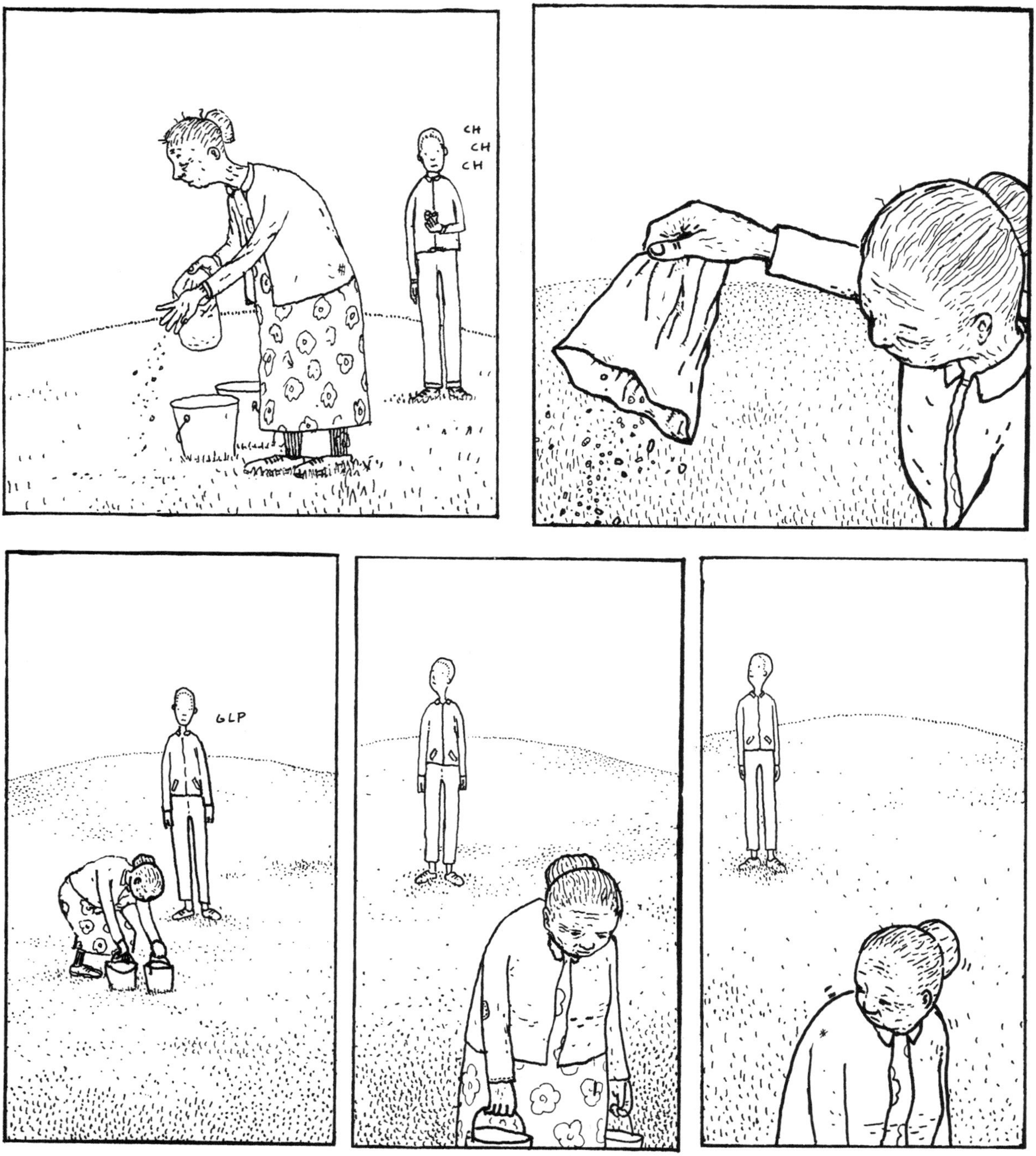
CH
CH
CH
GLP

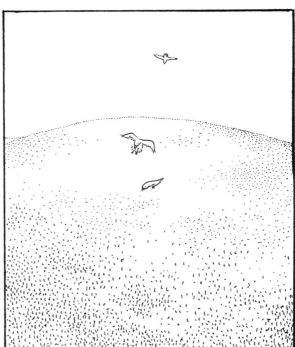

Algernon and the Snake

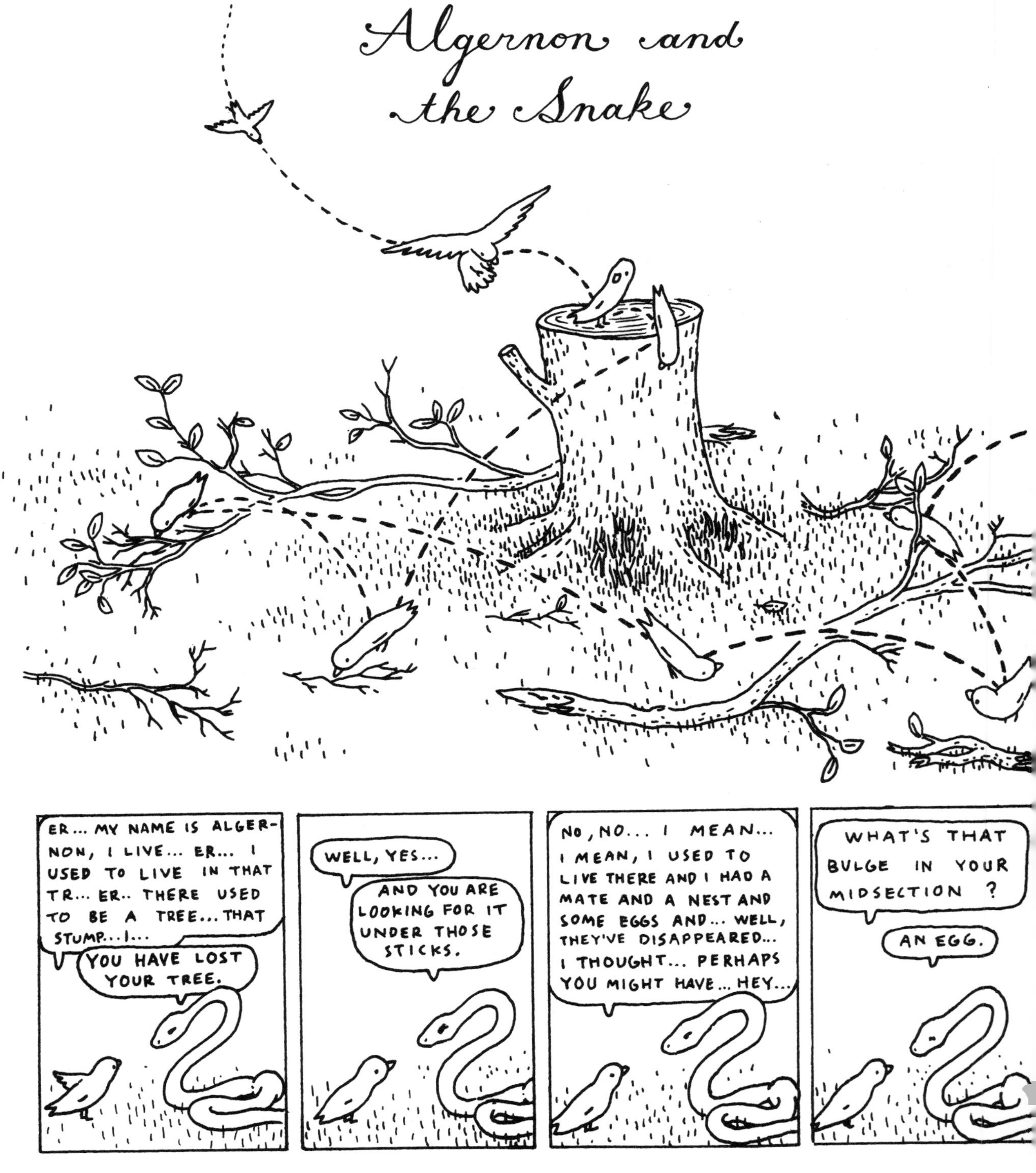
ER... MY NAME IS ALGERNON, I LIVE... ER... I USED TO LIVE IN THAT TR... ER.. THERE USED TO BE A TREE... THAT STUMP... I...
YOU HAVE LOST YOUR TREE.
WELL, YES...
AND YOU ARE LOOKING FOR IT UNDER THOSE STICKS.
NO, NO... I MEAN... I MEAN, I USED TO LIVE THERE AND I HAD A MATE AND A NEST AND SOME EGGS AND... WELL, THEY'VE DISAPPEARED... I THOUGHT... PERHAPS YOU MIGHT HAVE... HEY...
WHAT'S THAT BULGE IN YOUR MIDSECTION ?
AN EGG.

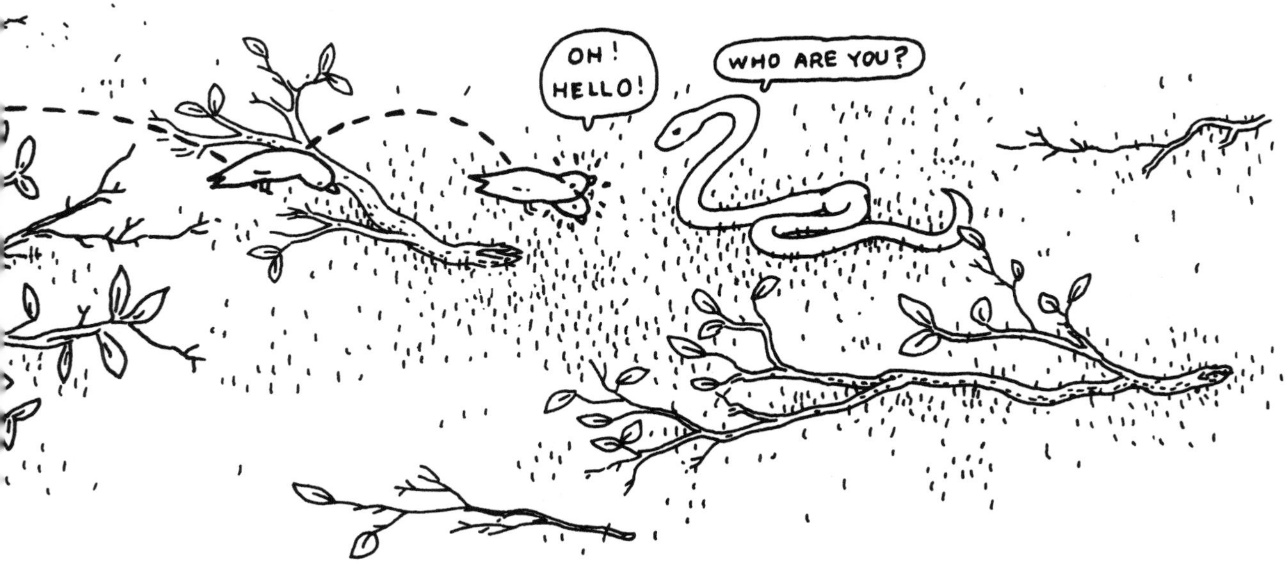
OH! HELLO!
WHO ARE YOU?

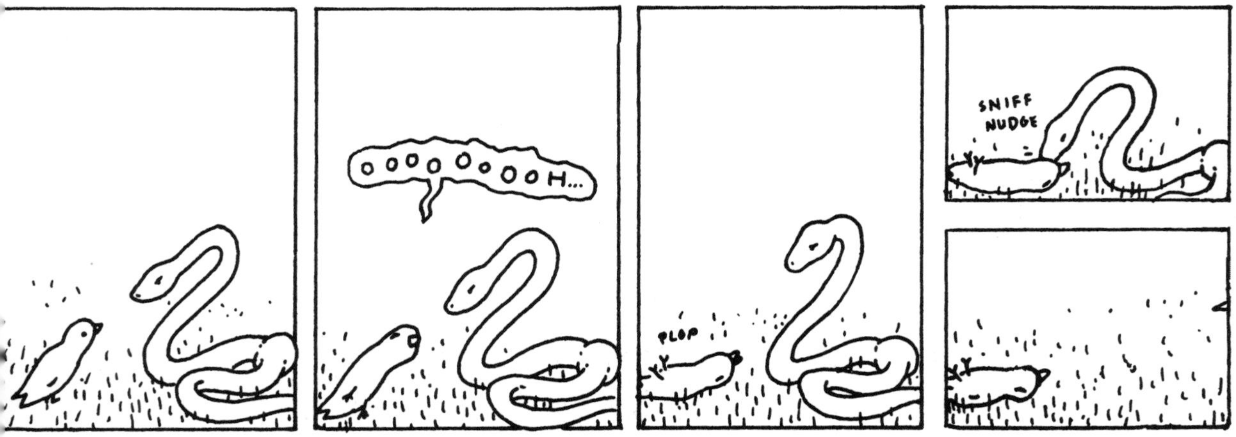
OOOOOOOOOH...
PLOP
SNIFF
NUDGE

Philo and Bayle

SIGH

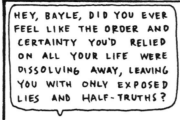

HEY, BAYLE, DID YOU EVER FEEL LIKE THE ORDER AND CERTAINTY YOU'D RELIED ON ALL YOUR LIFE WERE DISSOLVING AWAY, LEAVING YOU WITH ONLY EXPOSED LIES AND HALF-TRUTHS?

TODAY FOR LUNCH I HAD A PEANUT BUTTER AND JELLY SANDWICH.

YOU HAD A WHAT?

IT WAS SWEET YET SALTY, DRY AND CRUMBLY, YET STICKY.

BUT YOU AREN'T ANSWERING MY QUESTION!

WHEN I WAS DONE EATING I TRIED TO GET AHOLD OF ONE LAST PIECE TO BRING BACK TO THE NEST.

AS I BIT INTO THE SANDWICH, I WAS GRABBED BY A HUMAN HAND AND LIFTED INTO THE AIR.

WHAT?!

I TRIED TO TWIST OUT OF IT'S GRASP, BUT ALL I COULD DO, CONFRONTED WITH IT'S GAZE, WAS STARE BACK AND BLINK.

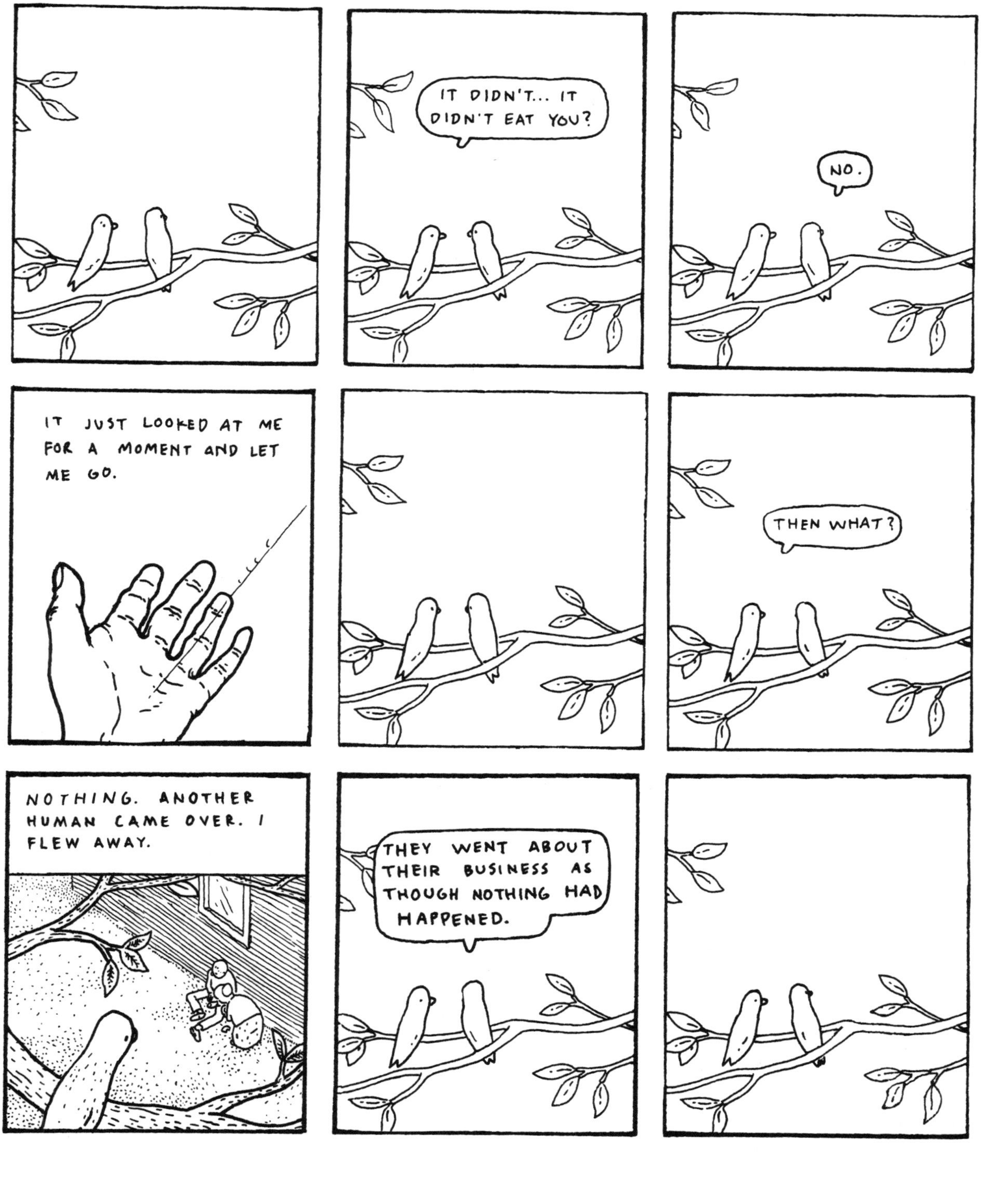
IT DIDN'T... IT DIDN'T EAT YOU?
NO.
IT JUST LOOKED AT ME FOR A MOMENT AND LET ME GO.
THEN WHAT?
NOTHING. ANOTHER HUMAN CAME OVER. I FLEW AWAY.
THEY WENT ABOUT THEIR BUSINESS AS THOUGH NOTHING HAD HAPPENED.

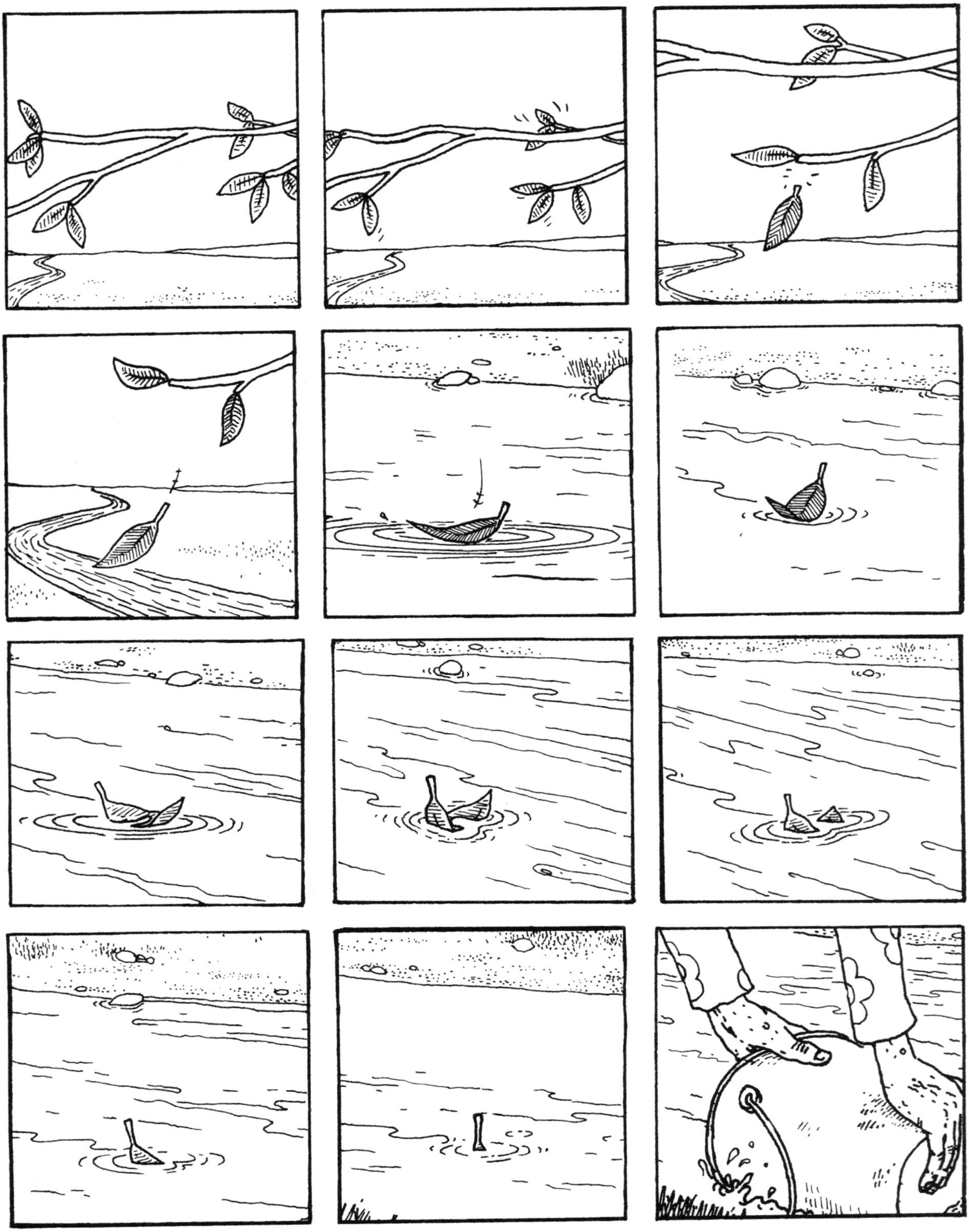

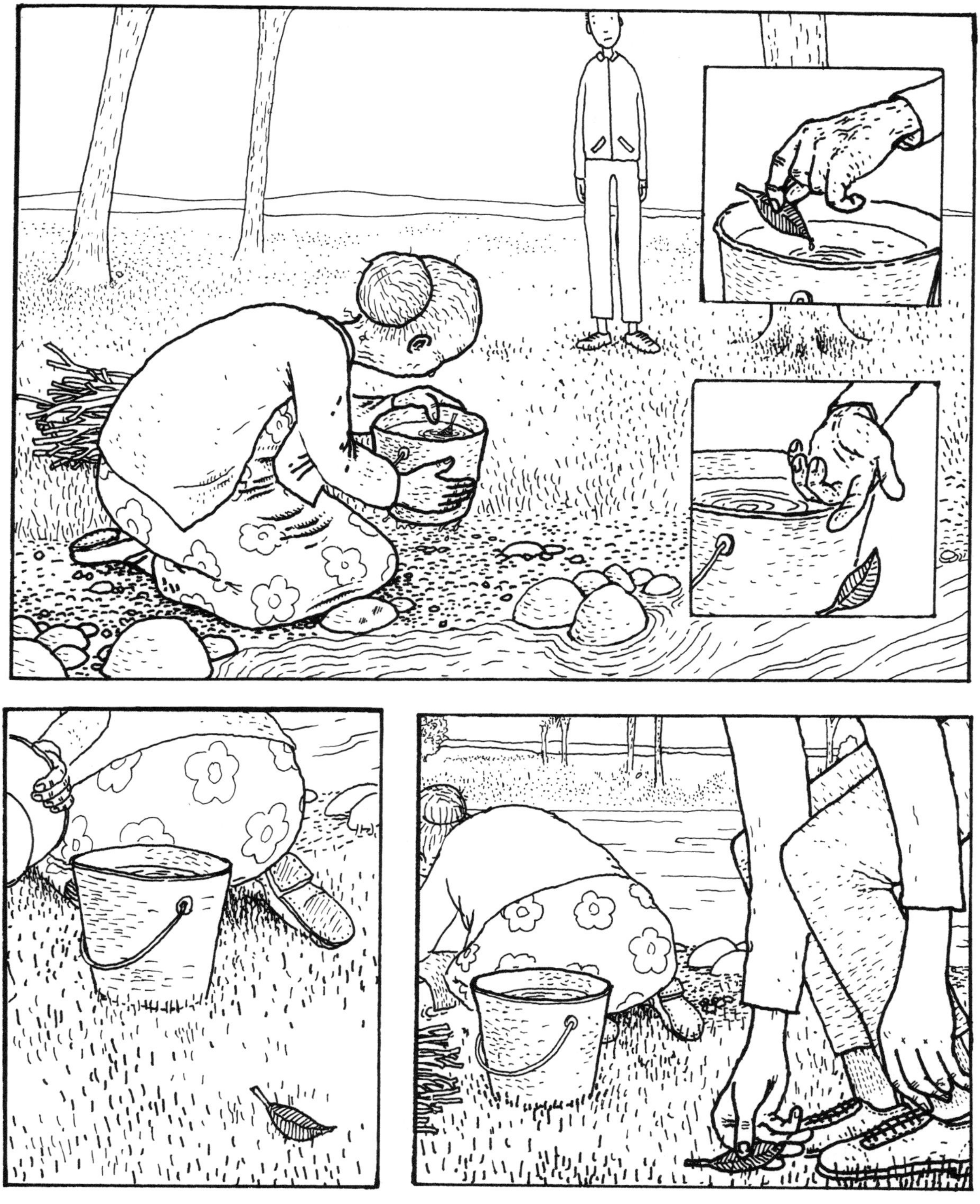

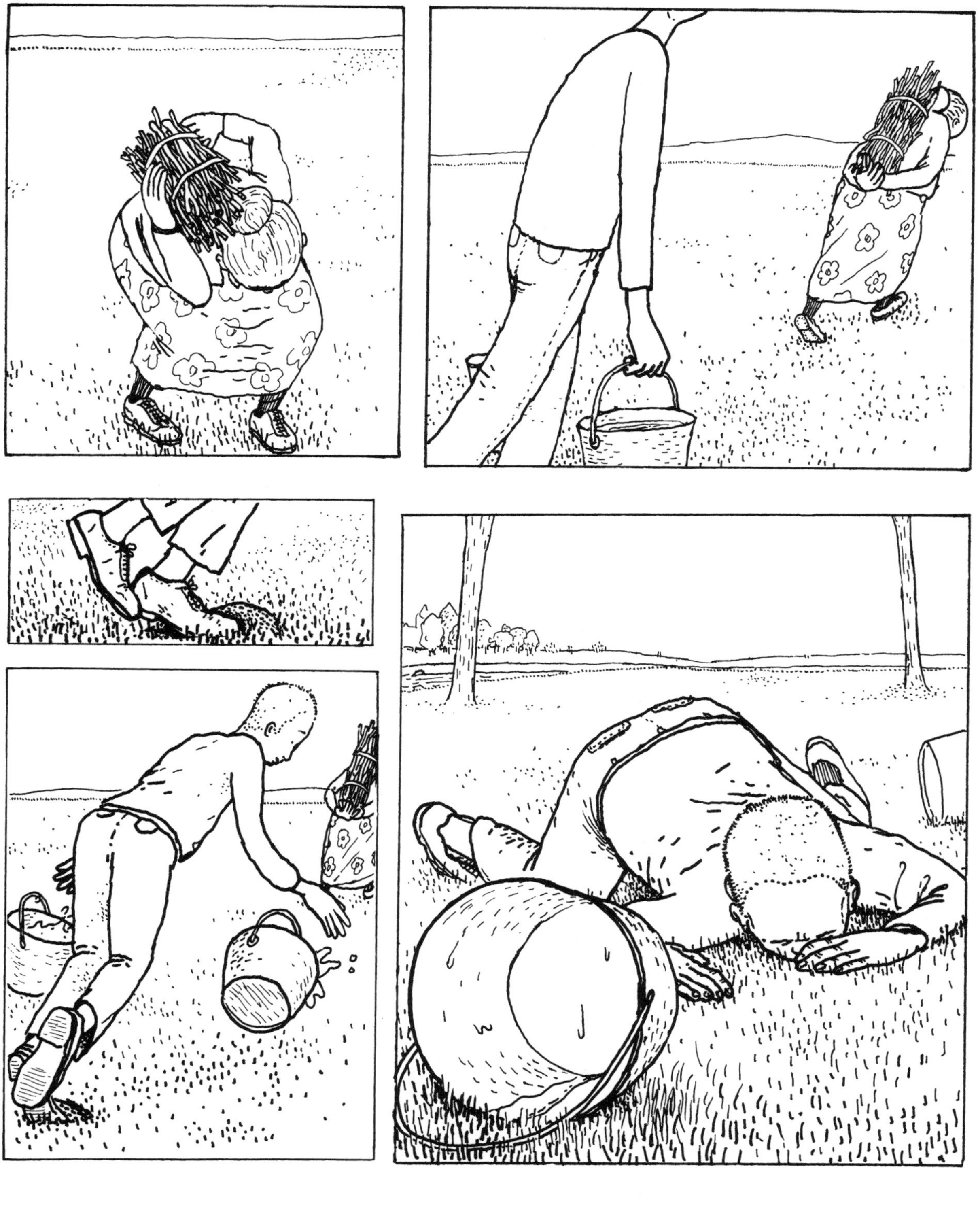

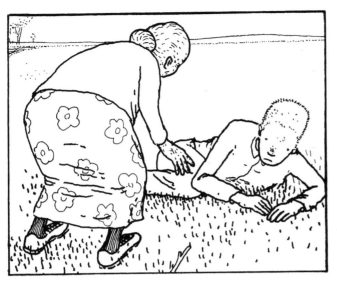

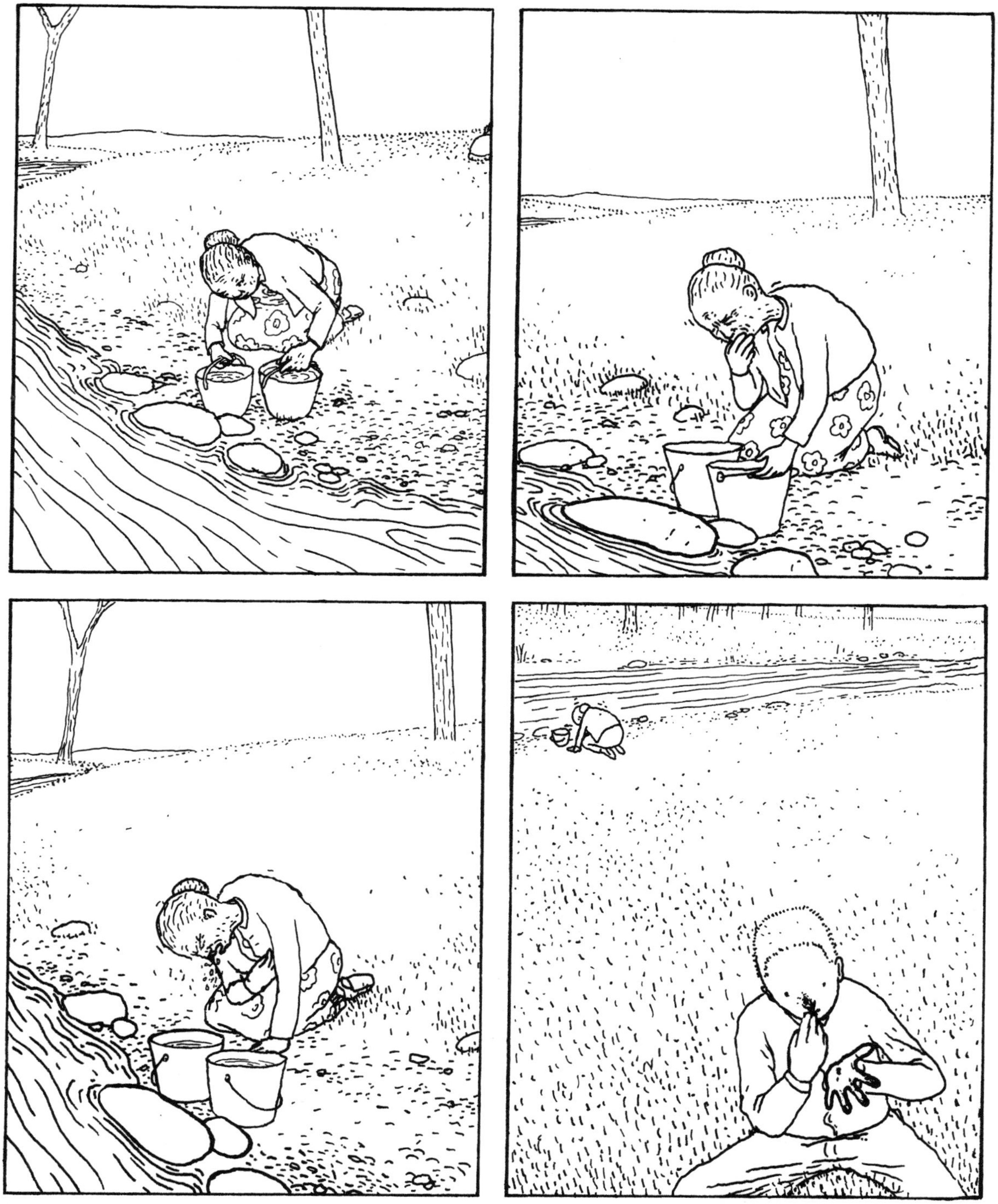

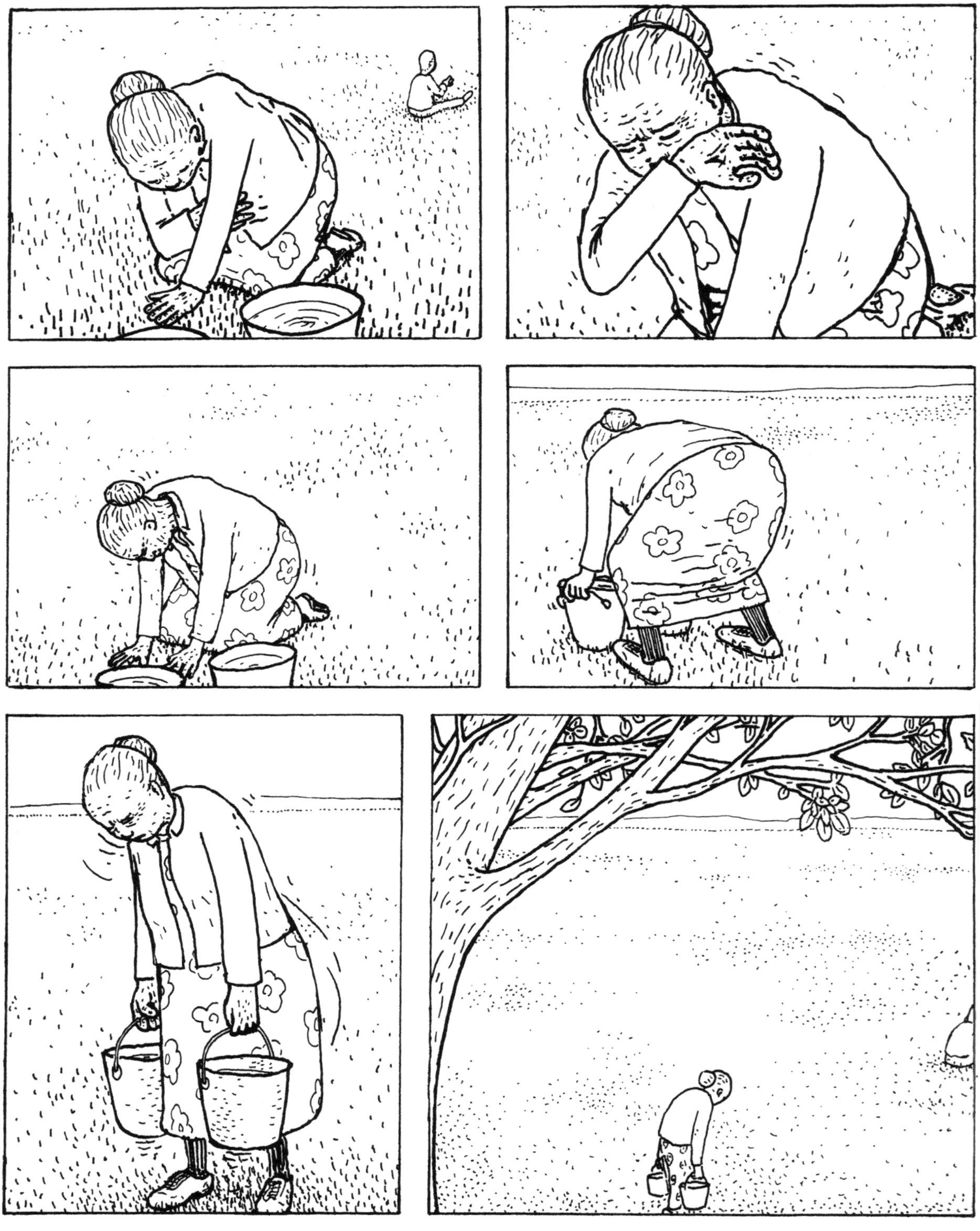

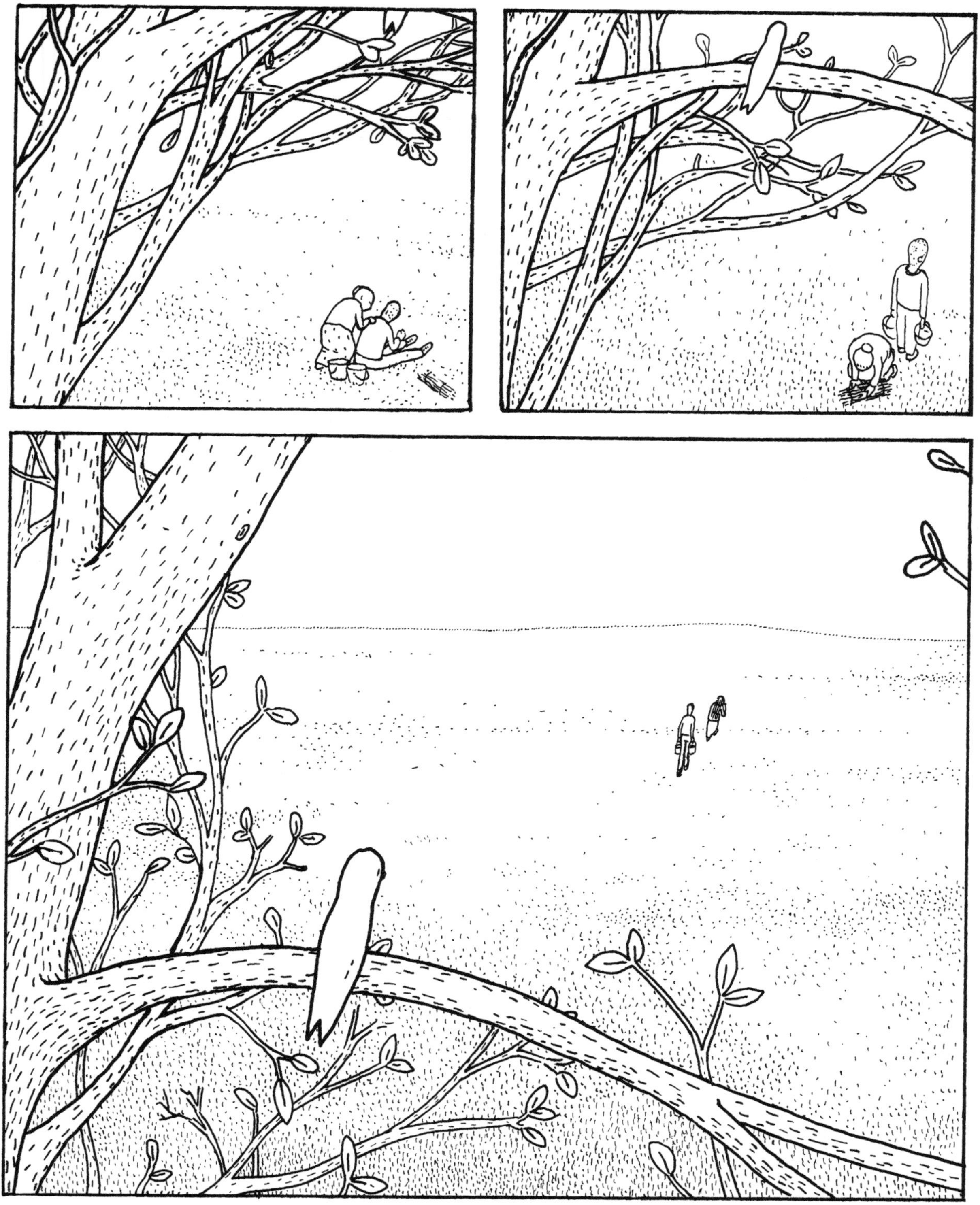

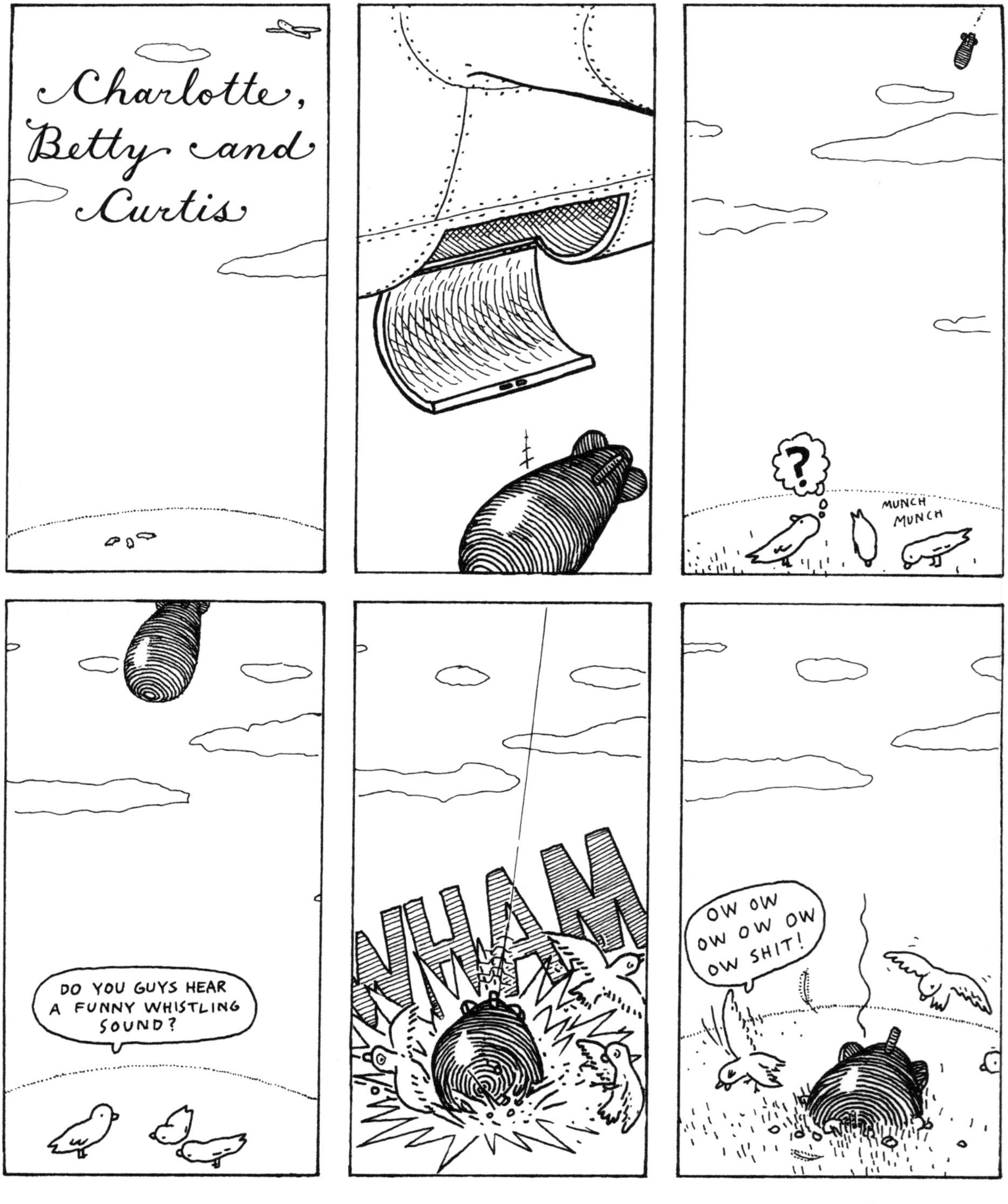
Charlotte, Betty and Curtis
?
MUNCH MUNCH
DO YOU GUYS HEAR A FUNNY WHISTLING SOUND?
WHAM
OW OW OW OW OW OW SHIT!

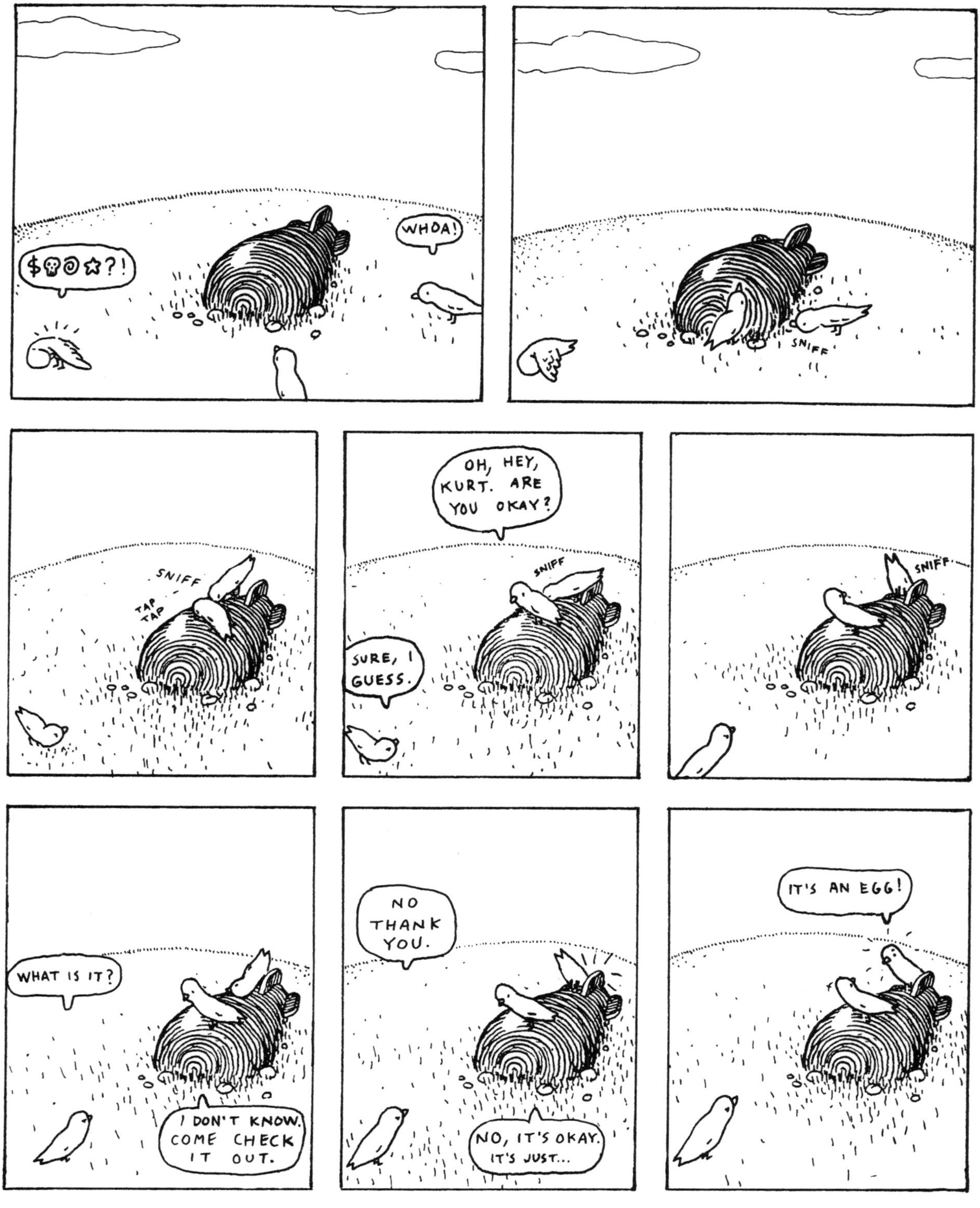
WHOA!
$💀@✩?!
SNIFF
SNIFF
TAP TAP
OH, HEY, KURT. ARE YOU OKAY?
SNIFF
SURE, I GUESS.
SNIFF
WHAT IS IT?
I DON'T KNOW. COME CHECK IT OUT.
NO THANK YOU.
NO, IT'S OKAY. IT'S JUST...
IT'S AN EGG!

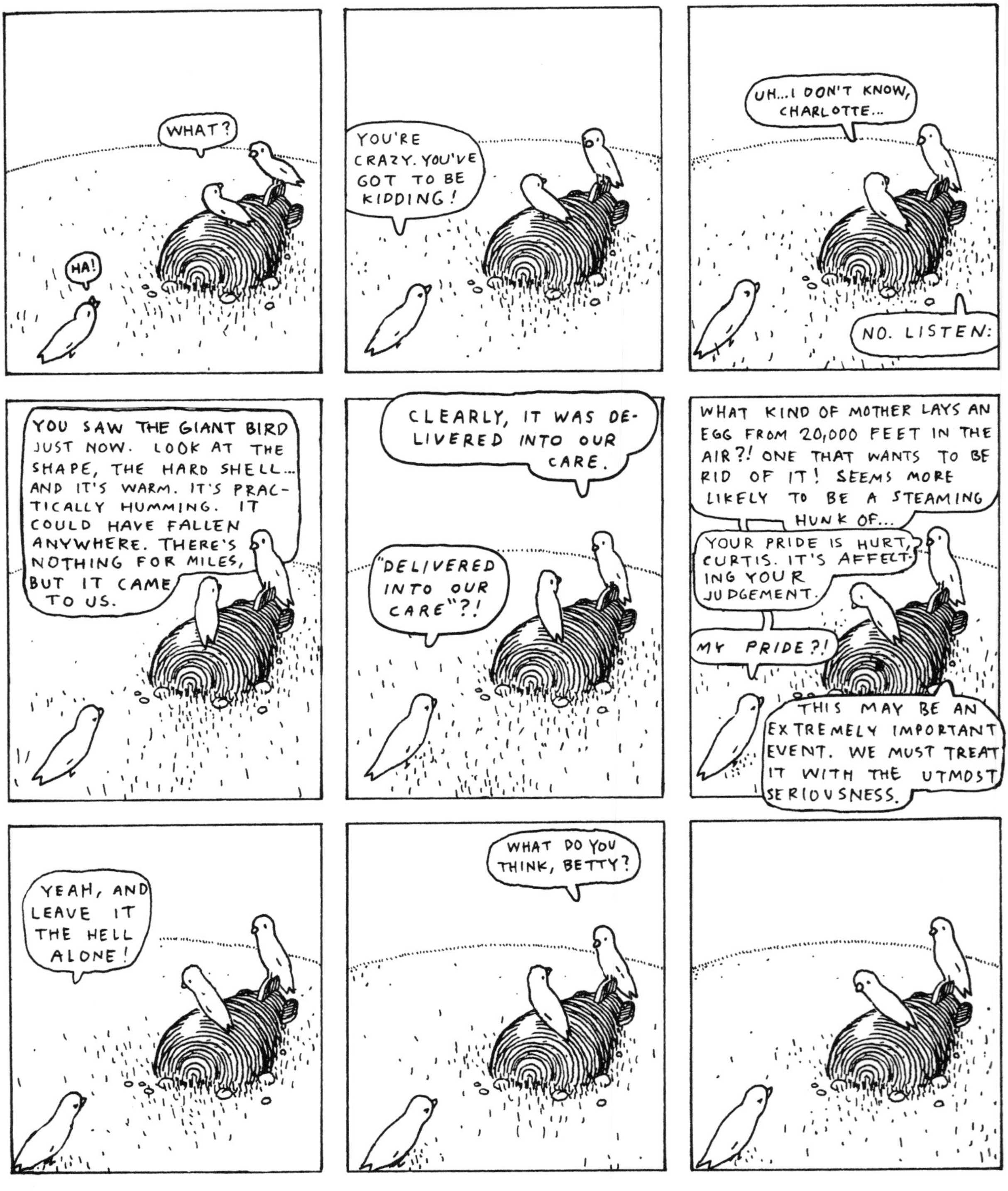
WHAT?
HA!
YOU'RE CRAZY. YOU'VE GOT TO BE KIDDING!
UH...I DON'T KNOW, CHARLOTTE...
NO. LISTEN:
YOU SAW THE GIANT BIRD JUST NOW. LOOK AT THE SHAPE, THE HARD SHELL... AND IT'S WARM. IT'S PRACTICALLY HUMMING. IT COULD HAVE FALLEN ANYWHERE. THERE'S NOTHING FOR MILES, BUT IT CAME TO US.
CLEARLY, IT WAS DELIVERED INTO OUR CARE.
"DELIVERED INTO OUR CARE"?!
WHAT KIND OF MOTHER LAYS AN EGG FROM 20,000 FEET IN THE AIR?! ONE THAT WANTS TO BE RID OF IT! SEEMS MORE LIKELY TO BE A STEAMING HUNK OF...
YOUR PRIDE IS HURT, CURTIS. IT'S AFFECTING YOUR JUDGEMENT.
MY PRIDE?!
THIS MAY BE AN EXTREMELY IMPORTANT EVENT. WE MUST TREAT IT WITH THE UTMOST SERIOUSNESS.
YEAH, AND LEAVE IT THE HELL ALONE!
WHAT DO YOU THINK, BETTY?

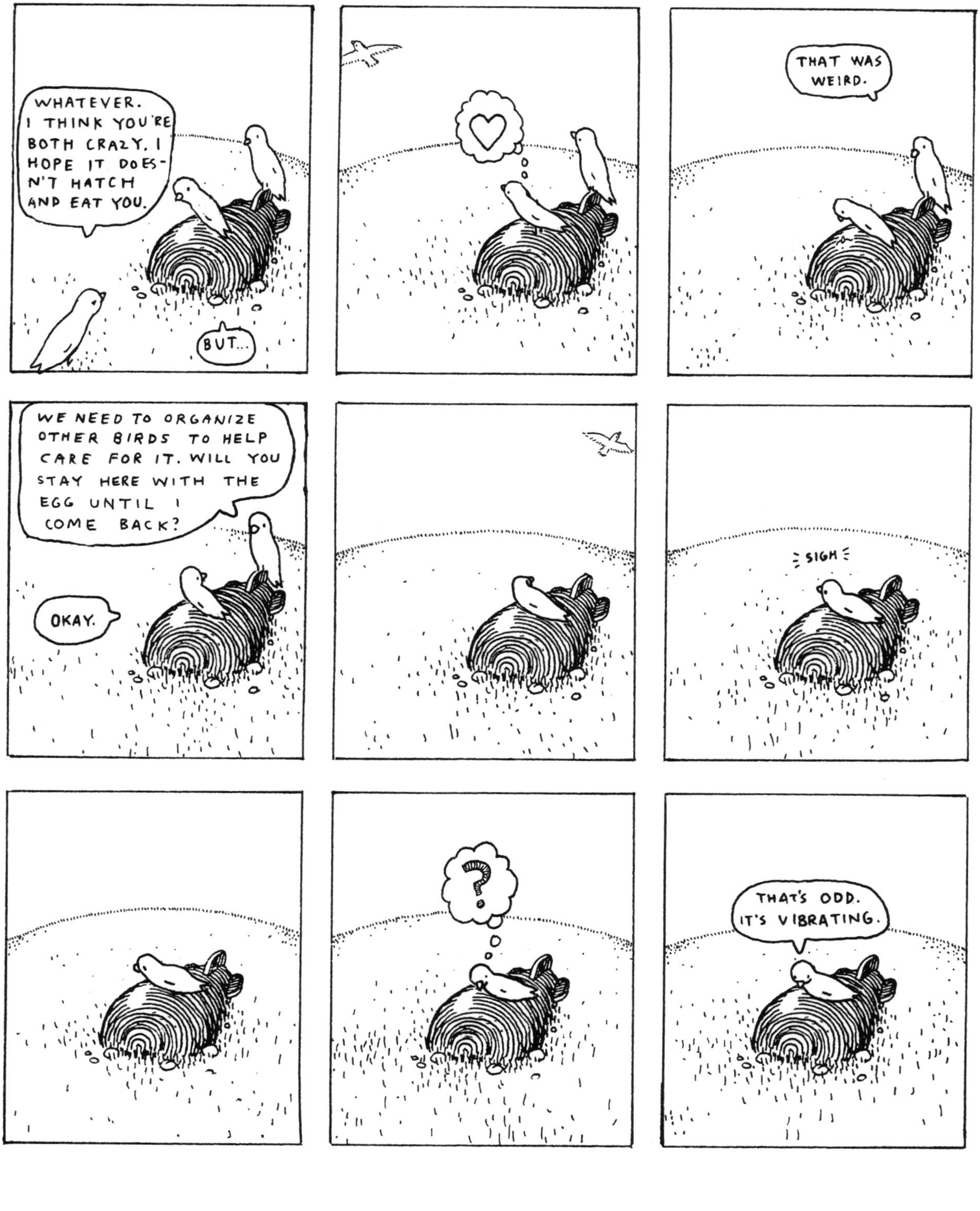
WHATEVER. I THINK YOU'RE BOTH CRAZY. I HOPE IT DOES-N'T HATCH AND EAT YOU.
BUT...
THAT WAS WEIRD.
WE NEED TO ORGANIZE OTHER BIRDS TO HELP CARE FOR IT. WILL YOU STAY HERE WITH THE EGG UNTIL I COME BACK?
OKAY.
SIGH
?
THAT'S ODD. IT'S VIBRATING.

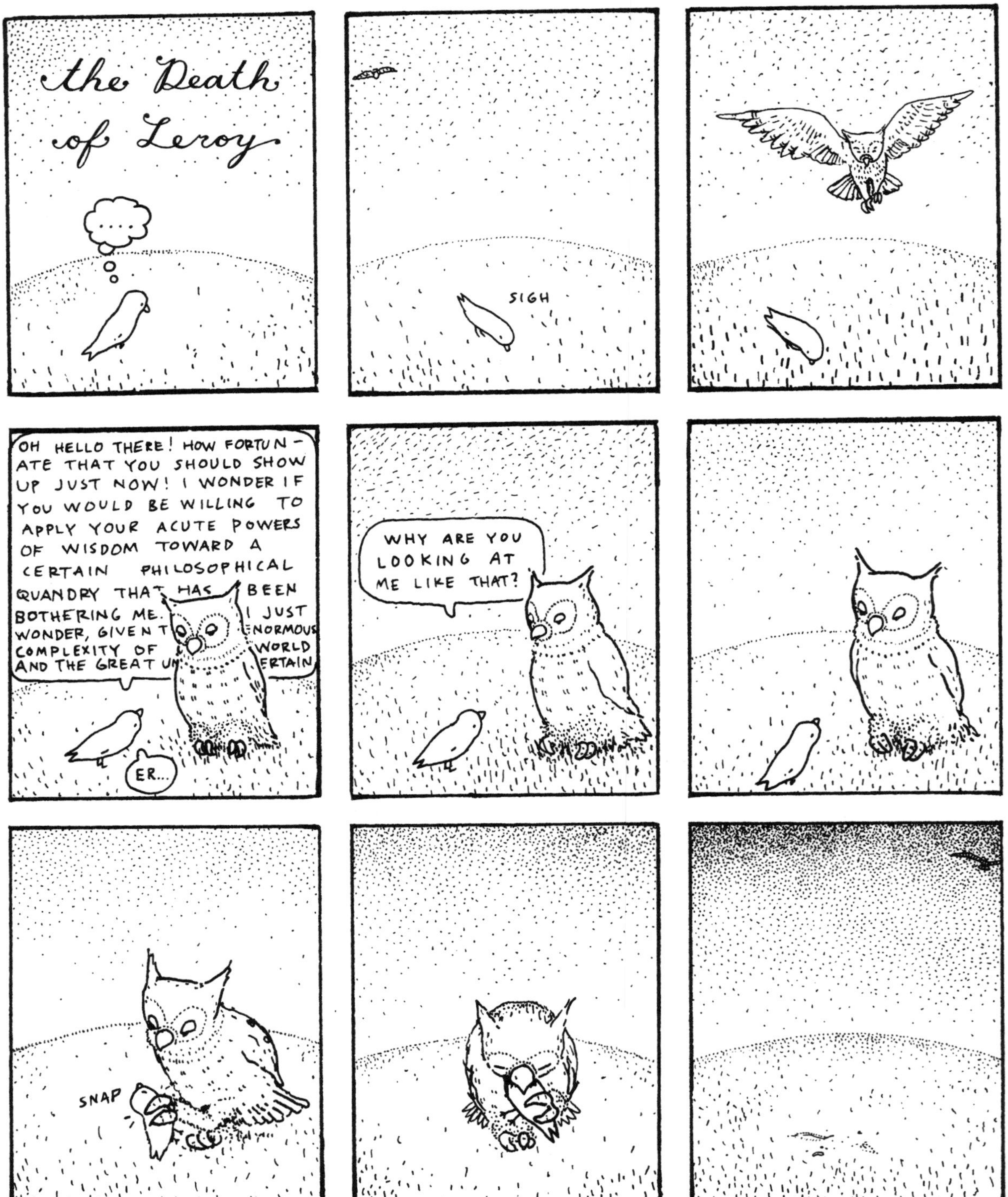
the Death of Leroy
SIGH
OH HELLO THERE! HOW FORTUNATE THAT YOU SHOULD SHOW UP JUST NOW! I WONDER IF YOU WOULD BE WILLING TO APPLY YOUR ACUTE POWERS OF WISDOM TOWARD A CERTAIN PHILOSOPHICAL QUANDRY THAT HAS BEEN BOTHERING ME. I JUST WONDER, GIVEN T NORMOUS COMPLEXITY OF WORLD AND THE GREAT U ERTAIN
ER...
WHY ARE YOU LOOKING AT ME LIKE THAT?
SNAP

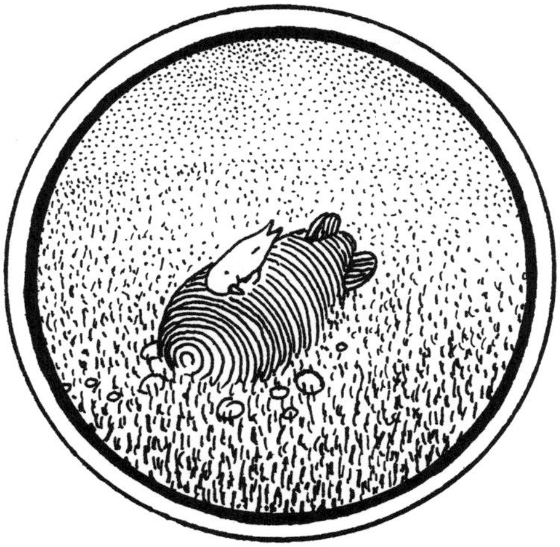

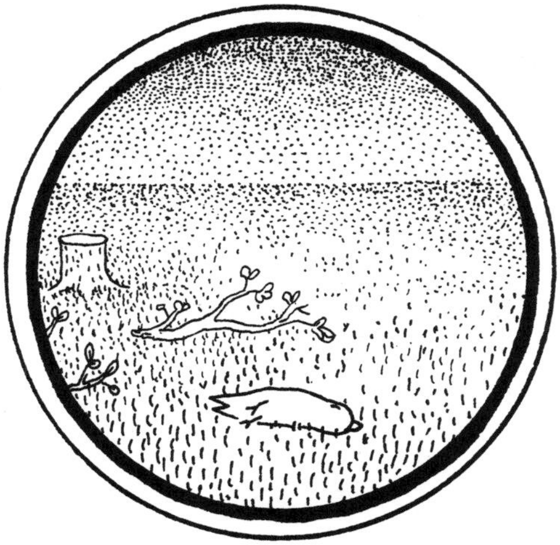

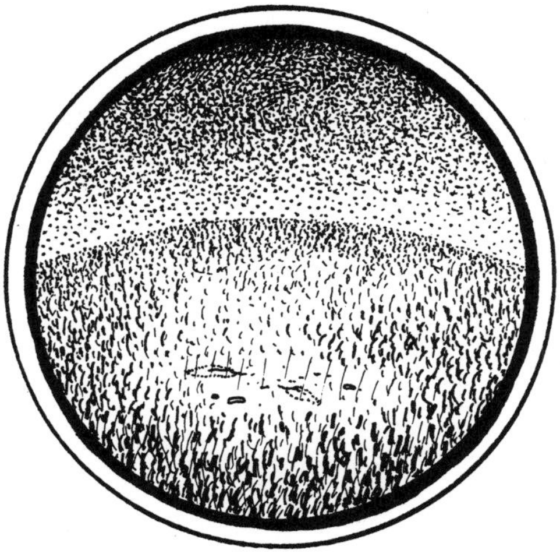

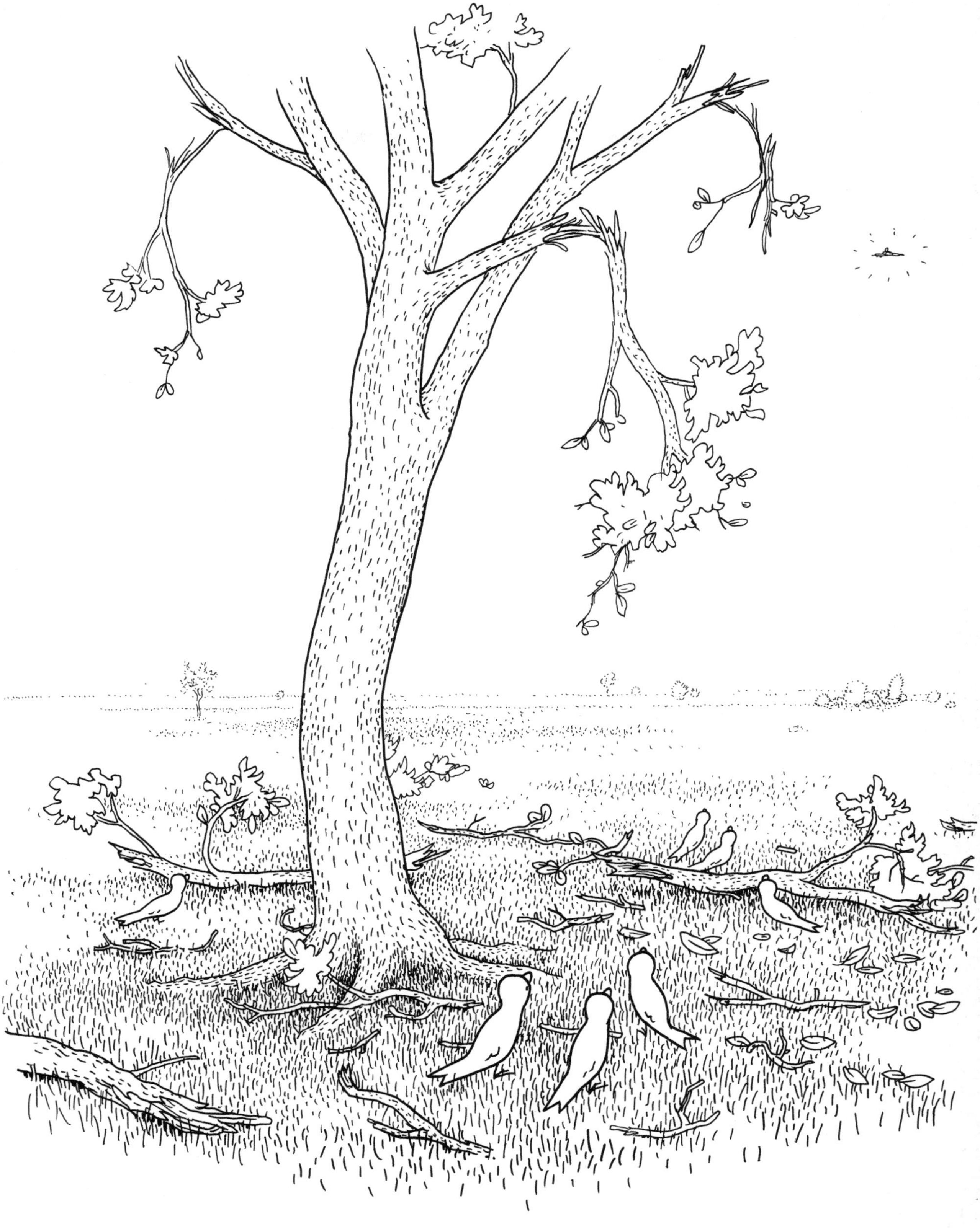

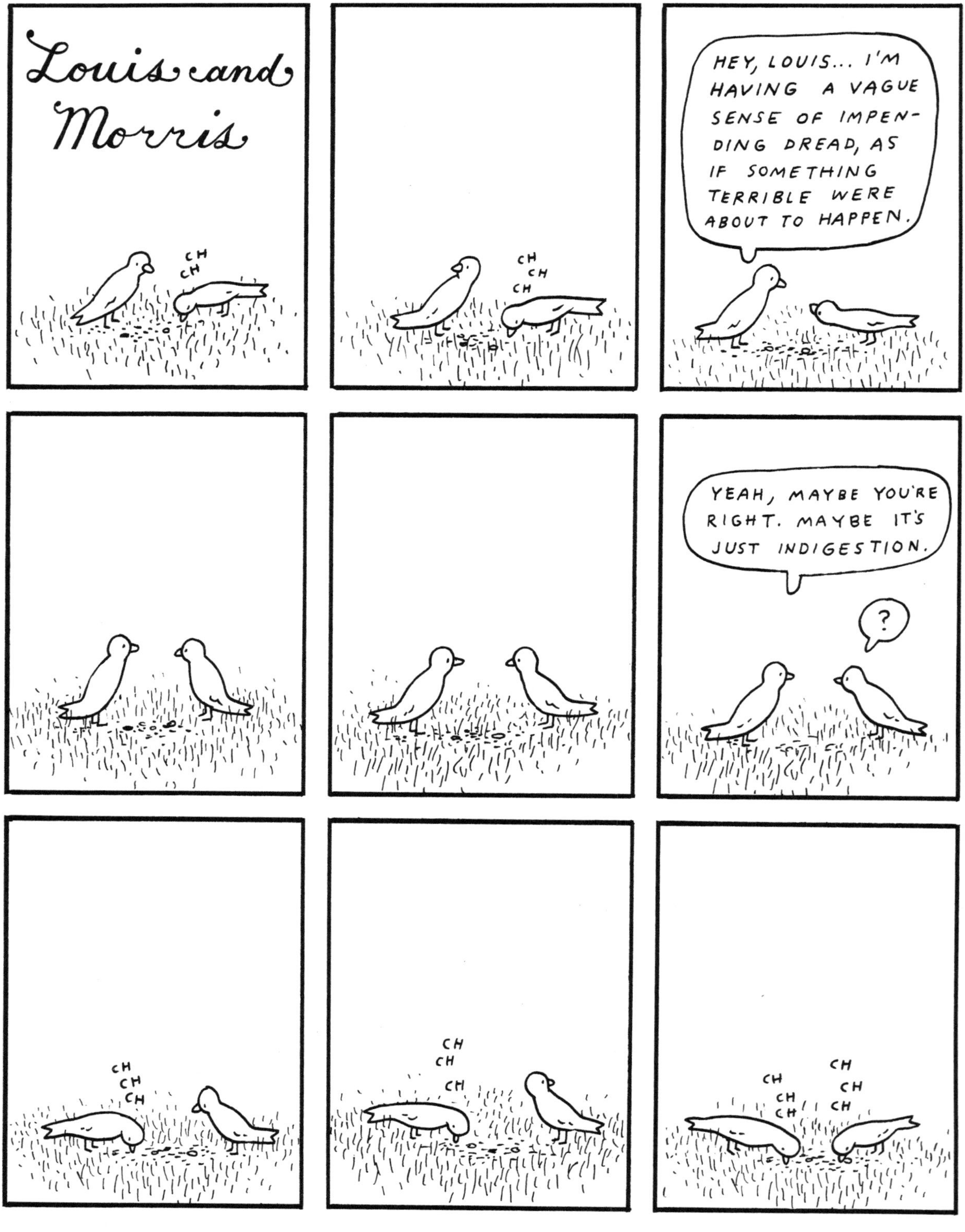
Louis and Morris
CH CH
CH CH CH
HEY, LOUIS... I'M HAVING A VAGUE SENSE OF IMPENDING DREAD, AS IF SOMETHING TERRIBLE WERE ABOUT TO HAPPEN.
YEAH, MAYBE YOU'RE RIGHT. MAYBE IT'S JUST INDIGESTION.
?
CH CH CH
CH CH CH
CH CH CH
CH CH CH

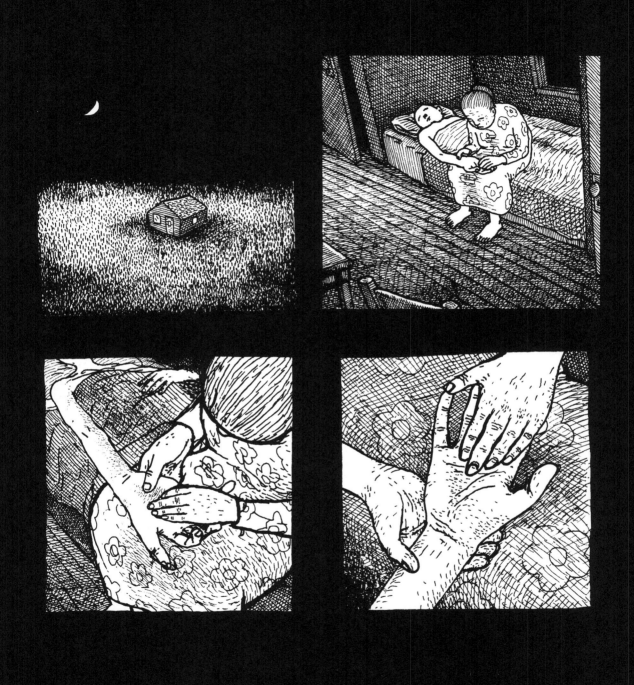

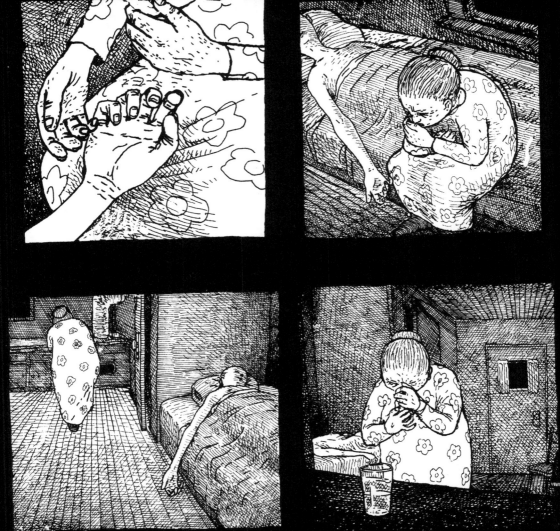

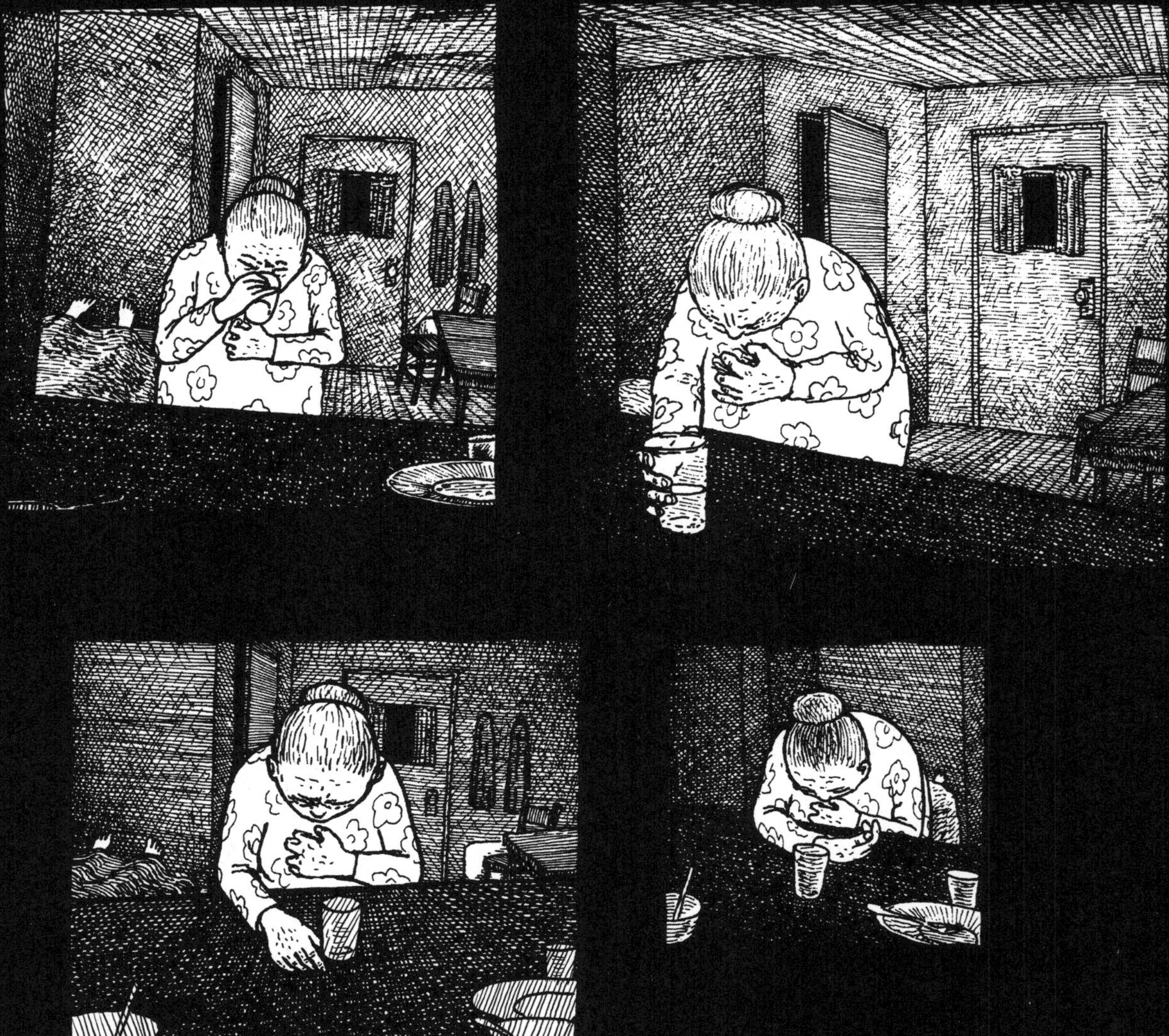

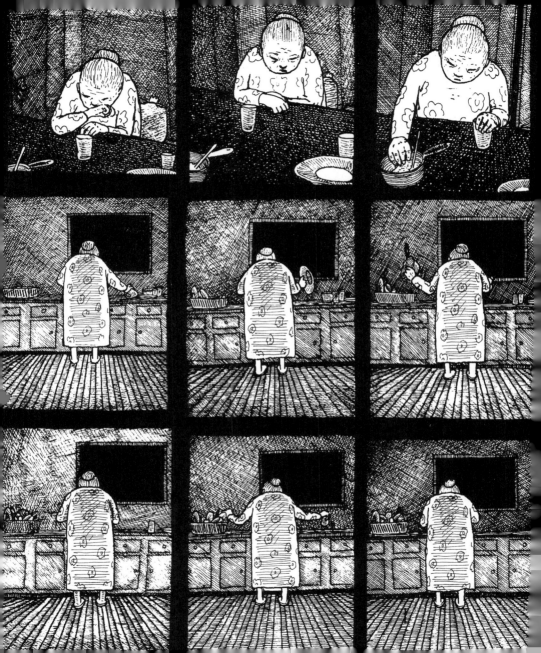

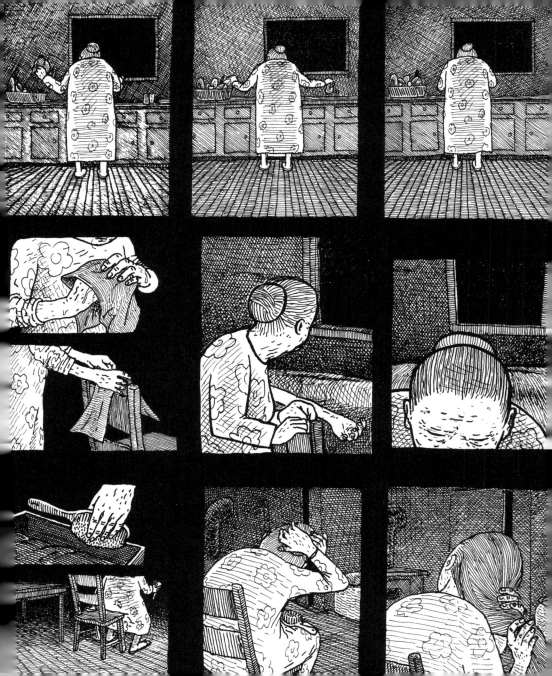

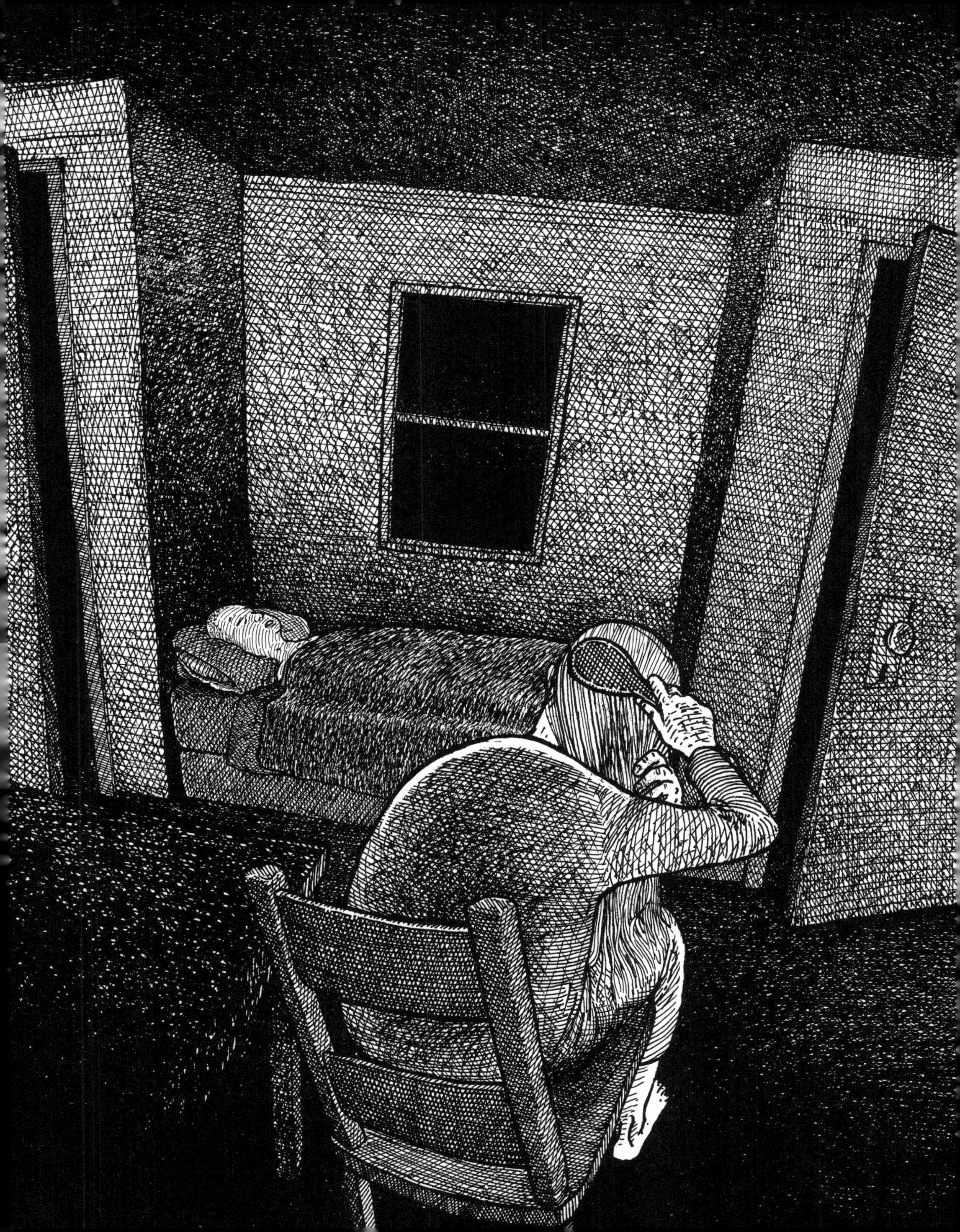

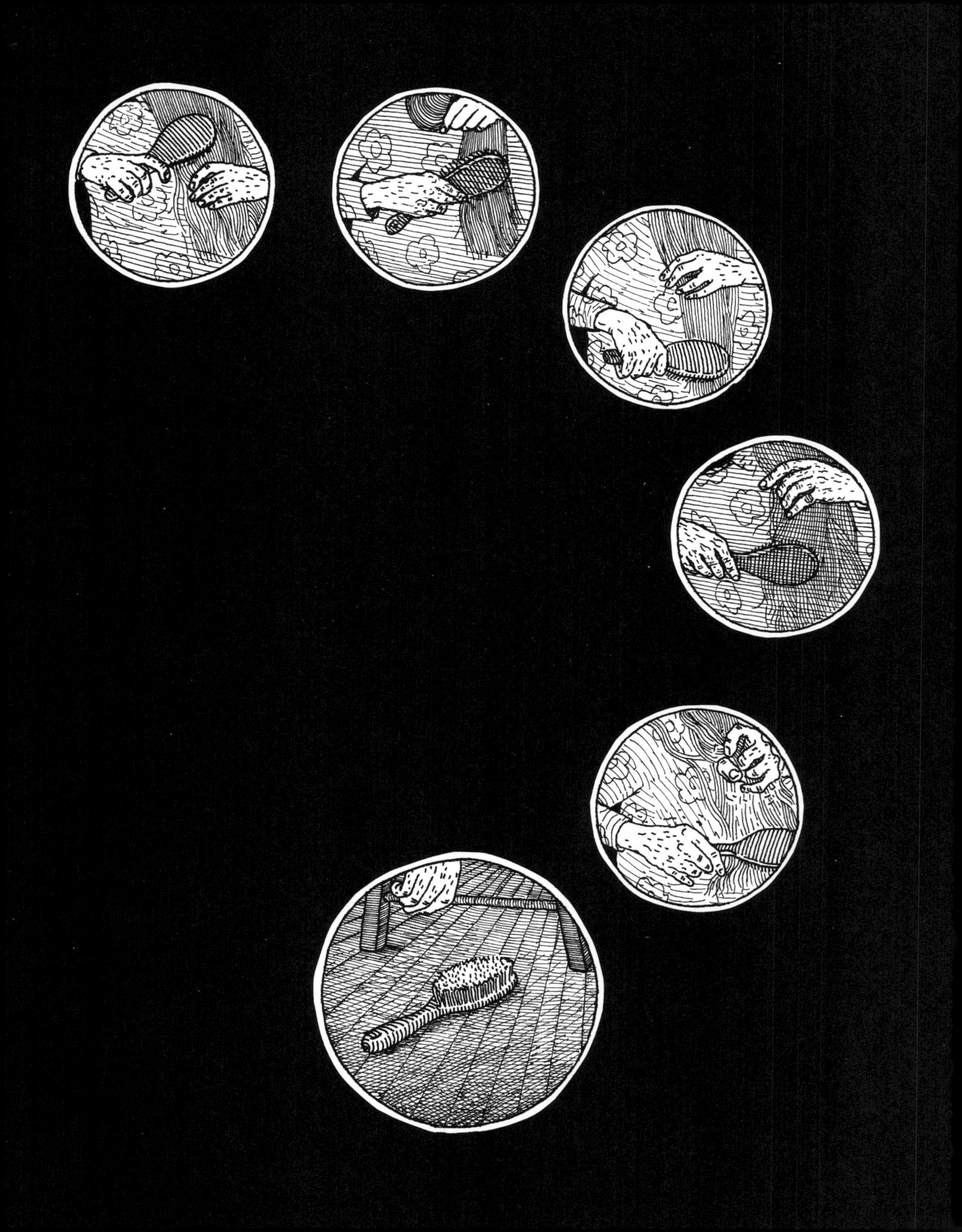

The Three Visitors of Betty Sentry

ONE: CURTIS

CURTIS!

HI, BETTY.

I BROUGHT YOU SOME FOOD. I THOUGHT YOU MIGHT BE HUNGRY.

OH THANKS! I AM. I'M STARVING.

MUNCH MNCH... IT'S SO NICE OF YOU TO COME OUT HERE, CURT. IT'S ACTUALLY KIND OF LONELY, YOU KNOW.

CHOMP CHOMP

UH-HUH.

BETTY... WHY ARE YOU STILL OUT HERE?

GUH-GUH

IF CHARLOTTE WANTS THIS THING GUARDED OR WHATEVER, SHE OUGHT TO DO IT HER-SELF. I DON'T THINK YOU BUY HER MUMBO JUMBO ANY MORE THAN I DO.

YOU KNOW, SHE'S BEEN TO EVERYONE WITH THIS "MIRACULOUS VISITATION" STUFF, HOLDING OUT SOME IMPLIED REWARD IF THEY DO AS SHE SAYS... IT'S ALL THIS NONESENSE ABOUT TESTS AND TRIALS AND DO-ING THE RIGHT THING.

YOU DON'T HONESTLY BELIEVE IN THAT STUFF, DO YOU?

I... I GUESS I DON'T REALLY KNOW.

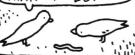

I MEAN...

YOU MIGHT BE RIGHT. CHARLOTTE MIGHT BE COMPLETELY OFF BASE ABOUT THIS THING... BUT... BUT THAT DOESN'T MEAN IT'S **NOTHING**, THAT WE SHOULD JUST WALK AWAY.

I DON'T KNOW IF IT'S GOOD OR BAD, BUT I HAVE A WEIRD FEELING ABOUT IT AND I JUST DON'T FEEL QUITE RIGHT LETTING IT ALONE. I GUESS I FEEL ...**RESPONSIBLE**... OR SOMETHING... AND...

AND SOMEWHAT CURIOUS TOO, I'LL ADMIT. AREN'T YOU, CURTIS? AREN'T YOU CURIOUS AT ALL? I MEAN IT CAME DOWN **OUT OF THE SKY**--FROM A **GIANT BIRD**. IT ALMOST **HIT** YOU!

IT **DID** HIT ME.

OH. YEAH.

YOU'RE NOT CURIOUS AT **ALL**?

YOU **DO** BELIEVE IN IT, DON'T YOU? YOU TRY TO PUSSY-FOOT AROUND IT, BUT REALLY YOU'RE EXPECTING SOME KIND OF **MIRACLE** TO HAPPEN-- AND A REWARD FOR YOUR 'GOOD BEHAVIOR'.

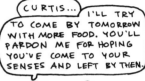

CURTIS... I'LL TRY TO COME BY TOMORROW WITH MORE FOOD. YOU'LL PARDON ME FOR HOPING YOU'VE COME TO YOUR SENSES AND LEFT BY THEN.

POKE POKE

SIGH

HEY!

SNAP!

SHIT.

HMPH

62

HI, BETTY.

HI, CHARLOTTE.

SO... HOW ARE THINGS GOING?

FINE, I GUESS.

IS THERE ANYTHING YOU NEED?

TWO: CHARLOTTE EVANGELISTA

UM...WELL, CURTIS BROUGHT ME SOME FOOD...BUT...

OH, THAT WAS NICE OF HIM.

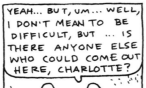

YEAH... BUT, UM... WELL, I DON'T MEAN TO BE DIFFICULT, BUT ... IS THERE ANYONE ELSE WHO COULD COME OUT HERE, CHARLOTTE?

I MEAN, IT'S BEEN TWO DAYS... IT'S JUST A LITTLE BIT CREEPY LONELY OUT HERE.

WE DON'T **REALLY** KNOW WHAT THIS THING IS. WHAT IF CURTIS IS RIGHT?

"WHAT IF"...?! WHOA, DON'T LOSE ME HERE, BETTY! -- THIS IS TOO IMPORTANT. IN THE SCHEME OF THINGS, THE JOB YOU'RE DOING IS HUMBLE, BUT IT'S VITALLY IMPORTANT.

YOU'RE RIGHT, YOU KNOW, WE CAN'T KNOW FOR **CERTAIN** WHAT THIS IS, BUT WHAT CAN ANYONE **EVER** KNOW WITH CERTAINTY? YOU AND I **BOTH** SAW WHERE THIS THING CAME FROM.

MAYBE IT WAS AN ACCIDENT, BUT **MAYBE** IT WAS A **TEST**. MAYBE IT'S A MESSAGE. AND IF WE DEAL WITH IT CORRECTLY, RESPECTFULLY...WELL IT'S NOT OUR JOB TO SPECULATE...

BUT WE CLEARLY HAVE AN OBLIGATION TO ACT WITH HUMILITY AND GRATITUDE FOR THE CHANCE WE'VE BEEN GIVEN.

I MEAN, WE LIVE IN A SPECIAL TIME, DON'T YOU THINK?

BASICALLY I'M TIRED, HUNGRY, SLIGHTLY CREEPED OUT AND ANNOYED AND I WANT TO GO HOME.

YOU'RE, YOU'RE PROBABLY RIGHT, IT'S JUST THAT I...

I KNOW HOW YOU FEEL, BETTY. IT'S EASY TO GET DISCOURAGED, BUT I'VE BEEN THINKING ABOUT THIS A LOT AND I FEEL LIKE MY WHOLE LIFE HAS LED TO THIS MOMENT.

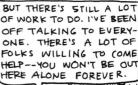

BUT THERE'S STILL A LOT OF WORK TO DO. I'VE BEEN OFF TALKING TO EVERYONE. THERE'S A LOT OF FOLKS WILLING TO COME HELP--YOU WON'T BE OUT HERE ALONE FOREVER.

YOU JUST HAVE TO TRUST ME A LITTLE BIT LONGER.
OKAY.
GREAT. THANKS, BETTY. YOU WON'T BE DISAPPOINTED.

THREE: LEROY BONES

"WILLING TO HELP"? HELP WHAT? SIT HERE AND STARE AT A BIG BLACK... WHAT-EVER-IT-IS?
EGG?
...EGG...
SHE DIDN'T EVEN SO MUCH AS LOOK AT IT THE WHOLE TIME SHE WAS HERE!
SHE TOLD BETTY GOD WAS GONNA HATCH OUT!
AND SHE BOUGHT IT! HA HA!
AUGH! BETTY, BETTY, BETTY. GET AHOLD OF YOURSELF. WHAT-EVER THIS THING IS, IT'S...IT'S...
EGG
MIRACLE
GIANT BIRD
TRUST ME
MUMBO JUMBO
CREEPY
SIGH
POKE
POKE
ONE MORE NIGHT. THEN I'M PUTTING MY FOOT DOWN.

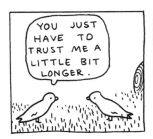

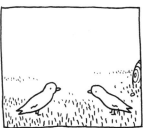

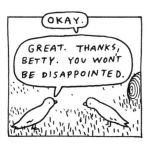

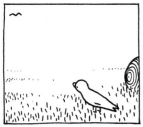

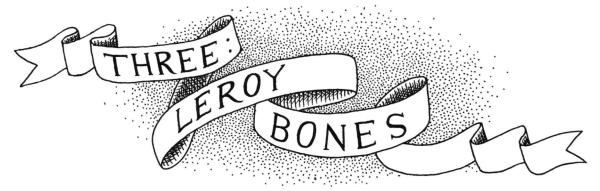

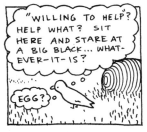

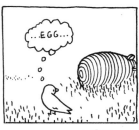

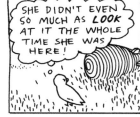

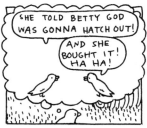

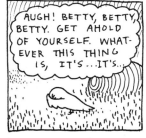

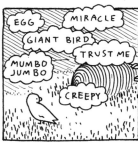

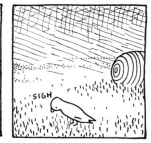

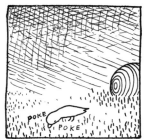

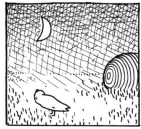

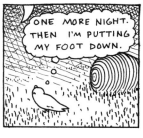

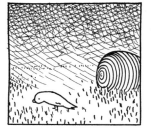

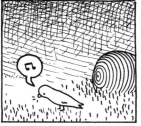

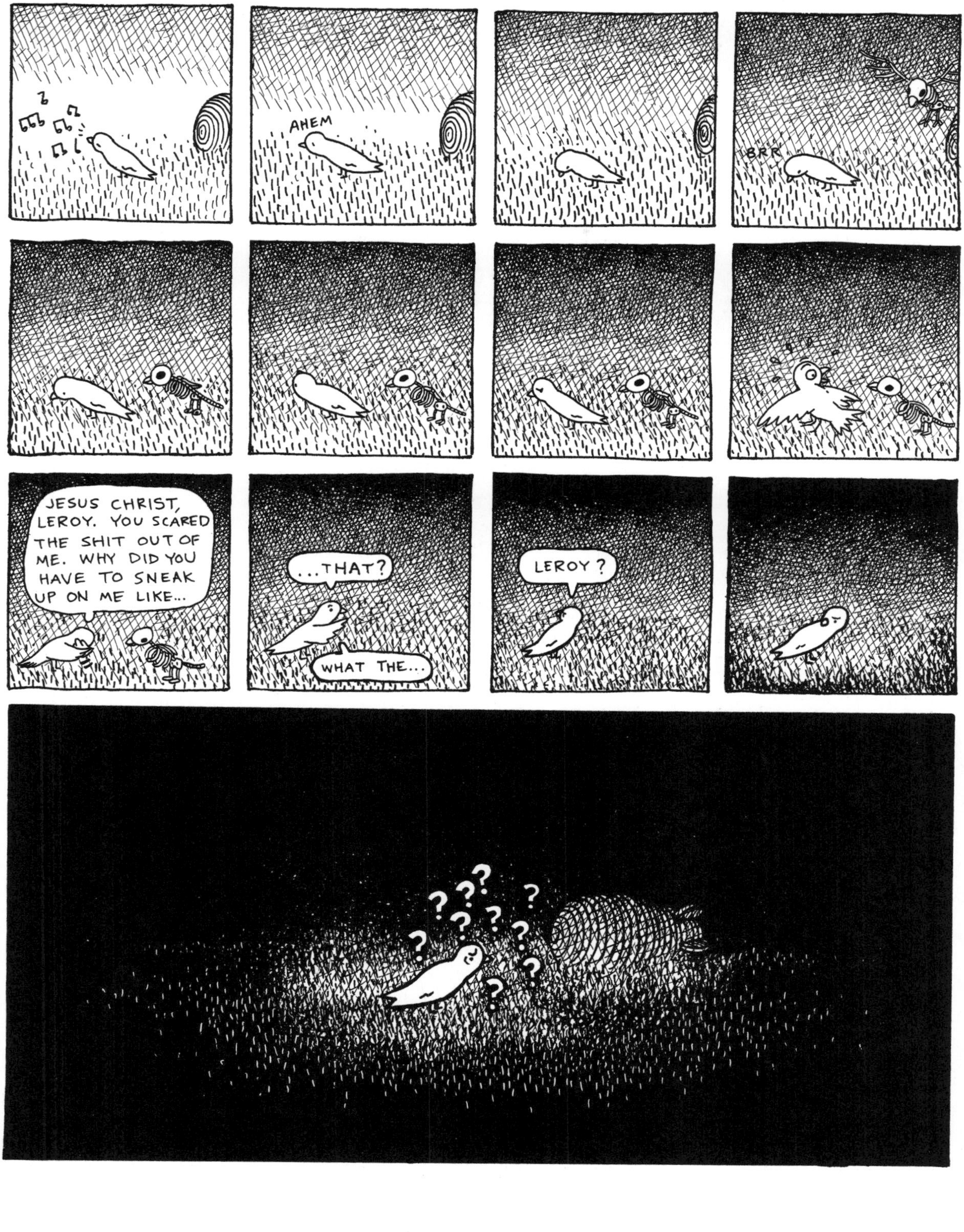
AHEM
BRR
JESUS CHRIST, LEROY. YOU SCARED THE SHIT OUT OF ME. WHY DID YOU HAVE TO SNEAK UP ON ME LIKE...
...THAT?
WHAT THE...
LEROY?

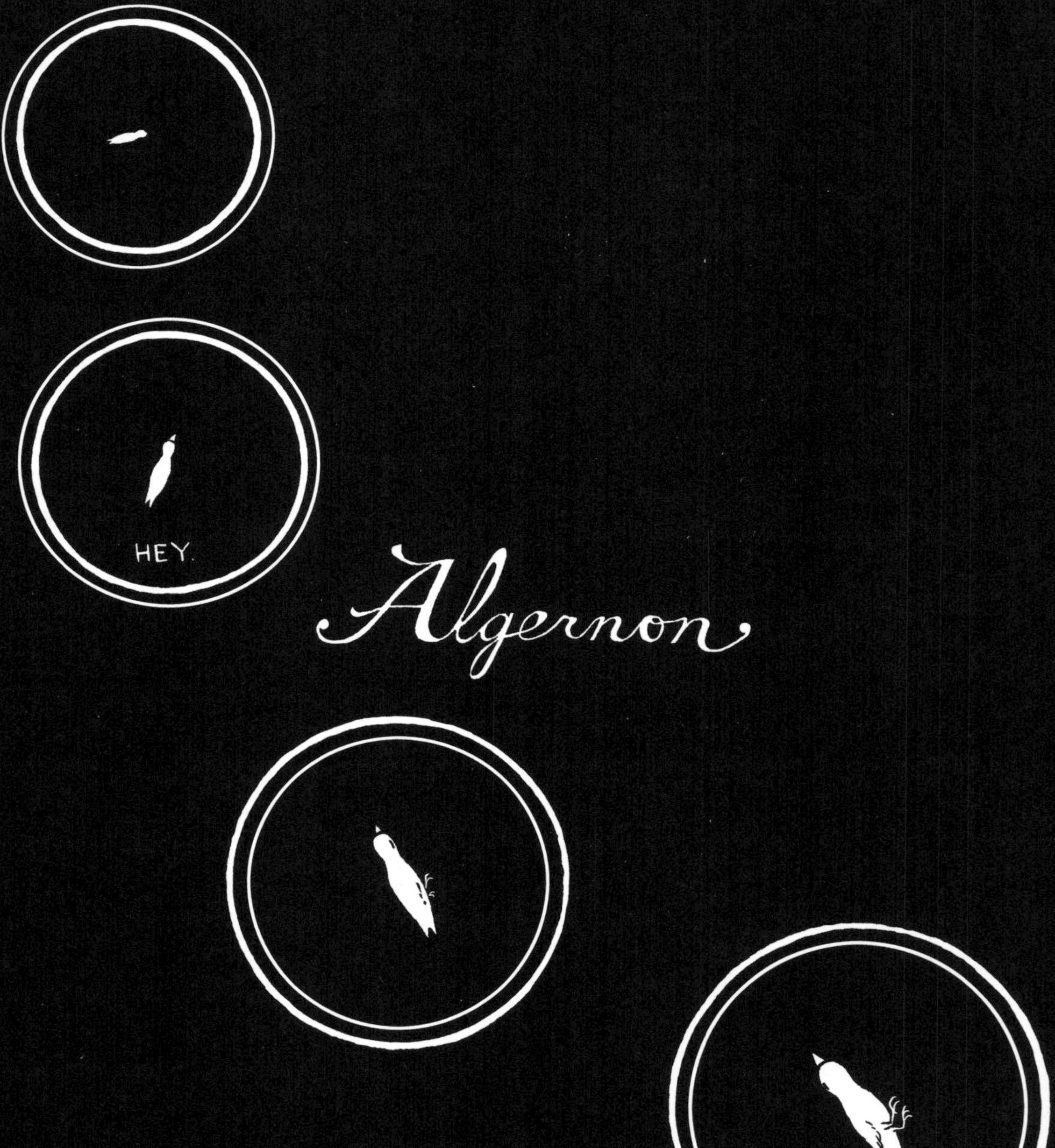
HEY.
Algernon
LOOK.

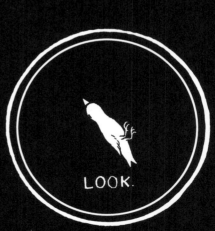

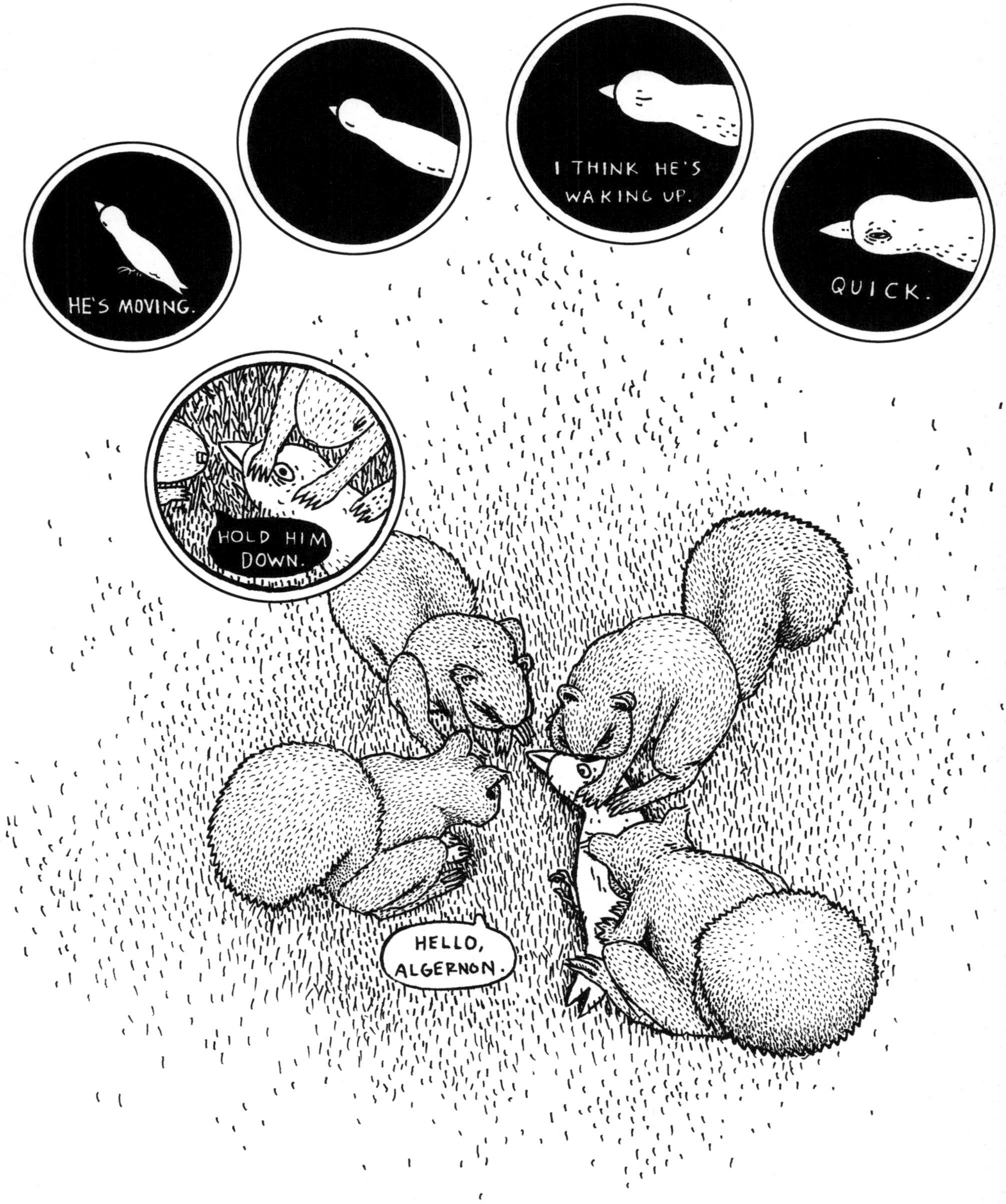
HE'S MOVING.
I THINK HE'S WAKING UP.
QUICK.
HOLD HIM DOWN.
HELLO, ALGERNON.

H...HI, EMMA.

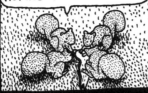

WE'RE SORRY TO HAVE TO **INCONVENIENCE** YOU LIKE THIS, ALGERNON, BUT WE SEEM TO HAVE A **PROBLEM** AND WE WERE HOPING YOU WOULD **HELP**.

YOU'VE PROBABLY NOTICED THAT THE TREE IS GONE. OUR ENTIRE STOCK OF **NUTS** WAS IN THAT TREE.

I.... YES, YES, YOU KNOW THIS. THEREIN LIES OUR PROBLEM.

YOU SEE, YOU AND THELMA WERE THE ONLY ONES WHO KNEW THIS.

WHICH MAKES YOU OUR PRIMARY SUSPECTS.

BUT, EMMA, WE'VE BEEN NEIGHBORS FOR...FOR..

YES, AND I LIKE YOU, ALGERNON. THAT'S WHY I'M GIVING YOU A CHANCE.

TELL US WHERE THE NUTS ARE AND WE'LL LET YOU GO.

EMMA, I...I SWEAR I DON'T KNOW ANY MORE THAN YOU...

DON'T LIE, ALGERNON. IT DOESN'T BECOME YOU.

BUT I...

WHACK **LOOK, BIRD, IT'S A SIMPLE QUESTION: WHAT DID YOU DO WITH OUR NUTS ?!**

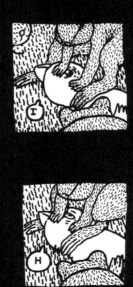

I

I

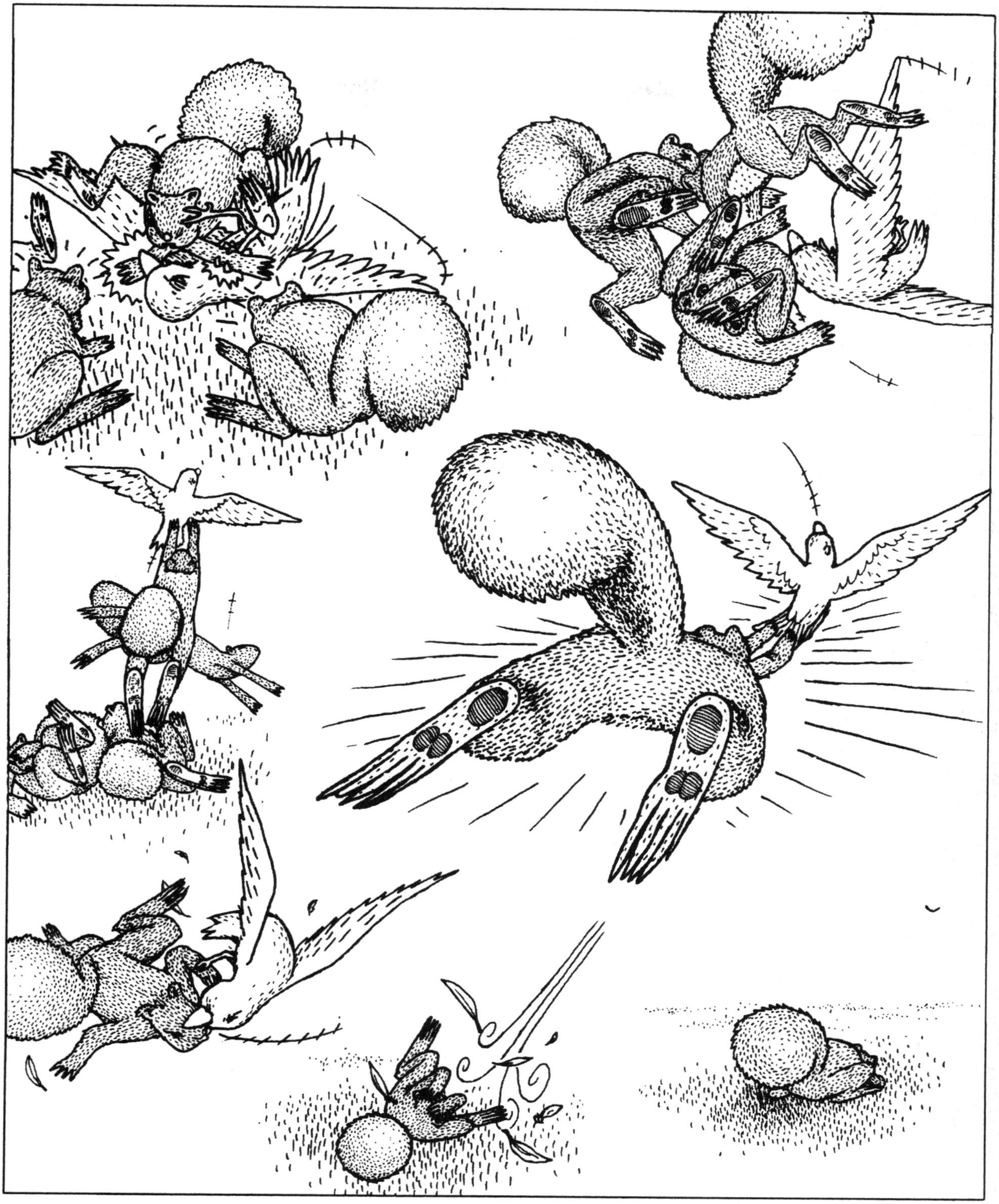

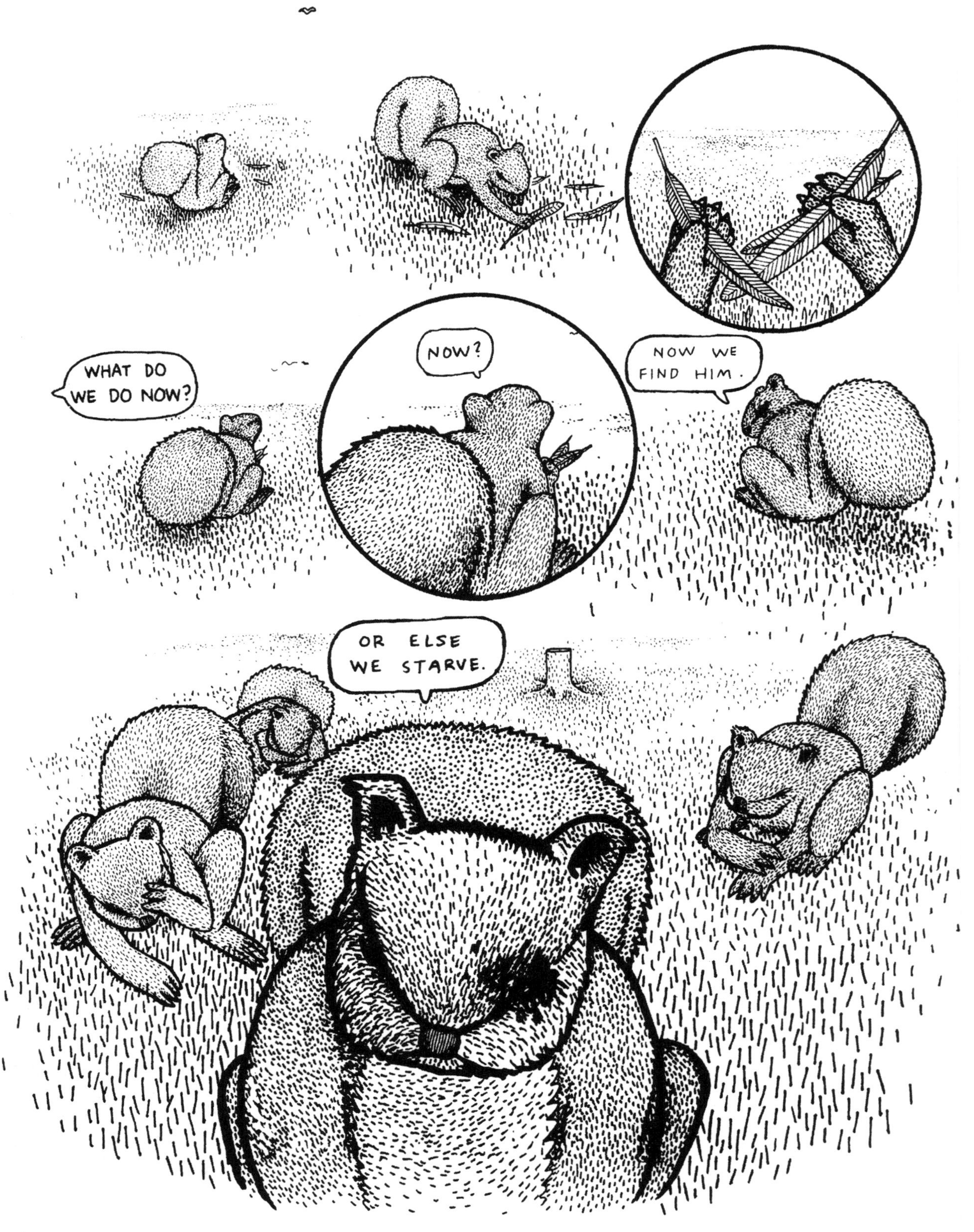
WHAT DO WE DO NOW?
NOW?
NOW WE FIND HIM.
OR ELSE WE STARVE.

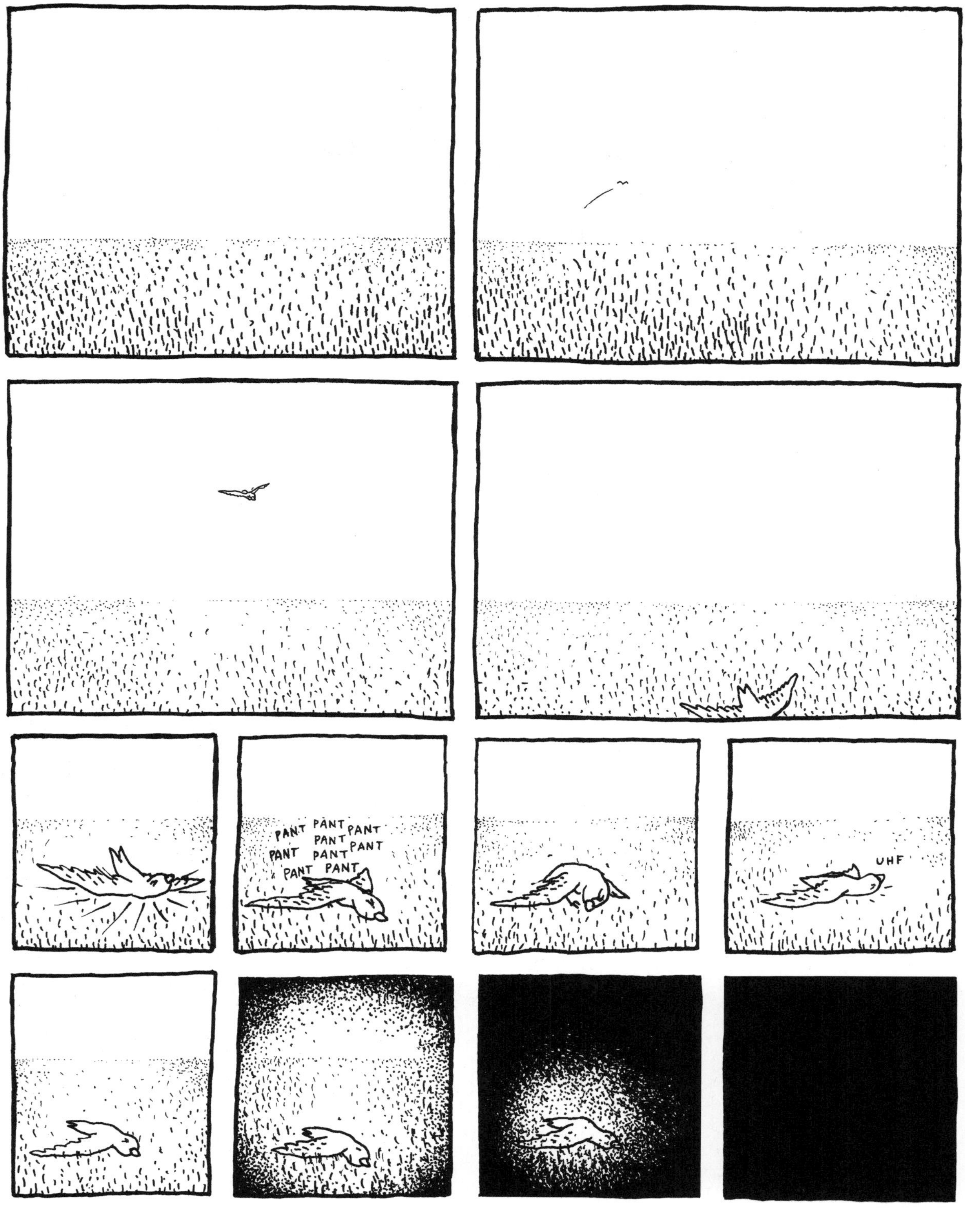
PANT PANT PANT
PANT PANT
PANT PANT PANT
PANT PANT
UHF

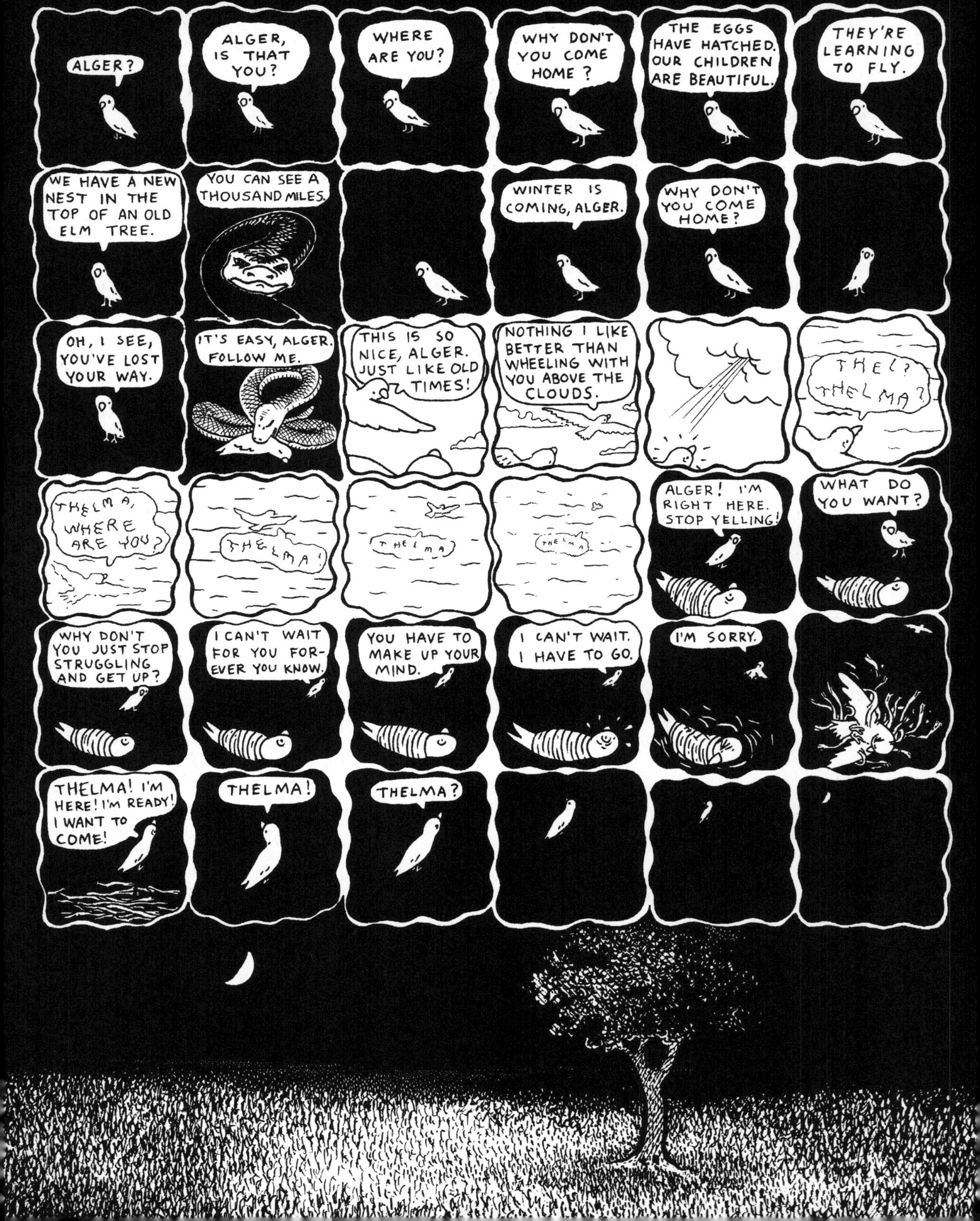
ALGER?
ALGER, IS THAT YOU?
WHERE ARE YOU?
WHY DON'T YOU COME HOME?
THE EGGS HAVE HATCHED. OUR CHILDREN ARE BEAUTIFUL.
THEY'RE LEARNING TO FLY.
WE HAVE A NEW NEST IN THE TOP OF AN OLD ELM TREE.
YOU CAN SEE A THOUSAND MILES.
WINTER IS COMING, ALGER.
WHY DON'T YOU COME HOME?
OH, I SEE, YOU'VE LOST YOUR WAY.
IT'S EASY, ALGER. FOLLOW ME.
THIS IS SO NICE, ALGER. JUST LIKE OLD TIMES!
NOTHING I LIKE BETTER THAN WHEELING WITH YOU ABOVE THE CLOUDS.
THEL? THELMA?
THELMA, WHERE ARE YOU?
THELMA!
THELMA
THELMA
ALGER! I'M RIGHT HERE. STOP YELLING!
WHAT DO YOU WANT?
WHY DON'T YOU JUST STOP STRUGGLING AND GET UP?
I CAN'T WAIT FOR YOU FOREVER YOU KNOW.
YOU HAVE TO MAKE UP YOUR MIND.
I CAN'T WAIT. I HAVE TO GO.
I'M SORRY.
THELMA! I'M HERE! I'M READY! I WANT TO COME!
THELMA!
THELMA?

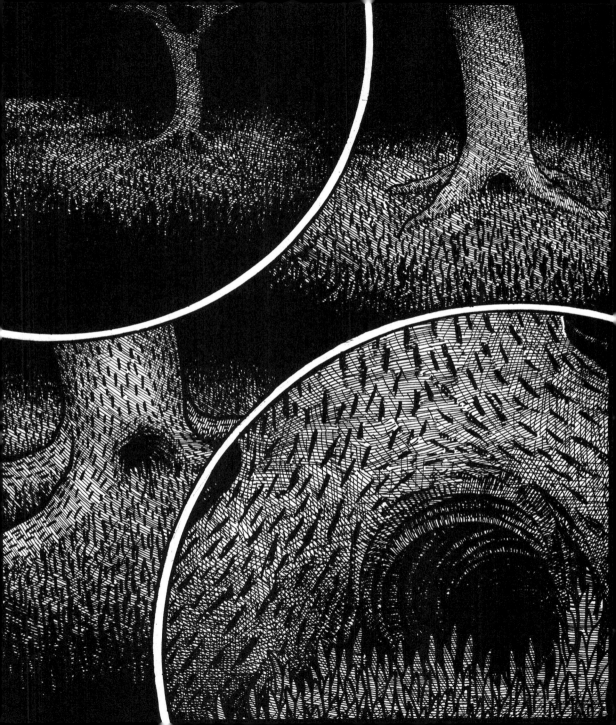

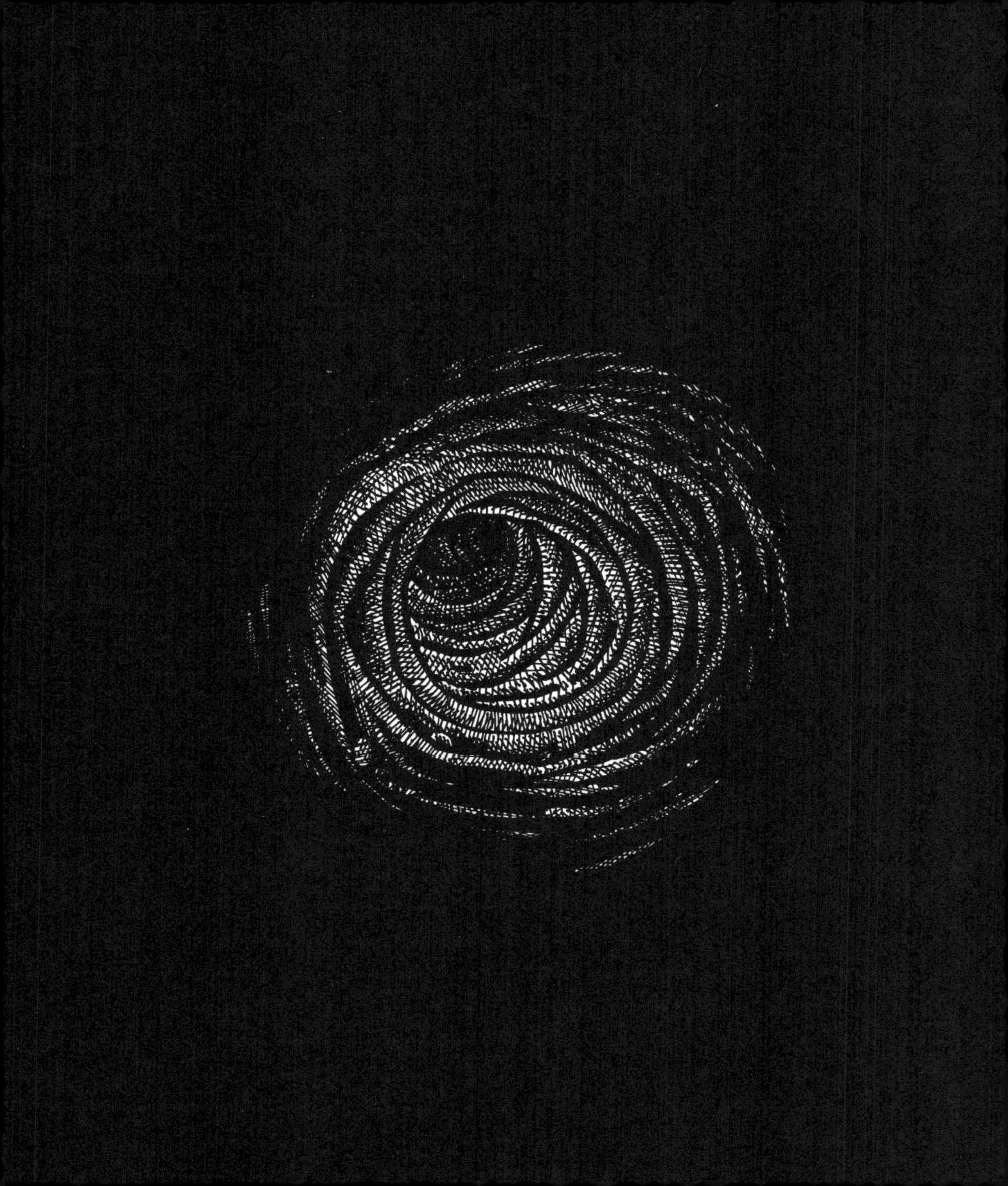

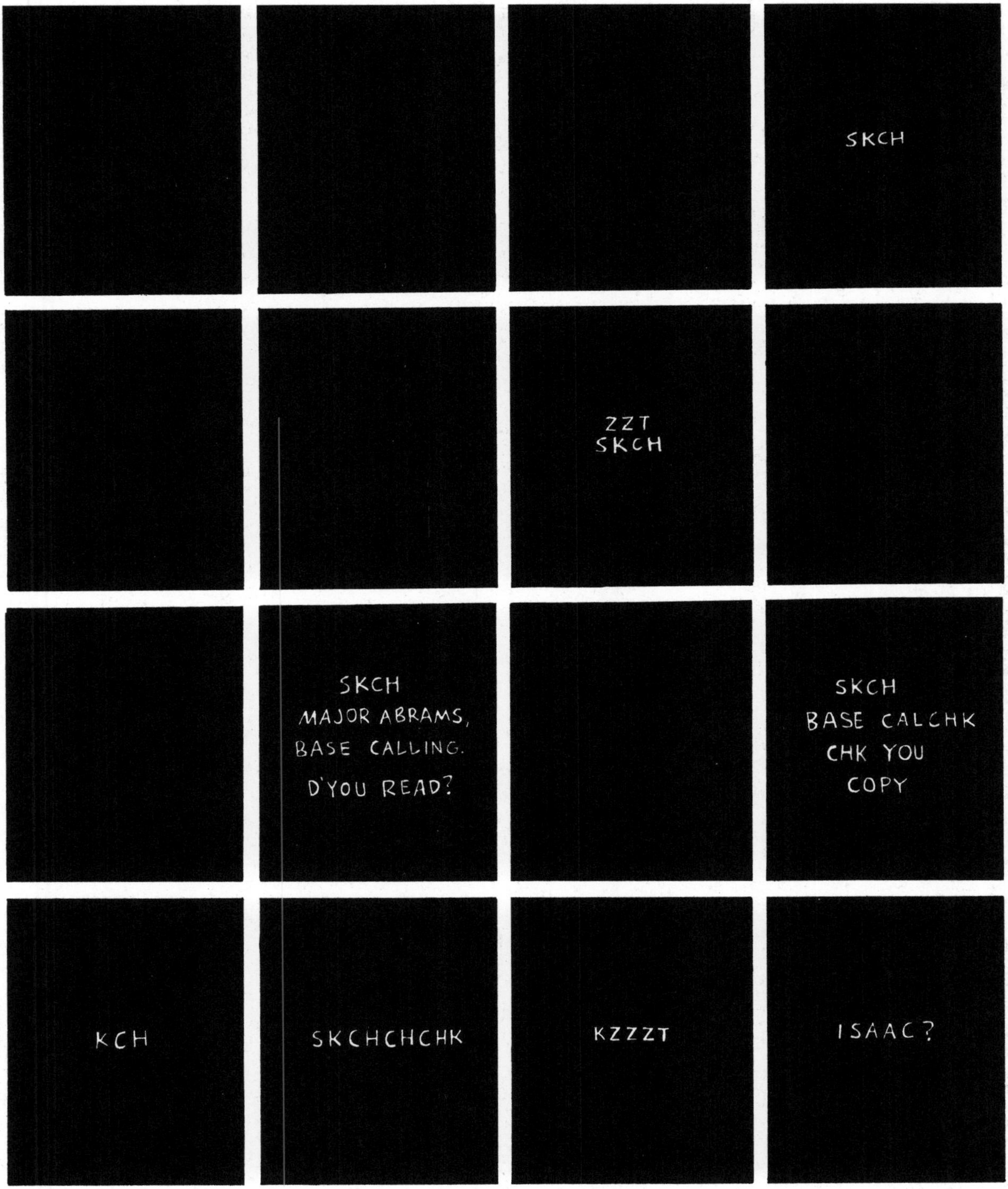
SKCH
ZZT
SKCH
SKCH
MAJOR ABRAMS, BASE CALLING.
D'YOU READ?
SKCH
BASE CALCHK
CHK YOU
COPY
KCH
SKCHCHCHK
KZZZT
ISAAC?

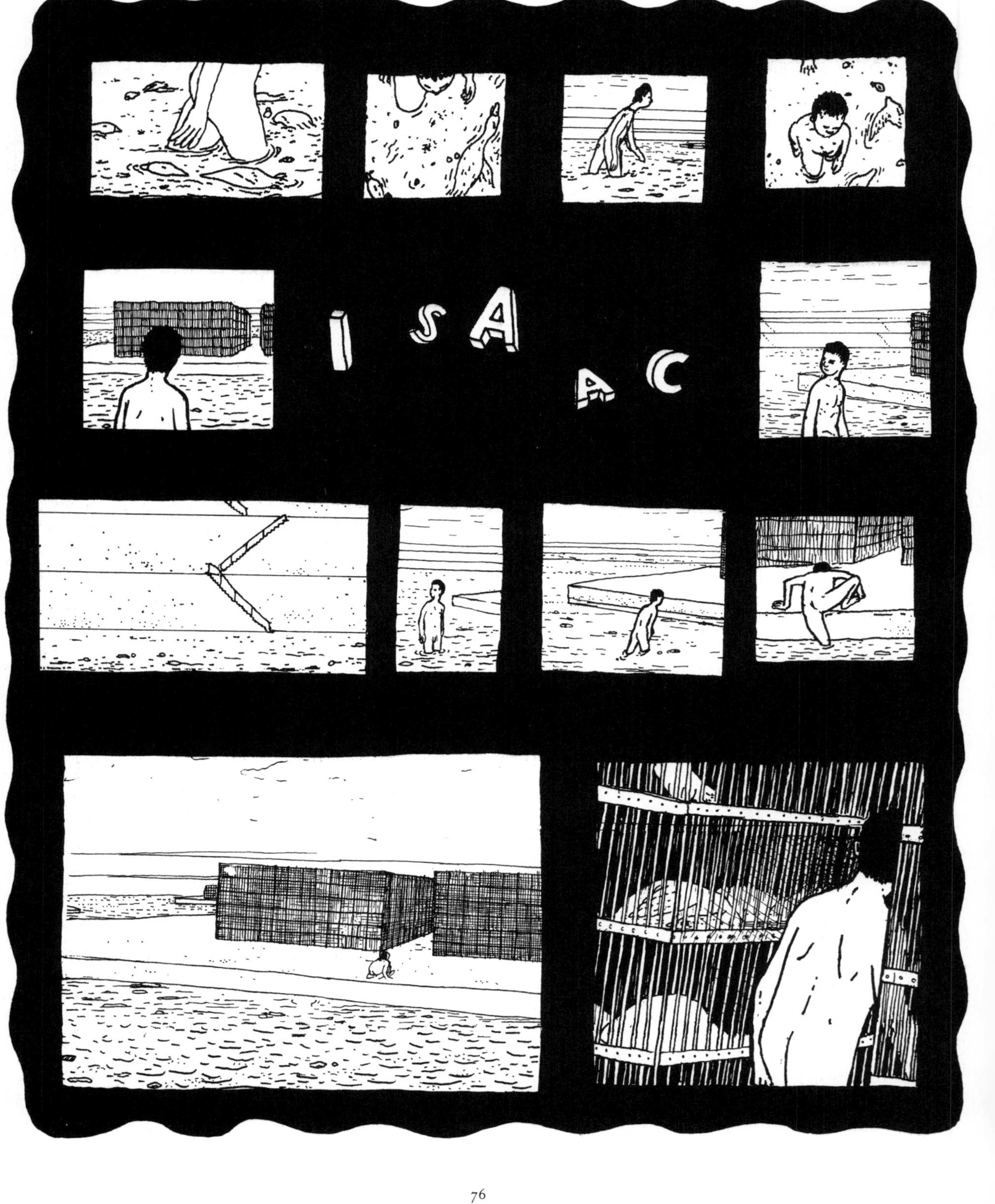
ISA
AC

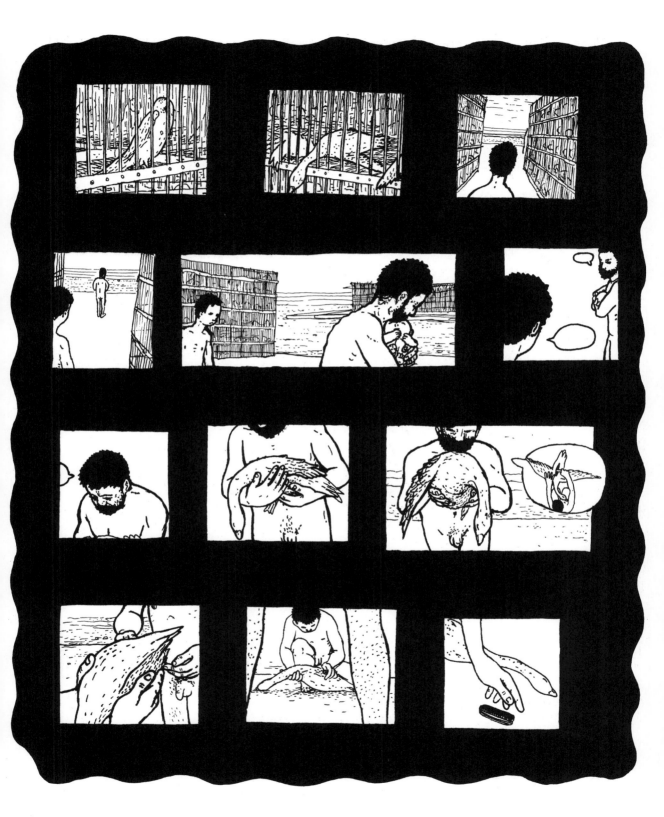

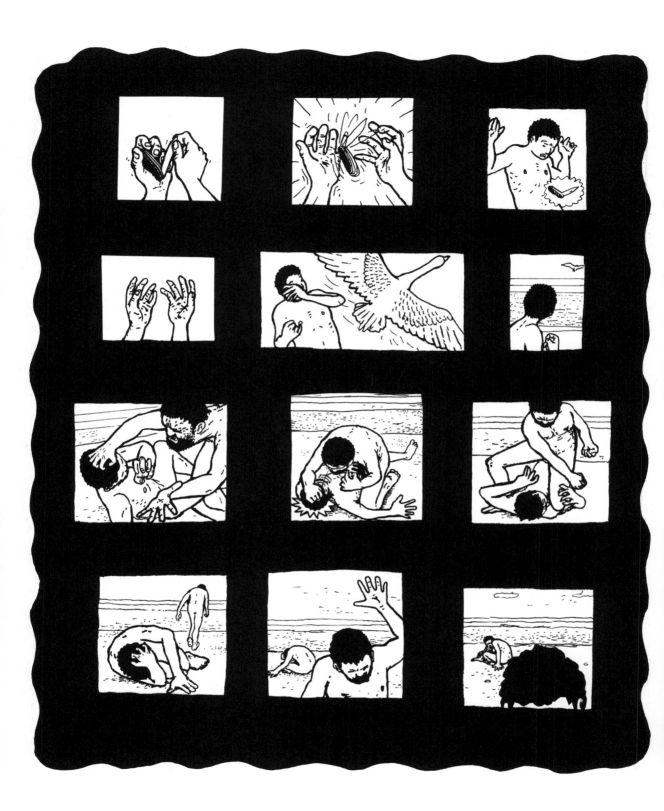

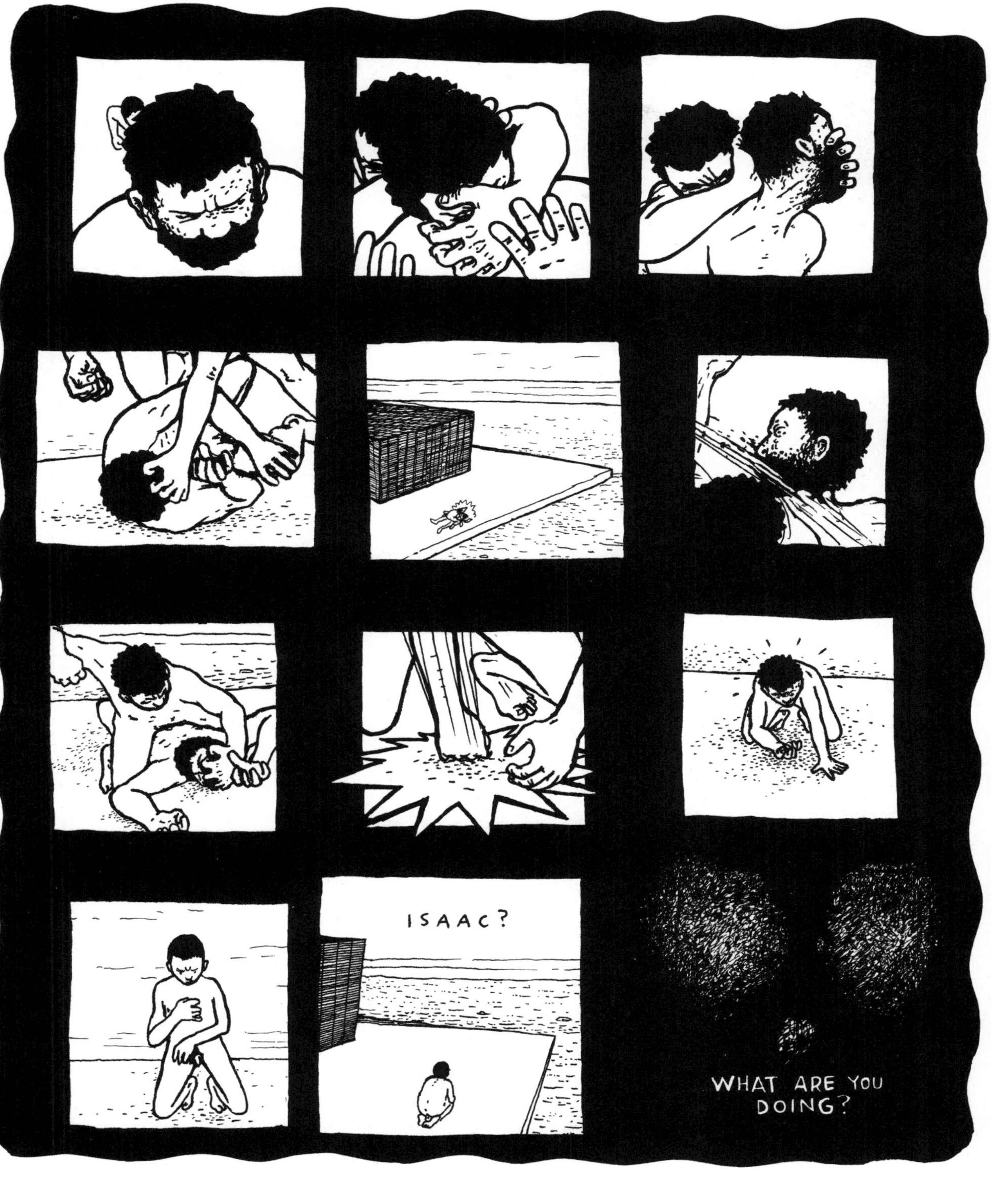
ISAAC?
WHAT ARE YOU DOING?

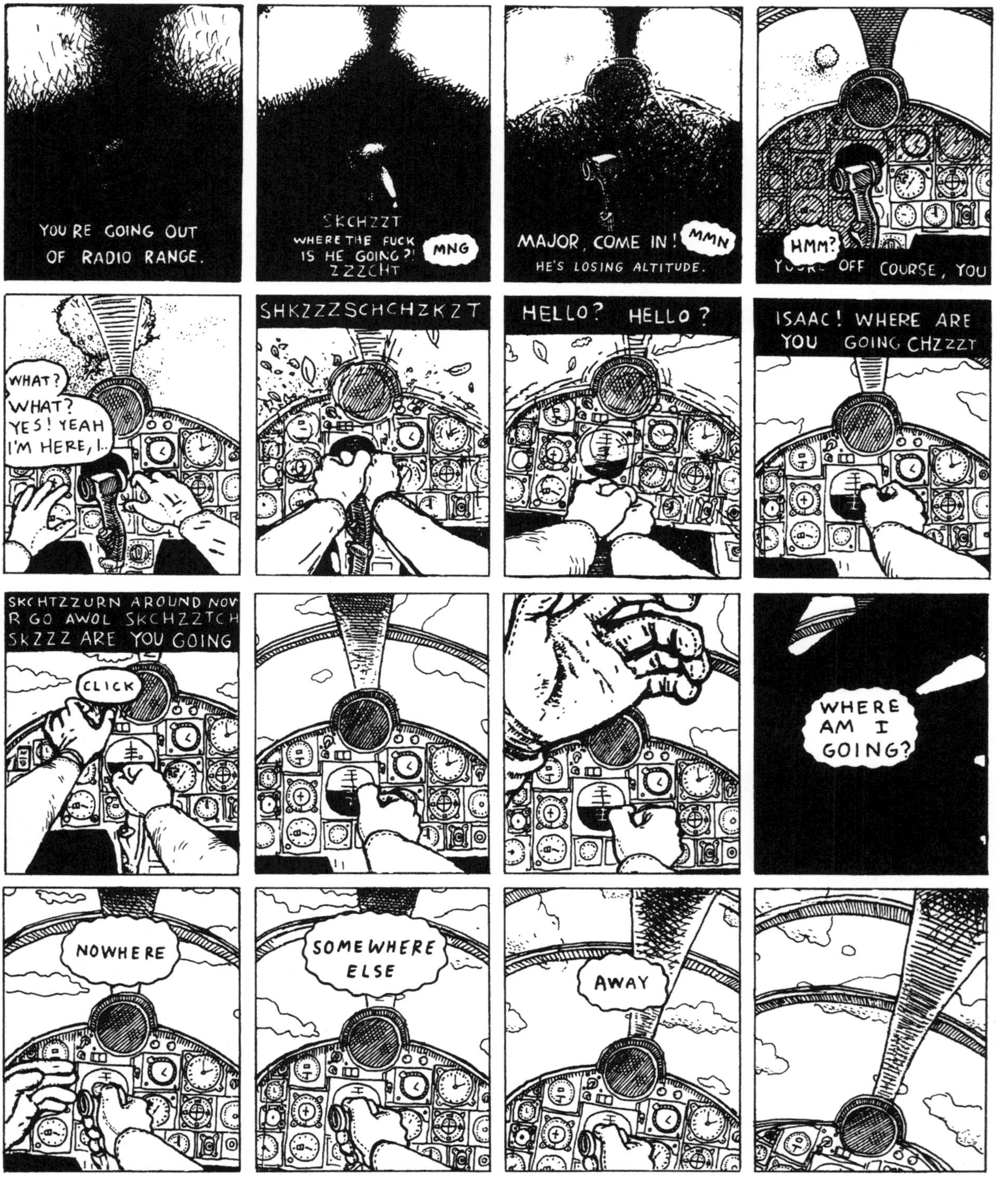
YOU'RE GOING OUT OF RADIO RANGE.
SKCHZZT WHERE THE FUCK IS HE GOING?! ZZZCHT
MNG
MAJOR, COME IN!
MMN
HE'S LOSING ALTITUDE.
HMM?
OFF COURSE, YOU
WHAT?
WHAT? YES! YEAH I'M HERE, I..
SHKZZZSCHCHZKZT
HELLO? HELLO?
ISAAC! WHERE ARE YOU GOING CHZzzT
SKCHTZZURN AROUND NOW R GO AWOL SKCHZZTCH SKZZZ ARE YOU GOING
CLICK
WHERE AM I GOING?
NOWHERE
SOMEWHERE ELSE
AWAY

Betty Visits Louis and Morris

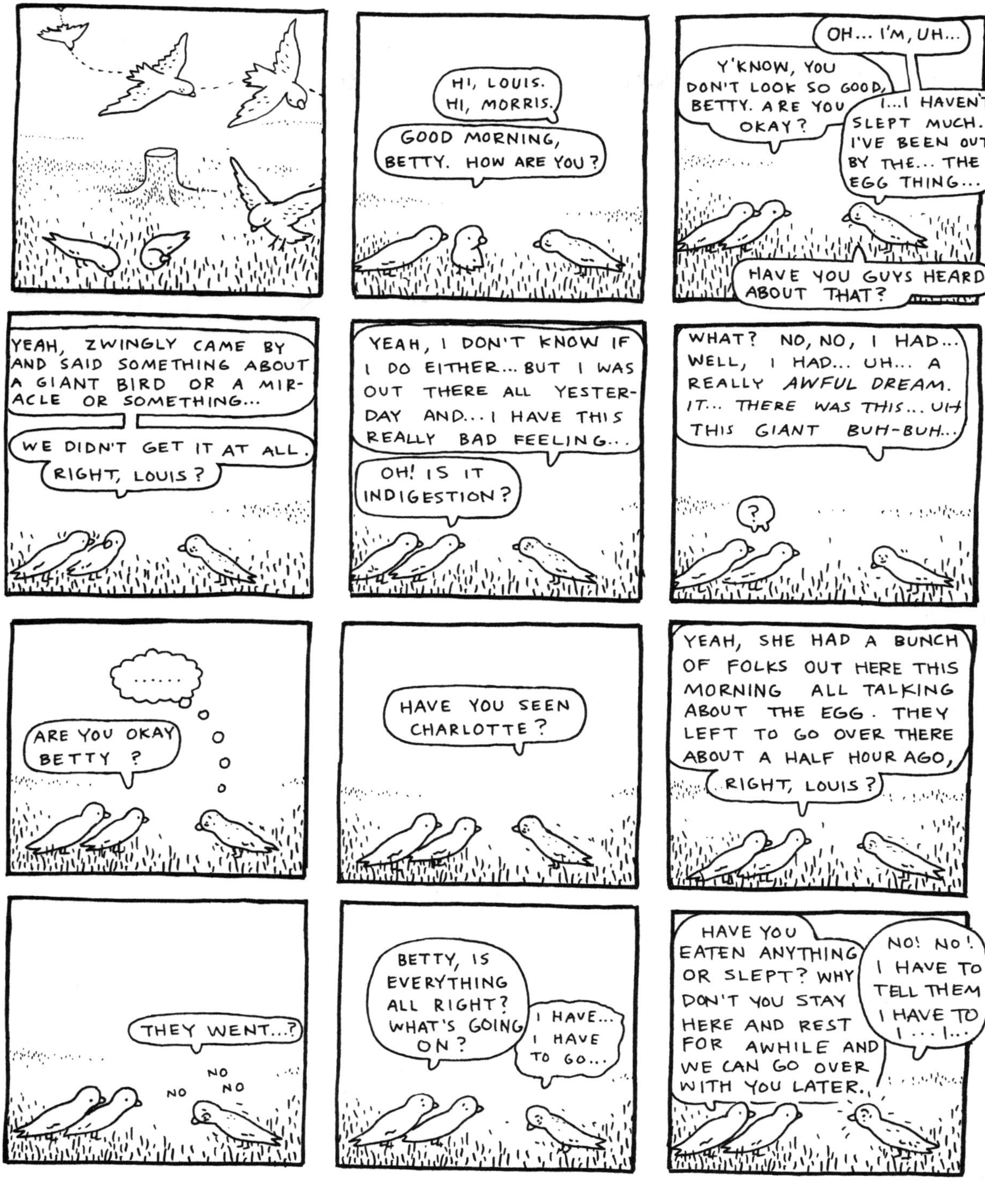

HI, LOUIS. HI, MORRIS.
GOOD MORNING, BETTY. HOW ARE YOU?
OH... I'M, UH...
Y'KNOW, YOU DON'T LOOK SO GOOD, BETTY. ARE YOU OKAY?
I...I HAVEN'T SLEPT MUCH. I'VE BEEN OUT BY THE... THE EGG THING...
HAVE YOU GUYS HEARD ABOUT THAT?
YEAH, ZWINGLY CAME BY AND SAID SOMETHING ABOUT A GIANT BIRD OR A MIRACLE OR SOMETHING...
WE DIDN'T GET IT AT ALL. RIGHT, LOUIS?
YEAH, I DON'T KNOW IF I DO EITHER... BUT I WAS OUT THERE ALL YESTERDAY AND... I HAVE THIS REALLY BAD FEELING...
OH! IS IT INDIGESTION?
WHAT? NO, NO, I HAD... WELL, I HAD... UH... A REALLY *AWFUL DREAM*. IT... THERE WAS THIS... UH THIS GIANT BUH-BUH...
?
......
ARE YOU OKAY BETTY ?
HAVE YOU SEEN CHARLOTTE?
YEAH, SHE HAD A BUNCH OF FOLKS OUT HERE THIS MORNING ALL TALKING ABOUT THE EGG. THEY LEFT TO GO OVER THERE ABOUT A HALF HOUR AGO,
RIGHT, LOUIS?
THEY WENT...?
NO NO NO
BETTY, IS EVERYTHING ALL RIGHT? WHAT'S GOING ON?
I HAVE... I HAVE TO GO...
HAVE YOU EATEN ANYTHING OR SLEPT? WHY DON'T YOU STAY HERE AND REST FOR AWHILE AND WE CAN GO OVER WITH YOU LATER.
NO! NO! I HAVE TO TELL THEM I HAVE TO I... I...

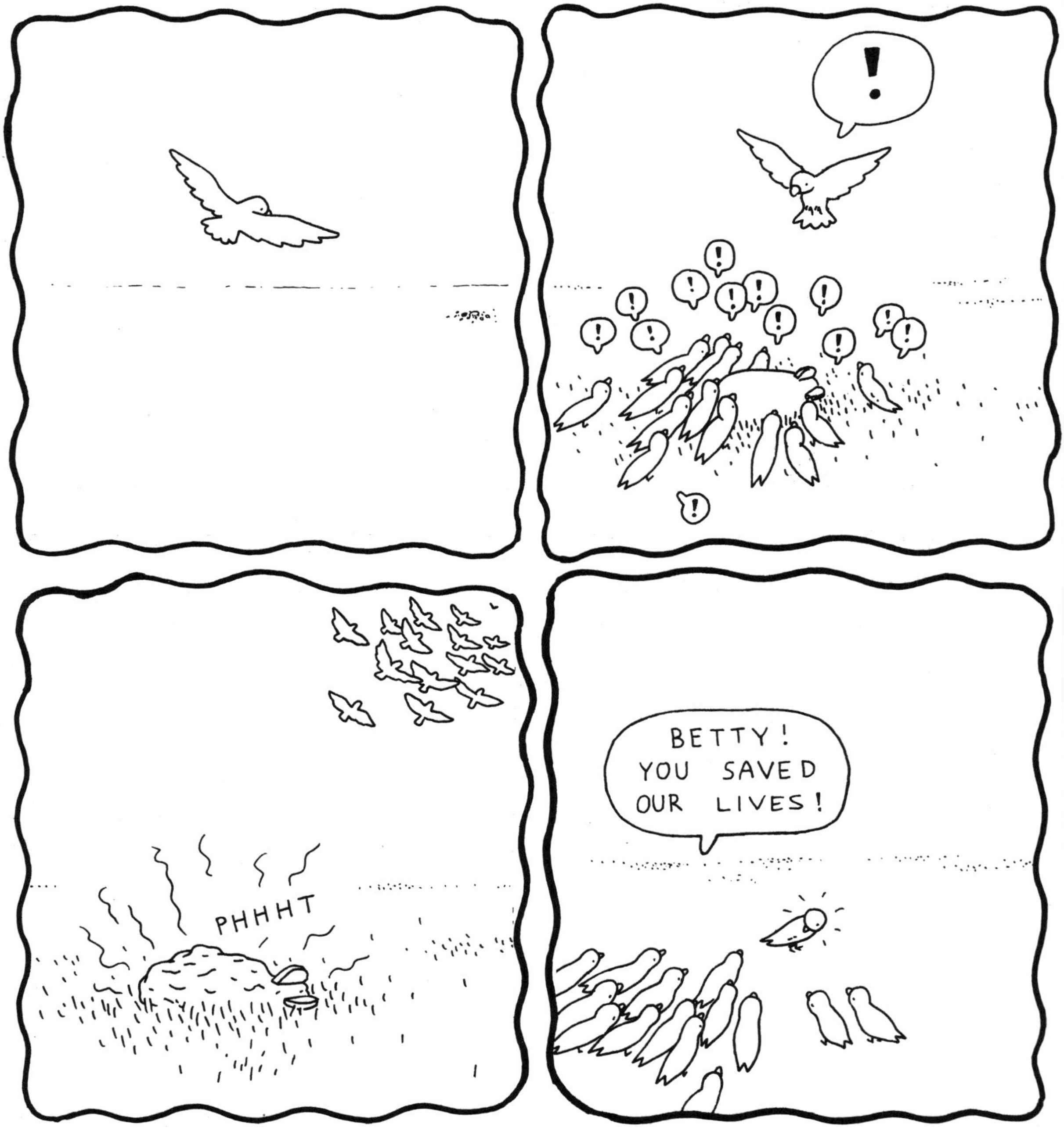
!
PHHHT
BETTY! YOU SAVED OUR LIVES!

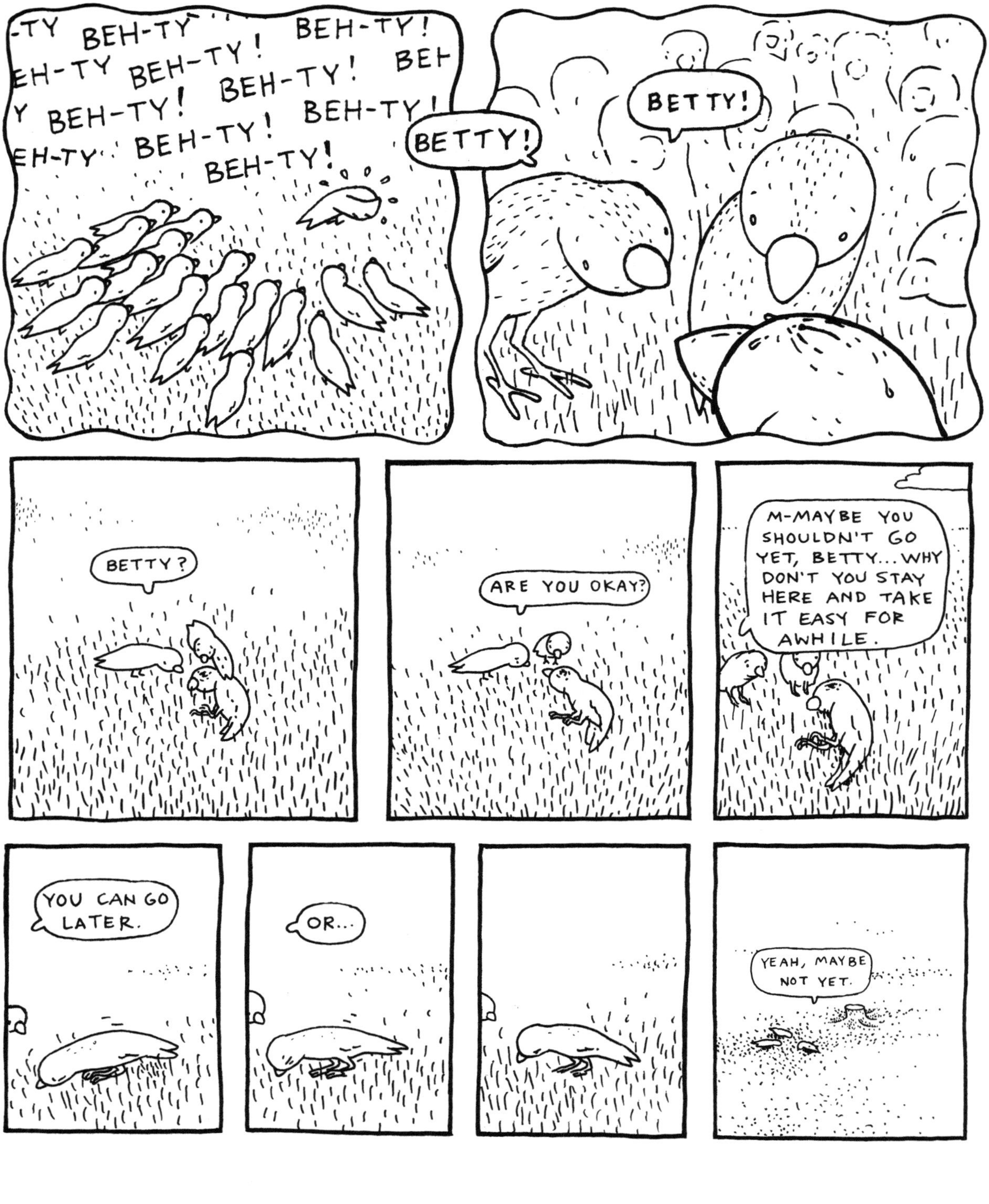
-TY BEH-TY BEH-TY!
EH-TY BEH-TY! BEH
Y BEH-TY! BEH-TY!
EH-TY BEH-TY! BEH-TY!
BEH-TY!
BETTY!
BETTY!
BETTY?
ARE YOU OKAY?
M-MAYBE YOU SHOULDN'T GO YET, BETTY... WHY DON'T YOU STAY HERE AND TAKE IT EASY FOR AWHILE.
YOU CAN GO LATER.
OR...
YEAH, MAYBE NOT YET.

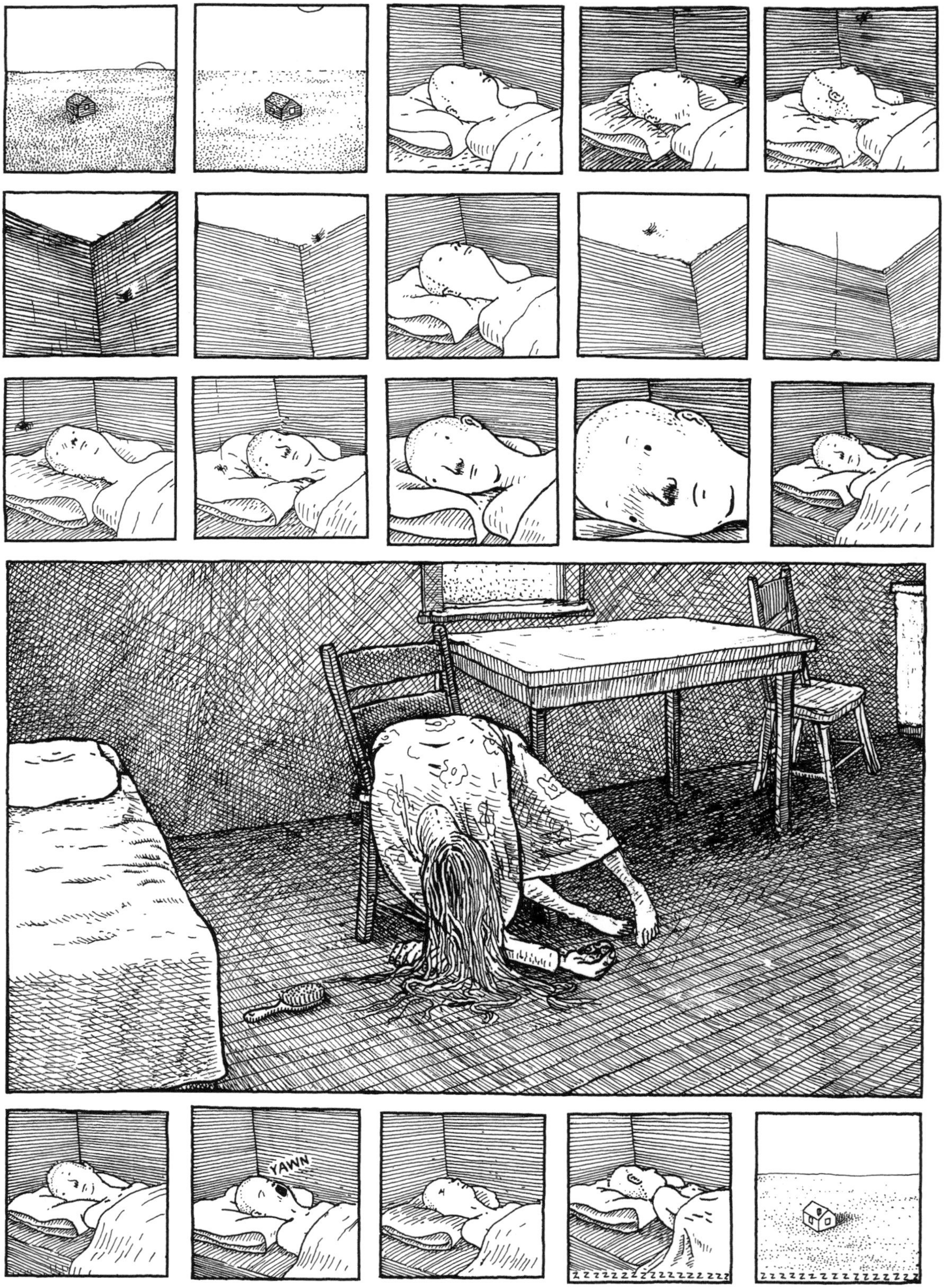
YAWN
zzzzzzzzzzzzzzzzzz
zzzzzzzzzzzzzzzzzz

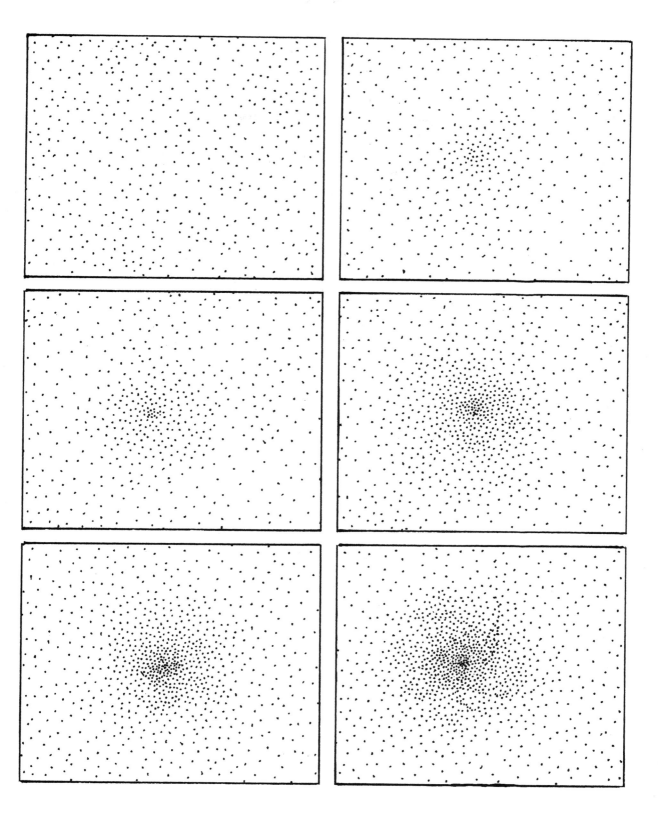

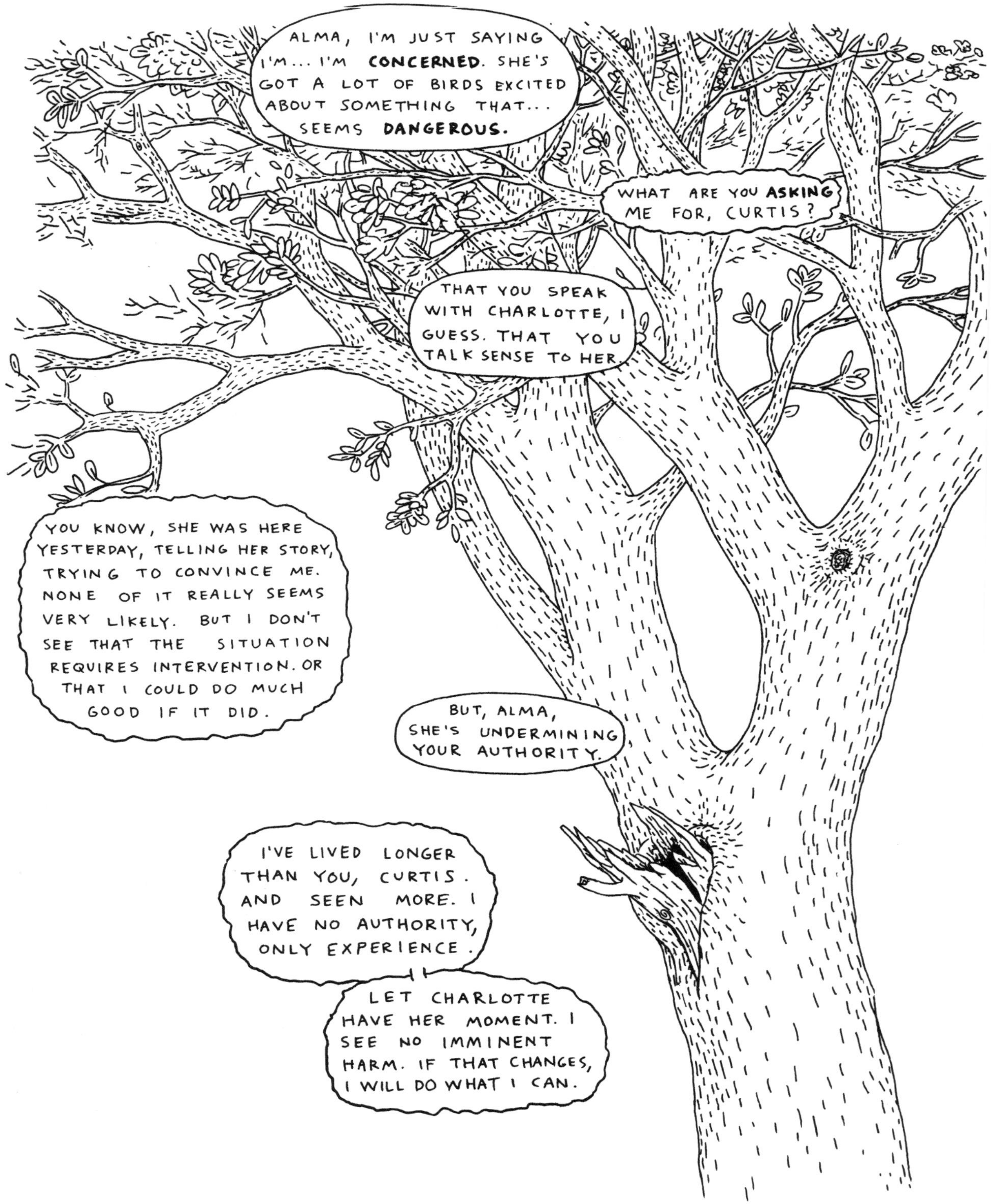
ALMA, I'M JUST SAYING I'M... I'M **CONCERNED**. SHE'S GOT A LOT OF BIRDS EXCITED ABOUT SOMETHING THAT... SEEMS **DANGEROUS**.
WHAT ARE YOU **ASKING** ME FOR, CURTIS?
THAT YOU SPEAK WITH CHARLOTTE, I GUESS. THAT YOU TALK SENSE TO HER.
YOU KNOW, SHE WAS HERE YESTERDAY, TELLING HER STORY, TRYING TO CONVINCE ME. NONE OF IT REALLY SEEMS VERY LIKELY. BUT I DON'T SEE THAT THE SITUATION REQUIRES INTERVENTION. OR THAT I COULD DO MUCH GOOD IF IT DID.
BUT, ALMA, SHE'S UNDERMINING YOUR AUTHORITY.
I'VE LIVED LONGER THAN YOU, CURTIS. AND SEEN MORE. I HAVE NO AUTHORITY, ONLY EXPERIENCE.
LET CHARLOTTE HAVE HER MOMENT. I SEE NO IMMINENT HARM. IF THAT CHANGES, I WILL DO WHAT I CAN.

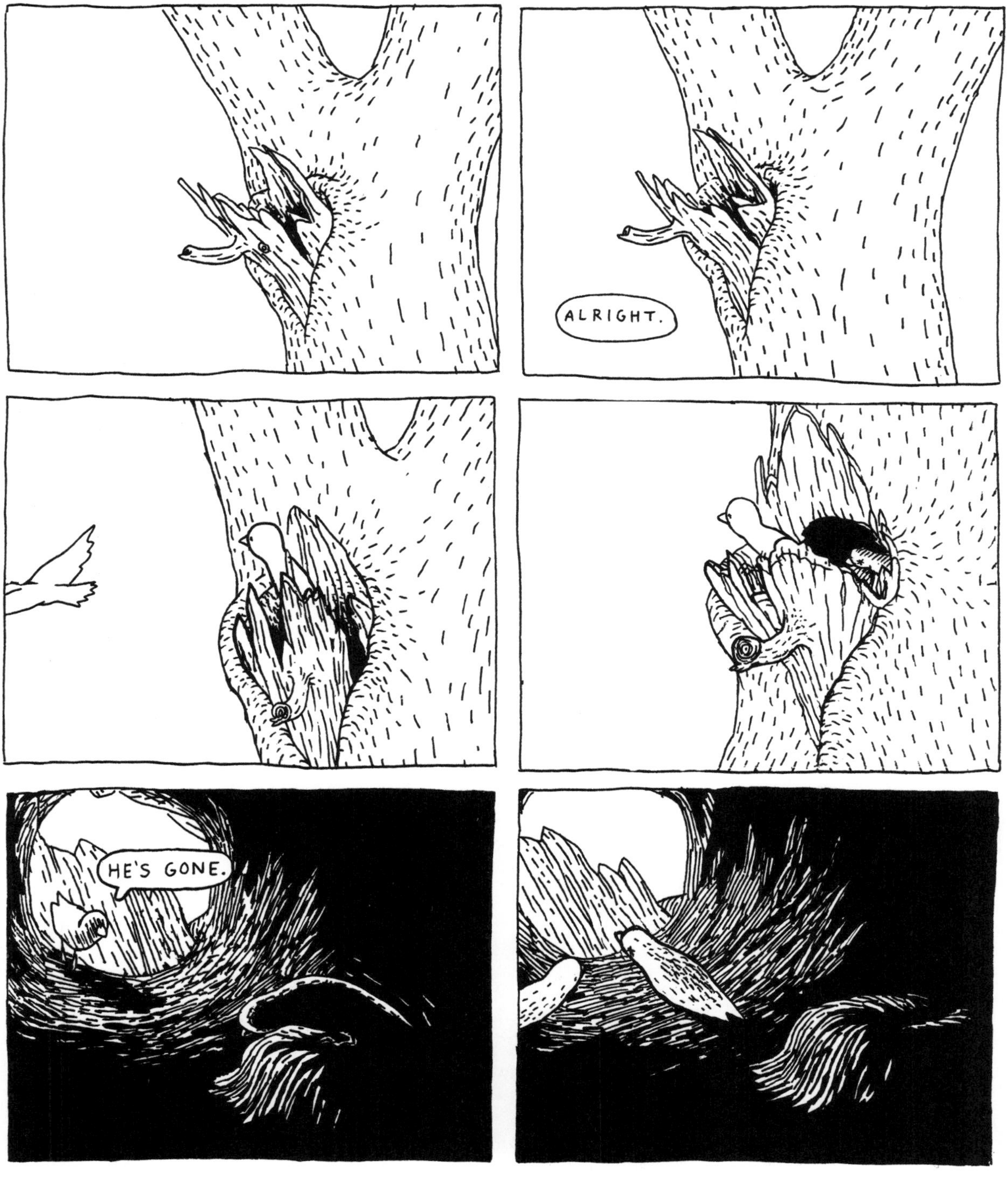
ALRIGHT.
HE'S GONE.

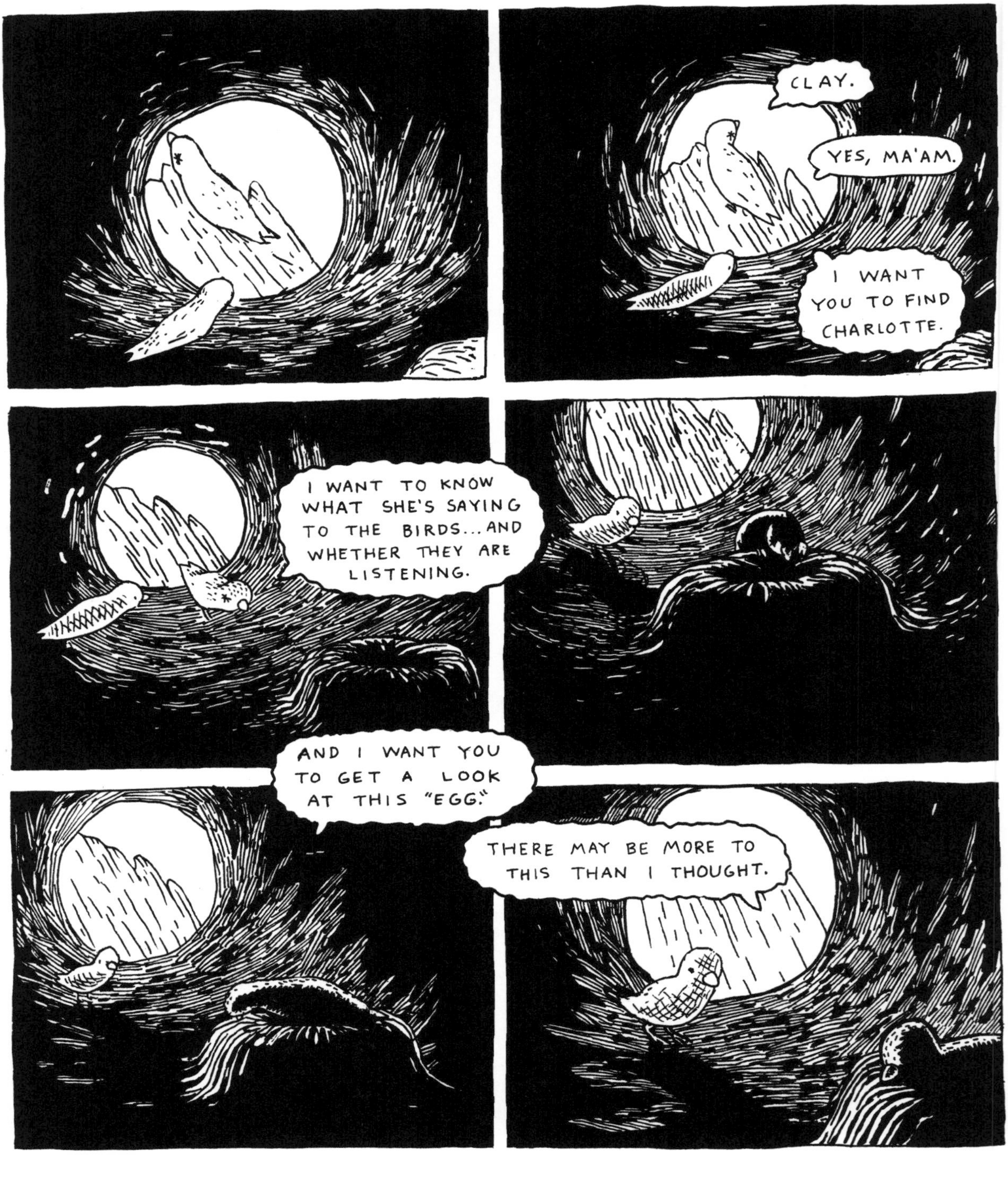
CLAY.
YES, MA'AM.
I WANT YOU TO FIND CHARLOTTE.
I WANT TO KNOW WHAT SHE'S SAYING TO THE BIRDS... AND WHETHER THEY ARE LISTENING.
AND I WANT YOU TO GET A LOOK AT THIS "EGG."
THERE MAY BE MORE TO THIS THAN I THOUGHT.

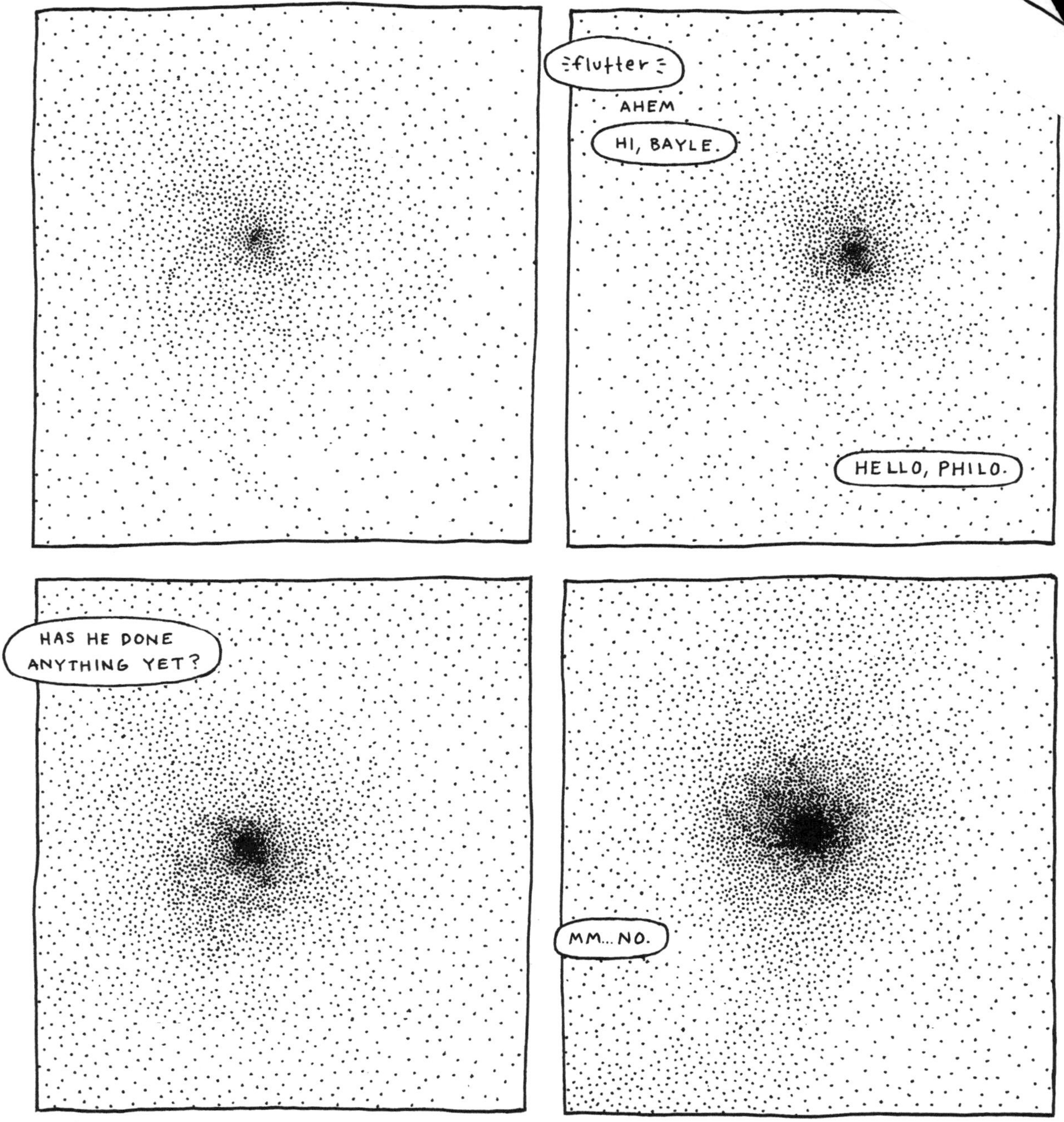
flutter
AHEM
HI, BAYLE.
HELLO, PHILO.
HAS HE DONE ANYTHING YET?
MM... NO.

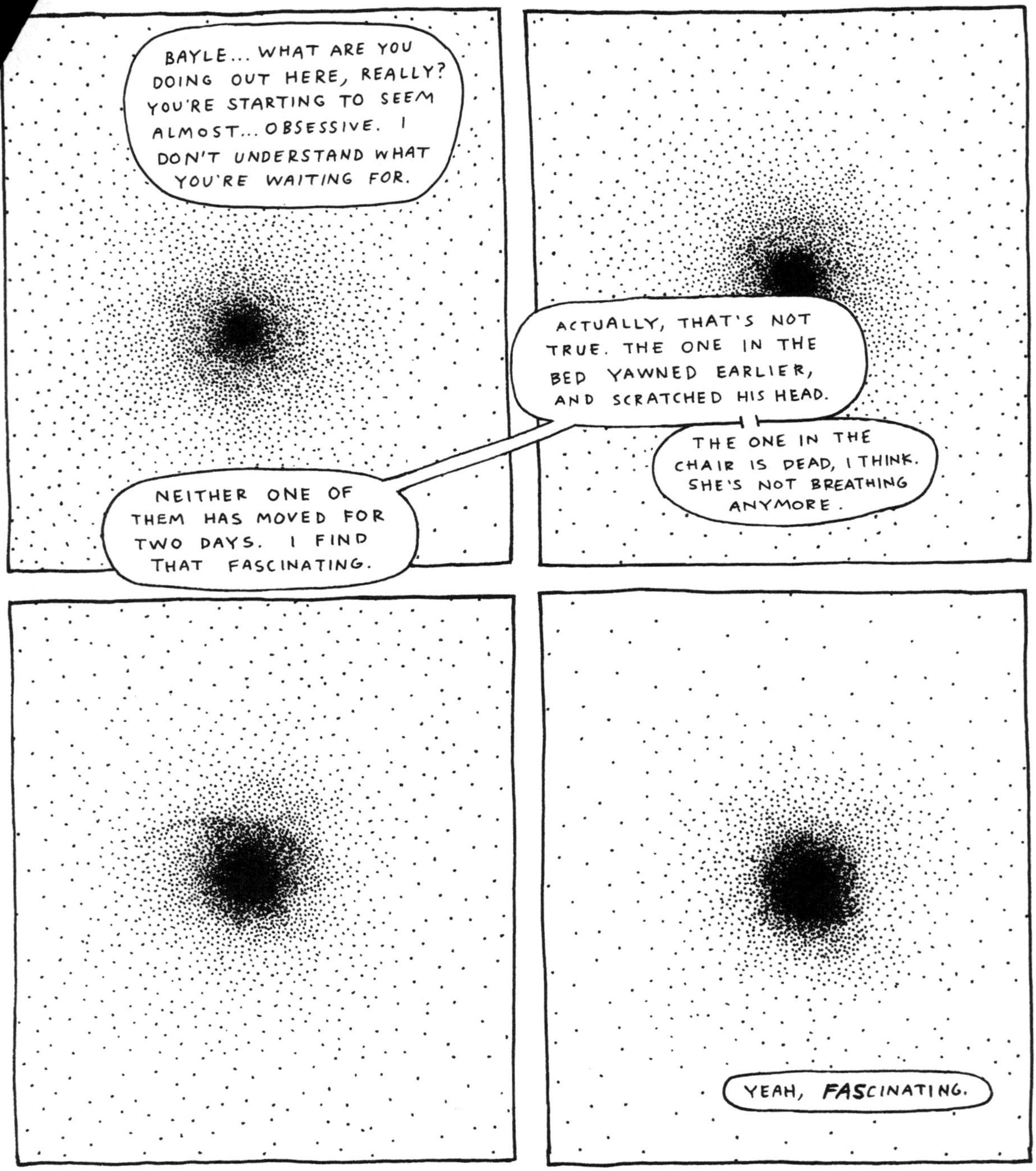
BAYLE... WHAT ARE YOU DOING OUT HERE, REALLY? YOU'RE STARTING TO SEEM ALMOST... OBSESSIVE. I DON'T UNDERSTAND WHAT YOU'RE WAITING FOR.
NEITHER ONE OF THEM HAS MOVED FOR TWO DAYS. I FIND THAT FASCINATING.
ACTUALLY, THAT'S NOT TRUE. THE ONE IN THE BED YAWNED EARLIER, AND SCRATCHED HIS HEAD.
THE ONE IN THE CHAIR IS DEAD, I THINK. SHE'S NOT BREATHING ANYMORE.
YEAH, **FAS**CINATING.

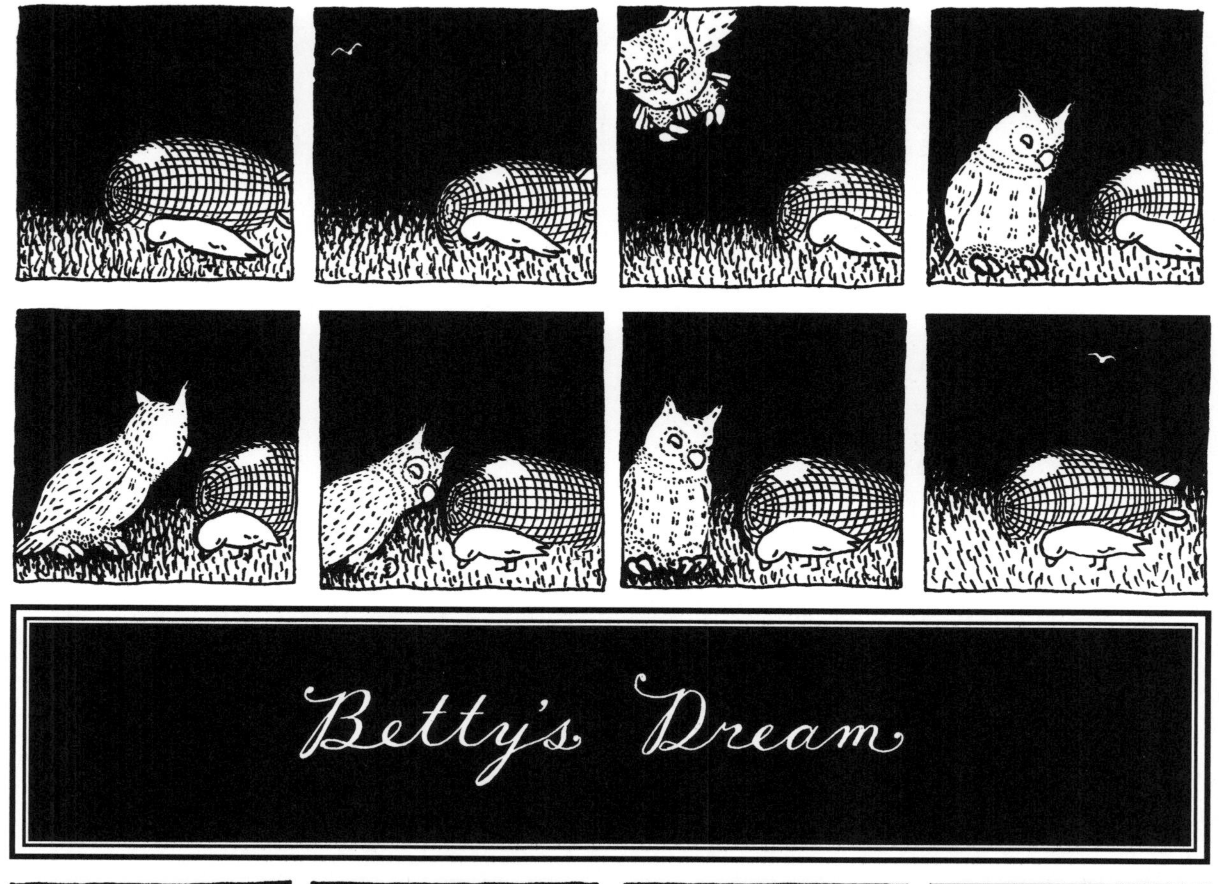

Betty's Dream

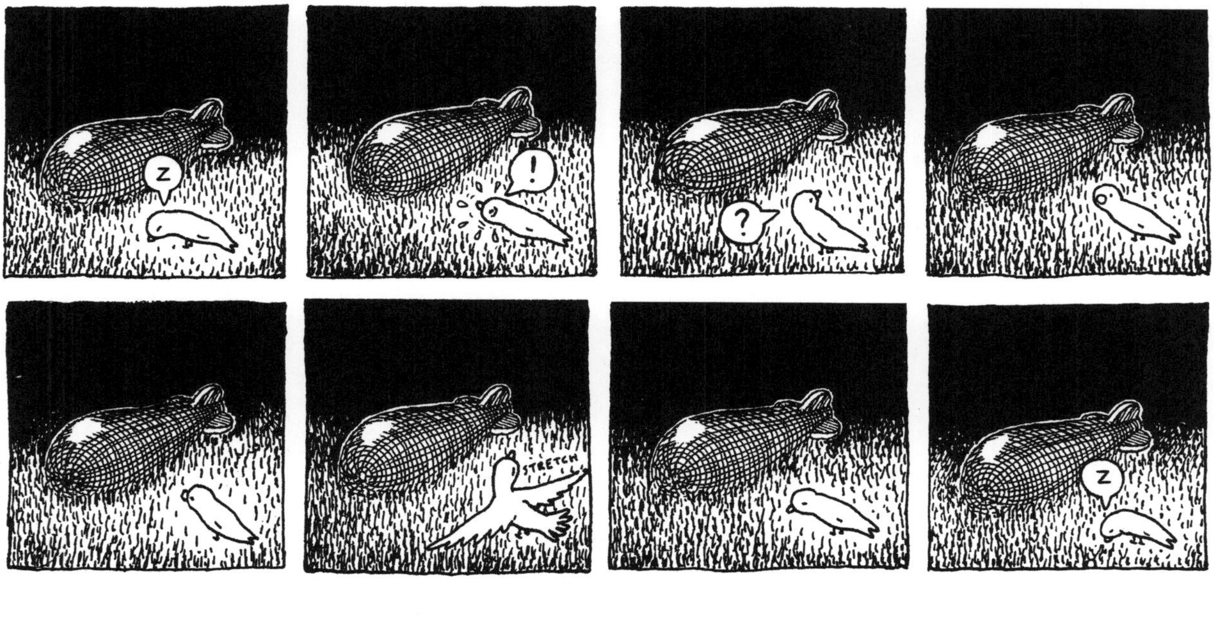
Z
!
?
STRETCH
Z

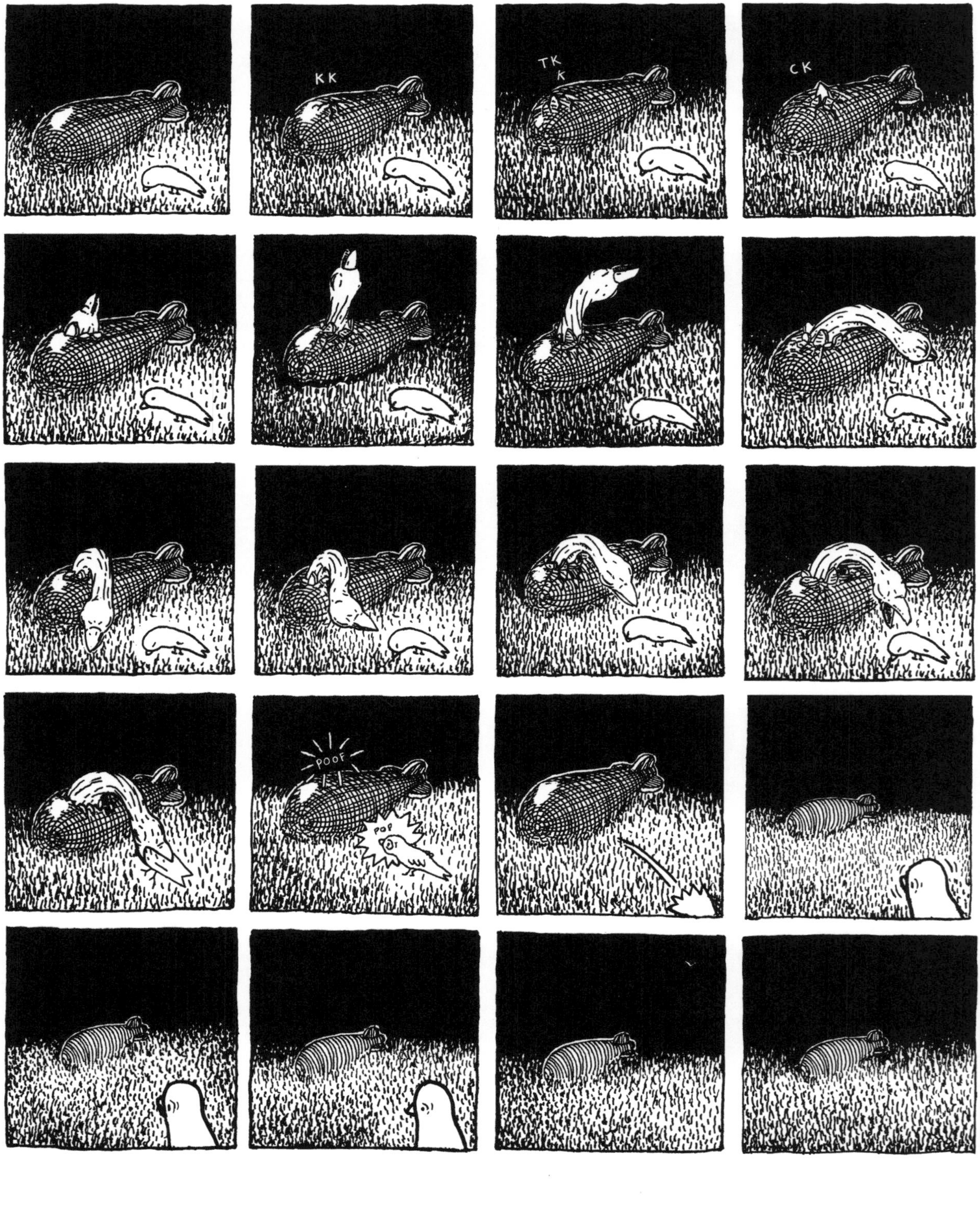
KK
TK
K
CK
POOF
POP

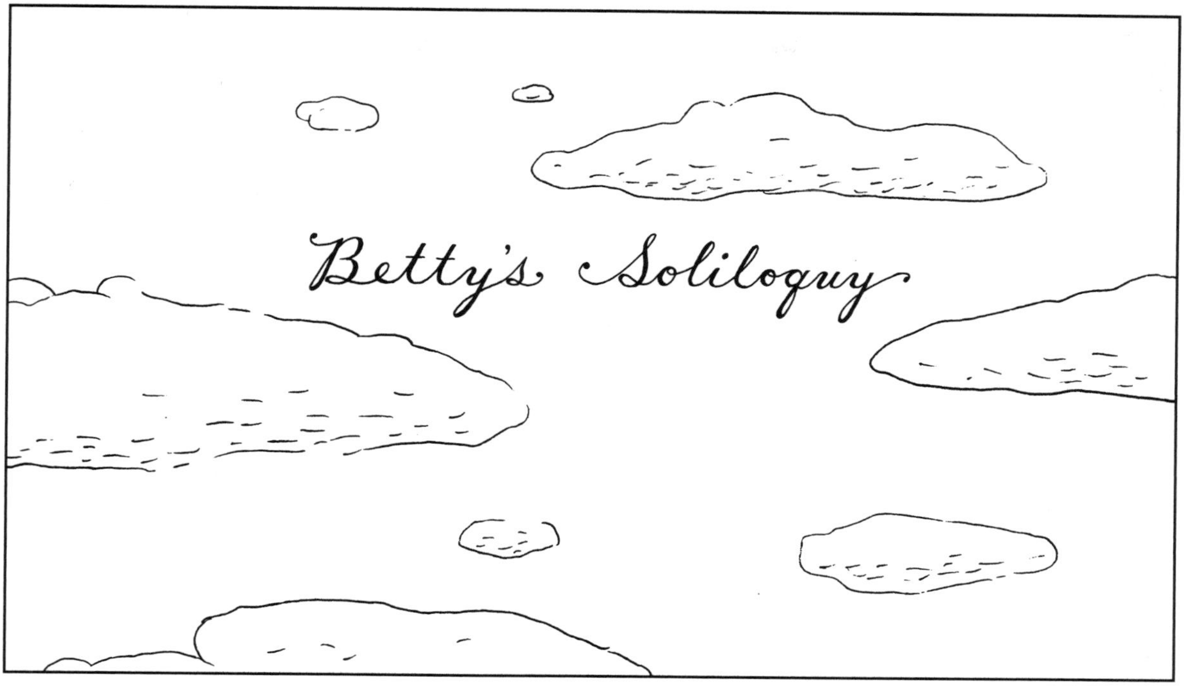
Betty's Soliloquy

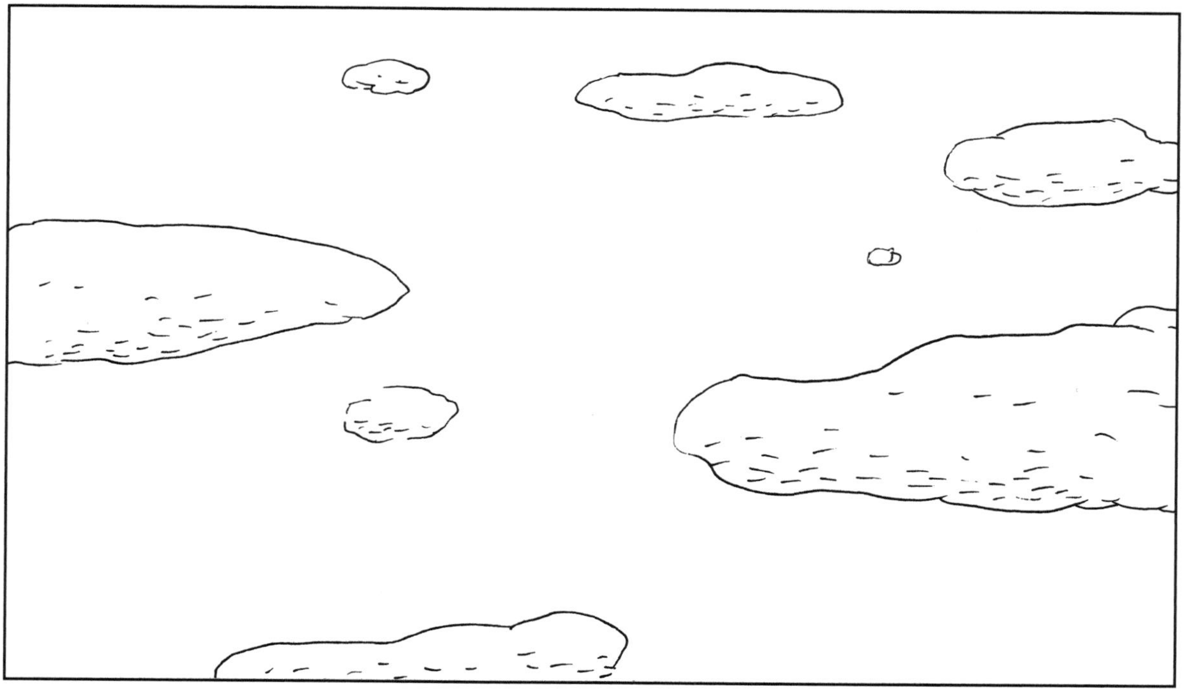

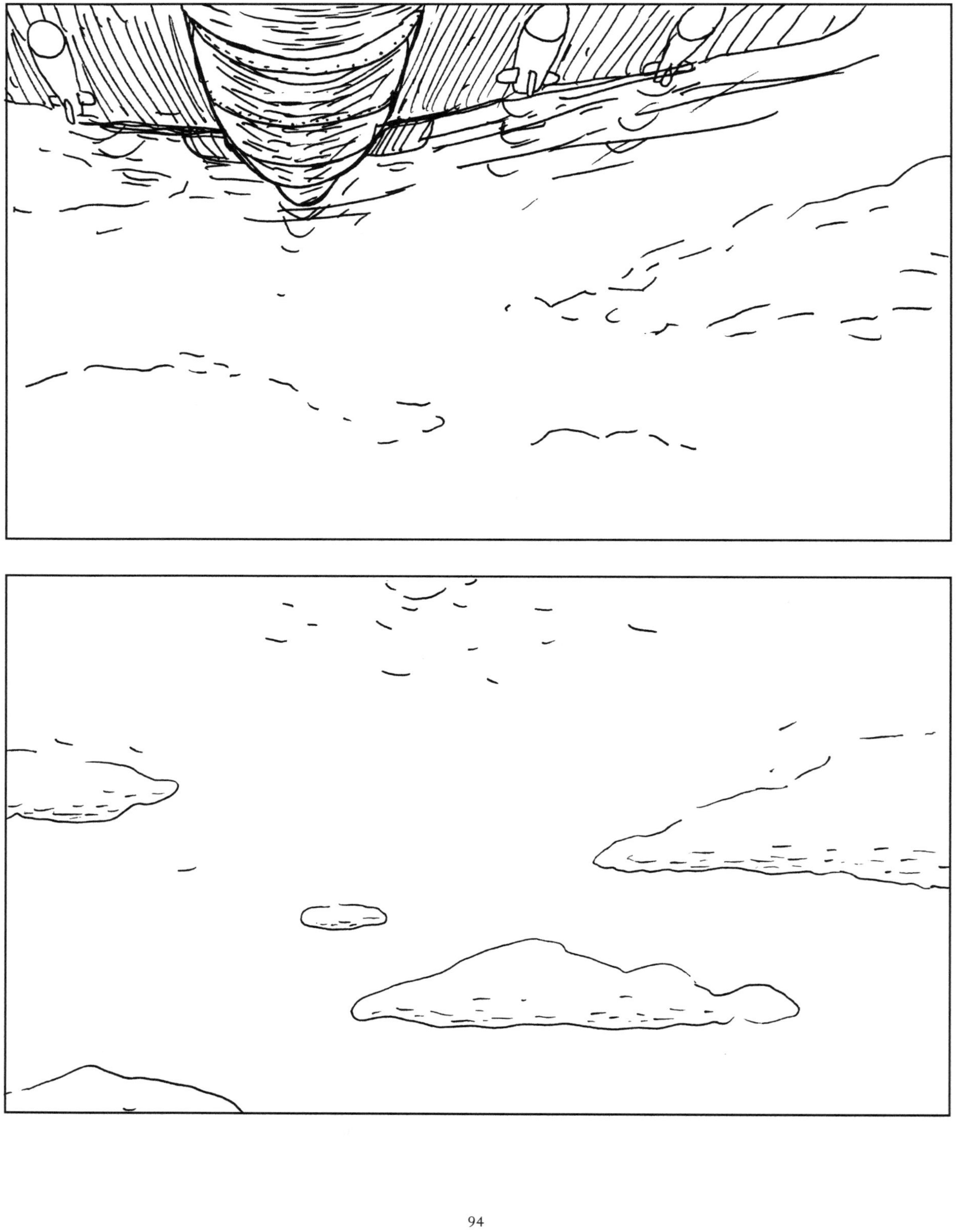

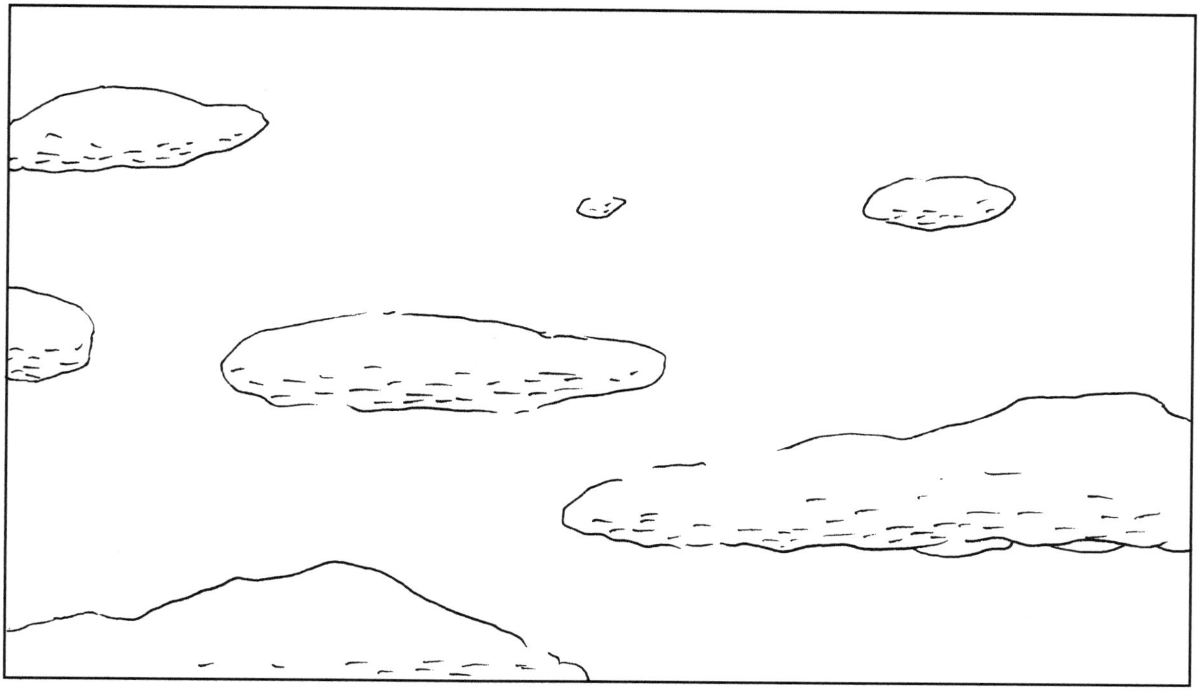

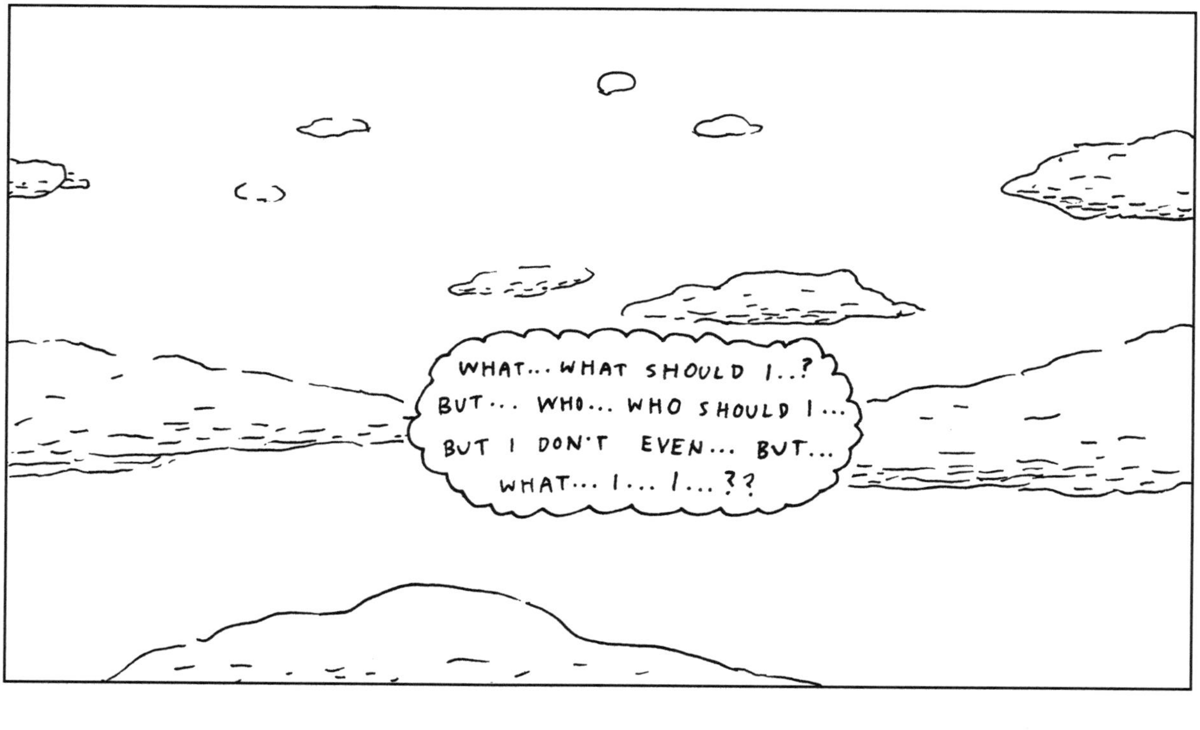
WHAT... WHAT SHOULD I..?
BUT... WHO... WHO SHOULD I...
BUT I DON'T EVEN... BUT...
WHAT... I... I...??

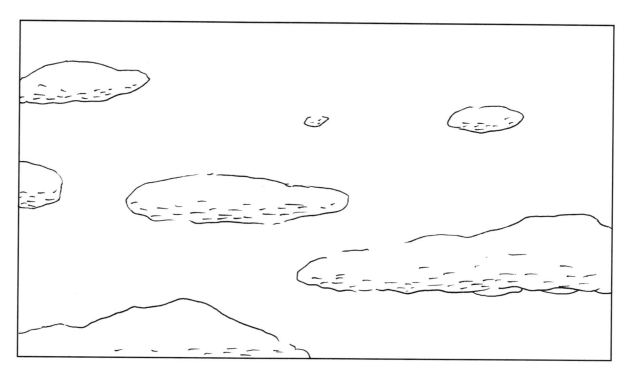

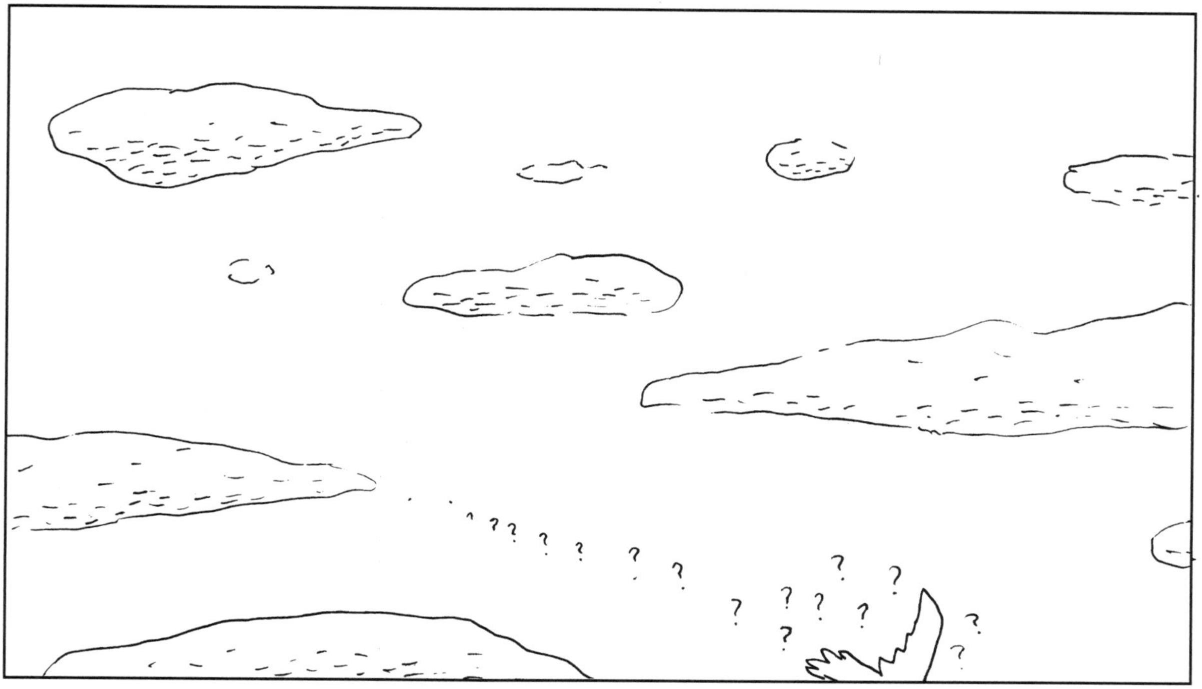

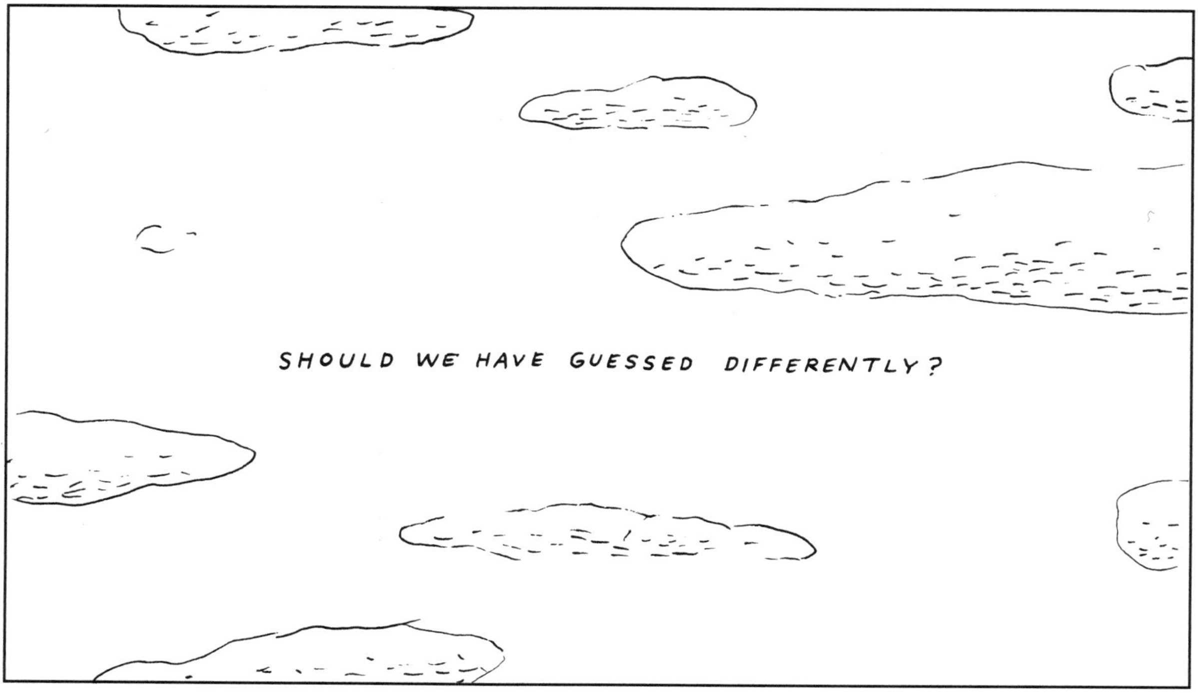
SHOULD WE HAVE GUESSED DIFFERENTLY?

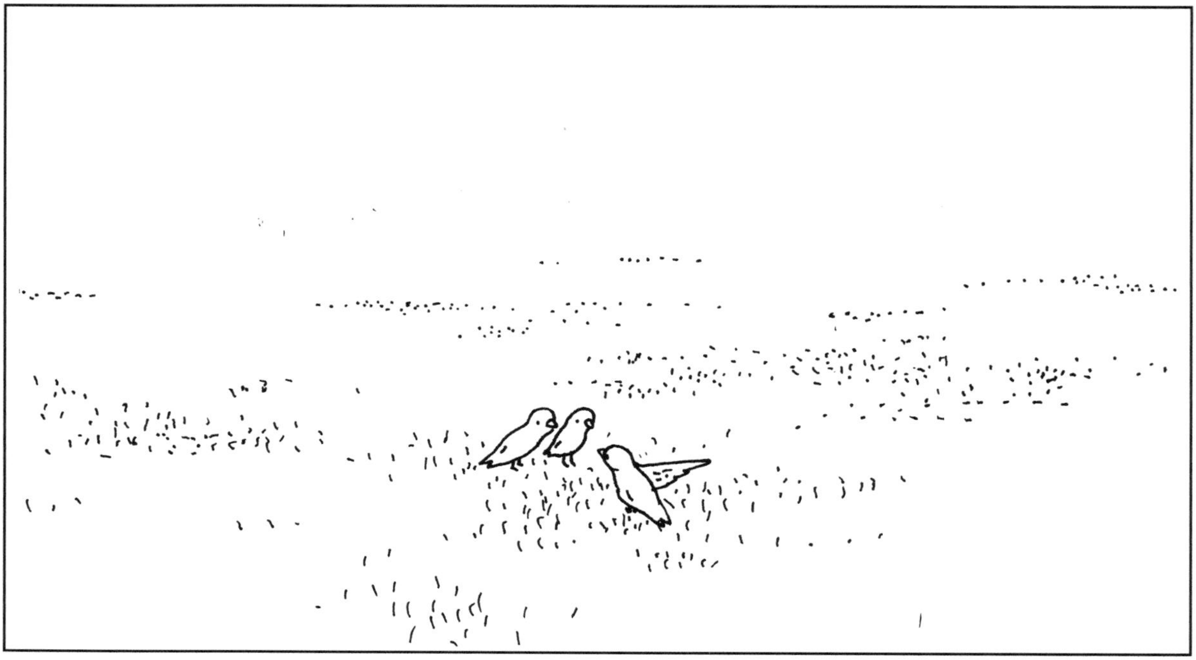

SHOULD WE HAVE KNOWN? WAS THERE SOME
CLUE WE MISSED? WAS OUR BLINDNESS LAUGHABLE?

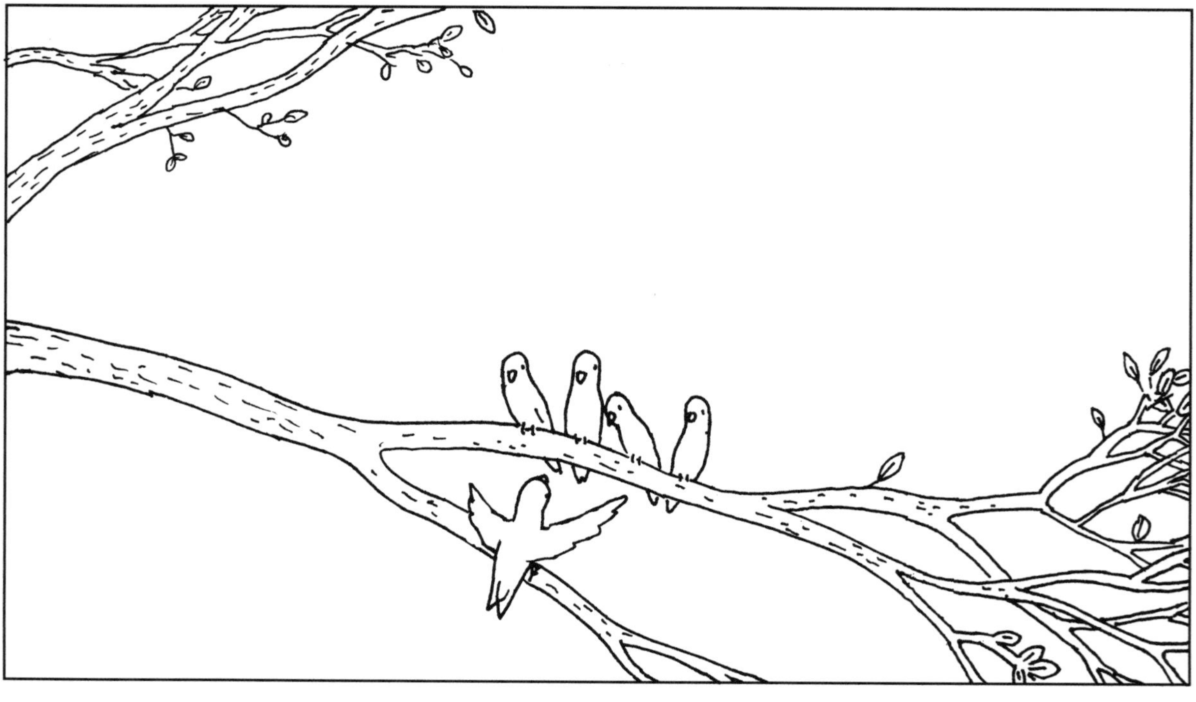

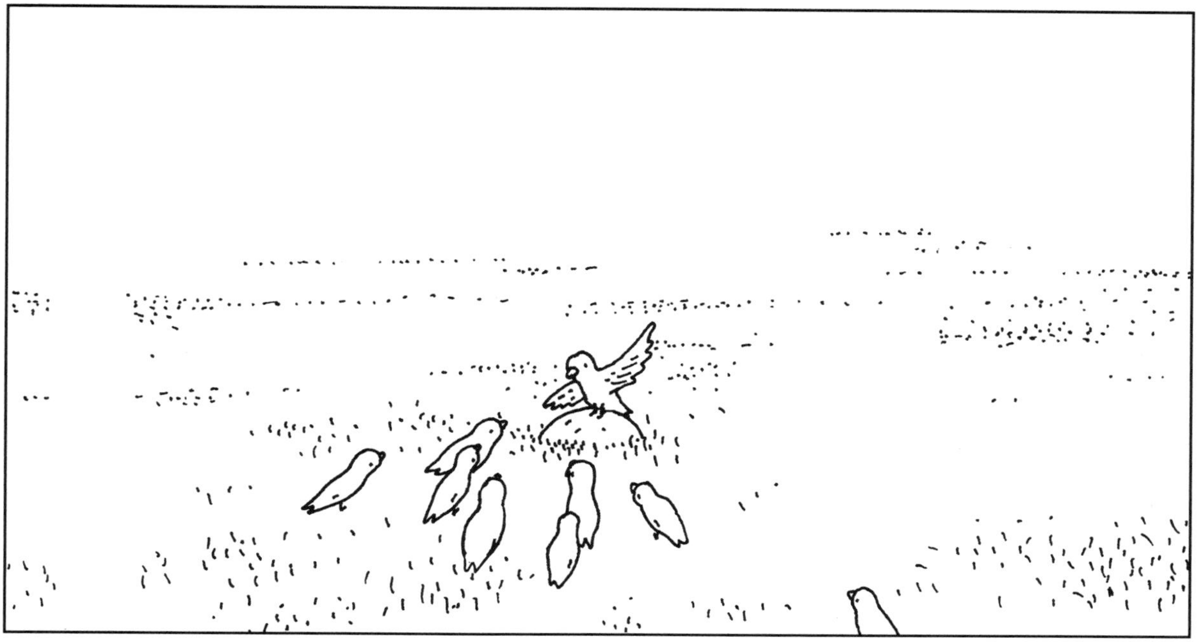

WE MUST HAVE SEEMED PITIFUL, COMICAL, TAKING THE THING FOR AN EGG. A THING TO SHEPHERD, TO PROTECT.

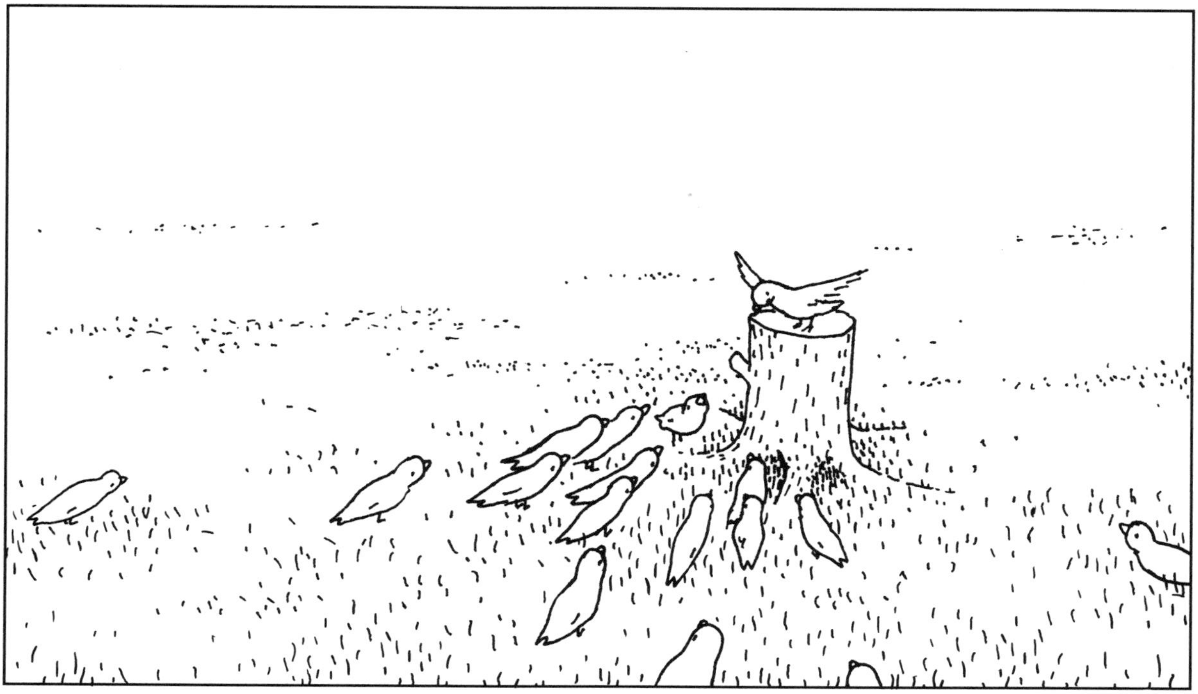

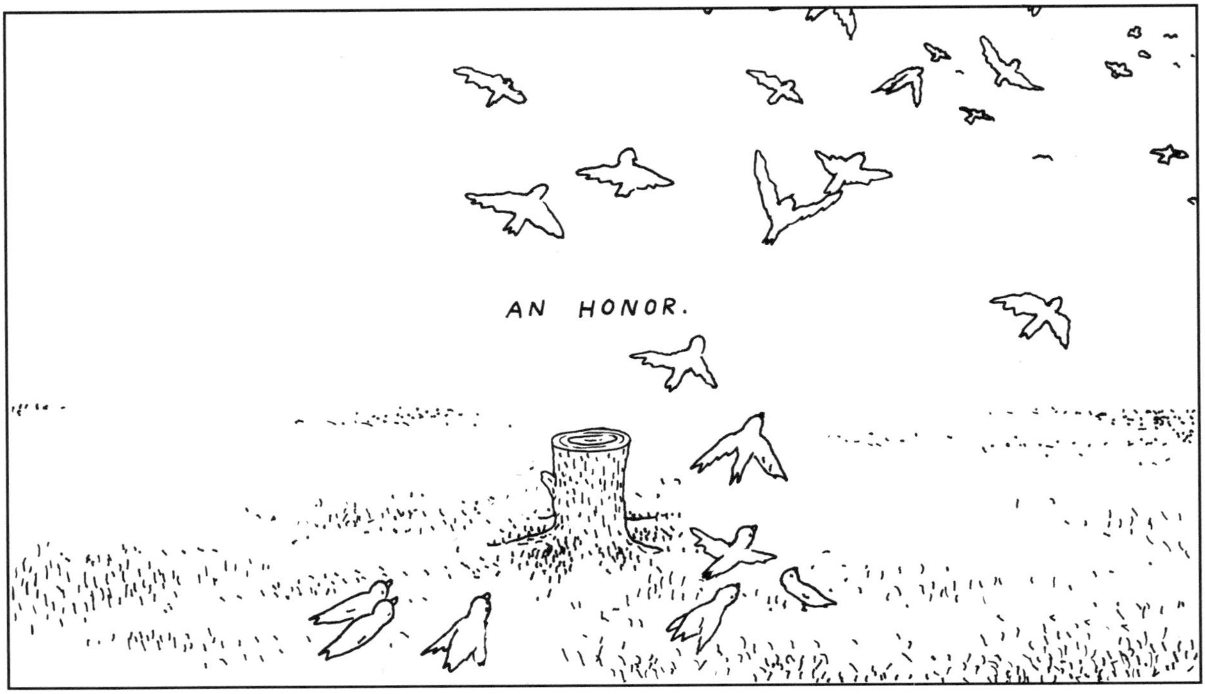
AN HONOR.

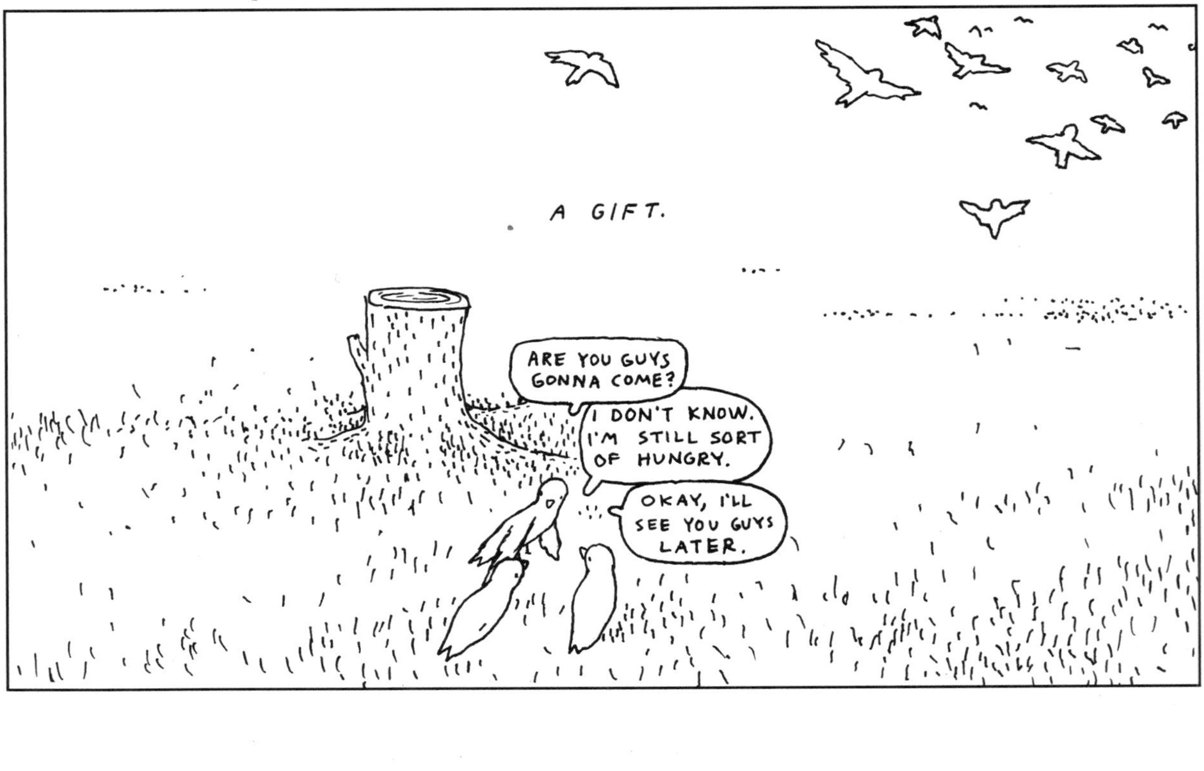
A GIFT.
ARE YOU GUYS GONNA COME?
I DON'T KNOW. I'M STILL SORT OF HUNGRY.
OKAY, I'LL SEE YOU GUYS LATER.

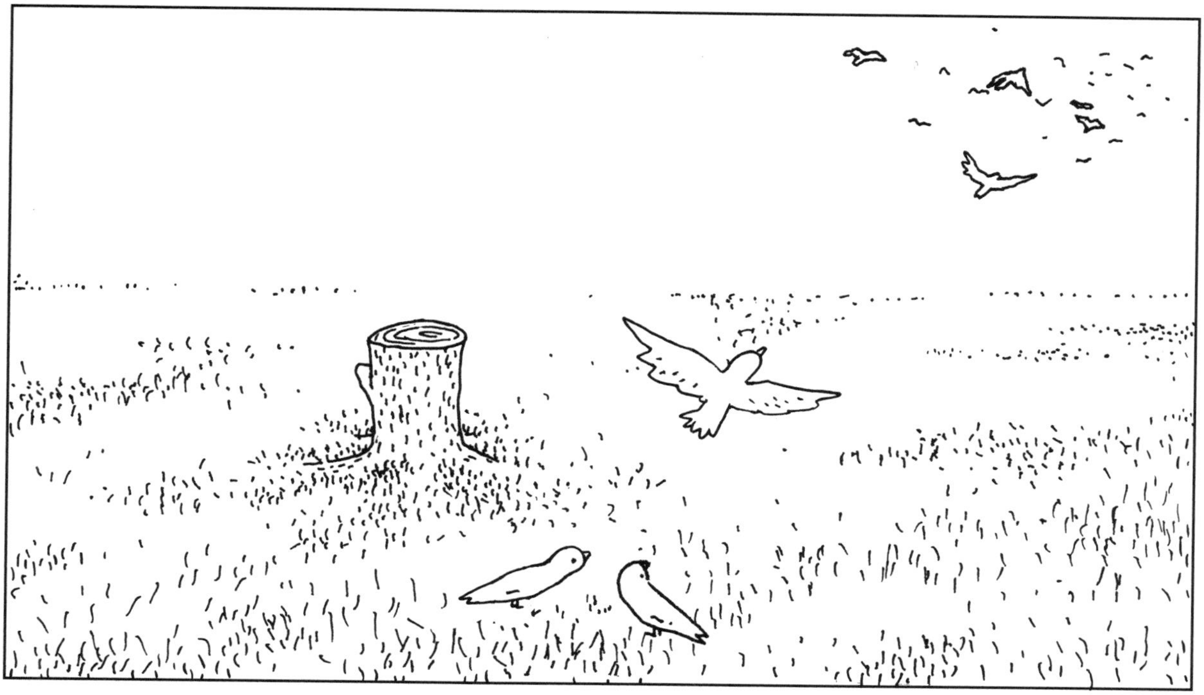

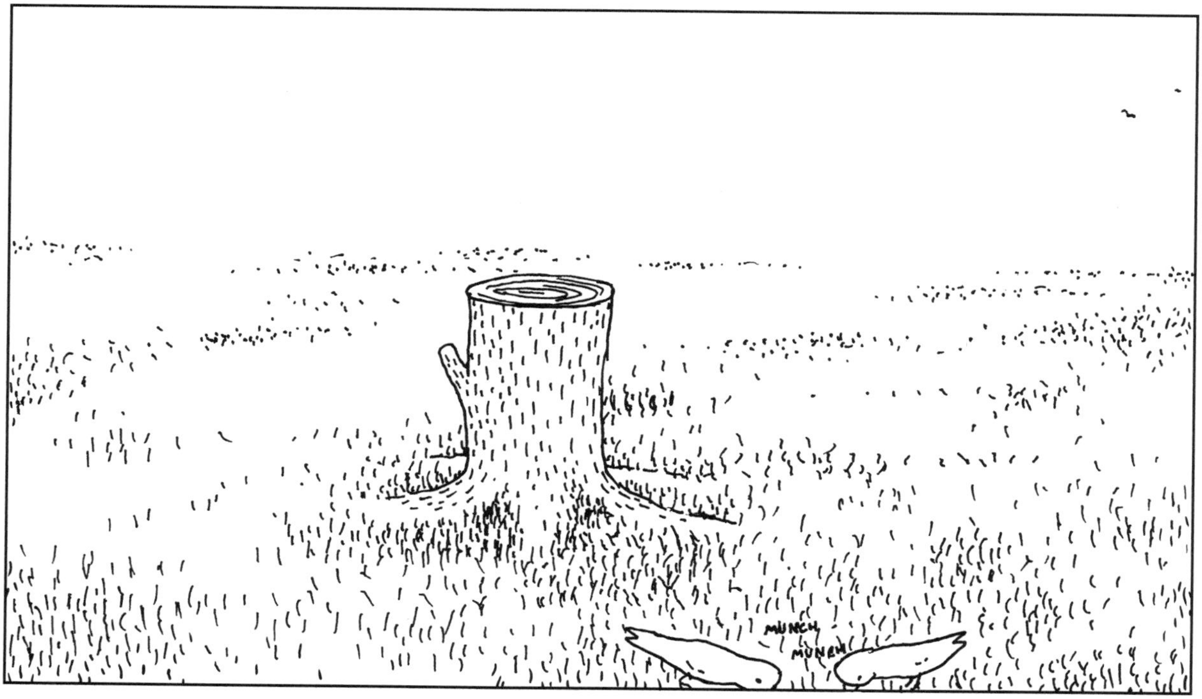
MUNCH
MUNCH

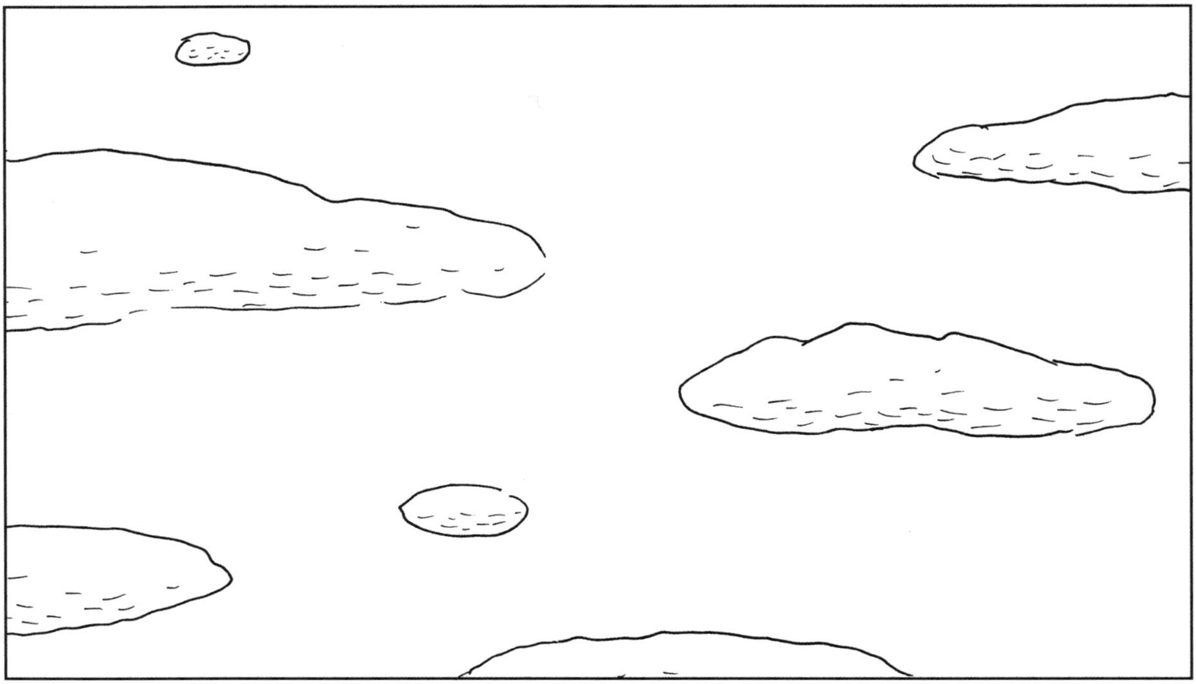

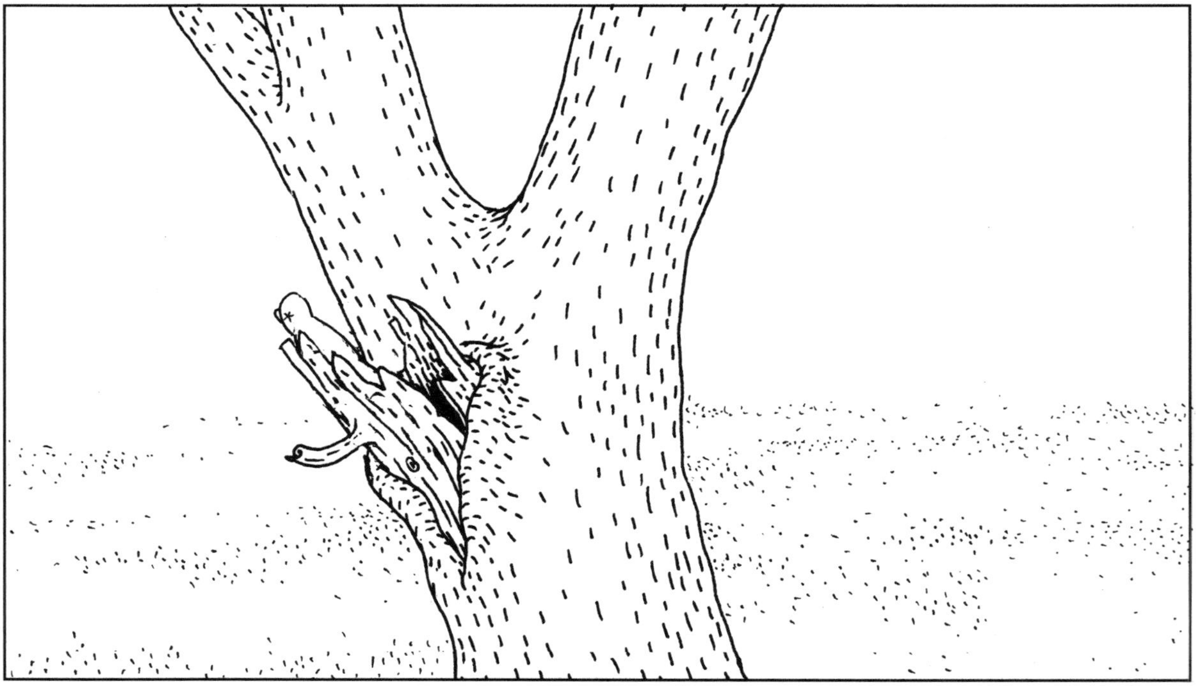

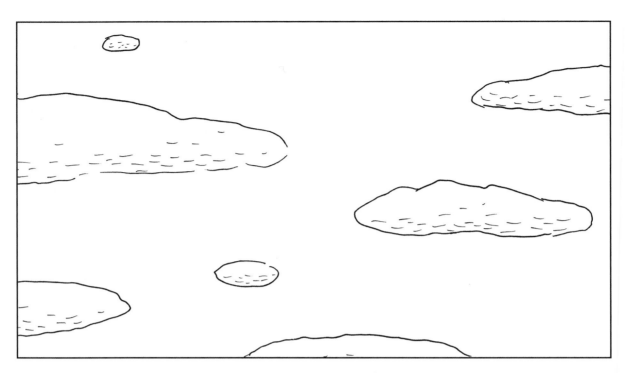

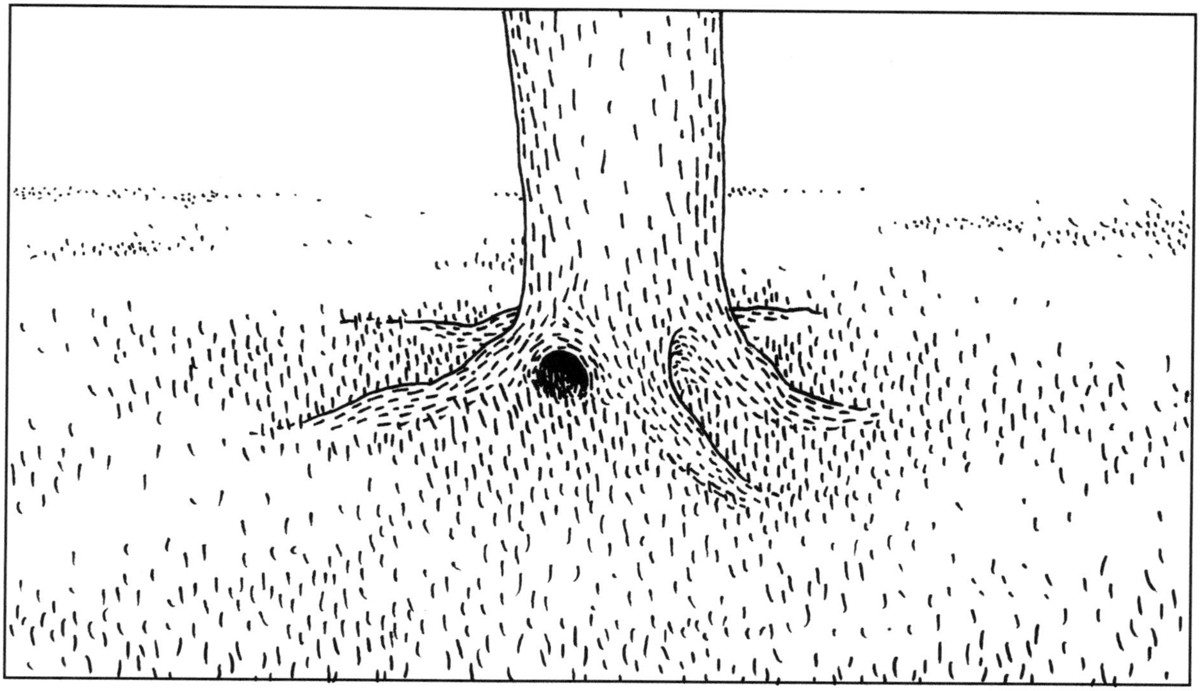

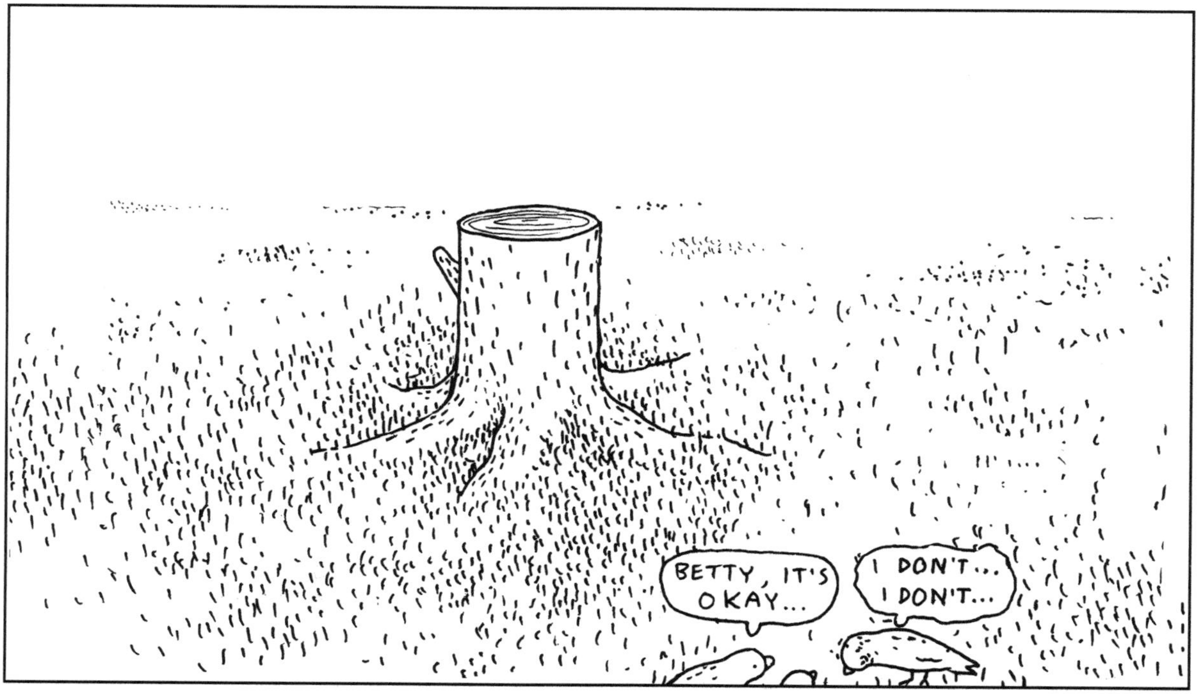
BETTY, IT'S OKAY...
I DON'T... I DON'T...

THE OTHERS COULD BE FORGIVEN.

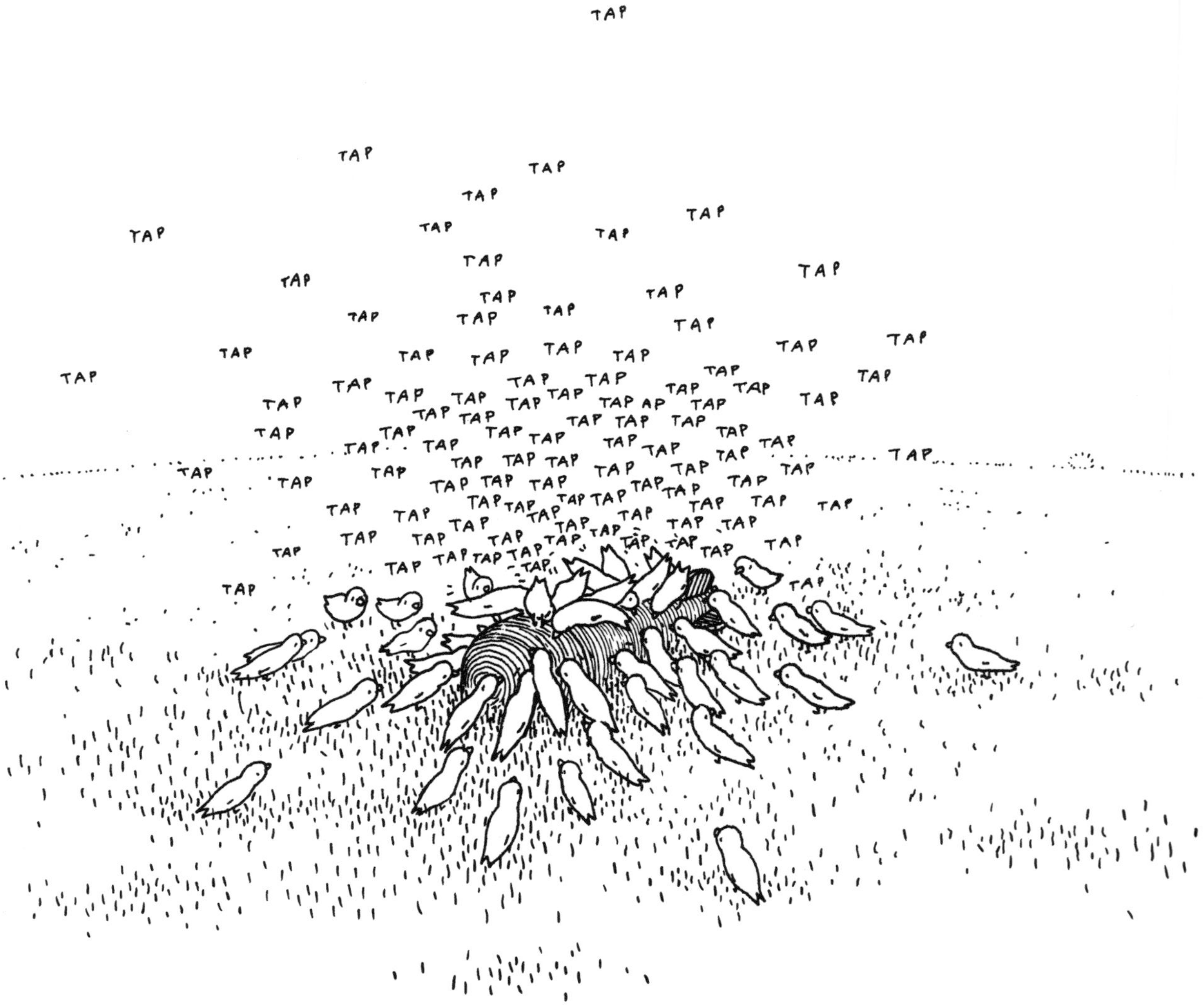
TAP
TAP
TAP
TAP
TAP
TAP
TAP
TAP
TAP
TAP
TAP
TAP
TAP
TAP
TAP
TAP TAP TAP TAP TAP
TAP
TAP TAP TAP TAP TAP TAP TAP TAP AP TAP TAP TAP TAP TAP
TAP TAP TAP TAP TAP TAP TAP TAP TAP
TAP TAP TAP TAP TAP TAP TAP TAP TAP TAP
TAP TAP TAP TAP TAP TAP TAP TAP TAP TAP TAP TAP
TAP TAP TAP TAP TAP TAP TAP TAP TAP TAP TAP TAP TAP
TAP TAP TAP TAP TAP TAP TAP TAP TAP TAP TAP
TAP TAP TAP TAP TAP TAP TAP TAP TAP TAP TAP TAP TAP
TAP TAP TAP TAP TAP TAP TAP
TAP

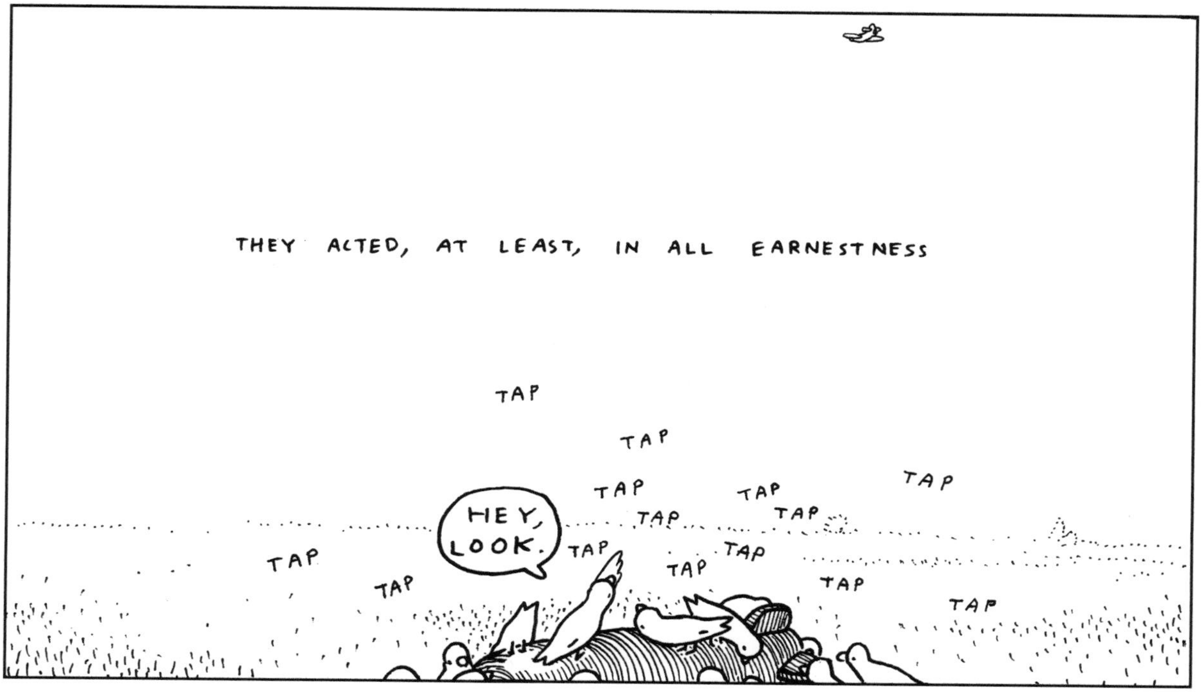
THEY ACTED, AT LEAST, IN ALL EARNESTNESS
TAP
TAP
TAP
TAP
TAP
TAP
HEY, LOOK.
TAP
TAP
TAP
TAP
TAP
TAP
TAP

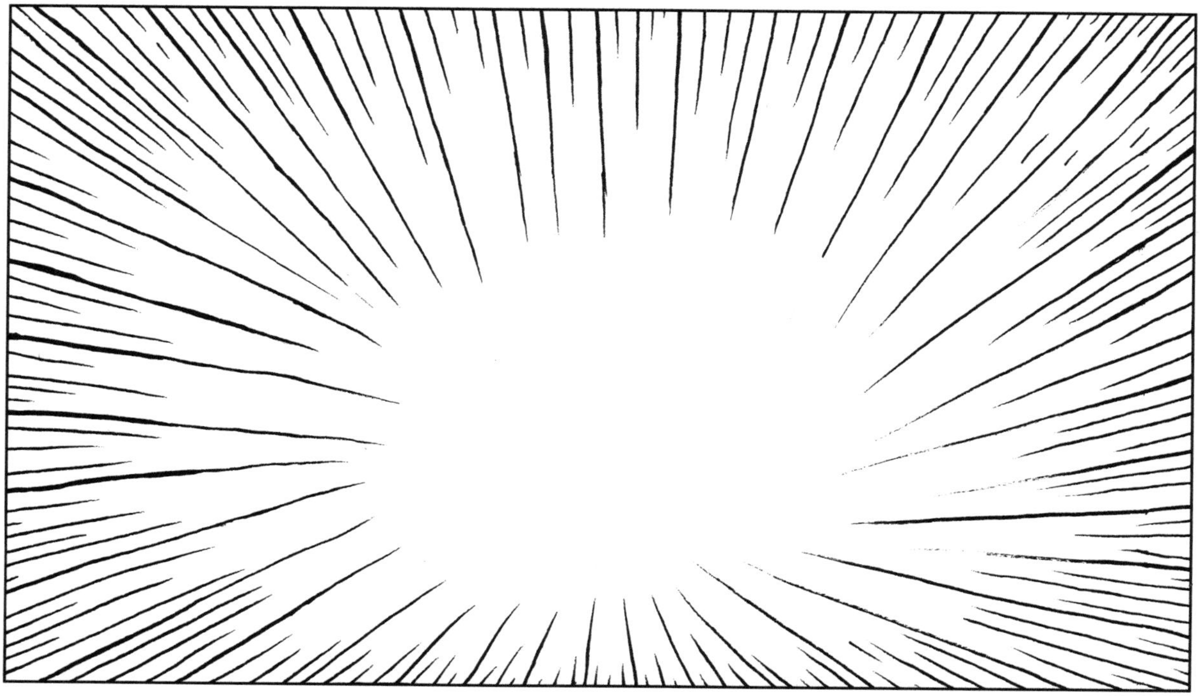

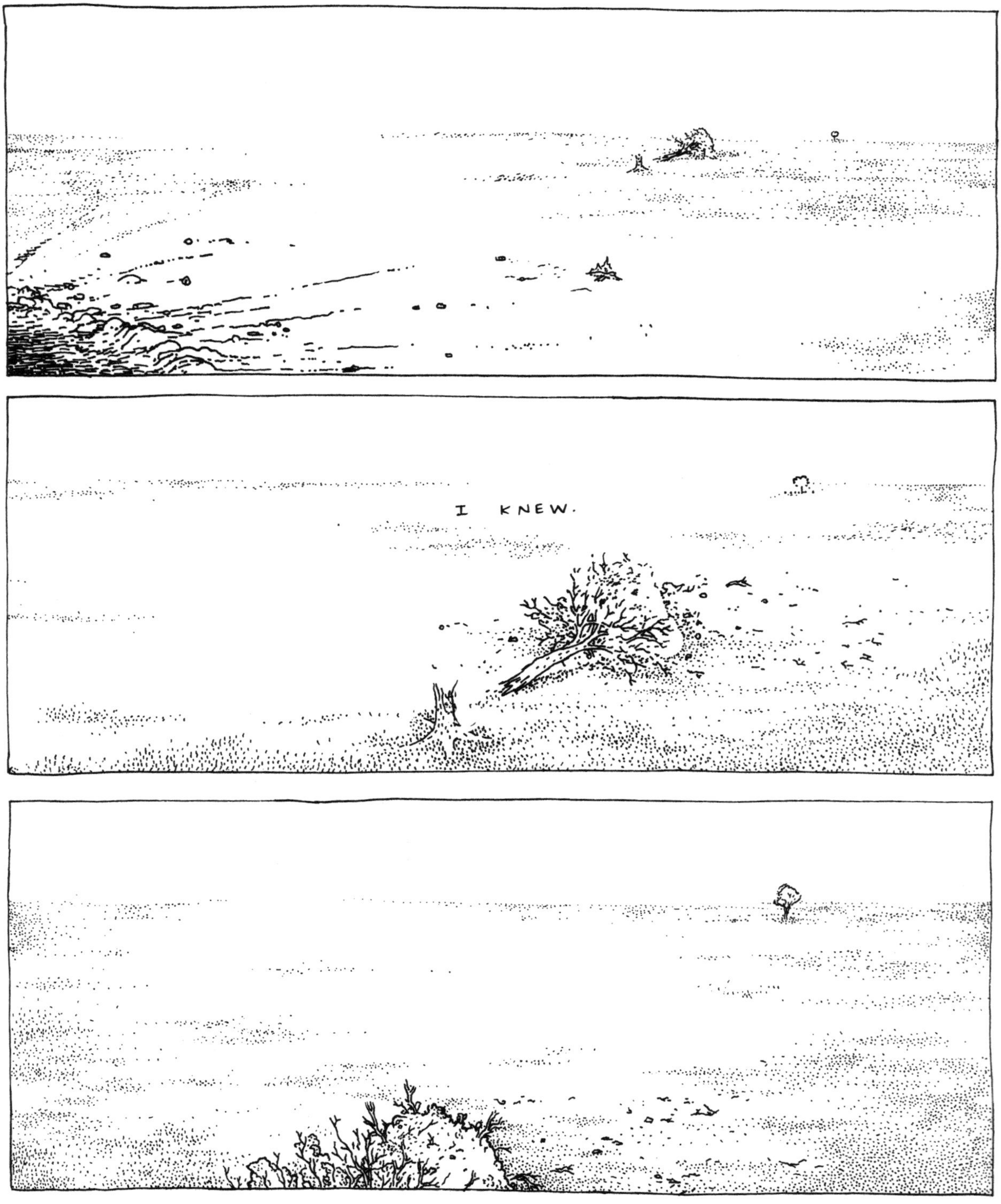
I KNEW.

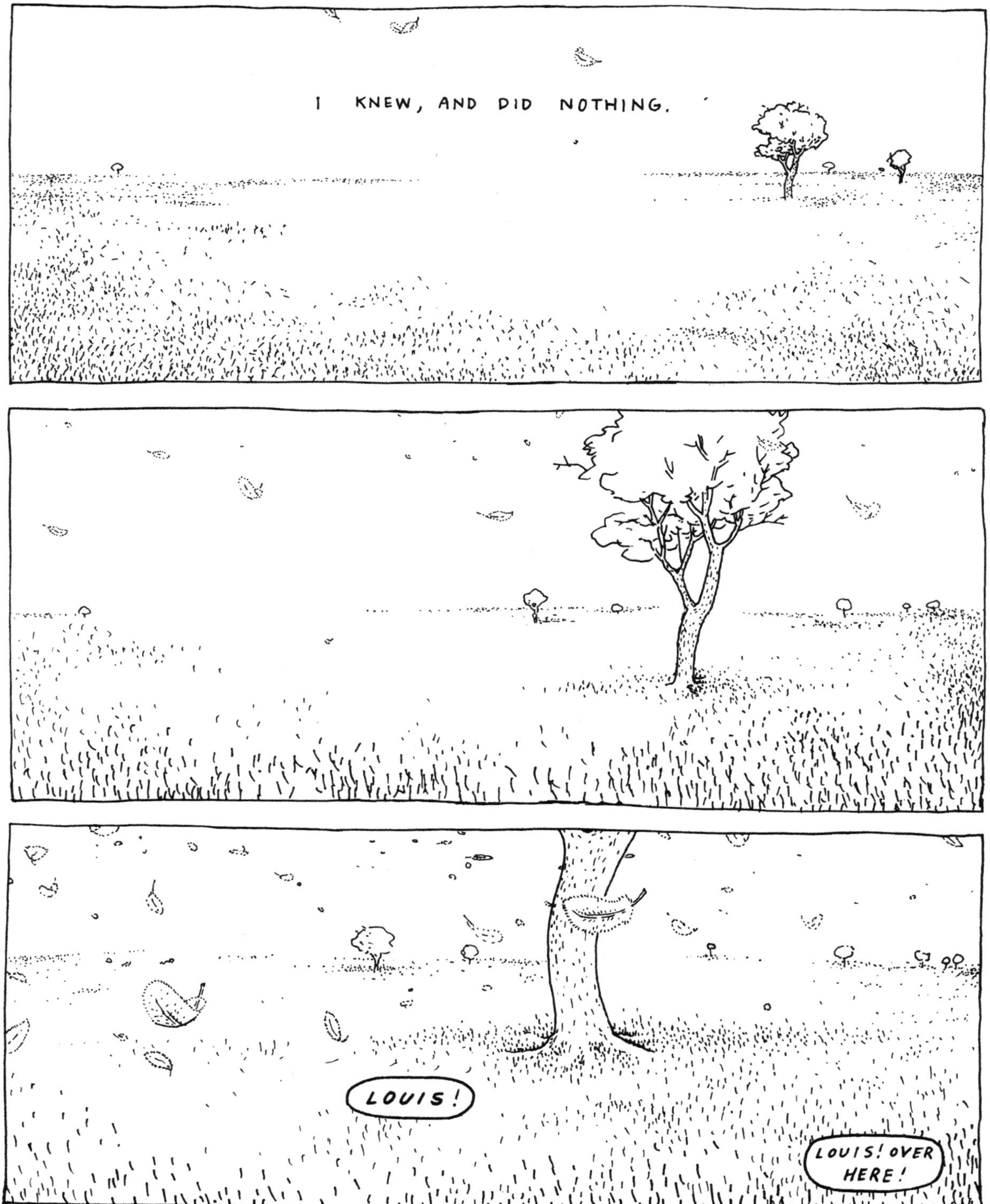
I KNEW, AND DID NOTHING.
LOUIS!
LOUIS! OVER HERE!

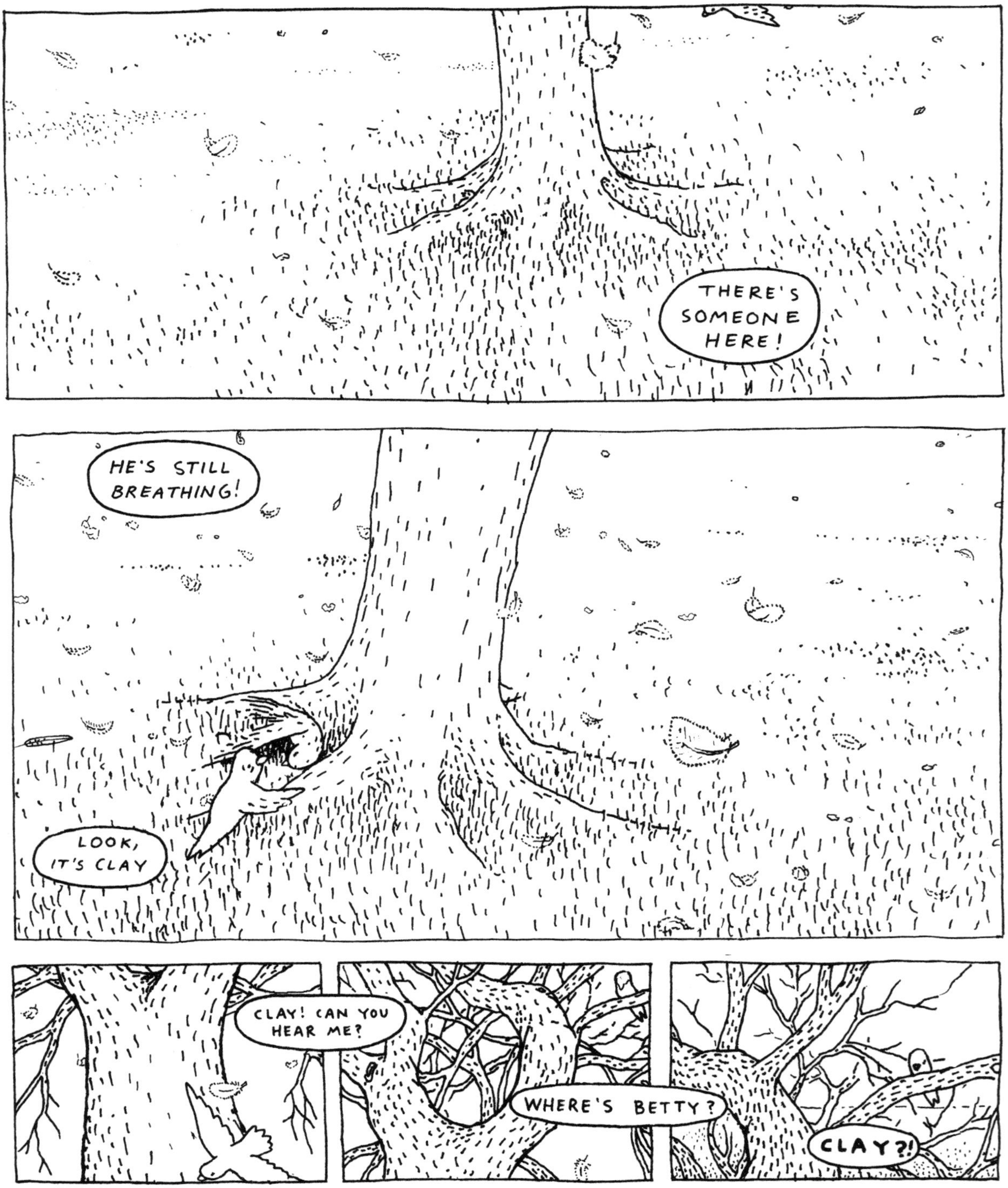
THERE'S SOMEONE HERE!
HE'S STILL BREATHING!
LOOK, IT'S CLAY
CLAY! CAN YOU HEAR ME?
WHERE'S BETTY?
CLAY?!

...ZZZZ...
...ZZZZ...
BAYLE...

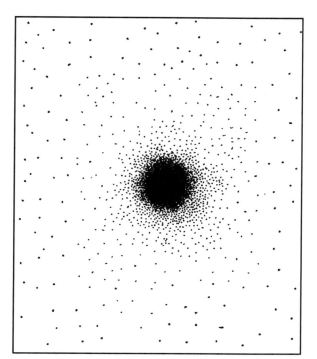

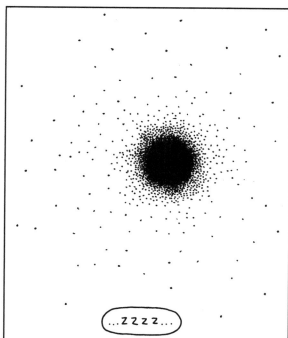

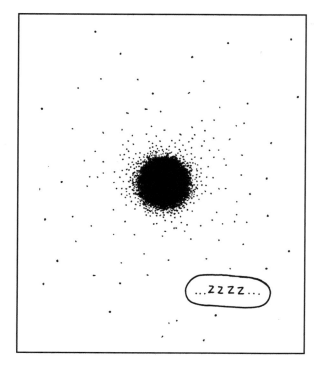

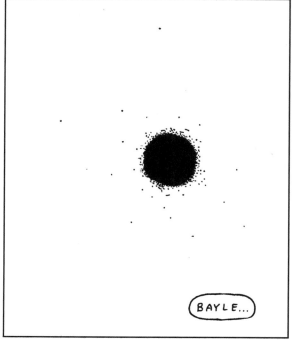

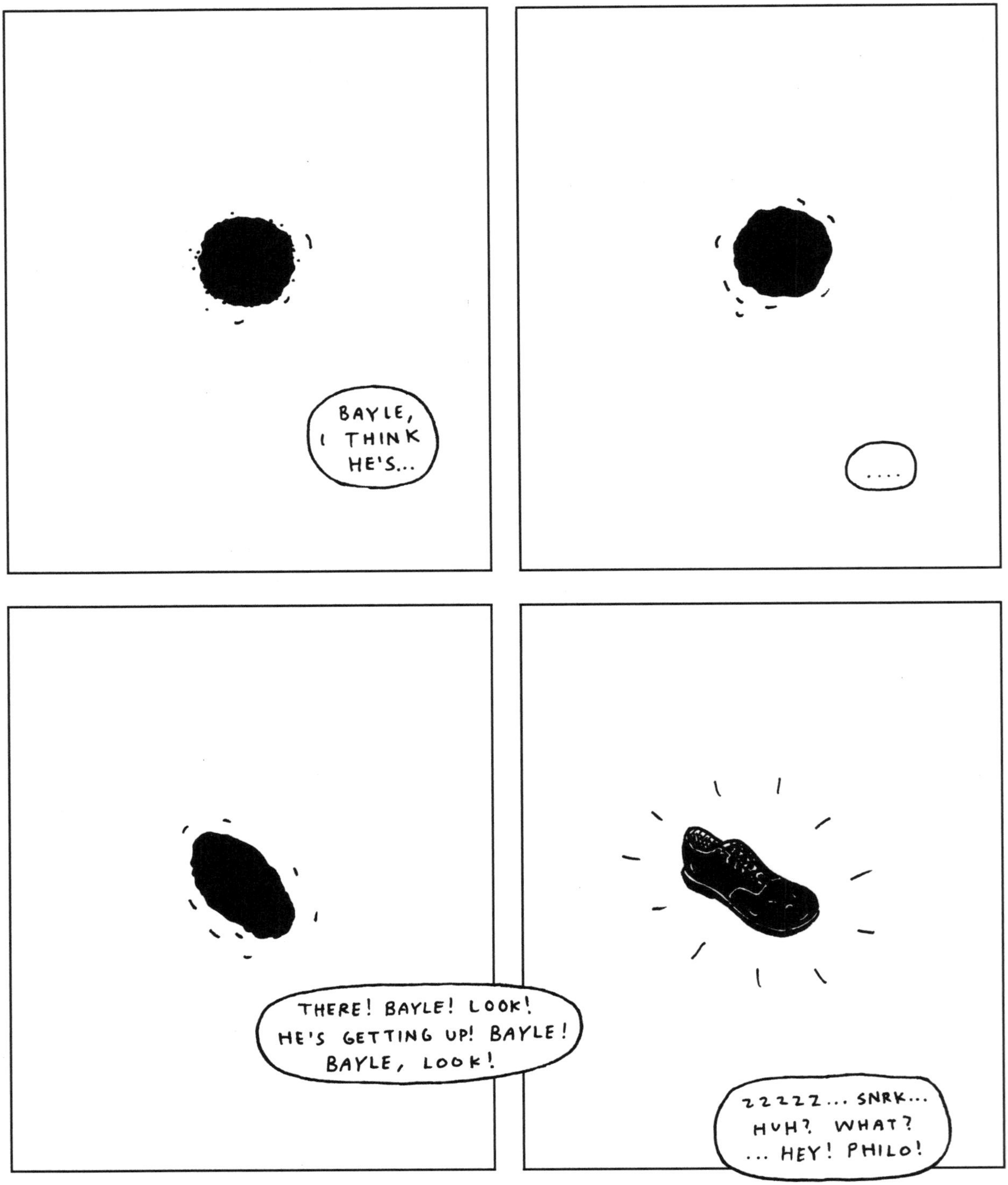
BAYLE, I THINK HE'S...
....
THERE! BAYLE! LOOK! HE'S GETTING UP! BAYLE! BAYLE, LOOK!
ZZZZZ... SNRK... HUH? WHAT? ... HEY! PHILO!

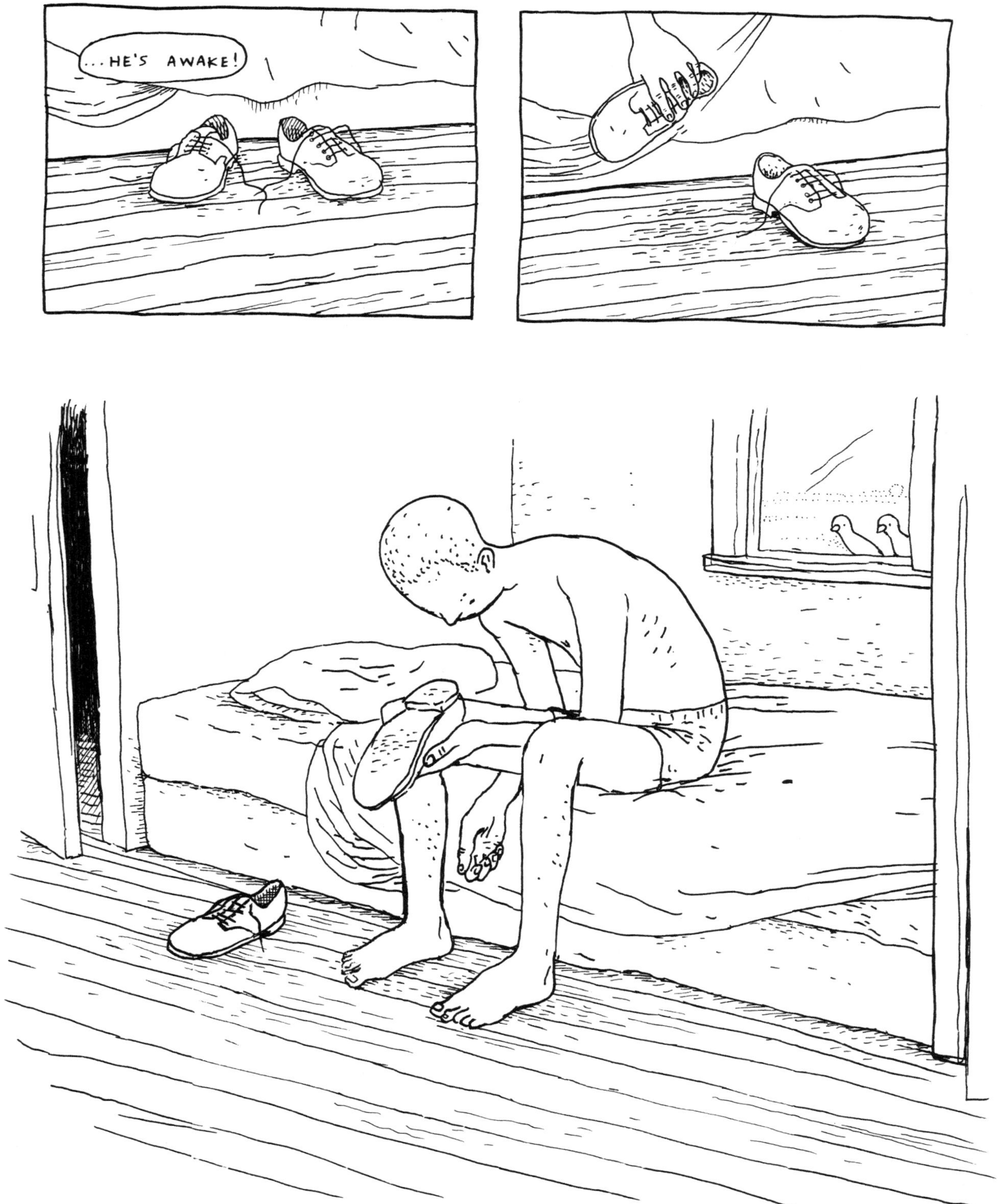
...HE'S AWAKE!

TAP
TAP

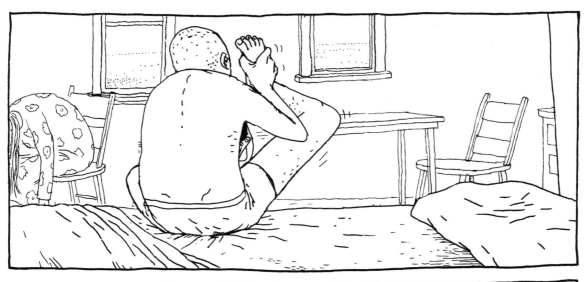

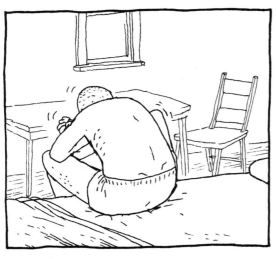

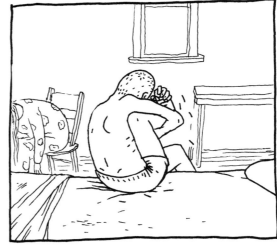

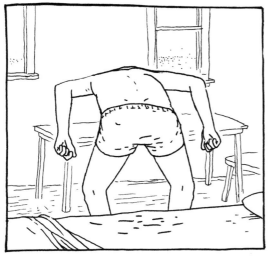

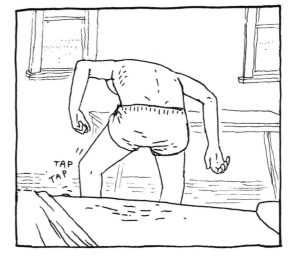

TAP
TAP
TAP

TAP
TAP
TAP

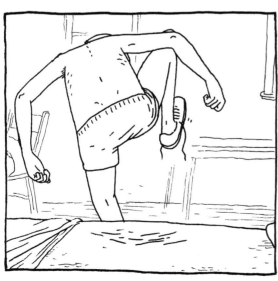

BANG
FFFFF FFFFF FFFFFF F-FFF FFFFFFFF
FFFFFFLLUMP
FFFLUMP
BANG
CRASH

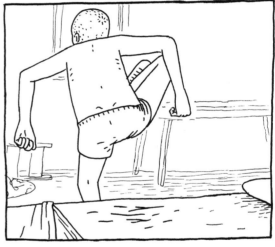

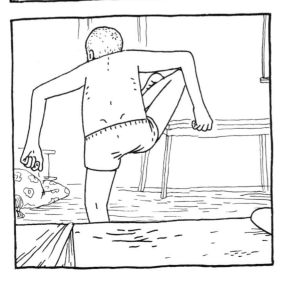

POKE
POKE

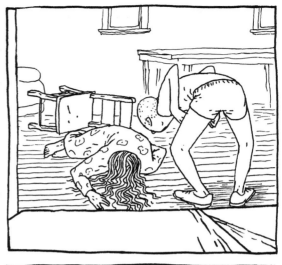

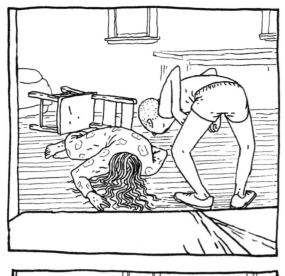

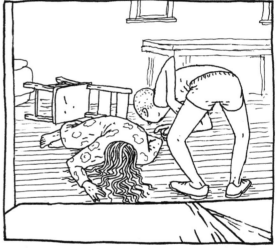

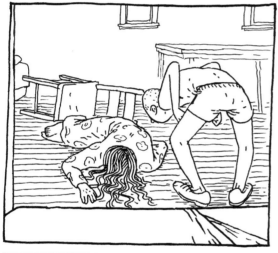

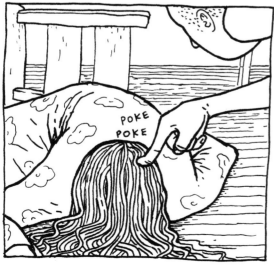

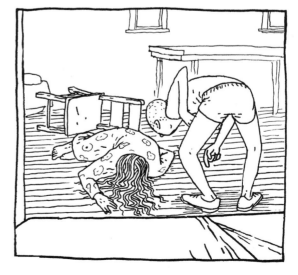

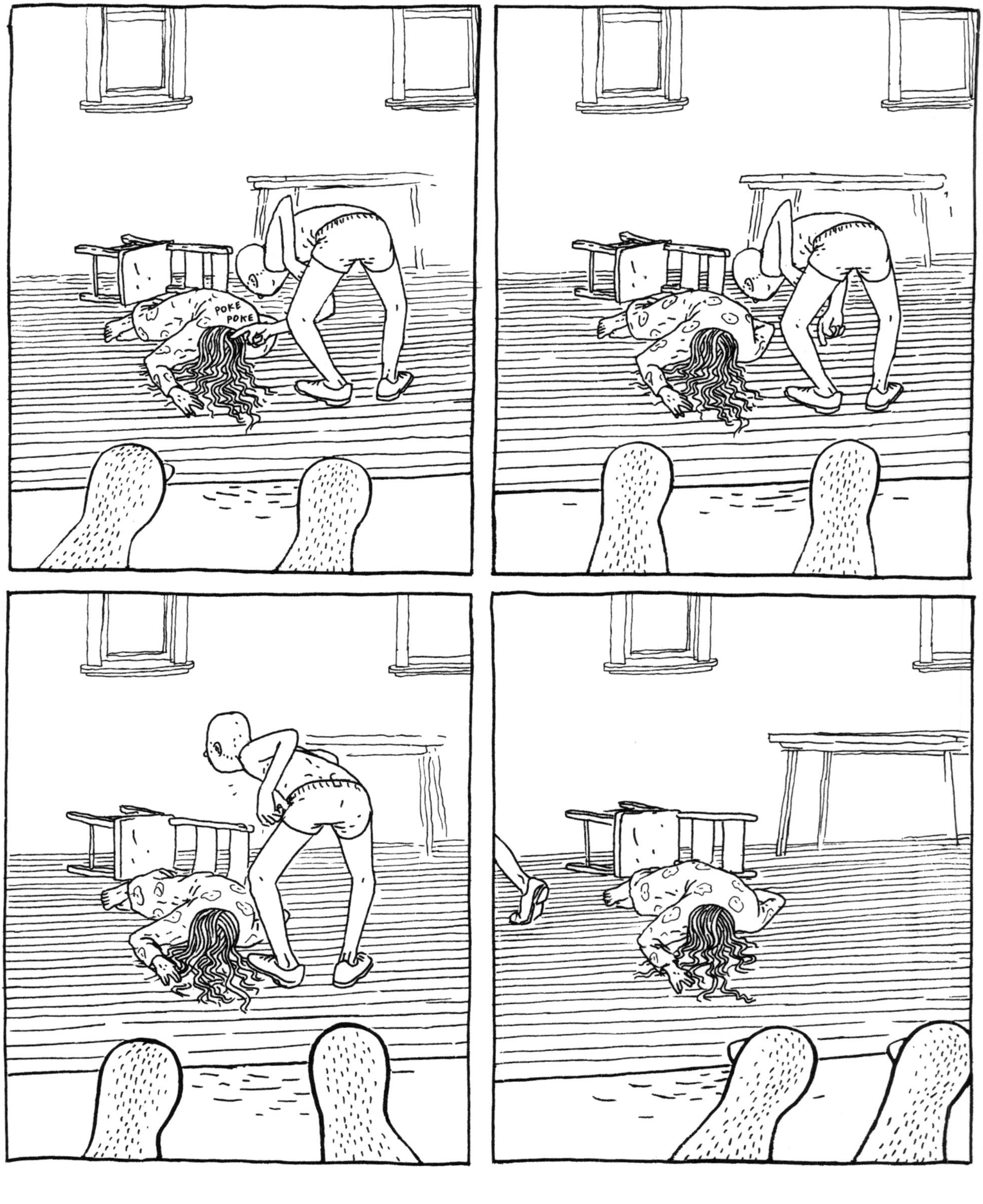
POKE
POKE

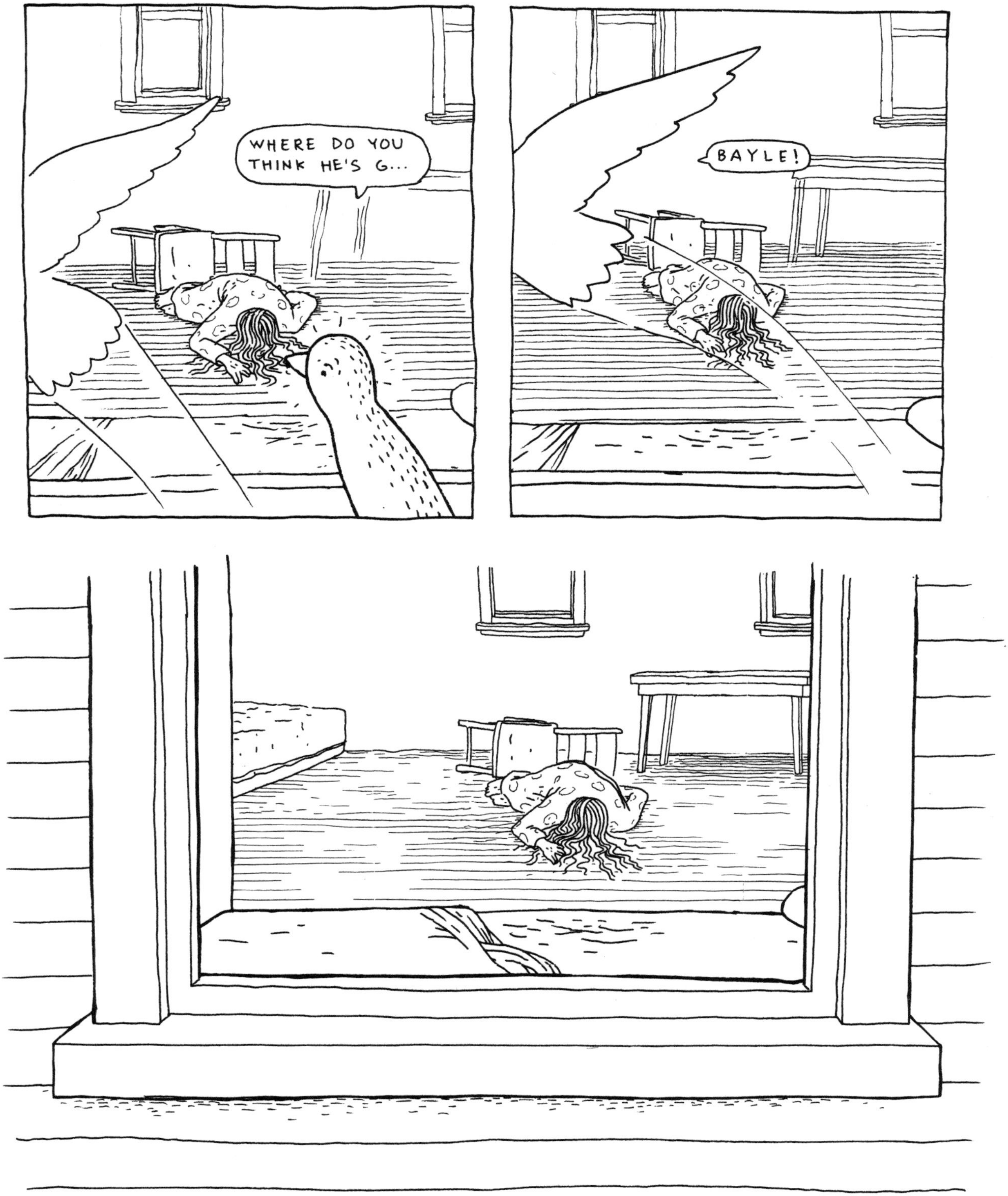
WHERE DO YOU THINK HE'S G...
BAYLE!

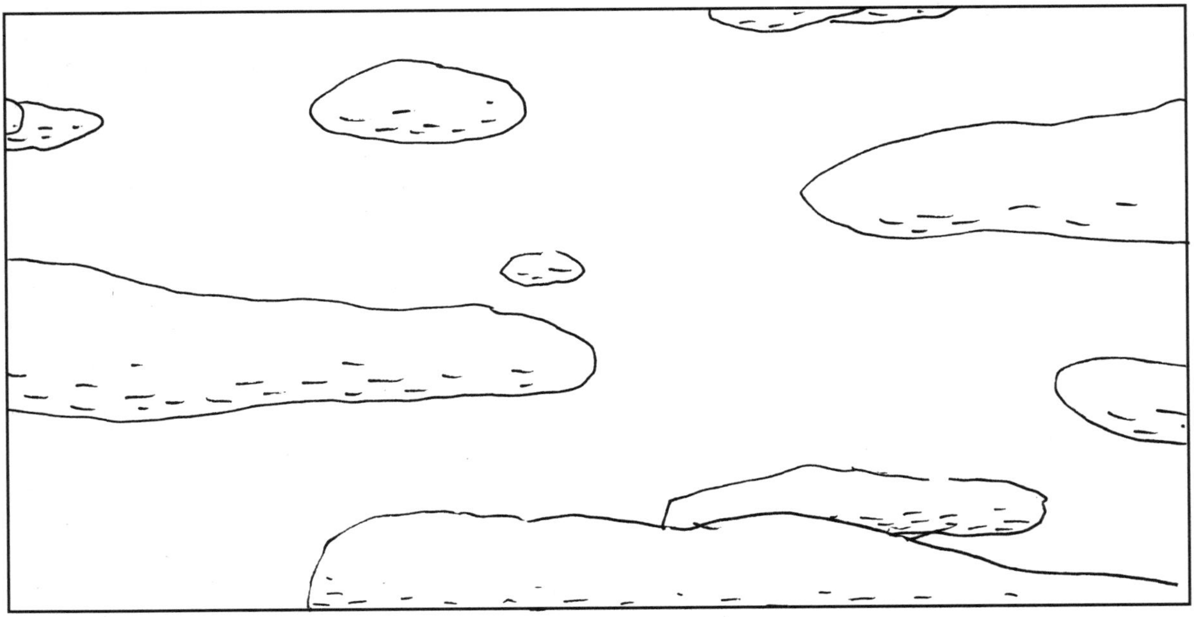

Algernon

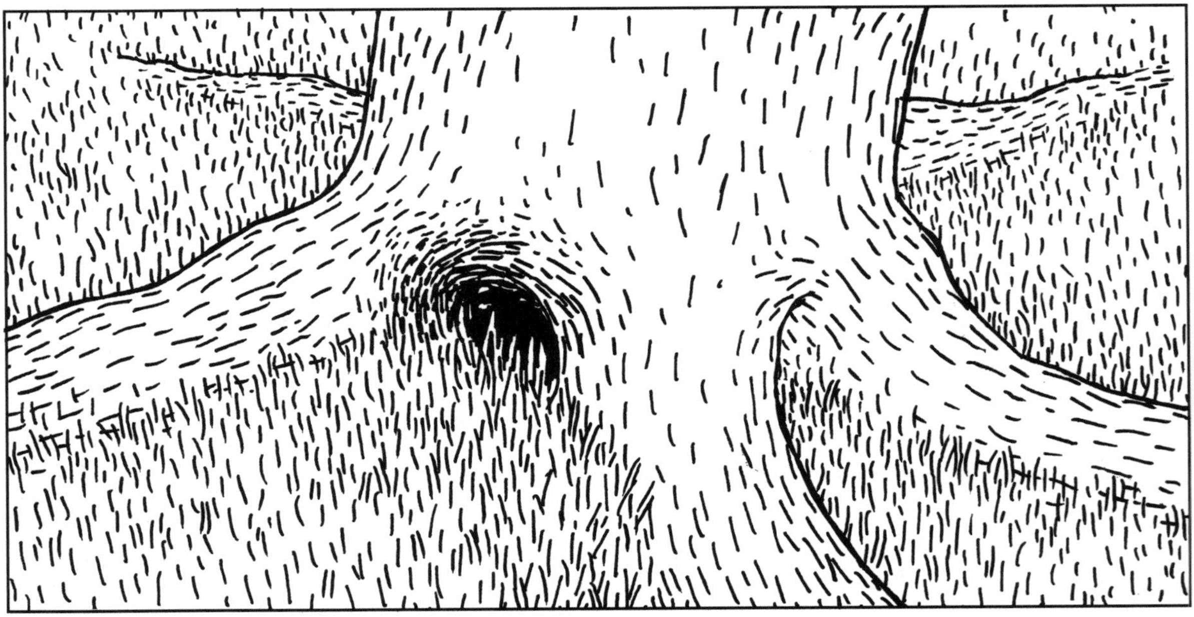

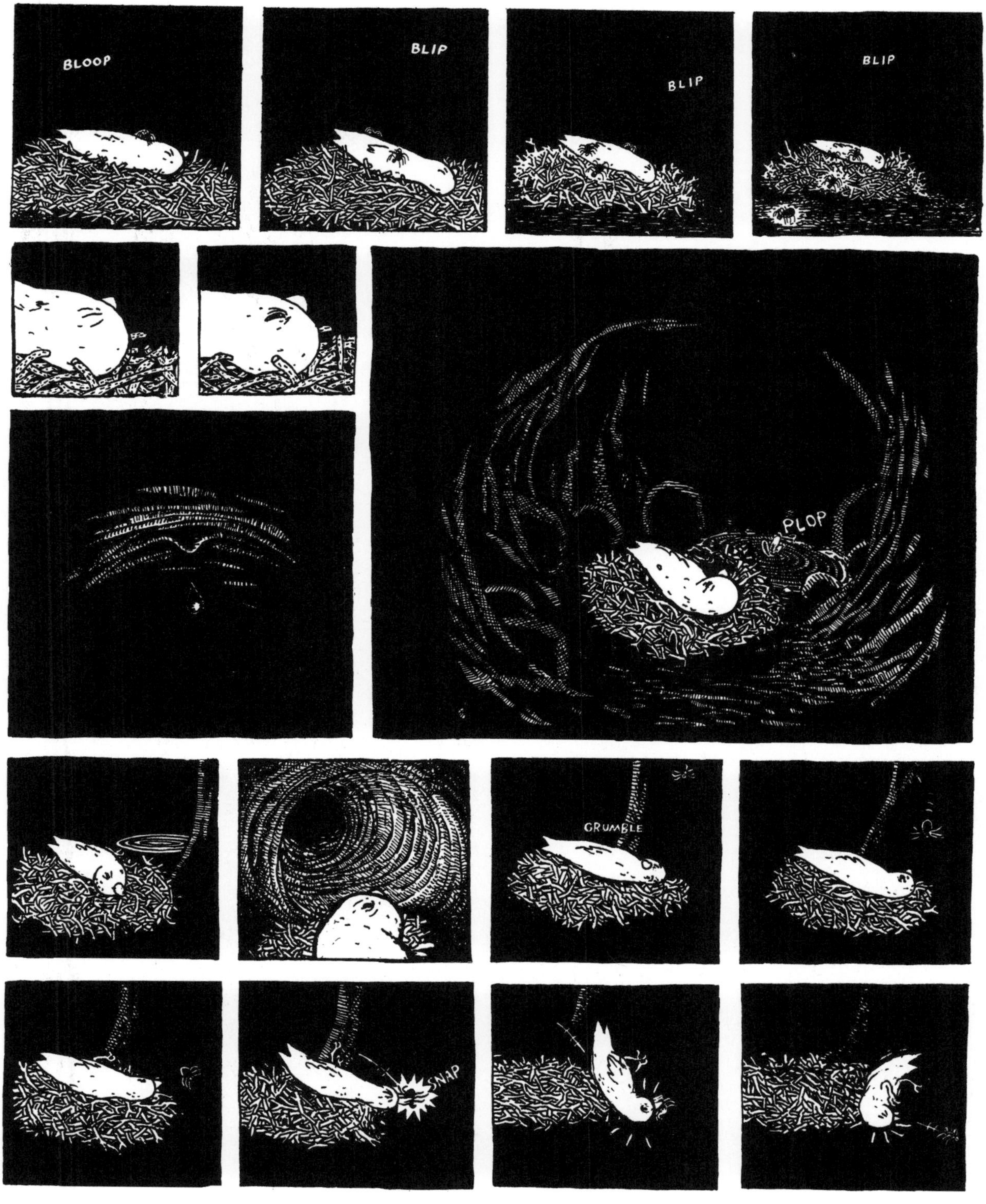
BLOOP
BLIP
BLIP
BLIP
PLOP
GRUMBLE
SNAP

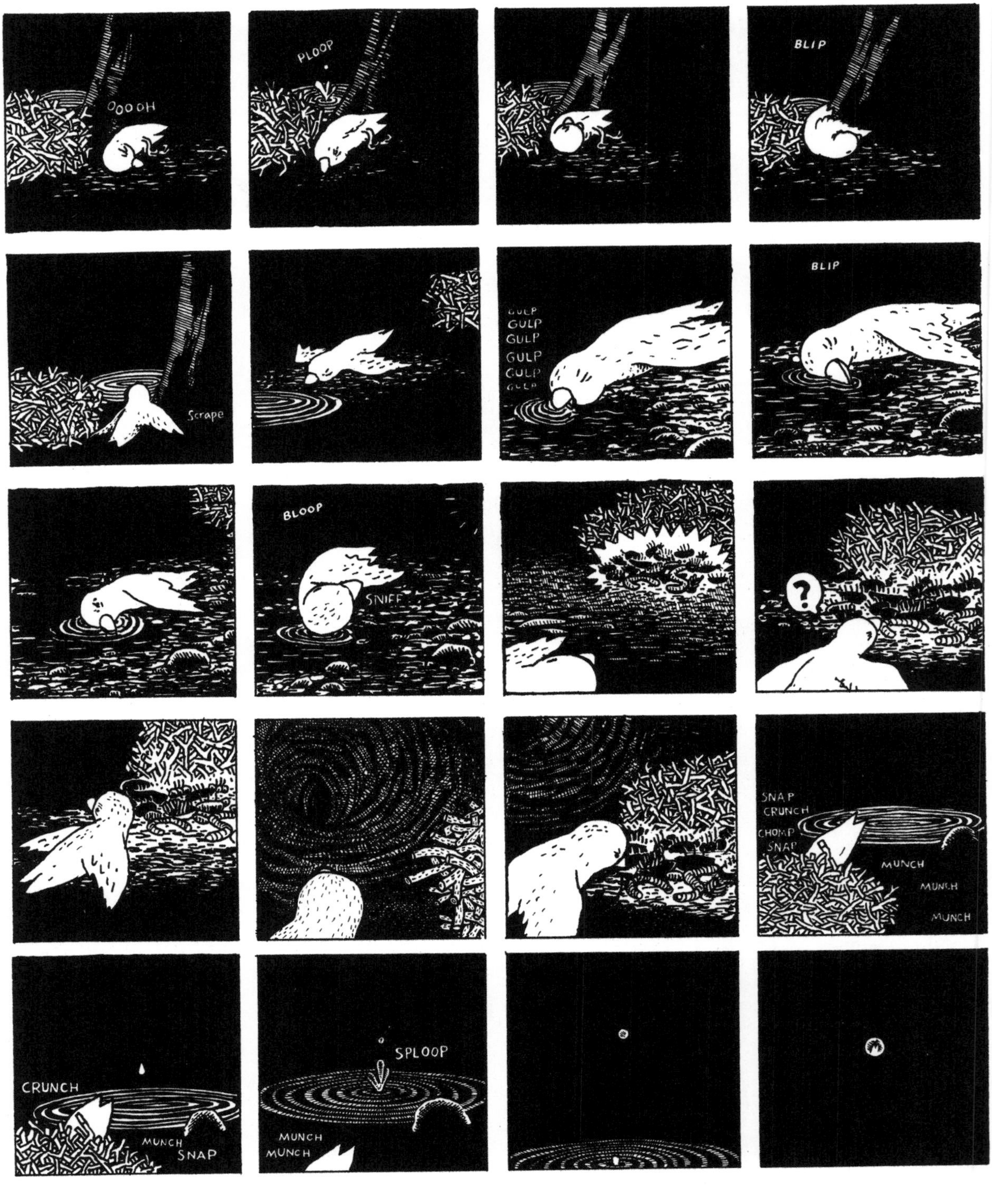
OOOOH
PLOOP
BLIP
Scrape
GULP
GULP
GULP
GULP
BLIP
BLOOP
SNIFF
?
SNAP
CRUNCH
CHOMP
SNAP
MUNCH
MUNCH
MUNCH
CRUNCH
MUNCH
SNAP
SPLOOP
MUNCH
MUNCH

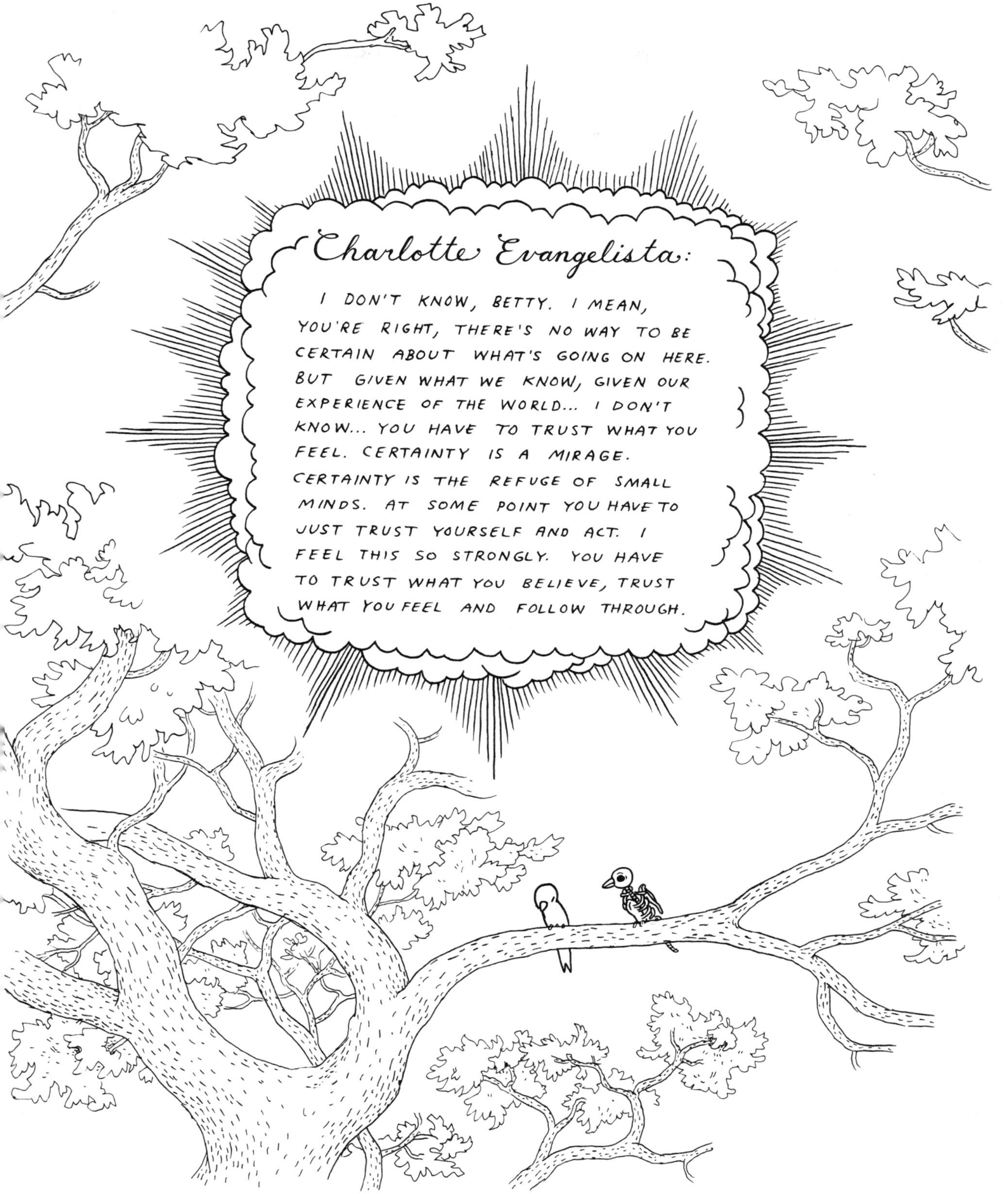
Charlotte Evangelista:
I DON'T KNOW, BETTY. I MEAN, YOU'RE RIGHT, THERE'S NO WAY TO BE CERTAIN ABOUT WHAT'S GOING ON HERE. BUT GIVEN WHAT WE KNOW, GIVEN OUR EXPERIENCE OF THE WORLD... I DON'T KNOW... YOU HAVE TO TRUST WHAT YOU FEEL. CERTAINTY IS A MIRAGE. CERTAINTY IS THE REFUGE OF SMALL MINDS. AT SOME POINT YOU HAVE TO JUST TRUST YOURSELF AND ACT. I FEEL THIS SO STRONGLY. YOU HAVE TO TRUST WHAT YOU BELIEVE, TRUST WHAT YOU FEEL AND FOLLOW THROUGH.

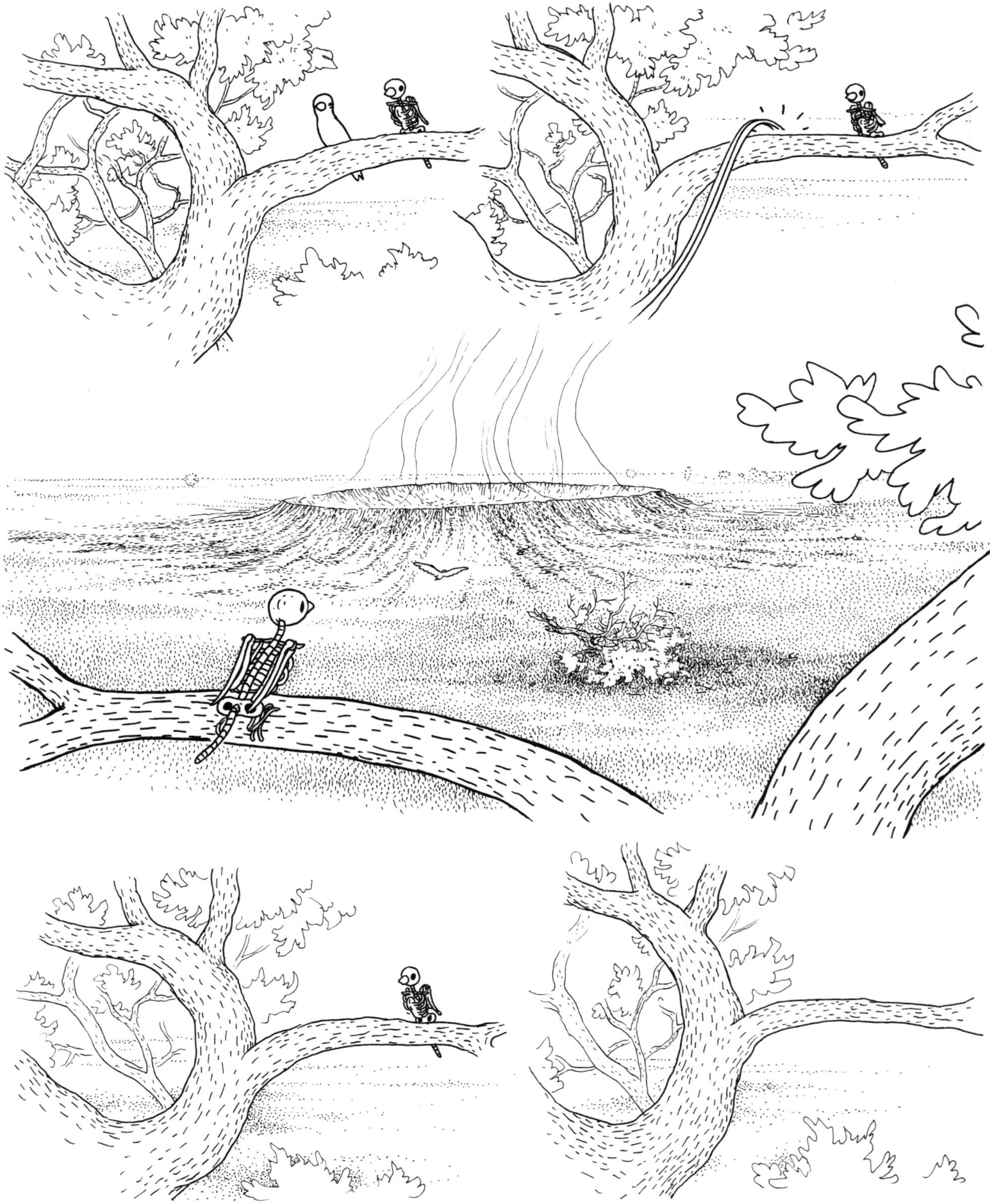

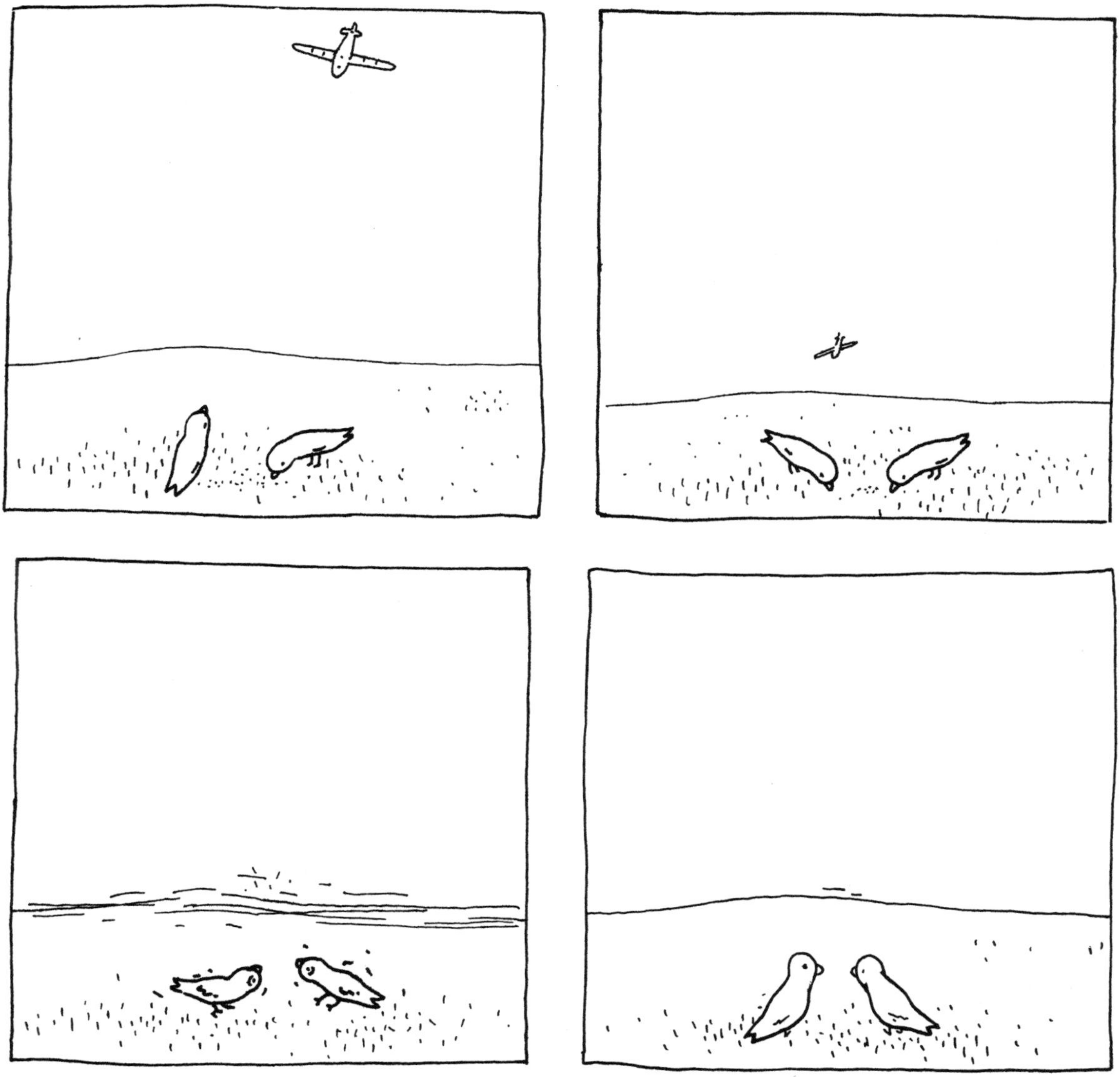

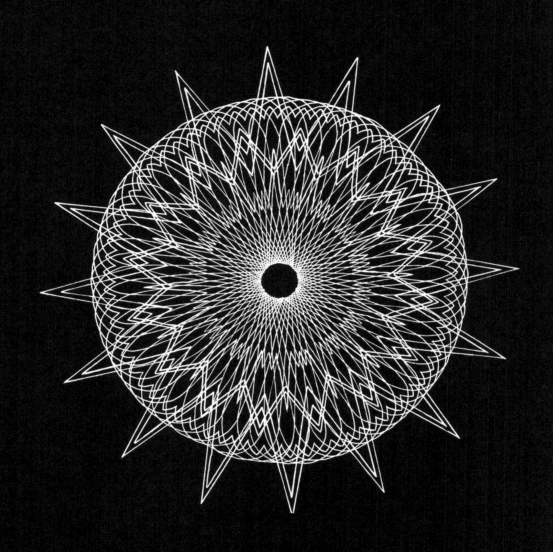

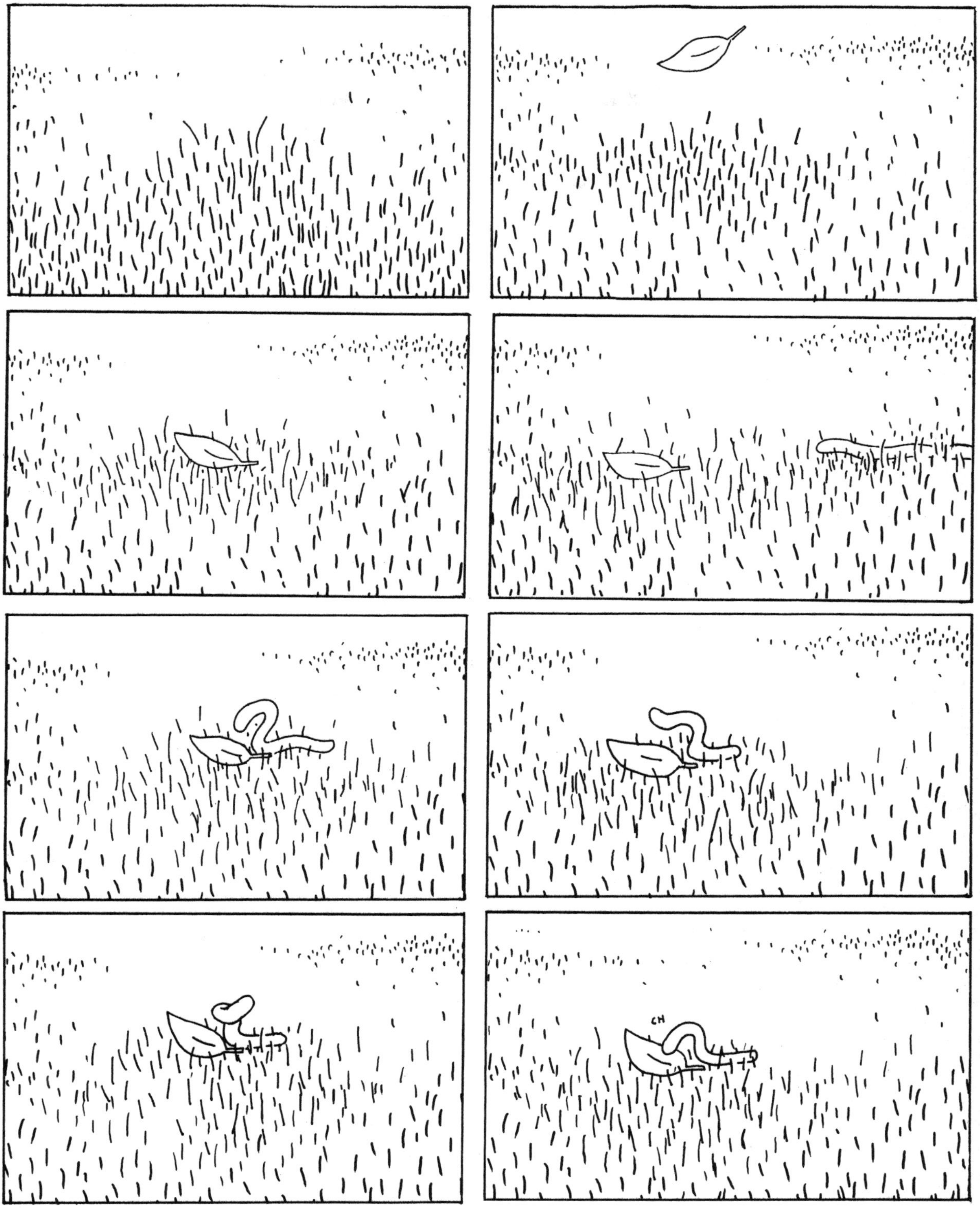
CH

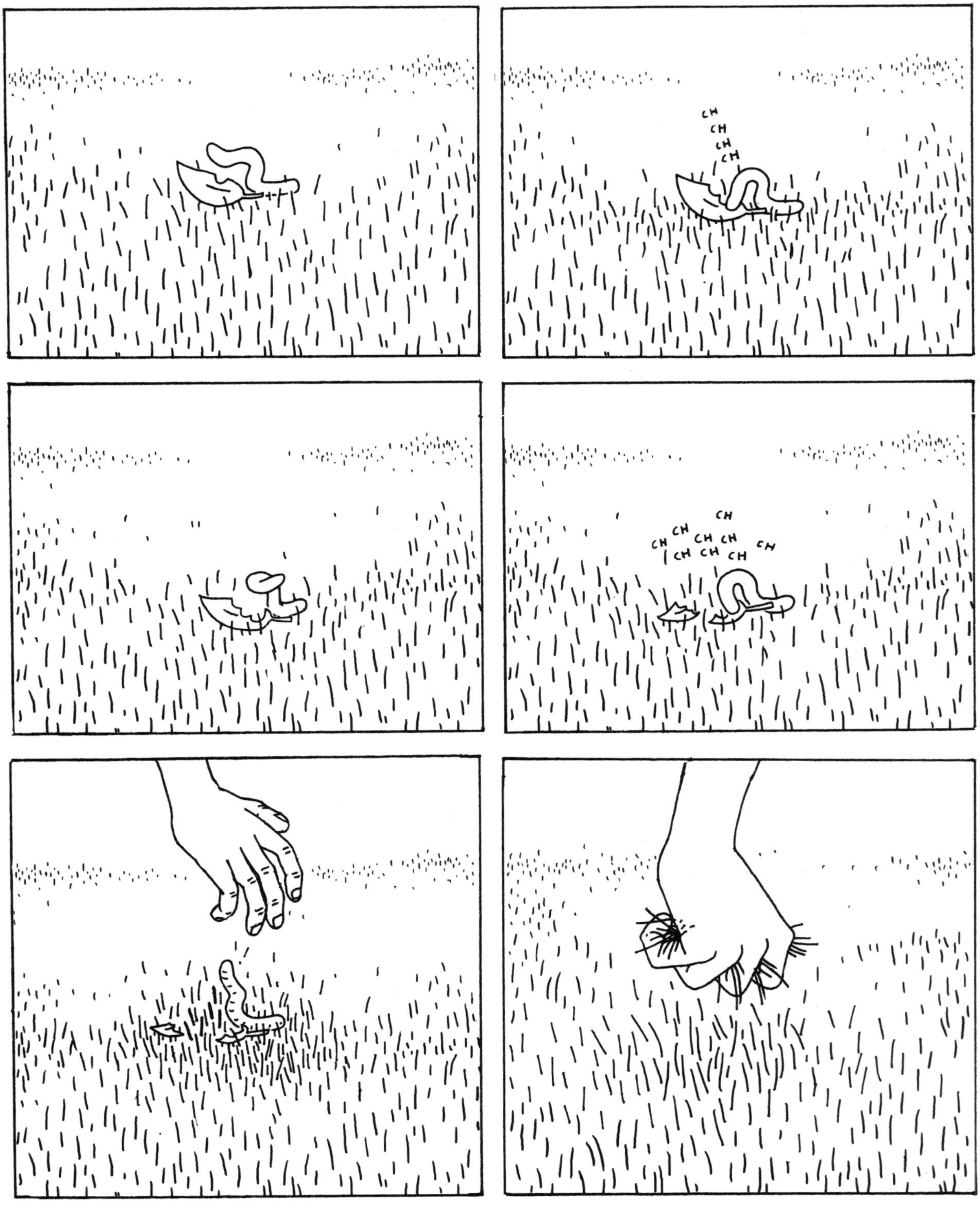
CH
CH
CH
CH
CH CH CH CH CH CH CH CH CH CH

SKCH
GN
CH
MN
CNCH
MCH
CHK
NN
NGM
MCH
NGN
CH
GLP

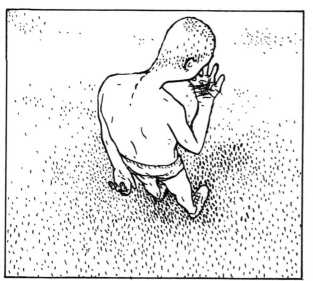

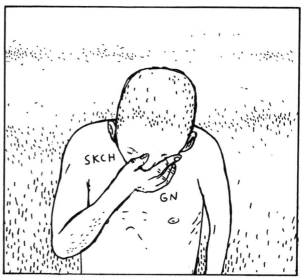

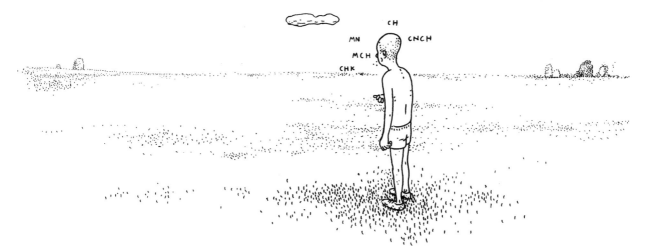

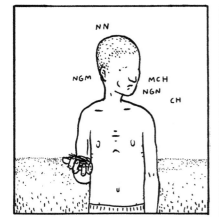

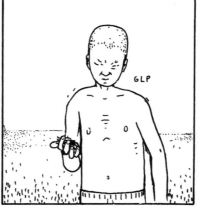

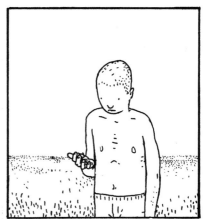

COFF
COFF
COFF
OFF
COFF
COFF
F
FF
GH
SNF
CHMP
NG
GNG
MCH
MNGM
MG
MN
CHK
CH
CKH
NCH
KT
MNG
SLP
SNK
CH

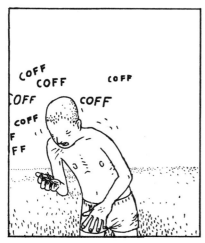

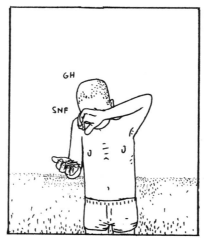

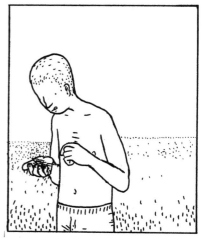

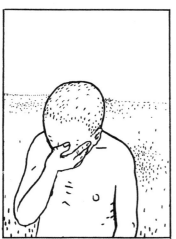

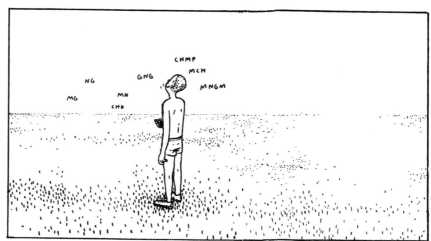

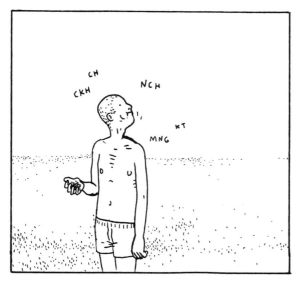

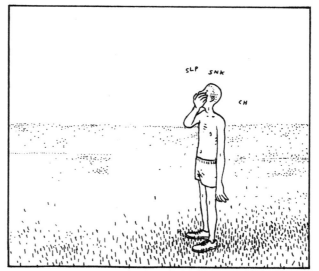

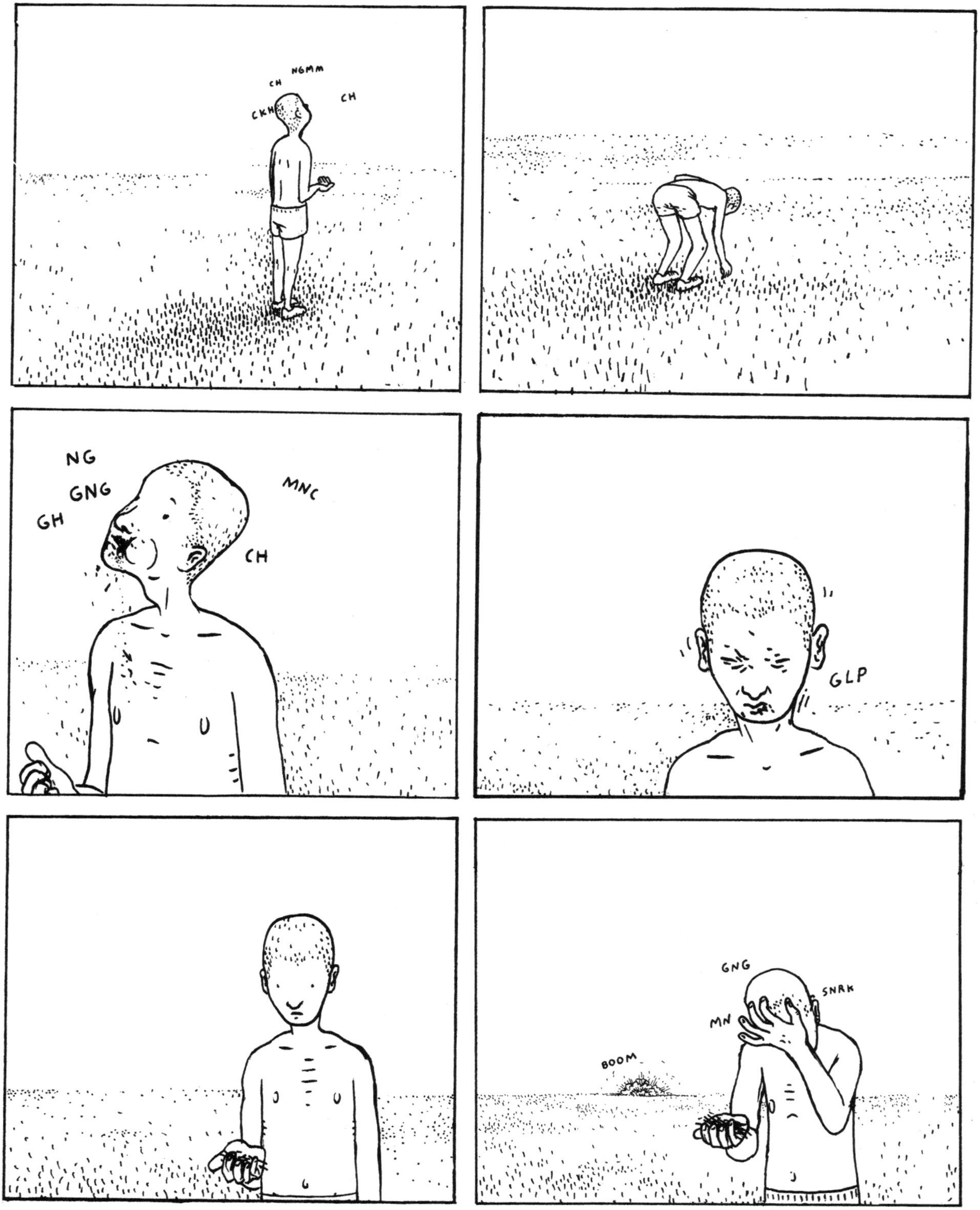
CH
NGMM
CKH
CH
NG
GNG
GH
MNC
CH
GLP
GNG
SNRK
MN
BOOM

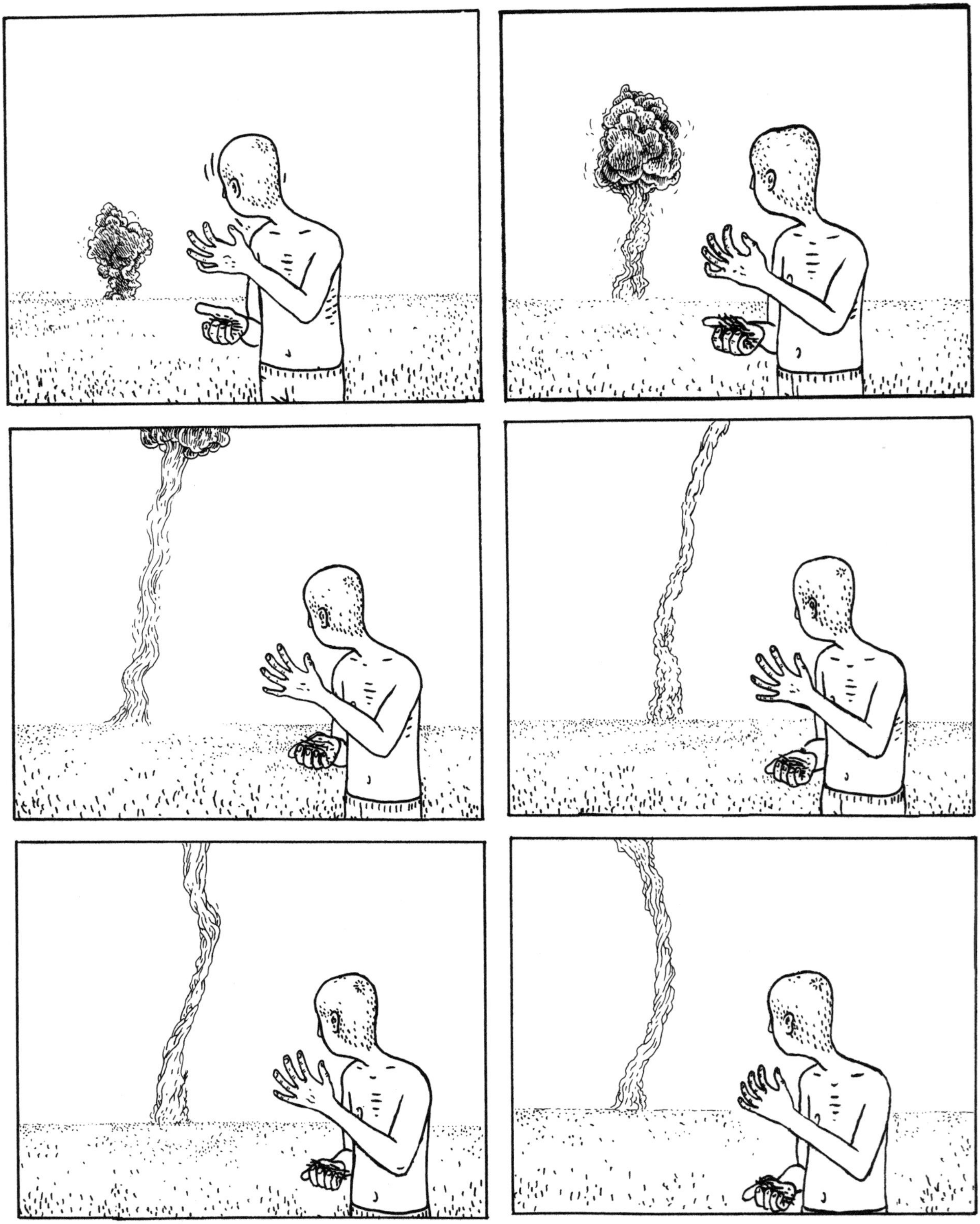

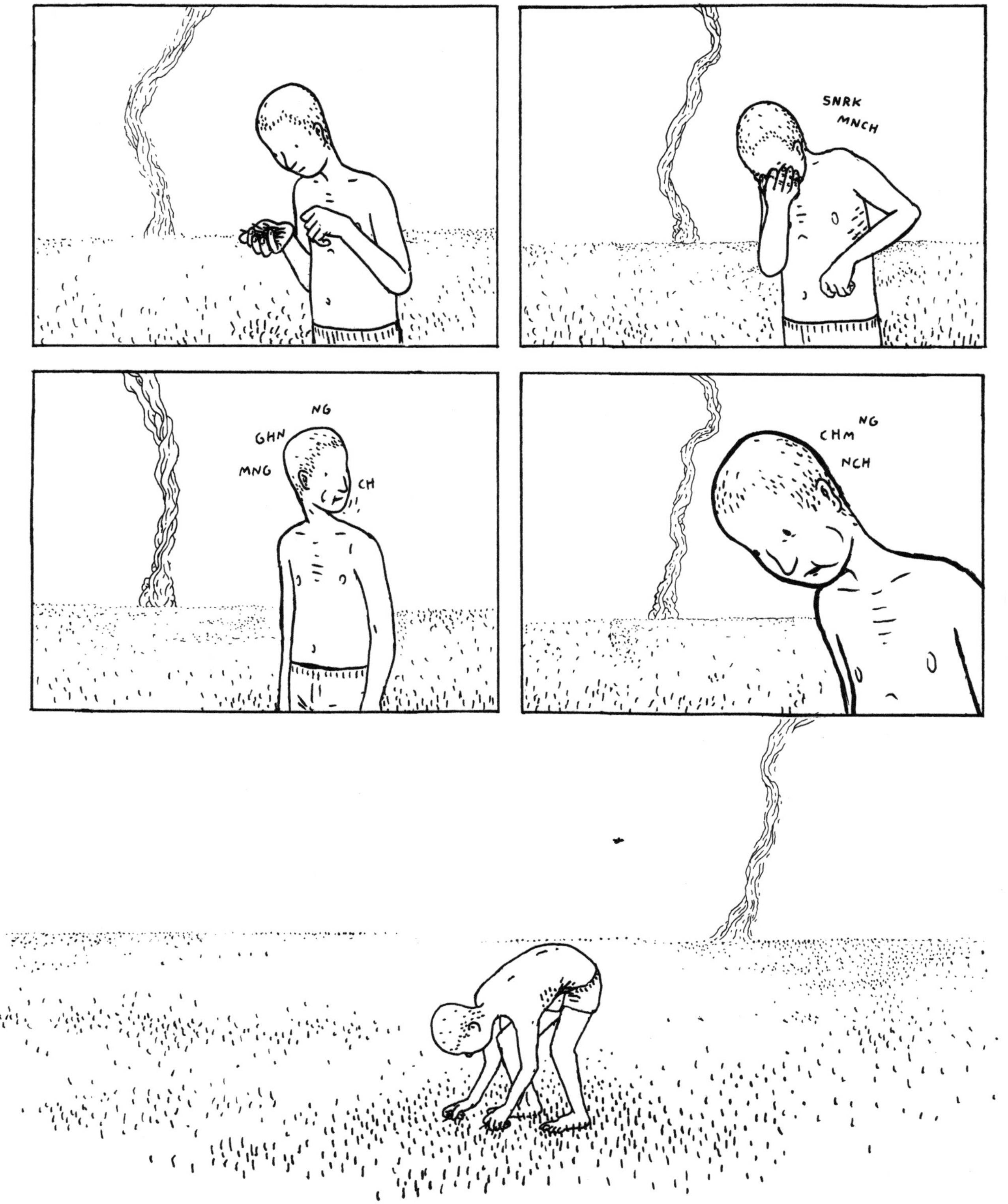
SNRK
MNCH
NG
GHN
MNG
CH
CHM
NG
NCH

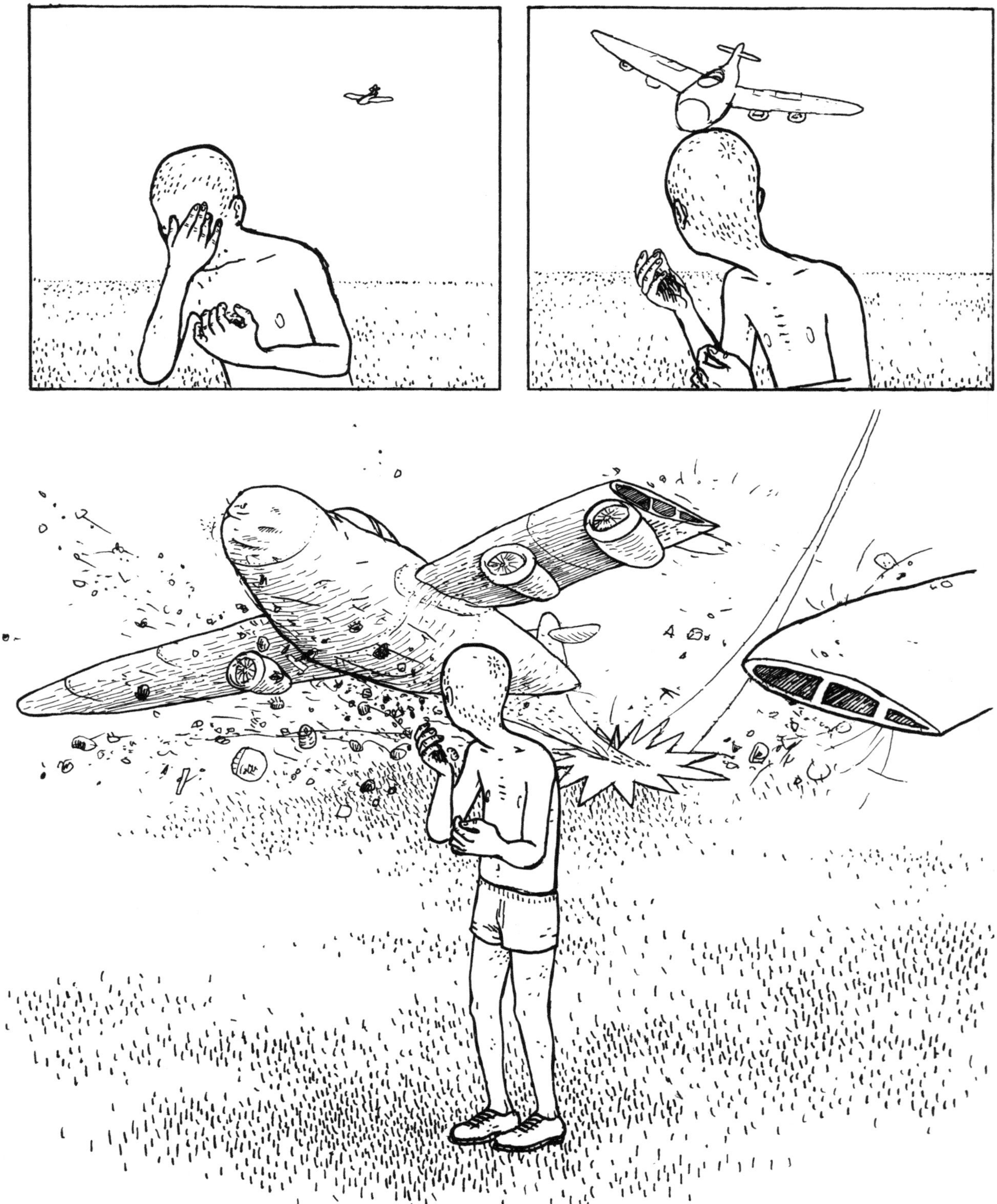

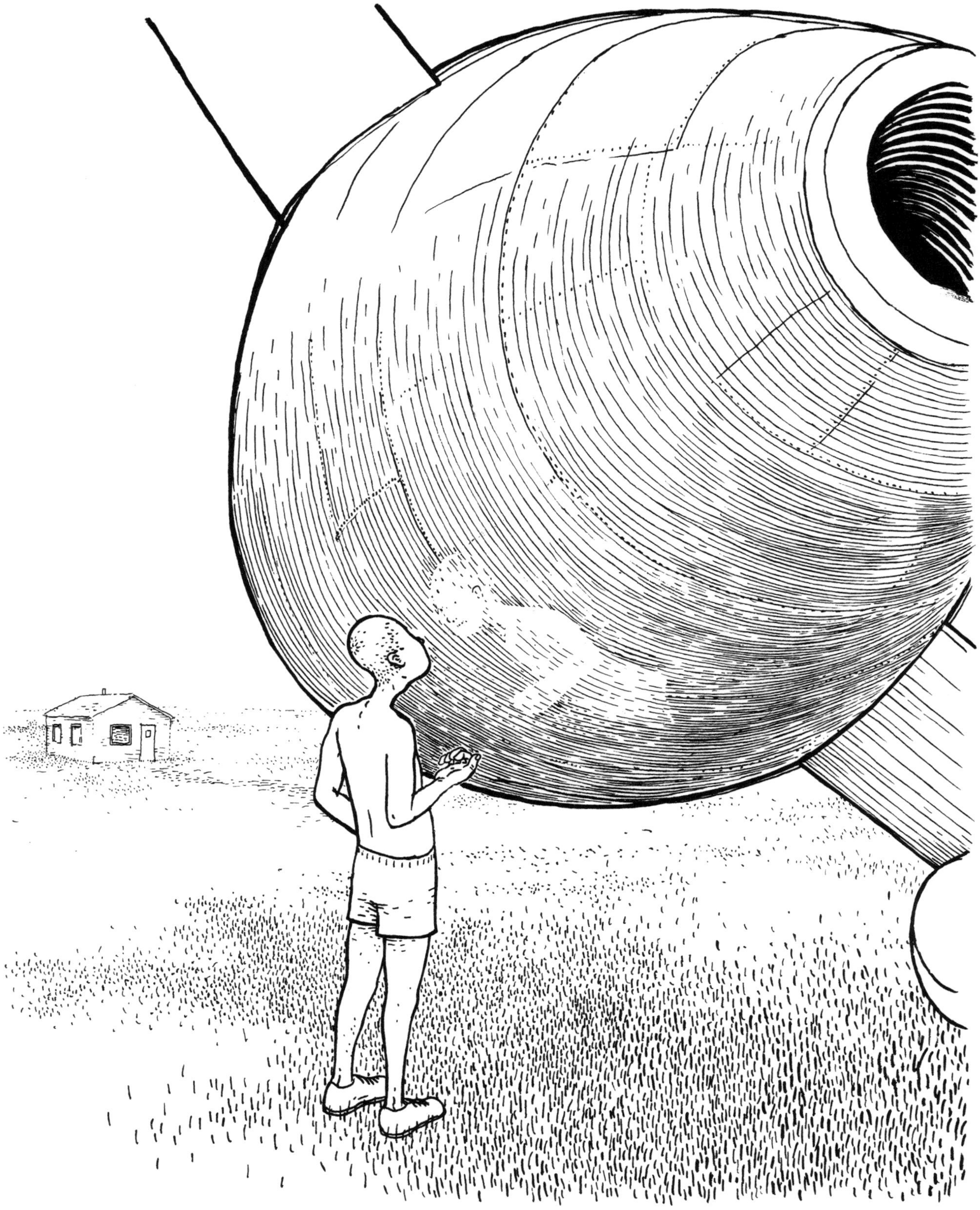

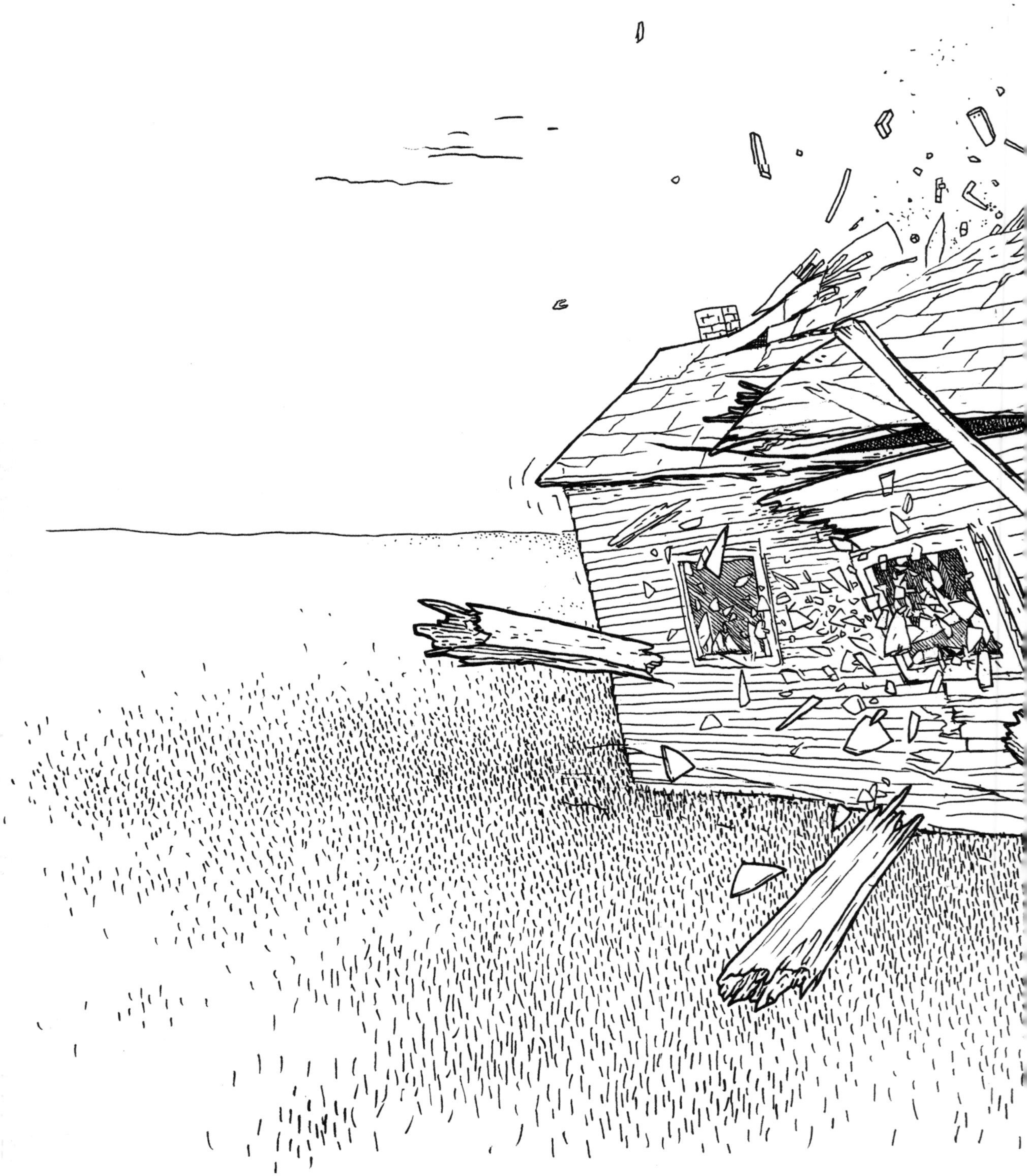

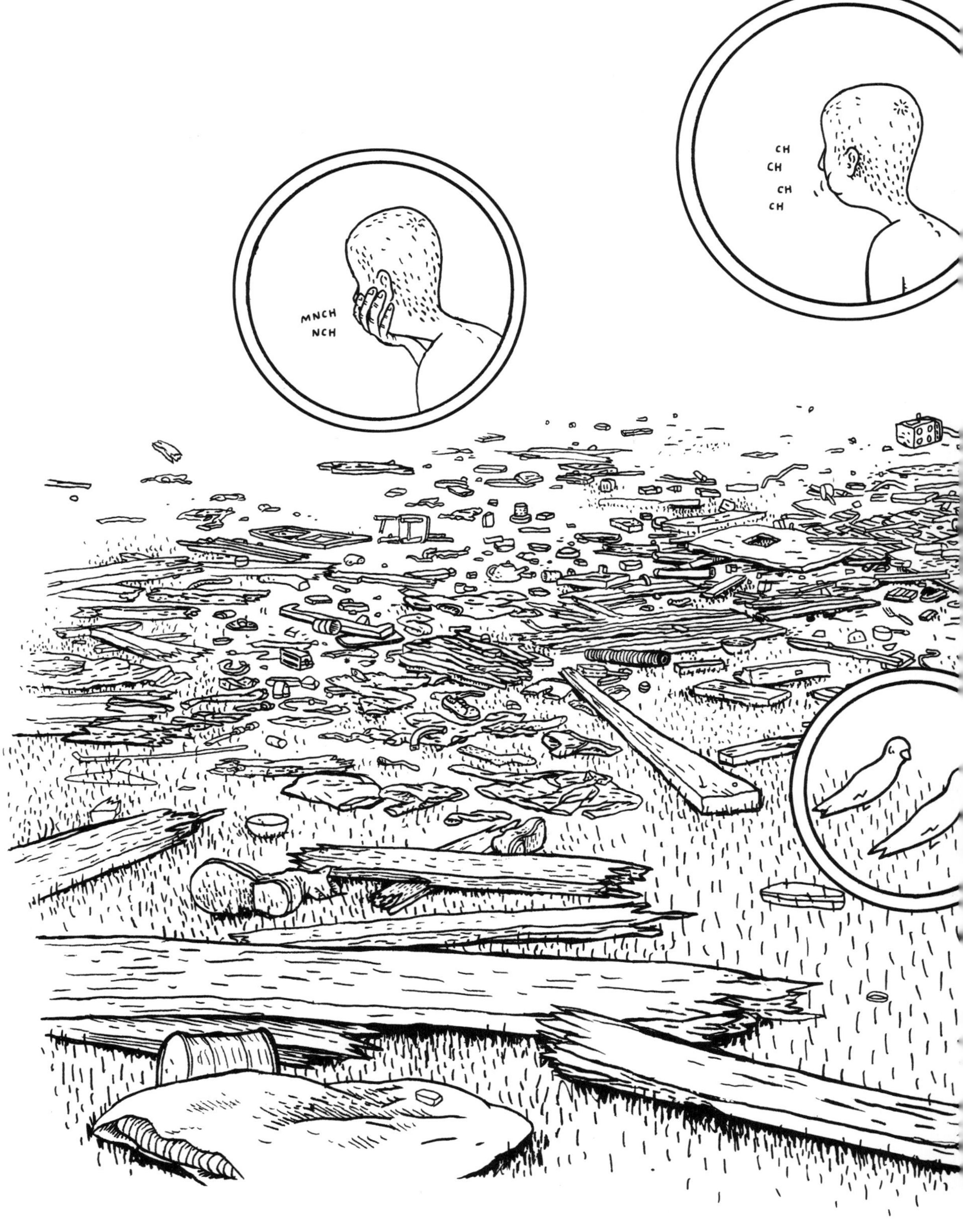
MNCH
NCH
CH
CH
CH
CH

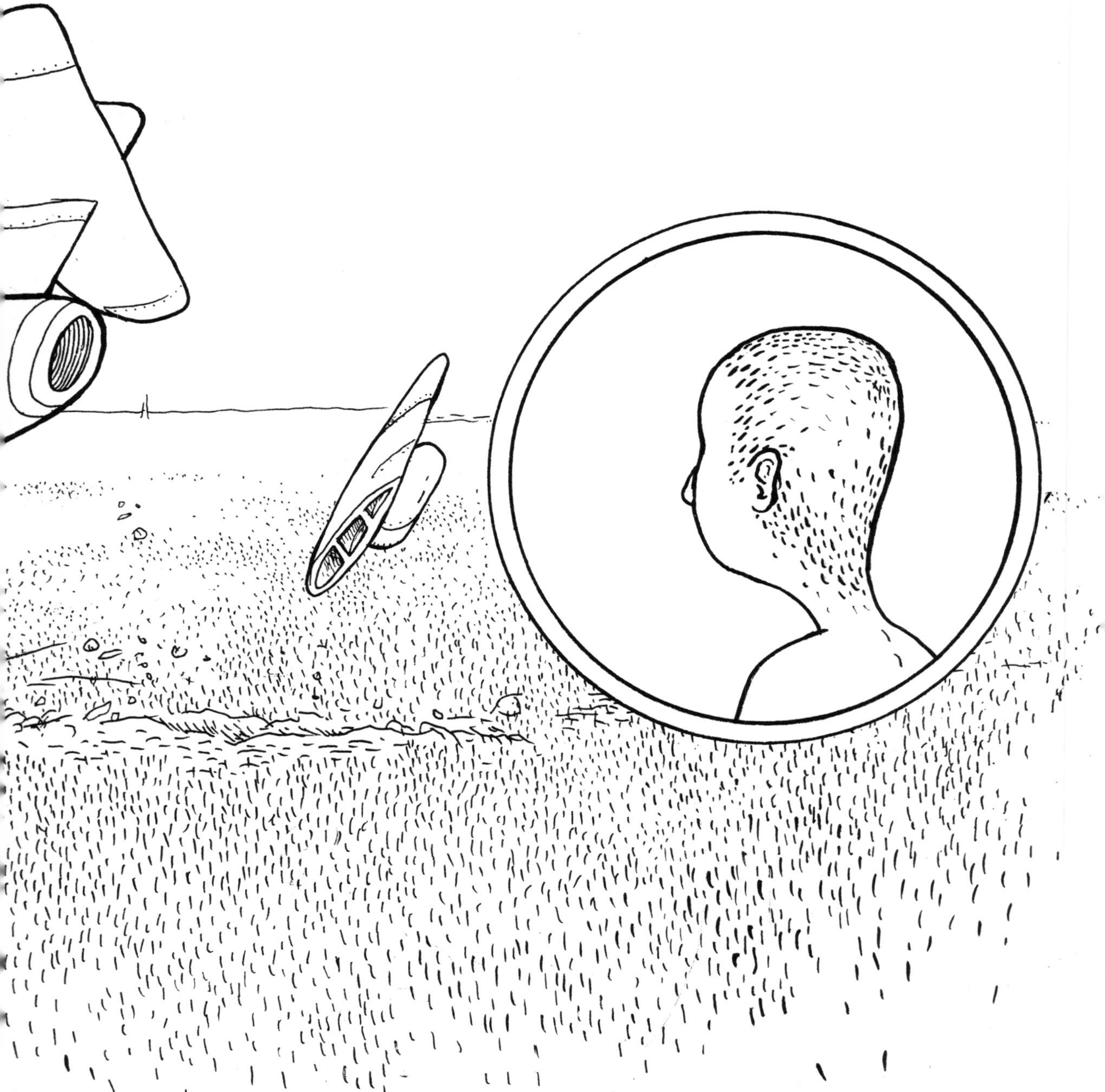

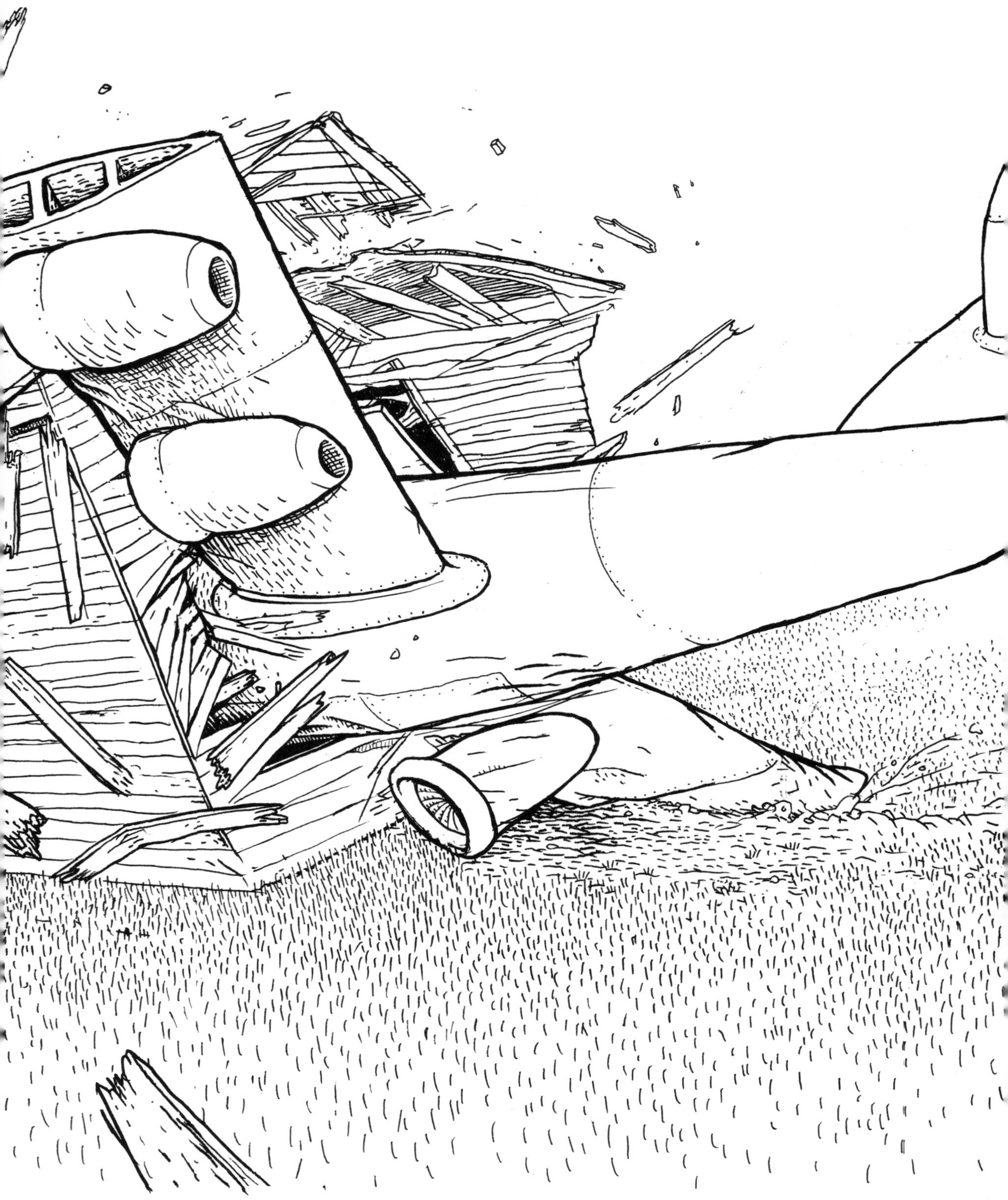

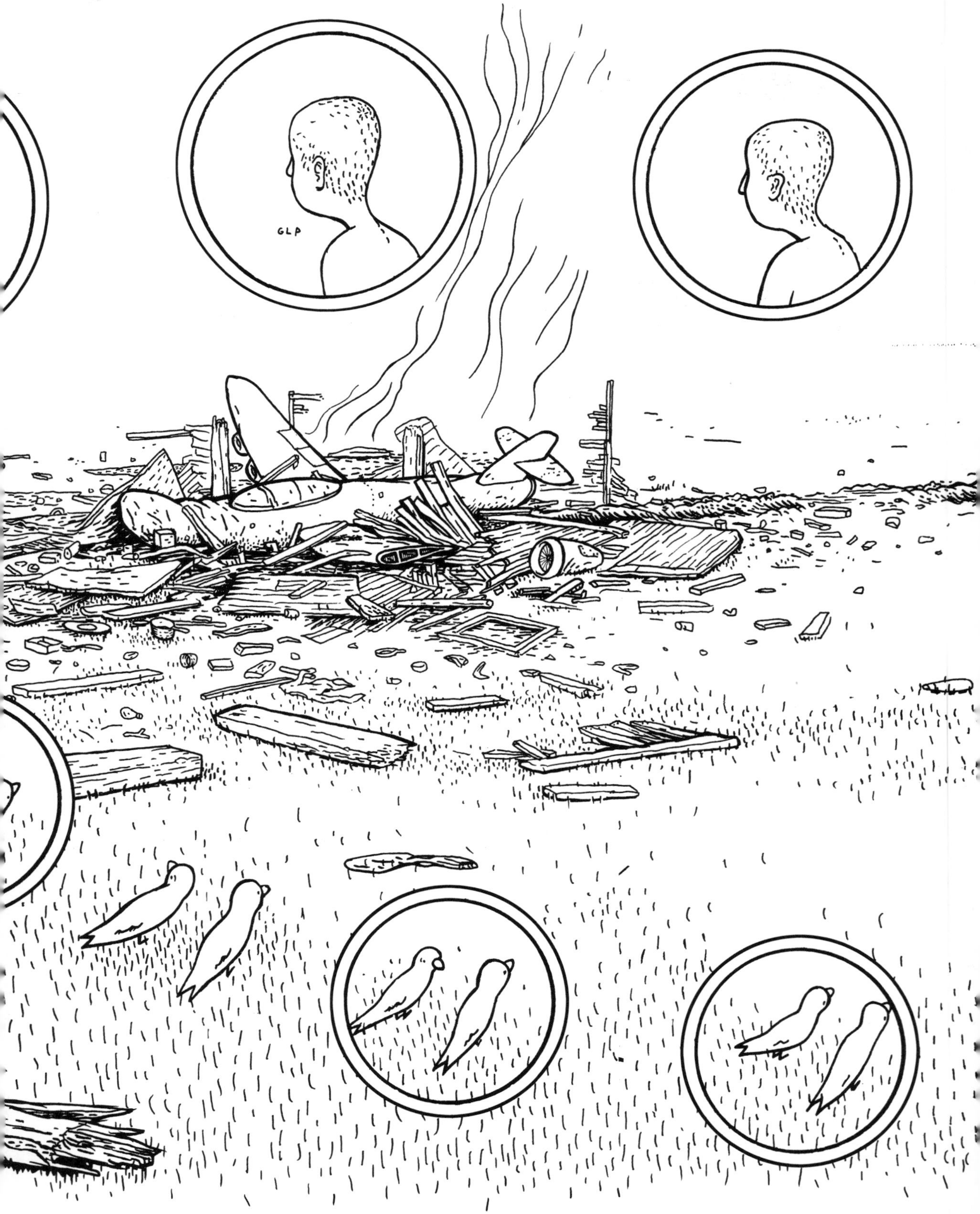
GLP

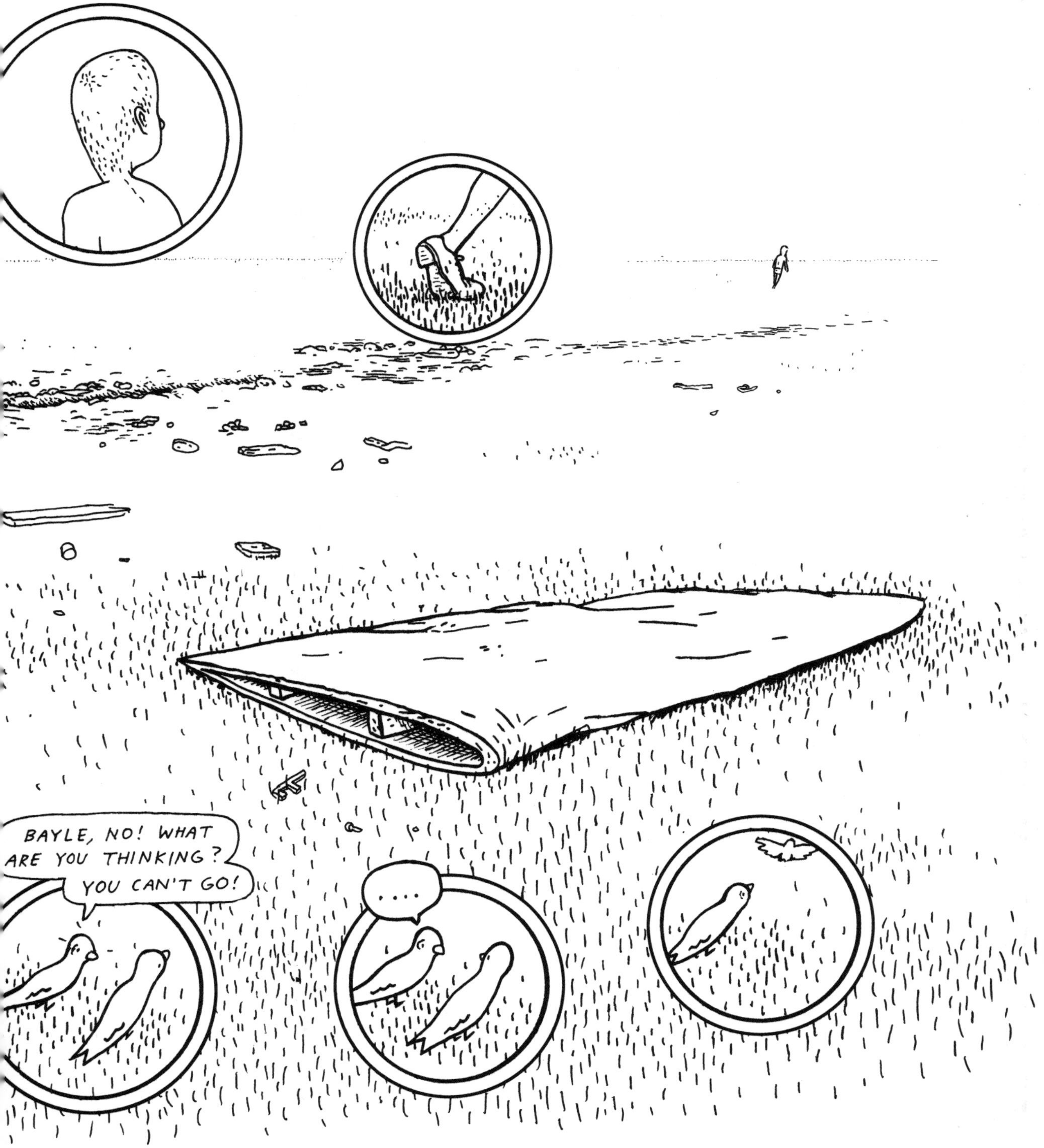
BAYLE, NO! WHAT ARE YOU THINKING? YOU CAN'T GO!
. . . .

BAYLE FOLLOWED HIM. I STAYED,
FEELING PARALYZED, MY HEAD SPINNING.
I DON'T KNOW EXACTLY WHAT I WAS
WORRIED ABOUT. THE EVENTS JUST
SEEMED SO INEXPLICABLE, SO
OMINOUS.

THERE HAD BEEN THE DISAPPEARANCES:
FIRST THELMA, THEN LEROY, THEN
ALGERNON. THERE WAS THE MISSING
TREE, AND THEN, OF COURSE,
THE EGG. SOME OF THE OTHER BIRDS
SEEMED CONCERNED AT FIRST, TOO, BUT
A DAY OR TWO LATER, THEY SEEMED
ALMOST TO FORGET.

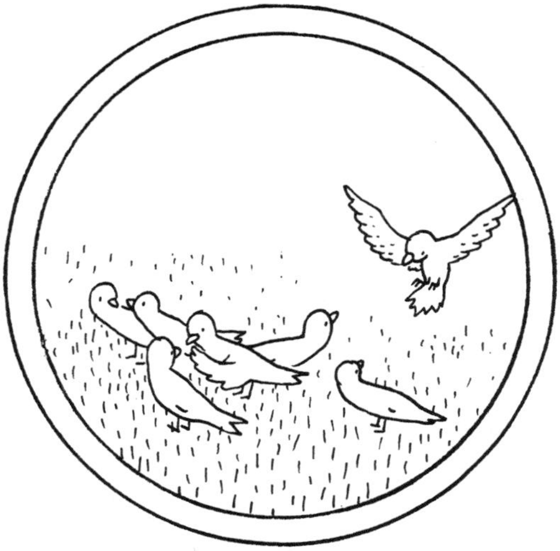

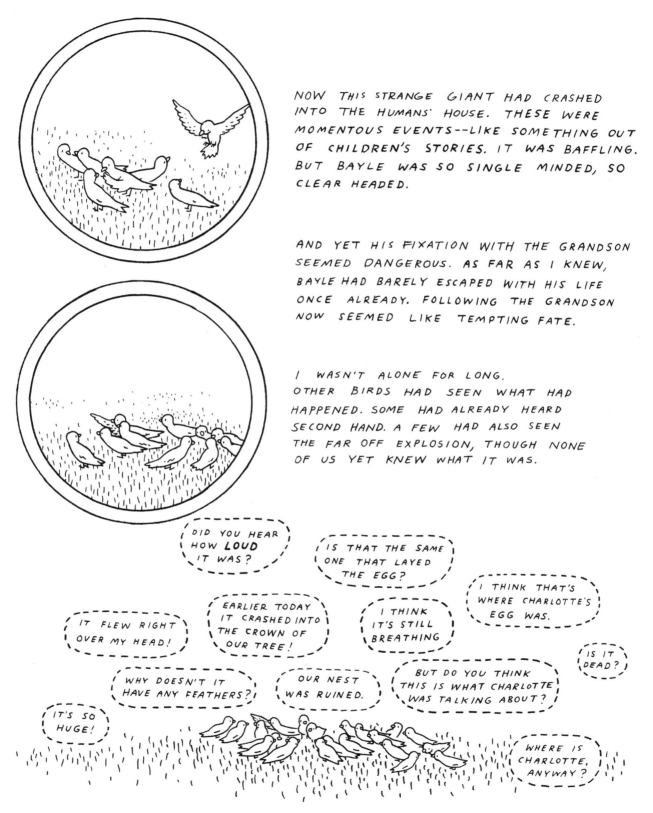

NOW THIS STRANGE GIANT HAD CRASHED INTO THE HUMANS' HOUSE. THESE WERE MOMENTOUS EVENTS--LIKE SOMETHING OUT OF CHILDREN'S STORIES. IT WAS BAFFLING. BUT BAYLE WAS SO SINGLE MINDED, SO CLEAR HEADED.

AND YET HIS FIXATION WITH THE GRANDSON SEEMED DANGEROUS. AS FAR AS I KNEW, BAYLE HAD BARELY ESCAPED WITH HIS LIFE ONCE ALREADY. FOLLOWING THE GRANDSON NOW SEEMED LIKE TEMPTING FATE.

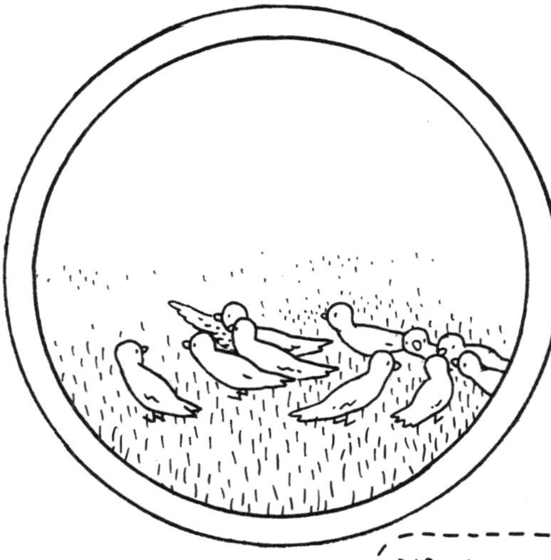

I WASN'T ALONE FOR LONG. OTHER BIRDS HAD SEEN WHAT HAD HAPPENED. SOME HAD ALREADY HEARD SECOND HAND. A FEW HAD ALSO SEEN THE FAR OFF EXPLOSION, THOUGH NONE OF US YET KNEW WHAT IT WAS.

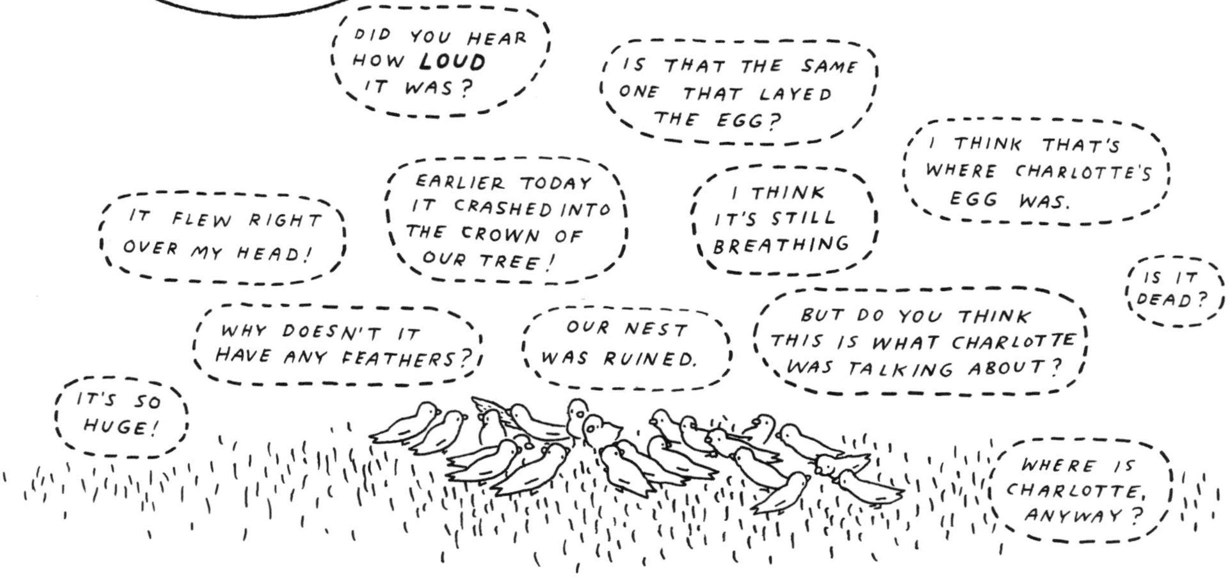
DID YOU HEAR HOW **LOUD** IT WAS?
IS THAT THE SAME ONE THAT LAYED THE EGG?
I THINK THAT'S WHERE CHARLOTTE'S EGG WAS.
EARLIER TODAY IT CRASHED INTO THE CROWN OF OUR TREE!
I THINK IT'S STILL BREATHING
IT FLEW RIGHT OVER MY HEAD!
IS IT DEAD?
WHY DOESN'T IT HAVE ANY FEATHERS?
OUR NEST WAS RUINED.
BUT DO YOU THINK THIS IS WHAT CHARLOTTE WAS TALKING ABOUT?
IT'S SO HUGE!
WHERE IS CHARLOTTE, ANYWAY?

I WAS JUST RECOUNTING FOR THE FOURTH TIME
THE INCREDIBLE SIGHT AND SOUND OF IT COMING
DOWN WHEN THE GIANT MADE A NOISE.

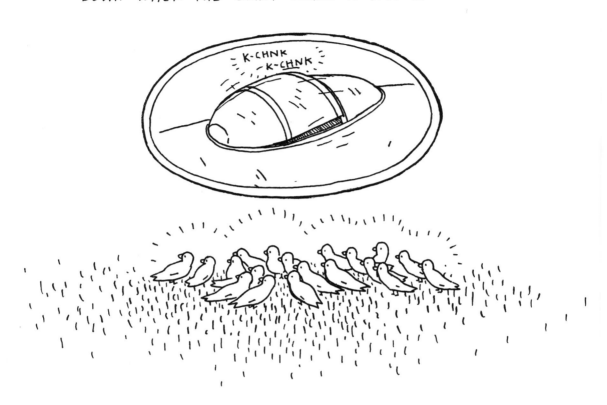

EVERYONE WAS QUIET, WATCHING.
FOR A MOMENT NOTHING HAPPENED.
THEN IT MADE THE SAME NOISE AGAIN.

AND THEN A MAN CAME OUT OF ITS HEAD.

CLICK
K-CHNK
K-CHUNK
K-CHNK
K-CHNK
K-CHNK
K-CHNK
TAP
TAP
TAP
TAP
KSH
KSH
KKSHSH

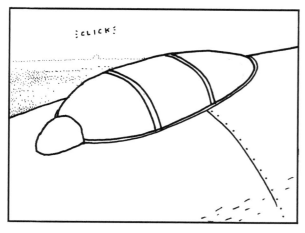

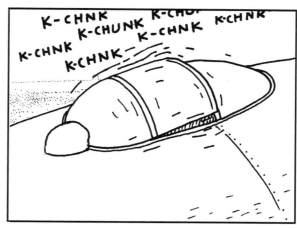

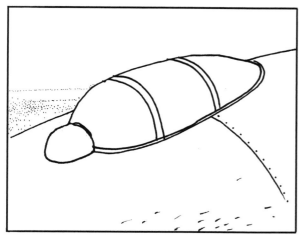

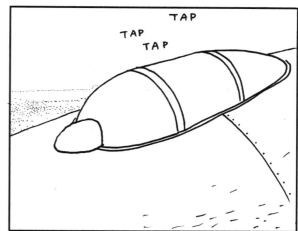

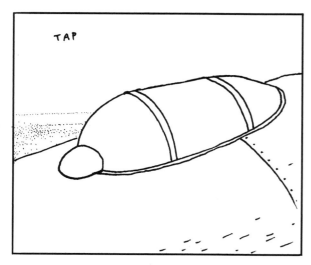

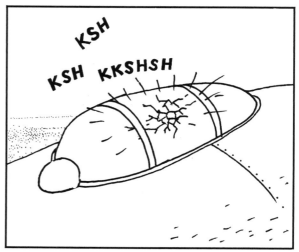

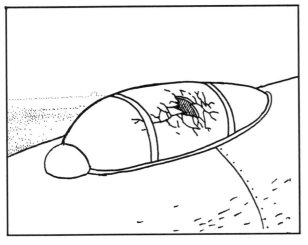

KSHSH!!

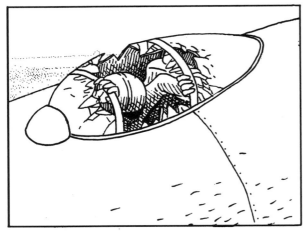

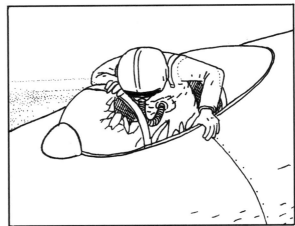

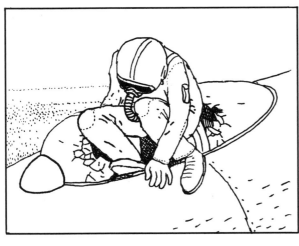

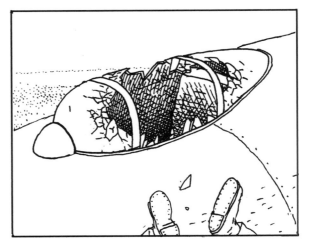

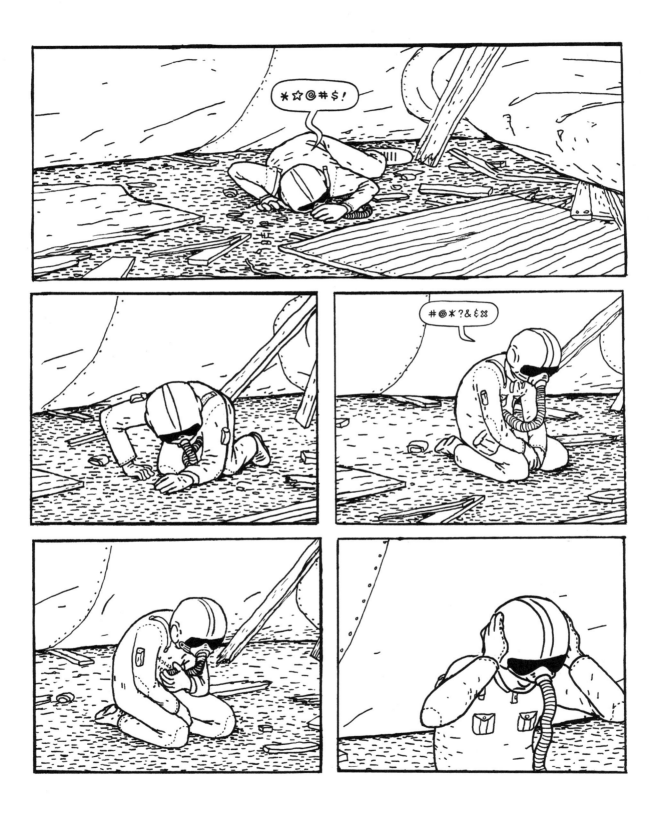

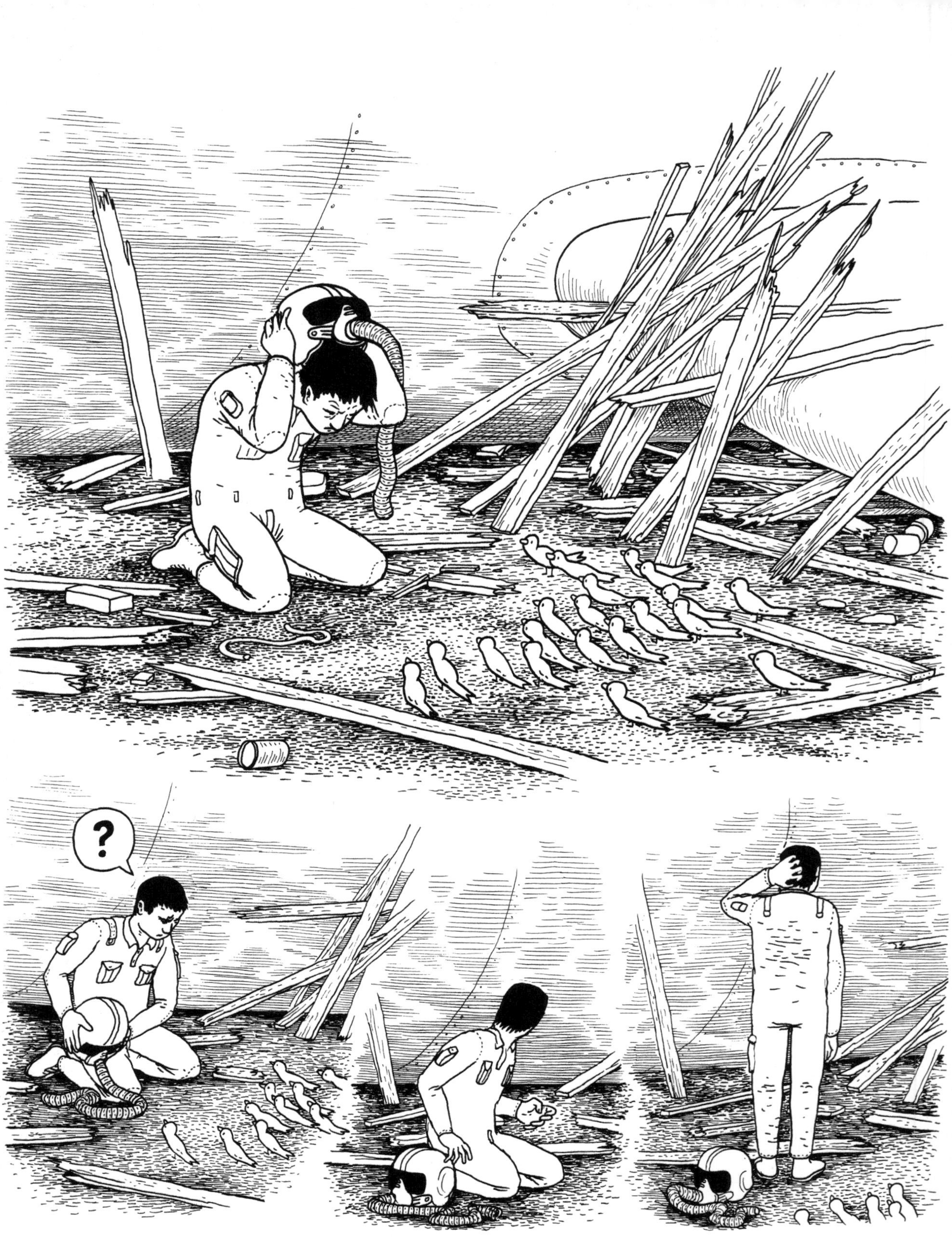
?

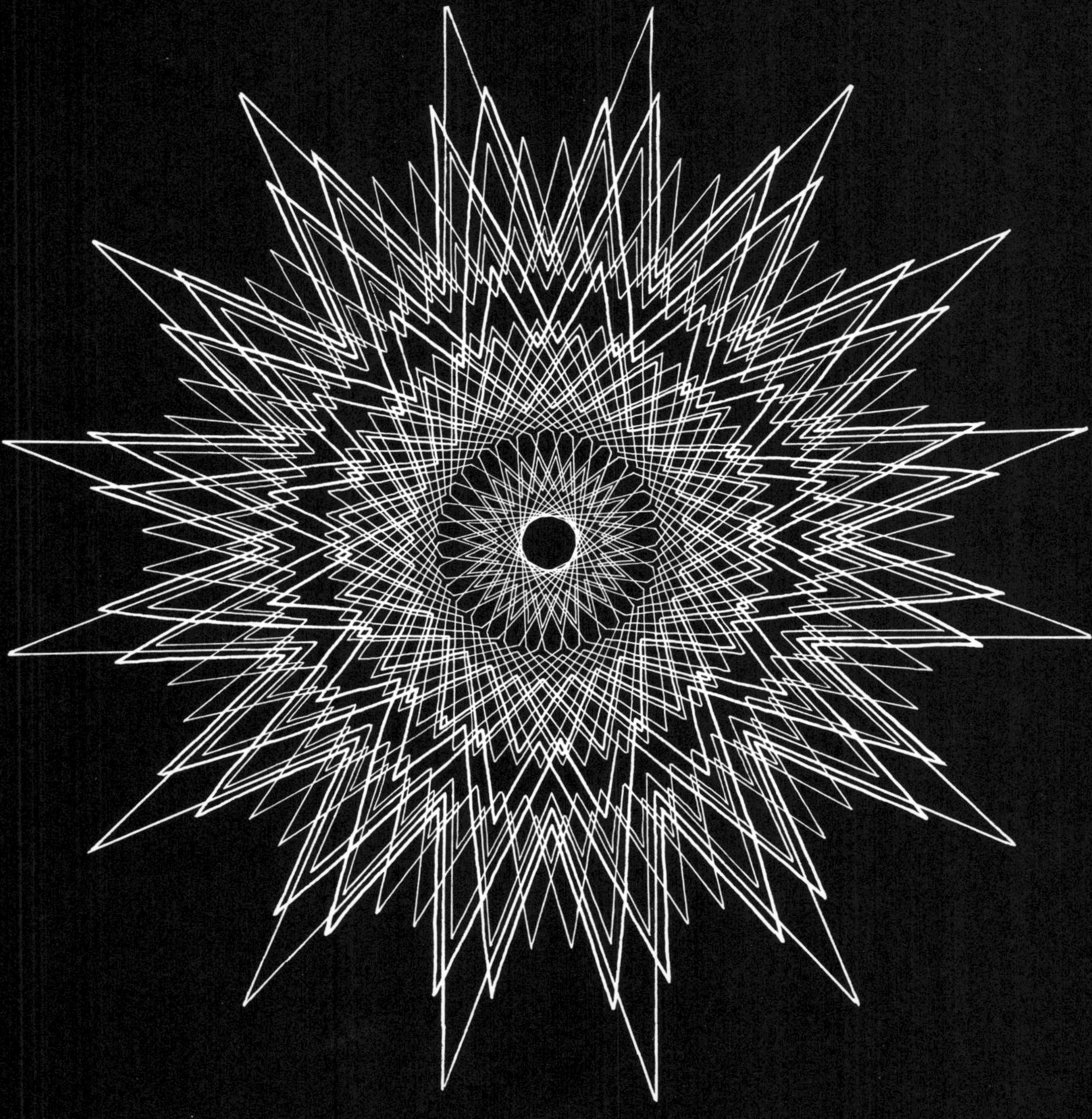

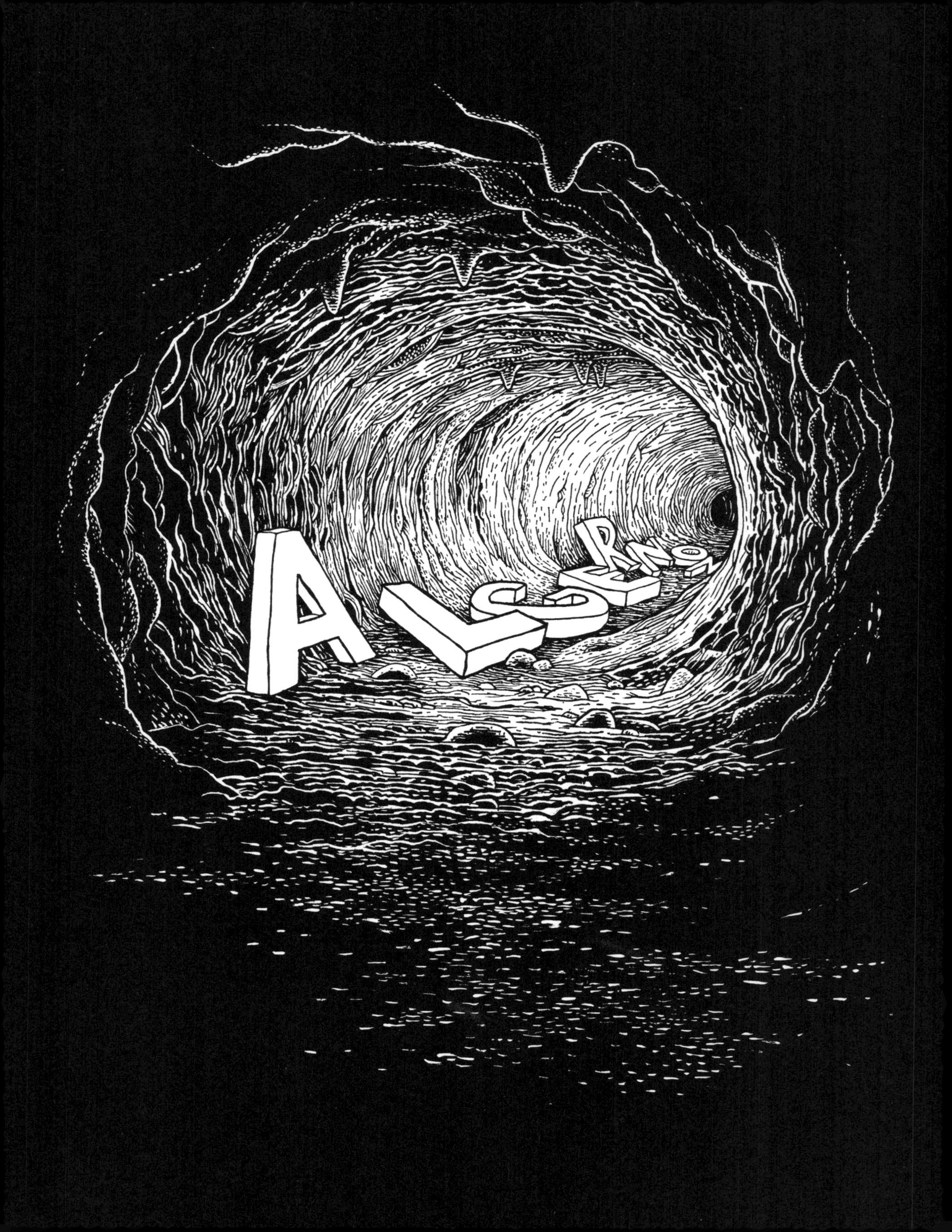
ALGERNON

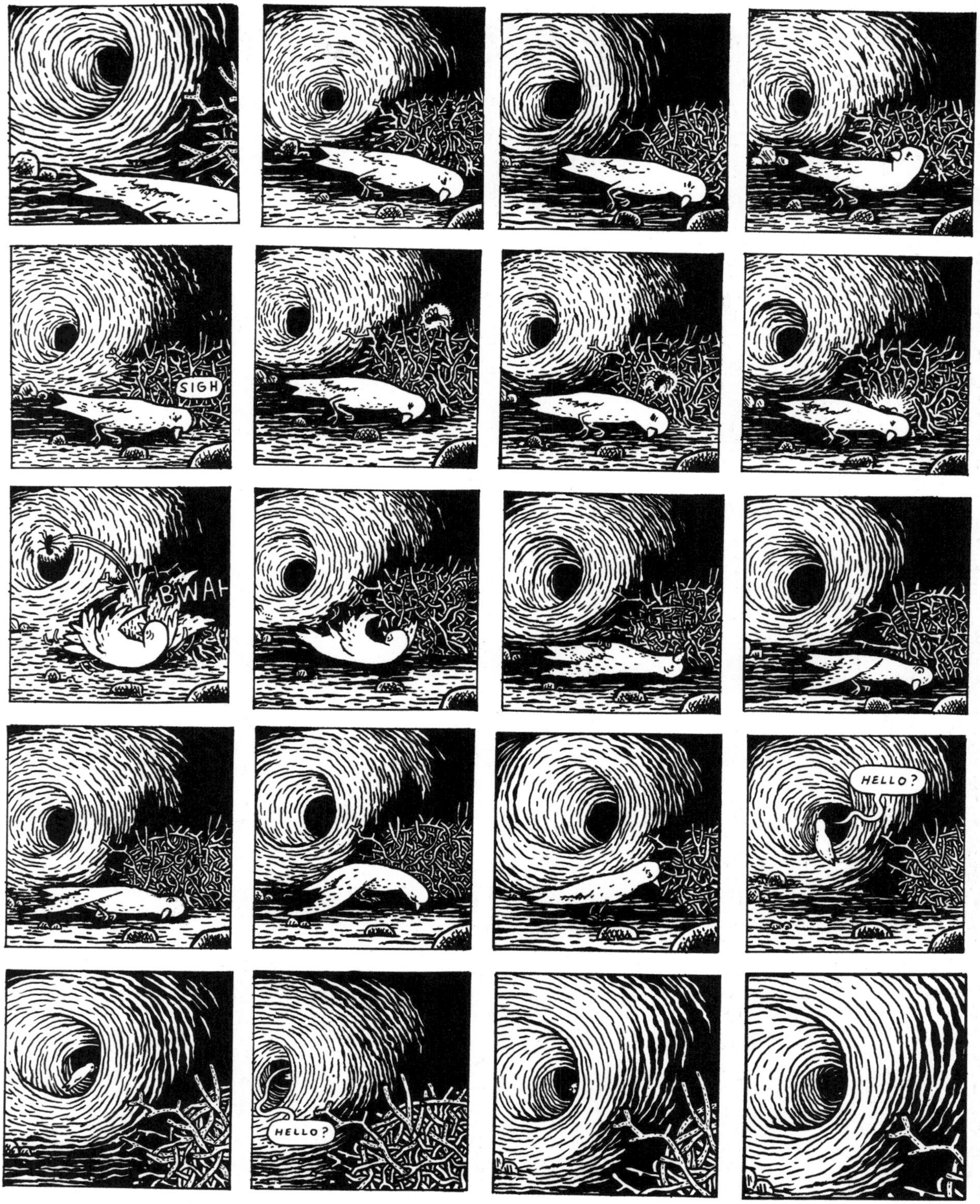
SIGH
BWAH
HELLO?
HELLO?

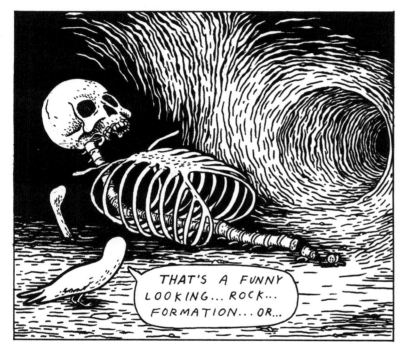

THAT'S A FUNNY LOOKING... ROCK... FORMATION... OR...

OH!

GUH-GUH

MM. THAT WAS EXQUISITE.

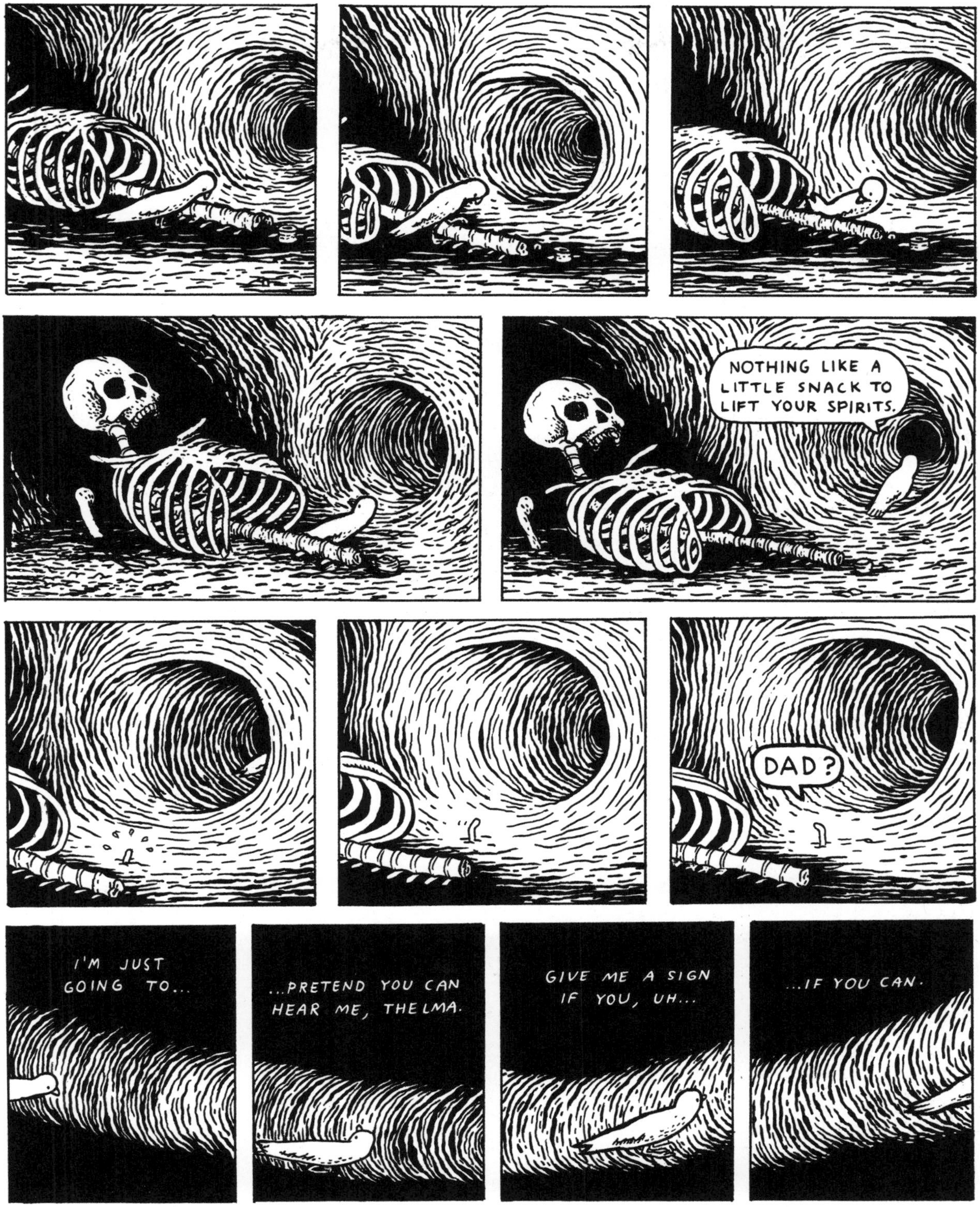
NOTHING LIKE A LITTLE SNACK TO LIFT YOUR SPIRITS.
DAD?
I'M JUST GOING TO...
...PRETEND YOU CAN HEAR ME, THELMA.
GIVE ME A SIGN IF YOU, UH...
...IF YOU CAN.

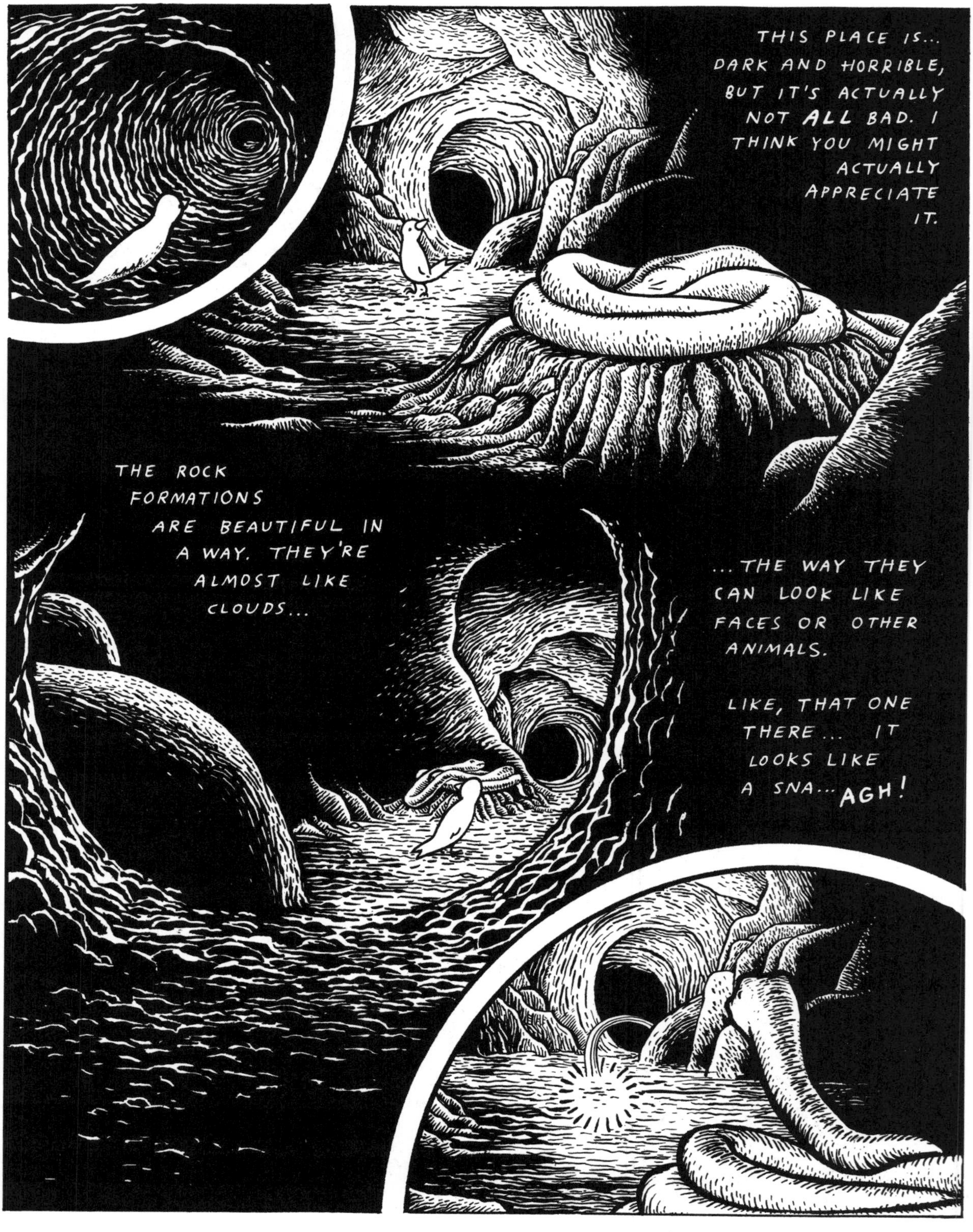
THIS PLACE IS... DARK AND HORRIBLE, BUT IT'S ACTUALLY NOT ALL BAD. I THINK YOU MIGHT ACTUALLY APPRECIATE IT.
THE ROCK FORMATIONS ARE BEAUTIFUL IN A WAY. THEY'RE ALMOST LIKE CLOUDS...
...THE WAY THEY CAN LOOK LIKE FACES OR OTHER ANIMALS.
LIKE, THAT ONE THERE... IT LOOKS LIKE A SNA... AGH!

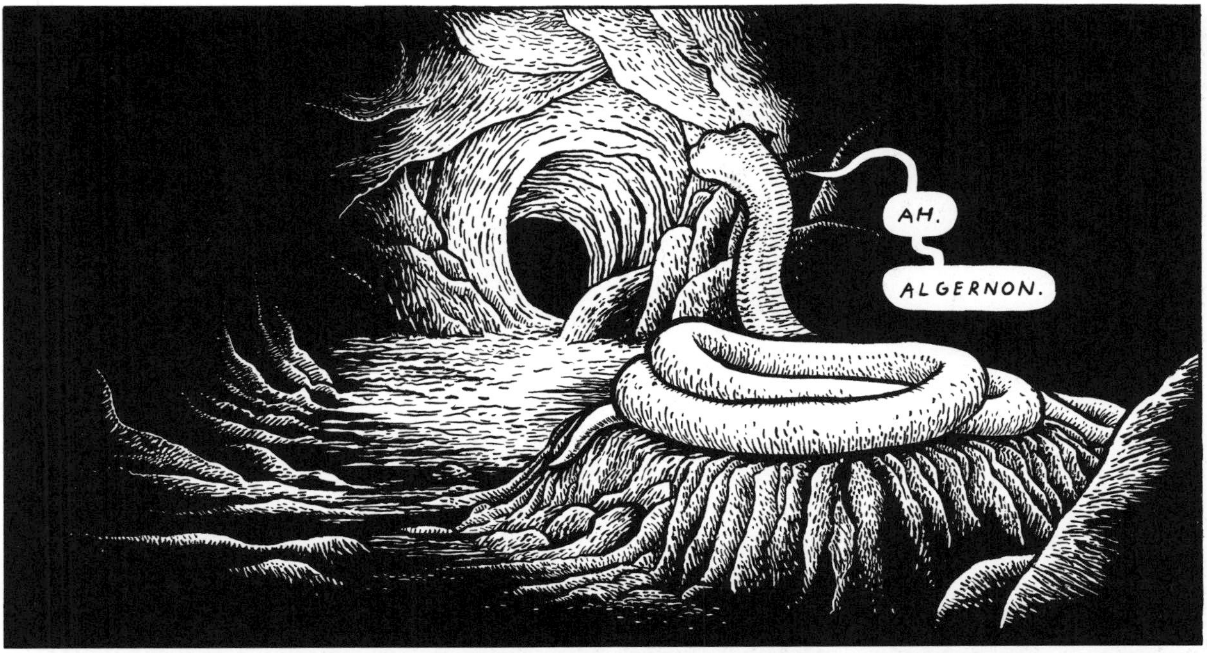
AH.
ALGERNON.
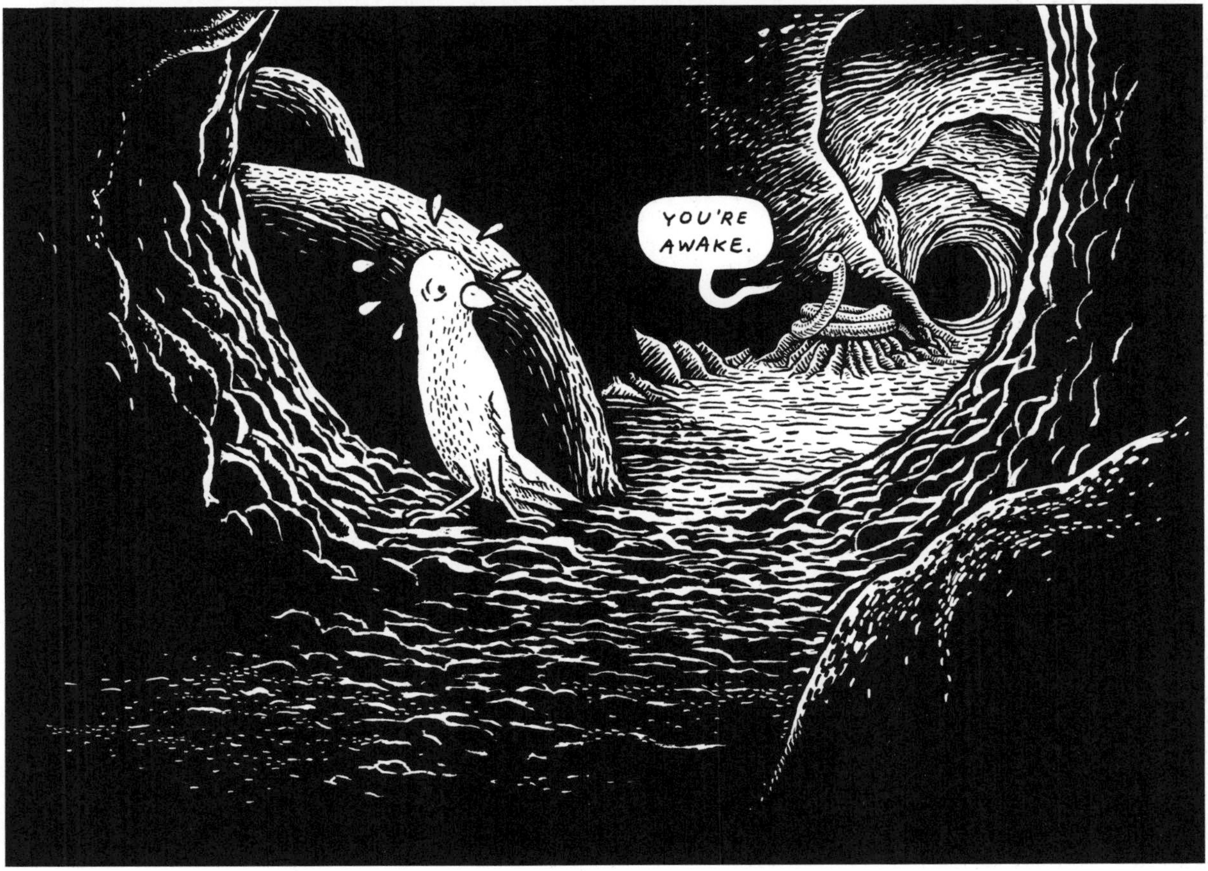
YOU'RE AWAKE.

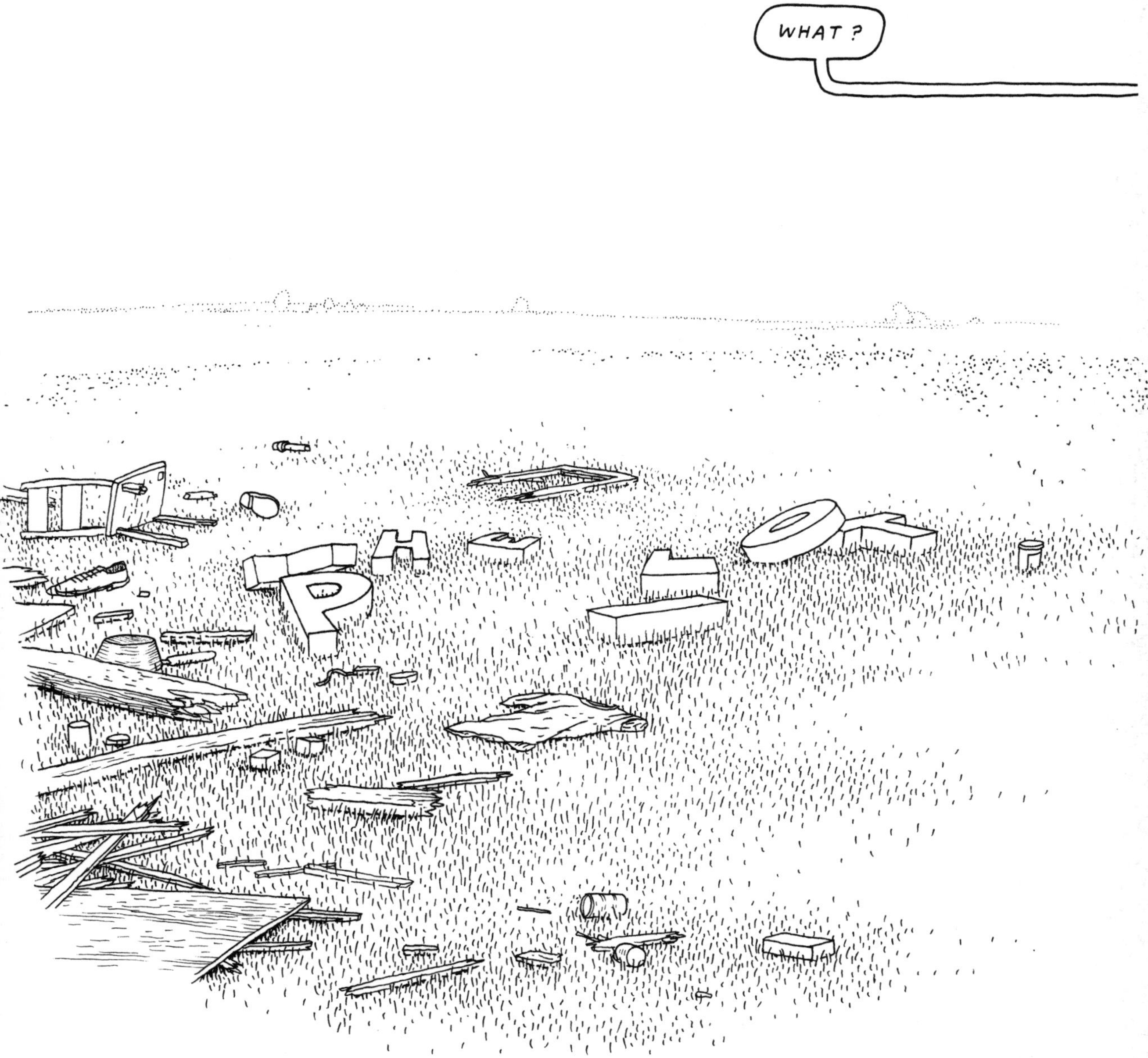
WHAT?

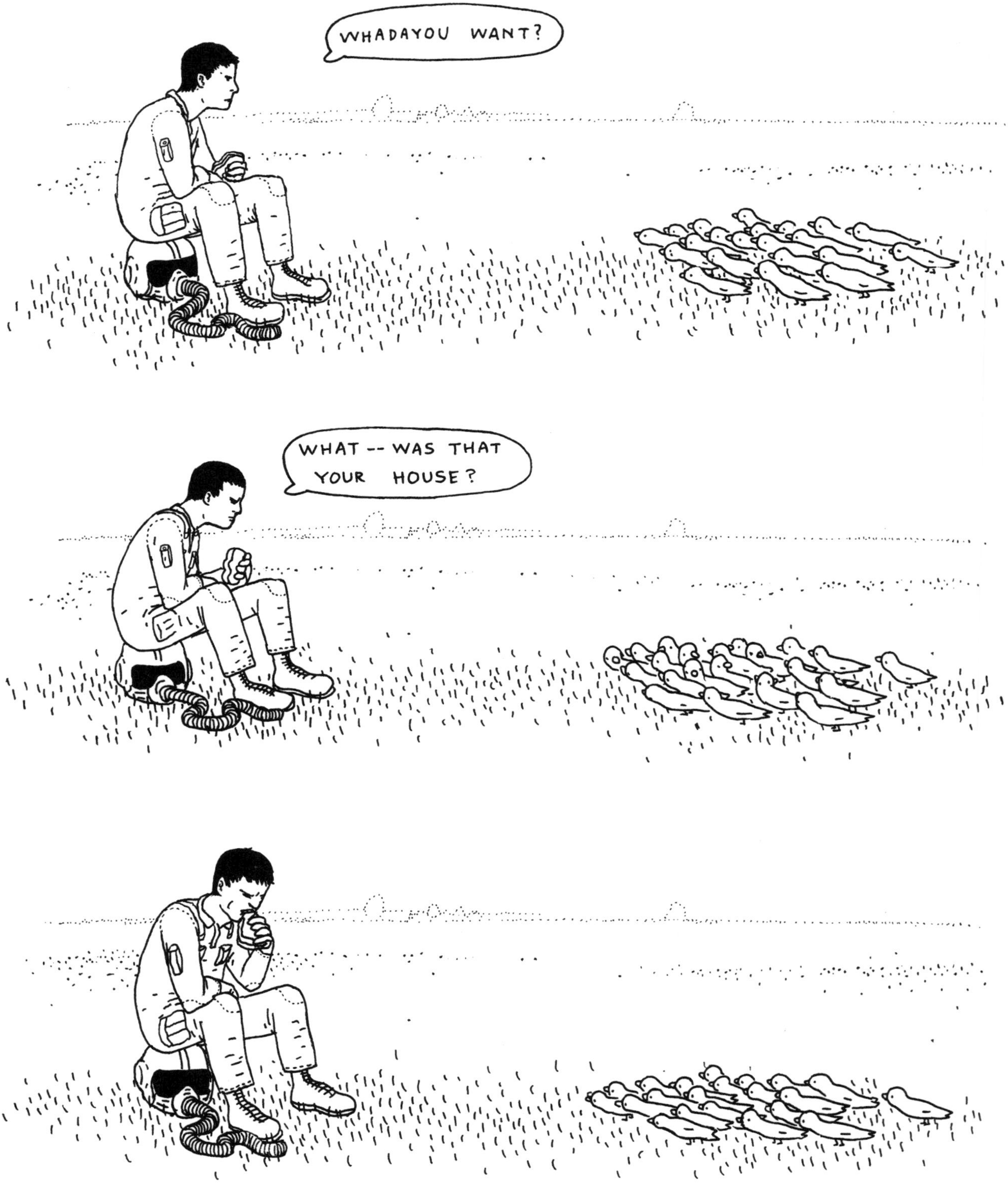
WHADAYOU WANT?
WHAT -- WAS THAT YOUR HOUSE?

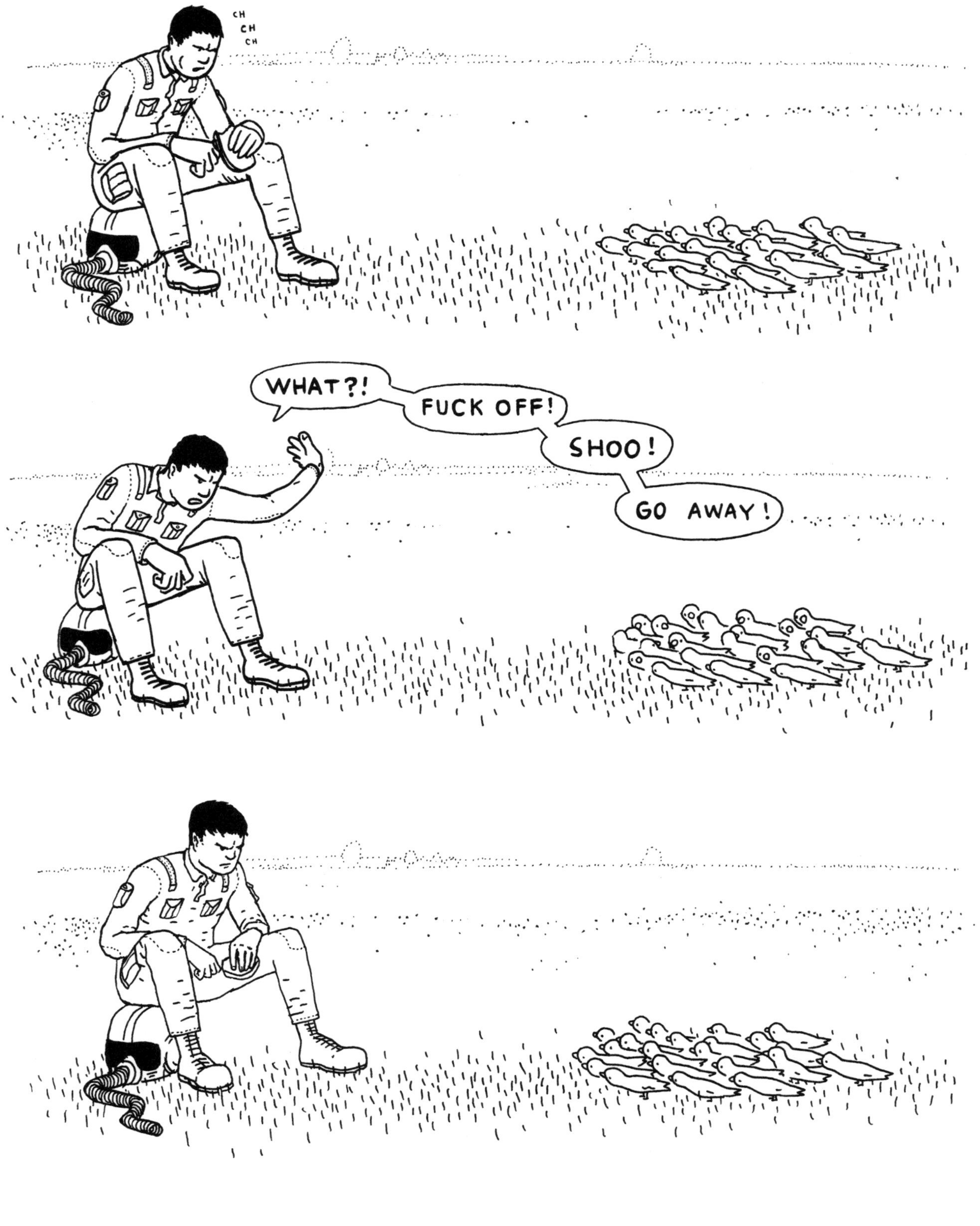
CH
CH
CH
WHAT?!
FUCK OFF!
SHOO!
GO AWAY!

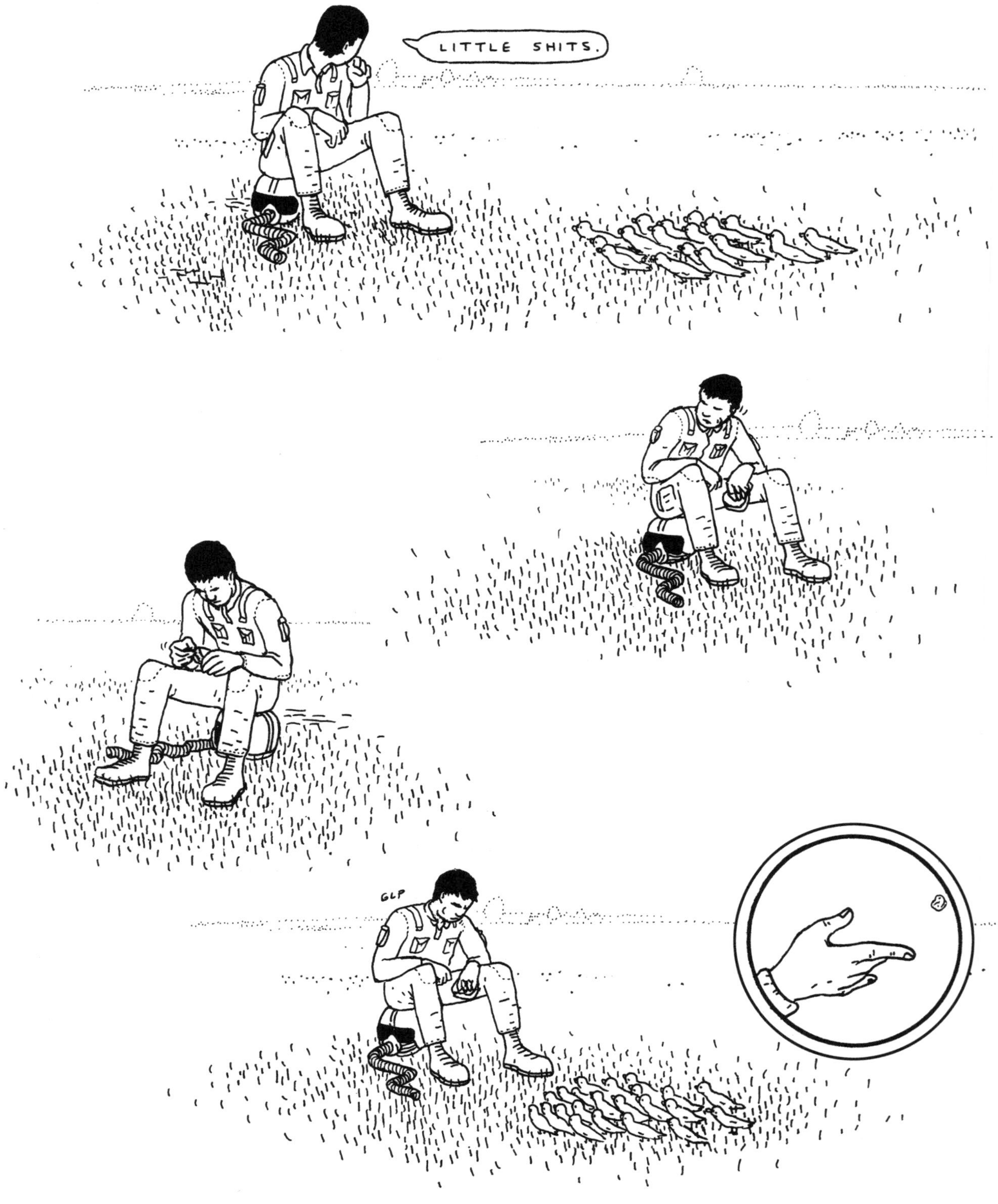
LITTLE SHITS.
GLP

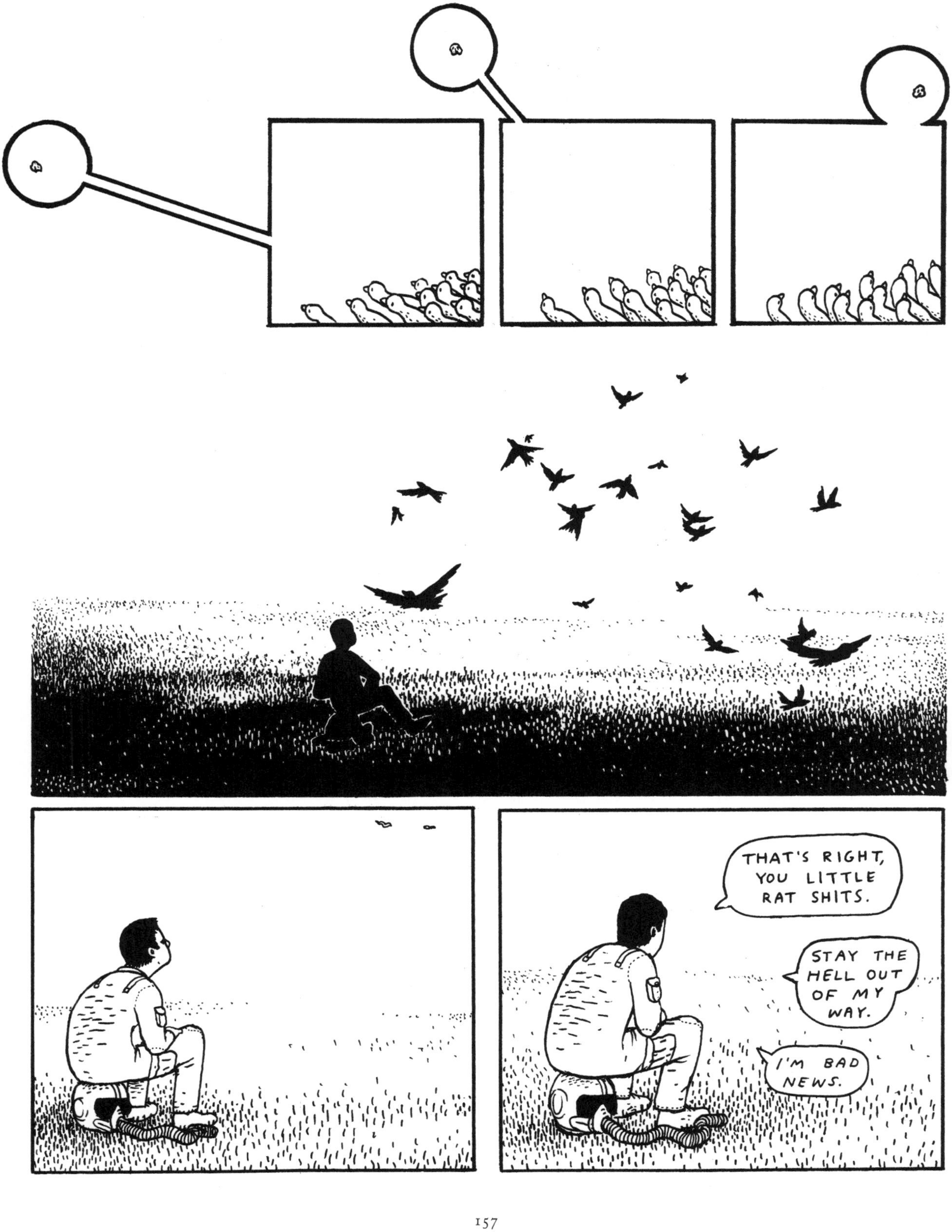
THAT'S RIGHT, YOU LITTLE RAT SHITS.
STAY THE HELL OUT OF MY WAY.
I'M BAD NEWS.

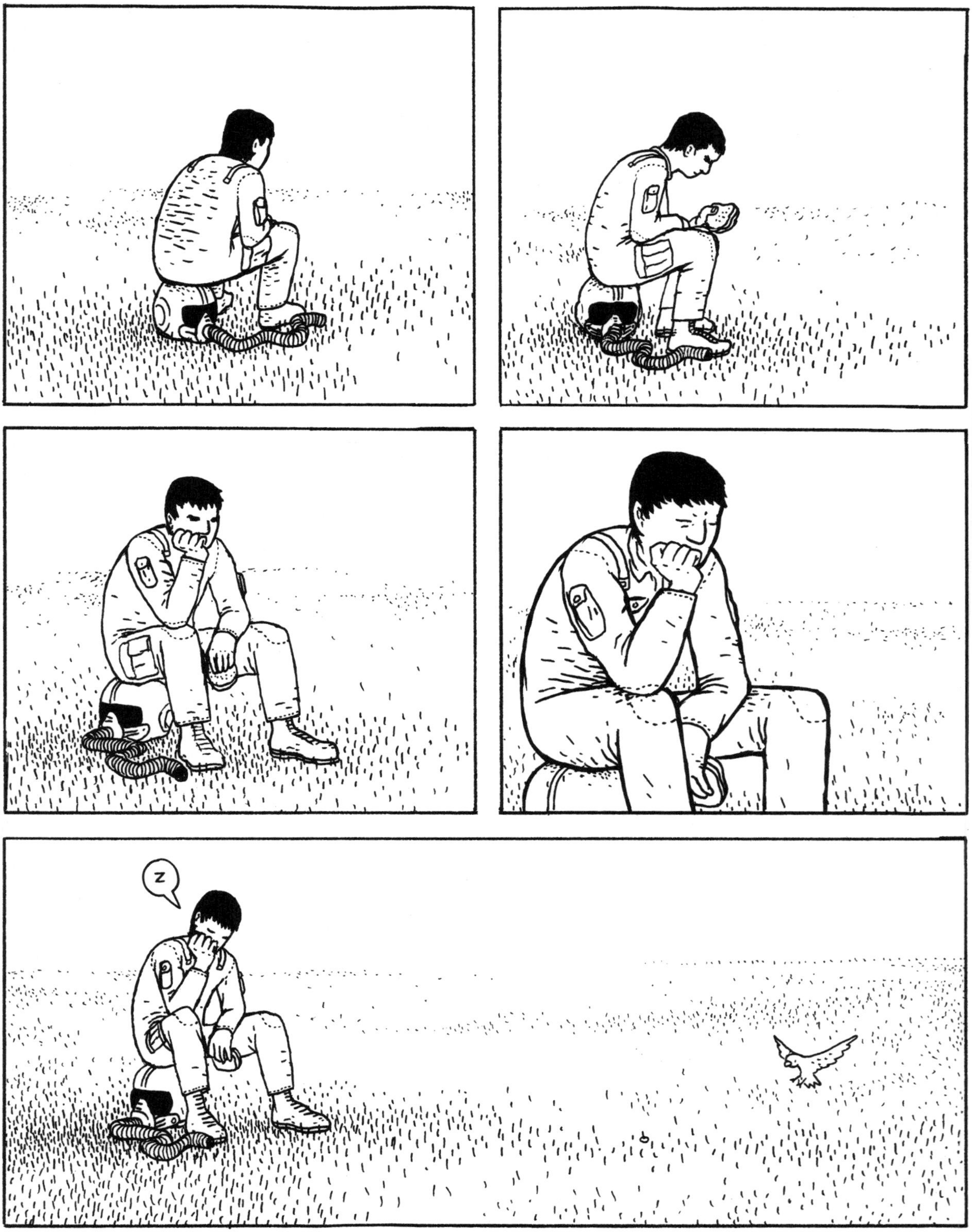
Z

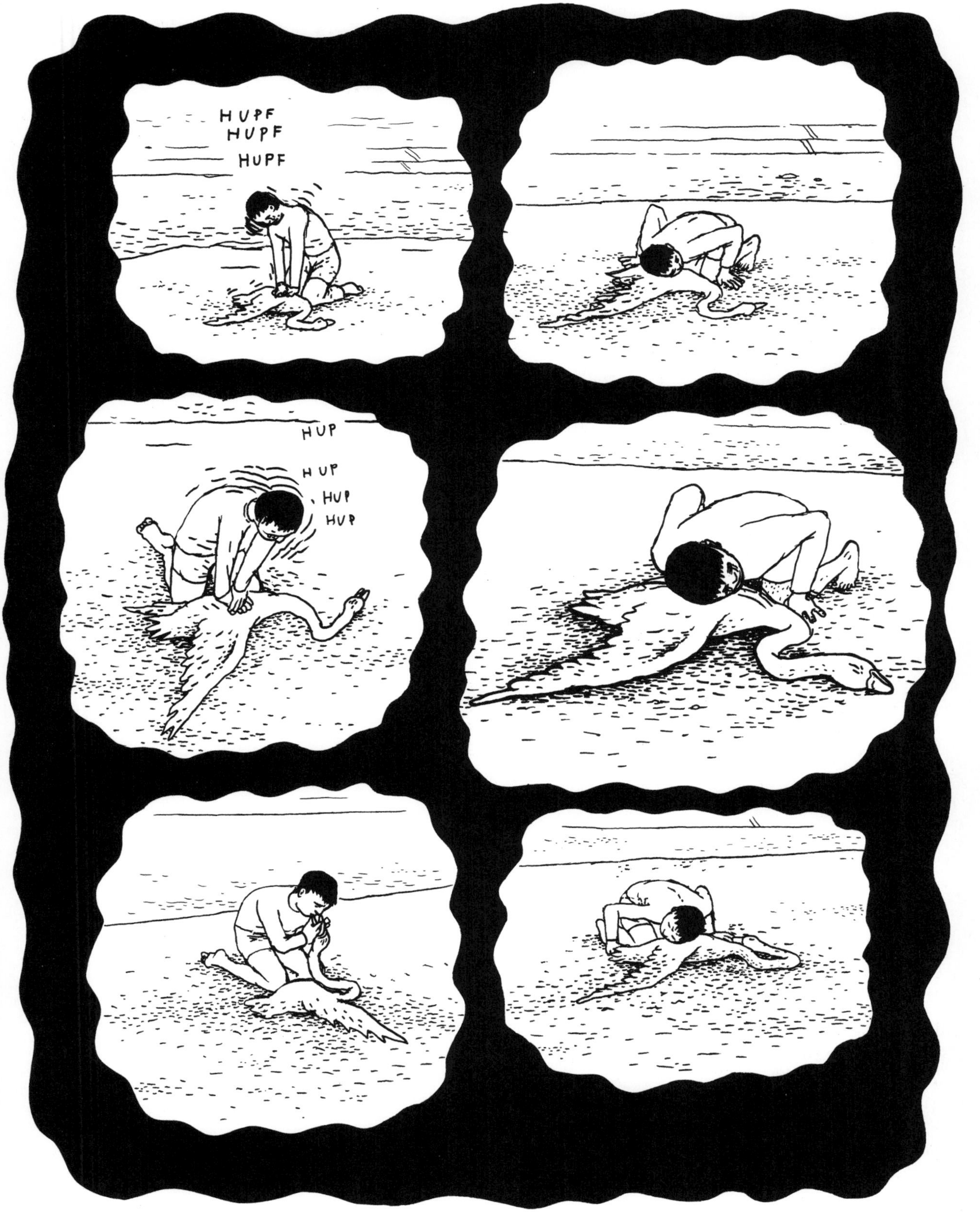
HUPF
HUPF
HUPF
HUP
HUP
HUP
HUP

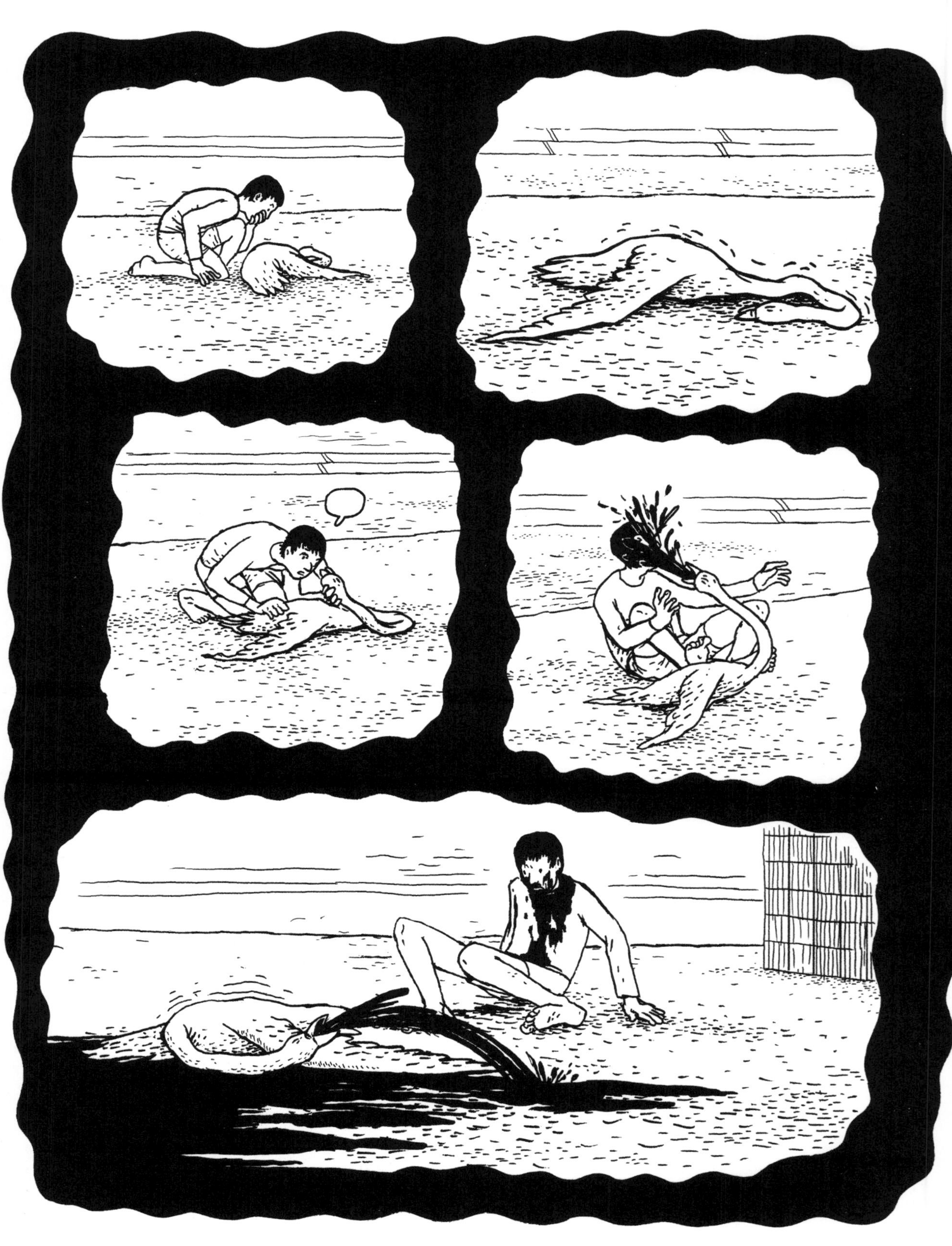

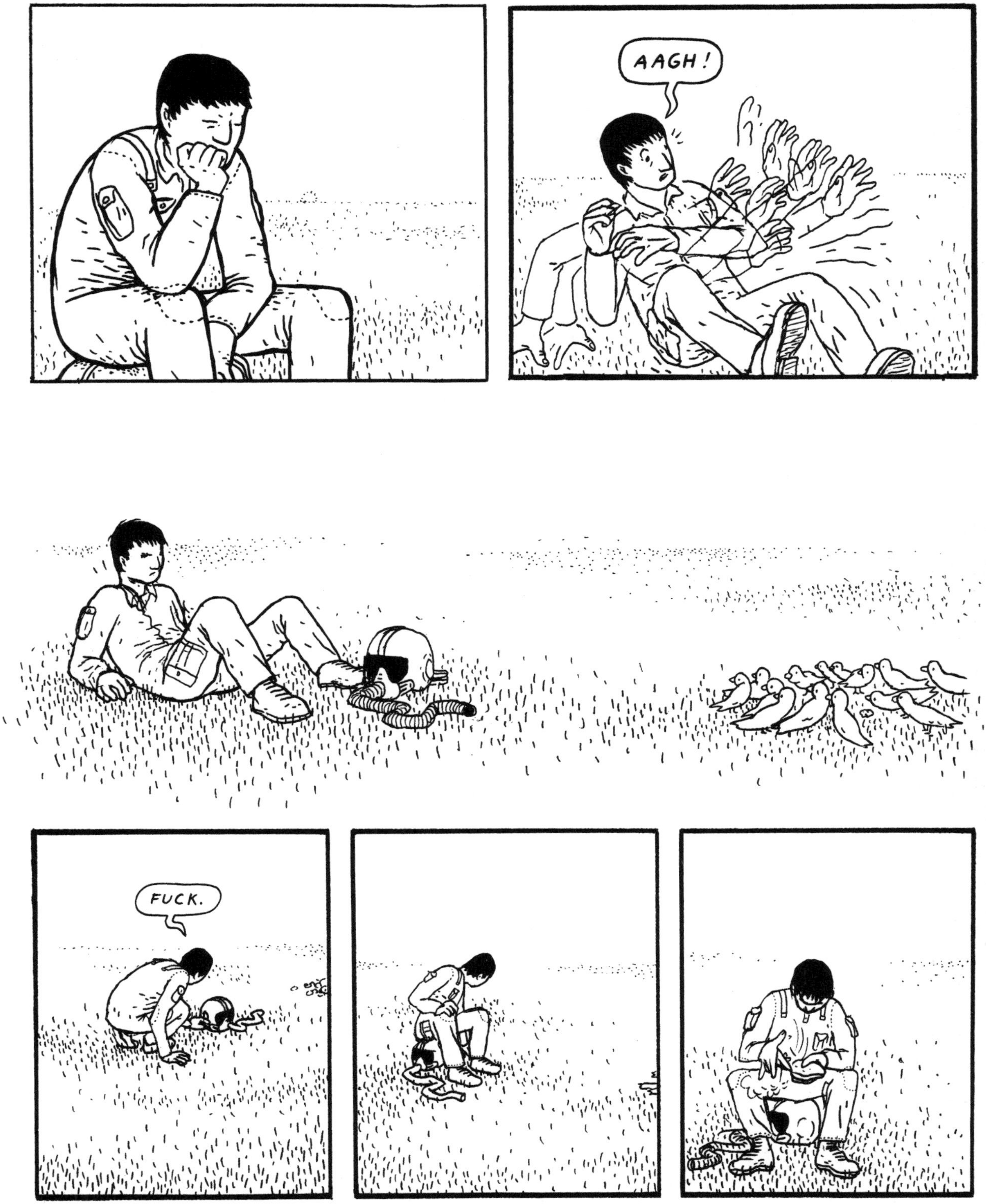
AAGH!
FUCK.

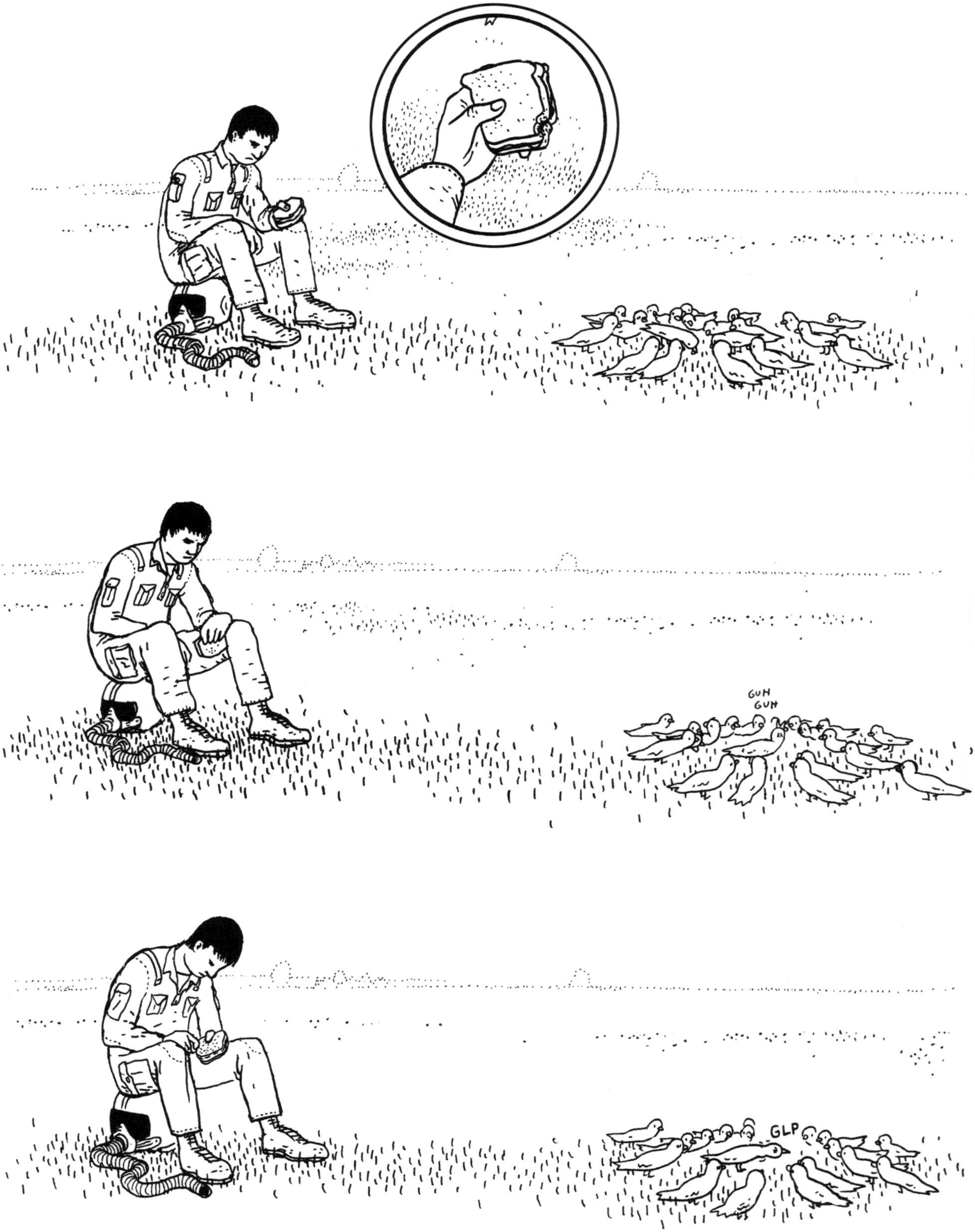
GUM
GUM
GLP

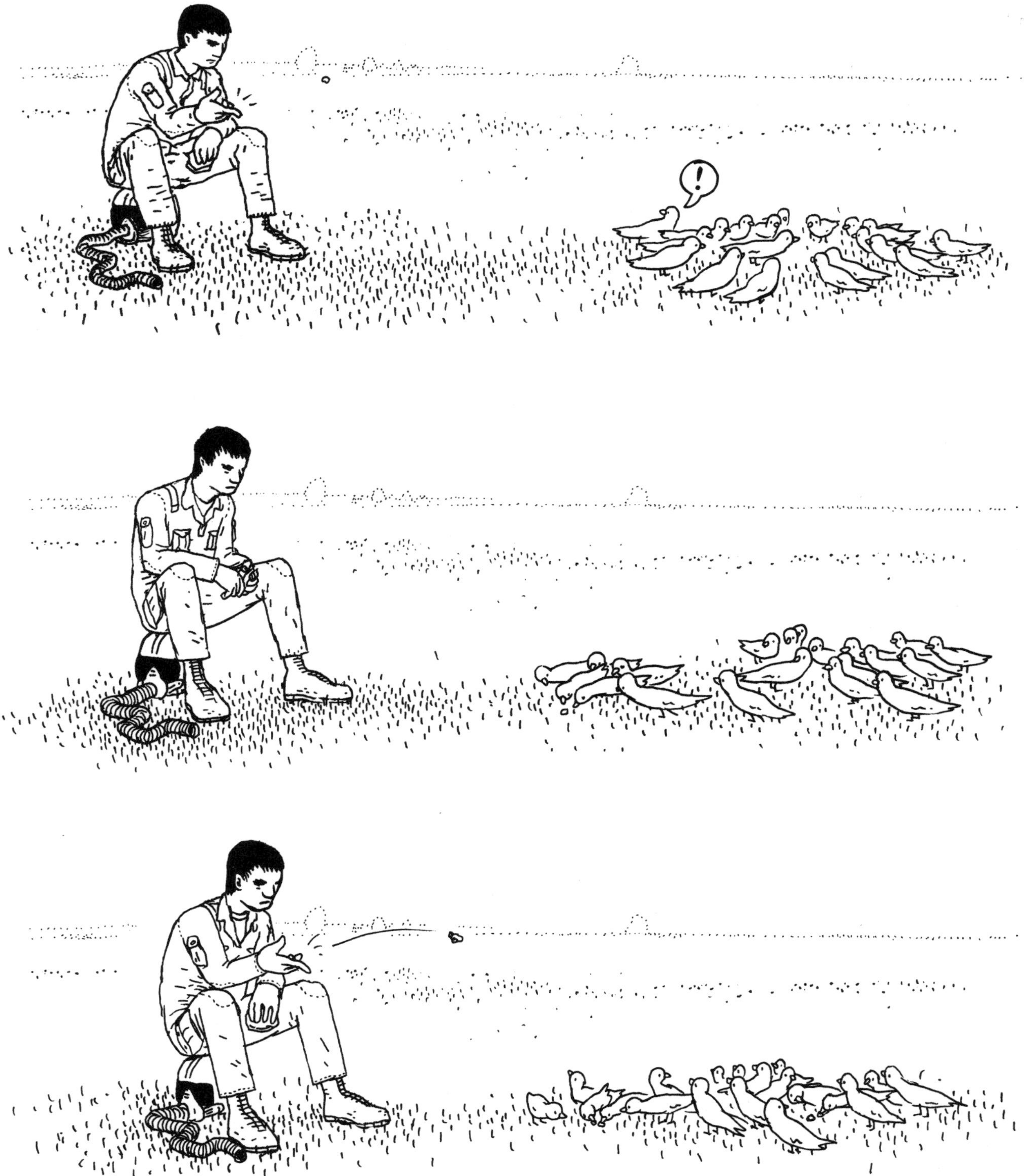
!

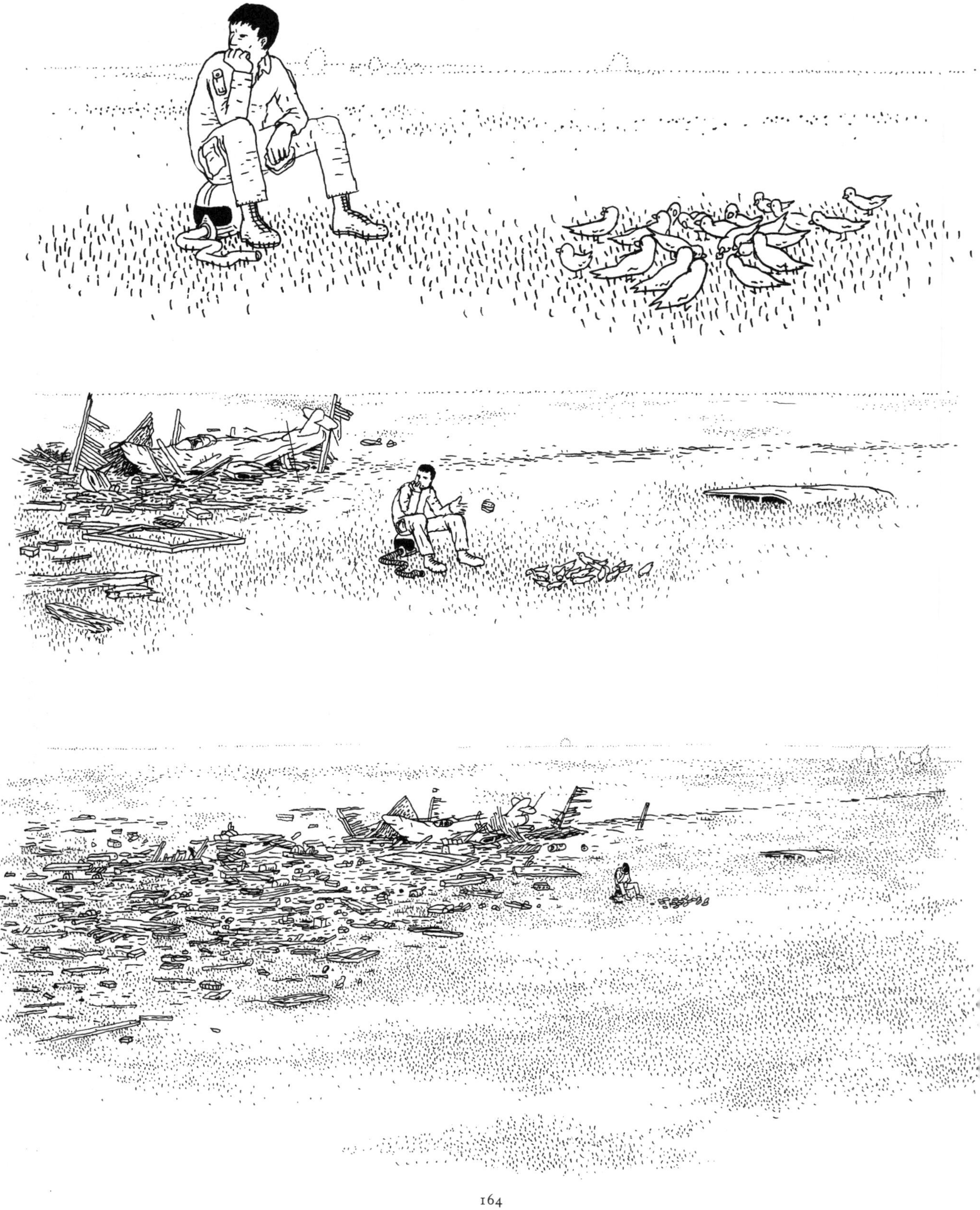

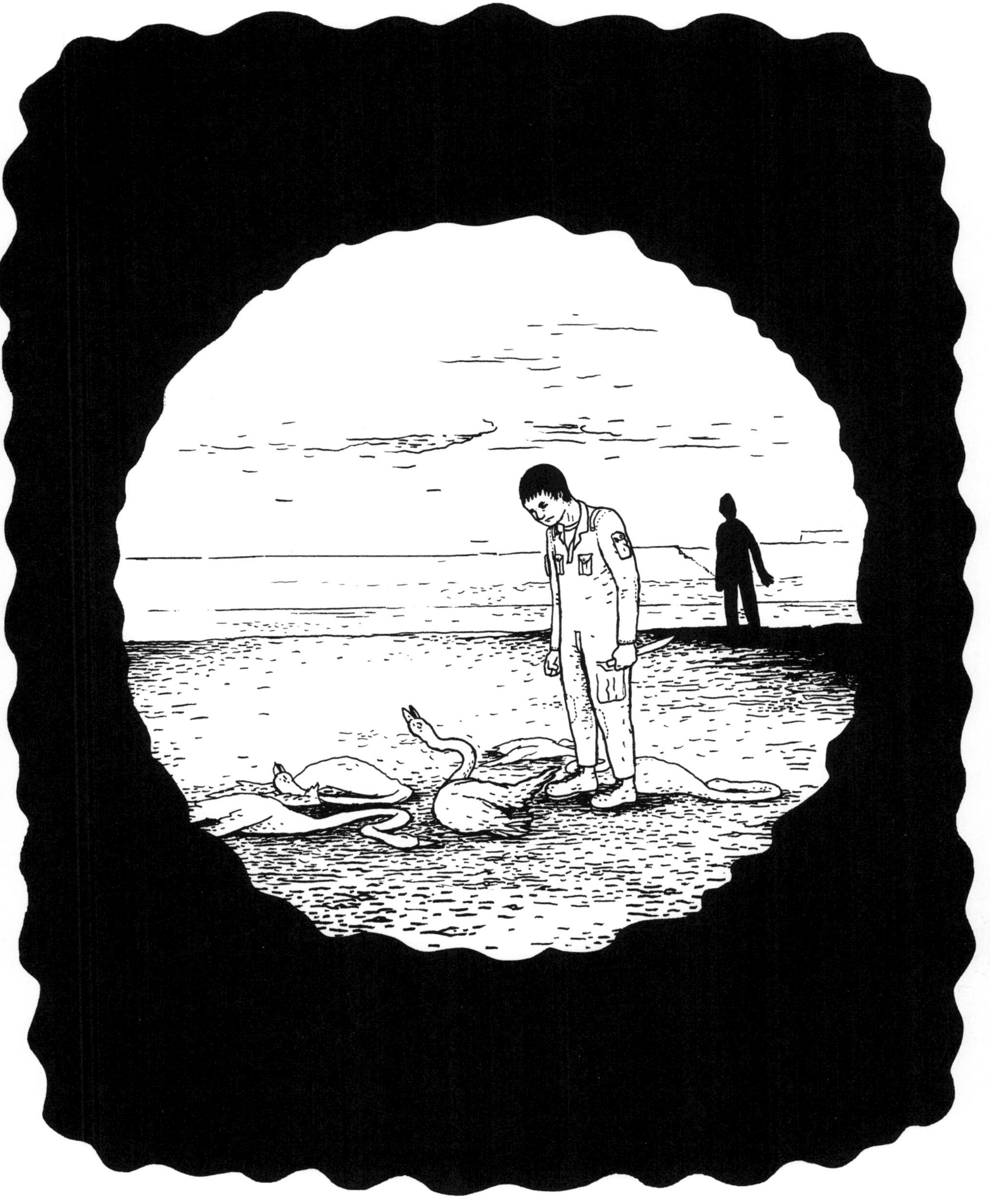

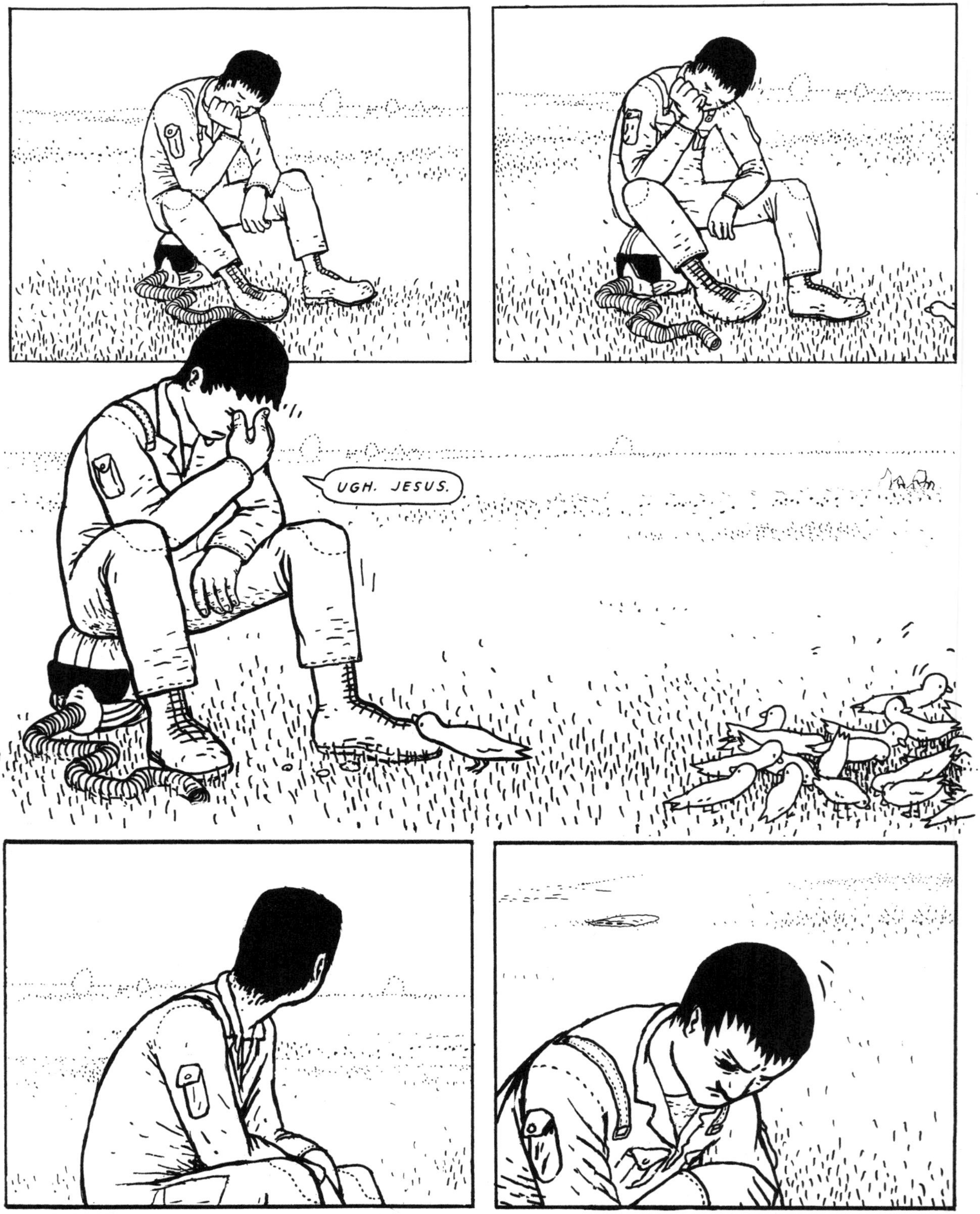
UGH. JESUS.

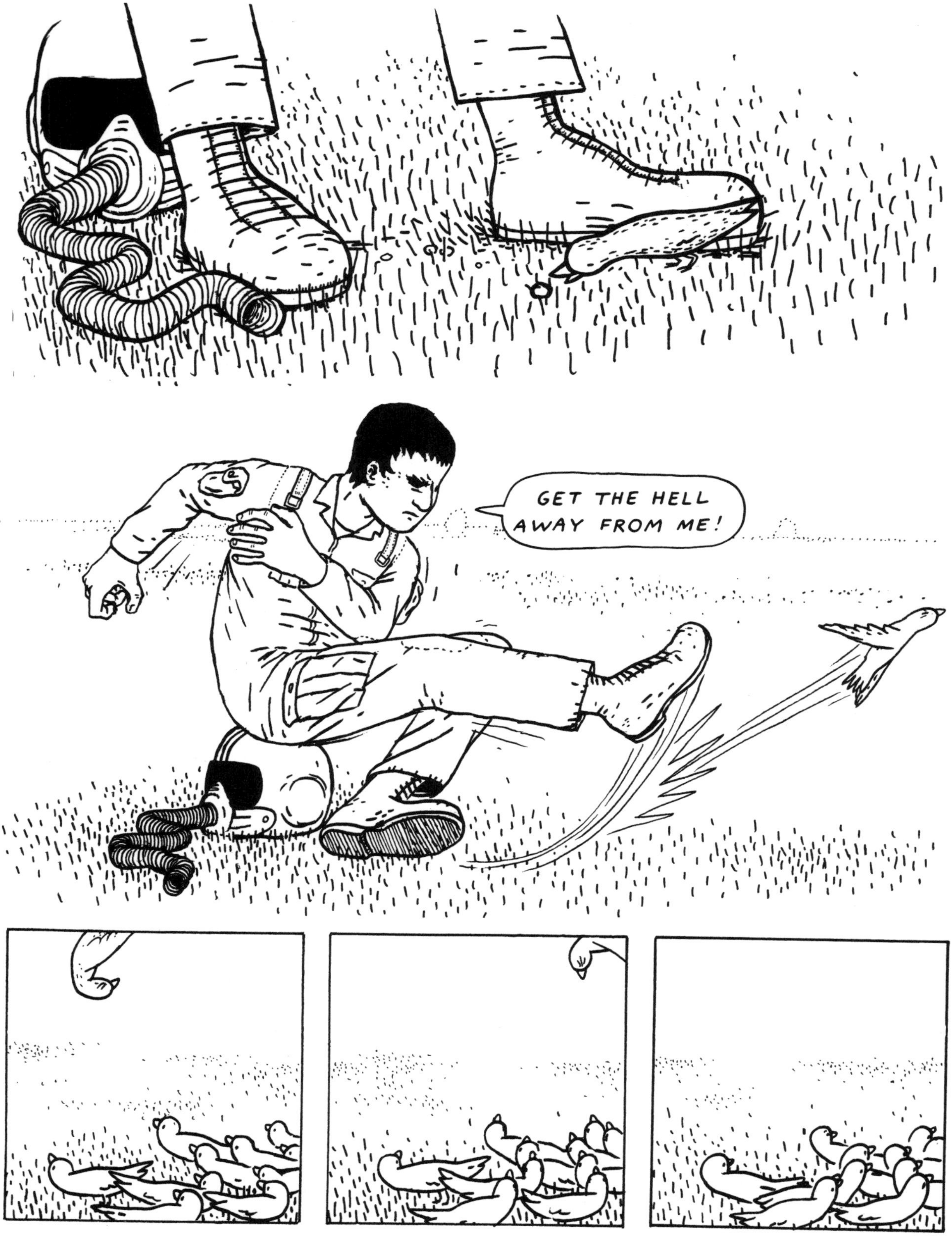
GET THE HELL AWAY FROM ME!

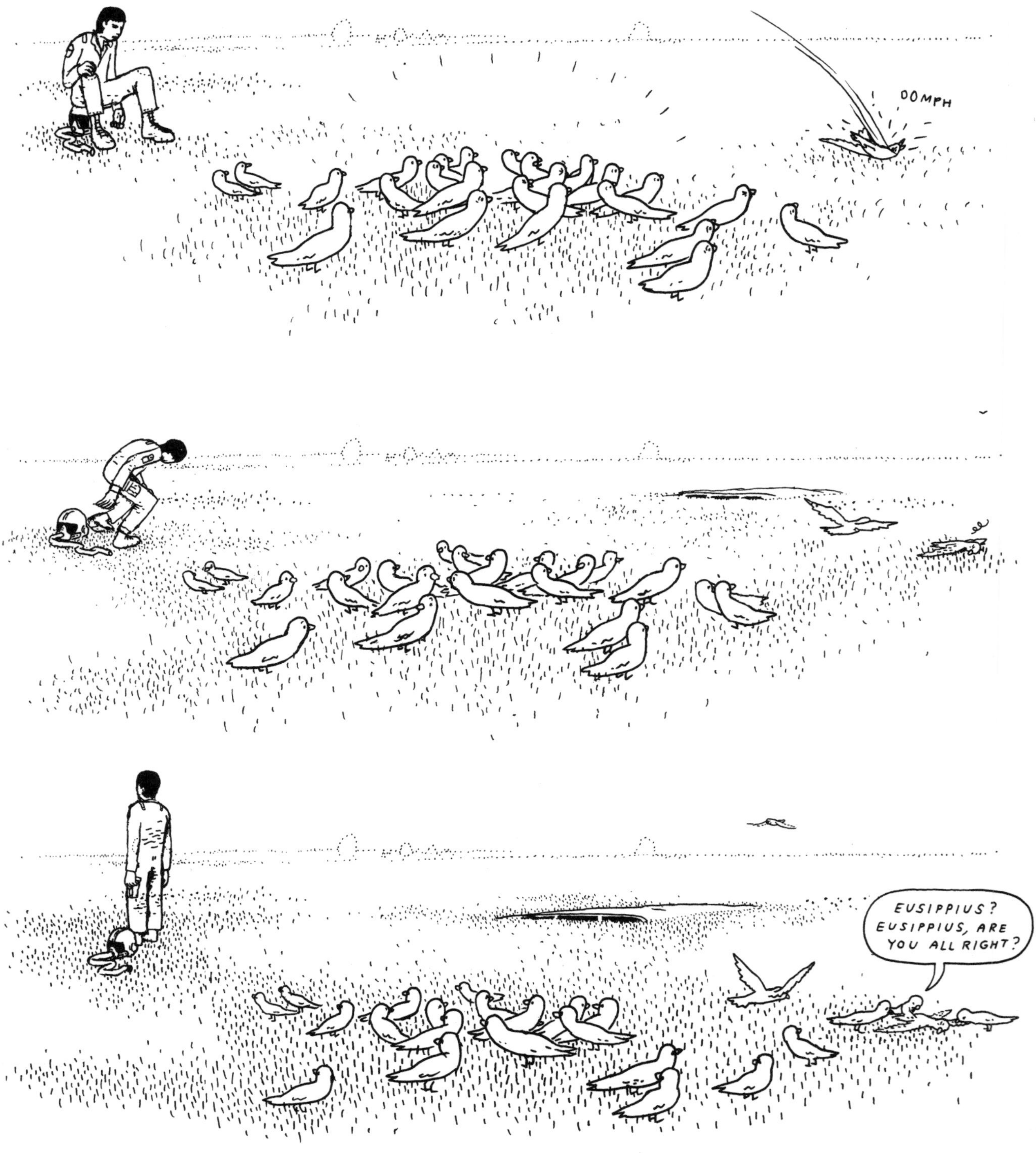
OOMPH
EUSIPPIUS?
EUSIPPIUS, ARE
YOU ALL RIGHT?

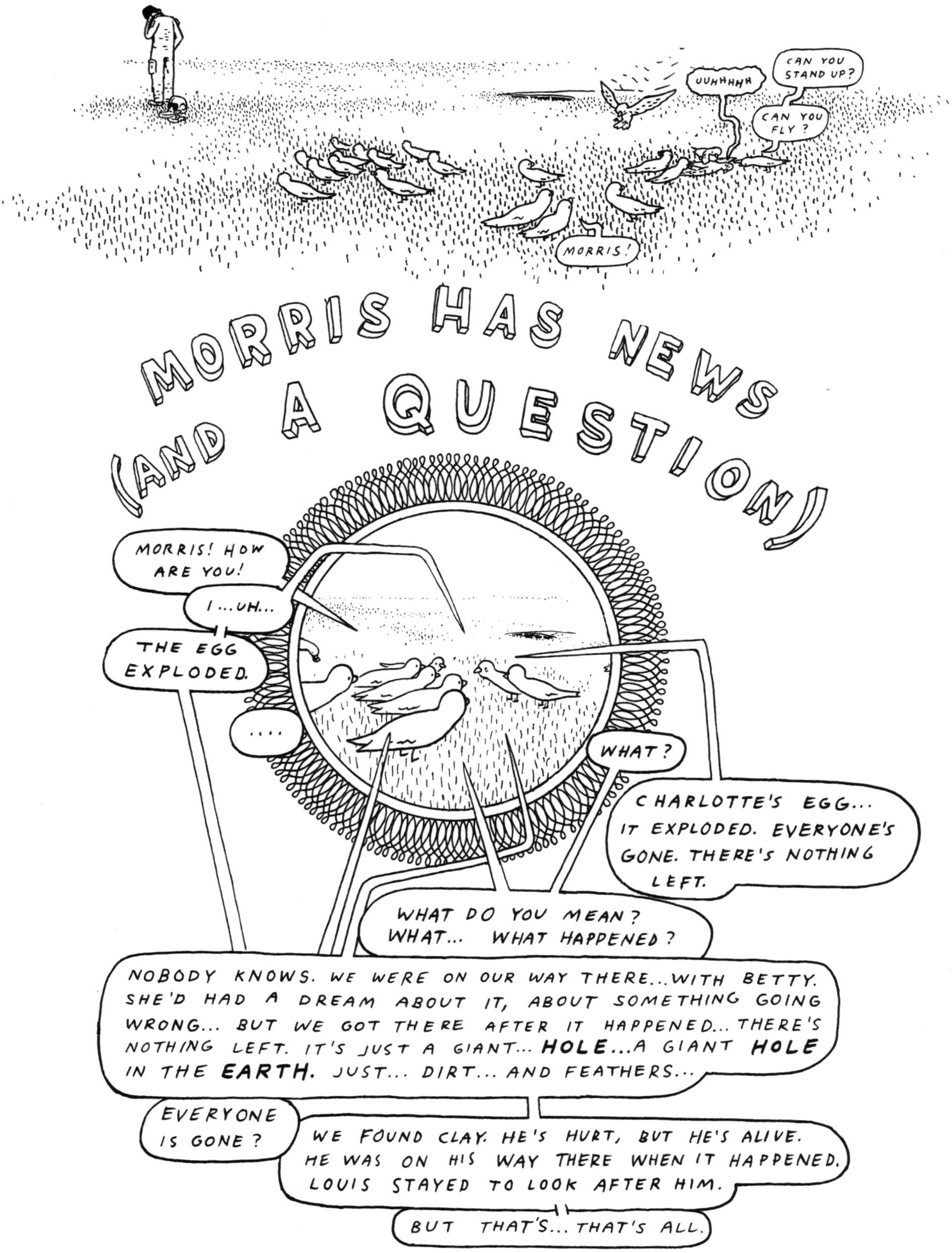
UUHHHHH
CAN YOU STAND UP?
CAN YOU FLY?
MORRIS!
MORRIS HAS NEWS (AND A QUESTION)
MORRIS! HOW ARE YOU!
I...UH...
THE EGG EXPLODED.
....
WHAT?
CHARLOTTE'S EGG... IT EXPLODED. EVERYONE'S GONE. THERE'S NOTHING LEFT.
WHAT DO YOU MEAN? WHAT... WHAT HAPPENED?
NOBODY KNOWS. WE WERE ON OUR WAY THERE...WITH BETTY. SHE'D HAD A DREAM ABOUT IT, ABOUT SOMETHING GOING WRONG... BUT WE GOT THERE AFTER IT HAPPENED... THERE'S NOTHING LEFT. IT'S JUST A GIANT... HOLE...A GIANT HOLE IN THE EARTH. JUST... DIRT... AND FEATHERS...
EVERYONE IS GONE?
WE FOUND CLAY. HE'S HURT, BUT HE'S ALIVE. HE WAS ON HIS WAY THERE WHEN IT HAPPENED. LOUIS STAYED TO LOOK AFTER HIM.
BUT THAT'S... THAT'S ALL.

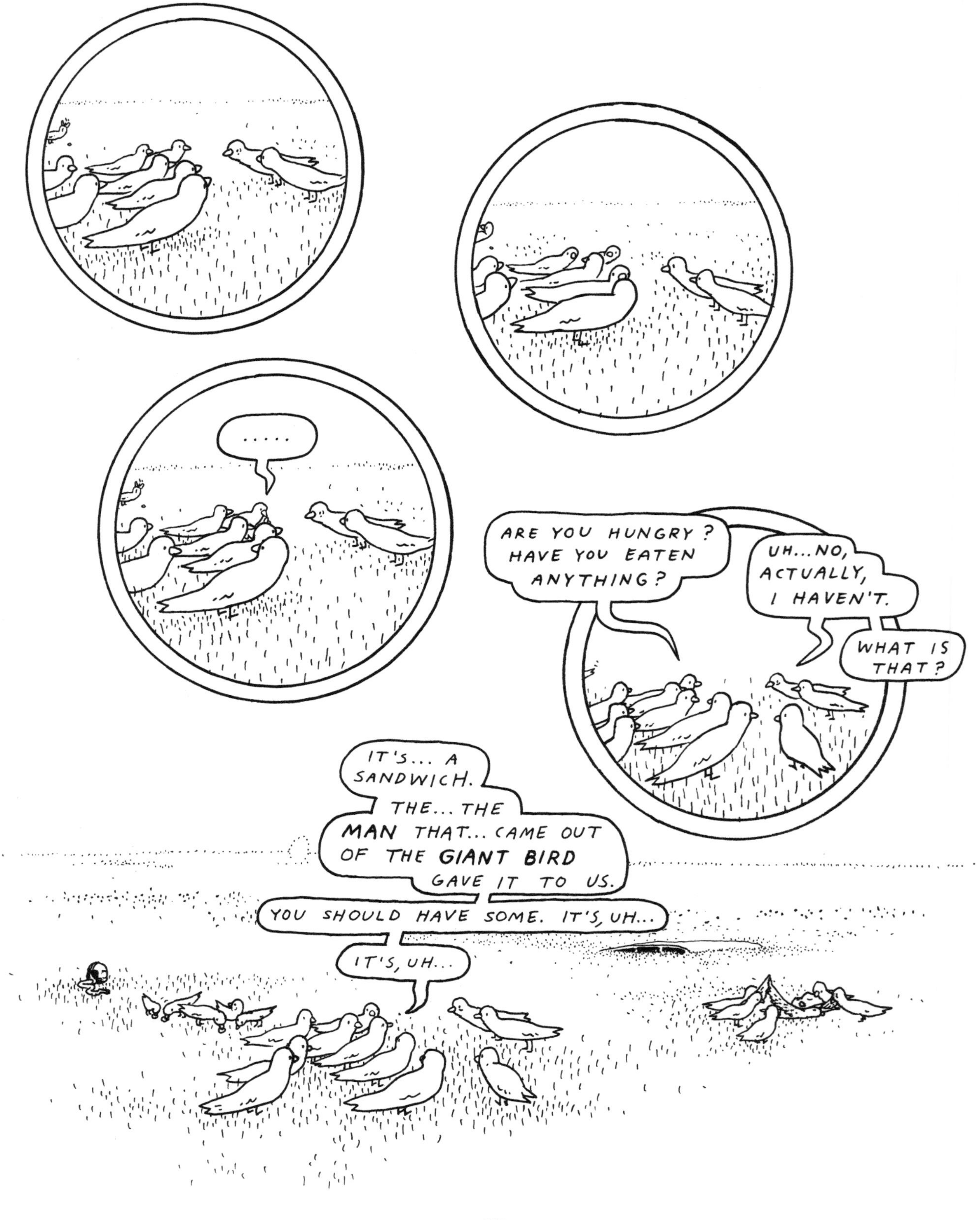
.....
ARE YOU HUNGRY? HAVE YOU EATEN ANYTHING?
UH...NO, ACTUALLY, I HAVEN'T.
WHAT IS THAT?
IT'S... A SANDWICH.
THE... THE MAN THAT... CAME OUT OF THE GIANT BIRD GAVE IT TO US.
YOU SHOULD HAVE SOME. IT'S, UH...
IT'S, UH...

...PEANUT BUTTER AND JELLY.

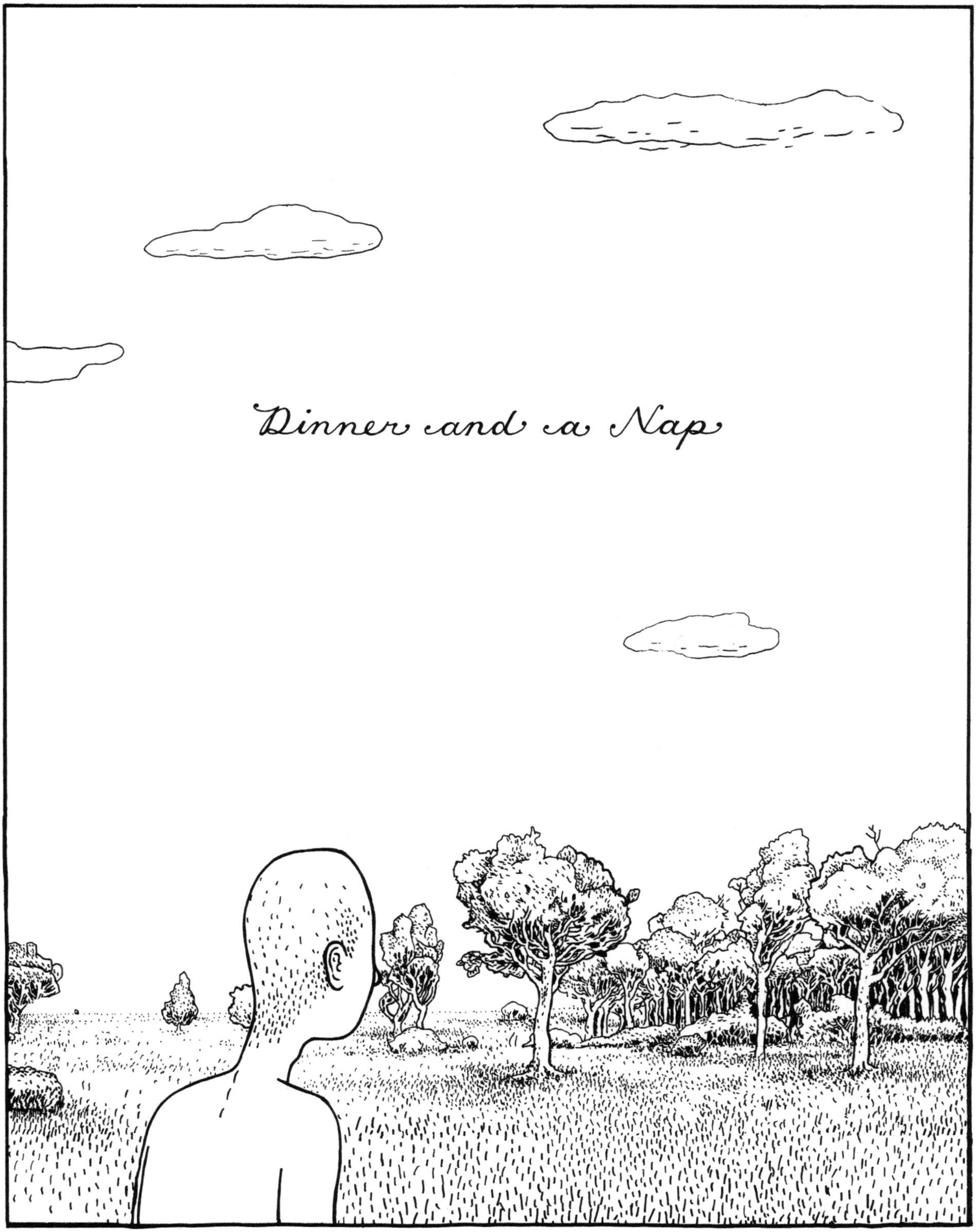
Dinner and a Nap

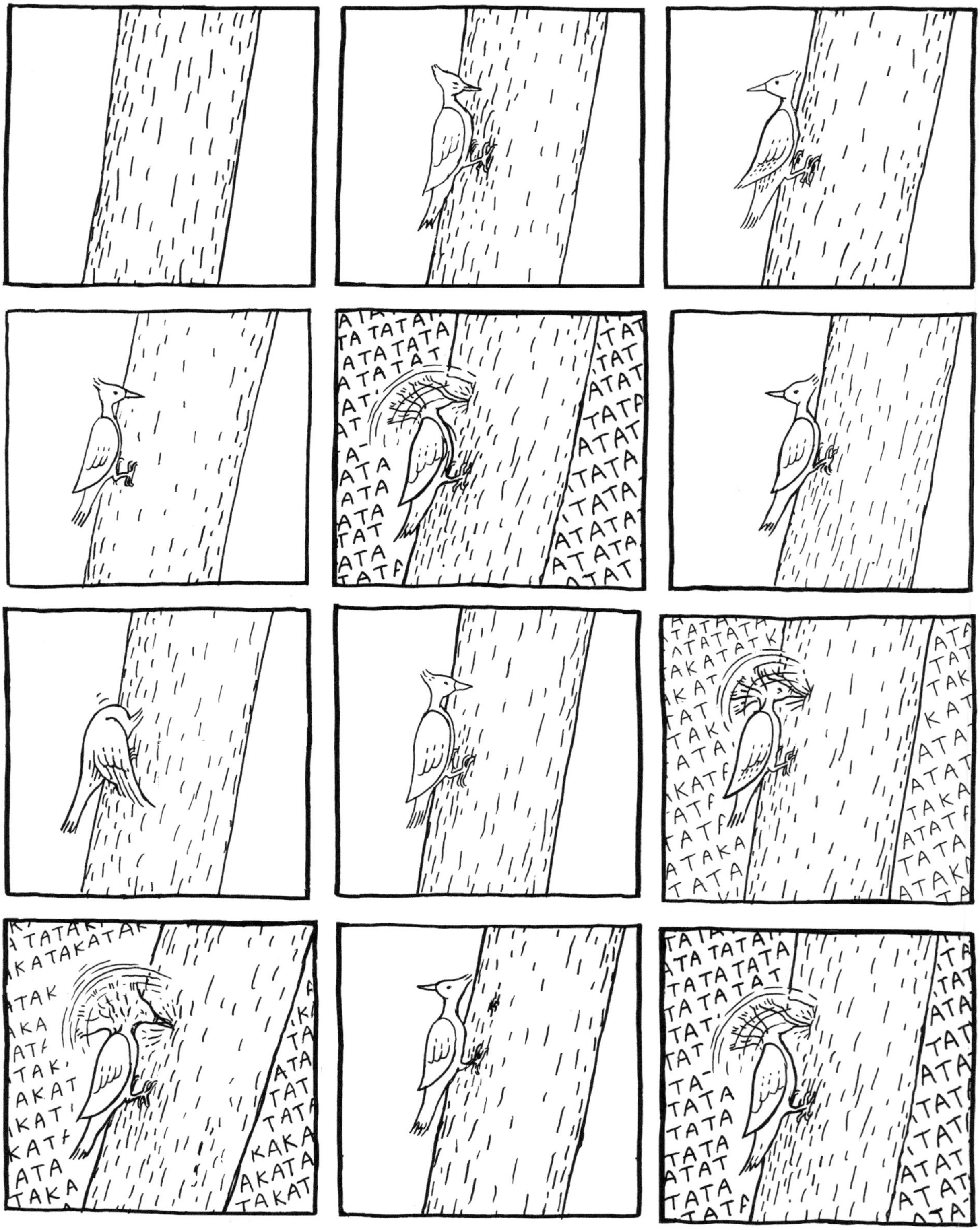
TA TATA
TA TATATA
ATATATA
ATATAT
TAT
ATAT
TATA
ATAT
TATATA
ATATAT
TATATAT
TAKAT
TAKATA
TAKATAK
KAT
TAKA
ATAKA
TATA
TATAKATAK
KATAKATAKAT
TAKAKA
TAKATA
TATA TATA
TATATAT

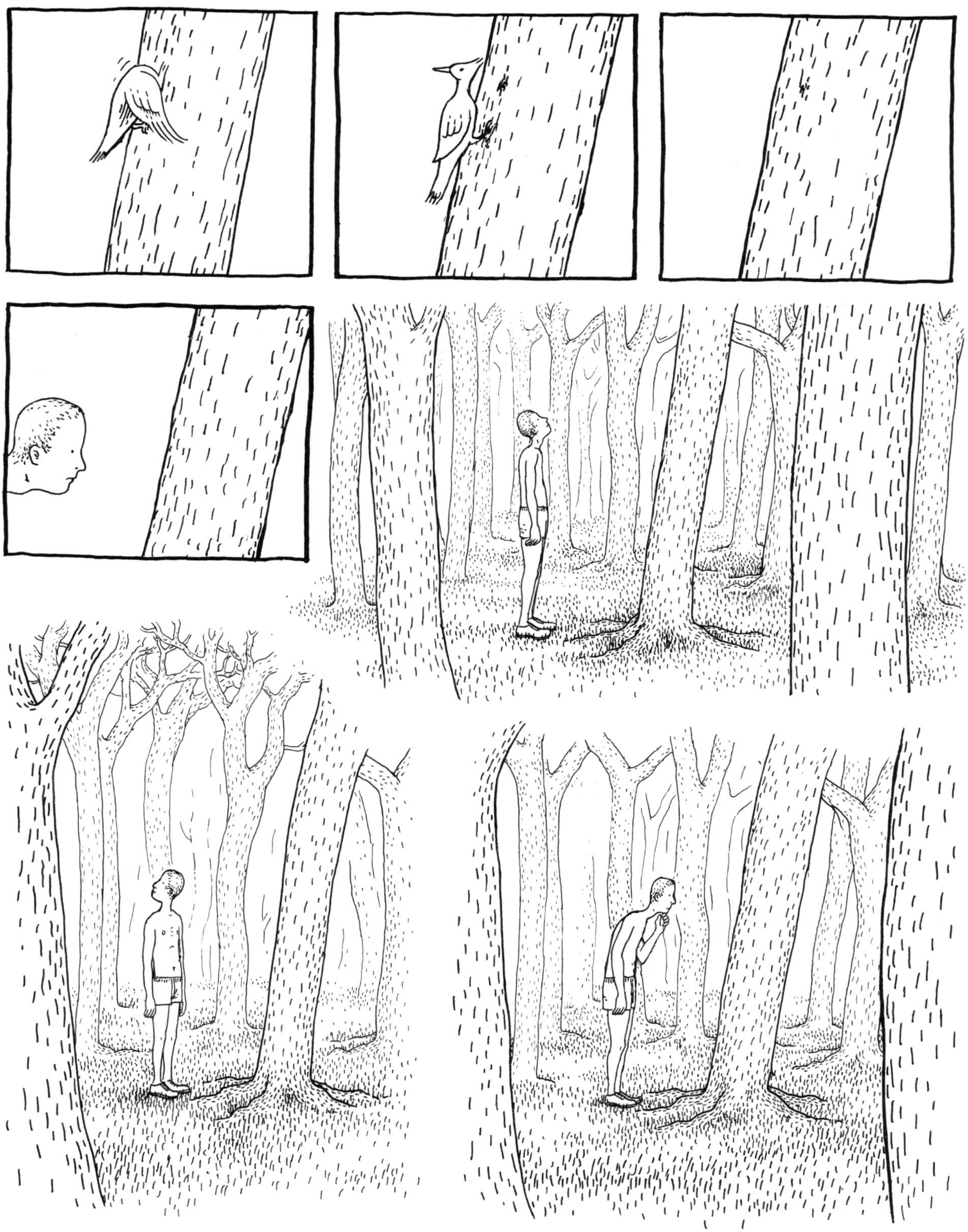

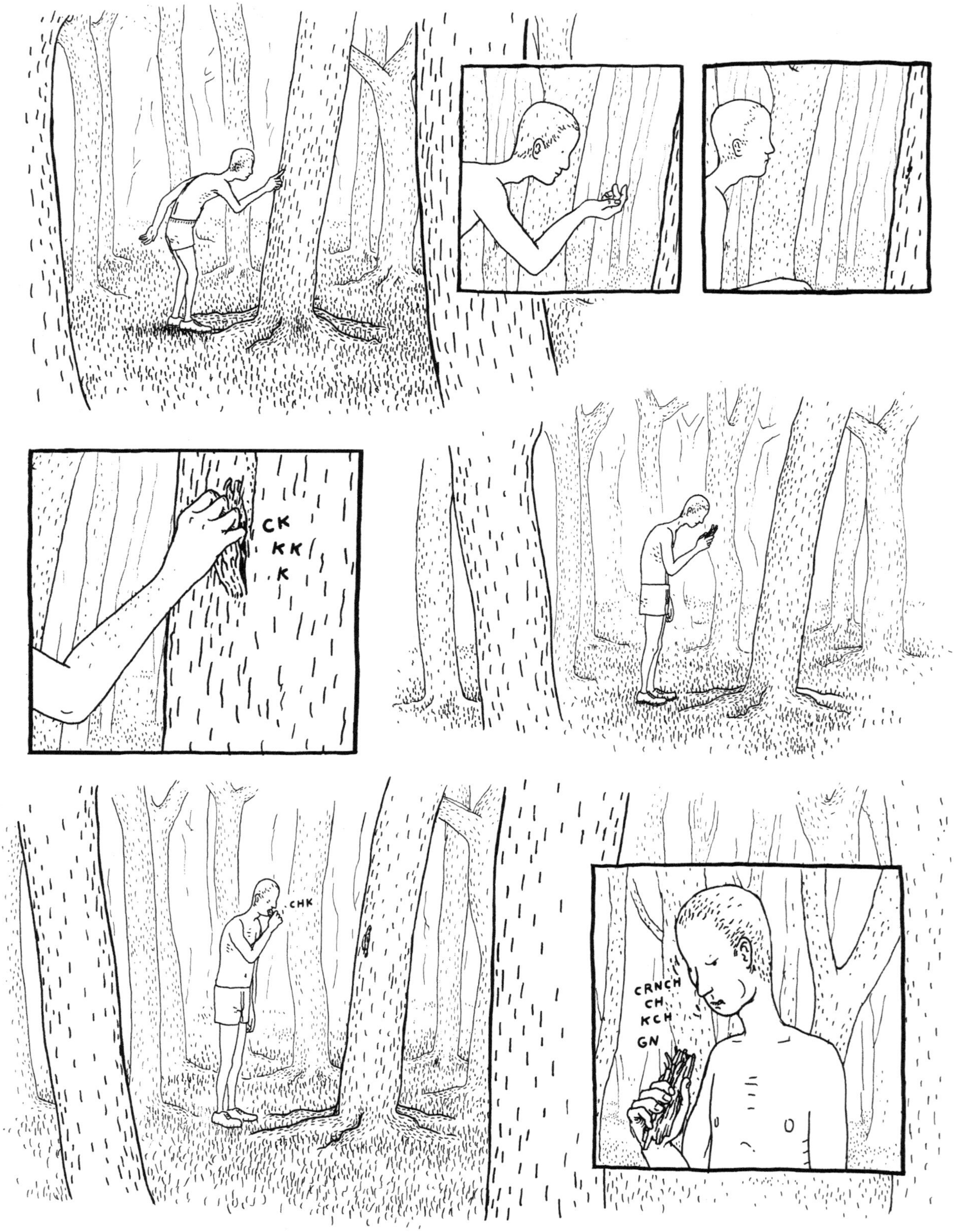
CK
KK
K
CHK
CRNCH
CH
KCH
GN

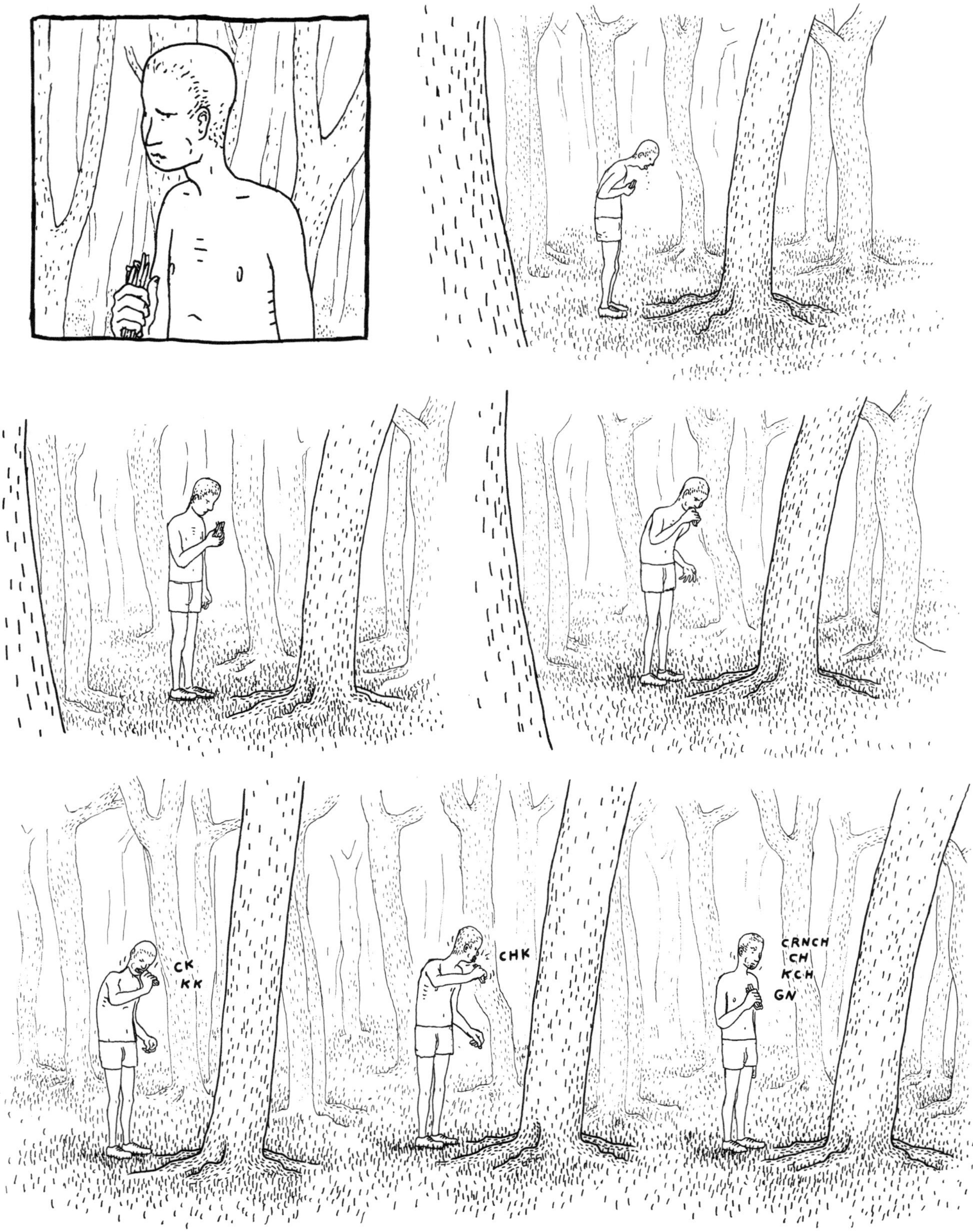
CK
KK
CHK
CRNCH
CH
KCH
GN

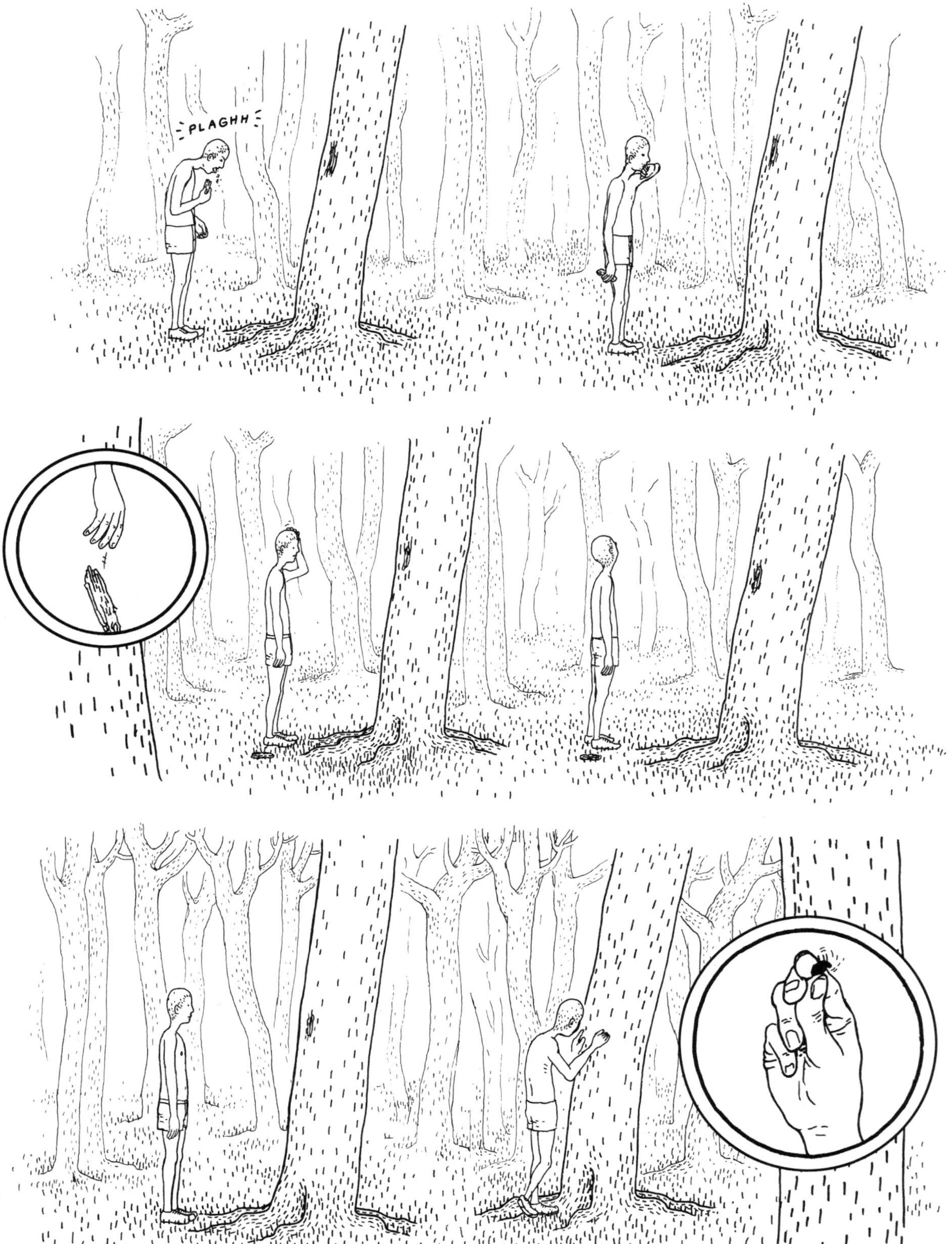
PLAGHH

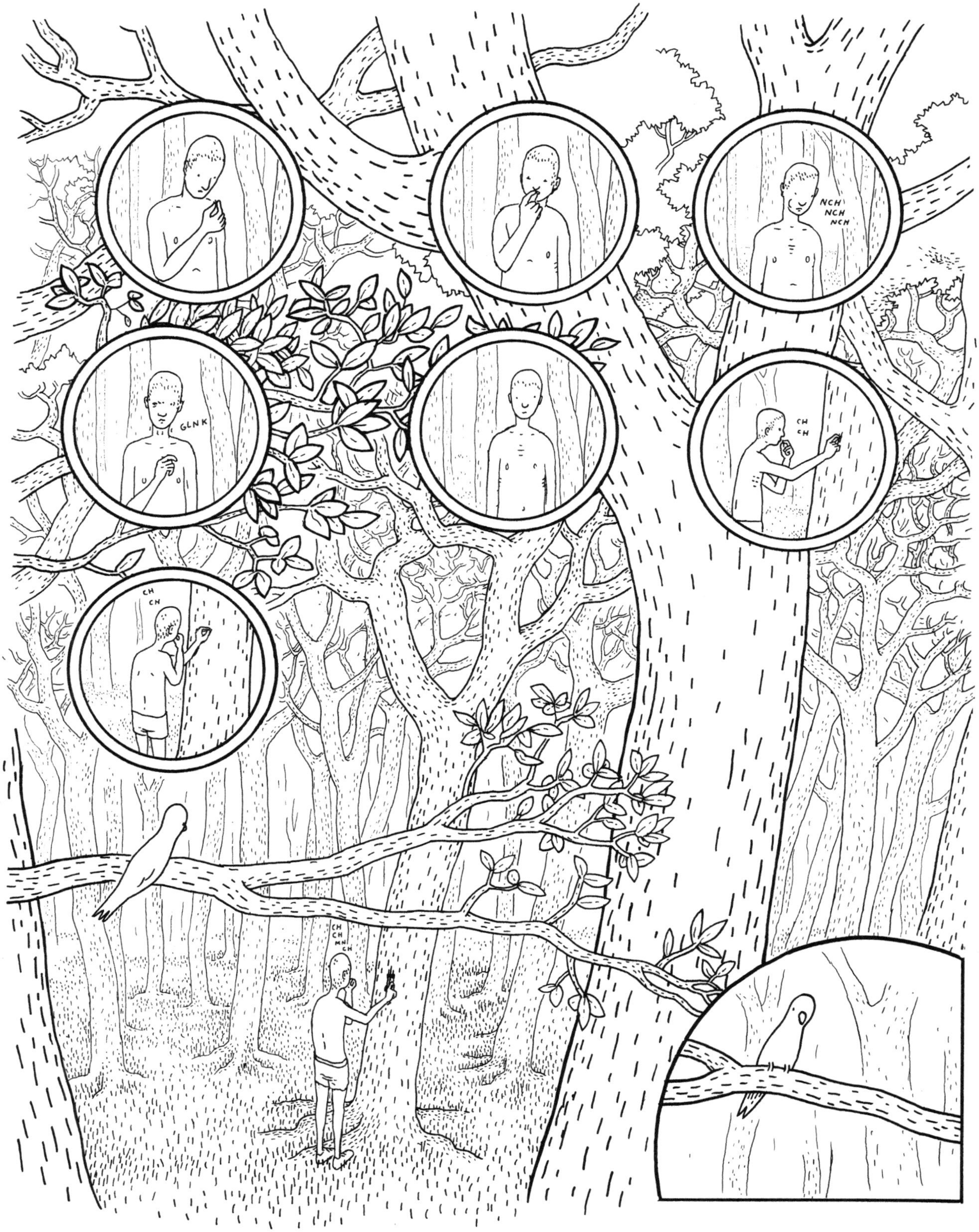
NCH
NCH
NCH
GLNK
CH
CH
CH
CH
CH
CH
MN
CH

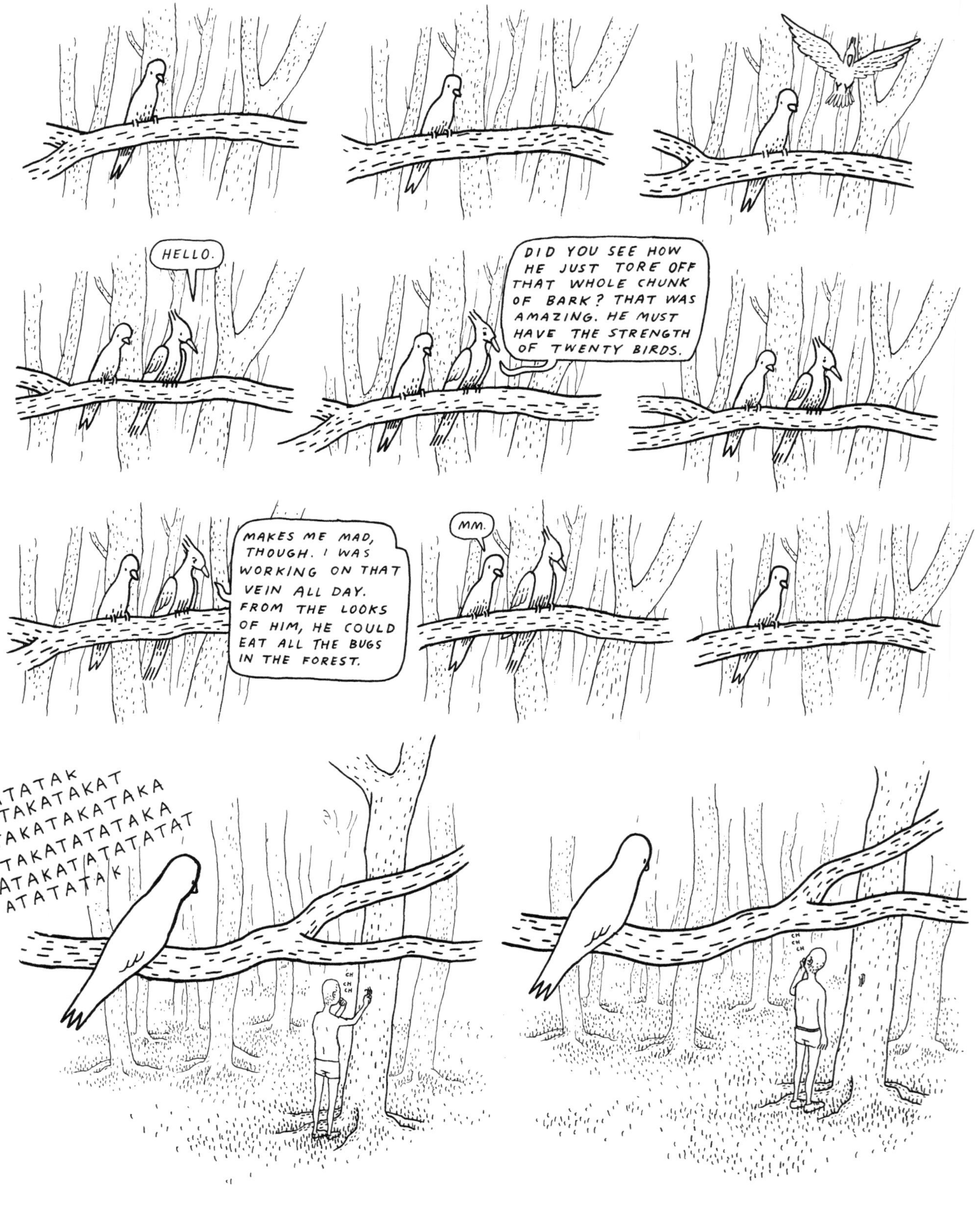
HELLO.
DID YOU SEE HOW HE JUST TORE OFF THAT WHOLE CHUNK OF BARK? THAT WAS AMAZING. HE MUST HAVE THE STRENGTH OF TWENTY BIRDS.
MAKES ME MAD, THOUGH. I WAS WORKING ON THAT VEIN ALL DAY. FROM THE LOOKS OF HIM, HE COULD EAT ALL THE BUGS IN THE FOREST.
MM.
ATATAK
TAKATAKAT
TAKATAKATAKA
TAKATATATAKA
TAKATATATATAT
ATAKATATATAK
ATATA
CH CH CH
CH CH CH

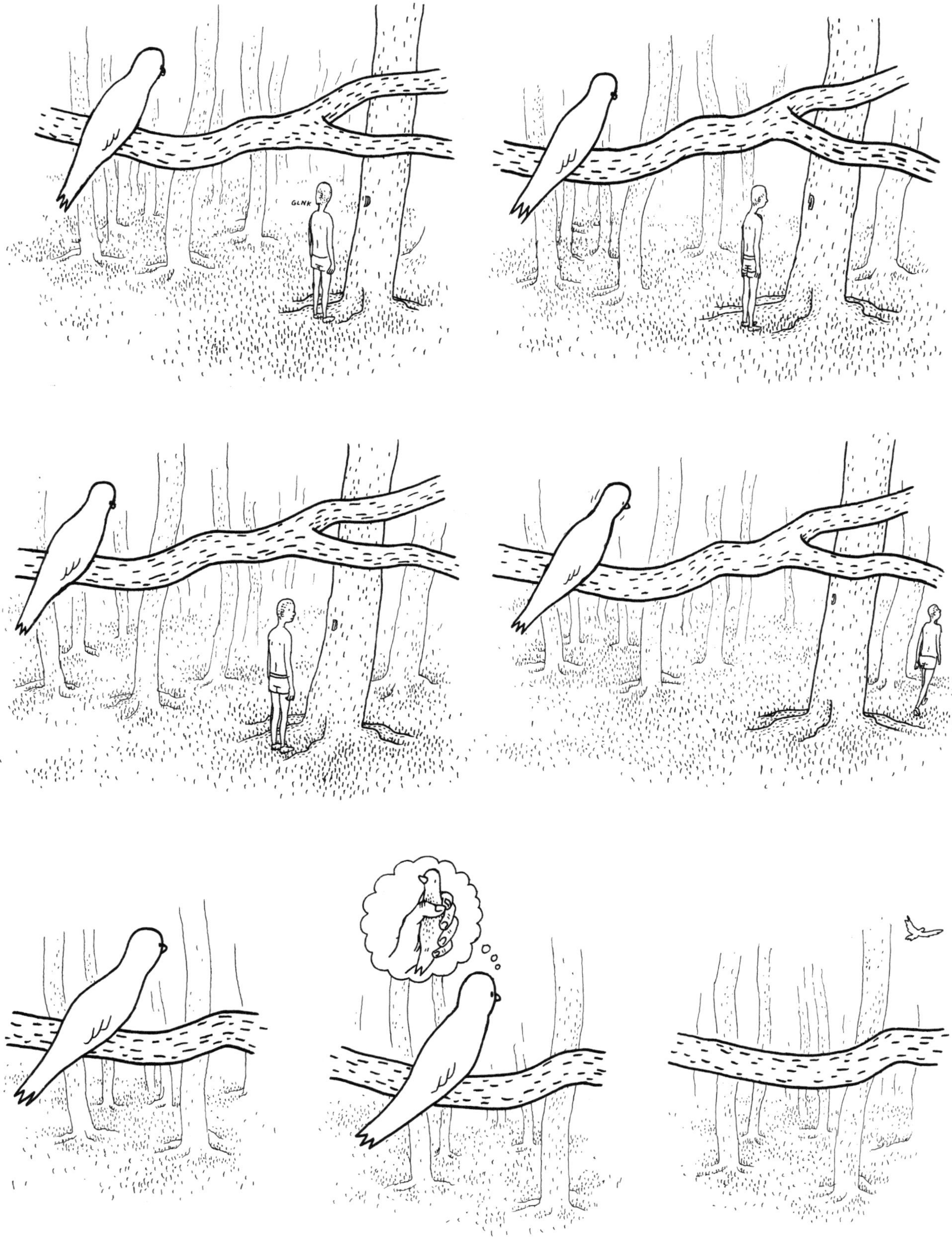
GLNK

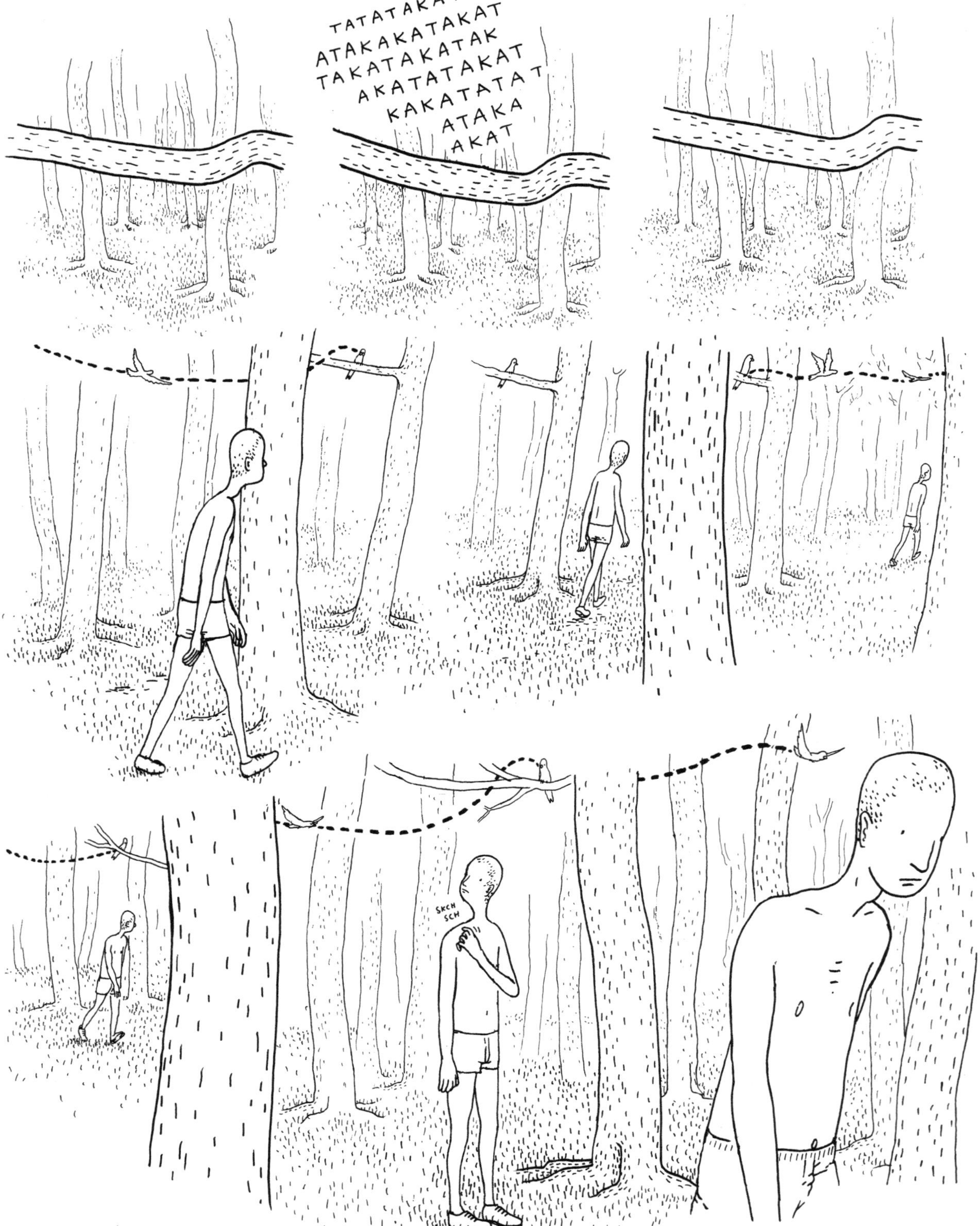
TATATAKAT
ATAKAKATAKAT
TAKATAKATAK
TAKATAKAT
AKATATAKAT
KAKATATAT
ATAKA
AKAT
SKCH SCH

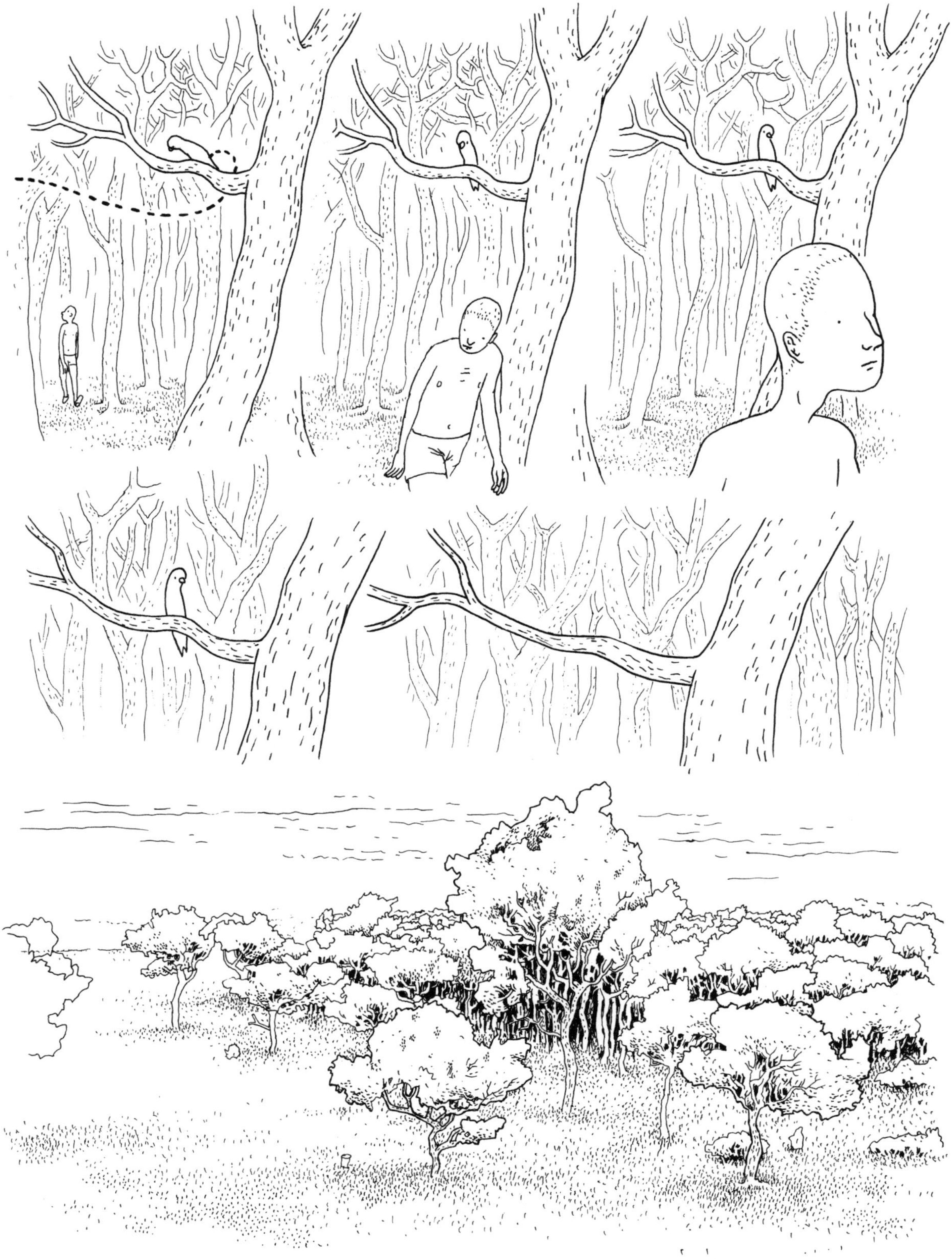

Algernon

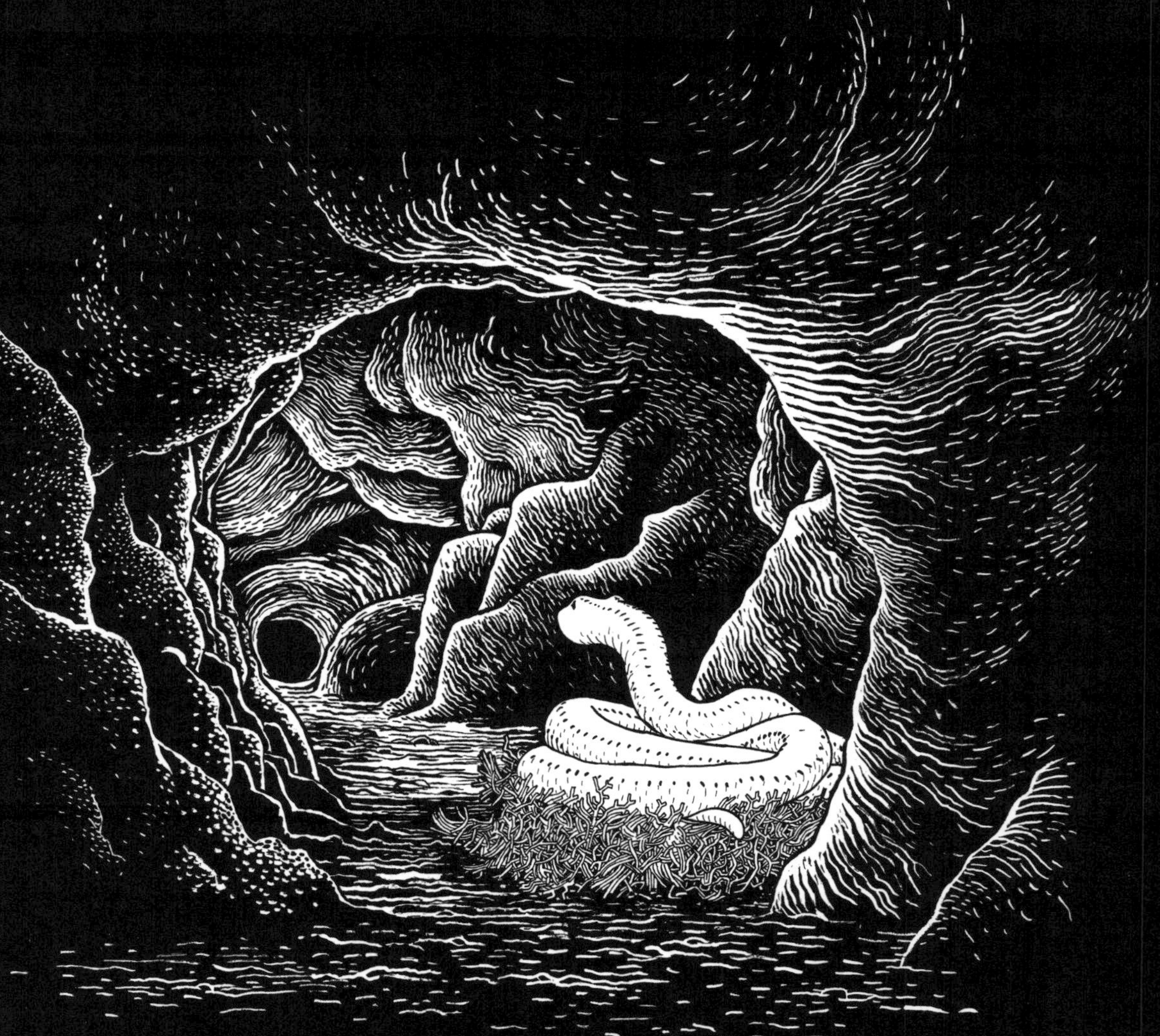

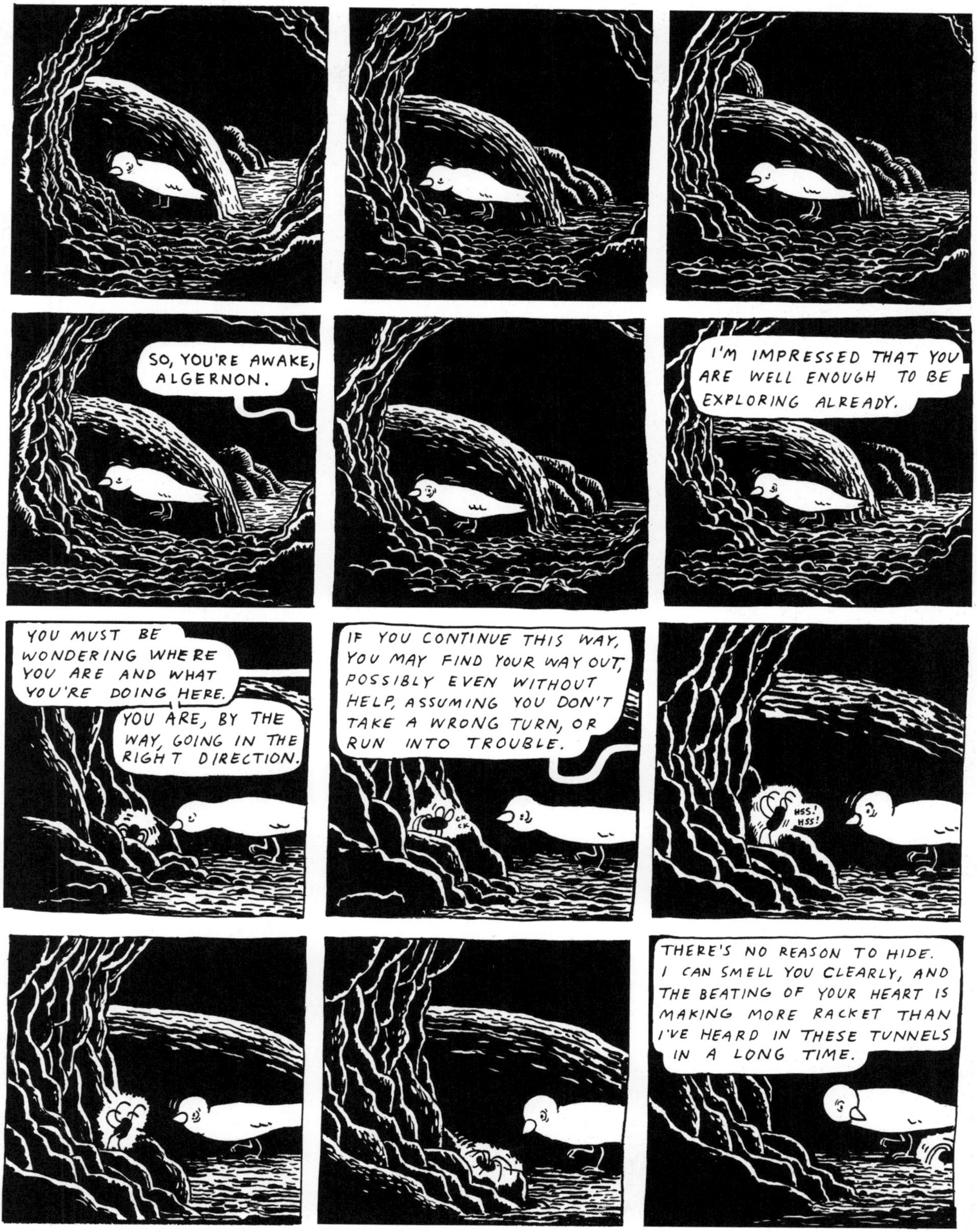
SO, YOU'RE AWAKE, ALGERNON.
I'M IMPRESSED THAT YOU ARE WELL ENOUGH TO BE EXPLORING ALREADY.
YOU MUST BE WONDERING WHERE YOU ARE AND WHAT YOU'RE DOING HERE.
YOU ARE, BY THE WAY, GOING IN THE RIGHT DIRECTION.
IF YOU CONTINUE THIS WAY, YOU MAY FIND YOUR WAY OUT, POSSIBLY EVEN WITHOUT HELP, ASSUMING YOU DON'T TAKE A WRONG TURN, OR RUN INTO TROUBLE.
CK CK
HSS! HSS!
THERE'S NO REASON TO HIDE. I CAN SMELL YOU CLEARLY, AND THE BEATING OF YOUR HEART IS MAKING MORE RACKET THAN I'VE HEARD IN THESE TUNNELS IN A LONG TIME.

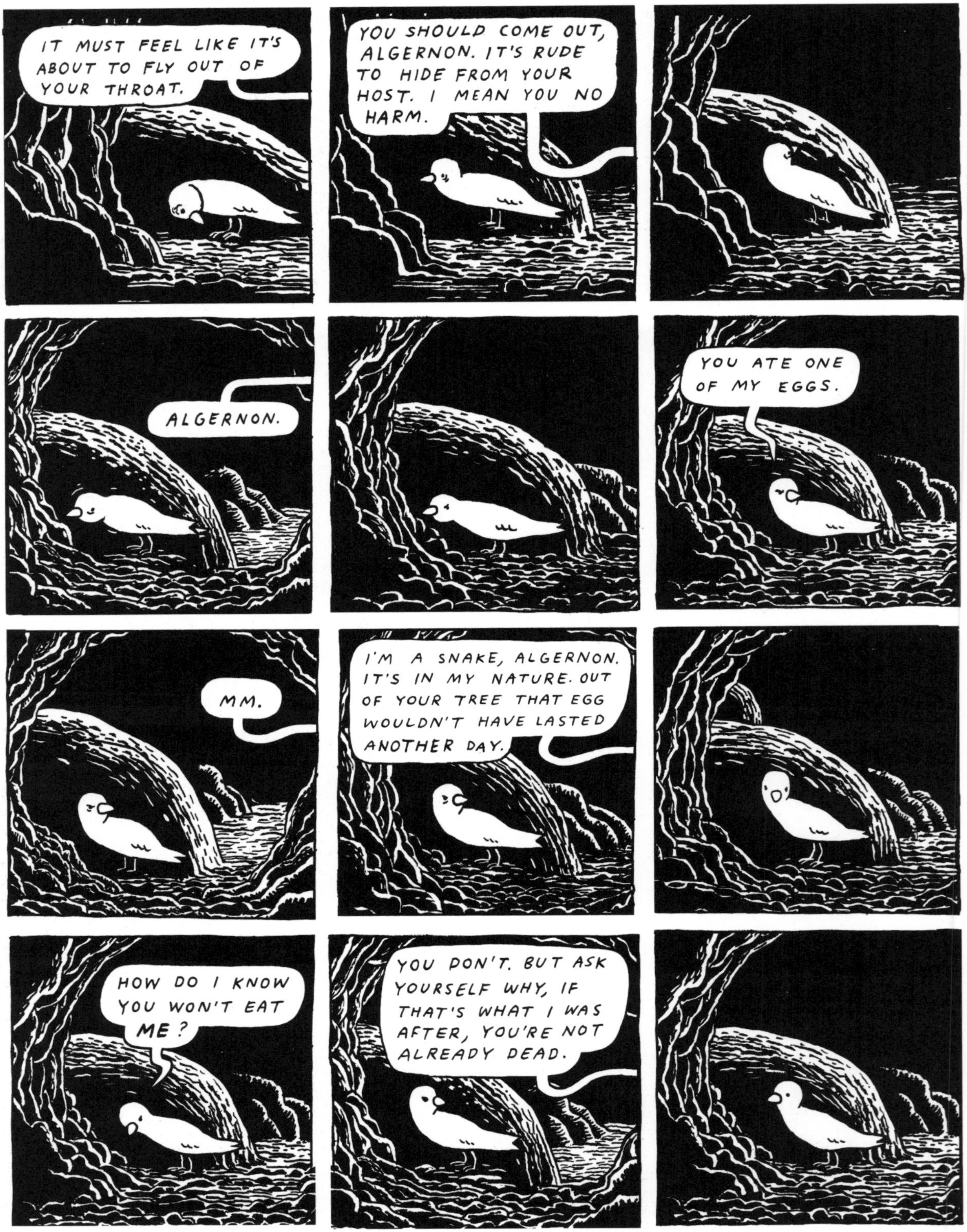
IT MUST FEEL LIKE IT'S ABOUT TO FLY OUT OF YOUR THROAT.
YOU SHOULD COME OUT, ALGERNON. IT'S RUDE TO HIDE FROM YOUR HOST. I MEAN YOU NO HARM.
ALGERNON.
YOU ATE ONE OF MY EGGS.
MM.
I'M A SNAKE, ALGERNON. IT'S IN MY NATURE. OUT OF YOUR TREE THAT EGG WOULDN'T HAVE LASTED ANOTHER DAY.
HOW DO I KNOW YOU WON'T EAT ME?
YOU DON'T. BUT ASK YOURSELF WHY, IF THAT'S WHAT I WAS AFTER, YOU'RE NOT ALREADY DEAD.

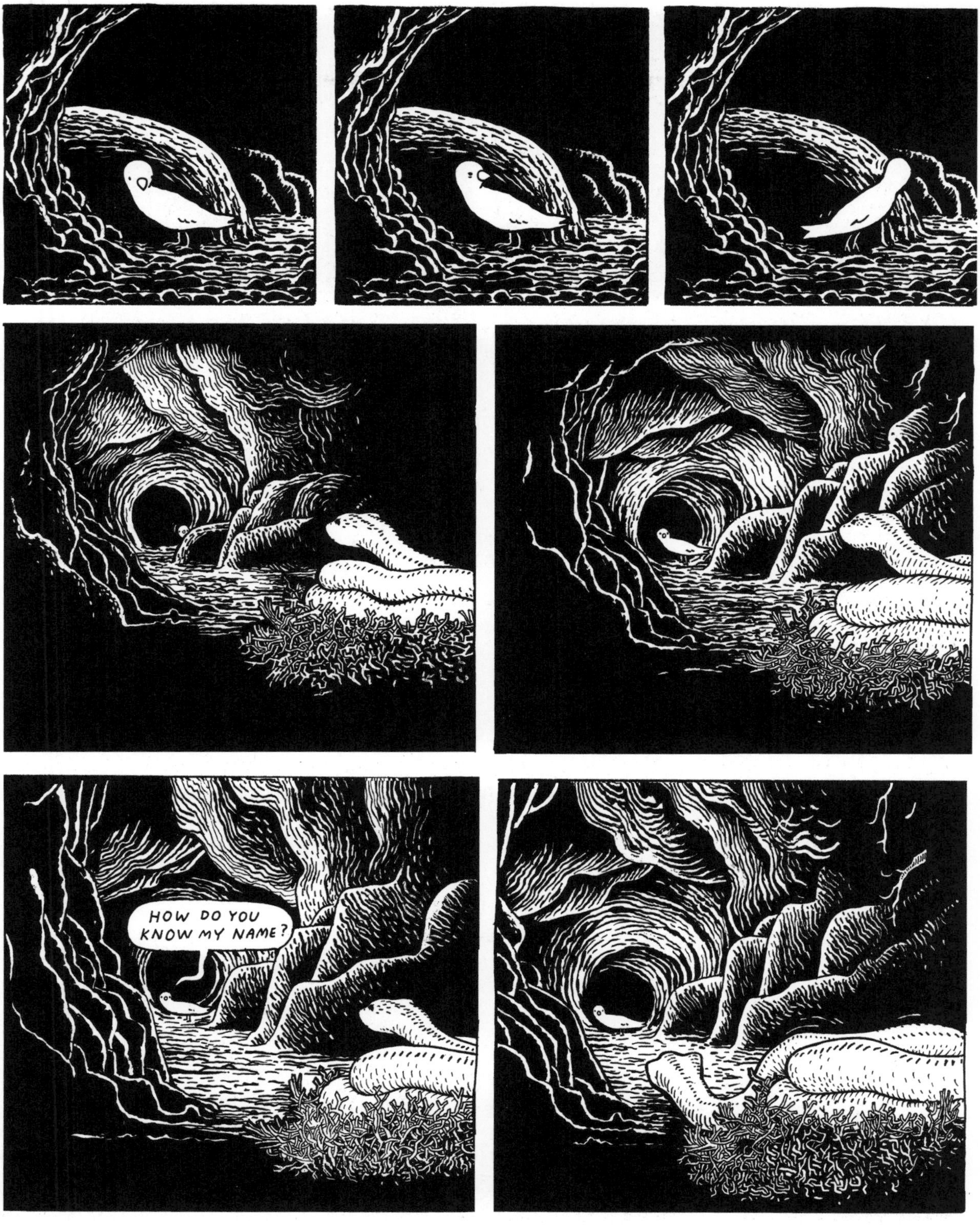
HOW DO YOU KNOW MY NAME?

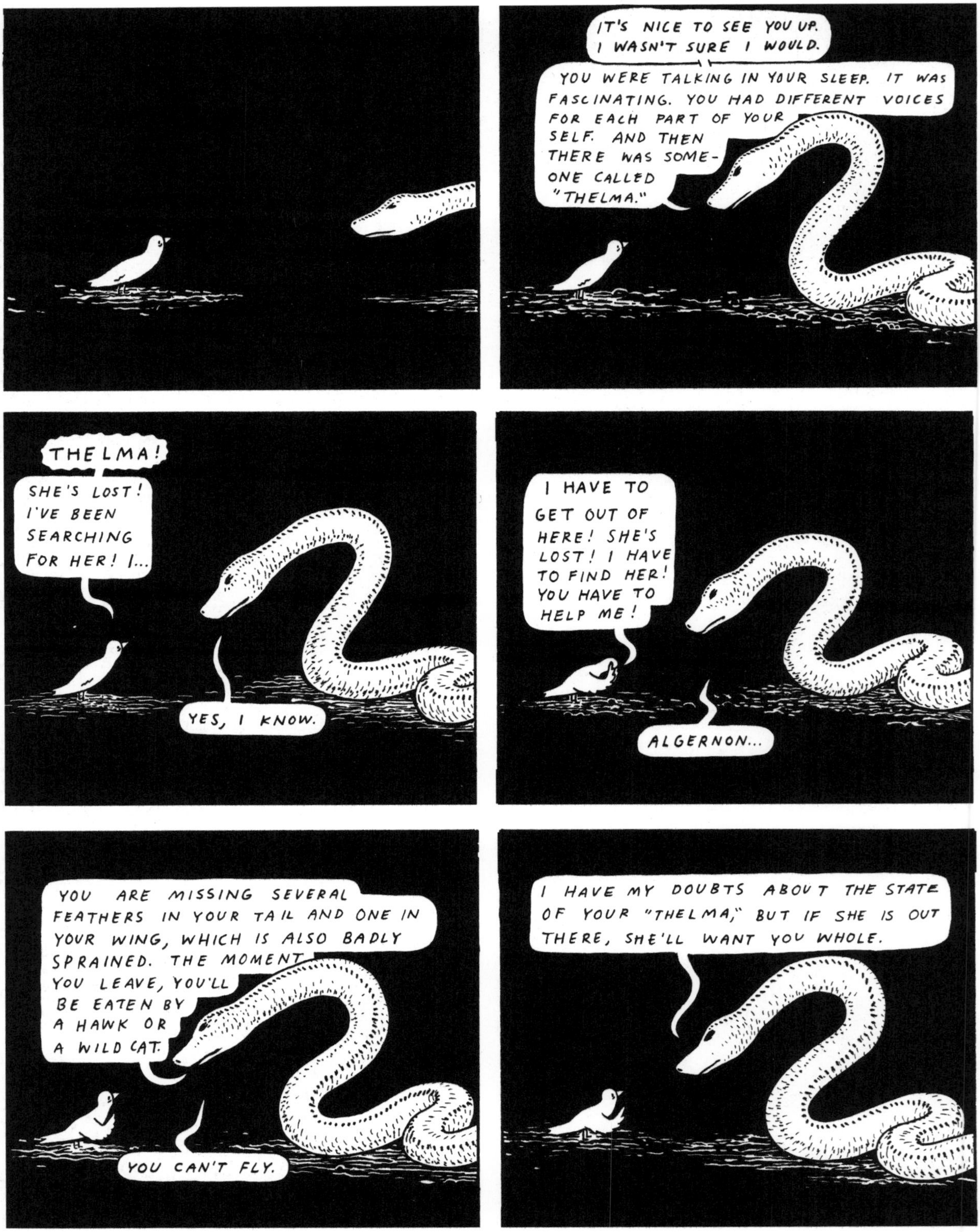
IT'S NICE TO SEE YOU UP. I WASN'T SURE I WOULD.
YOU WERE TALKING IN YOUR SLEEP. IT WAS FASCINATING. YOU HAD DIFFERENT VOICES FOR EACH PART OF YOUR SELF. AND THEN THERE WAS SOME-ONE CALLED "THELMA."
THELMA!
SHE'S LOST! I'VE BEEN SEARCHING FOR HER! I...
YES, I KNOW.
I HAVE TO GET OUT OF HERE! SHE'S LOST! I HAVE TO FIND HER! YOU HAVE TO HELP ME!
ALGERNON...
YOU ARE MISSING SEVERAL FEATHERS IN YOUR TAIL AND ONE IN YOUR WING, WHICH IS ALSO BADLY SPRAINED. THE MOMENT YOU LEAVE, YOU'LL BE EATEN BY A HAWK OR A WILD CAT.
YOU CAN'T FLY.
I HAVE MY DOUBTS ABOUT THE STATE OF YOUR "THELMA," BUT IF SHE IS OUT THERE, SHE'LL WANT YOU WHOLE.

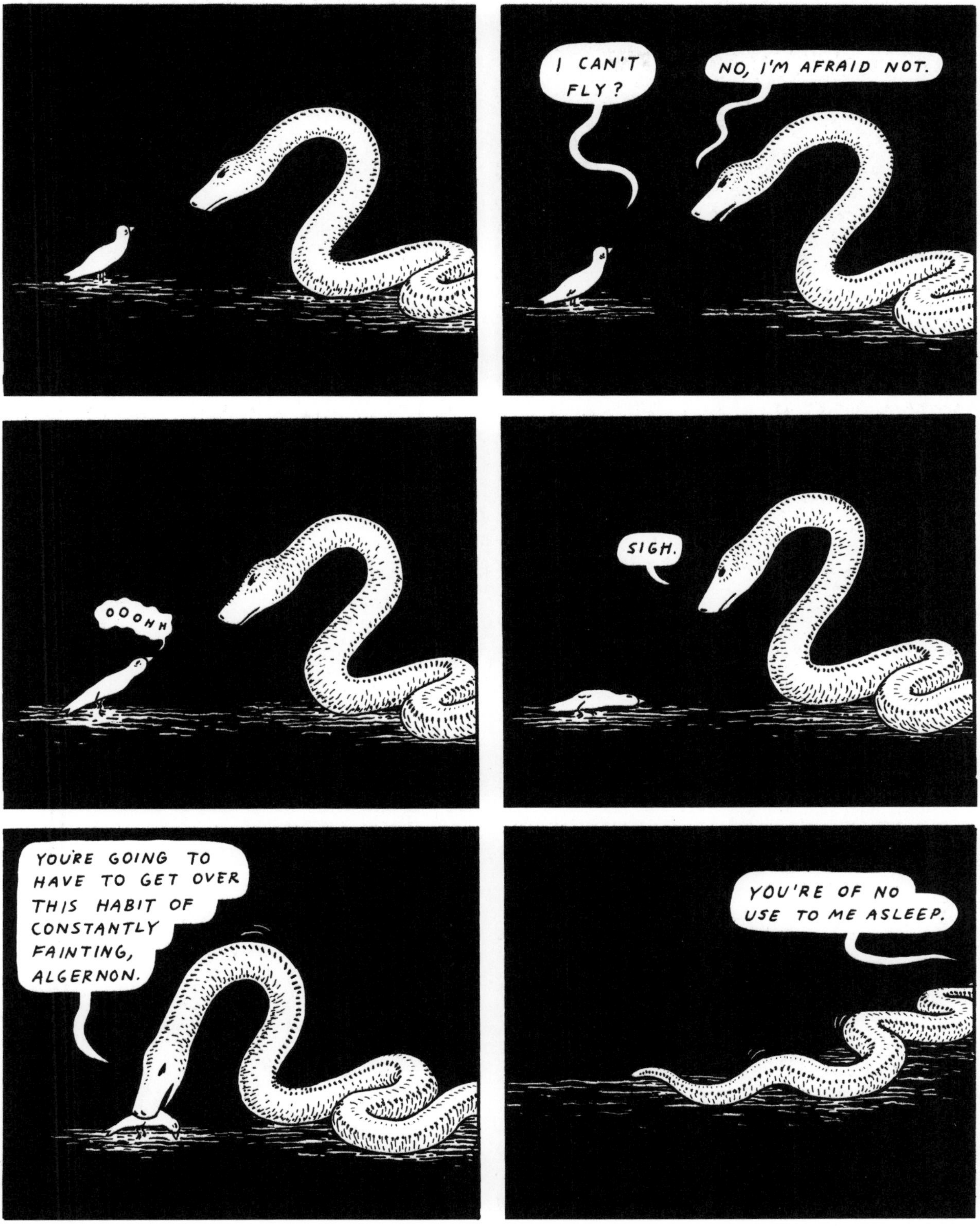
I CAN'T FLY?
NO, I'M AFRAID NOT.
OOOHH
SIGH.
YOU'RE GOING TO HAVE TO GET OVER THIS HABIT OF CONSTANTLY FAINTING, ALGERNON.
YOU'RE OF NO USE TO ME ASLEEP.

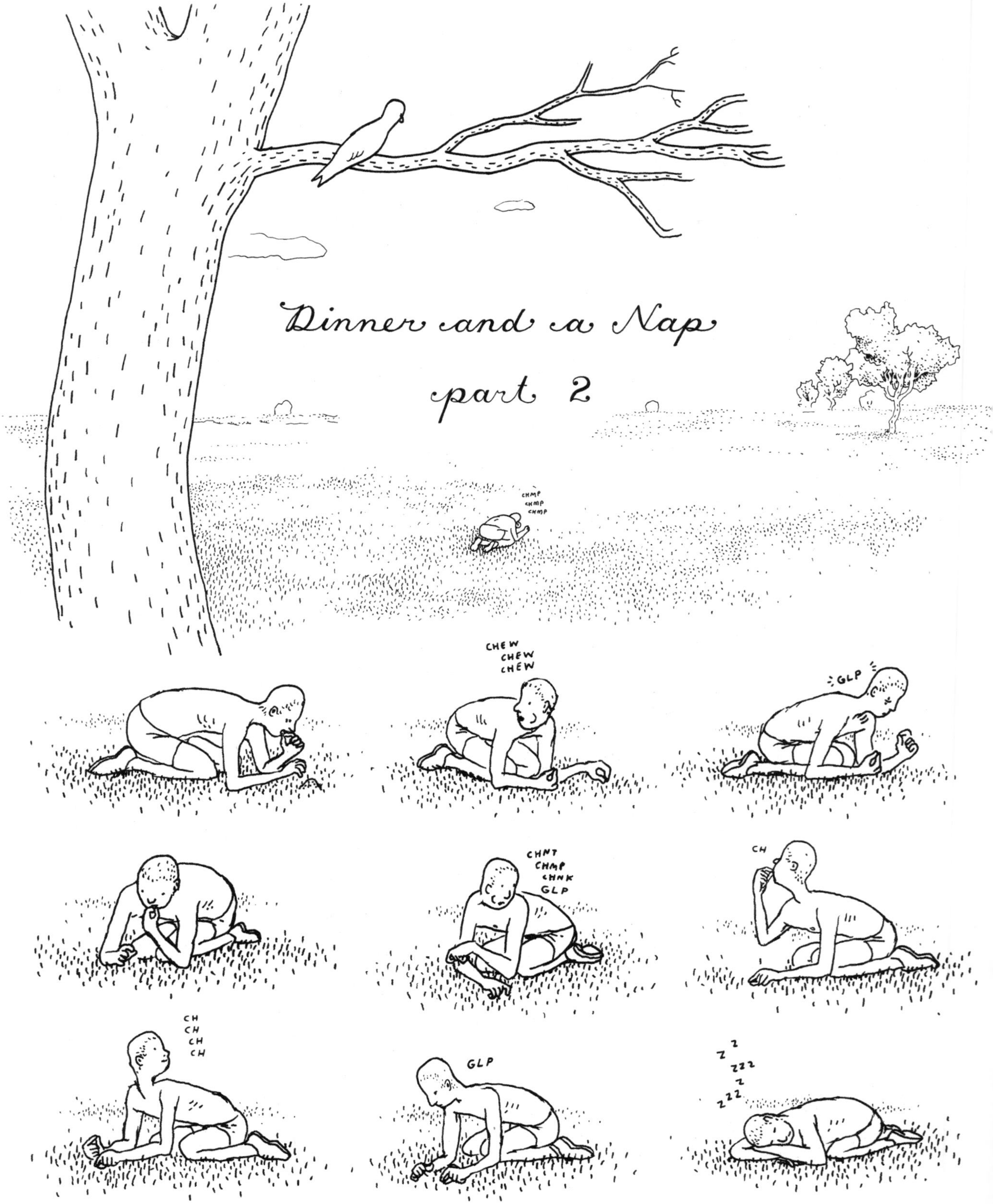
Dinner and a Nap
part 2
CHMP
CHMP
CHMP
CHEW
CHEW
CHEW
GLP
CHNT
CHMP
CHNK
GLP
CH
CH
CH
CH
CH
GLP
Z Z
ZZZ
Z
ZZZ

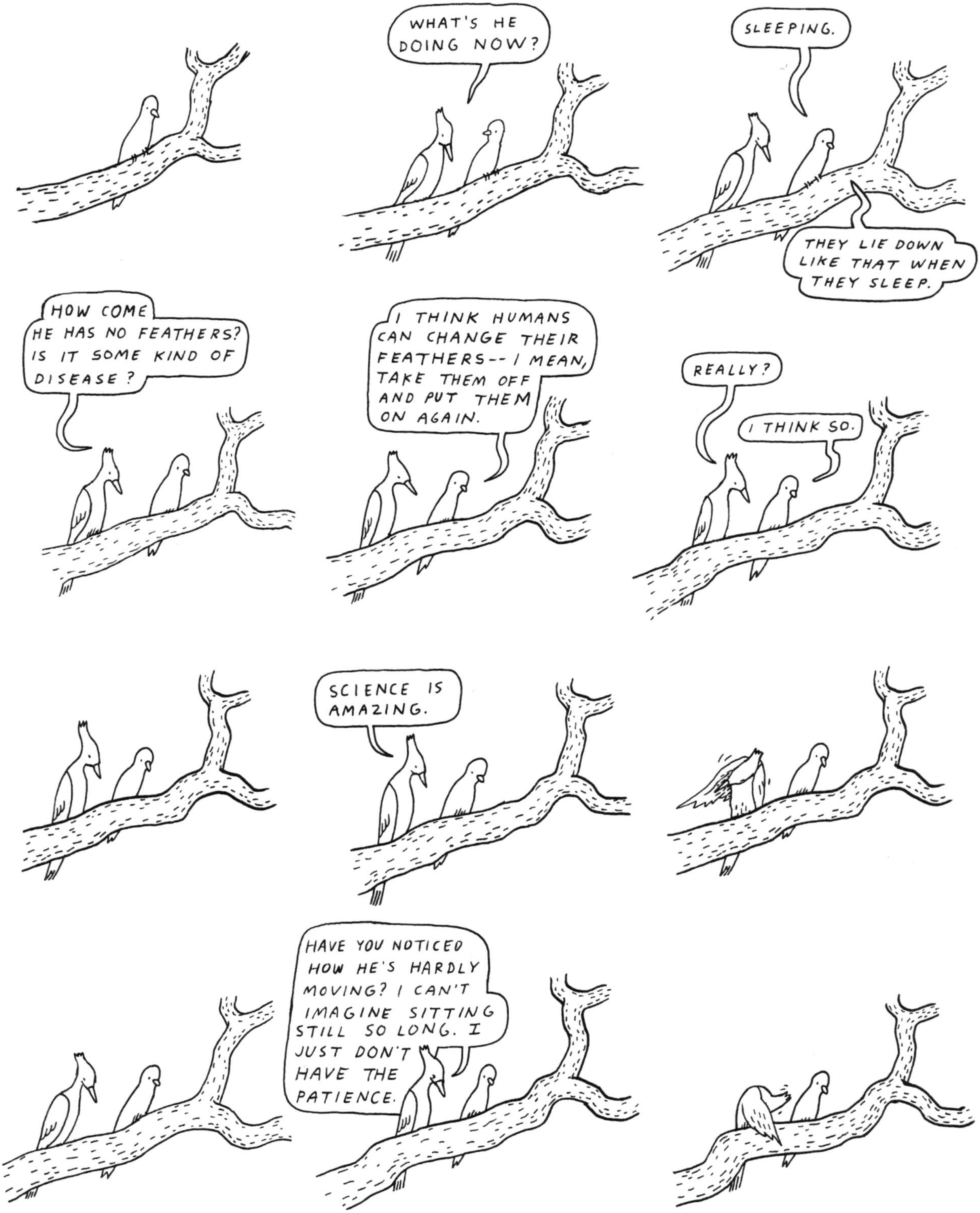
WHAT'S HE DOING NOW?
SLEEPING.
THEY LIE DOWN LIKE THAT WHEN THEY SLEEP.
HOW COME HE HAS NO FEATHERS? IS IT SOME KIND OF DISEASE?
I THINK HUMANS CAN CHANGE THEIR FEATHERS-- I MEAN, TAKE THEM OFF AND PUT THEM ON AGAIN.
REALLY?
I THINK SO.
SCIENCE IS AMAZING.
HAVE YOU NOTICED HOW HE'S HARDLY MOVING? I CAN'T IMAGINE SITTING STILL SO LONG. I JUST DON'T HAVE THE PATIENCE.

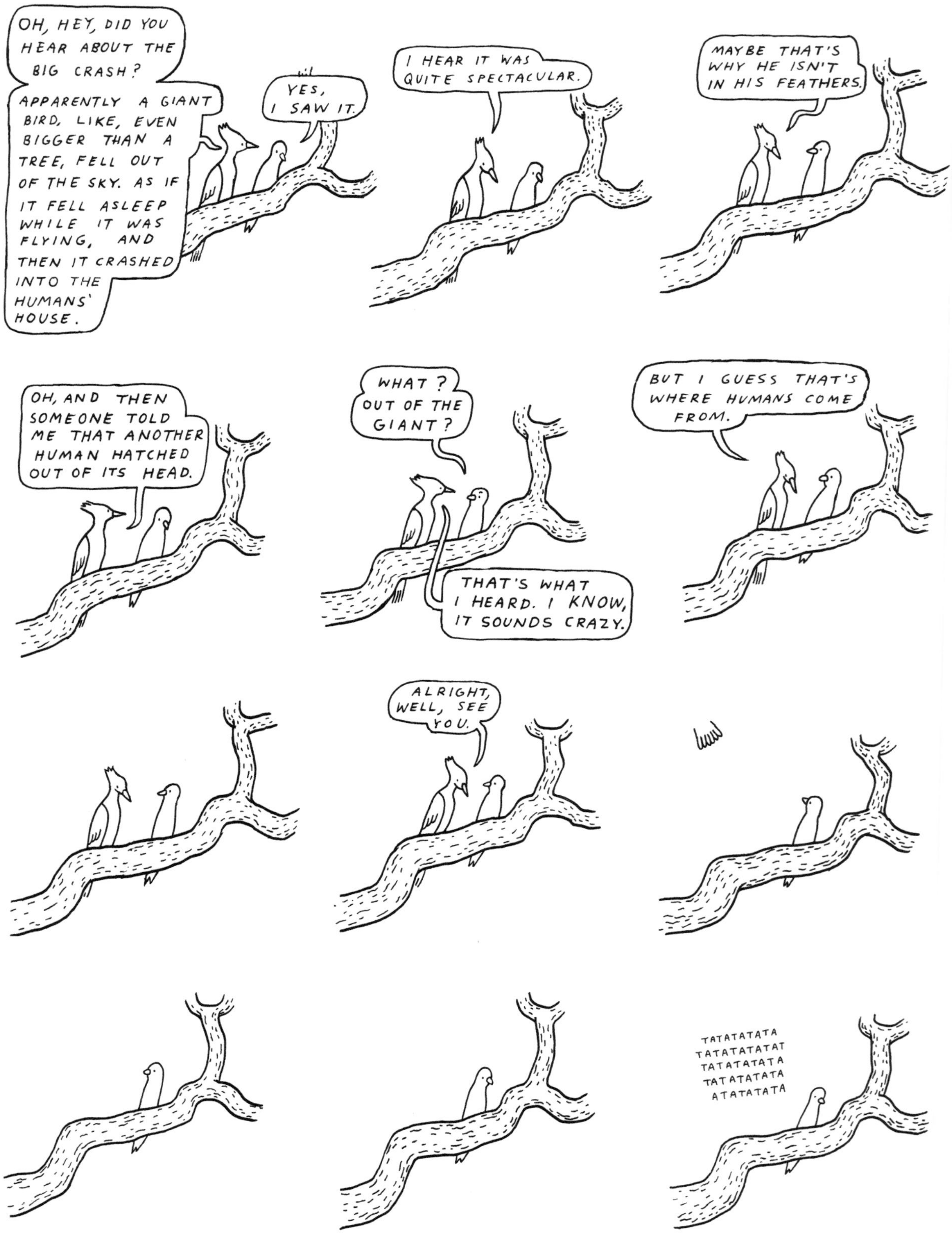
OH, HEY, DID YOU HEAR ABOUT THE BIG CRASH?
APPARENTLY A GIANT BIRD, LIKE, EVEN BIGGER THAN A TREE, FELL OUT OF THE SKY. AS IF IT FELL ASLEEP WHILE IT WAS FLYING, AND THEN IT CRASHED INTO THE HUMANS' HOUSE.
YES, I SAW IT.
I HEAR IT WAS QUITE SPECTACULAR.
MAYBE THAT'S WHY HE ISN'T IN HIS FEATHERS.
OH, AND THEN SOMEONE TOLD ME THAT ANOTHER HUMAN HATCHED OUT OF ITS HEAD.
WHAT? OUT OF THE GIANT?
THAT'S WHAT I HEARD. I KNOW, IT SOUNDS CRAZY.
BUT I GUESS THAT'S WHERE HUMANS COME FROM.
ALRIGHT, WELL, SEE YOU.
TATATATATA
TATATATATAT
TATATATATA
TATATATATA
ATATATATA

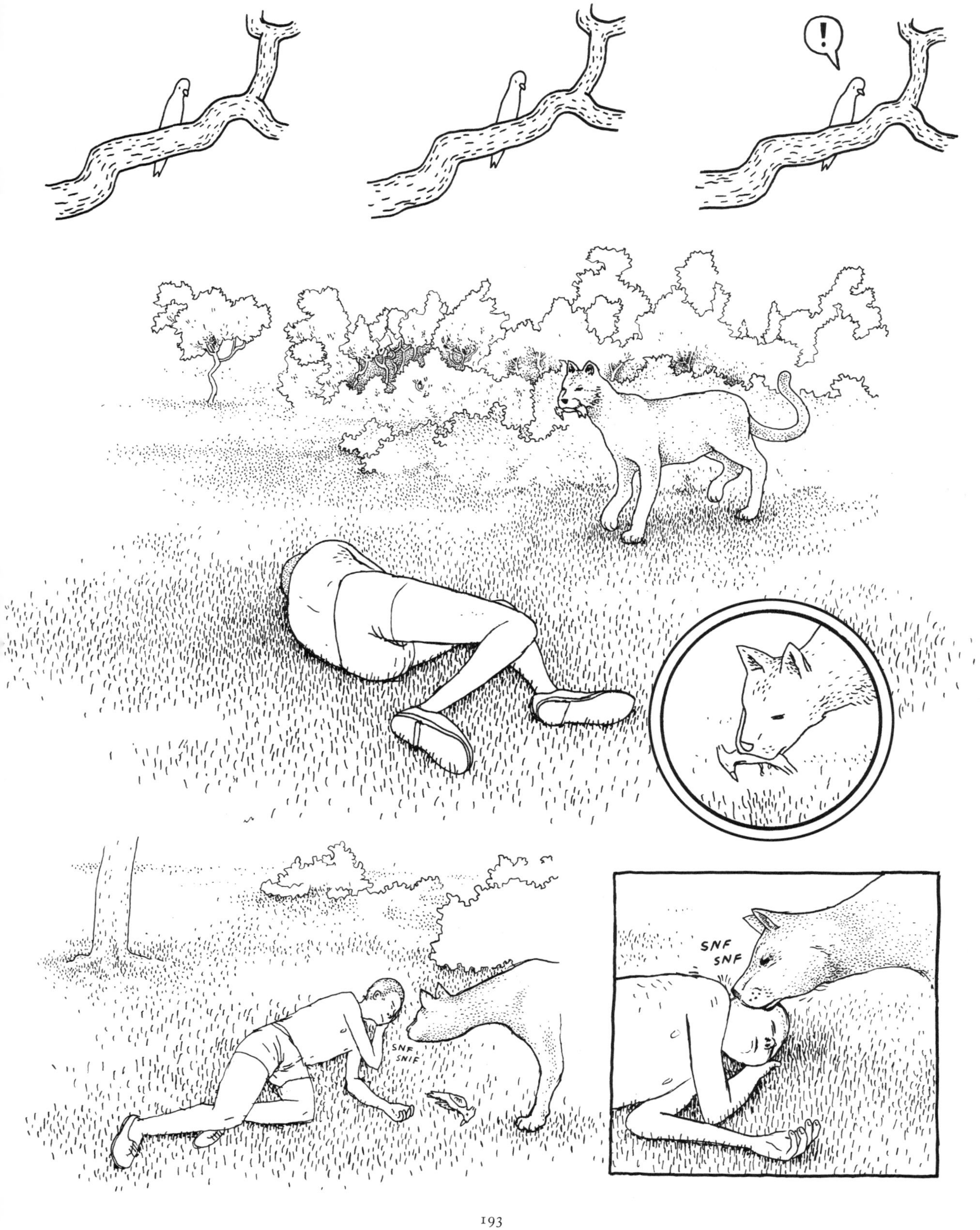
!
SNF
SNIF
SNF
SNF

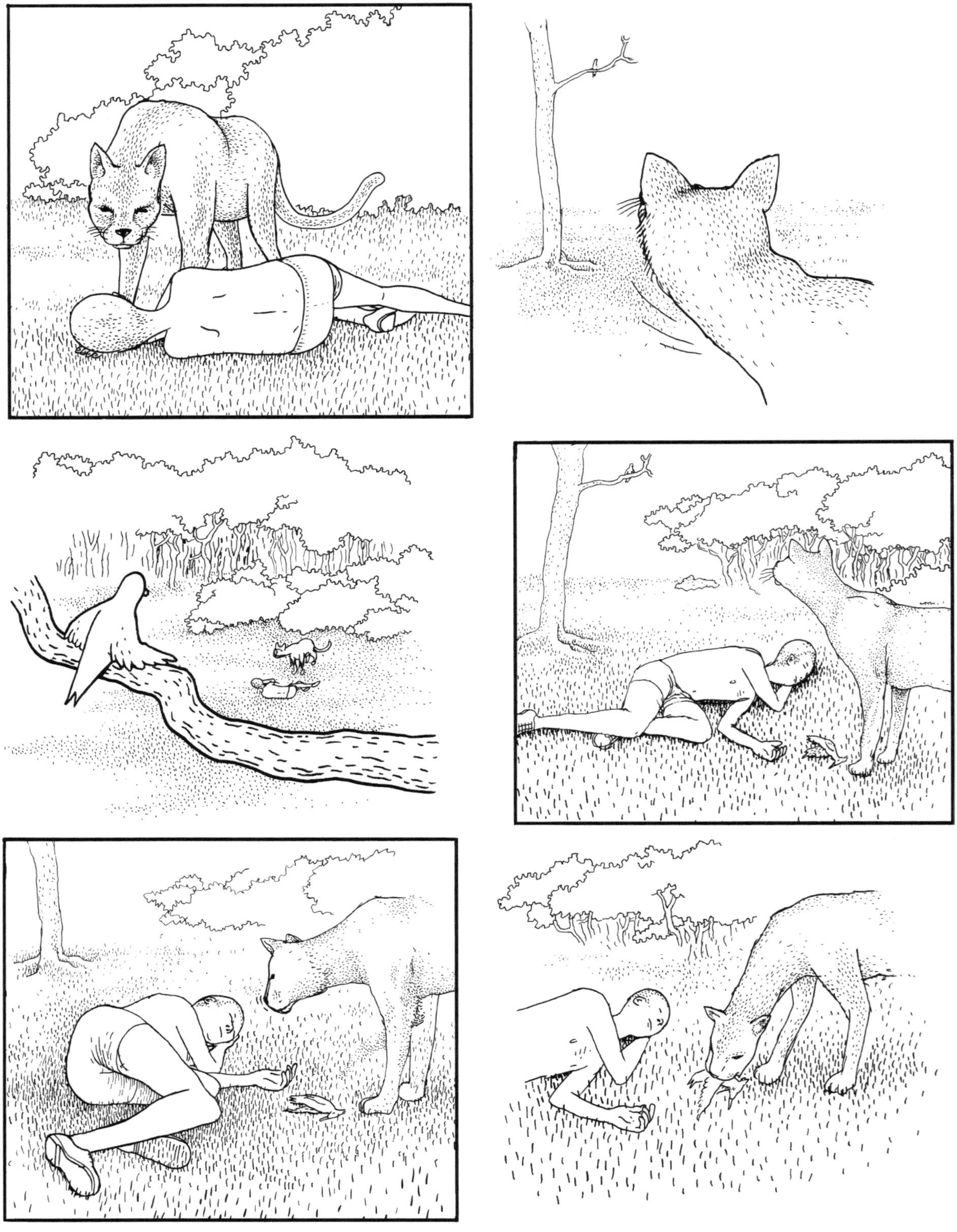

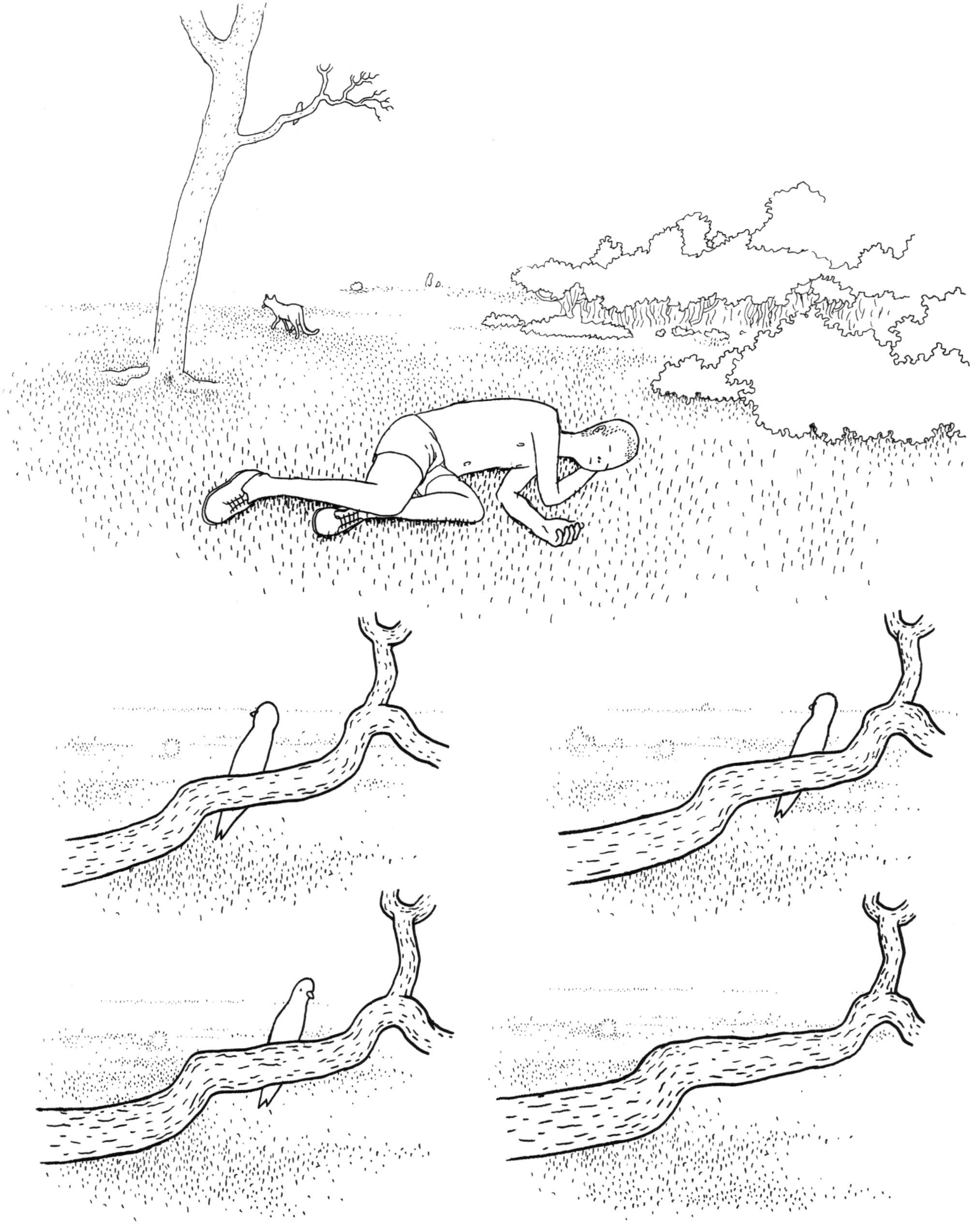

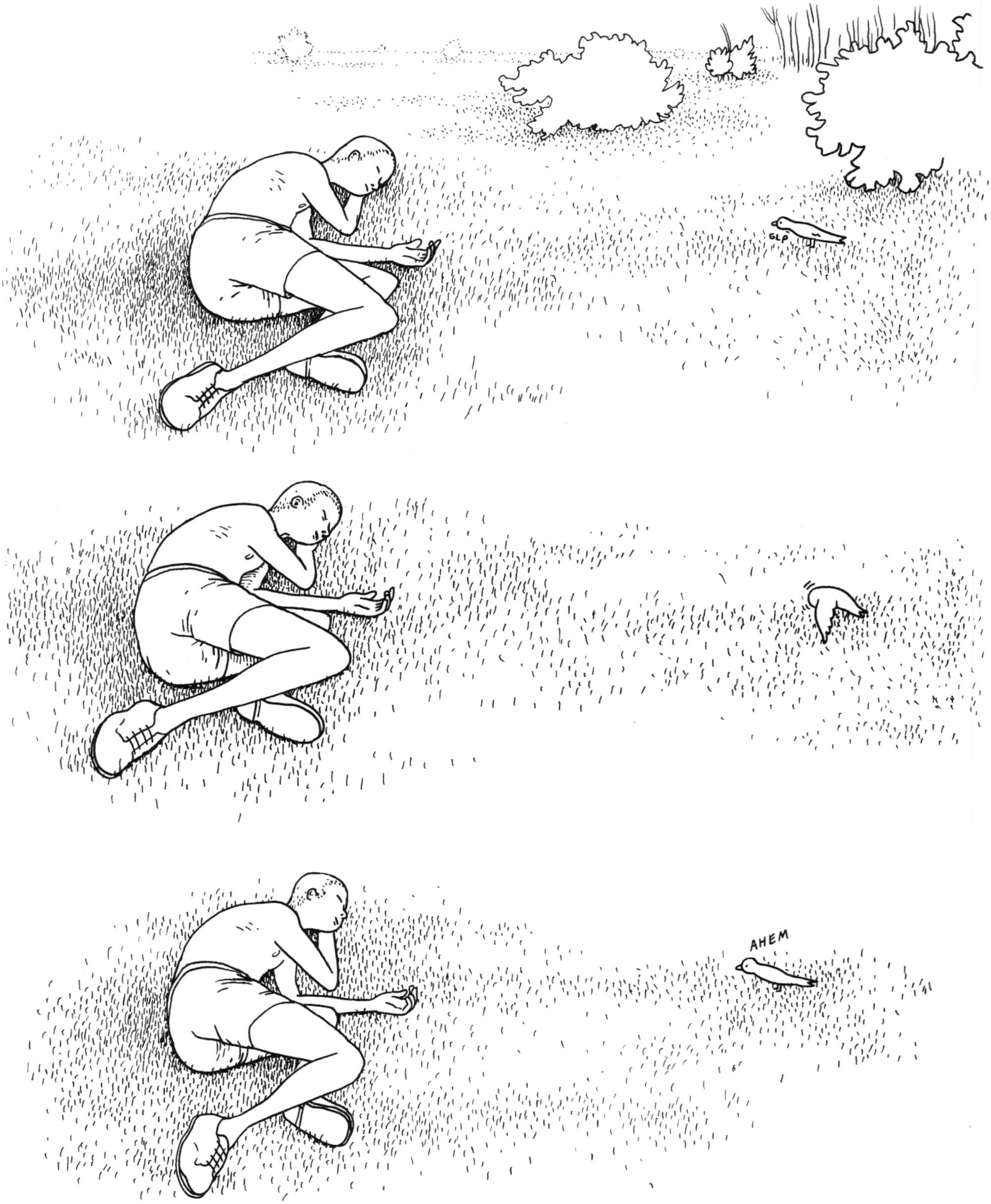
GLP
AHEM

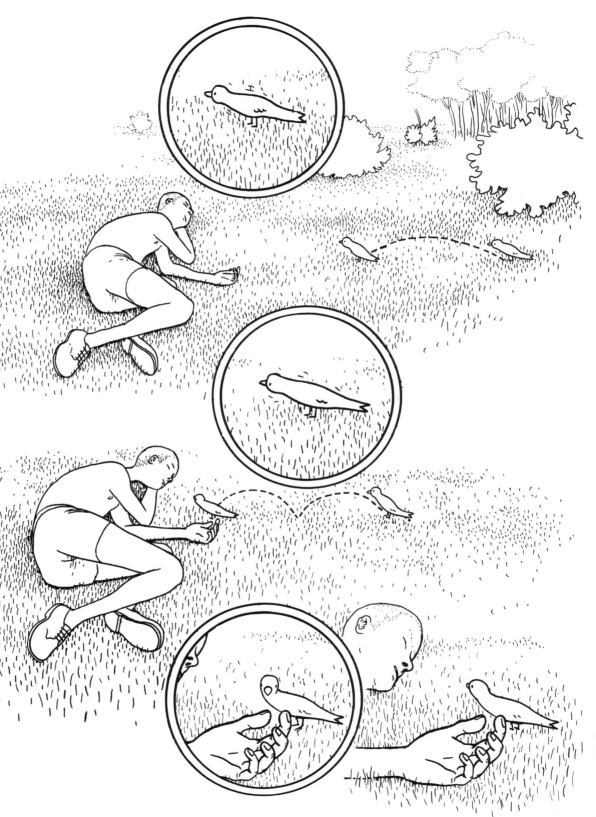

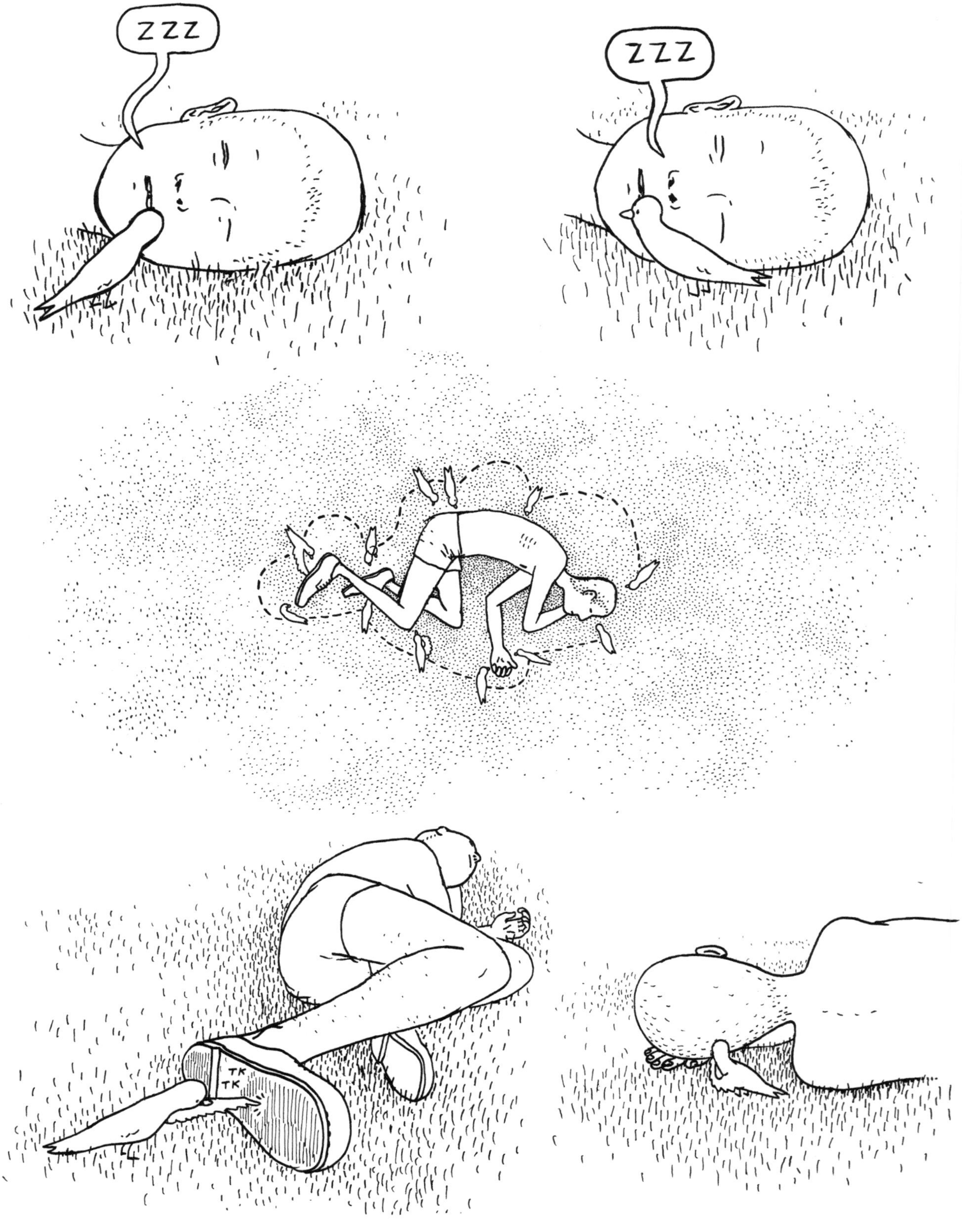
ZZZ
ZZZ
TK
TK

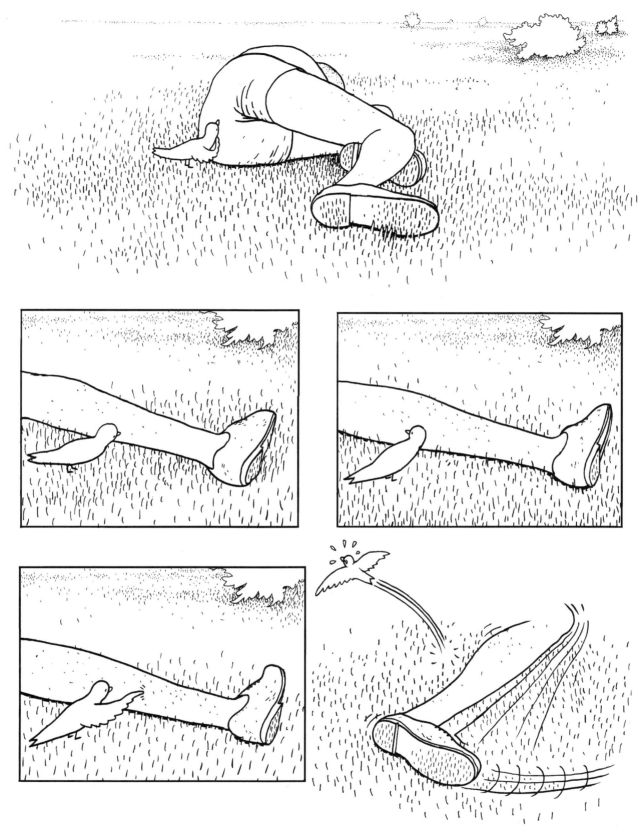

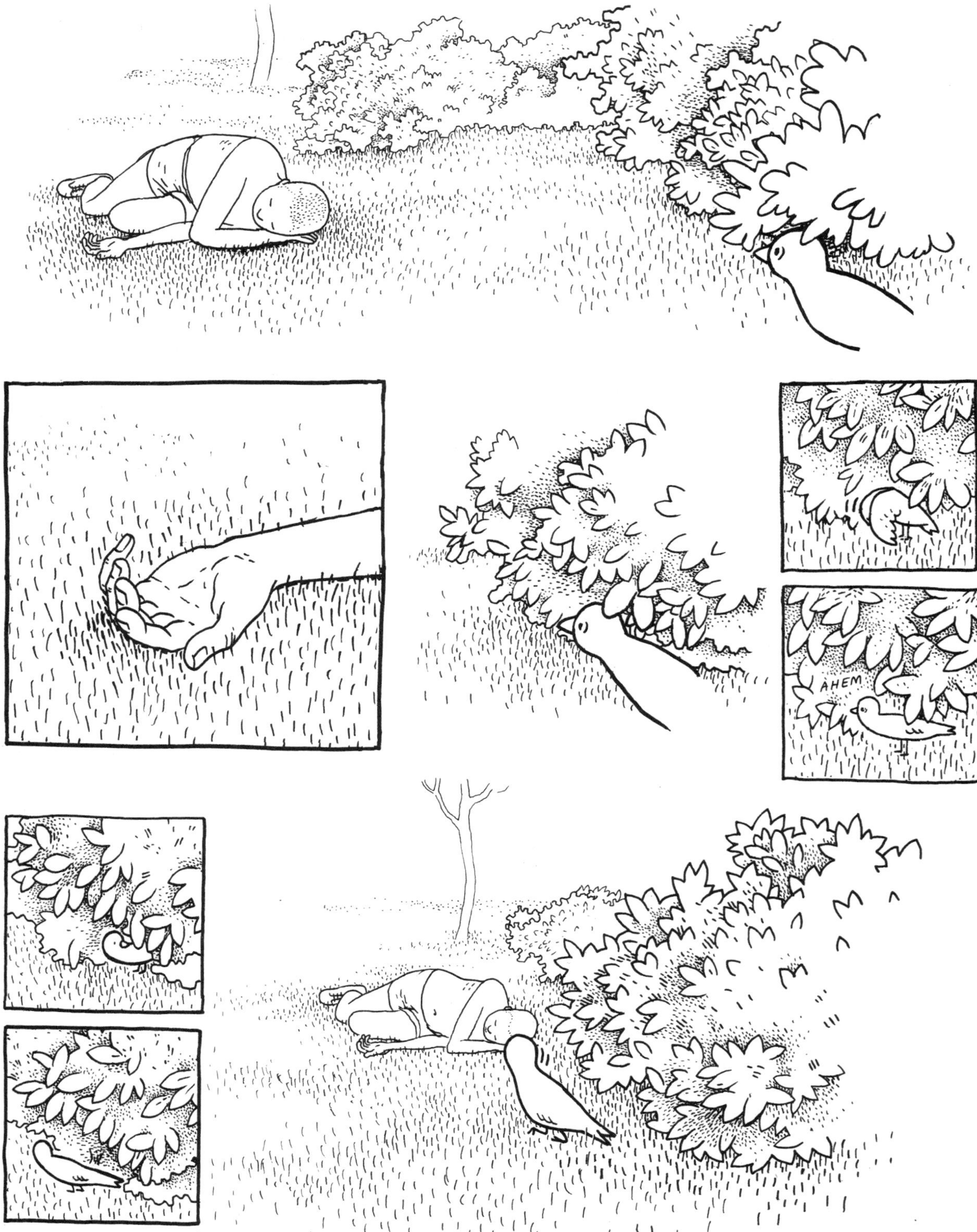
AHEM

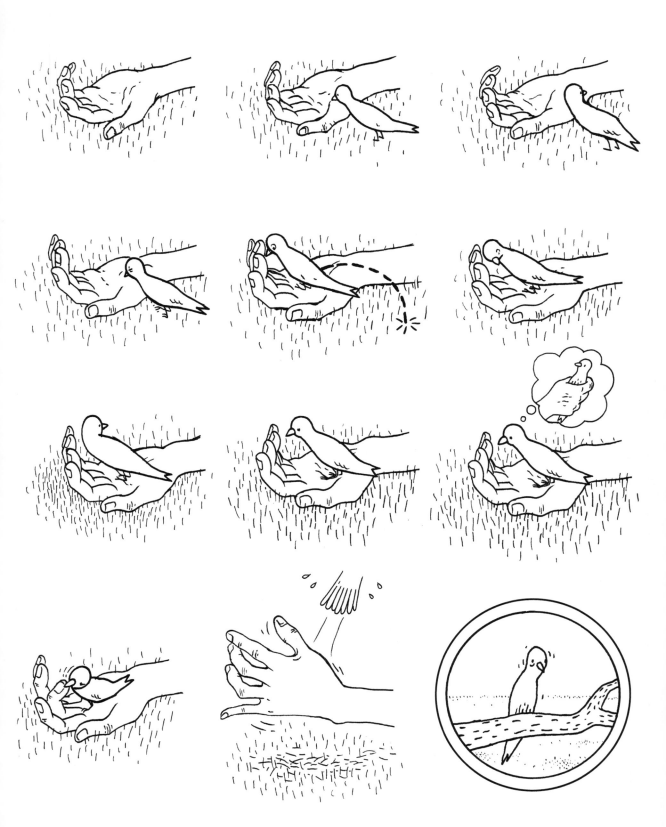

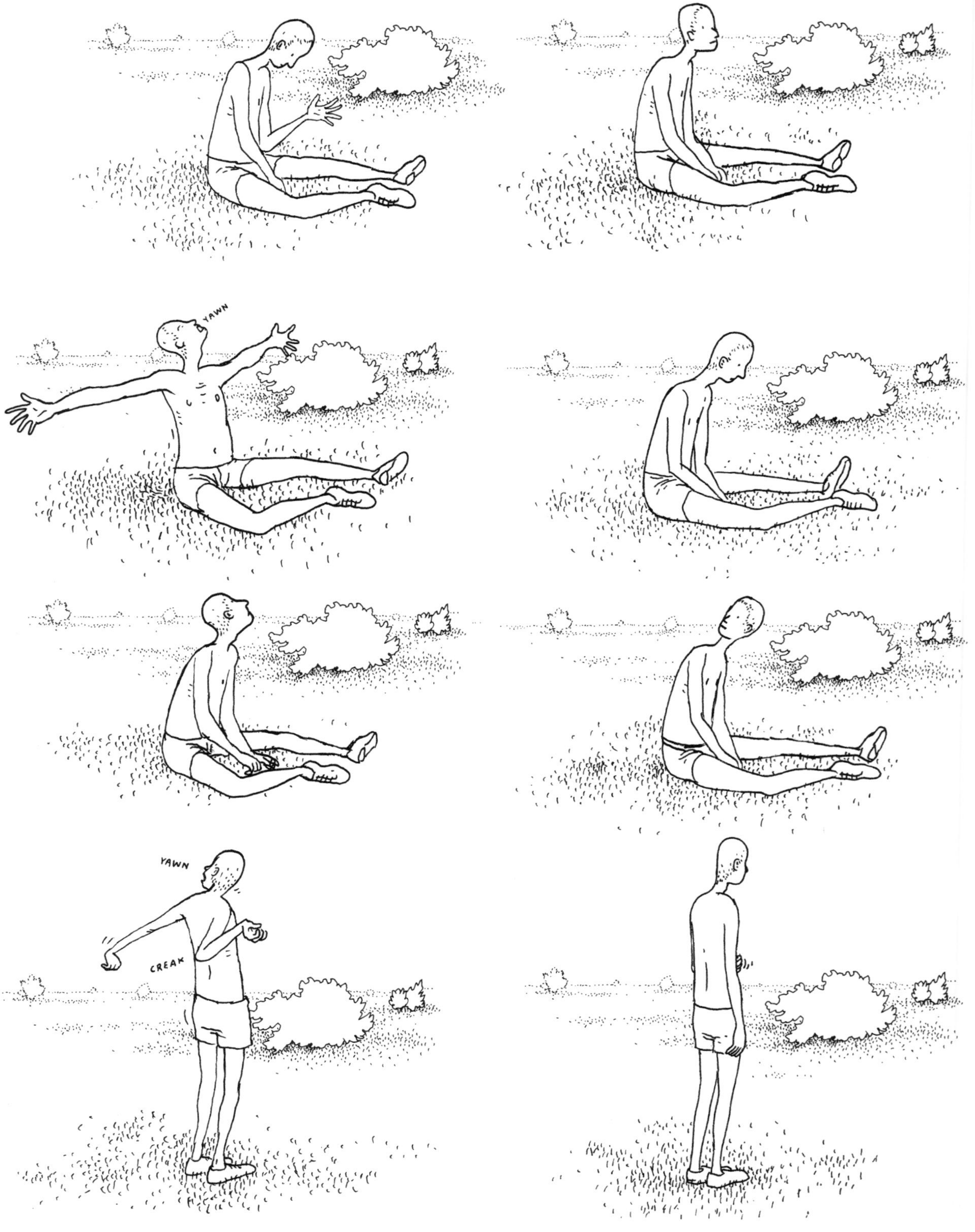
YAWN
YAWN
CREAK

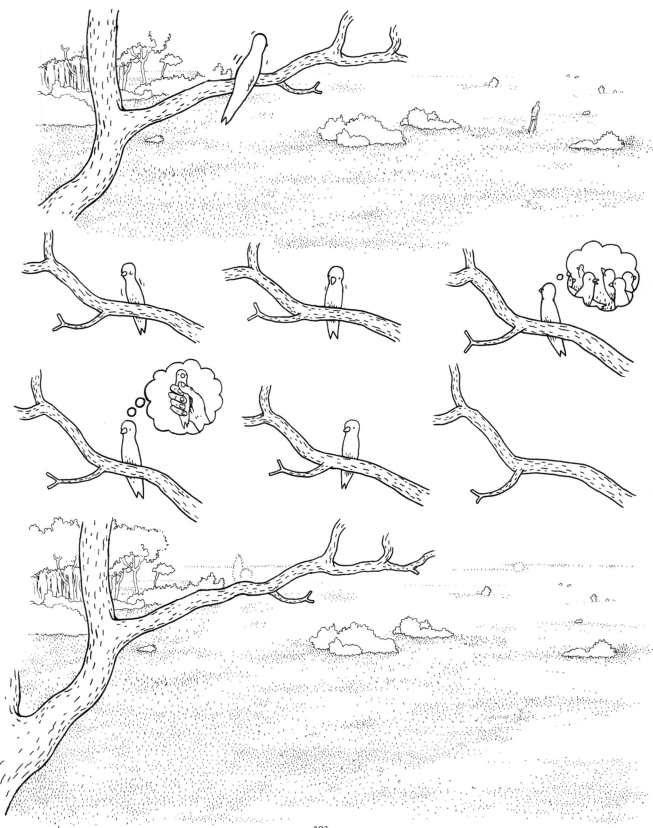

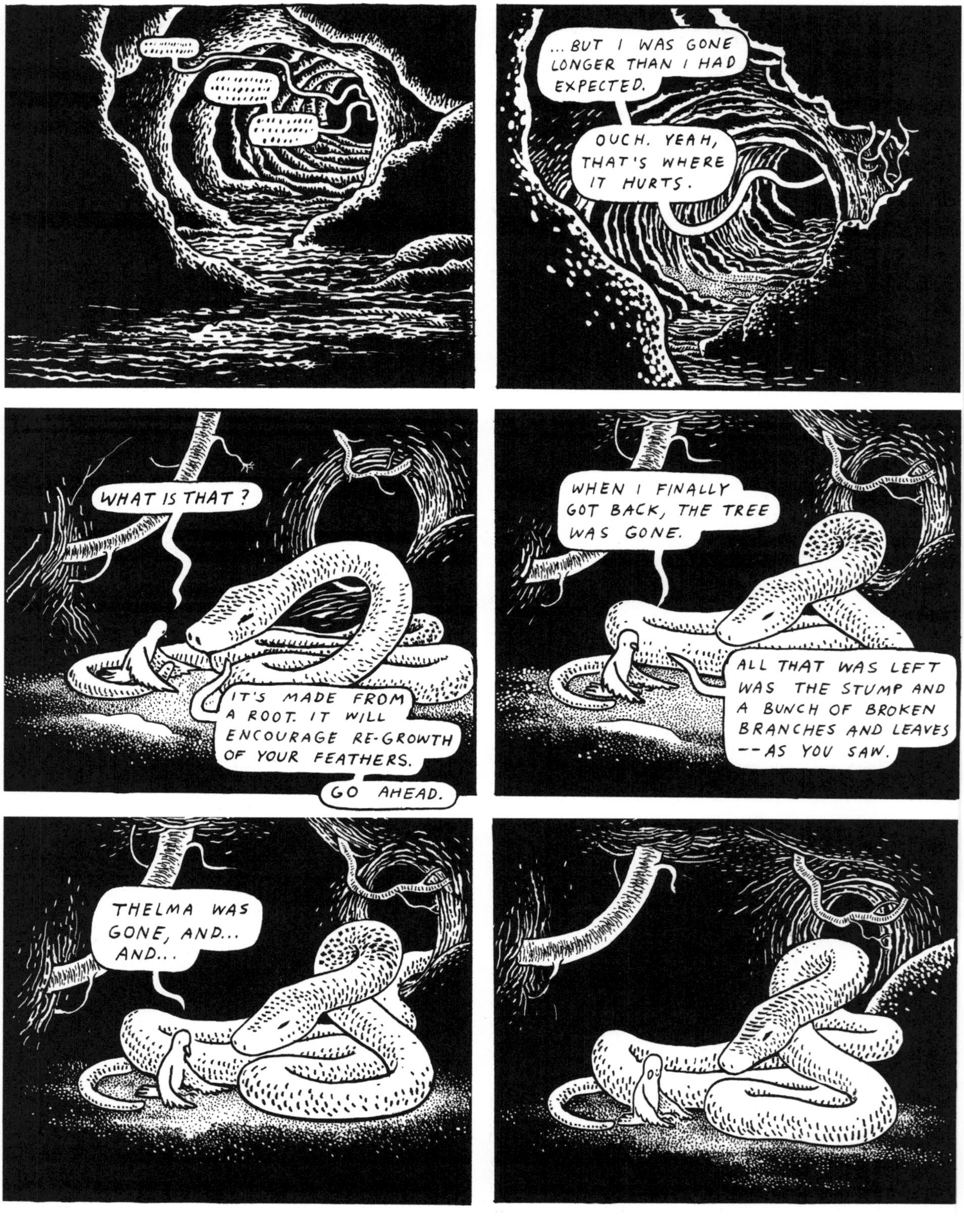

...BUT I WAS GONE LONGER THAN I HAD EXPECTED.
OUCH. YEAH, THAT'S WHERE IT HURTS.
WHAT IS THAT?
IT'S MADE FROM A ROOT. IT WILL ENCOURAGE RE-GROWTH OF YOUR FEATHERS.
GO AHEAD.
WHEN I FINALLY GOT BACK, THE TREE WAS GONE.
ALL THAT WAS LEFT WAS THE STUMP AND A BUNCH OF BROKEN BRANCHES AND LEAVES --AS YOU SAW.
THELMA WAS GONE, AND... AND...

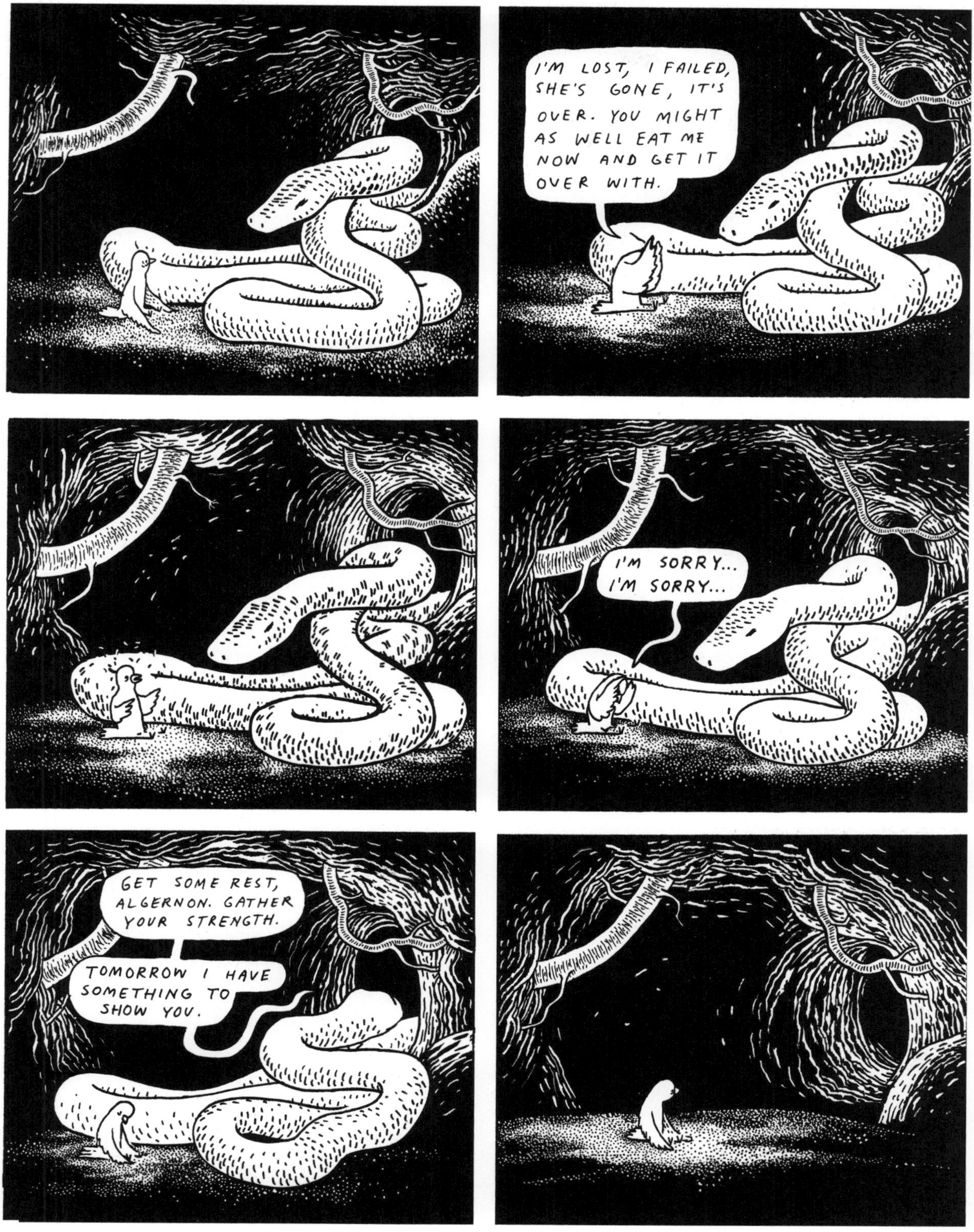
I'M LOST, I FAILED, SHE'S GONE, IT'S OVER. YOU MIGHT AS WELL EAT ME NOW AND GET IT OVER WITH.
I'M SORRY... I'M SORRY...
GET SOME REST, ALGERNON. GATHER YOUR STRENGTH.
TOMORROW I HAVE SOMETHING TO SHOW YOU.

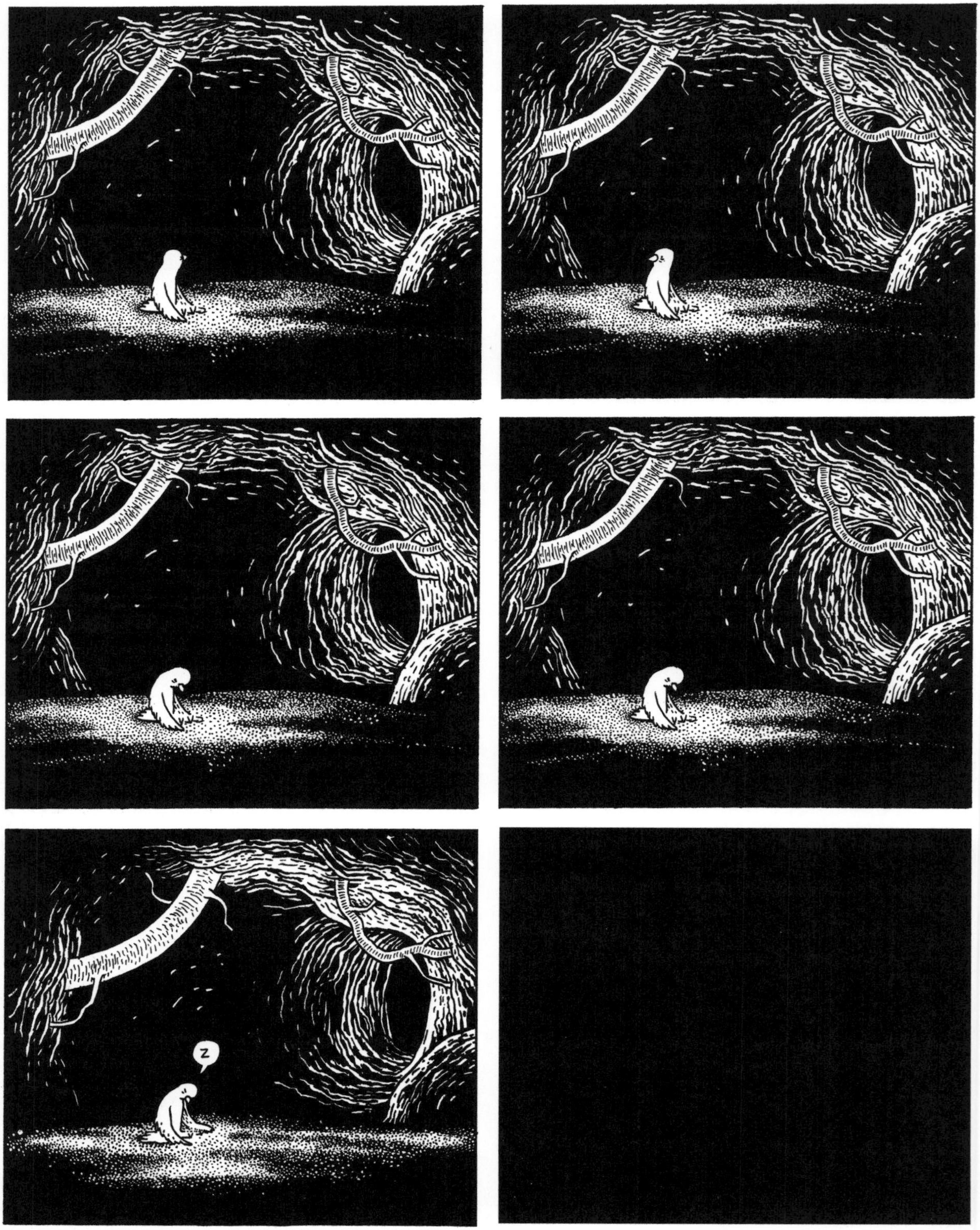
z

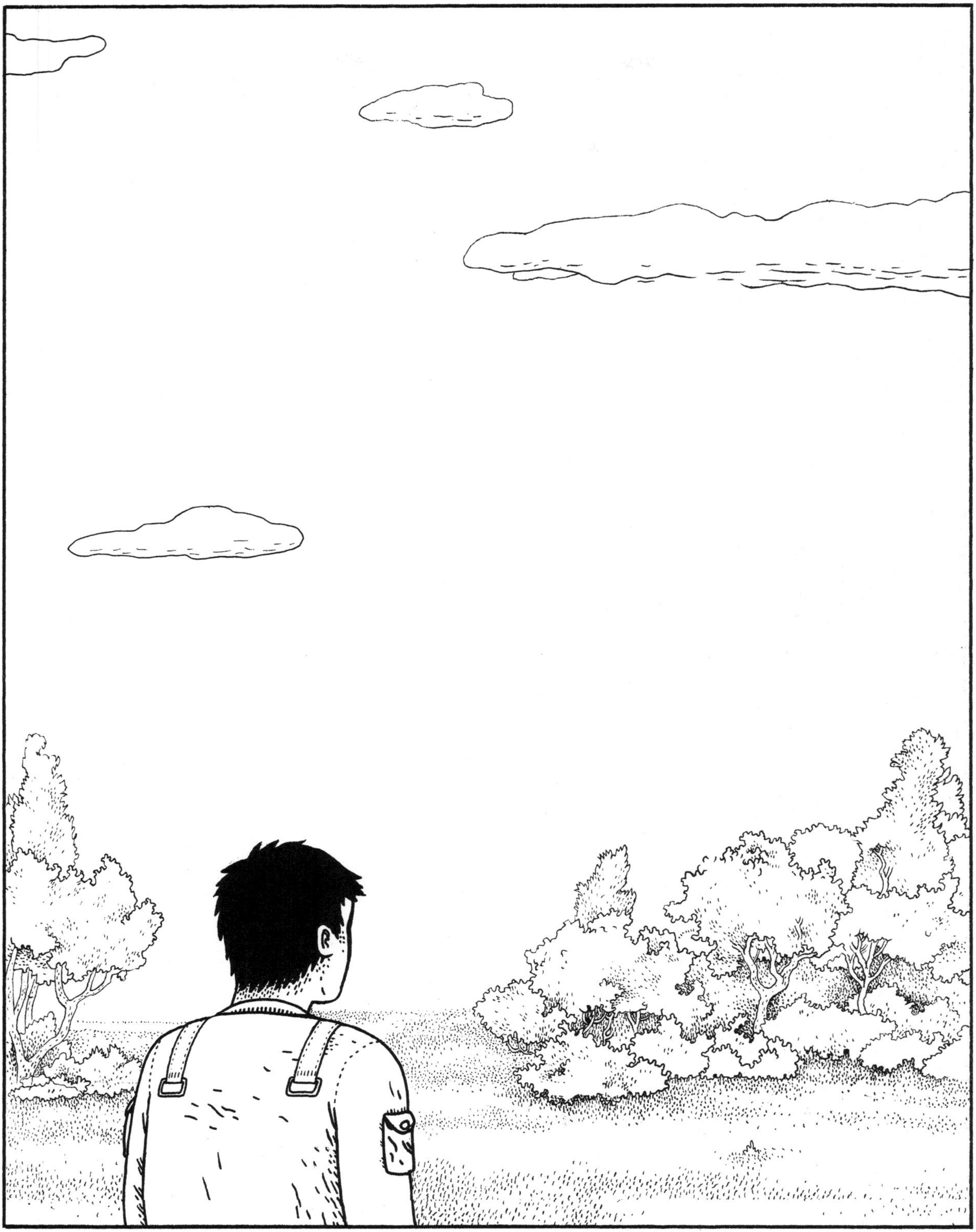

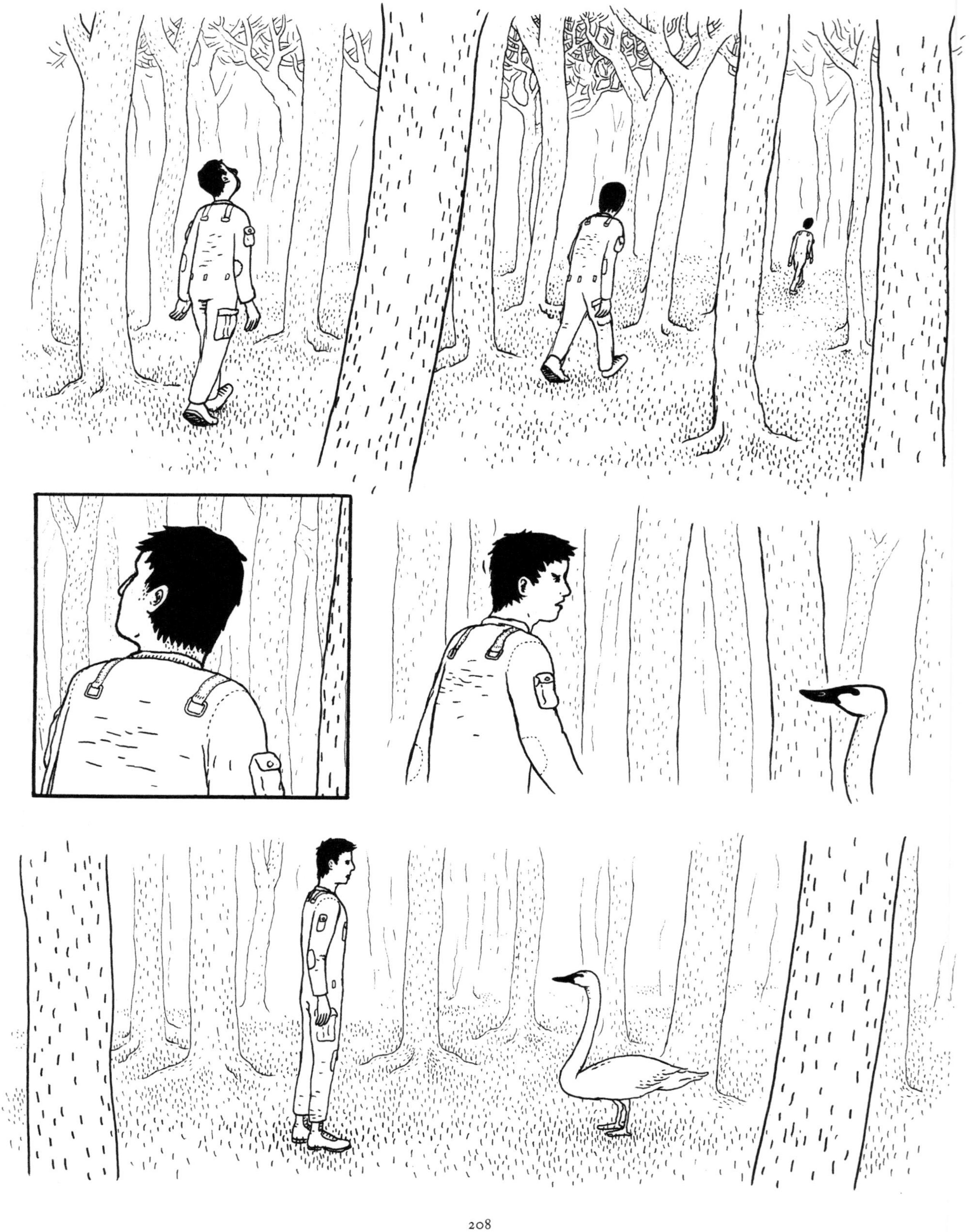

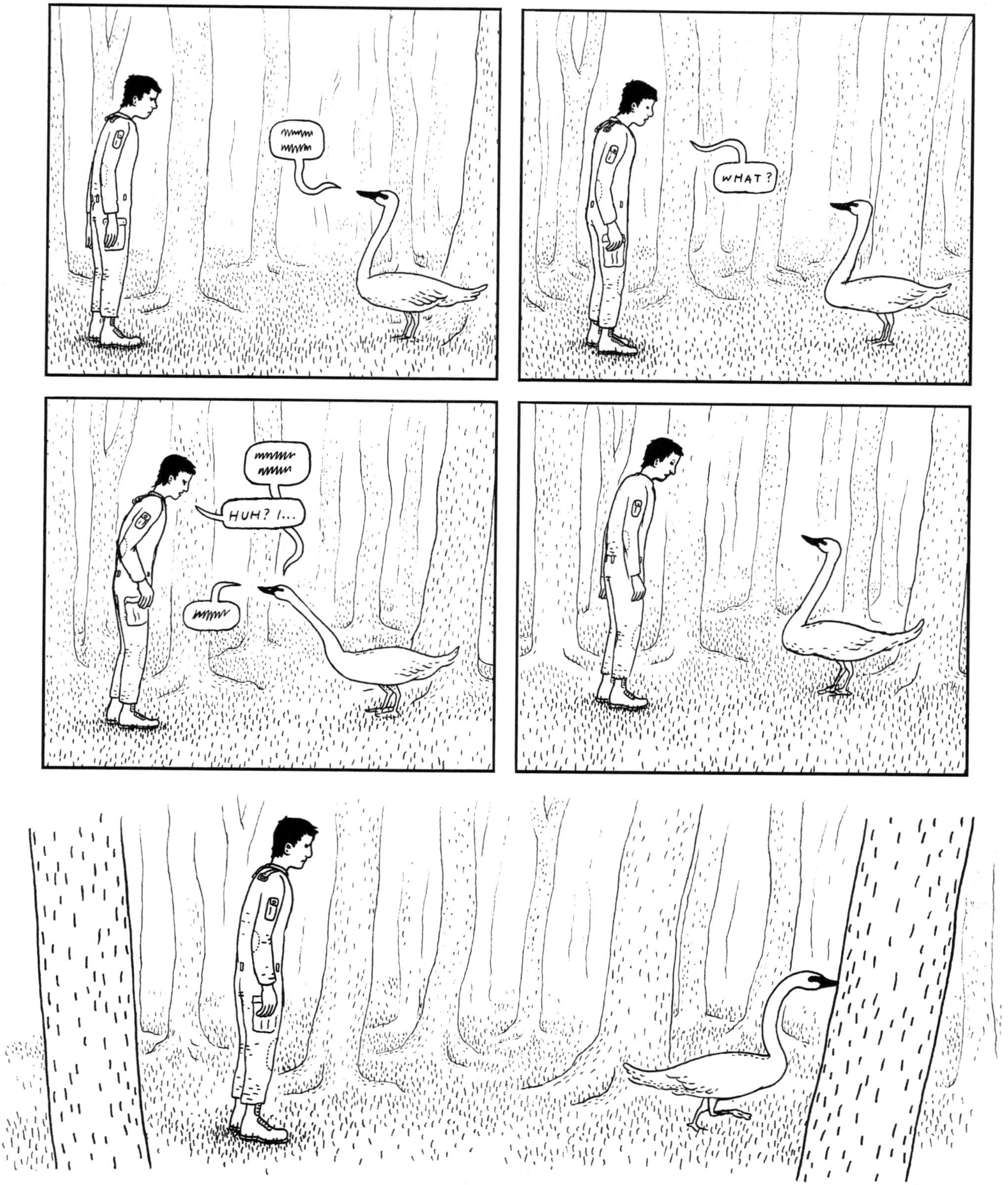
WHAT?
HUH? I...

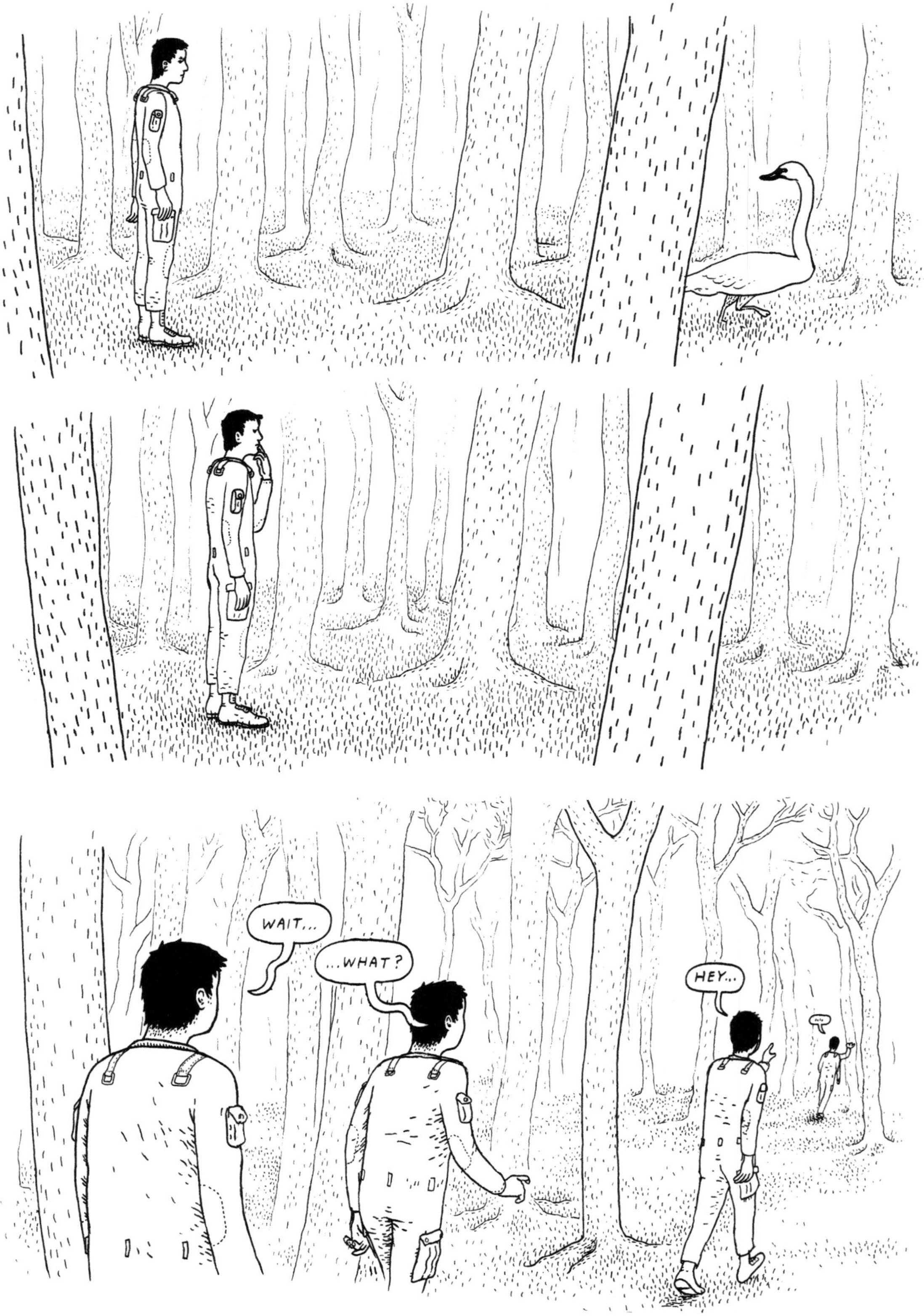
WAIT...
...WHAT?
HEY...

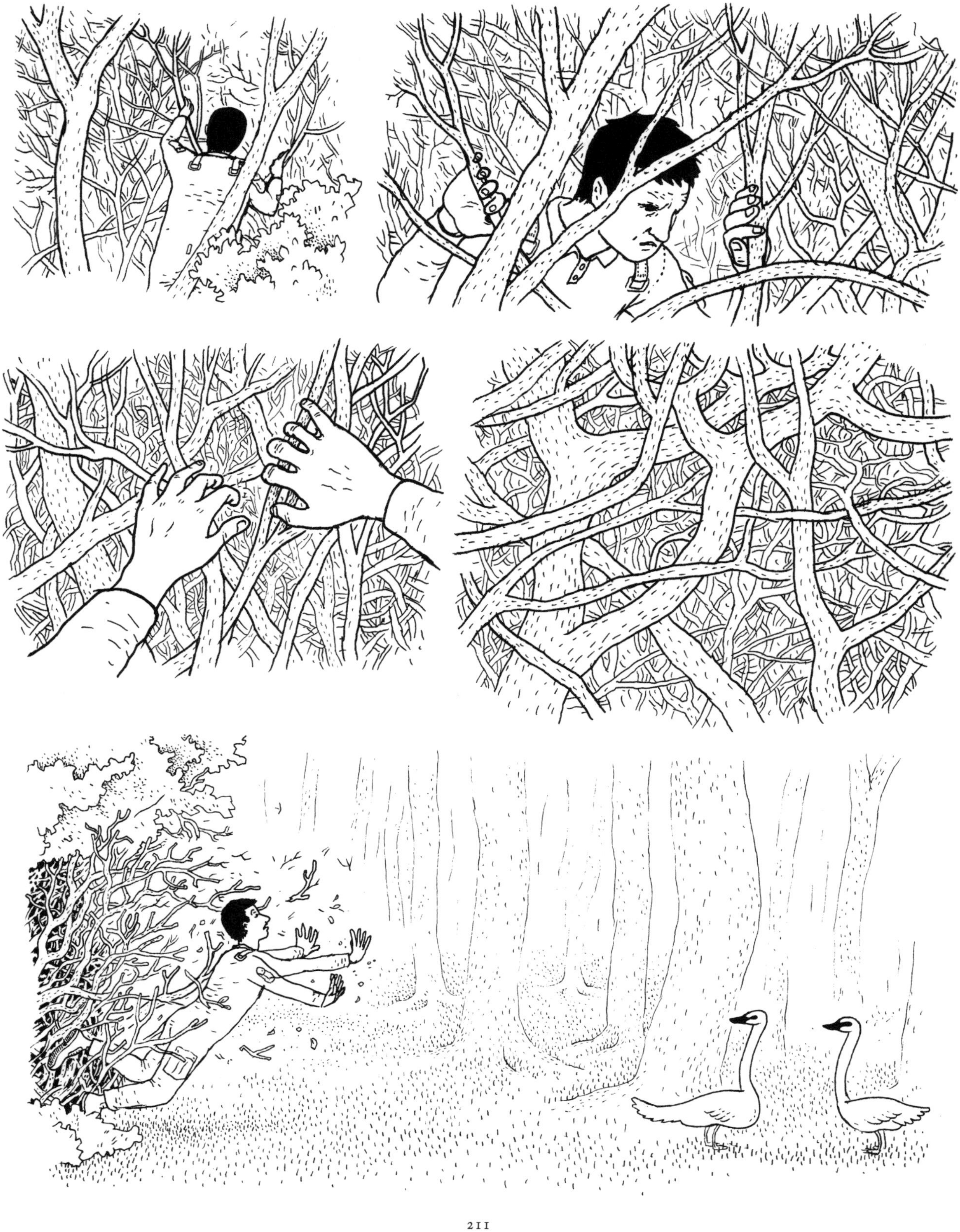

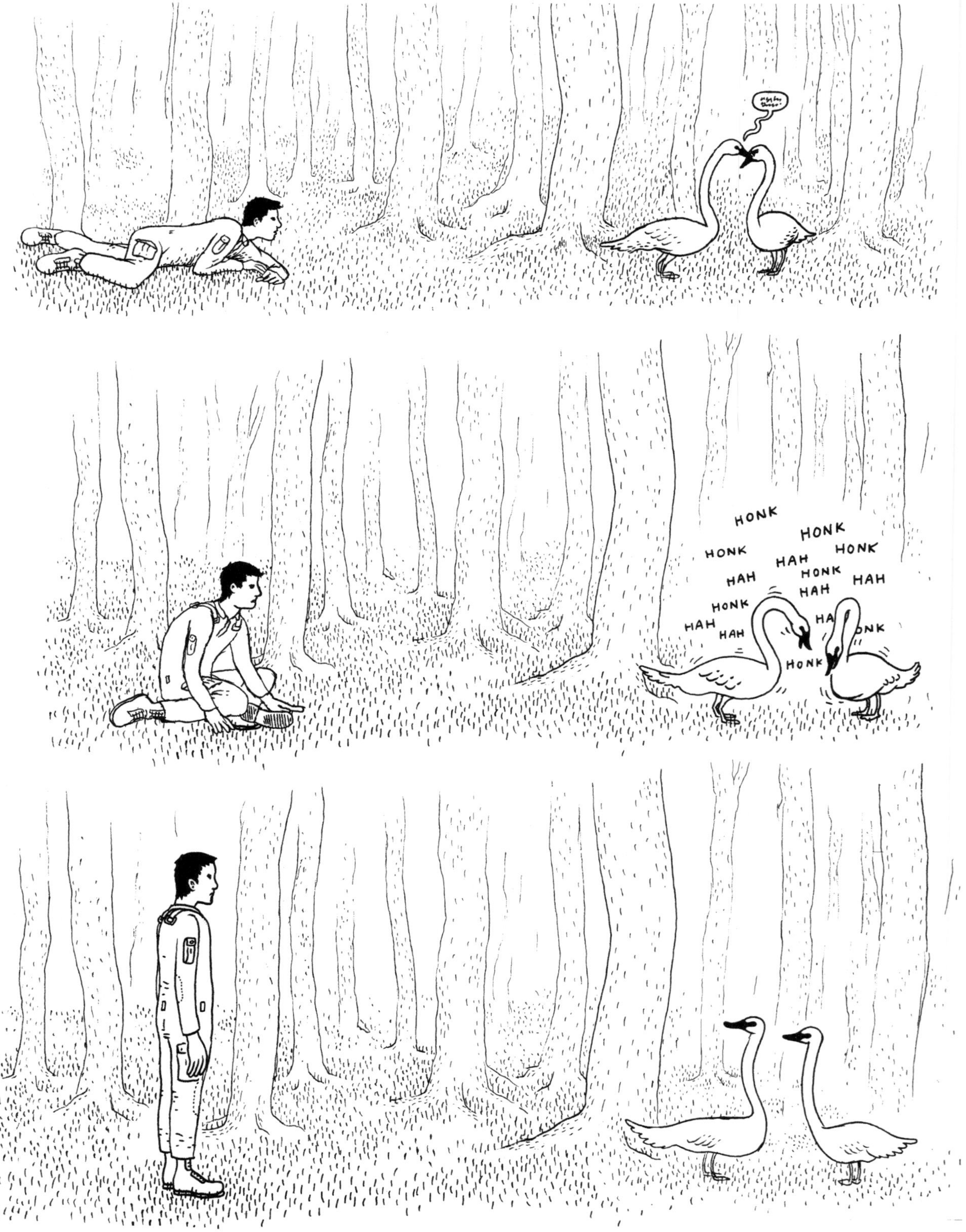
HONK
HONK
HONK
HAH
HONK
HAH
HONK
HAH
HONK
HAH
HAH
HA
ONK
HONK

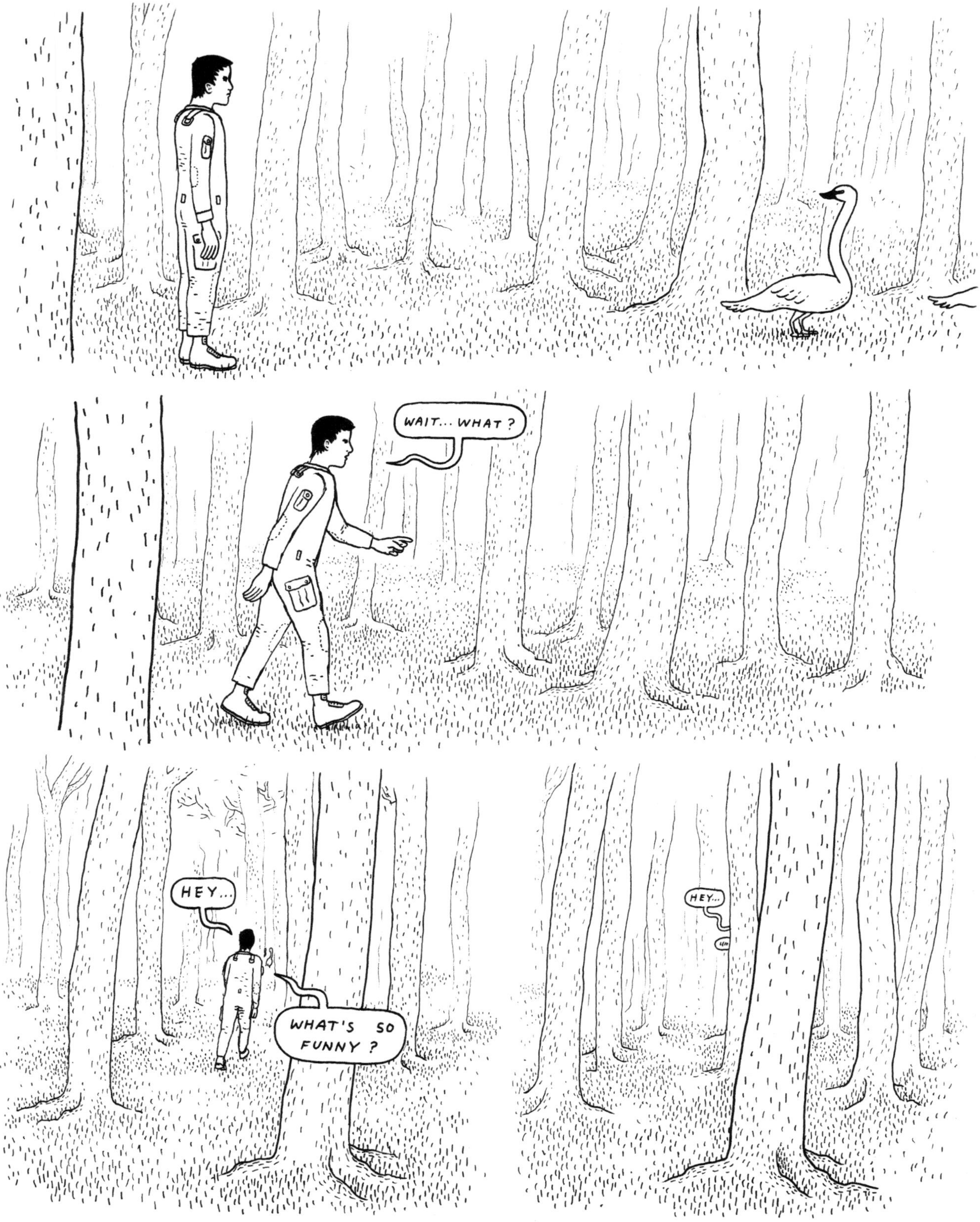
WAIT... WHAT?
HEY...
WHAT'S SO FUNNY?
HEY...

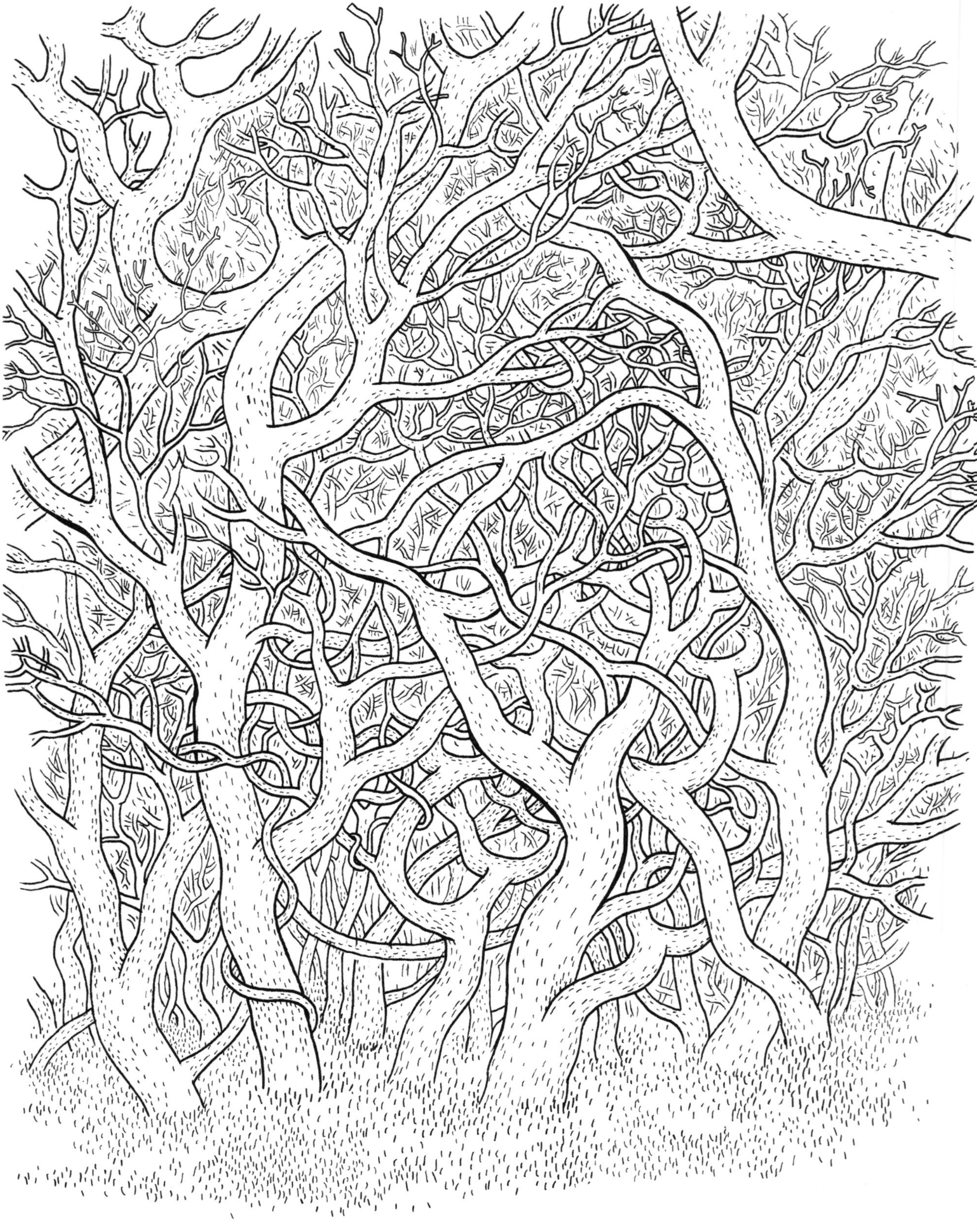

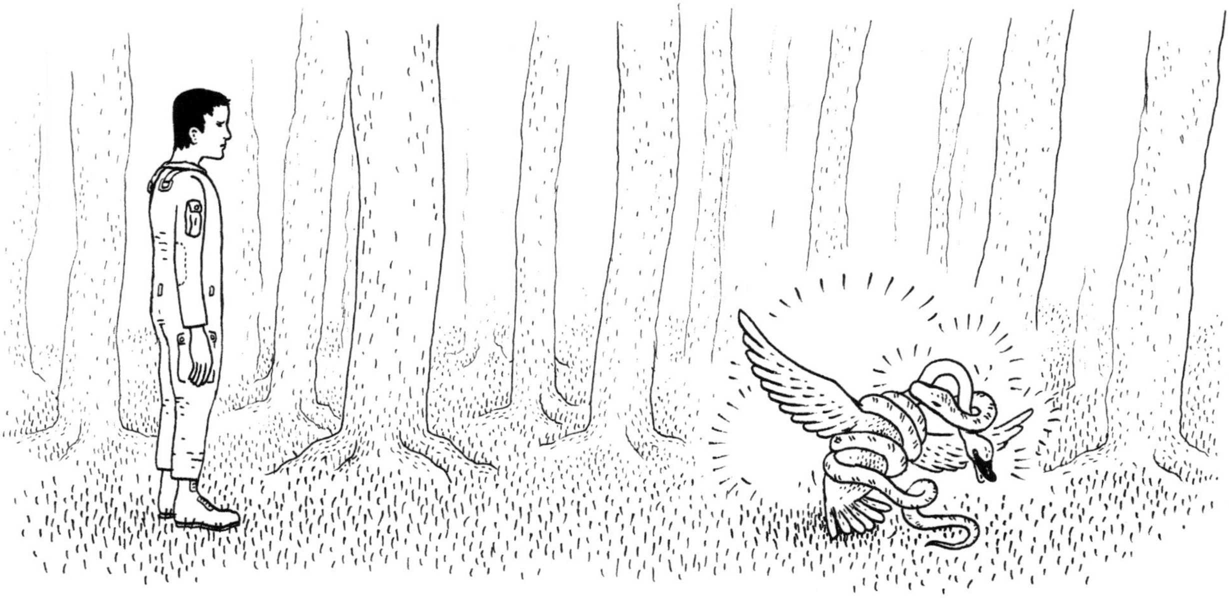

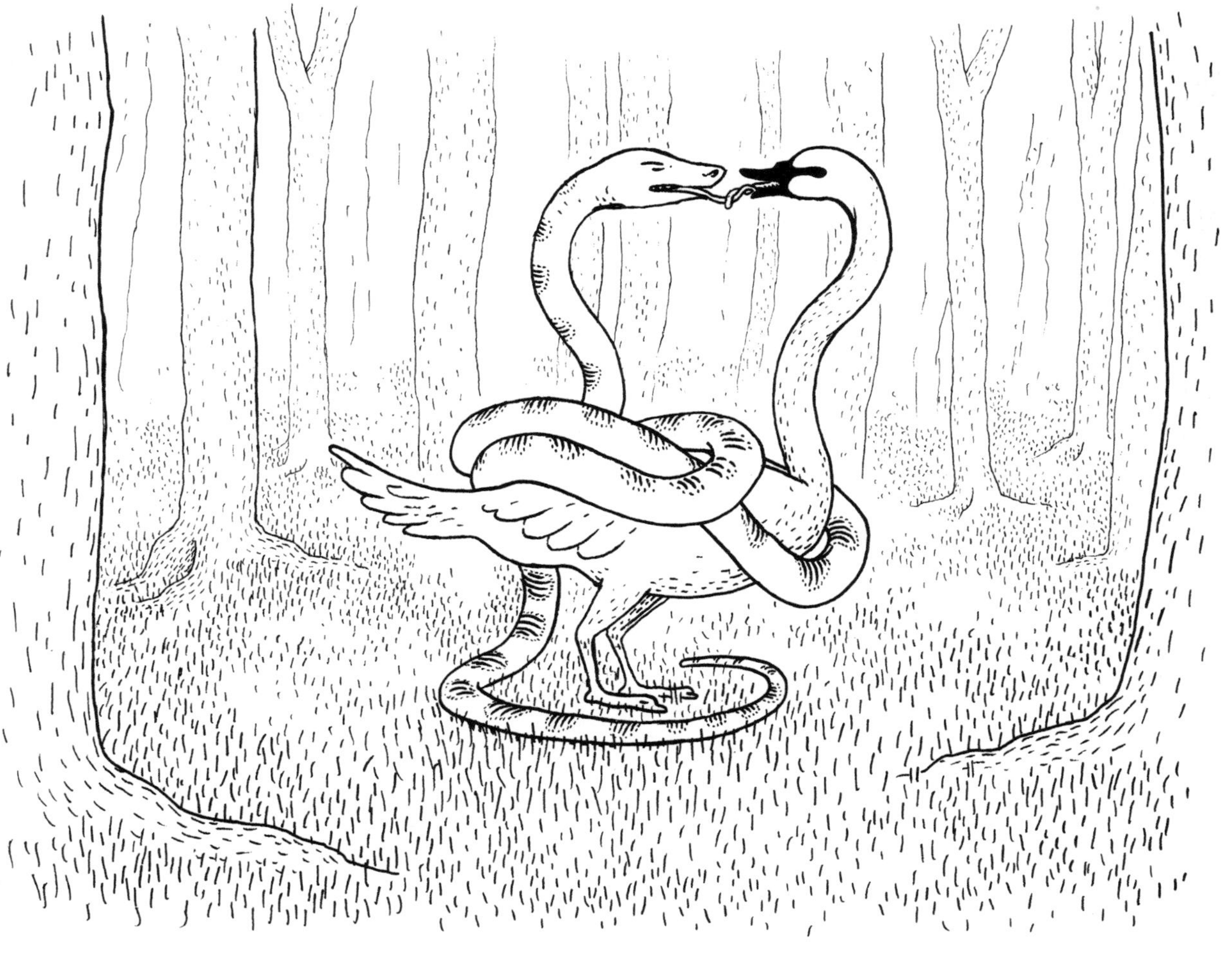

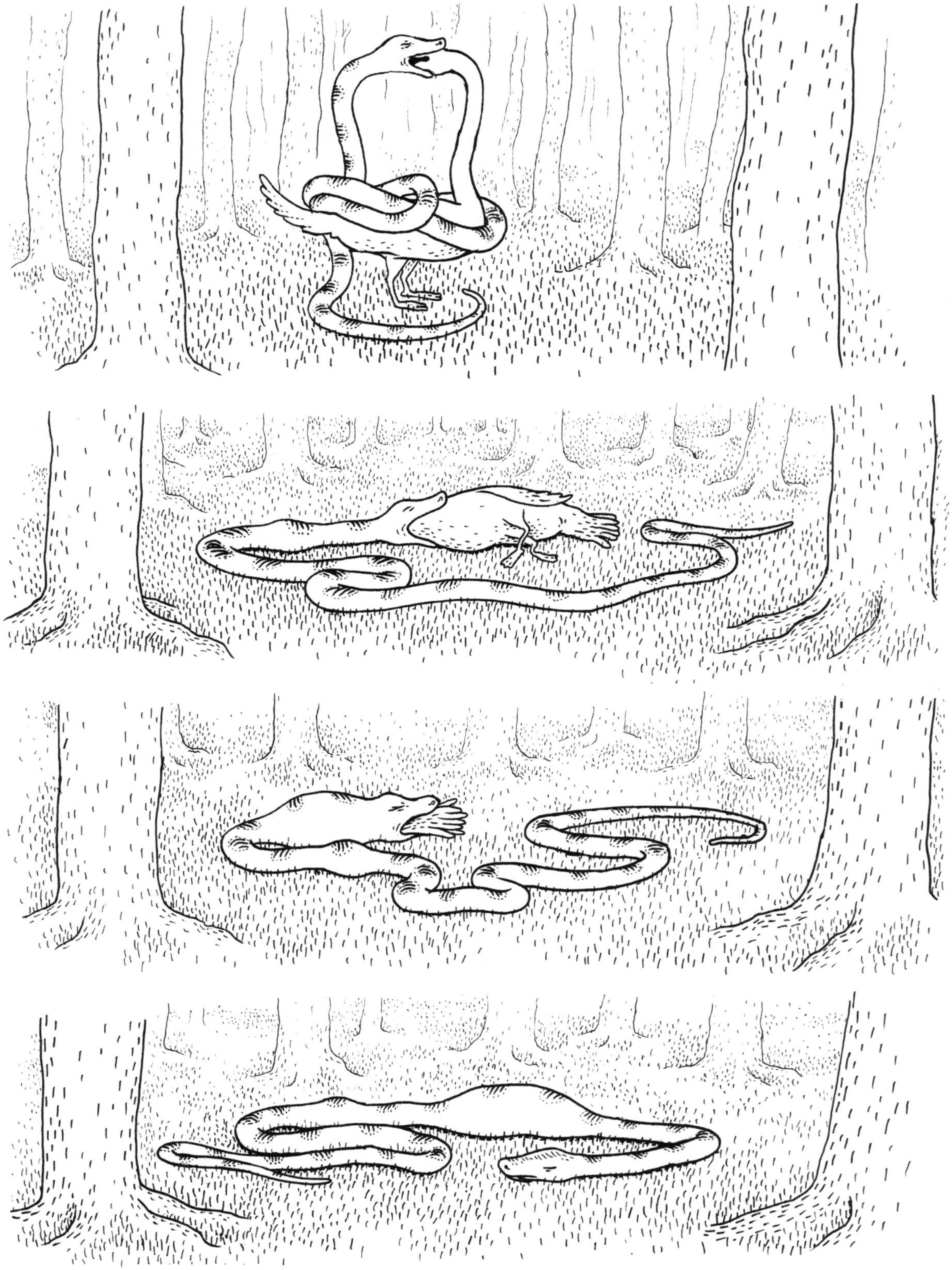

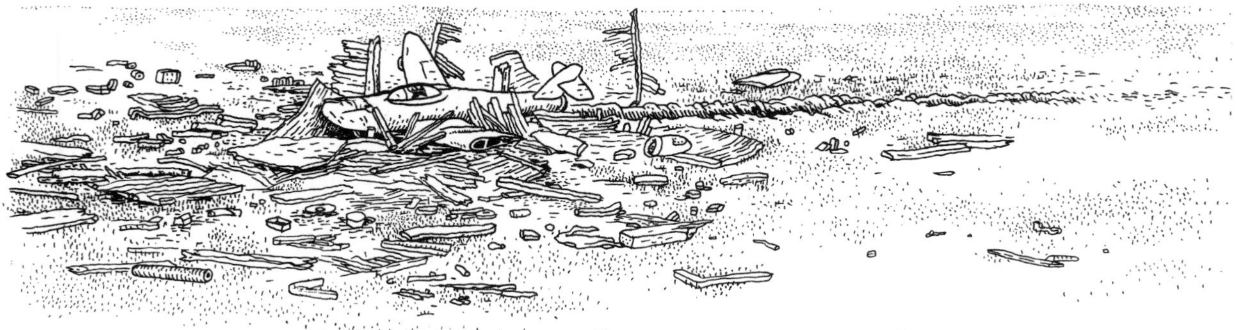

the Theophany According to Zwingly

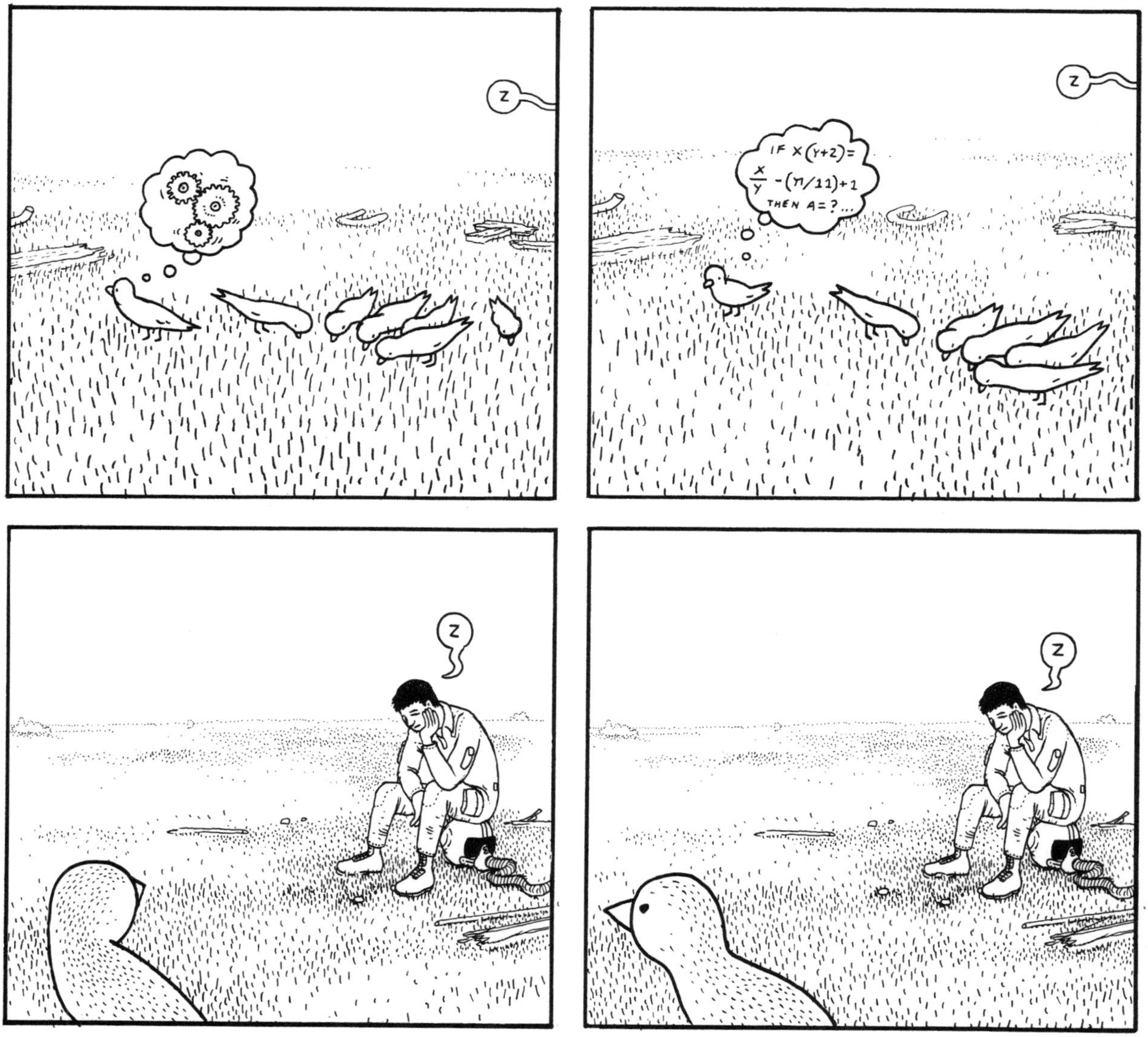
Z
Z
IF X(Y+Z)=
X/Y -(π/11)+1
THEN A=?...
Z
Z

TAP
TAP
TAP
TAP

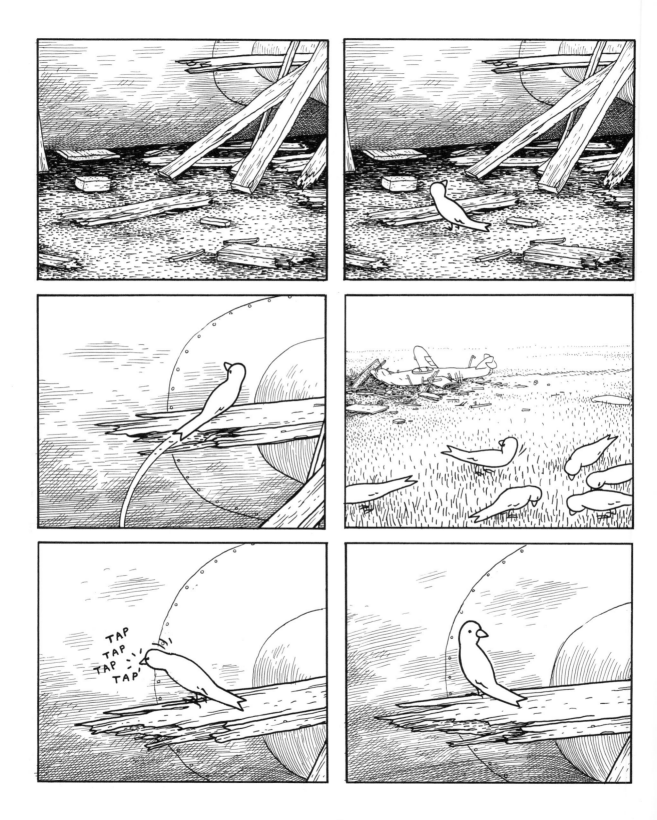

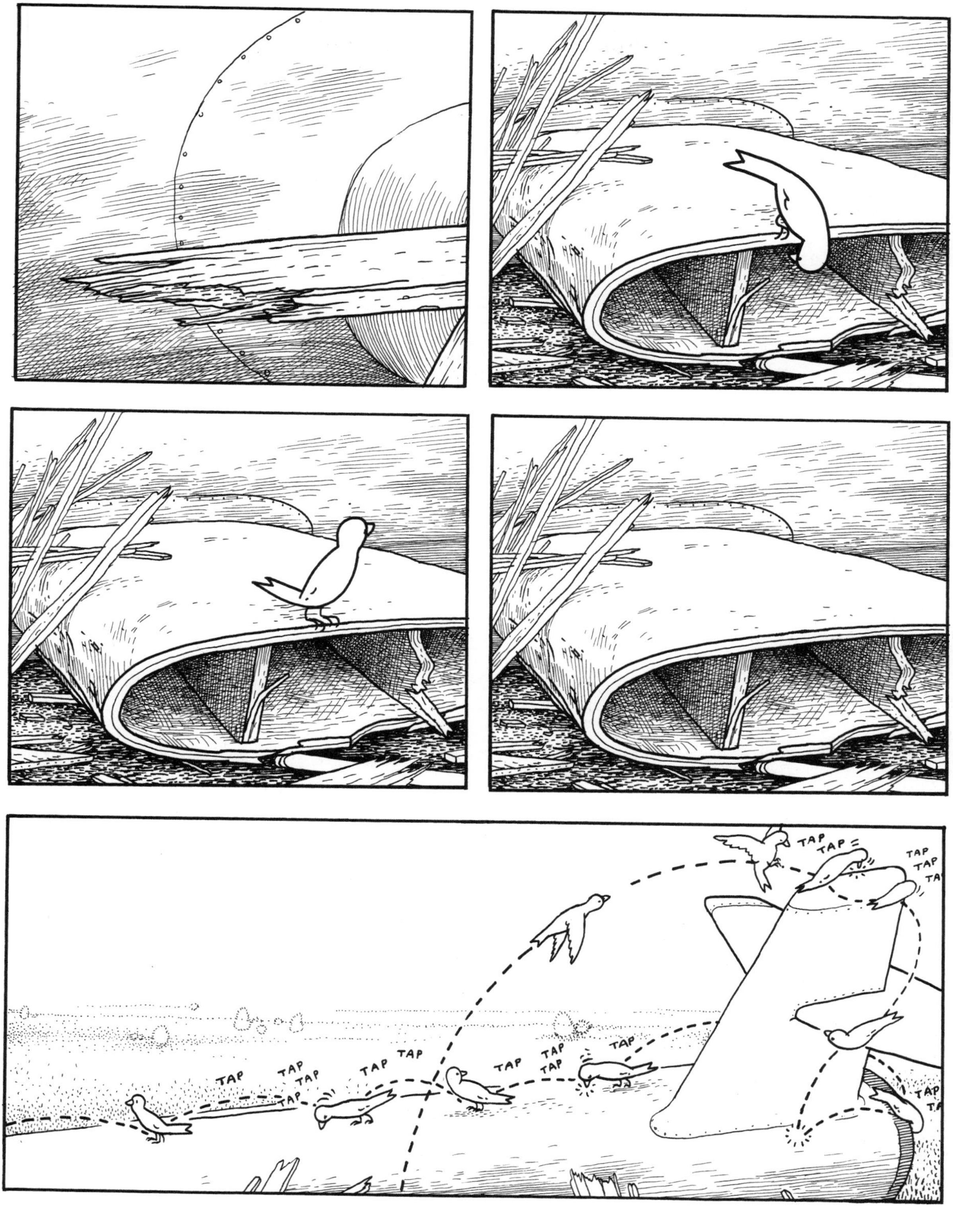
TAP
TAP
TAP
TAP
TAP TAP
TAP
TAP
TAP
TAP
TAP
TAP
TAP
TAP
TAP

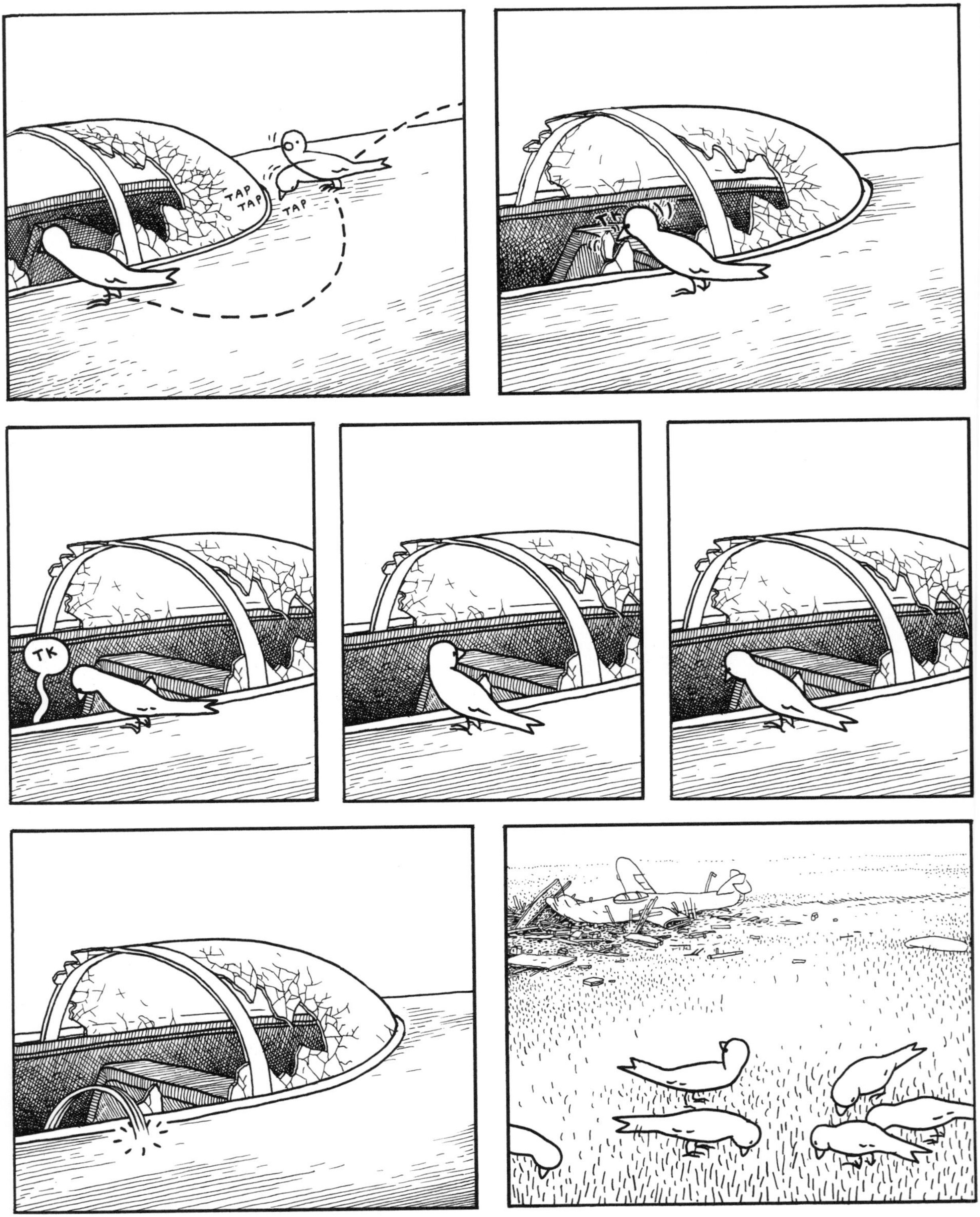
TAP
TAP
TAP
TK

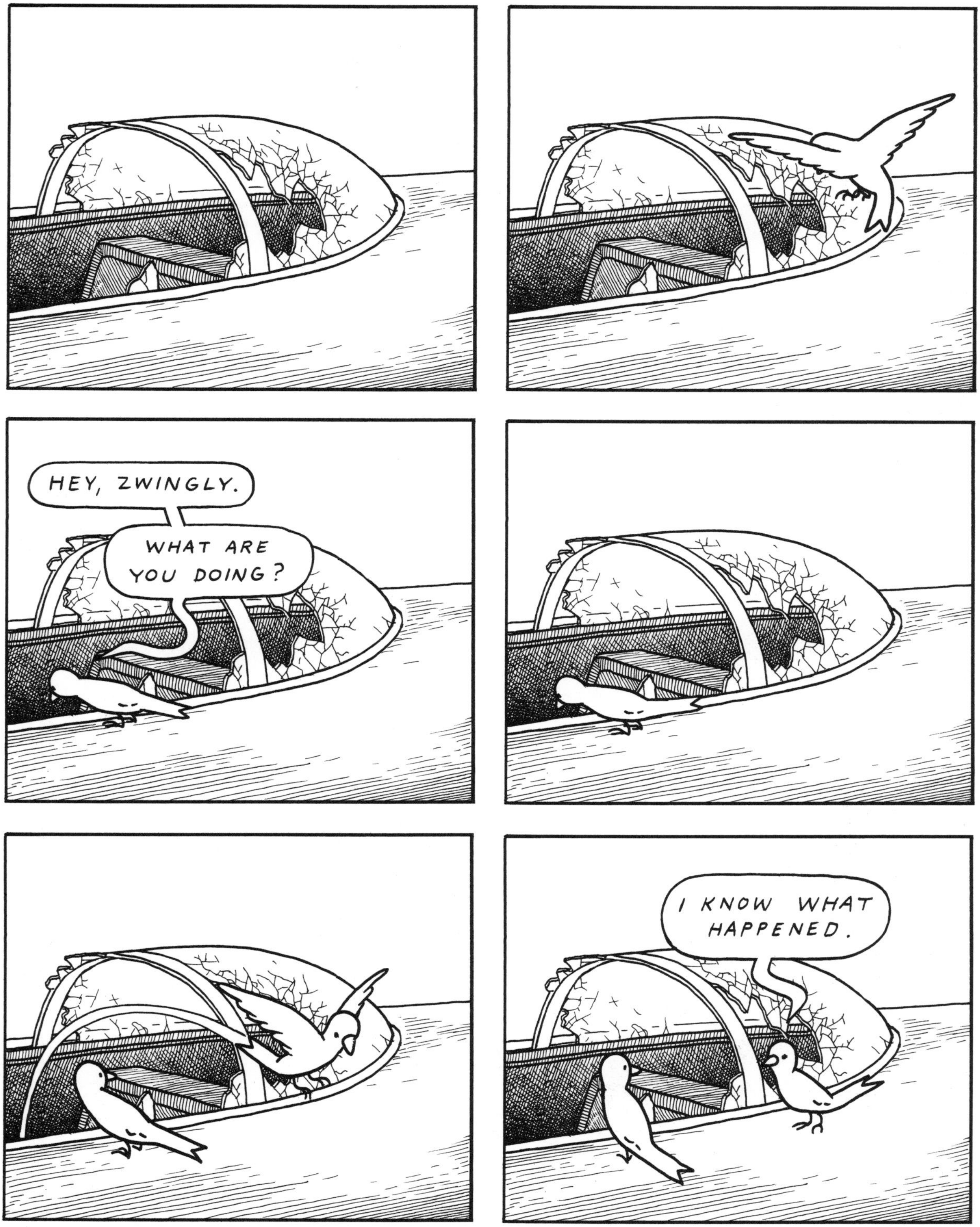
HEY, ZWINGLY.
WHAT ARE YOU DOING?
I KNOW WHAT HAPPENED.

Philo

ZWINGLY'S IDEA, AS I UNDERSTOOD IT, WAS THAT THE HATCHLING HAD SOMEHOW BROKEN FREE OF THE EGG WHILE IT WAS STILL **INSIDE** THE MOTHER. HE SAID IT HAD CRAWLED UP **THROUGH HER BODY** AND COME OUT THROUGH HER HEAD, KILLING HER AND CAUSING THE CRASH.

IF IT WAS TRUE, IT WAS KIND OF HORRIFYING.

BUT HE SEEMED ALMOST TO BE SAYING SHE'D DONE IT ON PURPOSE. FOR US.

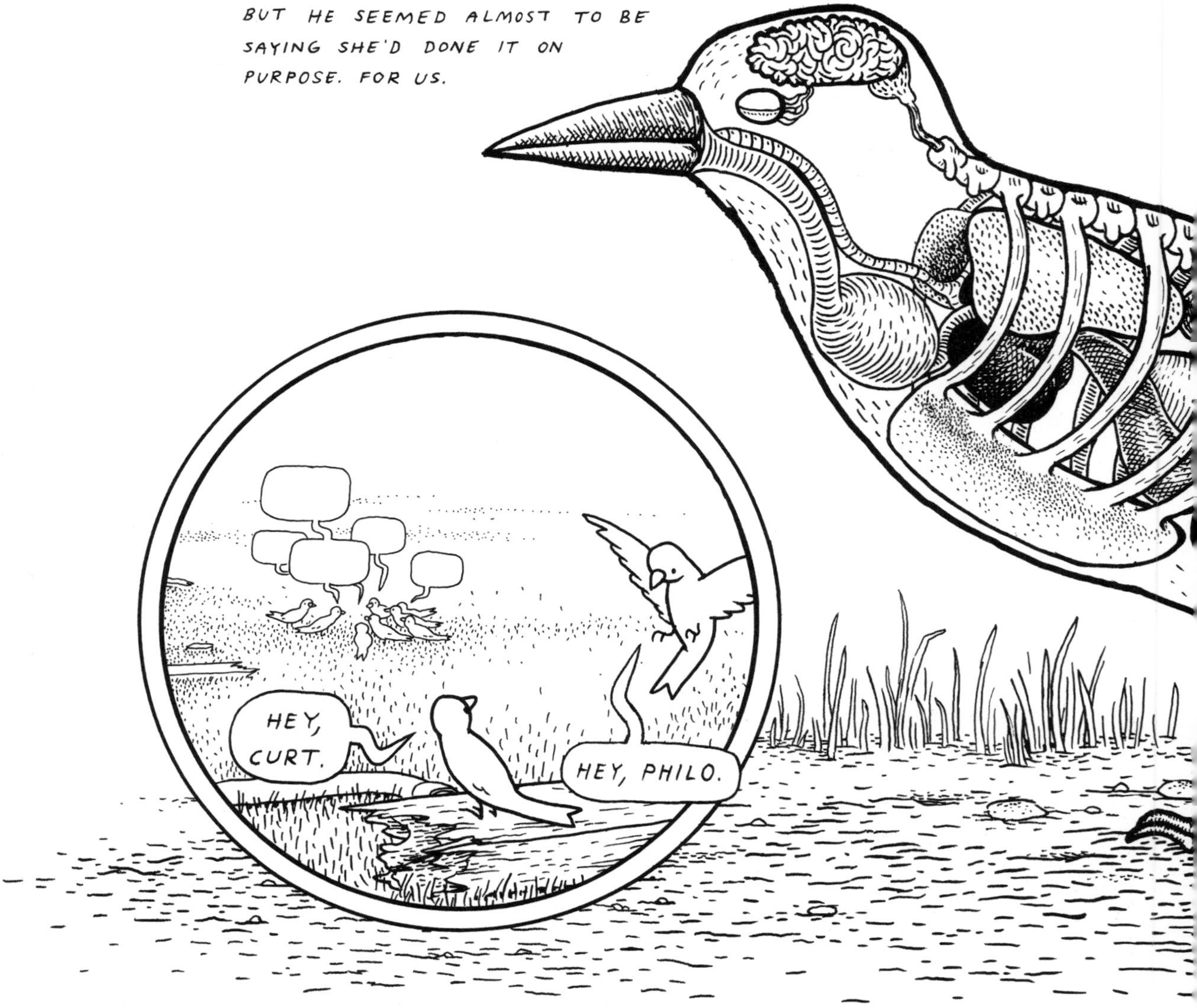
HEY, CURT.
HEY, PHILO.

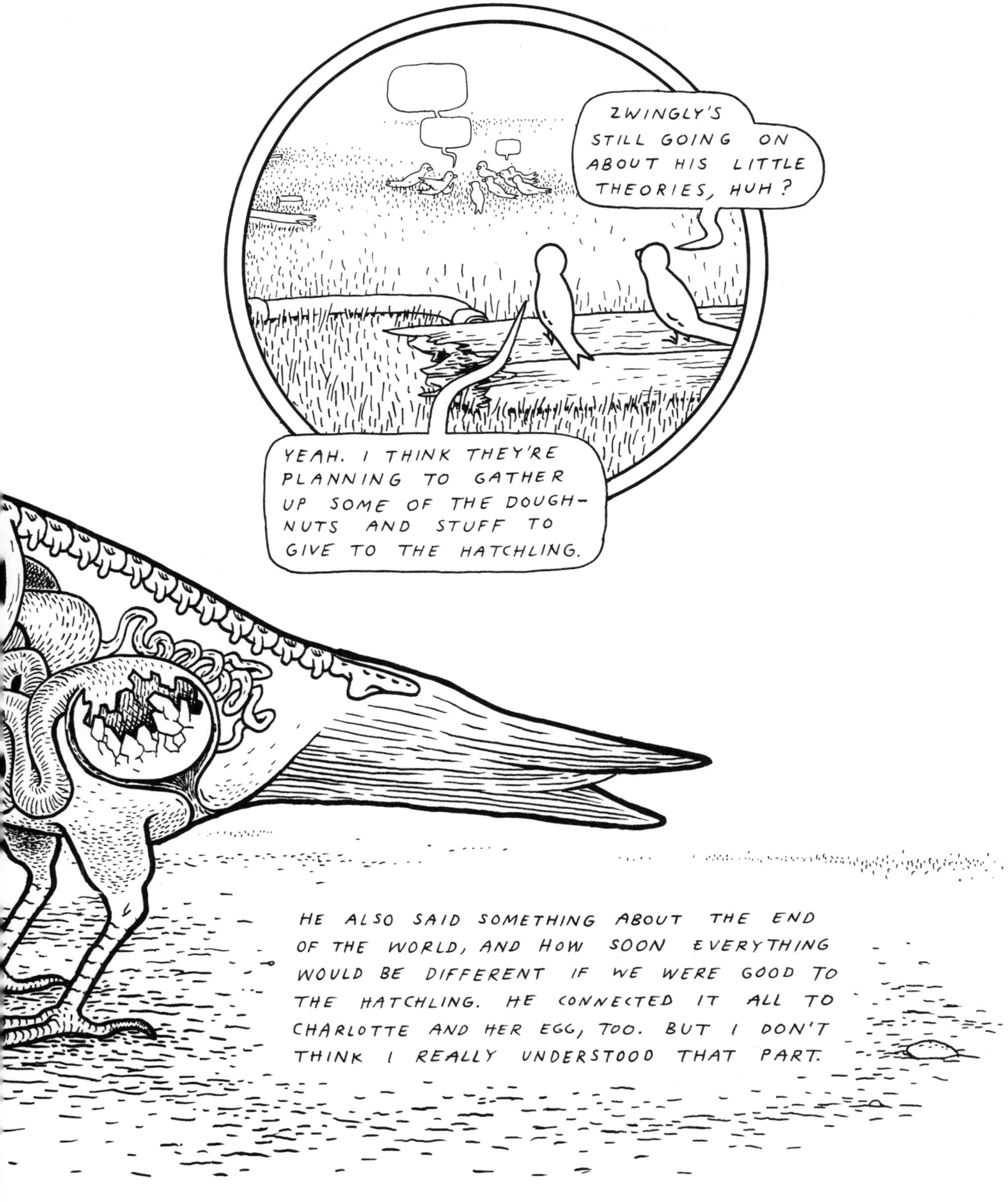
ZWINGLY'S STILL GOING ON ABOUT HIS LITTLE THEORIES, HUH?
YEAH. I THINK THEY'RE PLANNING TO GATHER UP SOME OF THE DOUGH-NUTS AND STUFF TO GIVE TO THE HATCHLING.
HE ALSO SAID SOMETHING ABOUT THE END OF THE WORLD, AND HOW SOON EVERYTHING WOULD BE DIFFERENT IF WE WERE GOOD TO THE HATCHLING. HE CONNECTED IT ALL TO CHARLOTTE AND HER EGG, TOO. BUT I DON'T THINK I REALLY UNDERSTOOD THAT PART.

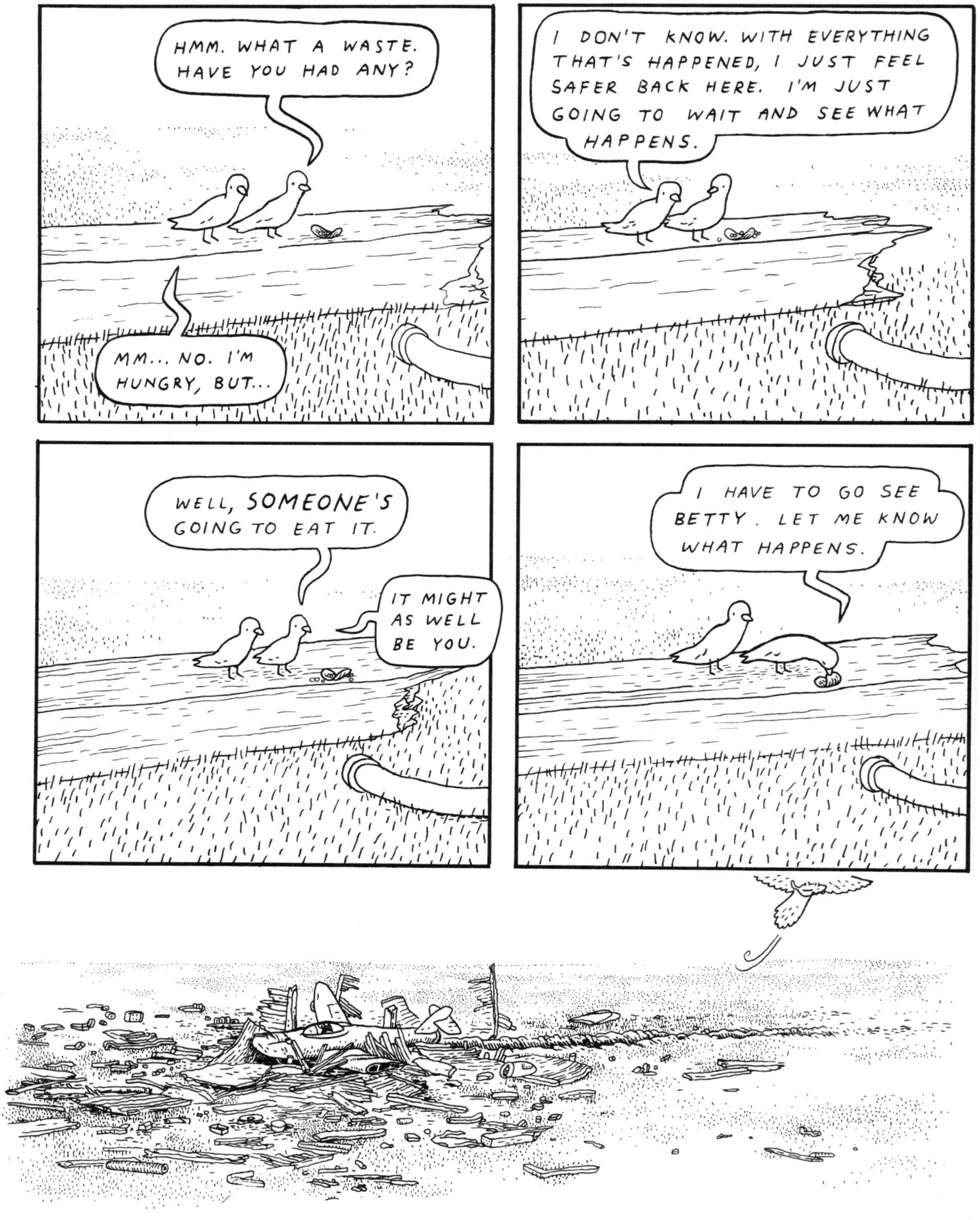
HMM. WHAT A WASTE. HAVE YOU HAD ANY?
MM... NO. I'M HUNGRY, BUT...
I DON'T KNOW. WITH EVERYTHING THAT'S HAPPENED, I JUST FEEL SAFER BACK HERE. I'M JUST GOING TO WAIT AND SEE WHAT HAPPENS.
WELL, SOMEONE'S GOING TO EAT IT.
IT MIGHT AS WELL BE YOU.
I HAVE TO GO SEE BETTY. LET ME KNOW WHAT HAPPENS.

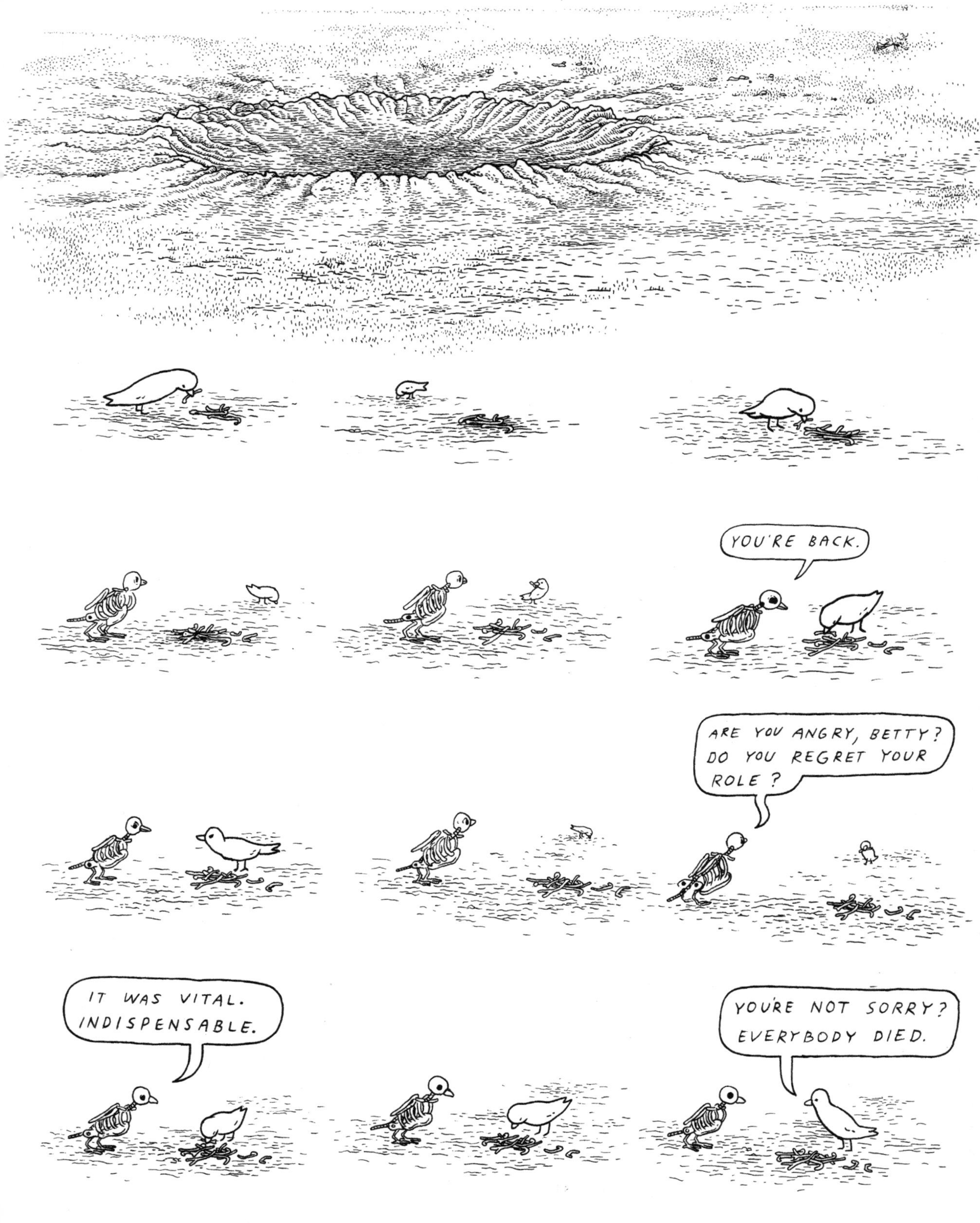
YOU'RE BACK.
ARE YOU ANGRY, BETTY? DO YOU REGRET YOUR ROLE?
IT WAS VITAL. INDISPENSABLE.
YOU'RE NOT SORRY? EVERYBODY DIED.

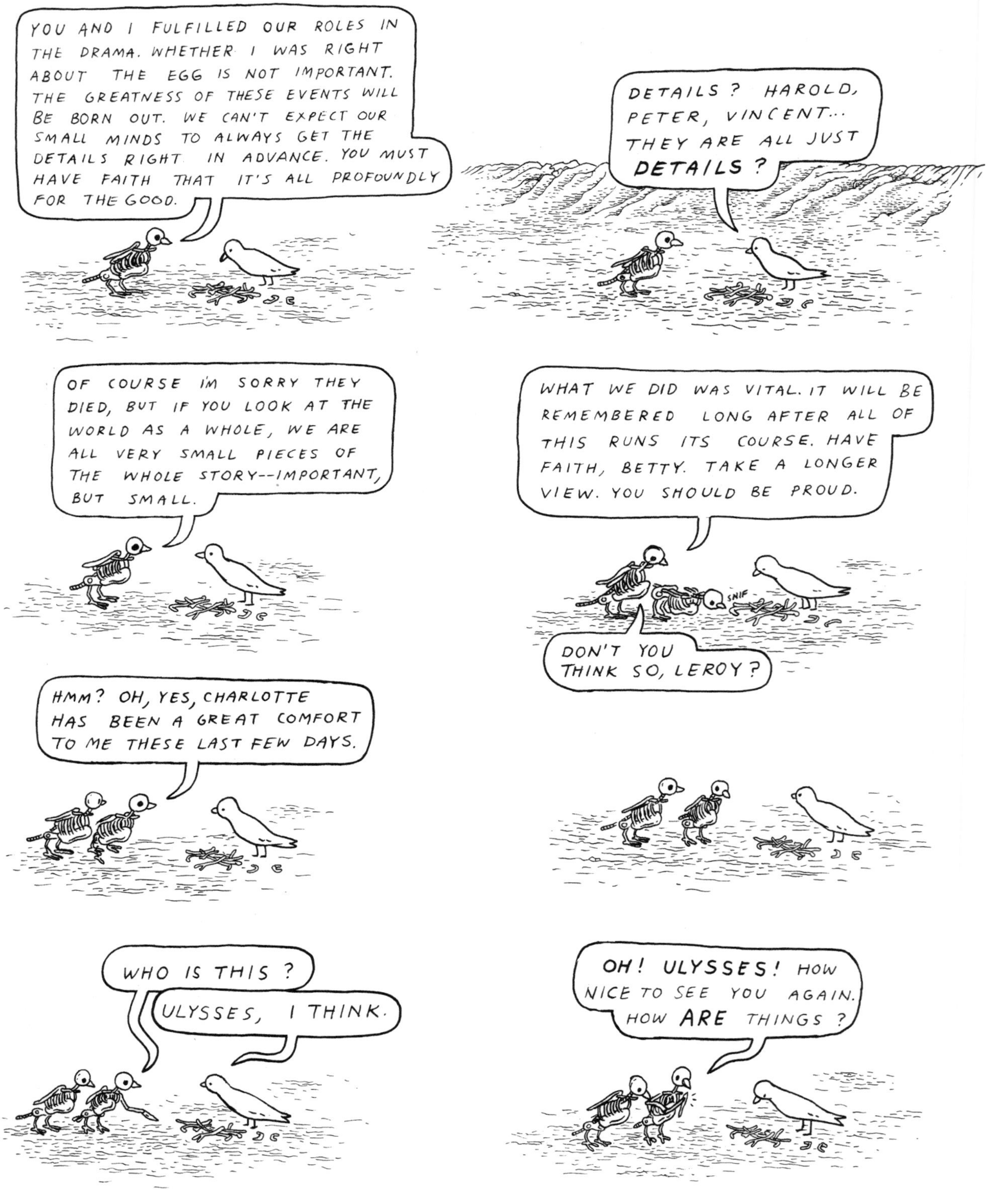
YOU AND I FULFILLED OUR ROLES IN THE DRAMA. WHETHER I WAS RIGHT ABOUT THE EGG IS NOT IMPORTANT. THE GREATNESS OF THESE EVENTS WILL BE BORN OUT. WE CAN'T EXPECT OUR SMALL MINDS TO ALWAYS GET THE DETAILS RIGHT IN ADVANCE. YOU MUST HAVE FAITH THAT IT'S ALL PROFOUNDLY FOR THE GOOD.
DETAILS? HAROLD, PETER, VINCENT... THEY ARE ALL JUST DETAILS?
OF COURSE I'M SORRY THEY DIED, BUT IF YOU LOOK AT THE WORLD AS A WHOLE, WE ARE ALL VERY SMALL PIECES OF THE WHOLE STORY--IMPORTANT, BUT SMALL.
WHAT WE DID WAS VITAL. IT WILL BE REMEMBERED LONG AFTER ALL OF THIS RUNS ITS COURSE. HAVE FAITH, BETTY. TAKE A LONGER VIEW. YOU SHOULD BE PROUD.
SNIF
DON'T YOU THINK SO, LEROY?
HMM? OH, YES, CHARLOTTE HAS BEEN A GREAT COMFORT TO ME THESE LAST FEW DAYS.
WHO IS THIS?
ULYSSES, I THINK.
OH! ULYSSES! HOW NICE TO SEE YOU AGAIN. HOW ARE THINGS?

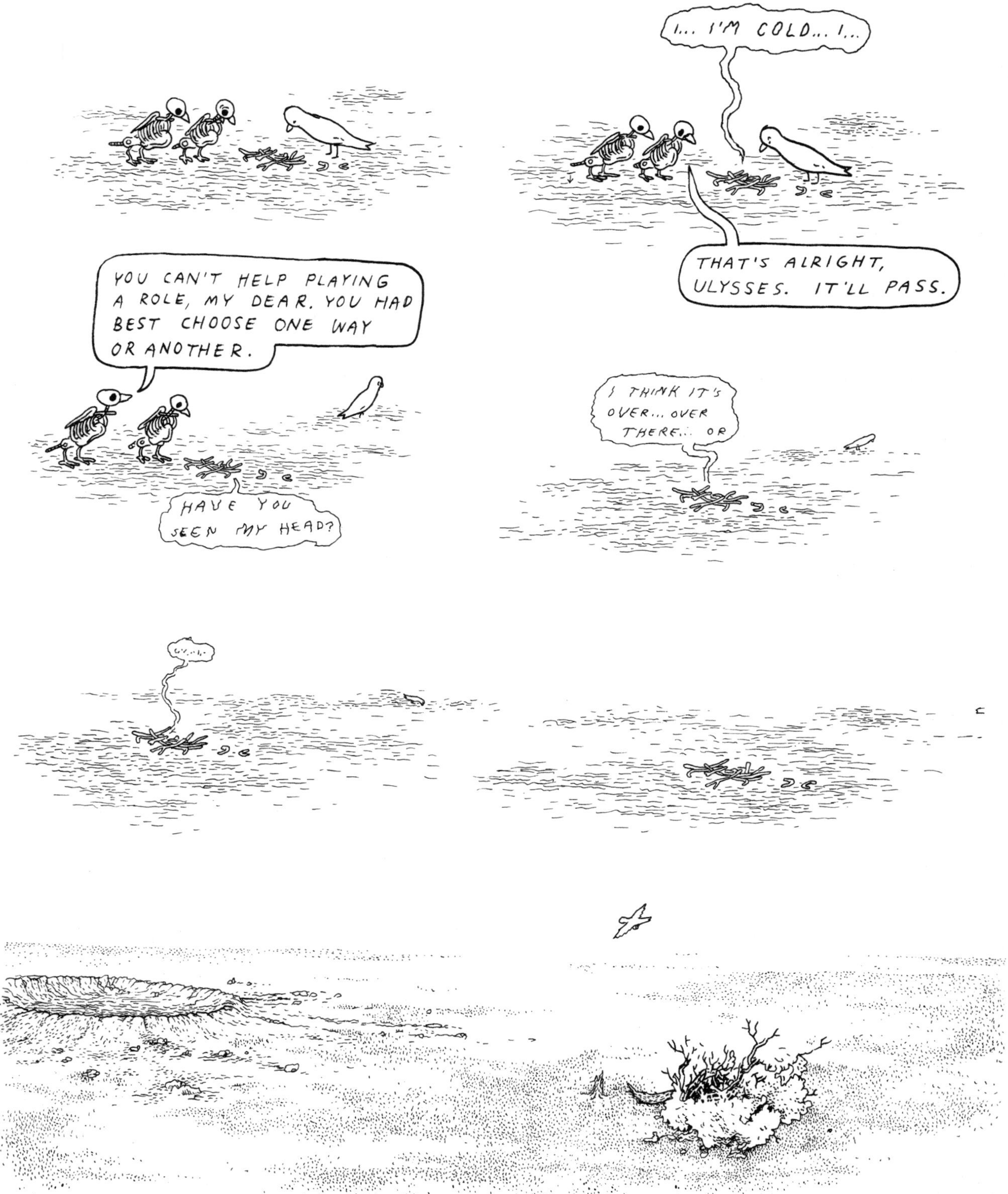
I... I'M COLD... I...
THAT'S ALRIGHT, ULYSSES. IT'LL PASS.
YOU CAN'T HELP PLAYING A ROLE, MY DEAR. YOU HAD BEST CHOOSE ONE WAY OR ANOTHER.
HAVE YOU SEEN MY HEAD?
I THINK IT'S OVER... OVER THERE... OR

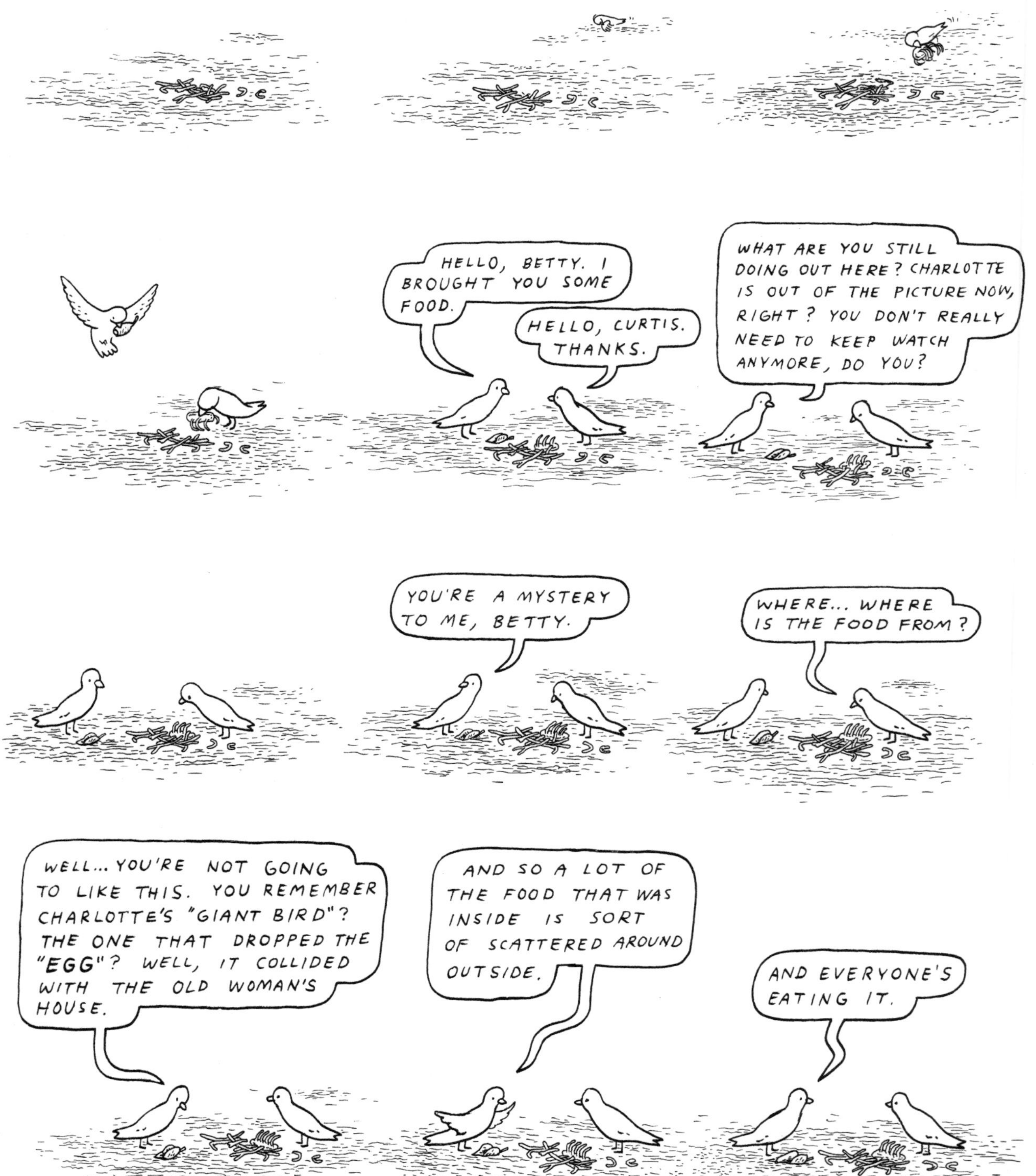
HELLO, BETTY. I BROUGHT YOU SOME FOOD.
HELLO, CURTIS. THANKS.
WHAT ARE YOU STILL DOING OUT HERE? CHARLOTTE IS OUT OF THE PICTURE NOW, RIGHT? YOU DON'T REALLY NEED TO KEEP WATCH ANYMORE, DO YOU?
YOU'RE A MYSTERY TO ME, BETTY.
WHERE... WHERE IS THE FOOD FROM?
WELL... YOU'RE NOT GOING TO LIKE THIS. YOU REMEMBER CHARLOTTE'S "GIANT BIRD"? THE ONE THAT DROPPED THE "EGG"? WELL, IT COLLIDED WITH THE OLD WOMAN'S HOUSE.
AND SO A LOT OF THE FOOD THAT WAS INSIDE IS SORT OF SCATTERED AROUND OUTSIDE.
AND EVERYONE'S EATING IT.

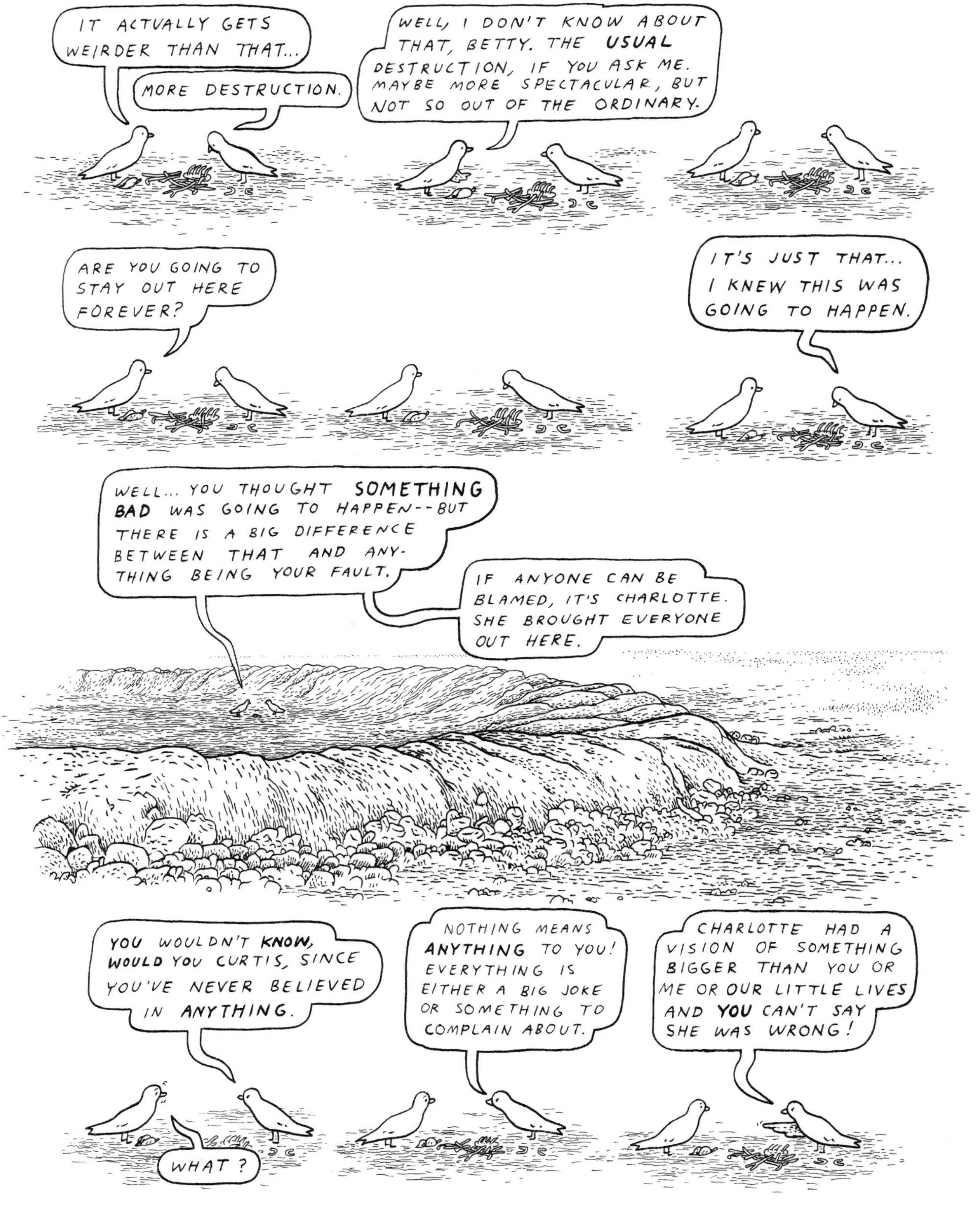
IT ACTUALLY GETS WEIRDER THAN THAT...
MORE DESTRUCTION.
WELL, I DON'T KNOW ABOUT THAT, BETTY. THE USUAL DESTRUCTION, IF YOU ASK ME. MAYBE MORE SPECTACULAR, BUT NOT SO OUT OF THE ORDINARY.
ARE YOU GOING TO STAY OUT HERE FOREVER?
IT'S JUST THAT... I KNEW THIS WAS GOING TO HAPPEN.
WELL... YOU THOUGHT SOMETHING BAD WAS GOING TO HAPPEN--BUT THERE IS A BIG DIFFERENCE BETWEEN THAT AND ANY-THING BEING YOUR FAULT.
IF ANYONE CAN BE BLAMED, IT'S CHARLOTTE. SHE BROUGHT EVERYONE OUT HERE.
YOU WOULDN'T KNOW, WOULD YOU CURTIS, SINCE YOU'VE NEVER BELIEVED IN ANYTHING.
WHAT?
NOTHING MEANS ANYTHING TO YOU! EVERYTHING IS EITHER A BIG JOKE OR SOMETHING TO COMPLAIN ABOUT.
CHARLOTTE HAD A VISION OF SOMETHING BIGGER THAN YOU OR ME OR OUR LITTLE LIVES AND YOU CAN'T SAY SHE WAS WRONG!

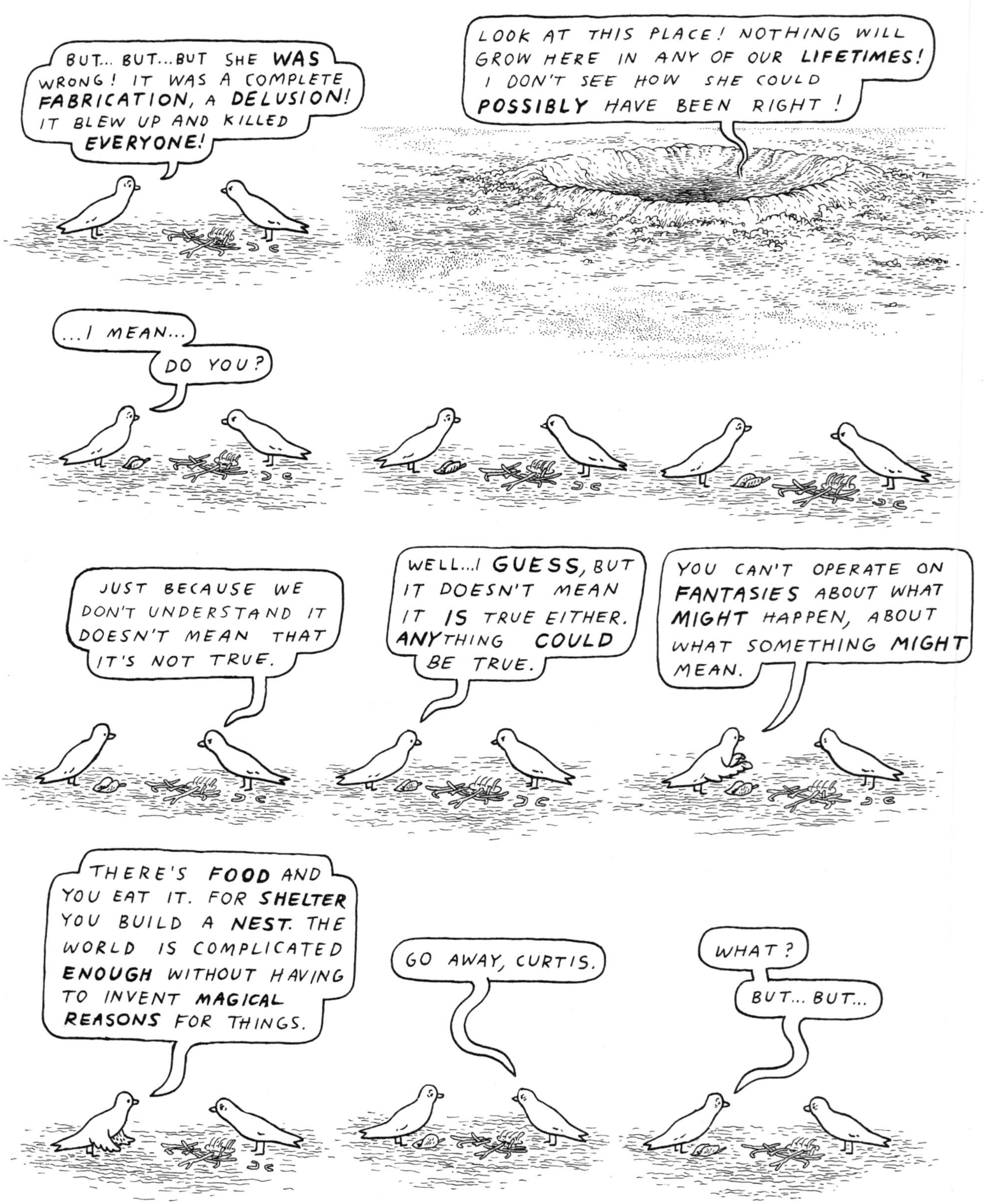
BUT... BUT... BUT SHE WAS WRONG! IT WAS A COMPLETE FABRICATION, A DELUSION! IT BLEW UP AND KILLED EVERYONE!
LOOK AT THIS PLACE! NOTHING WILL GROW HERE IN ANY OF OUR LIFETIMES! I DON'T SEE HOW SHE COULD POSSIBLY HAVE BEEN RIGHT!
...I MEAN...
DO YOU?
JUST BECAUSE WE DON'T UNDERSTAND IT DOESN'T MEAN THAT IT'S NOT TRUE.
WELL...I GUESS, BUT IT DOESN'T MEAN IT IS TRUE EITHER. ANYTHING COULD BE TRUE.
YOU CAN'T OPERATE ON FANTASIES ABOUT WHAT MIGHT HAPPEN, ABOUT WHAT SOMETHING MIGHT MEAN.
THERE'S FOOD AND YOU EAT IT. FOR SHELTER YOU BUILD A NEST. THE WORLD IS COMPLICATED ENOUGH WITHOUT HAVING TO INVENT MAGICAL REASONS FOR THINGS.
GO AWAY, CURTIS.
WHAT?
BUT... BUT...

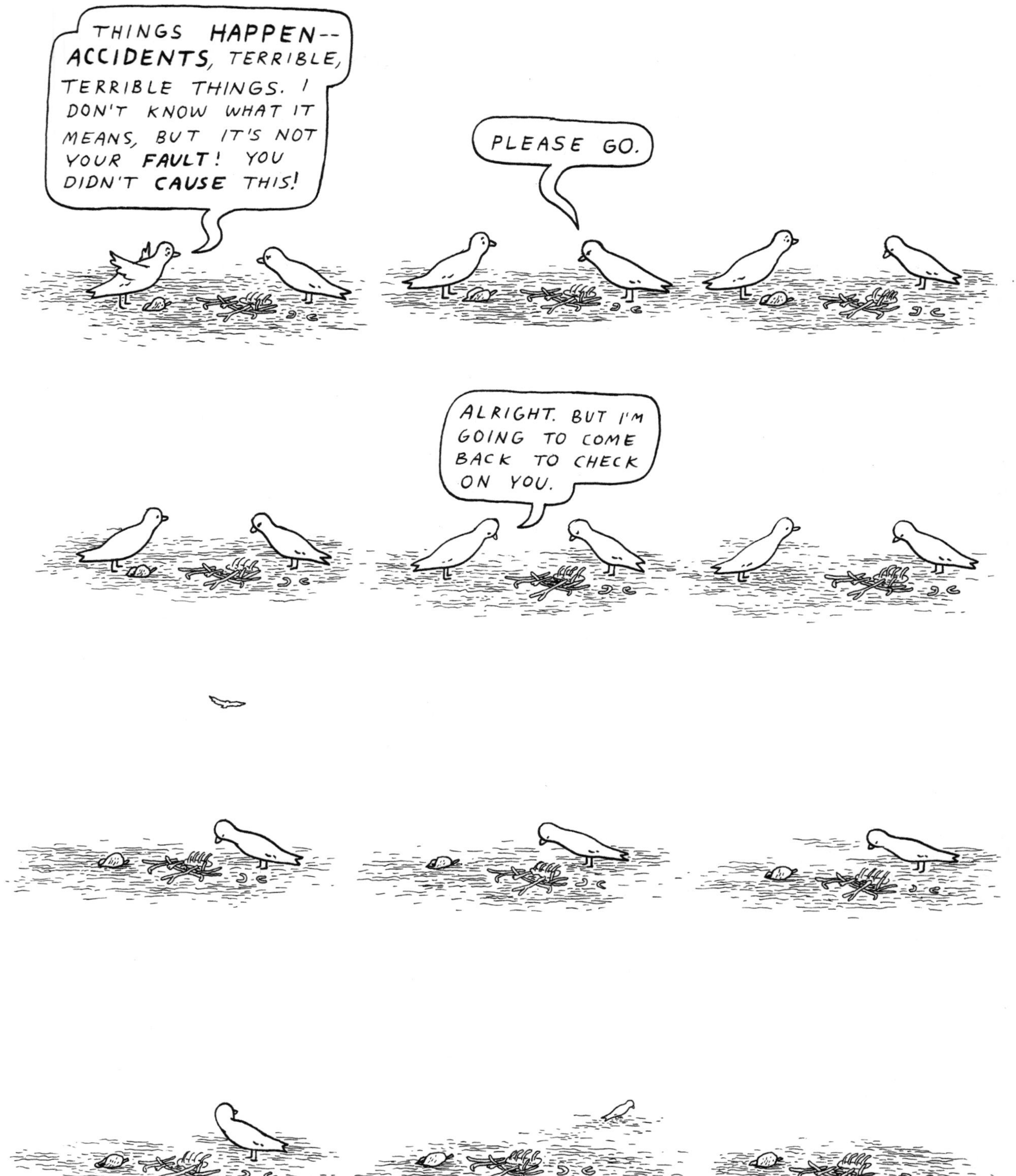
THINGS **HAPPEN**-- **ACCIDENTS**, TERRIBLE, TERRIBLE THINGS. I DON'T KNOW WHAT IT MEANS, BUT IT'S NOT YOUR **FAULT**! YOU DIDN'T **CAUSE** THIS!
PLEASE GO.
ALRIGHT. BUT I'M GOING TO COME BACK TO CHECK ON YOU.

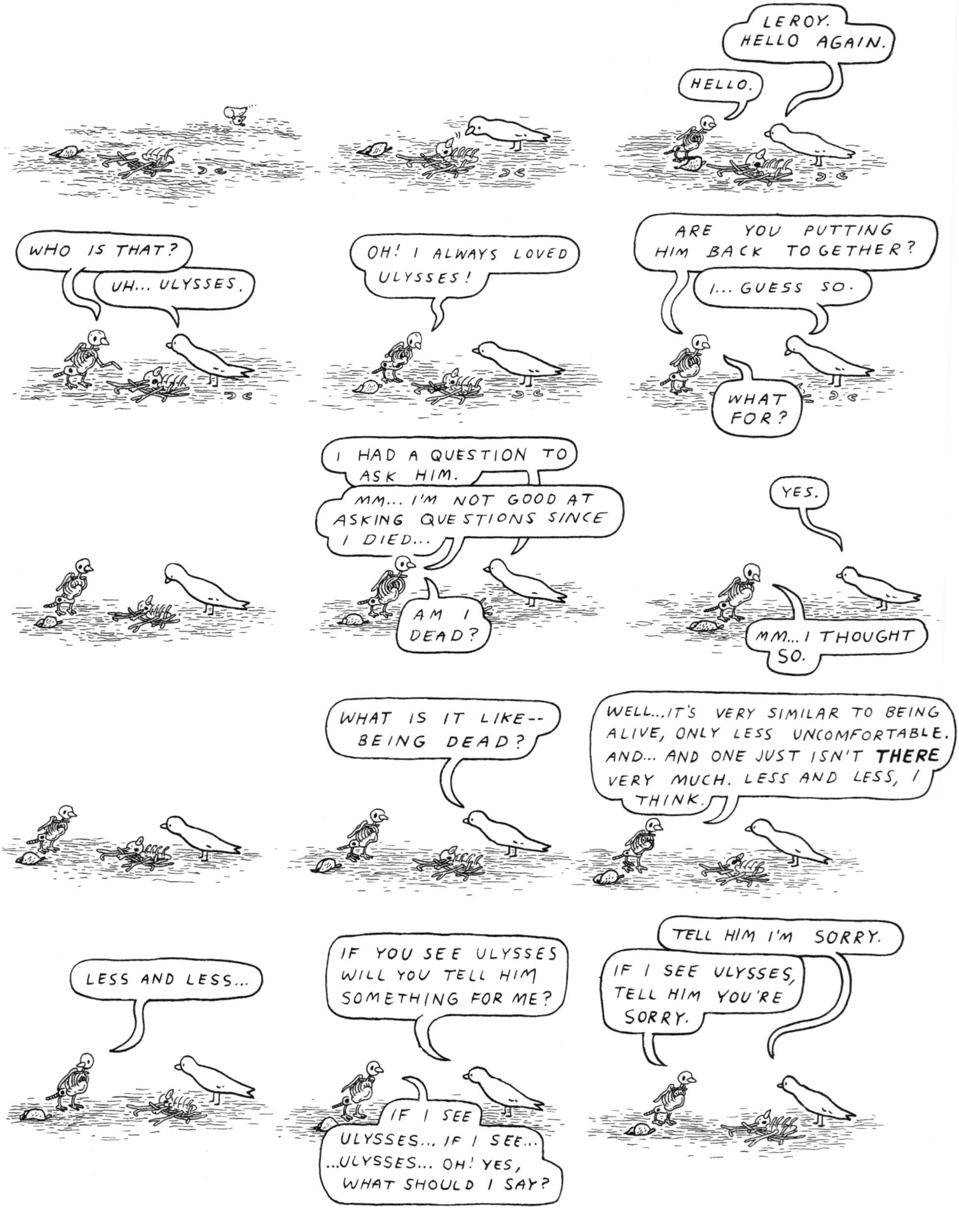
LEROY. HELLO AGAIN.
HELLO.
WHO IS THAT?
UH... ULYSSES.
OH! I ALWAYS LOVED ULYSSES!
ARE YOU PUTTING HIM BACK TOGETHER?
I... GUESS SO.
WHAT FOR?
I HAD A QUESTION TO ASK HIM.
MM... I'M NOT GOOD AT ASKING QUESTIONS SINCE I DIED...
AM I DEAD?
YES.
MM... I THOUGHT SO.
WHAT IS IT LIKE-- BEING DEAD?
WELL...IT'S VERY SIMILAR TO BEING ALIVE, ONLY LESS UNCOMFORTABLE. AND... AND ONE JUST ISN'T THERE VERY MUCH. LESS AND LESS, I THINK.
LESS AND LESS...
IF YOU SEE ULYSSES WILL YOU TELL HIM SOMETHING FOR ME?
IF I SEE ULYSSES... IF I SEE... ...ULYSSES... OH! YES, WHAT SHOULD I SAY?
TELL HIM I'M SORRY.
IF I SEE ULYSSES, TELL HIM YOU'RE SORRY.

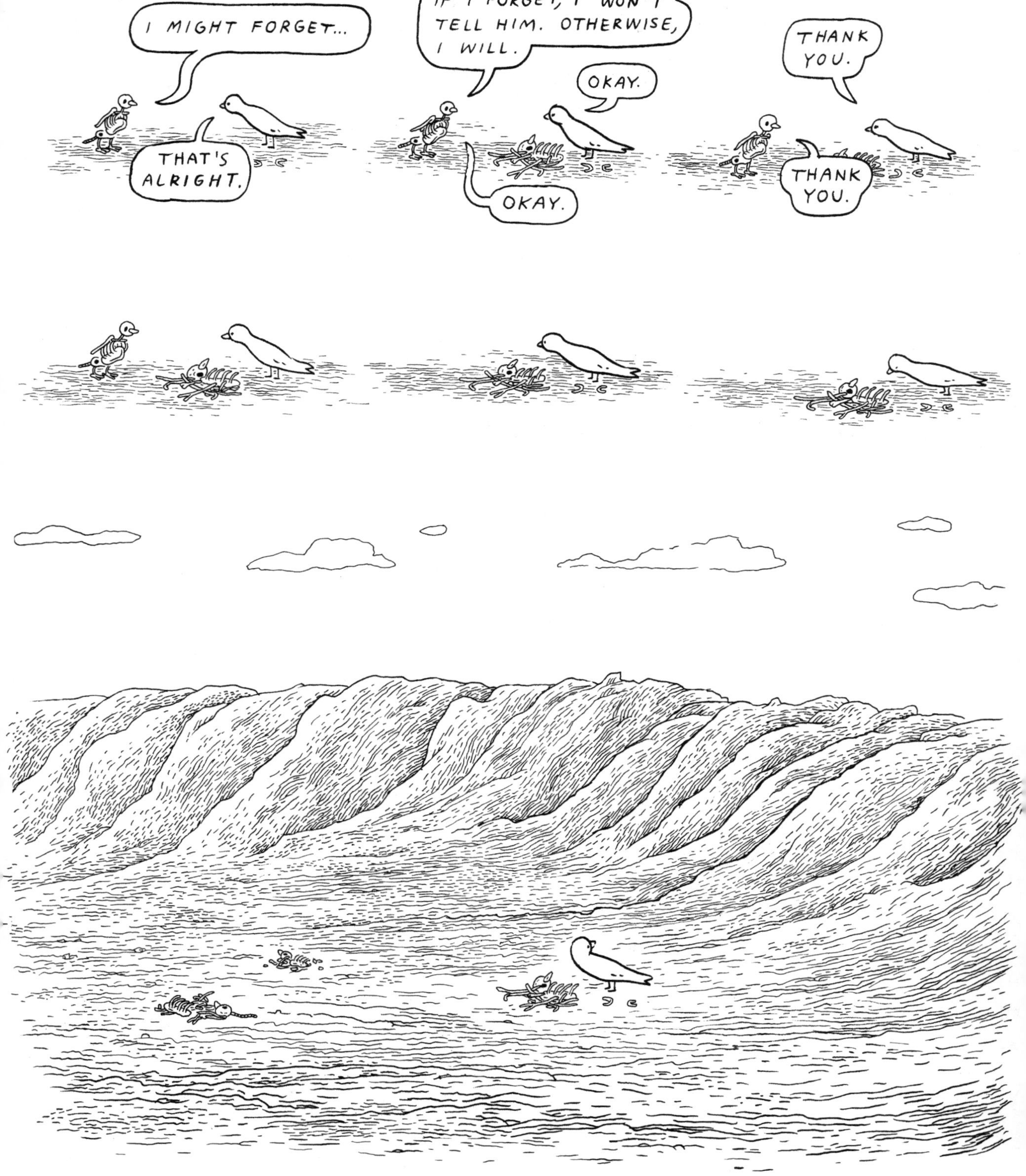
I MIGHT FORGET...
THAT'S ALRIGHT.
IF I FORGET, I WON'T TELL HIM. OTHERWISE, I WILL.
OKAY.
OKAY.
THANK YOU.
THANK YOU.

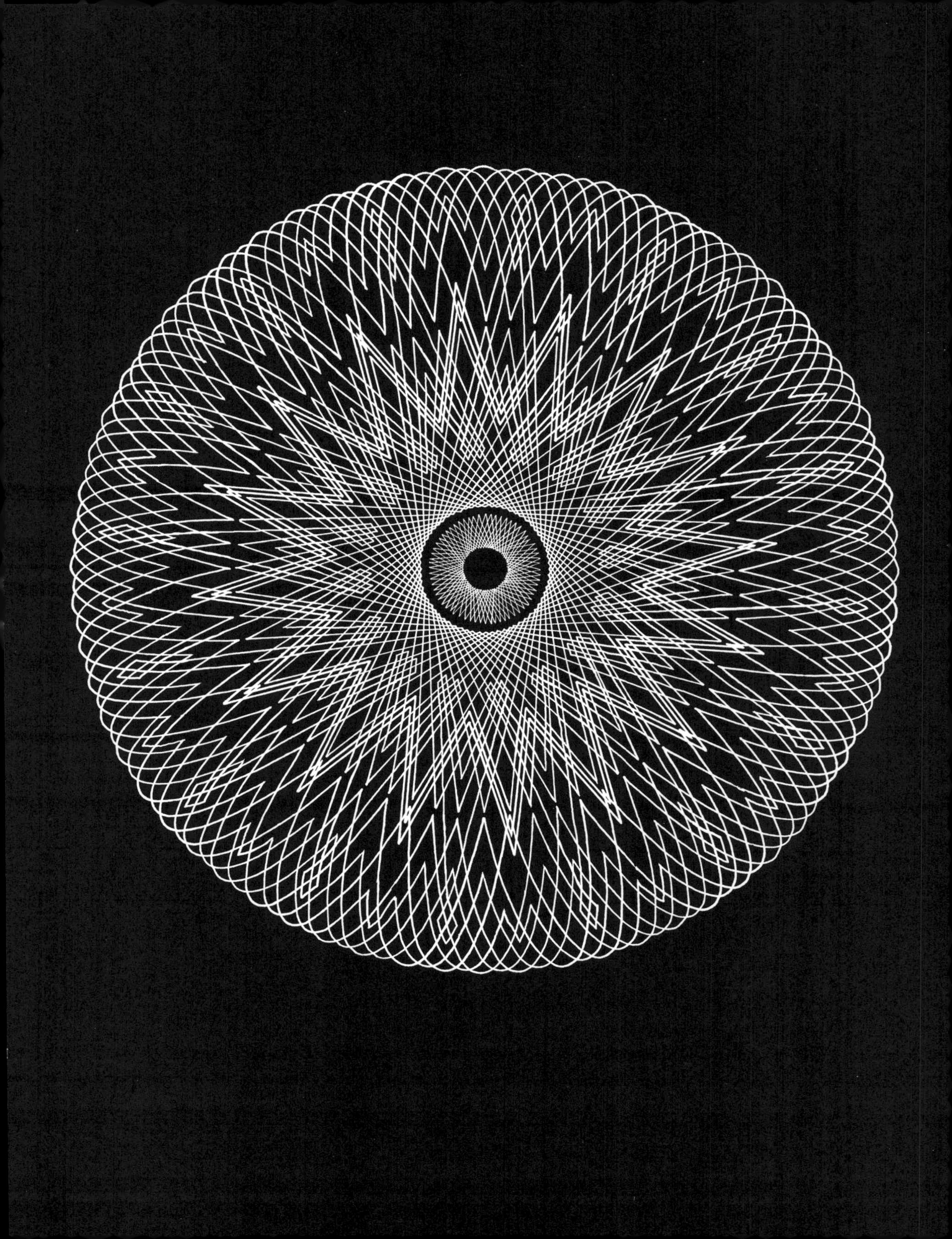

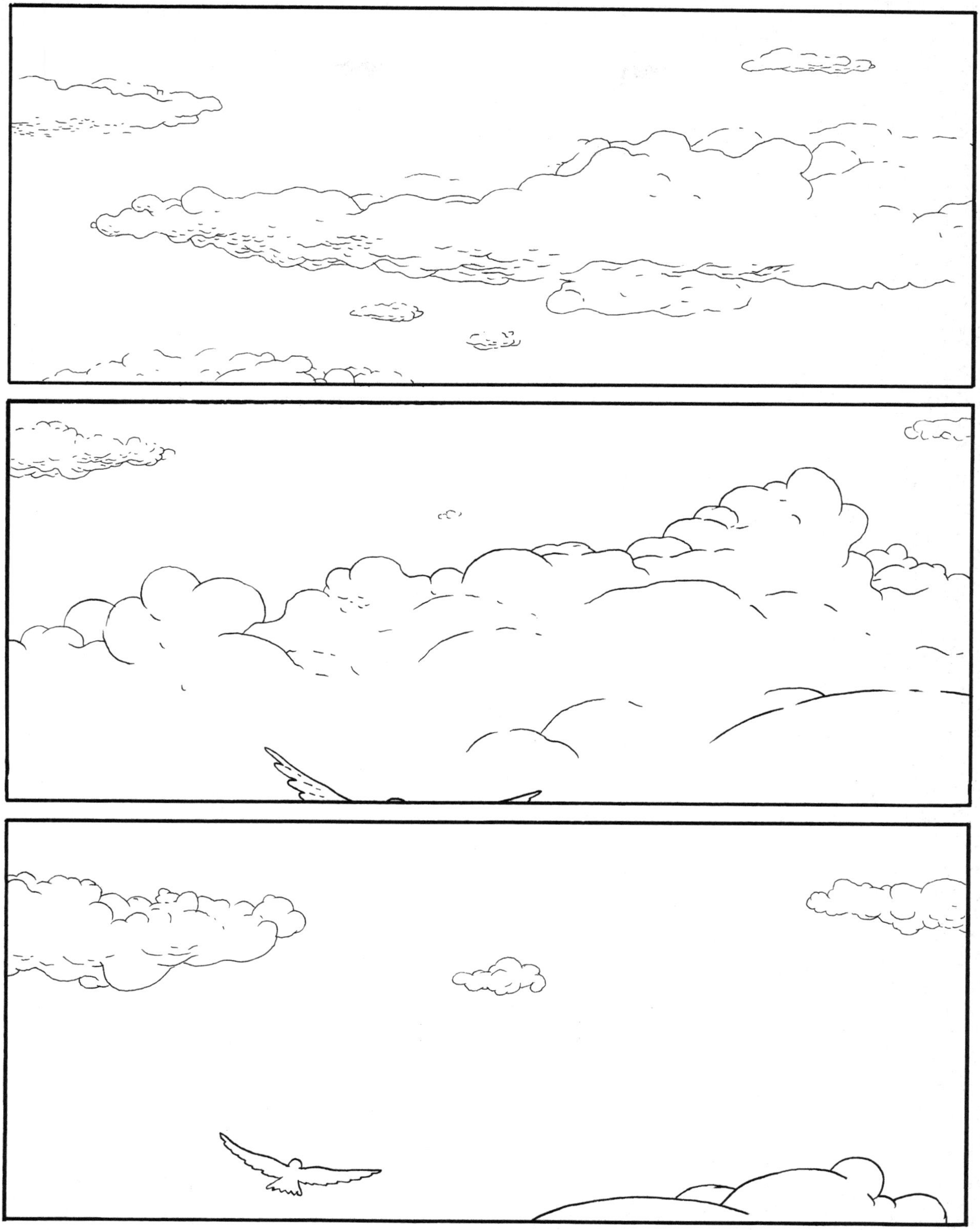

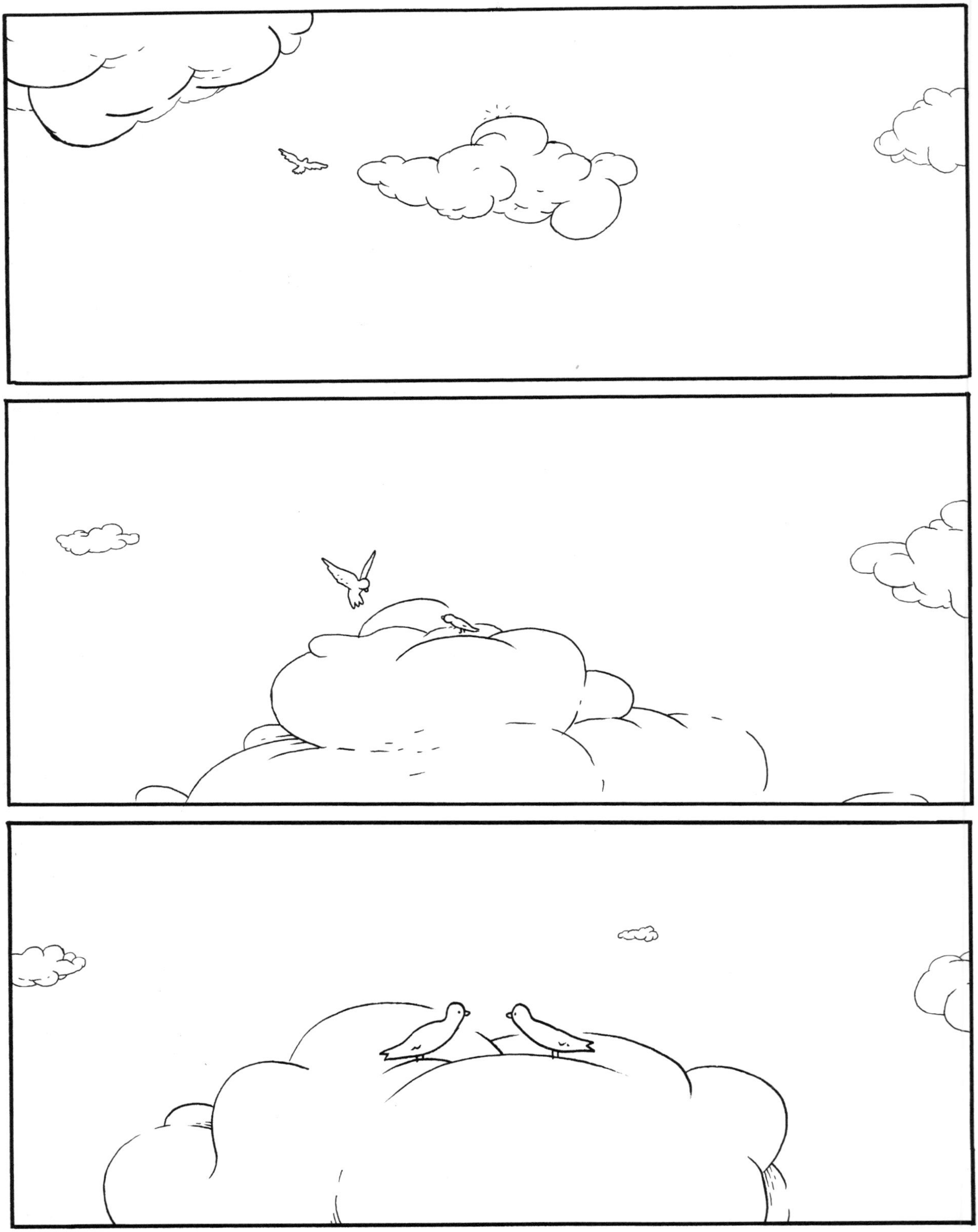

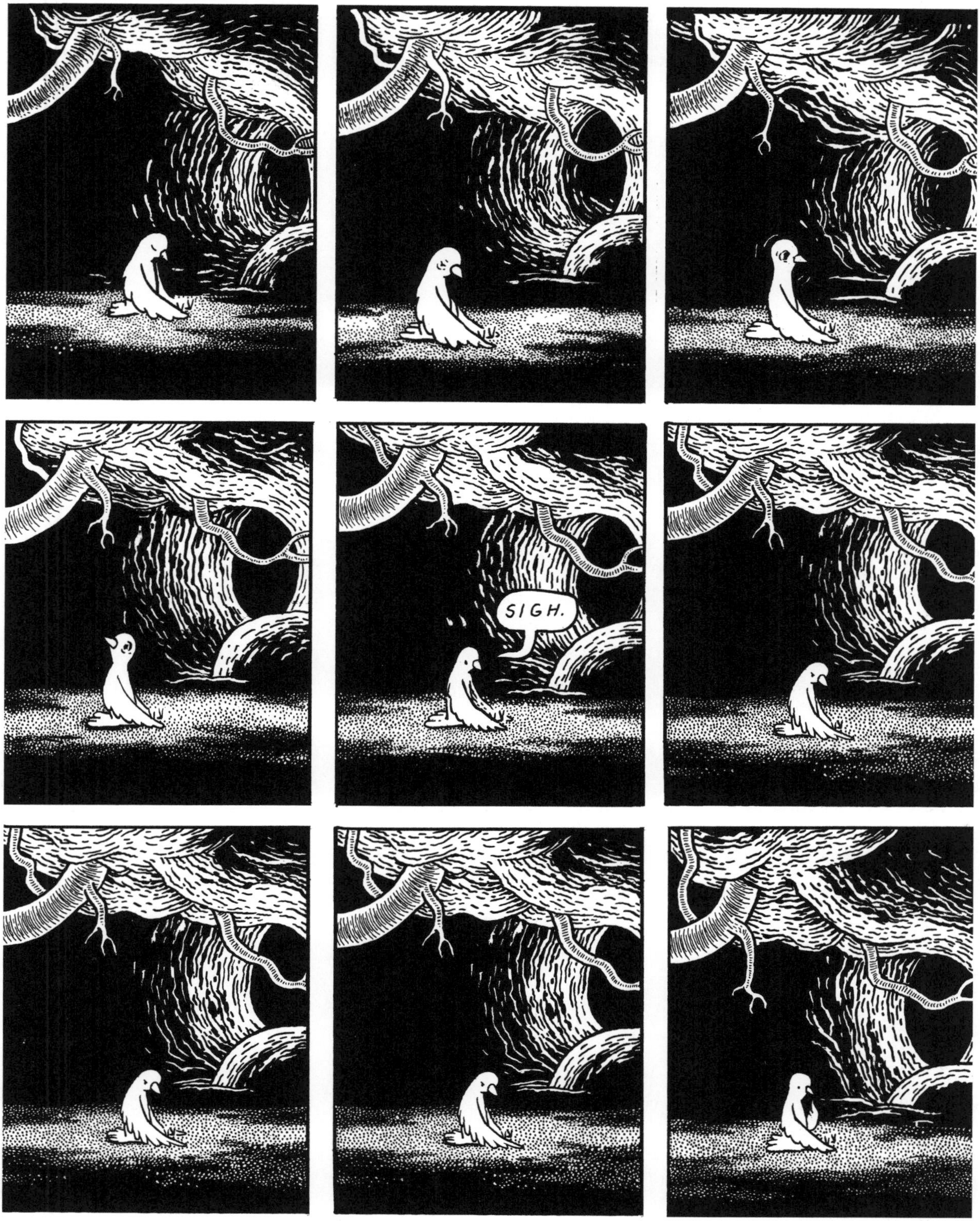
SIGH.

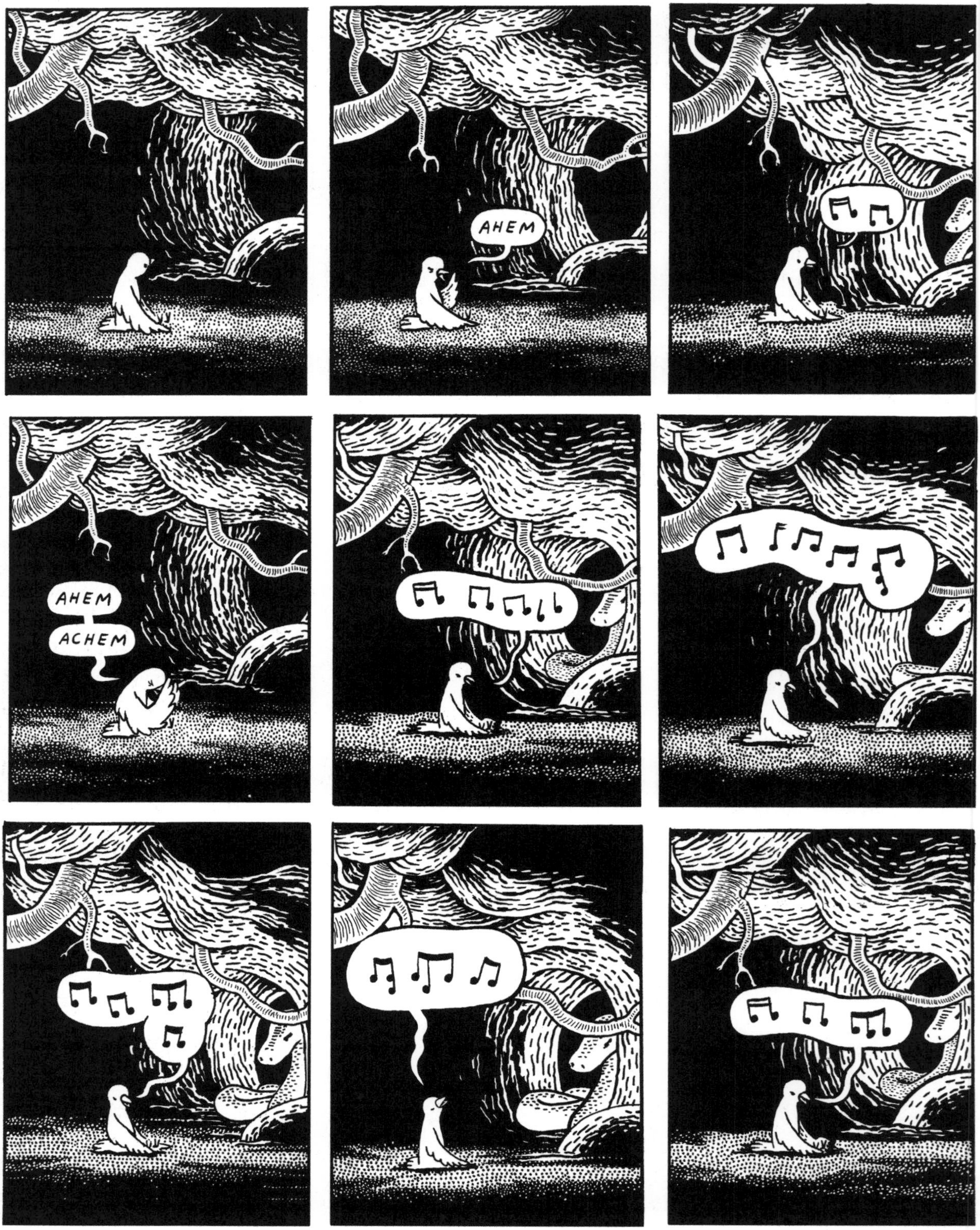
AHEM
AHEM
ACHEM

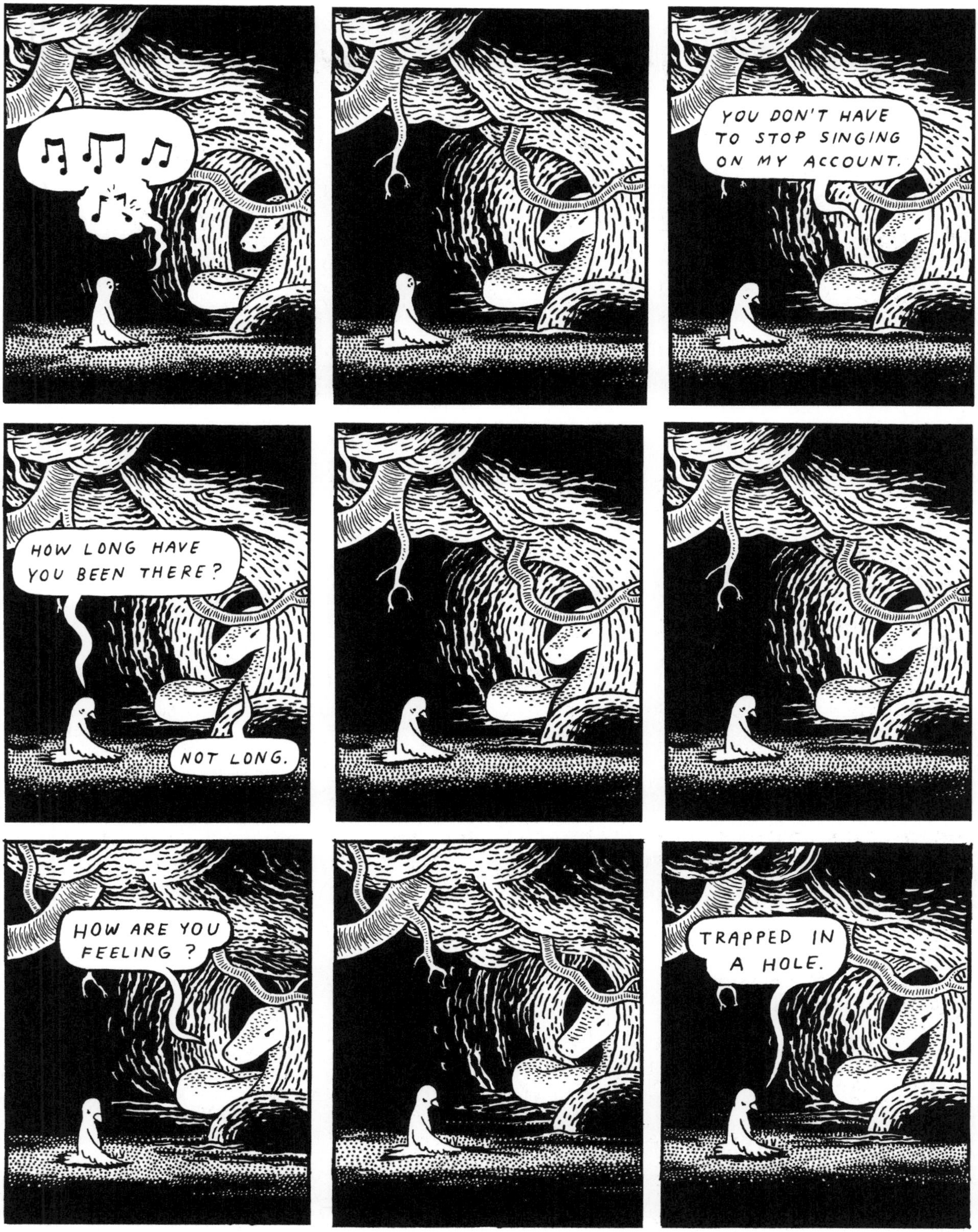
YOU DON'T HAVE TO STOP SINGING ON MY ACCOUNT.
HOW LONG HAVE YOU BEEN THERE?
NOT LONG.
HOW ARE YOU FEELING?
TRAPPED IN A HOLE.

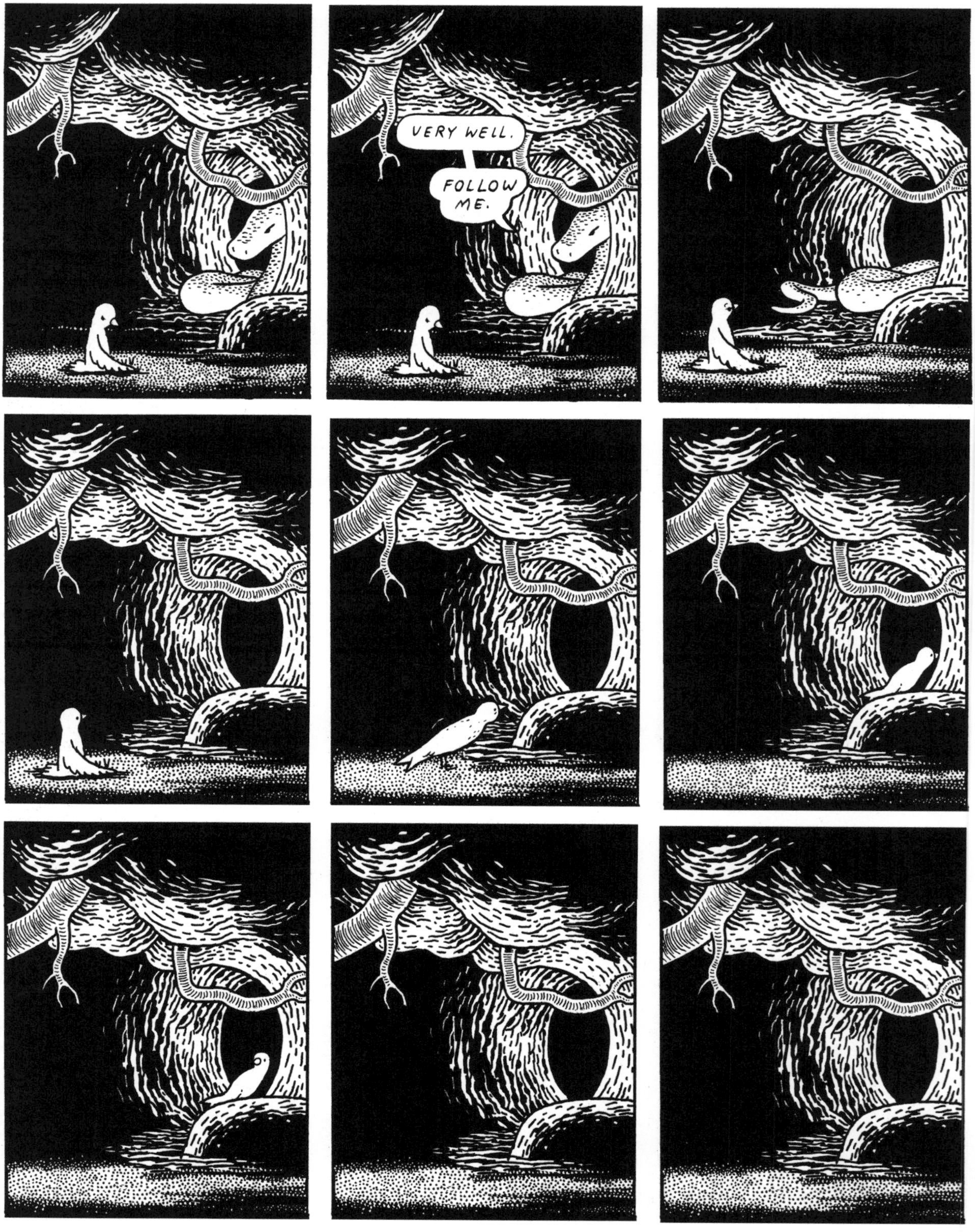
VERY WELL.
FOLLOW ME.

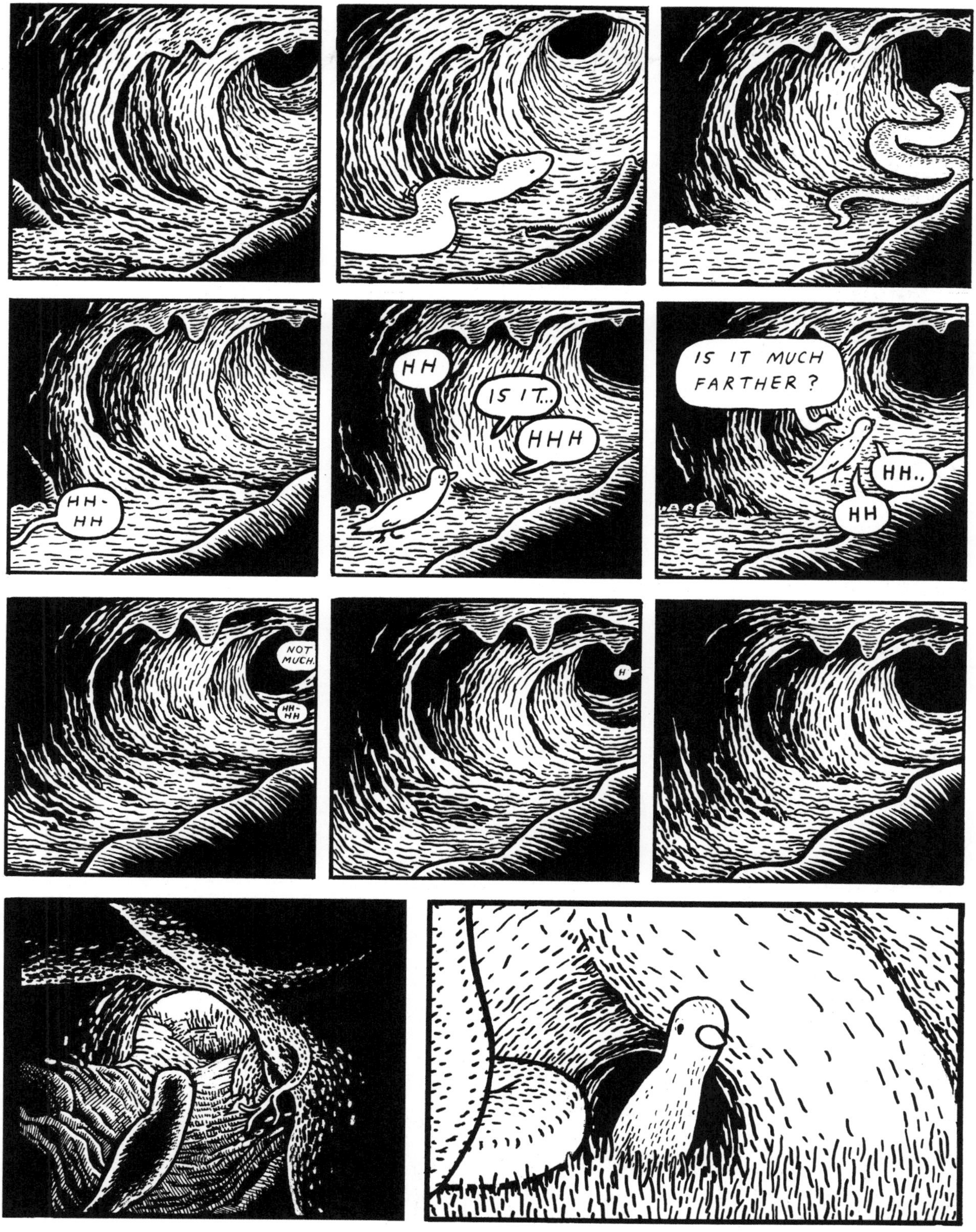
HH-HH
HH
IS IT...
HHH
IS IT MUCH FARTHER?
HH..
HH
NOT MUCH.
HH-HH
H

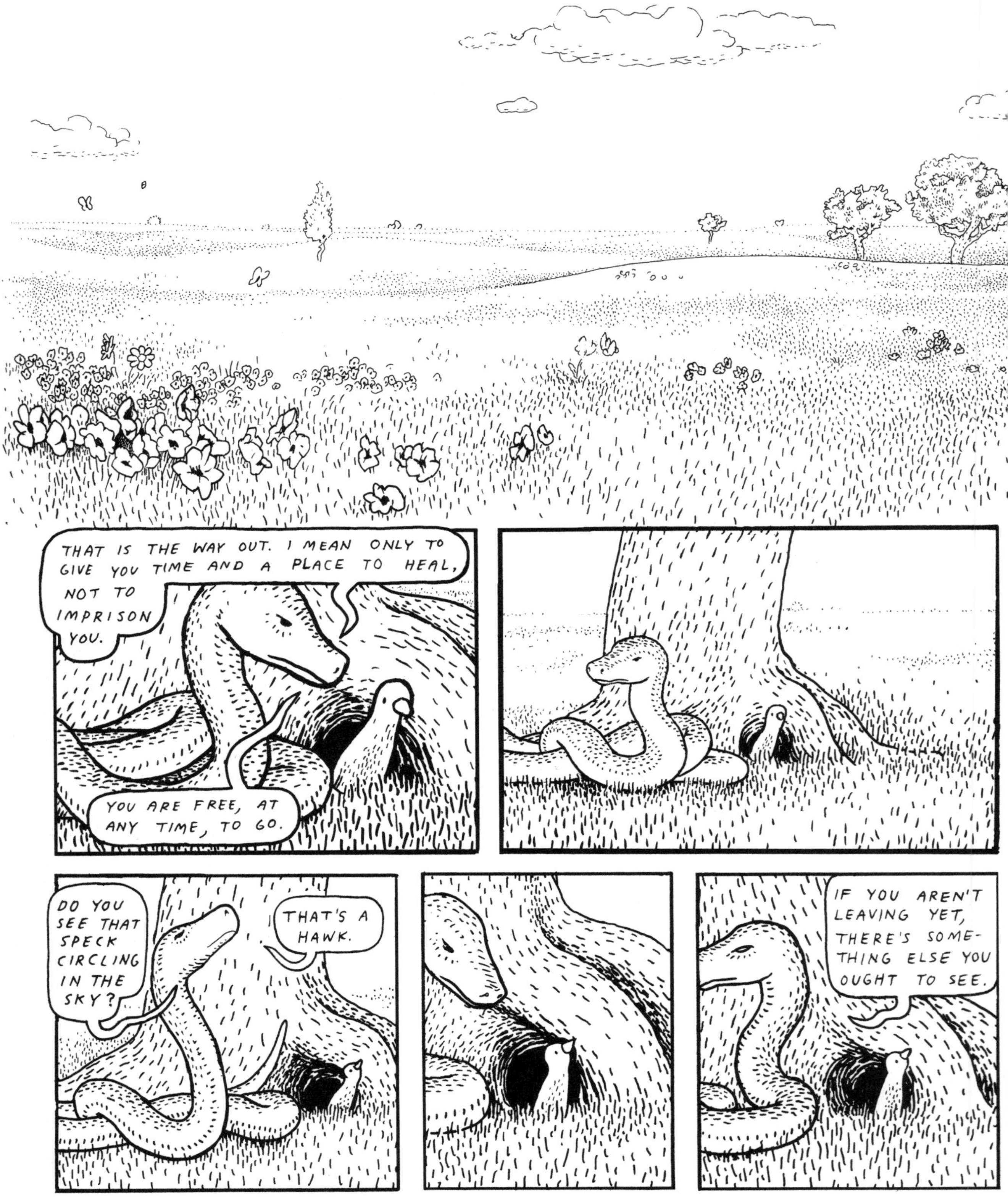
THAT IS THE WAY OUT. I MEAN ONLY TO GIVE YOU TIME AND A PLACE TO HEAL, NOT TO IMPRISON YOU.
YOU ARE FREE, AT ANY TIME, TO GO.
DO YOU SEE THAT SPECK CIRCLING IN THE SKY?
THAT'S A HAWK.
IF YOU AREN'T LEAVING YET, THERE'S SOMETHING ELSE YOU OUGHT TO SEE.

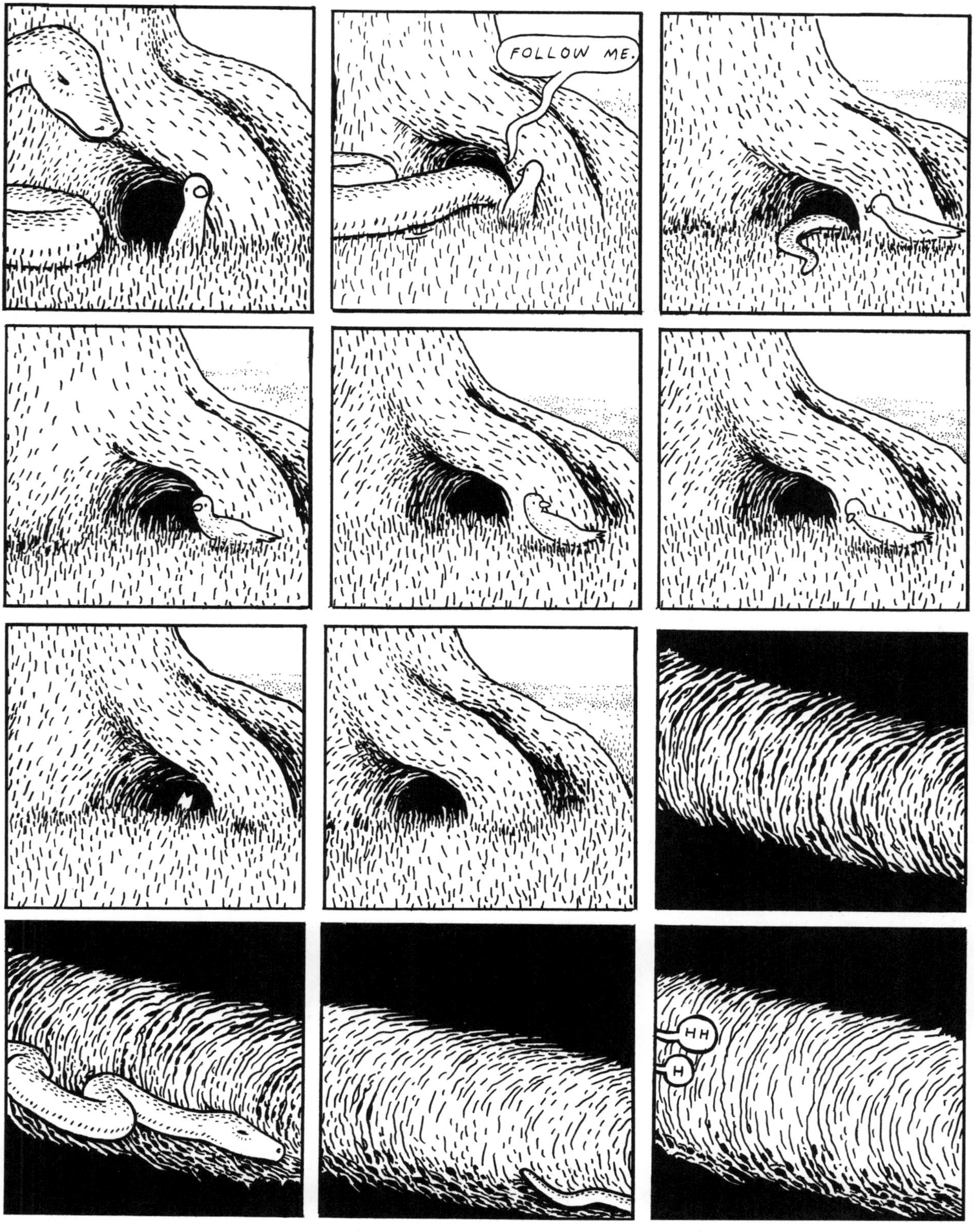
FOLLOW ME.
HH
H

HH
HH
H
H
SNAKE?
SNAKE?
I CAN'T SEE ANYTHING...
ARE YO..
BONK
OW.
WHAT'S WRONG?
THE MOLE IS COMING THIS WAY.
WHAT?
ARE MOLES DANGEROUS? SHOULD WE HIDE?
HELLO.
I WISH YOU'D STOP DIGGING NEW TUNNELS. IT'S VERY CONFUSING FOR VISITORS.

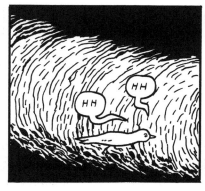

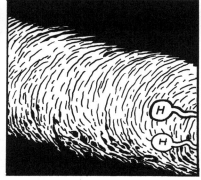

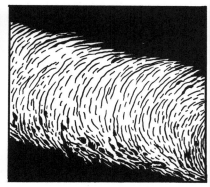

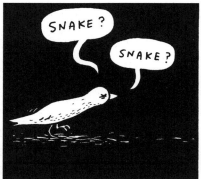

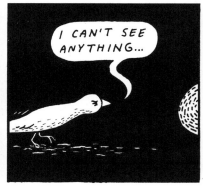

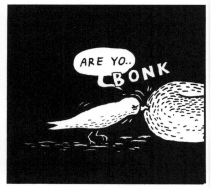

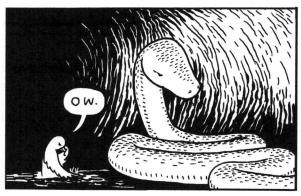

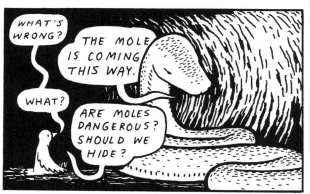

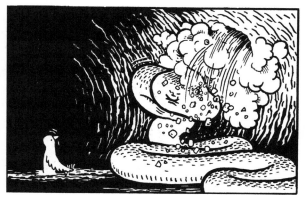

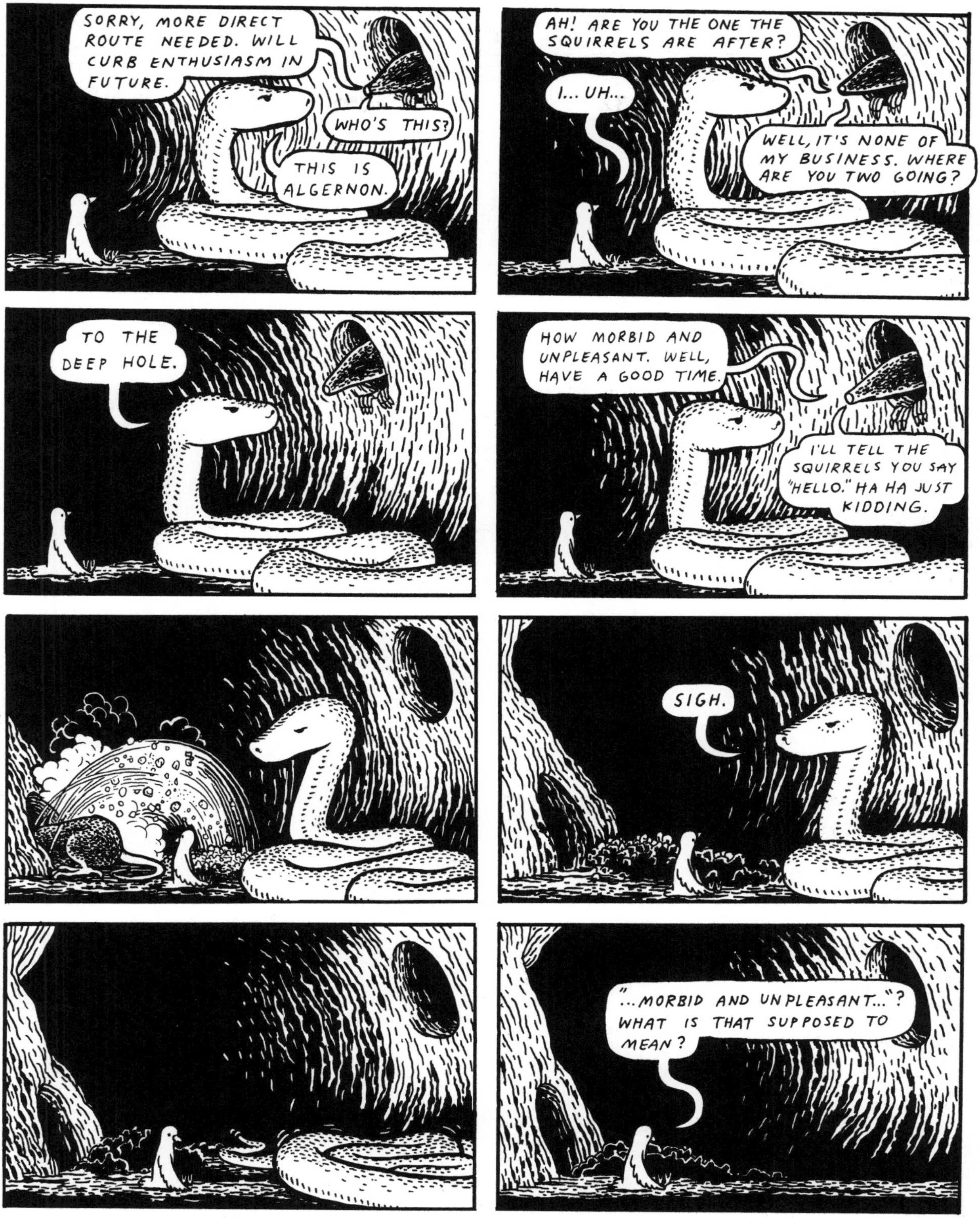
SORRY, MORE DIRECT ROUTE NEEDED. WILL CURB ENTHUSIASM IN FUTURE.
WHO'S THIS?
THIS IS ALGERNON.
AH! ARE YOU THE ONE THE SQUIRRELS ARE AFTER?
I... UH...
WELL, IT'S NONE OF MY BUSINESS. WHERE ARE YOU TWO GOING?
TO THE DEEP HOLE.
HOW MORBID AND UNPLEASANT. WELL, HAVE A GOOD TIME.
I'LL TELL THE SQUIRRELS YOU SAY "HELLO." HA HA JUST KIDDING.
SIGH.
"...MORBID AND UNPLEASANT..."? WHAT IS THAT SUPPOSED TO MEAN?

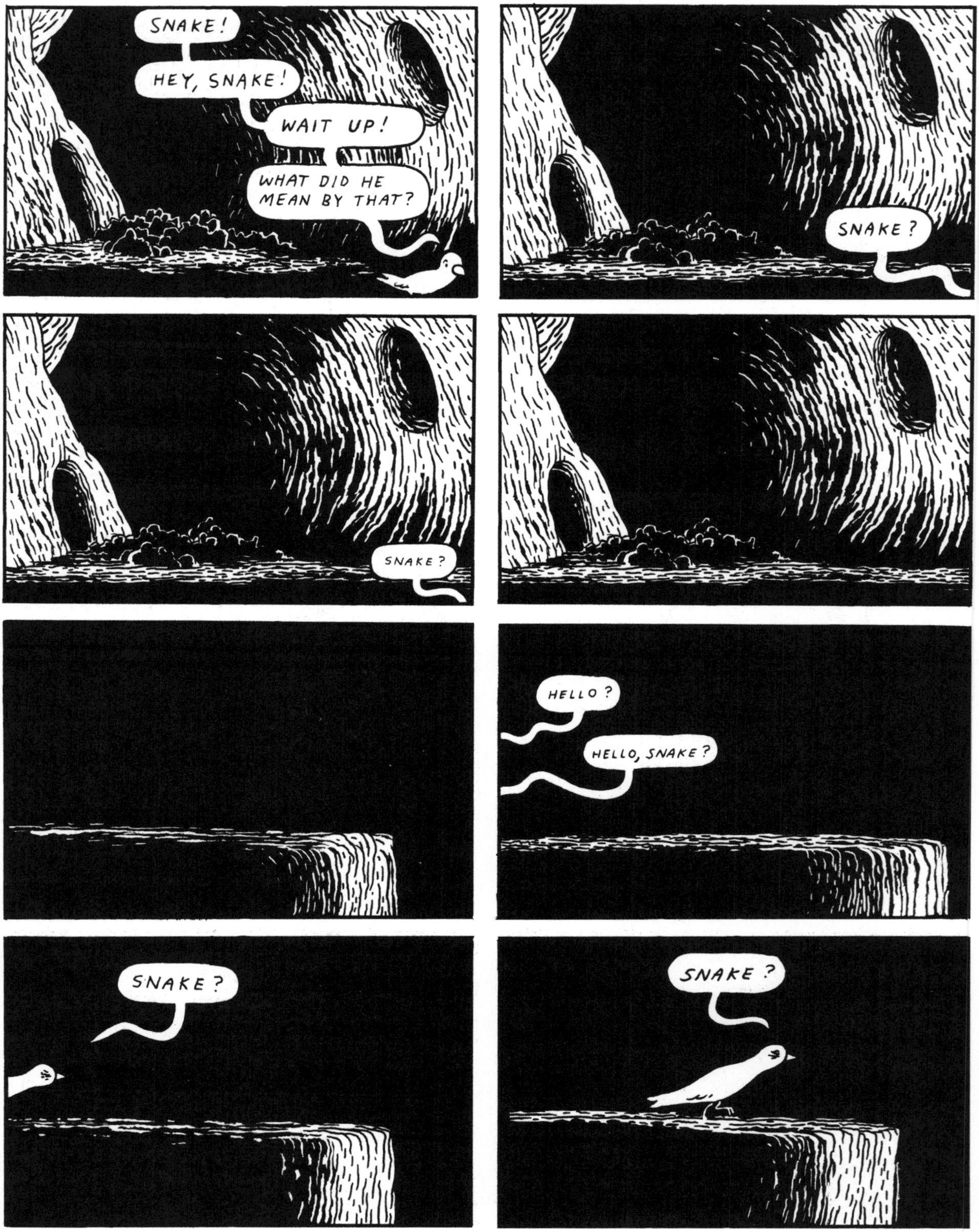
SNAKE!
HEY, SNAKE!
WAIT UP!
WHAT DID HE MEAN BY THAT?
SNAKE?
SNAKE?
HELLO?
HELLO, SNAKE?
SNAKE?
SNAKE?

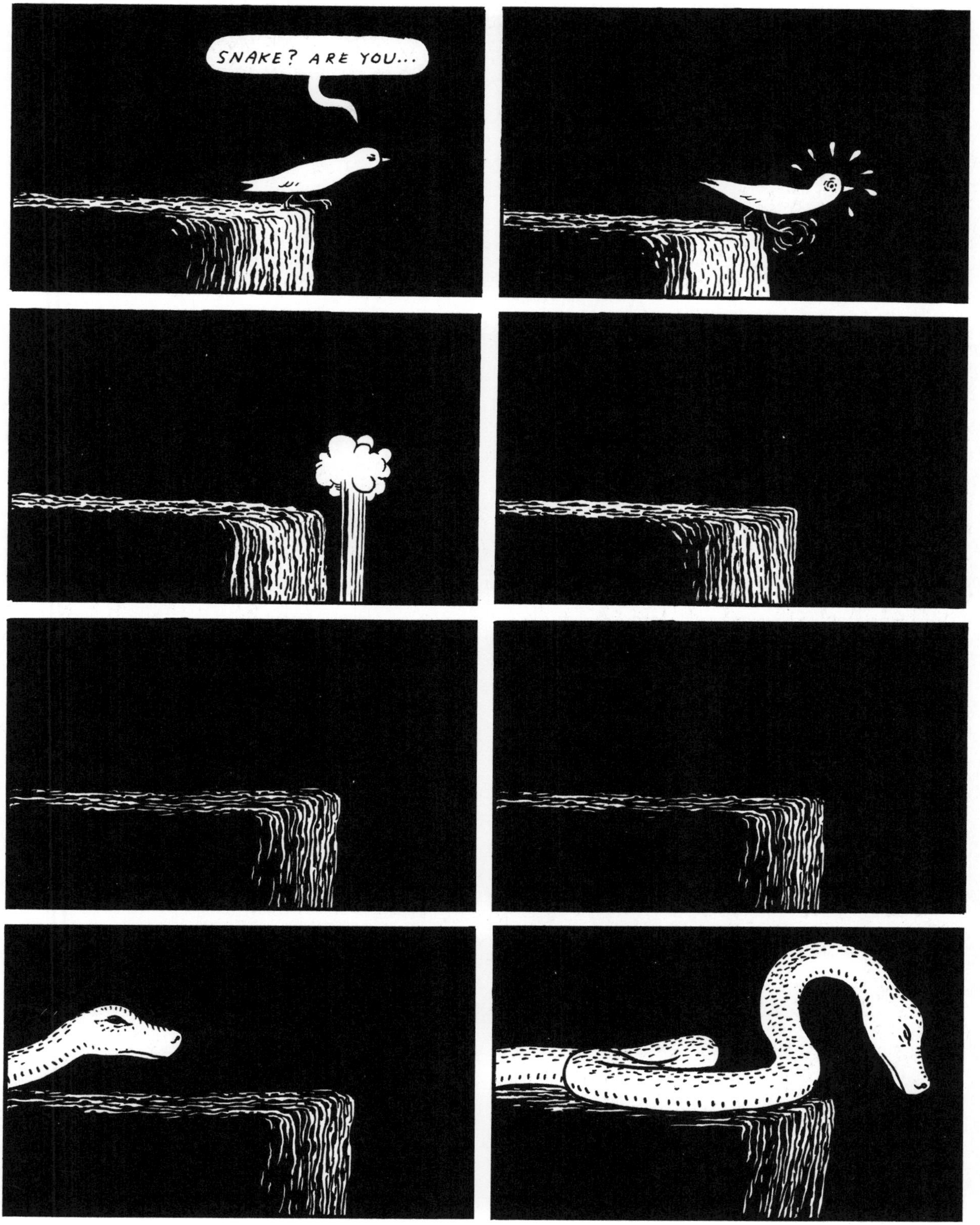
SNAKE? ARE YOU...

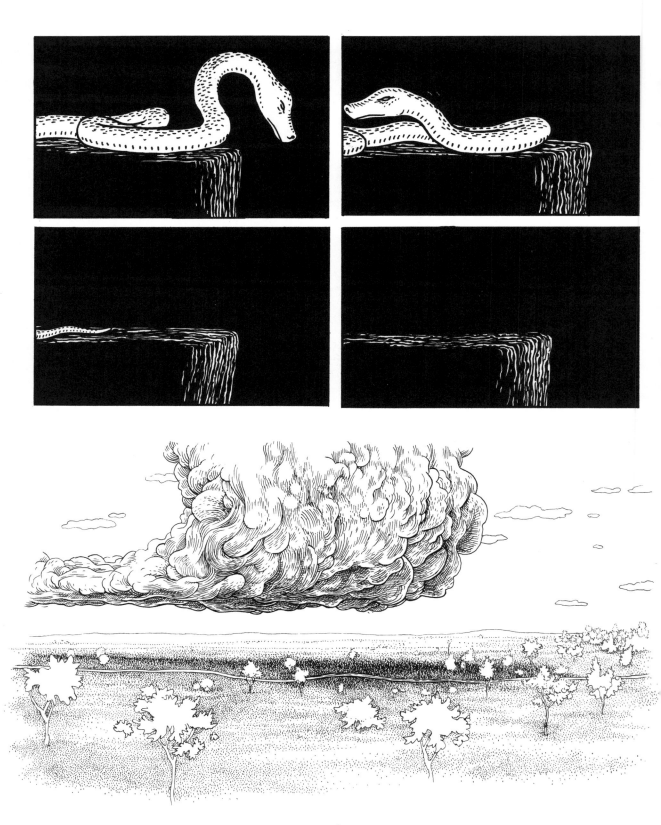

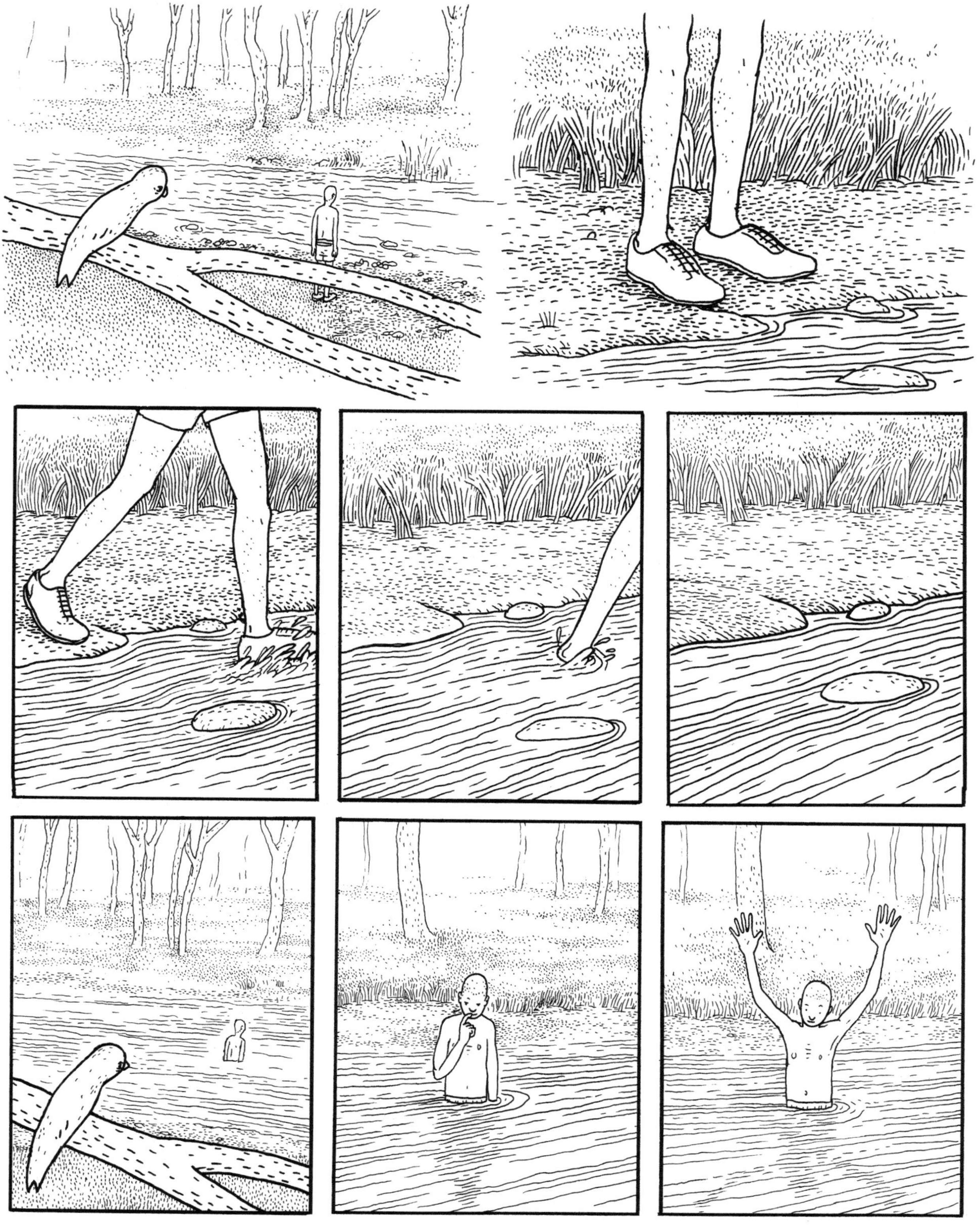

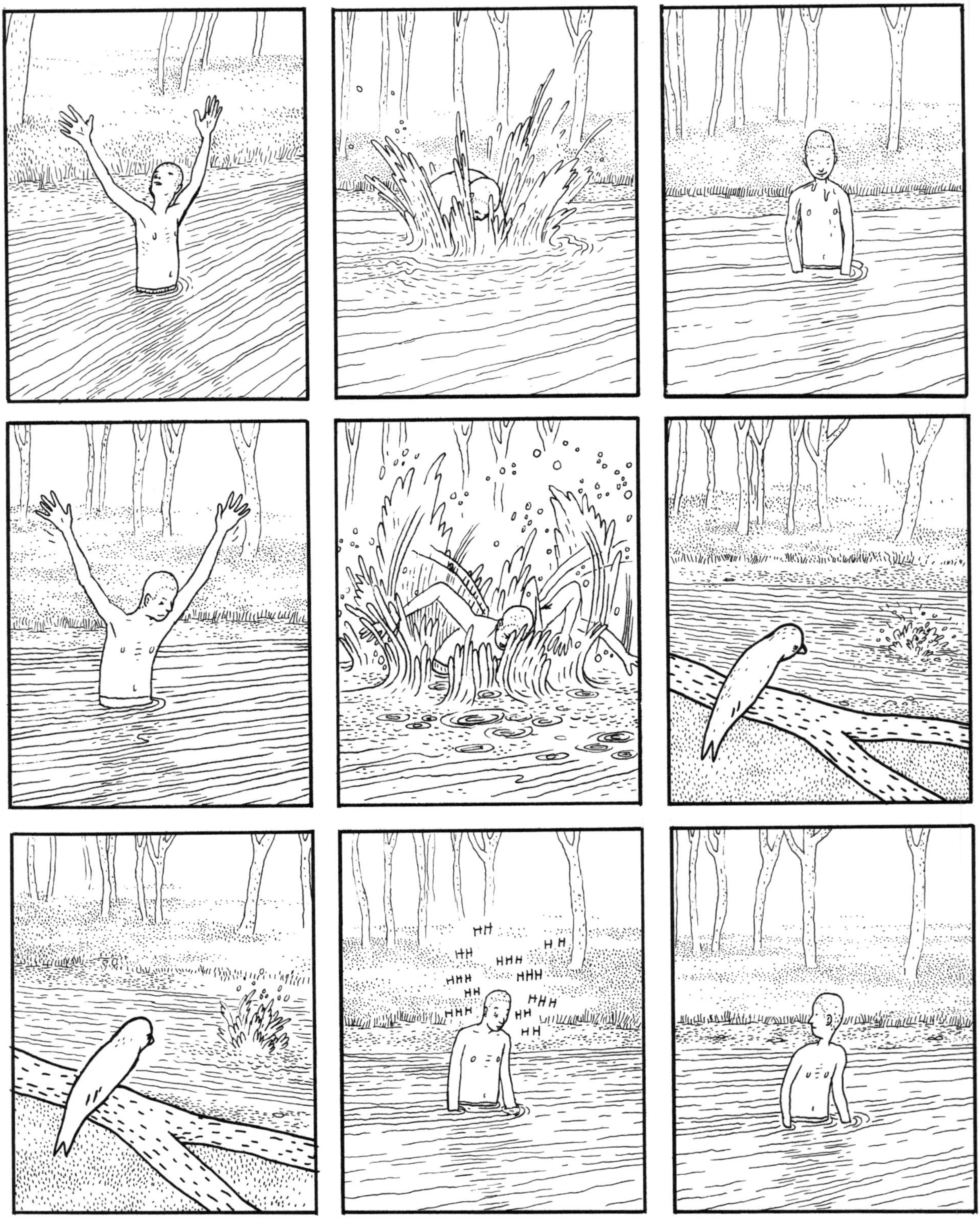
HH
H H
HH
HHH
HHH
HHH
HH
HHH
HHH
HH
HH
HH

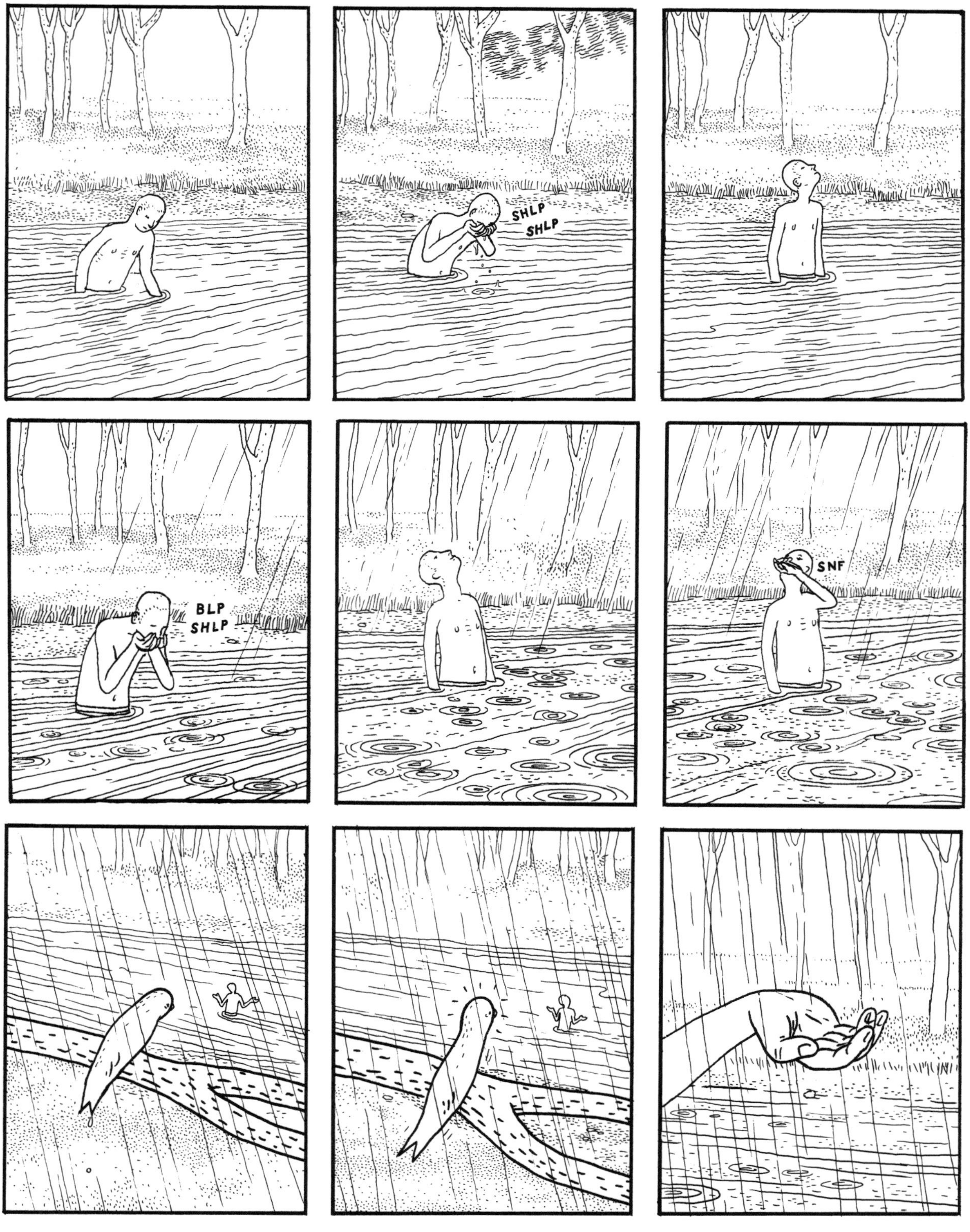
SHLP
SHLP
BLP
SHLP
SNF

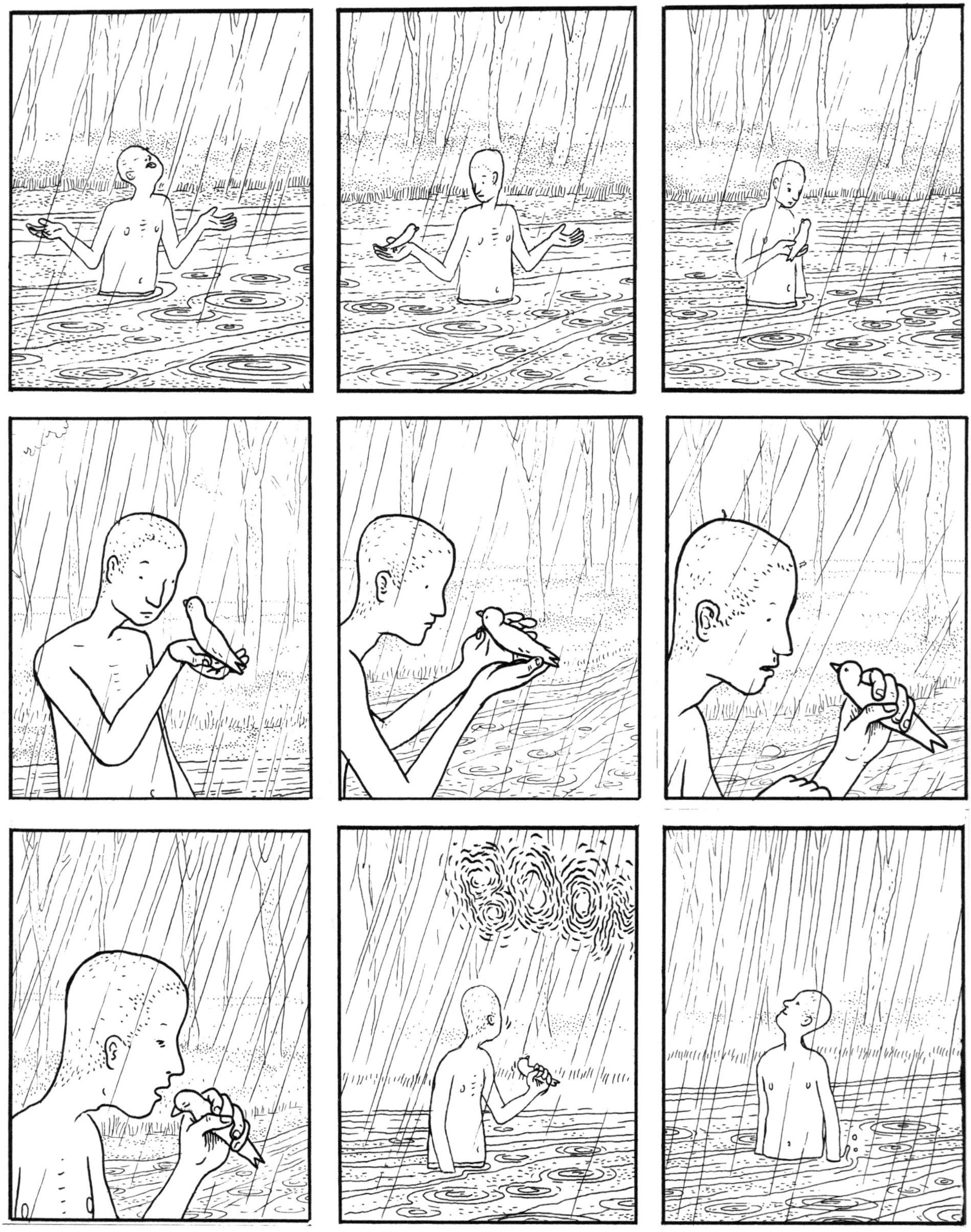

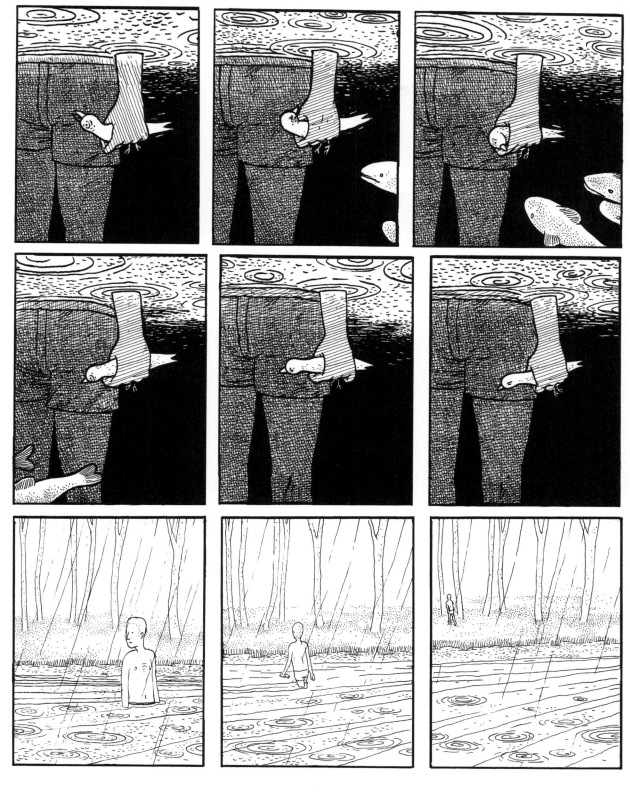

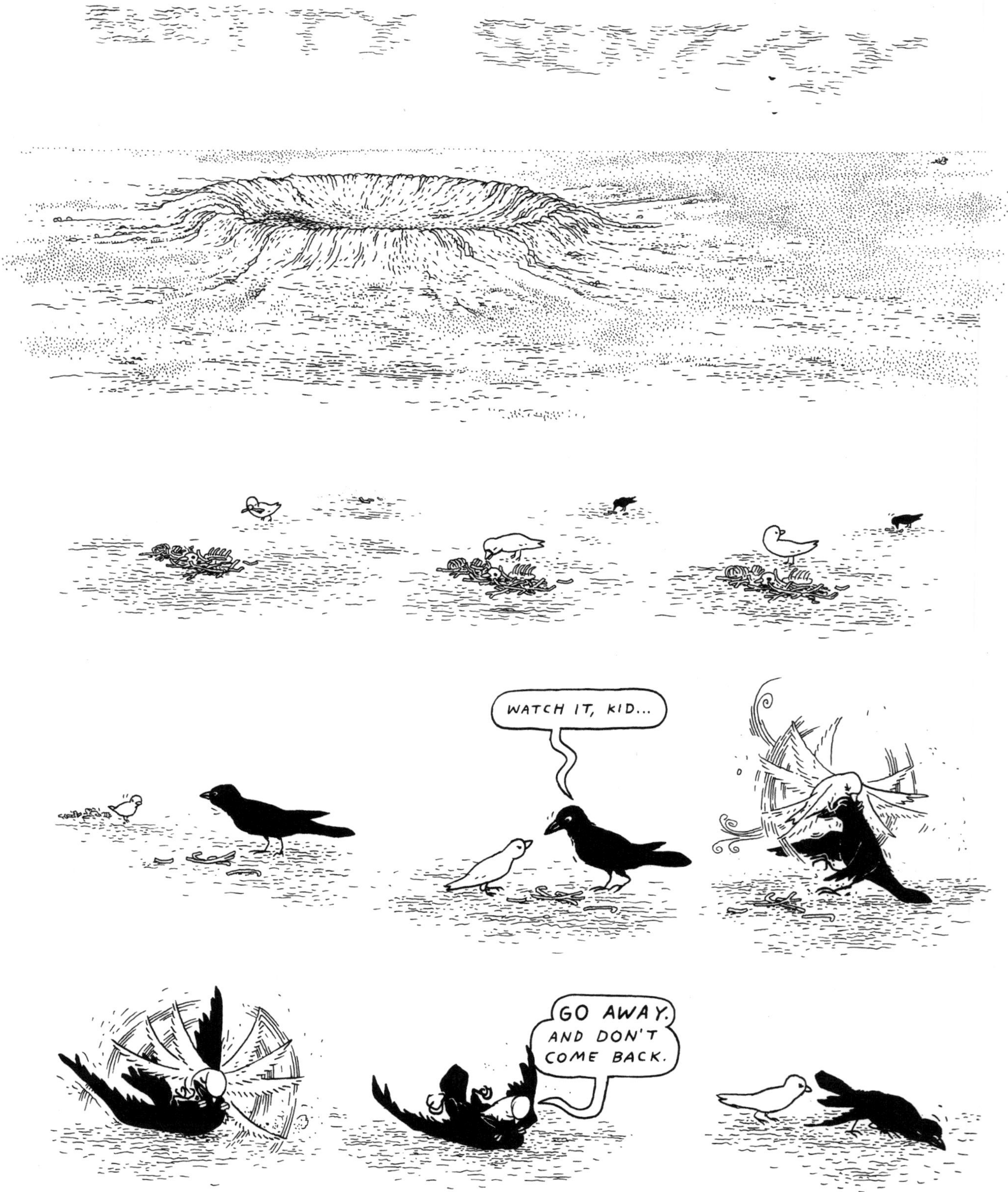
WATCH IT, KID...
GO AWAY. AND DON'T COME BACK.

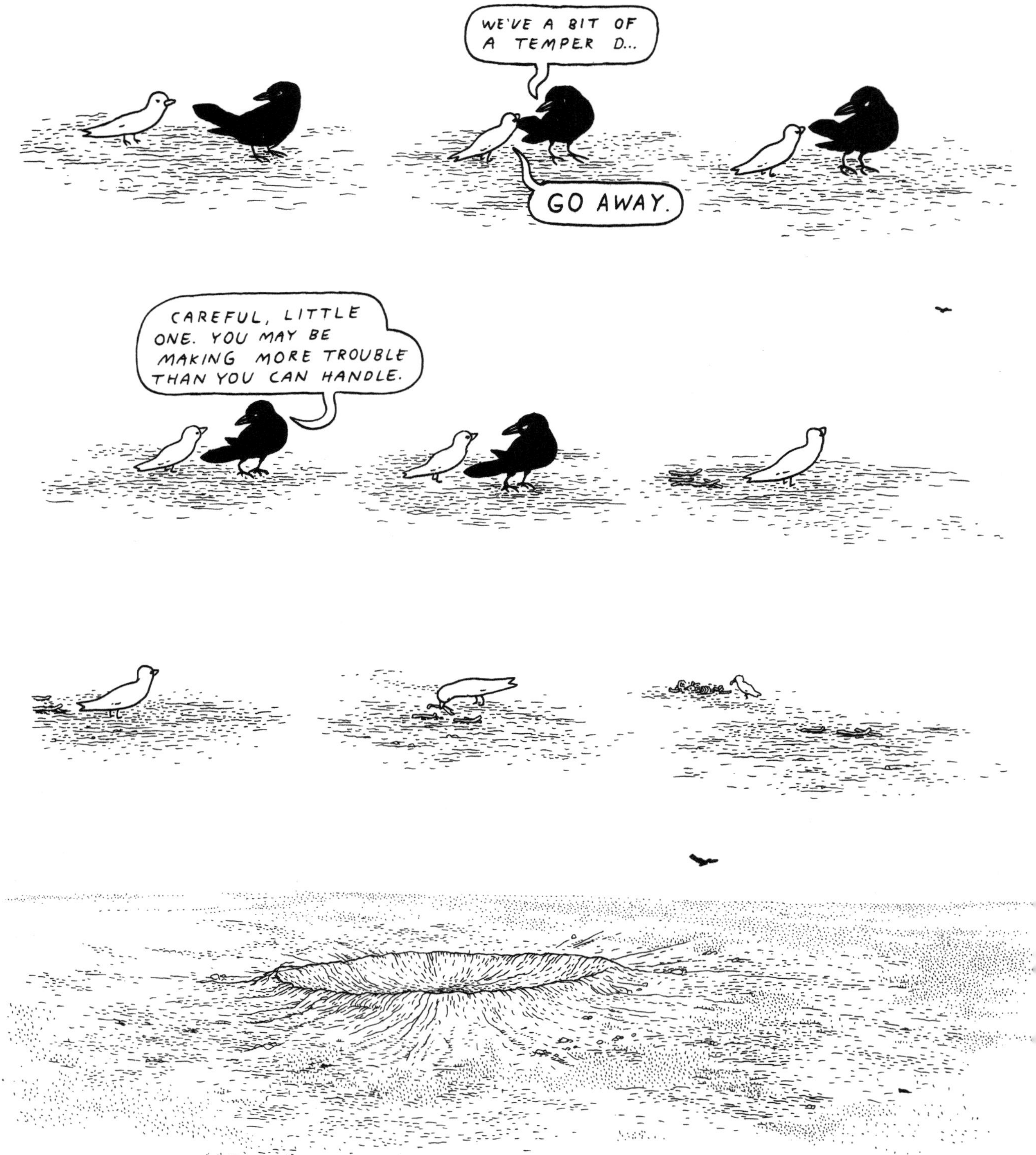
WE'VE A BIT OF A TEMPER D...
GO AWAY.
CAREFUL, LITTLE ONE. YOU MAY BE MAKING MORE TROUBLE THAN YOU CAN HANDLE.

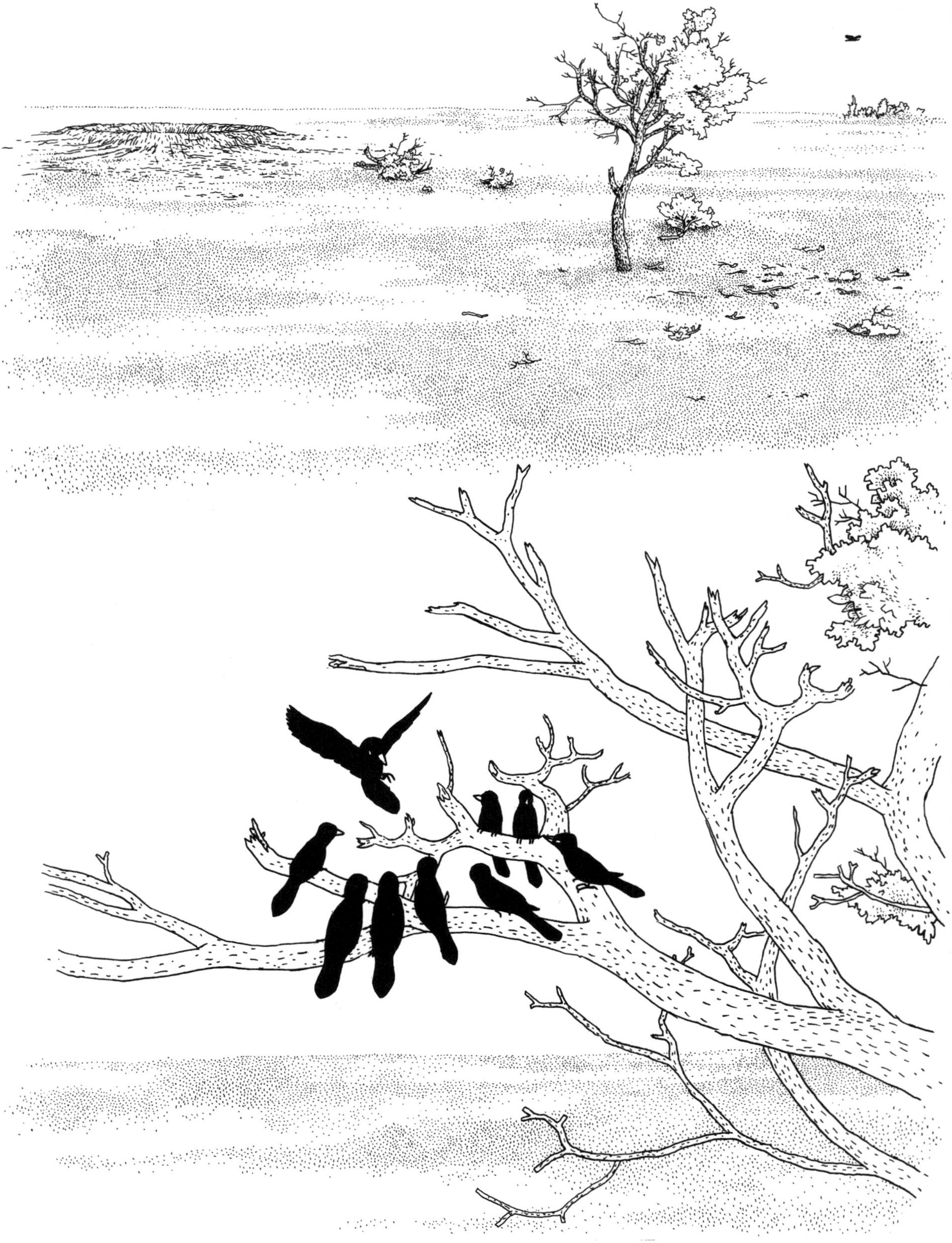

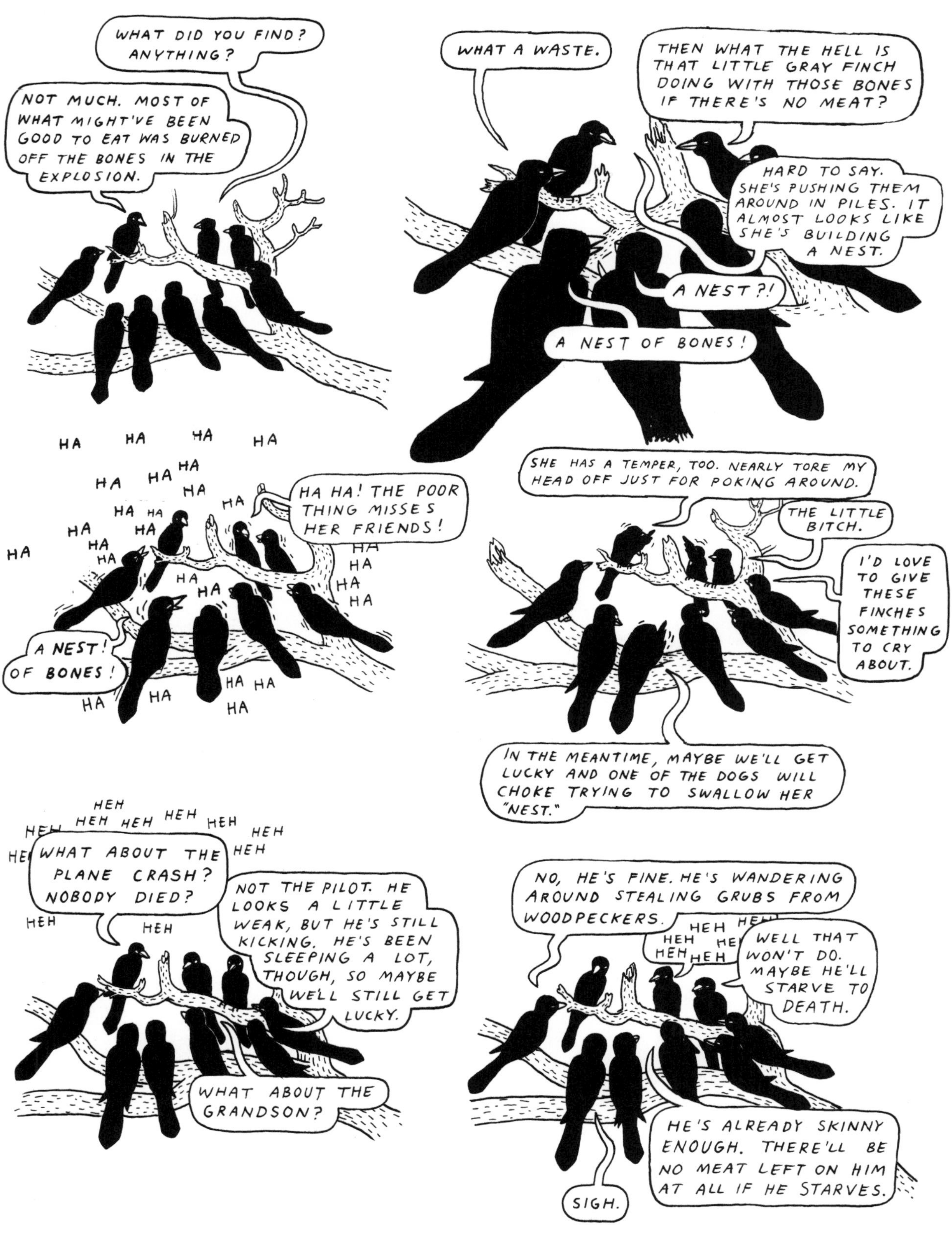
WHAT DID YOU FIND? ANYTHING?
NOT MUCH. MOST OF WHAT MIGHT'VE BEEN GOOD TO EAT WAS BURNED OFF THE BONES IN THE EXPLOSION.
WHAT A WASTE.
THEN WHAT THE HELL IS THAT LITTLE GRAY FINCH DOING WITH THOSE BONES IF THERE'S NO MEAT?
HARD TO SAY. SHE'S PUSHING THEM AROUND IN PILES. IT ALMOST LOOKS LIKE SHE'S BUILDING A NEST.
A NEST?!
A NEST OF BONES!
HA HA HA HA
HA HA HA HA HA HA HA HA HA HA HA HA HA
HA HA! THE POOR THING MISSES HER FRIENDS!
HA HA HA HA HA HA HA
A NEST! OF BONES!
HA HA HA HA HA
SHE HAS A TEMPER, TOO. NEARLY TORE MY HEAD OFF JUST FOR POKING AROUND.
THE LITTLE BITCH.
I'D LOVE TO GIVE THESE FINCHES SOMETHING TO CRY ABOUT.
IN THE MEANTIME, MAYBE WE'LL GET LUCKY AND ONE OF THE DOGS WILL CHOKE TRYING TO SWALLOW HER "NEST."
HEH HEH HEH HEH HEH HEH HEH HEH
WHAT ABOUT THE PLANE CRASH? NOBODY DIED?
HEH HEH
NOT THE PILOT. HE LOOKS A LITTLE WEAK, BUT HE'S STILL KICKING. HE'S BEEN SLEEPING A LOT, THOUGH, SO MAYBE WE'LL STILL GET LUCKY.
WHAT ABOUT THE GRANDSON?
NO, HE'S FINE. HE'S WANDERING AROUND STEALING GRUBS FROM WOODPECKERS.
HEH HEH HEH HEH
WELL THAT WON'T DO. MAYBE HE'LL STARVE TO DEATH.
HE'S ALREADY SKINNY ENOUGH. THERE'LL BE NO MEAT LEFT ON HIM AT ALL IF HE STARVES.
SIGH.

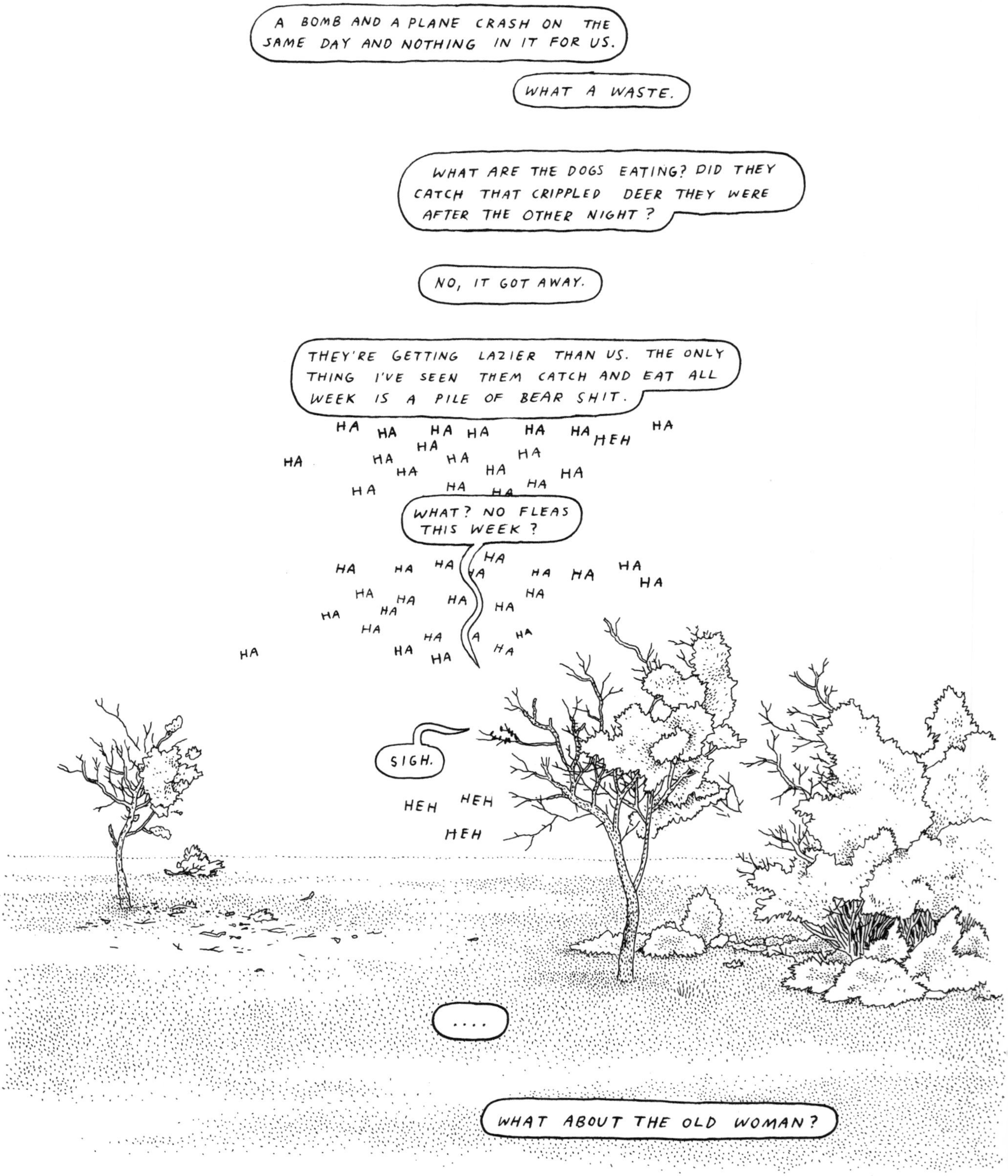
A BOMB AND A PLANE CRASH ON THE SAME DAY AND NOTHING IN IT FOR US.
WHAT A WASTE.
WHAT ARE THE DOGS EATING? DID THEY CATCH THAT CRIPPLED DEER THEY WERE AFTER THE OTHER NIGHT?
NO, IT GOT AWAY.
THEY'RE GETTING LAZIER THAN US. THE ONLY THING I'VE SEEN THEM CATCH AND EAT ALL WEEK IS A PILE OF BEAR SHIT.
HA HA HA HA HA HA HEH HA
HA HA HA HA HA HA HA HA
HA HA HA HA HA
WHAT? NO FLEAS THIS WEEK?
HA HA HA HA HA HA HA HA HA
HA HA HA HA HA HA
HA HA HA HA HA HA HA HA
SIGH.
HEH HEH HEH
....
WHAT ABOUT THE OLD WOMAN?

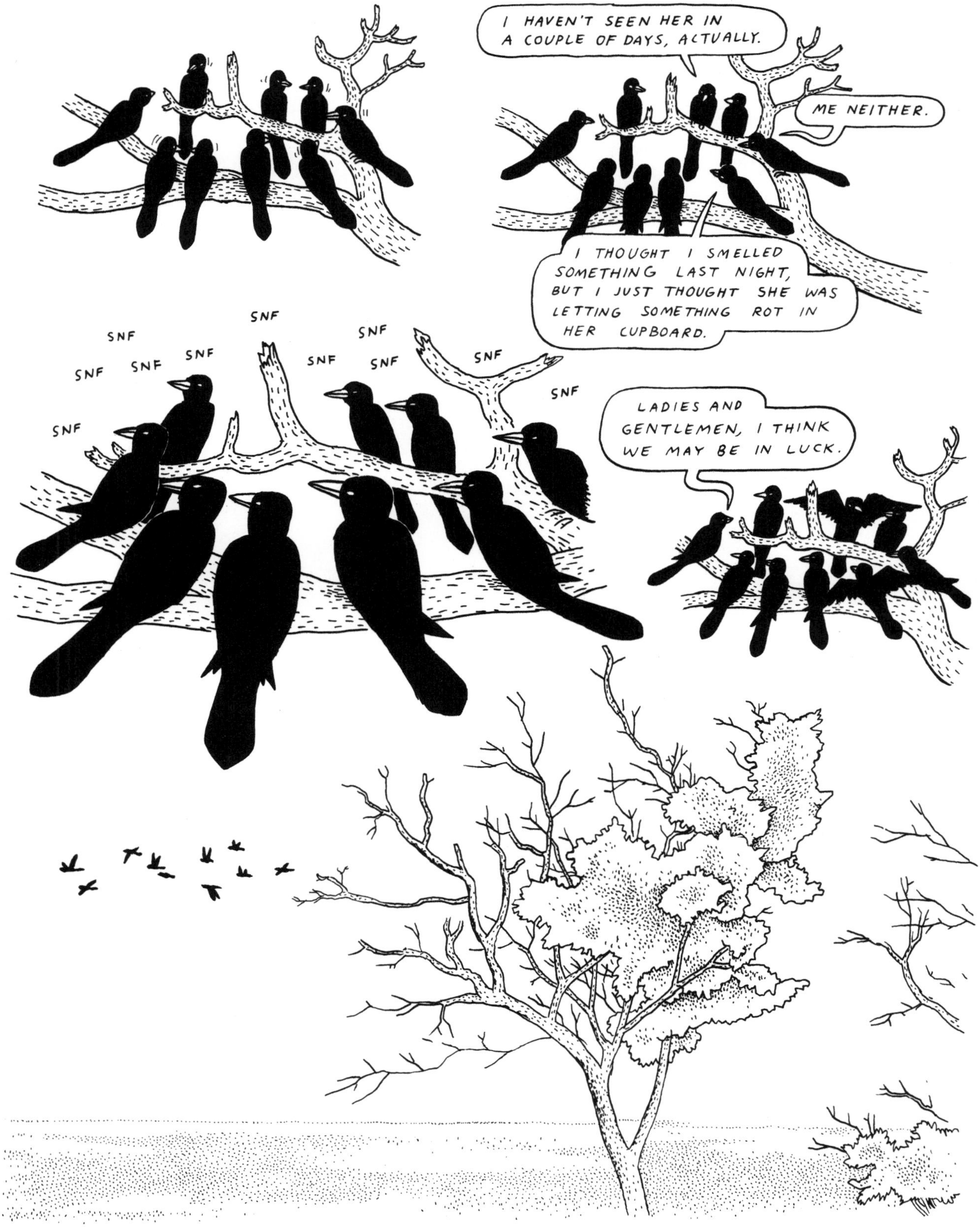
I HAVEN'T SEEN HER IN A COUPLE OF DAYS, ACTUALLY.
ME NEITHER.
I THOUGHT I SMELLED SOMETHING LAST NIGHT, BUT I JUST THOUGHT SHE WAS LETTING SOMETHING ROT IN HER CUPBOARD.
SNF
SNF
SNF
SNF
SNF
SNF
SNF
SNF
SNF
SNF
SNF
LADIES AND GENTLEMEN, I THINK WE MAY BE IN LUCK.

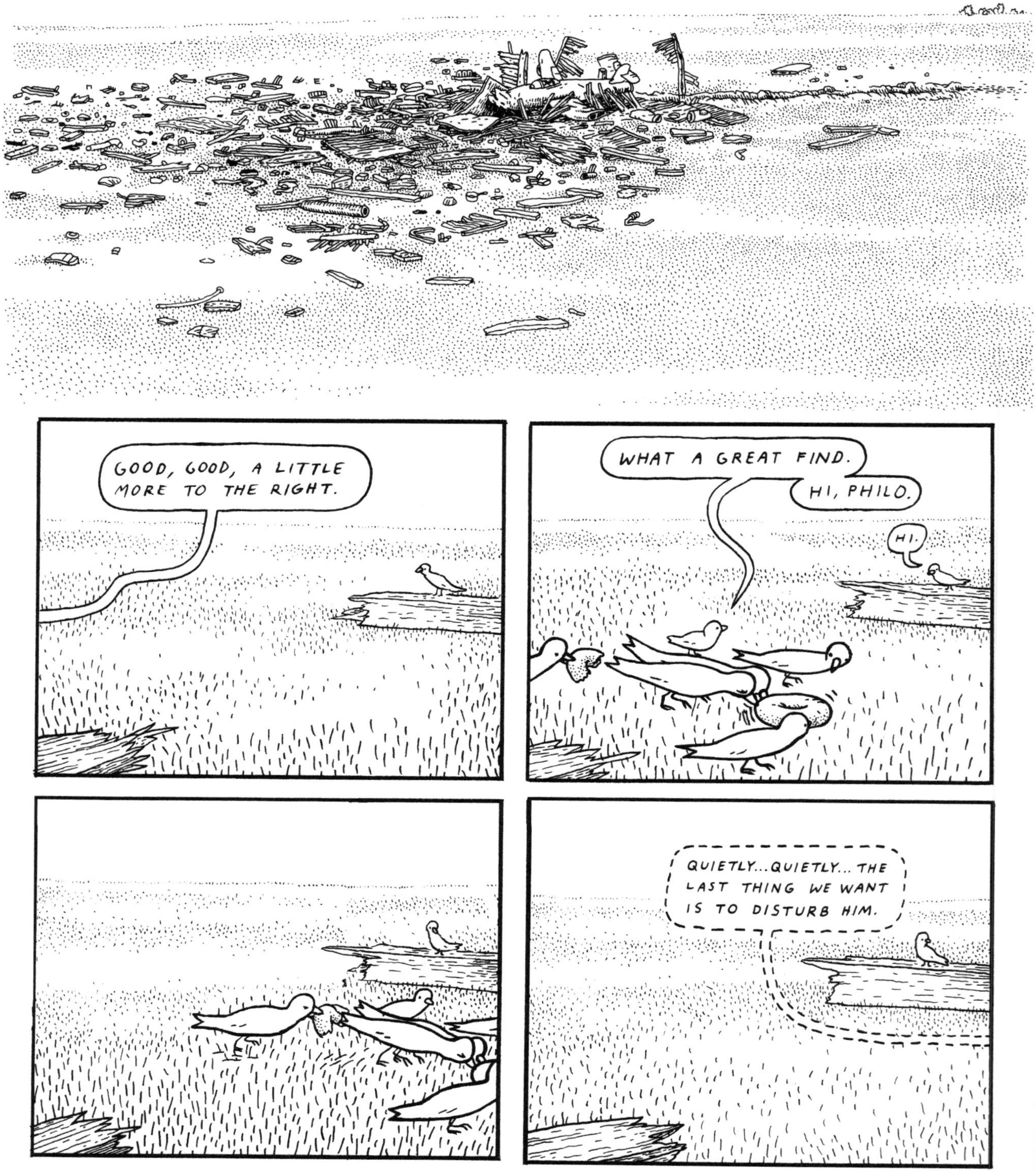
GOOD, GOOD, A LITTLE MORE TO THE RIGHT.
WHAT A GREAT FIND.
HI, PHILO.
HI.
QUIETLY... QUIETLY... THE LAST THING WE WANT IS TO DISTURB HIM.

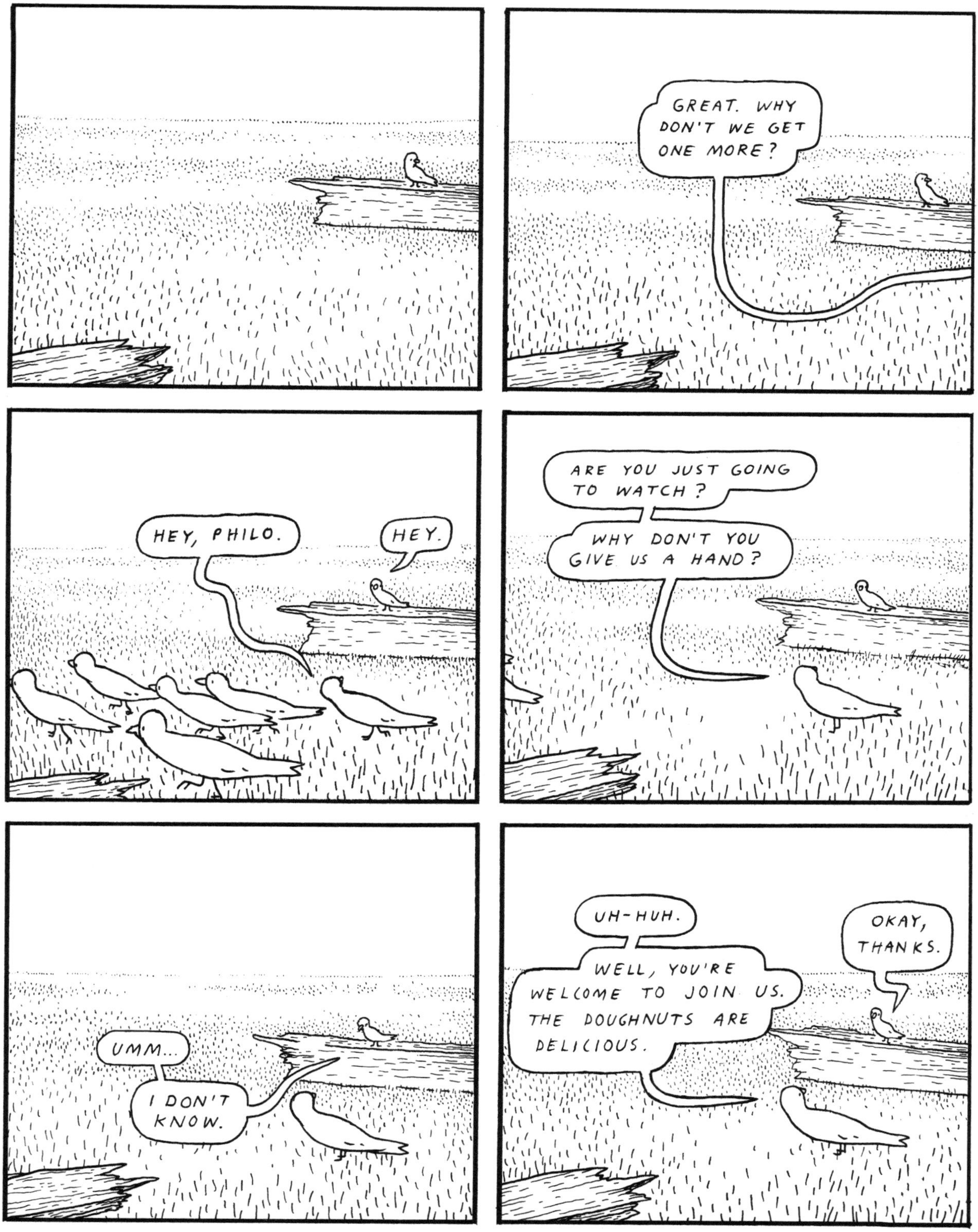
GREAT. WHY DON'T WE GET ONE MORE?
HEY, PHILO.
HEY.
ARE YOU JUST GOING TO WATCH?
WHY DON'T YOU GIVE US A HAND?
UMM...
I DON'T KNOW.
UH-HUH.
WELL, YOU'RE WELCOME TO JOIN US. THE DOUGHNUTS ARE DELICIOUS.
OKAY, THANKS.

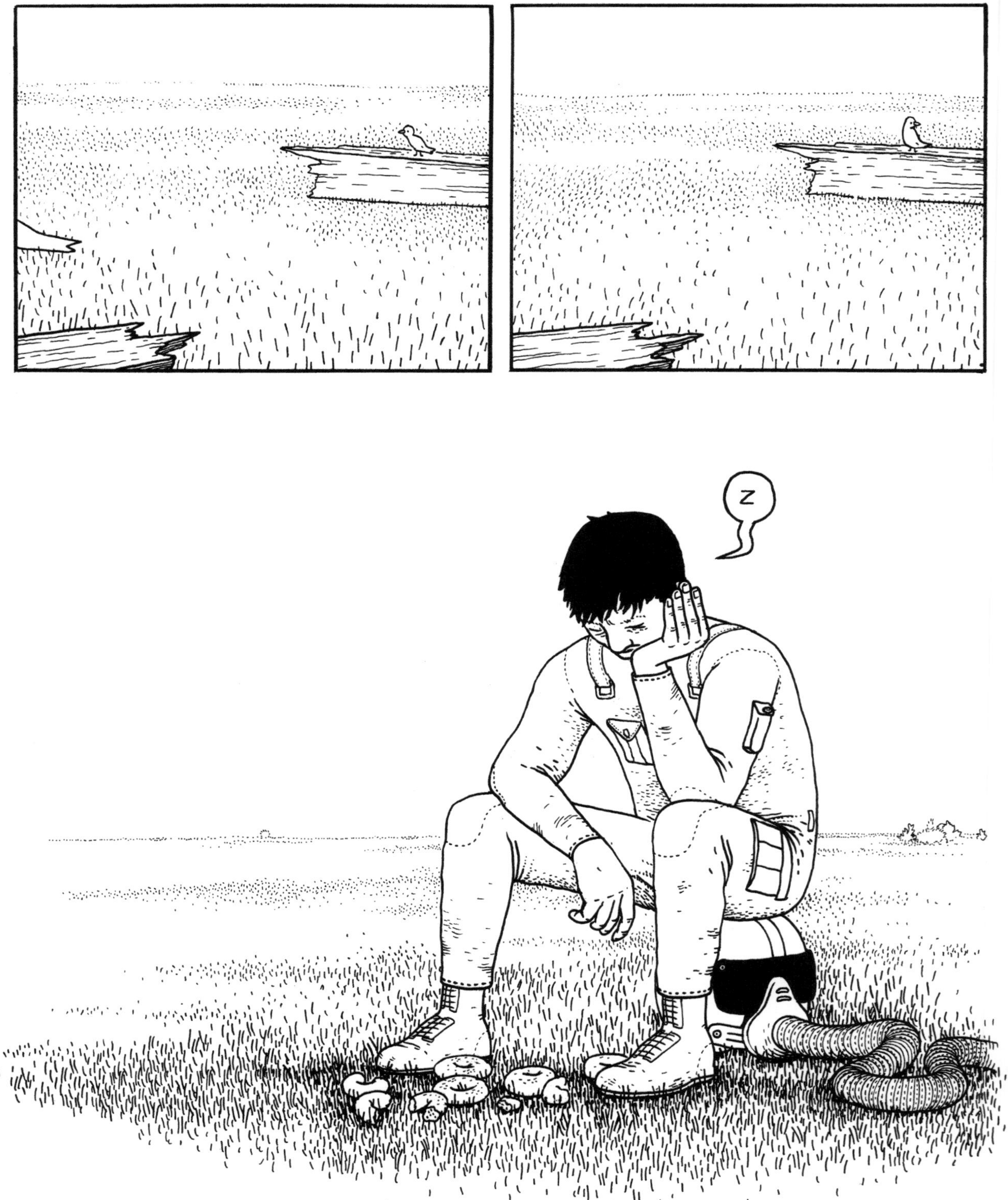
Z

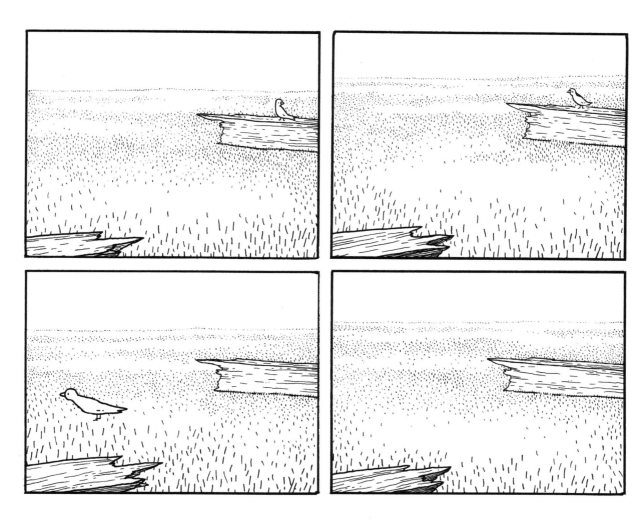

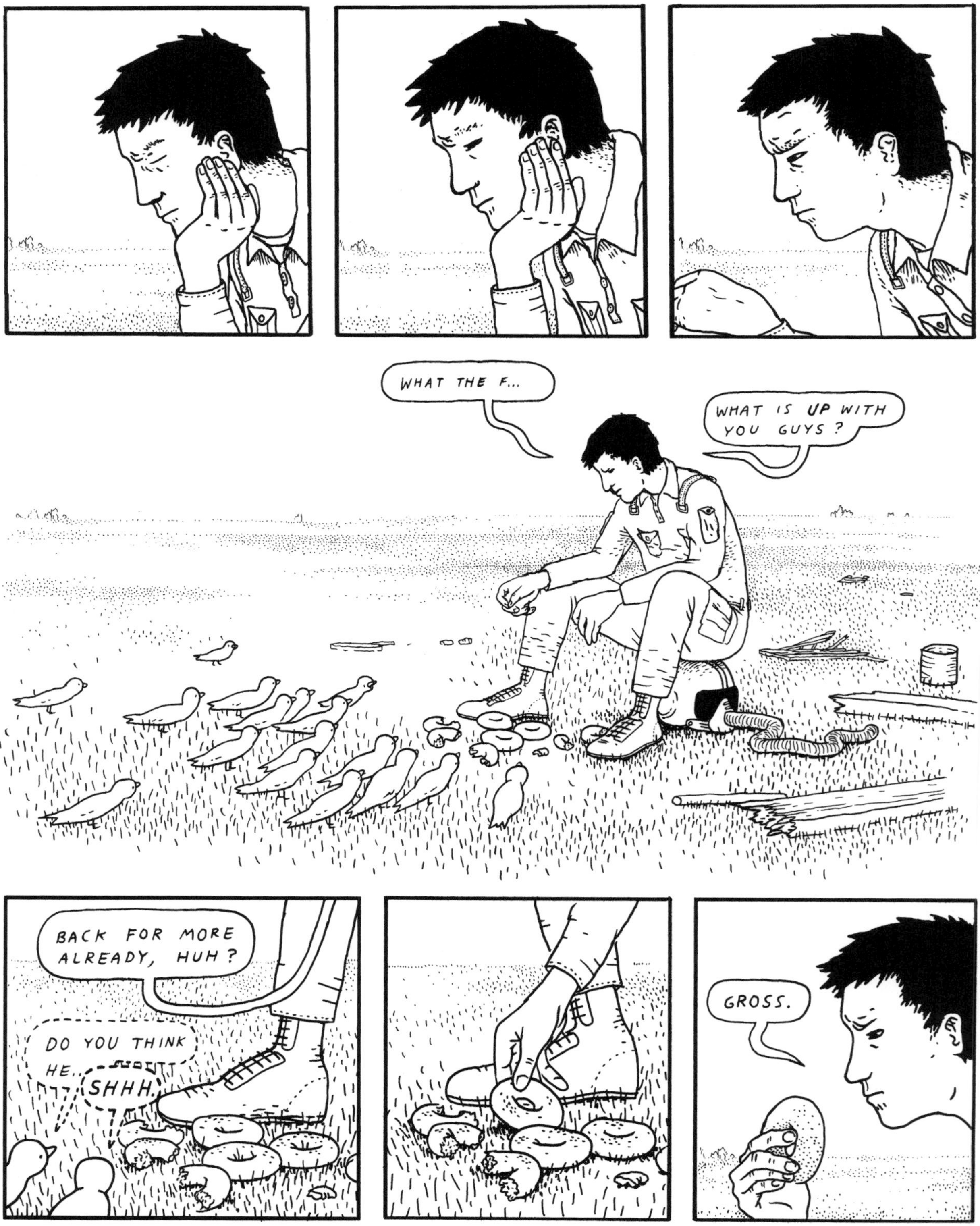
WHAT THE F...
WHAT IS UP WITH YOU GUYS?
BACK FOR MORE ALREADY, HUH?
DO YOU THINK HE...
SHHH.
GROSS.

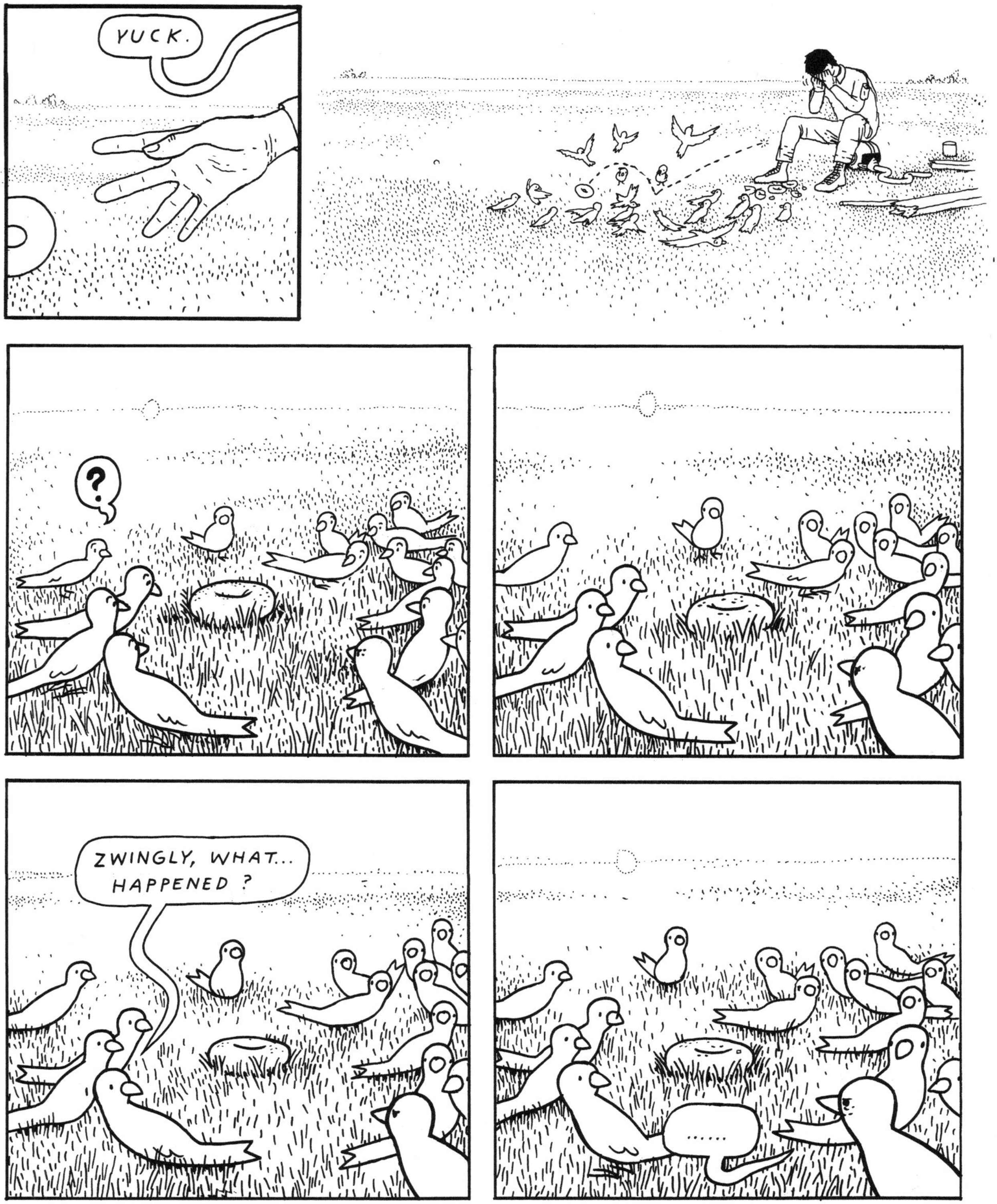
YUCK.
?
ZWINGLY, WHAT... HAPPENED ?
......

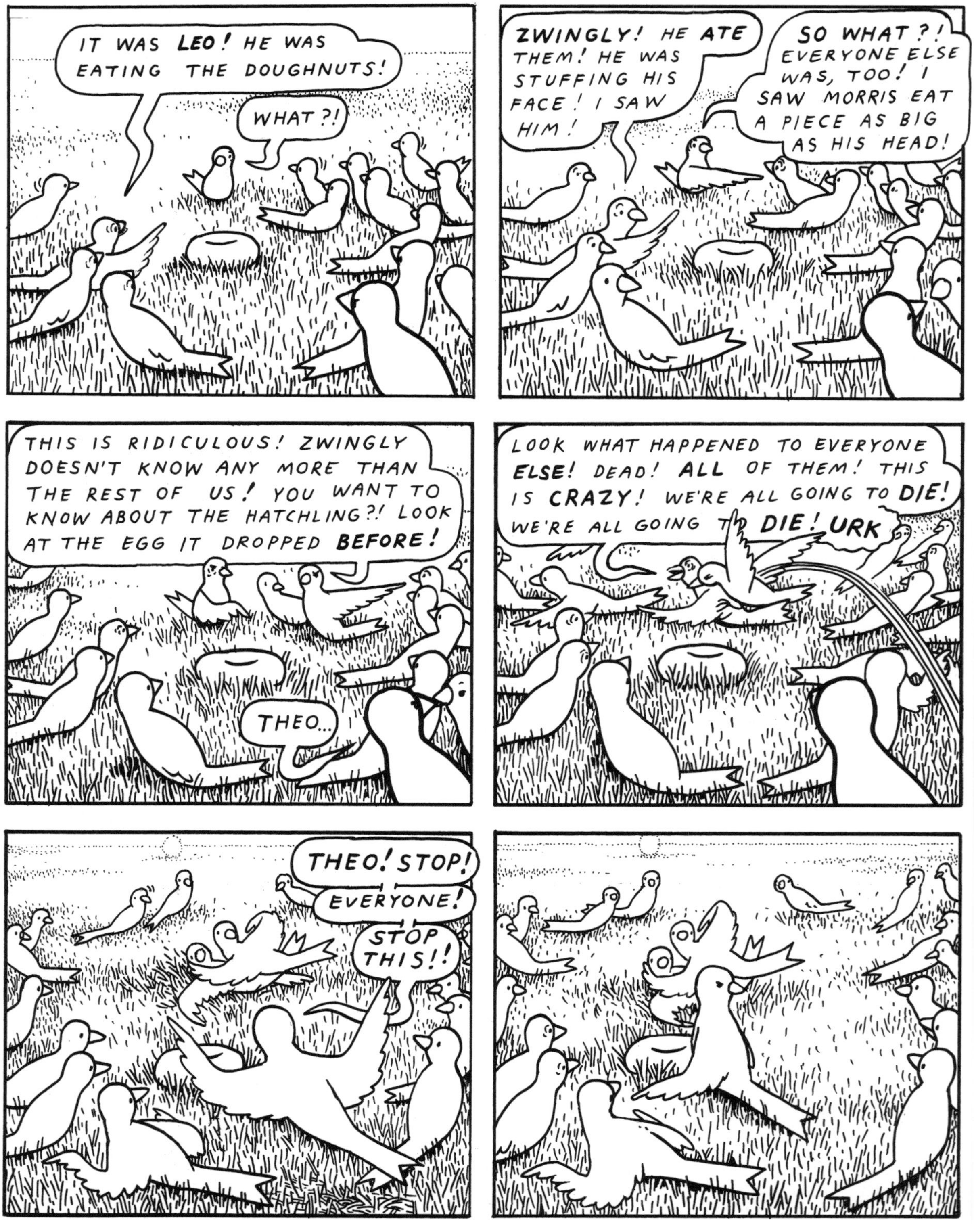
IT WAS LEO! HE WAS EATING THE DOUGHNUTS!
WHAT?!
ZWINGLY! HE ATE THEM! HE WAS STUFFING HIS FACE! I SAW HIM!
SO WHAT?! EVERYONE ELSE WAS, TOO! I SAW MORRIS EAT A PIECE AS BIG AS HIS HEAD!
THIS IS RIDICULOUS! ZWINGLY DOESN'T KNOW ANY MORE THAN THE REST OF US! YOU WANT TO KNOW ABOUT THE HATCHLING?! LOOK AT THE EGG IT DROPPED BEFORE!
THEO...
LOOK WHAT HAPPENED TO EVERYONE ELSE! DEAD! ALL OF THEM! THIS IS CRAZY! WE'RE ALL GOING TO DIE! WE'RE ALL GOING TO DIE! URK
THEO! STOP!
EVERYONE!
STOP THIS!!

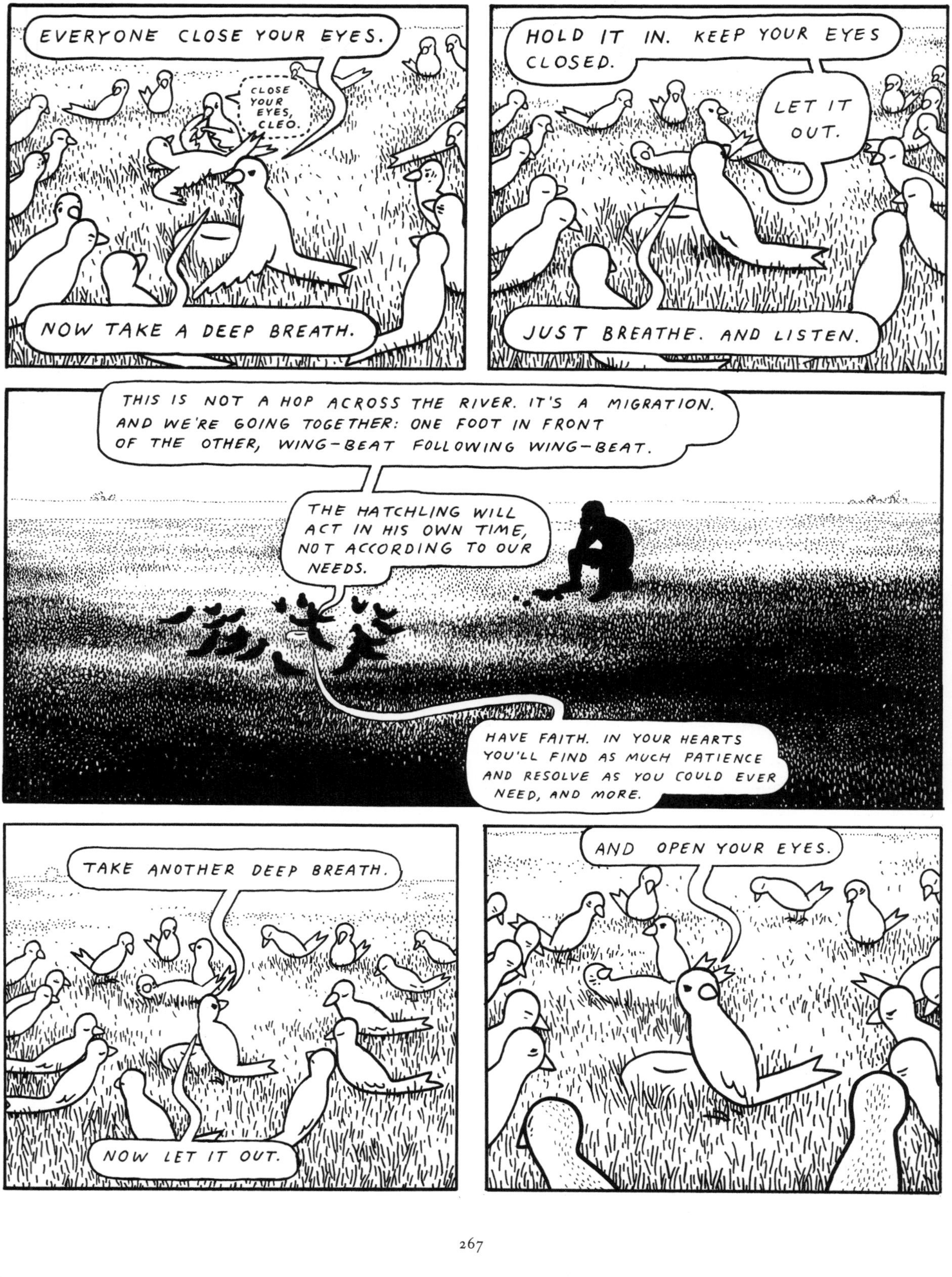
EVERYONE CLOSE YOUR EYES.
CLOSE YOUR EYES, CLEO.
NOW TAKE A DEEP BREATH.
HOLD IT IN. KEEP YOUR EYES CLOSED.
LET IT OUT.
JUST BREATHE. AND LISTEN.
THIS IS NOT A HOP ACROSS THE RIVER. IT'S A MIGRATION. AND WE'RE GOING TOGETHER: ONE FOOT IN FRONT OF THE OTHER, WING-BEAT FOLLOWING WING-BEAT.
THE HATCHLING WILL ACT IN HIS OWN TIME, NOT ACCORDING TO OUR NEEDS.
HAVE FAITH. IN YOUR HEARTS YOU'LL FIND AS MUCH PATIENCE AND RESOLVE AS YOU COULD EVER NEED, AND MORE.
TAKE ANOTHER DEEP BREATH.
NOW LET IT OUT.
AND OPEN YOUR EYES.

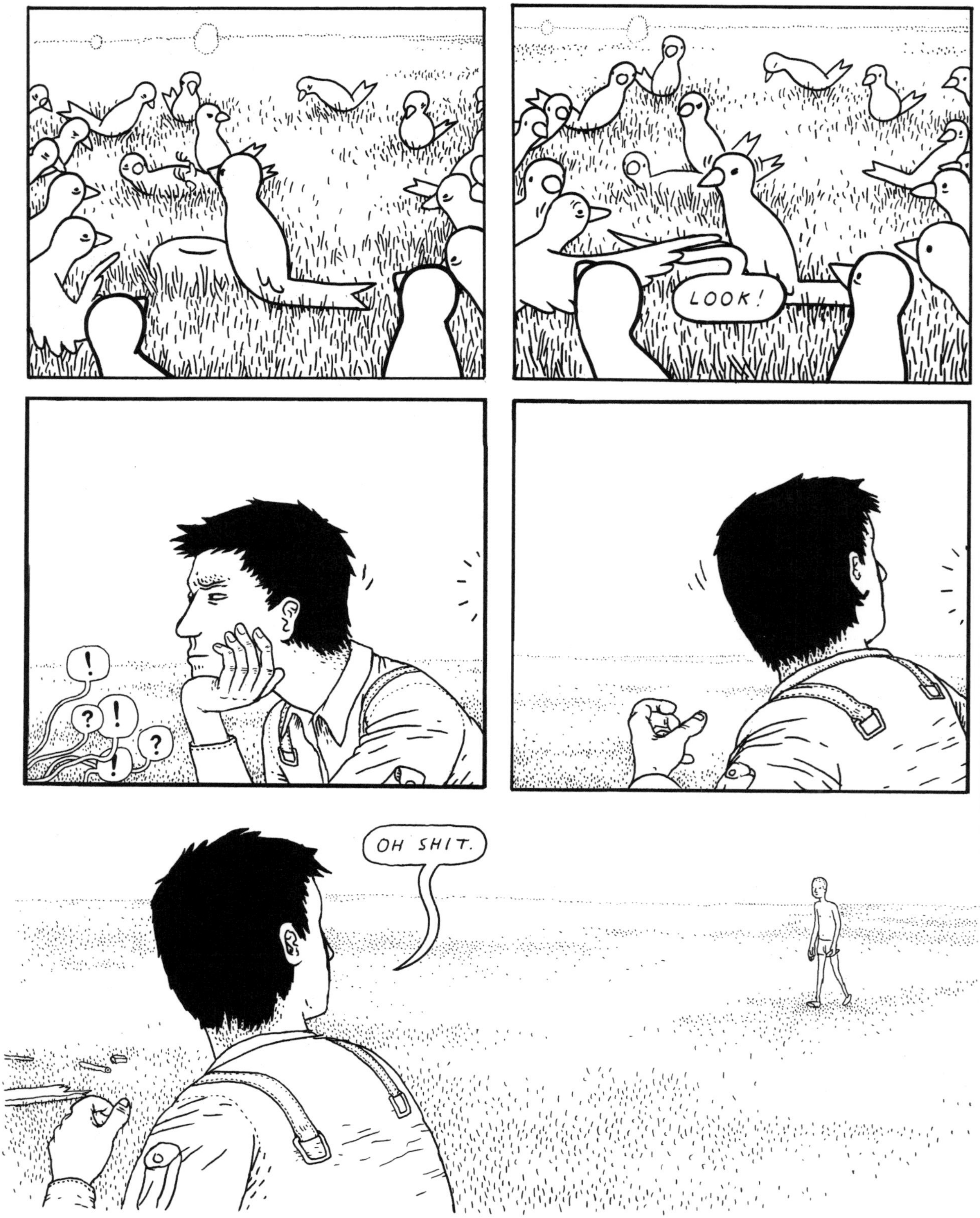
LOOK!
!
?
!
?
!
OH SHIT.

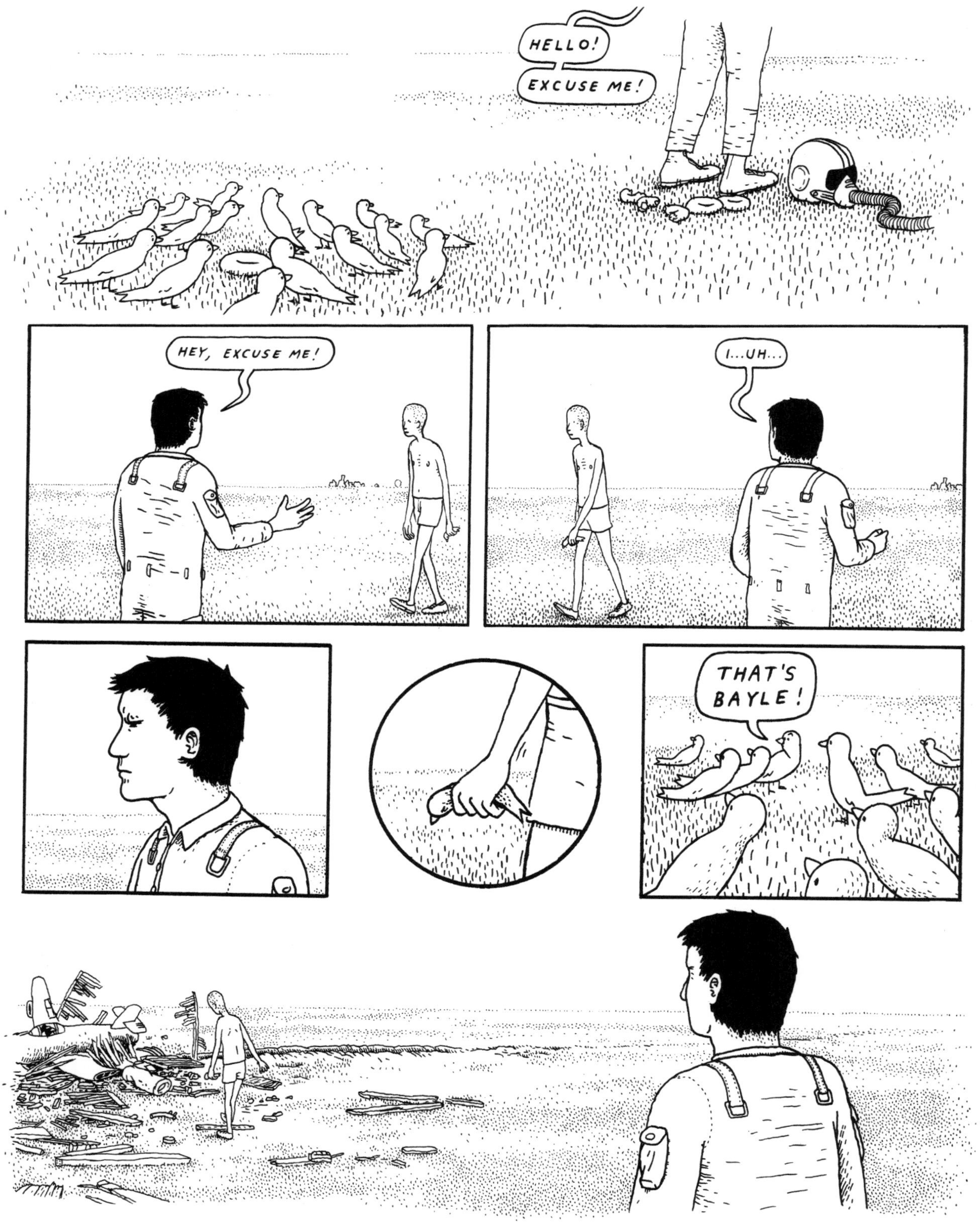
HELLO!
EXCUSE ME!
HEY, EXCUSE ME!
I...UH...
THAT'S BAYLE!

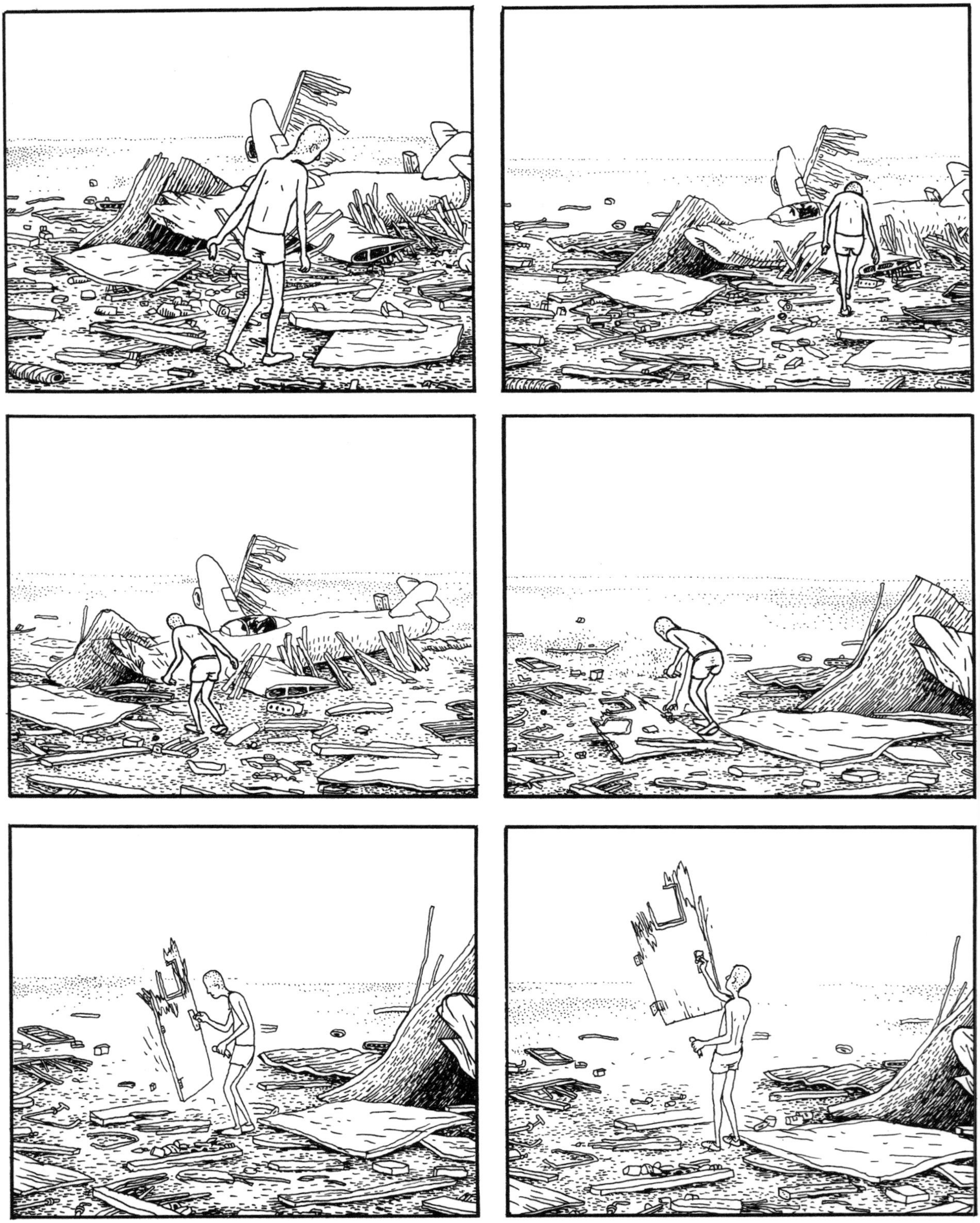

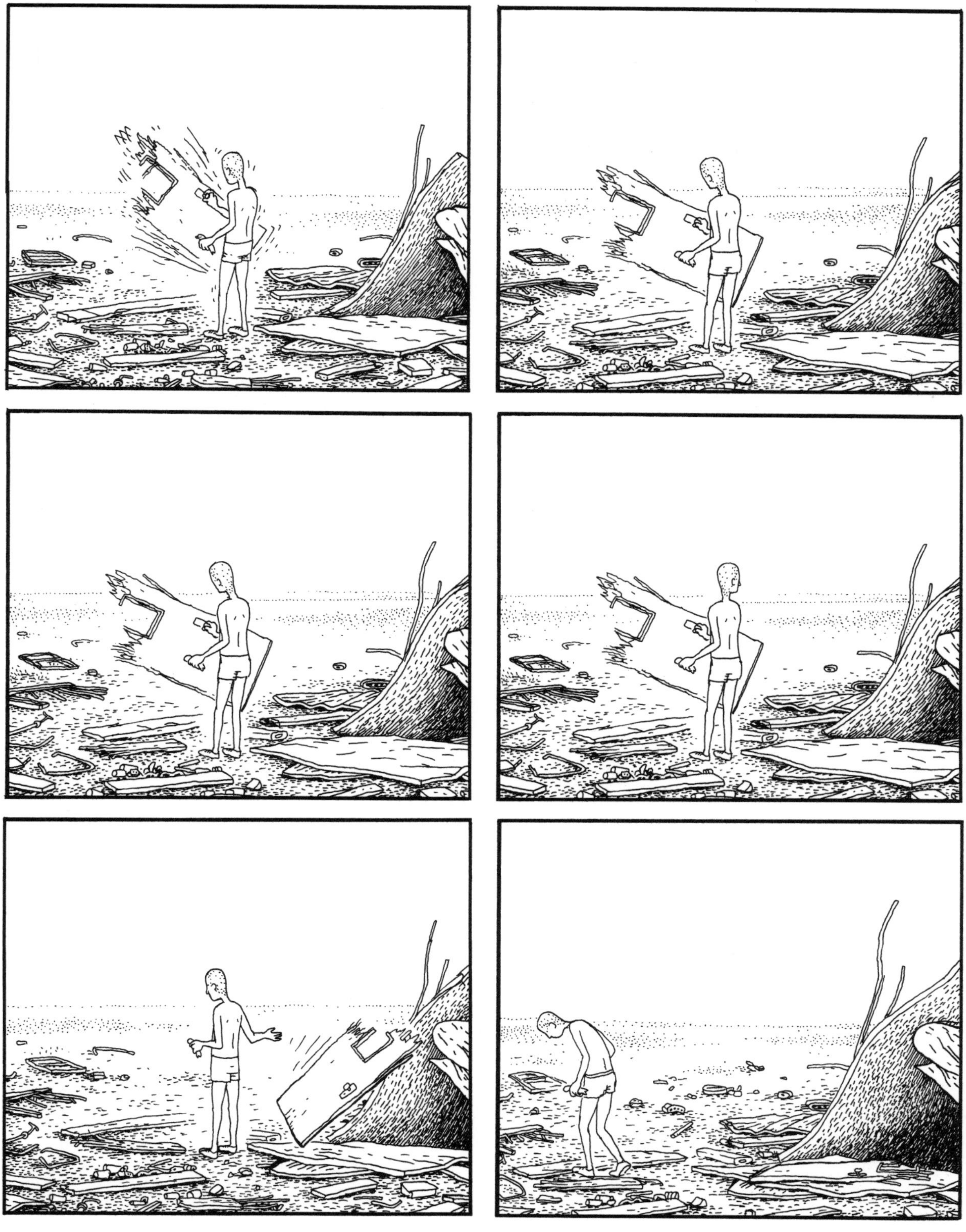

SHIT.
HEY.
HEY, IS THIS YOUR HOUSE?
I SAID, IS THIS YOUR HOUSE?

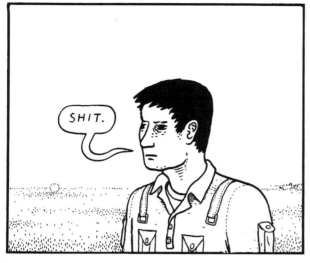

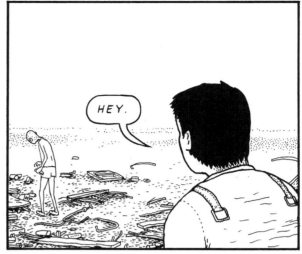

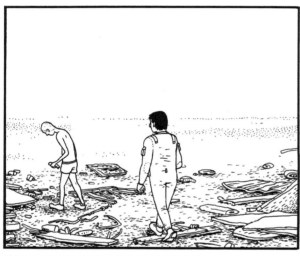

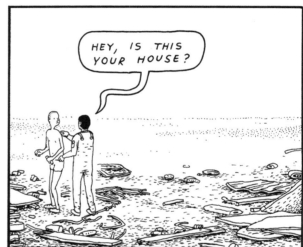

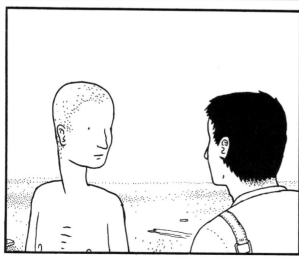

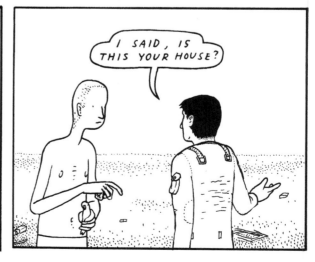

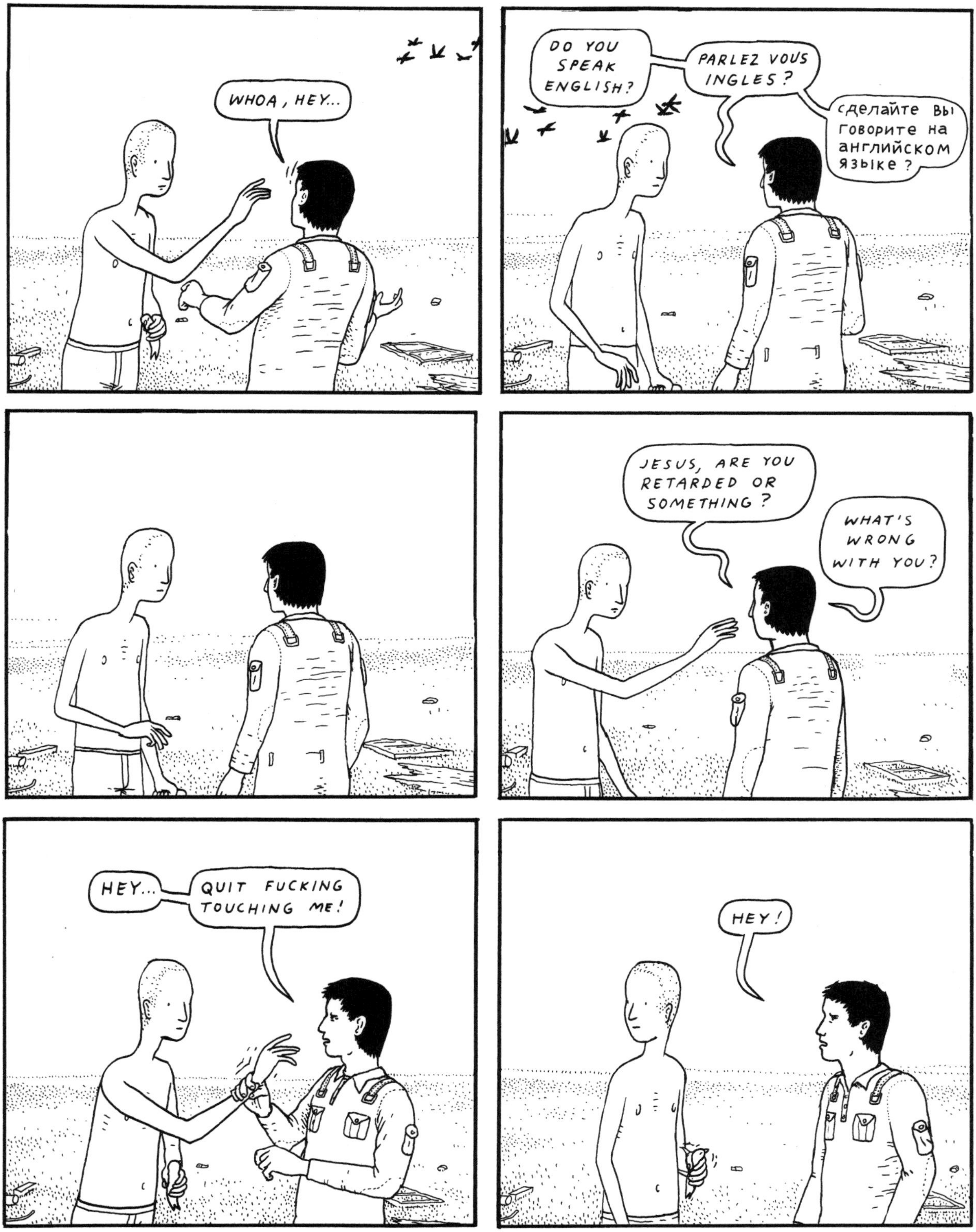
WHOA, HEY...
DO YOU SPEAK ENGLISH?
PARLEZ VOUS INGLES?
сделайте вы говорите на английском языке?
JESUS, ARE YOU RETARDED OR SOMETHING?
WHAT'S WRONG WITH YOU?
HEY...
QUIT FUCKING TOUCHING ME!
HEY!

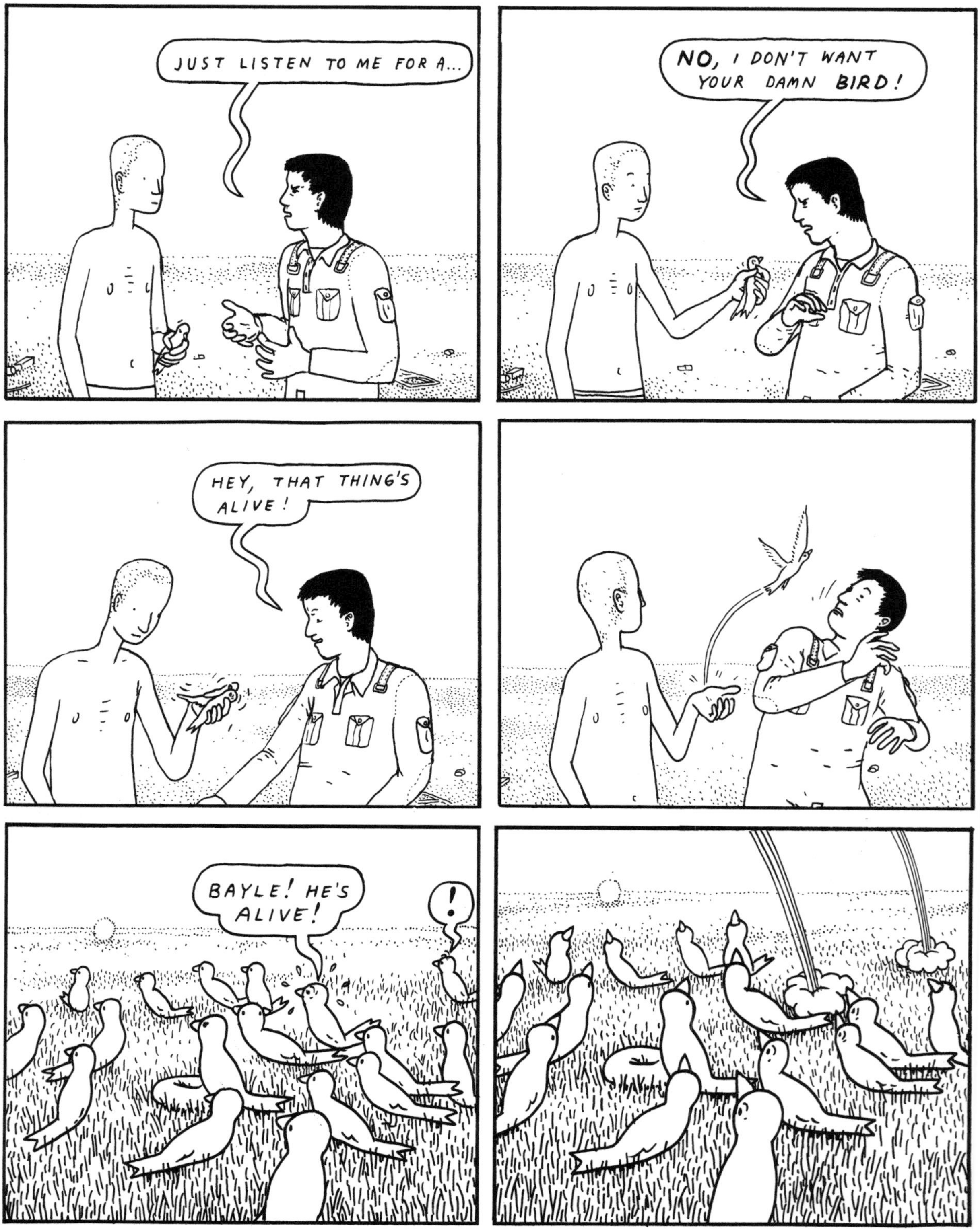
JUST LISTEN TO ME FOR A...
NO, I DON'T WANT YOUR DAMN BIRD!
HEY, THAT THING'S ALIVE!
BAYLE! HE'S ALIVE!
!

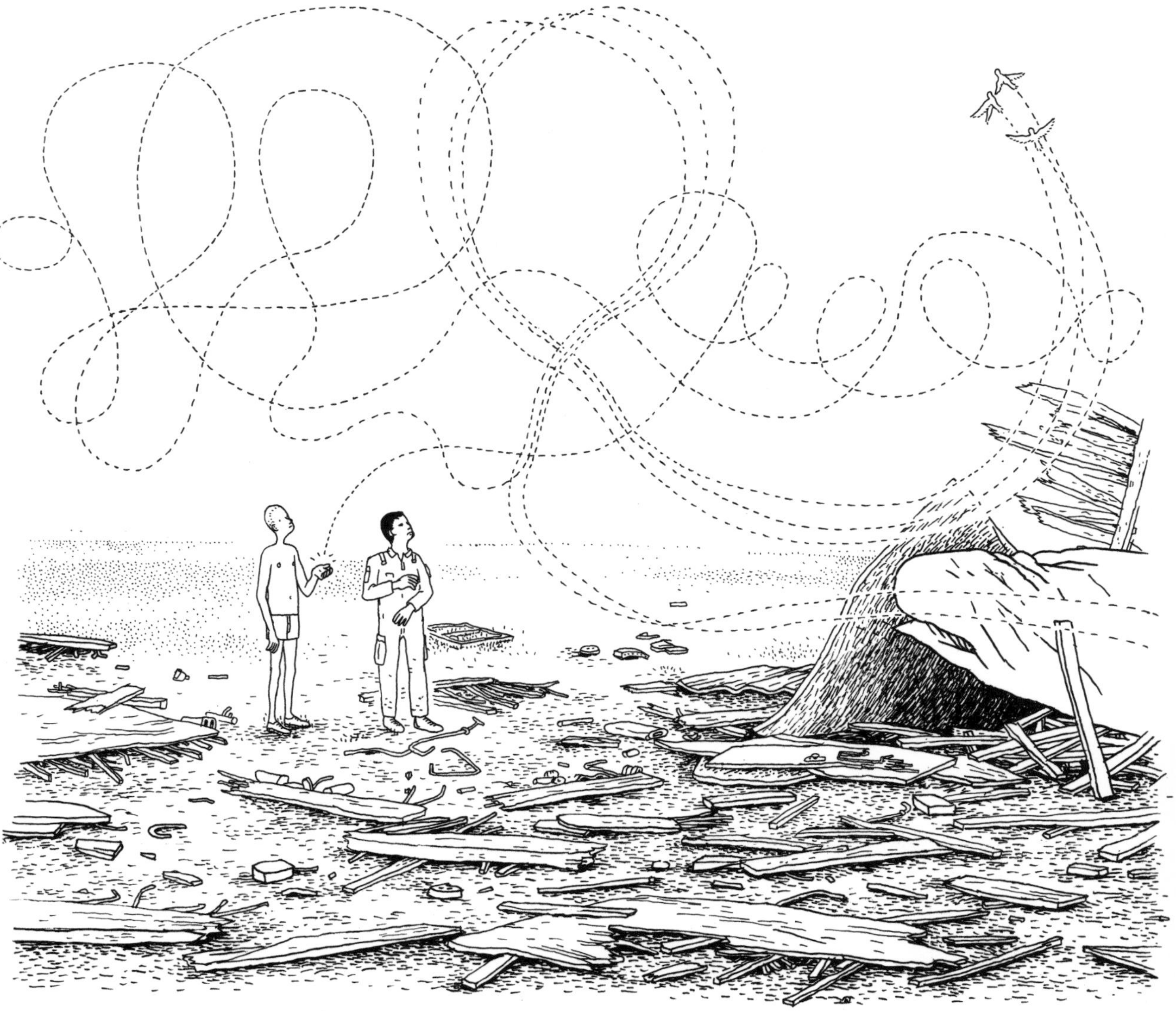

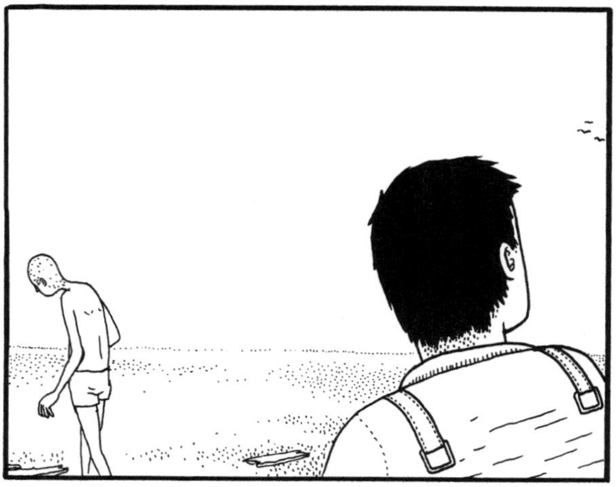

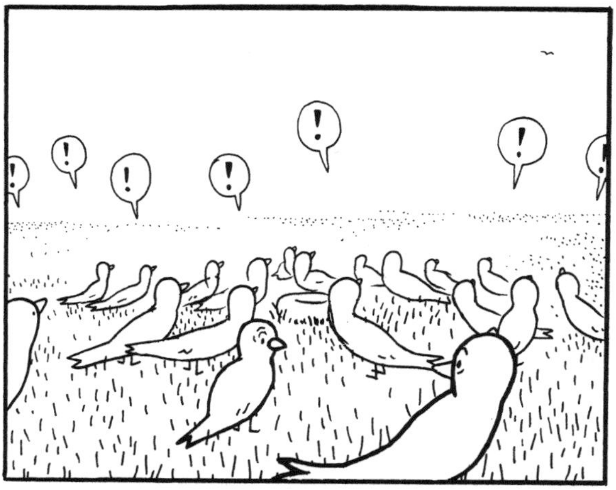
!
!
!
!
!
!
!

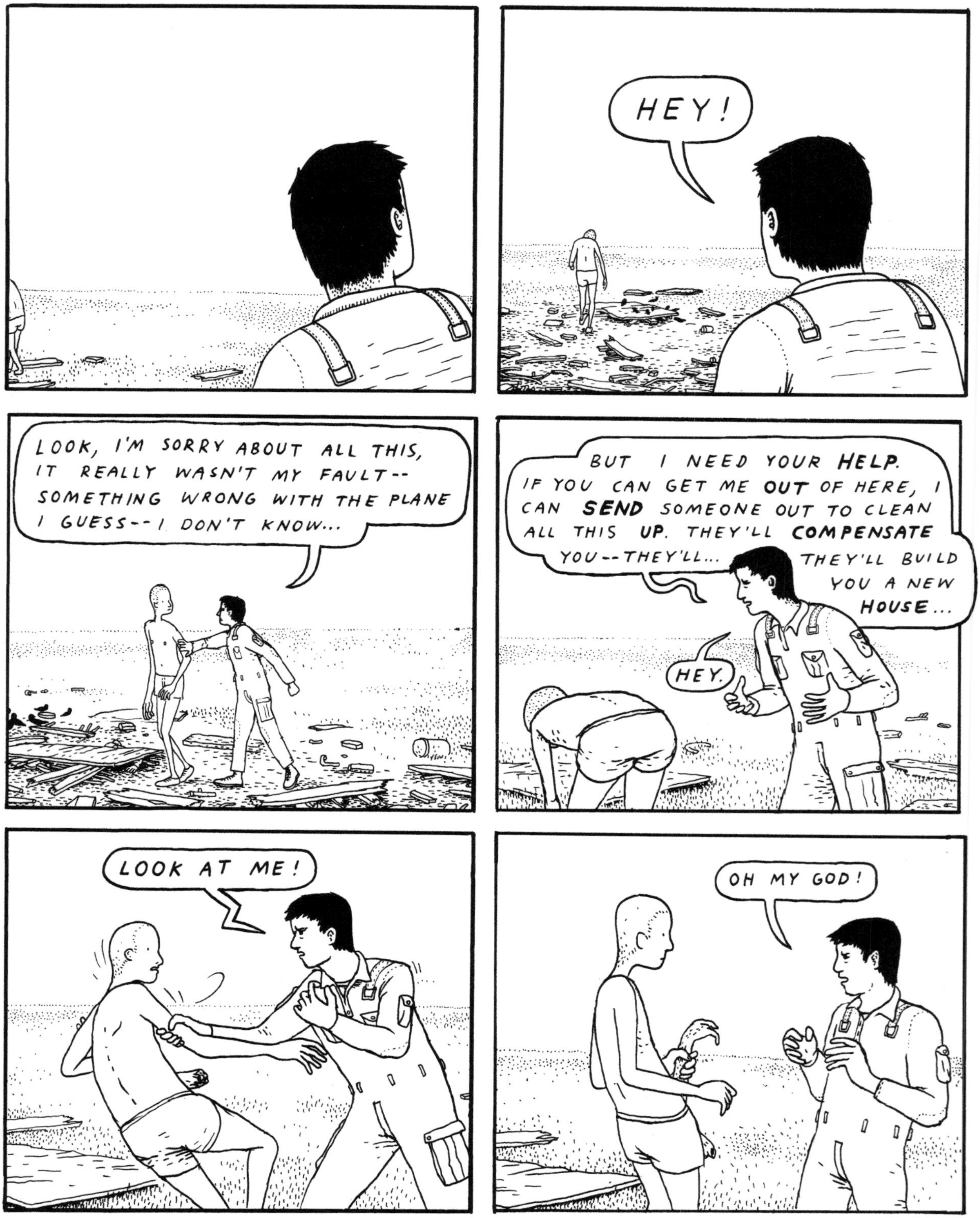
HEY!
LOOK, I'M SORRY ABOUT ALL THIS, IT REALLY WASN'T MY FAULT-- SOMETHING WRONG WITH THE PLANE I GUESS-- I DON'T KNOW...
BUT I NEED YOUR HELP. IF YOU CAN GET ME OUT OF HERE, I CAN SEND SOMEONE OUT TO CLEAN ALL THIS UP. THEY'LL COMPENSATE YOU--THEY'LL...
THEY'LL BUILD YOU A NEW HOUSE...
HEY.
LOOK AT ME!
OH MY GOD!

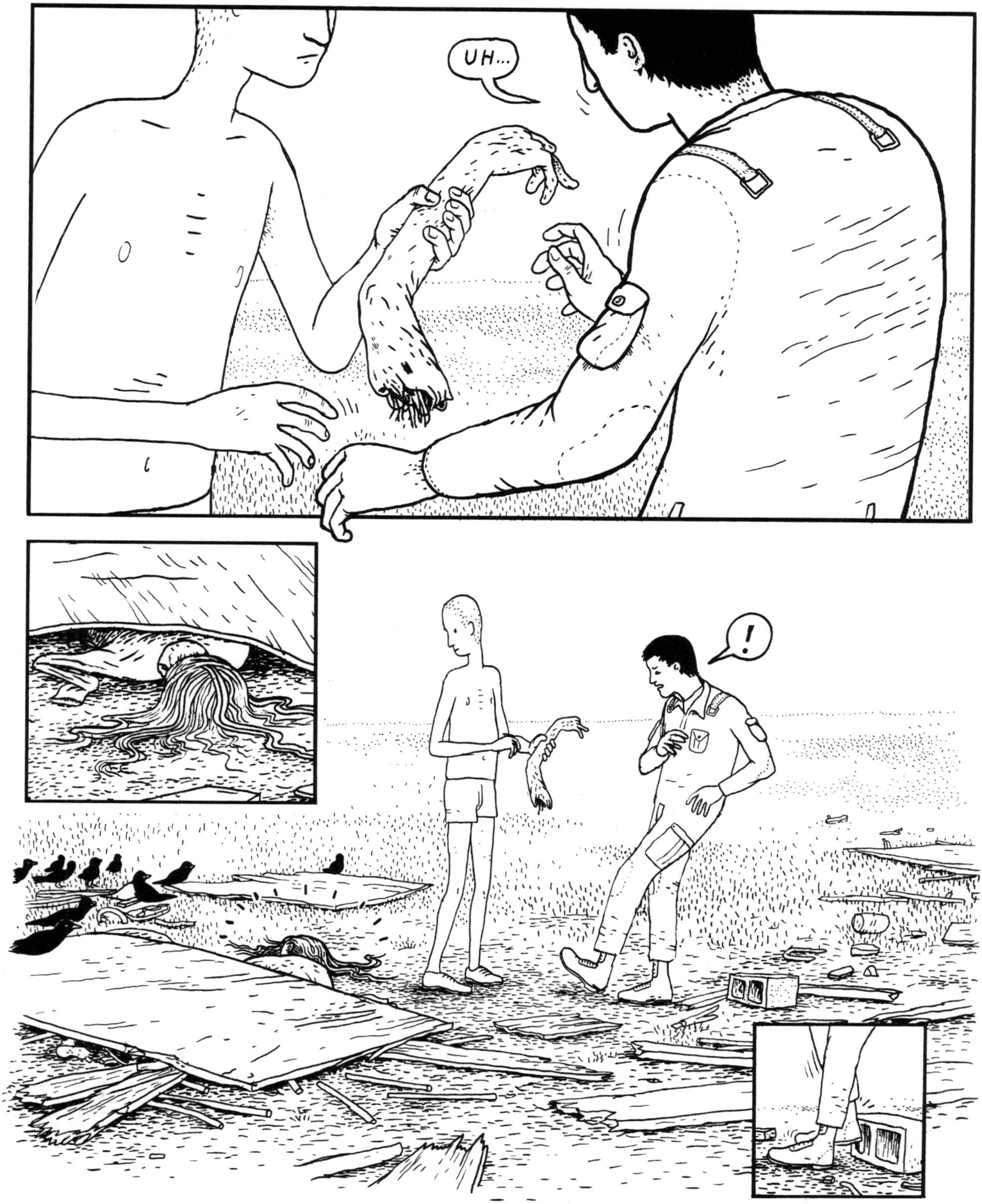
UH...
!

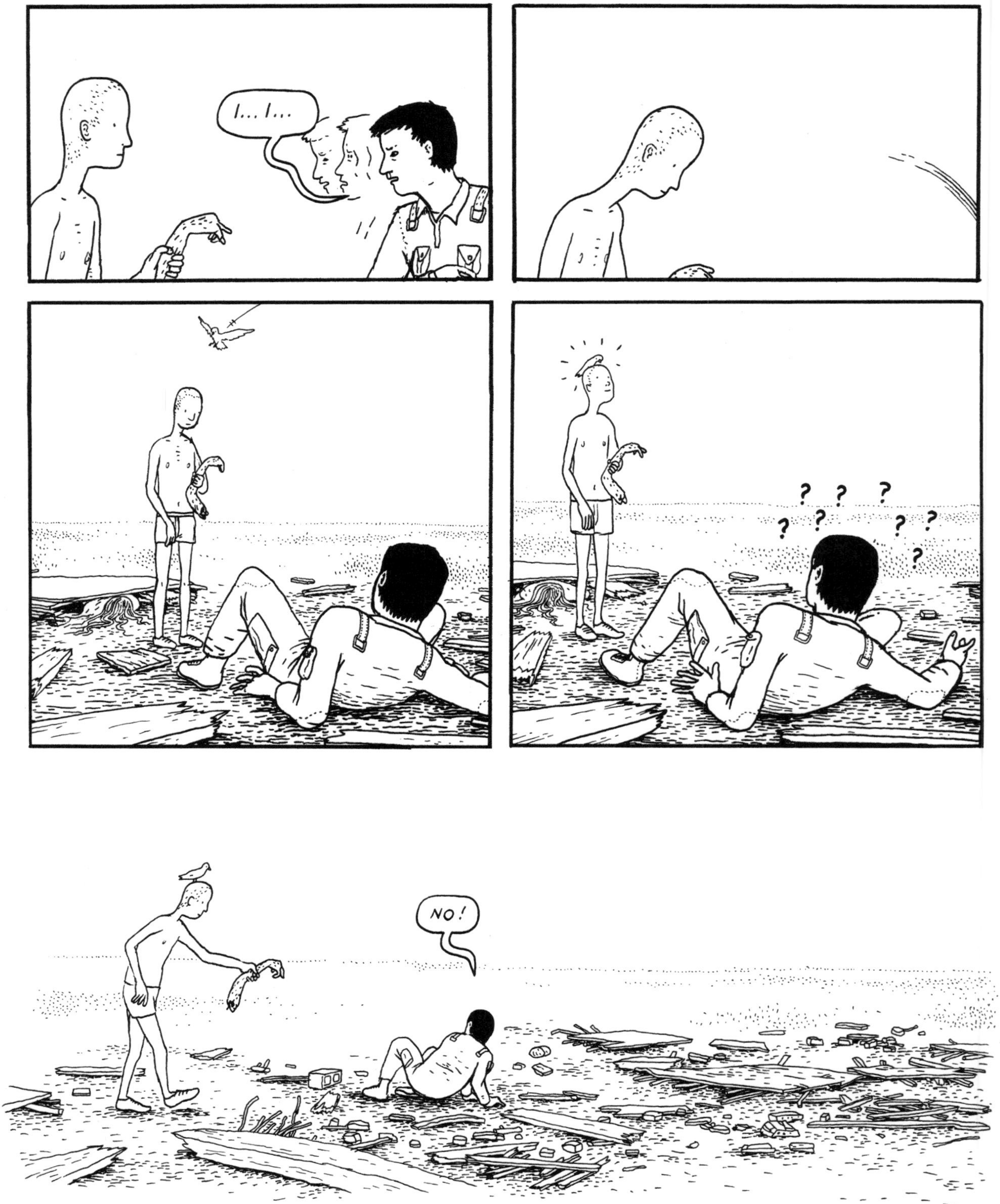
I... I...
NO!

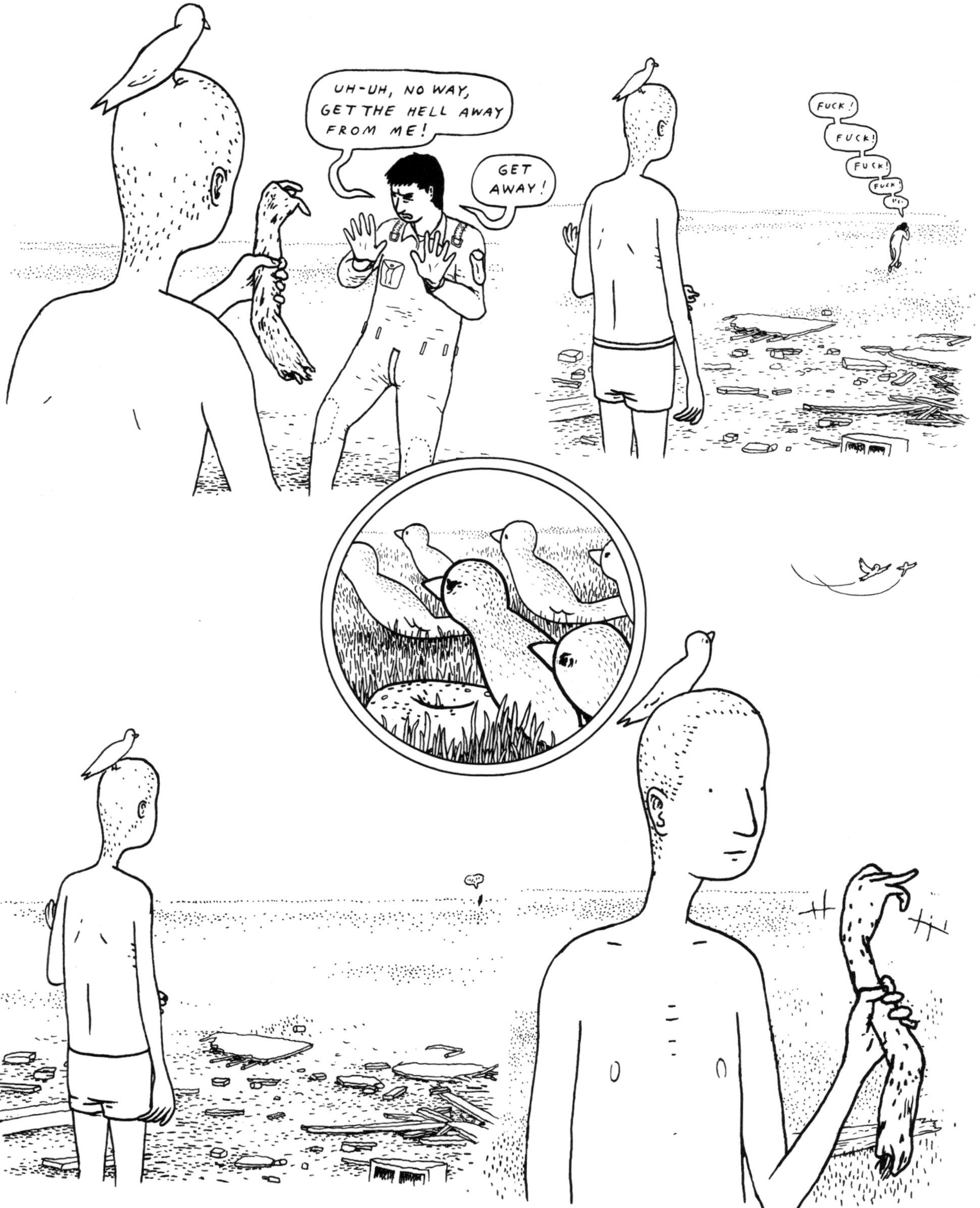
UH-UH, NO WAY, GET THE HELL AWAY FROM ME!
GET AWAY!
FUCK!
FUCK!
FUCK!
FUCK!

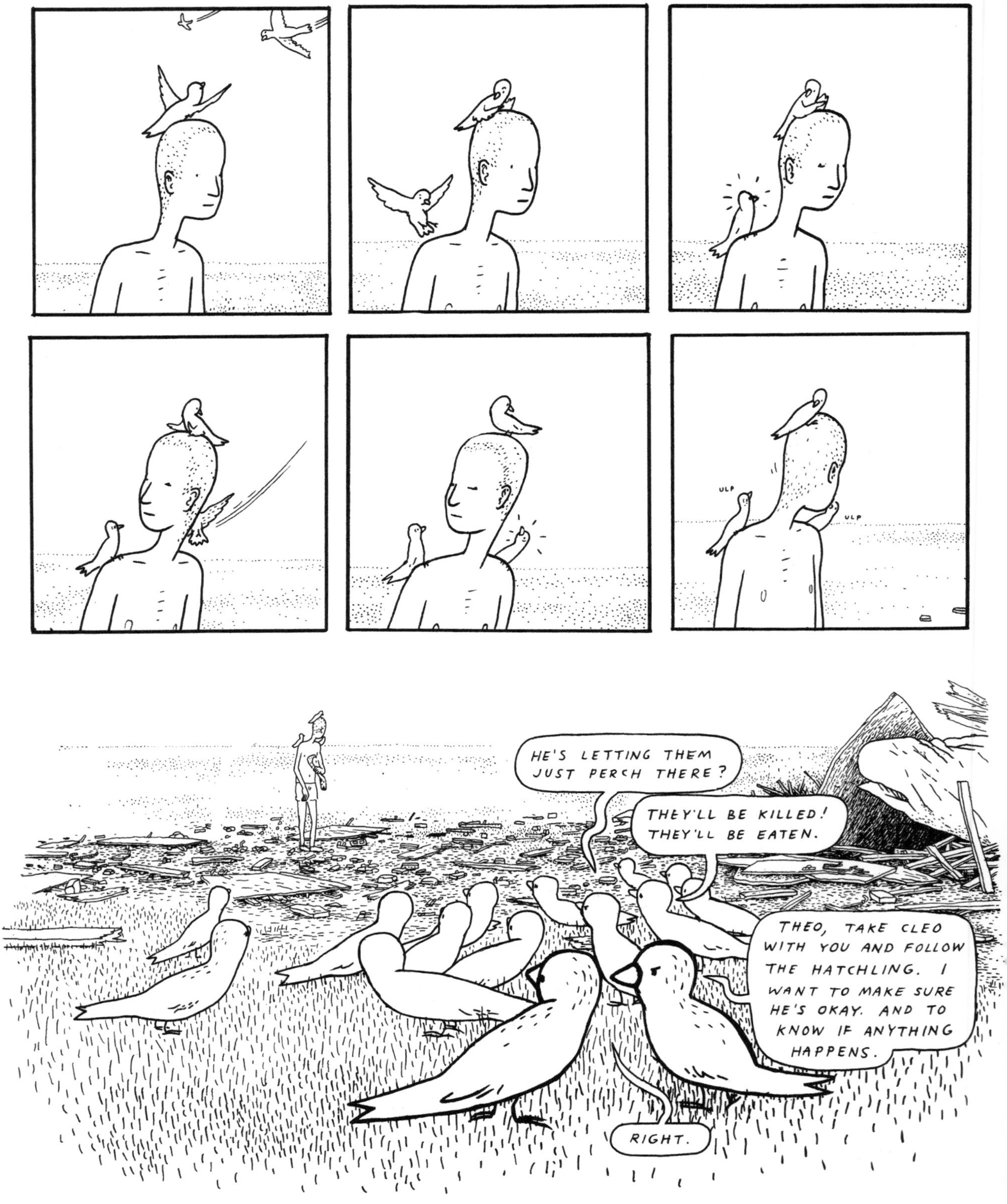
ULP
ULP
HE'S LETTING THEM JUST PERCH THERE?
THEY'LL BE KILLED! THEY'LL BE EATEN.
THEO, TAKE CLEO WITH YOU AND FOLLOW THE HATCHLING. I WANT TO MAKE SURE HE'S OKAY. AND TO KNOW IF ANYTHING HAPPENS.
RIGHT.

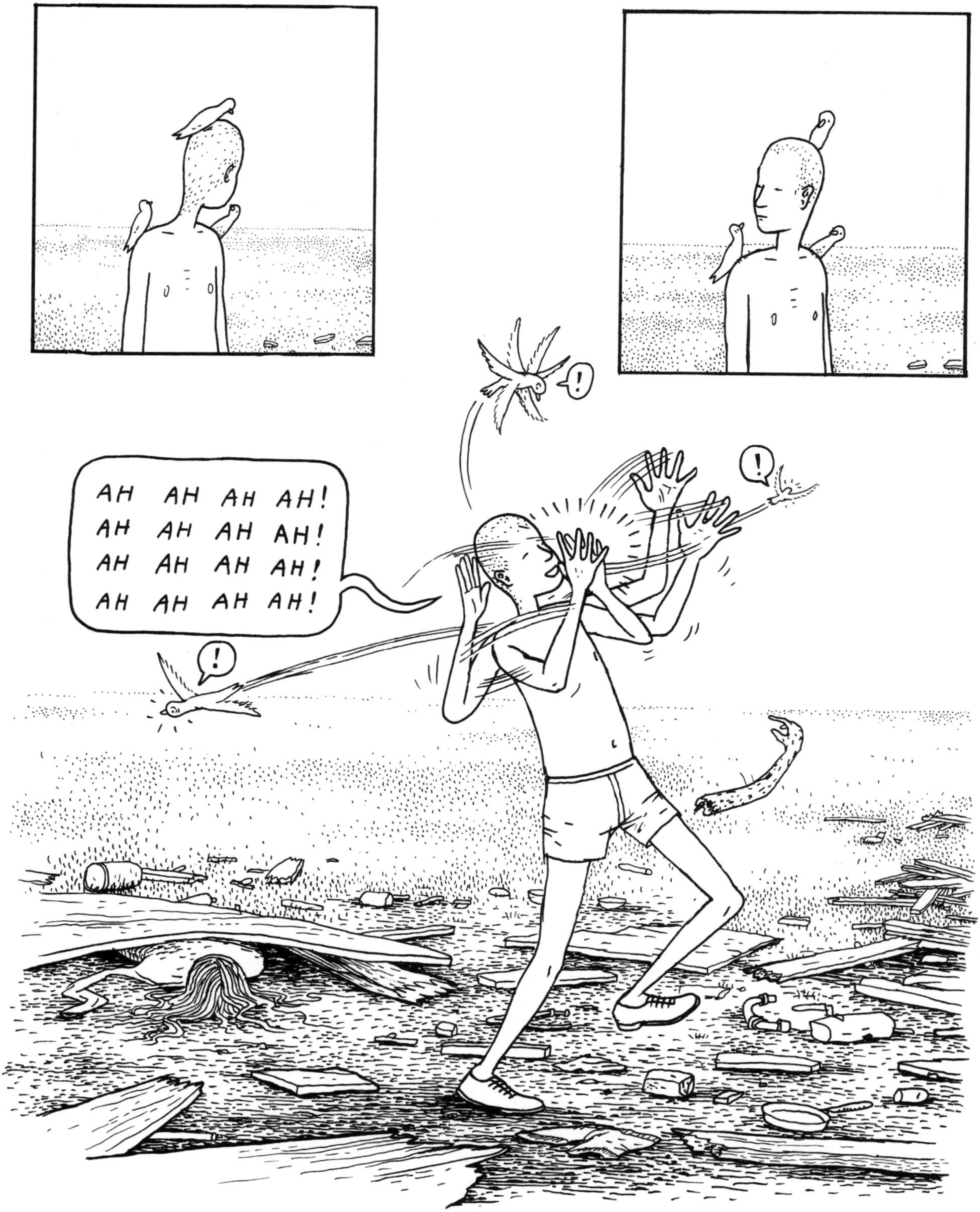
!
AH AH AH AH! AH AH AH AH! AH AH AH AH! AH AH AH AH!
!
!

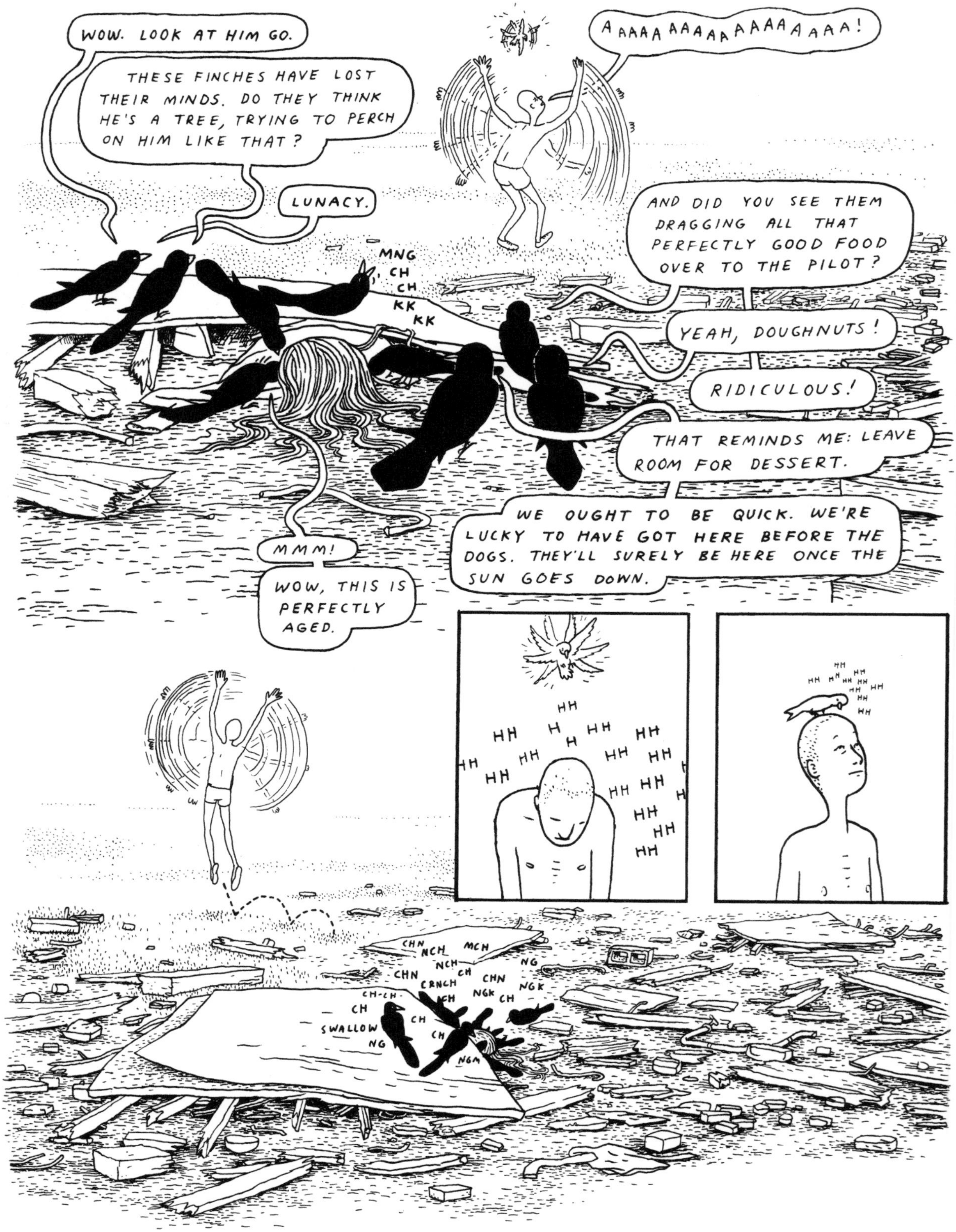
WOW. LOOK AT HIM GO.
THESE FINCHES HAVE LOST THEIR MINDS. DO THEY THINK HE'S A TREE, TRYING TO PERCH ON HIM LIKE THAT?
LUNACY.
AAAAAAAAAAAAAAAAAA!
MNG CH CH KK KK
AND DID YOU SEE THEM DRAGGING ALL THAT PERFECTLY GOOD FOOD OVER TO THE PILOT?
YEAH, DOUGHNUTS!
RIDICULOUS!
THAT REMINDS ME: LEAVE ROOM FOR DESSERT.
WE OUGHT TO BE QUICK. WE'RE LUCKY TO HAVE GOT HERE BEFORE THE DOGS. THEY'LL SURELY BE HERE ONCE THE SUN GOES DOWN.
MMM!
WOW, THIS IS PERFECTLY AGED.
CHN NCH MCH NCH NG CHN CH CHN CRNCH NGK NGK CH CH-CH CH SWALLOW CH NG CH NGM

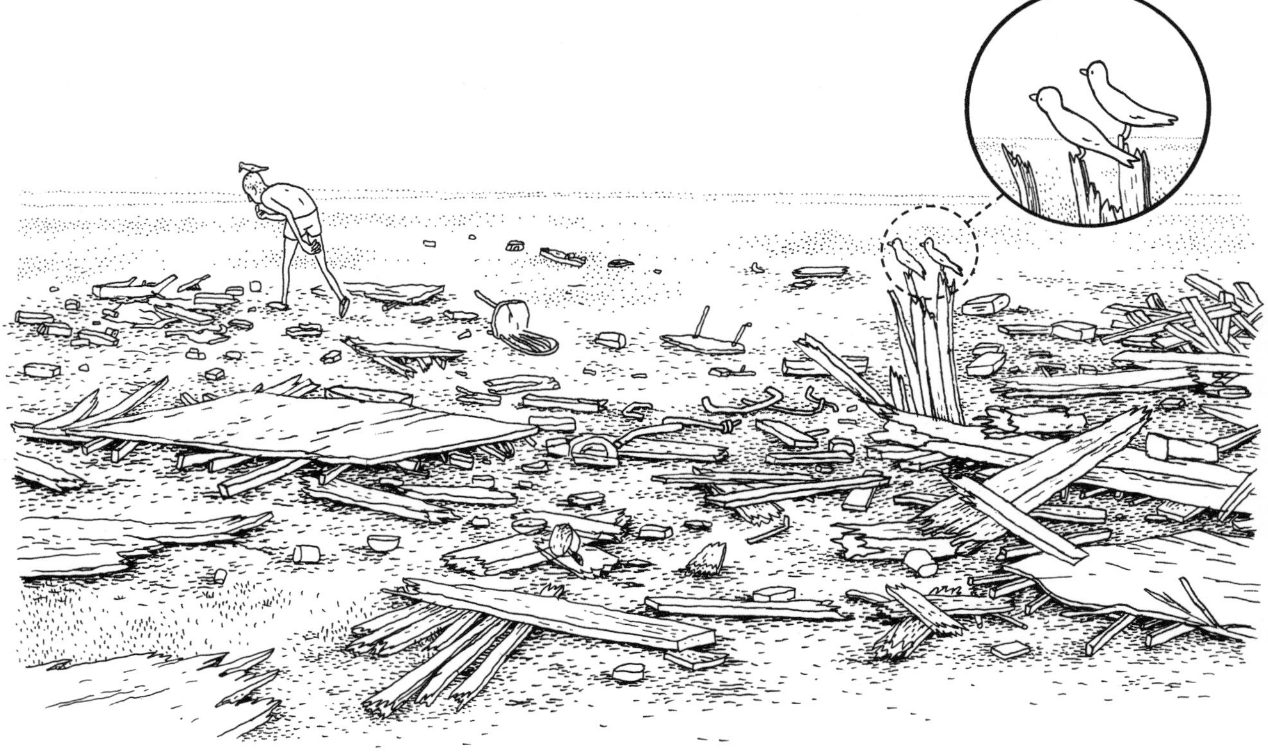

FOR THE REST OF THE DAY, ZWINGLY AND THE OTHERS AVOIDED ANY OVERTURES FROM HELEN AND I. WE BOTH STILL WANTED TO MAKE THE GIANT'S HATCHLING FEEL WELCOME, BUT THEY WEREN'T INTERESTED. APPARENTLY WE'D CROSSED SOME SORT OF LINE. BAYLE CONTINUED RIDING AROUND ON THE GRANDSON'S HEAD, INTERRUPTED ONLY OCCASIONALLY BY A BIT OF JUMPING AROUND. I WAS SYMPATHETIC--BAYLE REALLY SEEMED TO HAVE BEEN CHANGED--BUT PROXIMITY TO SUCH A LARGE ANIMAL MADE ME ANXIOUS. WE KEPT A CLOSE WATCH, BUT NEITHER OF US COULD GET THE NERVE UP TO JOIN HIM AGAIN. FOR THE MOMENT AT LEAST.

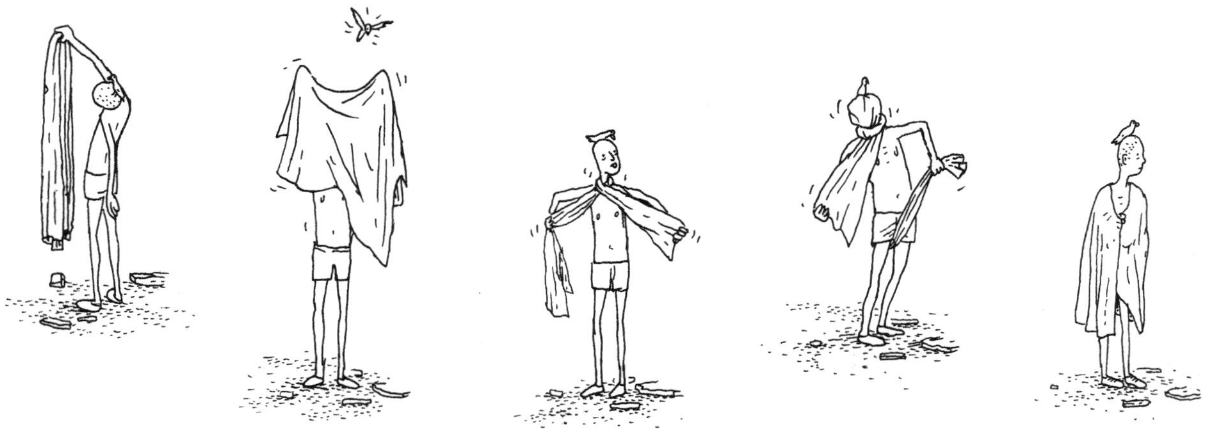

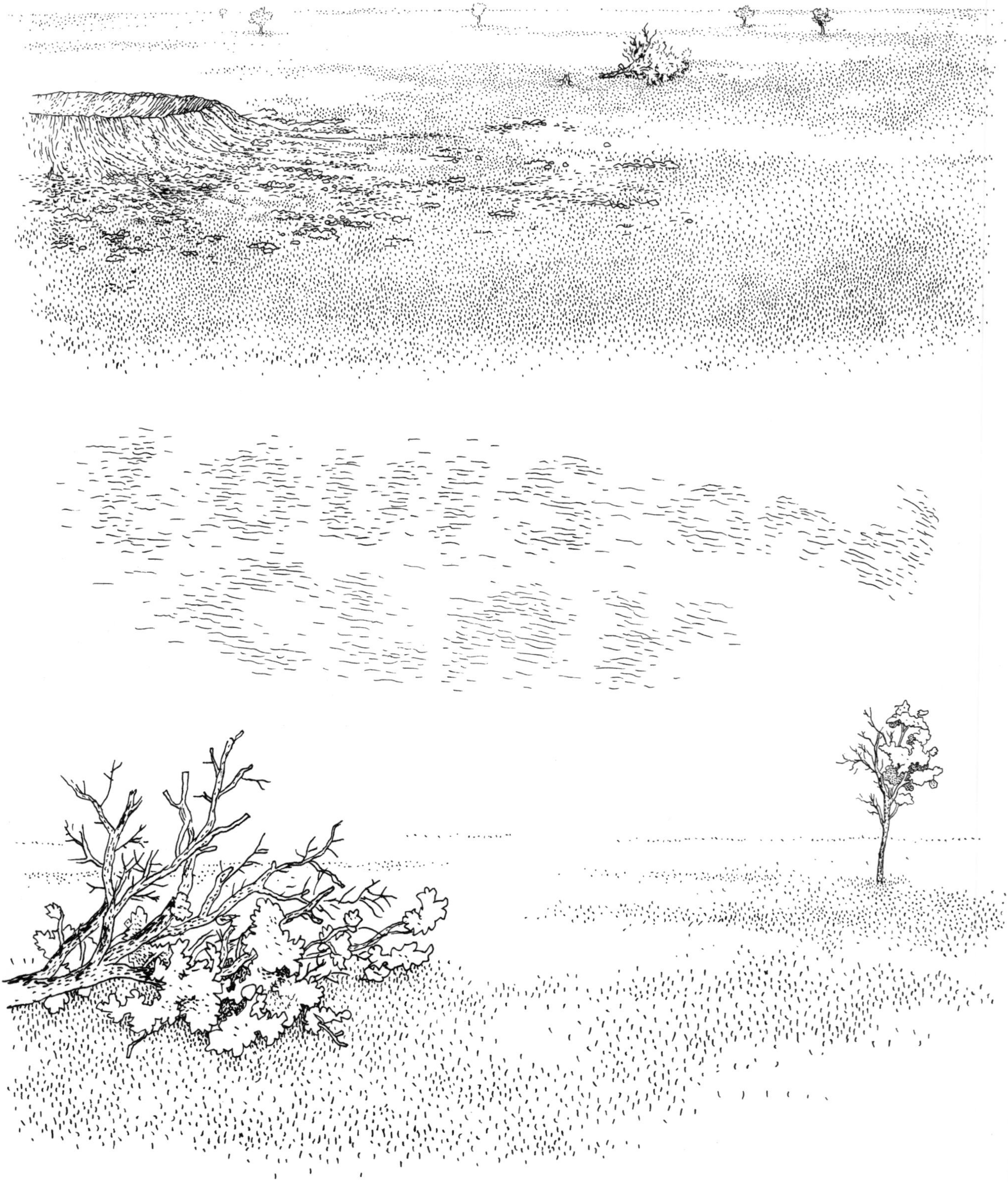

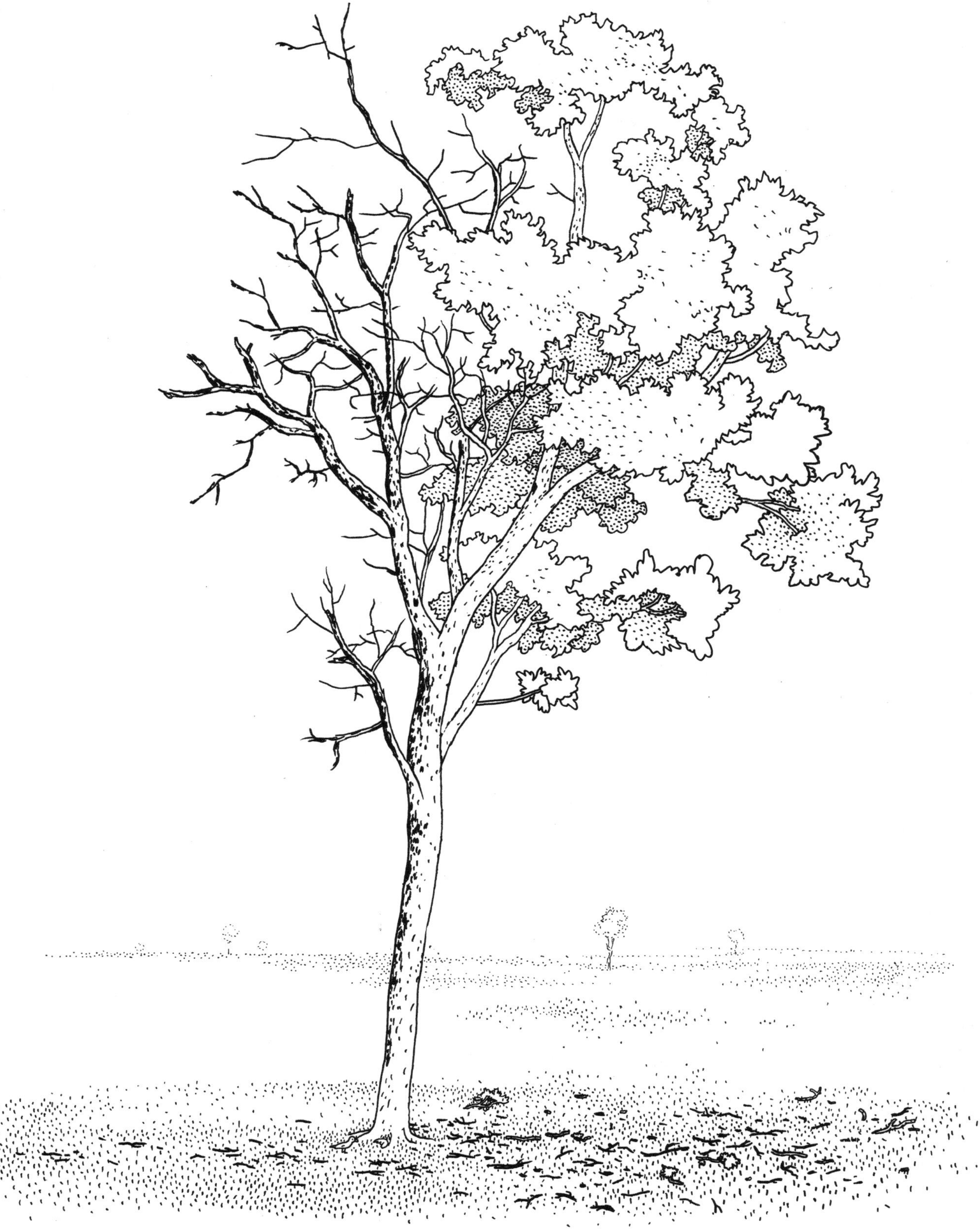

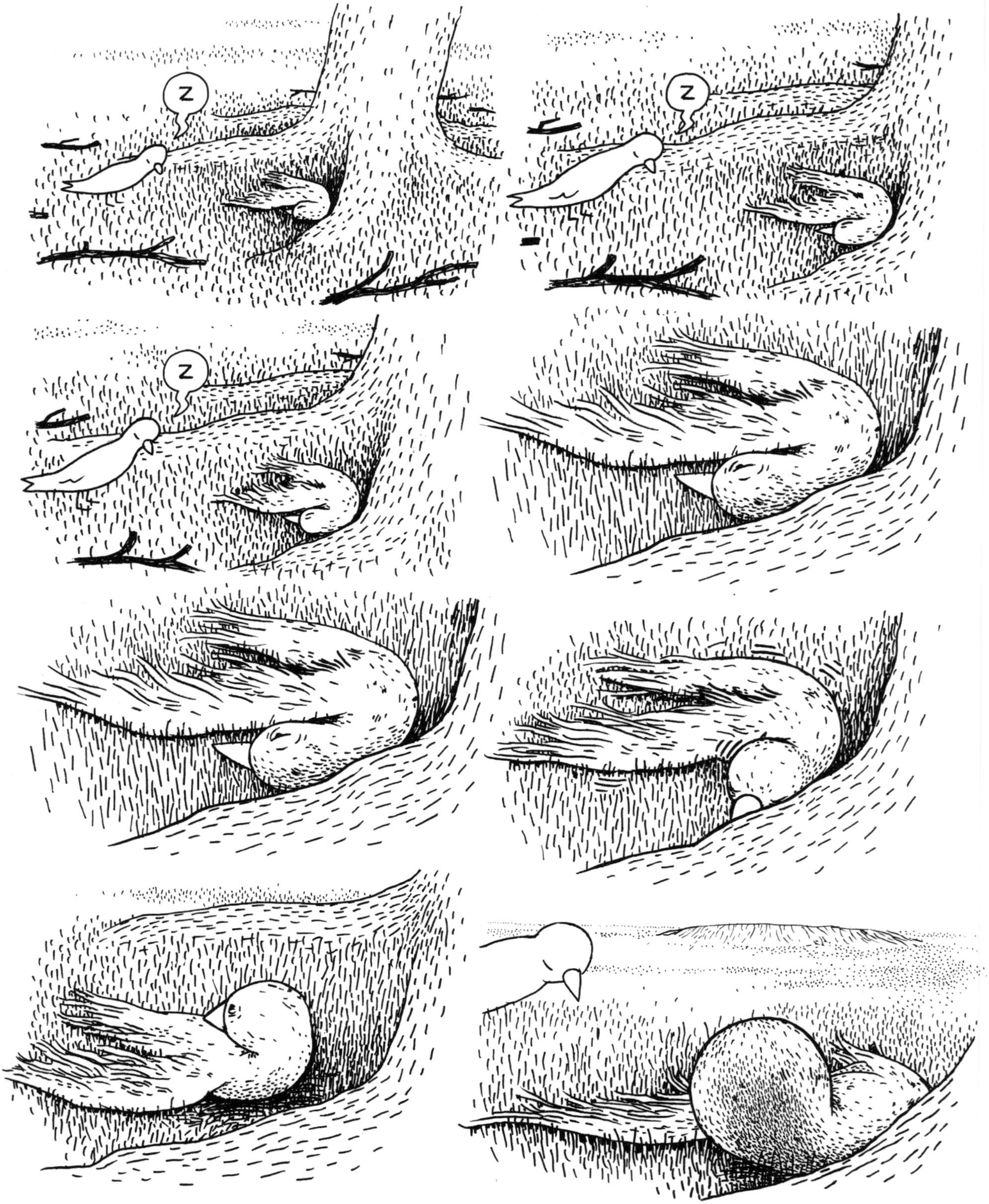
Z
Z
Z

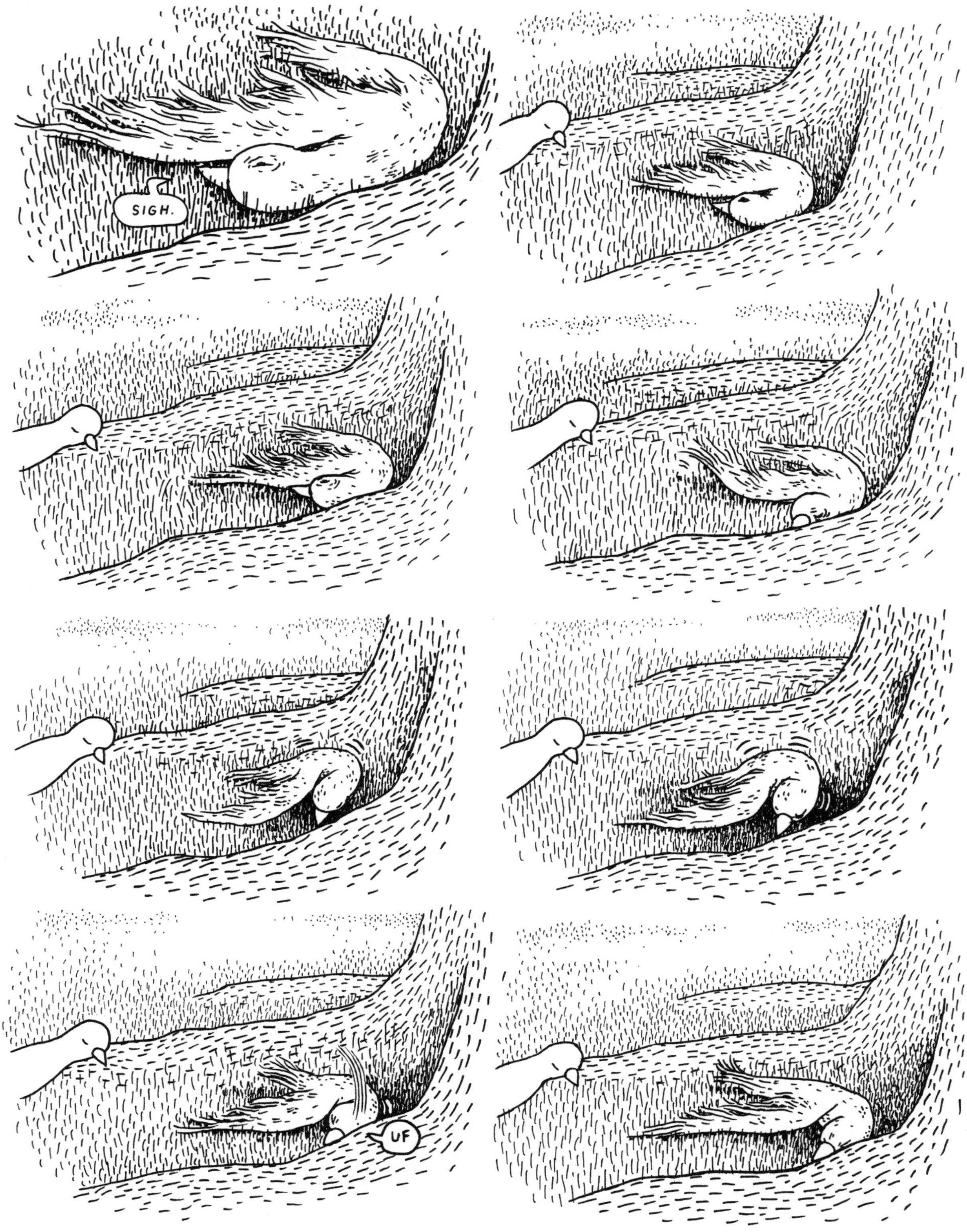
SIGH.
UF

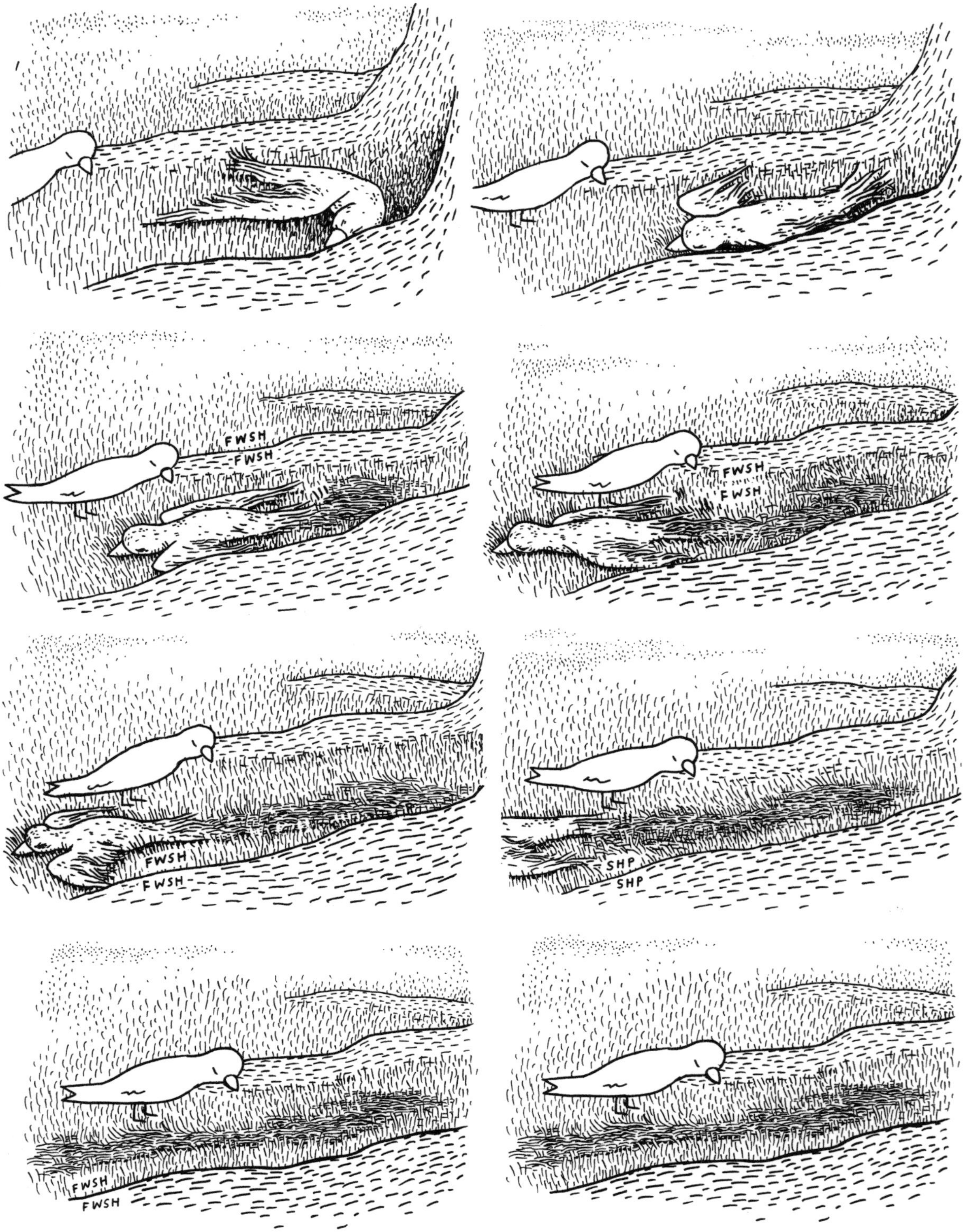
FWSH
FWSH
FWSH
FWSH
FWSH
FWSH
SHP
SHP
FWSH
FWSH

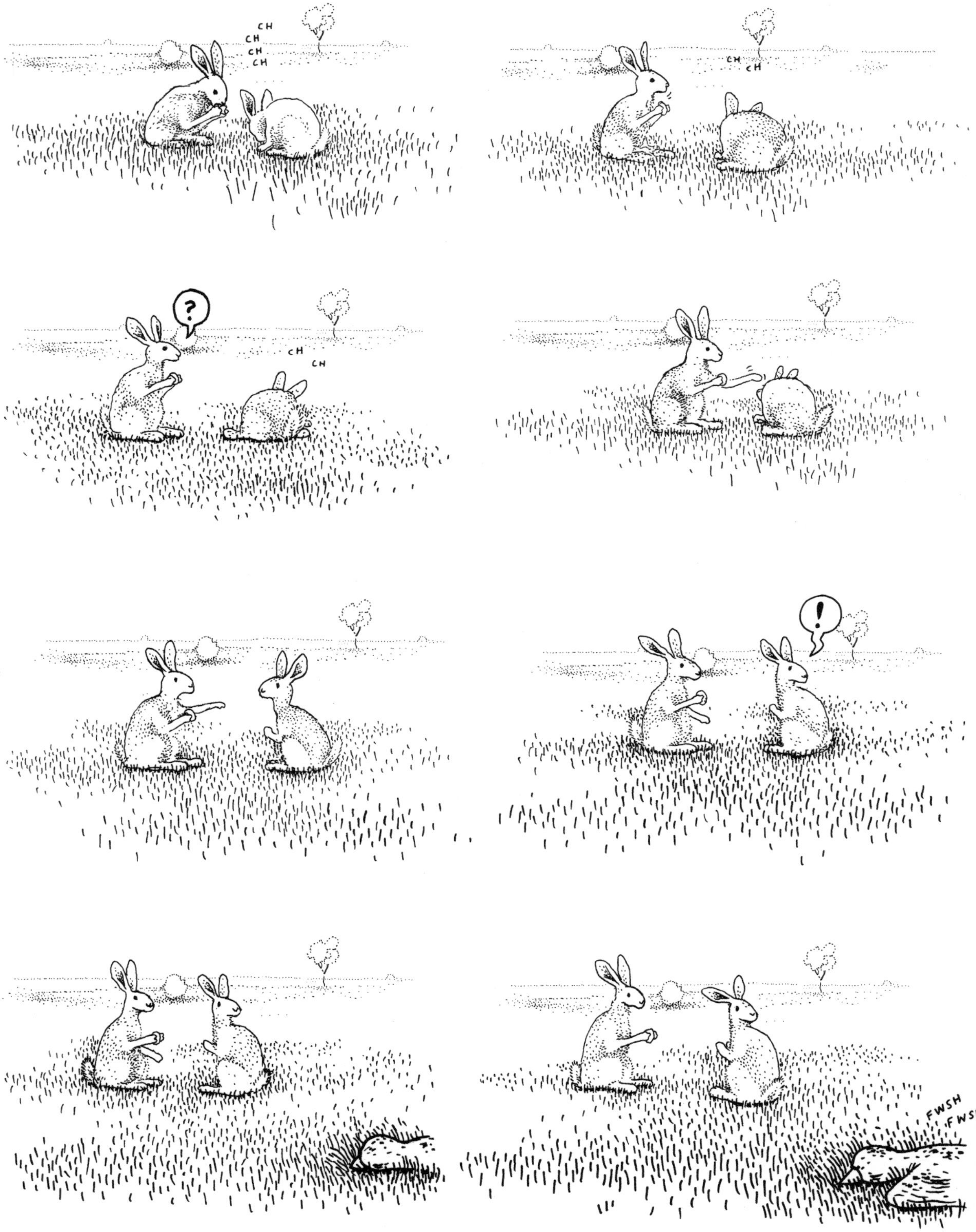

CH
CH
CH
CH
CH
CH
?
CH
CH
!
FWSH
FWSH

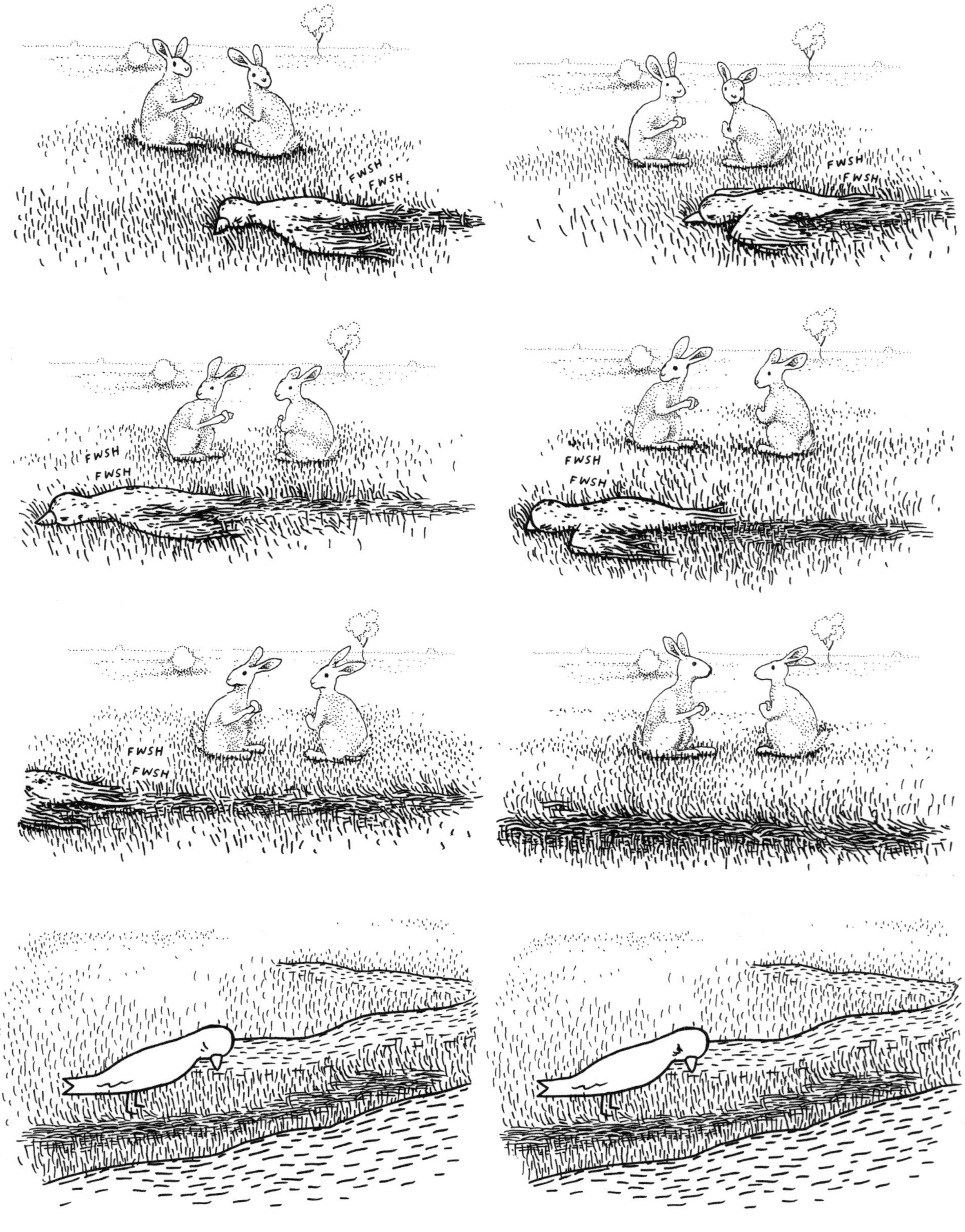
FWSH
FWSH
FWSH
FWSH
FWSH
FWSH
FWSH
FWSH
FWSH
FWSH

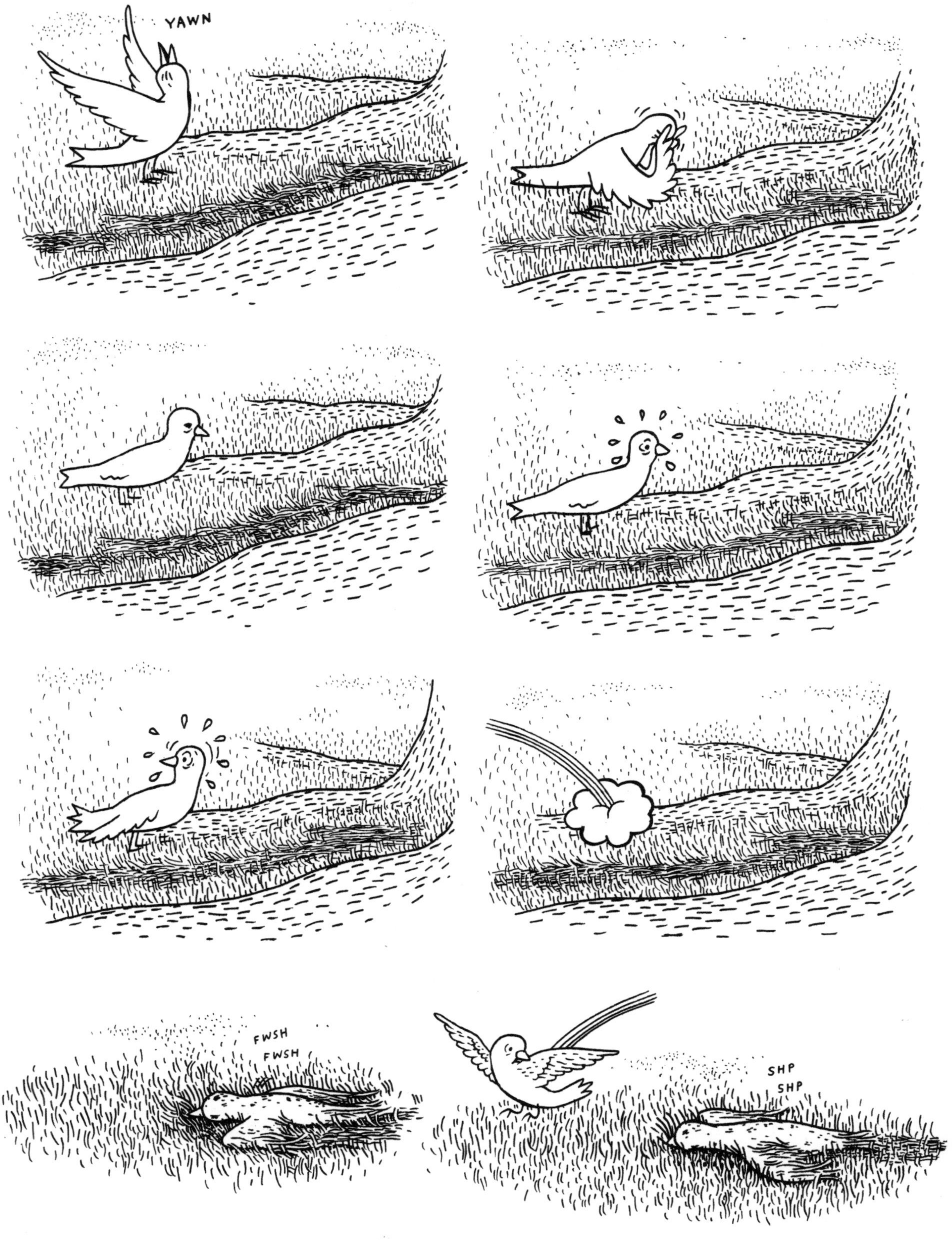
YAWN
FWSH
FWSH
SHP
SHP

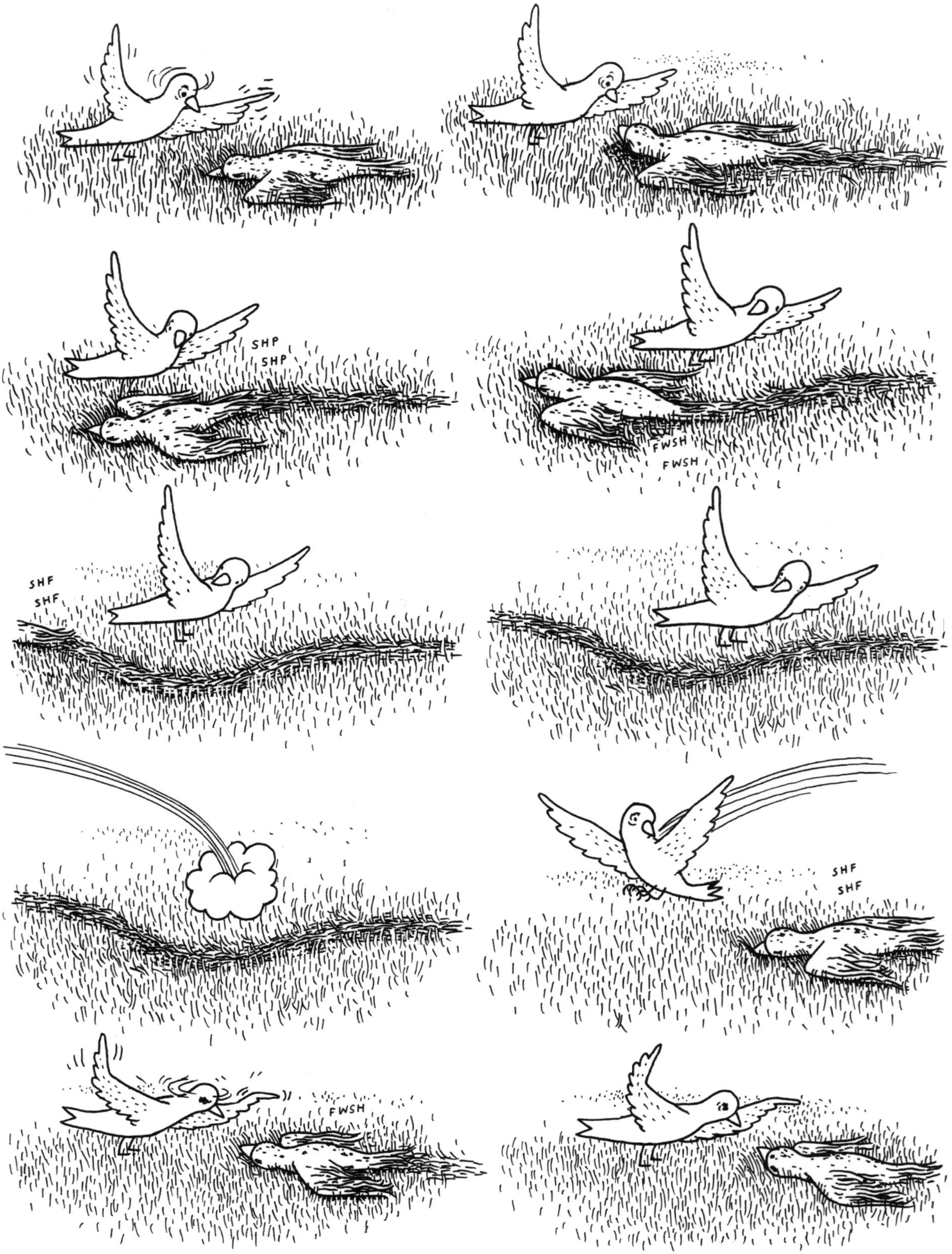
SHP
SHP
FWSH
FWSH
SHF
SHF
SHF
SHF
FWSH

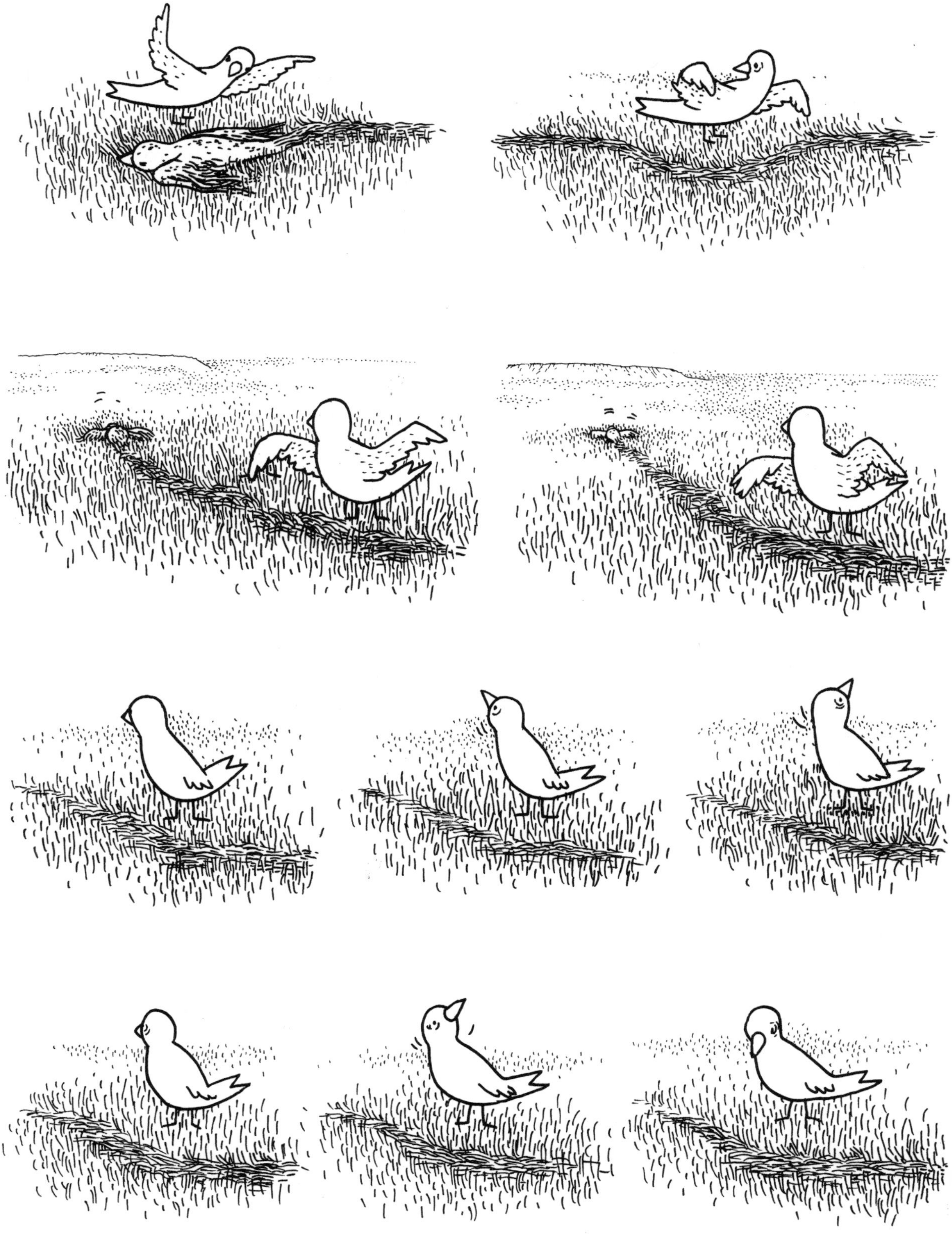

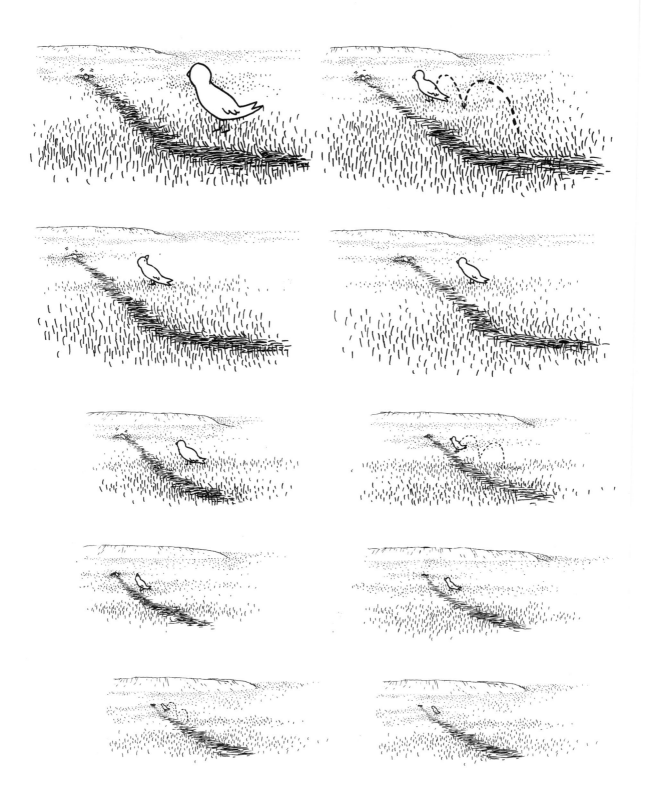

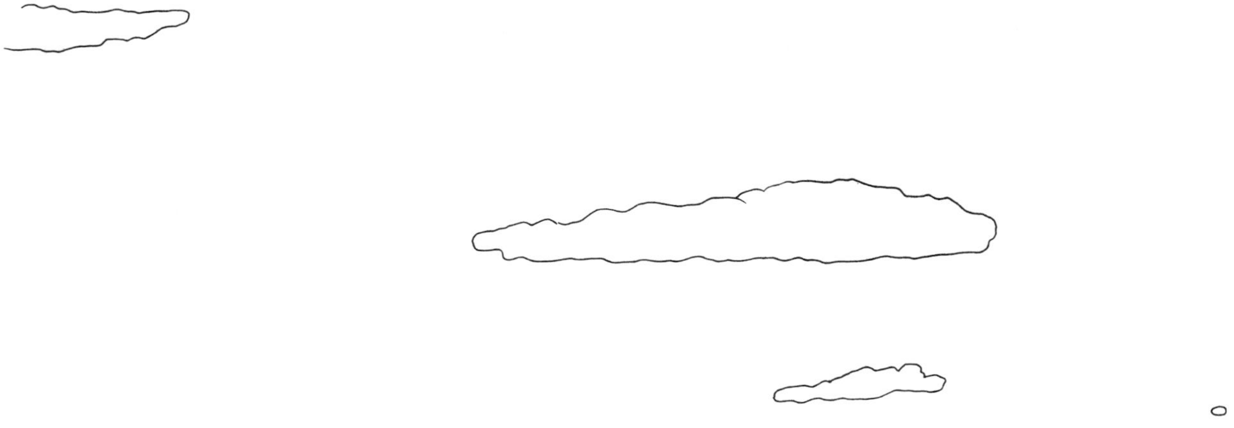

the Argument

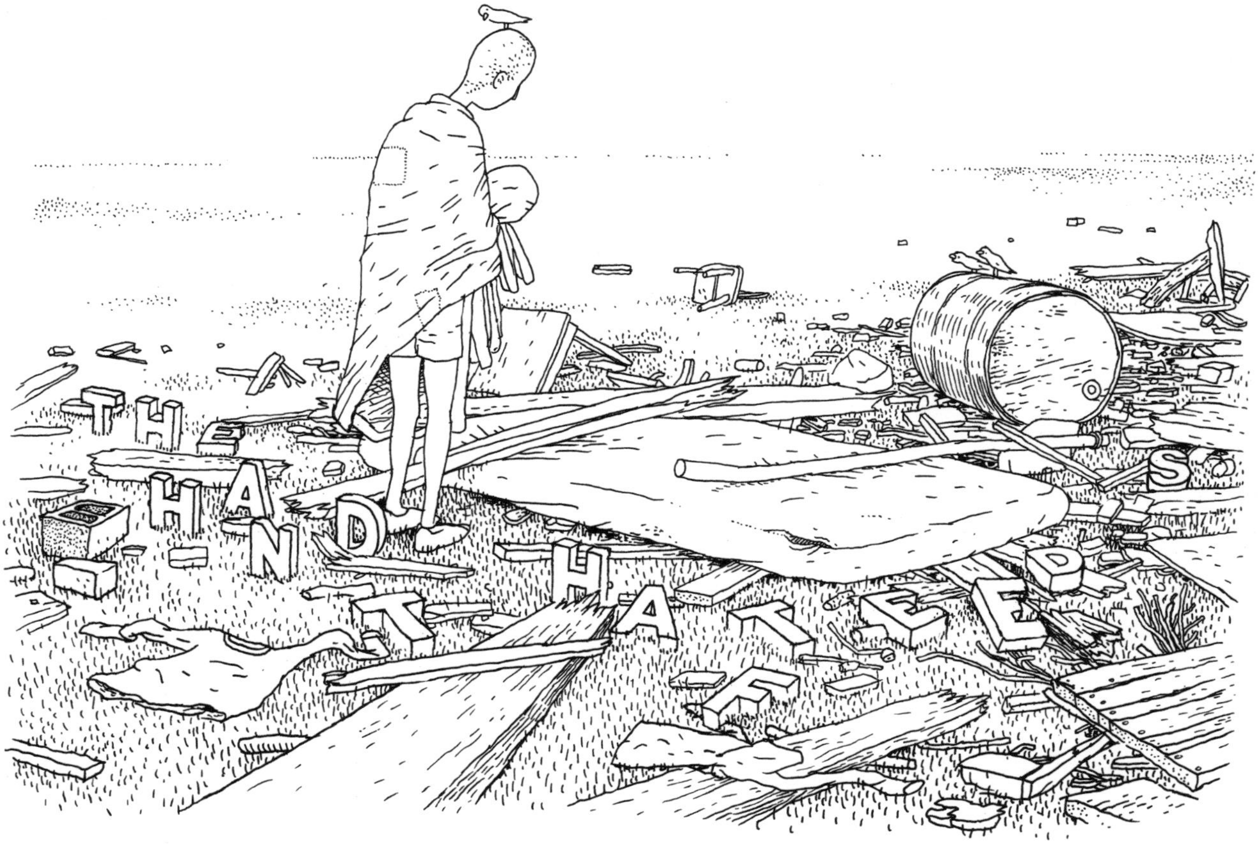
THE
HAND

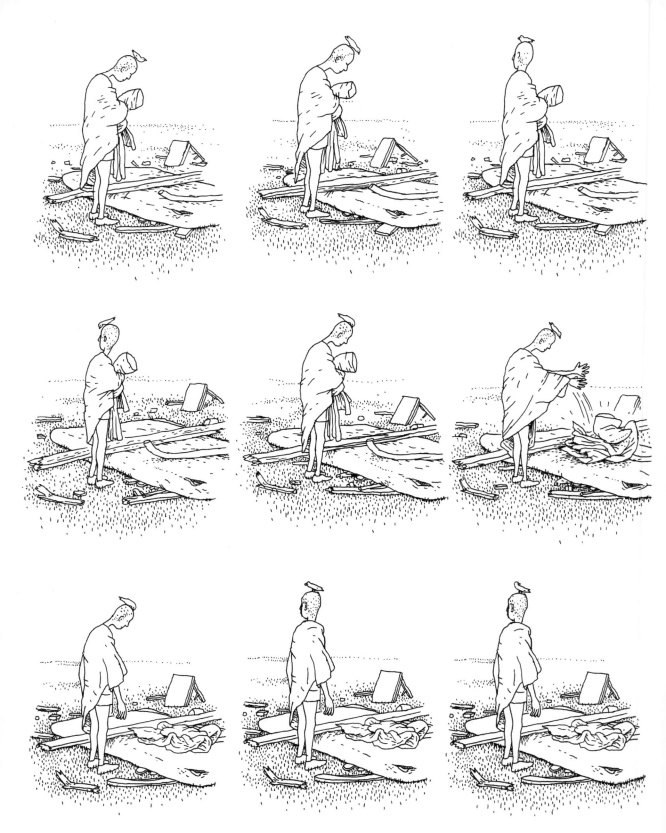

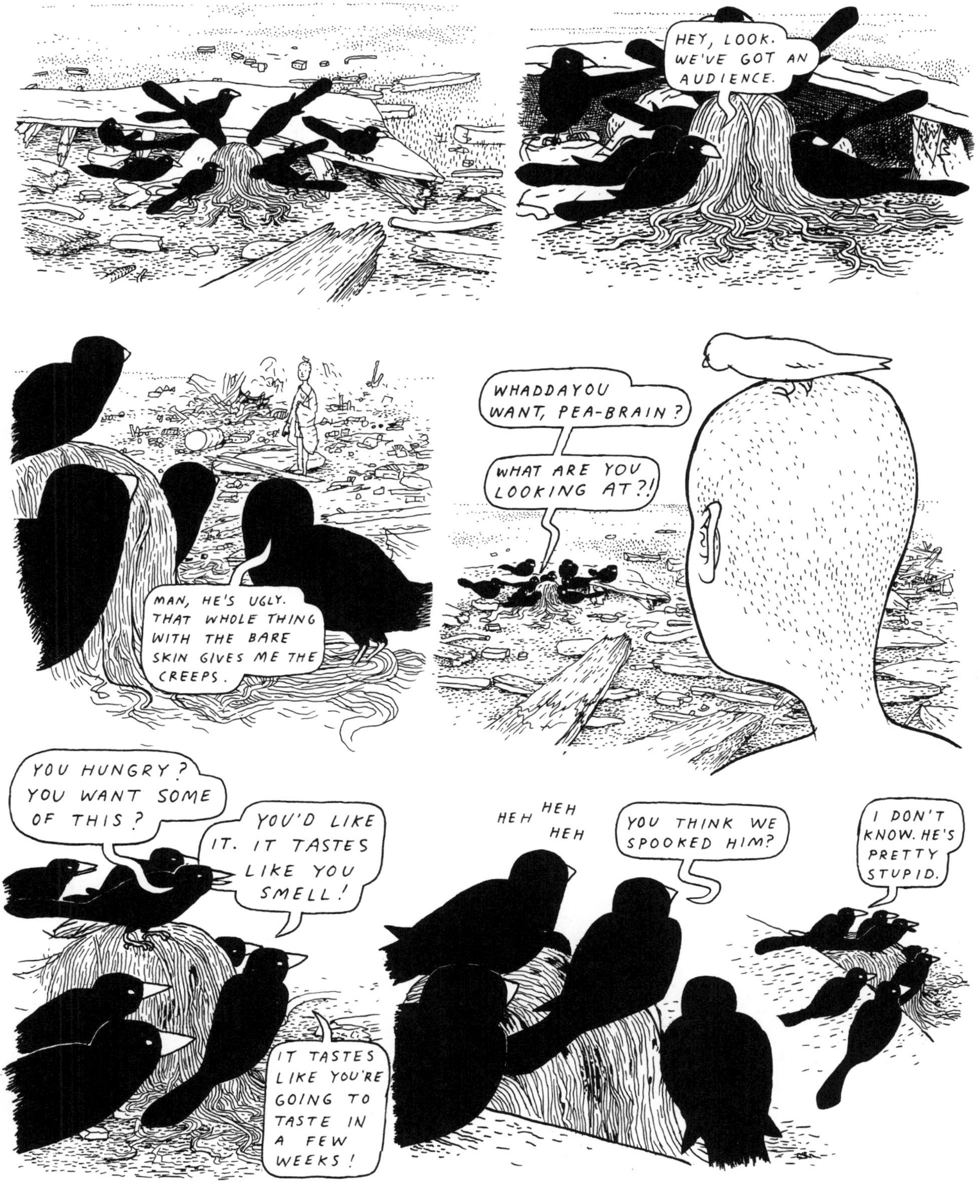

HEY, LOOK. WE'VE GOT AN AUDIENCE.
MAN, HE'S UGLY. THAT WHOLE THING WITH THE BARE SKIN GIVES ME THE CREEPS.
WHADDAYOU WANT, PEA-BRAIN?
WHAT ARE YOU LOOKING AT?!
YOU HUNGRY? YOU WANT SOME OF THIS?
YOU'D LIKE IT. IT TASTES LIKE YOU SMELL!
IT TASTES LIKE YOU'RE GOING TO TASTE IN A FEW WEEKS!
HEH HEH HEH
YOU THINK WE SPOOKED HIM?
I DON'T KNOW. HE'S PRETTY STUPID.

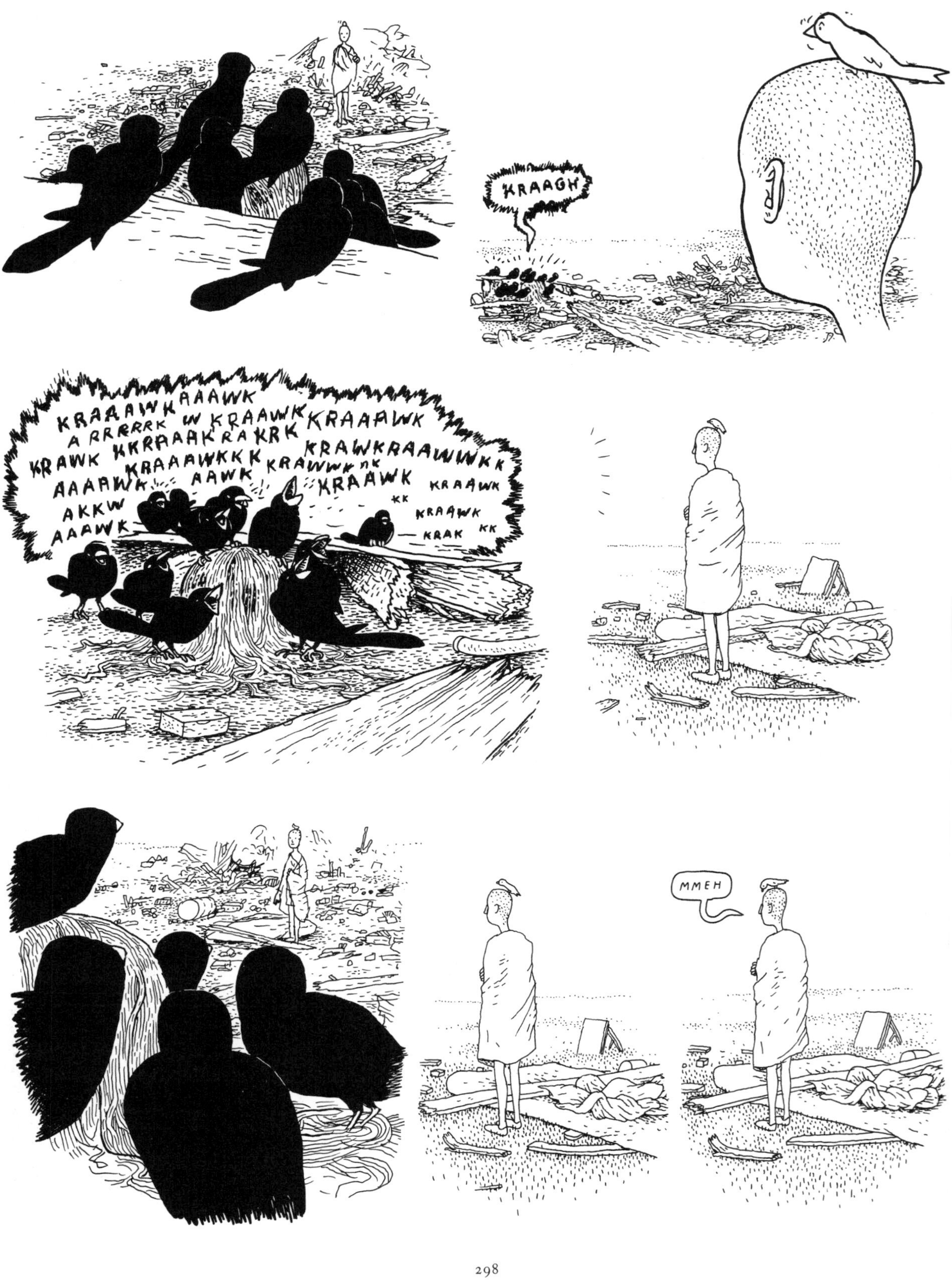
KRAAGH
KRAAAWK AAAWK
A RRRRRK W KRAAWK KRAAAAWK
KRAWK KKRAAAK RA KRK
KRAWKRAAWWKK
KRAAAAWKKK KRAWWK NK
AAAAWK AAWK KRAAWK KRAAWK
AKKW KK
AAAWK KRAAWK
KRAK KK
MMEH

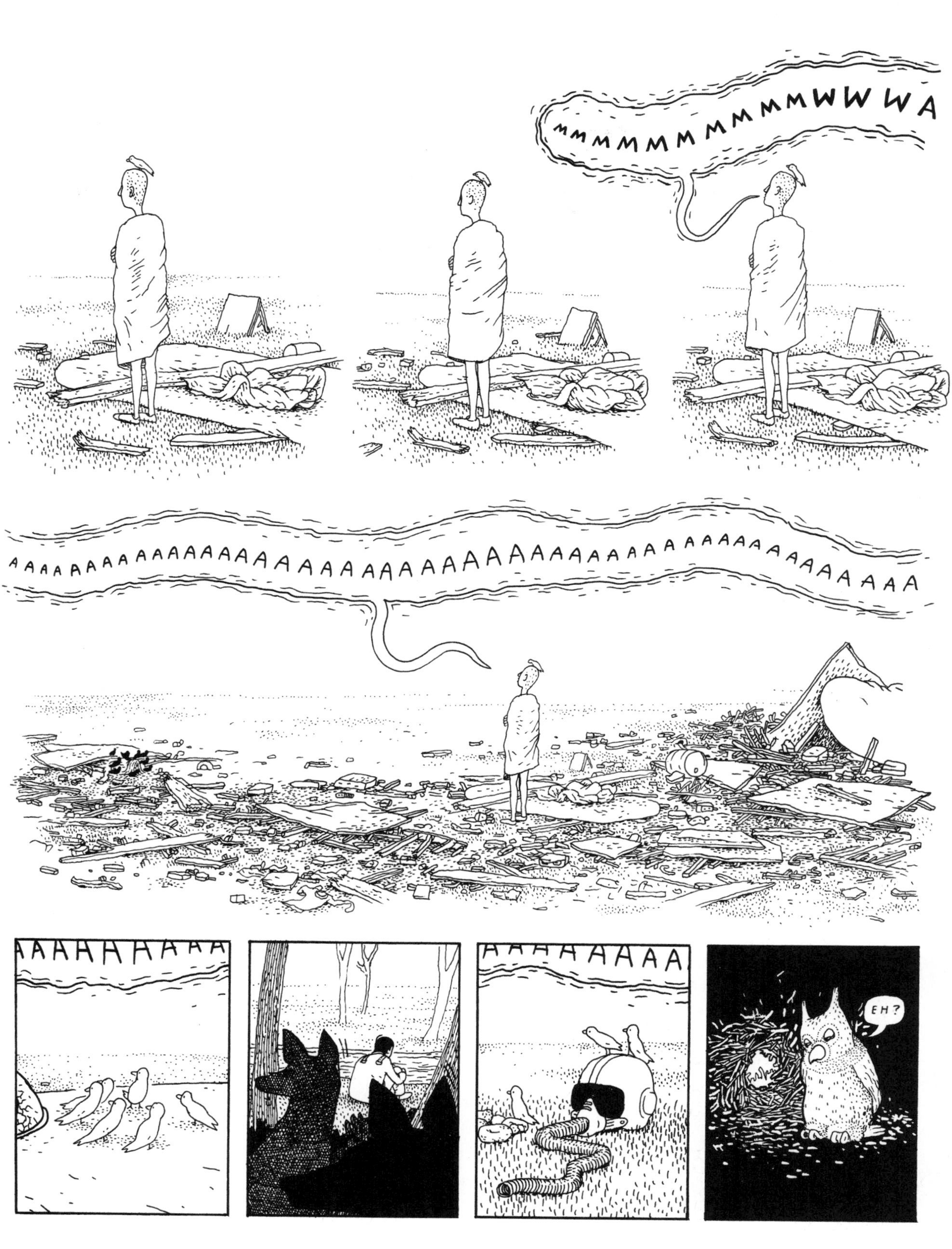
MMMMMMMMMMWWWA
AAAAAAAAAAAAAAAAAAAAAAAAAAAAAAAAAAAAAAAAAAAAAAAA
AAAAAAAAA
AAAAAAAA
EH?

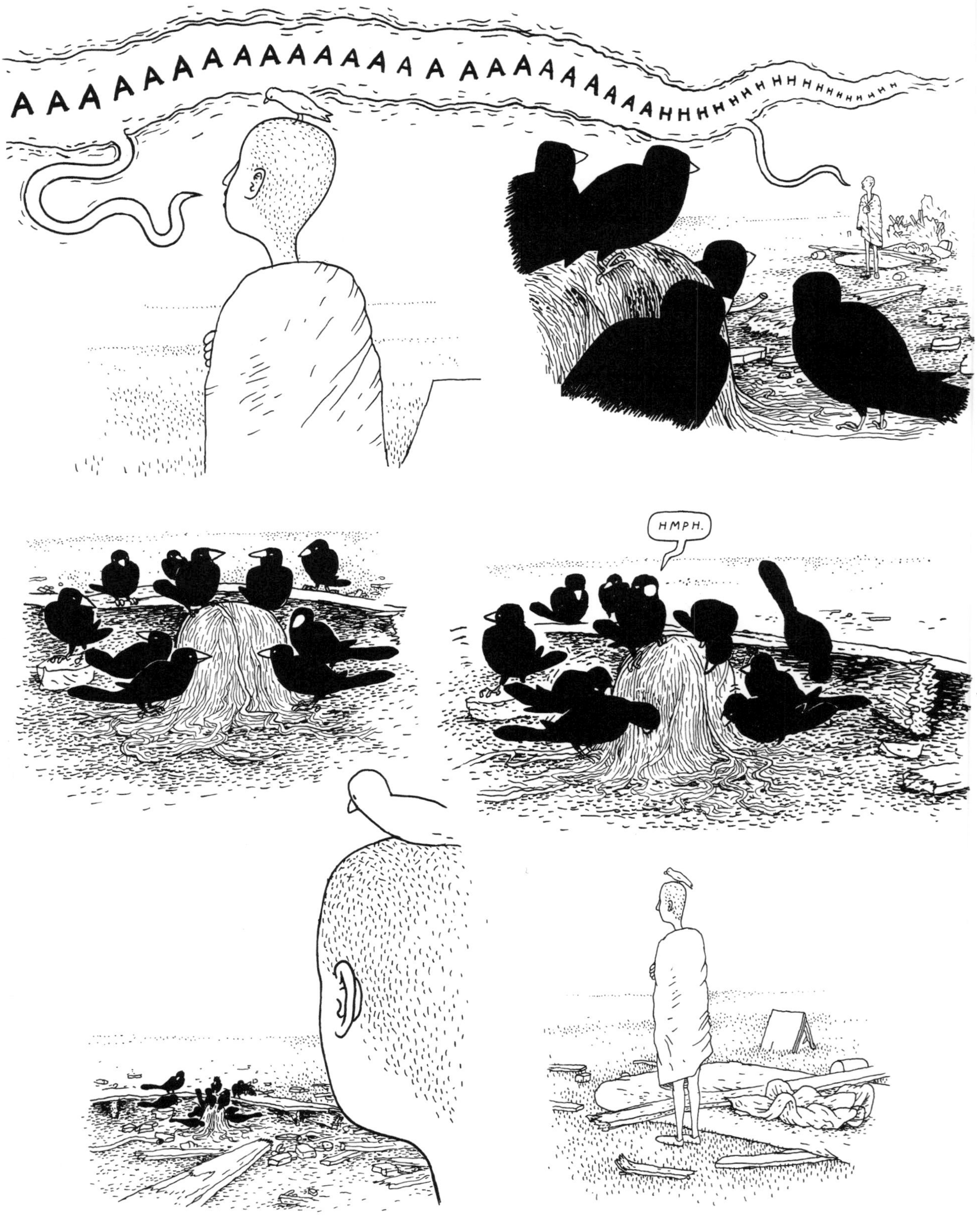
AAAAAAAAAAAAAAAAAAAAAAAHHHHHHHHHHHHHHHHHHH
HMPH.

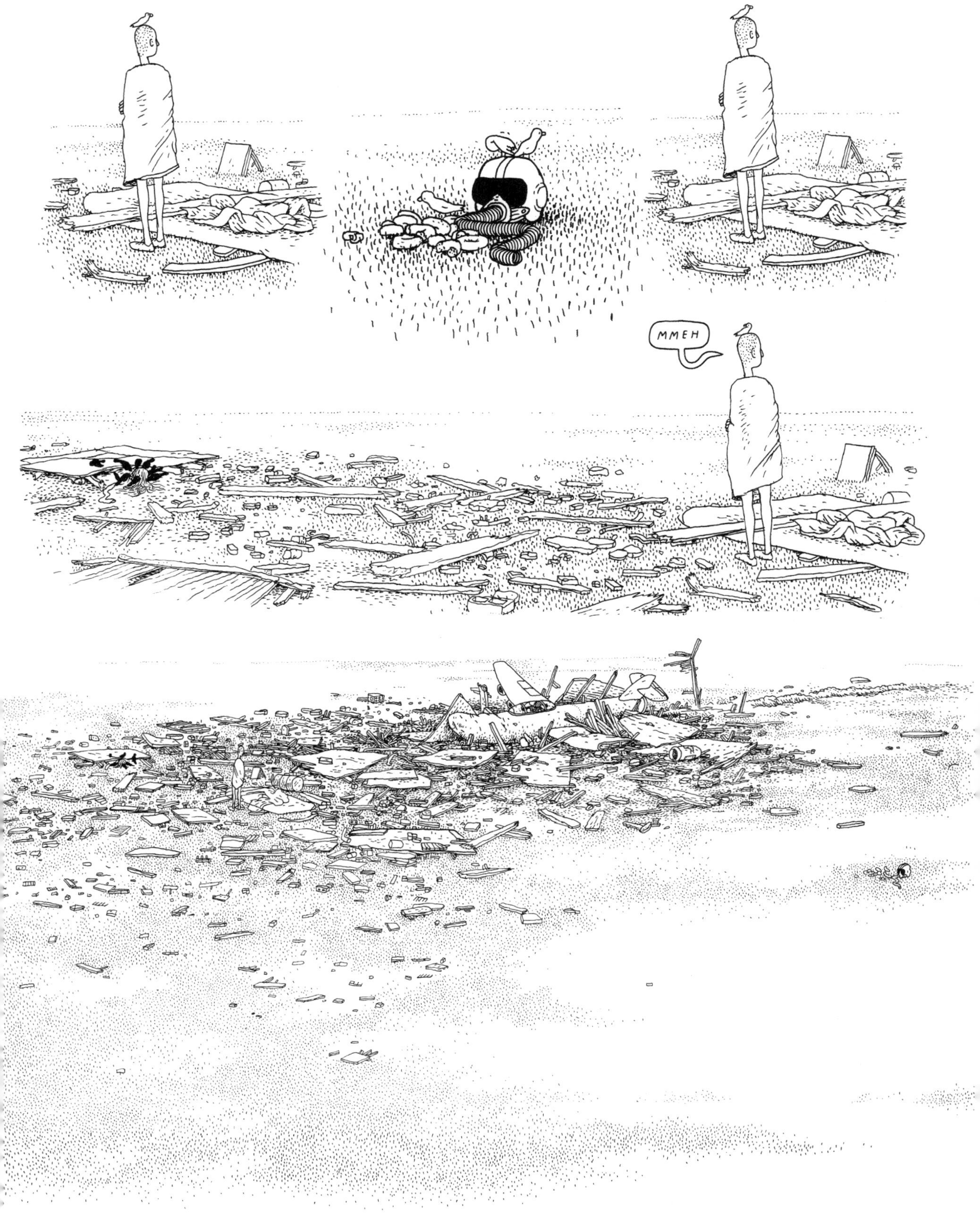
MMEH

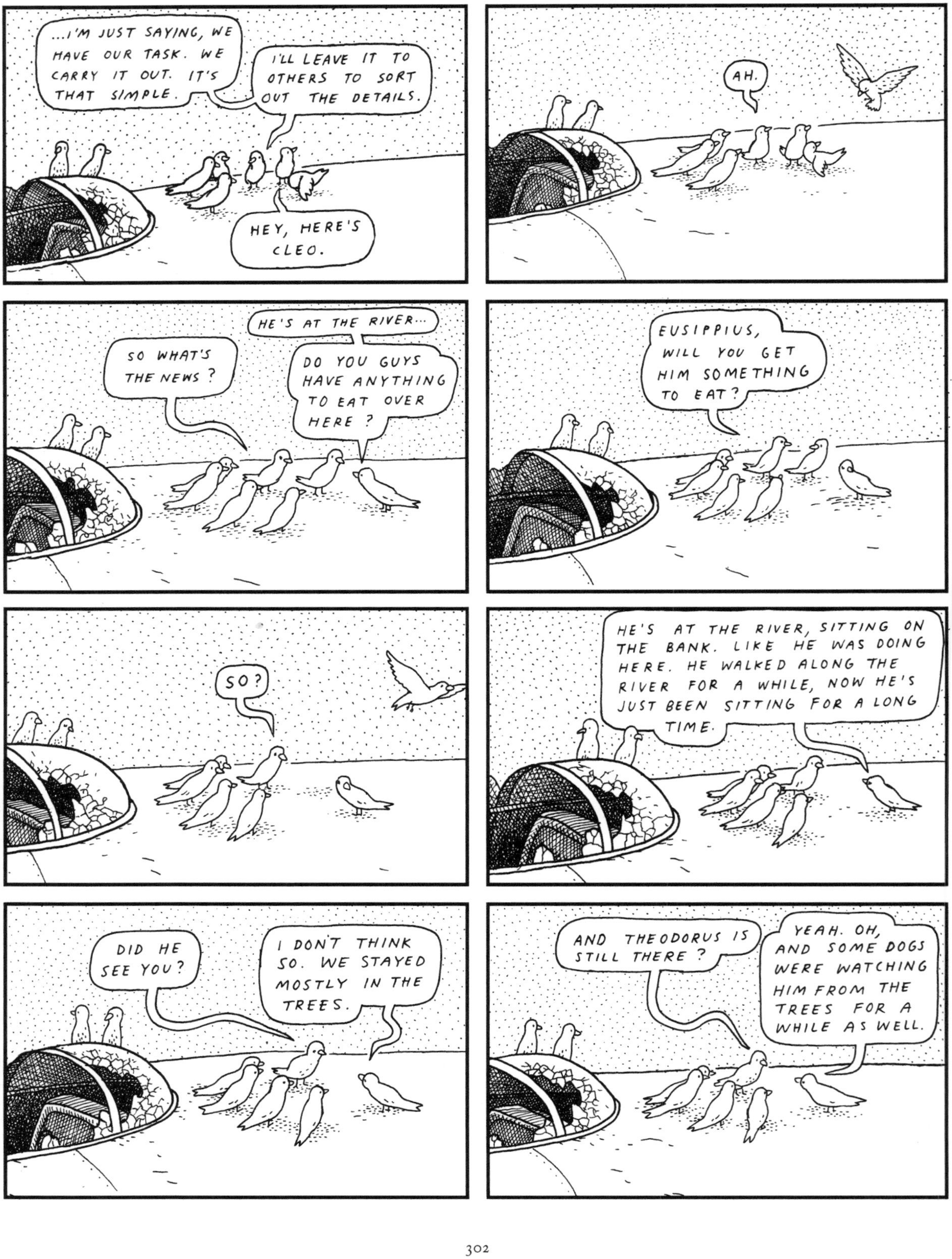
...I'M JUST SAYING, WE HAVE OUR TASK. WE CARRY IT OUT. IT'S THAT SIMPLE.
I'LL LEAVE IT TO OTHERS TO SORT OUT THE DETAILS.
HEY, HERE'S CLEO.
AH.
SO WHAT'S THE NEWS?
HE'S AT THE RIVER...
DO YOU GUYS HAVE ANYTHING TO EAT OVER HERE?
EUSIPPIUS, WILL YOU GET HIM SOMETHING TO EAT?
SO?
HE'S AT THE RIVER, SITTING ON THE BANK. LIKE HE WAS DOING HERE. HE WALKED ALONG THE RIVER FOR A WHILE, NOW HE'S JUST BEEN SITTING FOR A LONG TIME.
DID HE SEE YOU?
I DON'T THINK SO. WE STAYED MOSTLY IN THE TREES.
AND THEODORUS IS STILL THERE?
YEAH. OH, AND SOME DOGS WERE WATCHING HIM FROM THE TREES FOR A WHILE AS WELL.

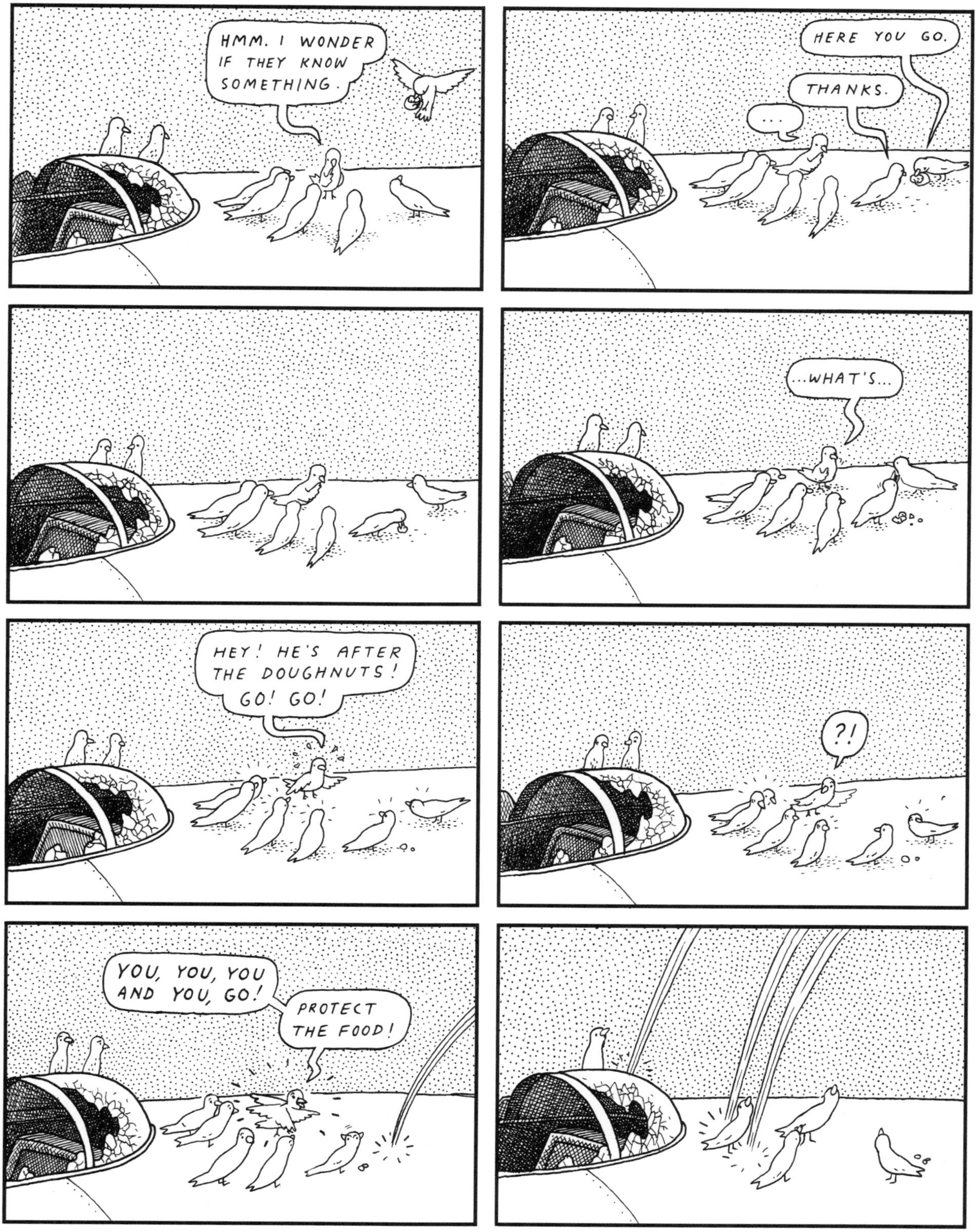
HMM. I WONDER IF THEY KNOW SOMETHING.
HERE YOU GO.
THANKS.
...
...WHAT'S...
HEY! HE'S AFTER THE DOUGHNUTS! GO! GO!
?!
YOU, YOU, YOU AND YOU, GO!
PROTECT THE FOOD!

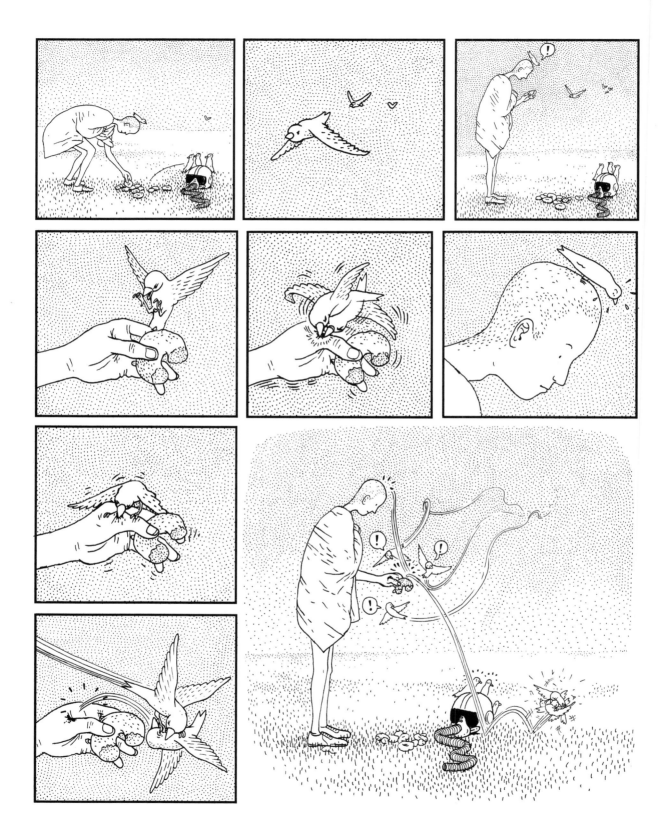

UGH. PLEASE GO GIVE THEM A HAND.
JUST... JUST...
...JUST PROTECT ...THE FOOD...

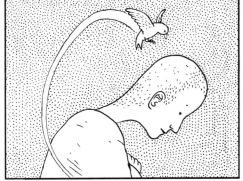

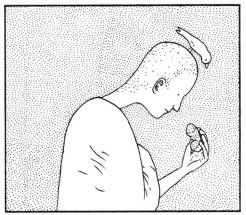

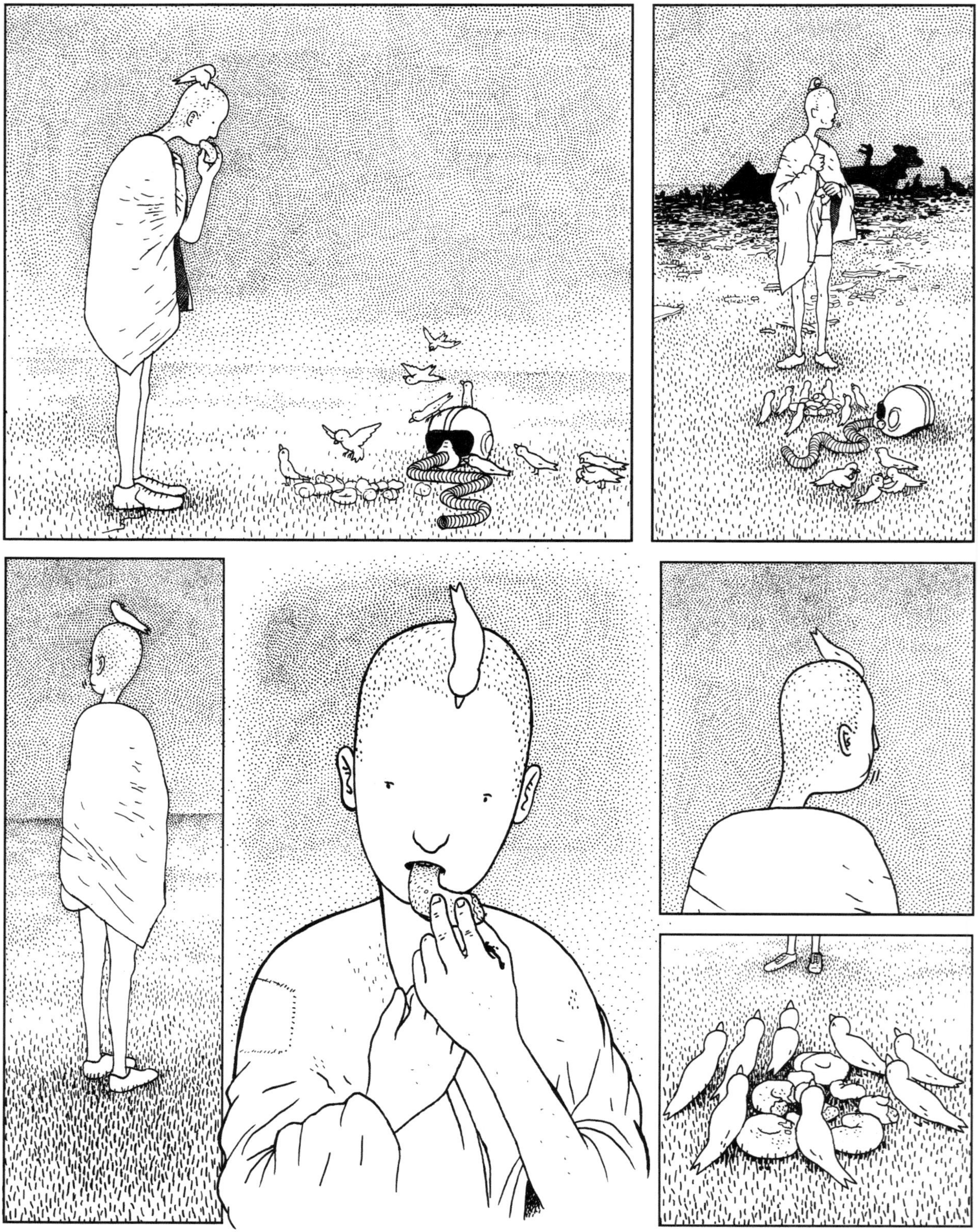

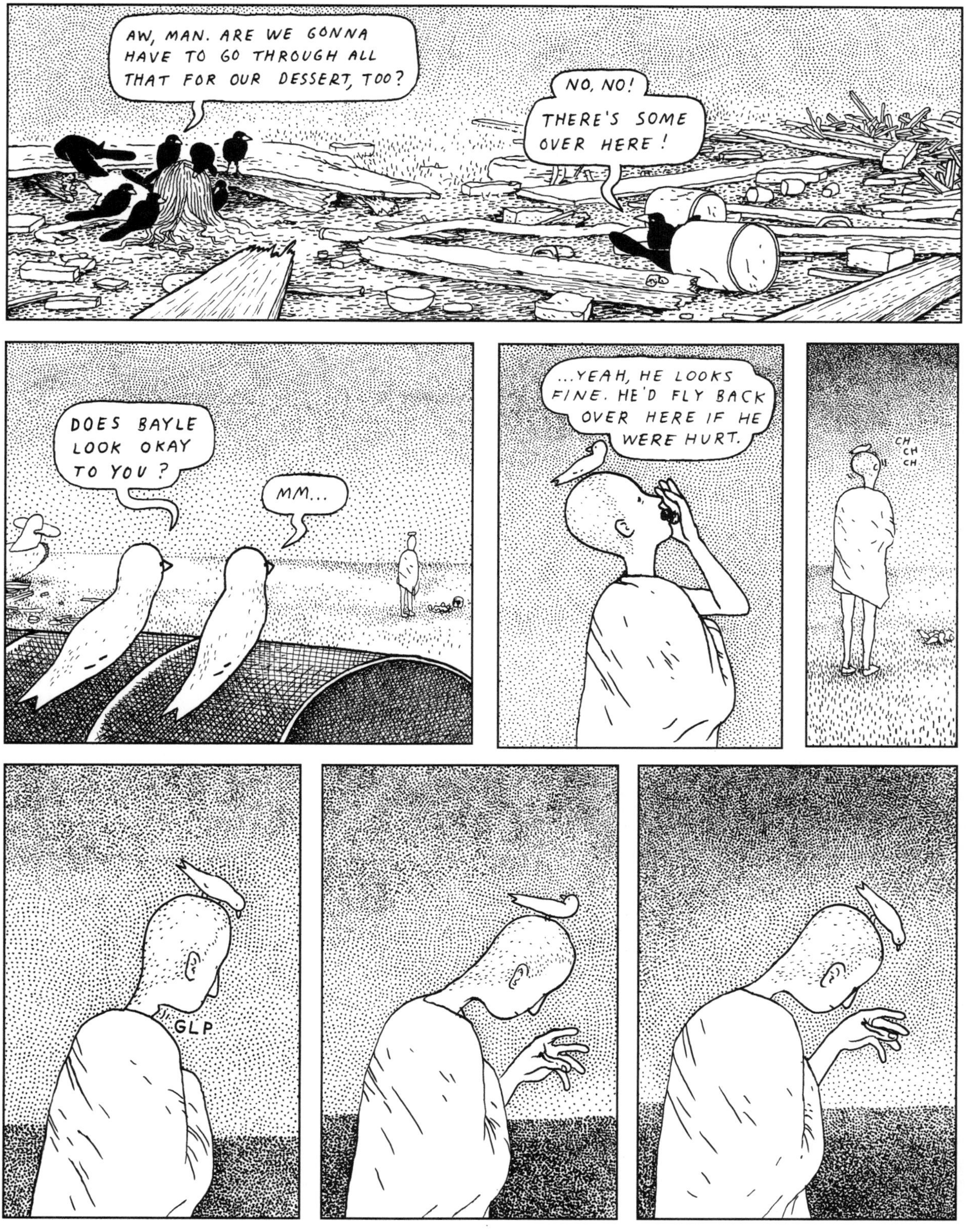
AW, MAN. ARE WE GONNA HAVE TO GO THROUGH ALL THAT FOR OUR DESSERT, TOO?
NO, NO! THERE'S SOME OVER HERE!
DOES BAYLE LOOK OKAY TO YOU?
MM...
...YEAH, HE LOOKS FINE. HE'D FLY BACK OVER HERE IF HE WERE HURT.
CH CH CH
GLP

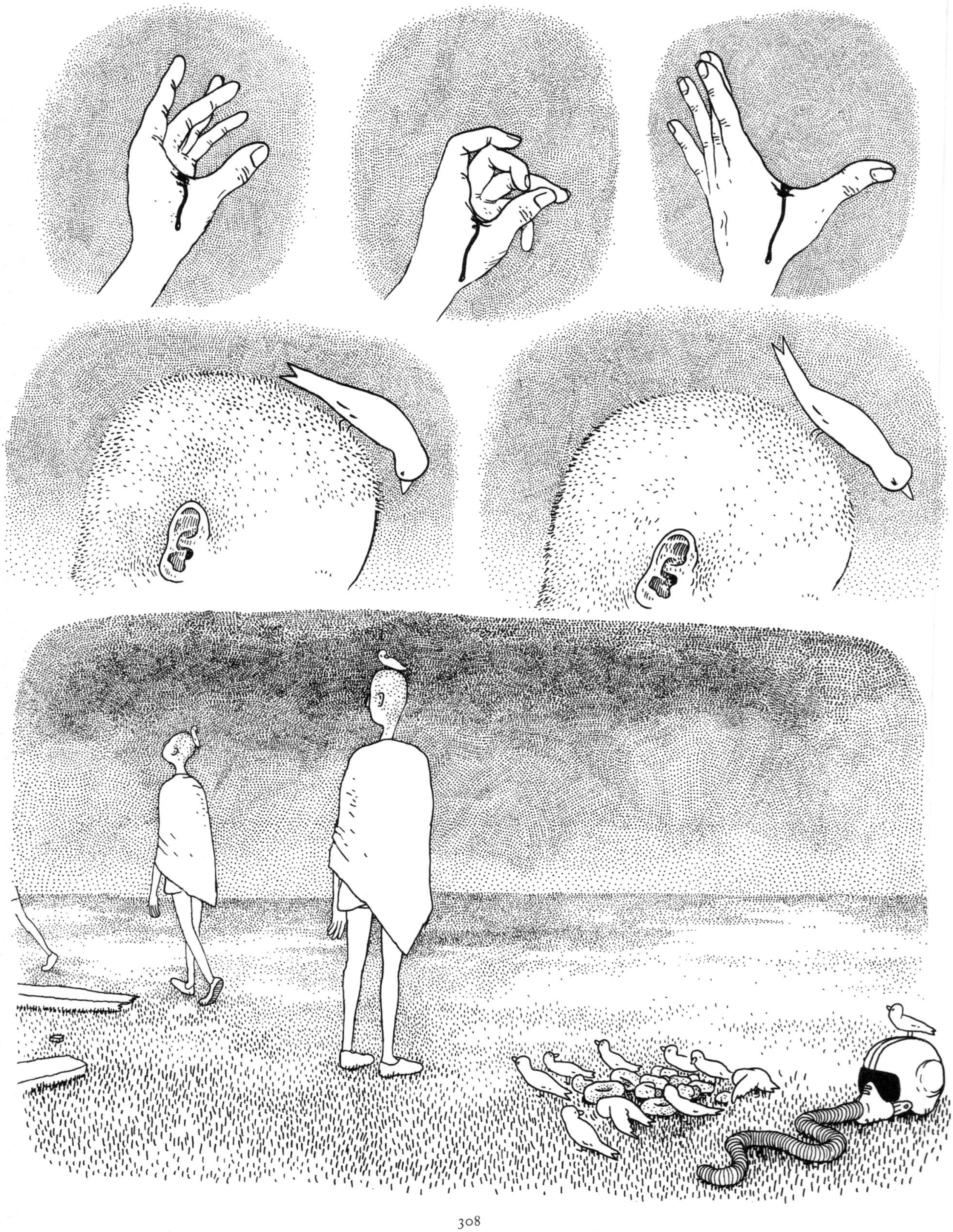

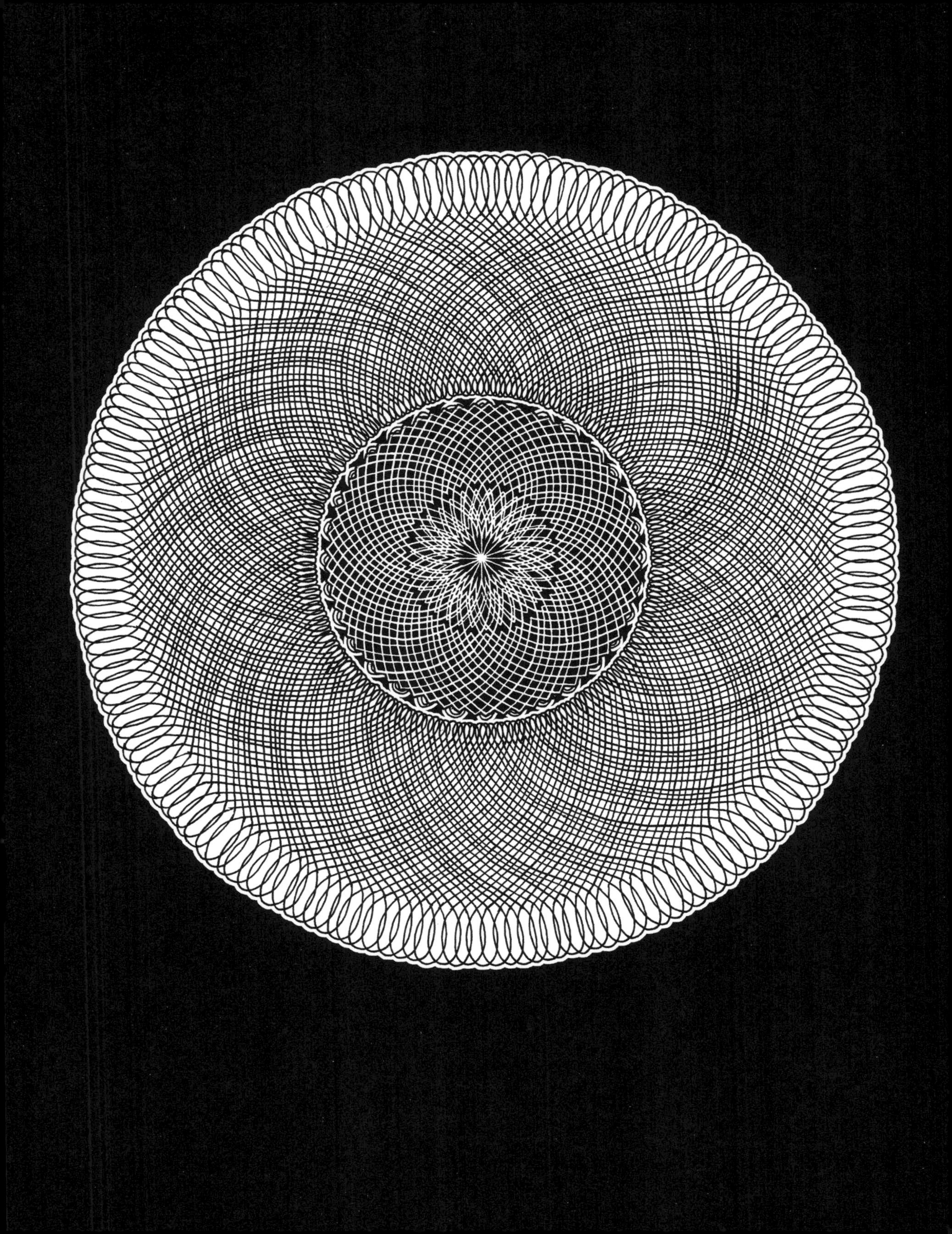

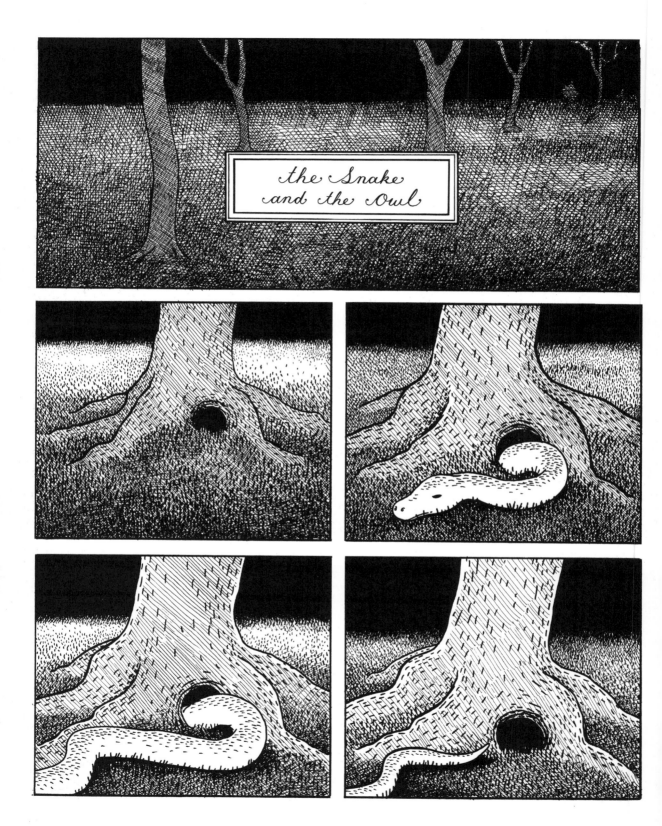

the Snake
and the Owl

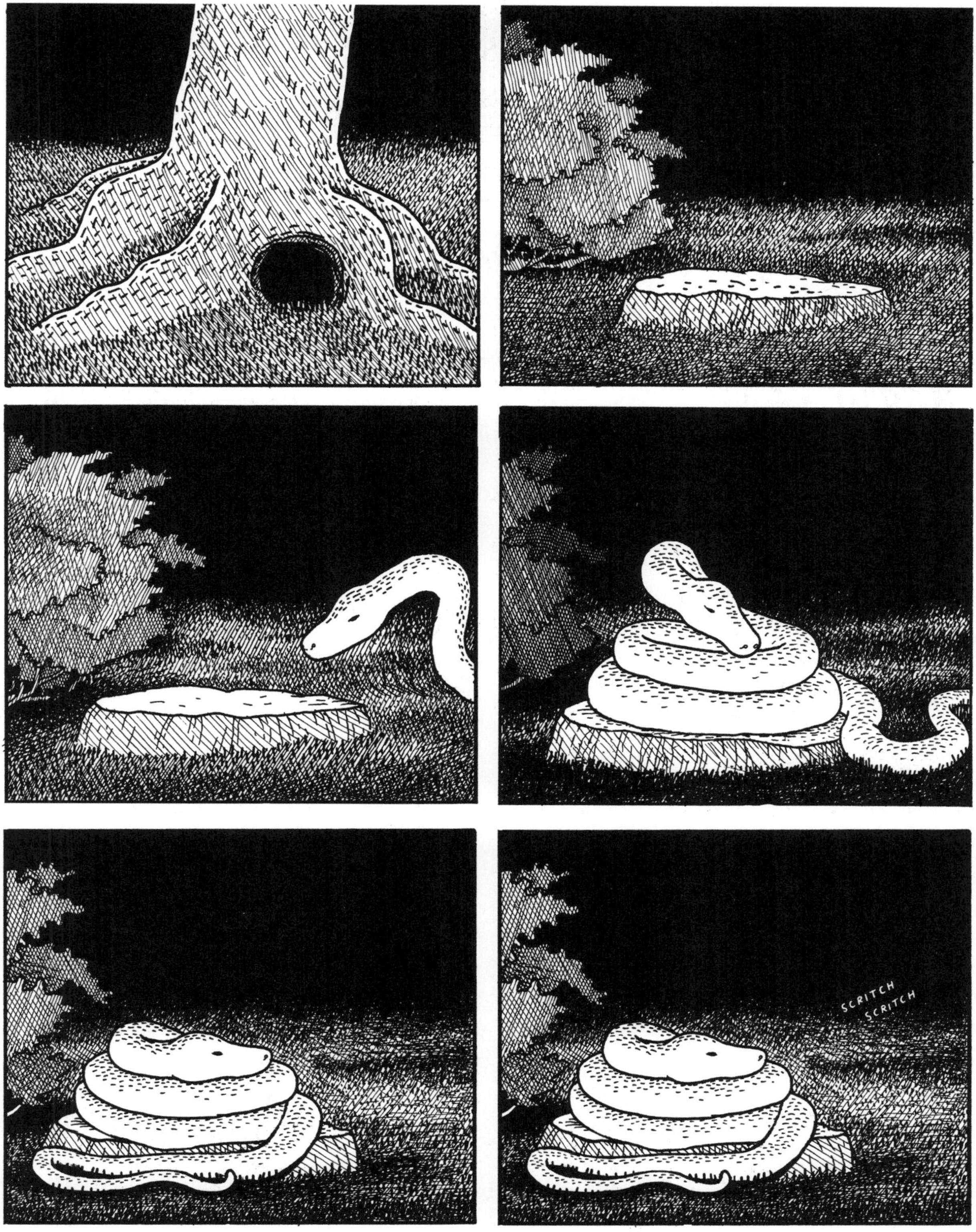
SCRITCH
SCRITCH

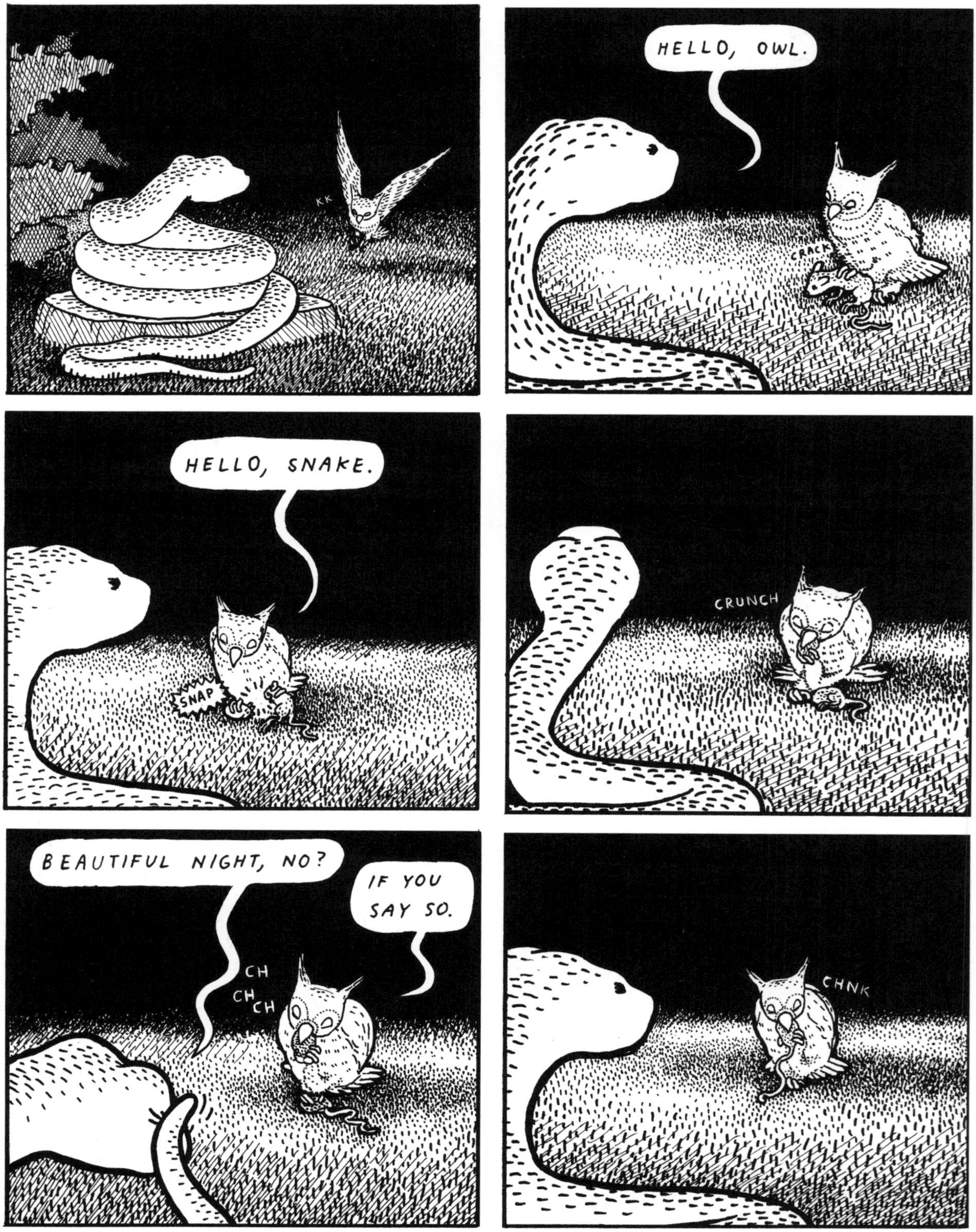
KK
HELLO, OWL.
CRACK
HELLO, SNAKE.
SNAP
CRUNCH
BEAUTIFUL NIGHT, NO?
IF YOU SAY SO.
CH CH CH
CHNK

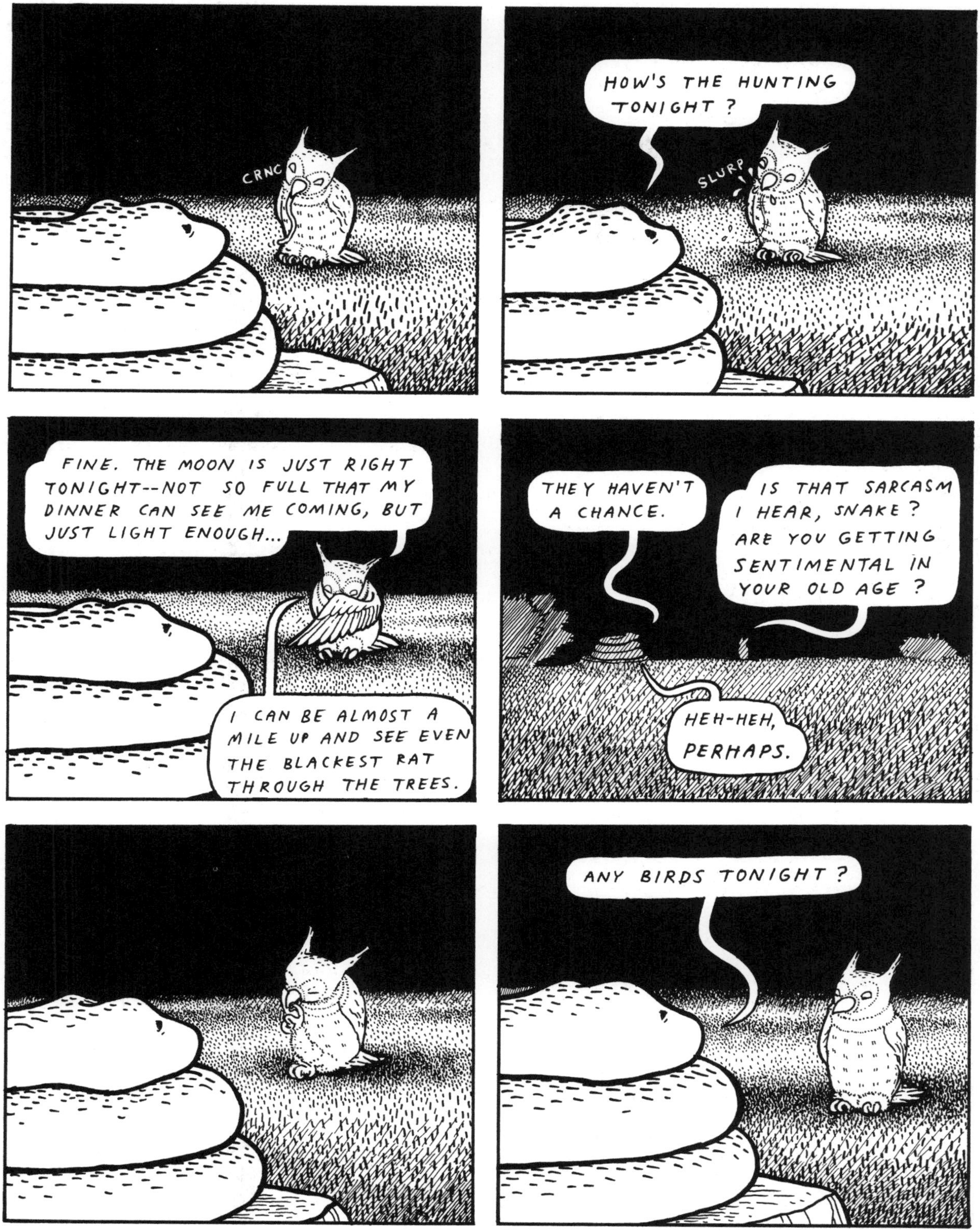
CRNC
HOW'S THE HUNTING TONIGHT?
SLURP
FINE. THE MOON IS JUST RIGHT TONIGHT--NOT SO FULL THAT MY DINNER CAN SEE ME COMING, BUT JUST LIGHT ENOUGH...
I CAN BE ALMOST A MILE UP AND SEE EVEN THE BLACKEST RAT THROUGH THE TREES.
THEY HAVEN'T A CHANCE.
IS THAT SARCASM I HEAR, SNAKE? ARE YOU GETTING SENTIMENTAL IN YOUR OLD AGE?
HEH-HEH, PERHAPS.
ANY BIRDS TONIGHT?

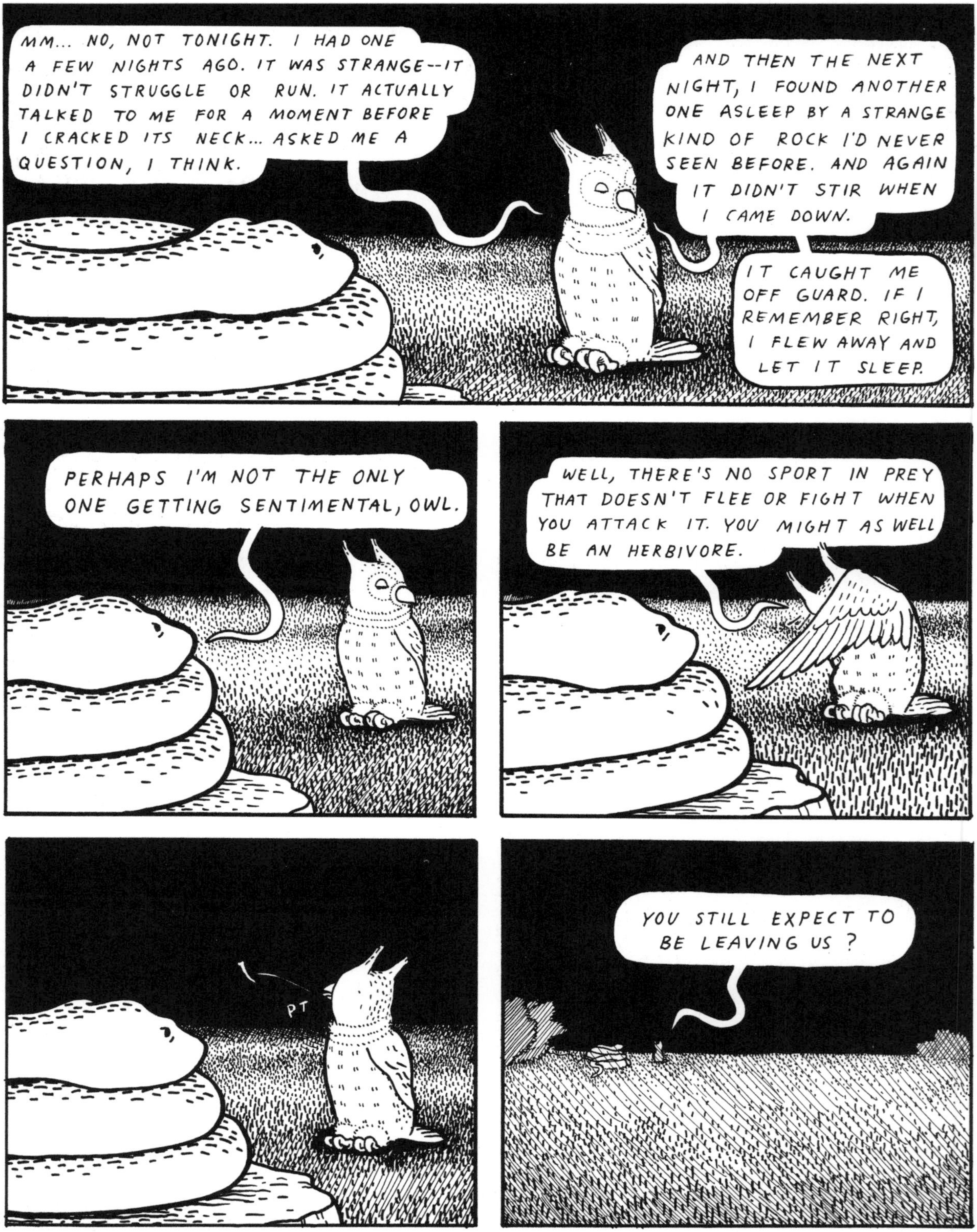
MM... NO, NOT TONIGHT. I HAD ONE A FEW NIGHTS AGO. IT WAS STRANGE--IT DIDN'T STRUGGLE OR RUN. IT ACTUALLY TALKED TO ME FOR A MOMENT BEFORE I CRACKED ITS NECK... ASKED ME A QUESTION, I THINK.
AND THEN THE NEXT NIGHT, I FOUND ANOTHER ONE ASLEEP BY A STRANGE KIND OF ROCK I'D NEVER SEEN BEFORE. AND AGAIN IT DIDN'T STIR WHEN I CAME DOWN.
IT CAUGHT ME OFF GUARD. IF I REMEMBER RIGHT, I FLEW AWAY AND LET IT SLEEP.
PERHAPS I'M NOT THE ONLY ONE GETTING SENTIMENTAL, OWL.
WELL, THERE'S NO SPORT IN PREY THAT DOESN'T FLEE OR FIGHT WHEN YOU ATTACK IT. YOU MIGHT AS WELL BE AN HERBIVORE.
PT
YOU STILL EXPECT TO BE LEAVING US ?

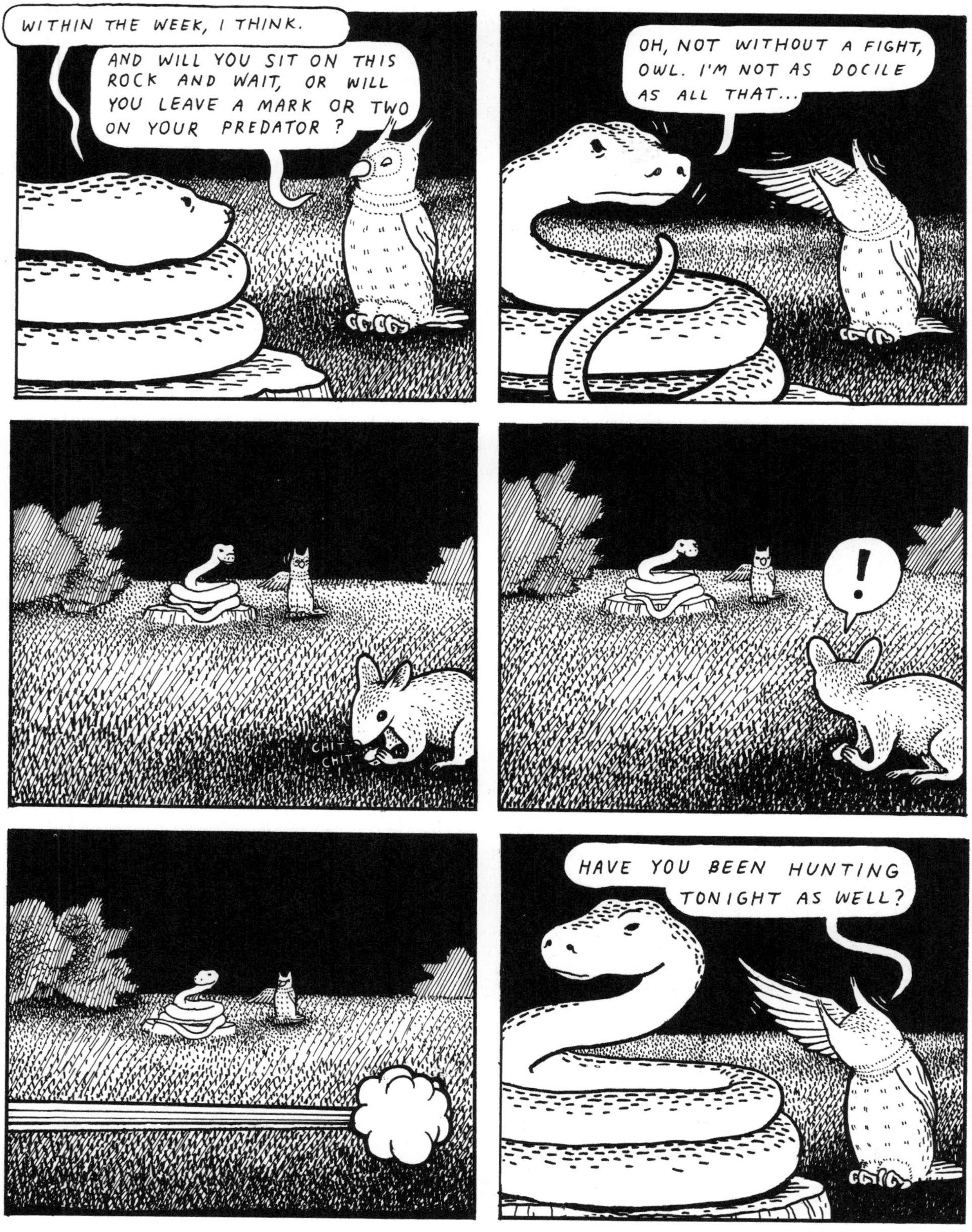
WITHIN THE WEEK, I THINK.
AND WILL YOU SIT ON THIS ROCK AND WAIT, OR WILL YOU LEAVE A MARK OR TWO ON YOUR PREDATOR ?
OH, NOT WITHOUT A FIGHT, OWL. I'M NOT AS DOCILE AS ALL THAT...
CHIT CHIT
!
HAVE YOU BEEN HUNTING TONIGHT AS WELL?

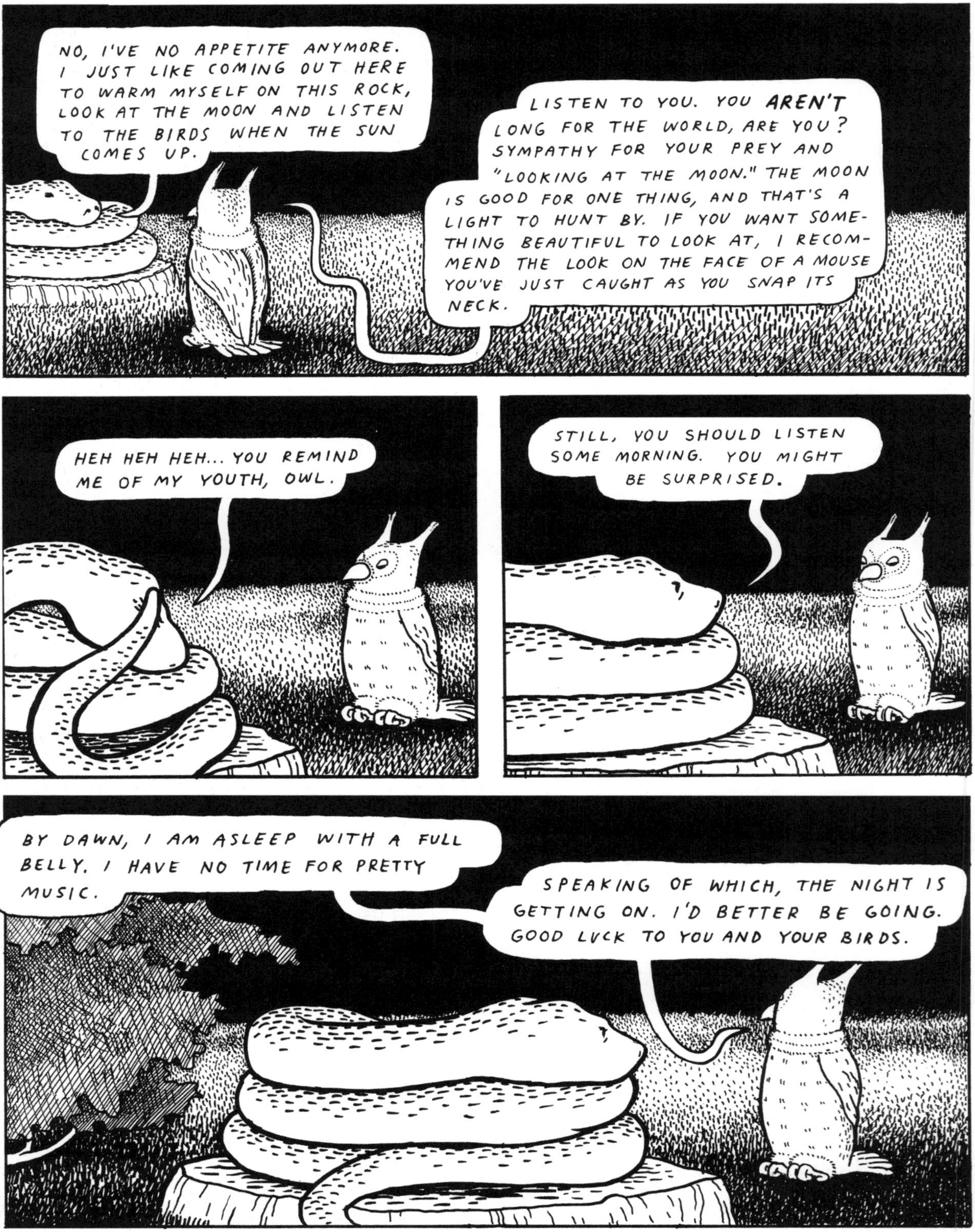
NO, I'VE NO APPETITE ANYMORE. I JUST LIKE COMING OUT HERE TO WARM MYSELF ON THIS ROCK, LOOK AT THE MOON AND LISTEN TO THE BIRDS WHEN THE SUN COMES UP.
LISTEN TO YOU. YOU **AREN'T** LONG FOR THE WORLD, ARE YOU? SYMPATHY FOR YOUR PREY AND "LOOKING AT THE MOON." THE MOON IS GOOD FOR ONE THING, AND THAT'S A LIGHT TO HUNT BY. IF YOU WANT SOMETHING BEAUTIFUL TO LOOK AT, I RECOMMEND THE LOOK ON THE FACE OF A MOUSE YOU'VE JUST CAUGHT AS YOU SNAP ITS NECK.
HEH HEH HEH... YOU REMIND ME OF MY YOUTH, OWL.
STILL, YOU SHOULD LISTEN SOME MORNING. YOU MIGHT BE SURPRISED.
BY DAWN, I AM ASLEEP WITH A FULL BELLY. I HAVE NO TIME FOR PRETTY MUSIC.
SPEAKING OF WHICH, THE NIGHT IS GETTING ON. I'D BETTER BE GOING. GOOD LUCK TO YOU AND YOUR BIRDS.

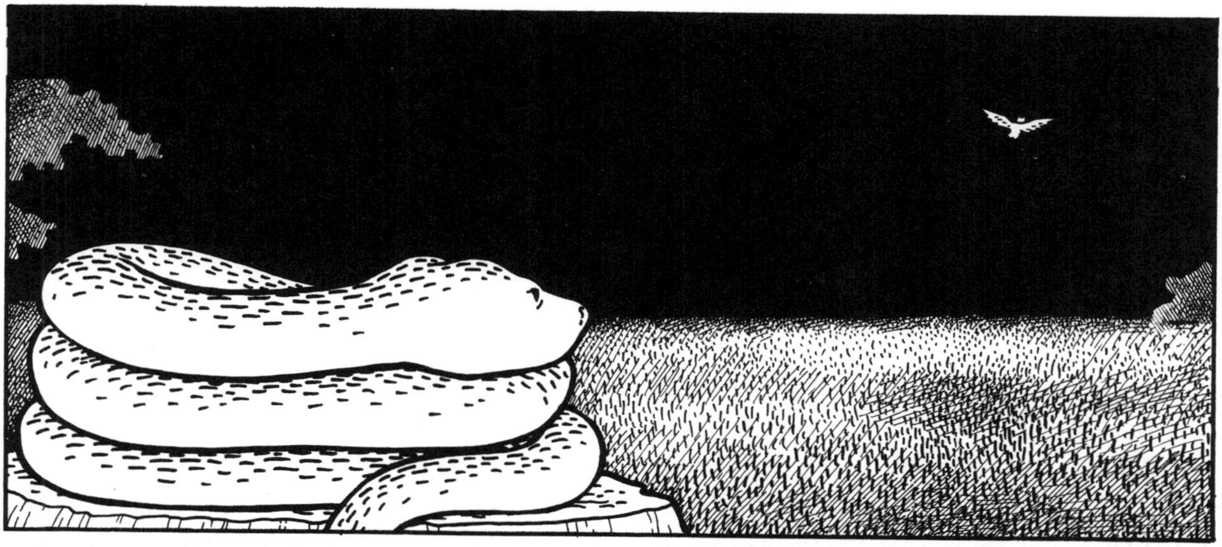

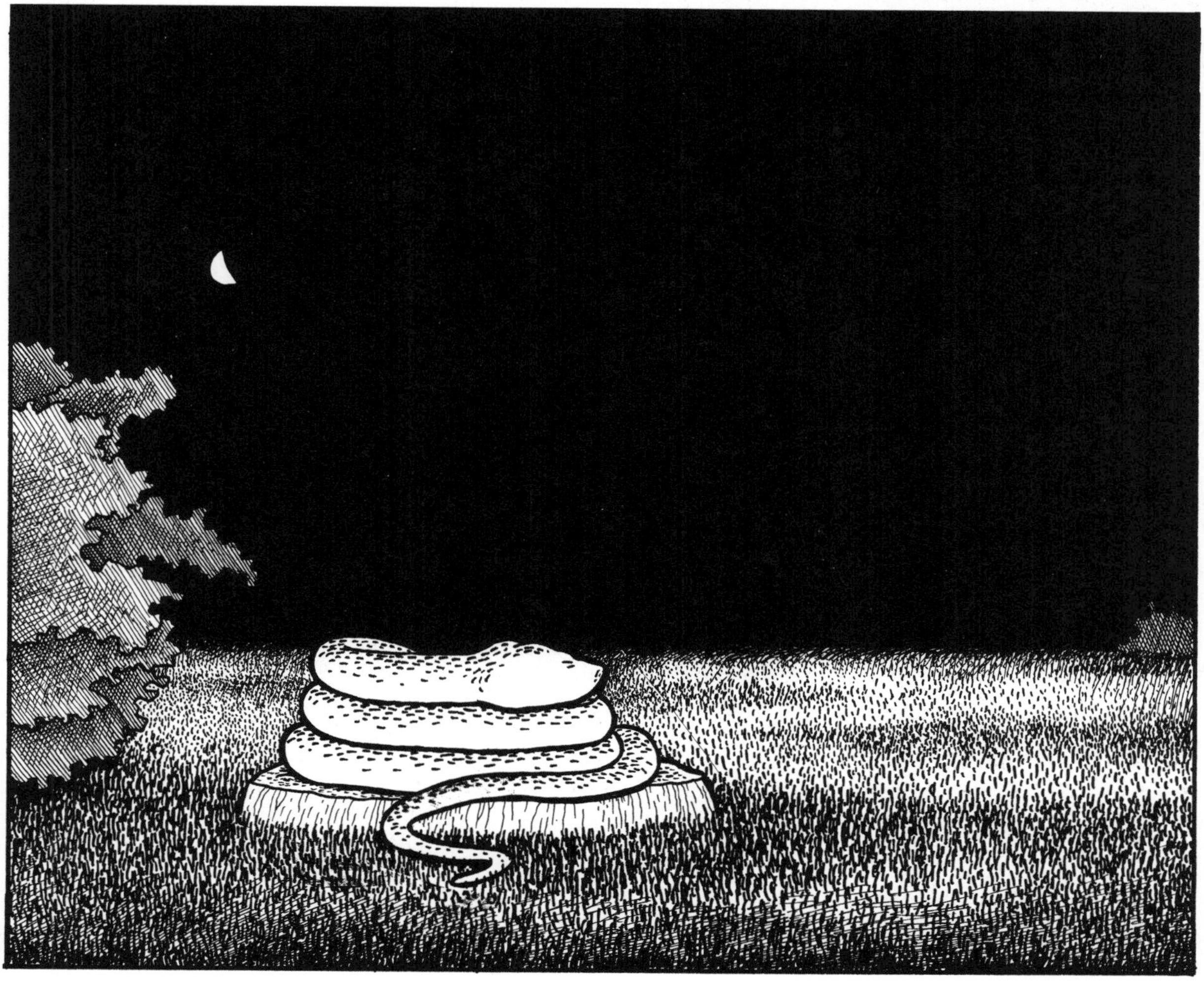

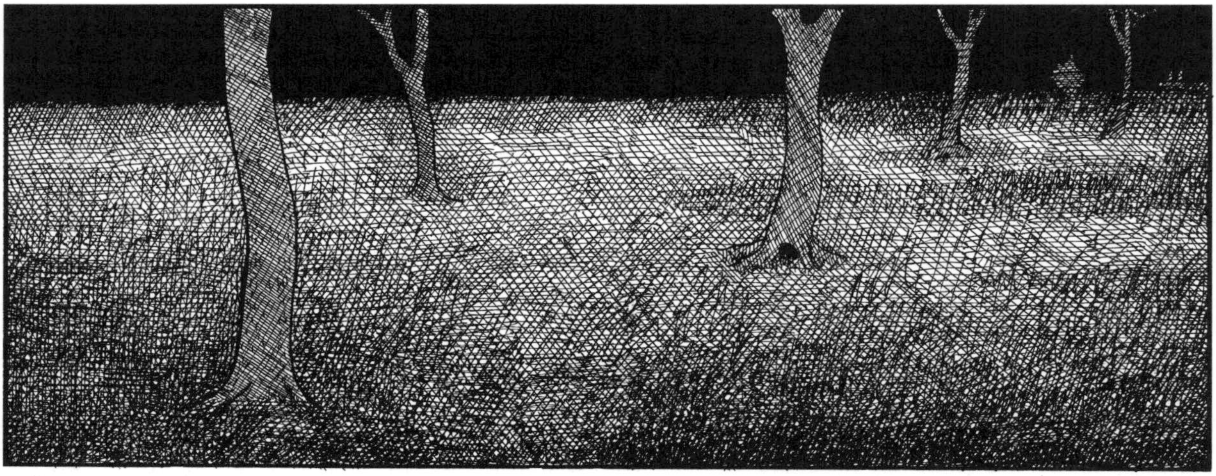

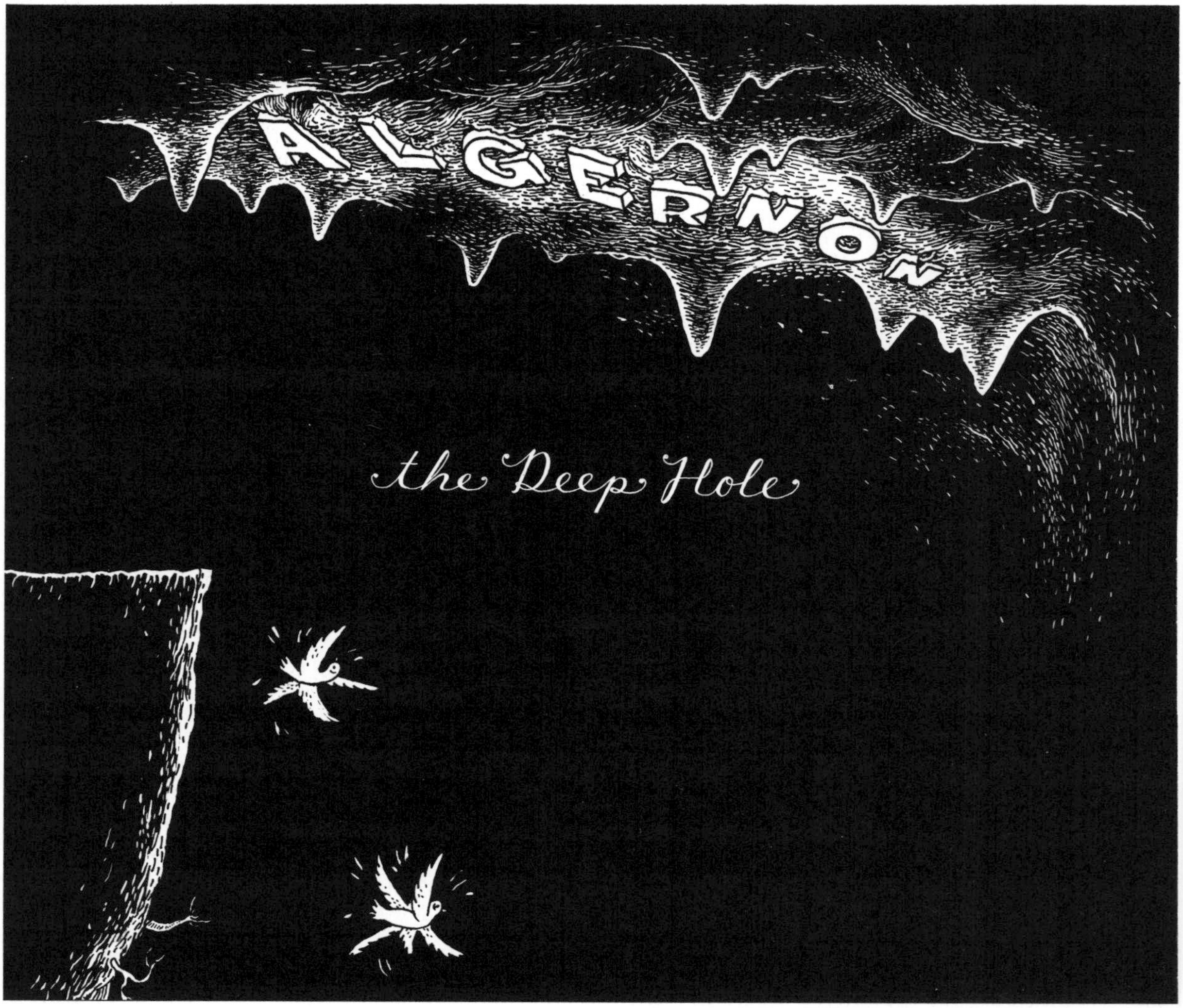
ALGERNON
the Deep Hole

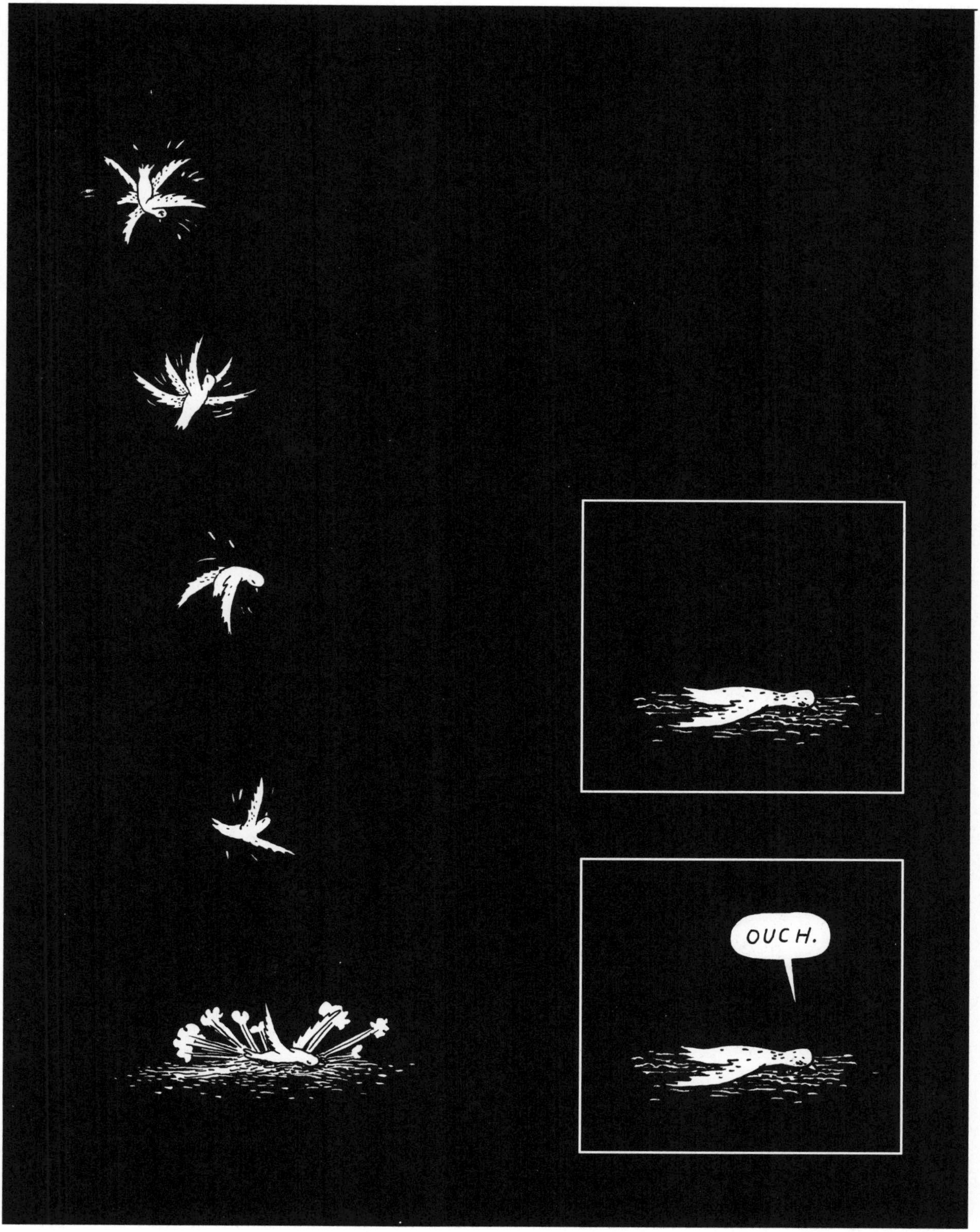
OUCH.

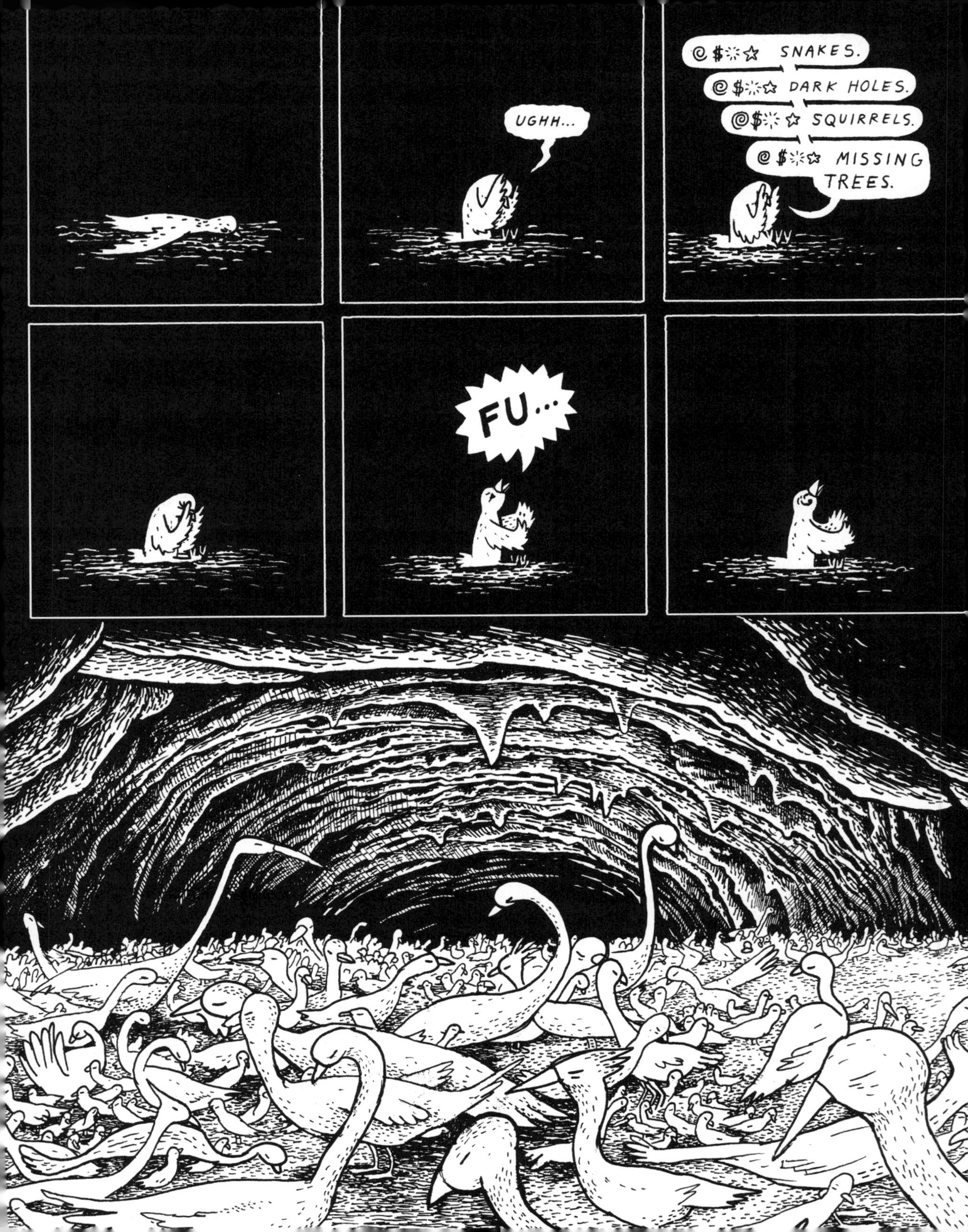

UGHH...
@$*☆ SNAKES.
@$*☆ DARK HOLES.
@$*☆ SQUIRRELS.
@$*☆ MISSING TREES.
FU...

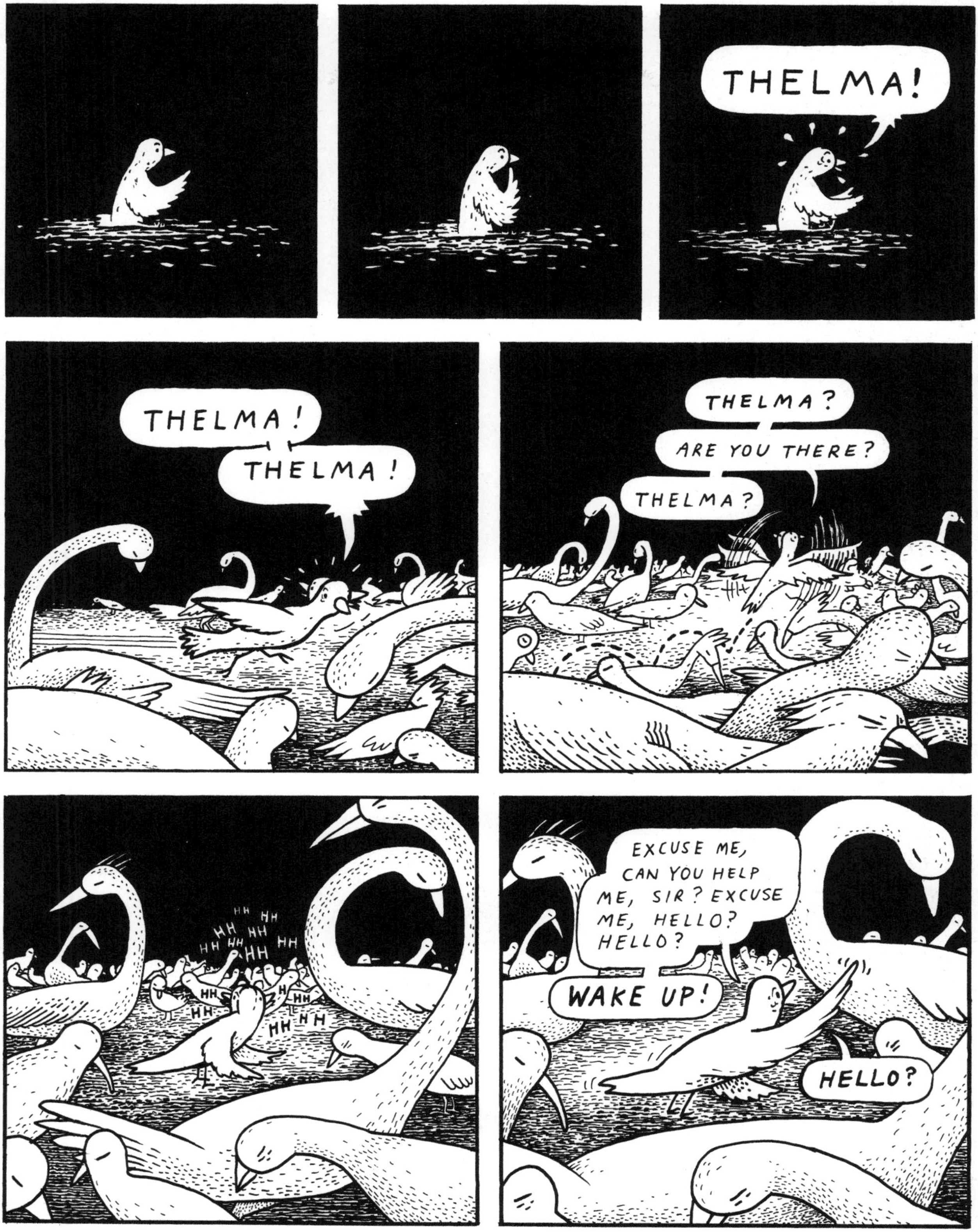
THELMA!
THELMA!
THELMA!
THELMA?
ARE YOU THERE?
THELMA?
HH HH HH HH HH HH HH HH HH HH HH HH HH HH HH
EXCUSE ME, CAN YOU HELP ME, SIR? EXCUSE ME, HELLO? HELLO?
WAKE UP!
HELLO?

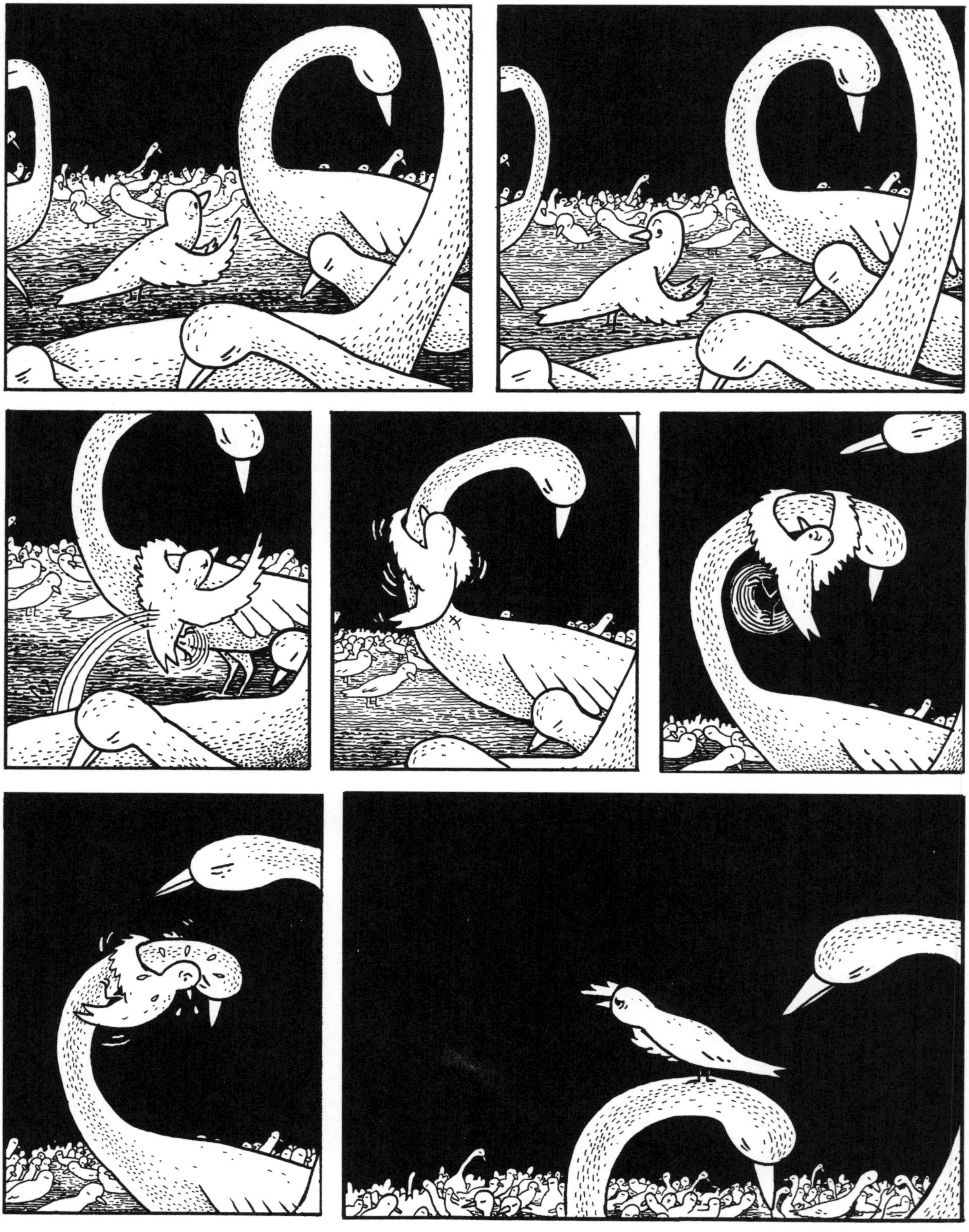

THELMA!
OOF!

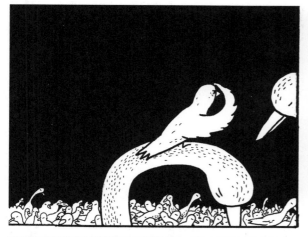

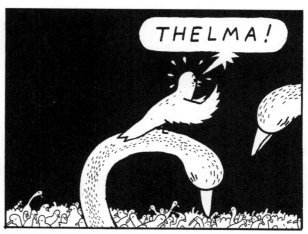

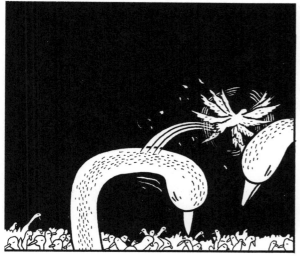

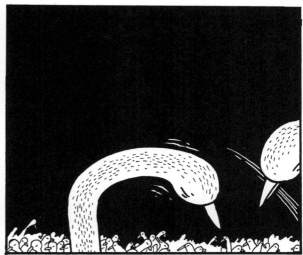

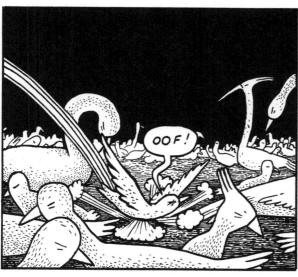

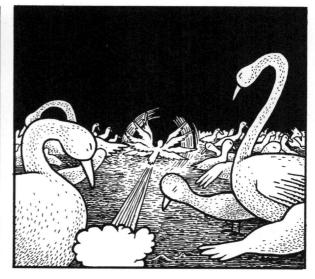

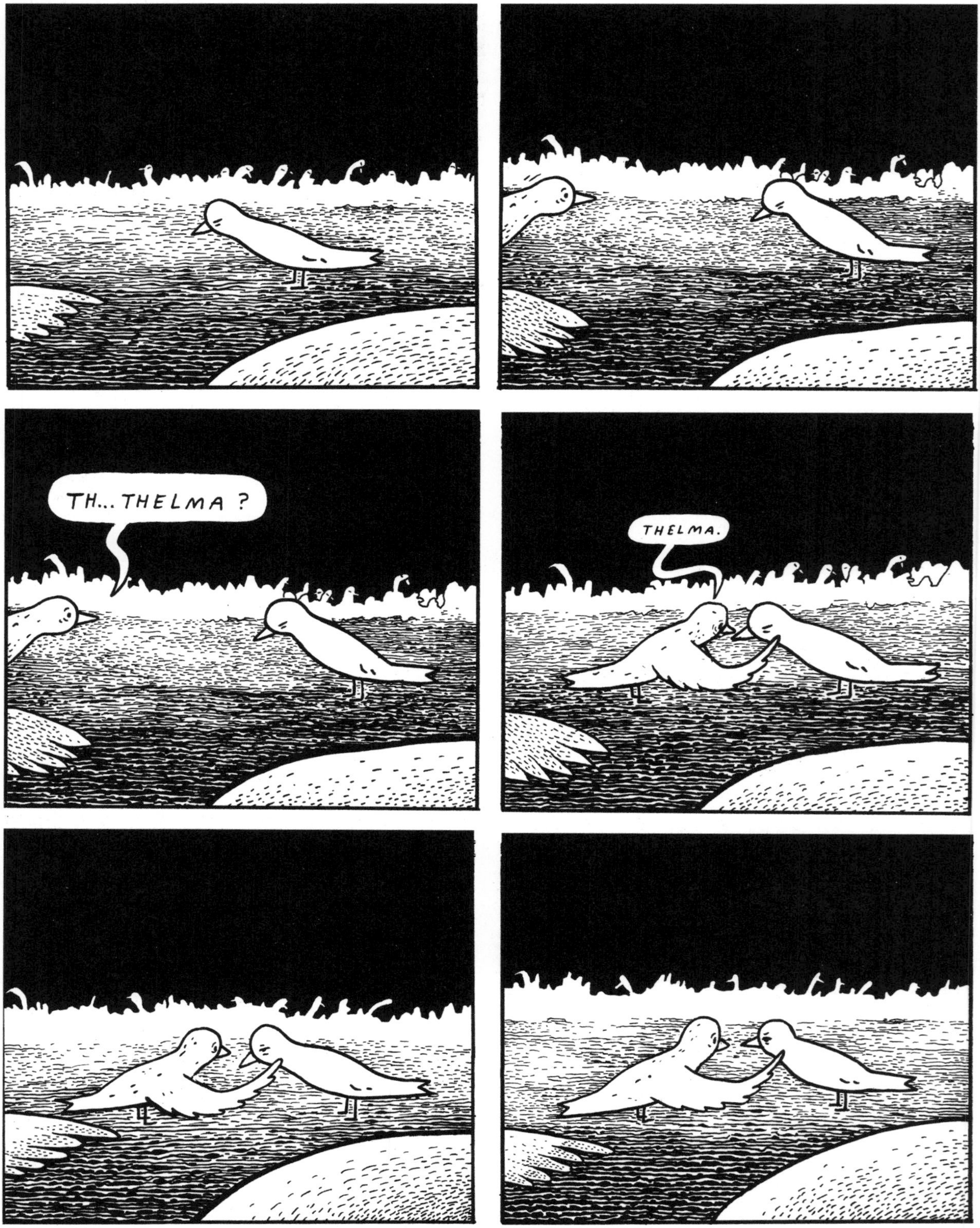
TH... THELMA ?
THELMA.

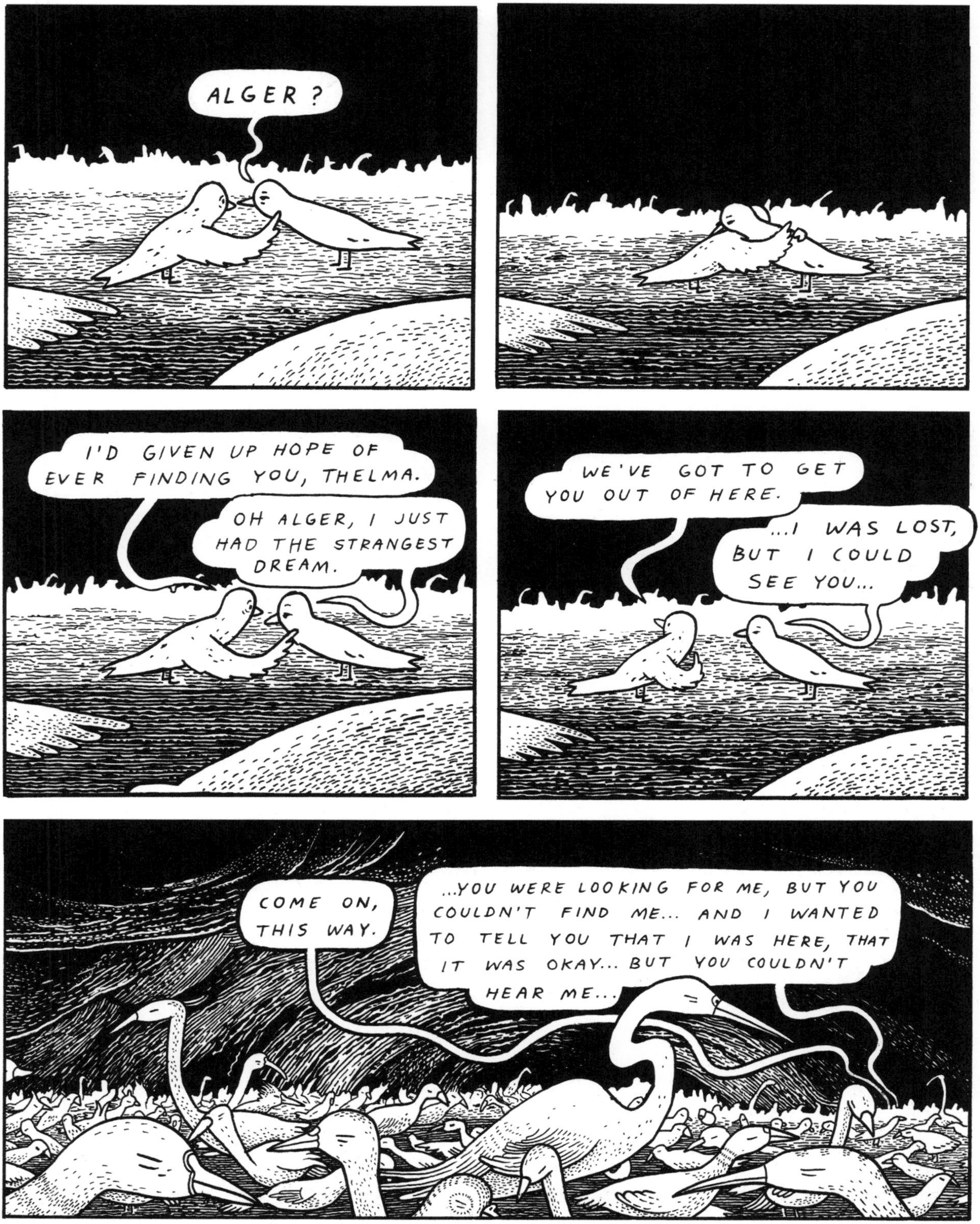
ALGER?
I'D GIVEN UP HOPE OF EVER FINDING YOU, THELMA.
OH ALGER, I JUST HAD THE STRANGEST DREAM.
WE'VE GOT TO GET YOU OUT OF HERE.
...I WAS LOST, BUT I COULD SEE YOU...
COME ON, THIS WAY.
...YOU WERE LOOKING FOR ME, BUT YOU COULDN'T FIND ME... AND I WANTED TO TELL YOU THAT I WAS HERE, THAT IT WAS OKAY... BUT YOU COULDN'T HEAR ME...

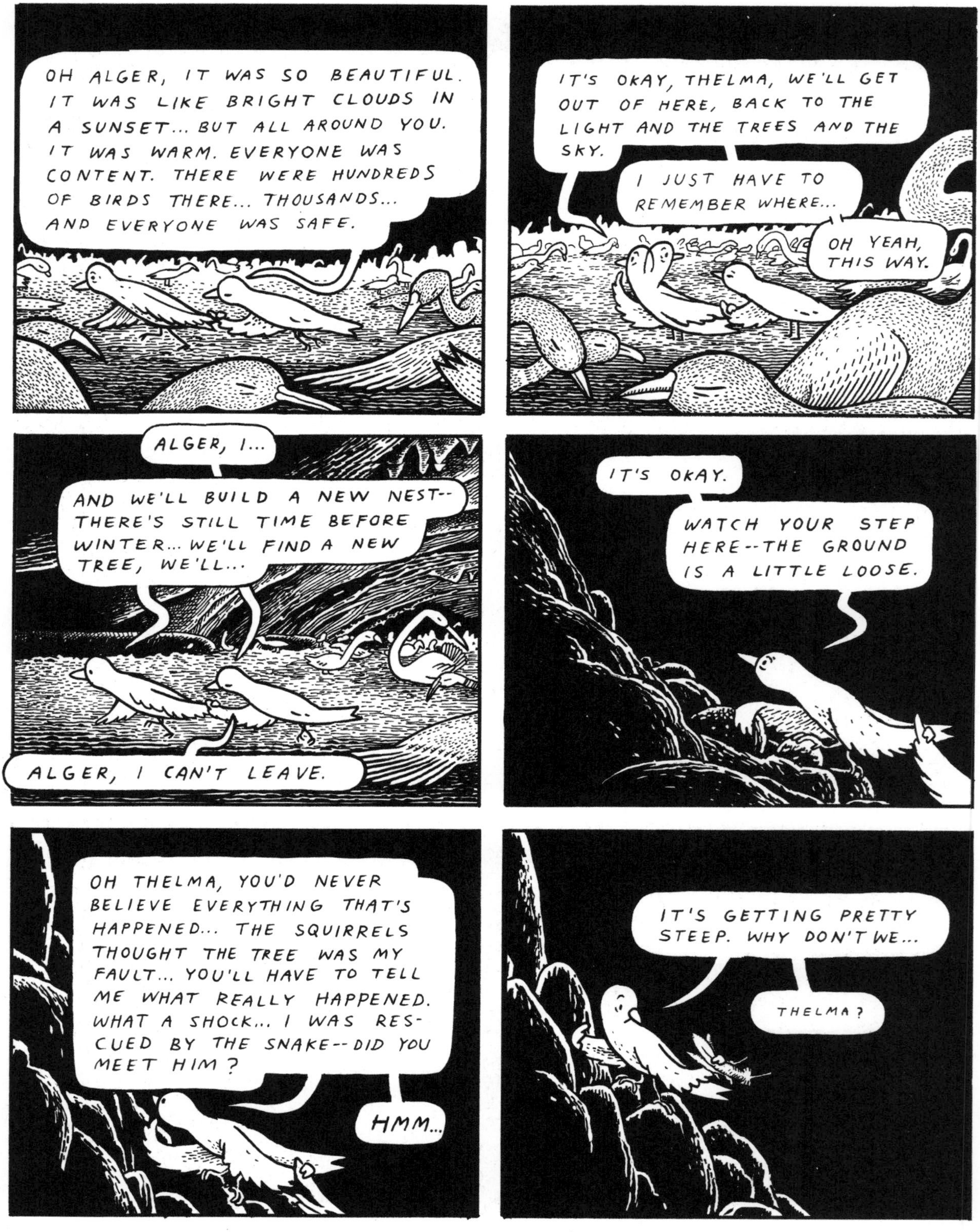
OH ALGER, IT WAS SO BEAUTIFUL. IT WAS LIKE BRIGHT CLOUDS IN A SUNSET... BUT ALL AROUND YOU. IT WAS WARM. EVERYONE WAS CONTENT. THERE WERE HUNDREDS OF BIRDS THERE... THOUSANDS... AND EVERYONE WAS SAFE.
IT'S OKAY, THELMA, WE'LL GET OUT OF HERE, BACK TO THE LIGHT AND THE TREES AND THE SKY.
I JUST HAVE TO REMEMBER WHERE...
OH YEAH, THIS WAY.
ALGER, I...
AND WE'LL BUILD A NEW NEST-- THERE'S STILL TIME BEFORE WINTER... WE'LL FIND A NEW TREE, WE'LL...
ALGER, I CAN'T LEAVE.
IT'S OKAY.
WATCH YOUR STEP HERE--THE GROUND IS A LITTLE LOOSE.
OH THELMA, YOU'D NEVER BELIEVE EVERYTHING THAT'S HAPPENED... THE SQUIRRELS THOUGHT THE TREE WAS MY FAULT... YOU'LL HAVE TO TELL ME WHAT REALLY HAPPENED. WHAT A SHOCK... I WAS RESCUED BY THE SNAKE--DID YOU MEET HIM?
HMM...
IT'S GETTING PRETTY STEEP. WHY DON'T WE...
THELMA?

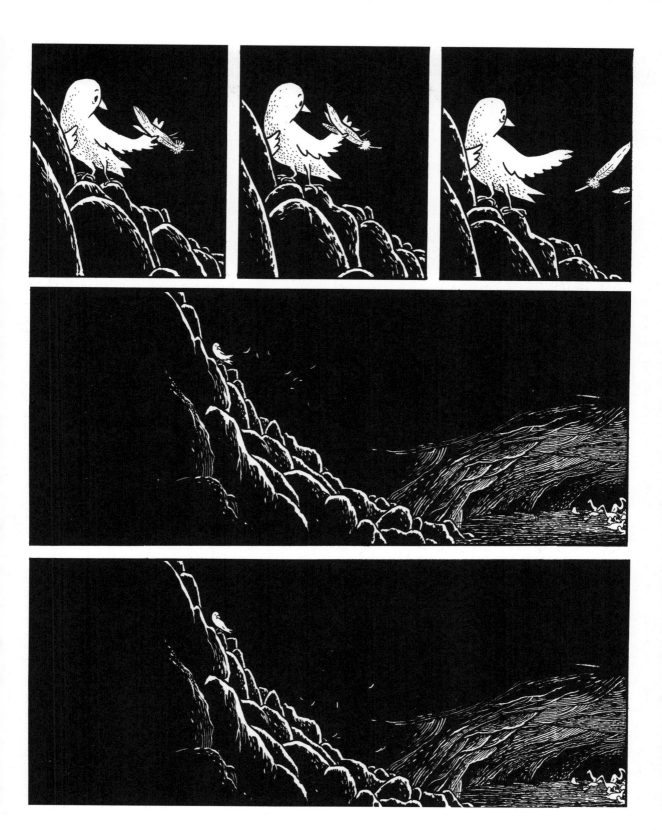

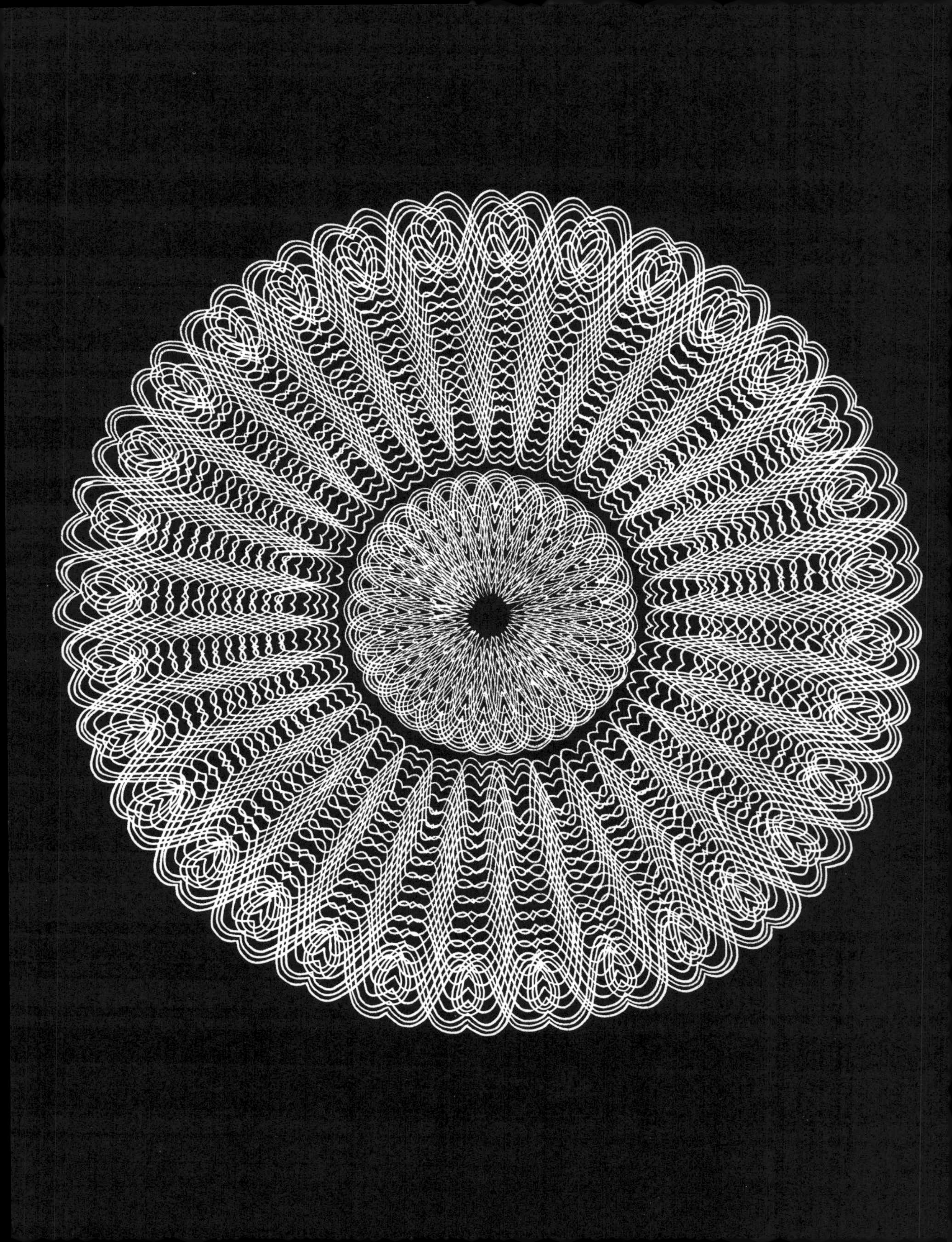

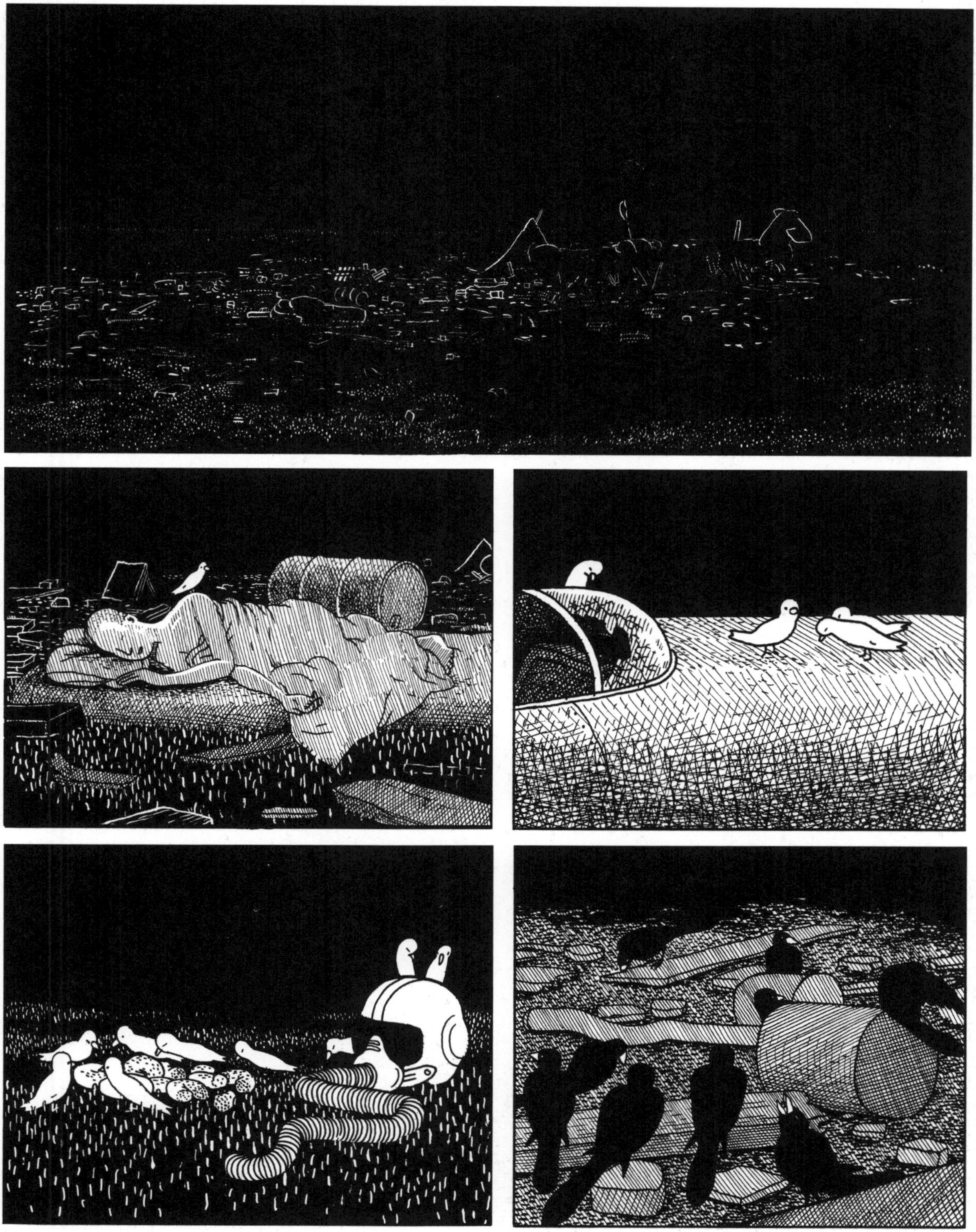

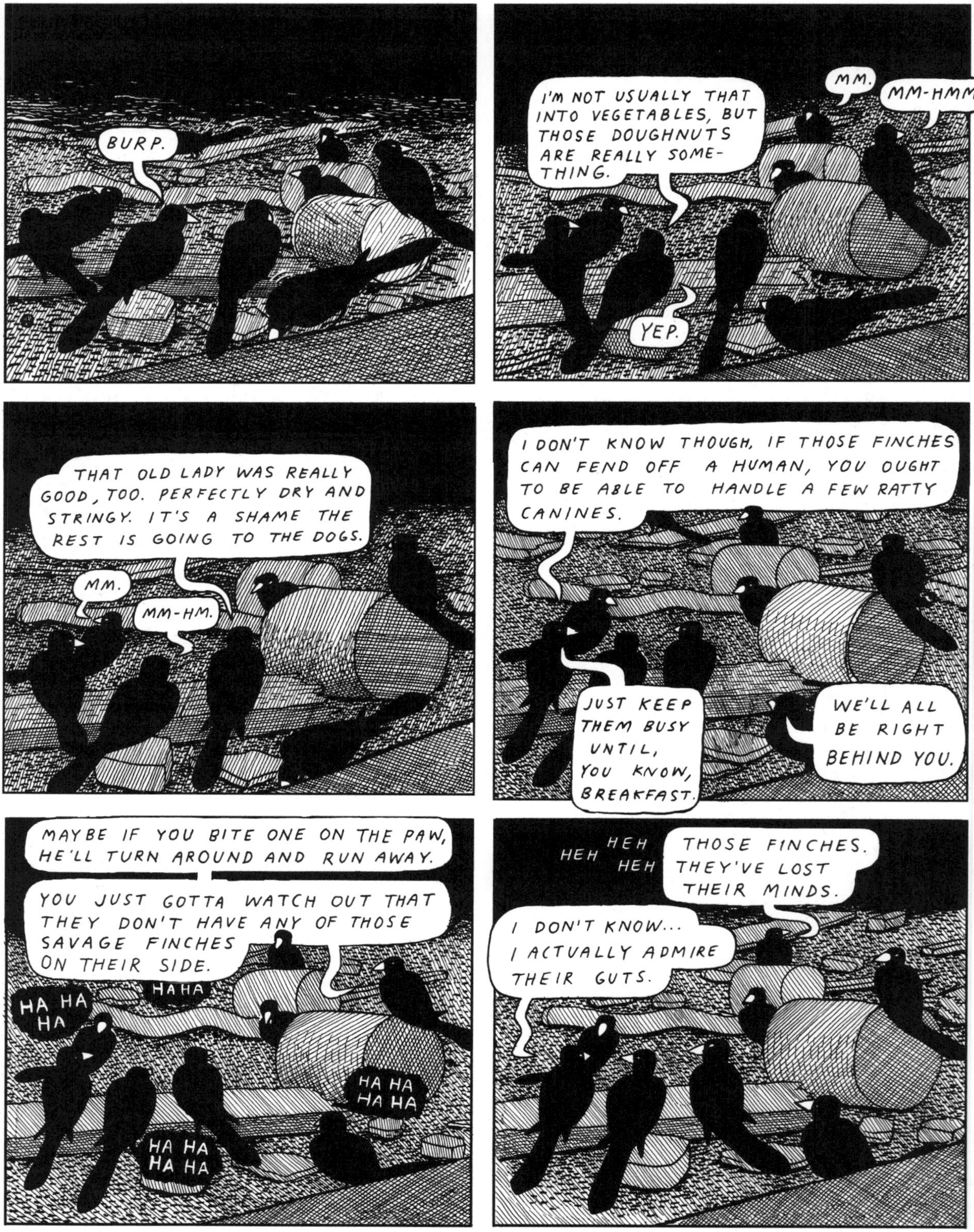
BURP.
I'M NOT USUALLY THAT INTO VEGETABLES, BUT THOSE DOUGHNUTS ARE REALLY SOME-THING.
MM.
MM-HMM.
YEP.
THAT OLD LADY WAS REALLY GOOD, TOO. PERFECTLY DRY AND STRINGY. IT'S A SHAME THE REST IS GOING TO THE DOGS.
MM.
MM-HM.
I DON'T KNOW THOUGH, IF THOSE FINCHES CAN FEND OFF A HUMAN, YOU OUGHT TO BE ABLE TO HANDLE A FEW RATTY CANINES.
JUST KEEP THEM BUSY UNTIL, YOU KNOW, BREAKFAST.
WE'LL ALL BE RIGHT BEHIND YOU.
MAYBE IF YOU BITE ONE ON THE PAW, HE'LL TURN AROUND AND RUN AWAY.
YOU JUST GOTTA WATCH OUT THAT THEY DON'T HAVE ANY OF THOSE SAVAGE FINCHES ON THEIR SIDE.
HA HA HA
HA HA
HA HA HA HA
HA HA HA HA
HEH HEH HEH
THOSE FINCHES. THEY'VE LOST THEIR MINDS.
I DON'T KNOW... I ACTUALLY ADMIRE THEIR GUTS.

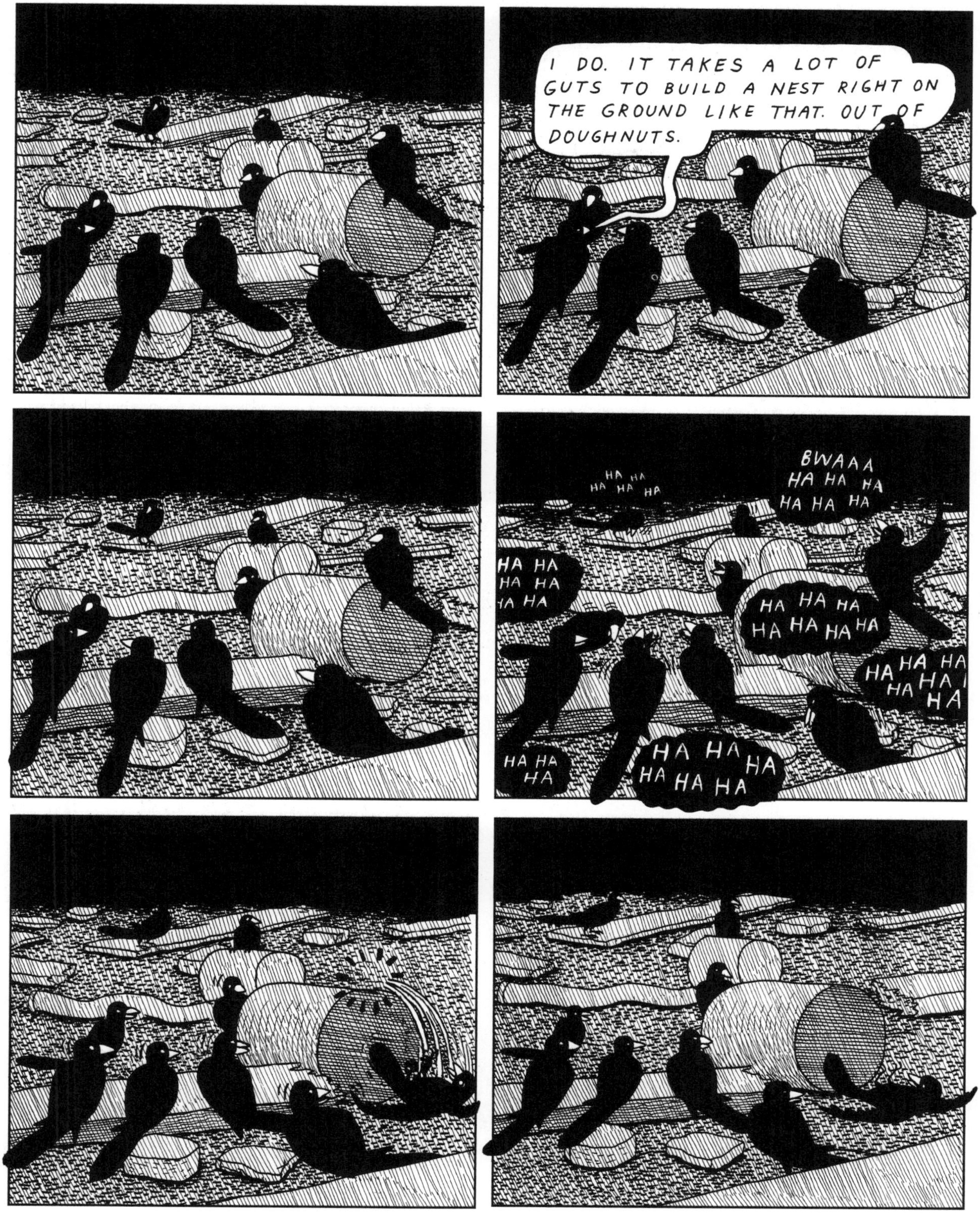
I DO. IT TAKES A LOT OF GUTS TO BUILD A NEST RIGHT ON THE GROUND LIKE THAT. OUT OF DOUGHNUTS.
HA HA HA HA HA
BWAAA HA HA HA HA HA HA
HA HA HA HA HA HA
HA HA HA HA HA HA HA
HA HA HA HA HA HA
HA HA HA
HA HA HA HA HA HA

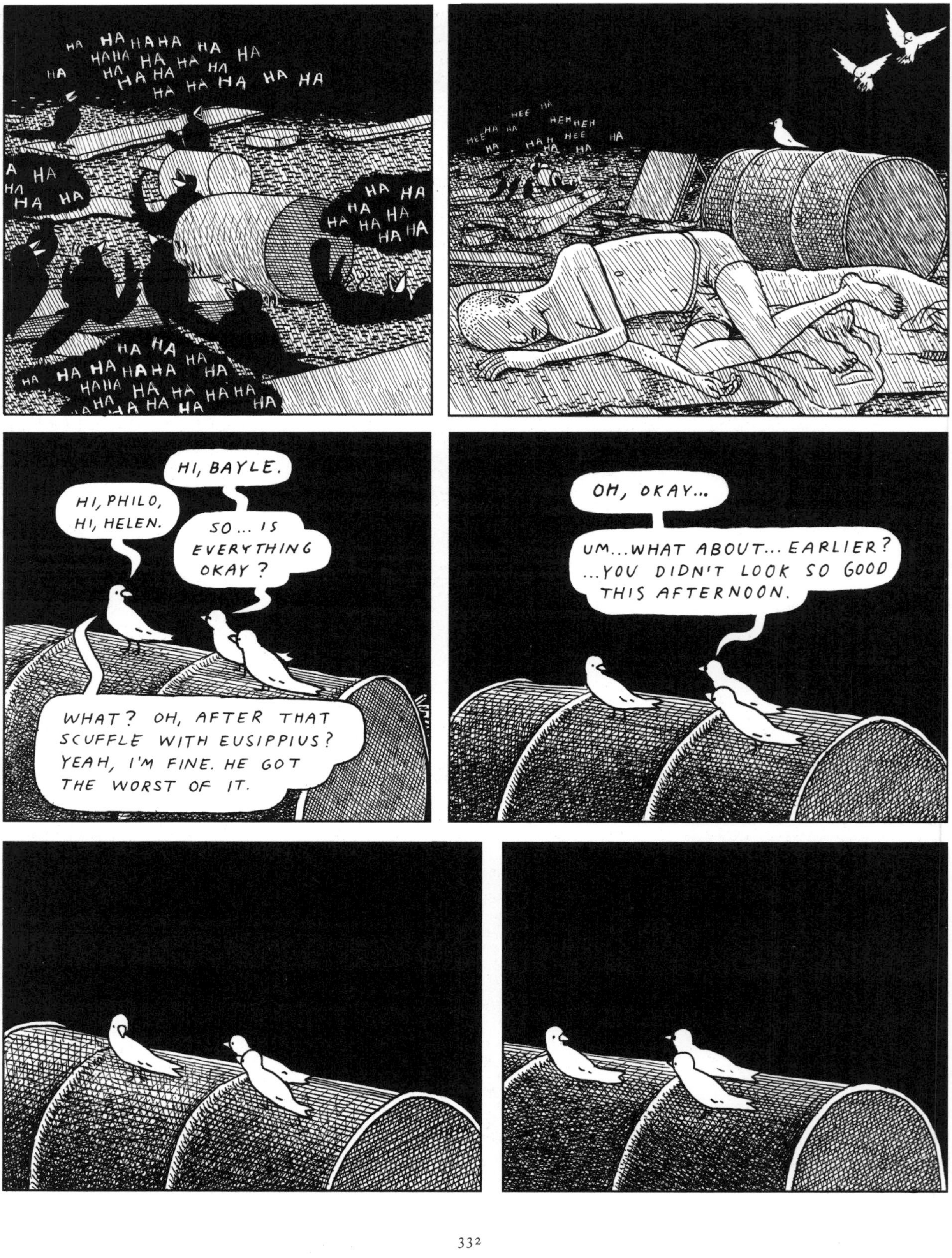
HA HA HAHA HA HA
HAHA HA HA HA HA
HA HA HA HA HA HA HA HA HA HA
HA HA HA HA
HA HA HA HA HA HA HA
HA HA HA HA HA HA HA HA HA HA HA HA HA HA HA HA HA HA
HEE HA HEE HA HA HEH HEH HEE HA HAH HA HA HA
HI, PHILO, HI, HELEN.
HI, BAYLE.
SO... IS EVERYTHING OKAY?
WHAT? OH, AFTER THAT SCUFFLE WITH EUSIPPIUS? YEAH, I'M FINE. HE GOT THE WORST OF IT.
OH, OKAY...
UM... WHAT ABOUT... EARLIER? ...YOU DIDN'T LOOK SO GOOD THIS AFTERNOON.

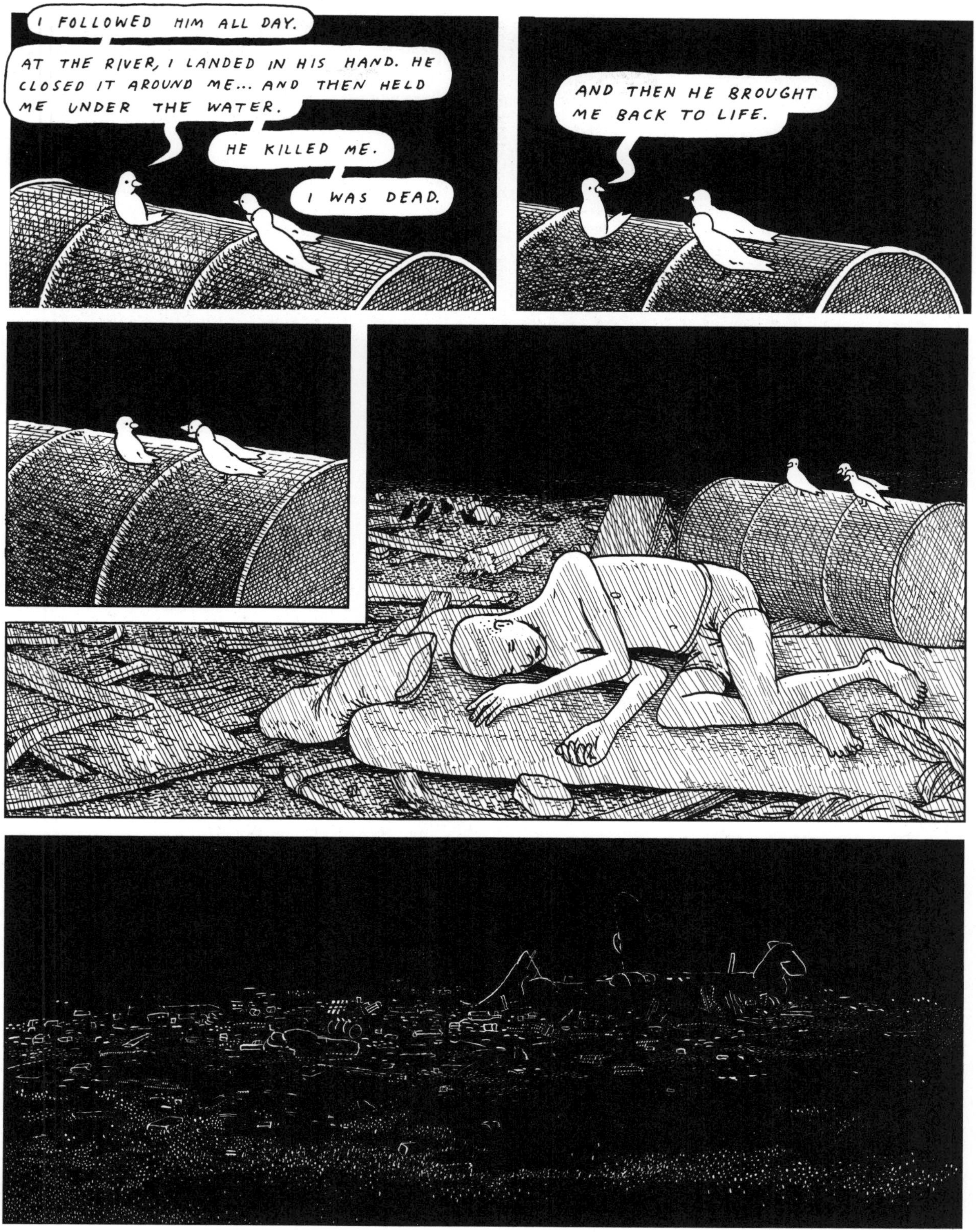
I FOLLOWED HIM ALL DAY.
AT THE RIVER, I LANDED IN HIS HAND. HE CLOSED IT AROUND ME... AND THEN HELD ME UNDER THE WATER.
HE KILLED ME.
I WAS DEAD.
AND THEN HE BROUGHT ME BACK TO LIFE.

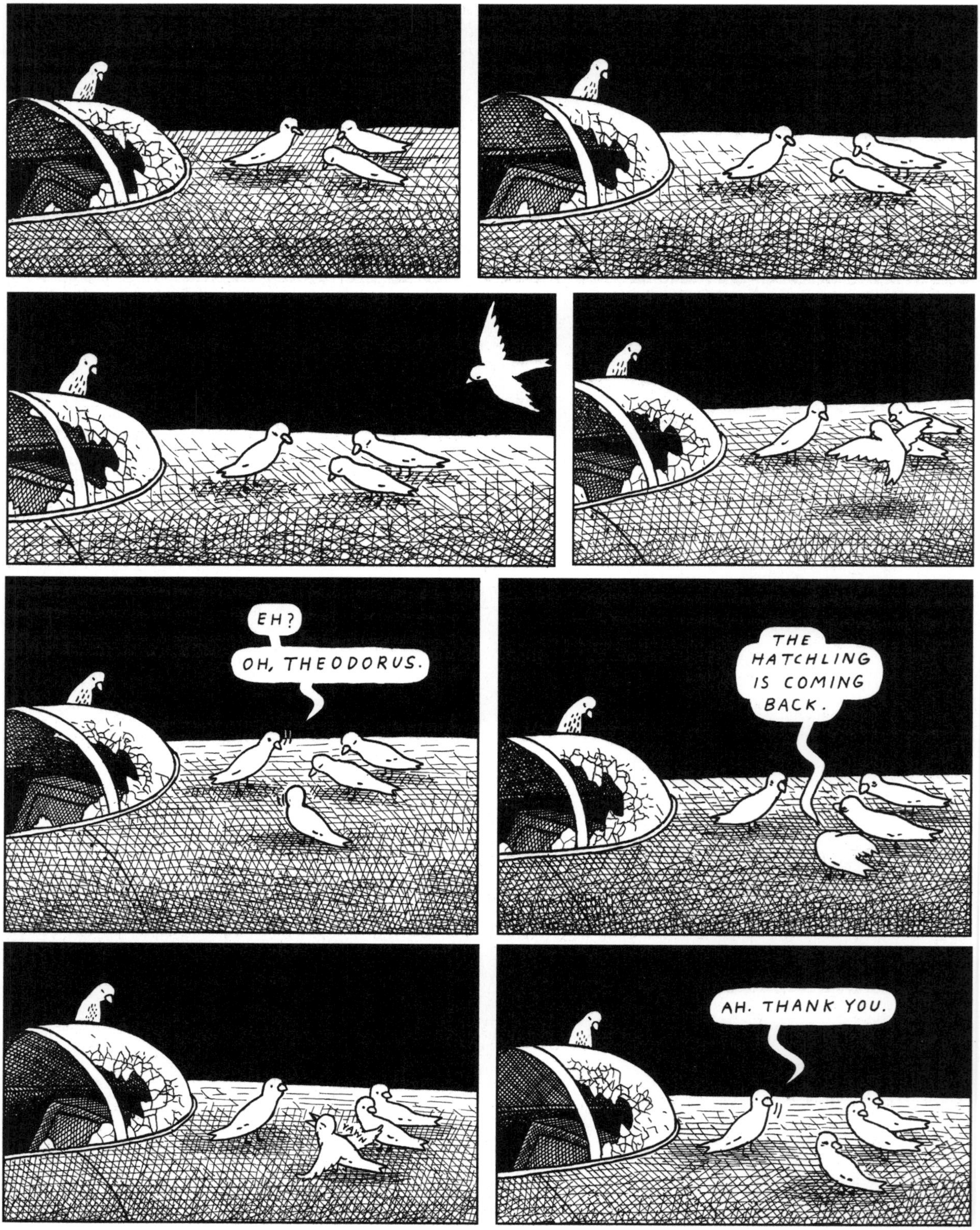
EH?
OH, THEODORUS.
THE HATCHLING IS COMING BACK.
YAWN
AH. THANK YOU.

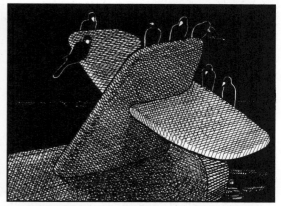

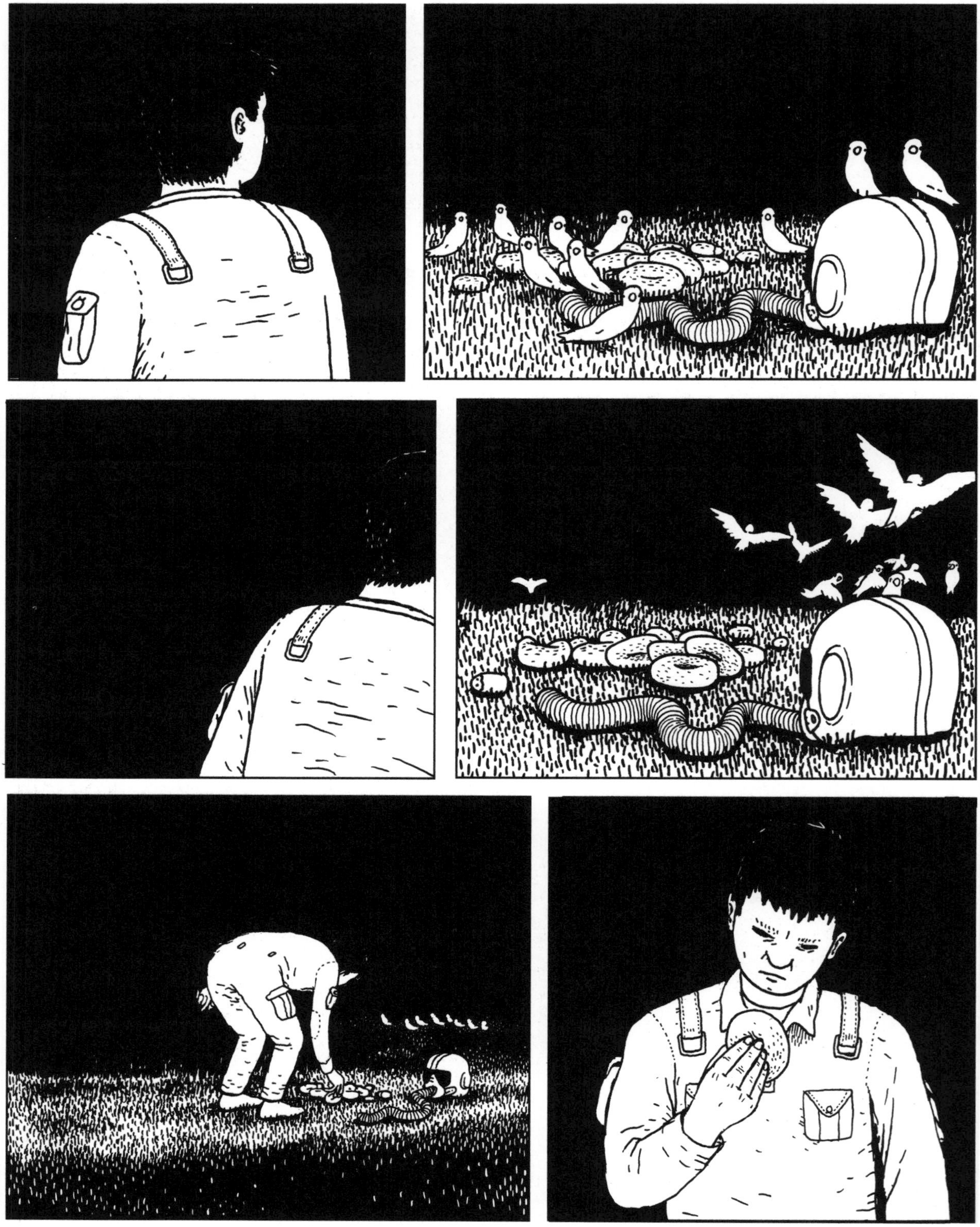

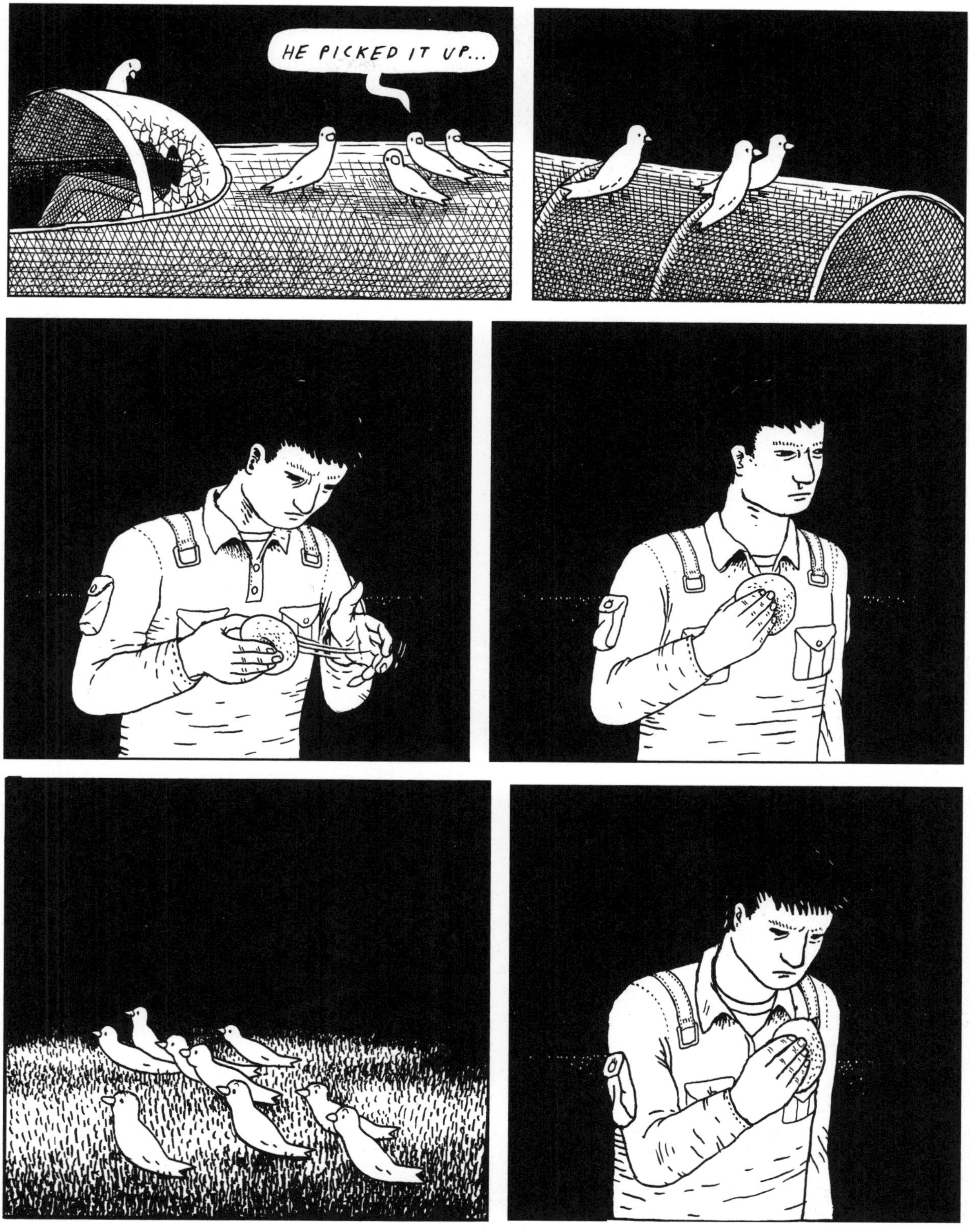
HE PICKED IT UP...

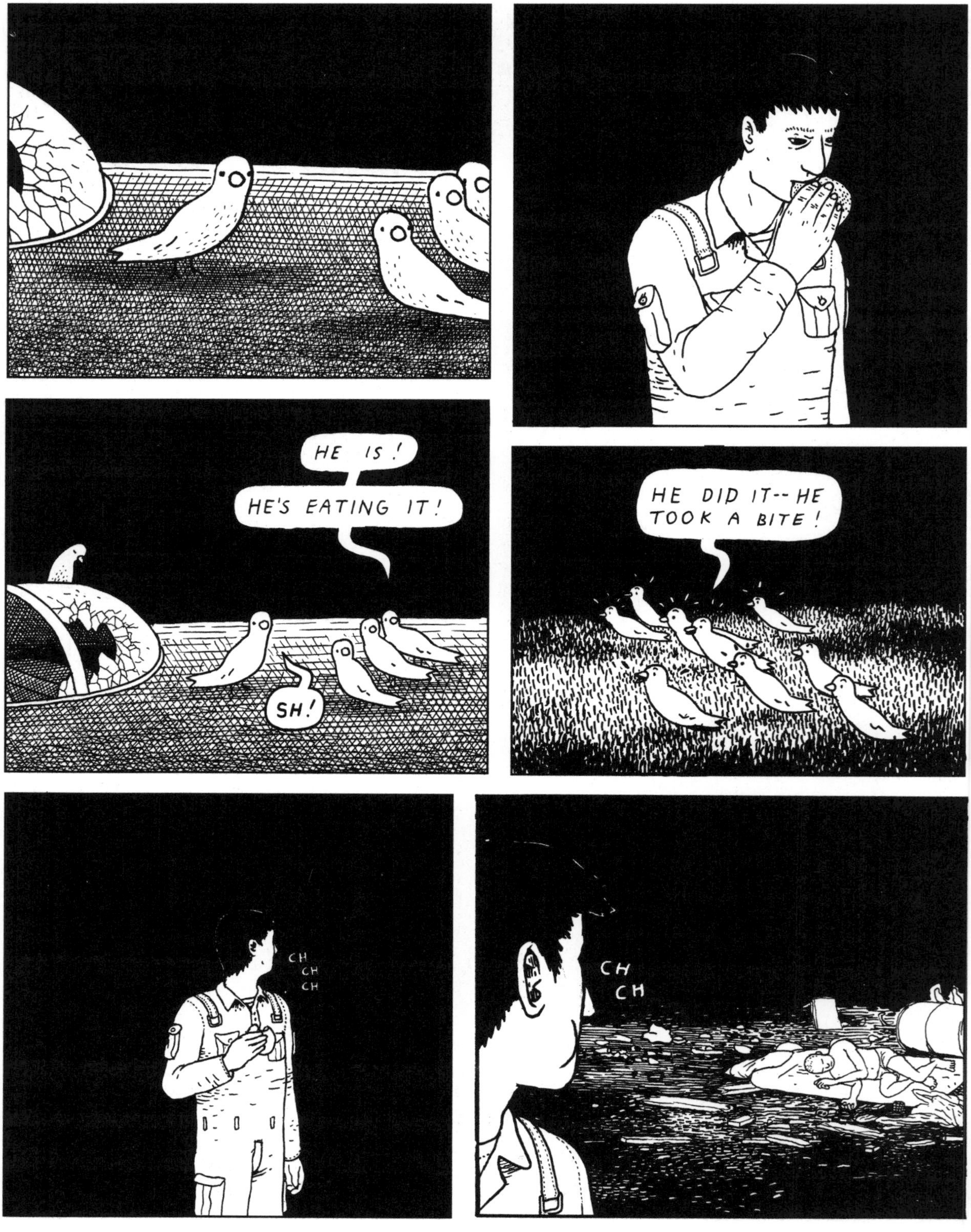
HE IS!
HE'S EATING IT!
SH!
HE DID IT-- HE TOOK A BITE!
CH CH CH
CH CH

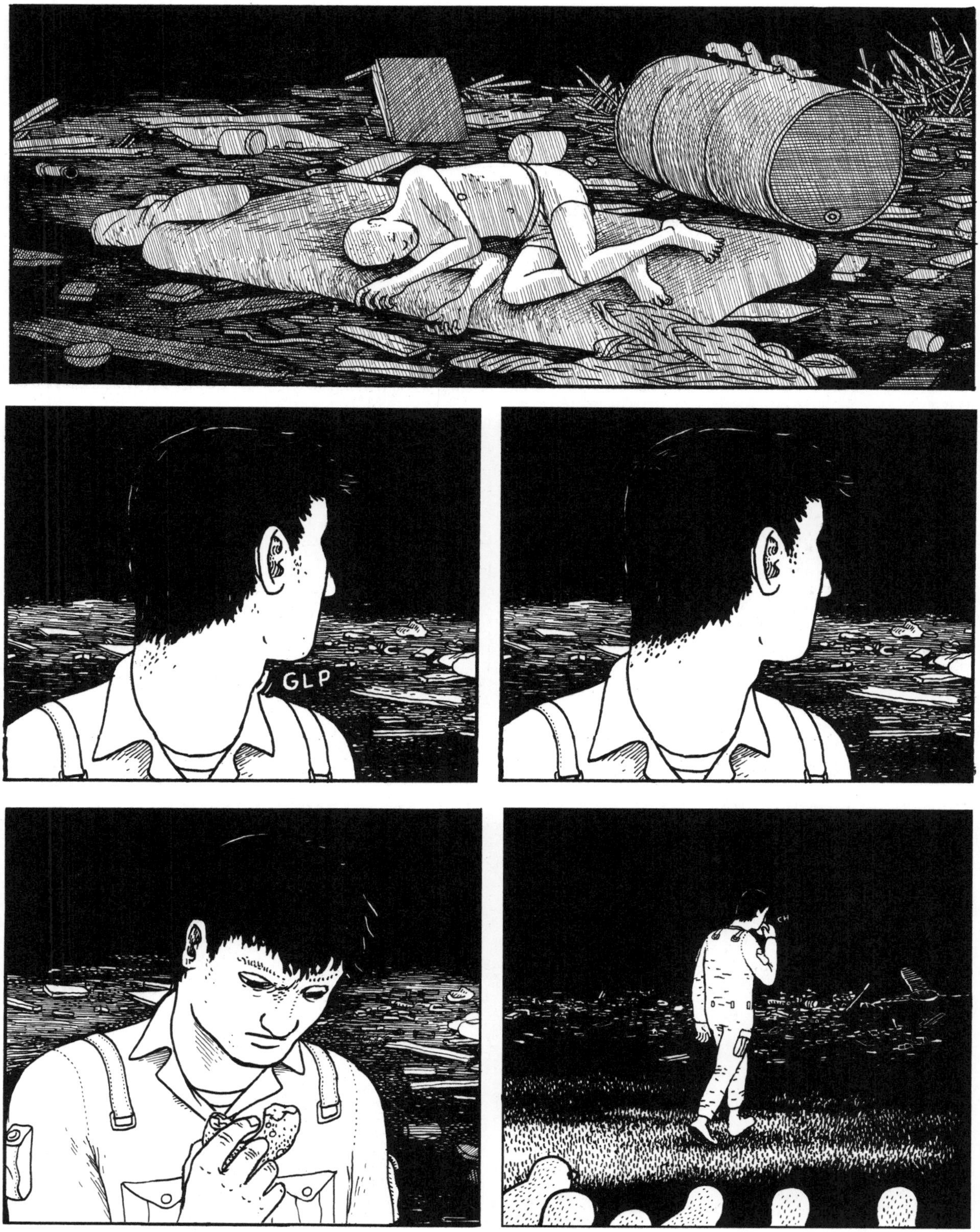
GLP
CH

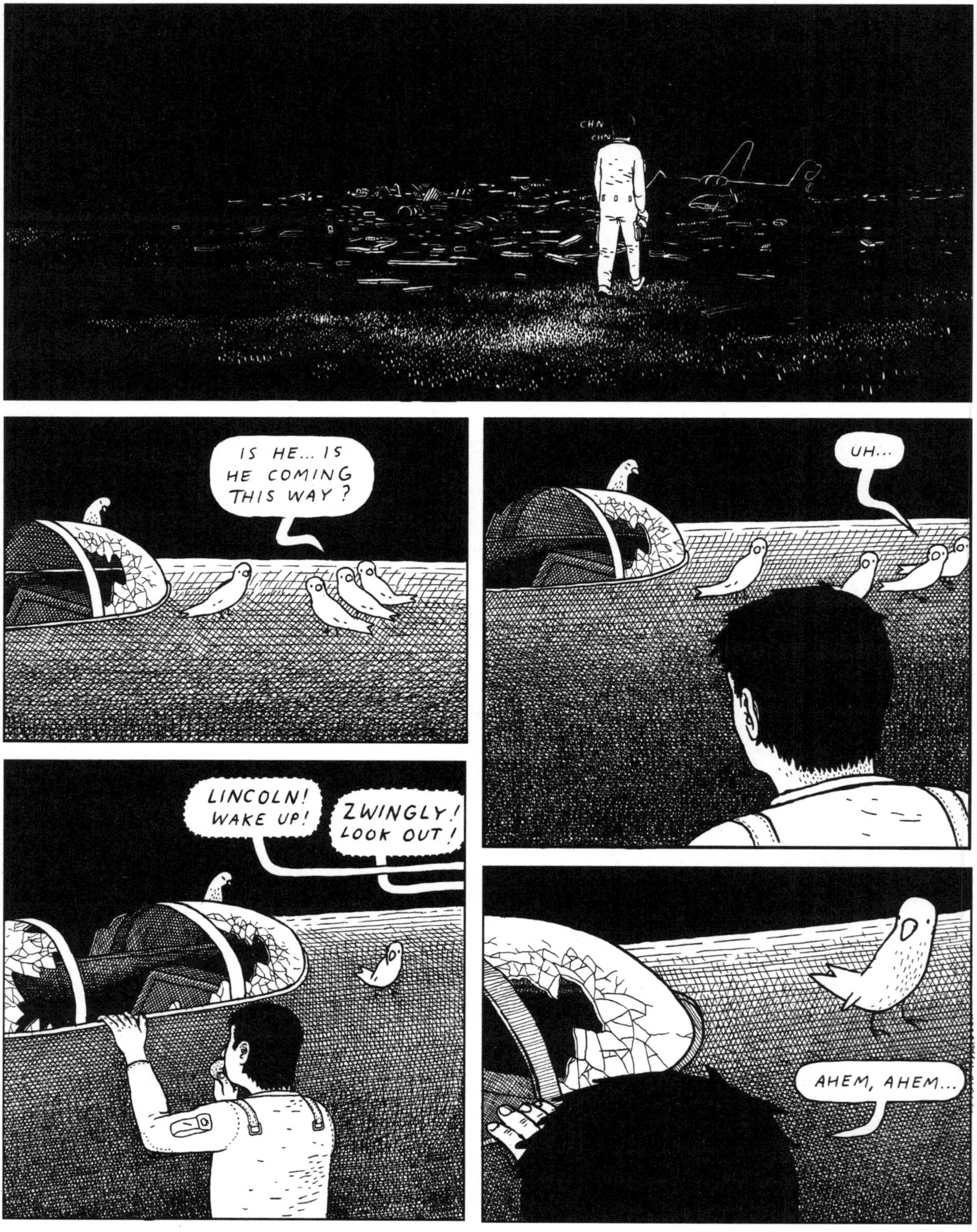
CHN CHN
IS HE... IS HE COMING THIS WAY?
UH...
LINCOLN! WAKE UP!
ZWINGLY! LOOK OUT!
AHEM, AHEM...

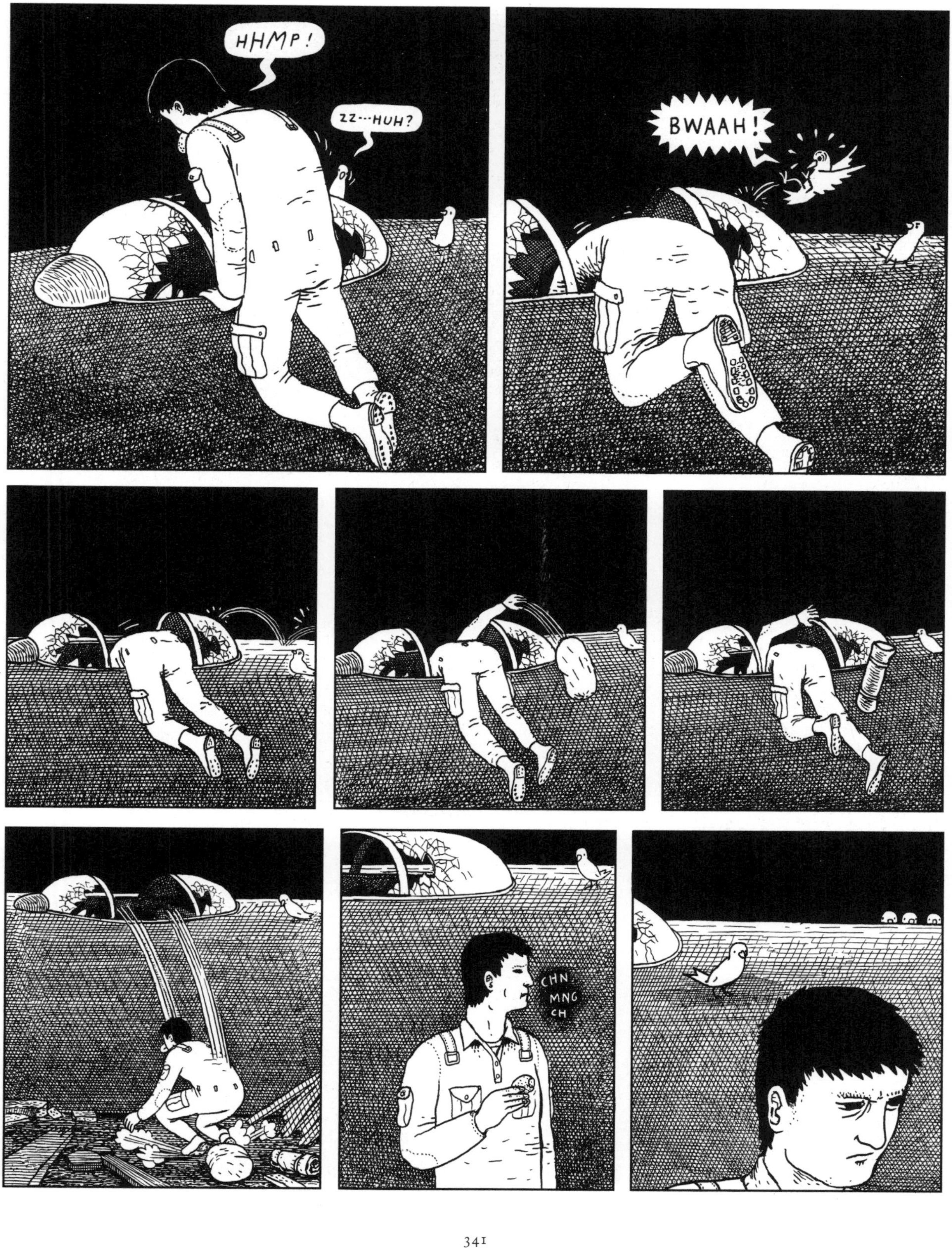
HHMP!
ZZ···HUH?
BWAAH!
CHN
MNG
CH

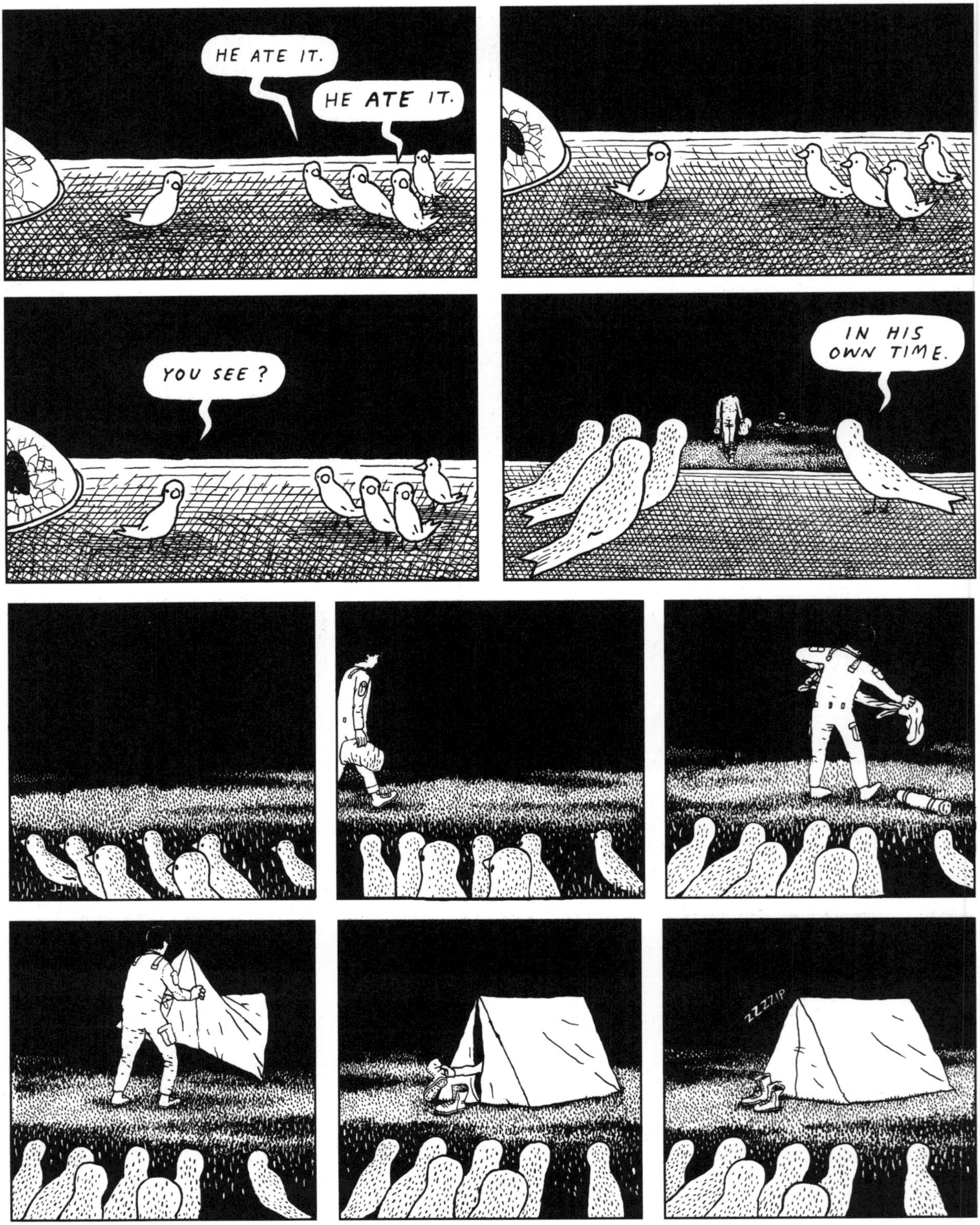
HE ATE IT.
HE ATE IT.
YOU SEE?
IN HIS OWN TIME.
ZZZZIP

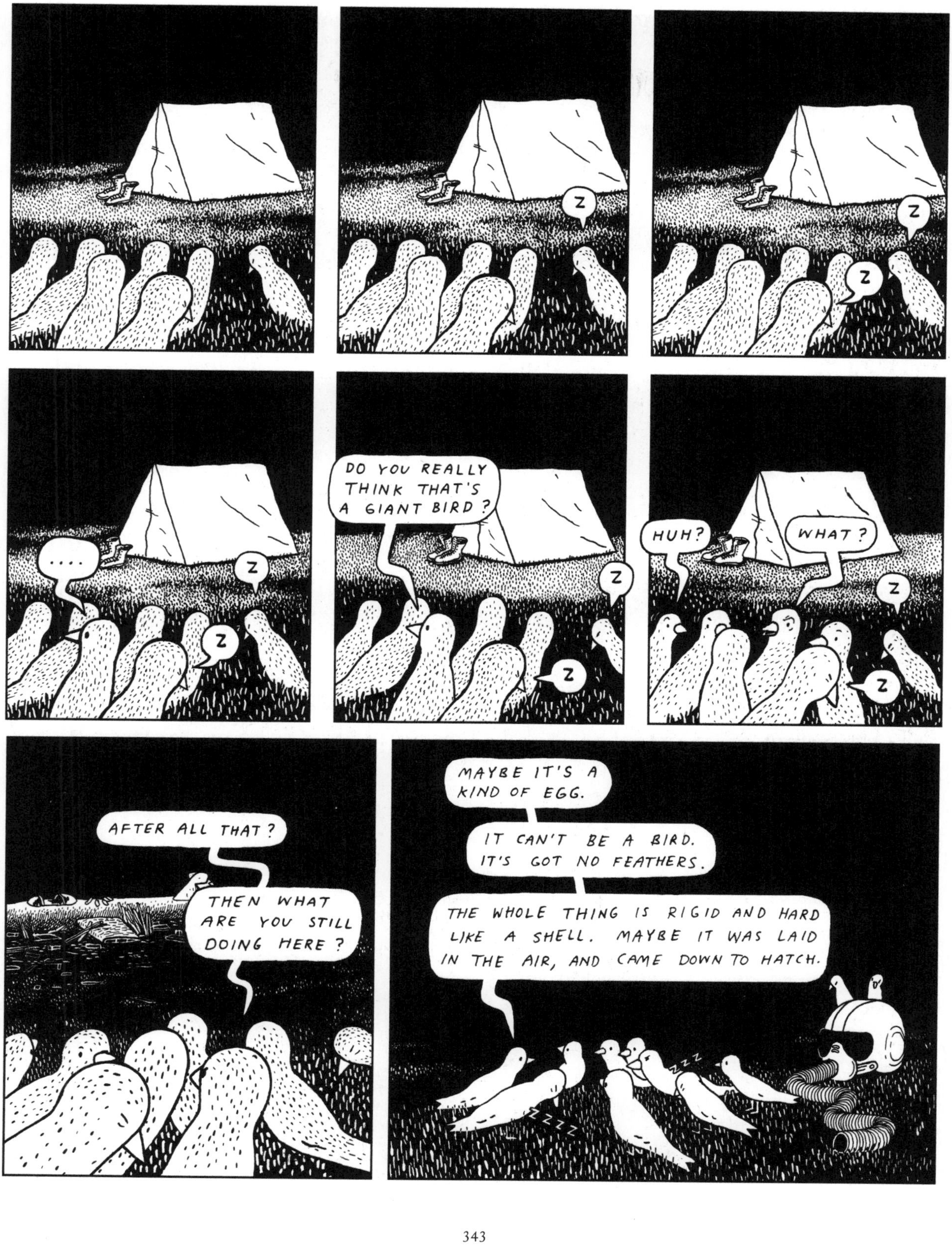
Z
Z
Z
....
Z
Z
DO YOU REALLY THINK THAT'S A GIANT BIRD?
Z
Z
HUH?
WHAT?
Z
Z
AFTER ALL THAT?
THEN WHAT ARE YOU STILL DOING HERE?
MAYBE IT'S A KIND OF EGG.
IT CAN'T BE A BIRD. IT'S GOT NO FEATHERS.
THE WHOLE THING IS RIGID AND HARD LIKE A SHELL. MAYBE IT WAS LAID IN THE AIR, AND CAME DOWN TO HATCH.

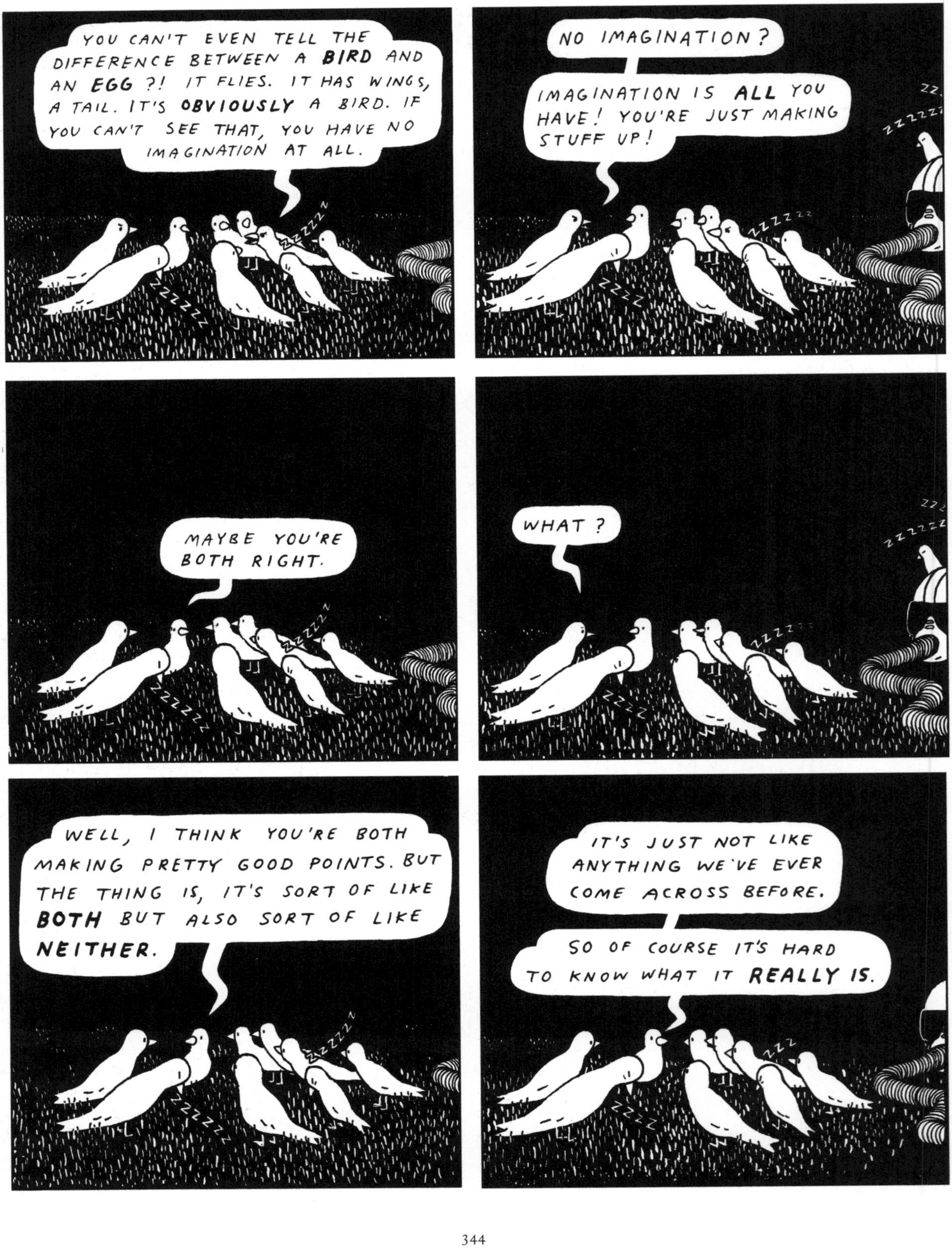
YOU CAN'T EVEN TELL THE DIFFERENCE BETWEEN A BIRD AND AN EGG ?! IT FLIES. IT HAS WINGS, A TAIL. IT'S OBVIOUSLY A BIRD. IF YOU CAN'T SEE THAT, YOU HAVE NO IMAGINATION AT ALL.
NO IMAGINATION?
IMAGINATION IS ALL YOU HAVE! YOU'RE JUST MAKING STUFF UP!
MAYBE YOU'RE BOTH RIGHT.
WHAT?
WELL, I THINK YOU'RE BOTH MAKING PRETTY GOOD POINTS. BUT THE THING IS, IT'S SORT OF LIKE BOTH BUT ALSO SORT OF LIKE NEITHER.
IT'S JUST NOT LIKE ANYTHING WE'VE EVER COME ACROSS BEFORE.
SO OF COURSE IT'S HARD TO KNOW WHAT IT REALLY IS.

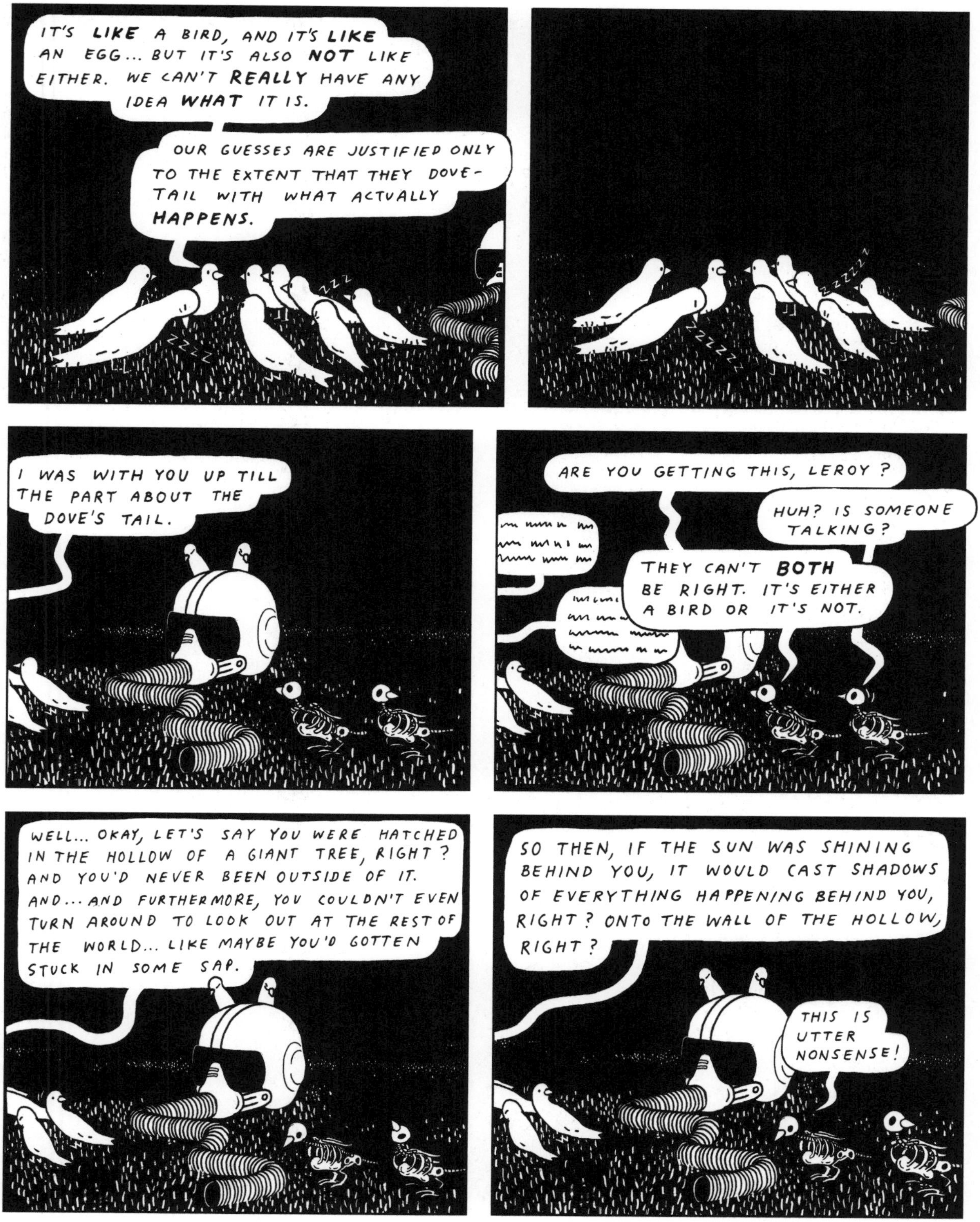

IT'S LIKE A BIRD, AND IT'S LIKE AN EGG... BUT IT'S ALSO NOT LIKE EITHER. WE CAN'T REALLY HAVE ANY IDEA WHAT IT IS.
OUR GUESSES ARE JUSTIFIED ONLY TO THE EXTENT THAT THEY DOVE-TAIL WITH WHAT ACTUALLY HAPPENS.
I WAS WITH YOU UP TILL THE PART ABOUT THE DOVE'S TAIL.
ARE YOU GETTING THIS, LEROY?
HUH? IS SOMEONE TALKING?
THEY CAN'T BOTH BE RIGHT. IT'S EITHER A BIRD OR IT'S NOT.
WELL... OKAY, LET'S SAY YOU WERE HATCHED IN THE HOLLOW OF A GIANT TREE, RIGHT? AND YOU'D NEVER BEEN OUTSIDE OF IT. AND... AND FURTHERMORE, YOU COULDN'T EVEN TURN AROUND TO LOOK OUT AT THE REST OF THE WORLD... LIKE MAYBE YOU'D GOTTEN STUCK IN SOME SAP.
SO THEN, IF THE SUN WAS SHINING BEHIND YOU, IT WOULD CAST SHADOWS OF EVERYTHING HAPPENING BEHIND YOU, RIGHT? ONTO THE WALL OF THE HOLLOW, RIGHT?
THIS IS UTTER NONSENSE!

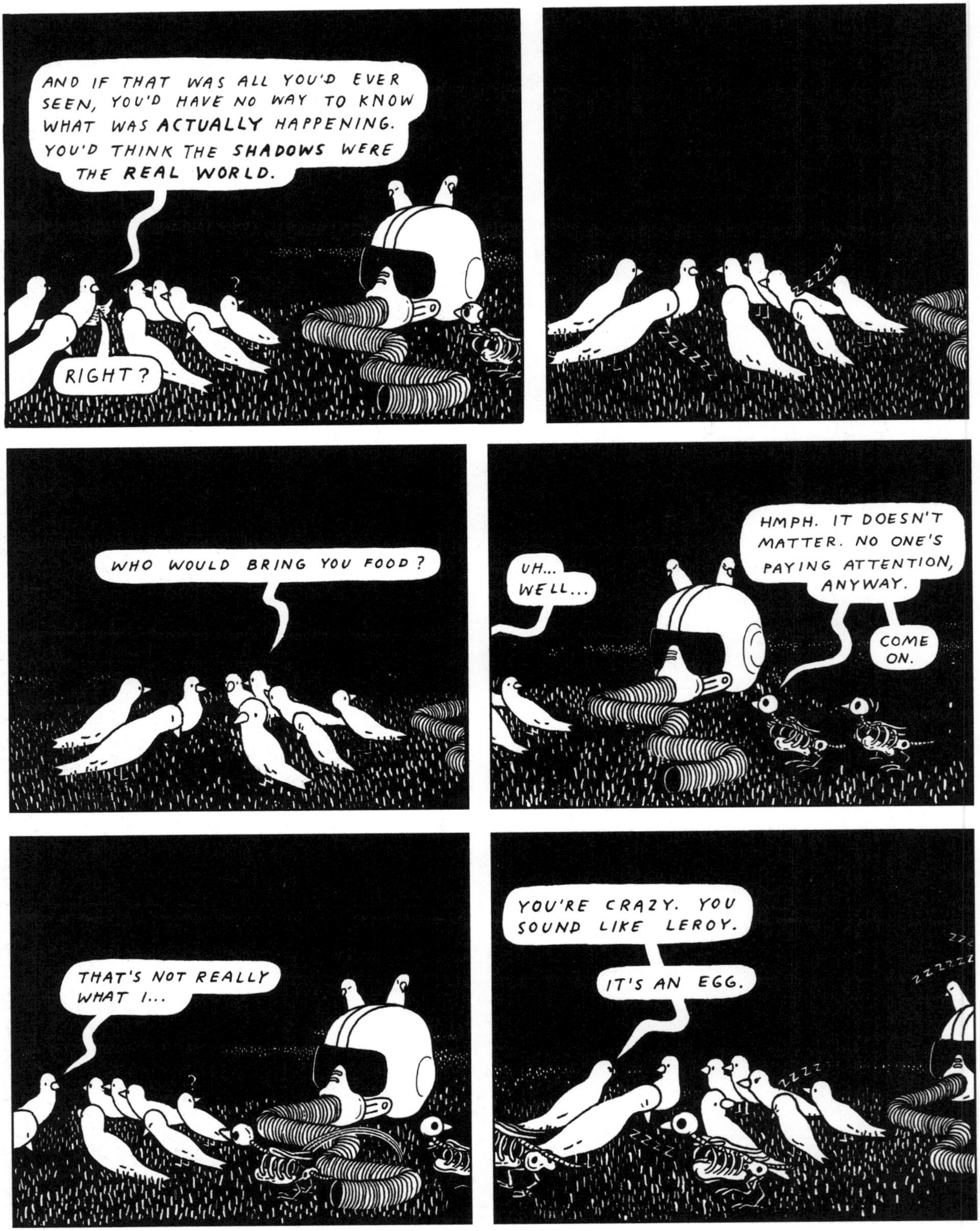
AND IF THAT WAS ALL YOU'D EVER SEEN, YOU'D HAVE NO WAY TO KNOW WHAT WAS ACTUALLY HAPPENING. YOU'D THINK THE SHADOWS WERE THE REAL WORLD.
RIGHT?
WHO WOULD BRING YOU FOOD?
UH... WELL...
HMPH. IT DOESN'T MATTER. NO ONE'S PAYING ATTENTION, ANYWAY.
COME ON.
THAT'S NOT REALLY WHAT I...
YOU'RE CRAZY. YOU SOUND LIKE LEROY.
IT'S AN EGG.

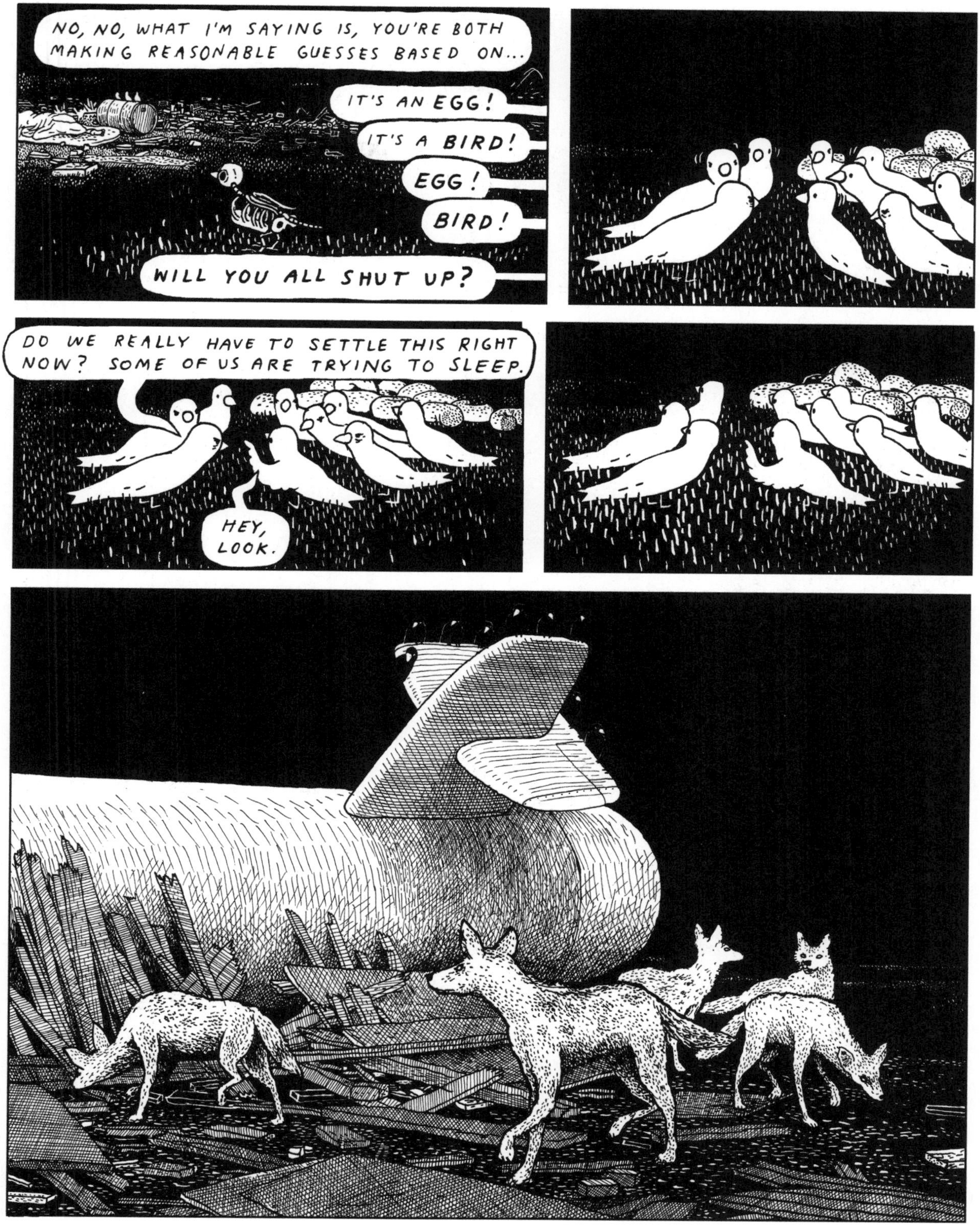
NO, NO, WHAT I'M SAYING IS, YOU'RE BOTH MAKING REASONABLE GUESSES BASED ON...
IT'S AN EGG!
IT'S A BIRD!
EGG!
BIRD!
WILL YOU ALL SHUT UP?
DO WE REALLY HAVE TO SETTLE THIS RIGHT NOW? SOME OF US ARE TRYING TO SLEEP.
HEY, LOOK.

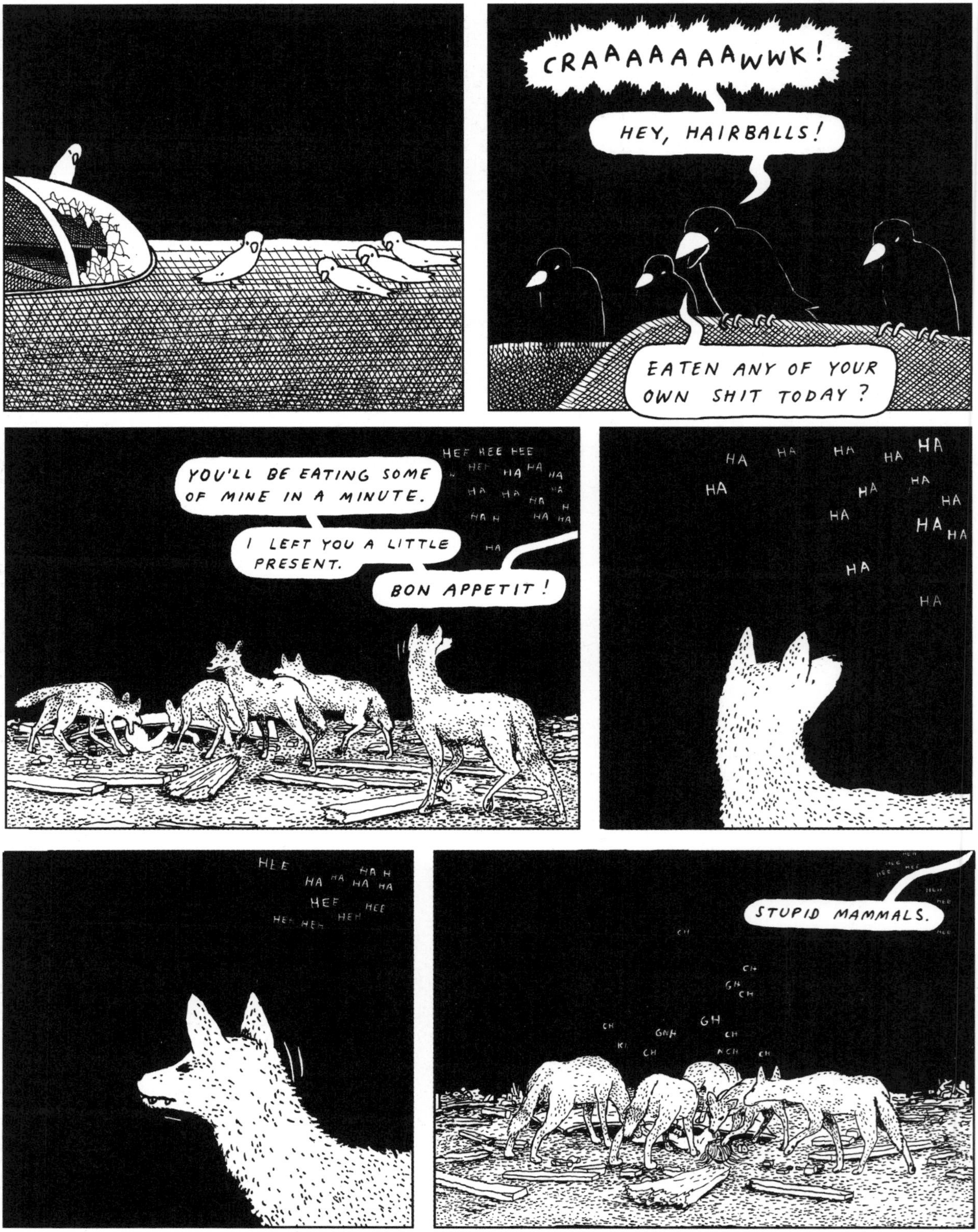
CRAAAAAAAWWK!
HEY, HAIRBALLS!
EATEN ANY OF YOUR OWN SHIT TODAY?
YOU'LL BE EATING SOME OF MINE IN A MINUTE.
I LEFT YOU A LITTLE PRESENT.
BON APPETIT!
HEE HEE HEE
HA HA HA HA HA
HA HA HA HA HA HA HA HA HA HA HA HA HA HA
HEE HA HA HA H HA HA HA
HEE HEE HEH HEH HEH
STUPID MAMMALS.
CH CH GH CH GH CH GNH CH CH NCH CH

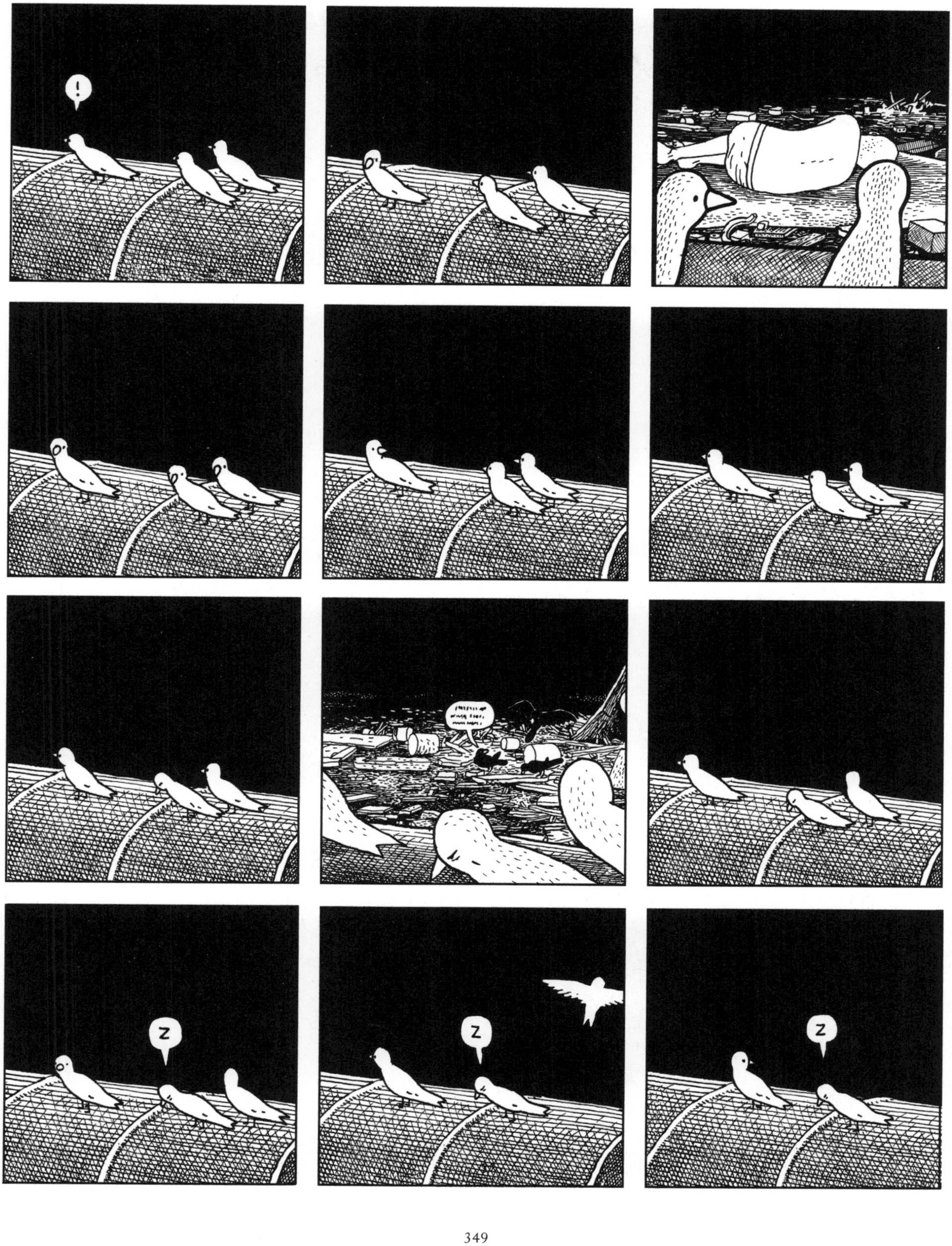
!
Z
Z
Z

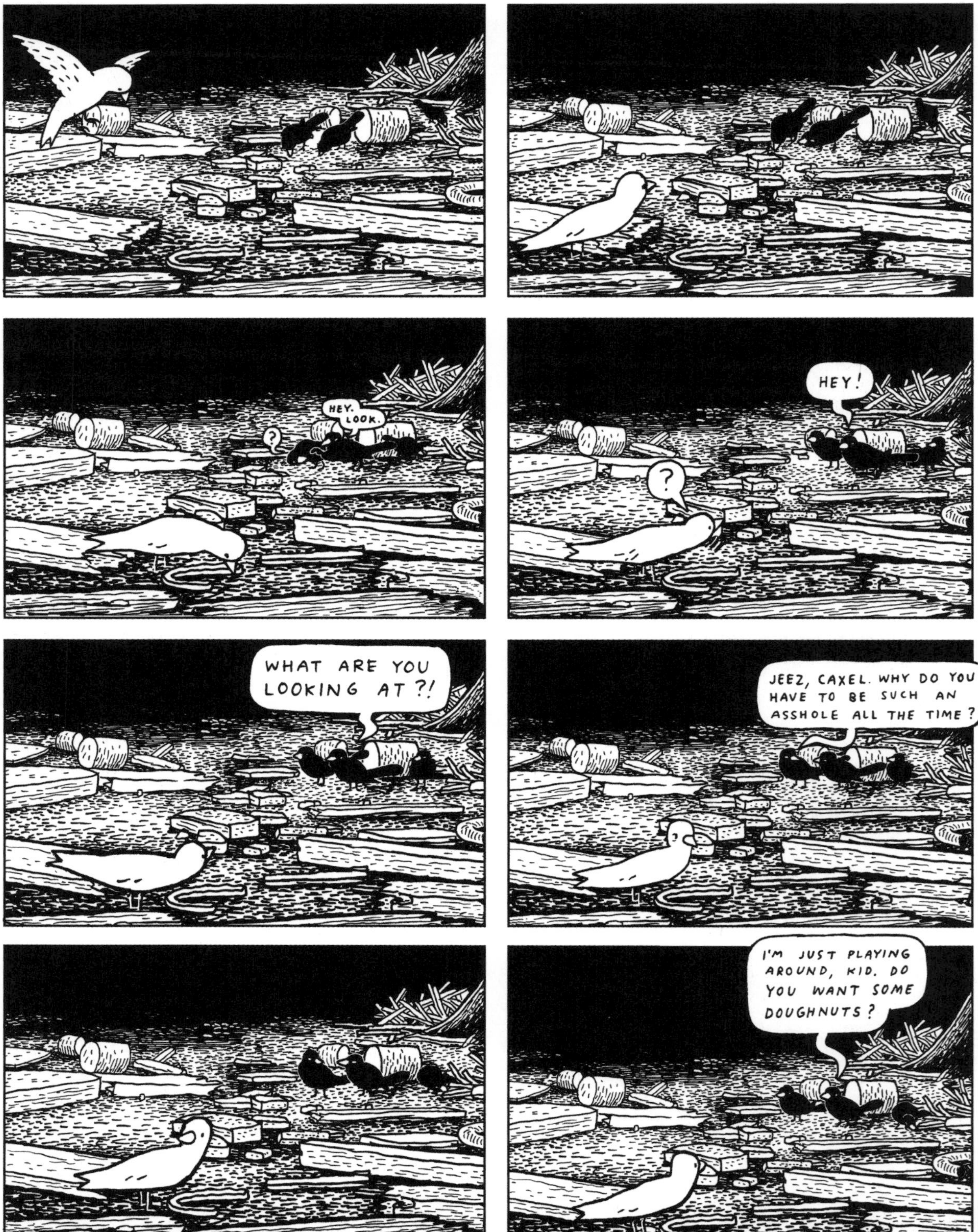
HEY. LOOK.
?
HEY!
?
WHAT ARE YOU LOOKING AT?!
JEEZ, CAXEL. WHY DO YOU HAVE TO BE SUCH AN ASSHOLE ALL THE TIME?
I'M JUST PLAYING AROUND, KID. DO YOU WANT SOME DOUGHNUTS?

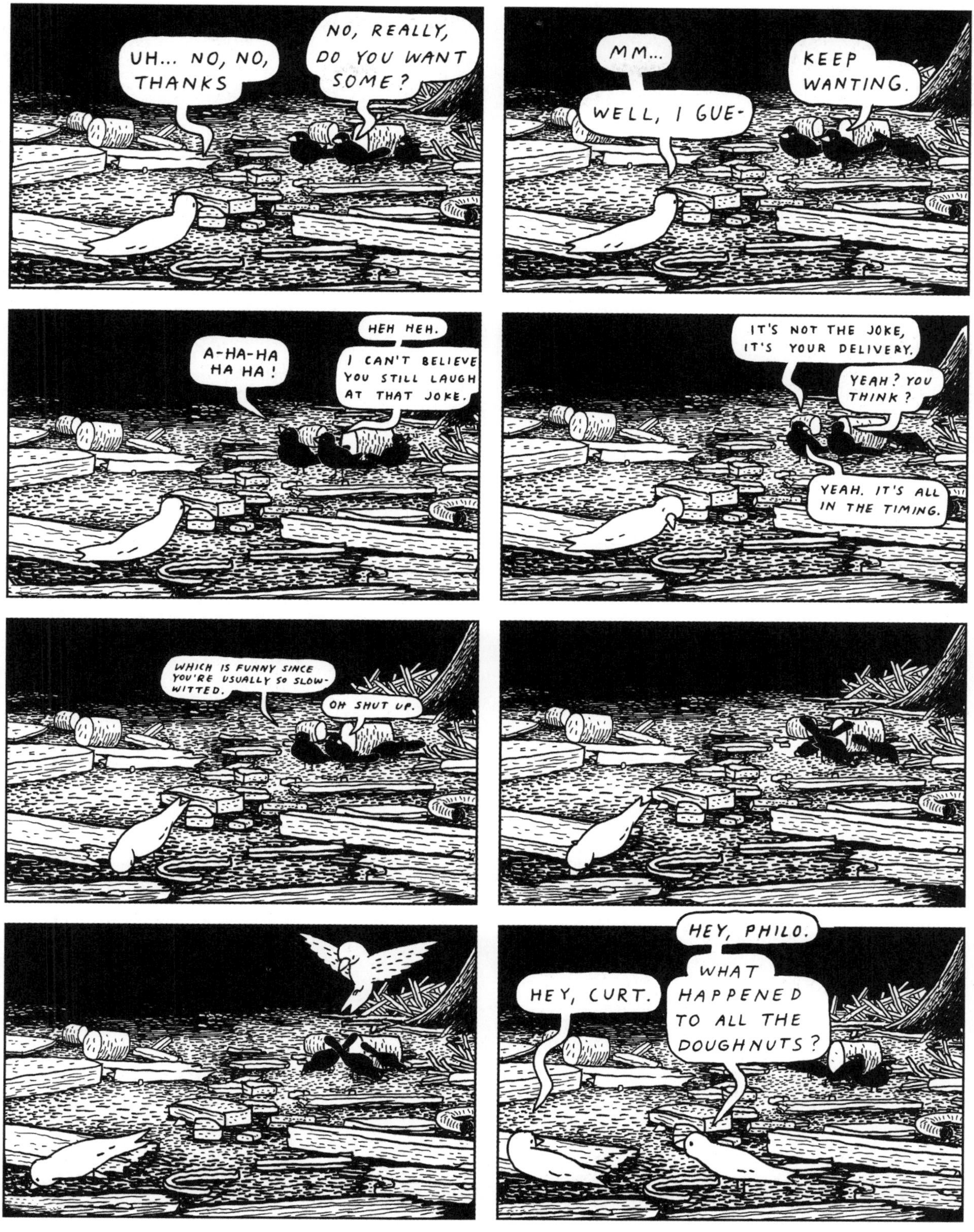
UH... NO, NO, THANKS
NO, REALLY, DO YOU WANT SOME?
MM...
WELL, I GUE-
KEEP WANTING.
A-HA-HA HA HA!
HEH HEH.
I CAN'T BELIEVE YOU STILL LAUGH AT THAT JOKE.
IT'S NOT THE JOKE, IT'S YOUR DELIVERY.
YEAH? YOU THINK?
YEAH. IT'S ALL IN THE TIMING.
WHICH IS FUNNY SINCE YOU'RE USUALLY SO SLOW-WITTED.
OH SHUT UP.
HEY, PHILO.
HEY, CURT.
WHAT HAPPENED TO ALL THE DOUGHNUTS?

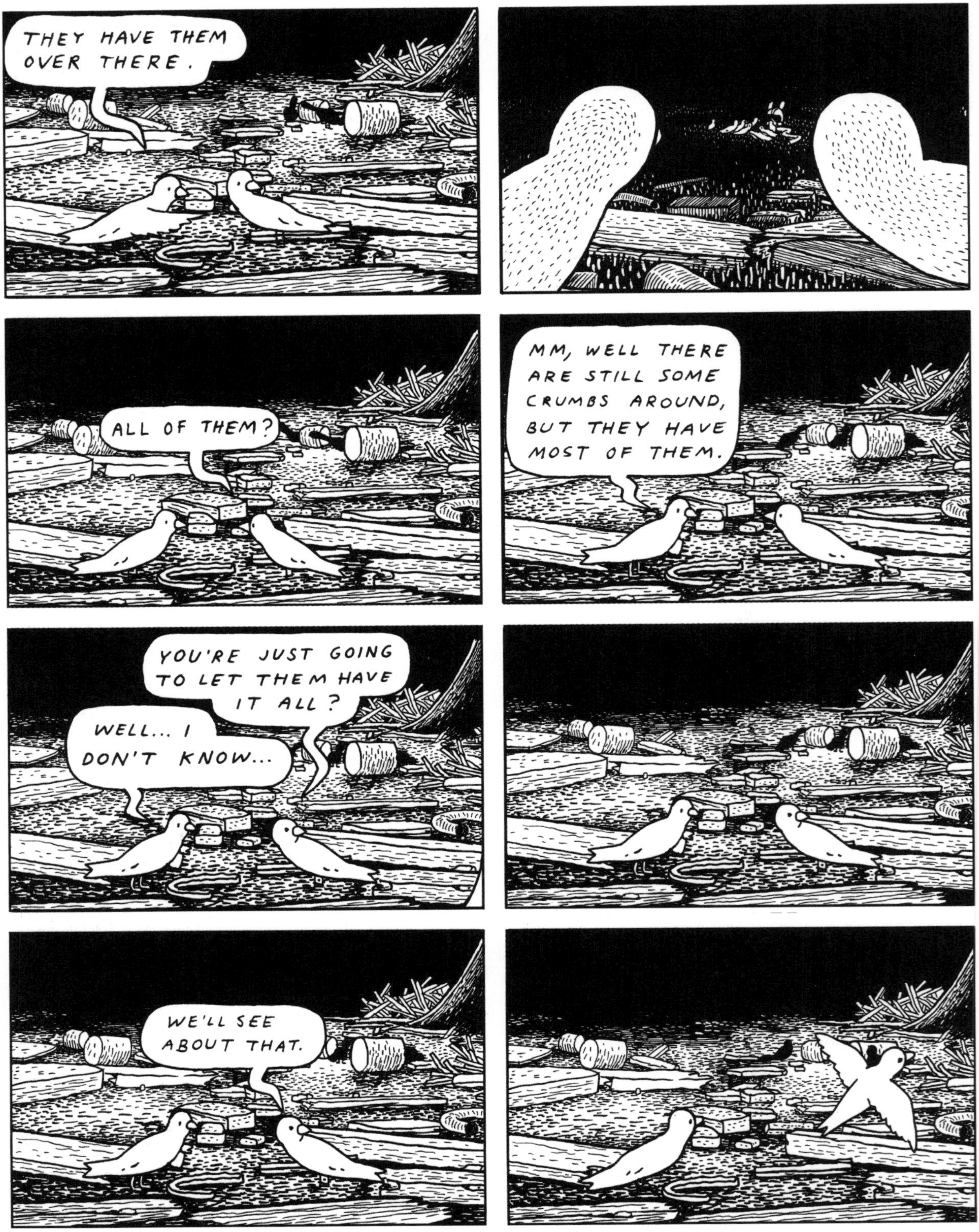
THEY HAVE THEM OVER THERE.
ALL OF THEM?
MM, WELL THERE ARE STILL SOME CRUMBS AROUND, BUT THEY HAVE MOST OF THEM.
YOU'RE JUST GOING TO LET THEM HAVE IT ALL?
WELL... I DON'T KNOW...
WE'LL SEE ABOUT THAT.

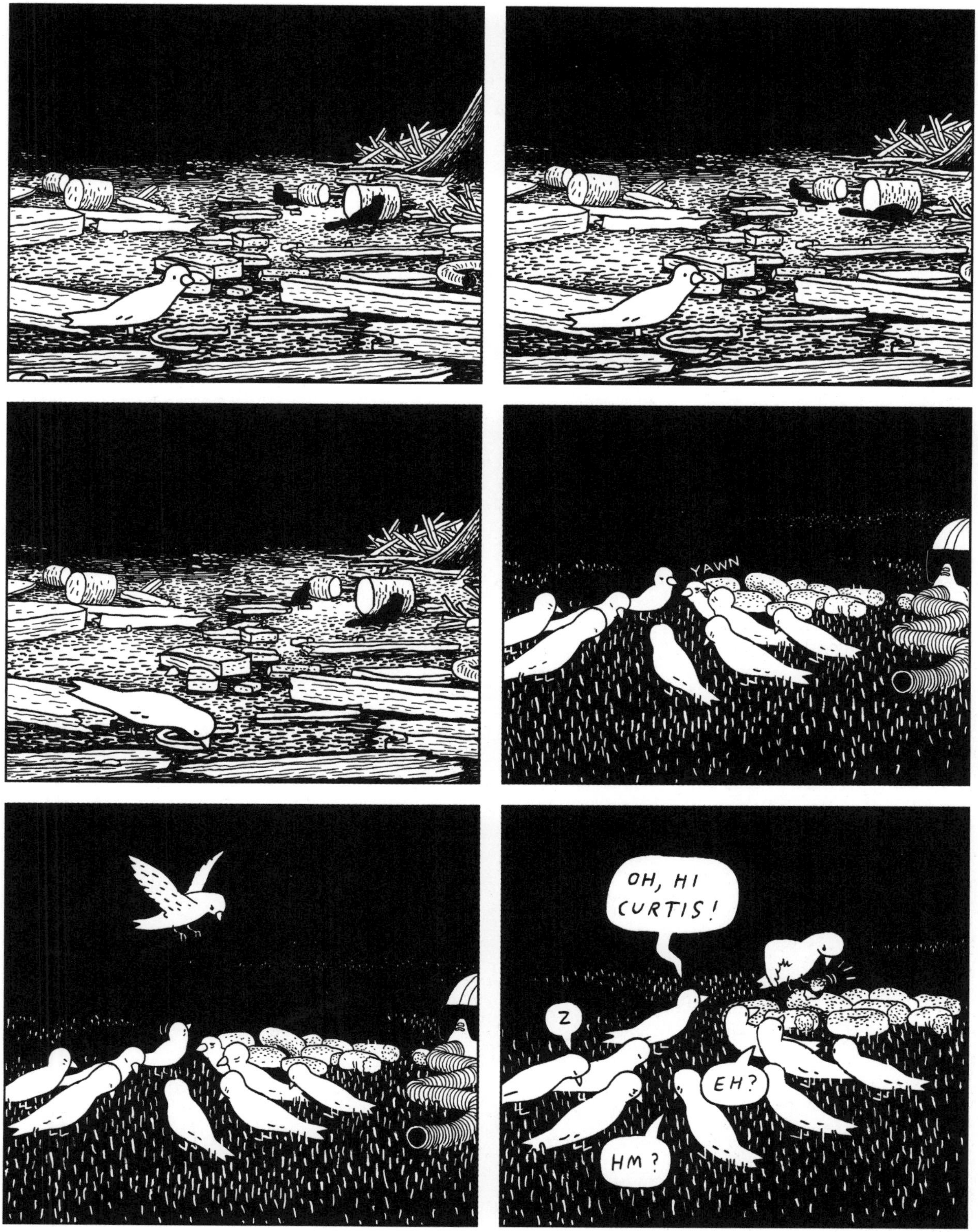
YAWN
OH, HI CURTIS!
Z
EH?
HM?

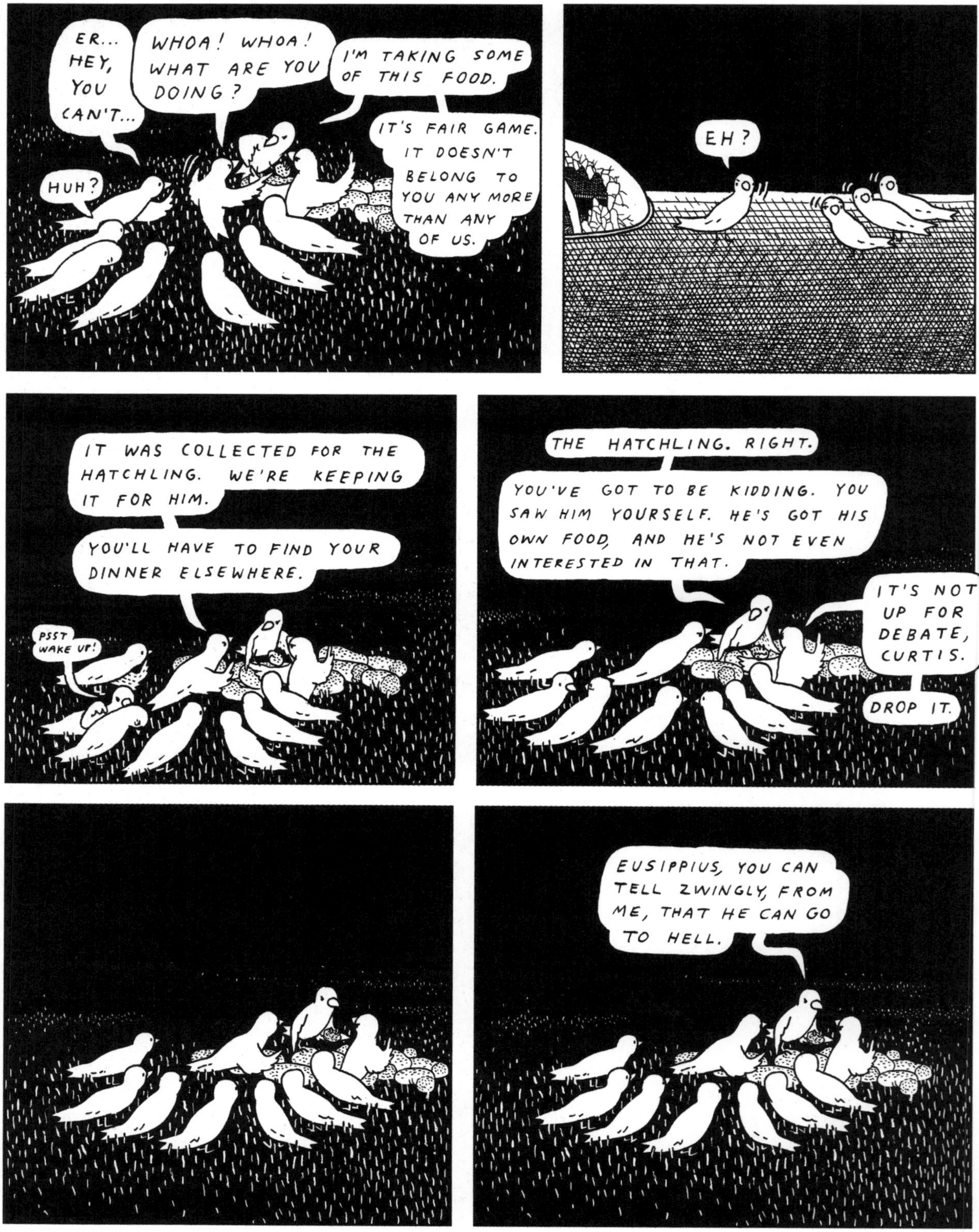
ER... HEY, YOU CAN'T...
WHOA! WHOA! WHAT ARE YOU DOING?
I'M TAKING SOME OF THIS FOOD.
IT'S FAIR GAME. IT DOESN'T BELONG TO YOU ANY MORE THAN ANY OF US.
HUH?
EH?
IT WAS COLLECTED FOR THE HATCHLING. WE'RE KEEPING IT FOR HIM.
YOU'LL HAVE TO FIND YOUR DINNER ELSEWHERE.
PSST WAKE UP!
THE HATCHLING. RIGHT.
YOU'VE GOT TO BE KIDDING. YOU SAW HIM YOURSELF. HE'S GOT HIS OWN FOOD, AND HE'S NOT EVEN INTERESTED IN THAT.
IT'S NOT UP FOR DEBATE, CURTIS.
DROP IT.
EUSIPPIUS, YOU CAN TELL ZWINGLY, FROM ME, THAT HE CAN GO TO HELL.

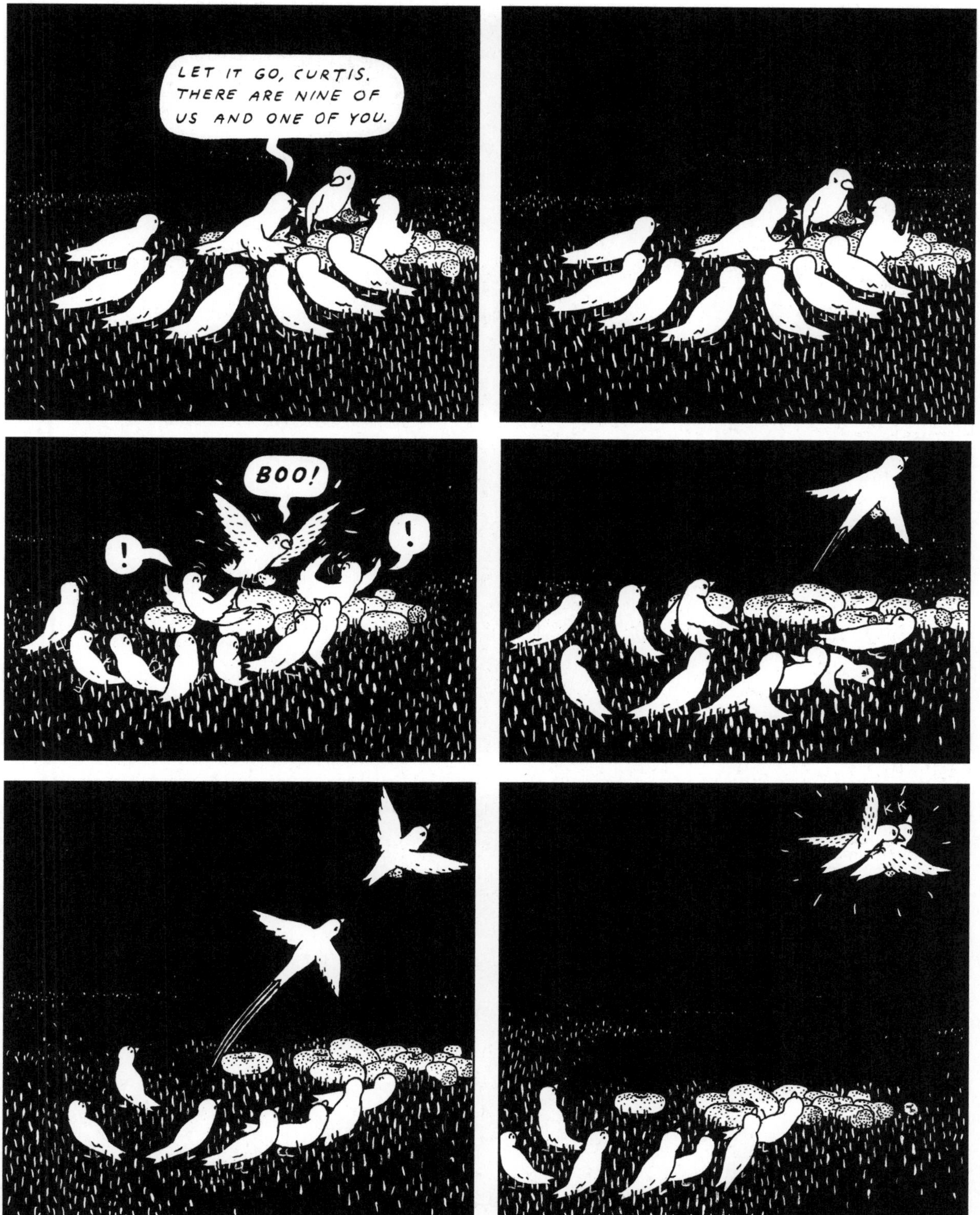
LET IT GO, CURTIS. THERE ARE NINE OF US AND ONE OF YOU.
BOO!
!
!
K K

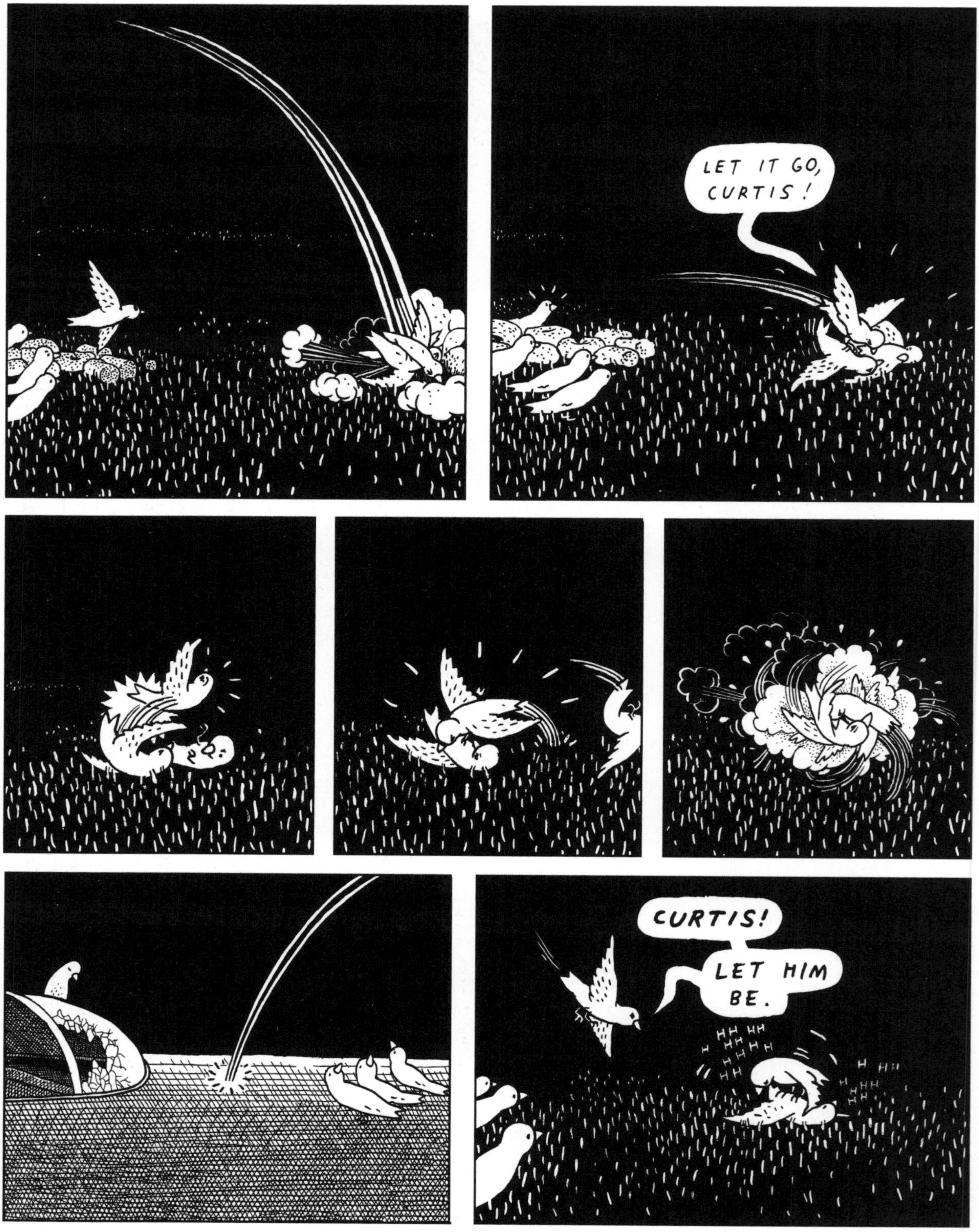
LET IT GO, CURTIS!
CURTIS!
LET HIM BE.

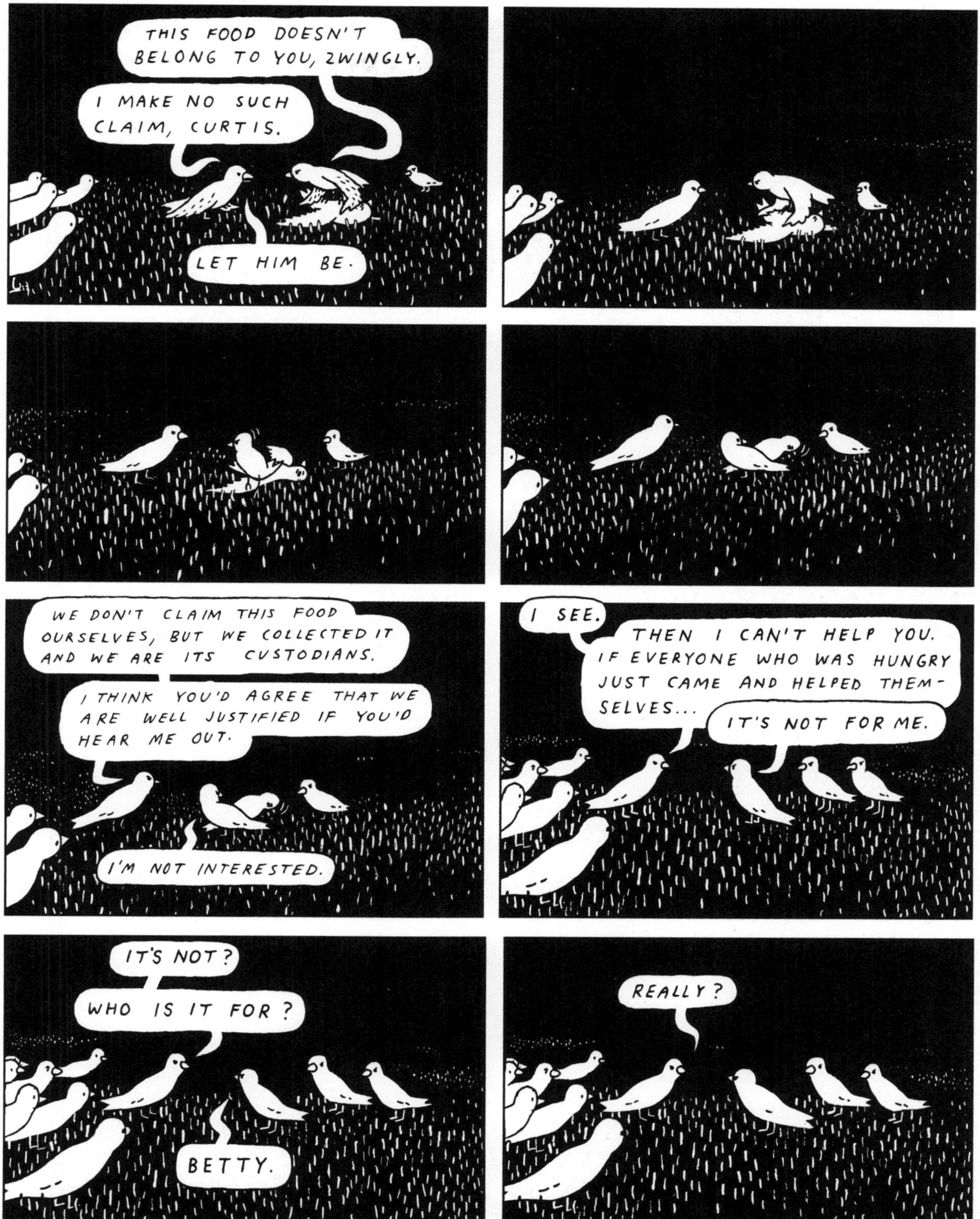
THIS FOOD DOESN'T BELONG TO YOU, ZWINGLY.
I MAKE NO SUCH CLAIM, CURTIS.
LET HIM BE.
WE DON'T CLAIM THIS FOOD OURSELVES, BUT WE COLLECTED IT AND WE ARE ITS CUSTODIANS.
I THINK YOU'D AGREE THAT WE ARE WELL JUSTIFIED IF YOU'D HEAR ME OUT.
I'M NOT INTERESTED.
I SEE.
THEN I CAN'T HELP YOU. IF EVERYONE WHO WAS HUNGRY JUST CAME AND HELPED THEMSELVES...
IT'S NOT FOR ME.
IT'S NOT?
WHO IS IT FOR?
BETTY.
REALLY?

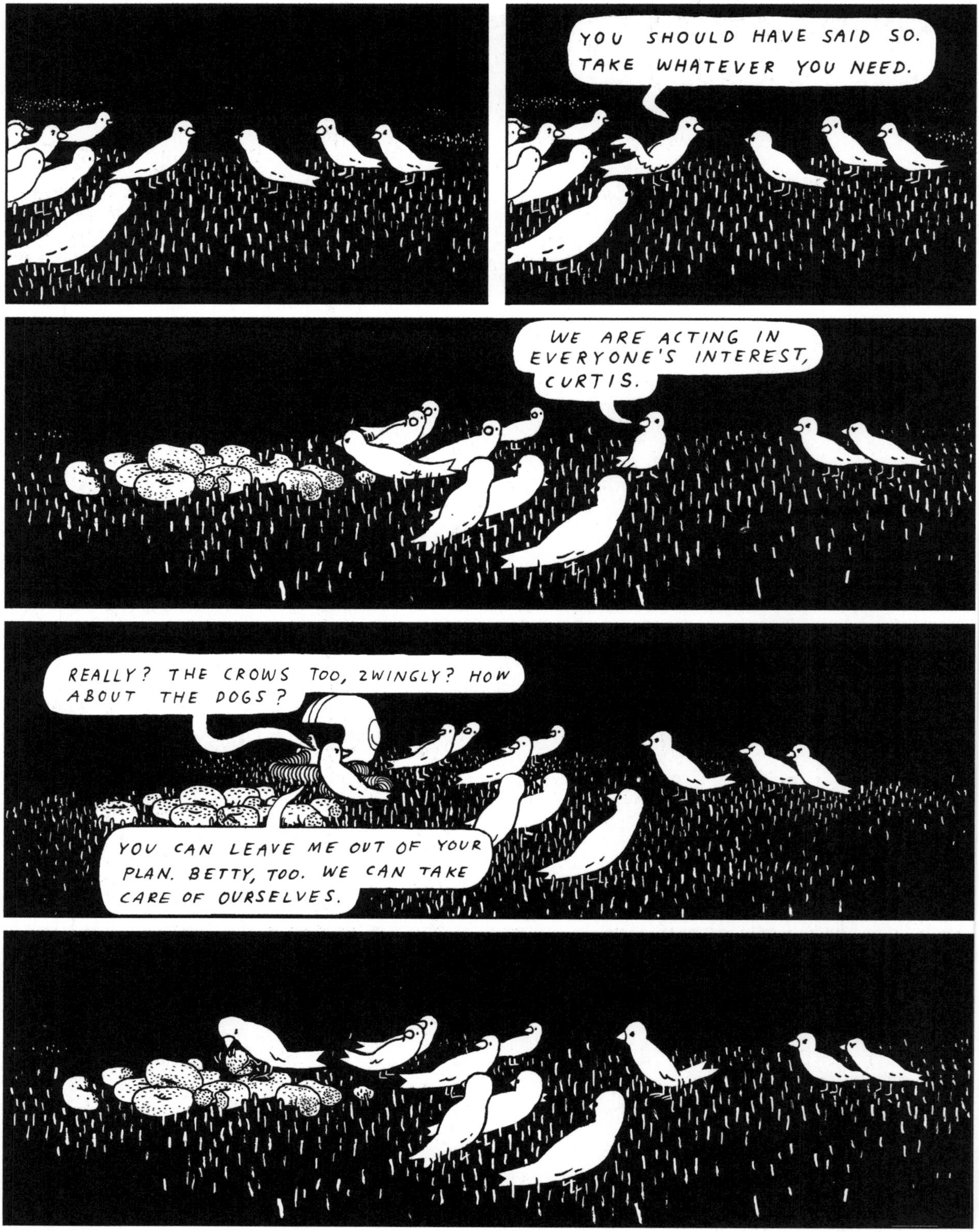
YOU SHOULD HAVE SAID SO. TAKE WHATEVER YOU NEED.
WE ARE ACTING IN EVERYONE'S INTEREST, CURTIS.
REALLY? THE CROWS TOO, ZWINGLY? HOW ABOUT THE DOGS?
YOU CAN LEAVE ME OUT OF YOUR PLAN. BETTY, TOO. WE CAN TAKE CARE OF OURSELVES.

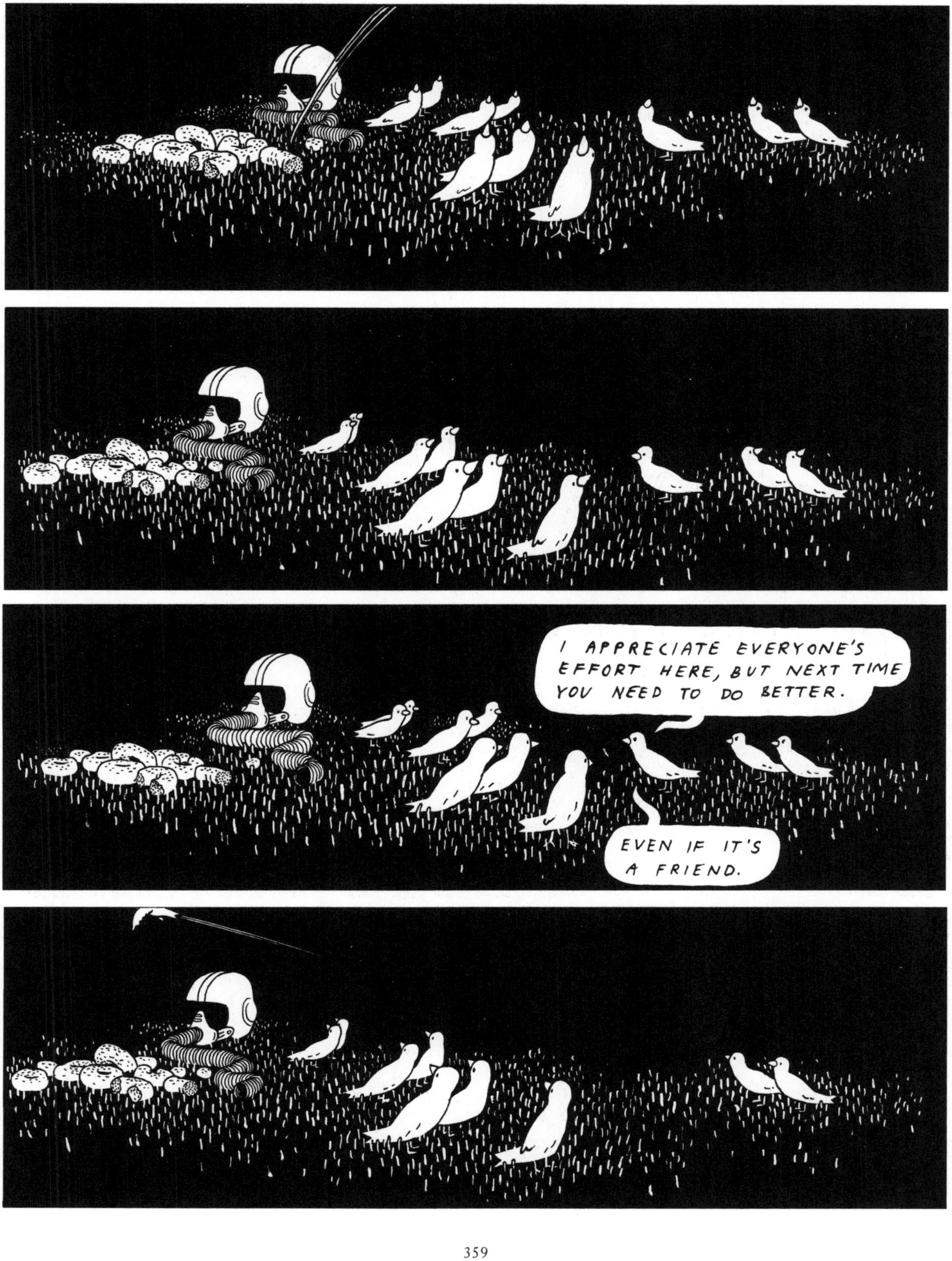
I APPRECIATE EVERYONE'S EFFORT HERE, BUT NEXT TIME YOU NEED TO DO BETTER.
EVEN IF IT'S A FRIEND.

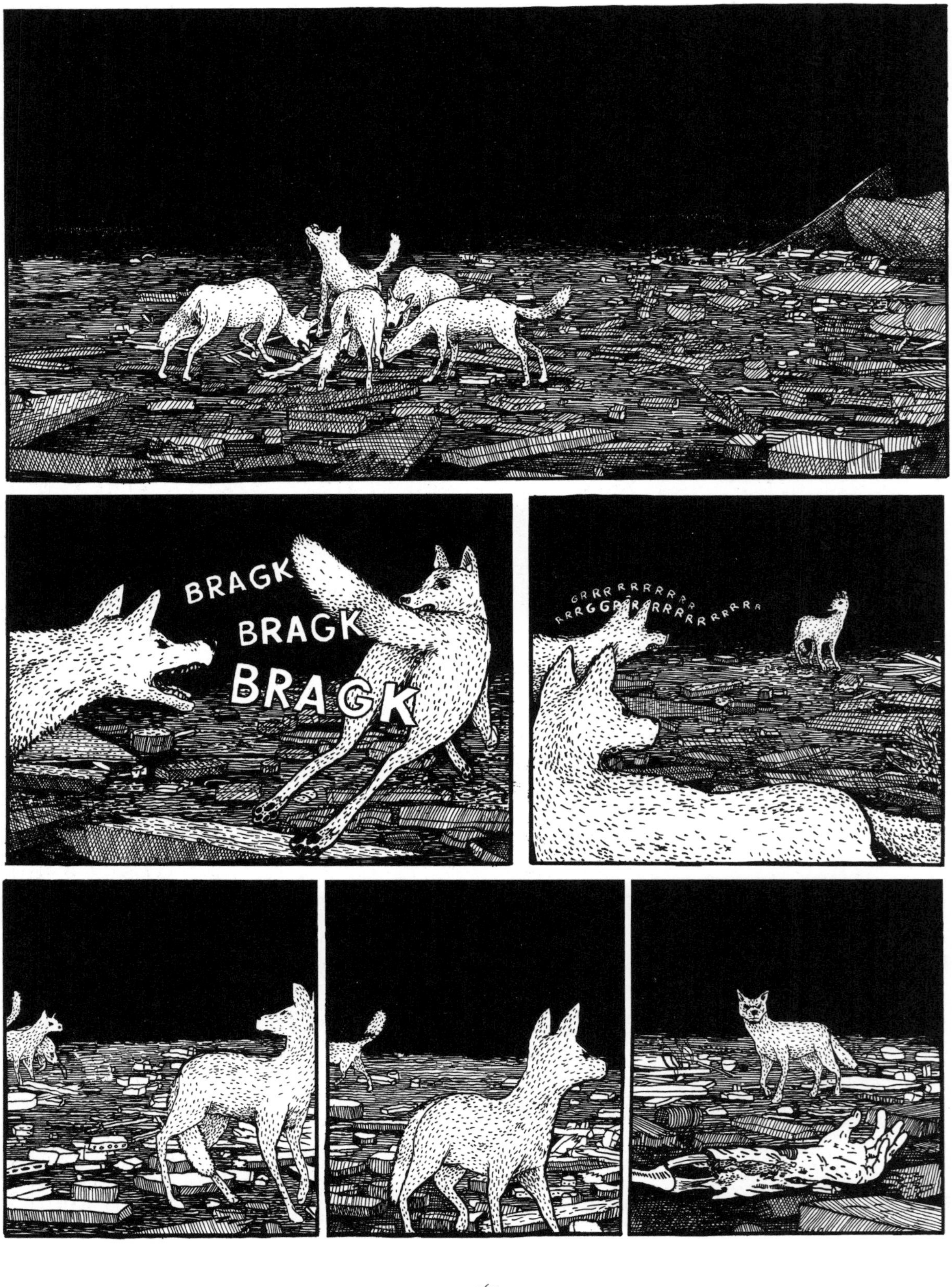
BRAGK
BRAGK
BRAGK
GRRRRRRRRRR
RRRGGRRRRRRRRRRR

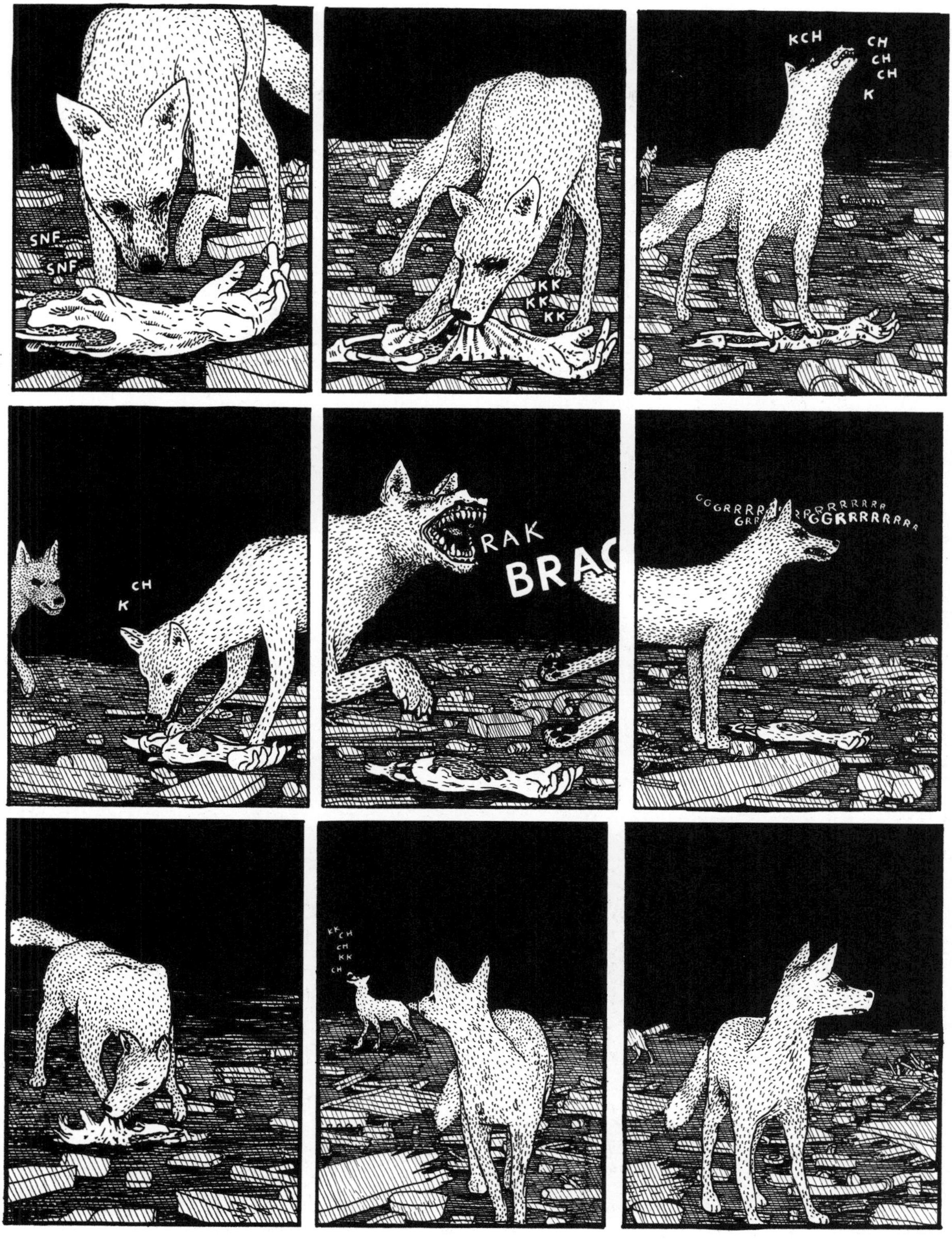
SNF
SNF
KK
KK
KK
KCH
CH
CH
CH
K
K
CH
RAK
BRAC
GGRRRRRRRRRRRRRR
GRR GGRRRRRRRRR
KKCH
CH
KK
CH

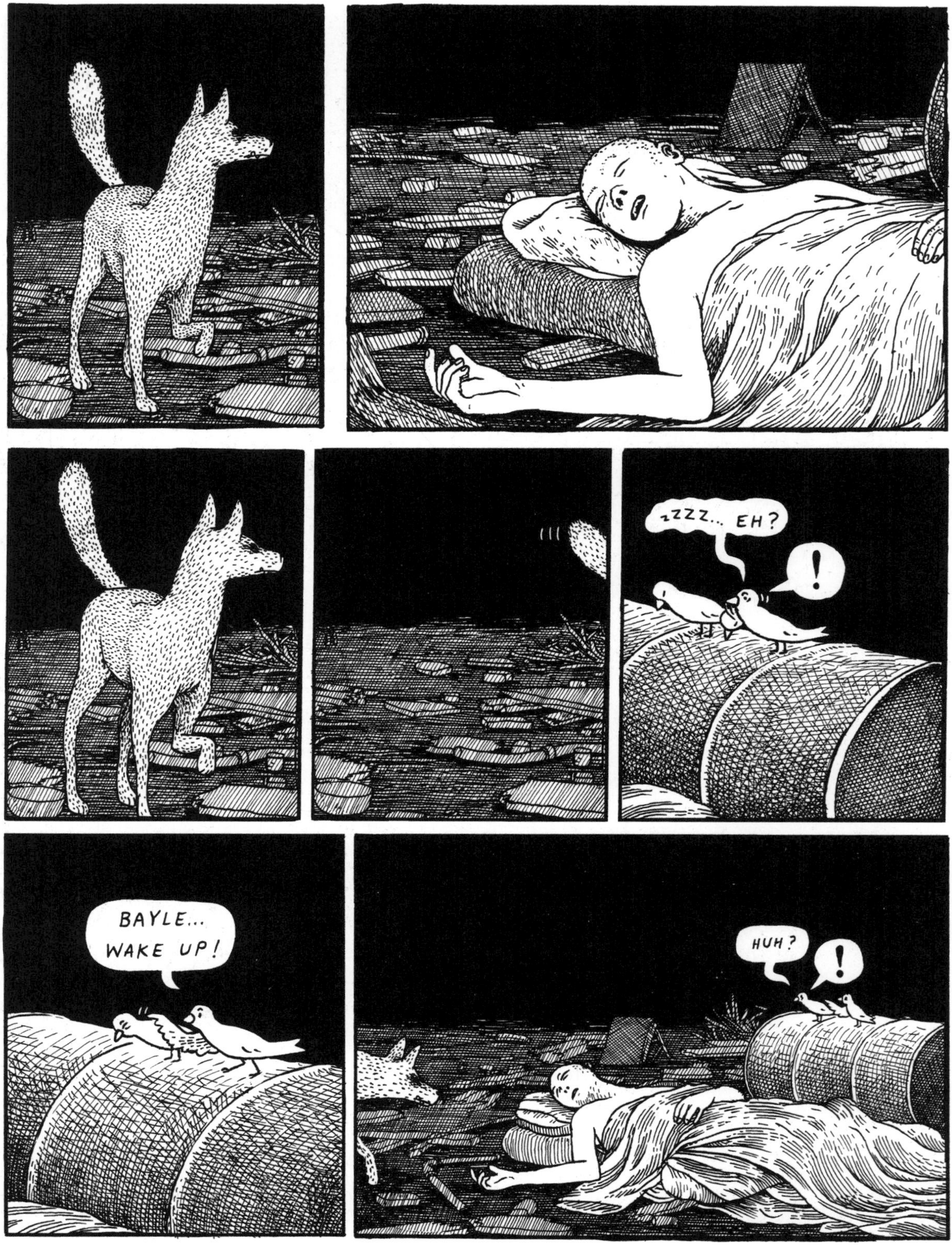
zZZZ... EH?
!
BAYLE...
WAKE UP!
HUH?
!

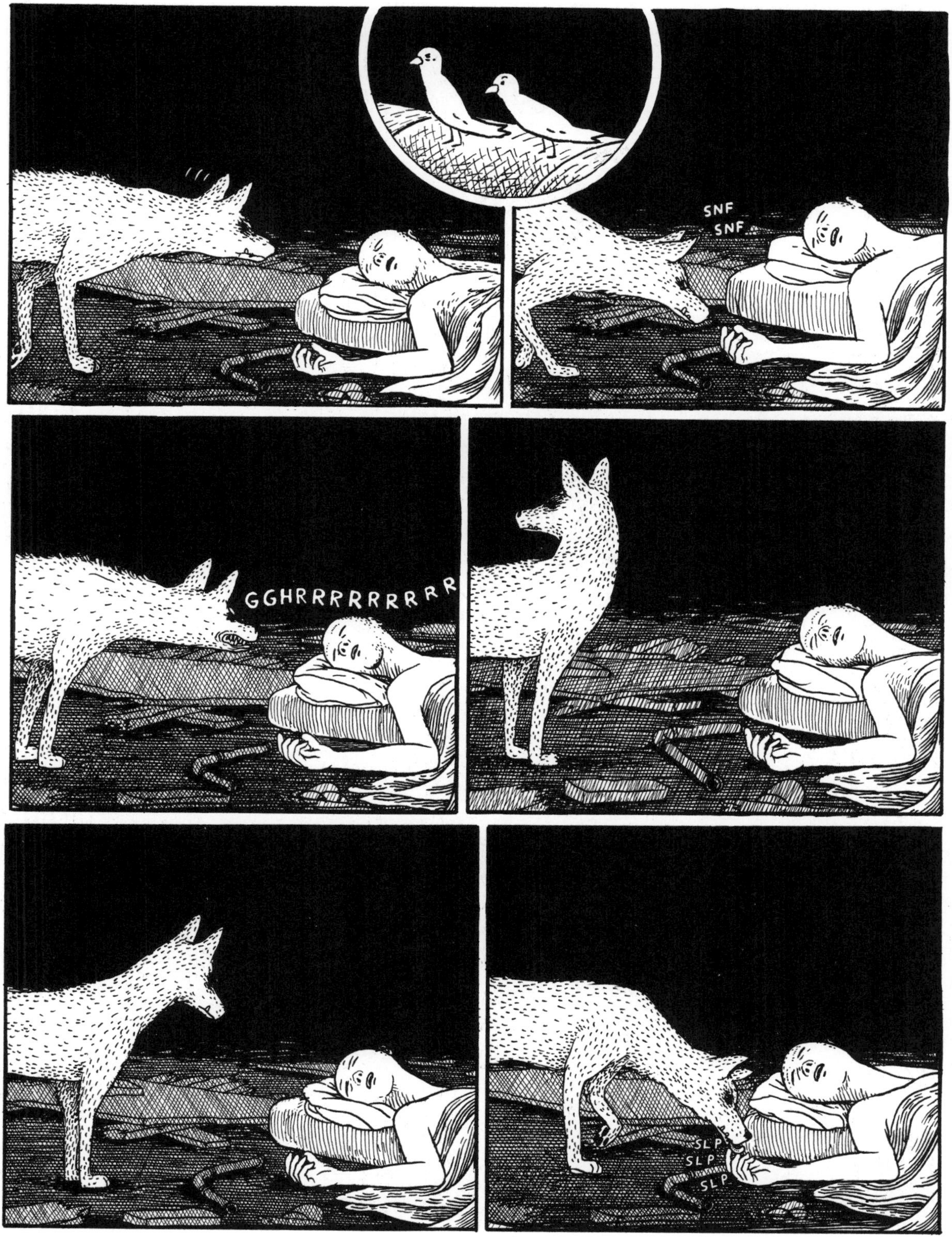
SNF
SNF
GGHRRRRRRRRR
SLP
SLP
SLP

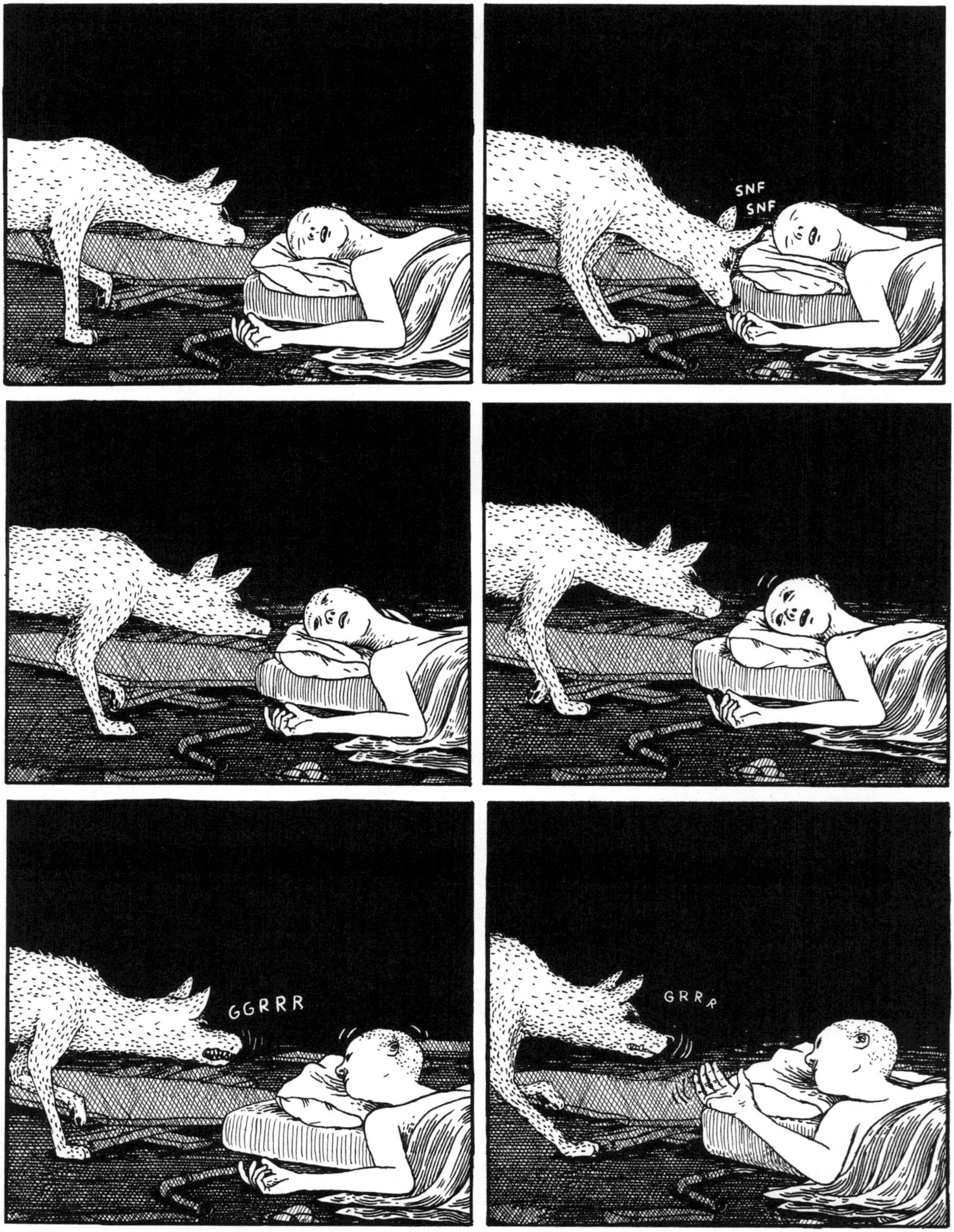
SNF
SNF
GGRRR
GRRR

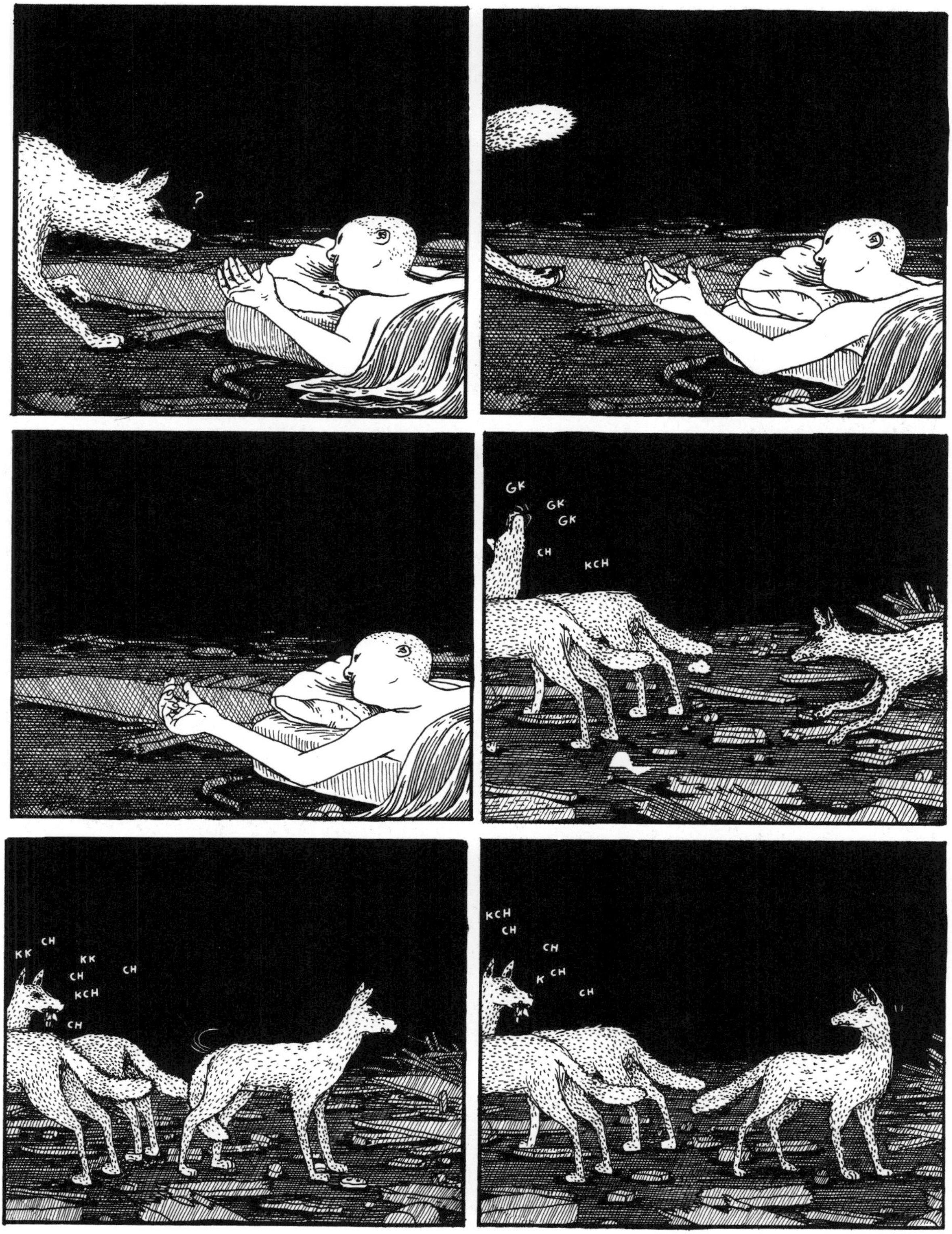
?
GK
GK
GK
CH
KCH
KK
CH
KK
CH
KCH
CH
CH
KCH
CH
CH
K
CH
CH

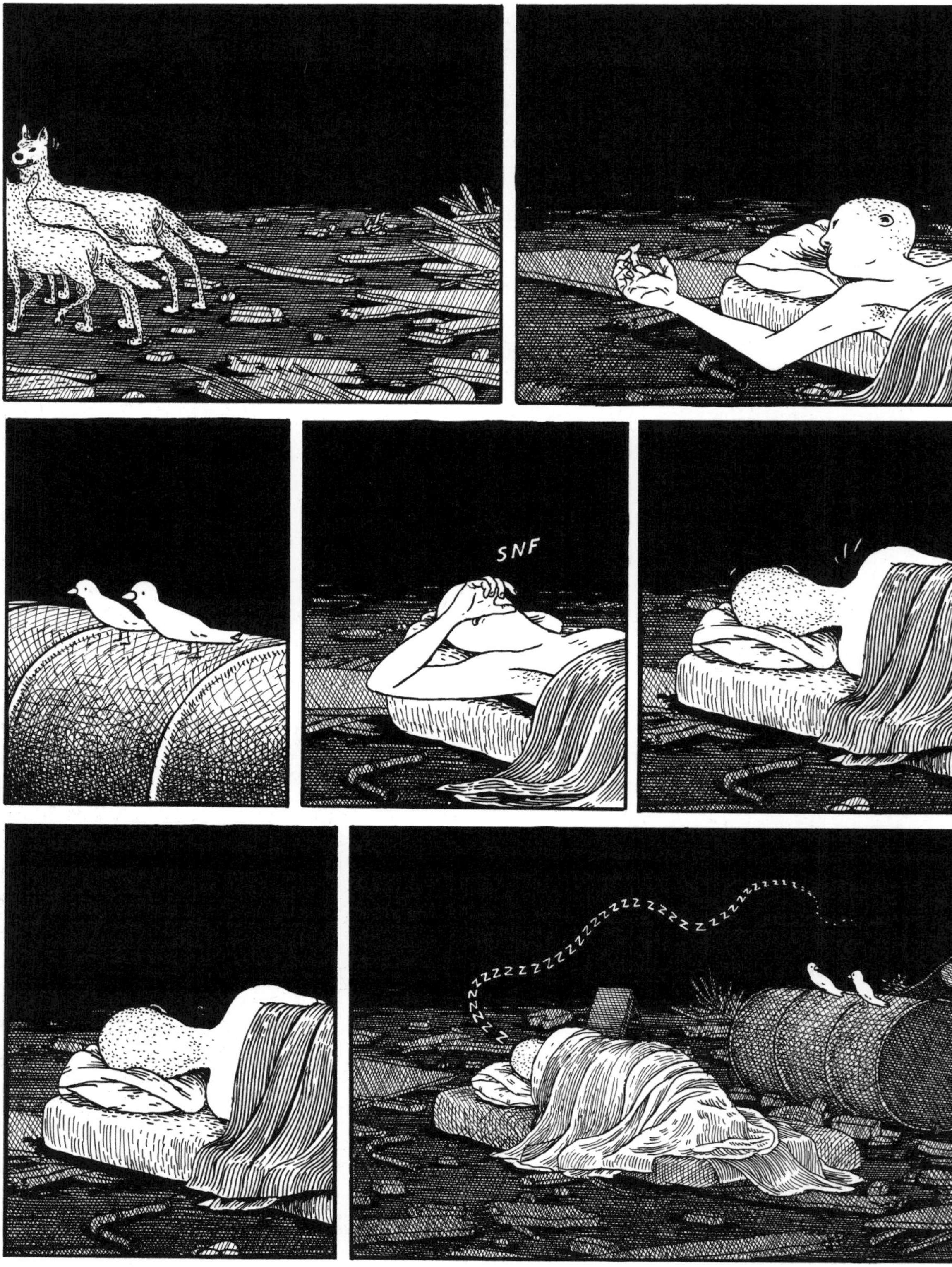
SNF
ZZZZZZZZZZZZZZZZZZZZZZZZZZZZZZZZZZZ

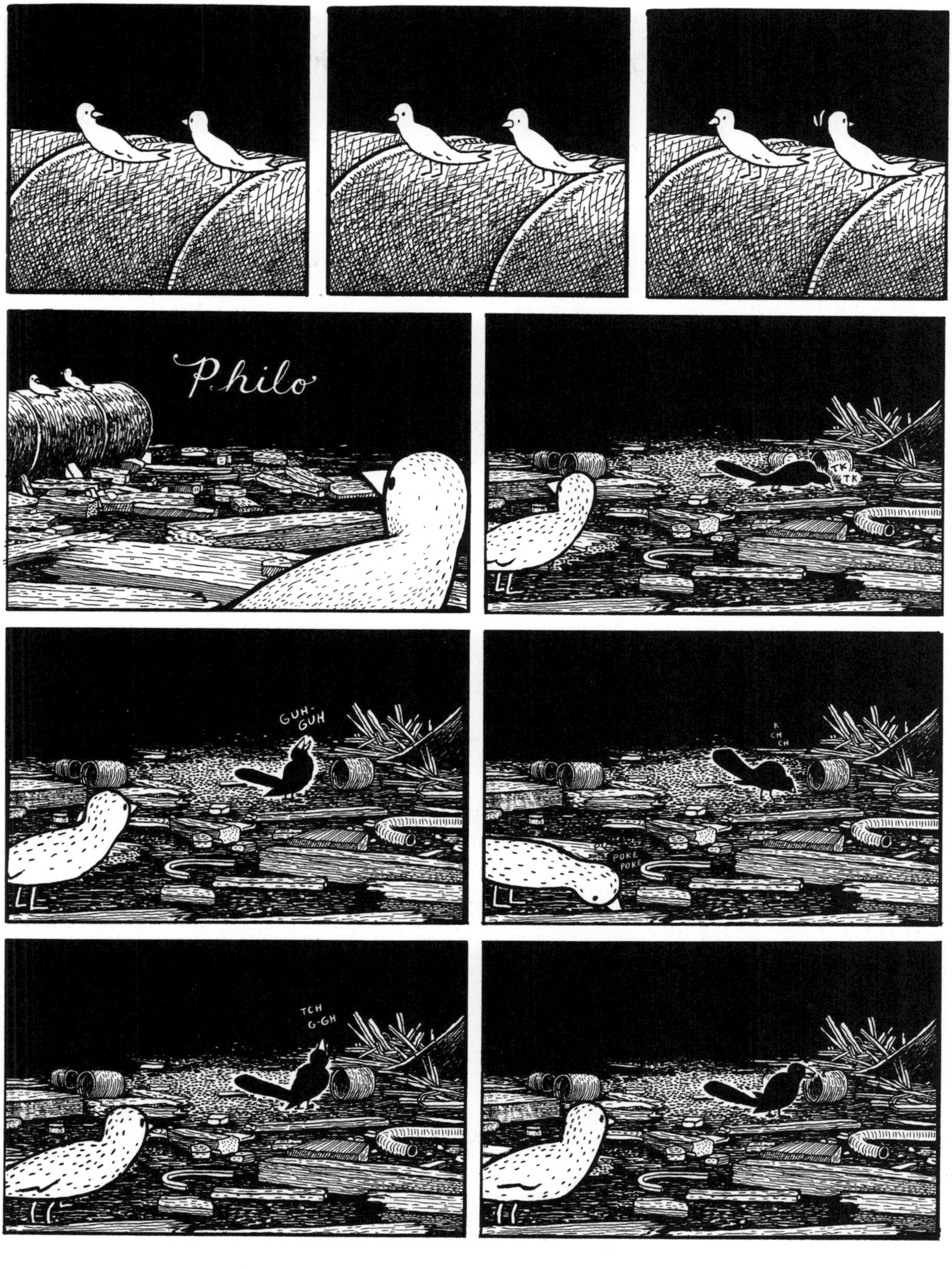
Philo
TK
TK
GUH-
GUH
K
CH
CH
POKE
POKE
TCH
G-GH

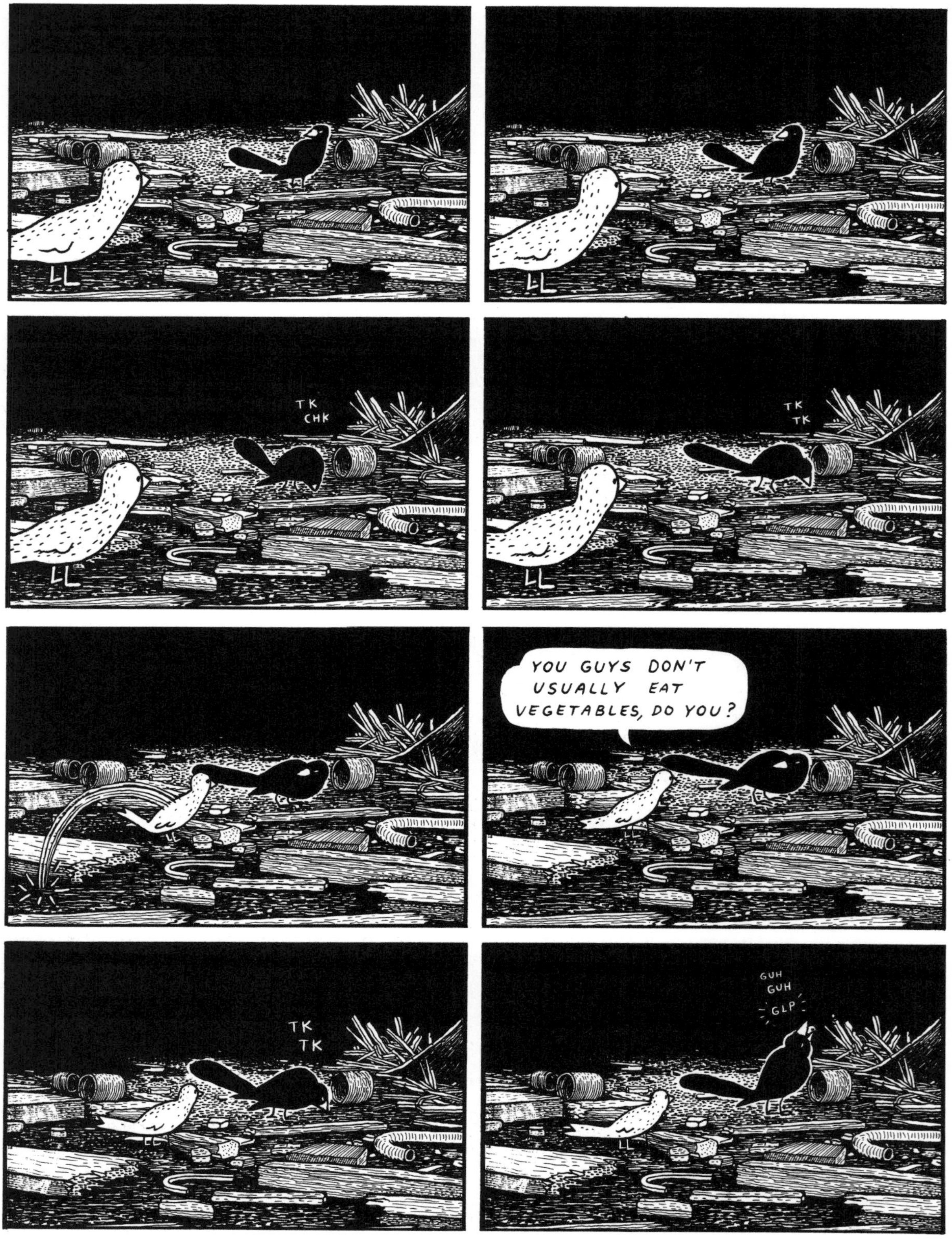
TK
CHK
TK
TK
YOU GUYS DON'T USUALLY EAT VEGETABLES, DO YOU?
TK
TK
GUH
GUH
GLP

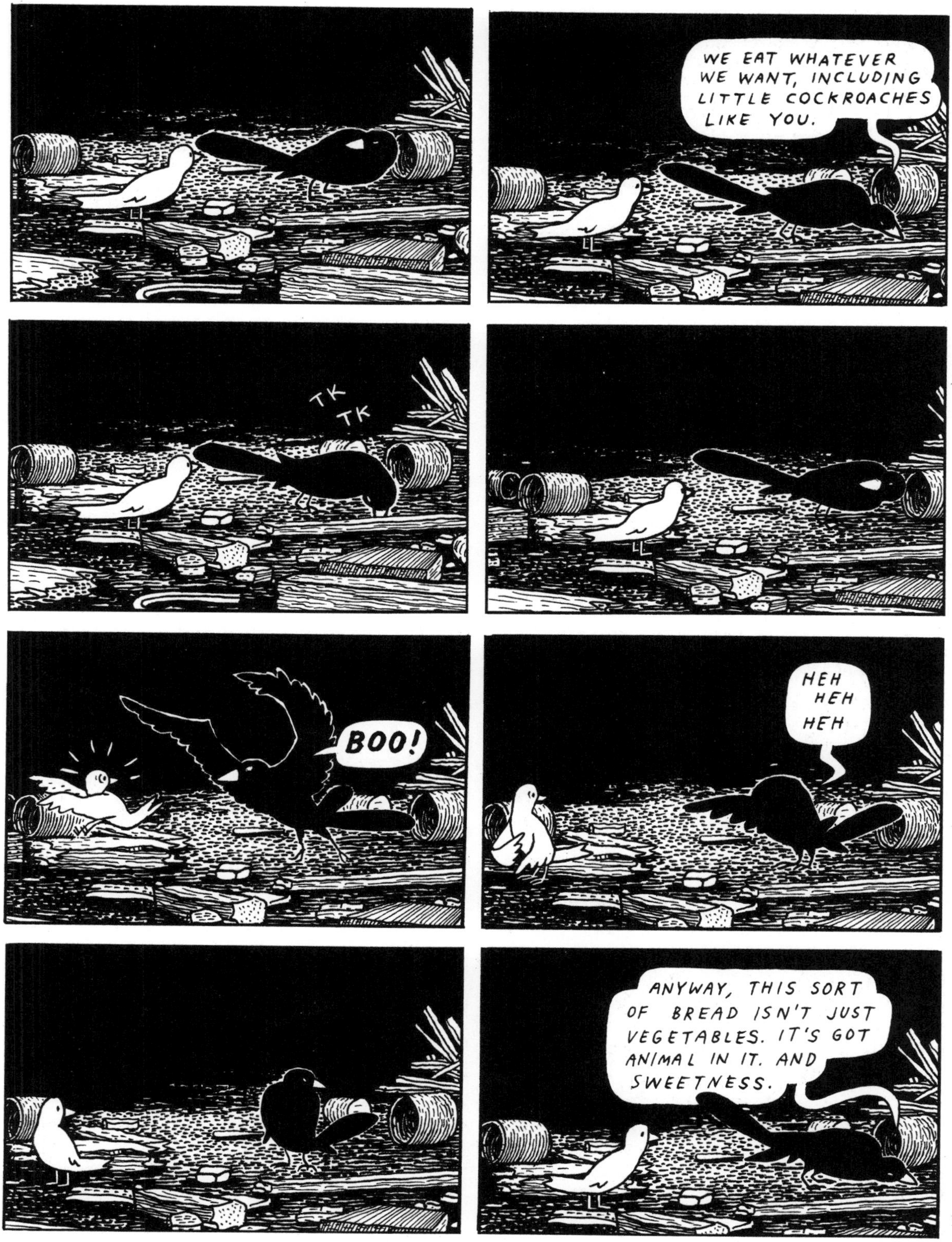
WE EAT WHATEVER WE WANT, INCLUDING LITTLE COCKROACHES LIKE YOU.
TK TK
BOO!
HEH HEH HEH
ANYWAY, THIS SORT OF BREAD ISN'T JUST VEGETABLES. IT'S GOT ANIMAL IN IT. AND SWEETNESS.

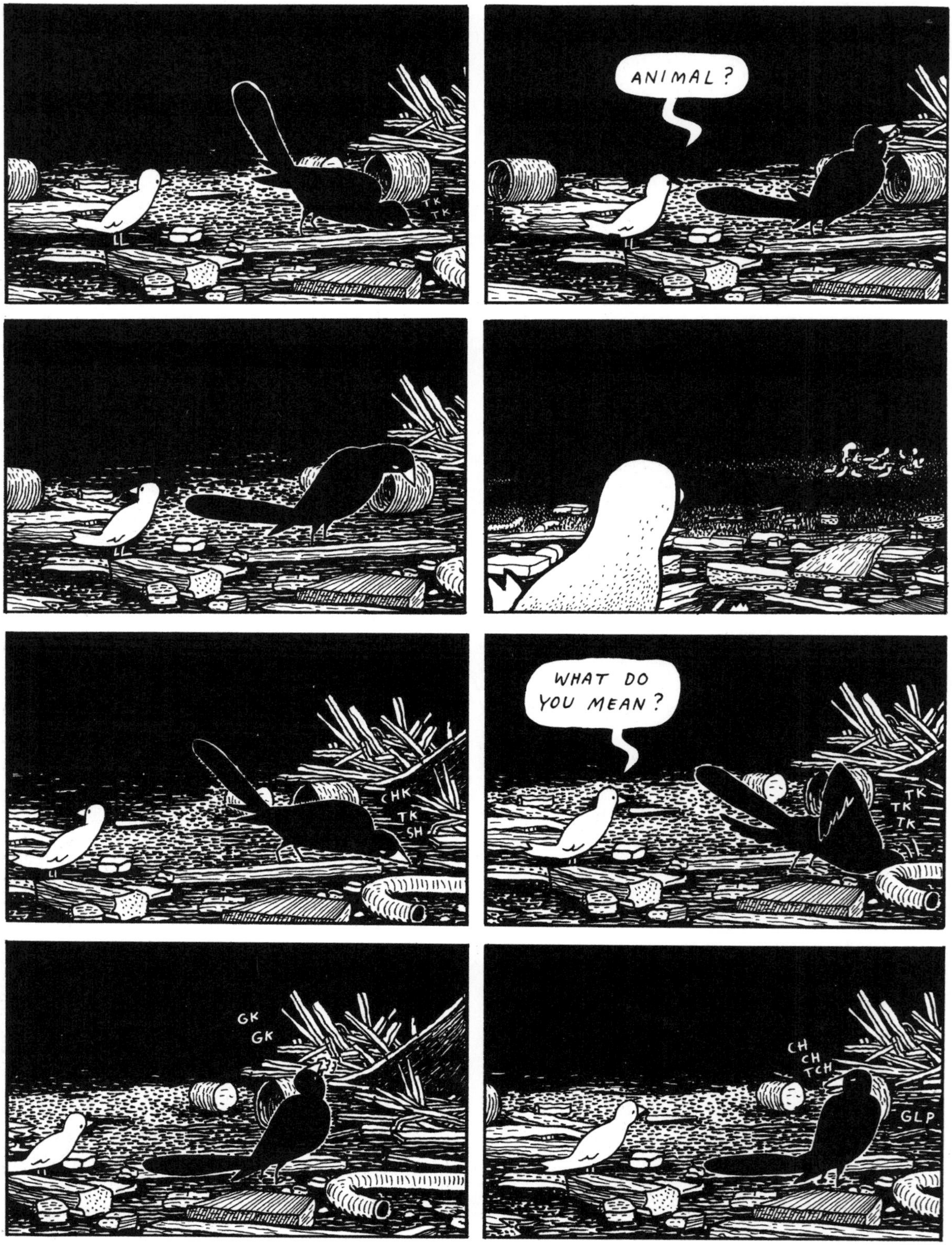
TK TK
ANIMAL?
CHK TK SH
WHAT DO YOU MEAN?
TK TK TK
GK GK
CH CH TCH
GLP

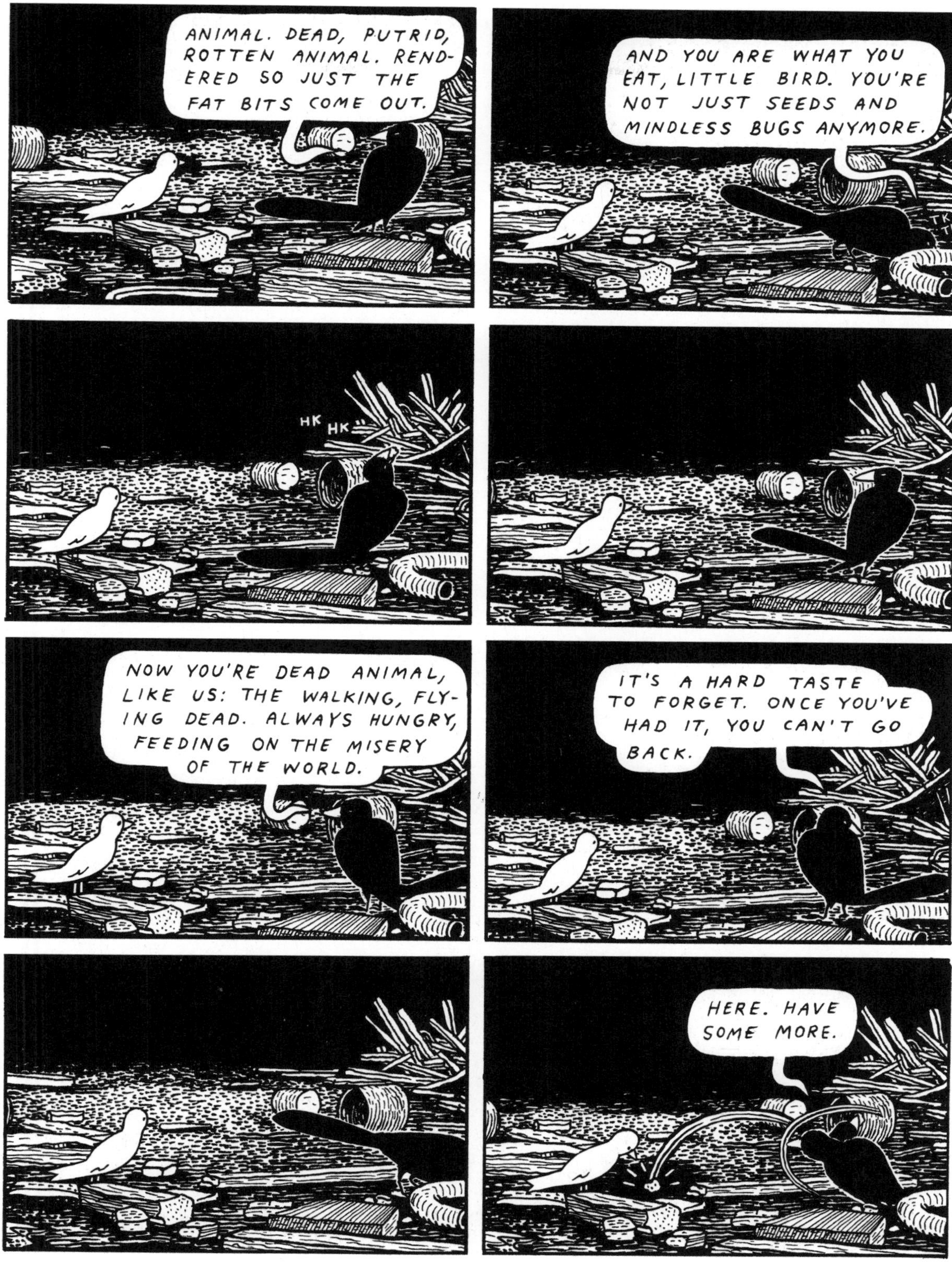

ANIMAL. DEAD, PUTRID, ROTTEN ANIMAL. RENDERED SO JUST THE FAT BITS COME OUT.
AND YOU ARE WHAT YOU EAT, LITTLE BIRD. YOU'RE NOT JUST SEEDS AND MINDLESS BUGS ANYMORE.
TK TK
HK HK"
NOW YOU'RE DEAD ANIMAL, LIKE US: THE WALKING, FLYING DEAD. ALWAYS HUNGRY, FEEDING ON THE MISERY OF THE WORLD.
IT'S A HARD TASTE TO FORGET. ONCE YOU'VE HAD IT, YOU CAN'T GO BACK.
HERE. HAVE SOME MORE.

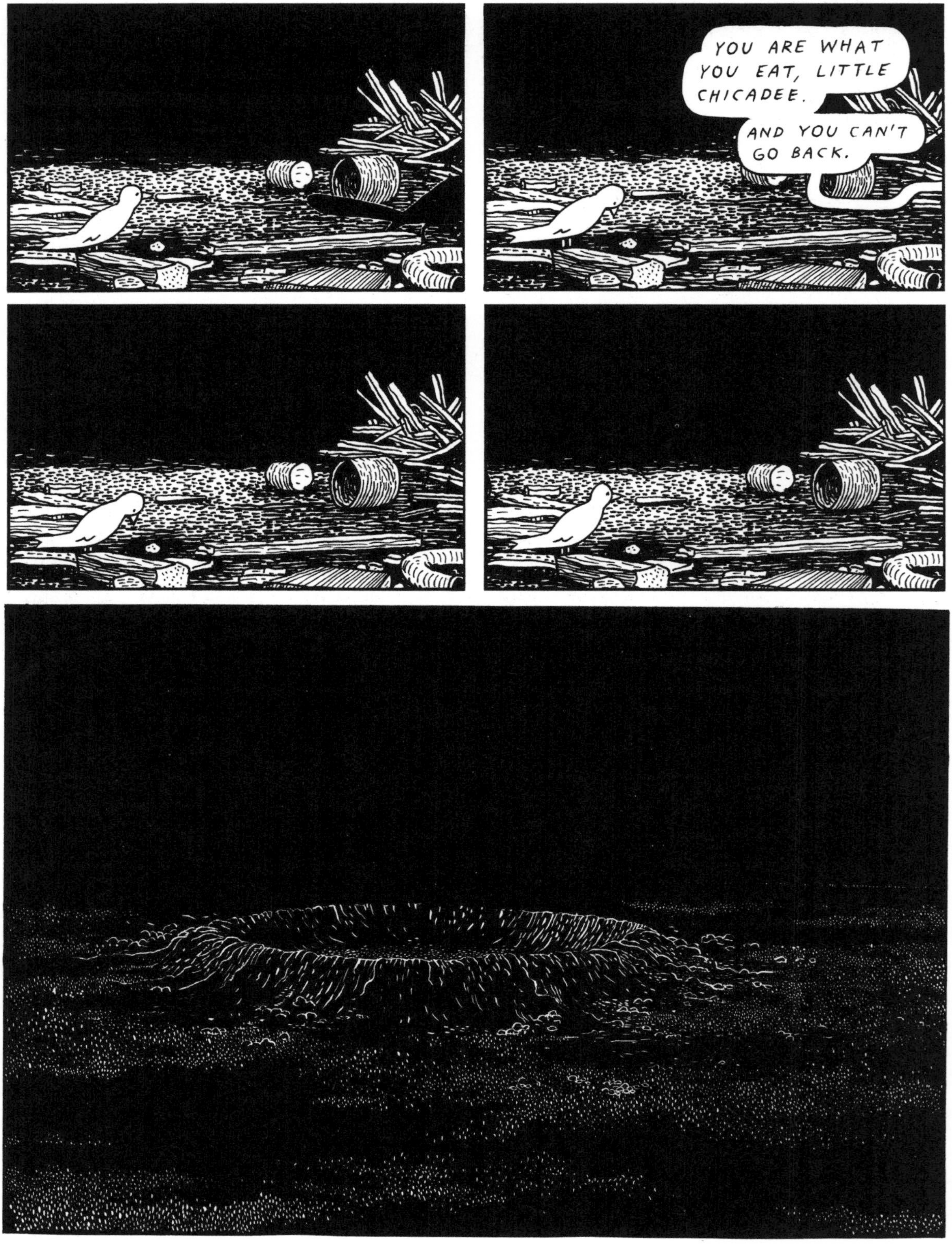
YOU ARE WHAT YOU EAT, LITTLE CHICADEE.
AND YOU CAN'T GO BACK.

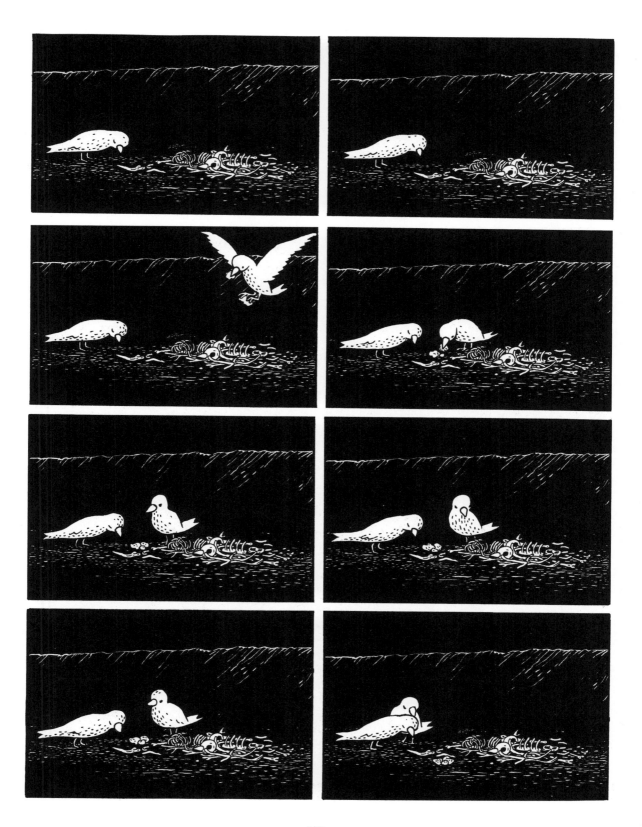

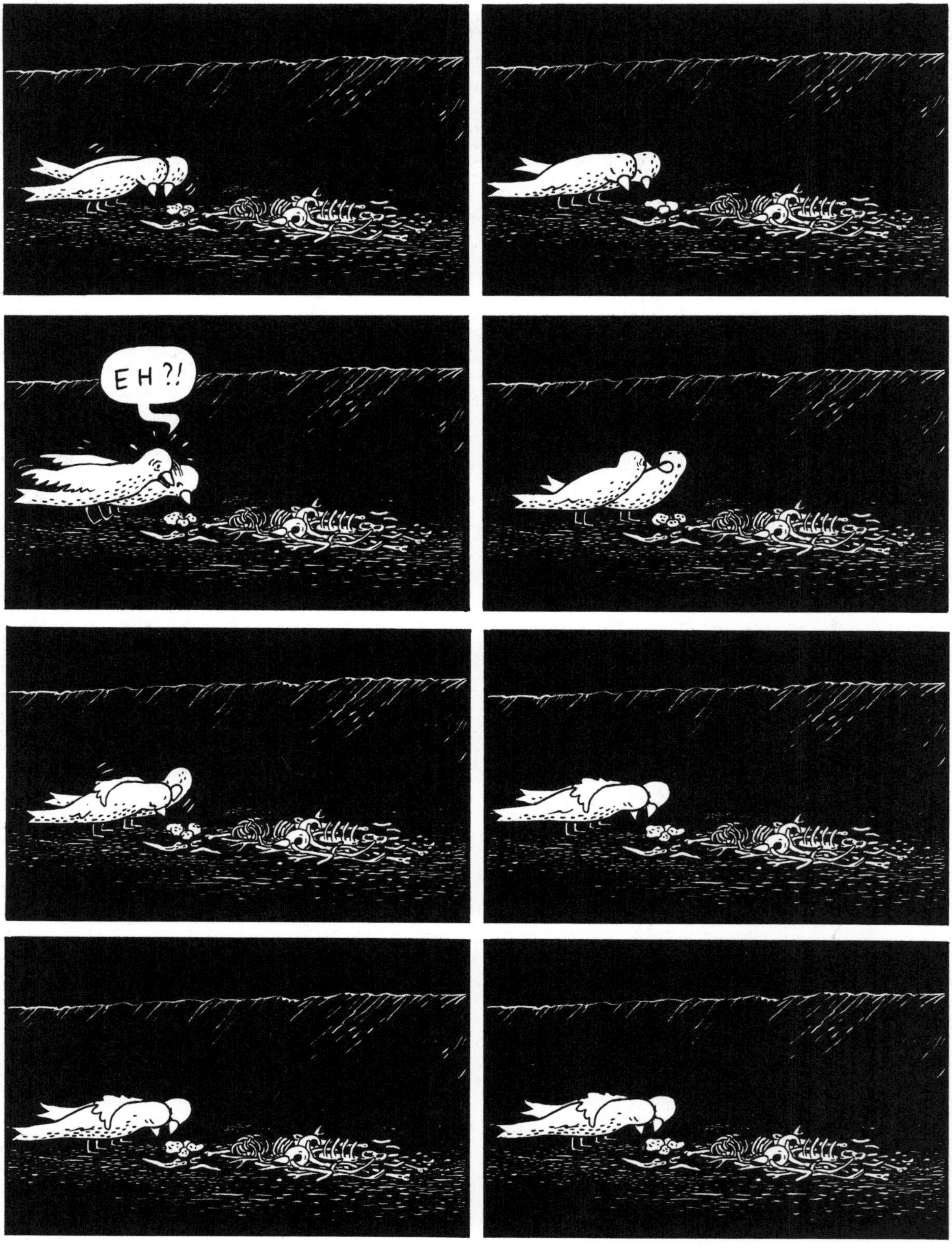
EH ?!

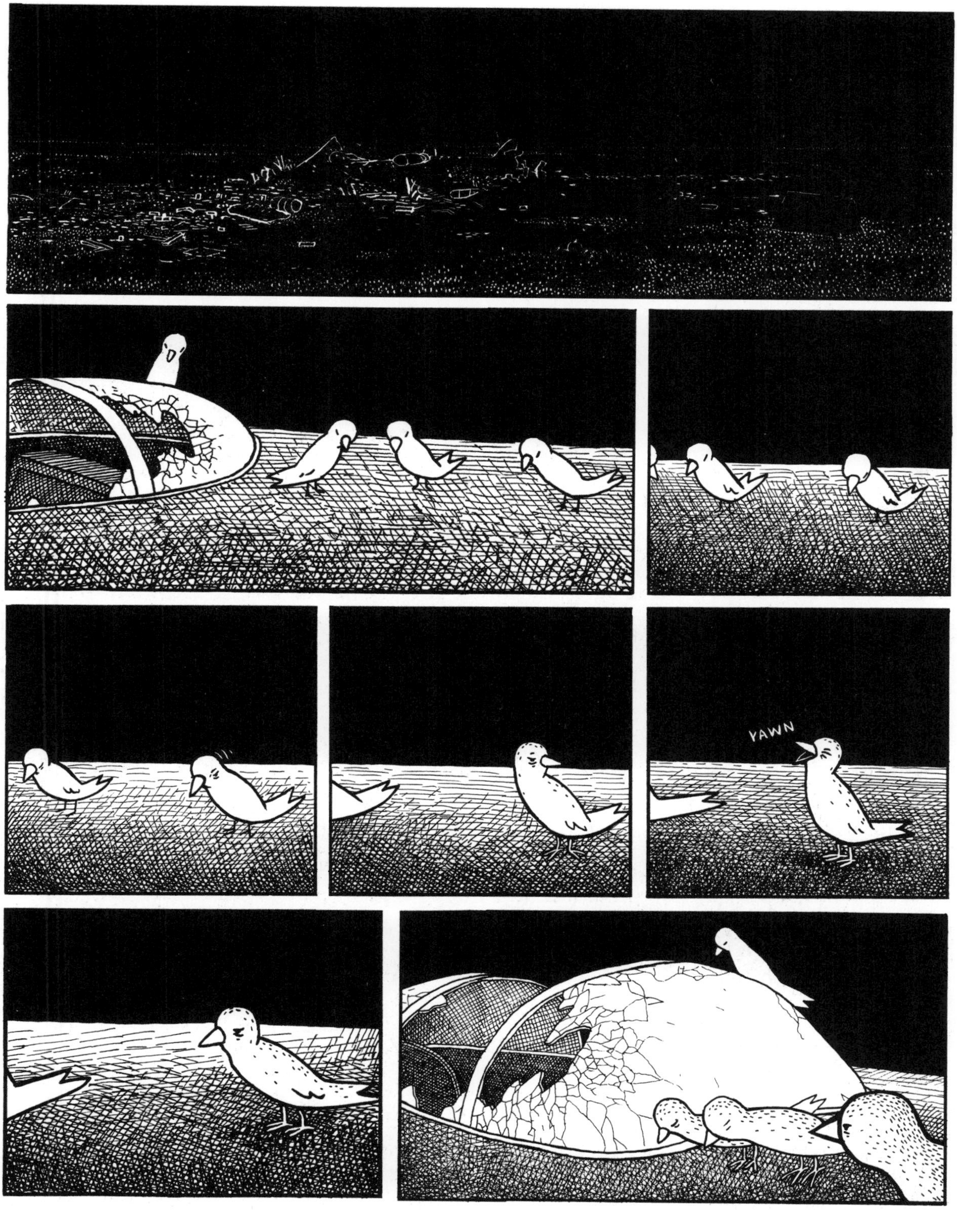
YAWN

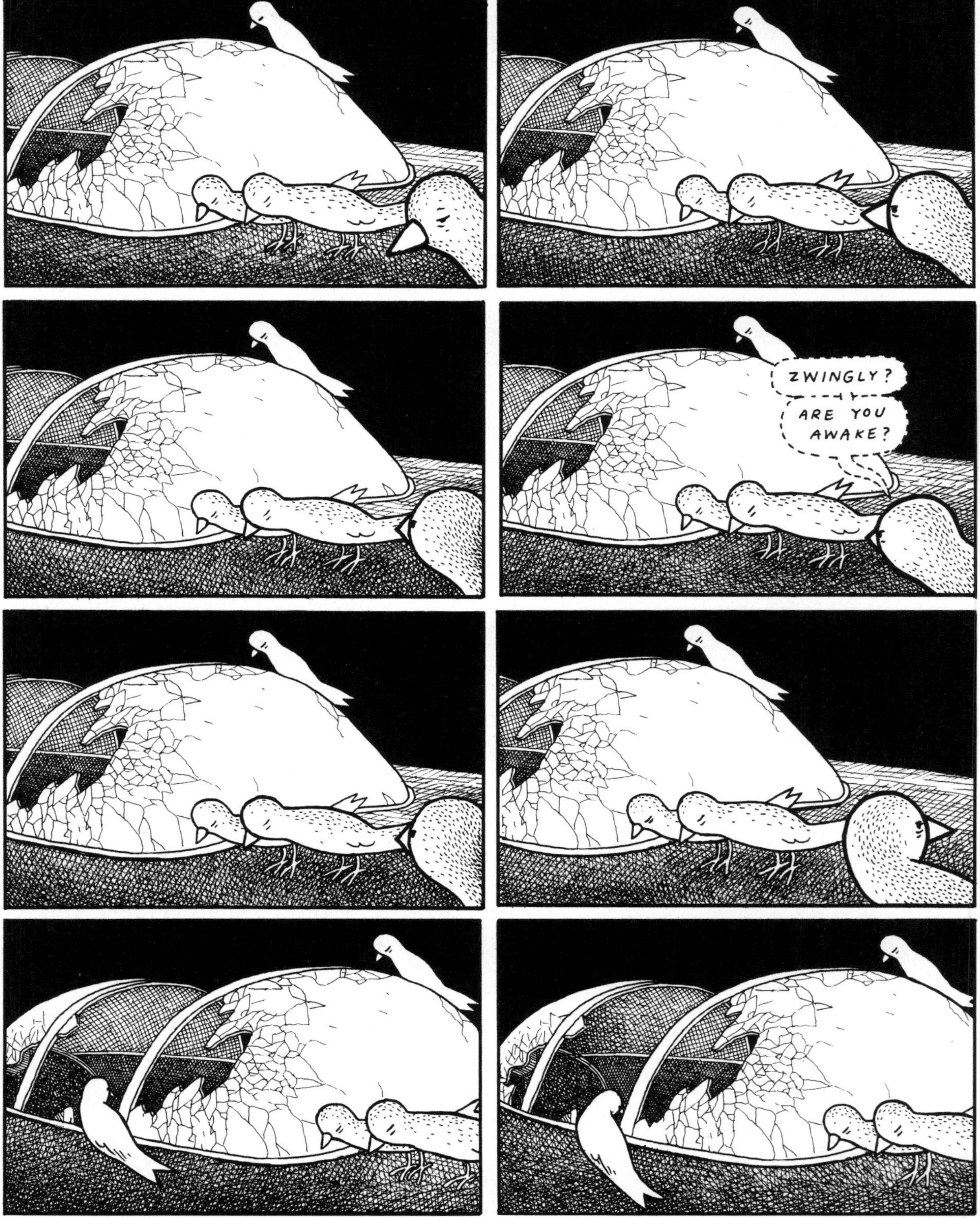
ZWINGLY?
ARE YOU AWAKE?

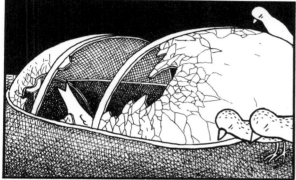
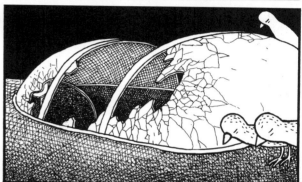

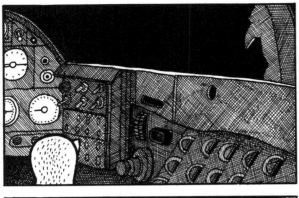

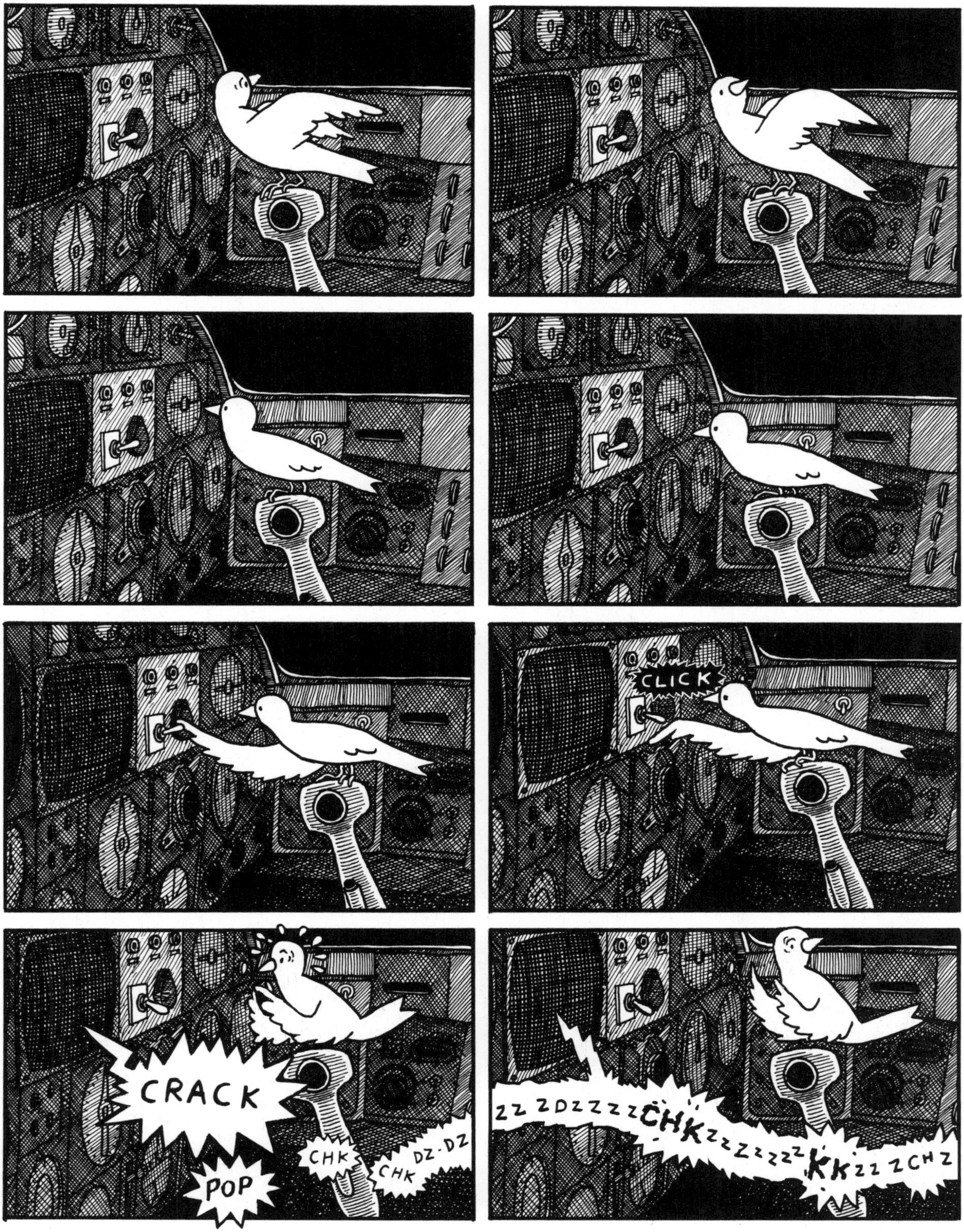
CLICK
CRACK
POP
CHK
CHK
DZ-DZ
ZZ ZDZZZZZCHKZZZZZZZKKZZZCHZ

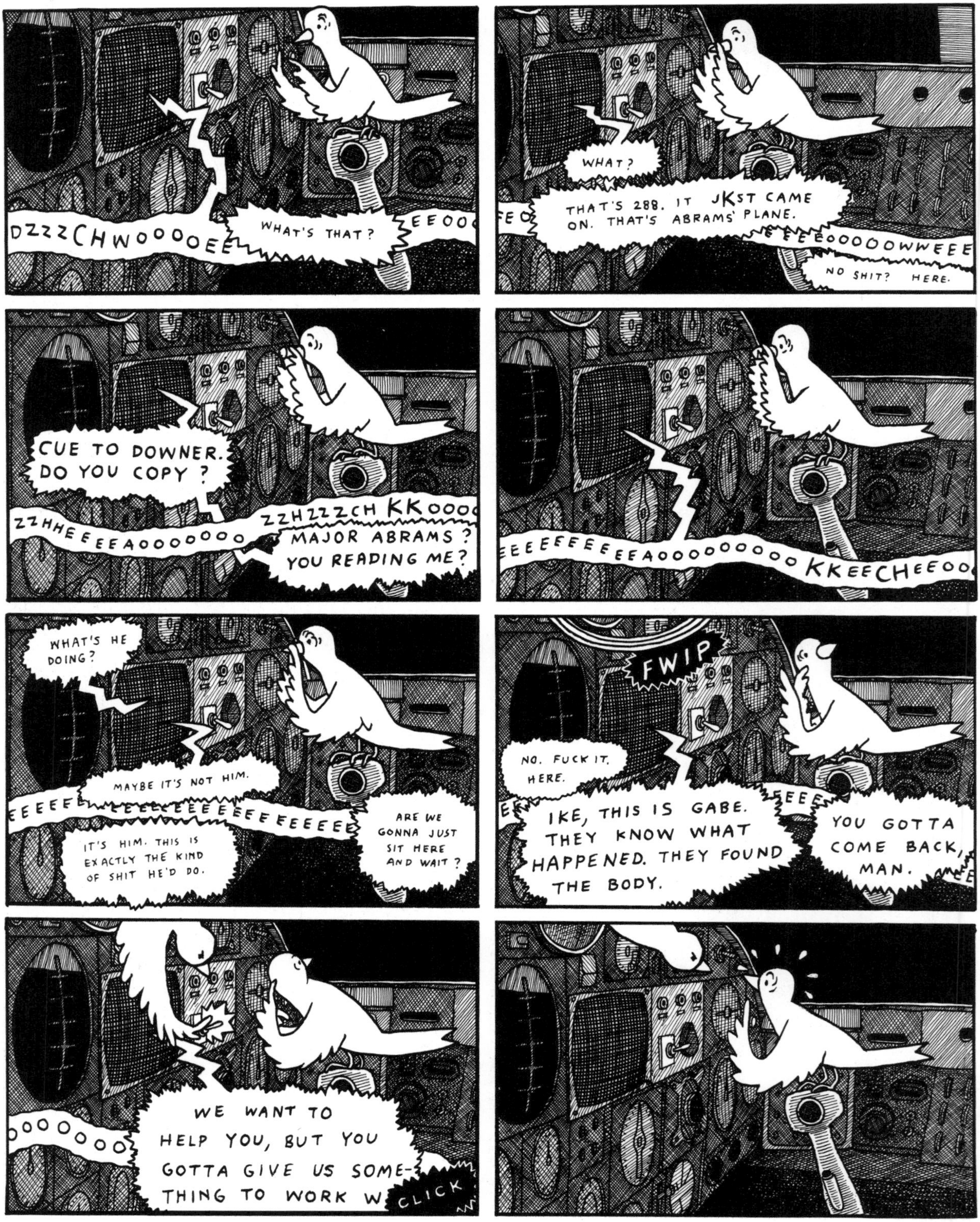
DZZZCHWOOOOEE
WHAT'S THAT?
EEOO
WHAT?
THAT'S 288. IT JUST CAME ON. THAT'S ABRAMS' PLANE.
EEEEOOOOOWWEEE
NO SHIT? HERE.
CUE TO DOWNER. DO YOU COPY?
ZZHHEEEEAOOOOOOO
ZZHZZZCH KKOOOO
MAJOR ABRAMS? YOU READING ME?
EEEEEEEEEAOOOOOOOOOO KKEECHEEOO
WHAT'S HE DOING?
MAYBE IT'S NOT HIM.
EEEEEEEEEEEEEEEEEEEEEE
IT'S HIM. THIS IS EXACTLY THE KIND OF SHIT HE'D DO.
ARE WE GONNA JUST SIT HERE AND WAIT?
FWIP
NO. FUCK IT. HERE.
IKE, THIS IS GABE. THEY KNOW WHAT HAPPENED. THEY FOUND THE BODY.
EEEE
YOU GOTTA COME BACK, MAN.
OOOOOOO
WE WANT TO HELP YOU, BUT YOU GOTTA GIVE US SOME-THING TO WORK W
CLICK

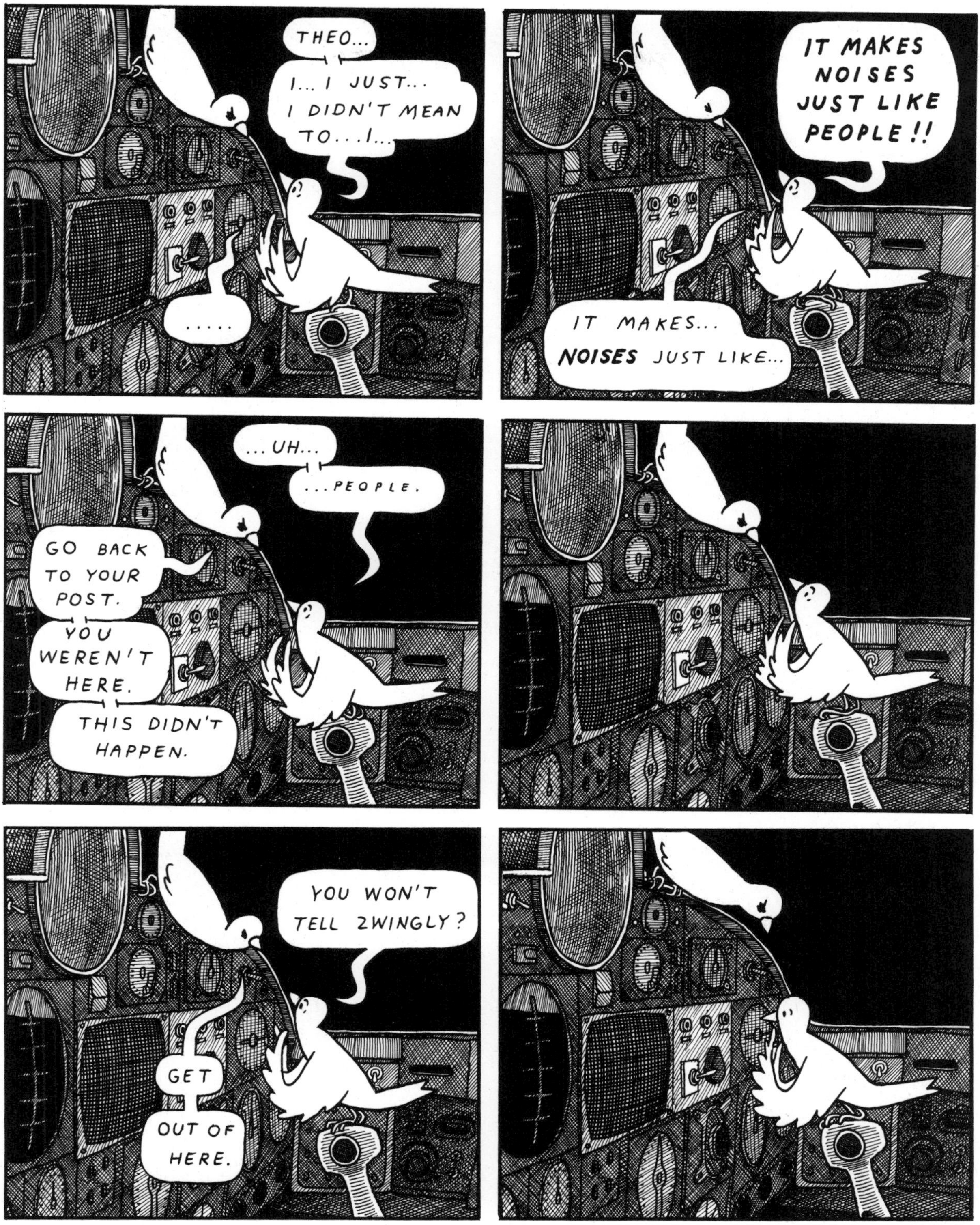
THEO...
I... I JUST... I DIDN'T MEAN TO...I...
.....
IT MAKES NOISES JUST LIKE PEOPLE!!
IT MAKES... NOISES JUST LIKE...
...UH...
...PEOPLE.
GO BACK TO YOUR POST.
YOU WEREN'T HERE.
THIS DIDN'T HAPPEN.
YOU WON'T TELL ZWINGLY?
GET
OUT OF HERE.

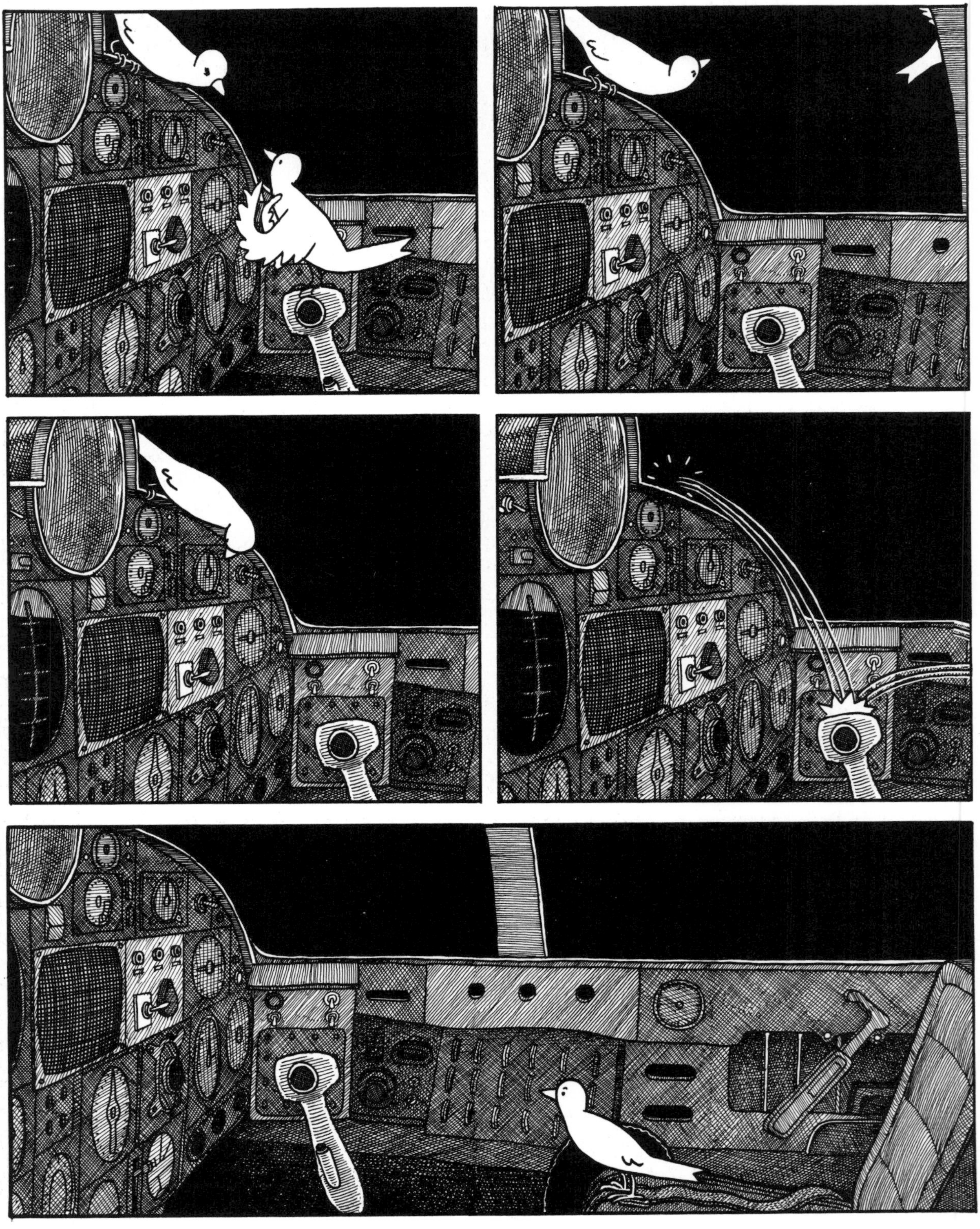

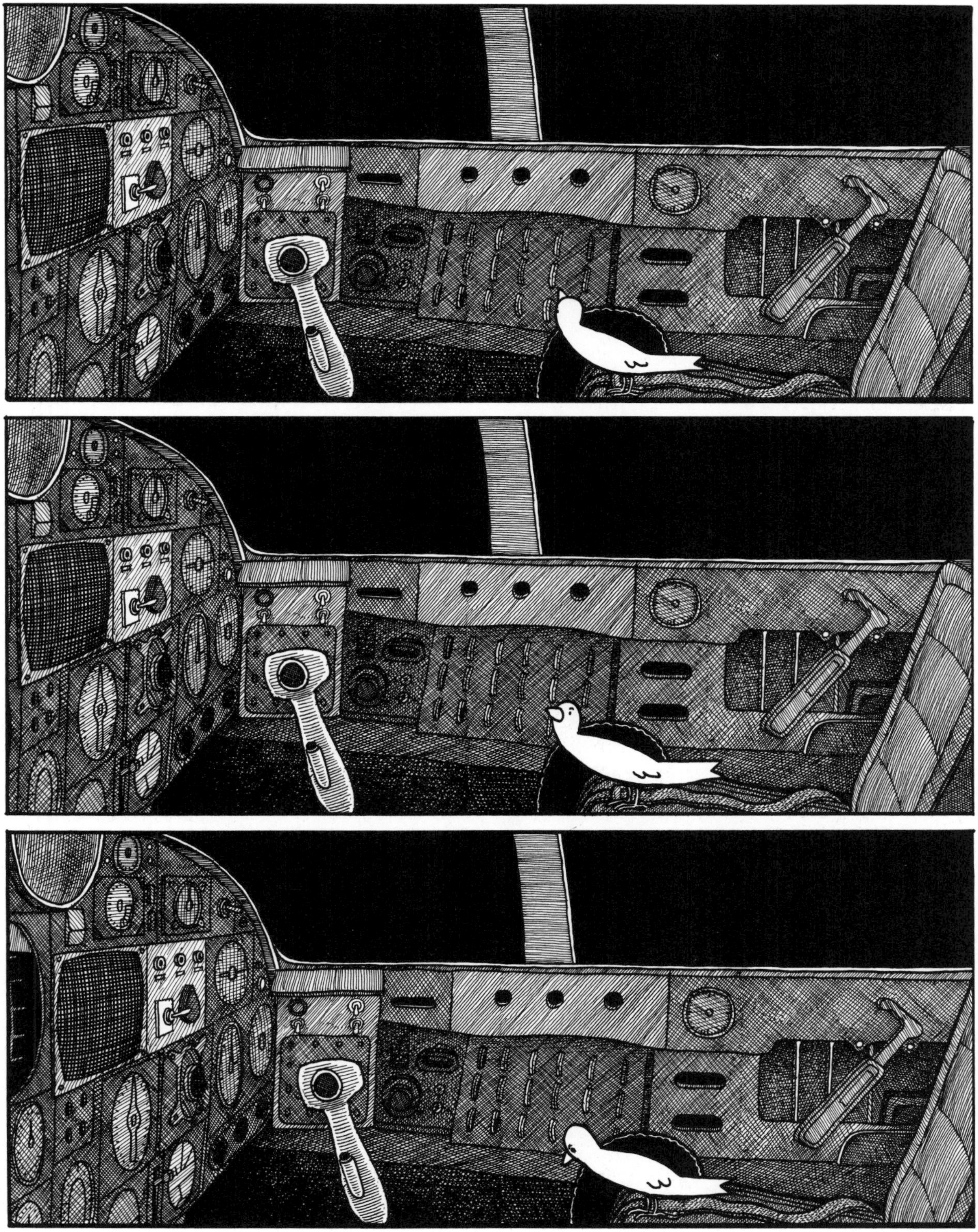

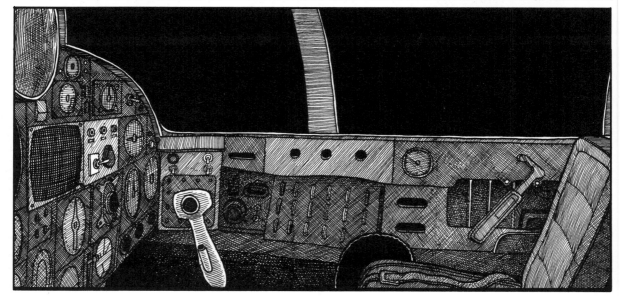

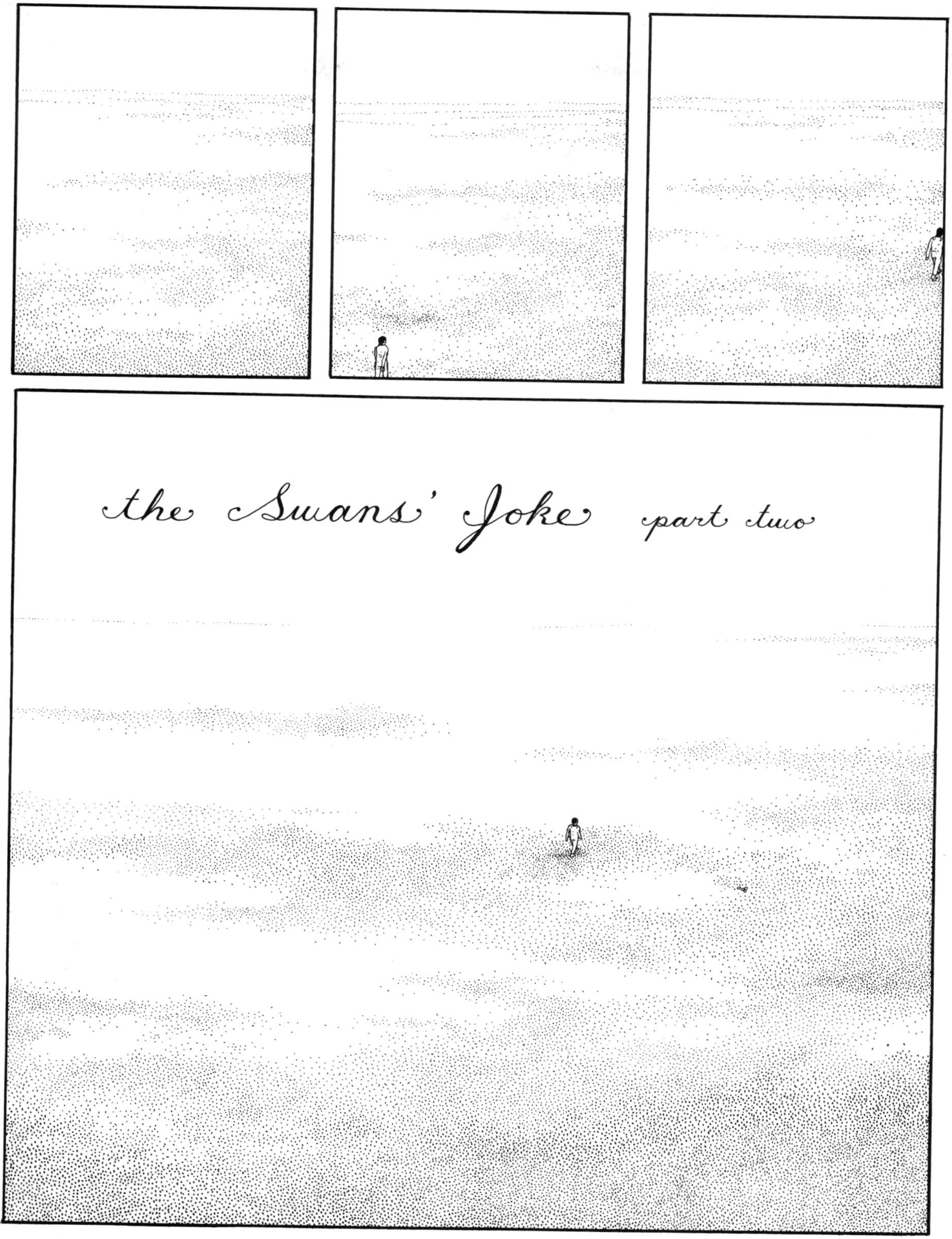
the Swans' Joke part two

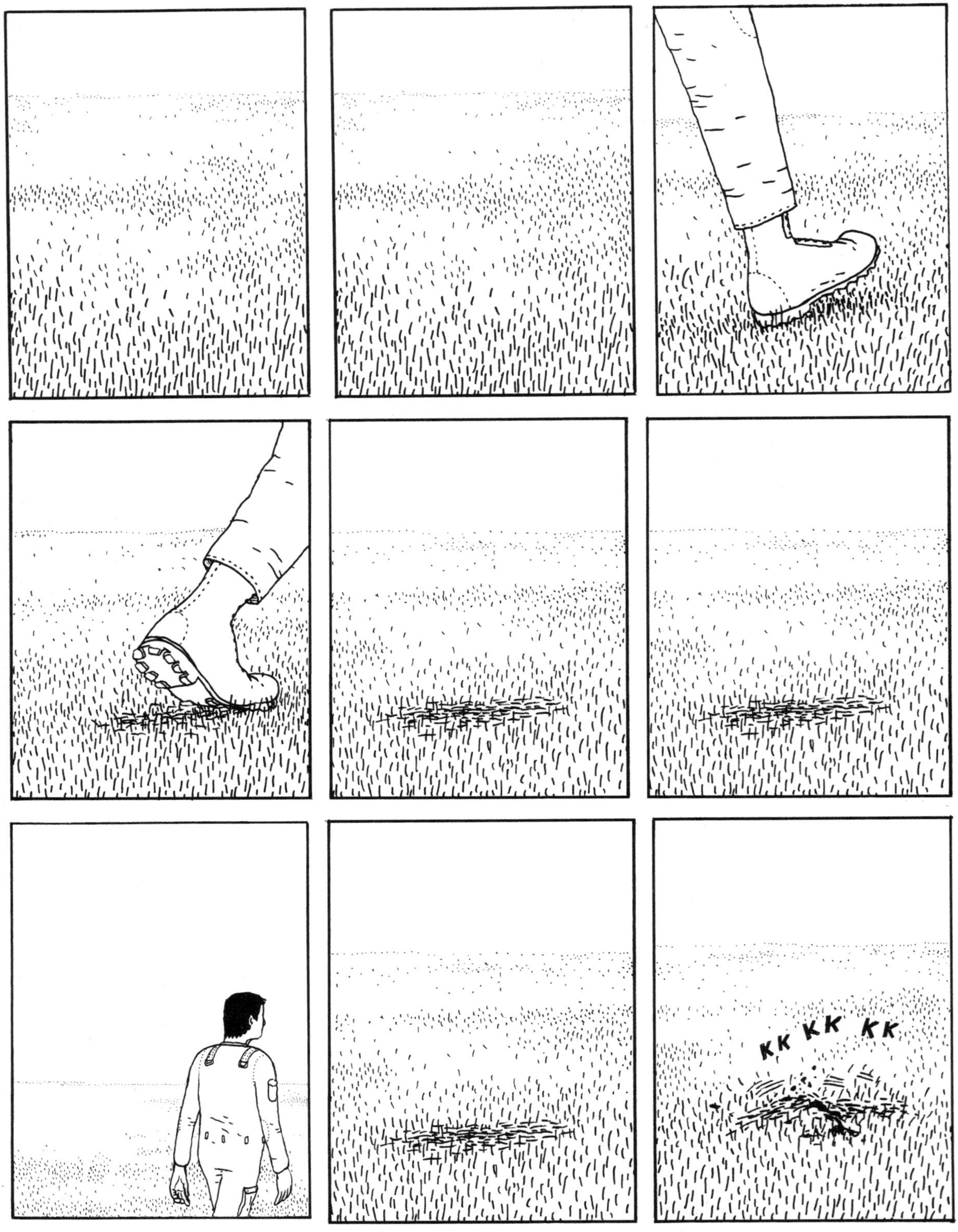
KK KK KK

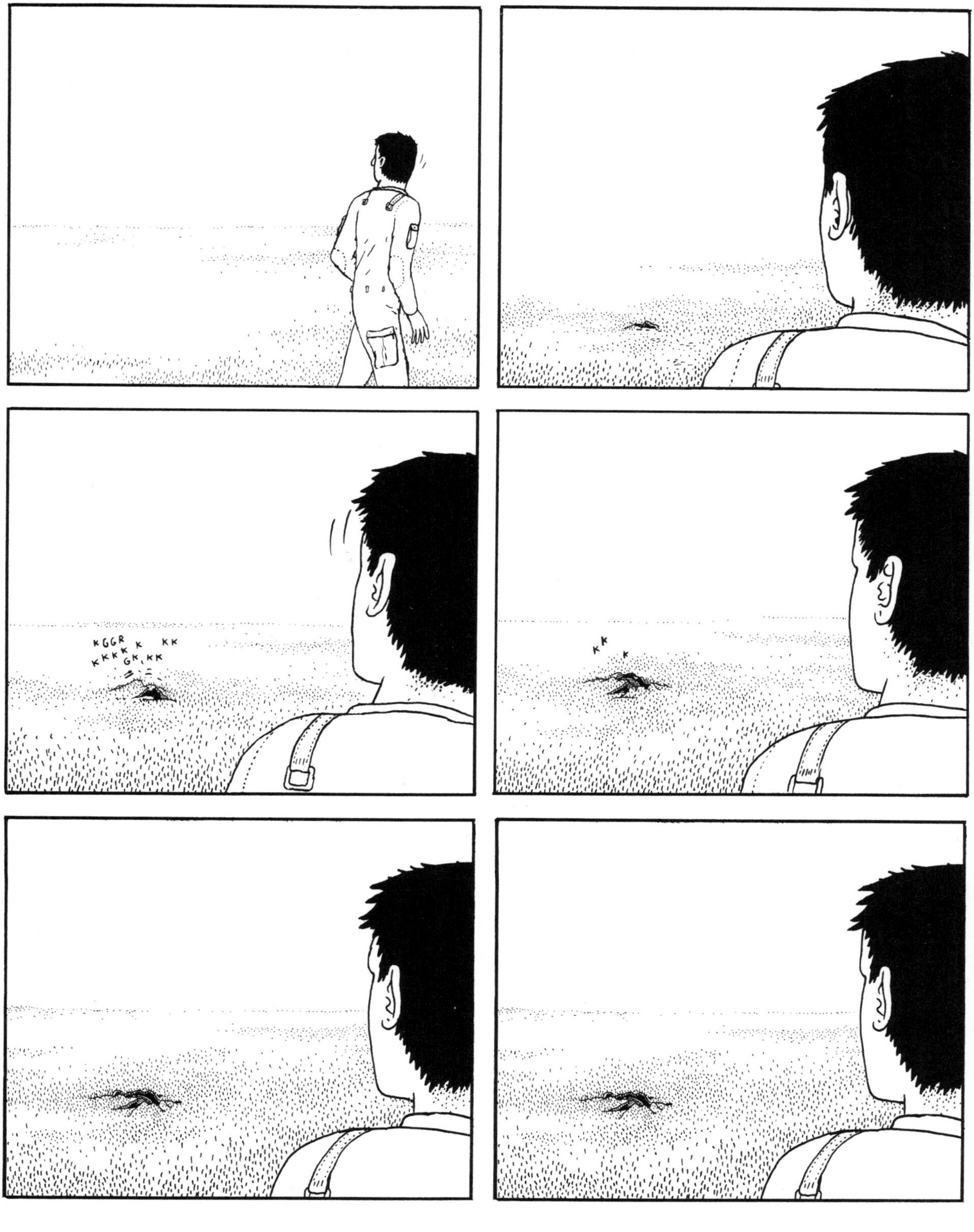
KGGR
KKKKK K KK
GK KK
KK
K

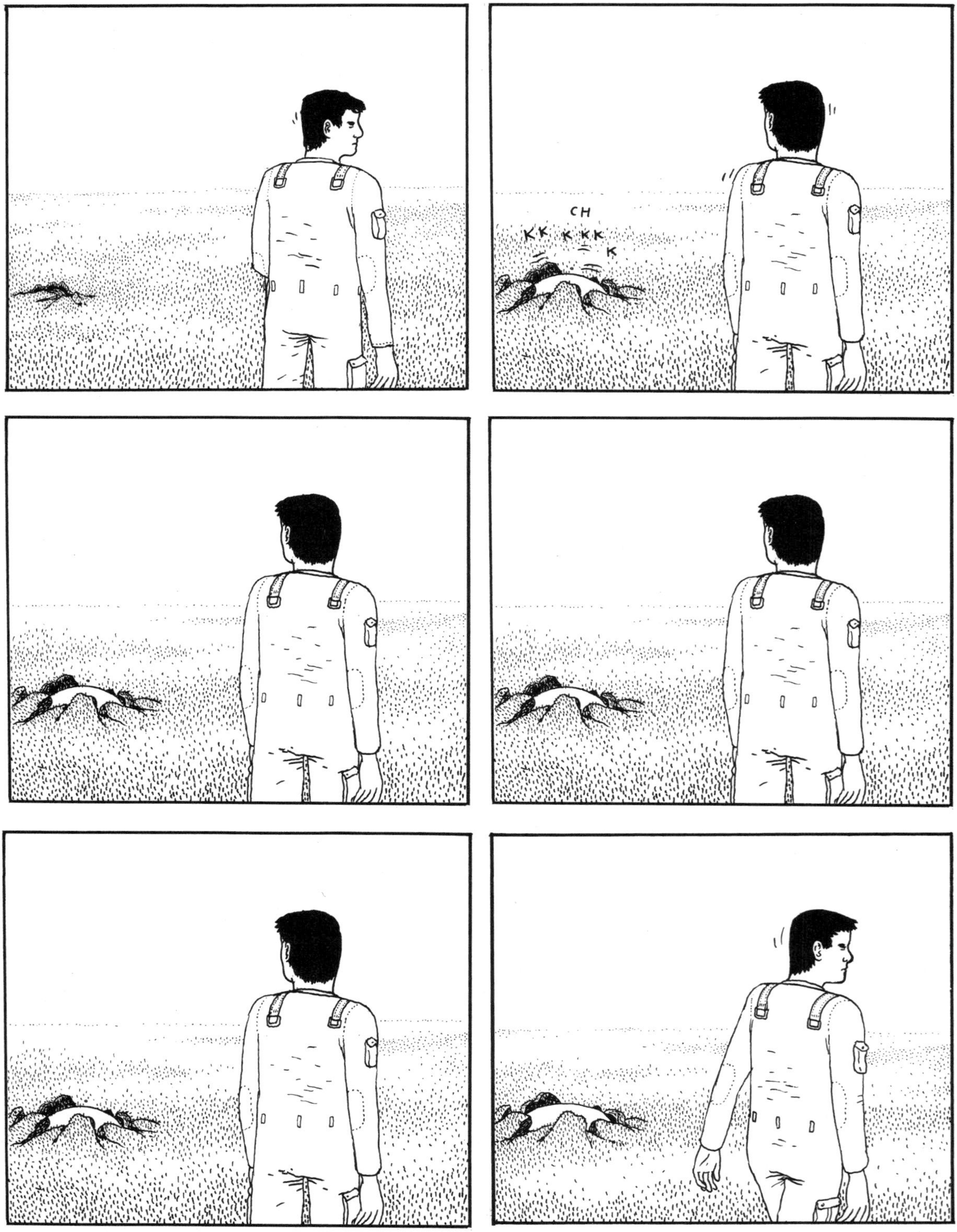
CH
KK KKK K

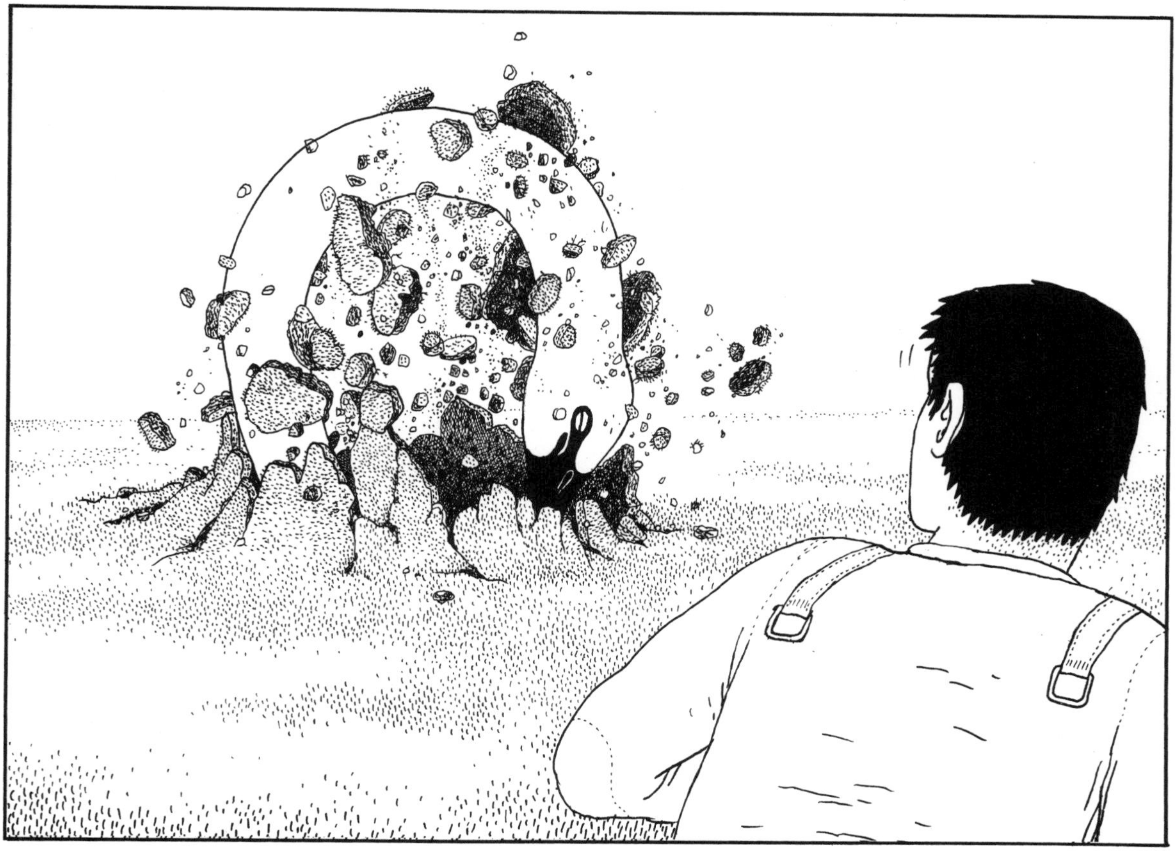

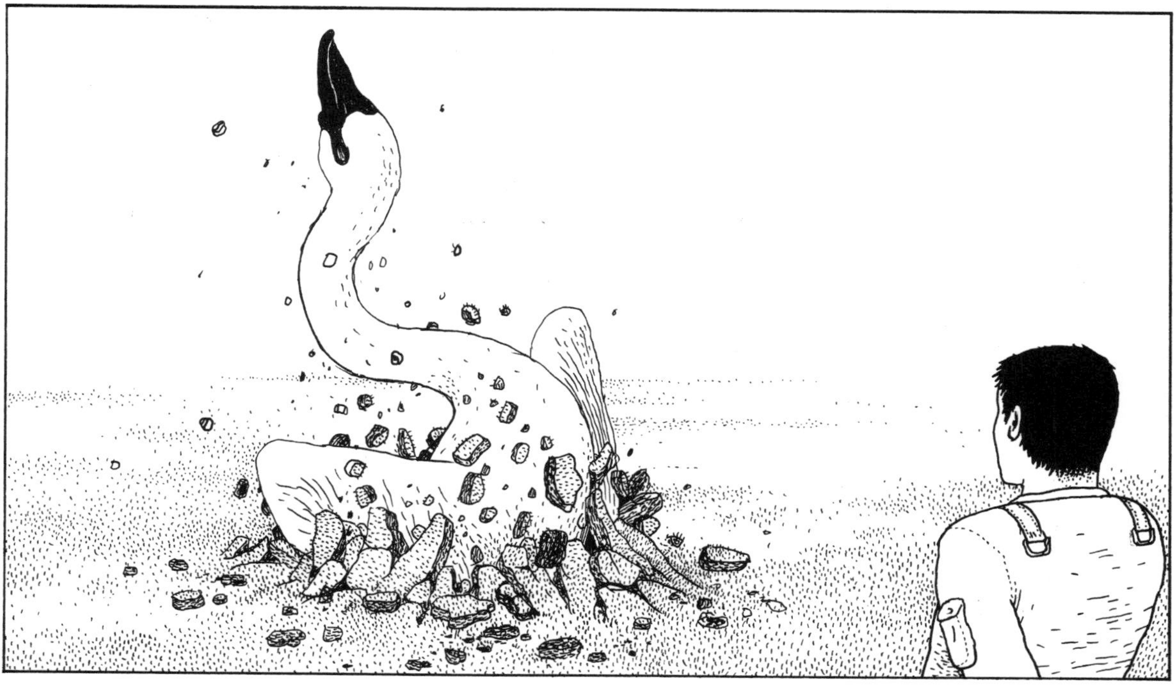

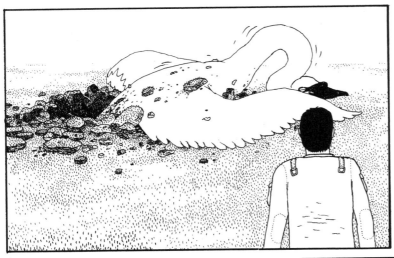

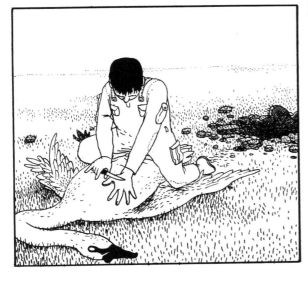
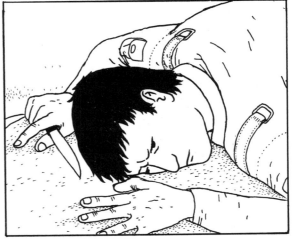

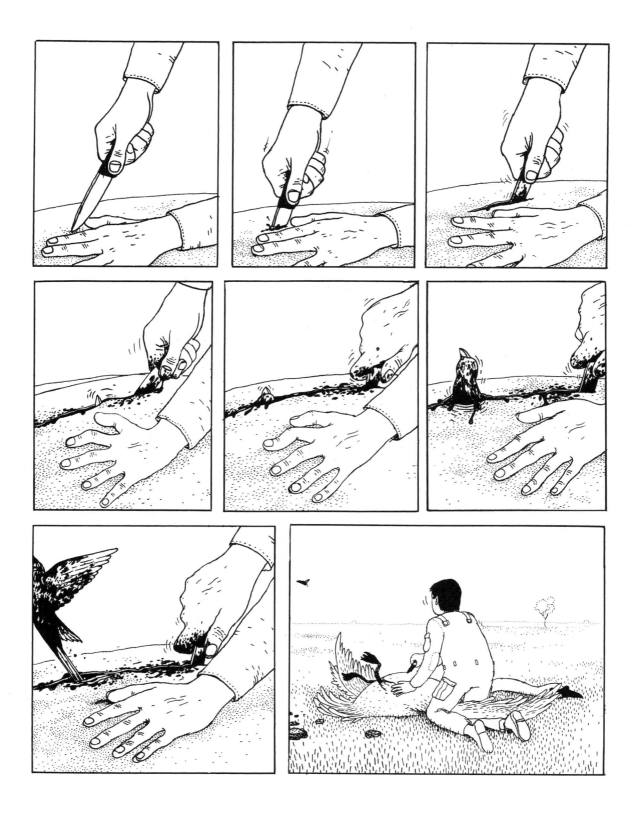

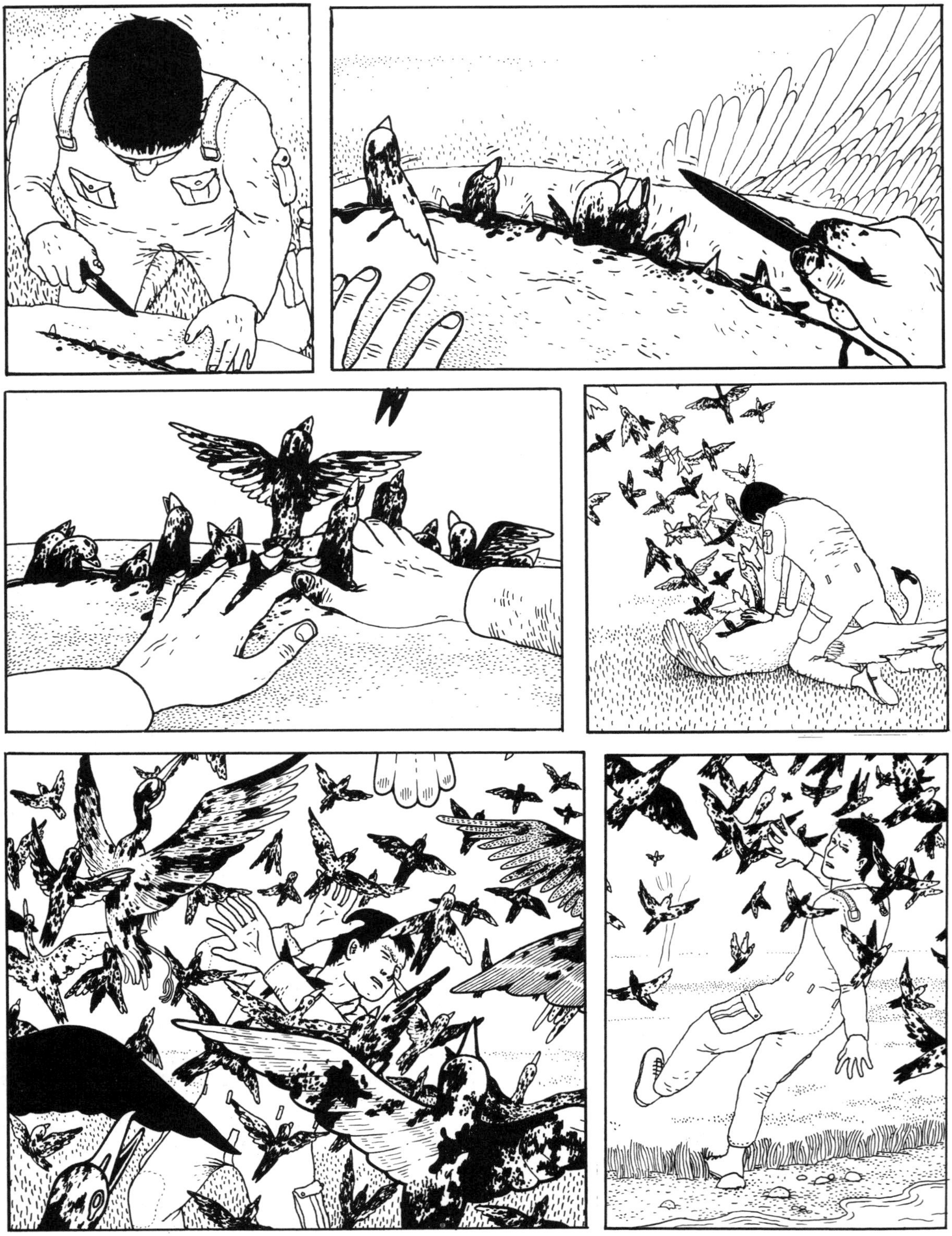

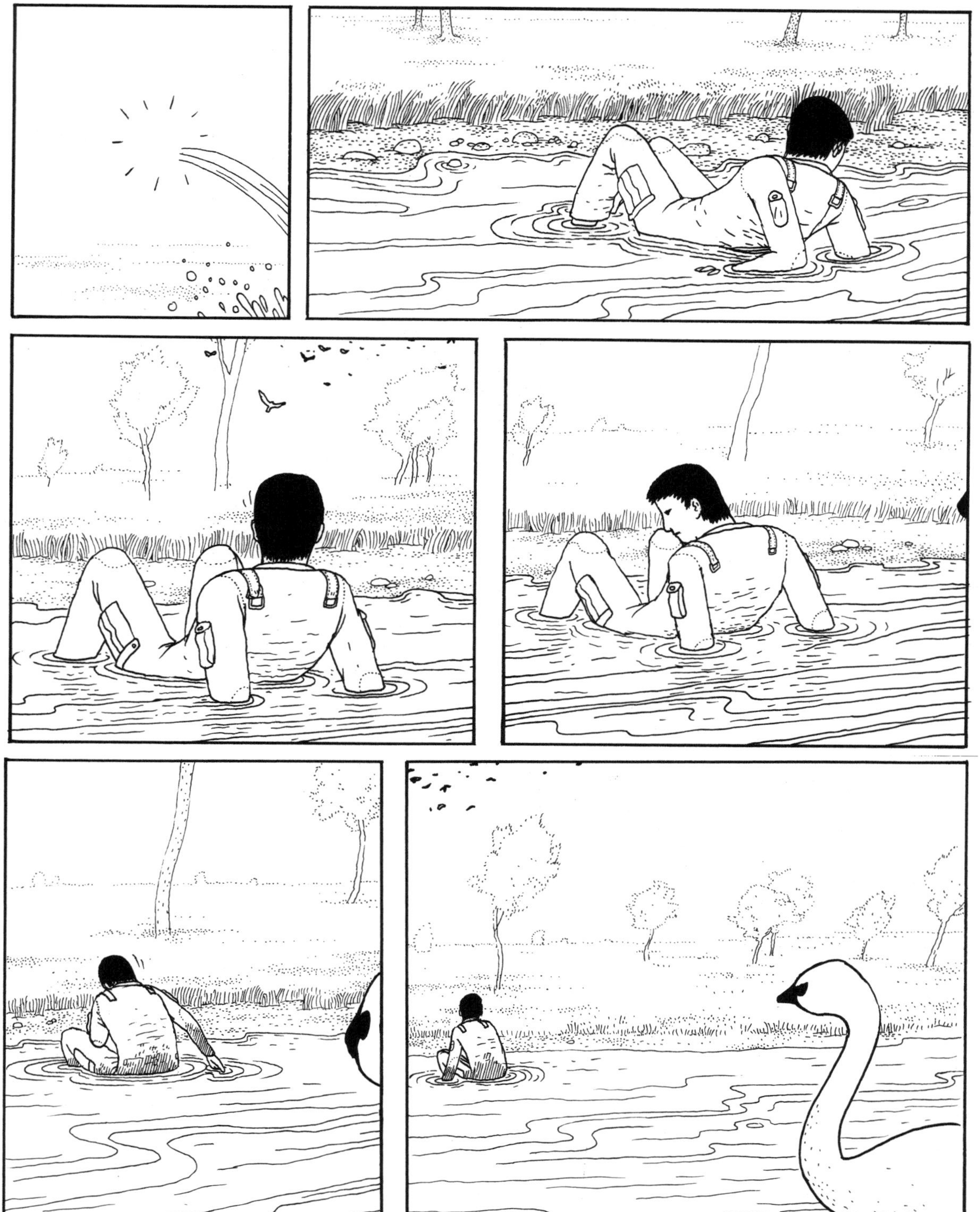

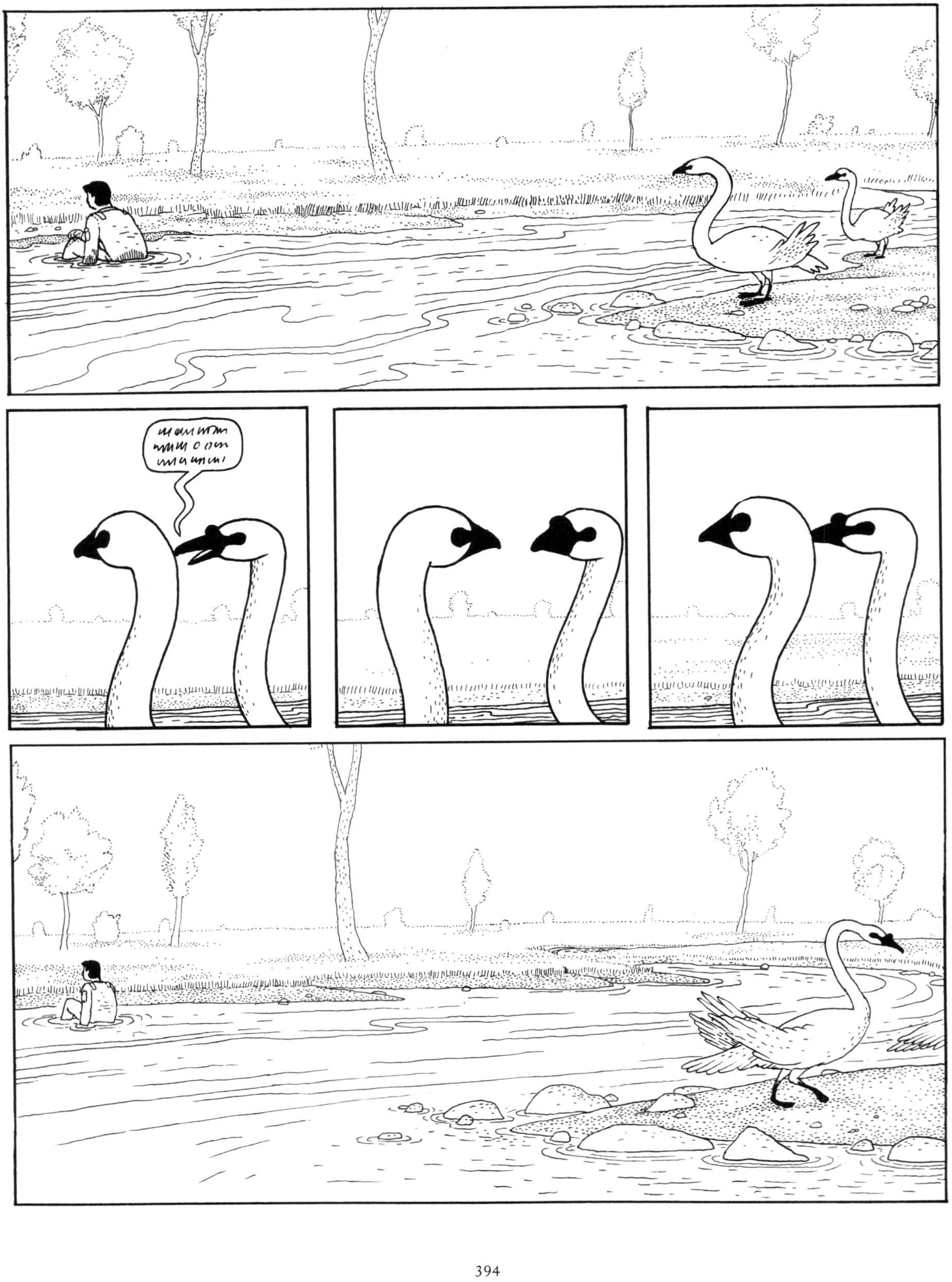

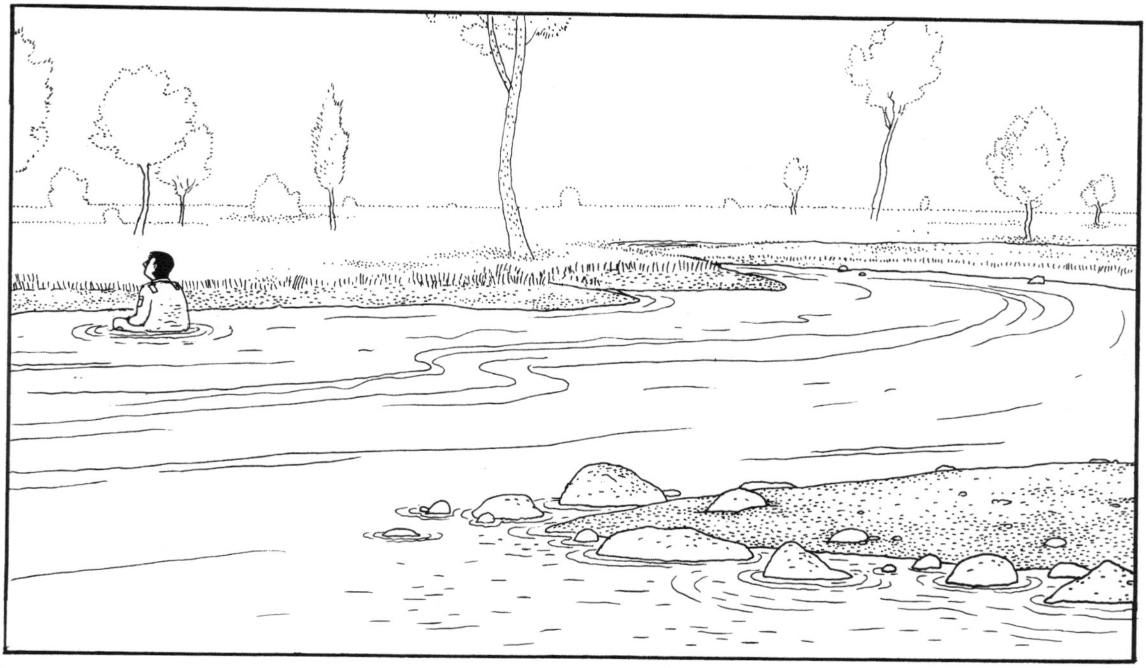

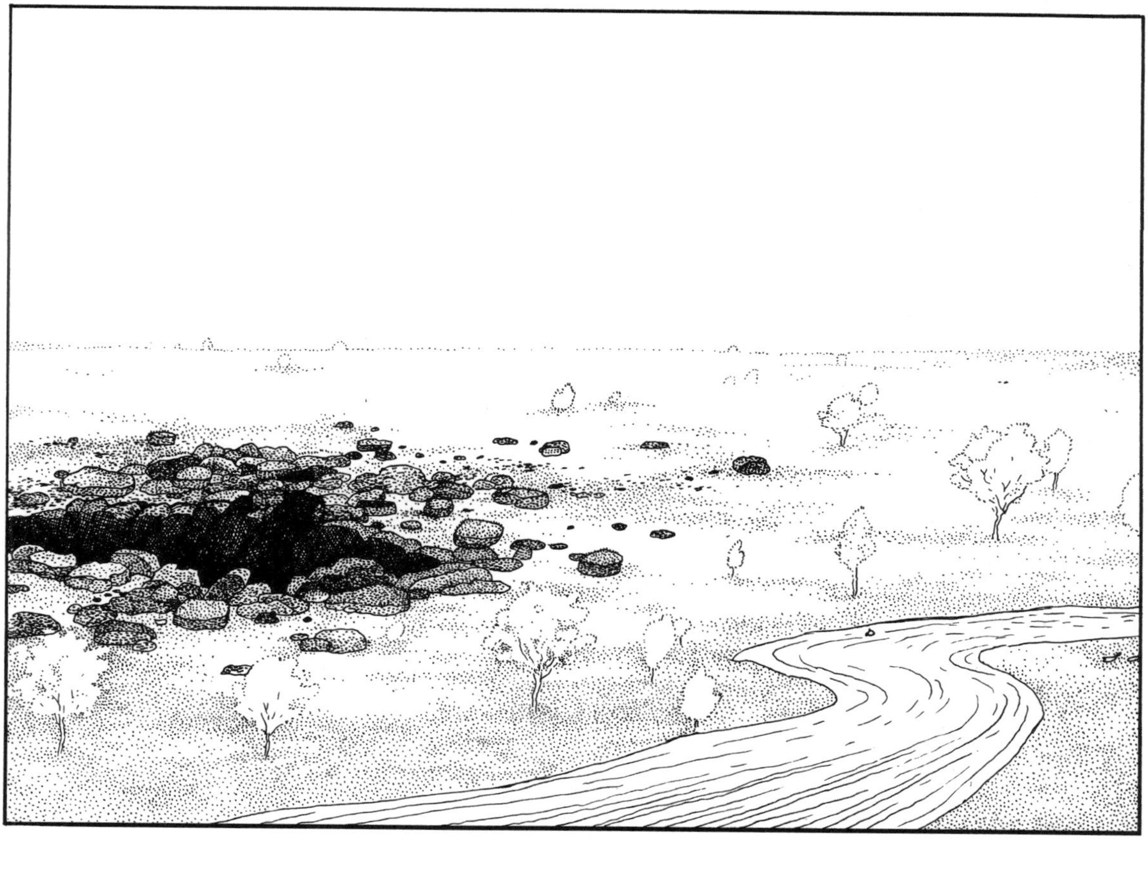

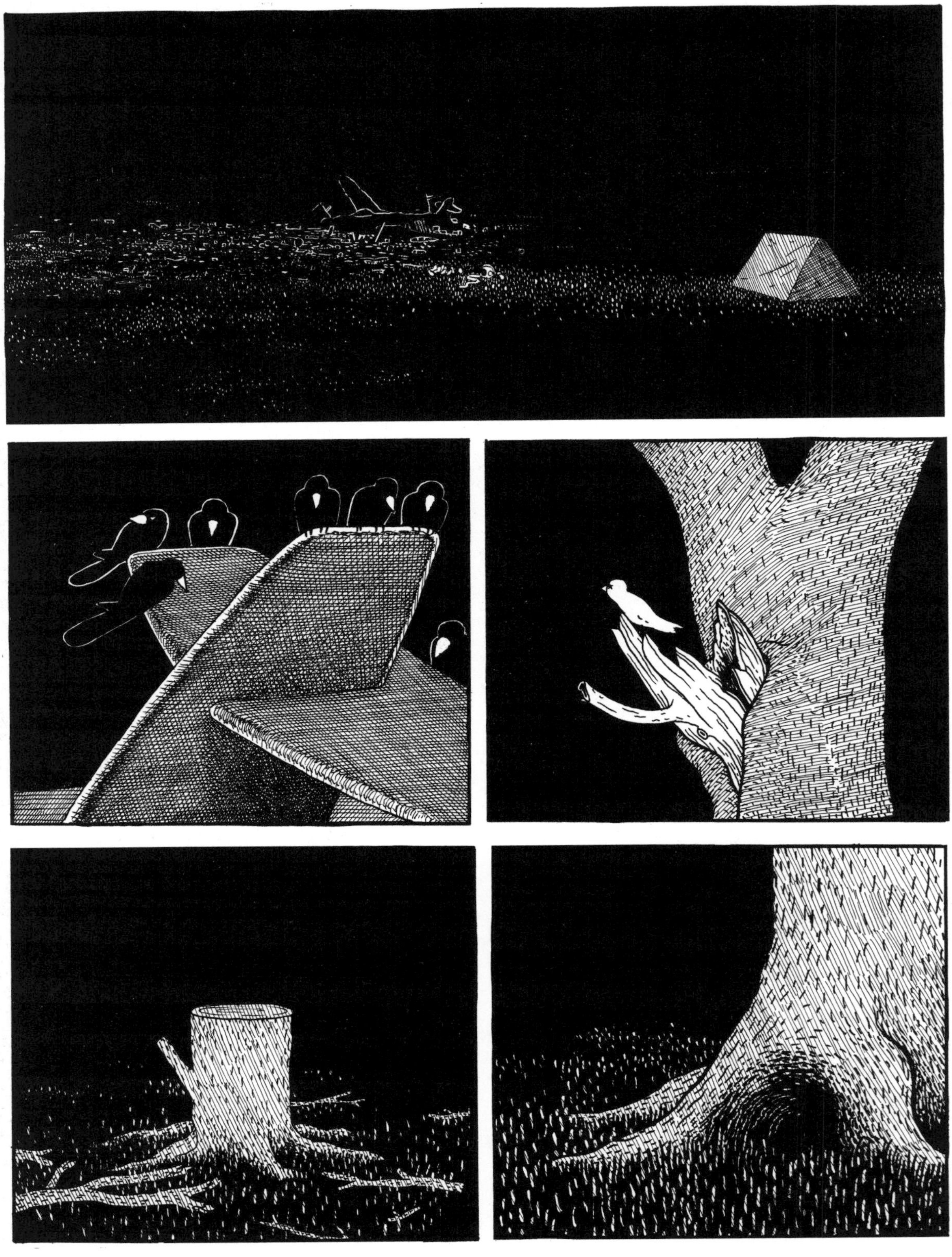

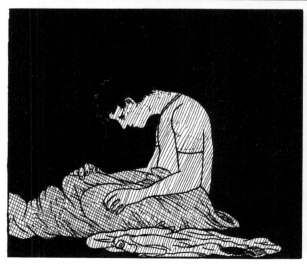
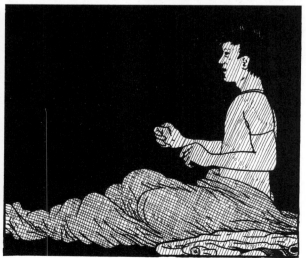

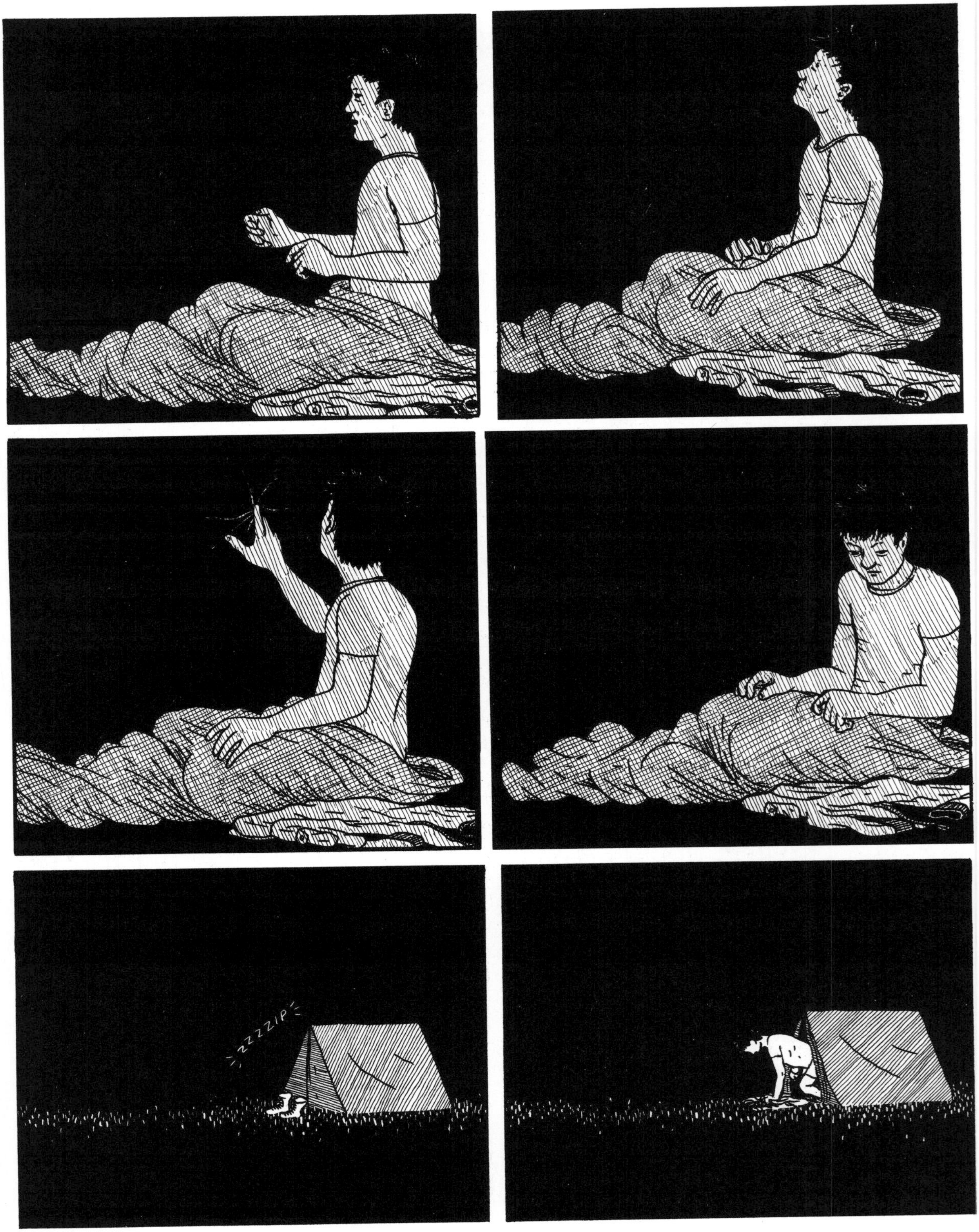
ZZZZIP

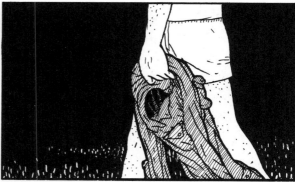

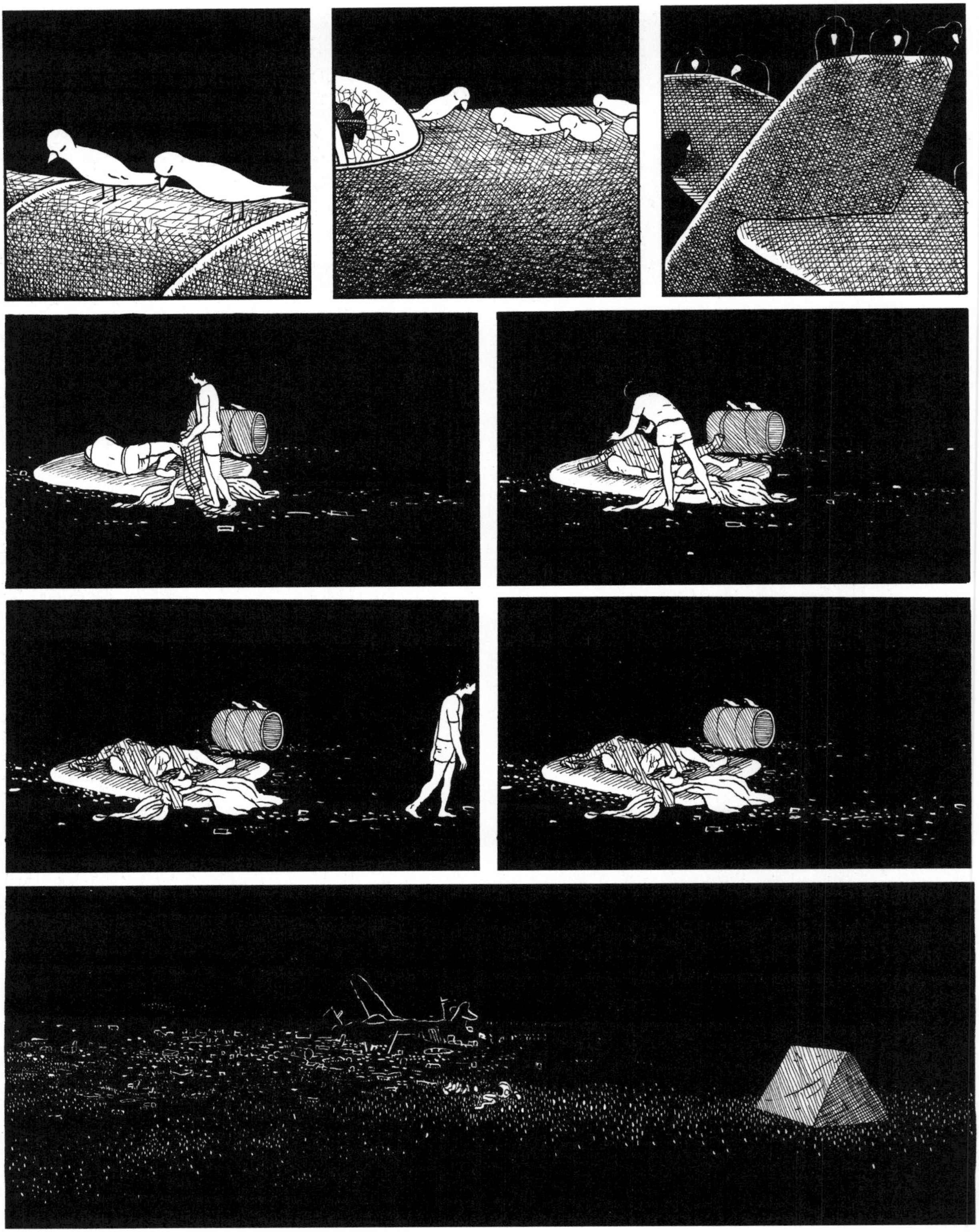

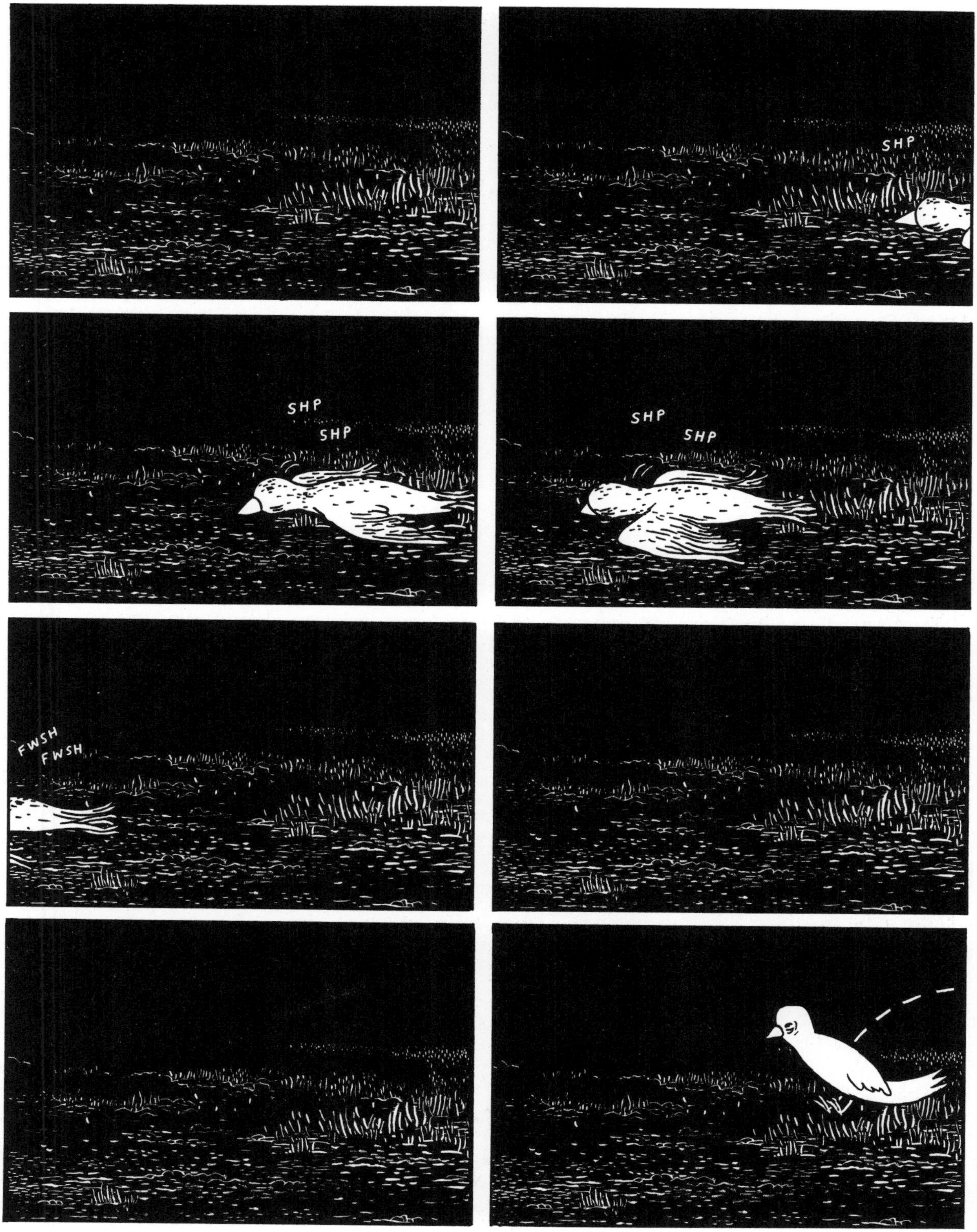
SHP
SHP
SHP
SHP
SHP
FWSH
FWSH

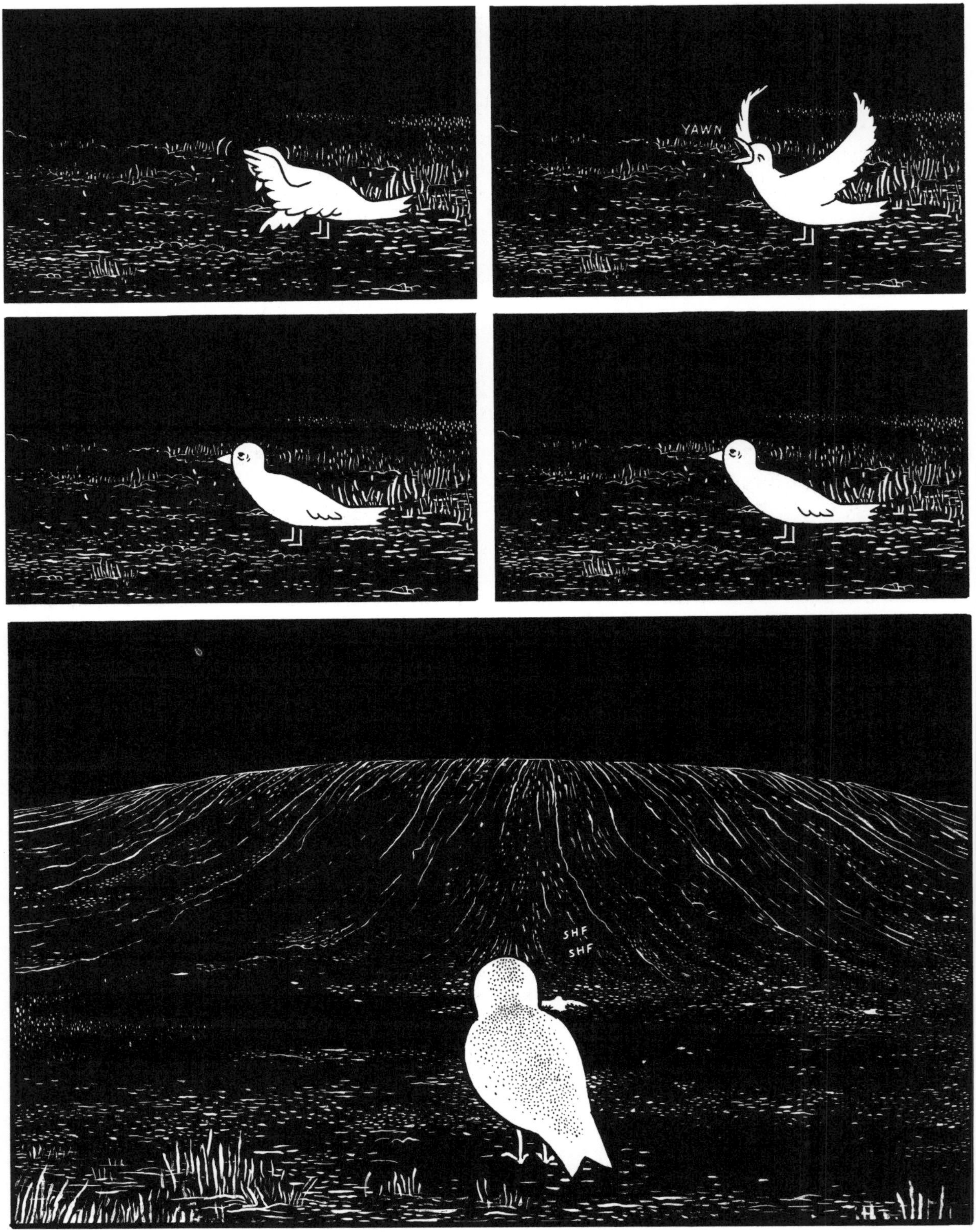
YAWN
SHF
SHF

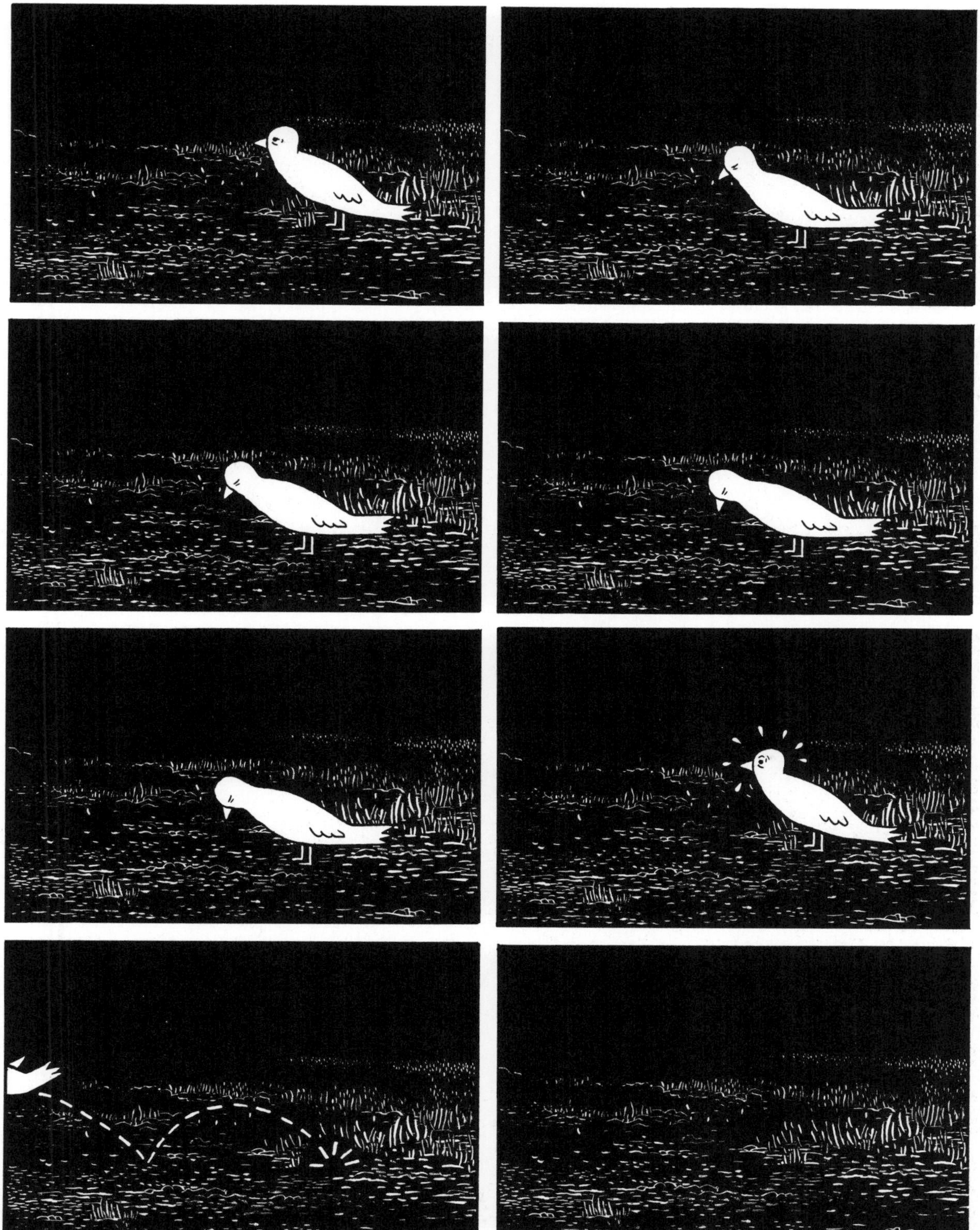

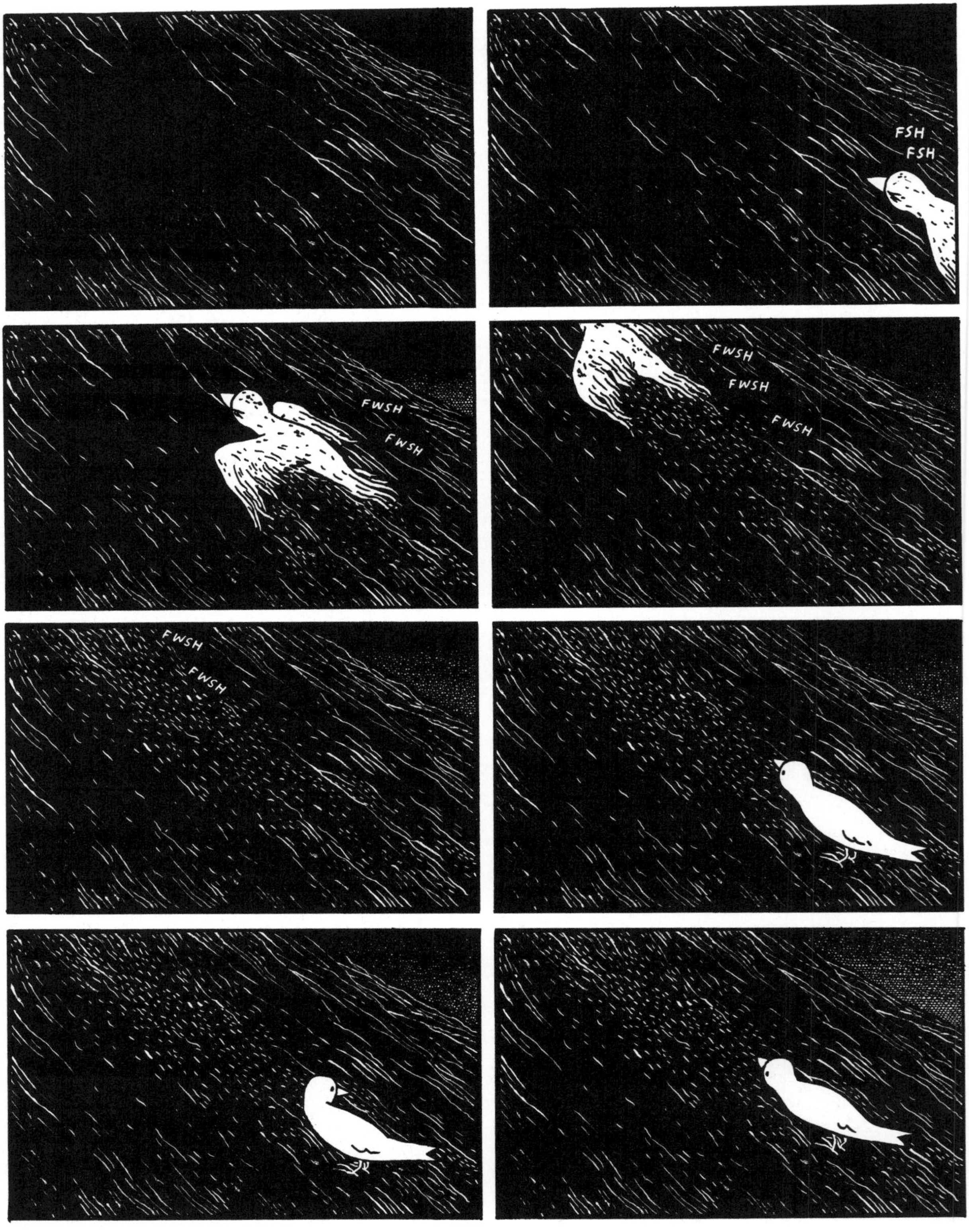
FSH
FSH
FWSH
FWSH
FWSH
FWSH
FWSH
FWSH
FWSH

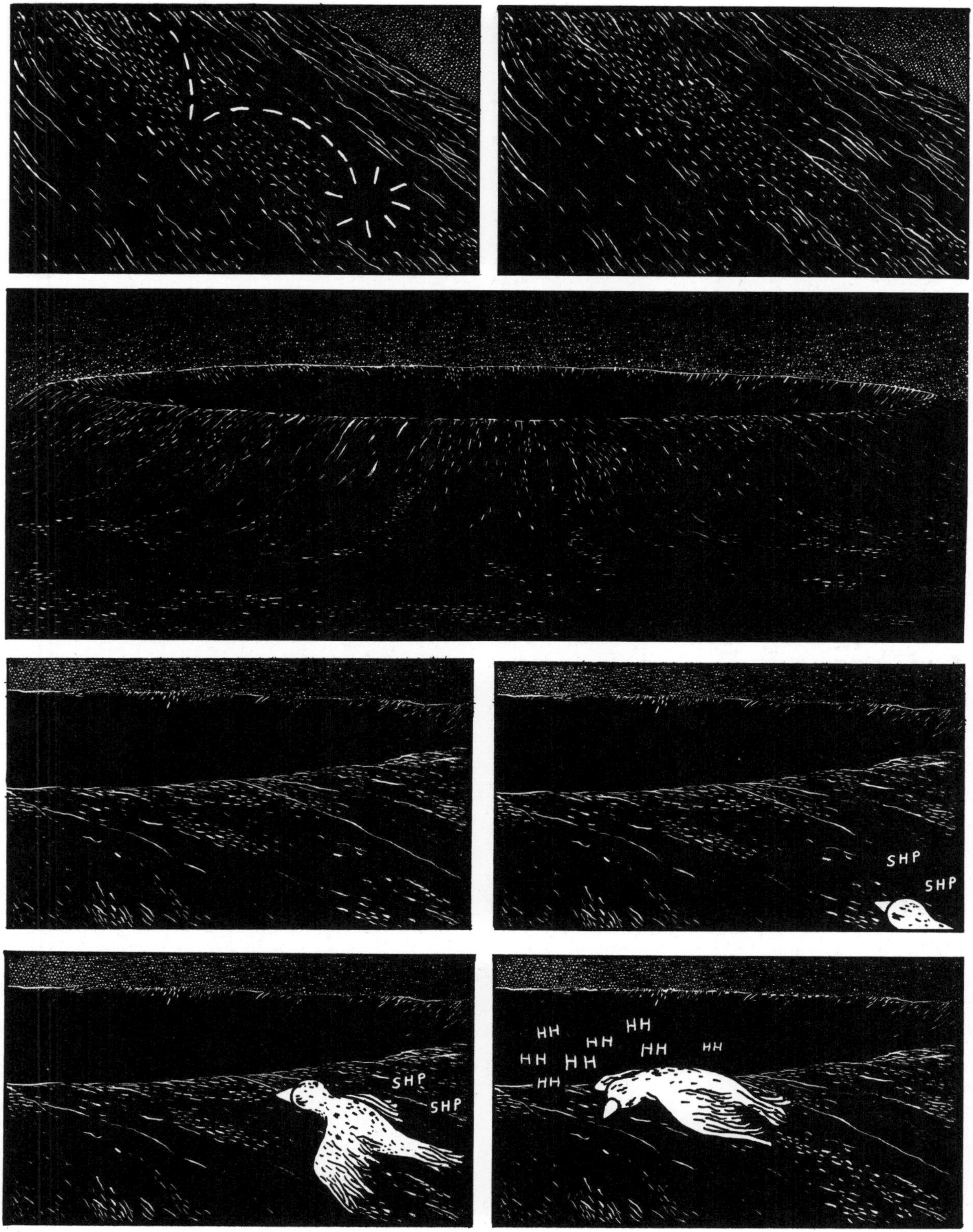
SHP
SHP
SHP
SHP
HH
HH
HH
HH
HH
HH
HH
HH

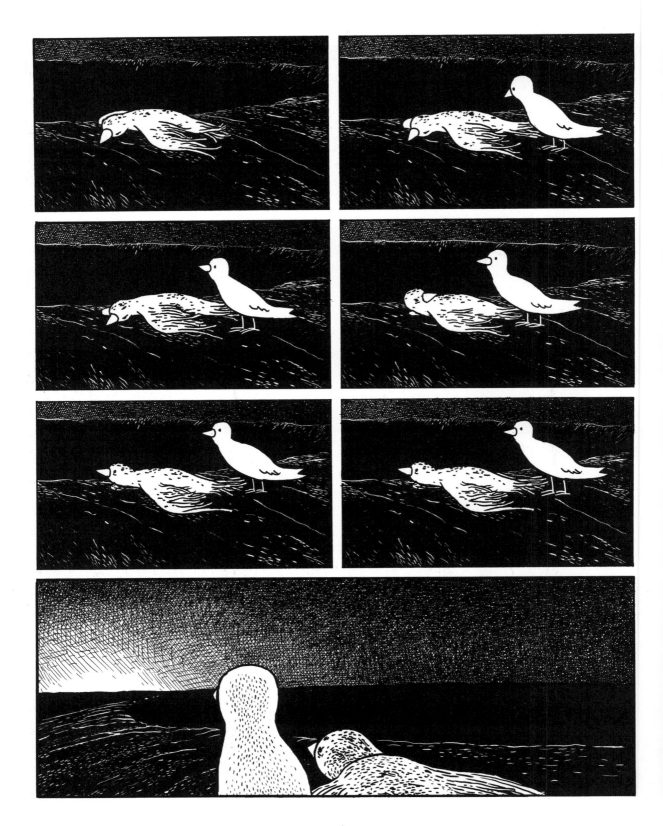

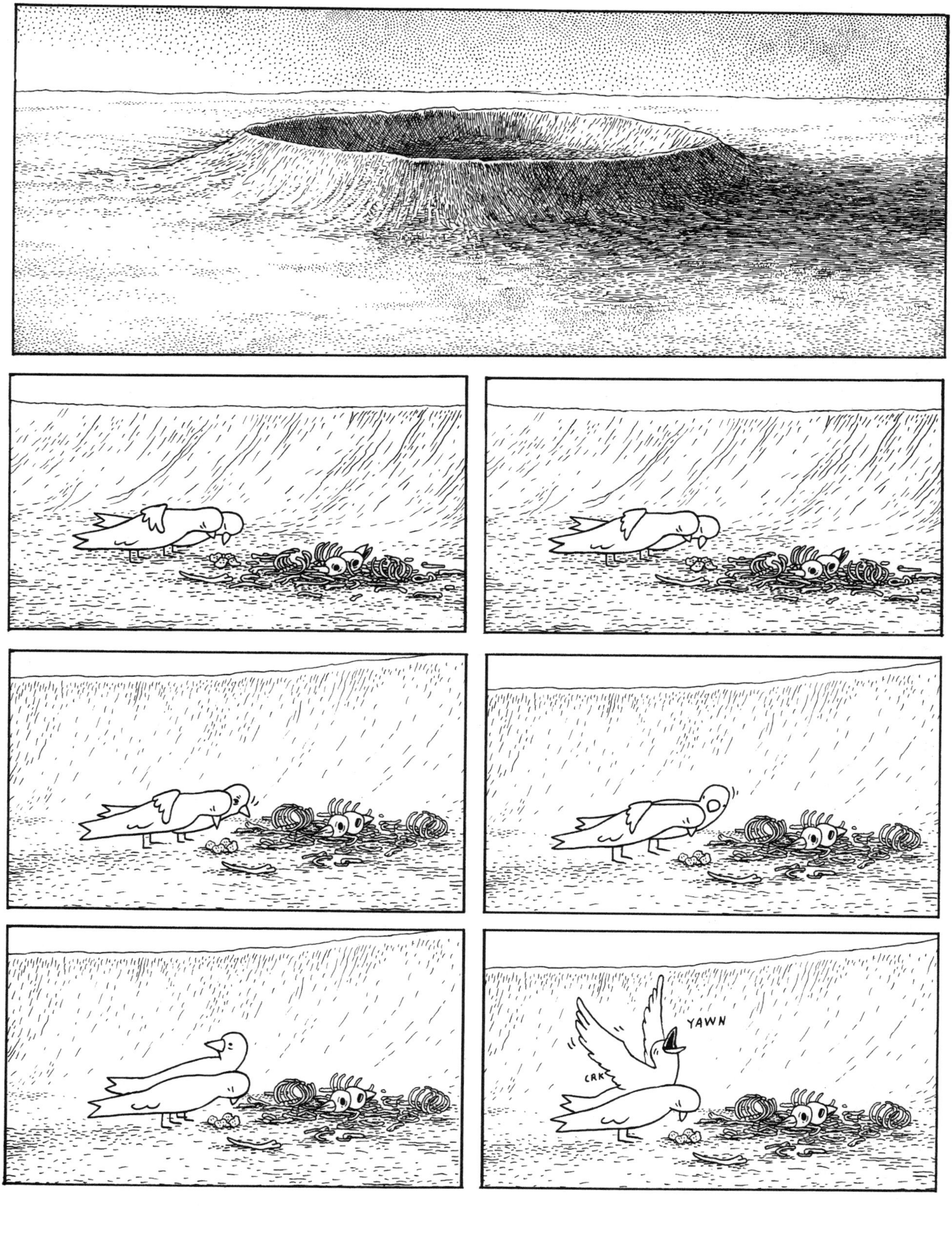
YAWN
CRK

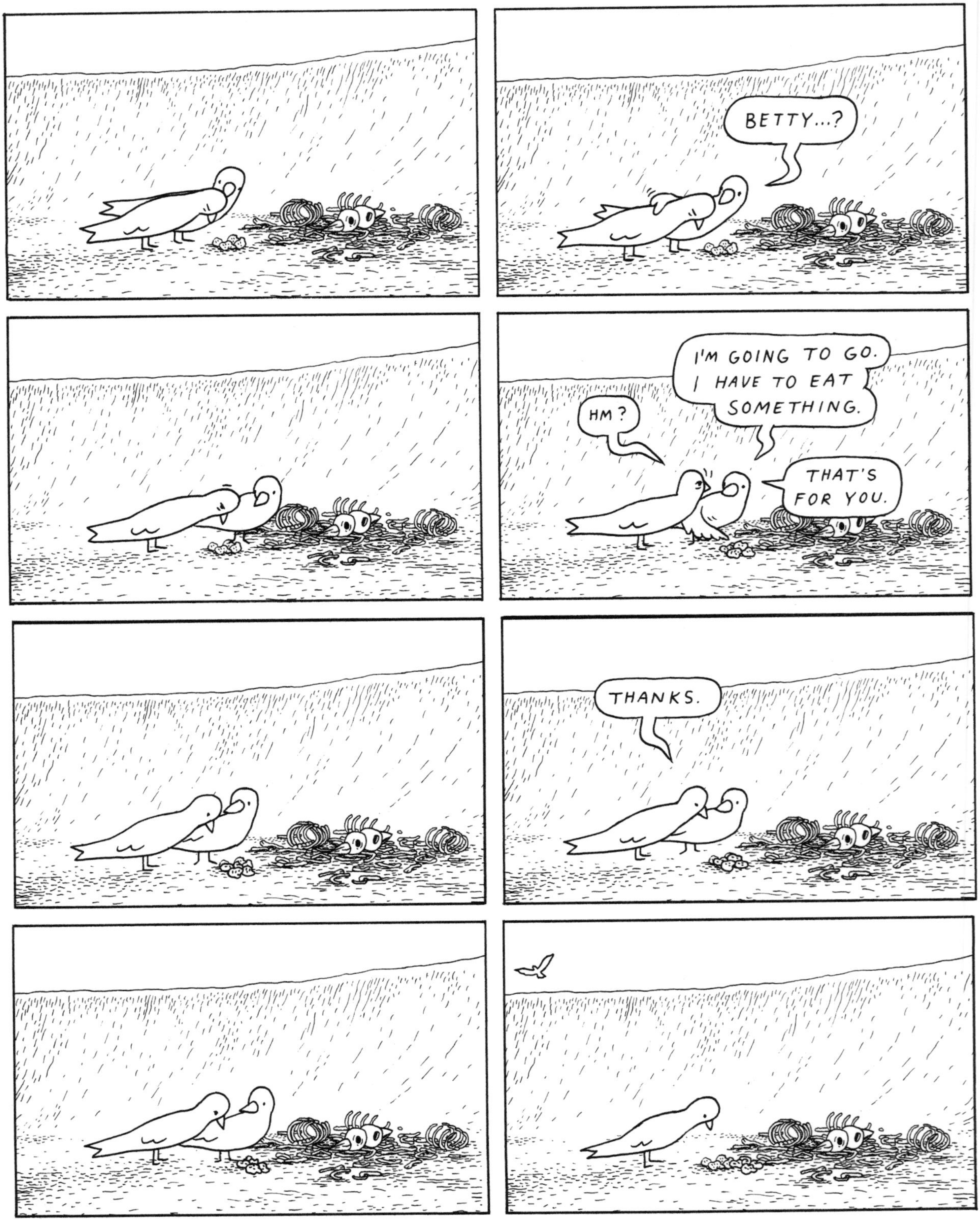
BETTY...?
HM?
I'M GOING TO GO. I HAVE TO EAT SOMETHING.
THAT'S FOR YOU.
THANKS.

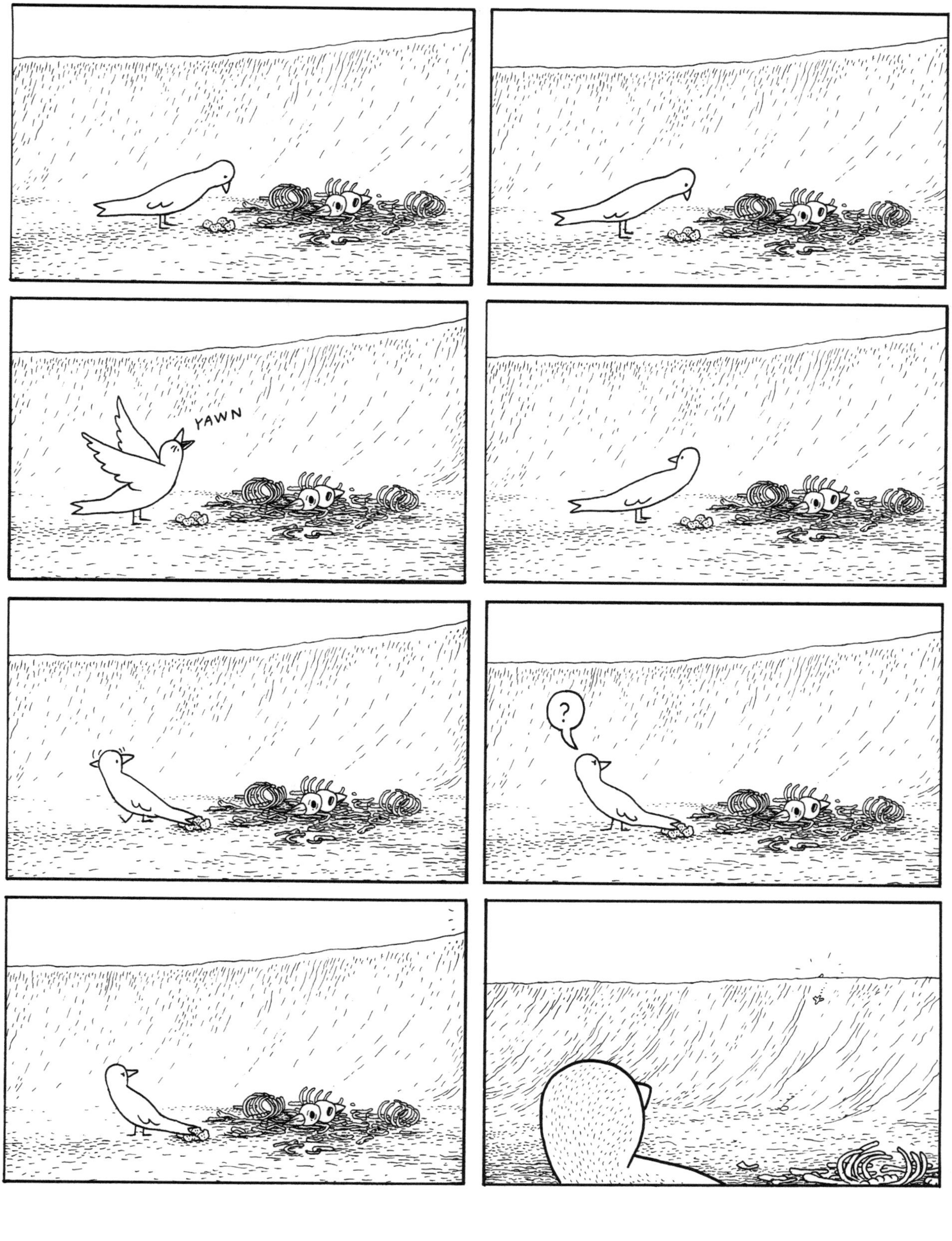
YAWN
?

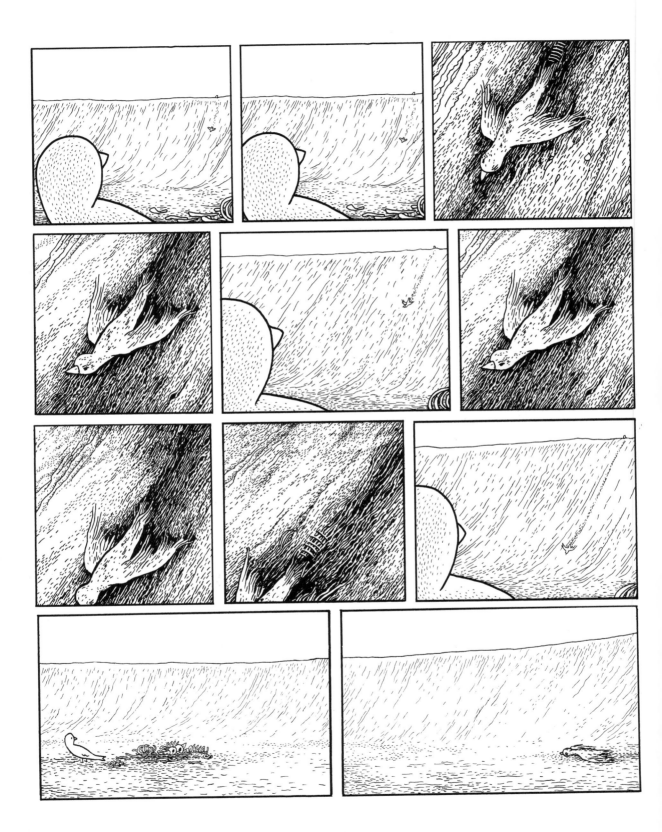

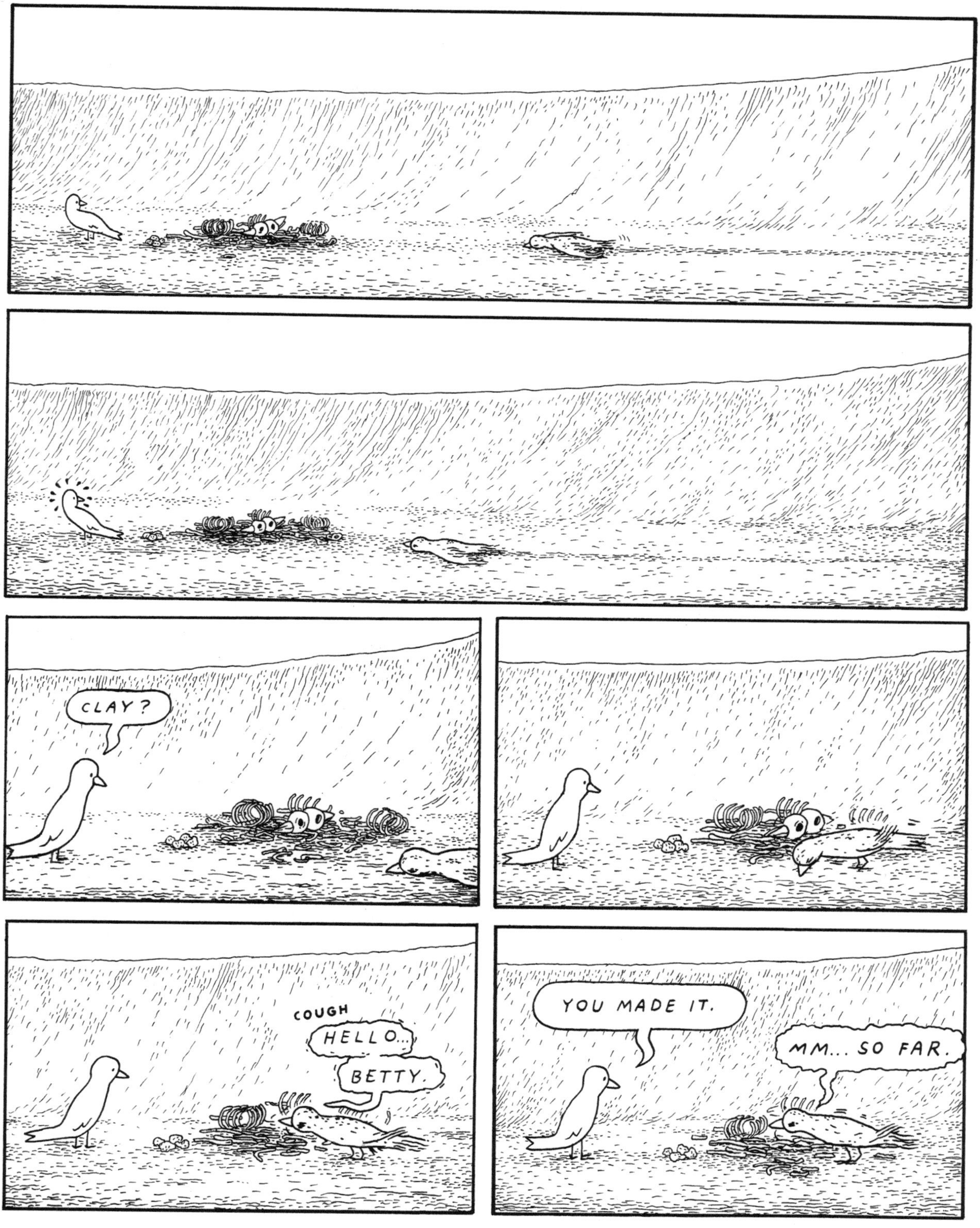
CLAY?
COUGH
HELLO...
BETTY.
YOU MADE IT.
MM... SO FAR.

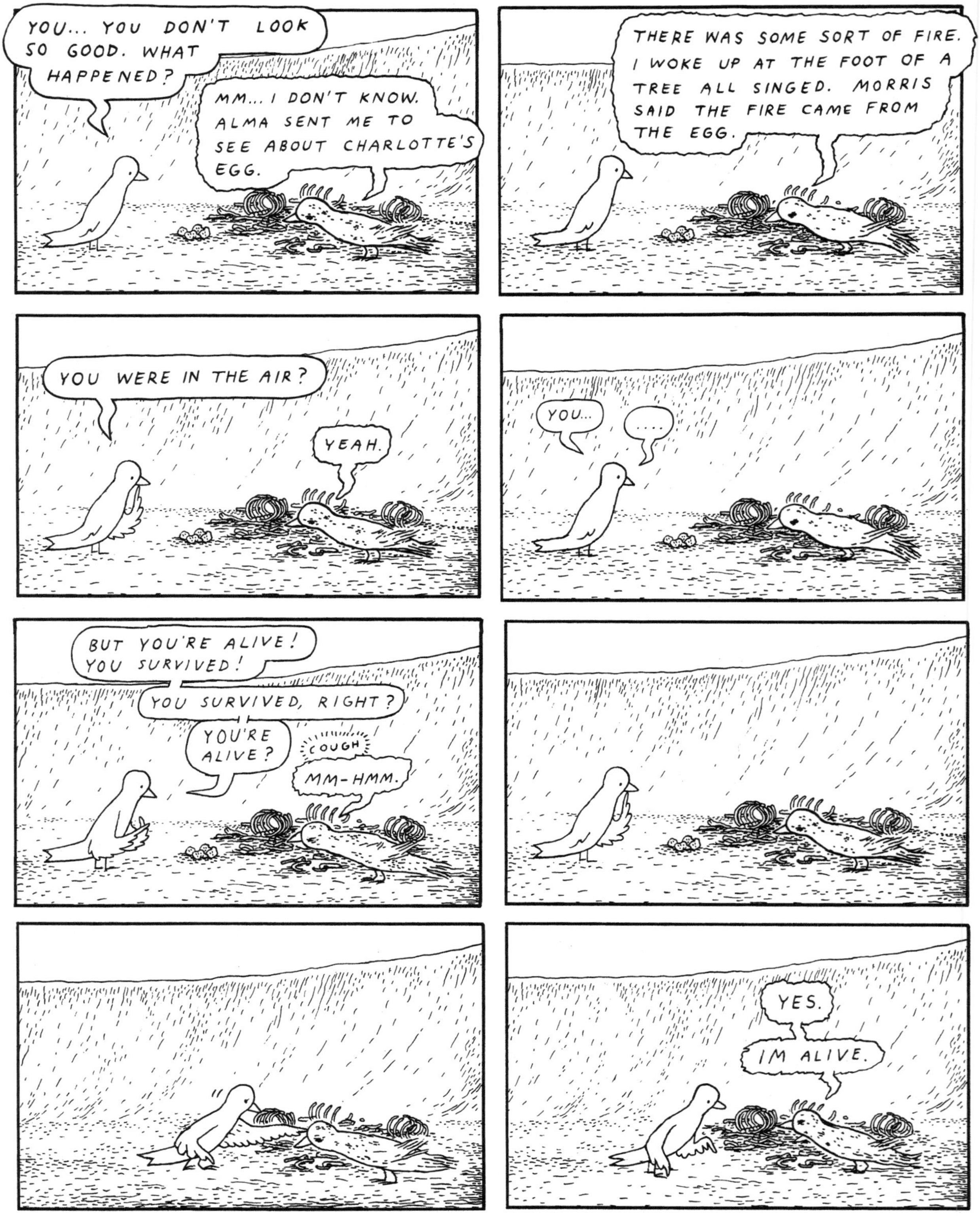
YOU... YOU DON'T LOOK SO GOOD. WHAT HAPPENED?
MM... I DON'T KNOW. ALMA SENT ME TO SEE ABOUT CHARLOTTE'S EGG.
THERE WAS SOME SORT OF FIRE. I WOKE UP AT THE FOOT OF A TREE ALL SINGED. MORRIS SAID THE FIRE CAME FROM THE EGG.
YOU WERE IN THE AIR?
YEAH.
YOU...
....
BUT YOU'RE ALIVE! YOU SURVIVED!
YOU SURVIVED, RIGHT?
YOU'RE ALIVE?
COUGH
MM-HMM.
YES.
IM ALIVE.

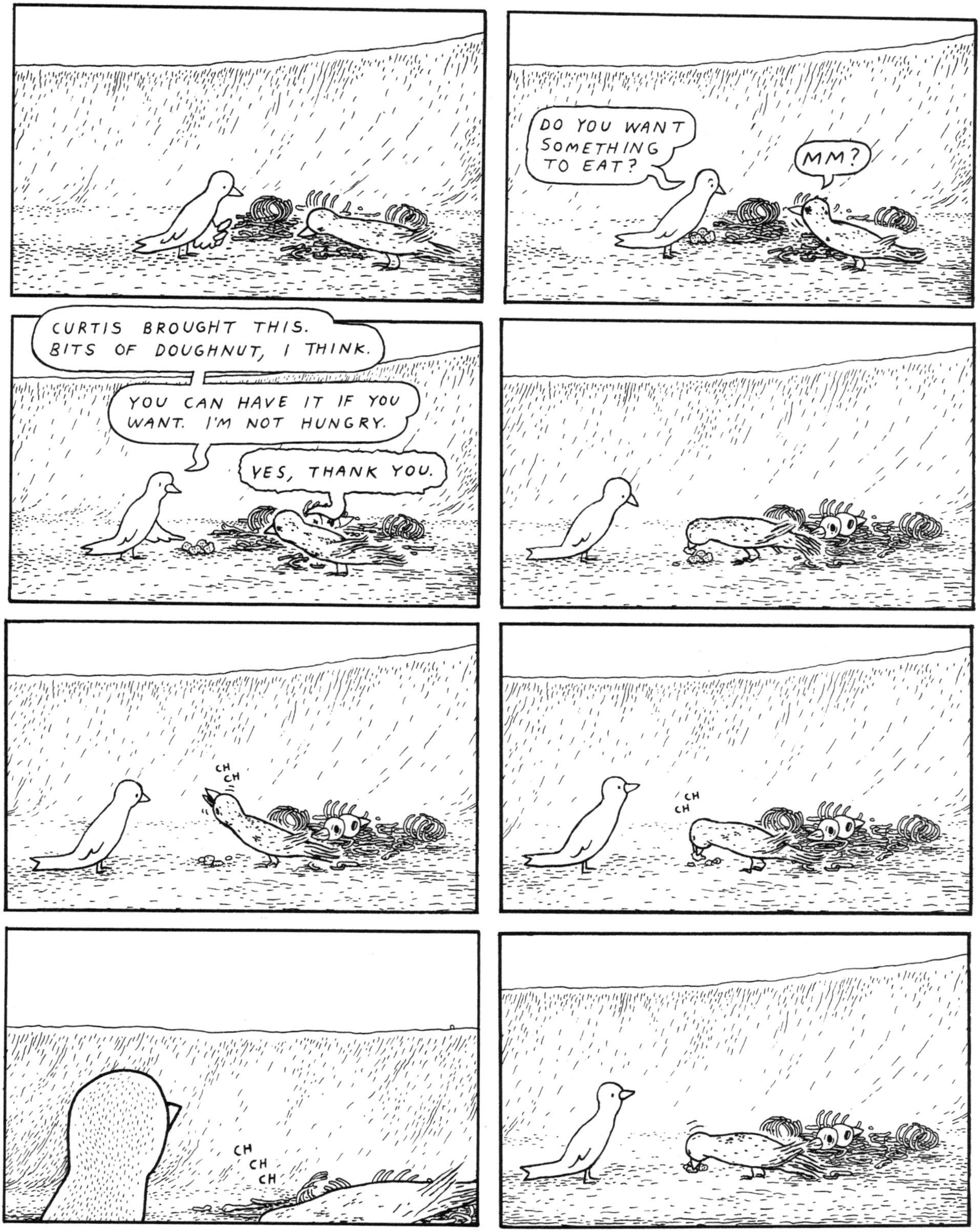
DO YOU WANT SOMETHING TO EAT?
MM?
CURTIS BROUGHT THIS. BITS OF DOUGHNUT, I THINK.
YOU CAN HAVE IT IF YOU WANT. I'M NOT HUNGRY.
YES, THANK YOU.
CH CH
CH CH
CH CH CH

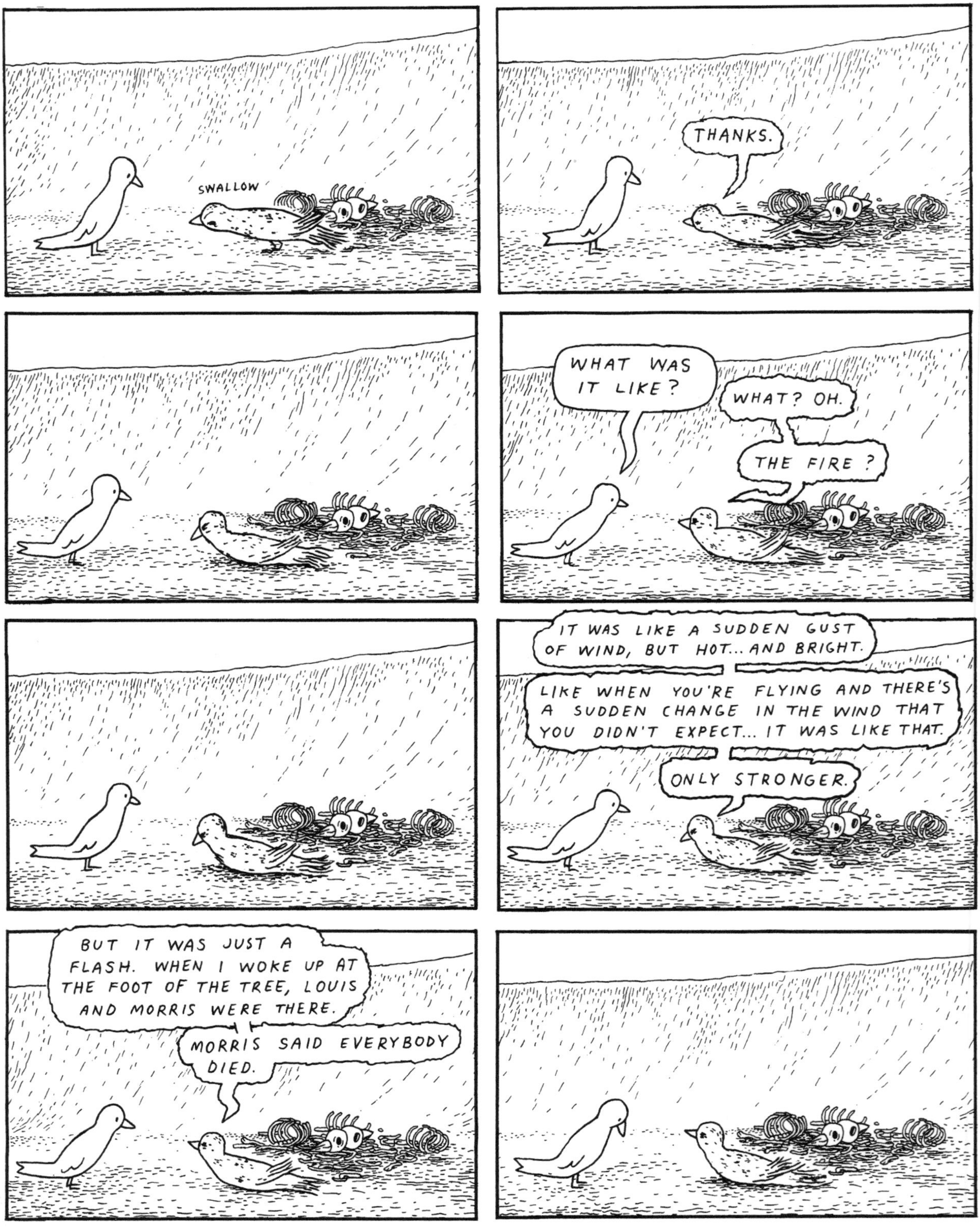
SWALLOW
THANKS.
WHAT WAS IT LIKE?
WHAT? OH.
THE FIRE?
IT WAS LIKE A SUDDEN GUST OF WIND, BUT HOT... AND BRIGHT.
LIKE WHEN YOU'RE FLYING AND THERE'S A SUDDEN CHANGE IN THE WIND THAT YOU DIDN'T EXPECT... IT WAS LIKE THAT.
ONLY STRONGER.
BUT IT WAS JUST A FLASH. WHEN I WOKE UP AT THE FOOT OF THE TREE, LOUIS AND MORRIS WERE THERE.
MORRIS SAID EVERYBODY DIED.

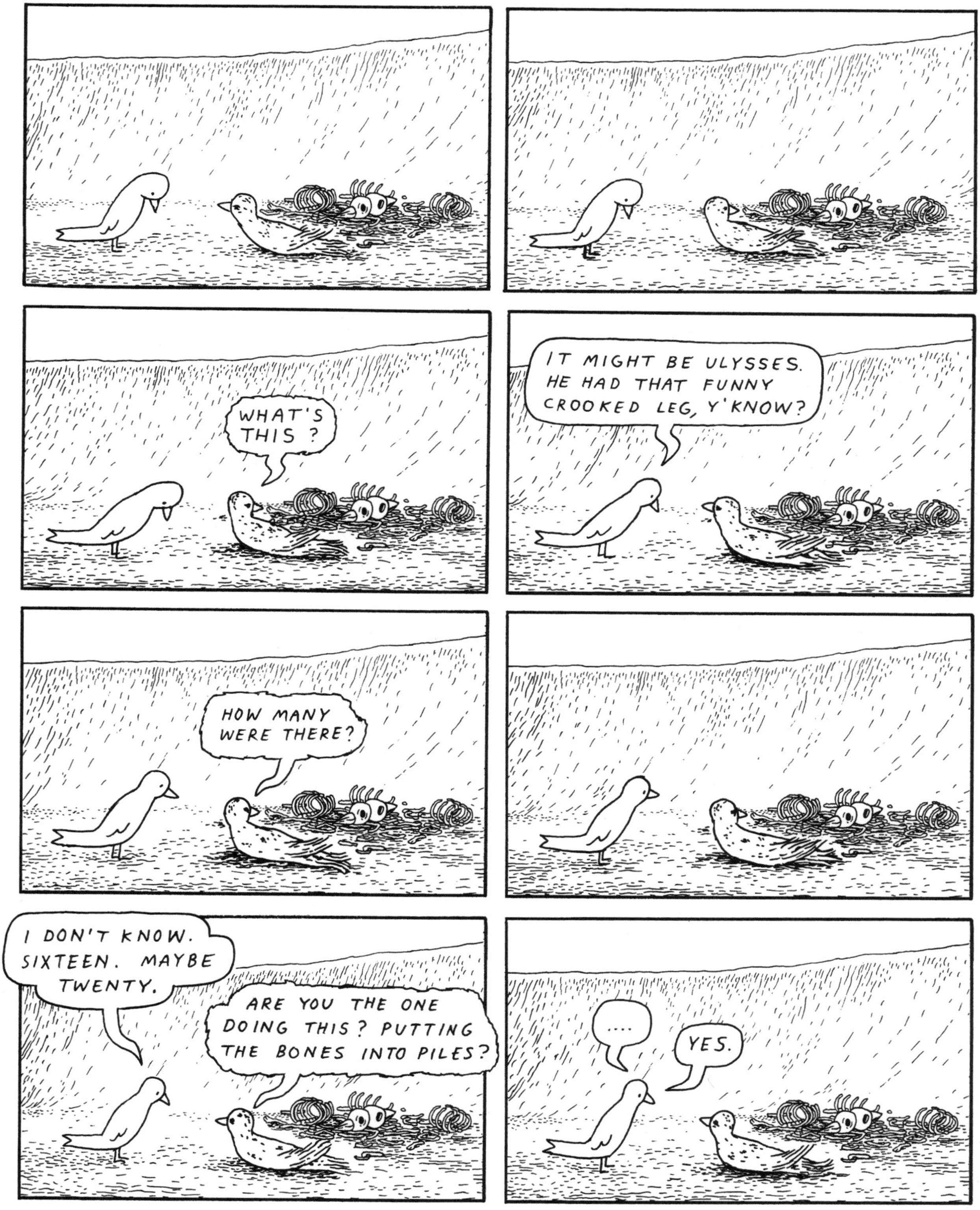
WHAT'S THIS ?
IT MIGHT BE ULYSSES. HE HAD THAT FUNNY CROOKED LEG, Y'KNOW?
HOW MANY WERE THERE?
I DON'T KNOW. SIXTEEN. MAYBE TWENTY.
ARE YOU THE ONE DOING THIS? PUTTING THE BONES INTO PILES?
....
YES.

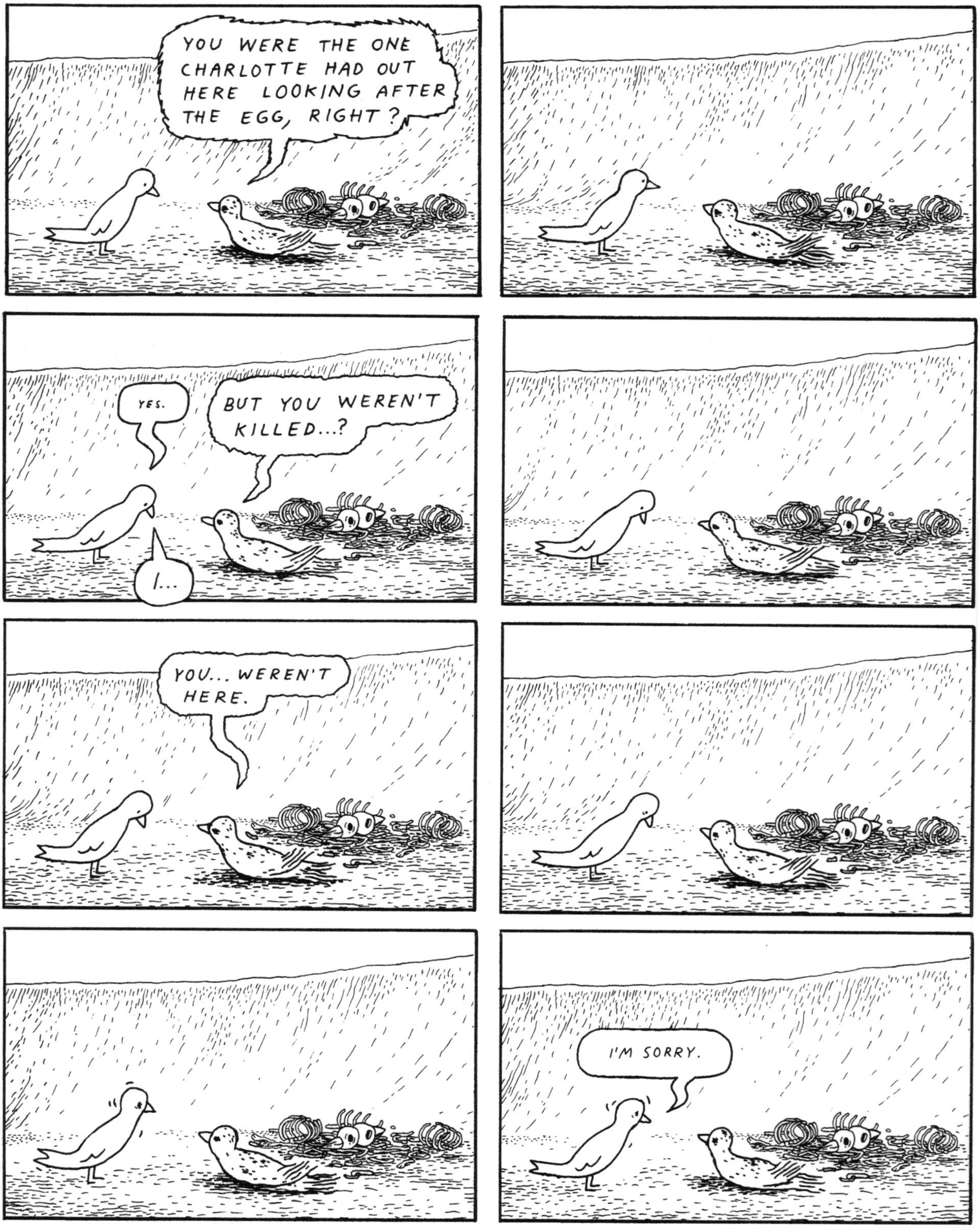
YOU WERE THE ONE CHARLOTTE HAD OUT HERE LOOKING AFTER THE EGG, RIGHT?
YES.
BUT YOU WEREN'T KILLED...?
I...
YOU... WEREN'T HERE.
I'M SORRY.

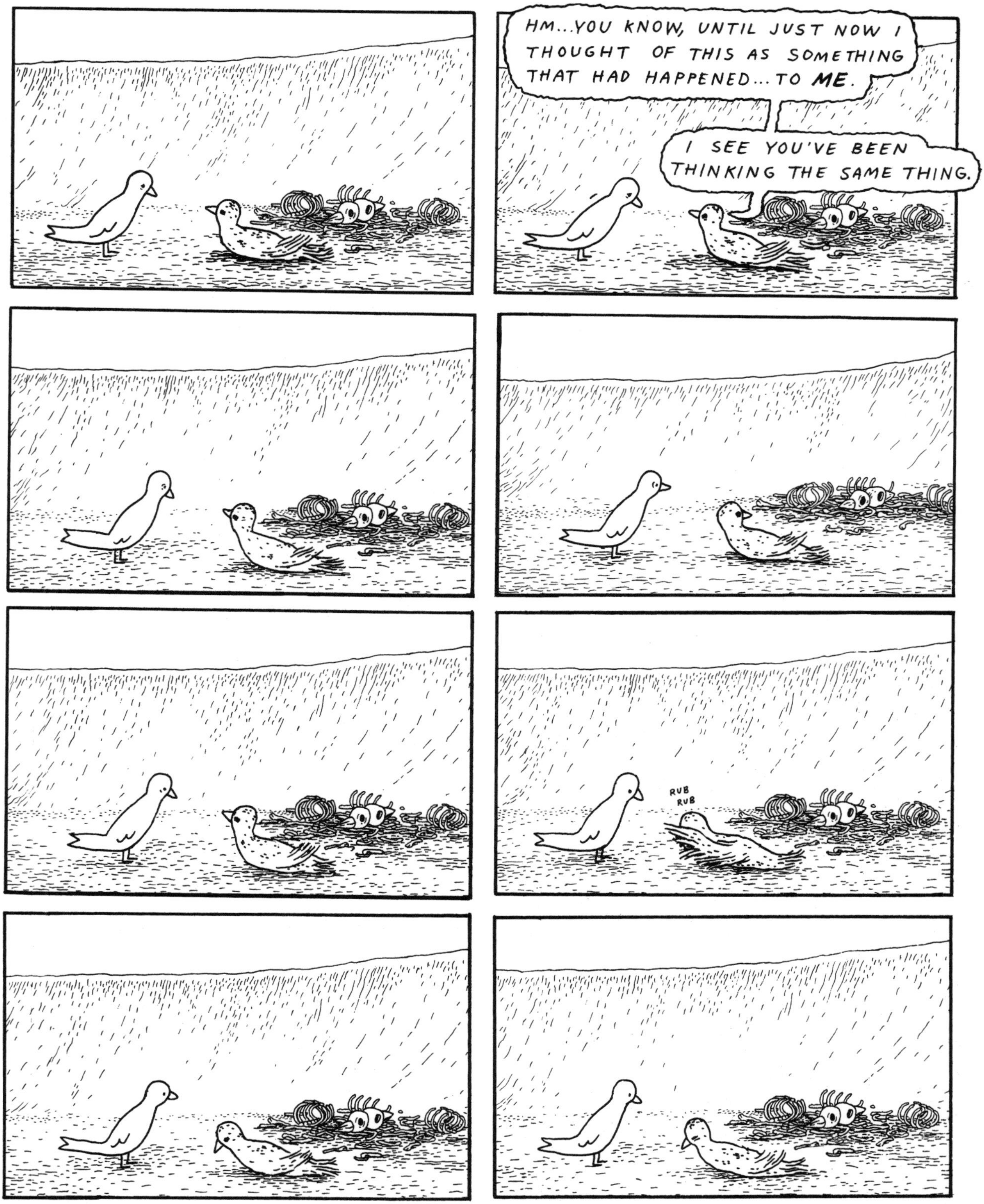
HM...YOU KNOW, UNTIL JUST NOW I THOUGHT OF THIS AS SOMETHING THAT HAD HAPPENED... TO **ME**.
I SEE YOU'VE BEEN THINKING THE SAME THING.
RUB RUB

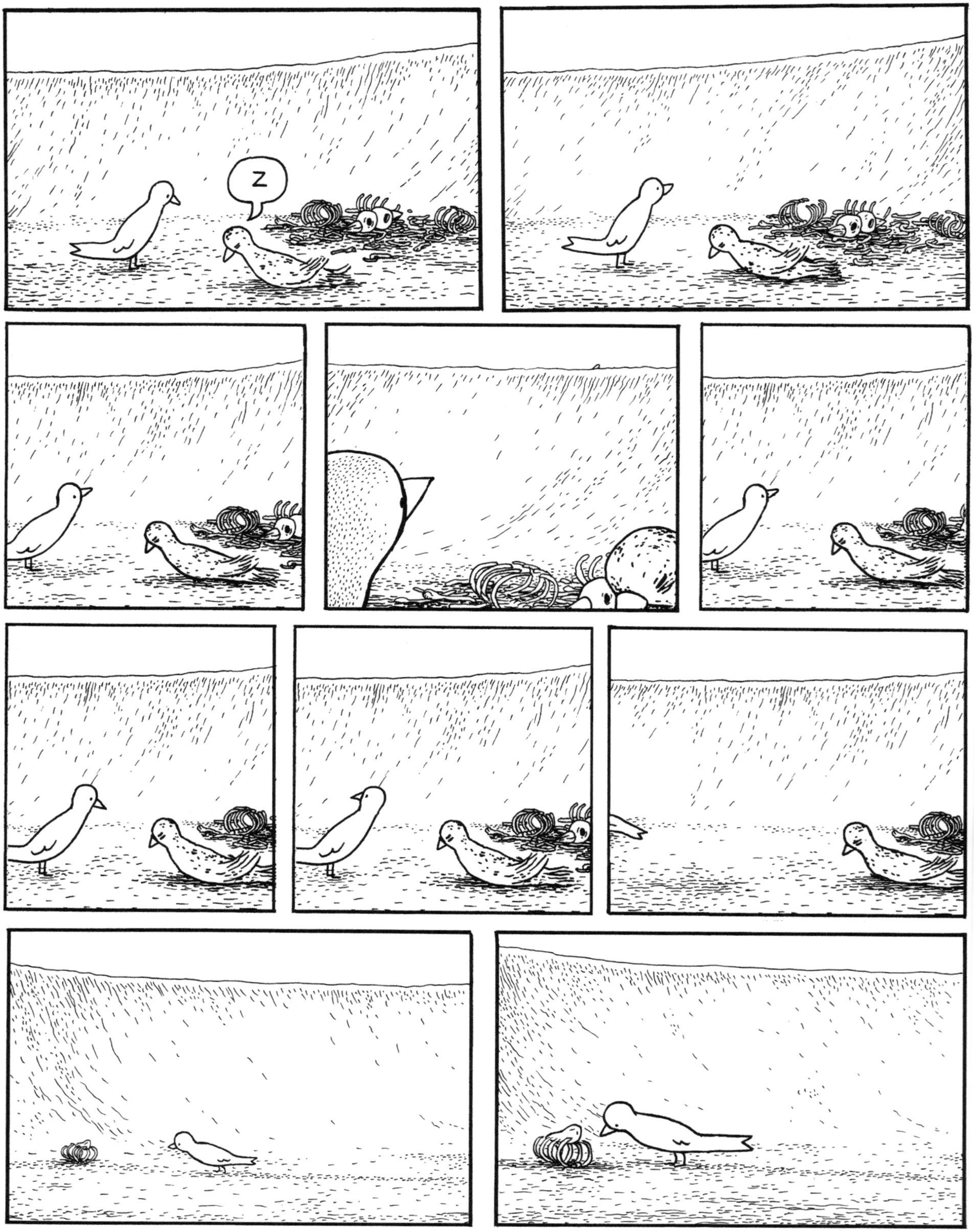
Z

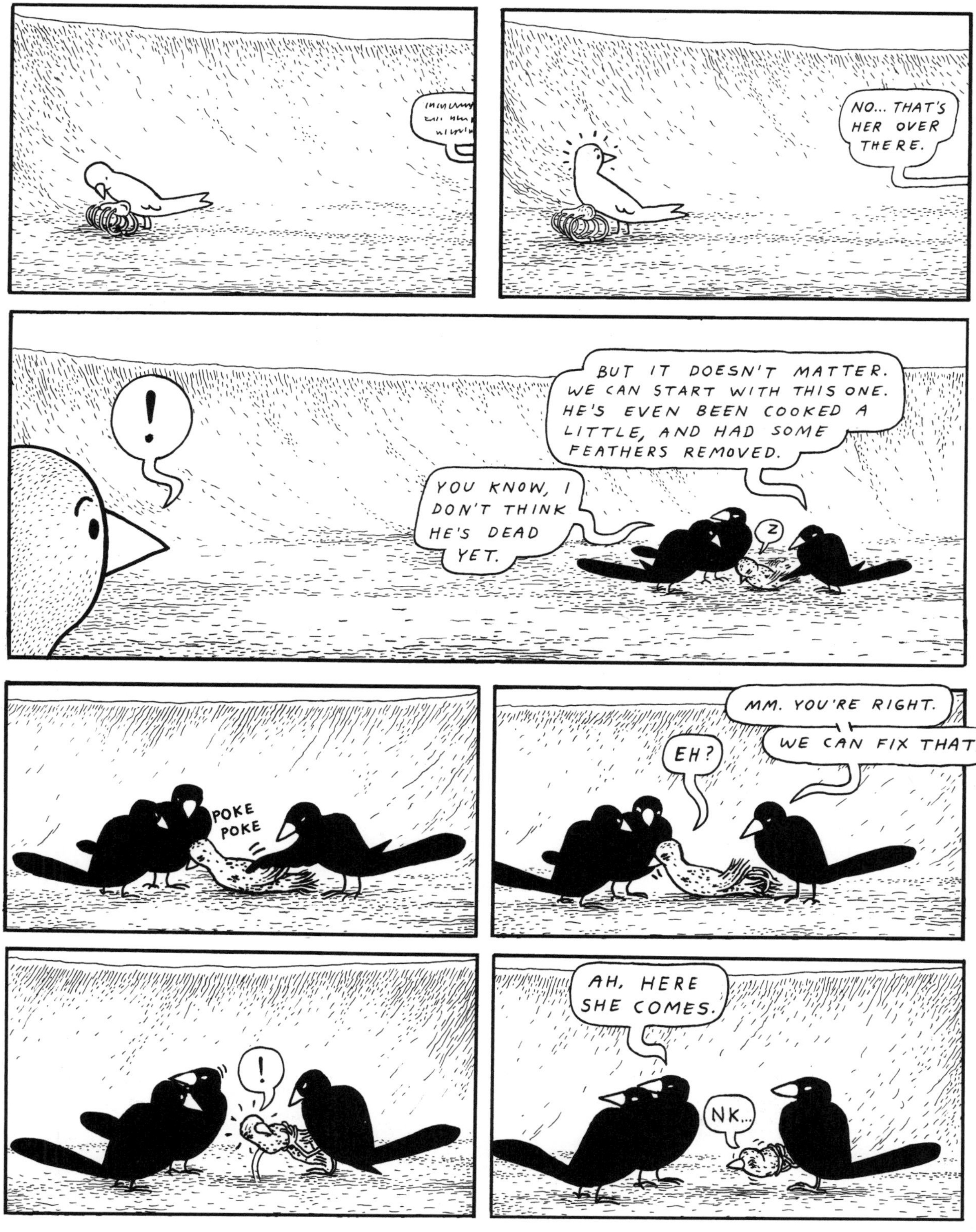
NO... THAT'S HER OVER THERE.
!
BUT IT DOESN'T MATTER. WE CAN START WITH THIS ONE. HE'S EVEN BEEN COOKED A LITTLE, AND HAD SOME FEATHERS REMOVED.
YOU KNOW, I DON'T THINK HE'S DEAD YET.
Z
POKE POKE
EH?
MM. YOU'RE RIGHT.
WE CAN FIX THAT.
!
AH, HERE SHE COMES.
NK...

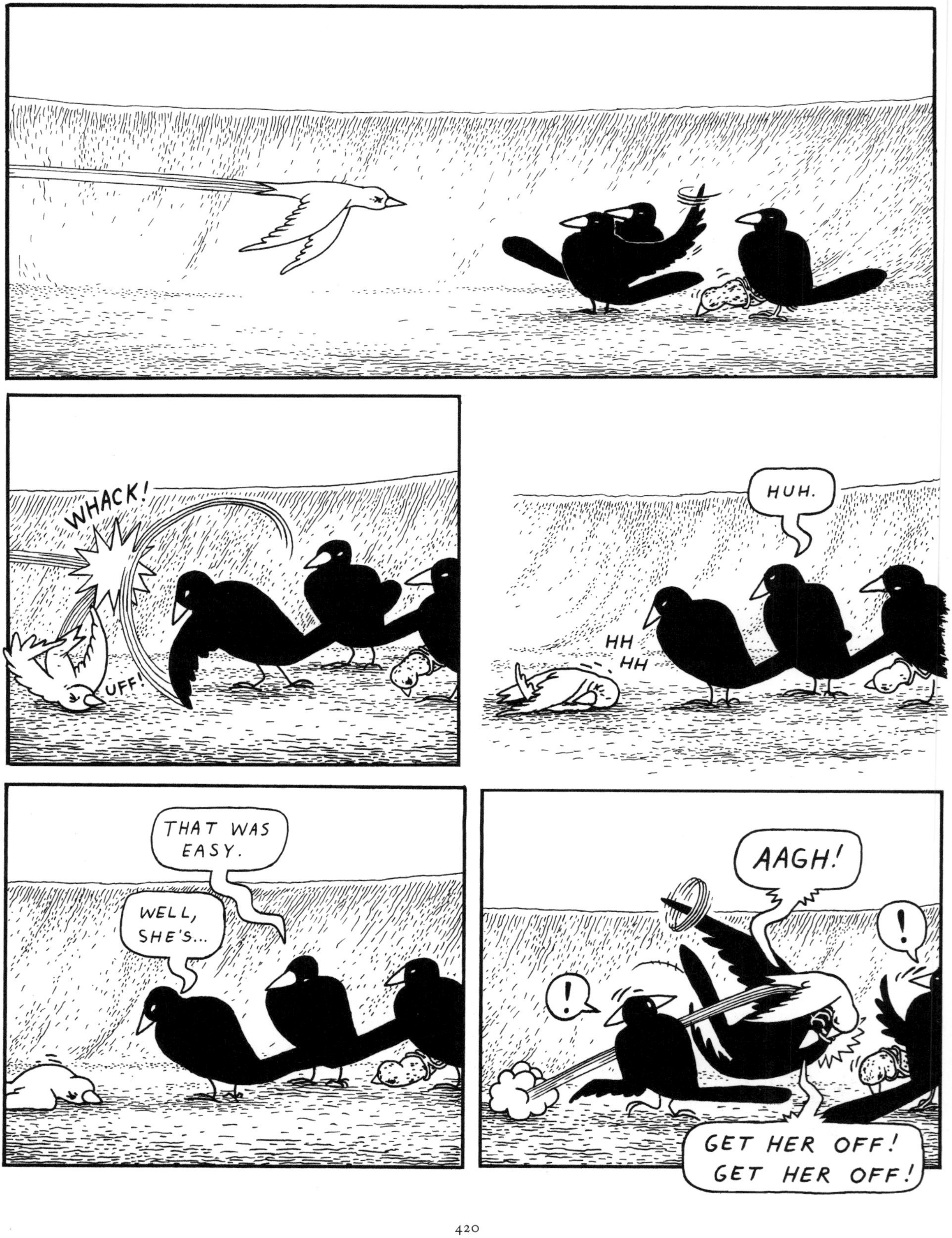
WHACK!
UFF!
HH
HH
HUH.
THAT WAS EASY.
WELL, SHE'S...
AAGH!
!
!
GET HER OFF! GET HER OFF!

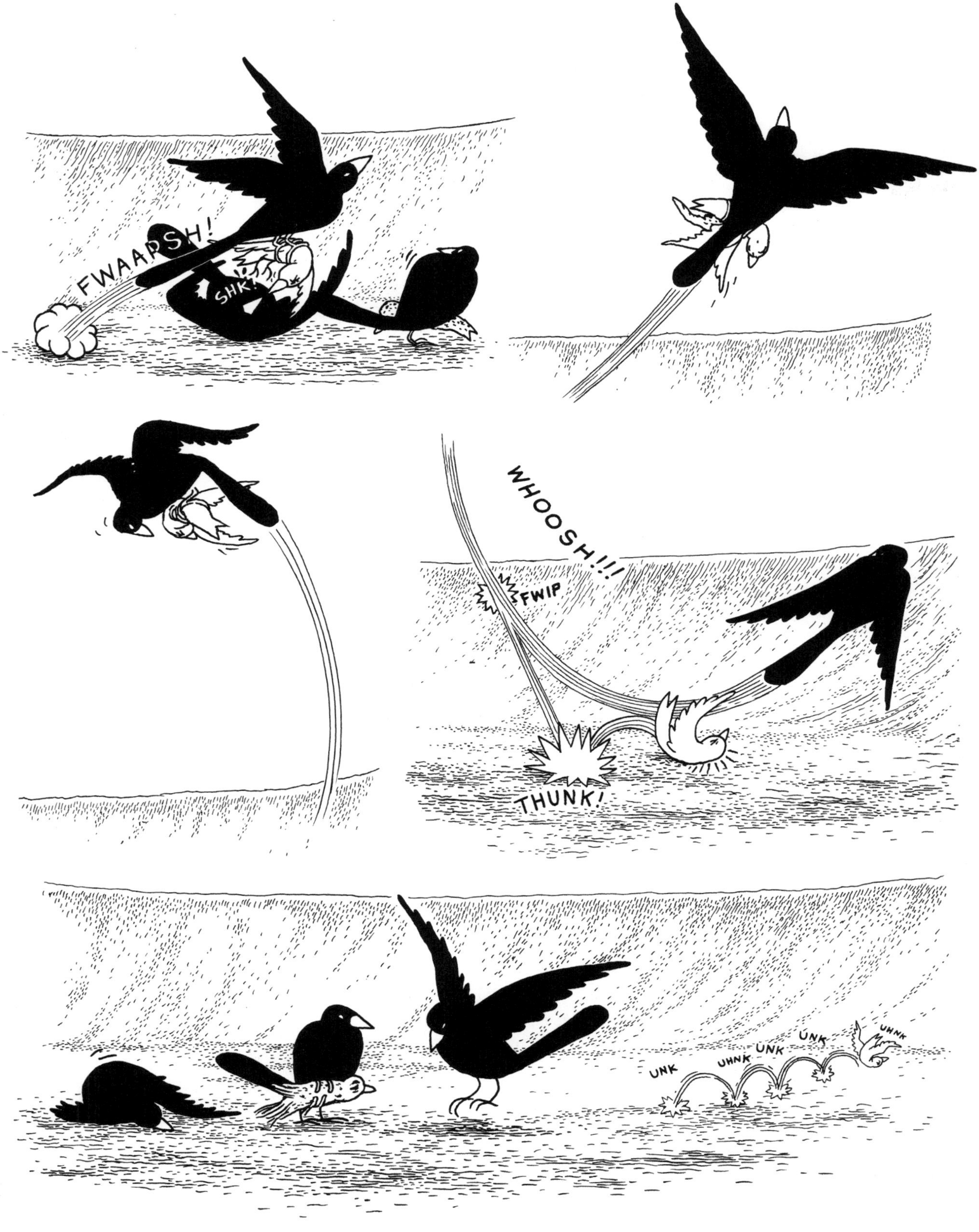
FWAAPSH!
SHK!
WHOOSH!!!!
FWIP
THUNK!
UNK
UHNK
UNK
UNK
UHNK

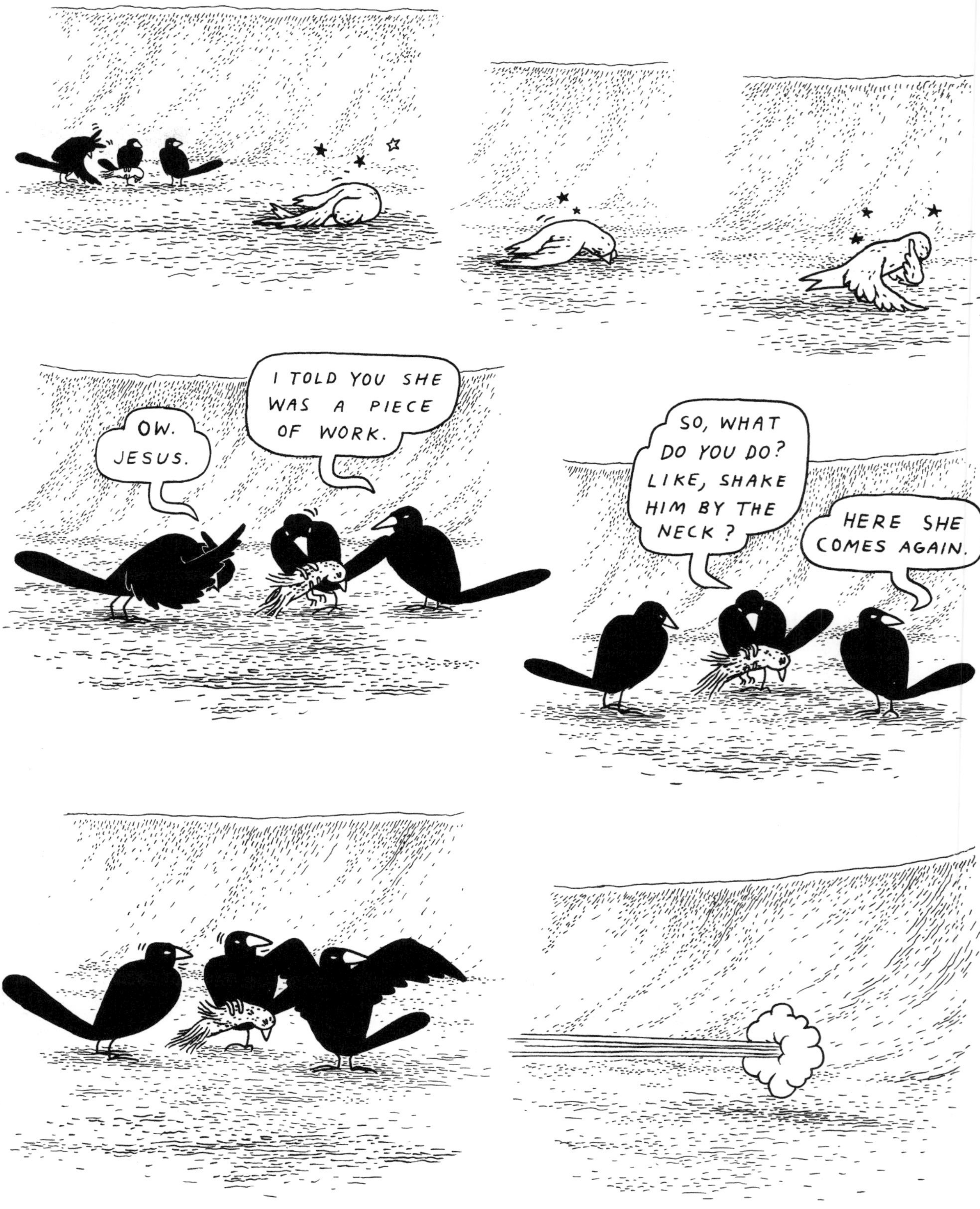
OW. JESUS.
I TOLD YOU SHE WAS A PIECE OF WORK.
SO, WHAT DO YOU DO? LIKE, SHAKE HIM BY THE NECK?
HERE SHE COMES AGAIN.

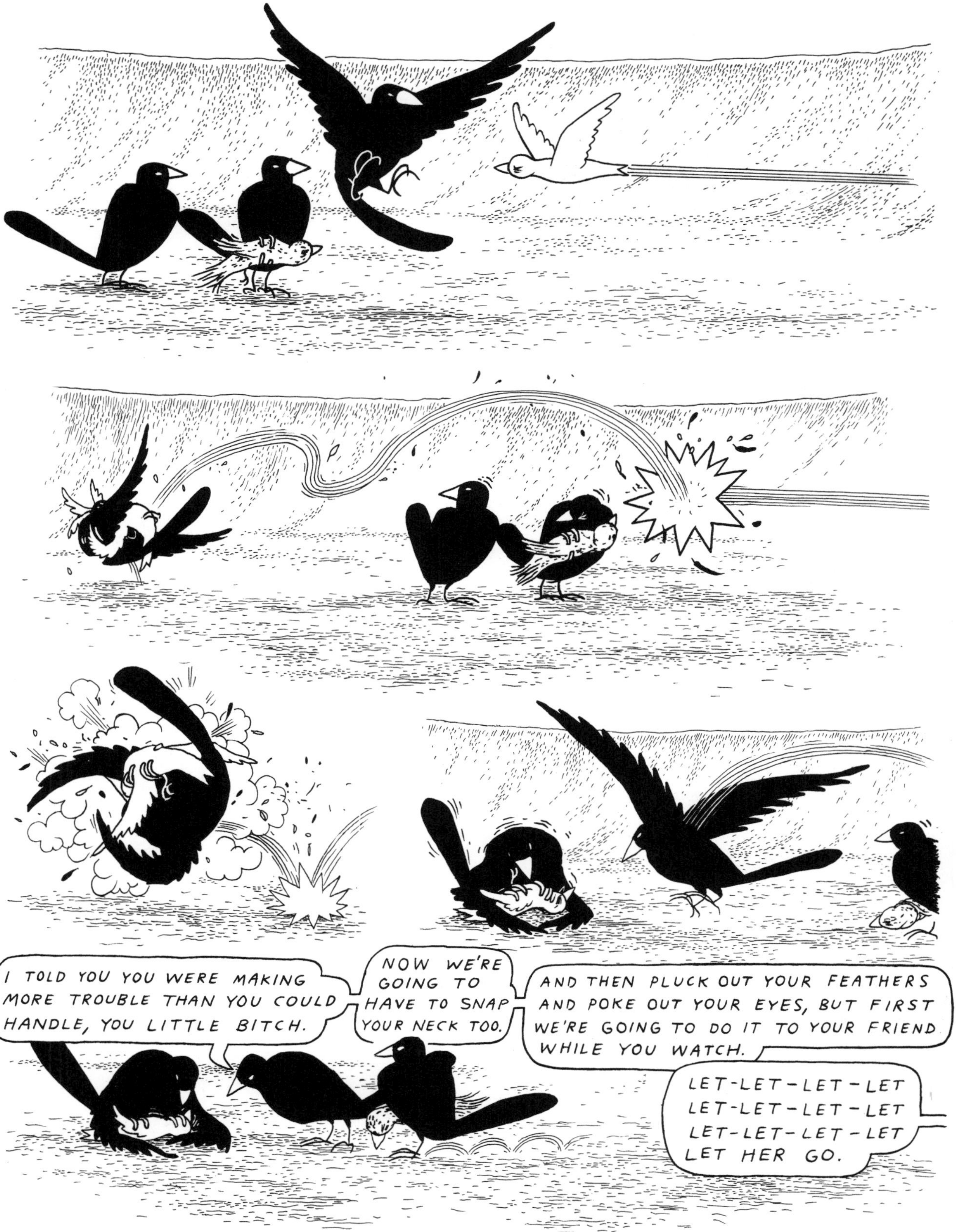
I TOLD YOU YOU WERE MAKING MORE TROUBLE THAN YOU COULD HANDLE, YOU LITTLE BITCH.
NOW WE'RE GOING TO HAVE TO SNAP YOUR NECK TOO.
AND THEN PLUCK OUT YOUR FEATHERS AND POKE OUT YOUR EYES, BUT FIRST WE'RE GOING TO DO IT TO YOUR FRIEND WHILE YOU WATCH.
LET-LET-LET-LET LET-LET-LET-LET LET-LET-LET-LET LET HER GO.

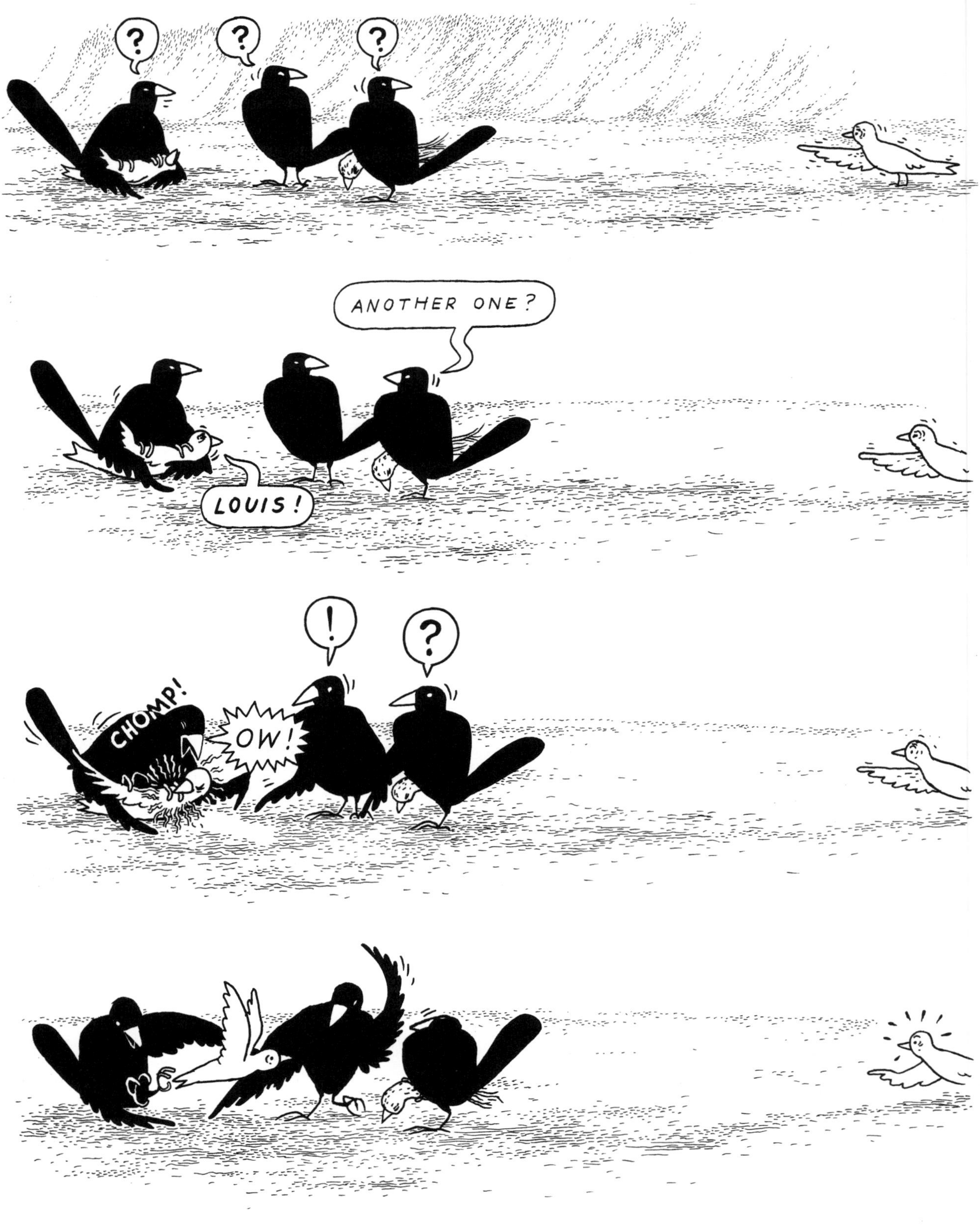
?
?
?
ANOTHER ONE?
LOUIS!
!
?
CHOMP!
OW!

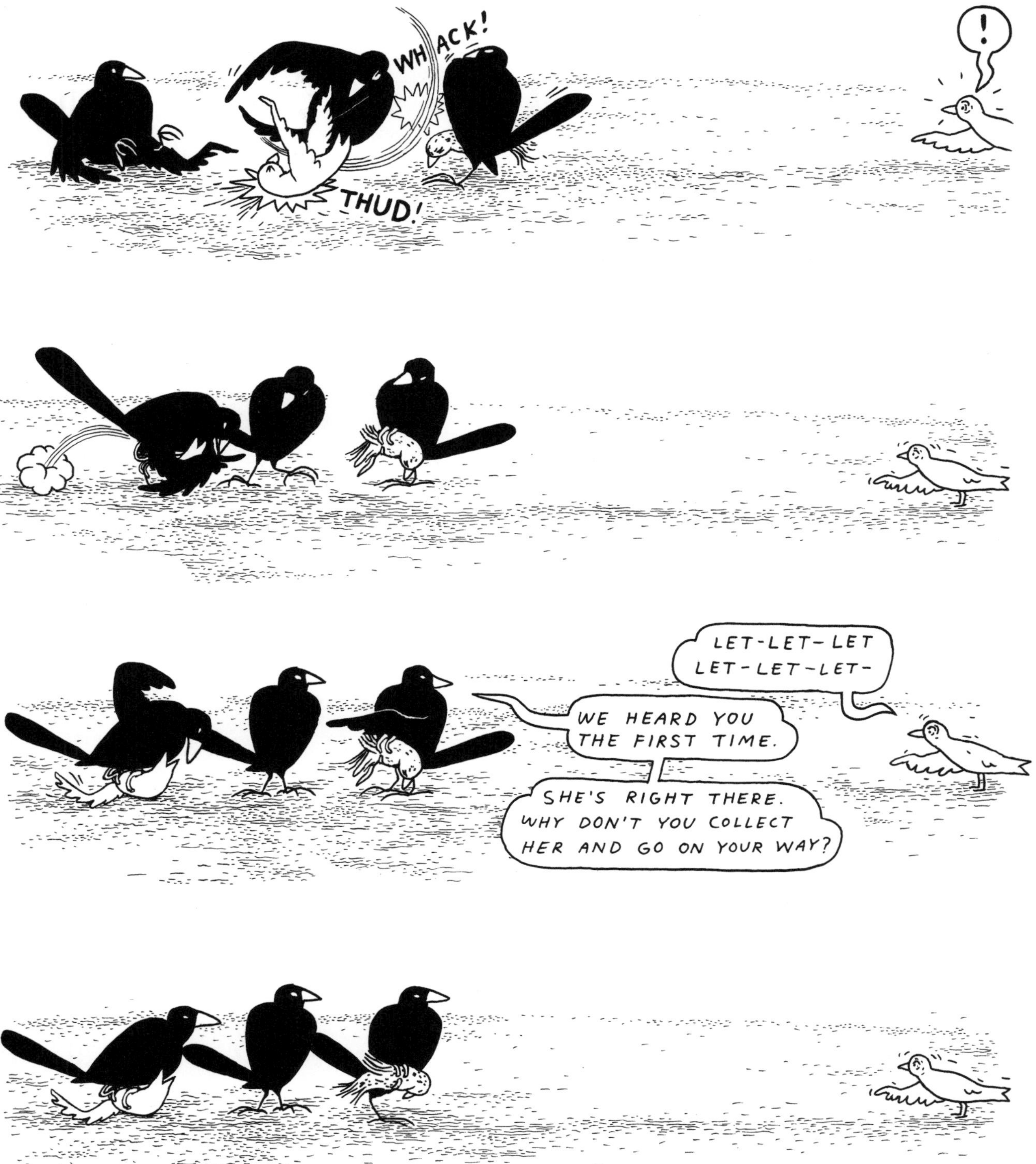
WHACK!
THUD!
!
LET-LET-LET
LET-LET-LET-
WE HEARD YOU THE FIRST TIME.
SHE'S RIGHT THERE. WHY DON'T YOU COLLECT HER AND GO ON YOUR WAY?

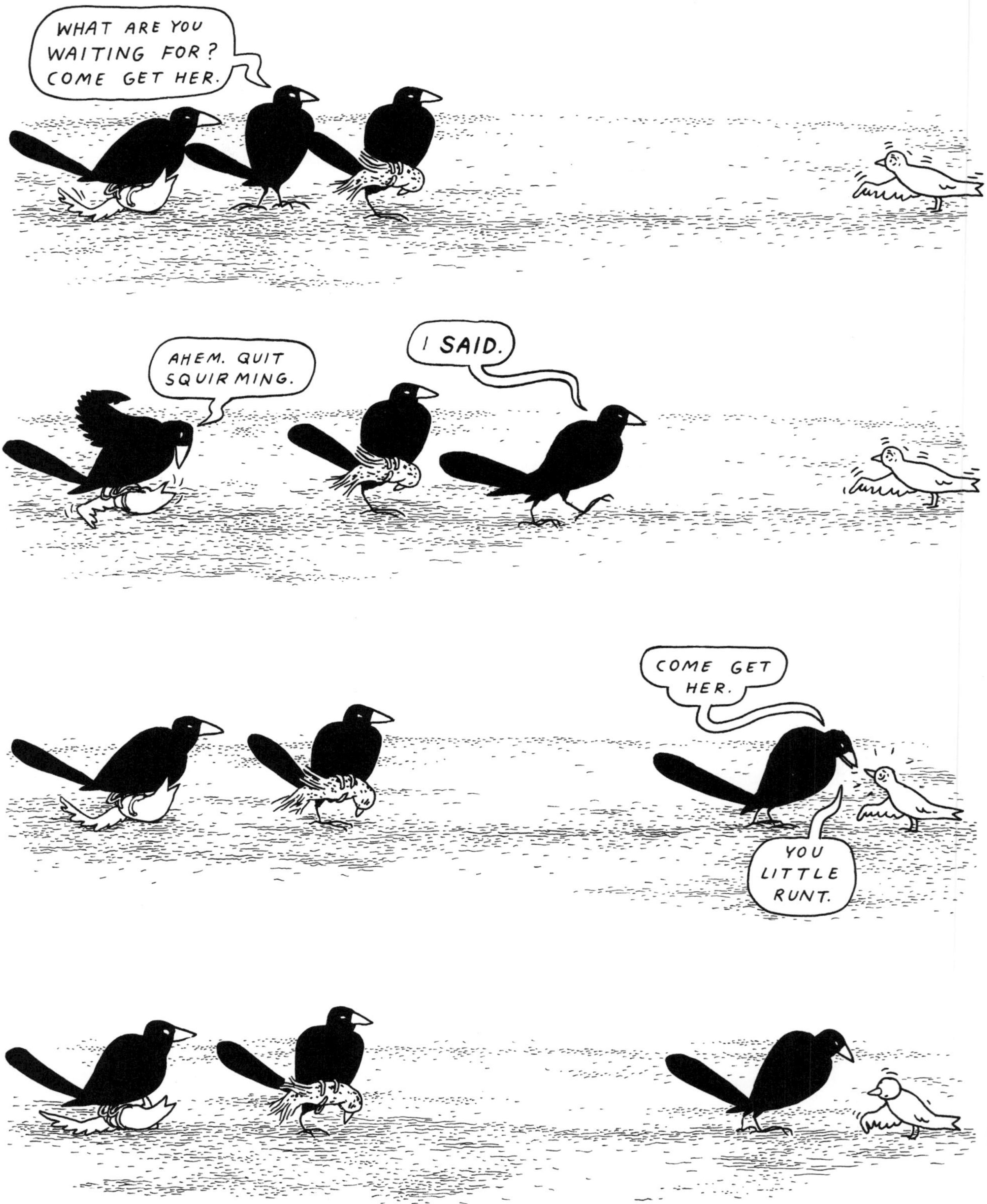
WHAT ARE YOU WAITING FOR? COME GET HER.
AHEM. QUIT SQUIRMING.
I SAID.
COME GET HER.
YOU LITTLE RUNT.

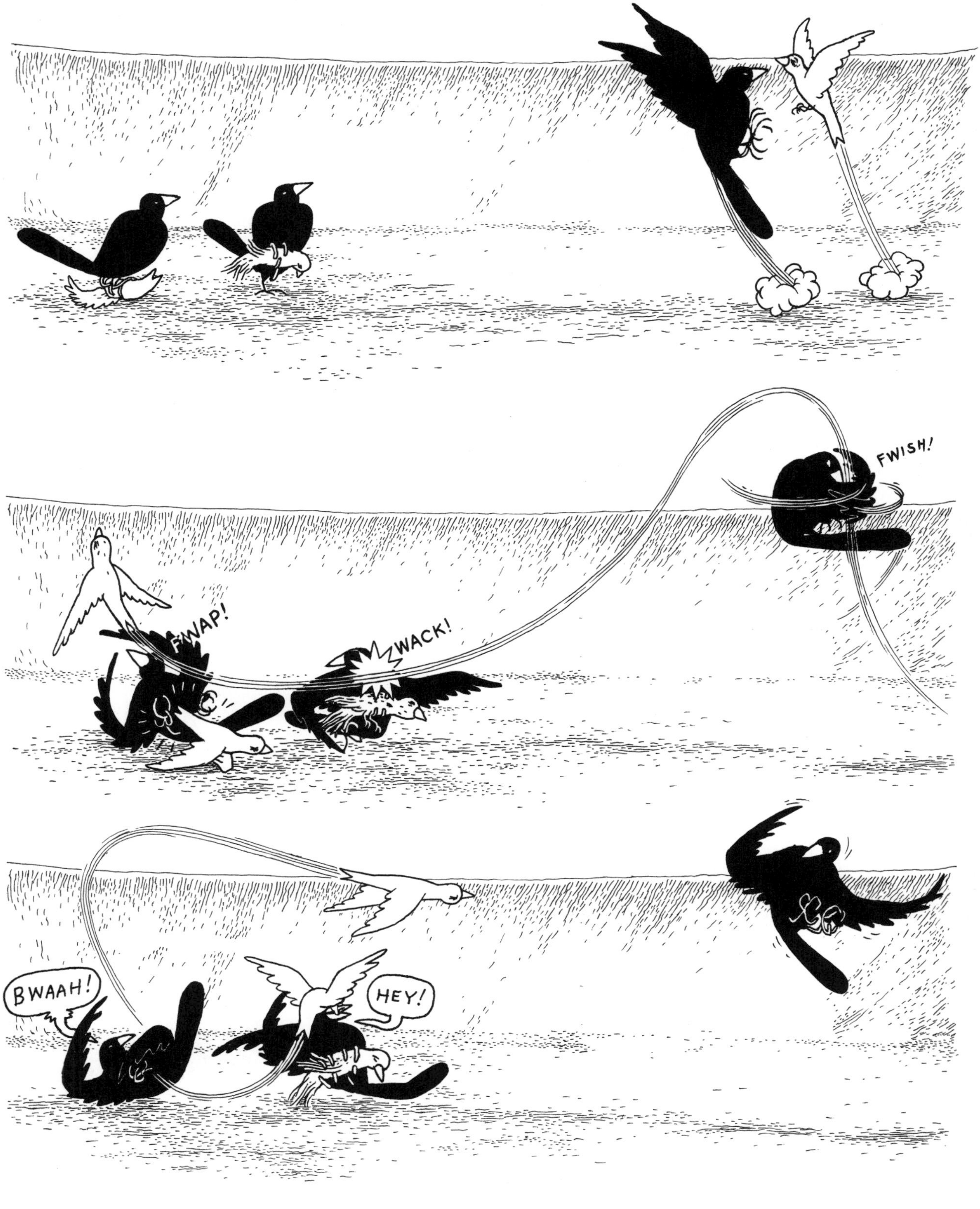
FWISH!
FWAP!
WACK!
BWAAH!
HEY!

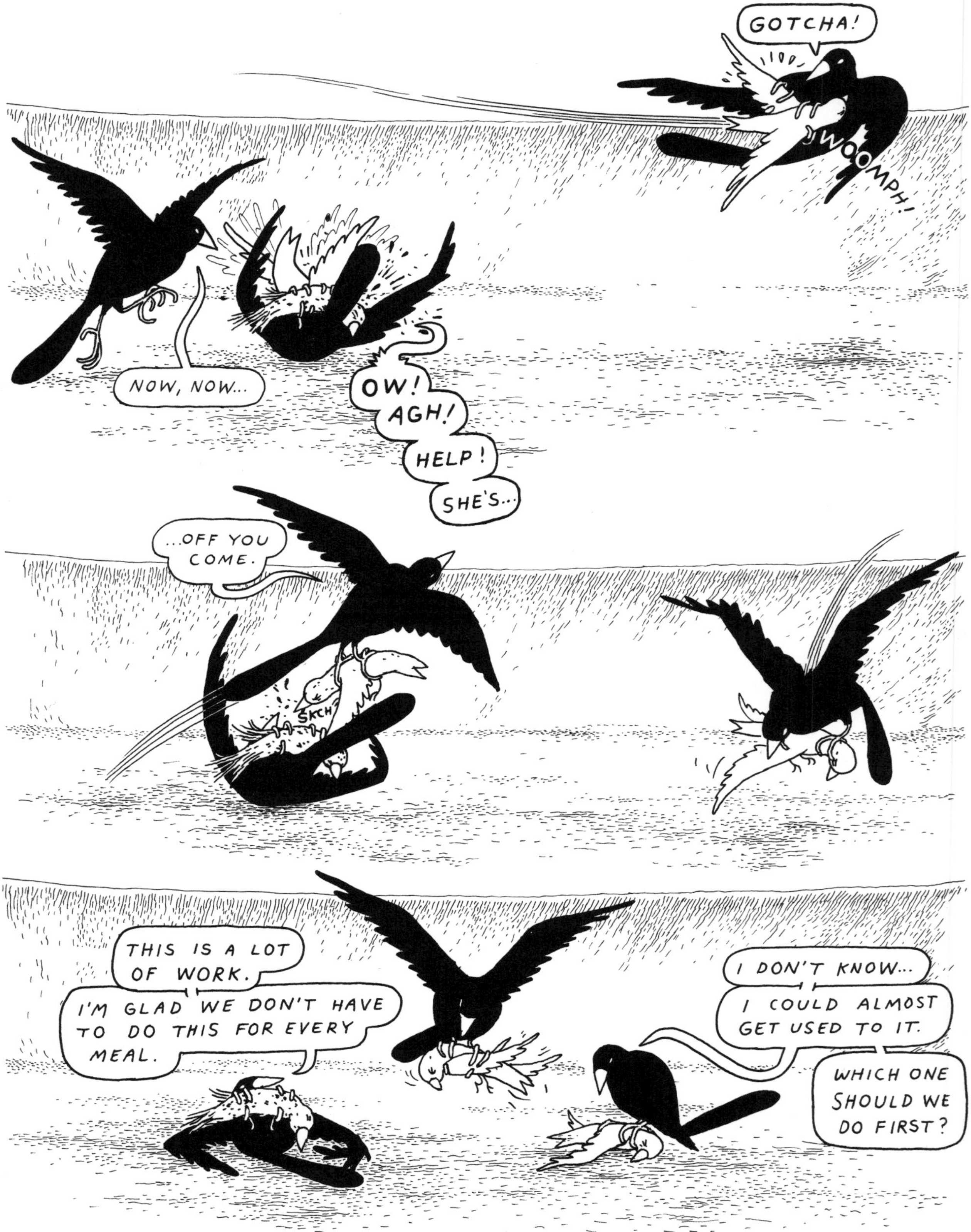
GOTCHA!
WOOMPH!
NOW, NOW...
OW!
AGH!
HELP!
SHE'S...
...OFF YOU COME.
SKCH
THIS IS A LOT OF WORK.
I'M GLAD WE DON'T HAVE TO DO THIS FOR EVERY MEAL.
I DON'T KNOW...
I COULD ALMOST GET USED TO IT.
WHICH ONE SHOULD WE DO FIRST?

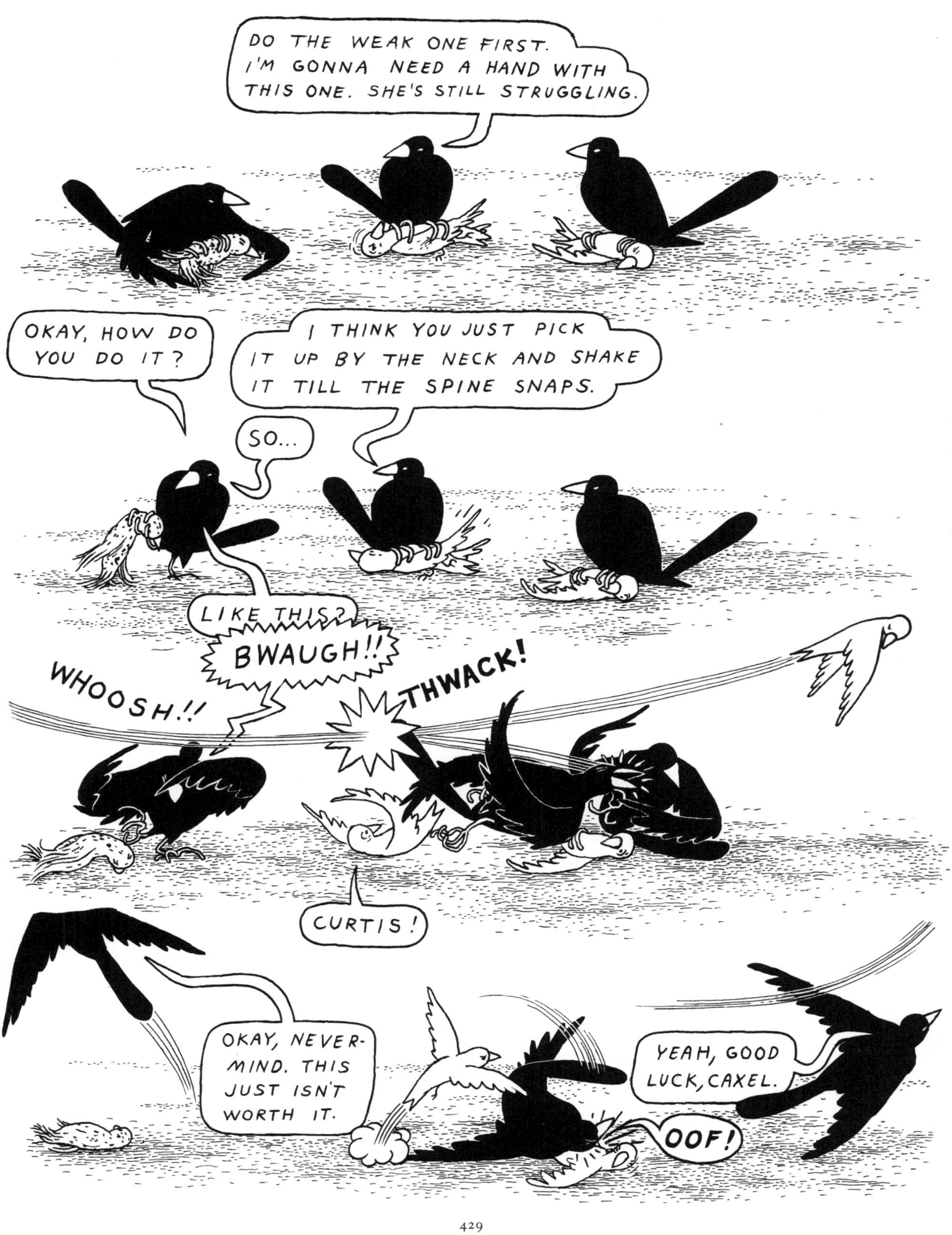
DO THE WEAK ONE FIRST. I'M GONNA NEED A HAND WITH THIS ONE. SHE'S STILL STRUGGLING.
OKAY, HOW DO YOU DO IT?
I THINK YOU JUST PICK IT UP BY THE NECK AND SHAKE IT TILL THE SPINE SNAPS.
SO...
LIKE THIS?
BWAUGH!!
WHOOSH!!
THWACK!
CURTIS!
OKAY, NEVER-MIND. THIS JUST ISN'T WORTH IT.
YEAH, GOOD LUCK, CAXEL.
OOF!

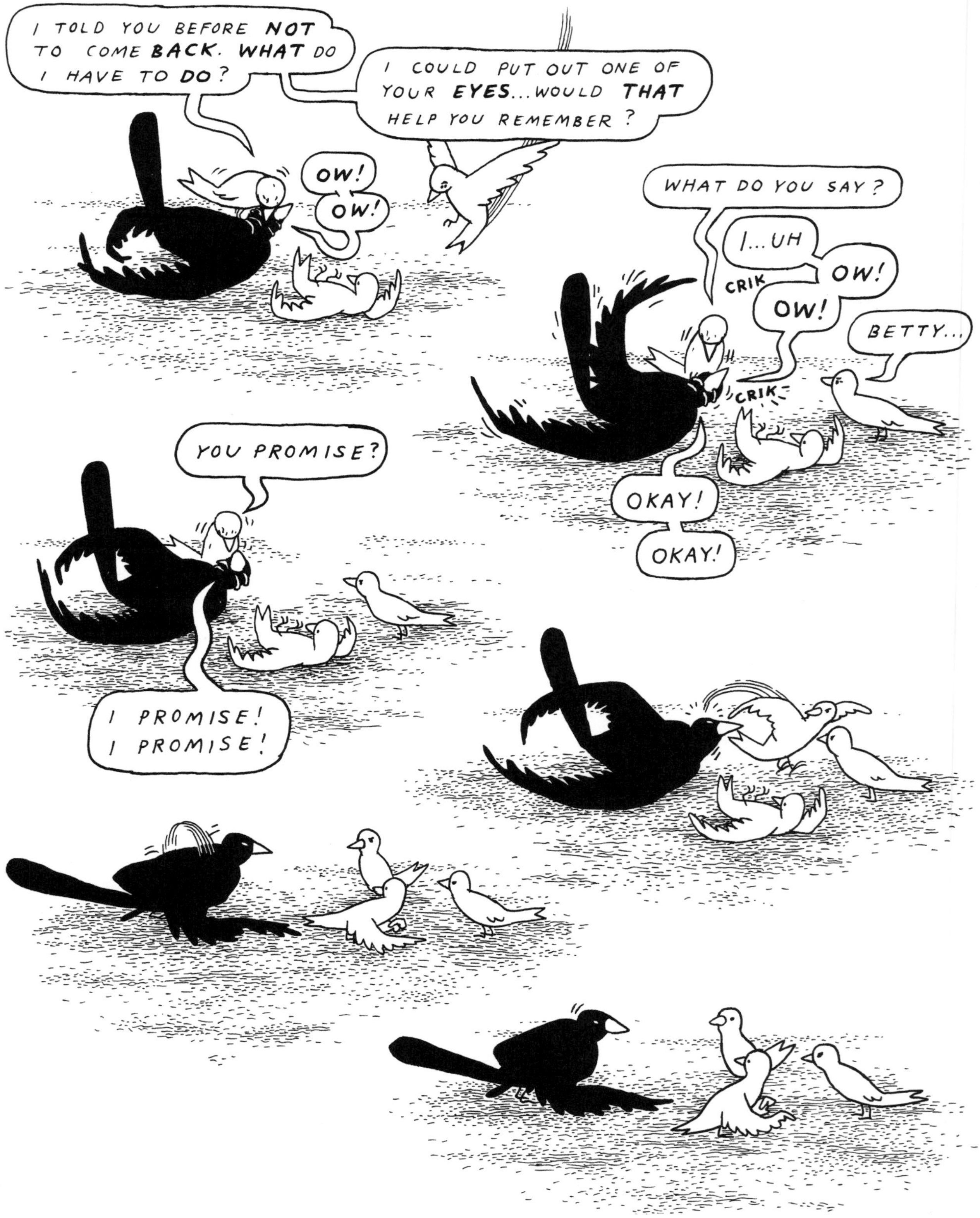
I TOLD YOU BEFORE NOT TO COME BACK. WHAT DO I HAVE TO DO?
I COULD PUT OUT ONE OF YOUR EYES... WOULD THAT HELP YOU REMEMBER?
OW!
OW!
WHAT DO YOU SAY?
I... UH
CRIK
OW!
OW!
BETTY...
CRIK
OKAY!
OKAY!
YOU PROMISE?
I PROMISE! I PROMISE!

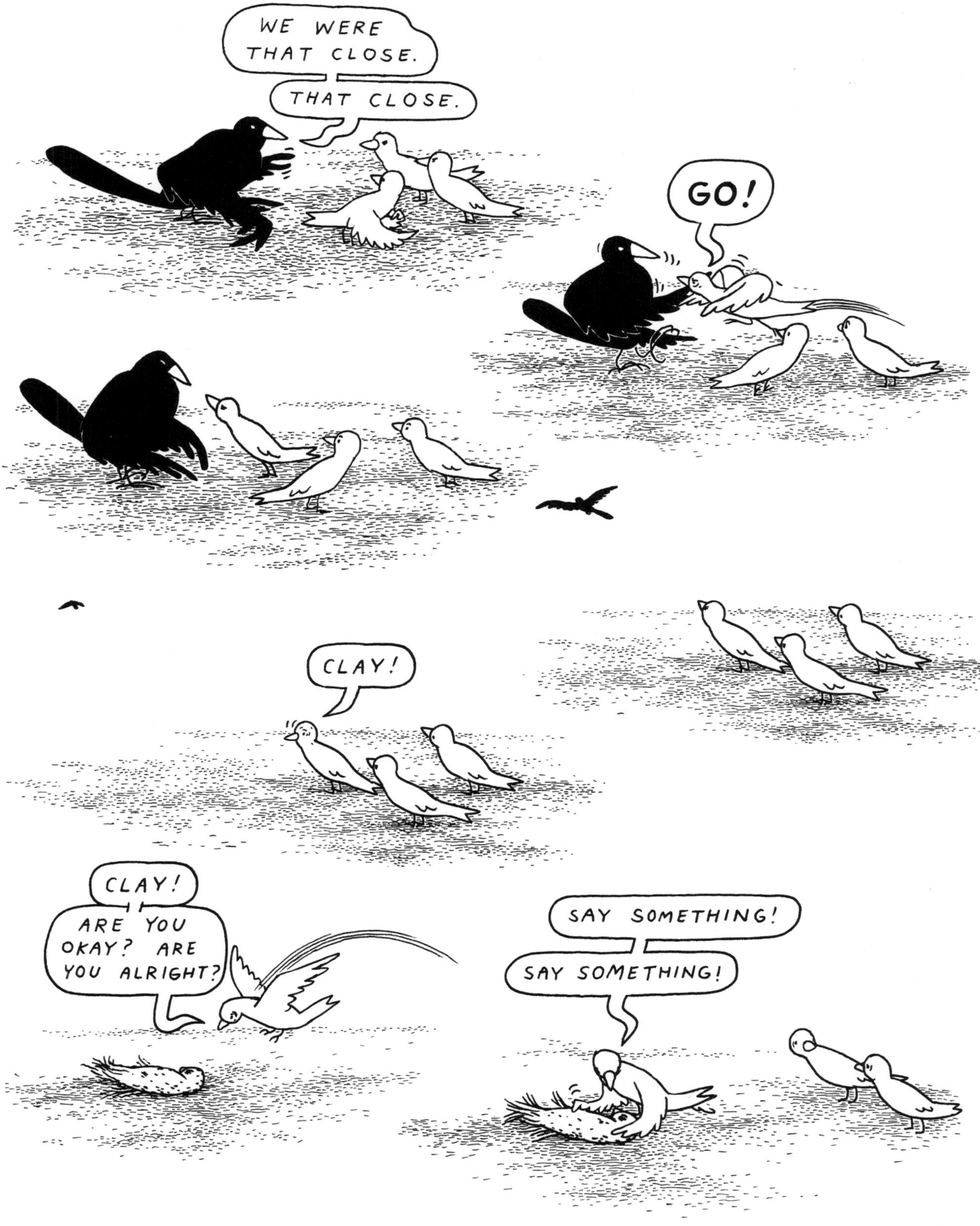
WE WERE THAT CLOSE.
THAT CLOSE.
GO!
CLAY!
CLAY!
ARE YOU OKAY? ARE YOU ALRIGHT?
SAY SOMETHING!
SAY SOMETHING!

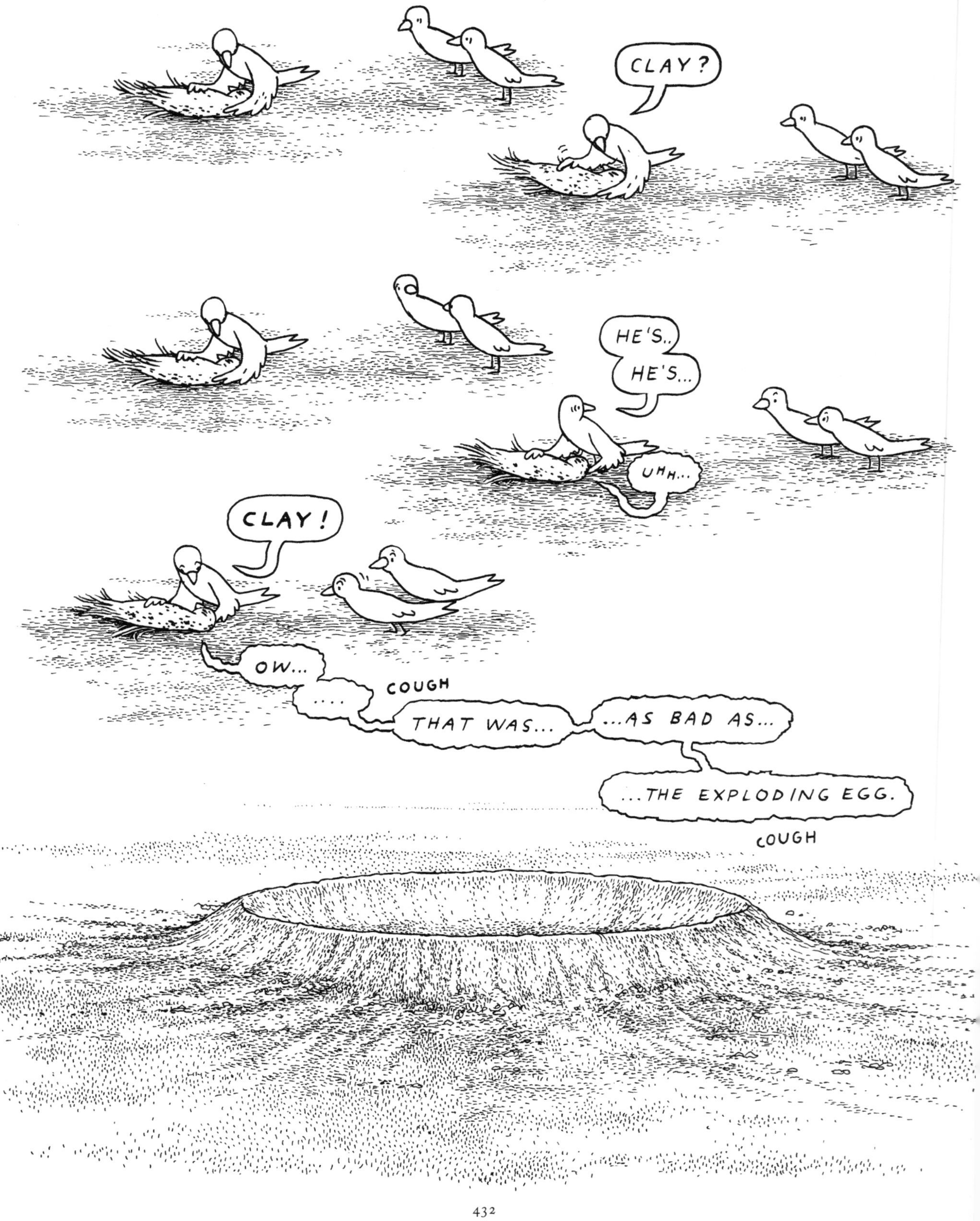
CLAY?
HE'S..
HE'S...
UHH...
CLAY!
OW...
....
COUGH
THAT WAS...
...AS BAD AS...
...THE EXPLODING EGG.
COUGH

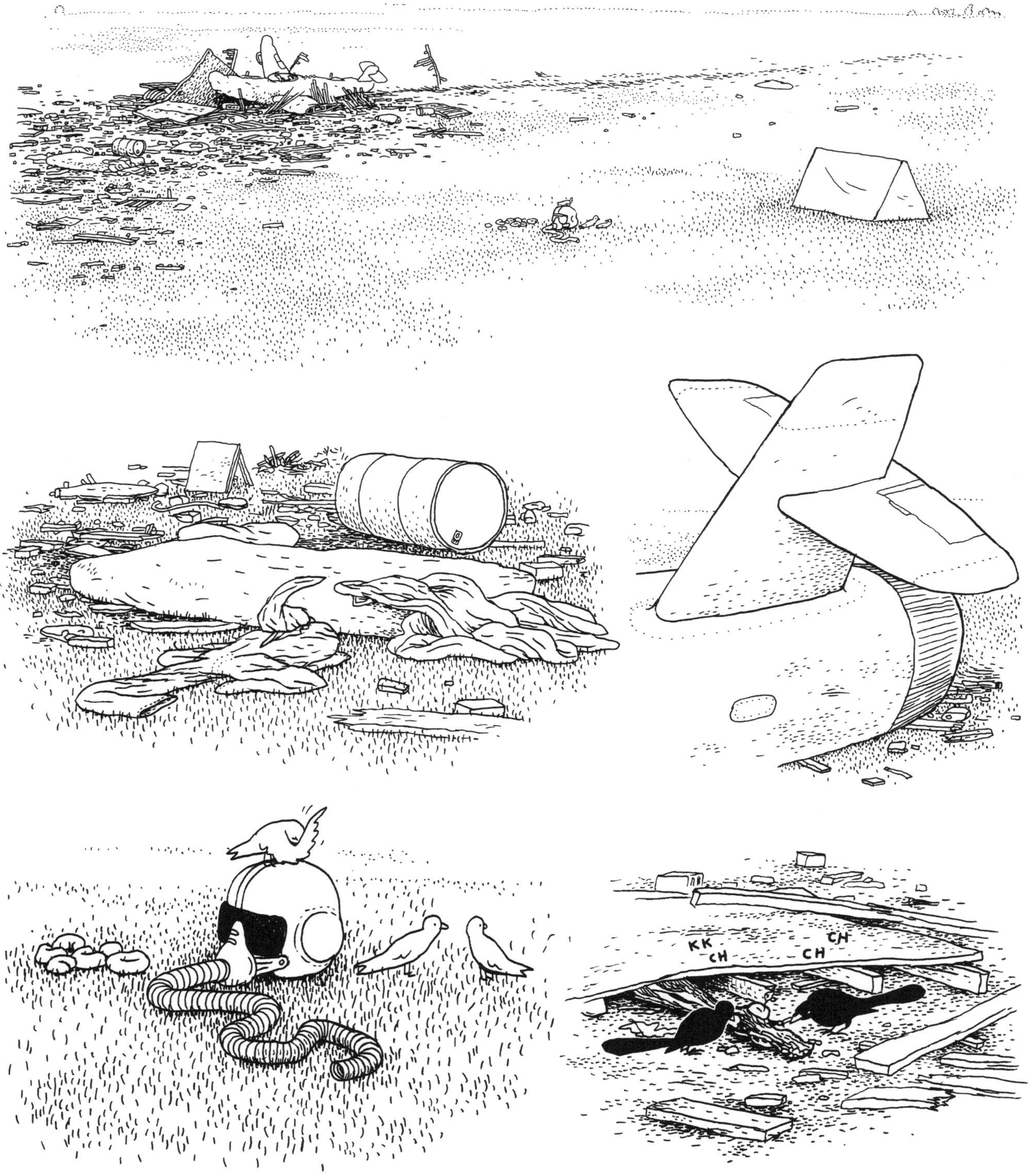
KK
CH
CH
CH

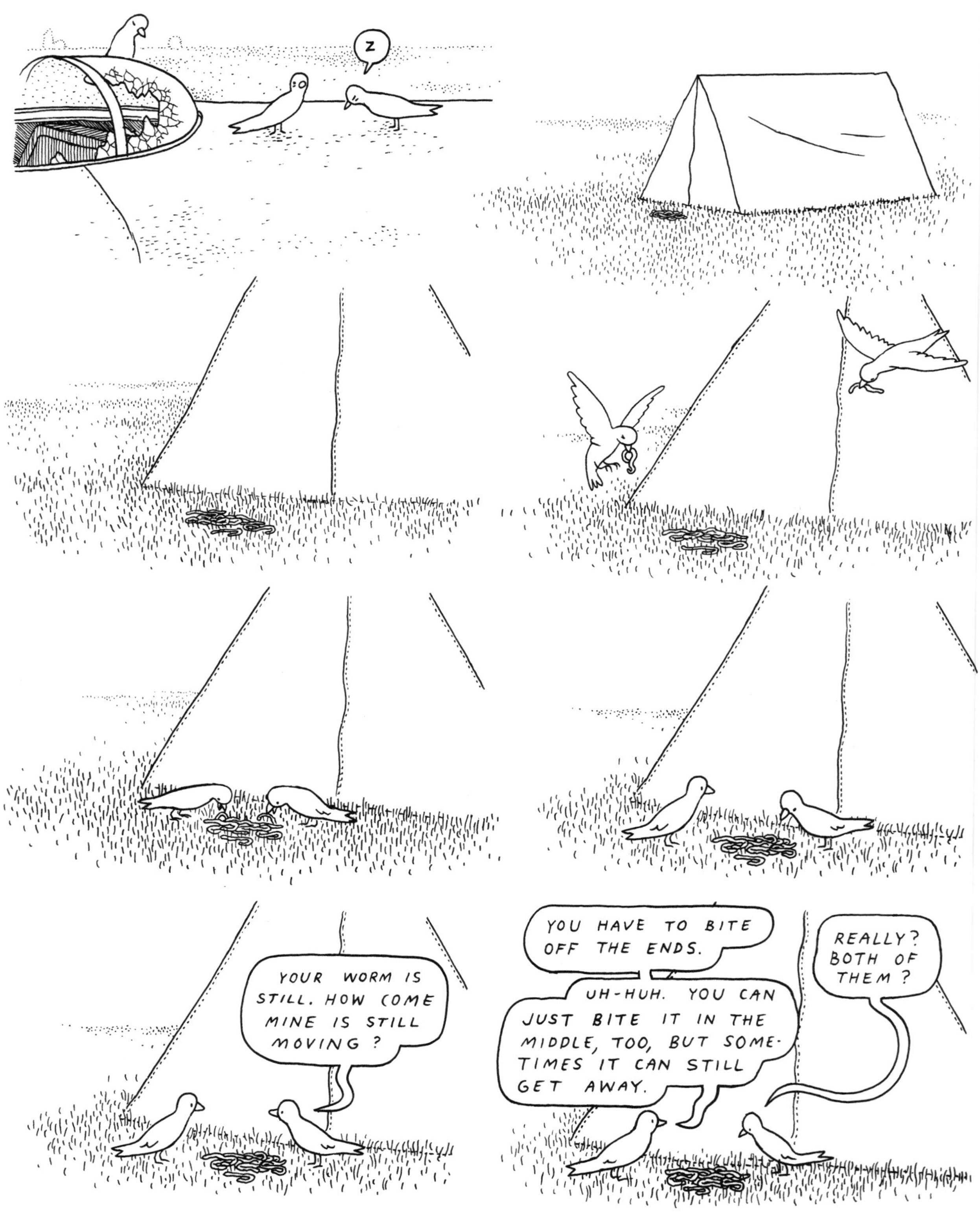
Z
YOUR WORM IS STILL. HOW COME MINE IS STILL MOVING?
YOU HAVE TO BITE OFF THE ENDS.
REALLY? BOTH OF THEM?
UH-HUH. YOU CAN JUST BITE IT IN THE MIDDLE, TOO, BUT SOMETIMES IT CAN STILL GET AWAY.

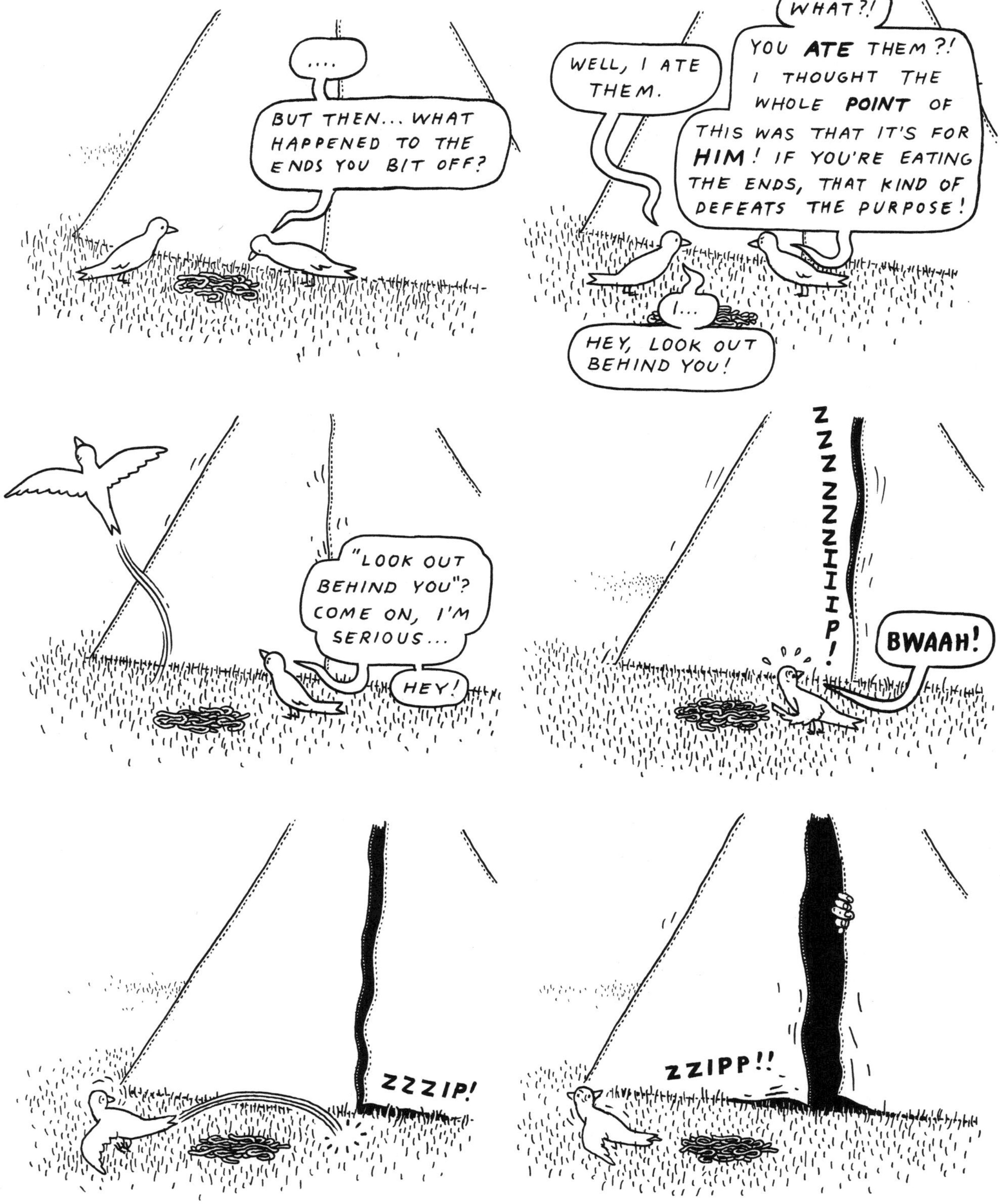
....
BUT THEN... WHAT HAPPENED TO THE ENDS YOU BIT OFF?
WELL, I ATE THEM.
WHAT?!
YOU ATE THEM?! I THOUGHT THE WHOLE POINT OF THIS WAS THAT IT'S FOR HIM! IF YOU'RE EATING THE ENDS, THAT KIND OF DEFEATS THE PURPOSE!
I...
HEY, LOOK OUT BEHIND YOU!
"LOOK OUT BEHIND YOU"? COME ON, I'M SERIOUS...
HEY!
ZZZZZZIIIIP!
BWAAH!
ZZZIP!
ZZIPP!!

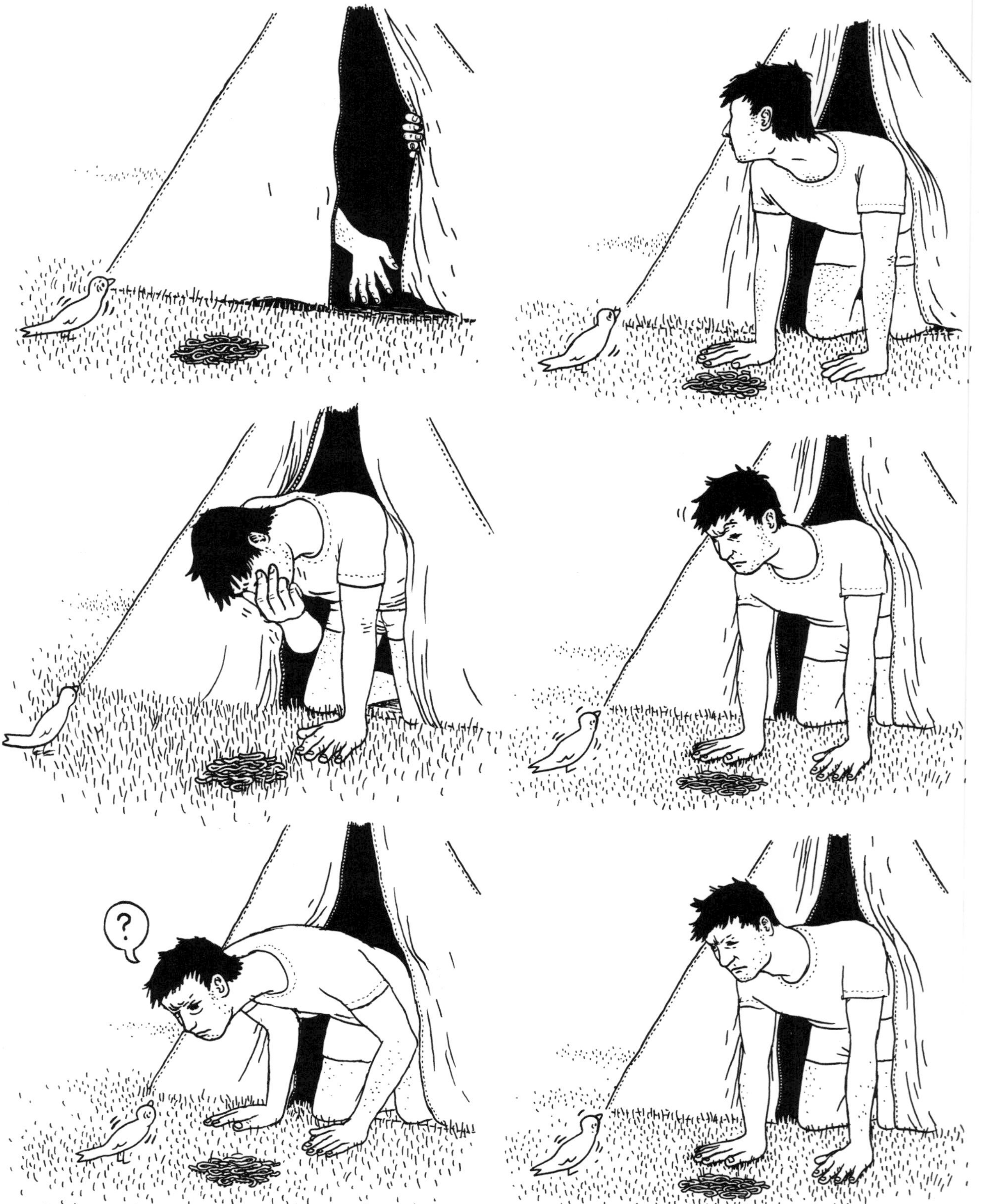
?

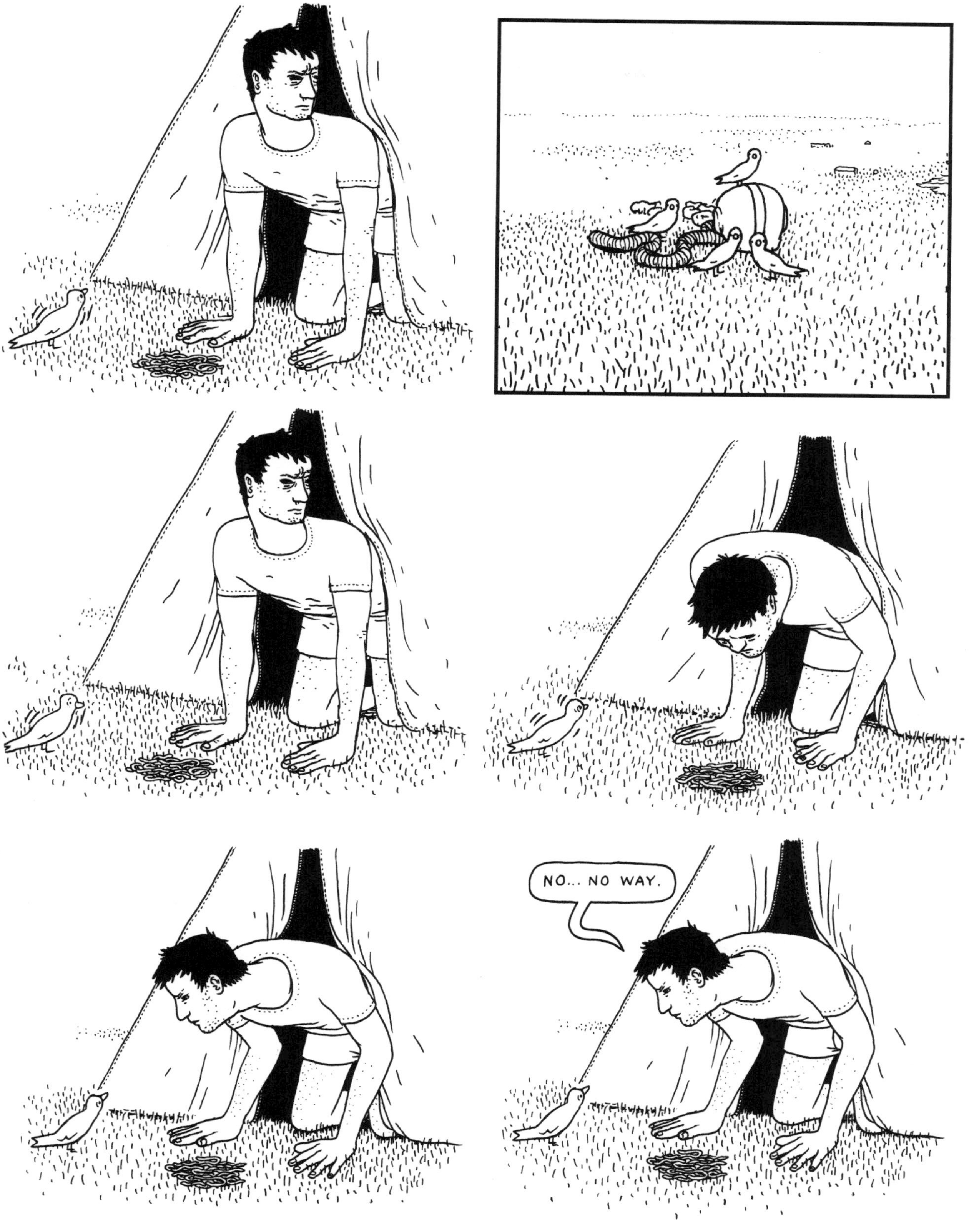
NO... NO WAY.

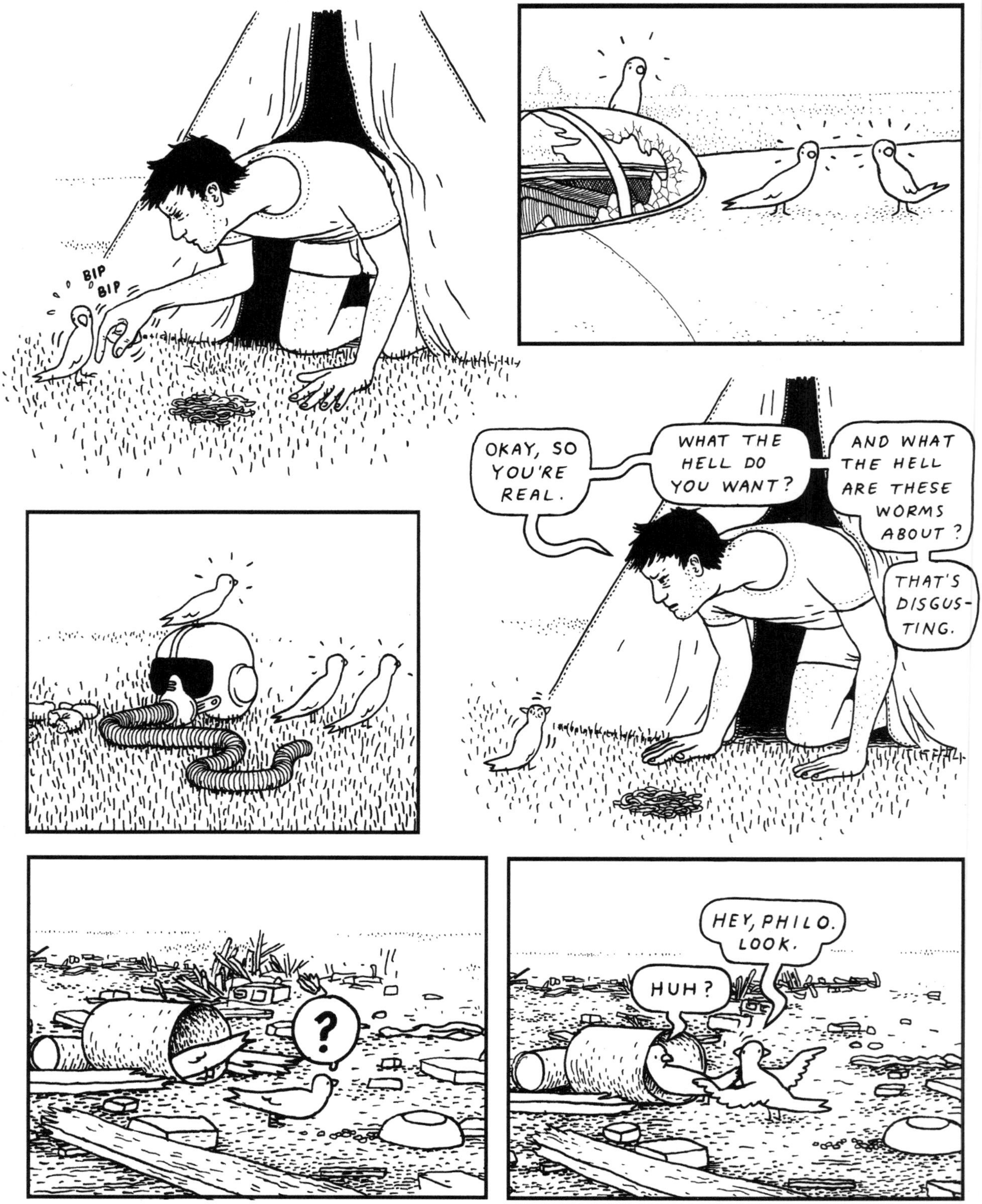
BIP
BIP
OKAY, SO YOU'RE REAL.
WHAT THE HELL DO YOU WANT?
AND WHAT THE HELL ARE THESE WORMS ABOUT?
THAT'S DISGUSTING.
?
HEY, PHILO. LOOK.
HUH?

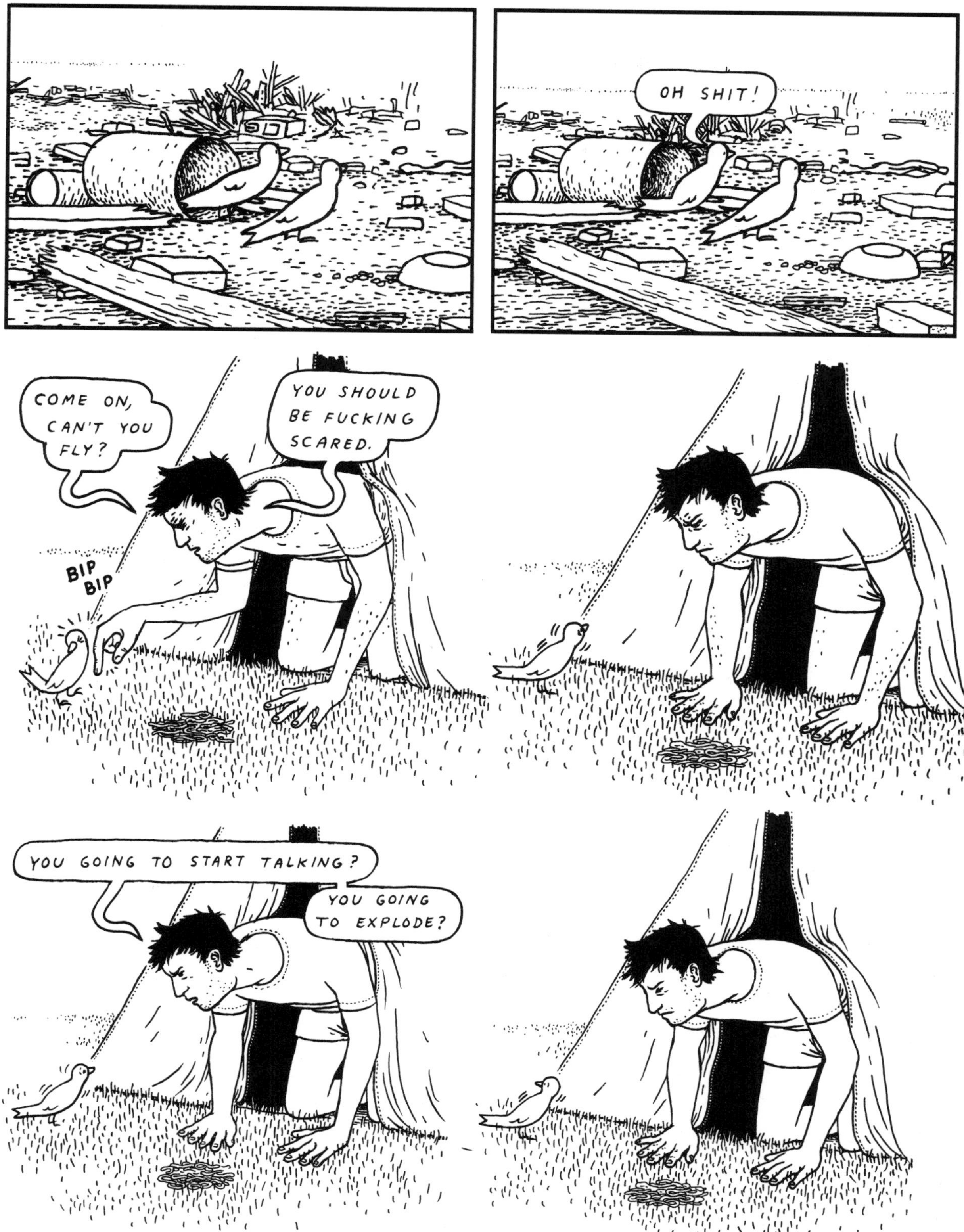
OH SHIT!
COME ON, CAN'T YOU FLY?
YOU SHOULD BE FUCKING SCARED.
BIP BIP
YOU GOING TO START TALKING?
YOU GOING TO EXPLODE?

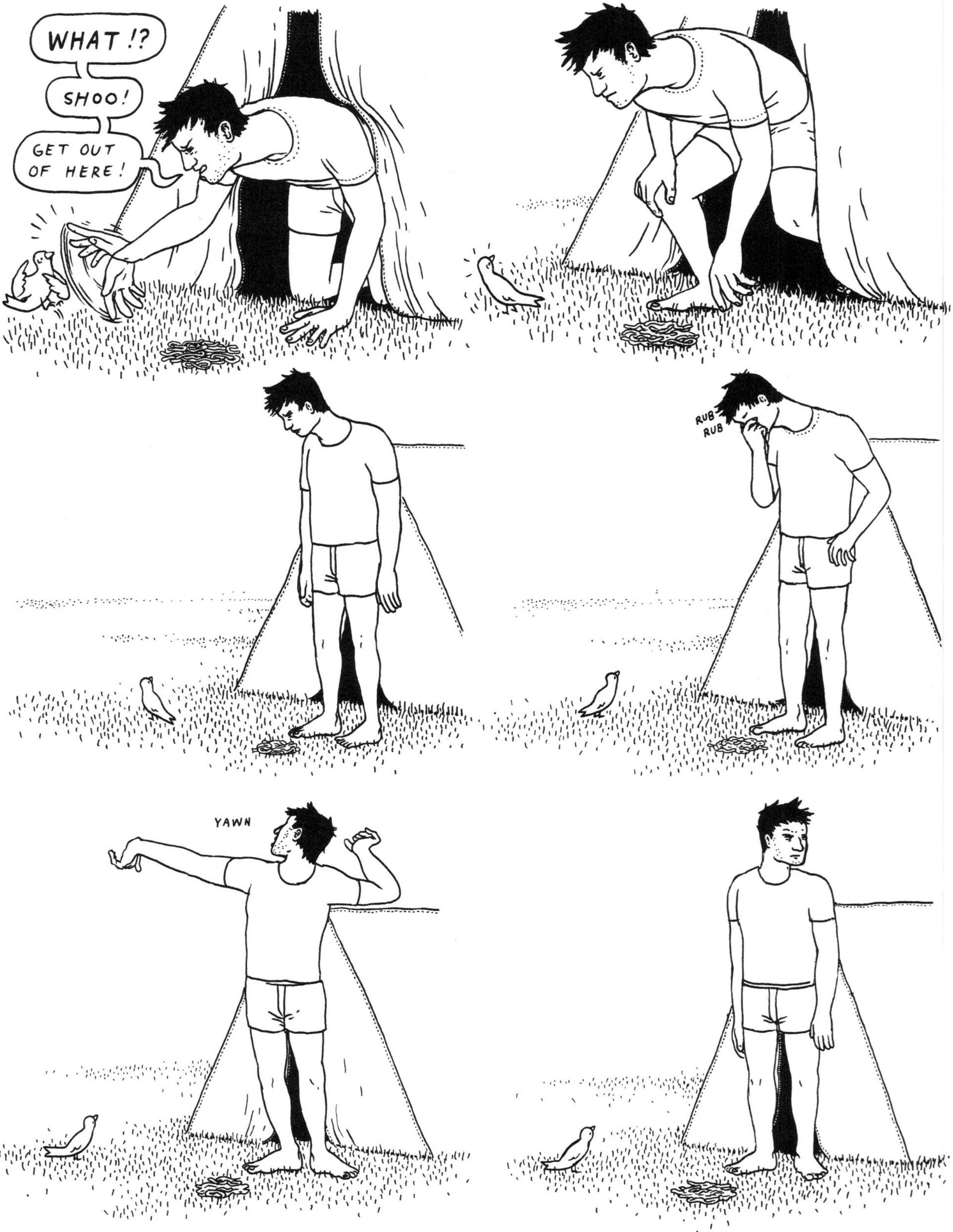
WHAT !?
SHOO!
GET OUT OF HERE!
RUB RUB
YAWN

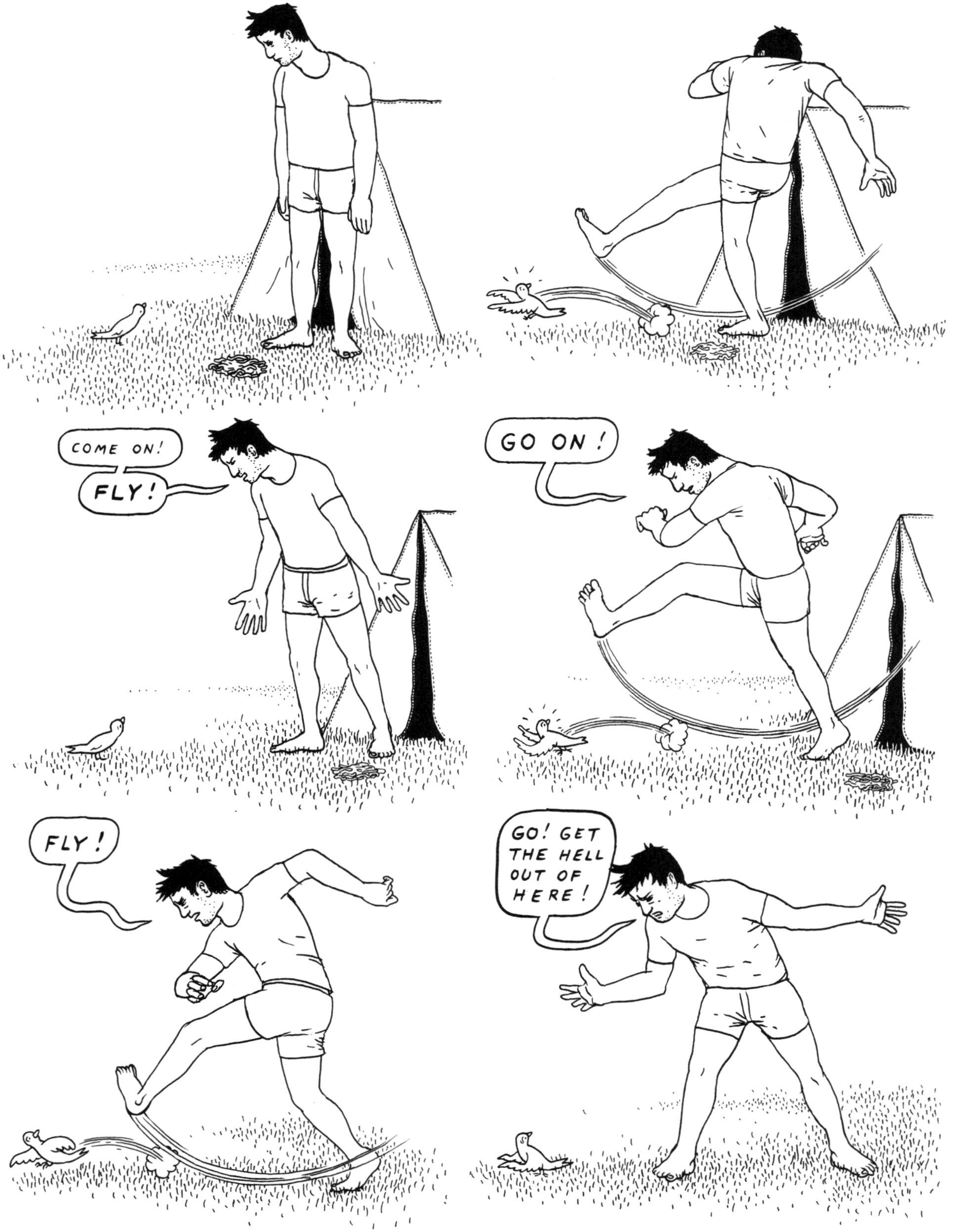
COME ON!
FLY!
GO ON!
FLY!
GO! GET THE HELL OUT OF HERE!

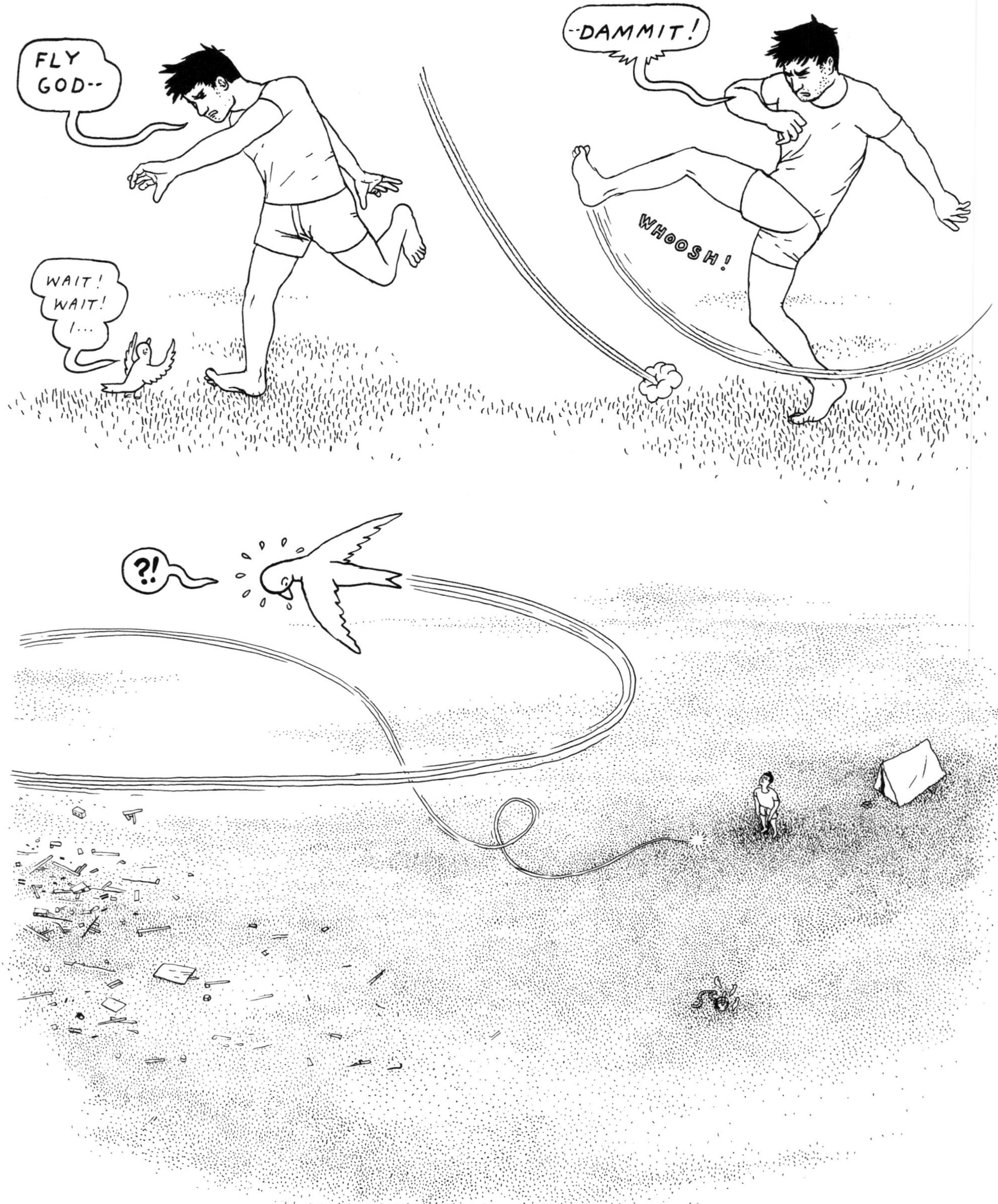
FLY GOD--
WAIT! WAIT! I...
--DAMMIT!
WHOOSH!
?!

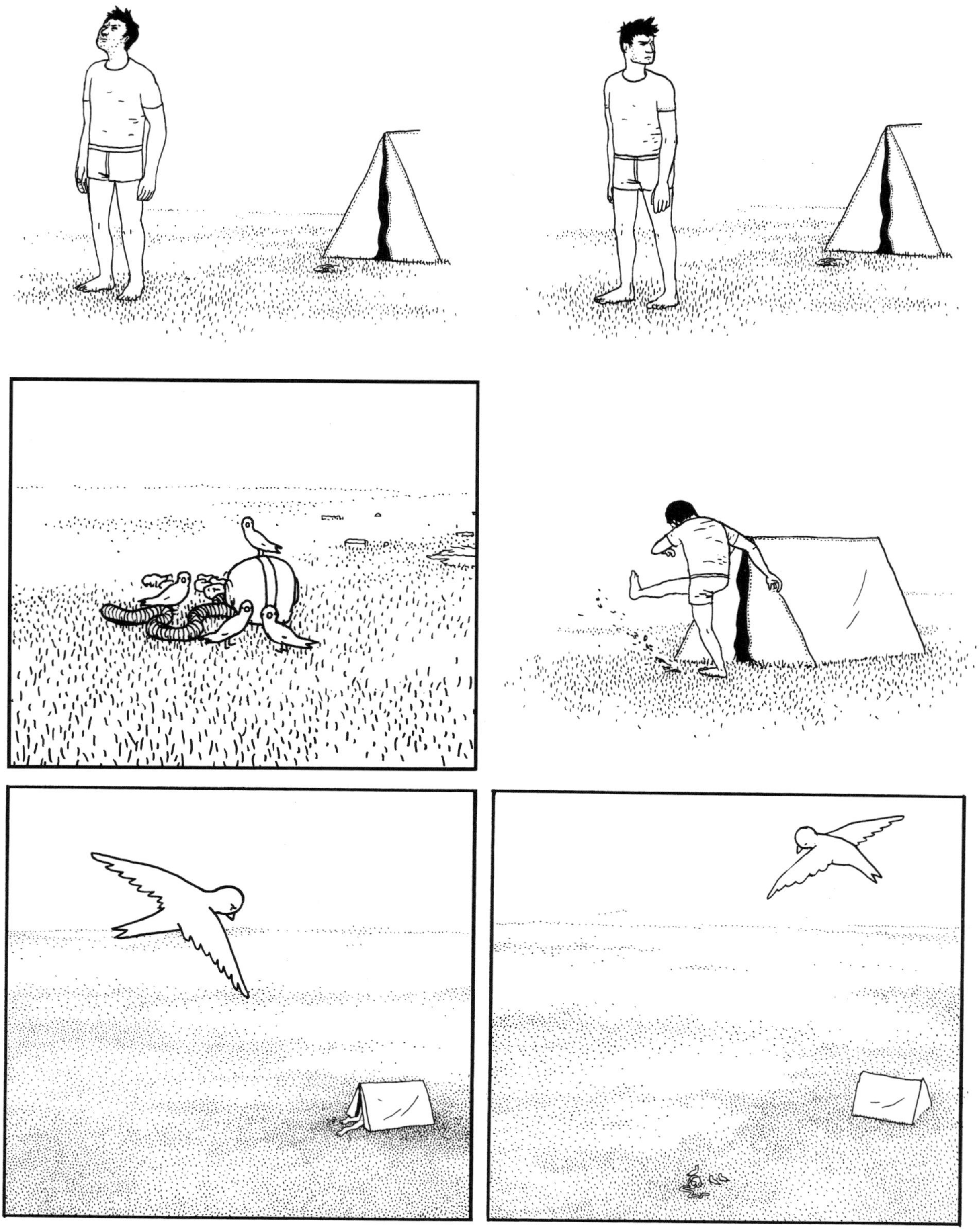

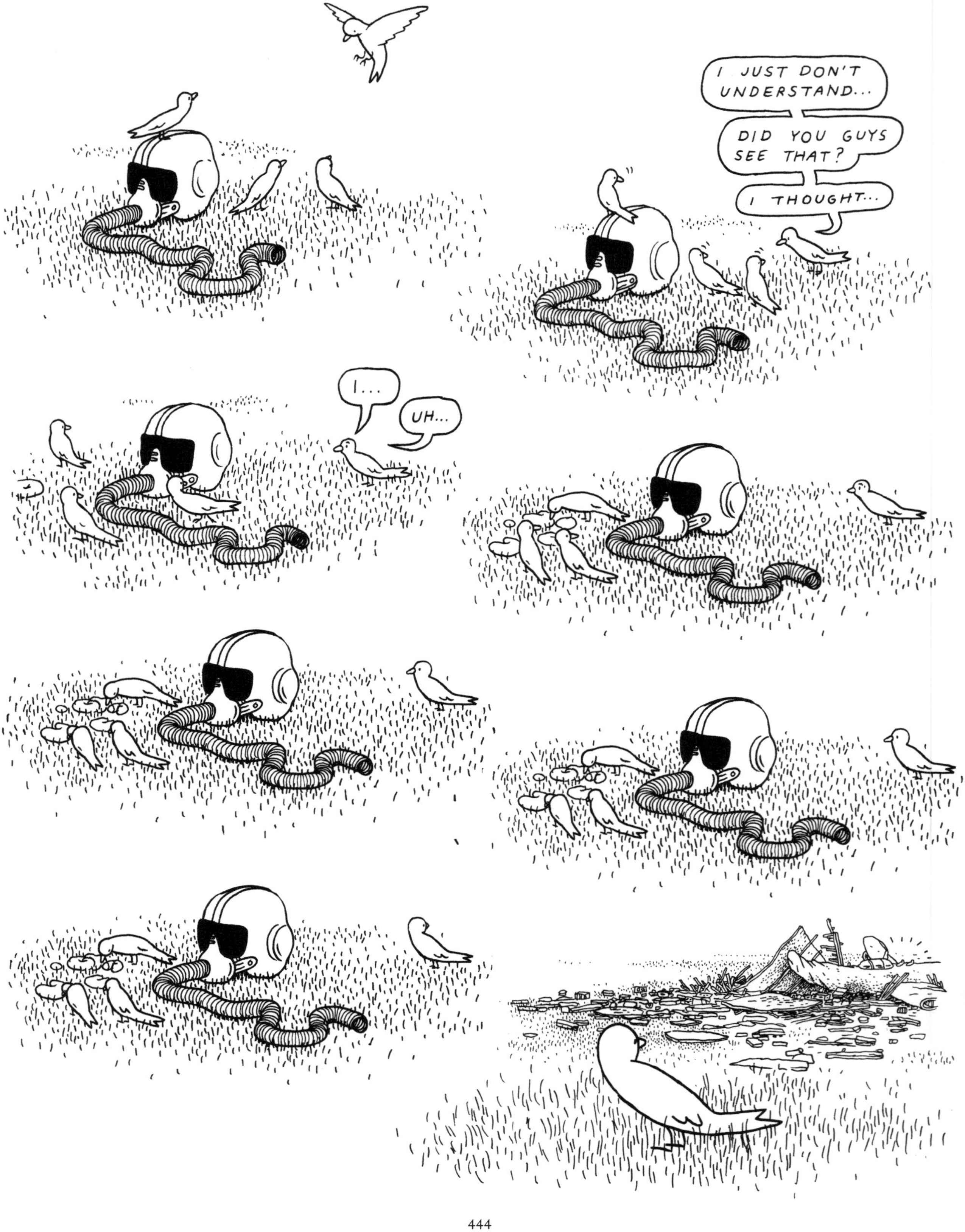
I JUST DON'T UNDERSTAND...
DID YOU GUYS SEE THAT?
I THOUGHT...
I...
UH...

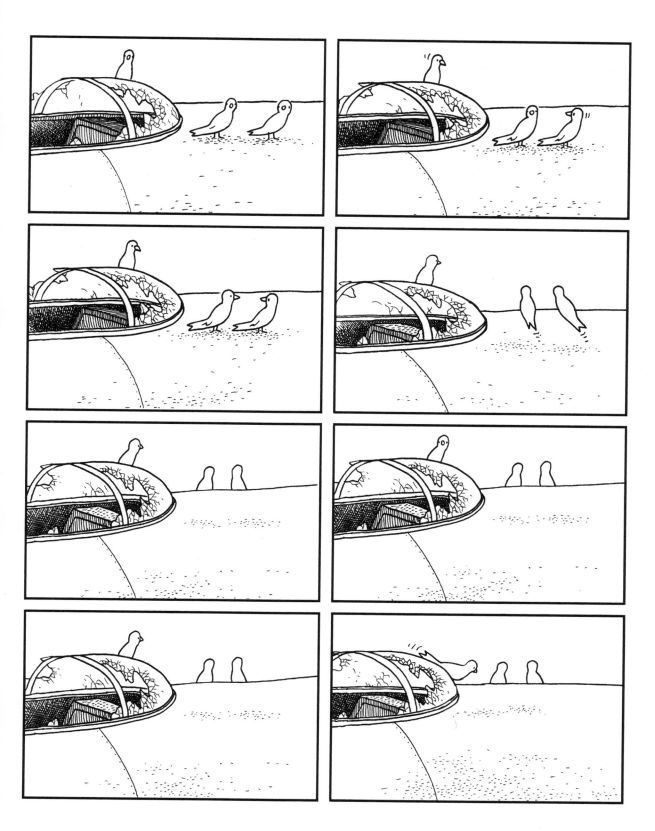

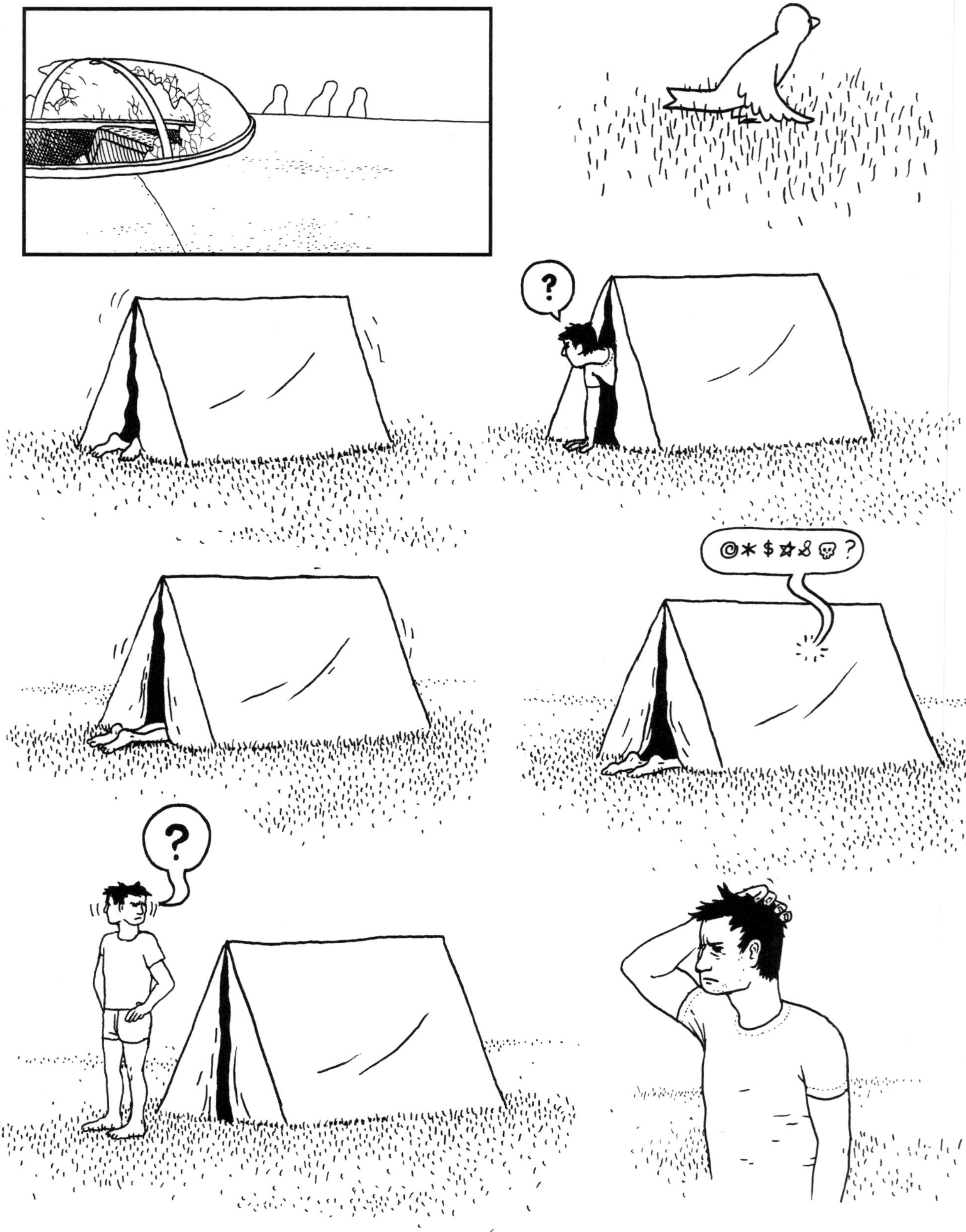
?
@*$☆ಽ☠?
?

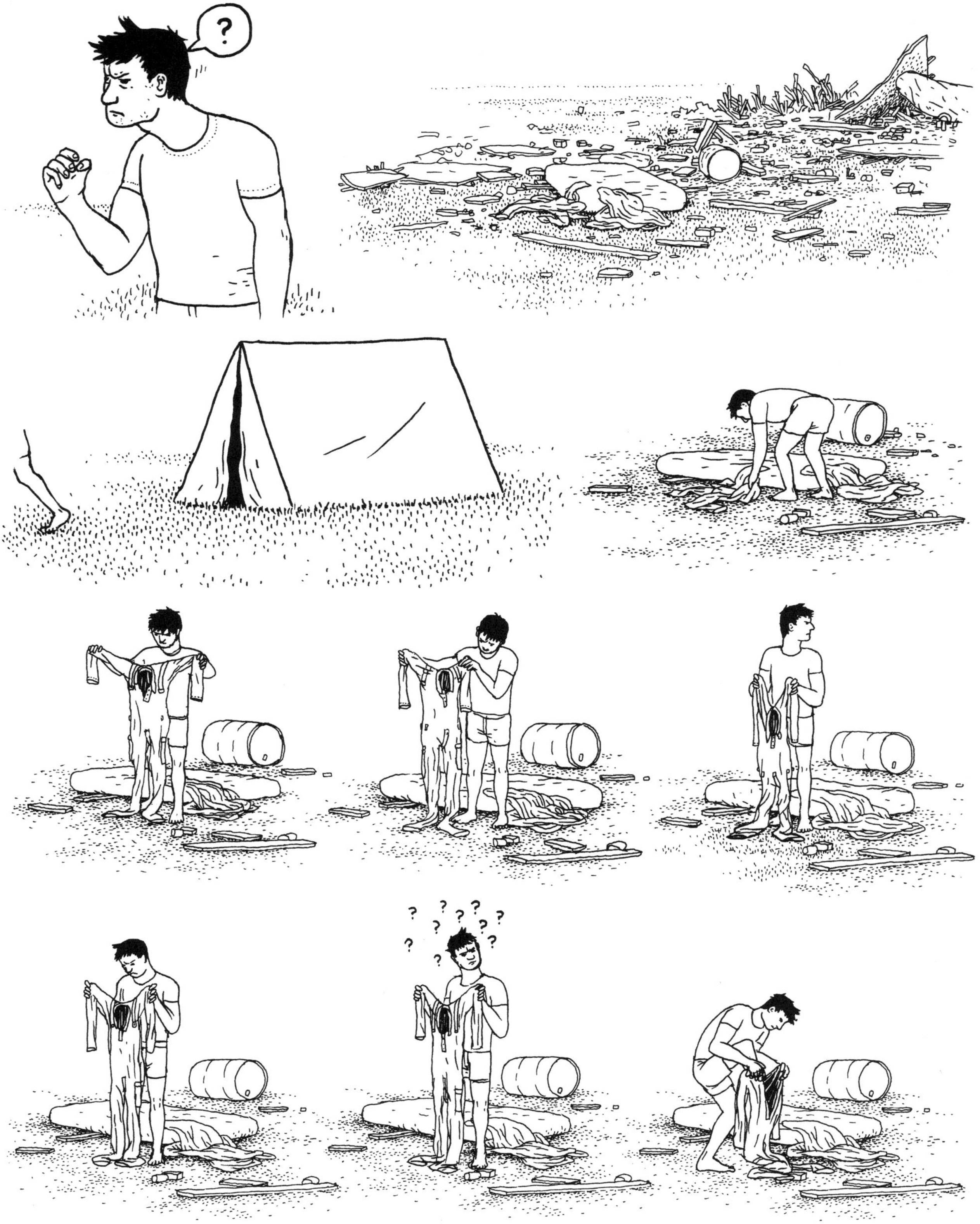
?

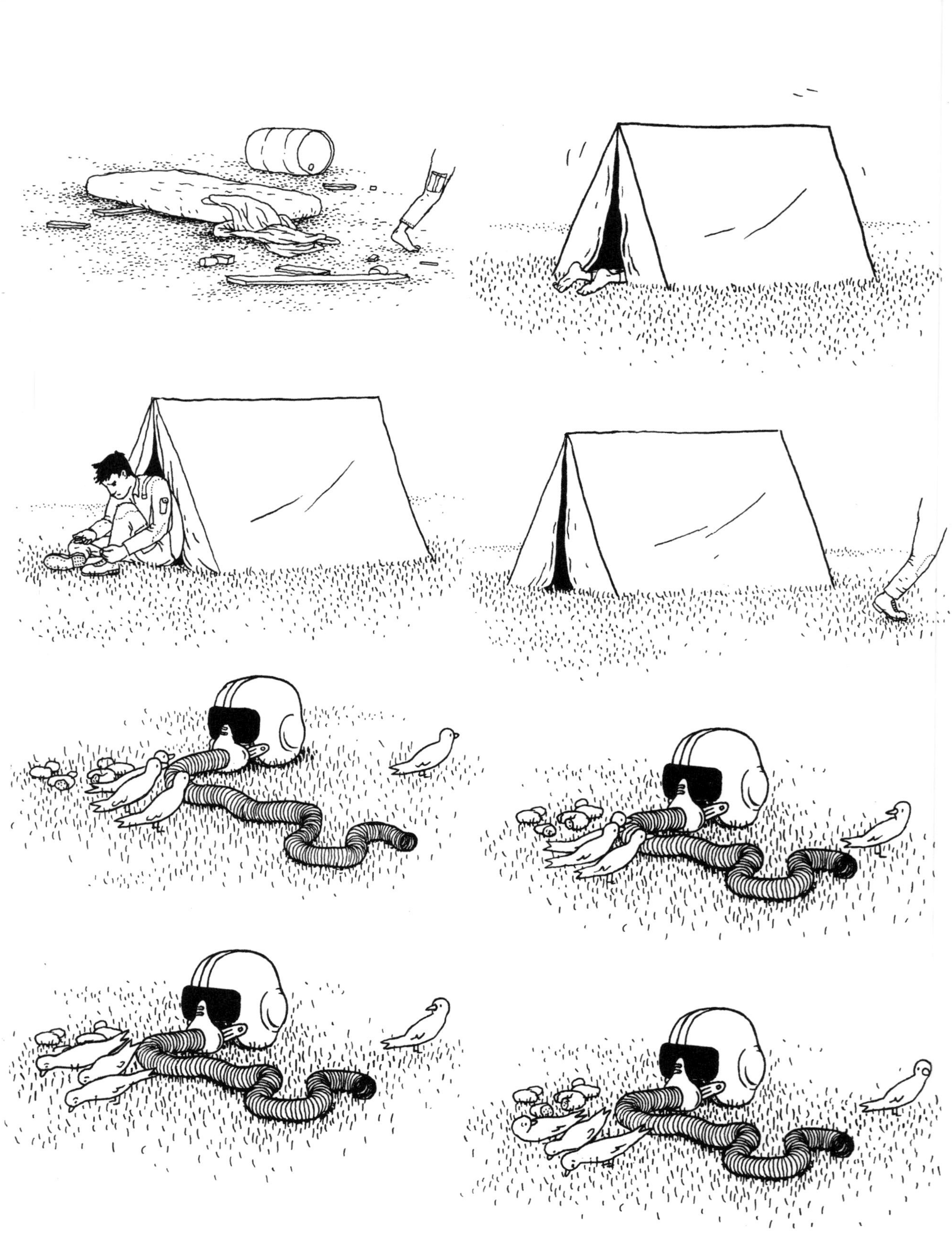

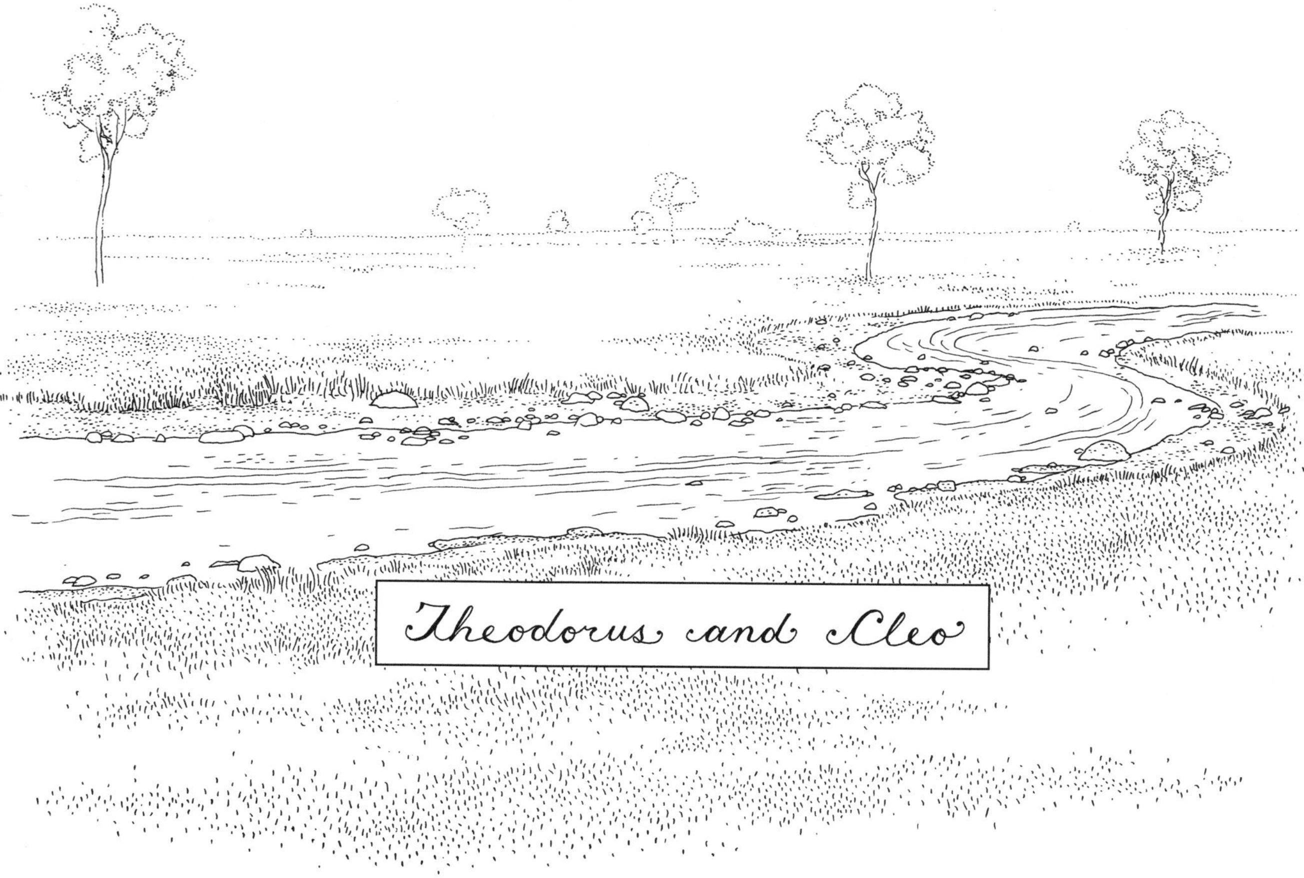
Theodorus and Cleo

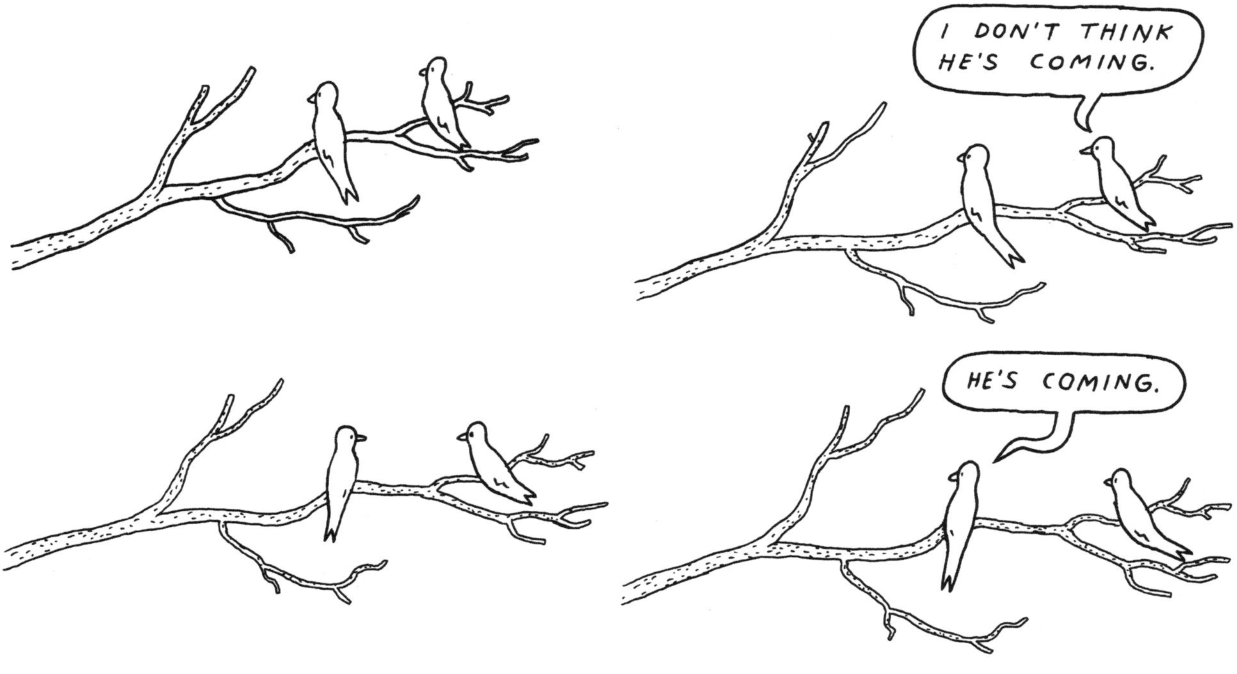
I DON'T THINK HE'S COMING.
HE'S COMING.

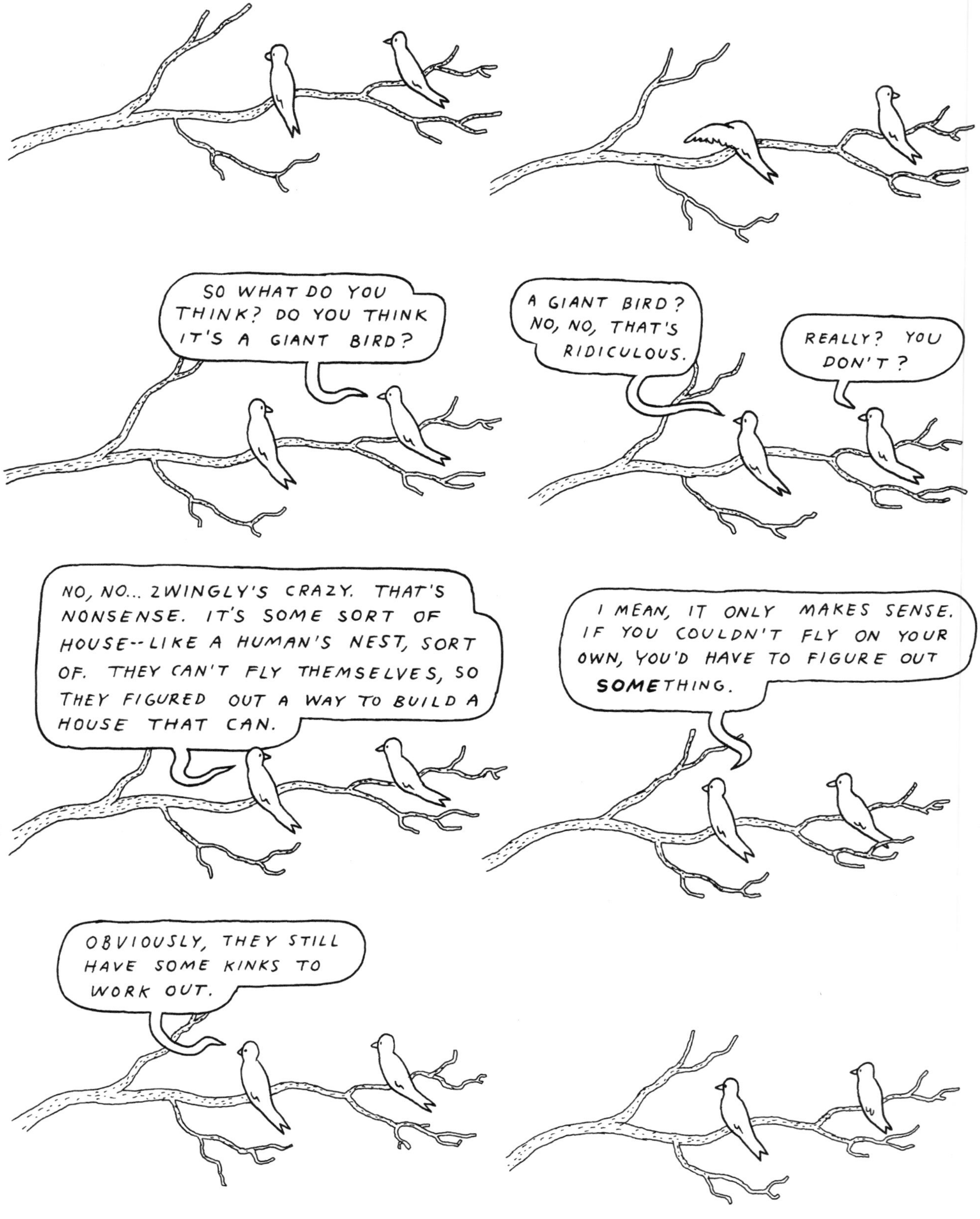
SO WHAT DO YOU THINK? DO YOU THINK IT'S A GIANT BIRD?
A GIANT BIRD? NO, NO, THAT'S RIDICULOUS.
REALLY? YOU DON'T?
NO, NO... ZWINGLY'S CRAZY. THAT'S NONSENSE. IT'S SOME SORT OF HOUSE--LIKE A HUMAN'S NEST, SORT OF. THEY CAN'T FLY THEMSELVES, SO THEY FIGURED OUT A WAY TO BUILD A HOUSE THAT CAN.
I MEAN, IT ONLY MAKES SENSE. IF YOU COULDN'T FLY ON YOUR OWN, YOU'D HAVE TO FIGURE OUT SOMETHING.
OBVIOUSLY, THEY STILL HAVE SOME KINKS TO WORK OUT.

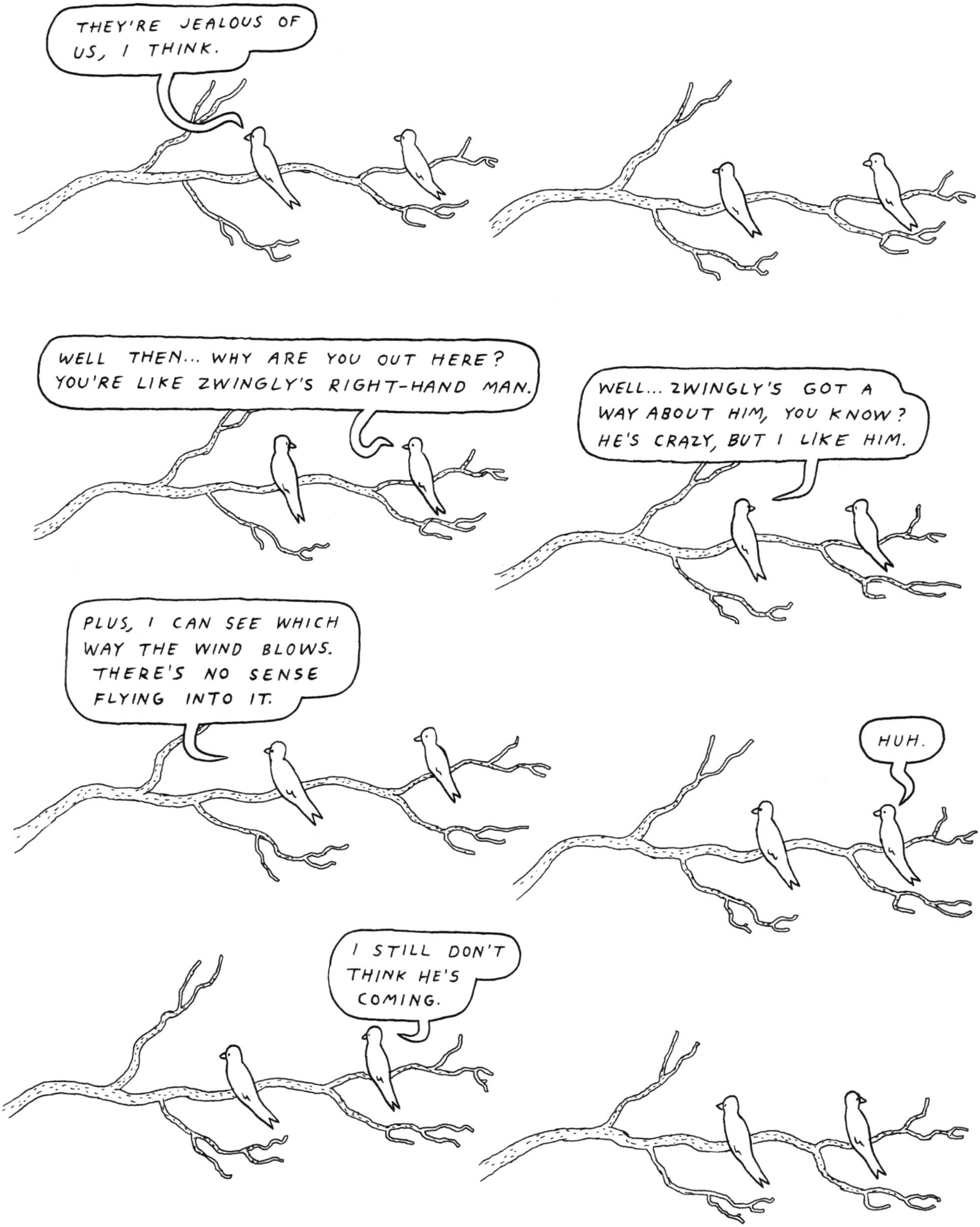
THEY'RE JEALOUS OF US, I THINK.
WELL THEN... WHY ARE YOU OUT HERE? YOU'RE LIKE ZWINGLY'S RIGHT-HAND MAN.
WELL... ZWINGLY'S GOT A WAY ABOUT HIM, YOU KNOW? HE'S CRAZY, BUT I LIKE HIM.
PLUS, I CAN SEE WHICH WAY THE WIND BLOWS. THERE'S NO SENSE FLYING INTO IT.
HUH.
I STILL DON'T THINK HE'S COMING.

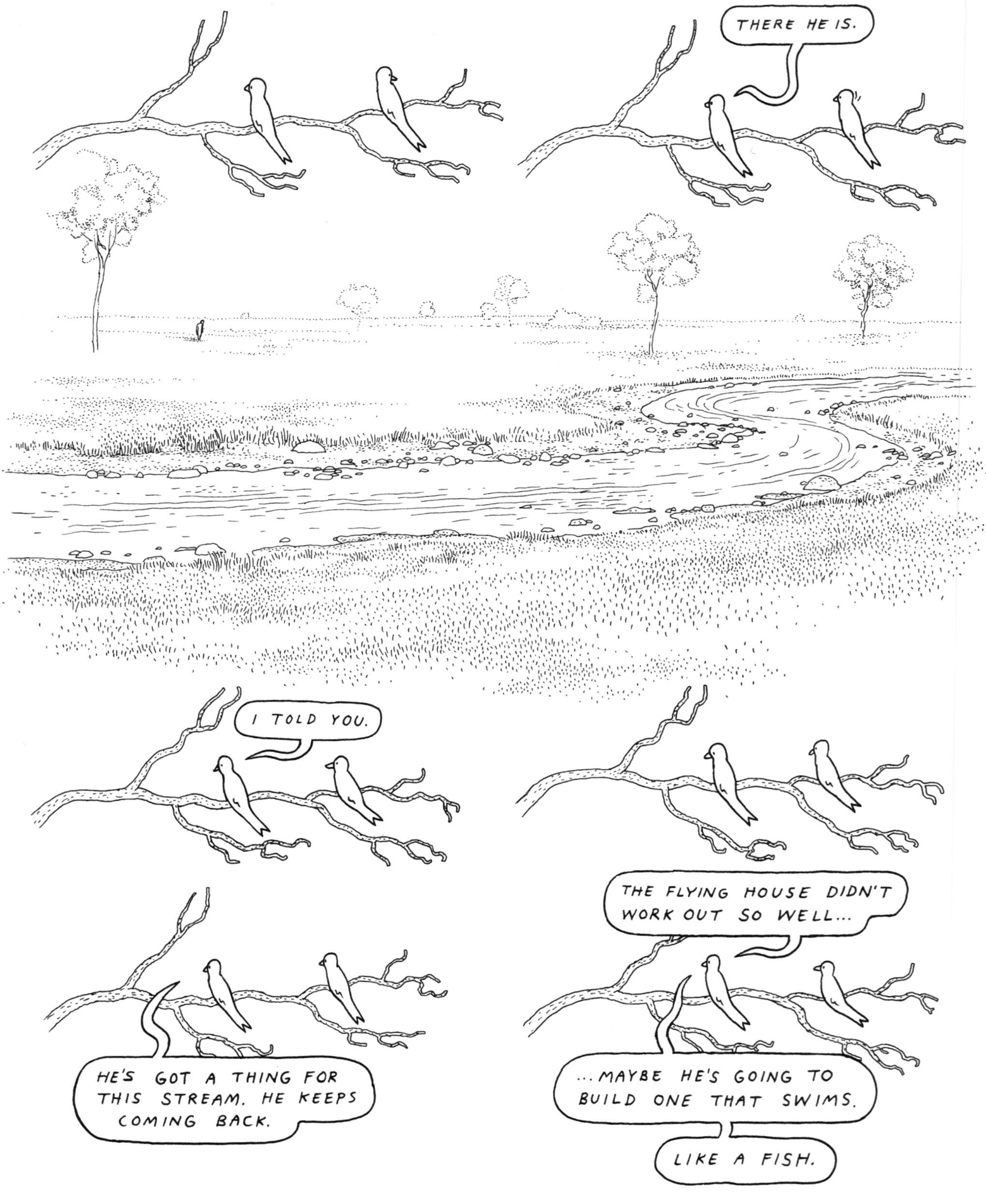
THERE HE IS.
I TOLD YOU.
HE'S GOT A THING FOR THIS STREAM. HE KEEPS COMING BACK.
THE FLYING HOUSE DIDN'T WORK OUT SO WELL...
...MAYBE HE'S GOING TO BUILD ONE THAT SWIMS.
LIKE A FISH.

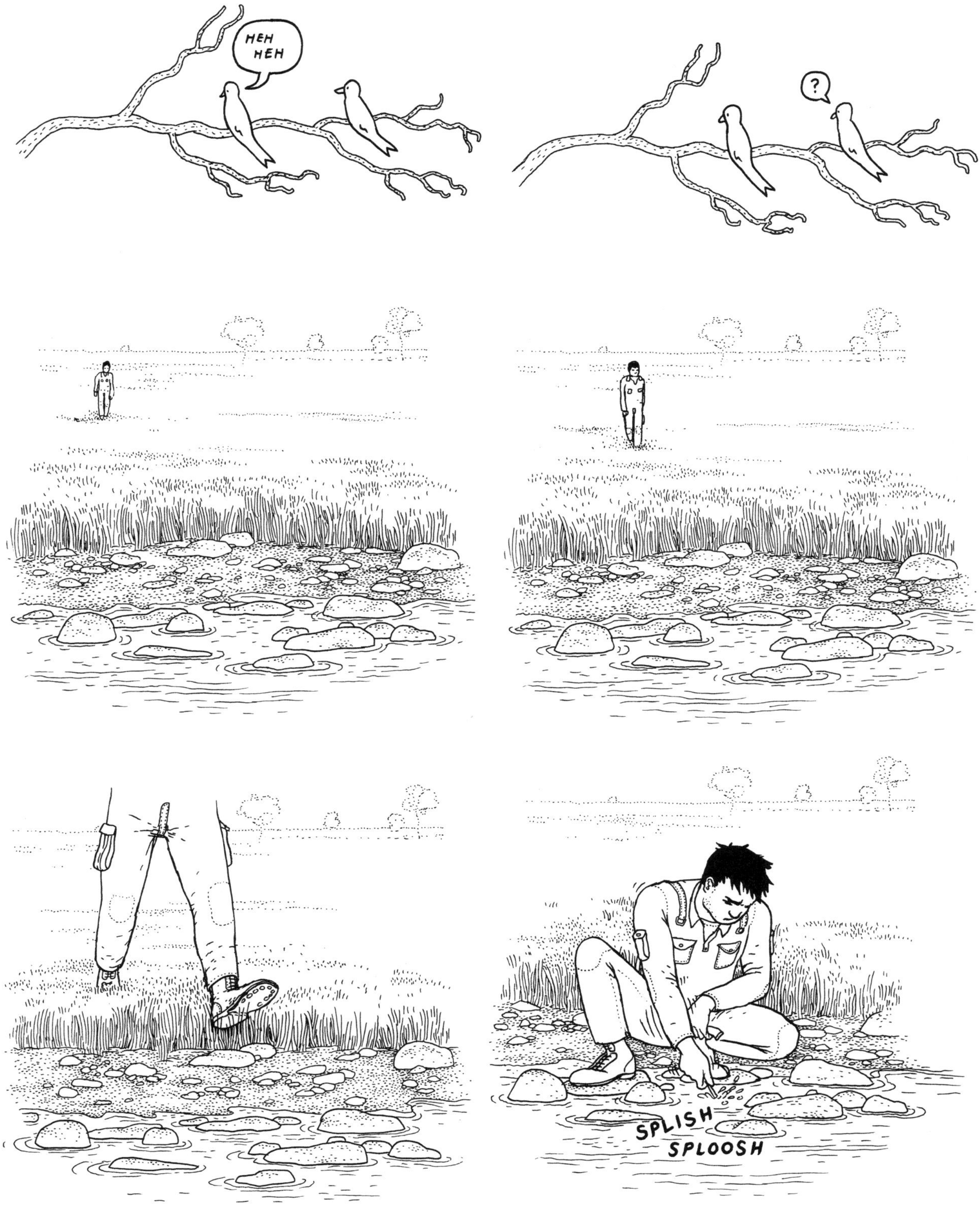
HEH HEH
?
SPLISH
SPLOOSH

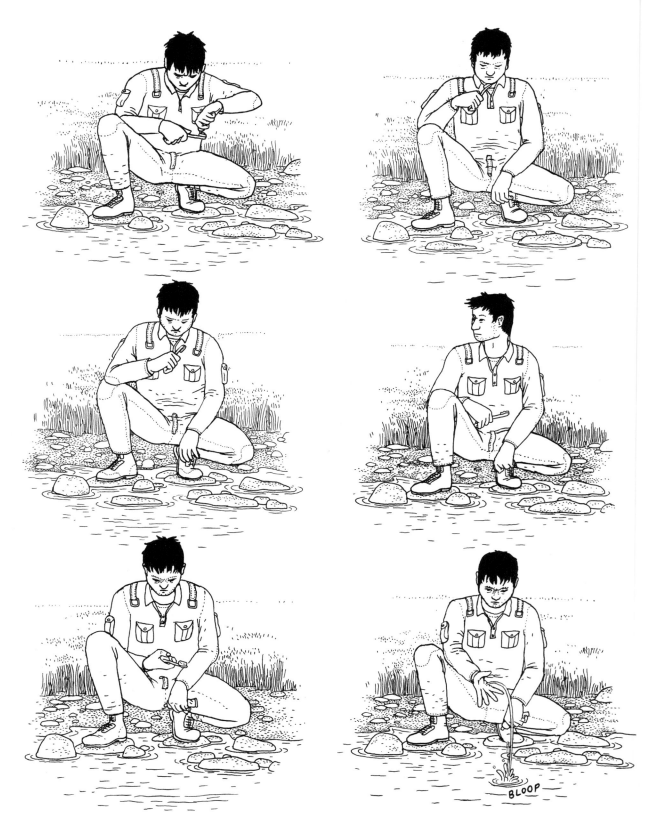

BLOOP

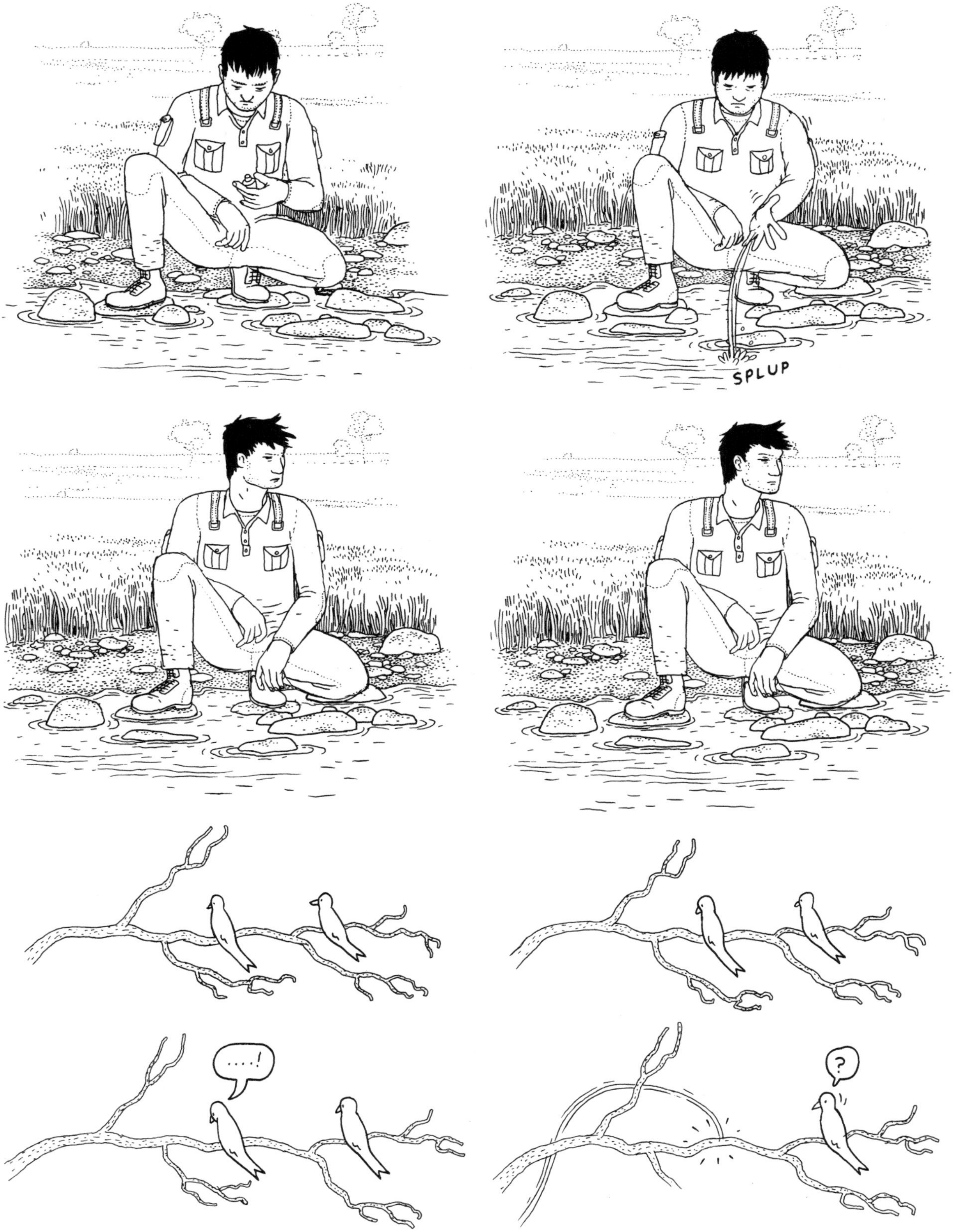
SPLUP
....!
?

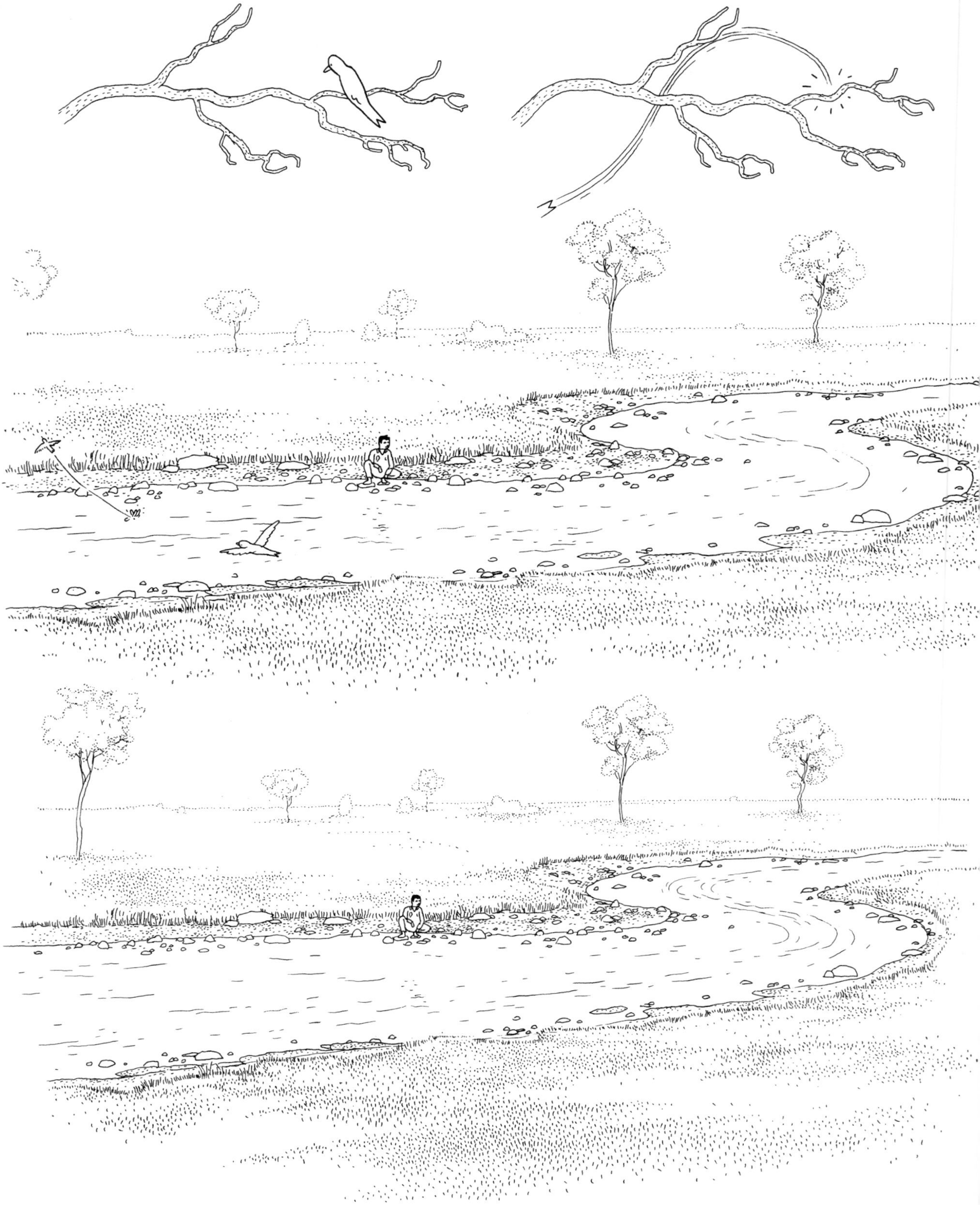

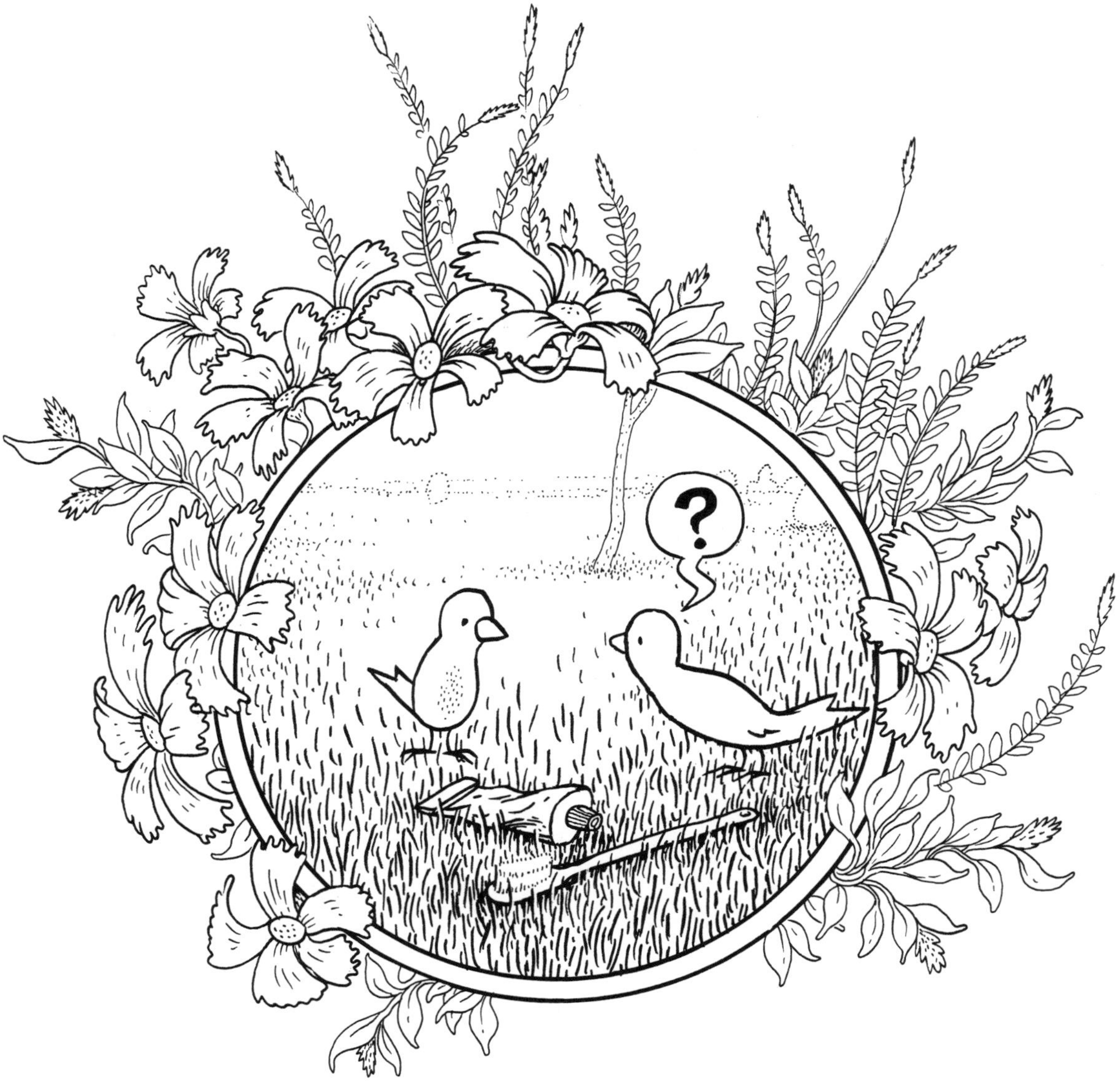
?

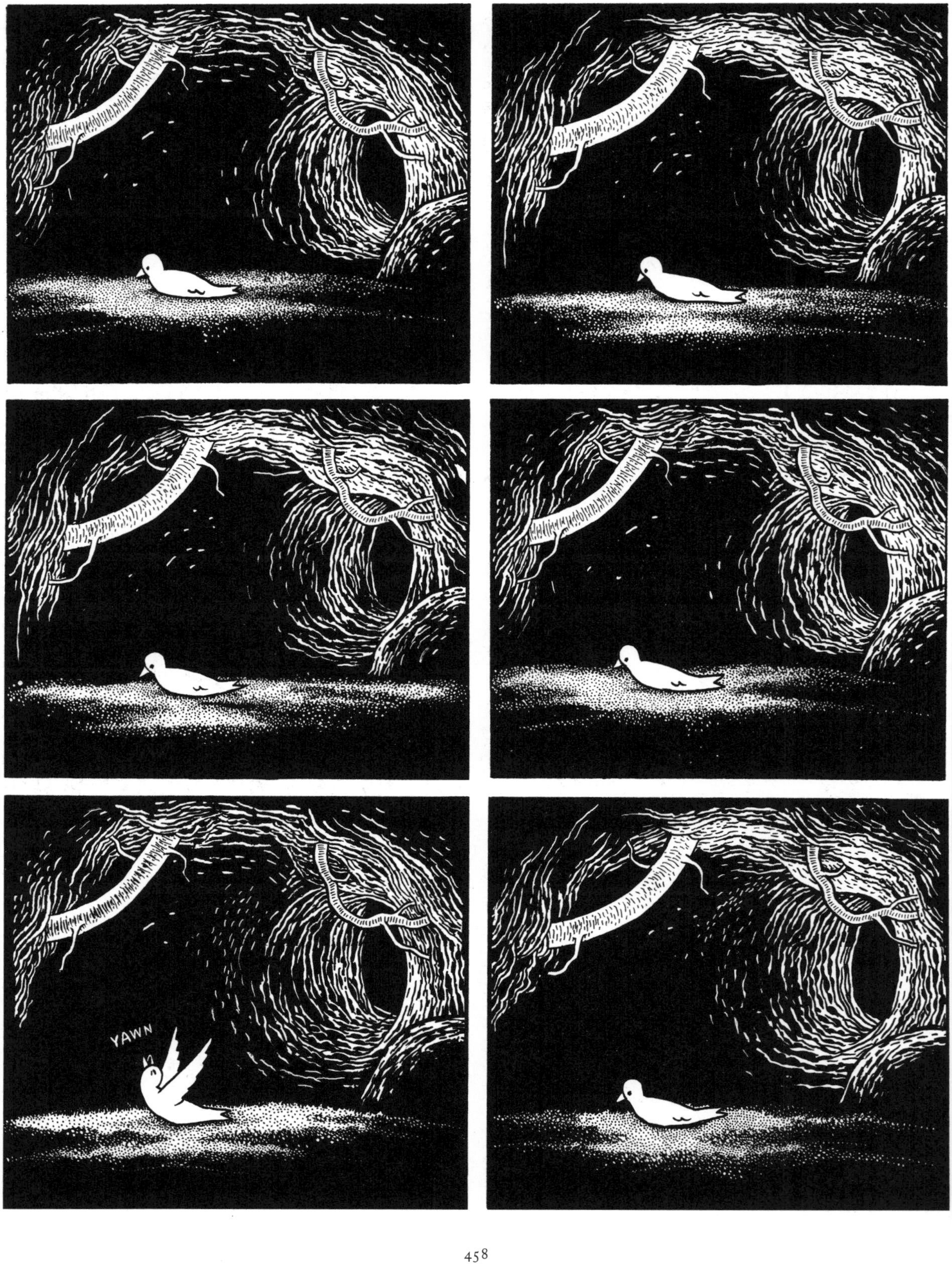
YAWN

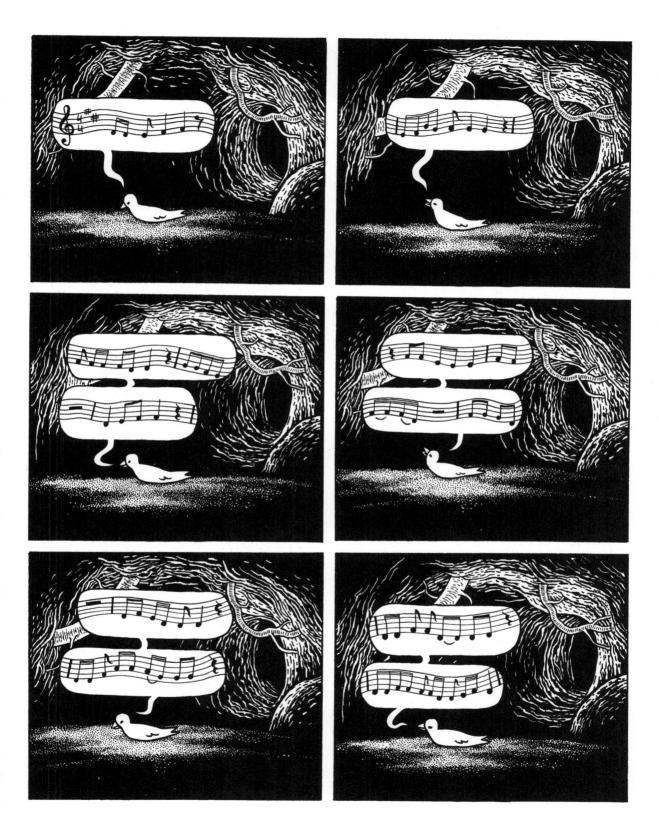

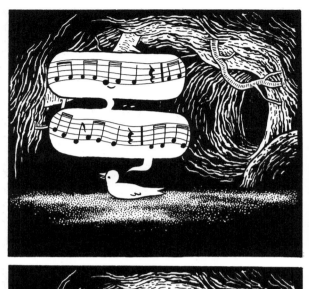

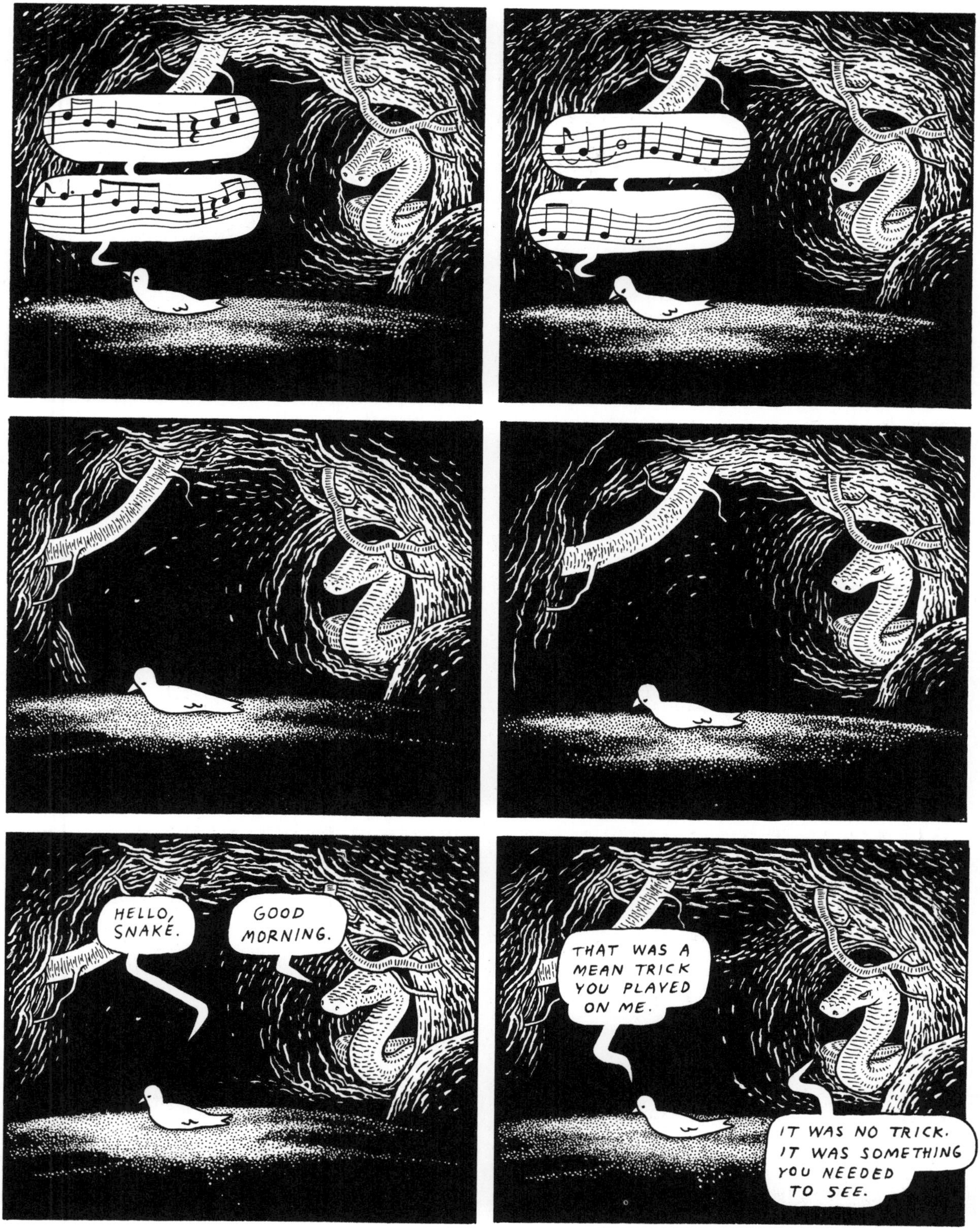
HELLO, SNAKE.
GOOD MORNING.
THAT WAS A MEAN TRICK YOU PLAYED ON ME.
IT WAS NO TRICK. IT WAS SOMETHING YOU NEEDED TO SEE.

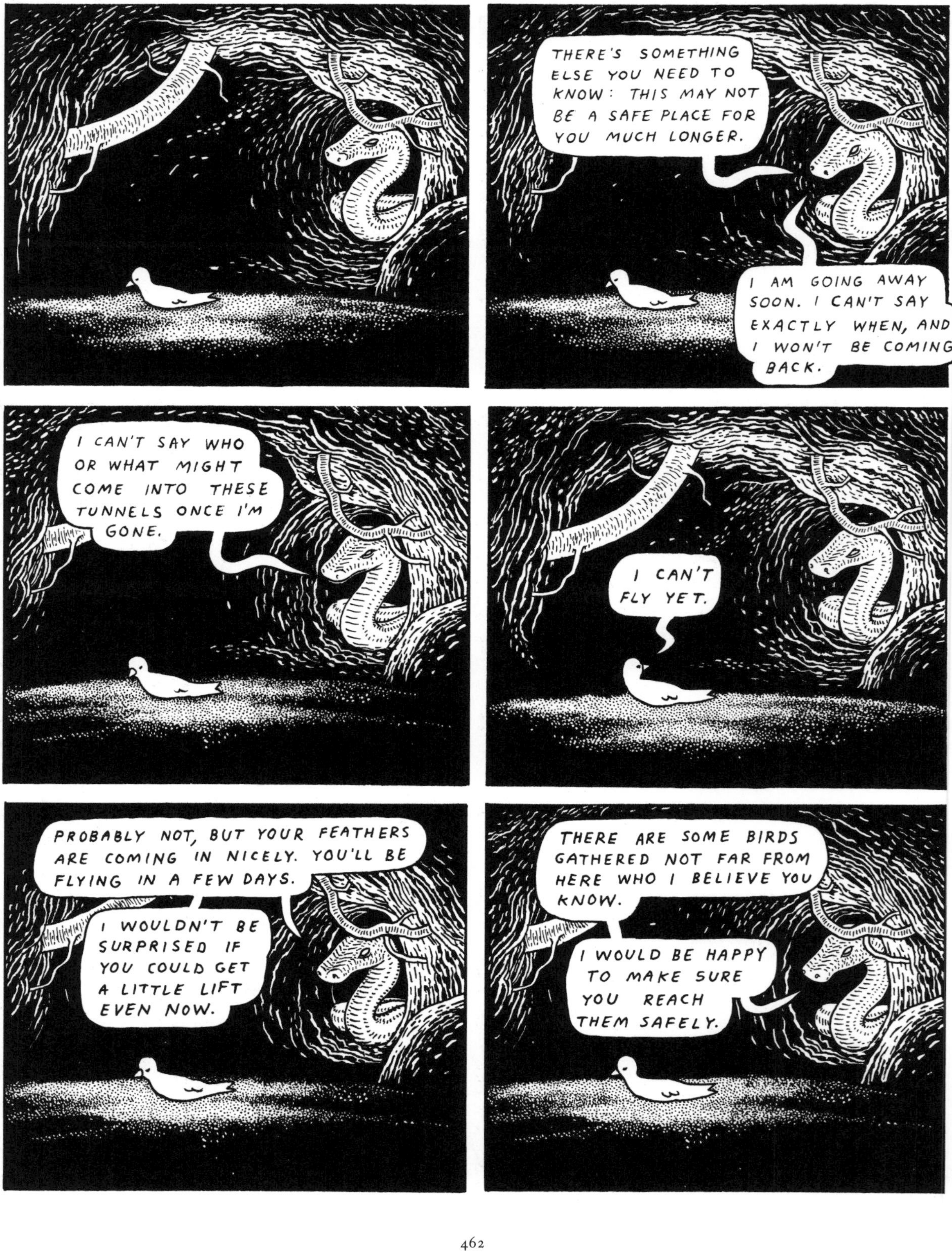
THERE'S SOMETHING ELSE YOU NEED TO KNOW: THIS MAY NOT BE A SAFE PLACE FOR YOU MUCH LONGER.
I AM GOING AWAY SOON. I CAN'T SAY EXACTLY WHEN, AND I WON'T BE COMING BACK.
I CAN'T SAY WHO OR WHAT MIGHT COME INTO THESE TUNNELS ONCE I'M GONE.
I CAN'T FLY YET.
PROBABLY NOT, BUT YOUR FEATHERS ARE COMING IN NICELY. YOU'LL BE FLYING IN A FEW DAYS.
I WOULDN'T BE SURPRISED IF YOU COULD GET A LITTLE LIFT EVEN NOW.
THERE ARE SOME BIRDS GATHERED NOT FAR FROM HERE WHO I BELIEVE YOU KNOW.
I WOULD BE HAPPY TO MAKE SURE YOU REACH THEM SAFELY.

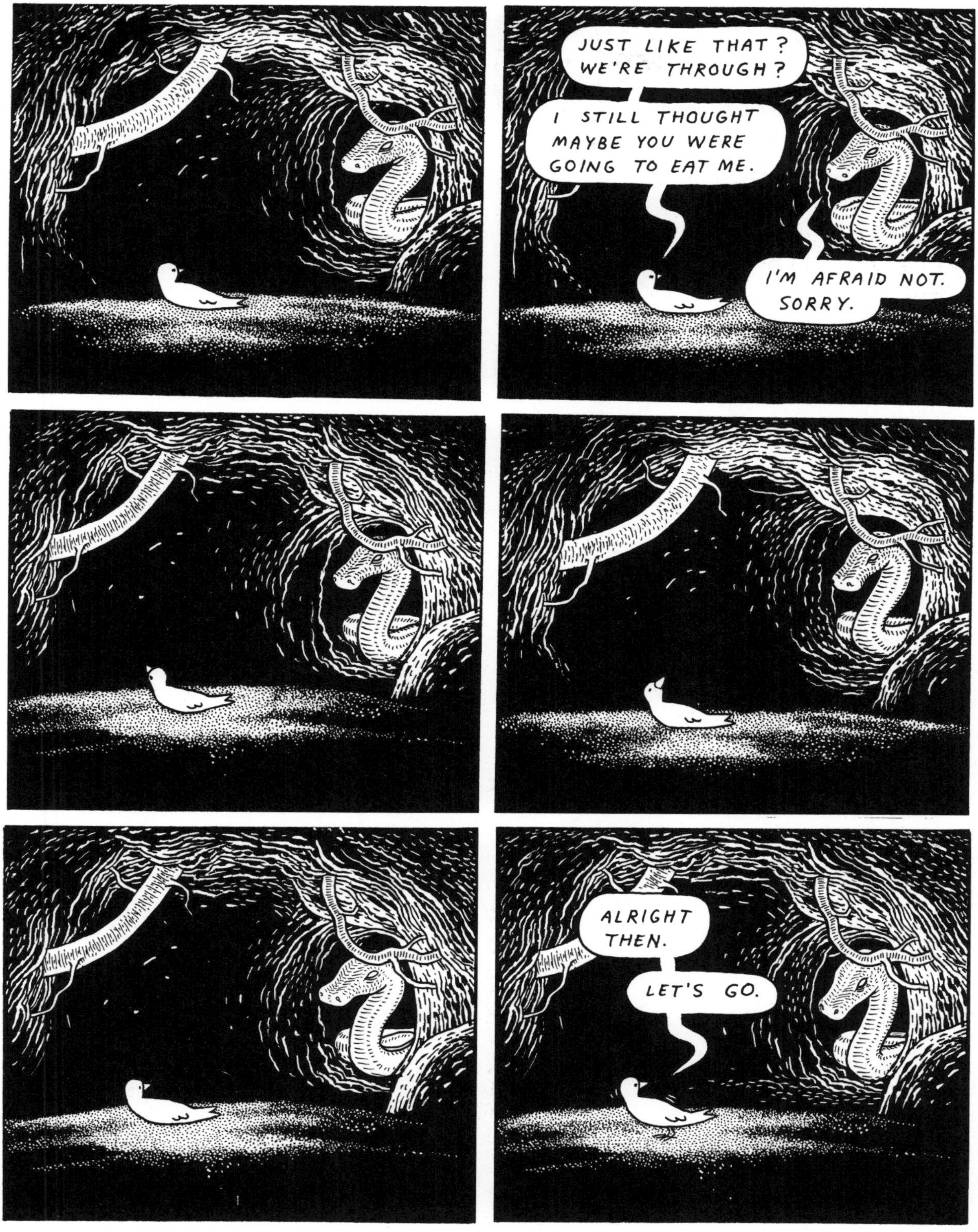
JUST LIKE THAT? WE'RE THROUGH?
I STILL THOUGHT MAYBE YOU WERE GOING TO EAT ME.
I'M AFRAID NOT. SORRY.
ALRIGHT THEN.
LET'S GO.

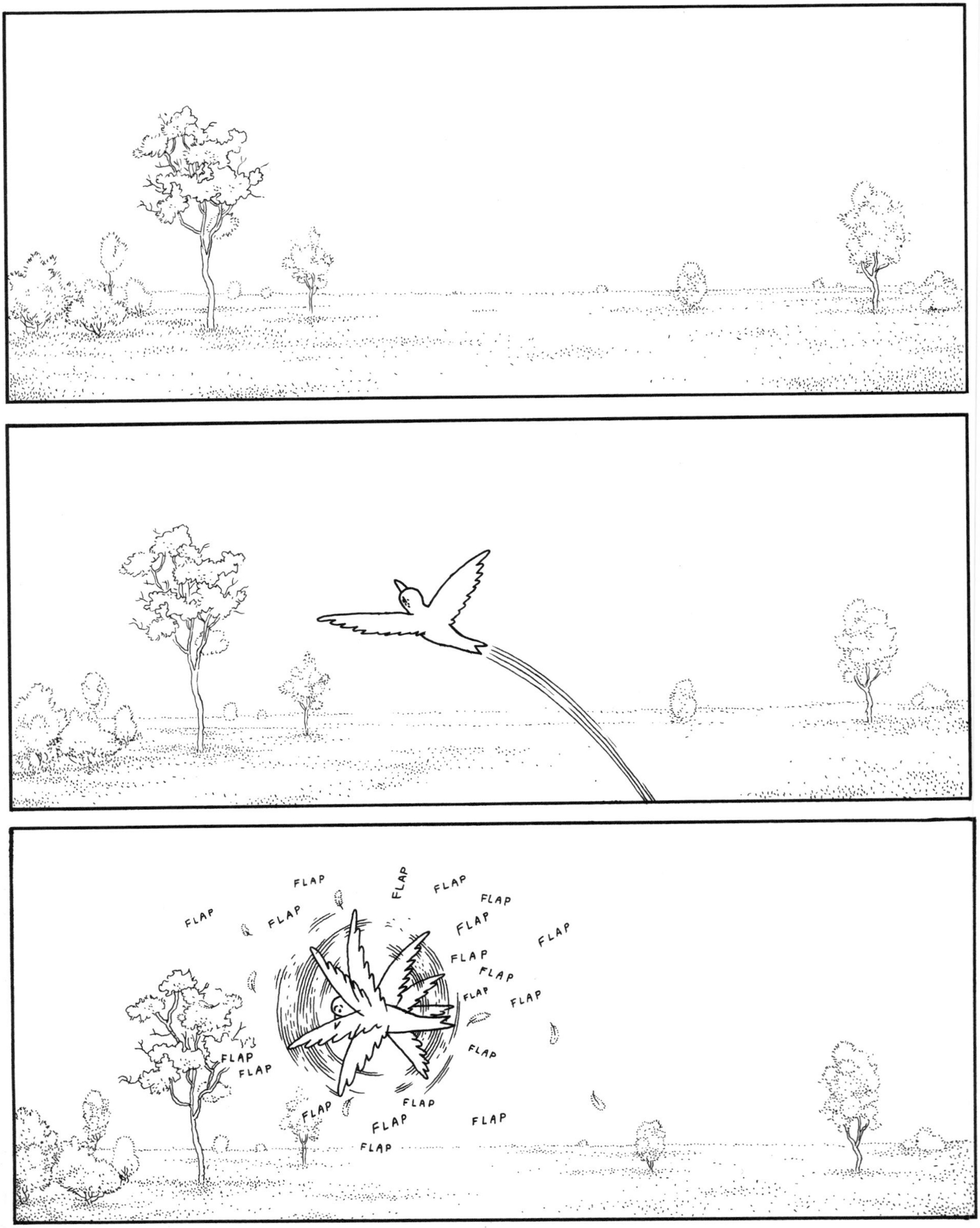
FLAP
FLAP
FLAP
FLAP
FLAP
FLAP
FLAP
FLAP
FLAP
FLAP
FLAP
FLAP
FLAP
FLAP
FLAP
FLAP
FLAP
FLAP
FLAP
FLAP

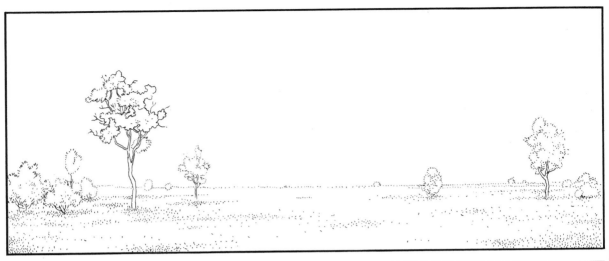

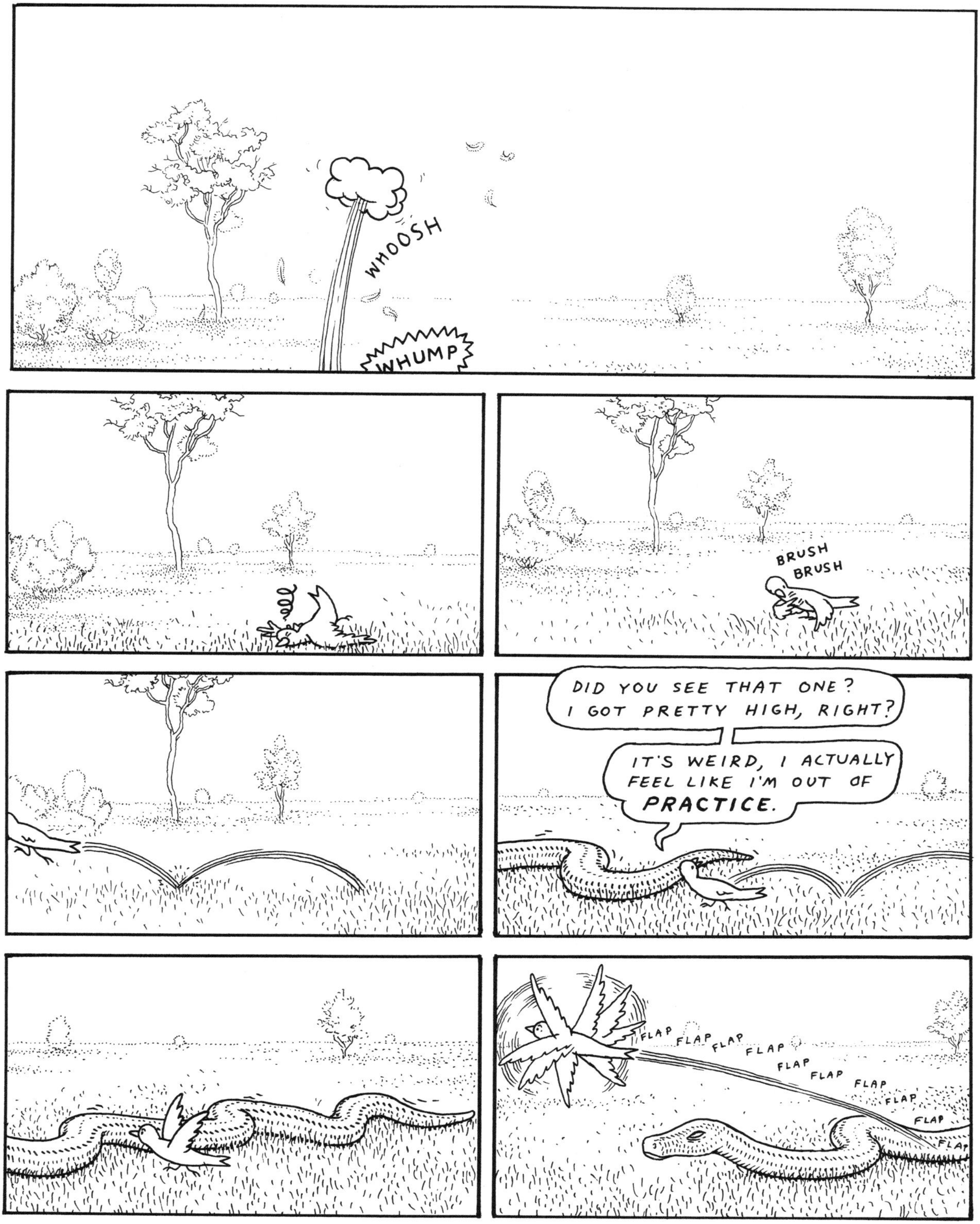
WHOOSH
WHUMP
BRUSH BRUSH
DID YOU SEE THAT ONE? I GOT PRETTY HIGH, RIGHT?
IT'S WEIRD, I ACTUALLY FEEL LIKE I'M OUT OF PRACTICE.
FLAP FLAP FLAP FLAP FLAP FLAP FLAP FLAP FLAP FLAP

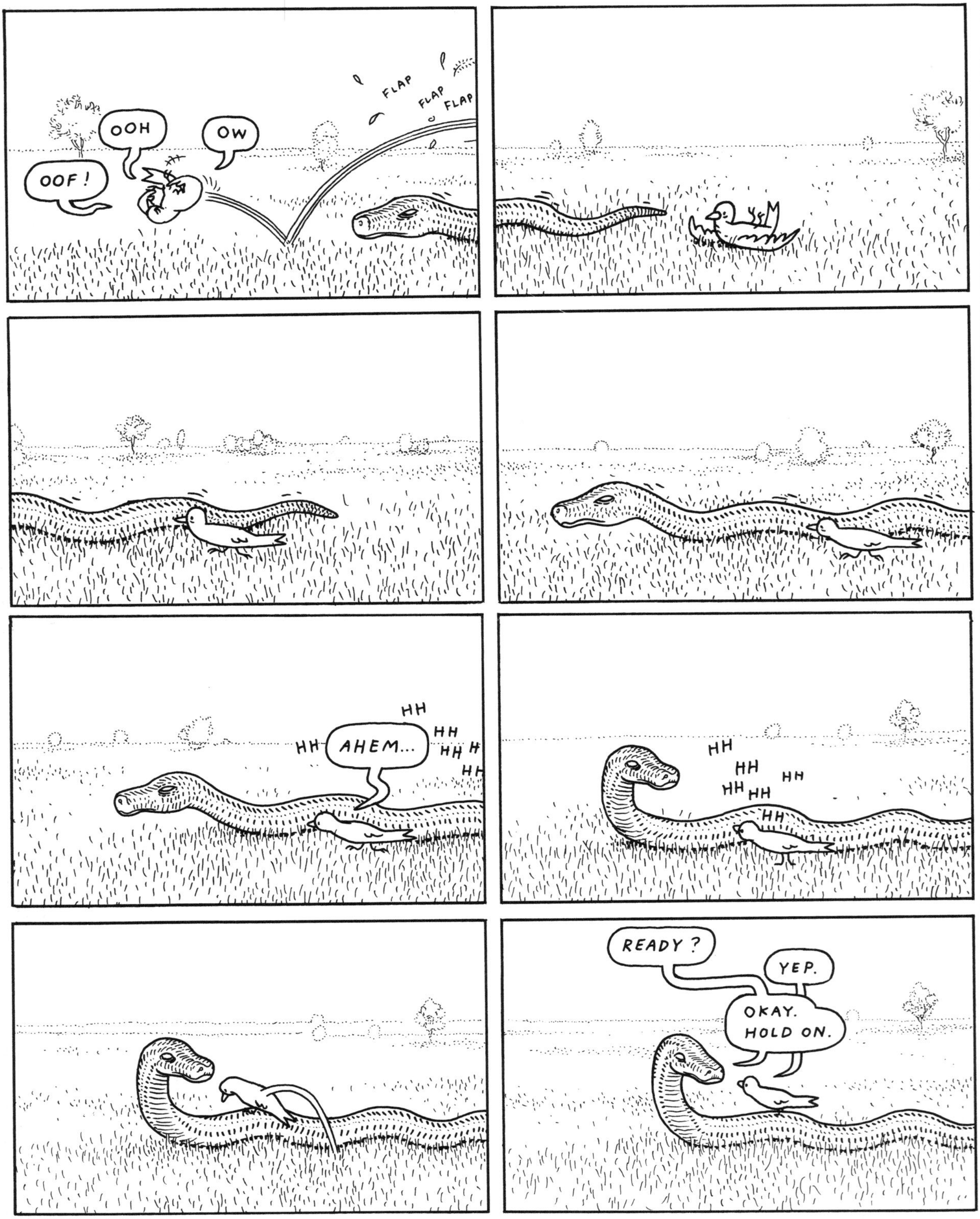
OOF!
OOH
OW
FLAP
FLAP
FLAP
HH
AHEM...
HH
HH
HH
HH
HH
HH
HH
HH
HH
HH
HH
READY?
YEP.
OKAY.
HOLD ON.

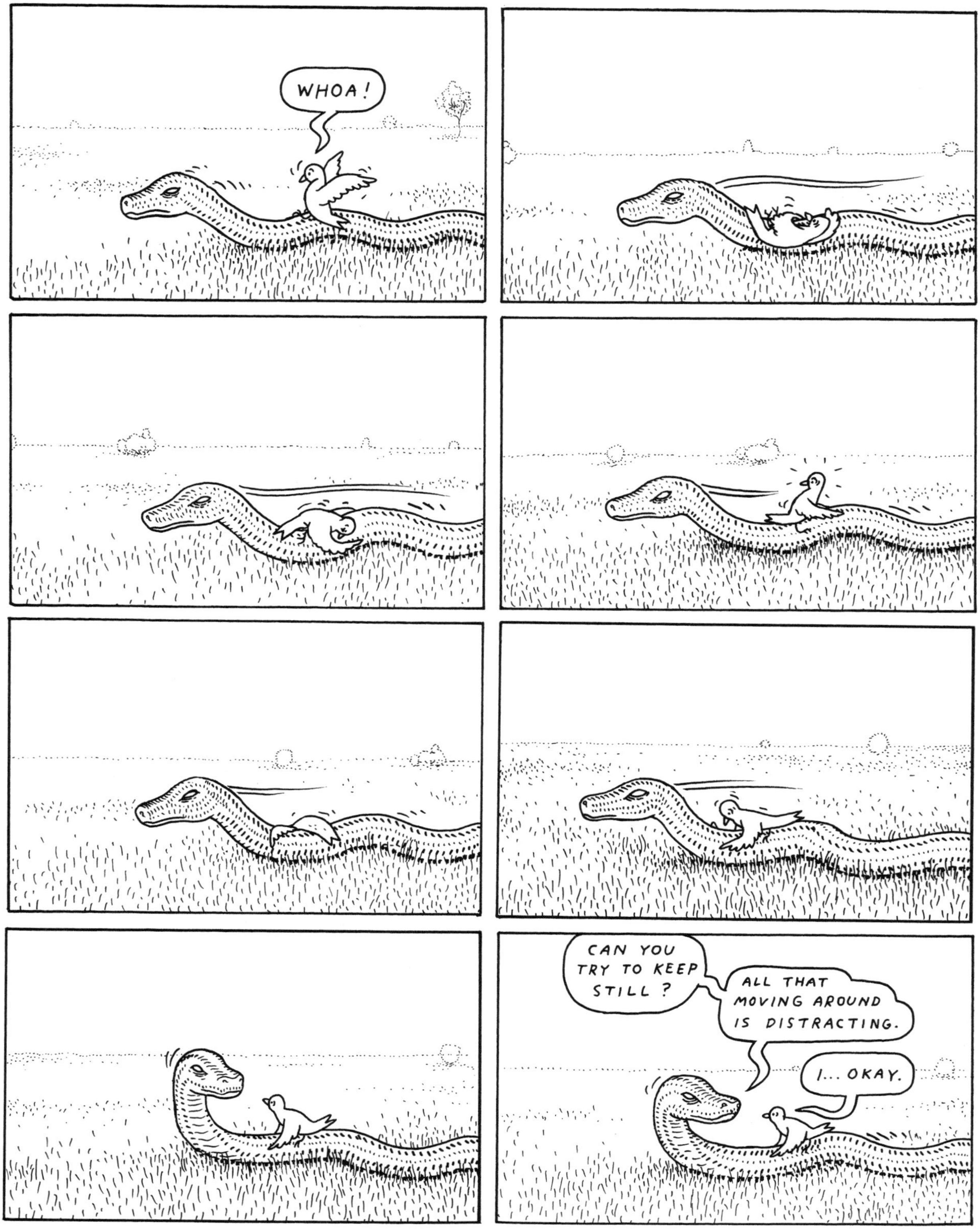
WHOA!
CAN YOU TRY TO KEEP STILL?
ALL THAT MOVING AROUND IS DISTRACTING.
I... OKAY.

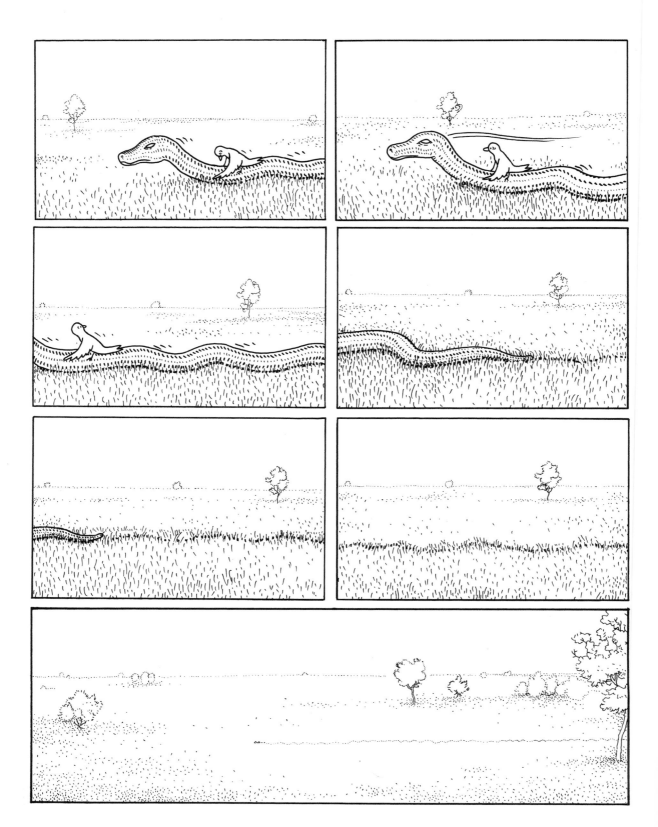

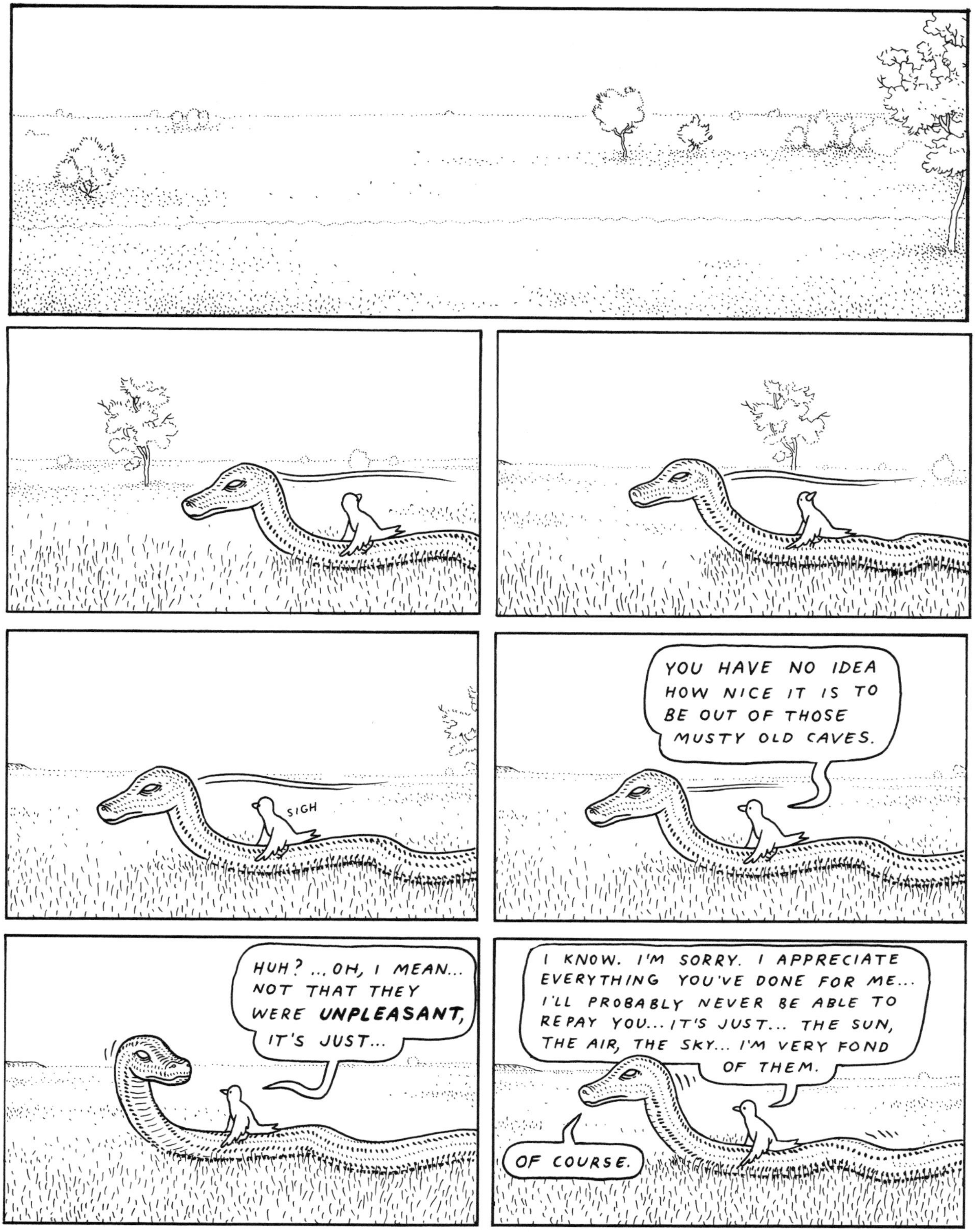
SIGH
YOU HAVE NO IDEA HOW NICE IT IS TO BE OUT OF THOSE MUSTY OLD CAVES.
HUH? ...OH, I MEAN... NOT THAT THEY WERE **UNPLEASANT,** IT'S JUST...
I KNOW. I'M SORRY. I APPRECIATE EVERYTHING YOU'VE DONE FOR ME... I'LL PROBABLY NEVER BE ABLE TO REPAY YOU... IT'S JUST... THE SUN, THE AIR, THE SKY... I'M VERY FOND OF THEM.
OF COURSE.

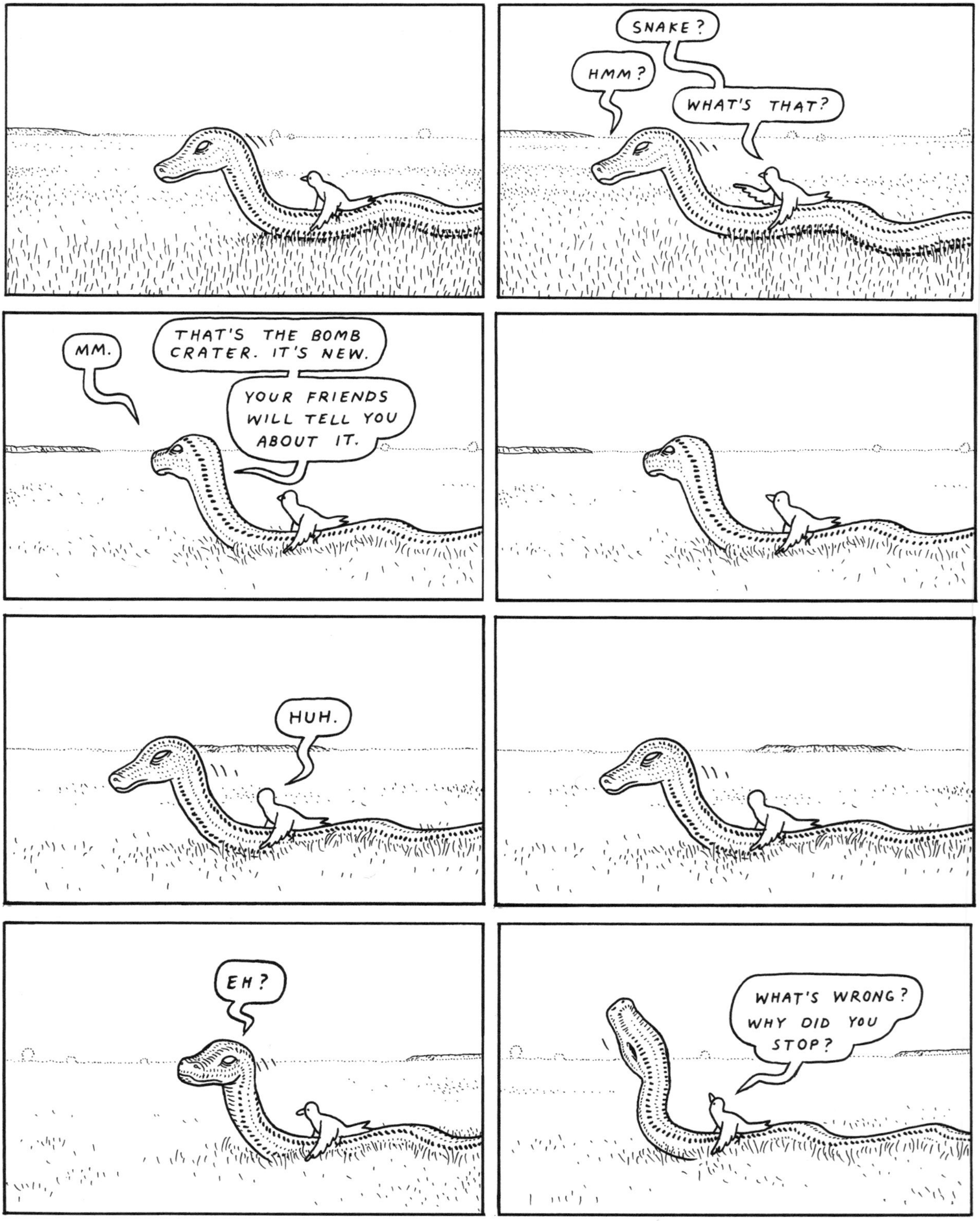
HMM?
SNAKE?
WHAT'S THAT?
MM.
THAT'S THE BOMB CRATER. IT'S NEW.
YOUR FRIENDS WILL TELL YOU ABOUT IT.
HUH.
EH?
WHAT'S WRONG? WHY DID YOU STOP?

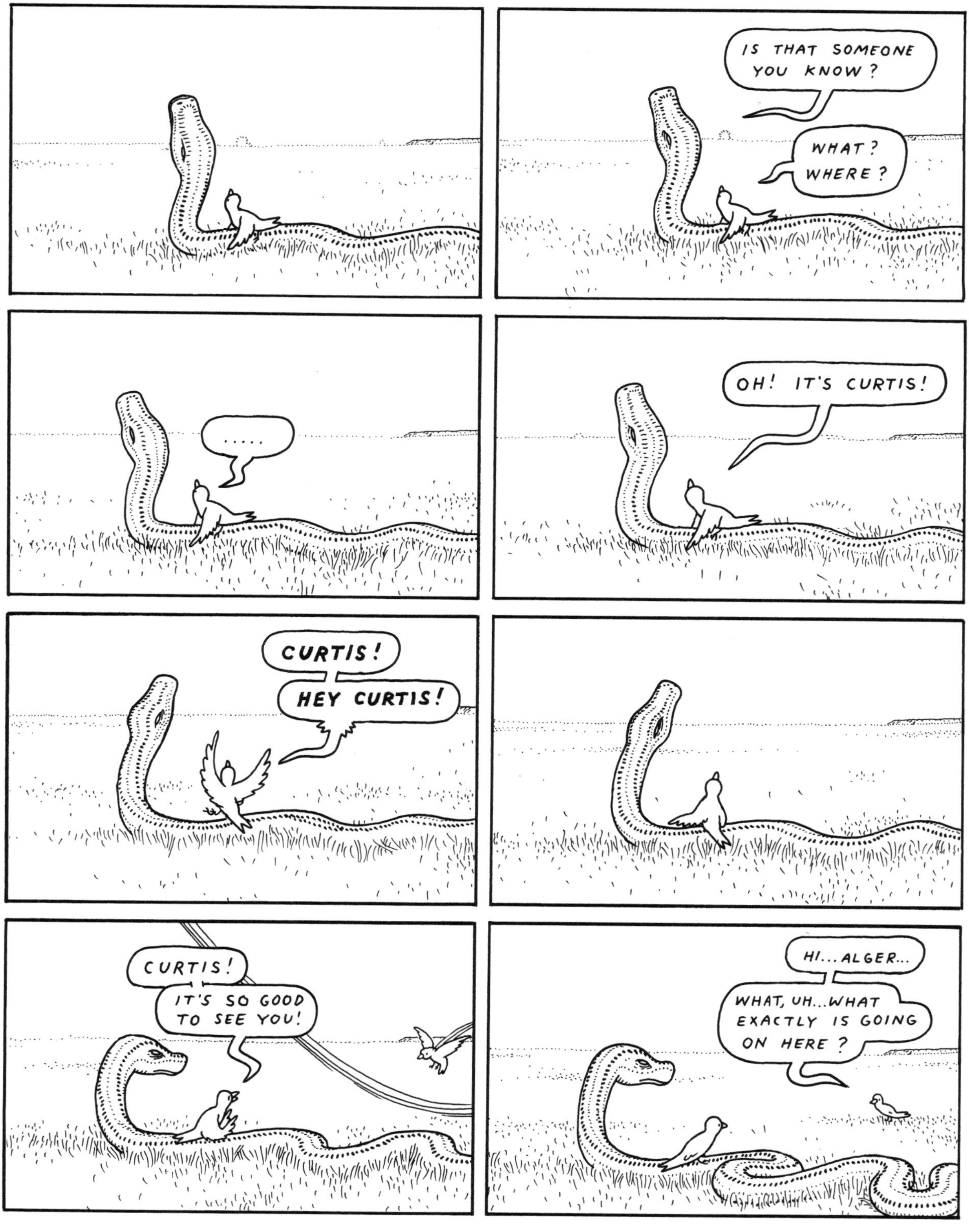
IS THAT SOMEONE YOU KNOW?
WHAT? WHERE?
.....
OH! IT'S CURTIS!
CURTIS!
HEY CURTIS!
CURTIS!
IT'S SO GOOD TO SEE YOU!
HI... ALGER...
WHAT, UH... WHAT EXACTLY IS GOING ON HERE?

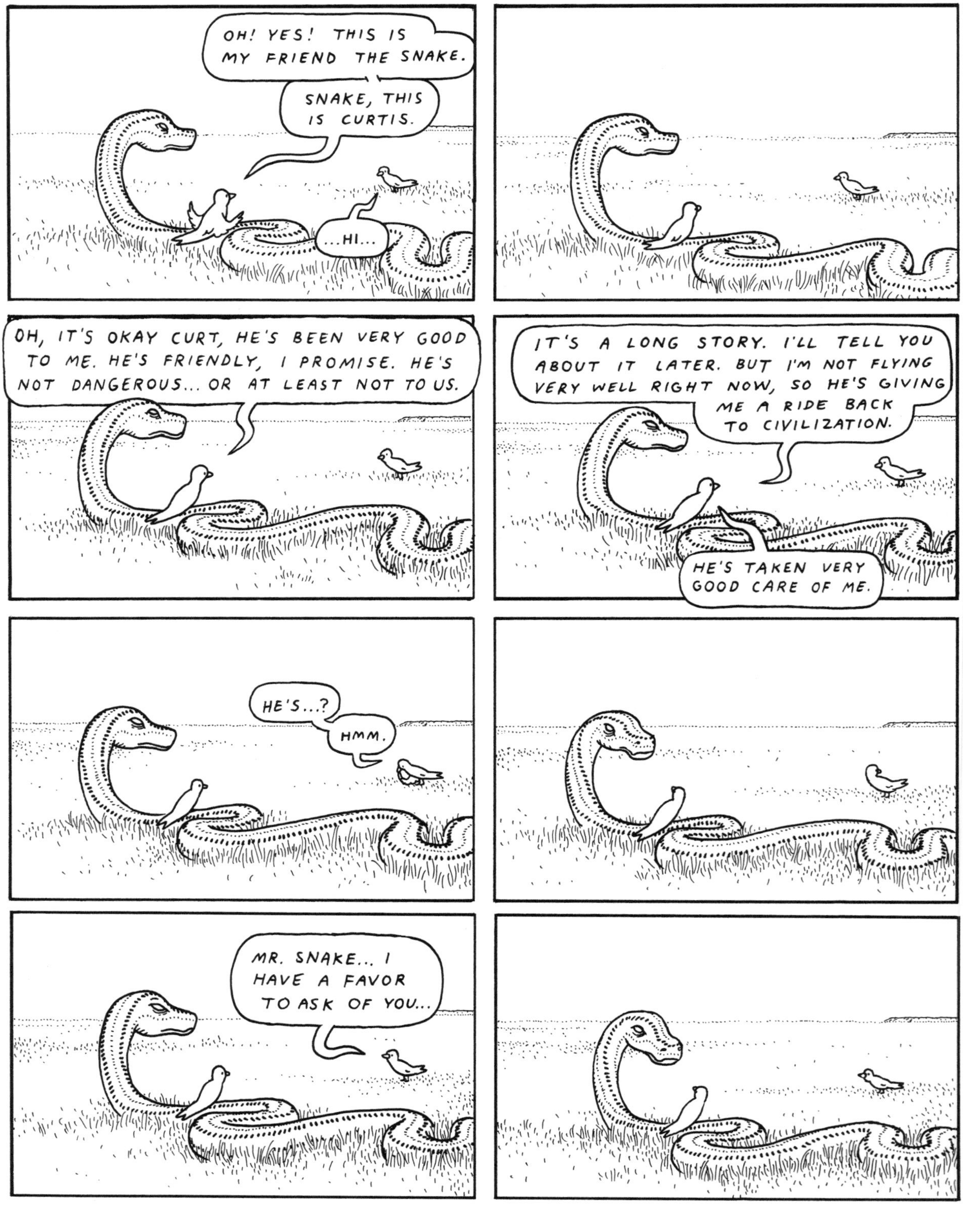
OH! YES! THIS IS MY FRIEND THE SNAKE.
SNAKE, THIS IS CURTIS.
...HI...
OH, IT'S OKAY CURT, HE'S BEEN VERY GOOD TO ME. HE'S FRIENDLY, I PROMISE. HE'S NOT DANGEROUS... OR AT LEAST NOT TO US.
IT'S A LONG STORY. I'LL TELL YOU ABOUT IT LATER. BUT I'M NOT FLYING VERY WELL RIGHT NOW, SO HE'S GIVING ME A RIDE BACK TO CIVILIZATION.
HE'S TAKEN VERY GOOD CARE OF ME.
HE'S...?
HMM.
MR. SNAKE... I HAVE A FAVOR TO ASK OF YOU...

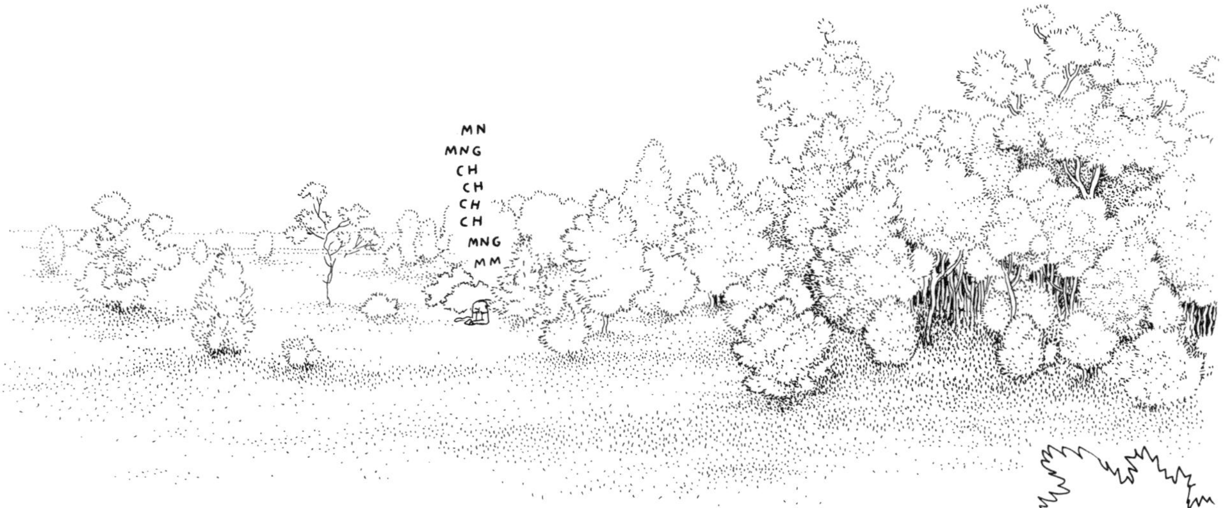
MN
MNG
CH
CH
CH
CH
MNG
MM

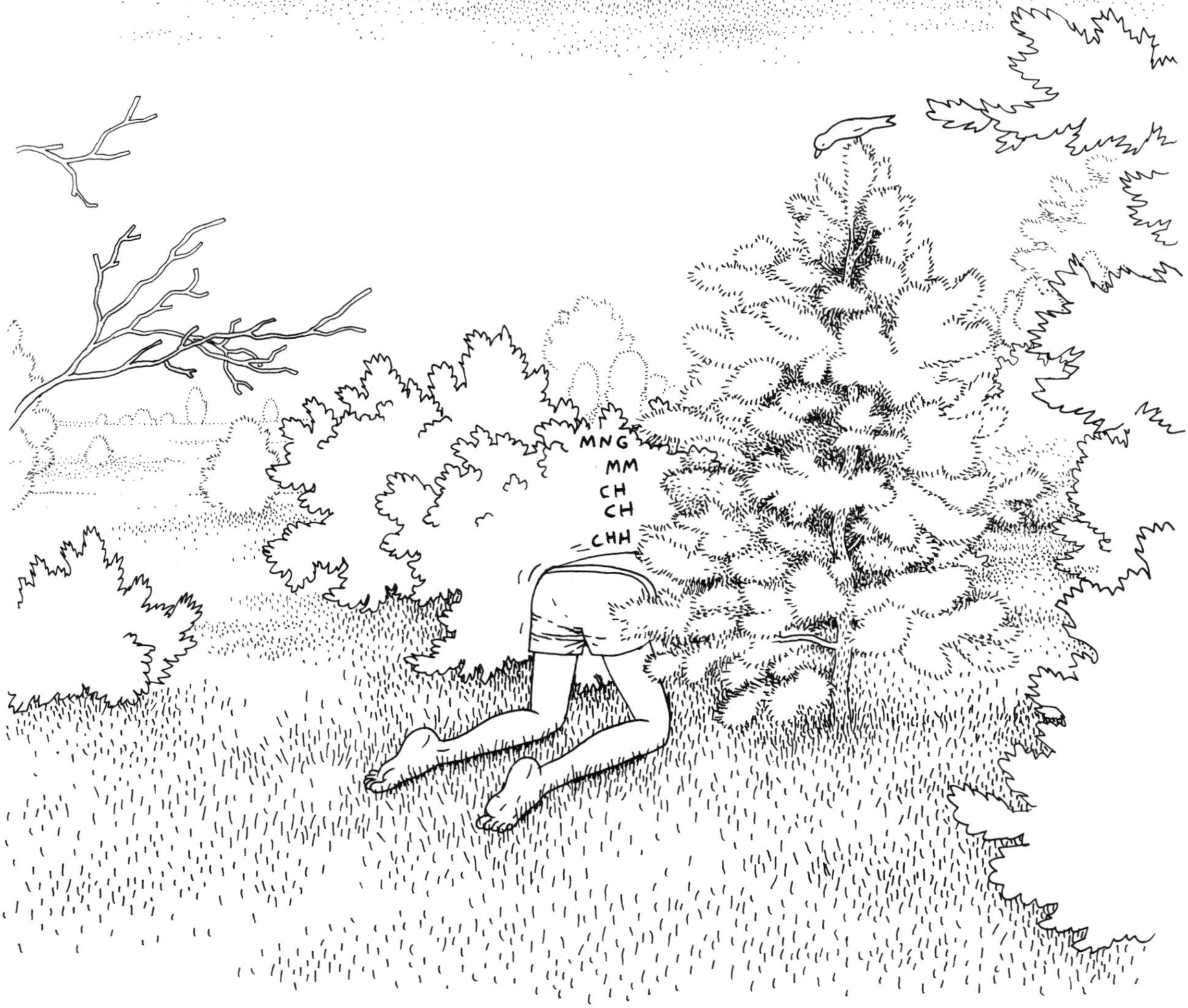
MNG
MM
CH
CH
CHH

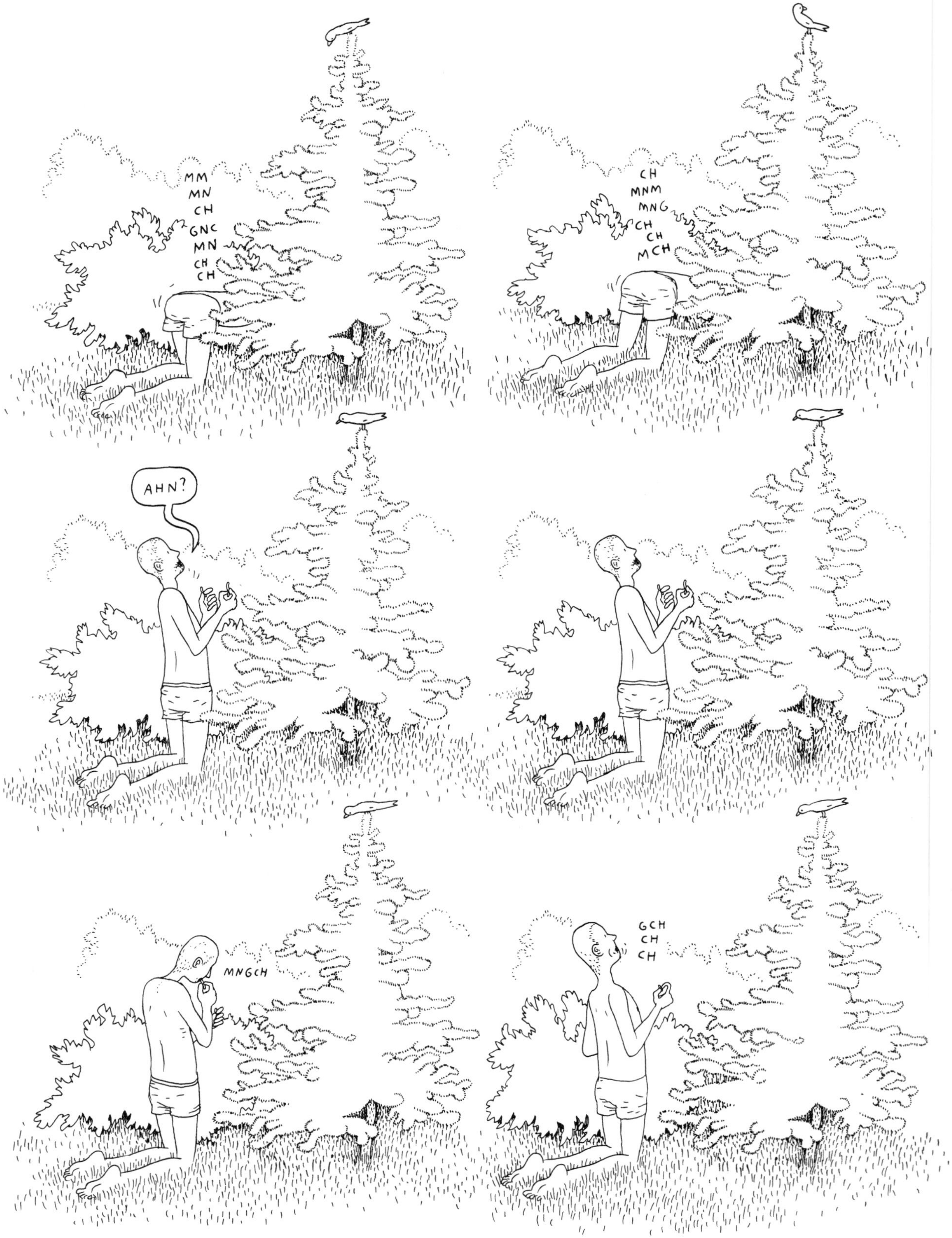
MM
MN
CH
GNC
MN
CH
CH
CH
MNM
MNG
CH
CH
MCH
AHN?
MNGCH
GCH
CH
CH

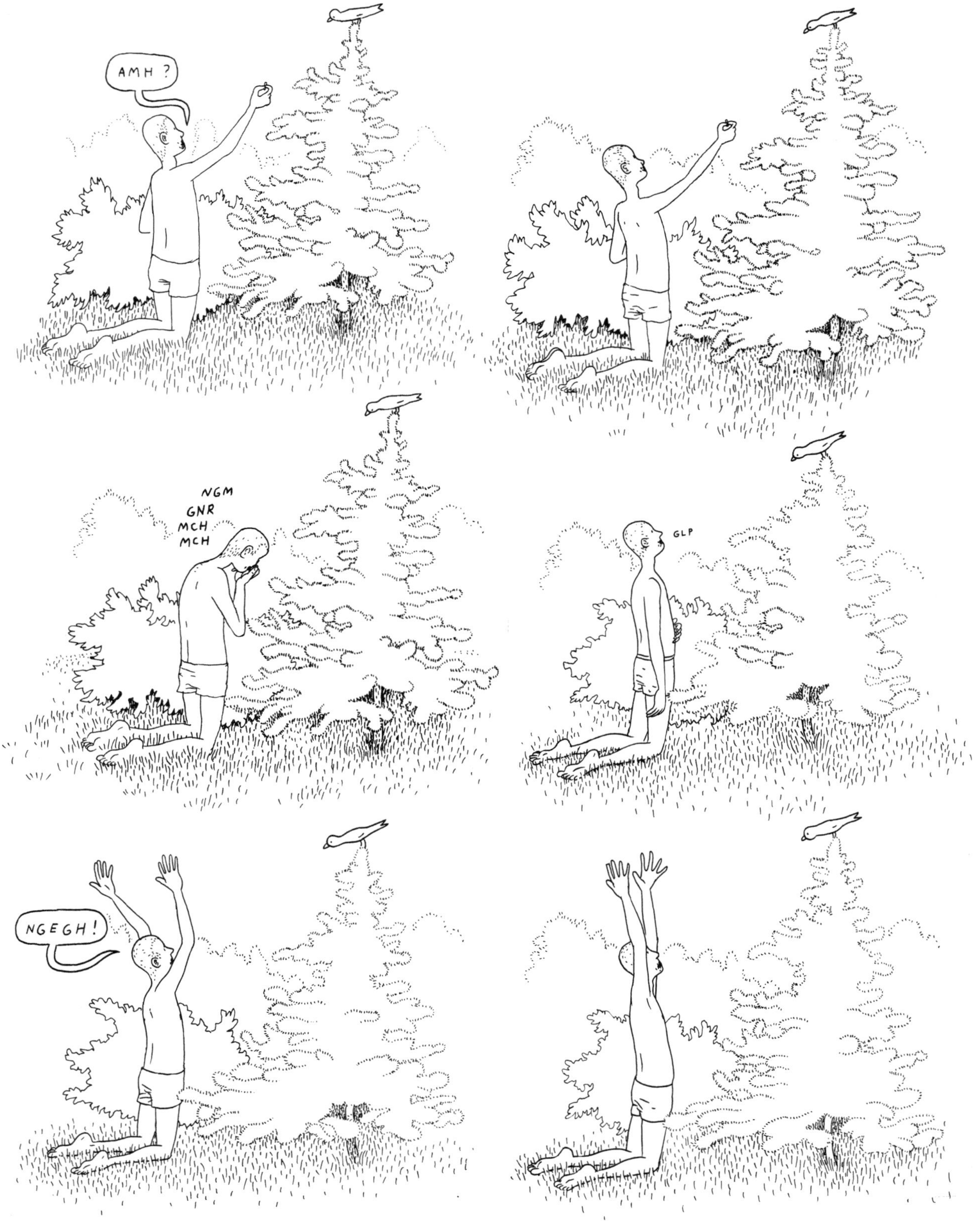
AMH?
NGM
GNR
MCH
MCH
GLP
NGEGH!

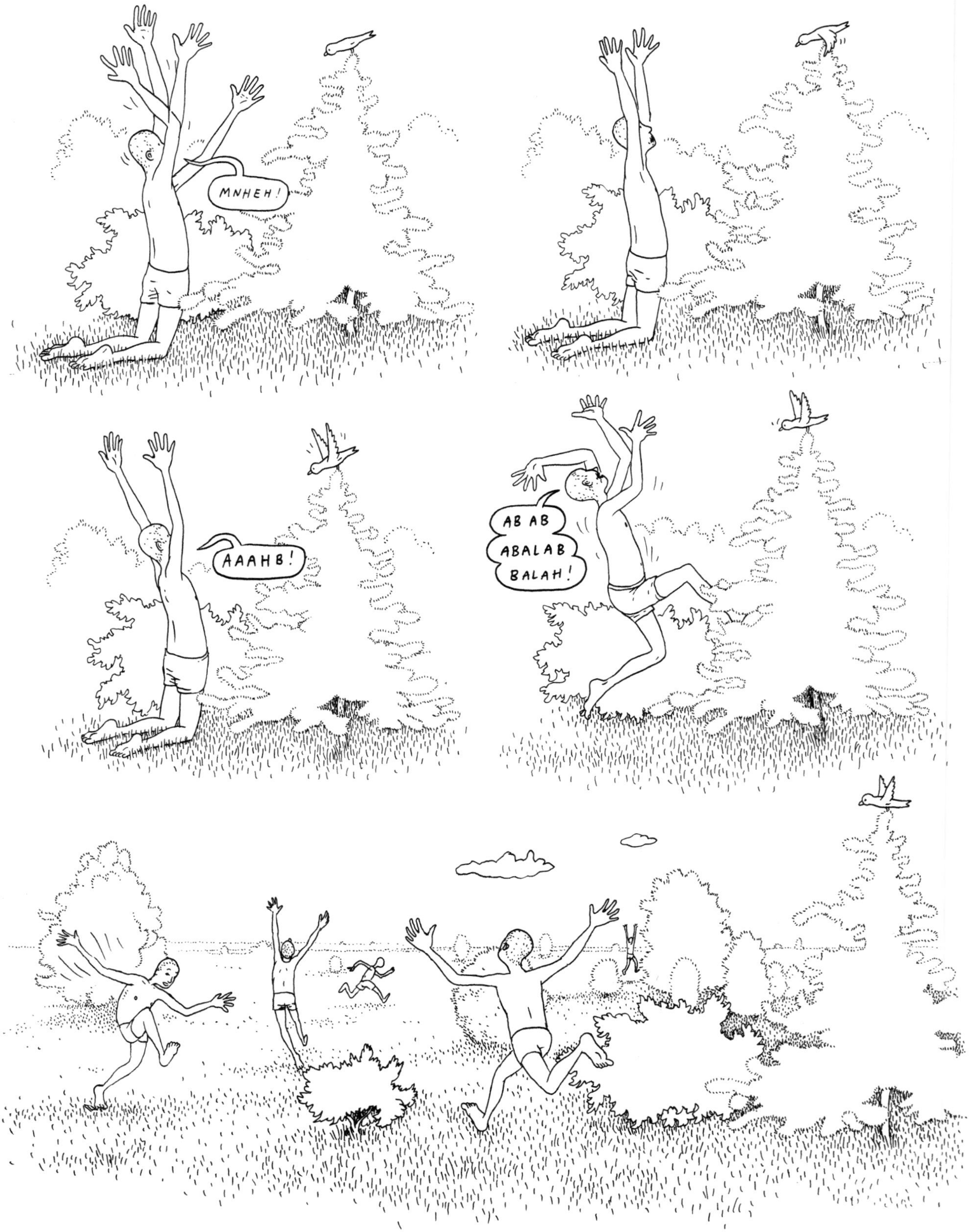
MNHEH!
AAAHB!
AB AB ABALAB BALAH!

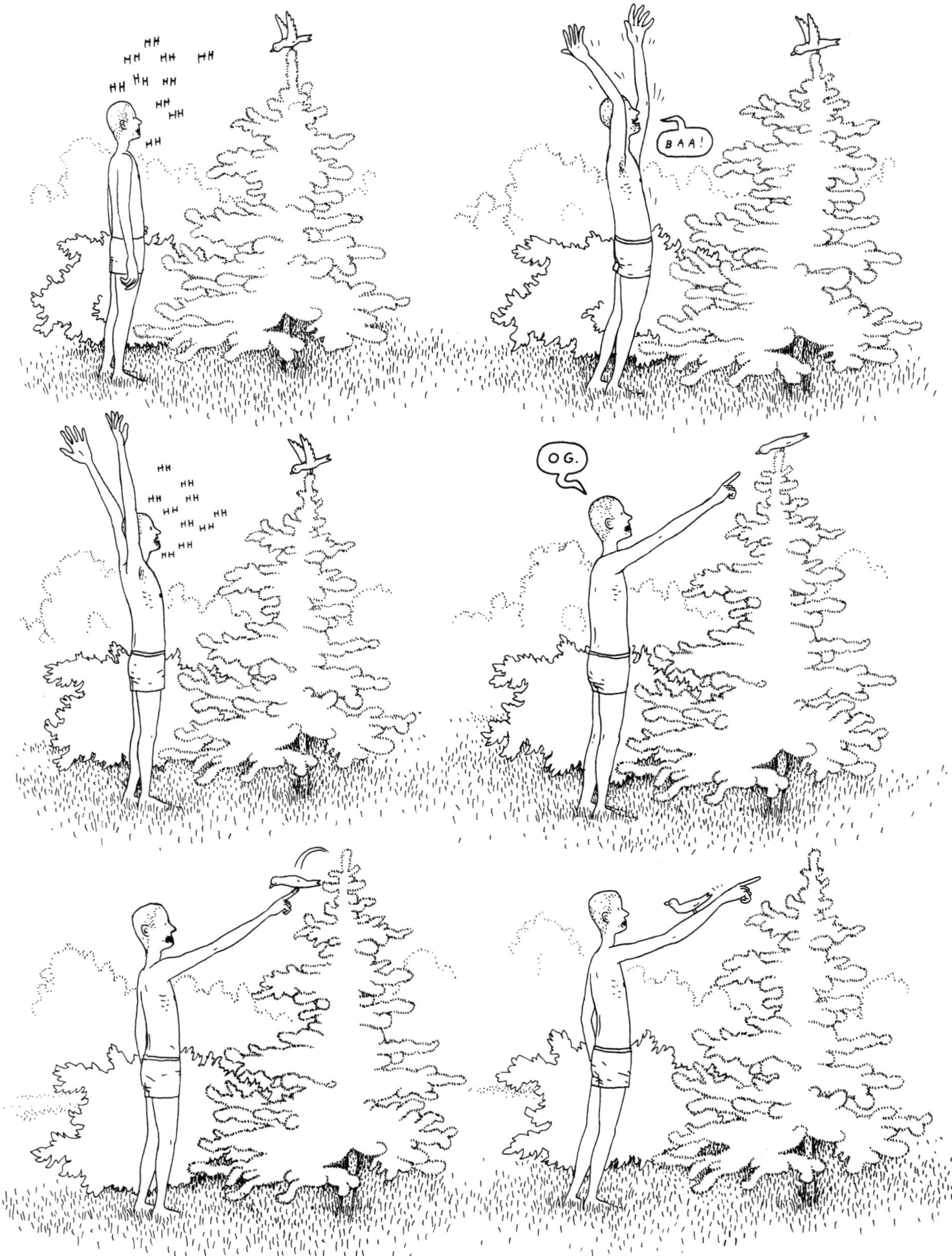
HH HH HH HH HH HH HH HH HH HH HH
BAA!
HH HH HH HH HH HH HH HH HH
OG.

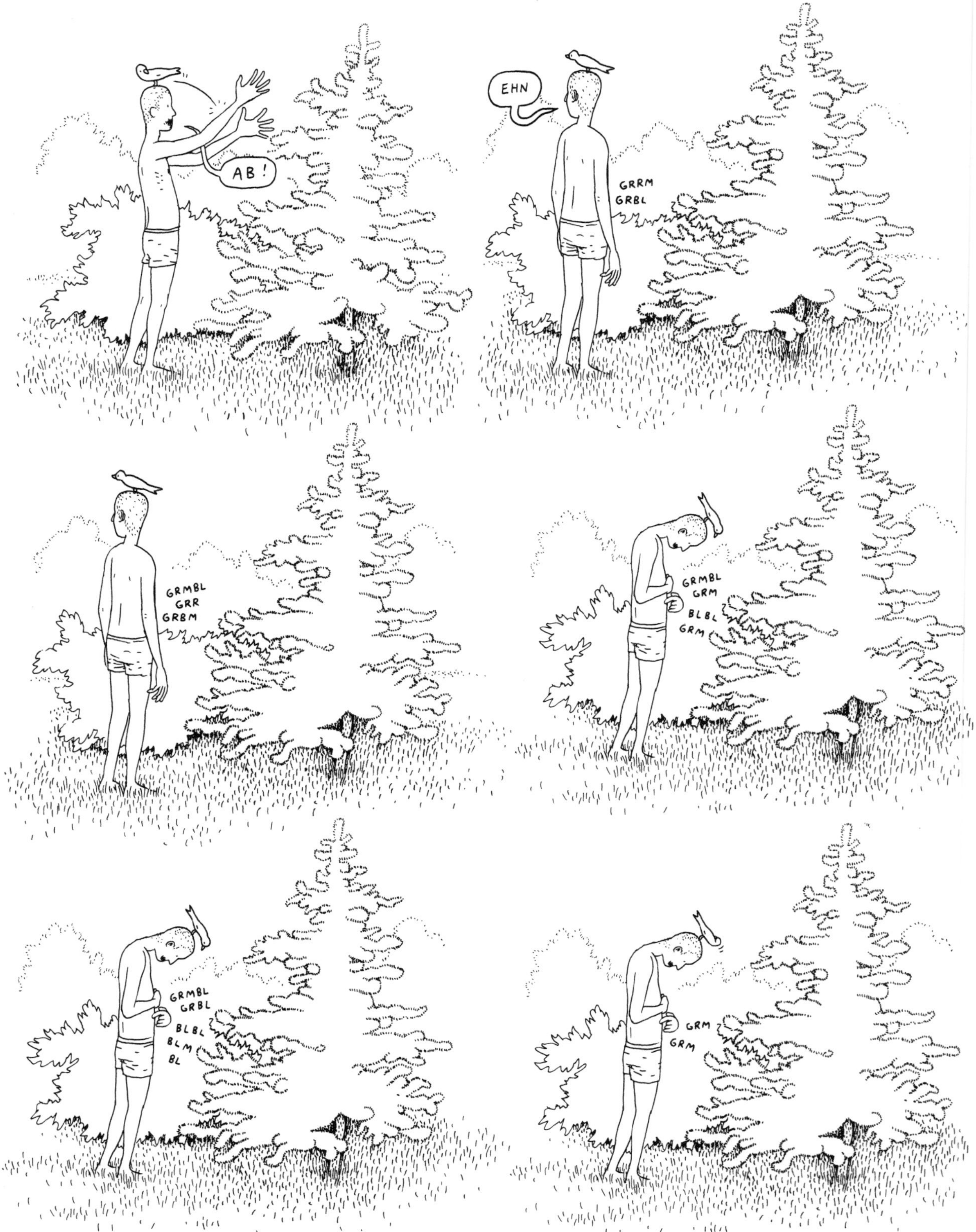
AB!
EHN
GRRM
GRBL
GRMBL
GRR
GRBM
GRMBL
GRM
BLBL
GRM
GRMBL
GRBL
BLBL
BLM
BL
GRM
GRM

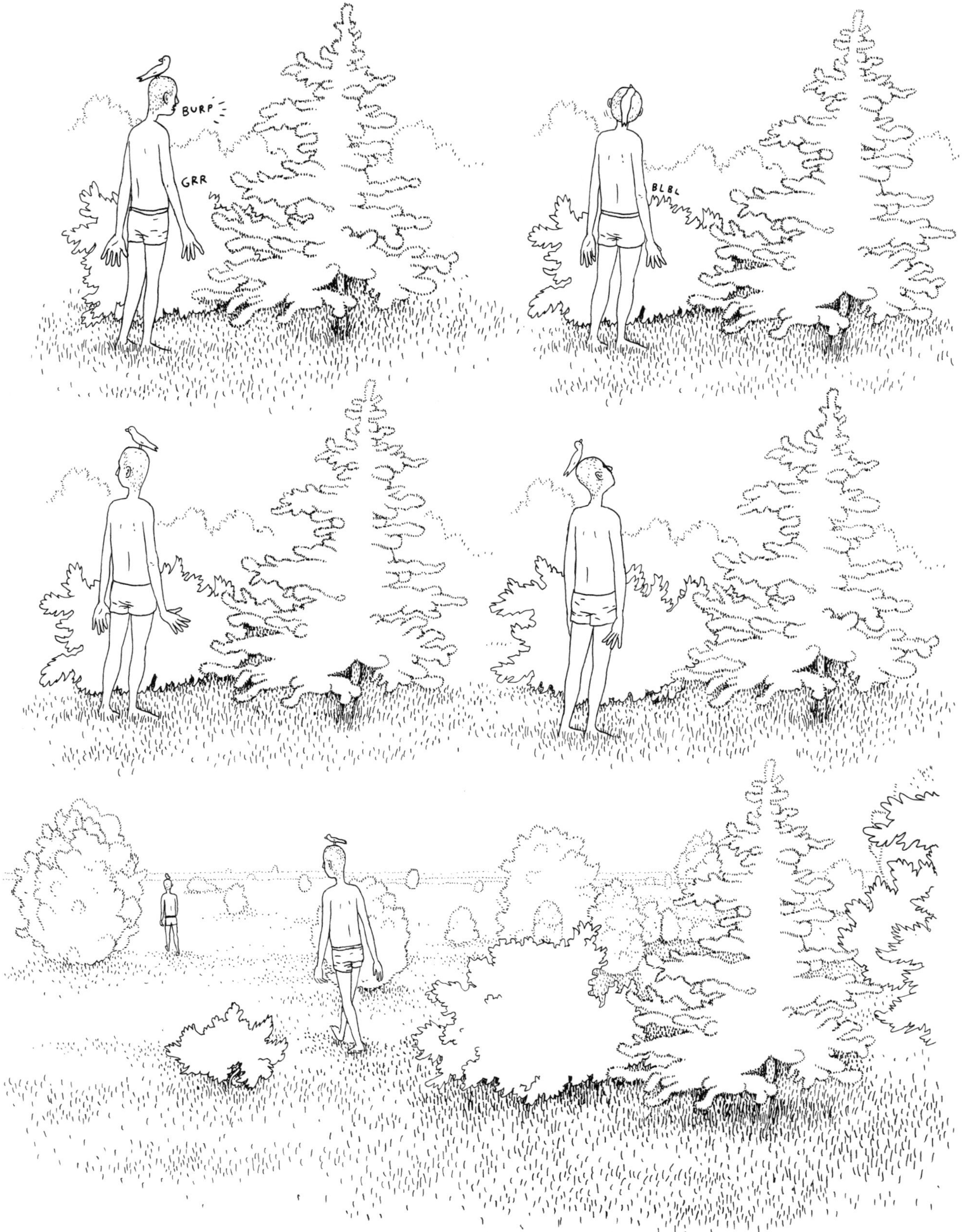
BURP
GRR
BLBL

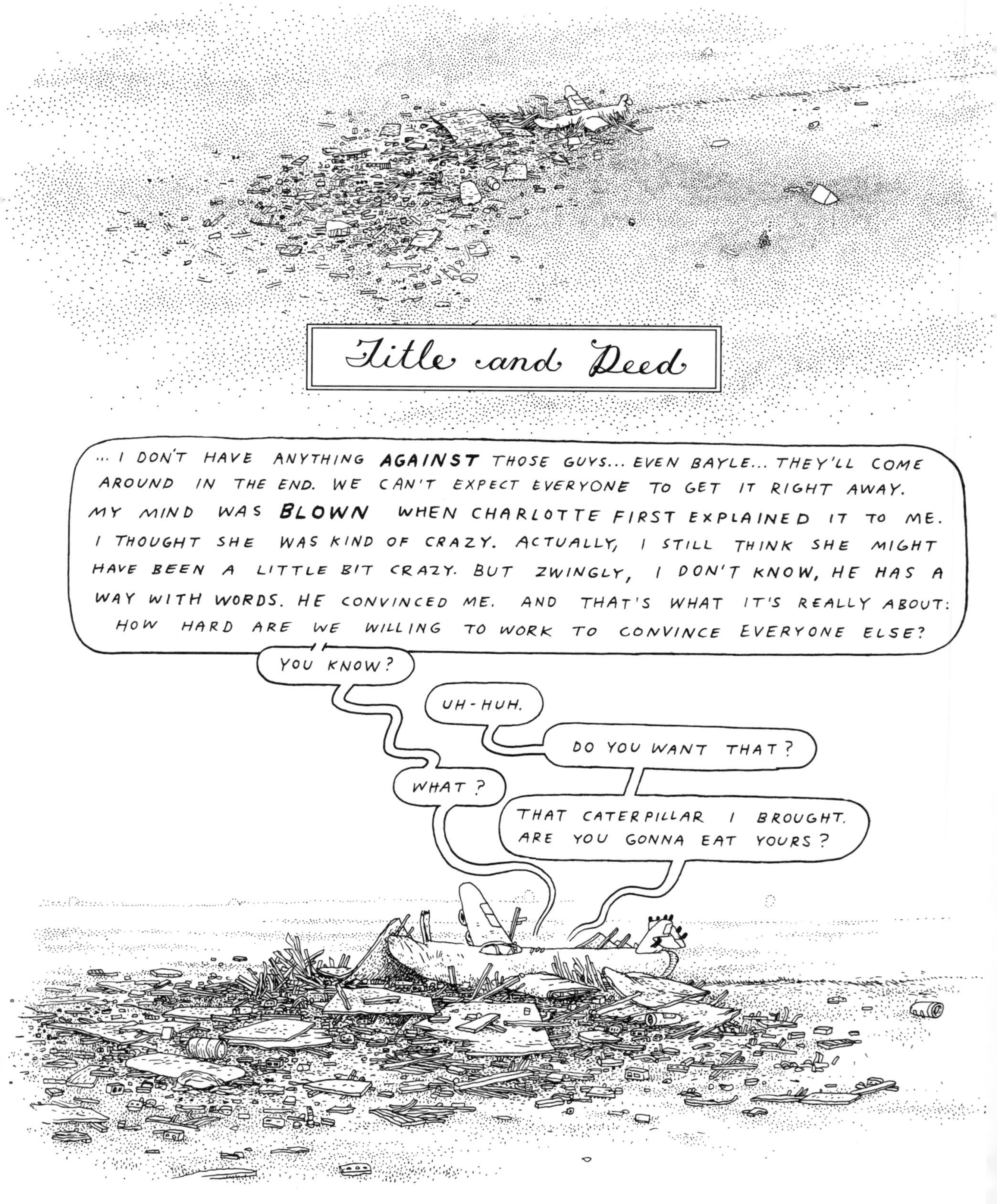
Title and Deed
... I DON'T HAVE ANYTHING AGAINST THOSE GUYS... EVEN BAYLE... THEY'LL COME AROUND IN THE END. WE CAN'T EXPECT EVERYONE TO GET IT RIGHT AWAY. MY MIND WAS BLOWN WHEN CHARLOTTE FIRST EXPLAINED IT TO ME. I THOUGHT SHE WAS KIND OF CRAZY. ACTUALLY, I STILL THINK SHE MIGHT HAVE BEEN A LITTLE BIT CRAZY. BUT ZWINGLY, I DON'T KNOW, HE HAS A WAY WITH WORDS. HE CONVINCED ME. AND THAT'S WHAT IT'S REALLY ABOUT: HOW HARD ARE WE WILLING TO WORK TO CONVINCE EVERYONE ELSE?
YOU KNOW?
UH-HUH.
DO YOU WANT THAT?
WHAT?
THAT CATERPILLAR I BROUGHT. ARE YOU GONNA EAT YOURS?

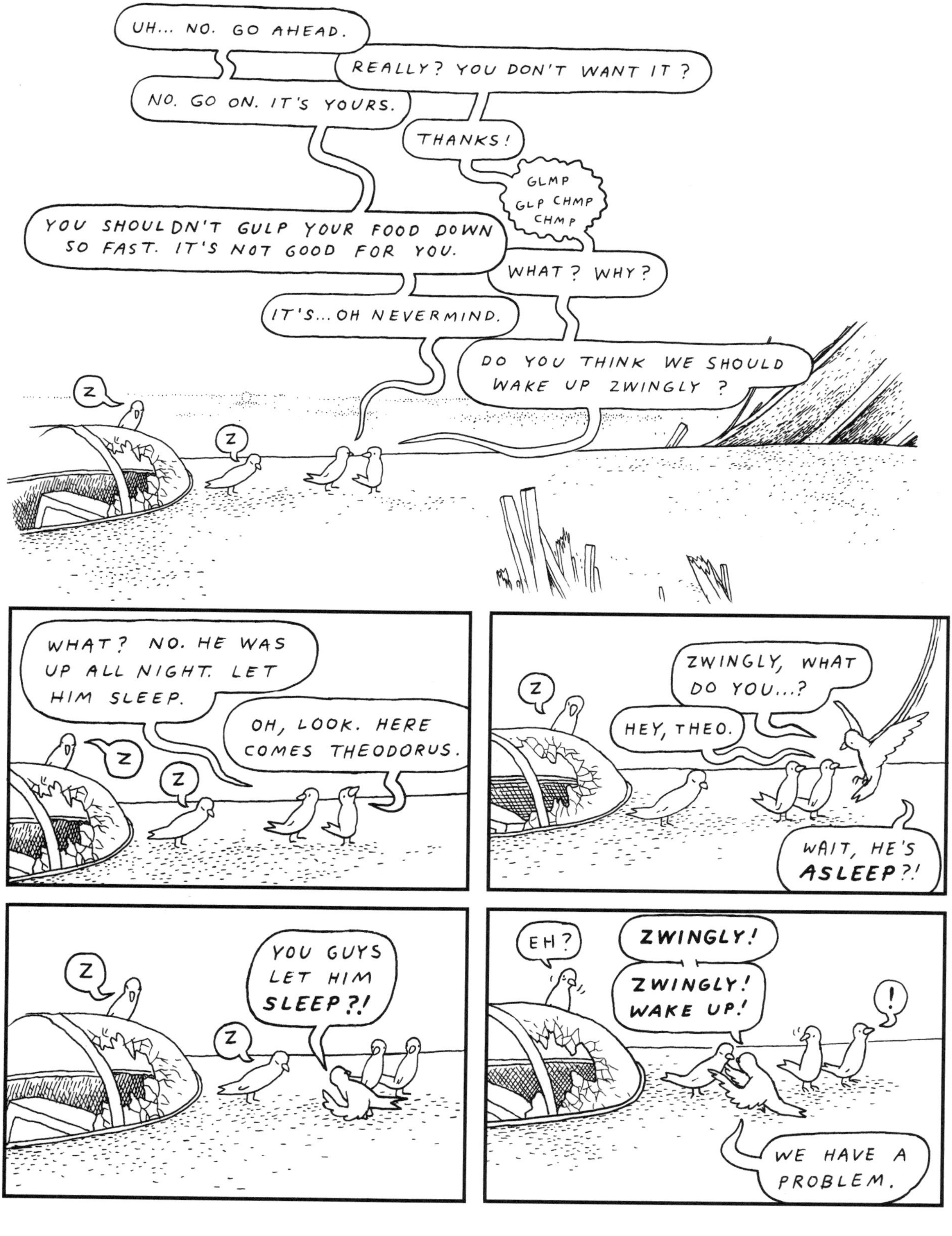
UH... NO. GO AHEAD.
REALLY? YOU DON'T WANT IT?
NO. GO ON. IT'S YOURS.
THANKS!
GLMP GLP CHMP CHMP
YOU SHOULDN'T GULP YOUR FOOD DOWN SO FAST. IT'S NOT GOOD FOR YOU.
WHAT? WHY?
IT'S... OH NEVERMIND.
DO YOU THINK WE SHOULD WAKE UP ZWINGLY?
Z
Z
WHAT? NO. HE WAS UP ALL NIGHT. LET HIM SLEEP.
OH, LOOK. HERE COMES THEODORUS.
Z
Z
ZWINGLY, WHAT DO YOU...?
HEY, THEO.
Z
WAIT, HE'S **ASLEEP**?!
Z
Z
YOU GUYS LET HIM **SLEEP?!**
EH?
ZWINGLY!
ZWINGLY! WAKE UP!
!
WE HAVE A PROBLEM.

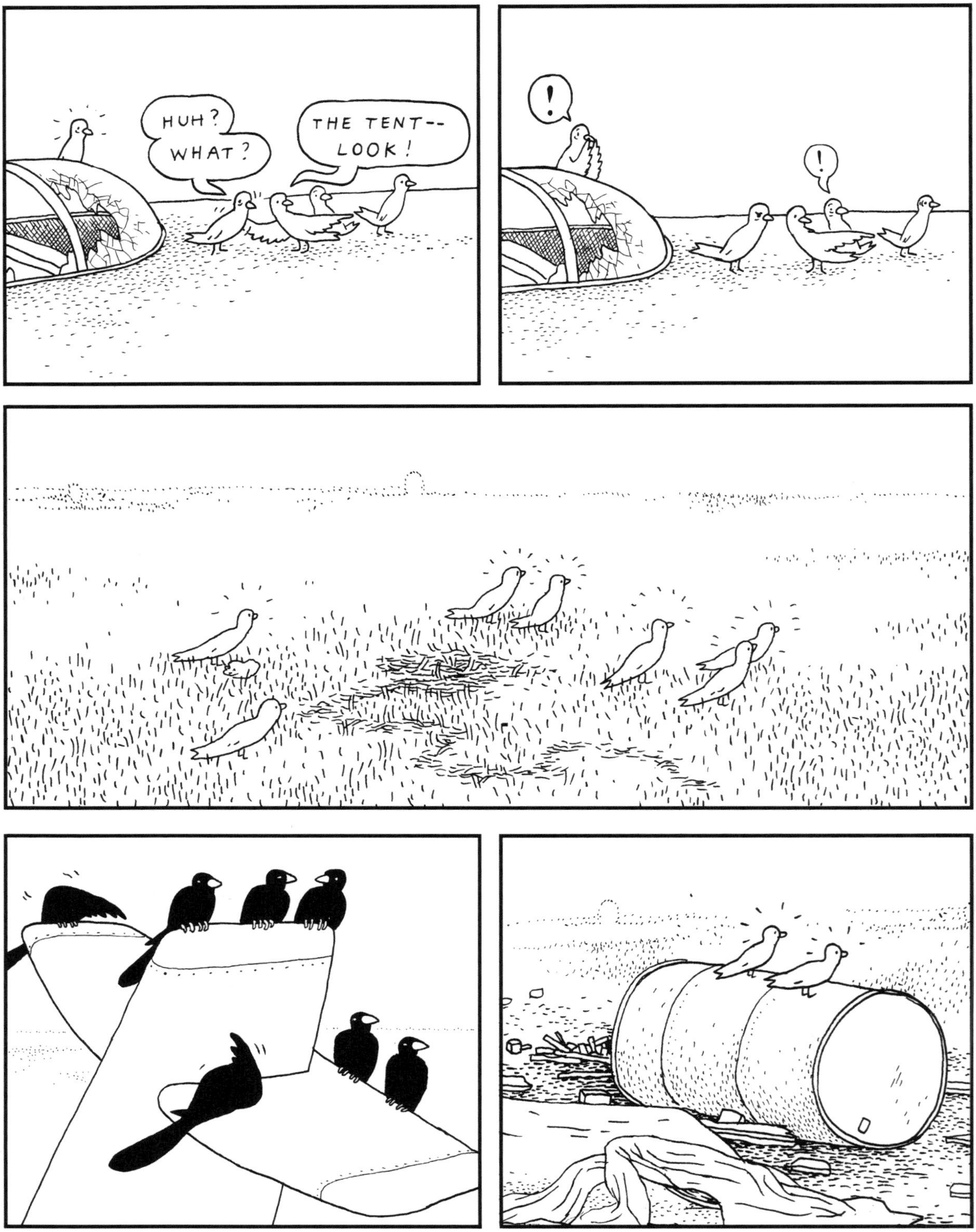
HUH? WHAT?
THE TENT-- LOOK!
!
!

YOU SHOULD HAVE WOKEN ME EARLIER.

I'LL GO BITE HIM IF YOU WANT.

BUT SOMEONE IS GOING TO HAVE TO TAKE CARE OF BAYLE.

IT'S GOING TO TAKE ALL OF YOU. ORGANIZE EVERY-ONE. GET HIM OUT OF THERE. DO WHAT YOU HAVE TO DO.

AND BE QUICK.

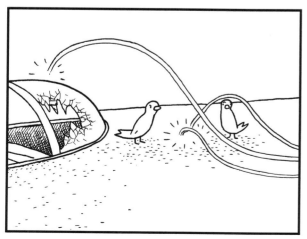

YOU TOO. WHAT ARE YOU WAITING FOR?

I... UH... SHOULDN'T SOMEONE STAY HERE IN CASE YOU HAVE A MESSAGE TO CONVEY?

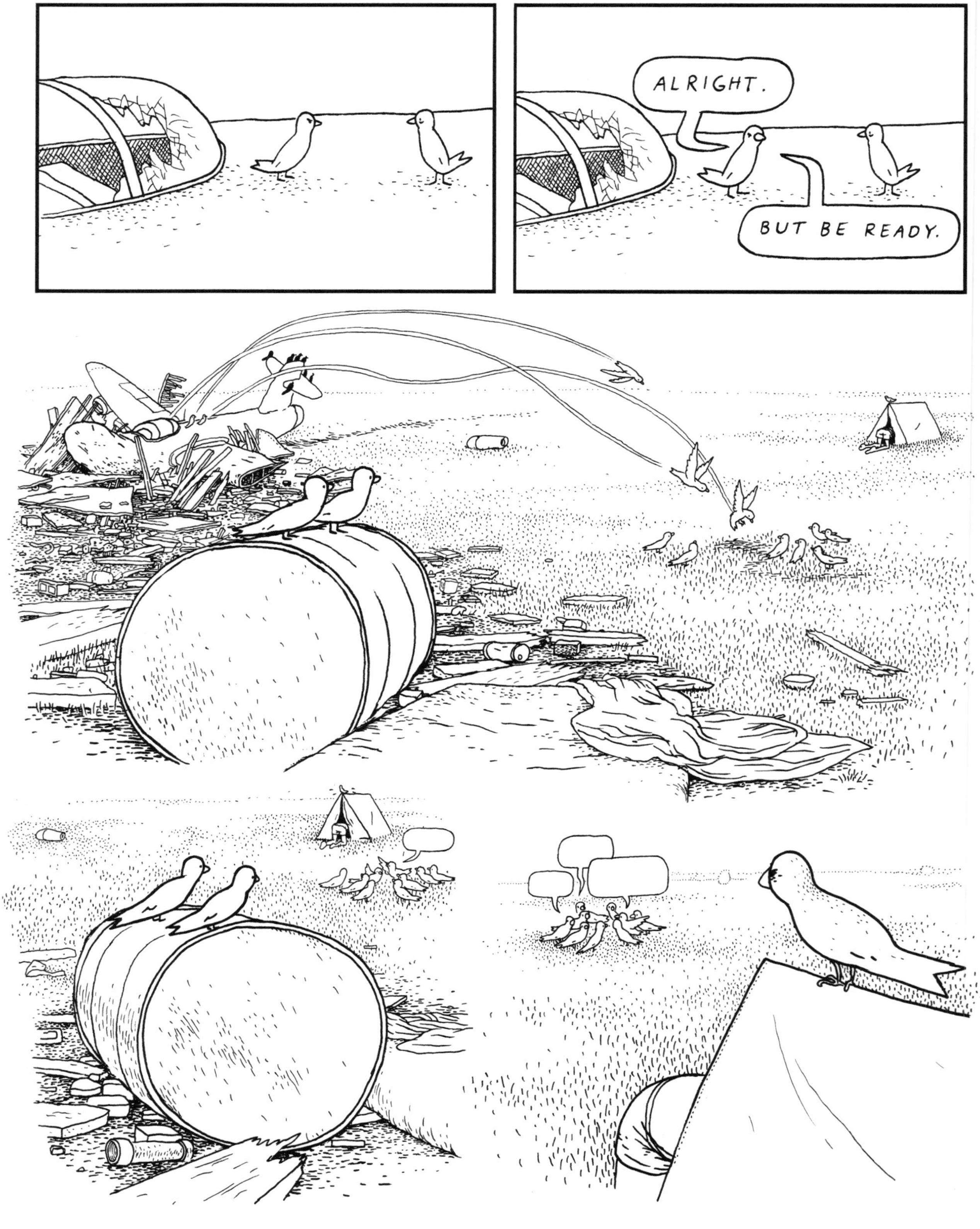
ALRIGHT.
BUT BE READY.

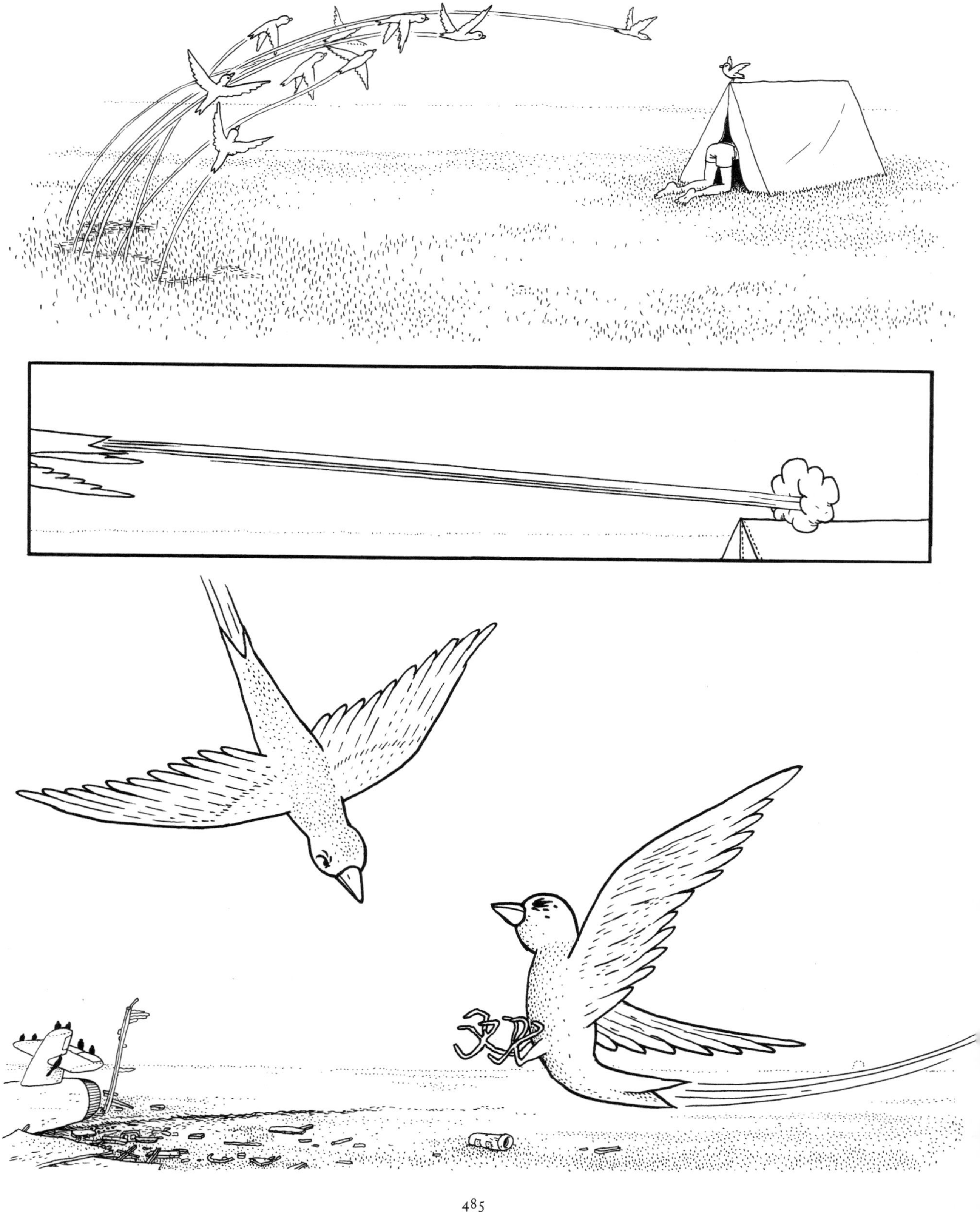

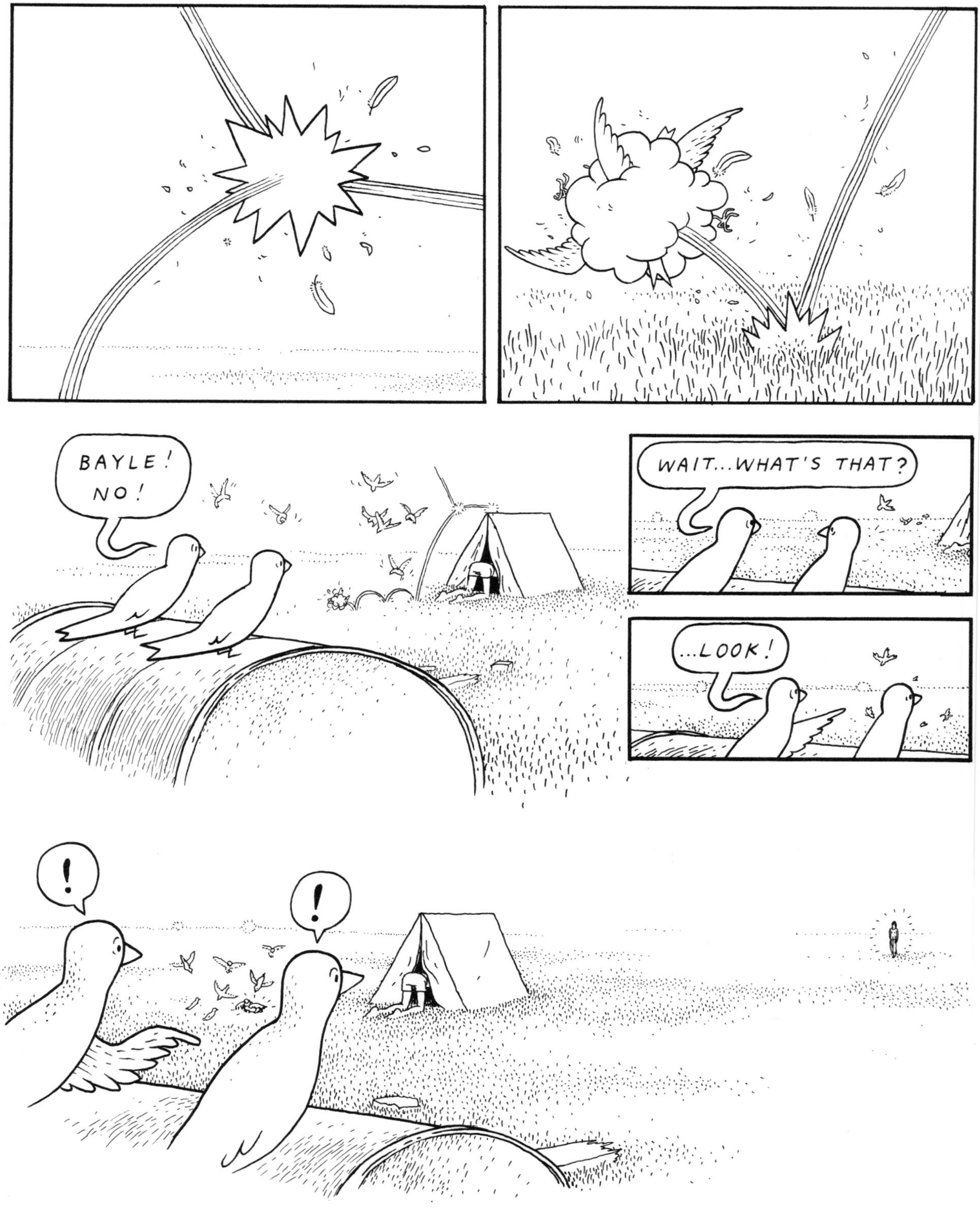
BAYLE! NO!
WAIT...WHAT'S THAT?
...LOOK!
!
!

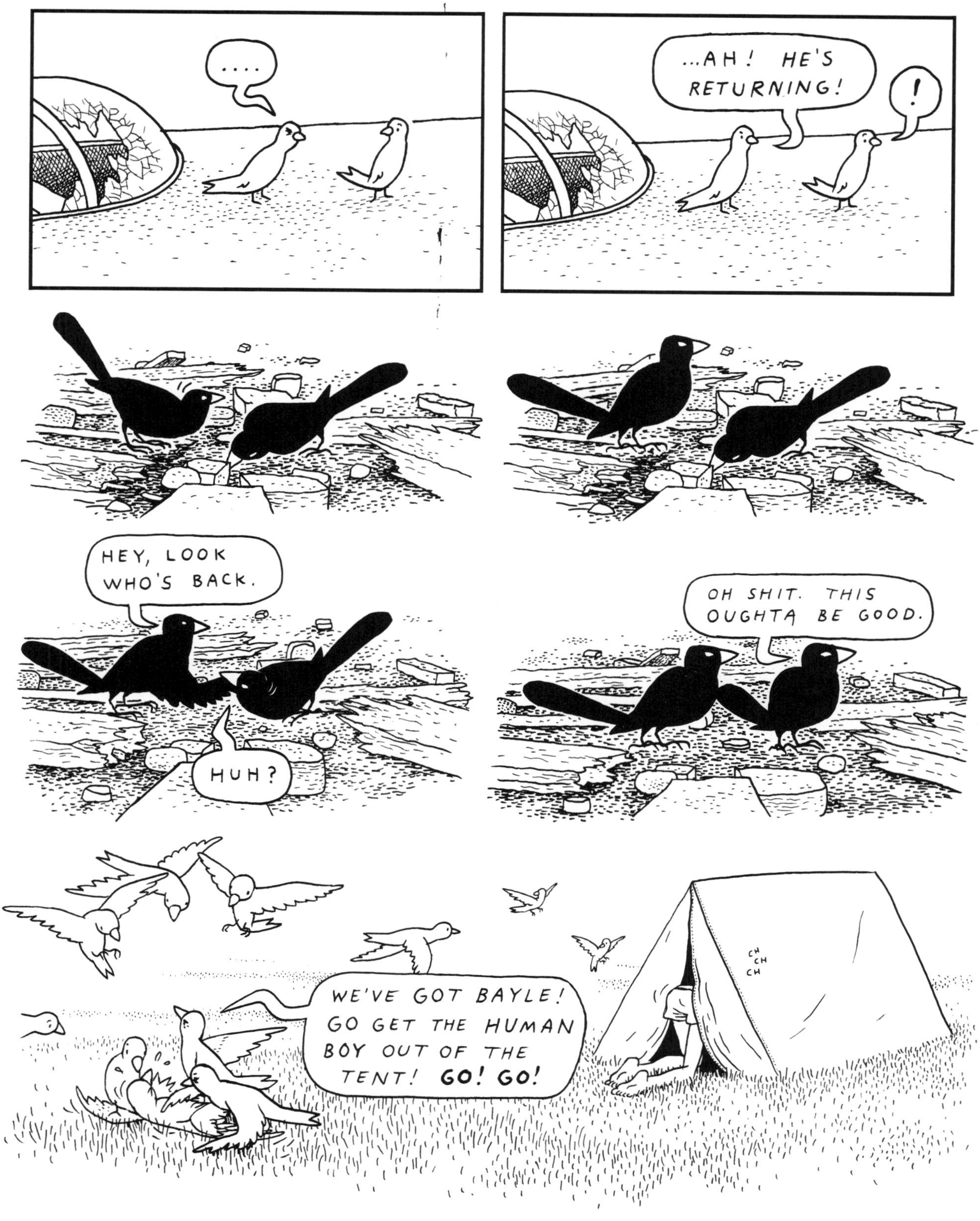
....
...AH! HE'S RETURNING!
!
HEY, LOOK WHO'S BACK.
HUH?
OH SHIT. THIS OUGHTA BE GOOD.
WE'VE GOT BAYLE! GO GET THE HUMAN BOY OUT OF THE TENT! GO! GO!
CH CH CH

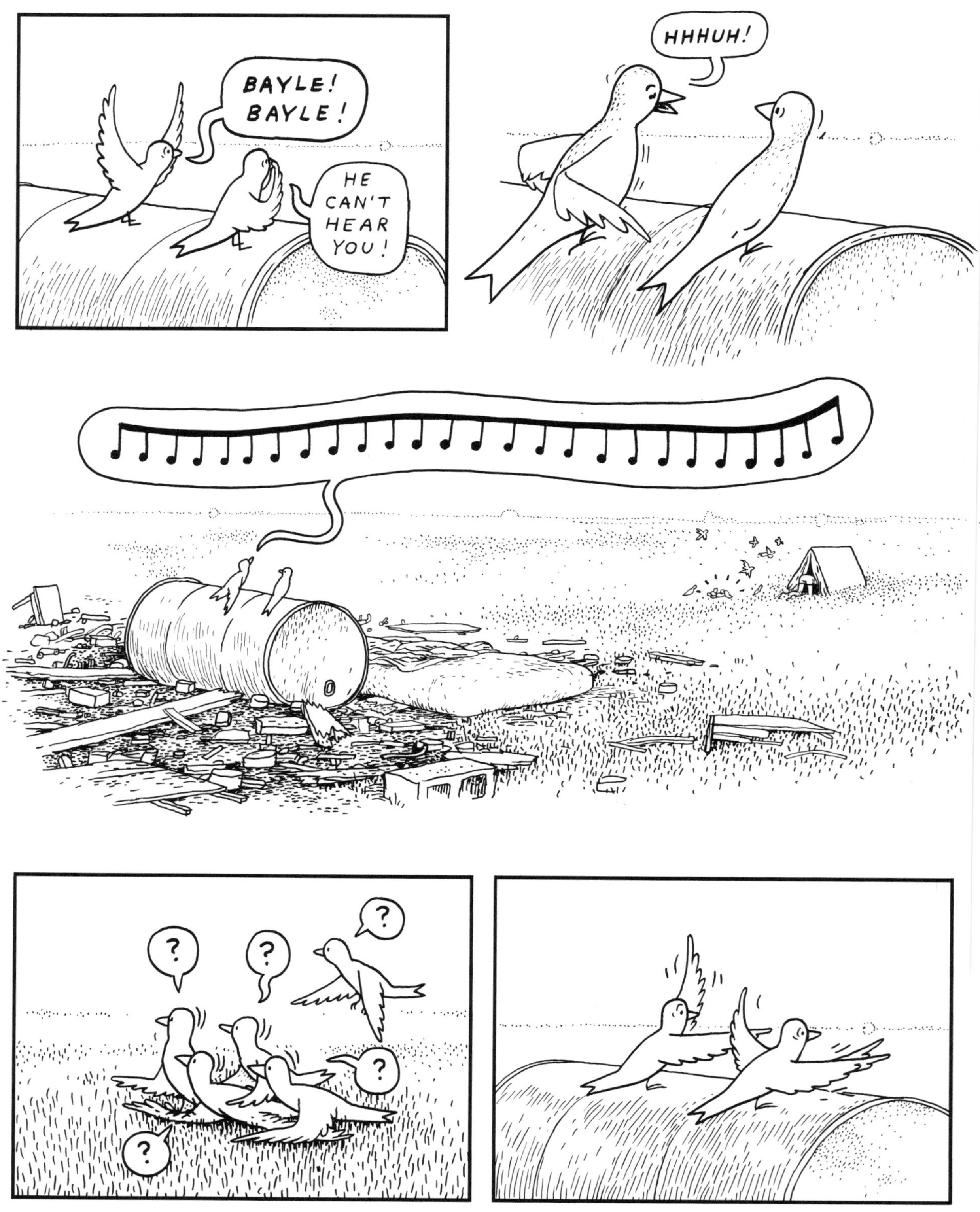
BAYLE! BAYLE!
HE CAN'T HEAR YOU!
HHHUH!
?
?
?
?
?

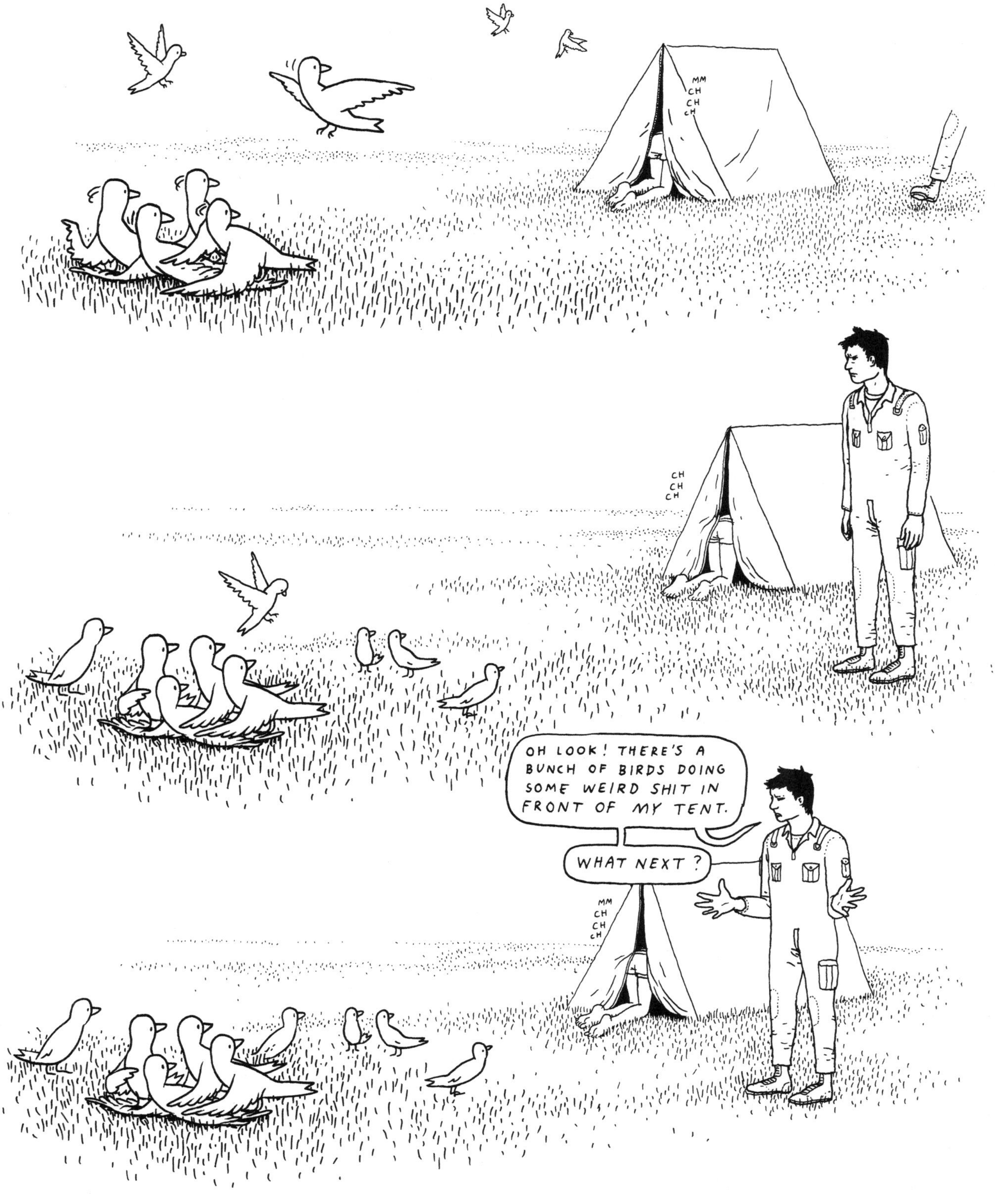
MM CH CH CH
CH CH CH
OH LOOK! THERE'S A BUNCH OF BIRDS DOING SOME WEIRD SHIT IN FRONT OF MY TENT.
WHAT NEXT?
MM CH CH CH

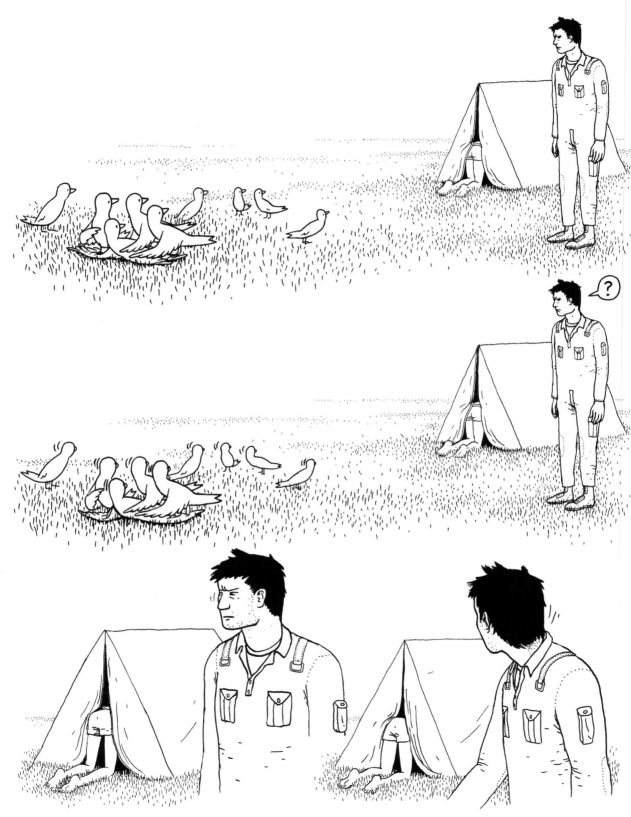

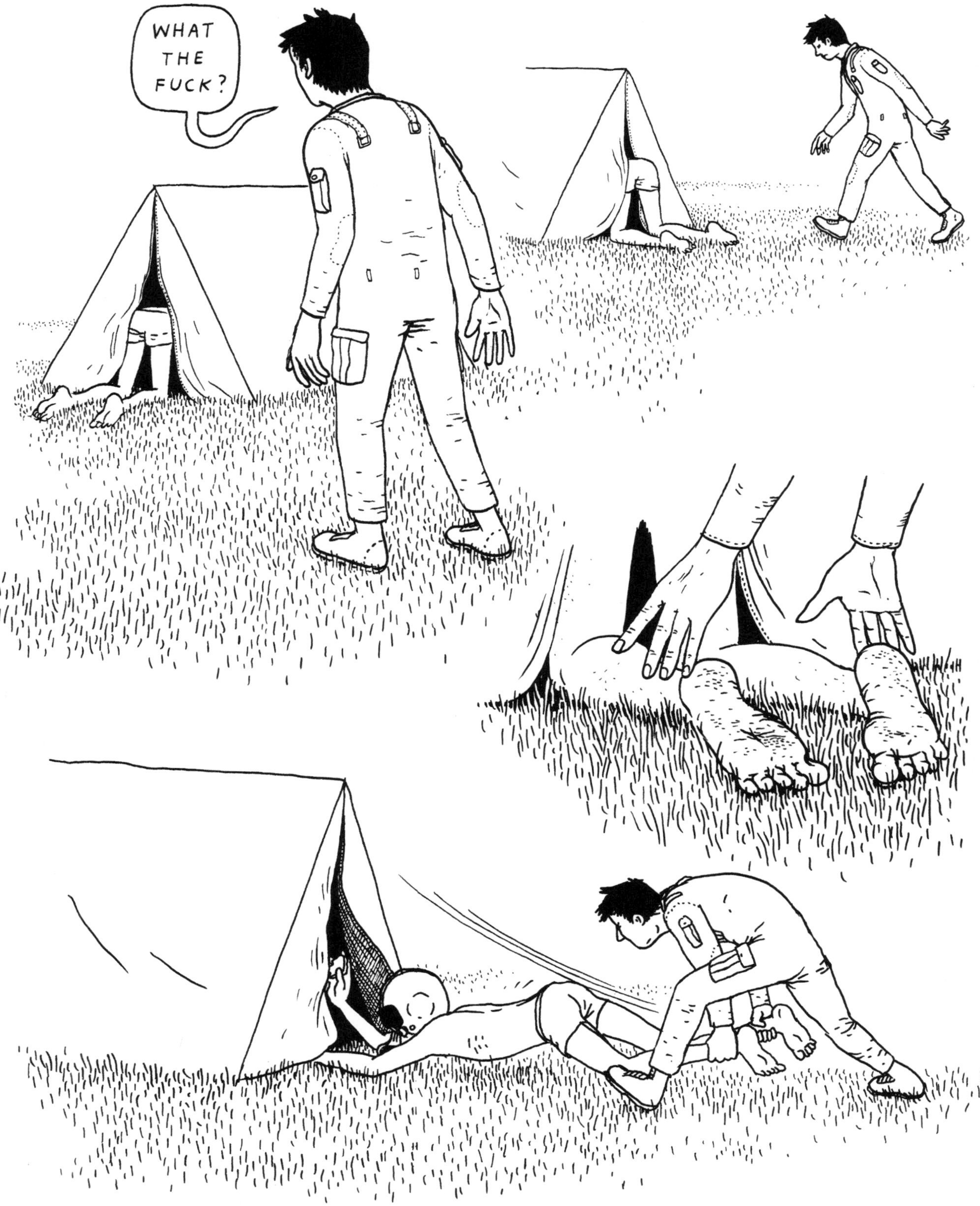
WHAT THE FUCK?

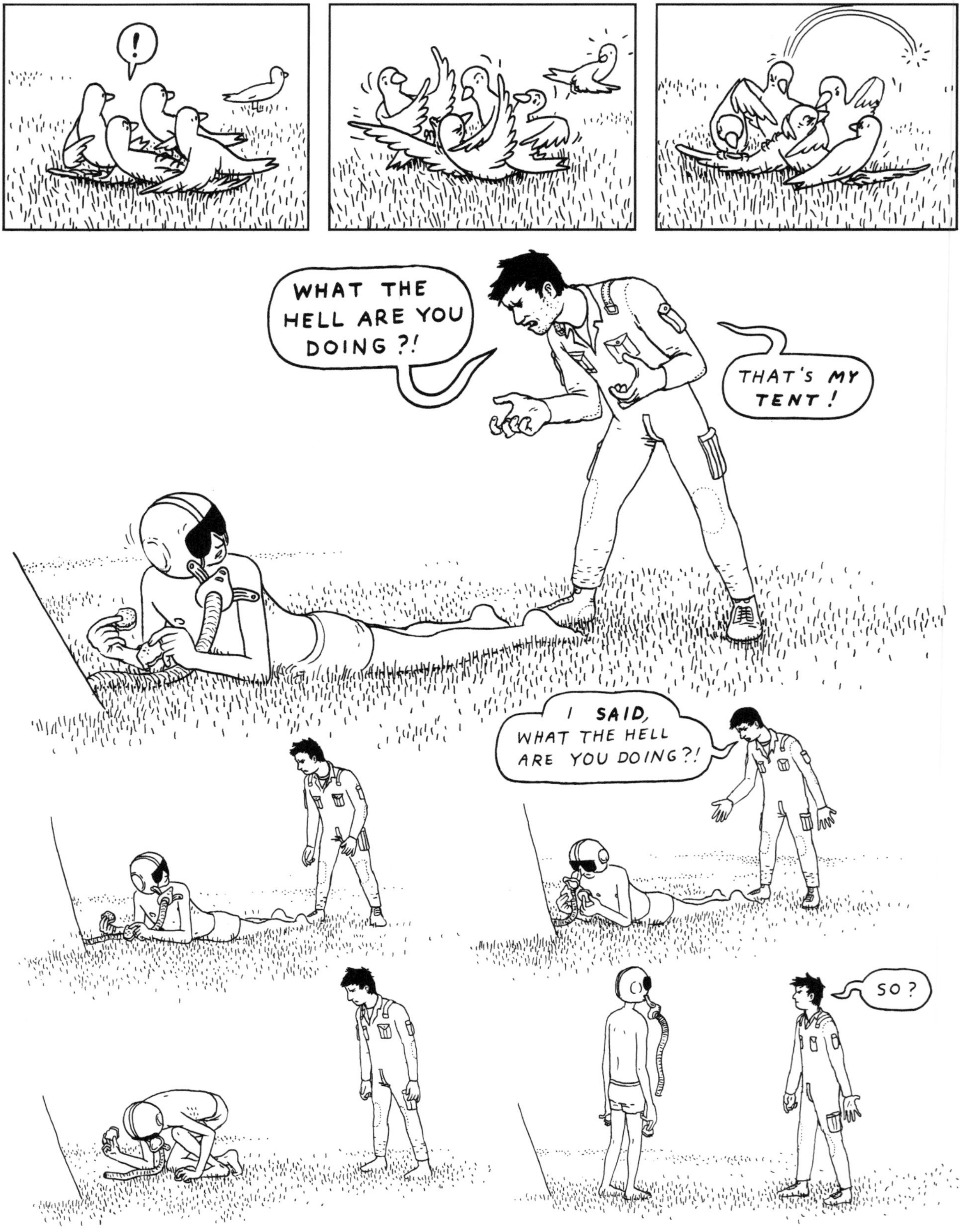
!
WHAT THE HELL ARE YOU DOING ?!
THAT'S MY TENT !
I SAID, WHAT THE HELL ARE YOU DOING ?!
SO ?

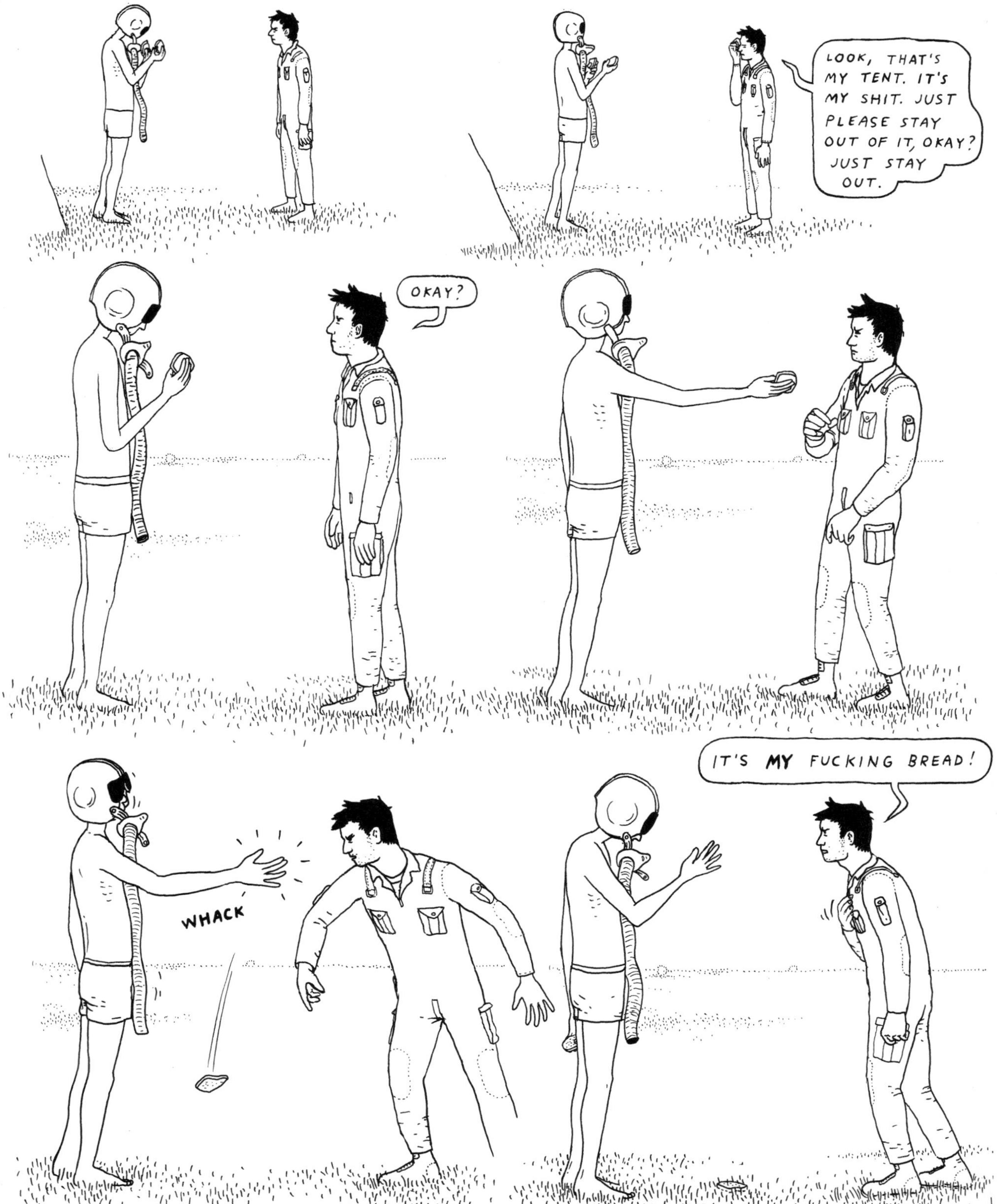
LOOK, THAT'S MY TENT. IT'S MY SHIT. JUST PLEASE STAY OUT OF IT, OKAY? JUST STAY OUT.
OKAY?
WHACK
IT'S **MY** FUCKING BREAD!

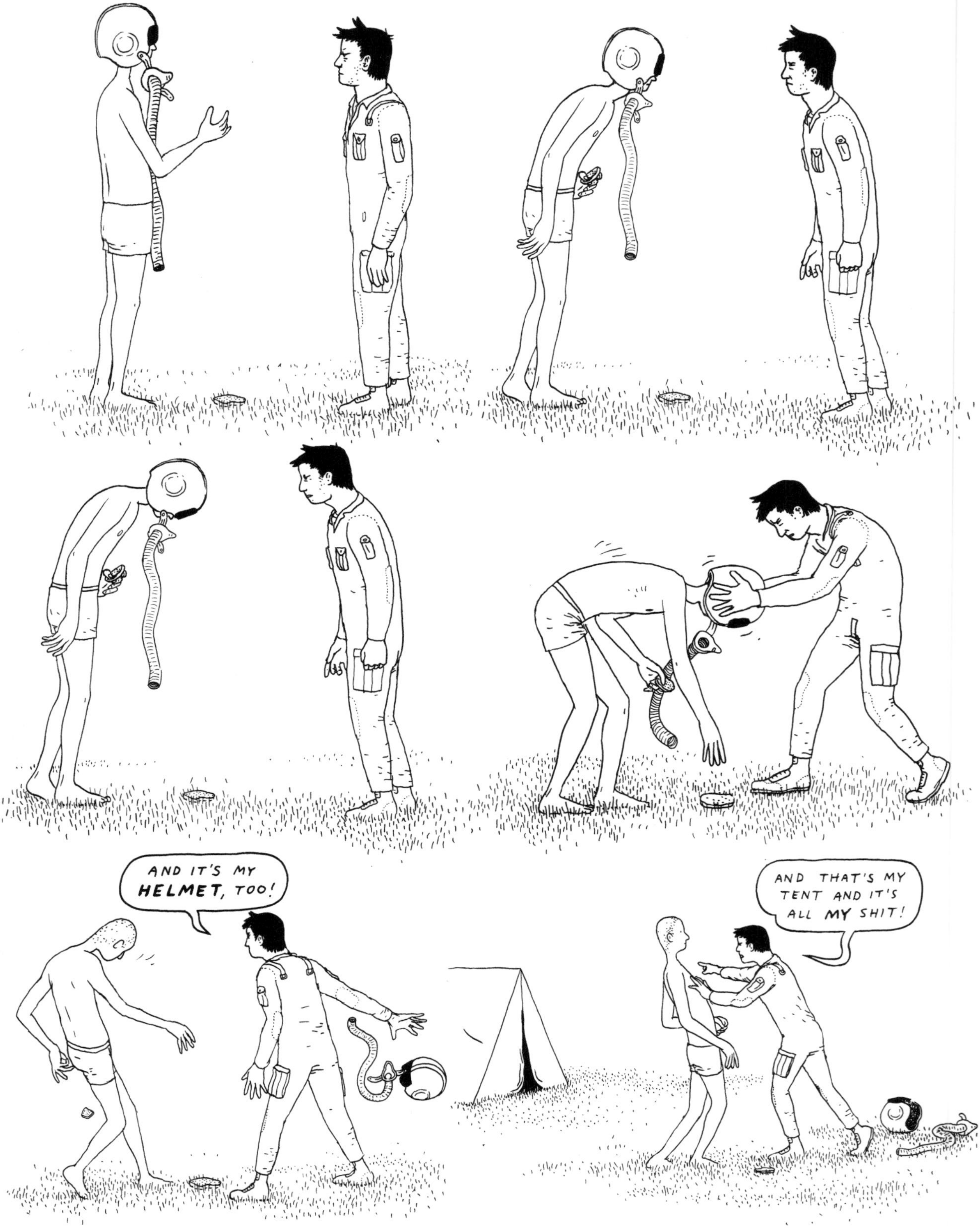
AND IT'S MY HELMET, TOO!
AND THAT'S MY TENT AND IT'S ALL MY SHIT!

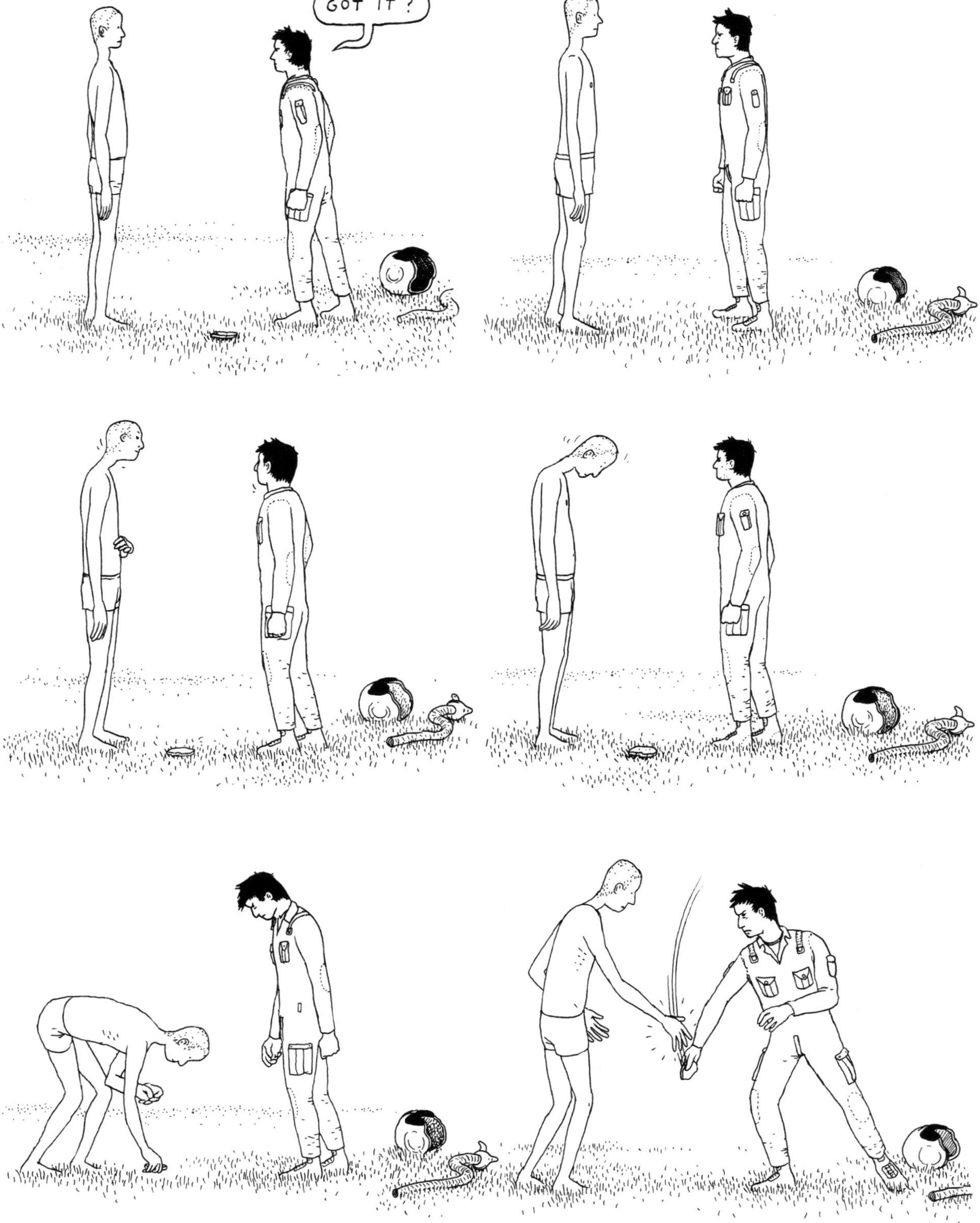
GOT IT ?

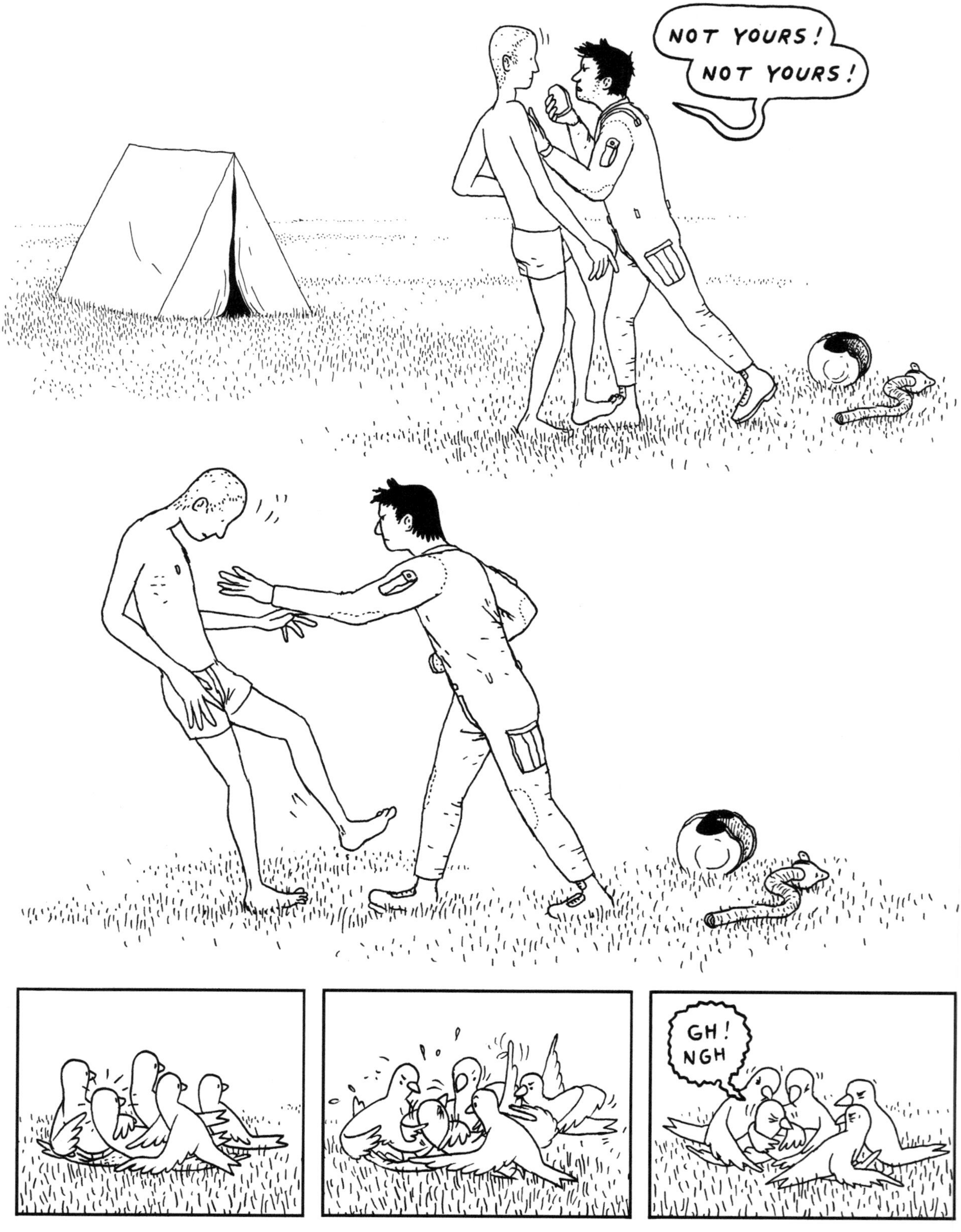
NOT YOURS!
NOT YOURS!
GH!
NGH

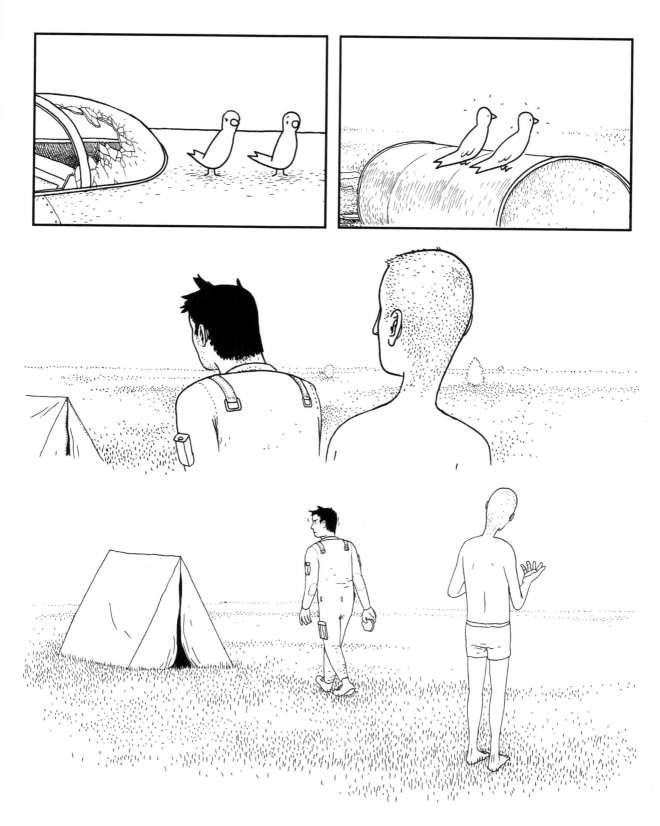

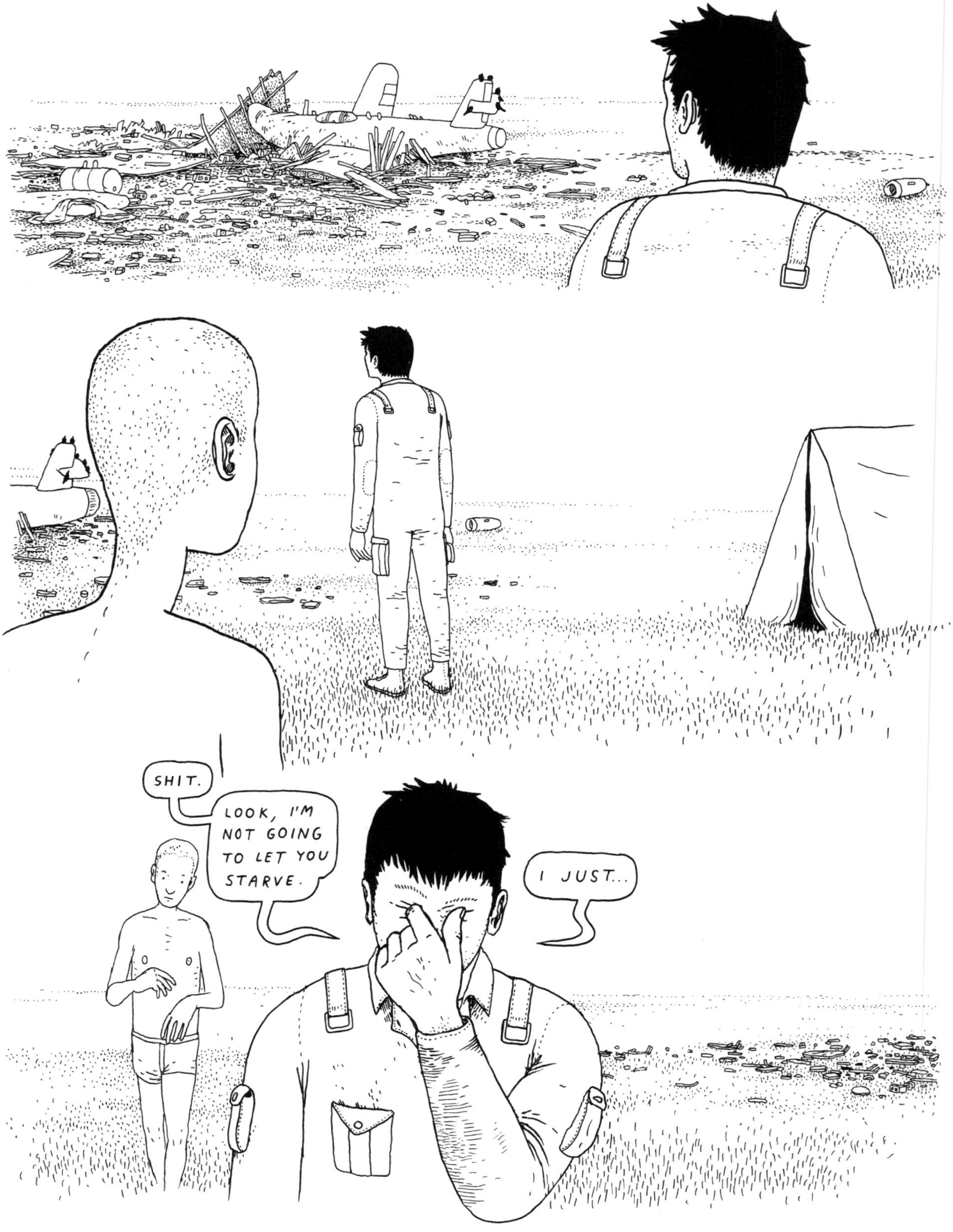
SHIT.
LOOK, I'M NOT GOING TO LET YOU STARVE.
I JUST...

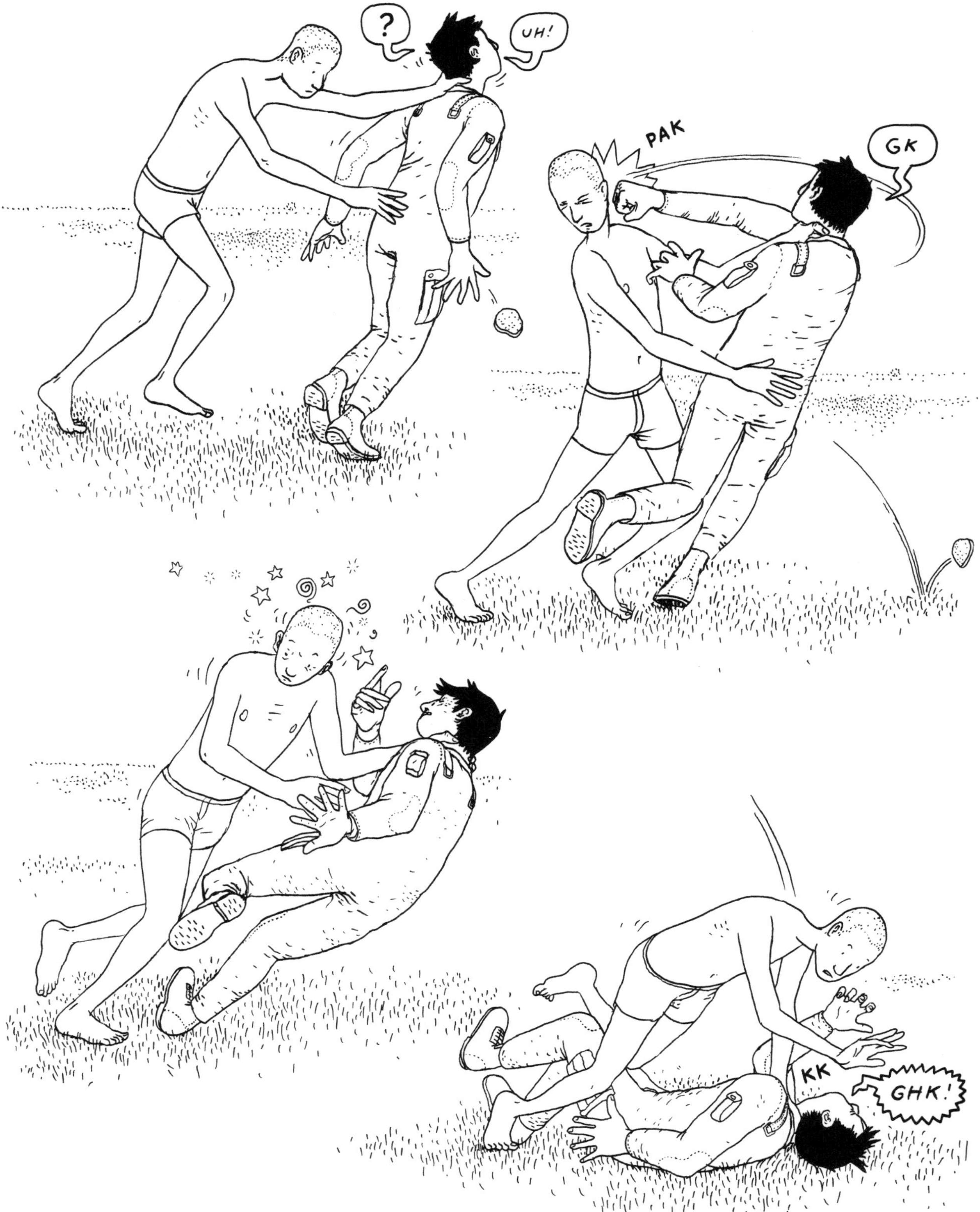
?
UH!
PAK
GK
KK
GHK!

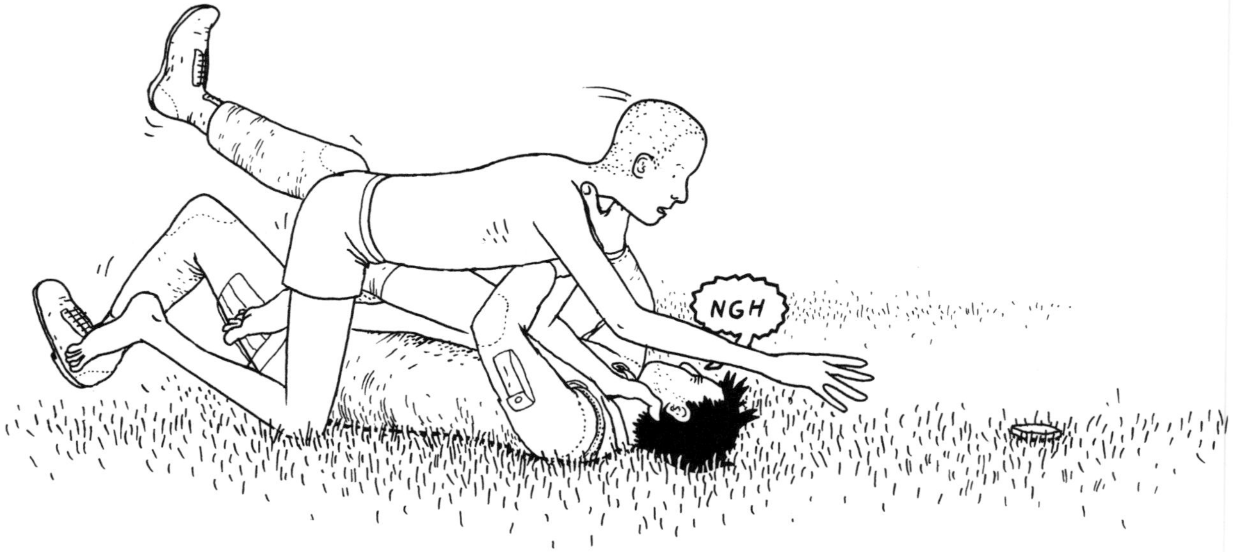
NGH
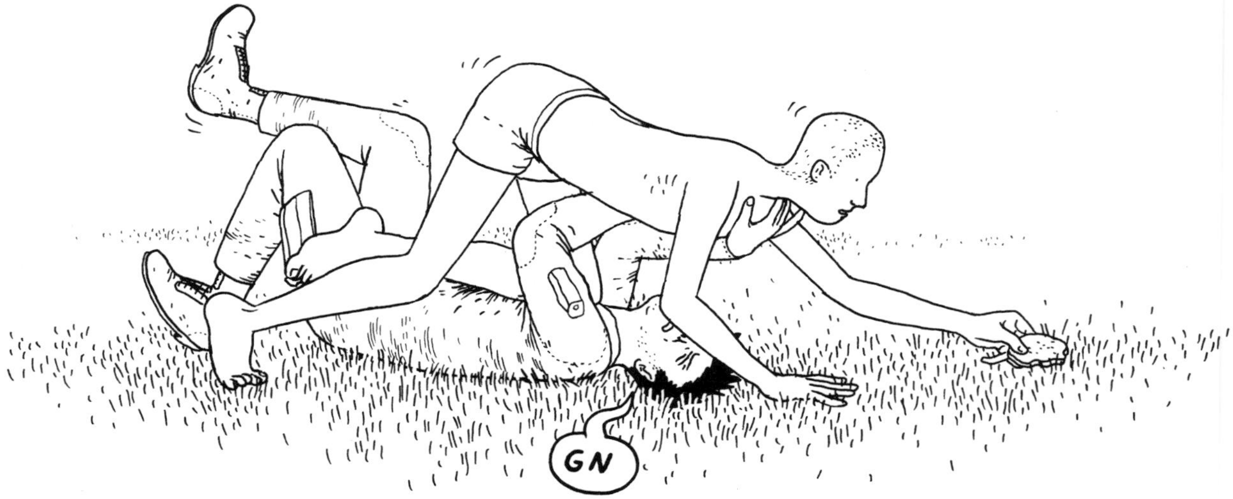
GN
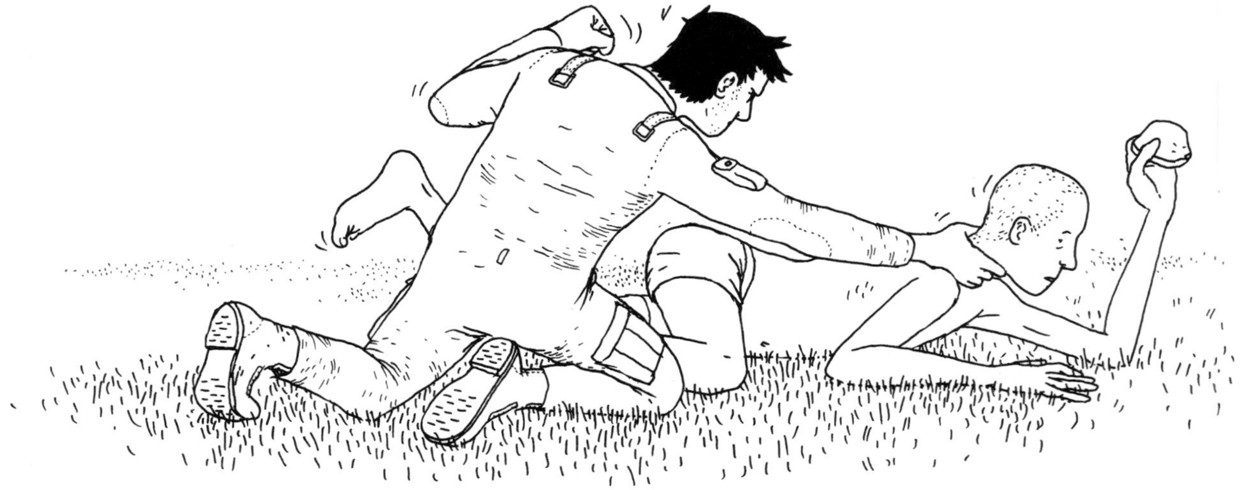

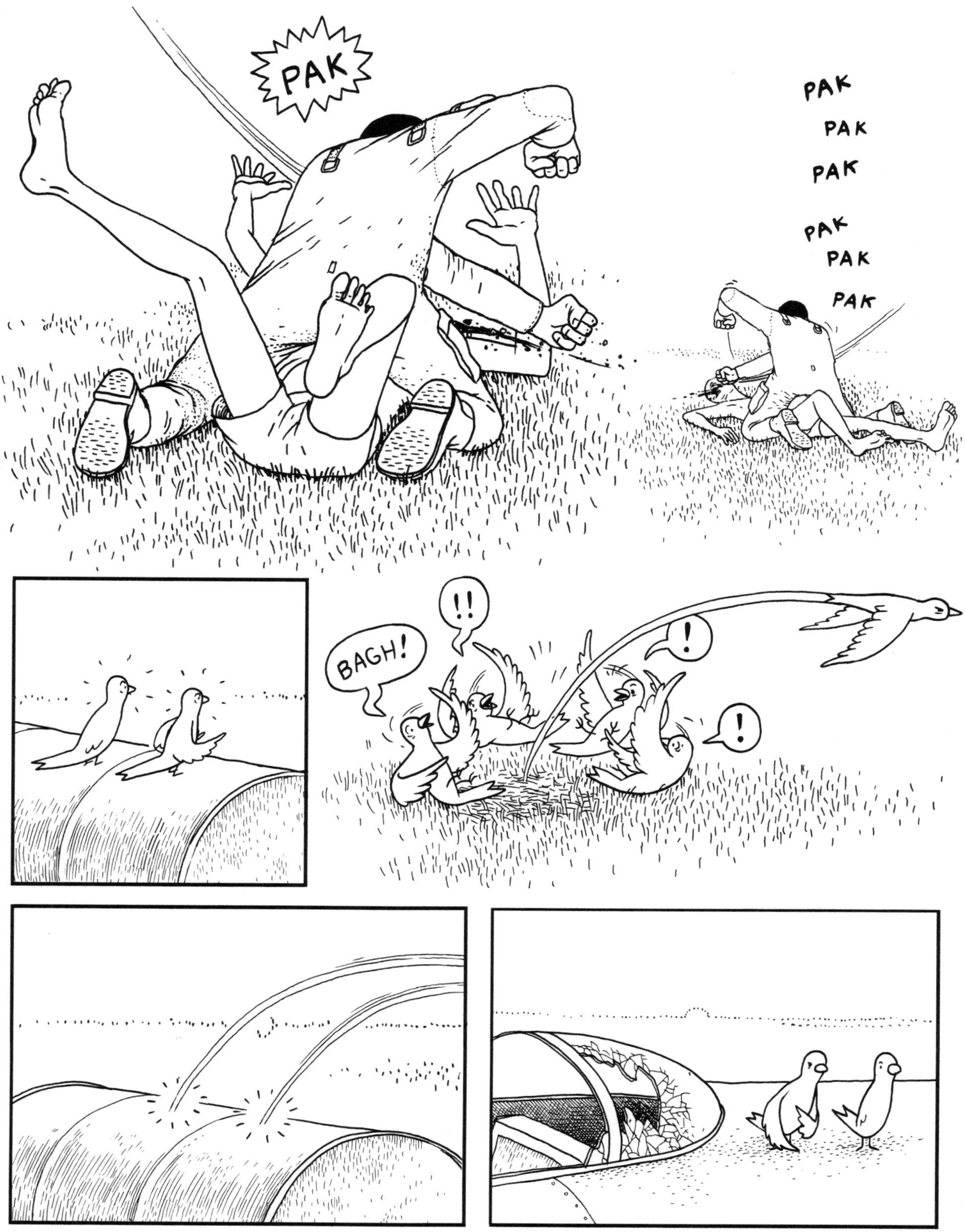
PAK
PAK
PAK
PAK
PAK
PAK
PAK
BAGH!
!!
!
!

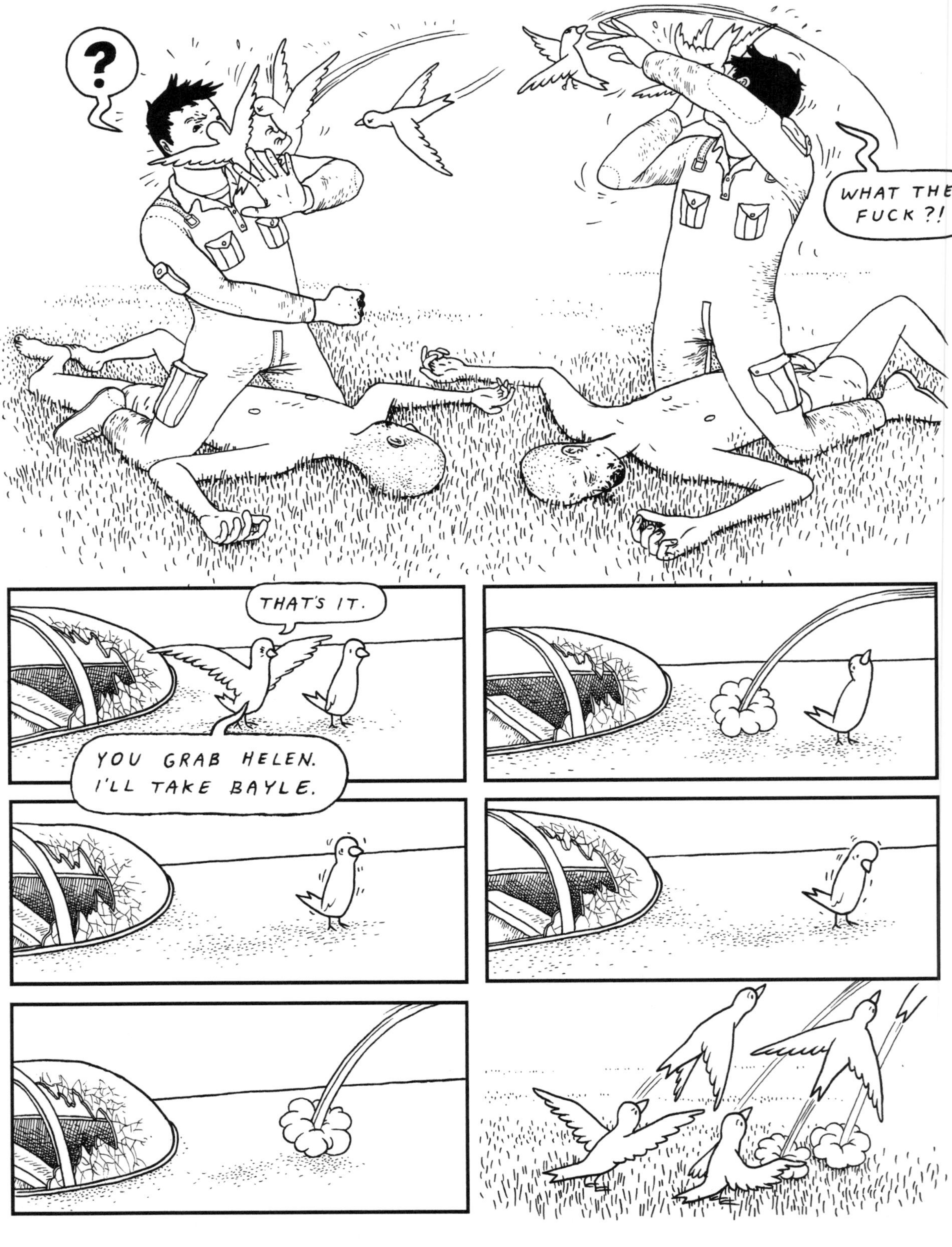
?
WHAT THE FUCK?!
THAT'S IT.
YOU GRAB HELEN. I'LL TAKE BAYLE.

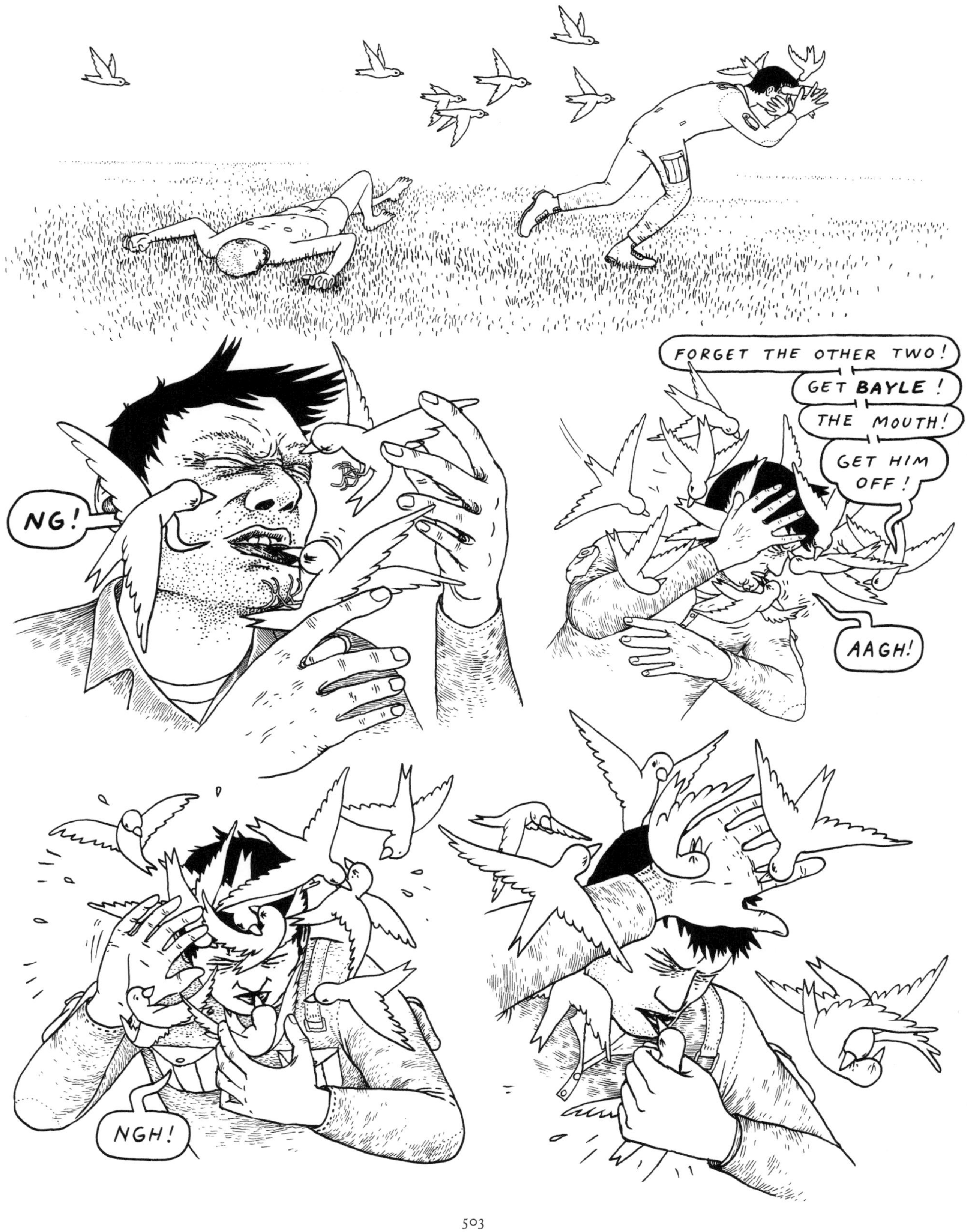
NG!
FORGET THE OTHER TWO!
GET BAYLE!
THE MOUTH!
GET HIM OFF!
AAGH!
NGH!

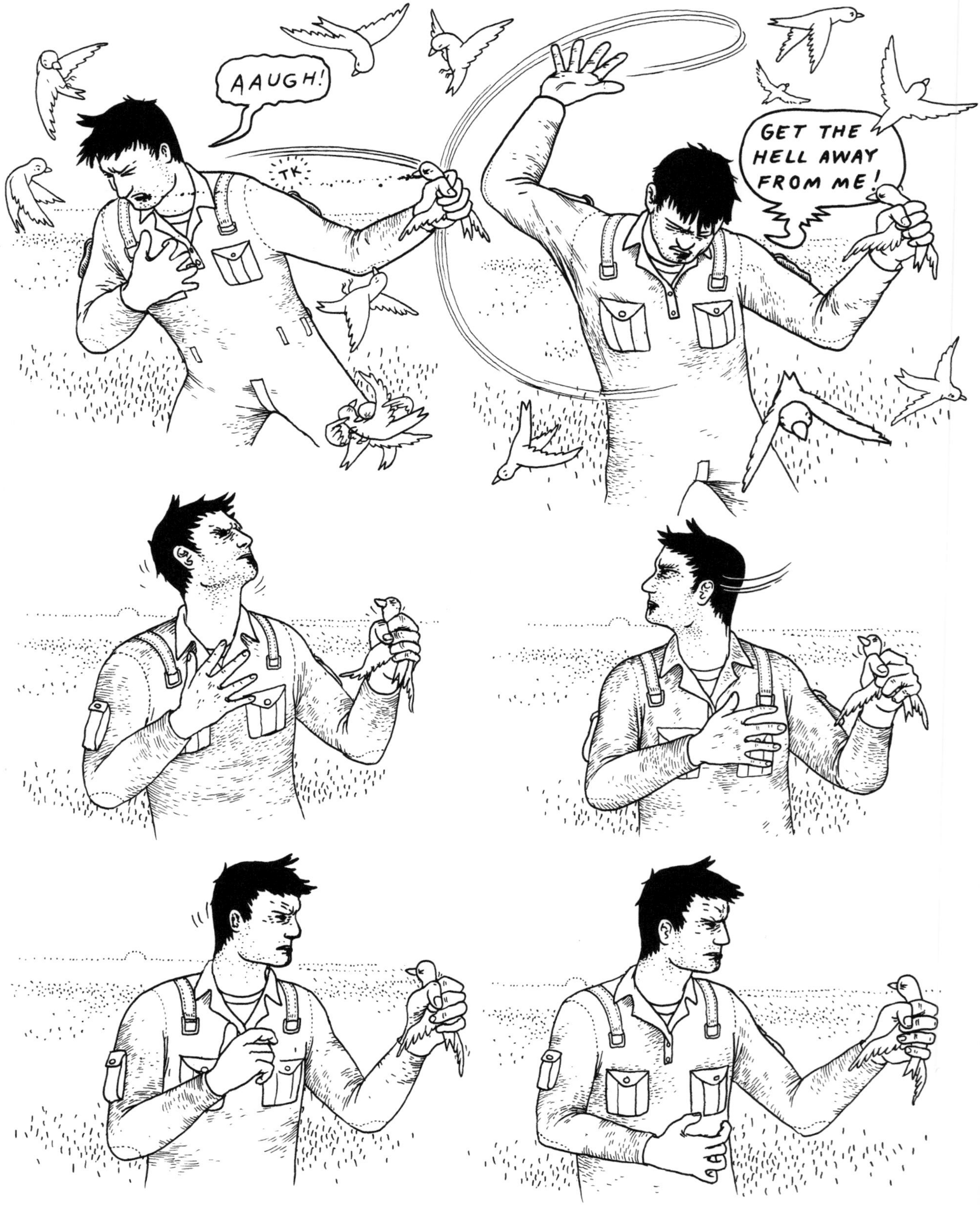
AAUGH!
TK
GET THE HELL AWAY FROM ME!

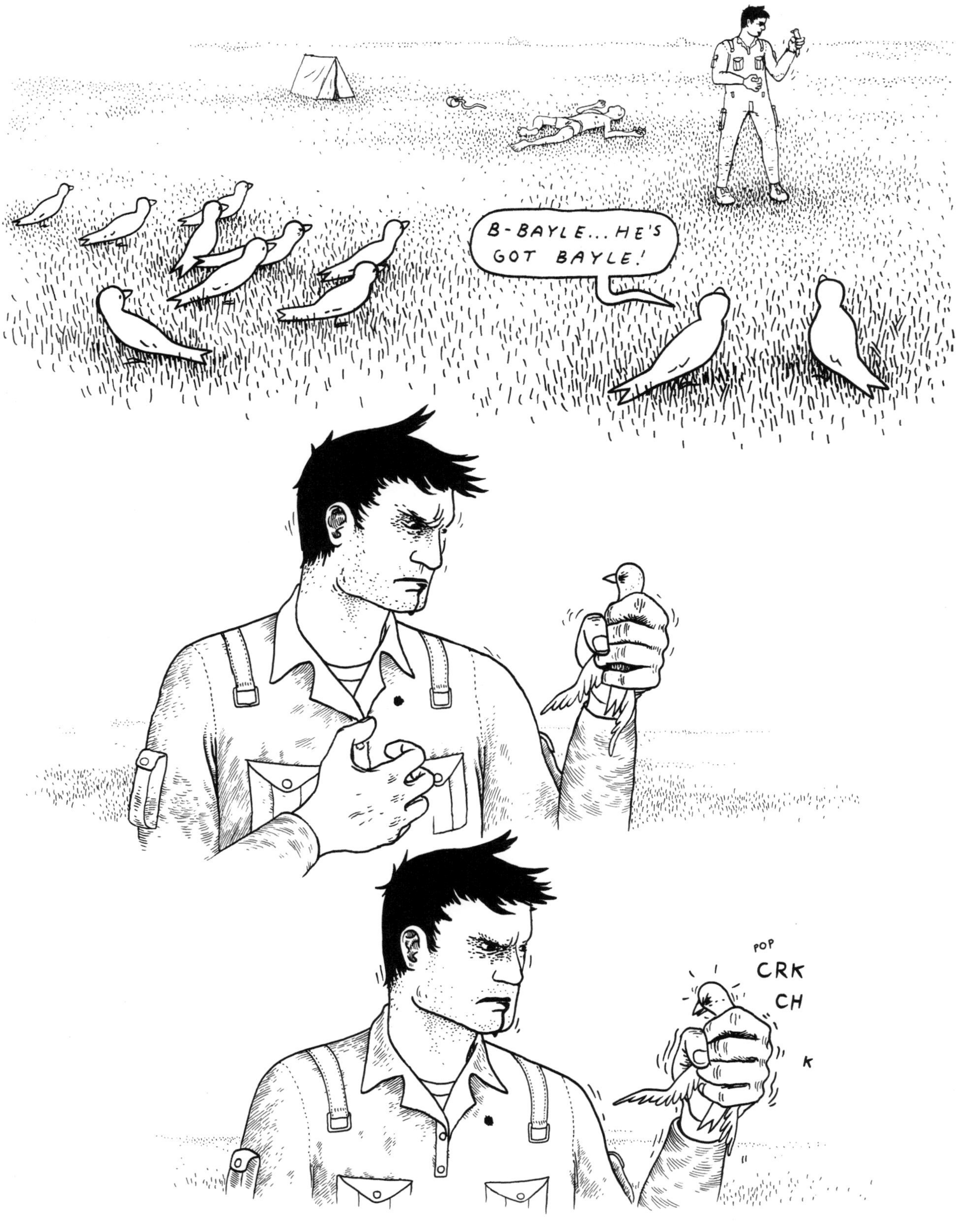
B-BAYLE... HE'S GOT BAYLE!
POP
CRK
CH
K

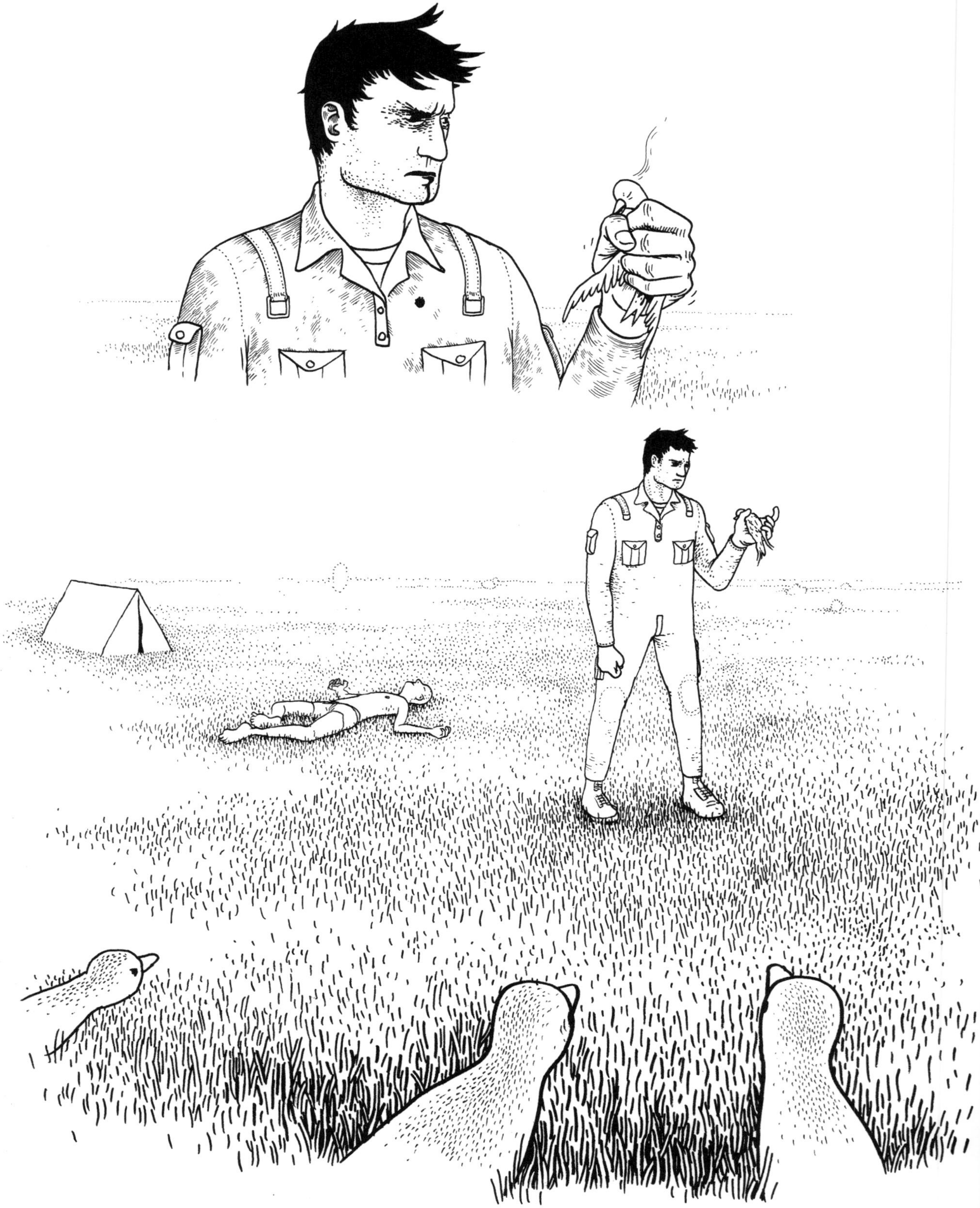

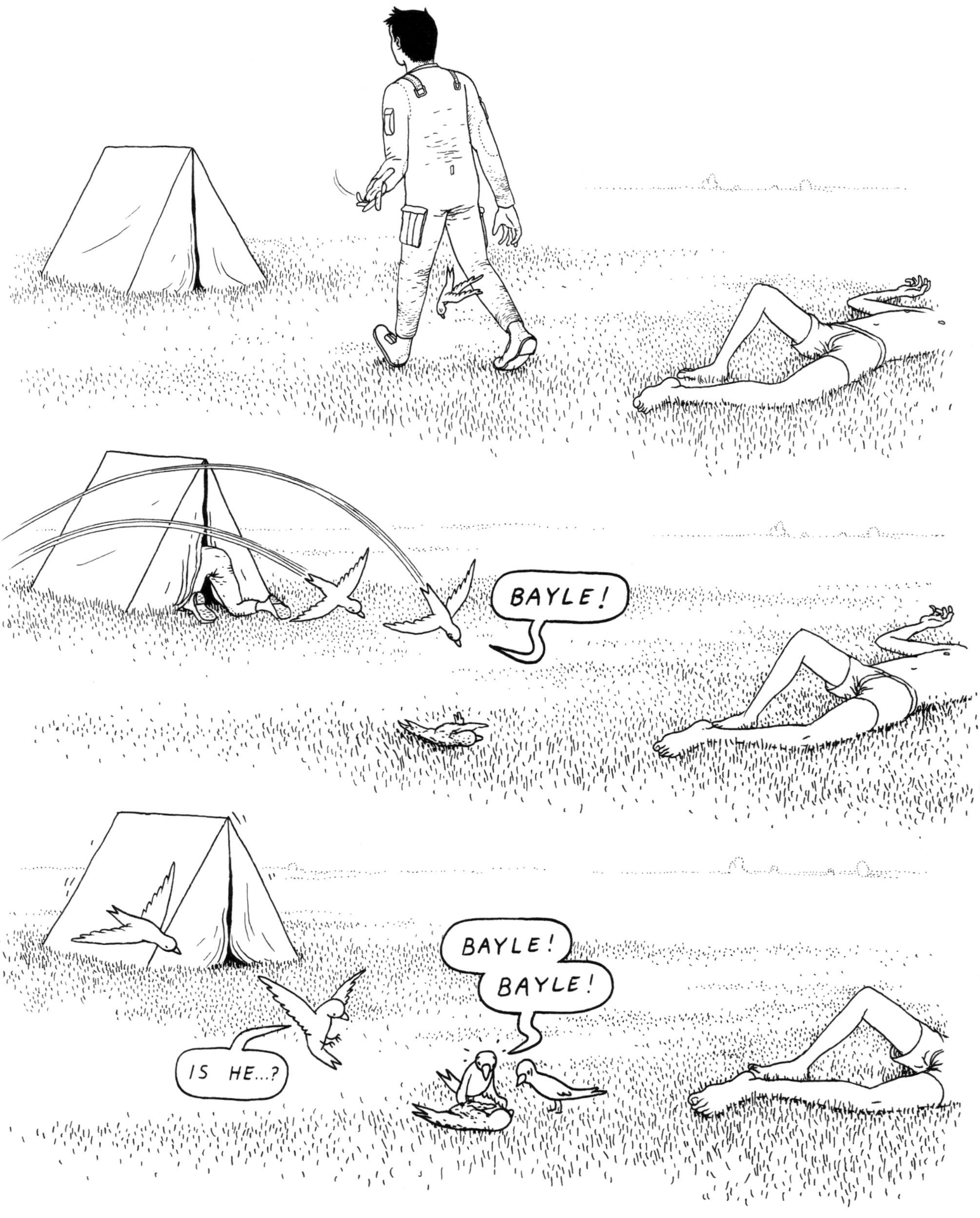
BAYLE!
IS HE...?
BAYLE!
BAYLE!

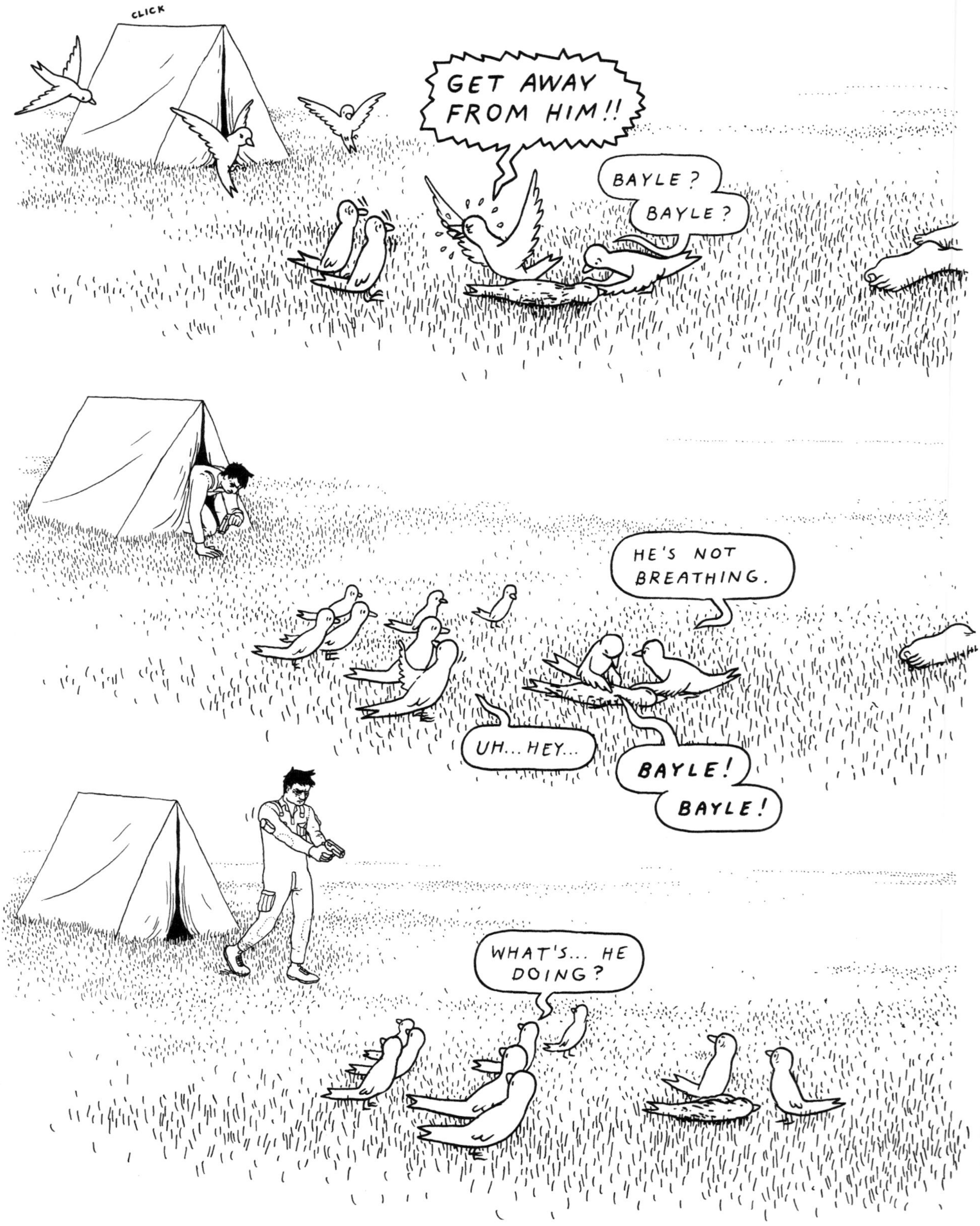
CLICK
GET AWAY FROM HIM!!
BAYLE?
BAYLE?
HE'S NOT BREATHING.
UH... HEY...
BAYLE!
BAYLE!
WHAT'S... HE DOING?

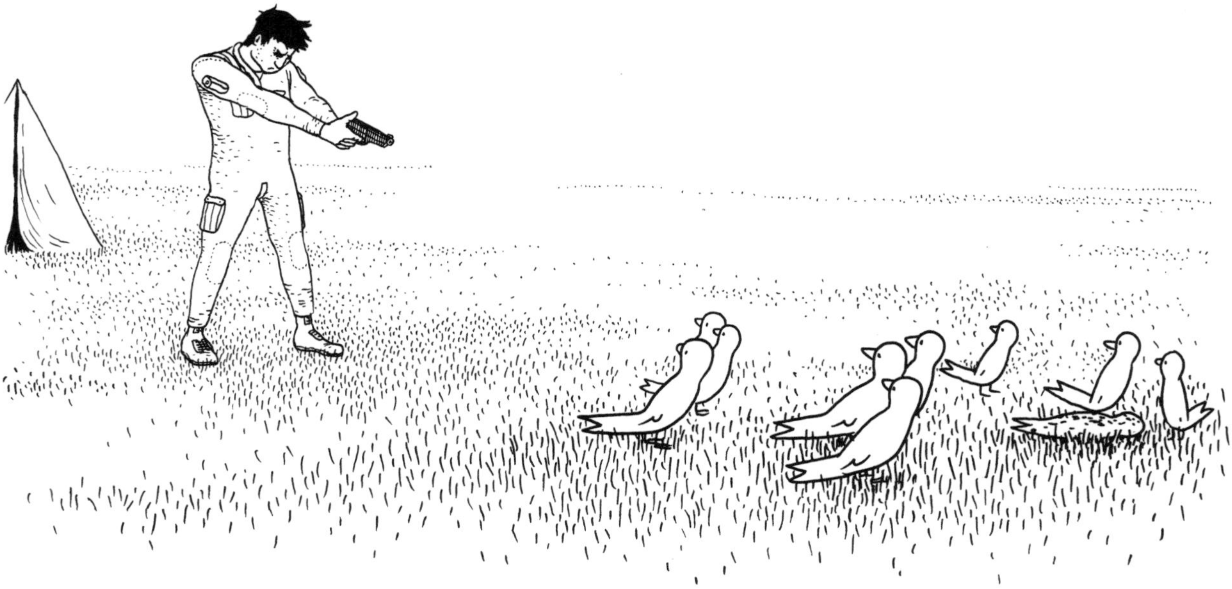

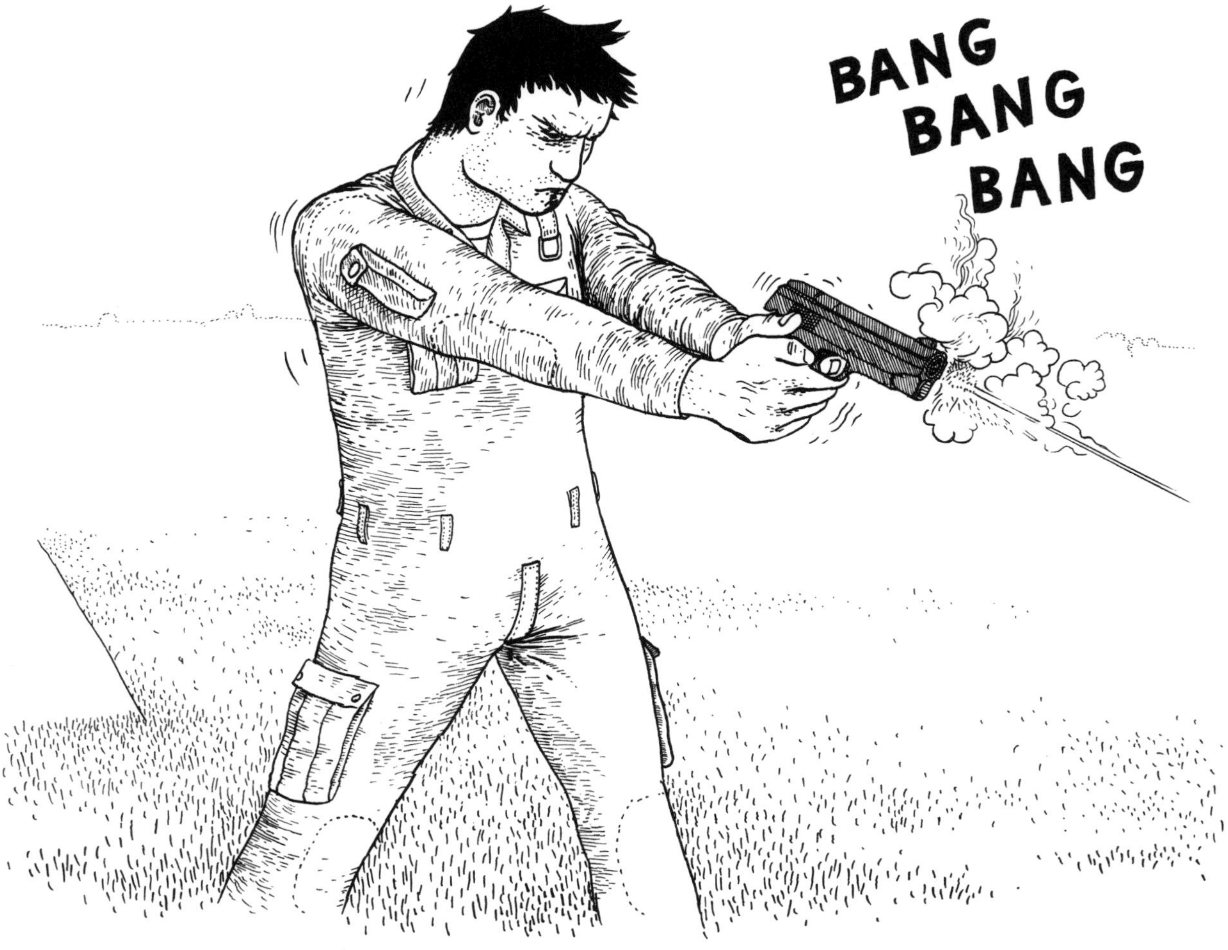
BANG
BANG
BANG

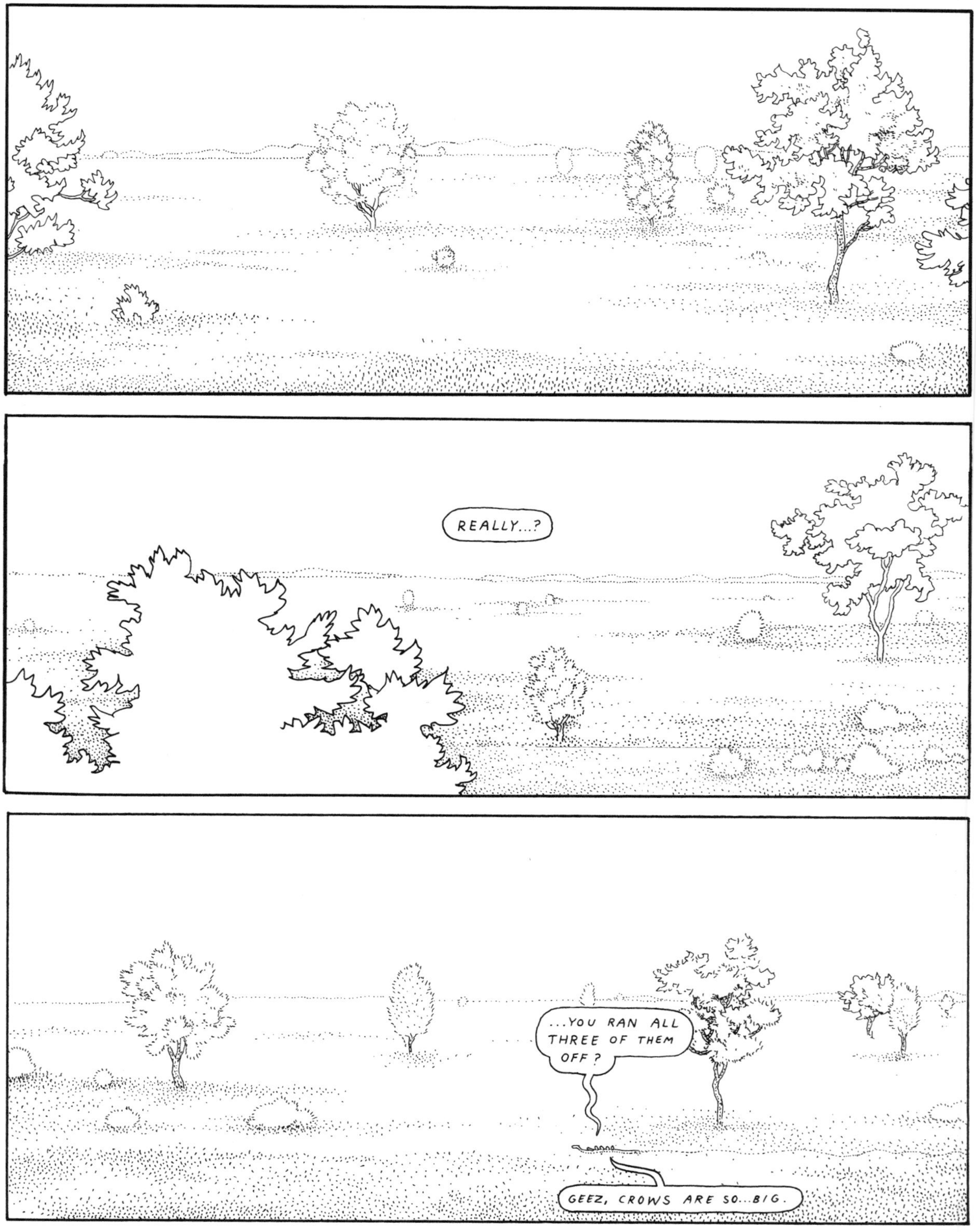
REALLY...?
...YOU RAN ALL THREE OF THEM OFF?
GEEZ, CROWS ARE SO...BIG.

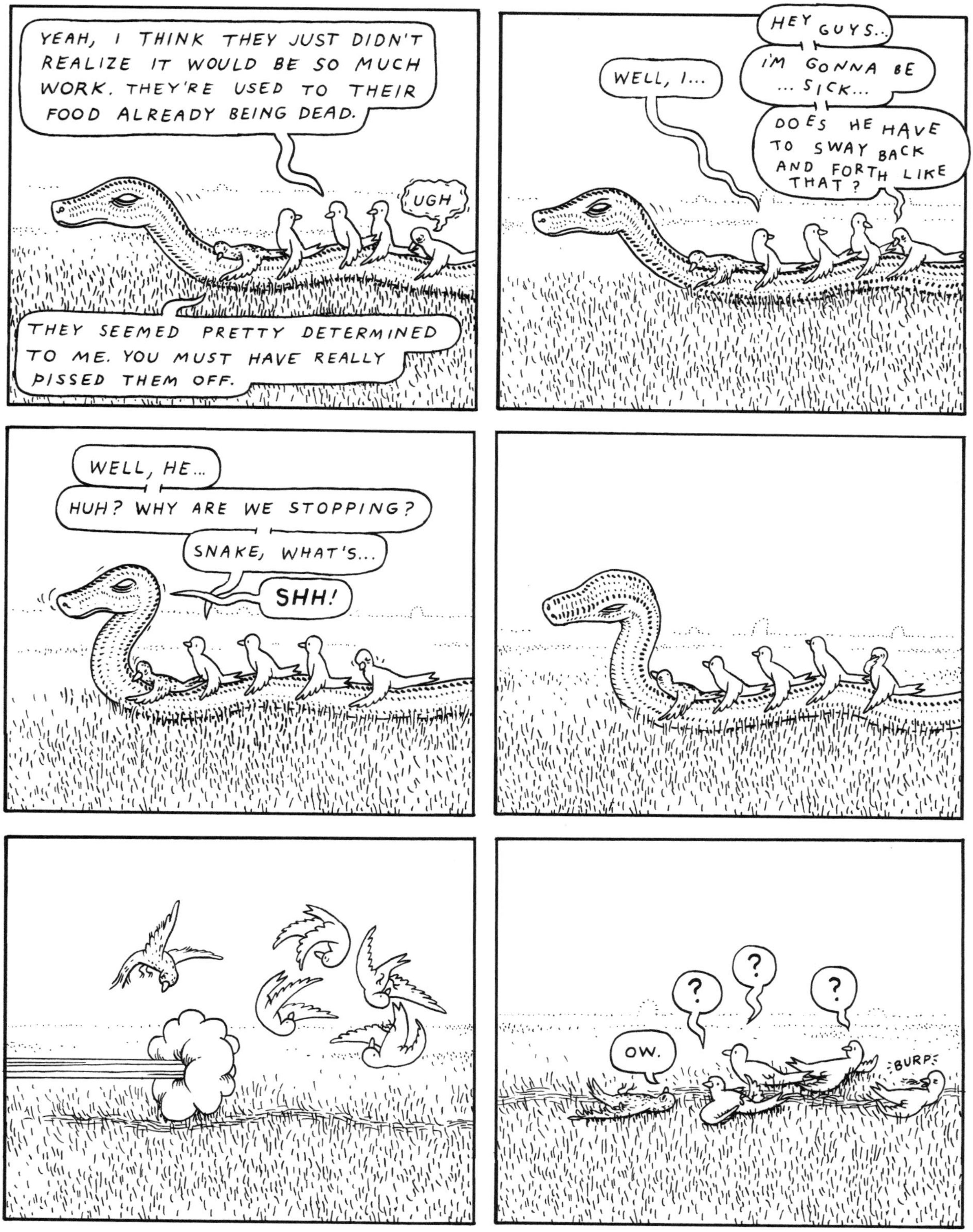
YEAH, I THINK THEY JUST DIDN'T REALIZE IT WOULD BE SO MUCH WORK. THEY'RE USED TO THEIR FOOD ALREADY BEING DEAD.
UGH
THEY SEEMED PRETTY DETERMINED TO ME. YOU MUST HAVE REALLY PISSED THEM OFF.
WELL, I...
HEY GUYS...
I'M GONNA BE ... SICK...
DOES HE HAVE TO SWAY BACK AND FORTH LIKE THAT?
WELL, HE...
HUH? WHY ARE WE STOPPING?
SNAKE, WHAT'S...
SHH!
?
?
?
OW.
BURP

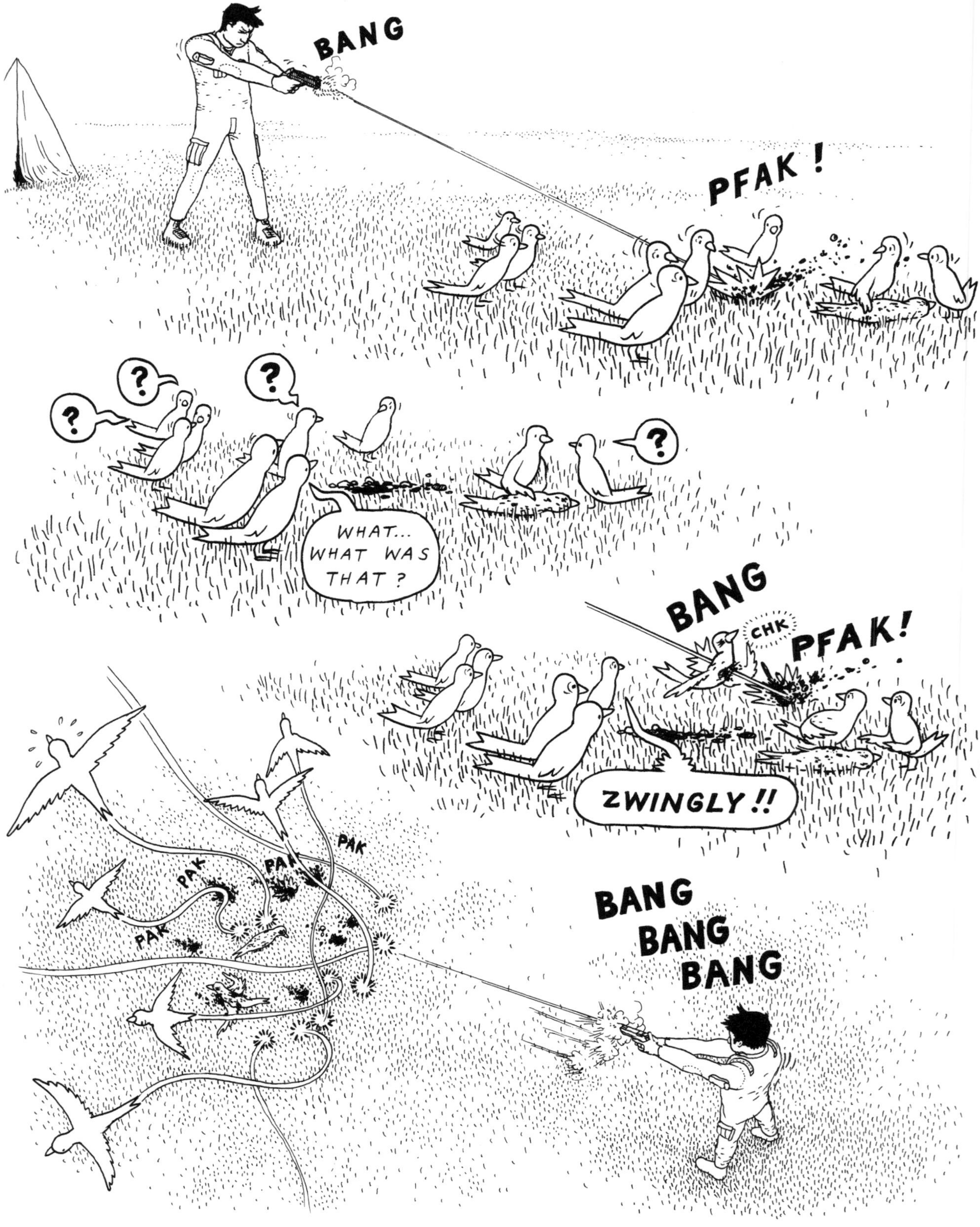
BANG
PFAK!
?
?
?
?
WHAT... WHAT WAS THAT?
BANG
CHK
PFAK!
ZWINGLY!!
PAK
PAK
PAK
PAK
BANG
BANG
BANG

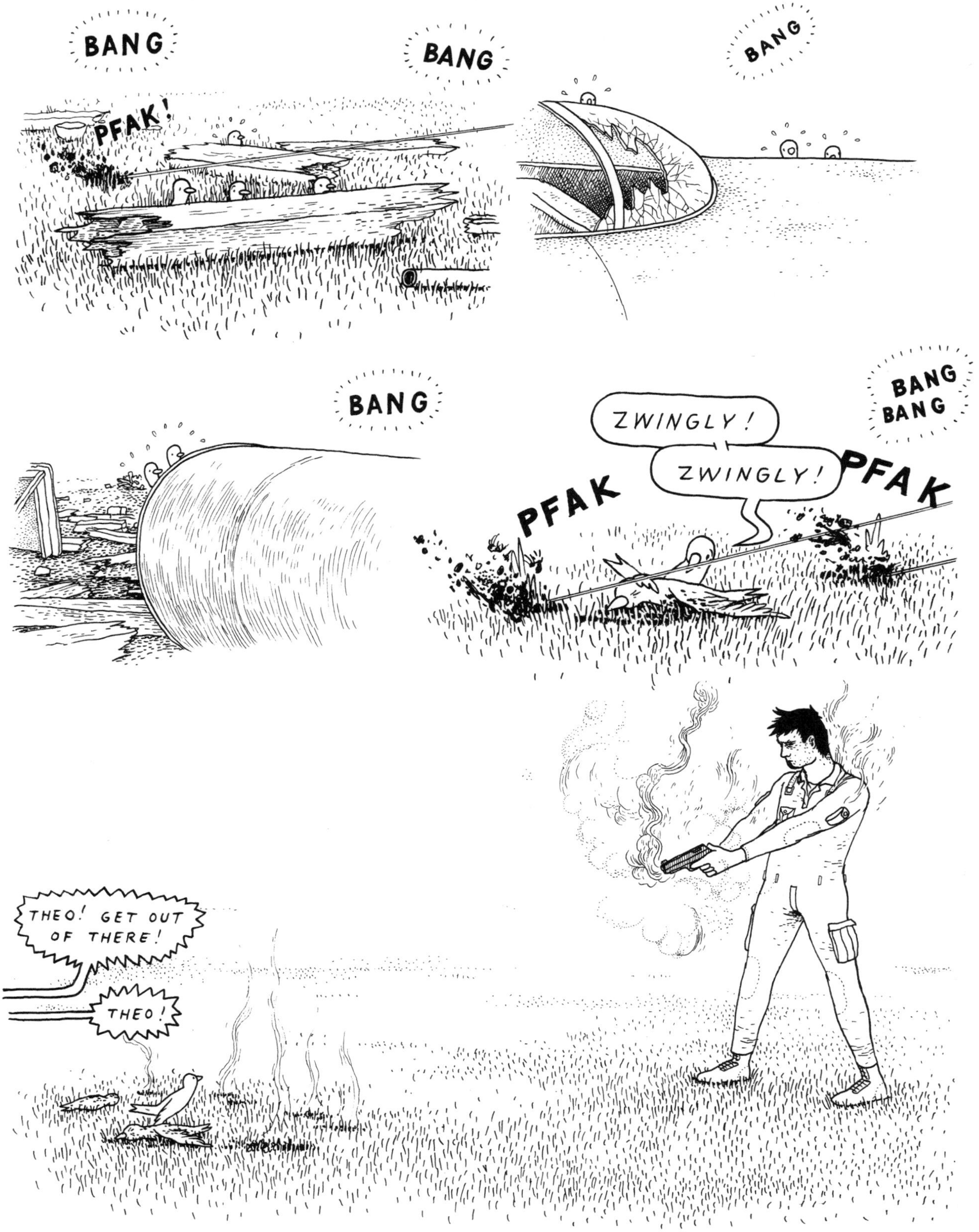
BANG
PFAK!
BANG
BANG
BANG
ZWINGLY!
ZWINGLY!
BANG
BANG
PFAK
PFAK
THEO! GET OUT OF THERE!
THEO!

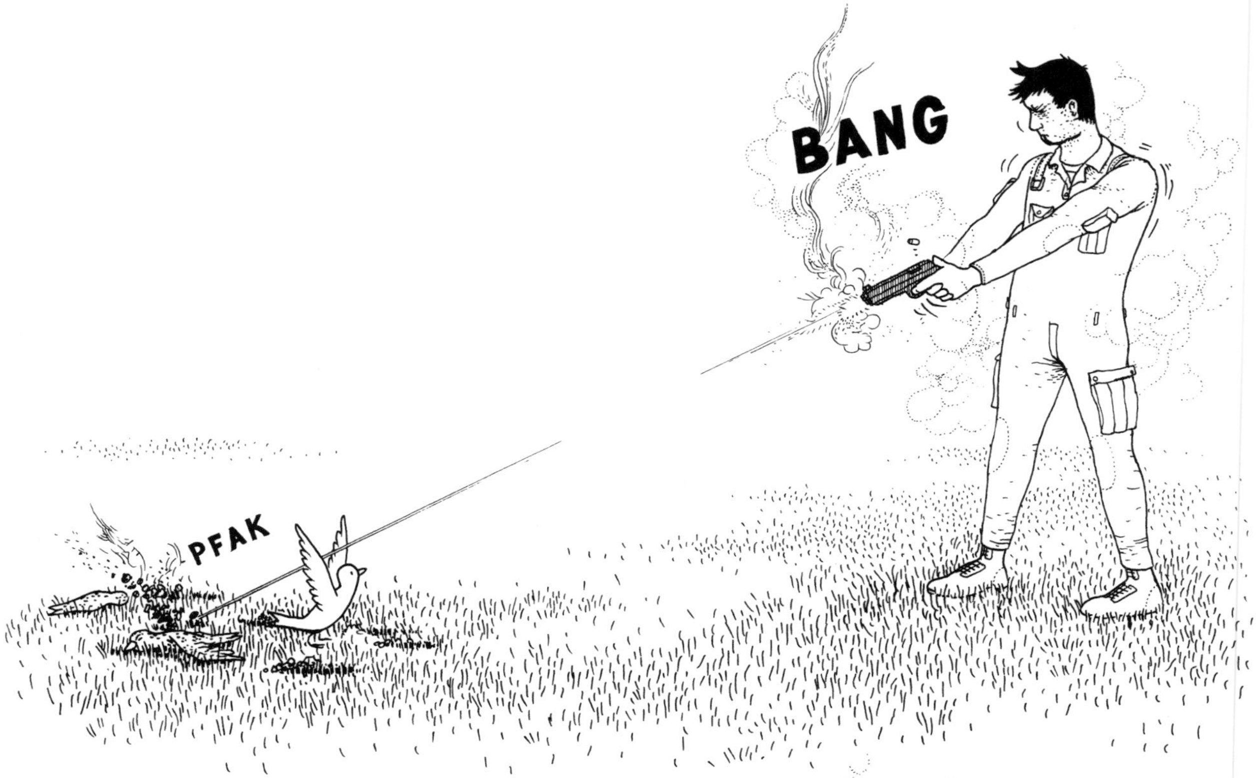
BANG
PFAK
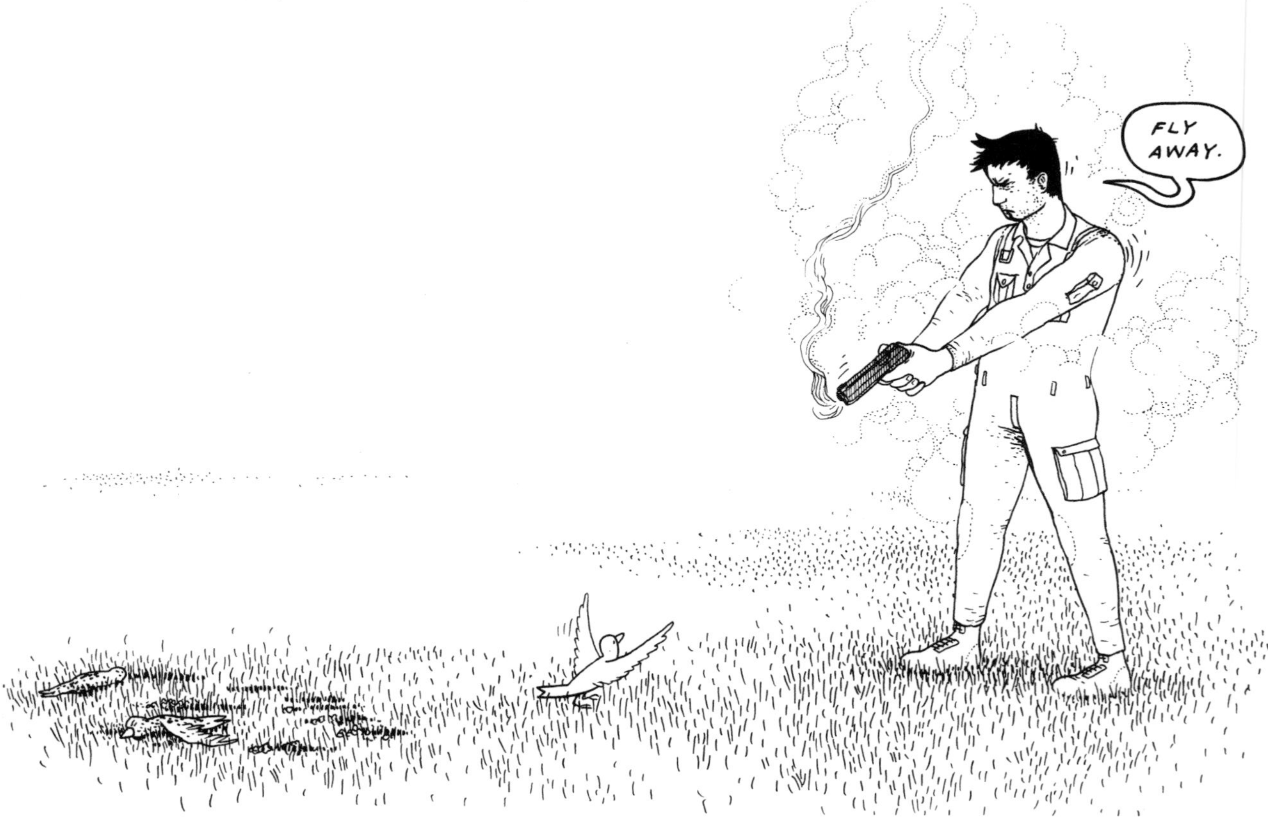
FLY AWAY.

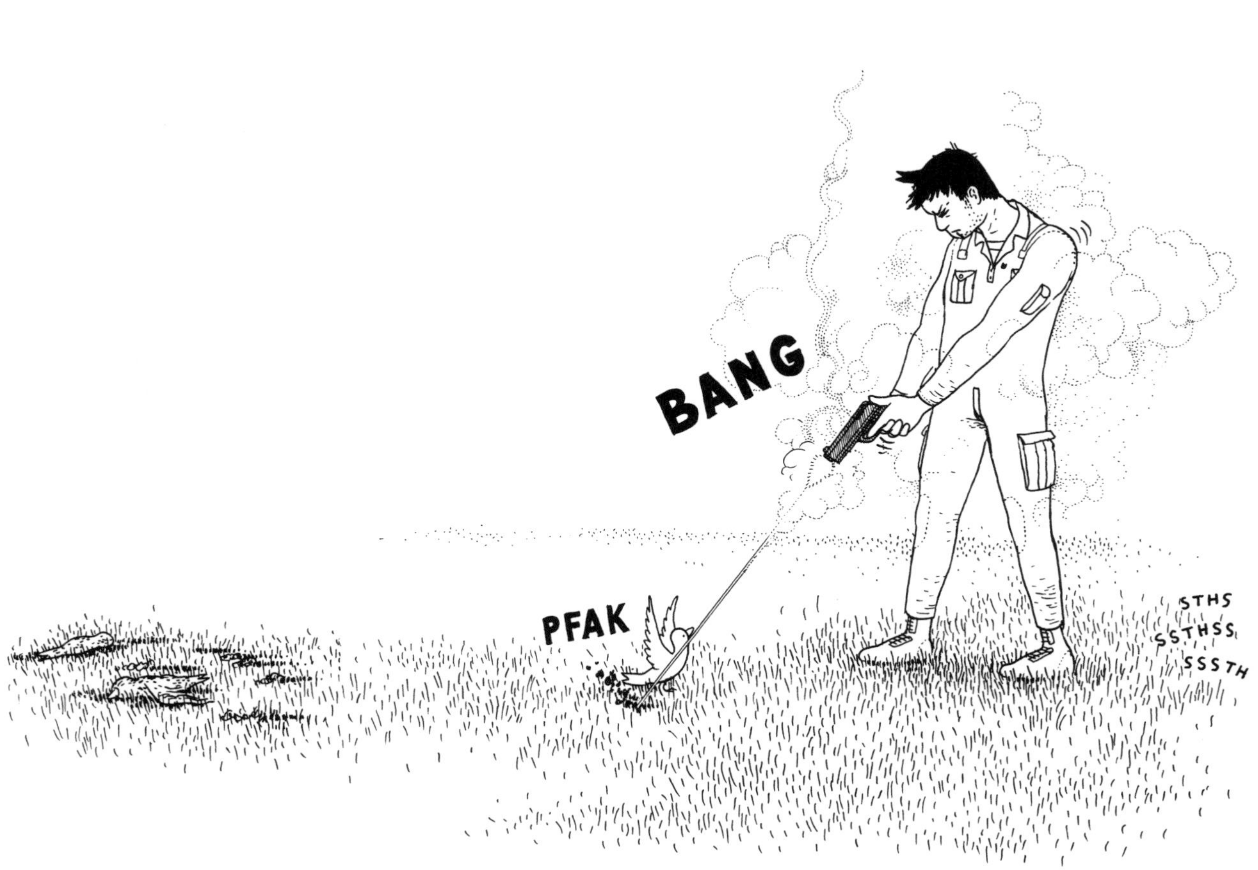
BANG
PFAK
STHS
SSTHSS
SSSTH

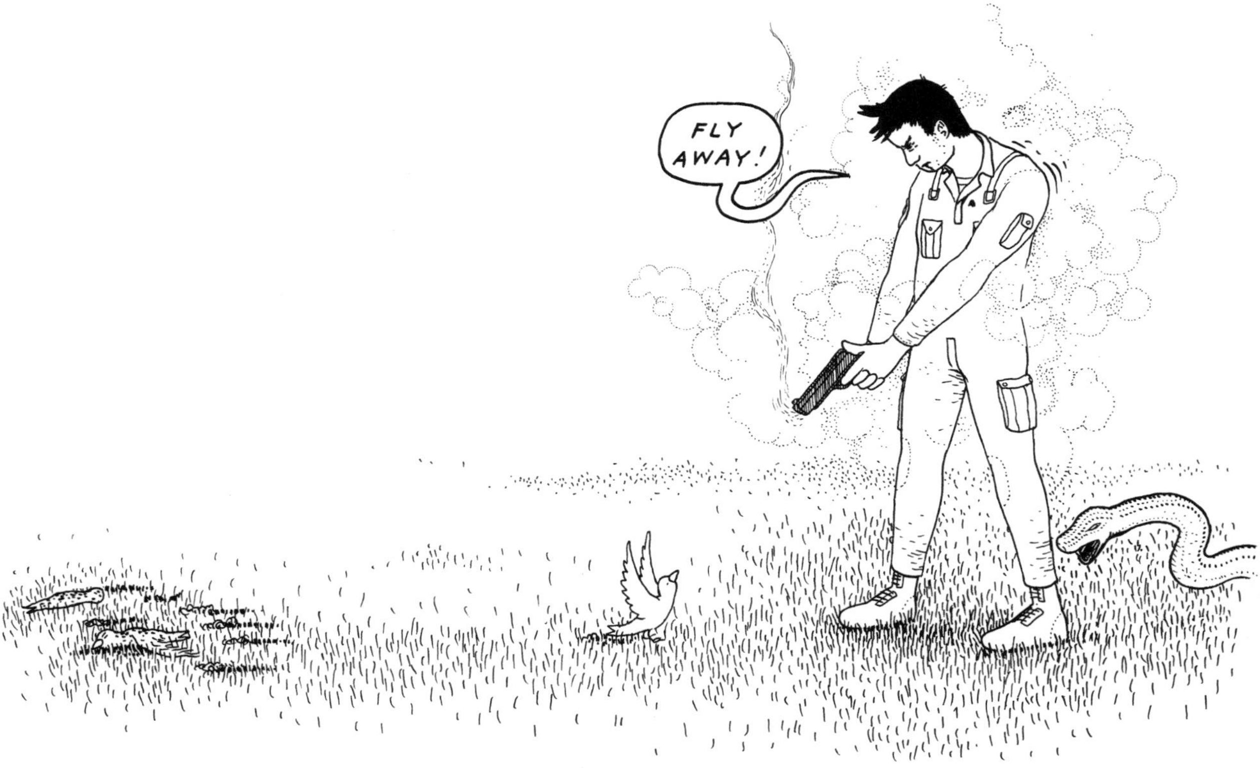
FLY AWAY!

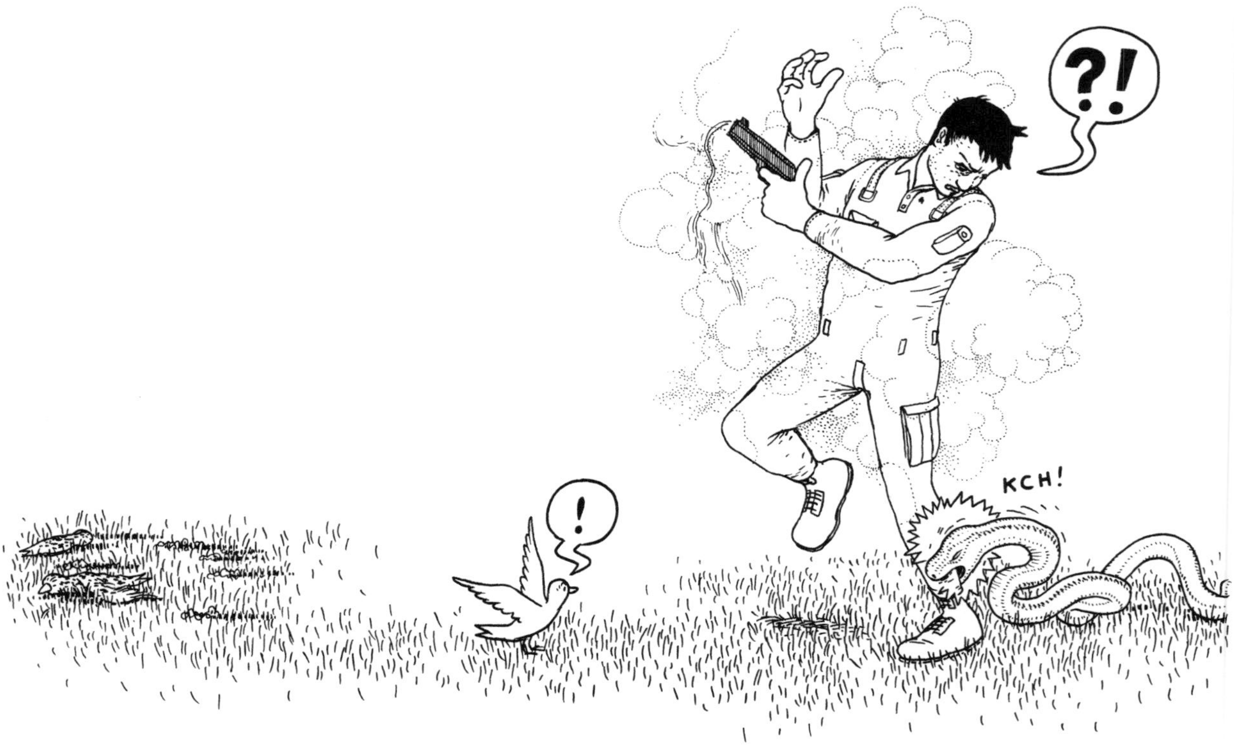
?!
KCH!
!

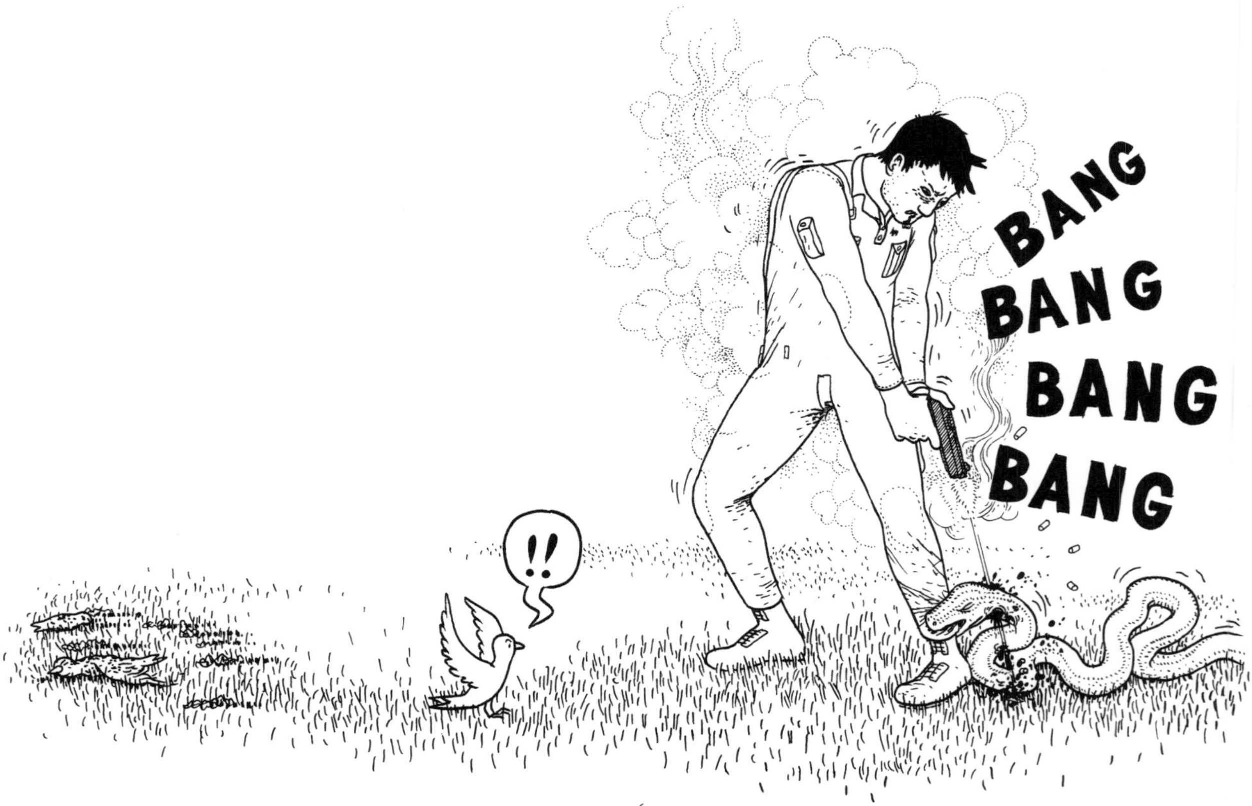
BANG
BANG
BANG
BANG
!!

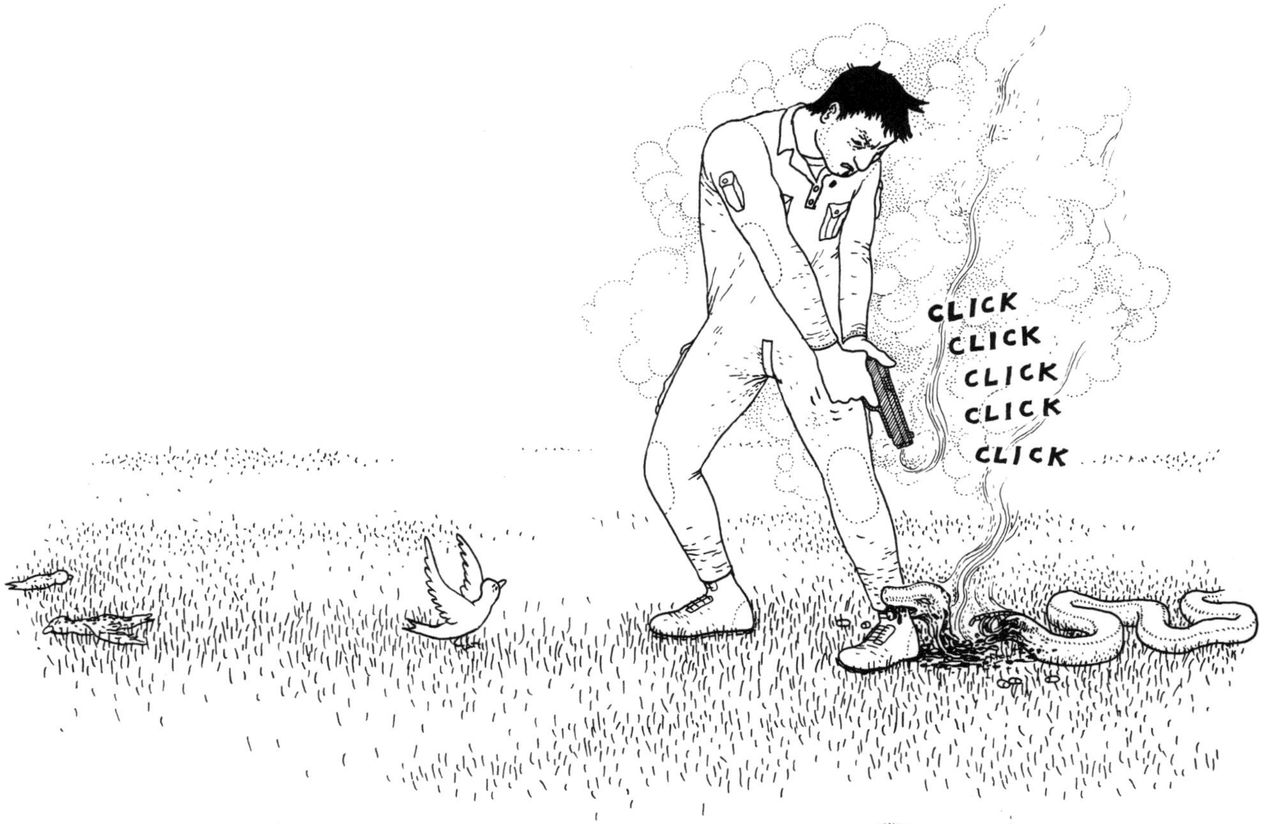
CLICK
CLICK
CLICK
CLICK
CLICK

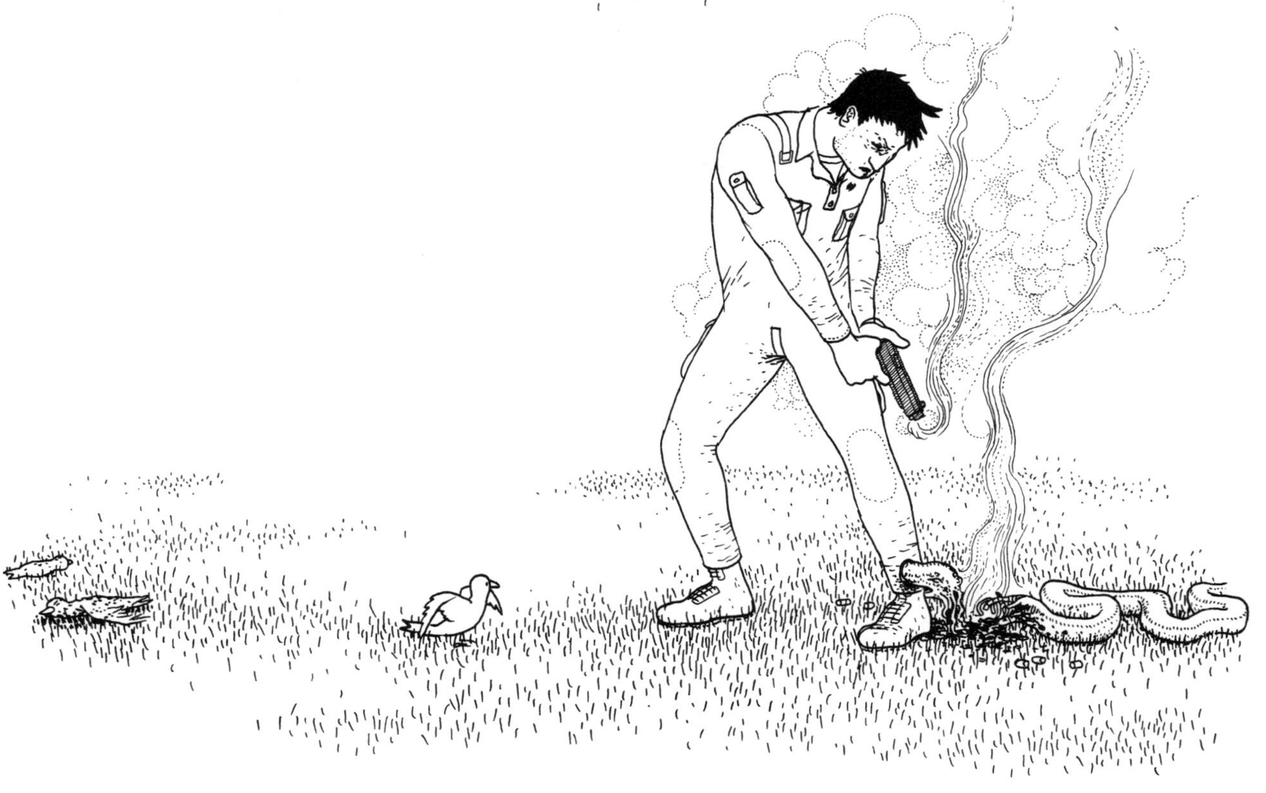

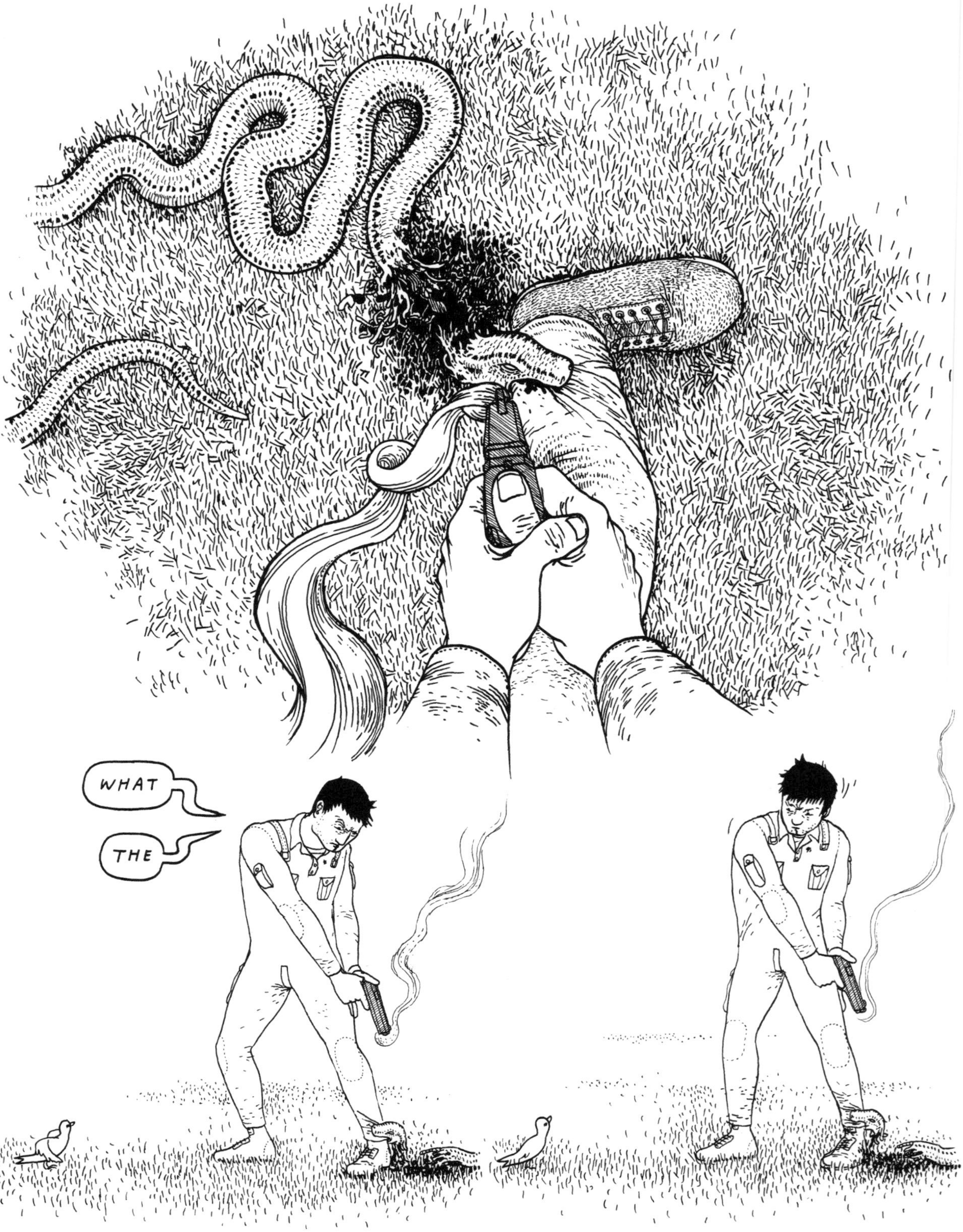
WHAT
THE

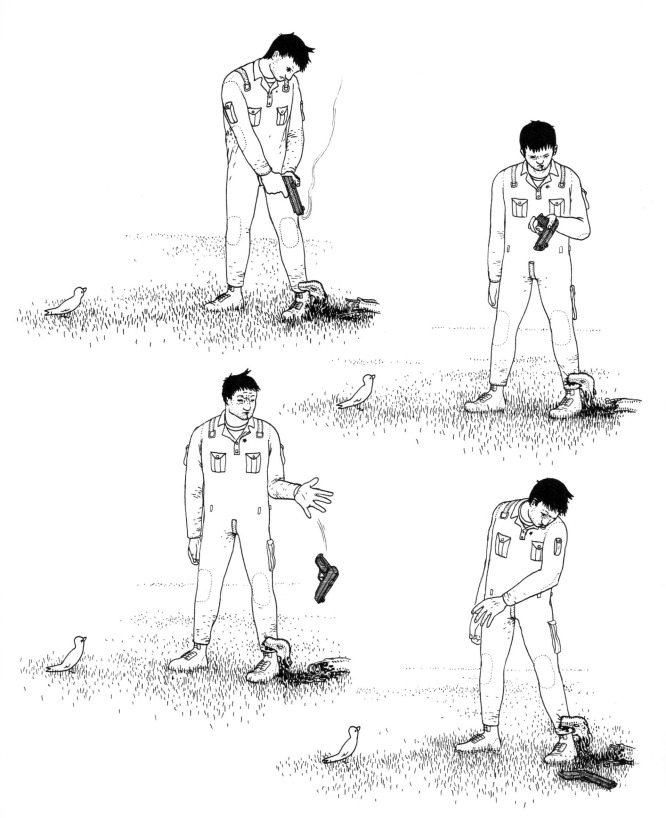

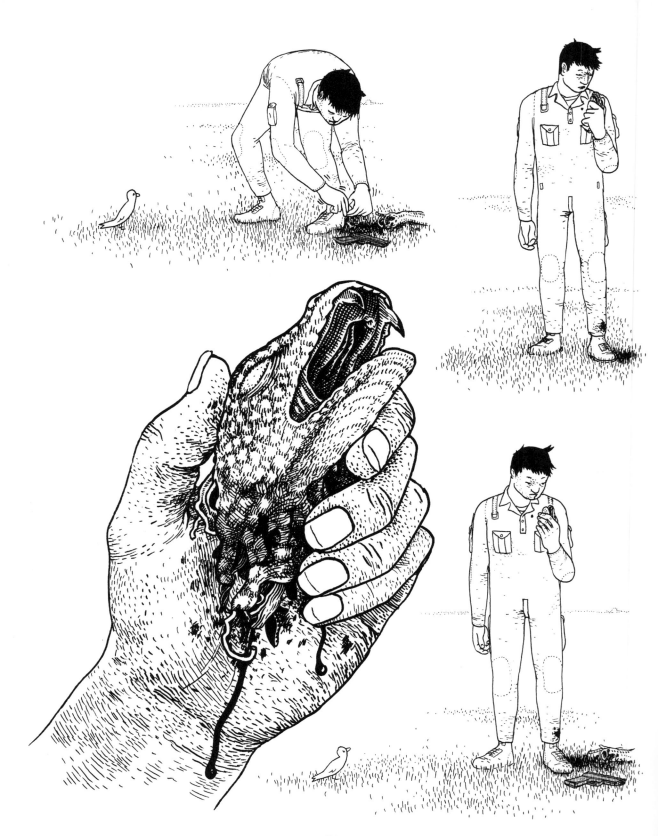

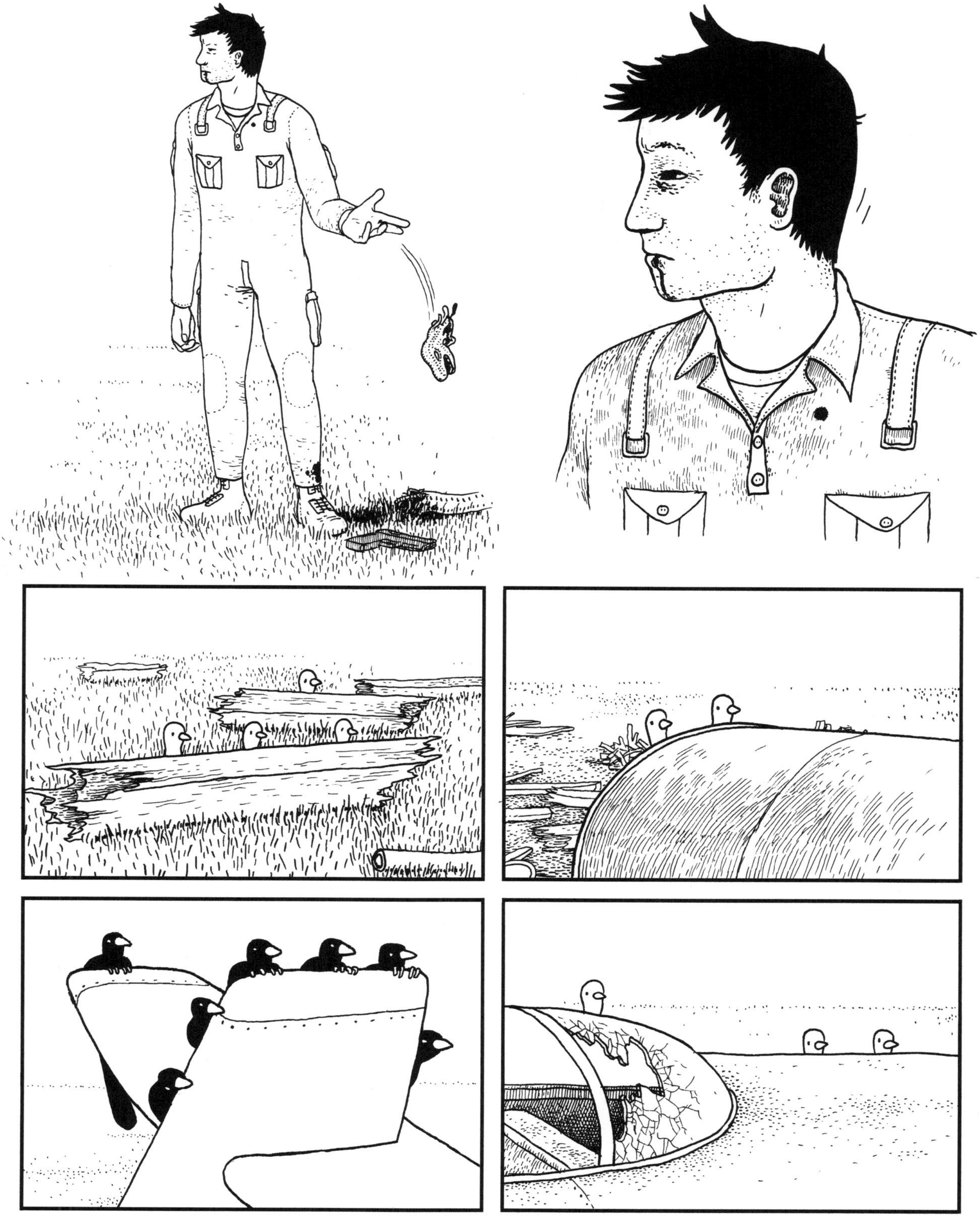

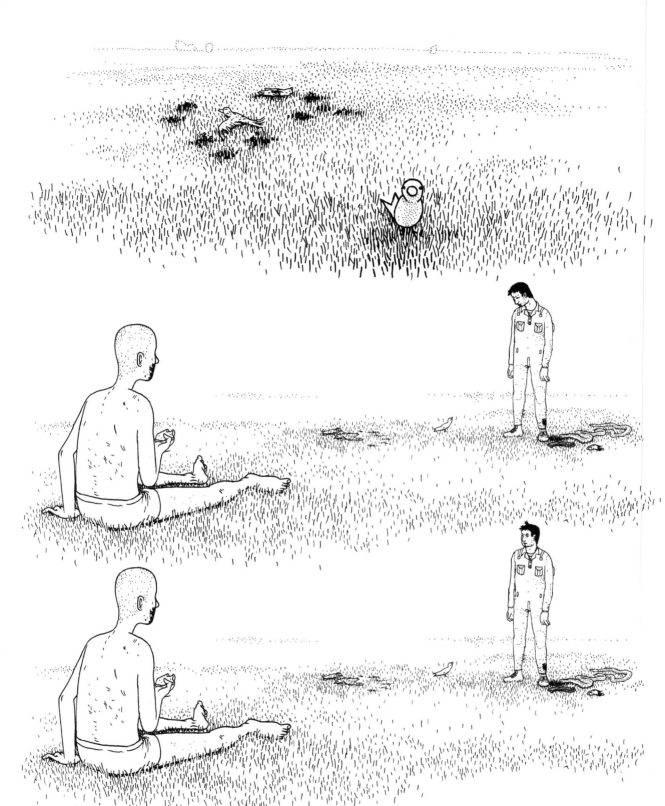

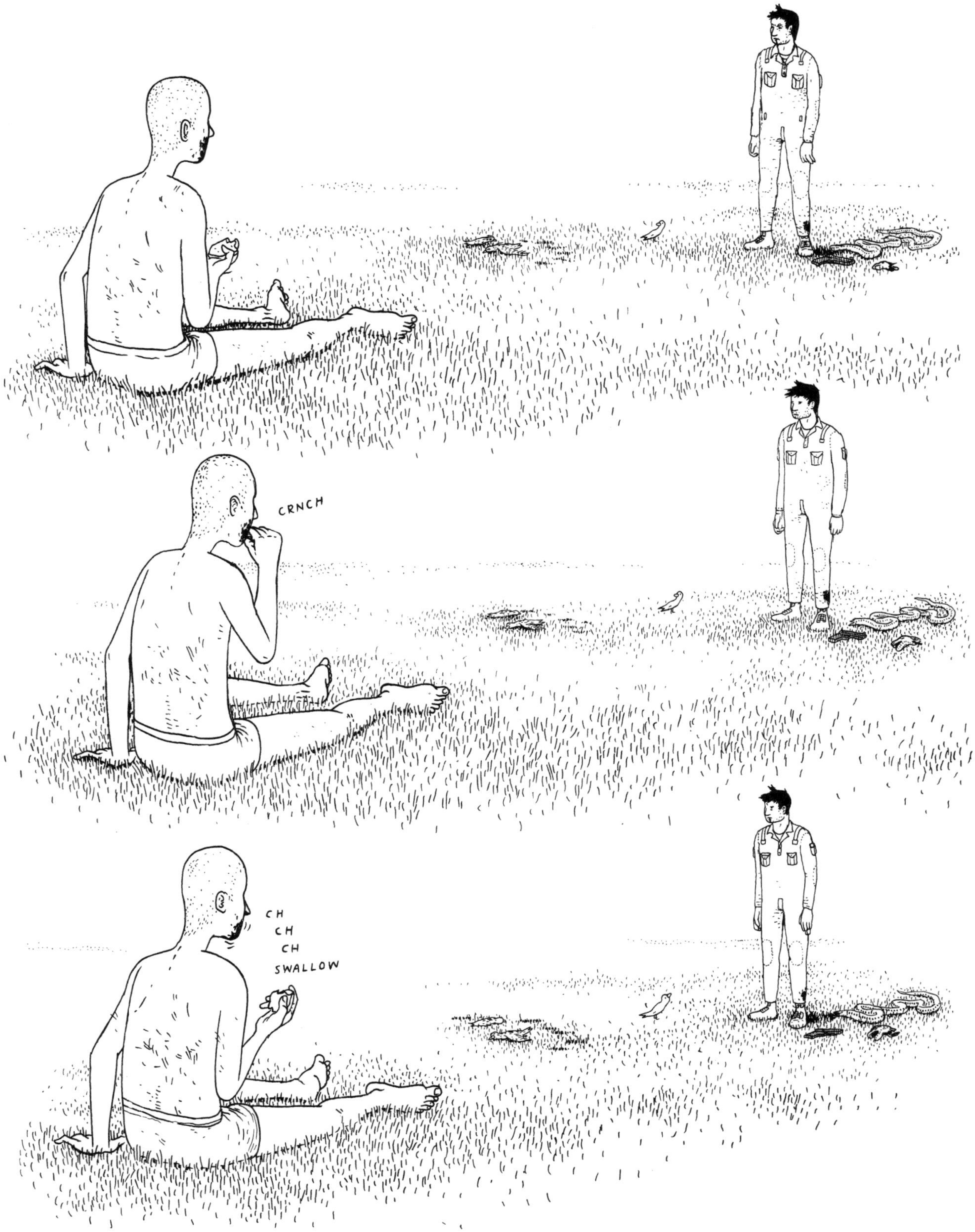
CRNCH
CH
CH
CH
SWALLOW

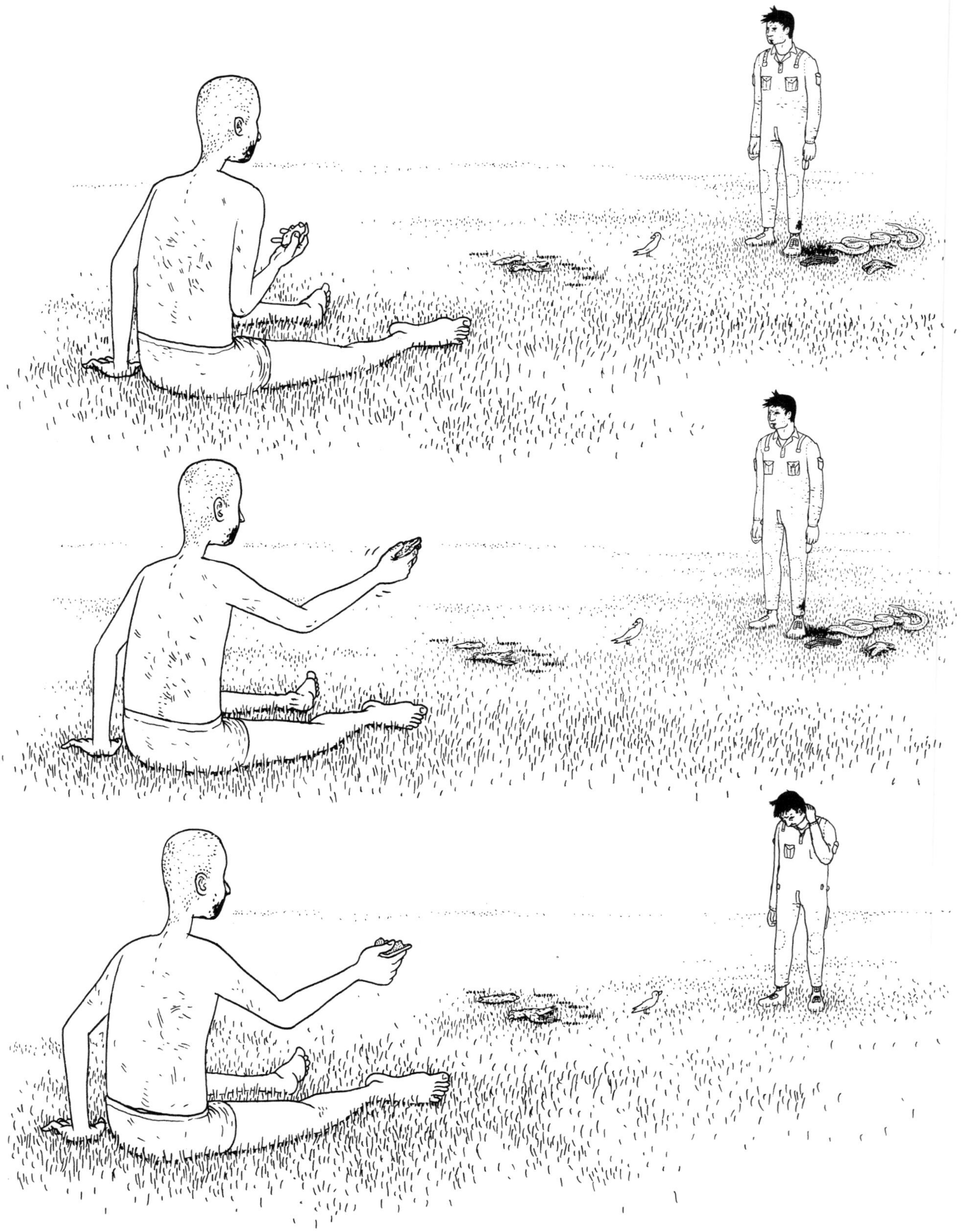

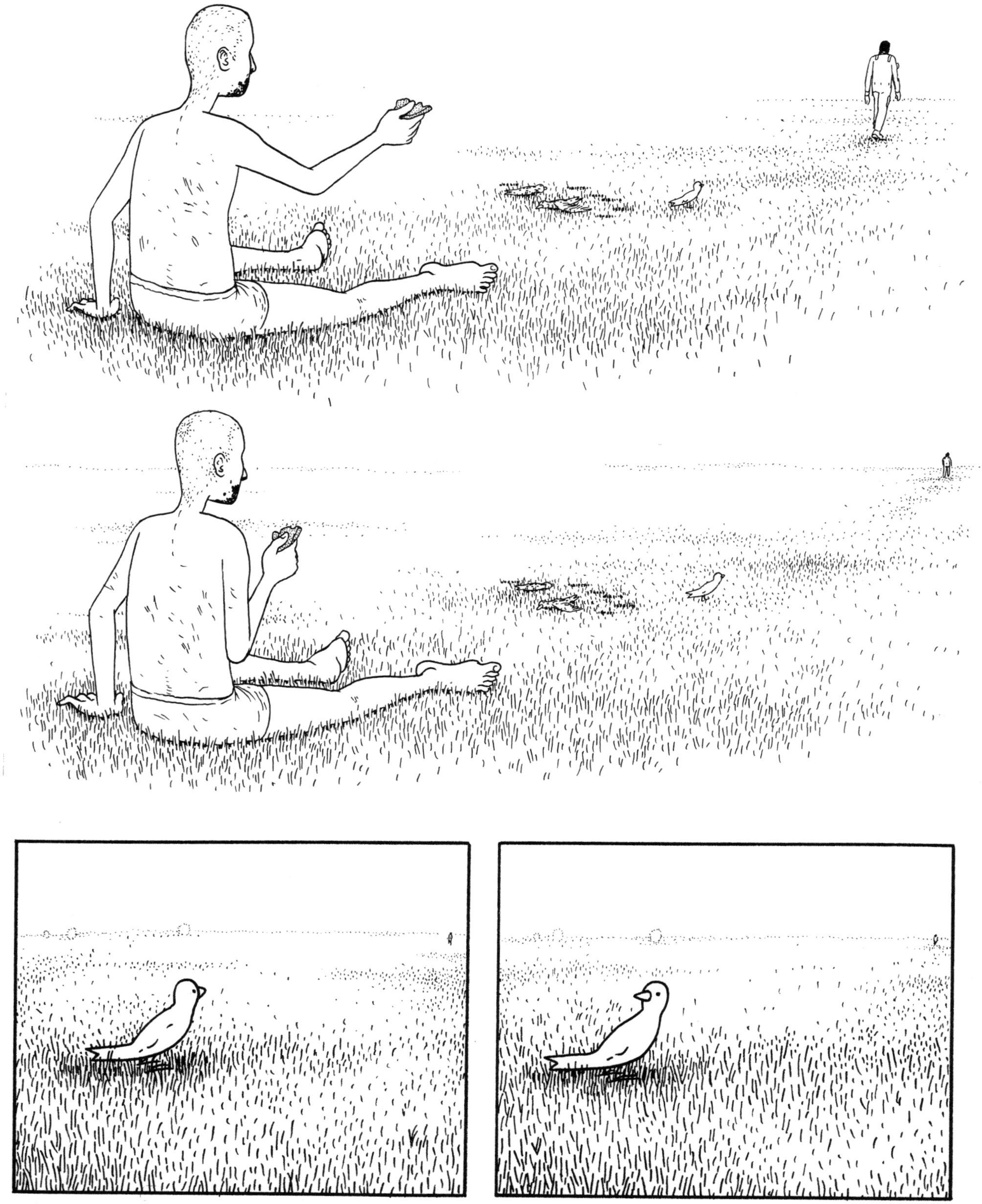

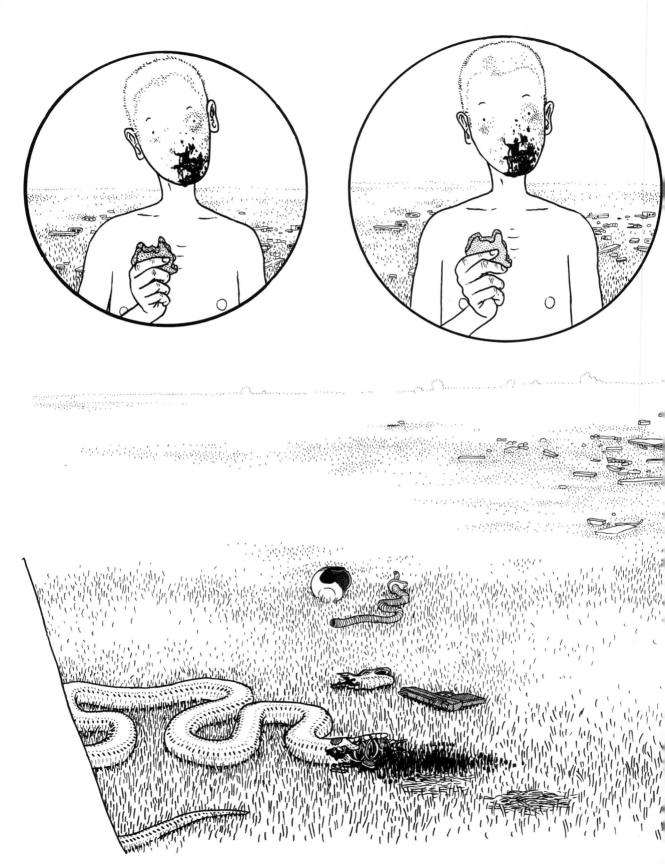

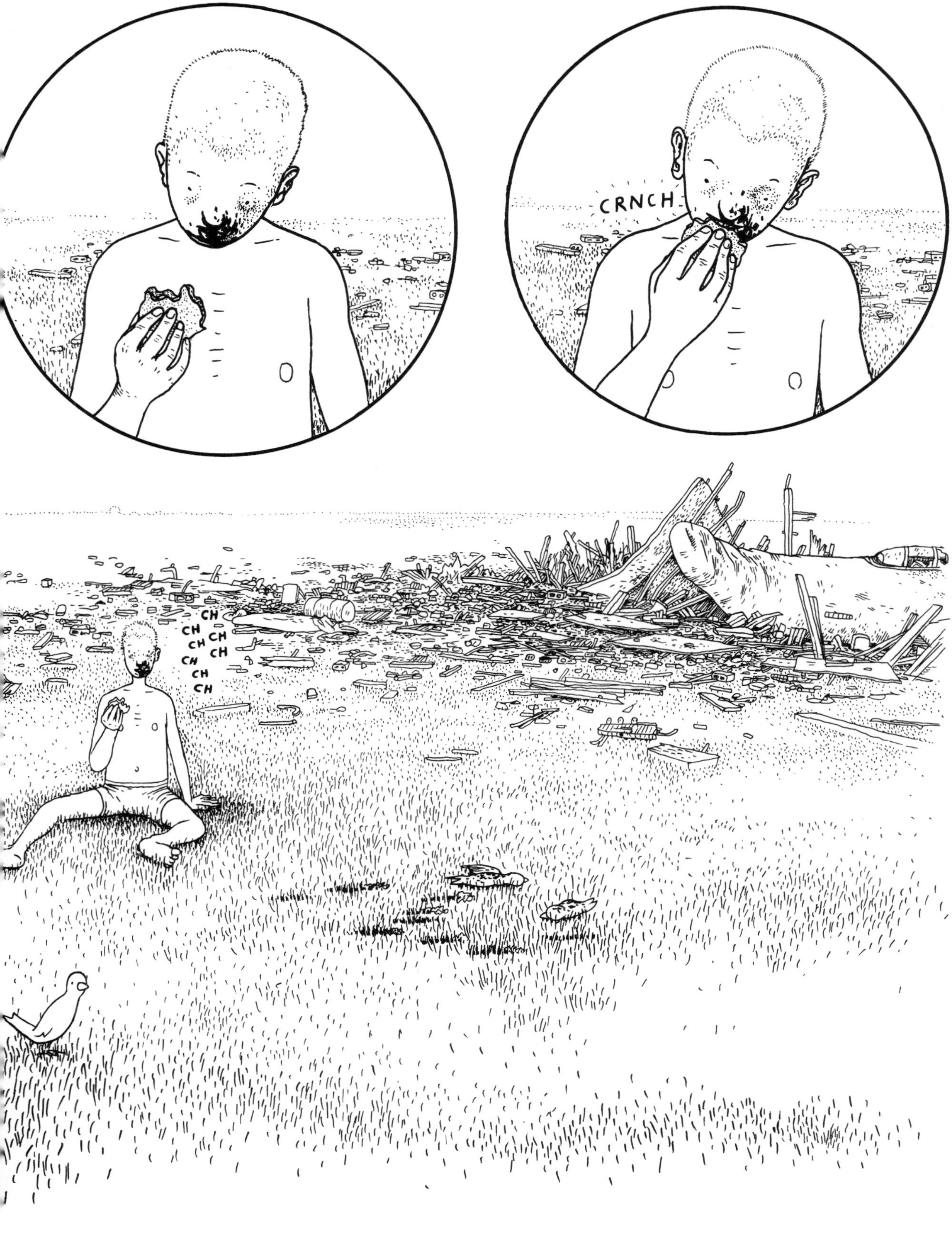
CRNCH
CH
CH
CH
CH
CH
CH
CH
CH
CH

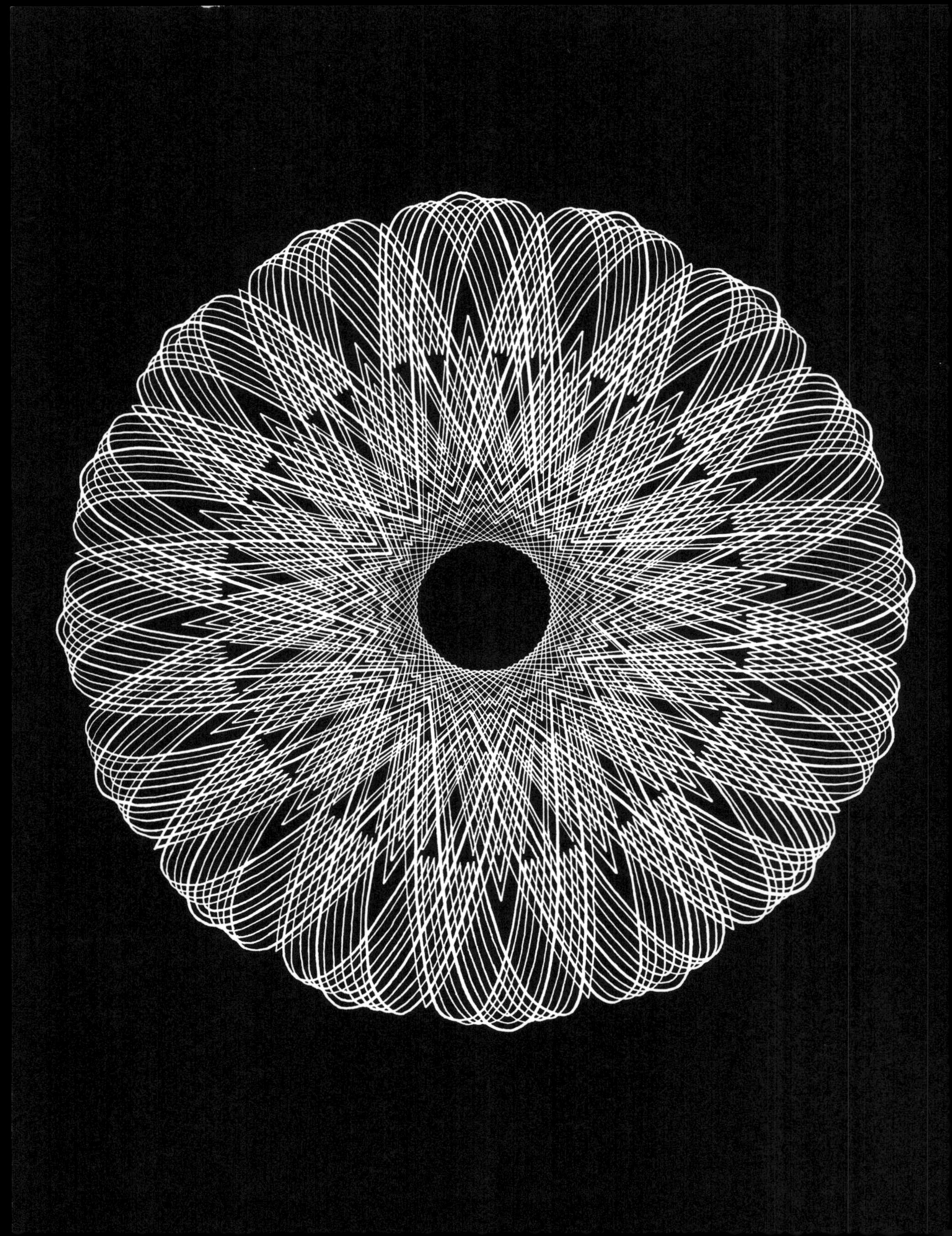

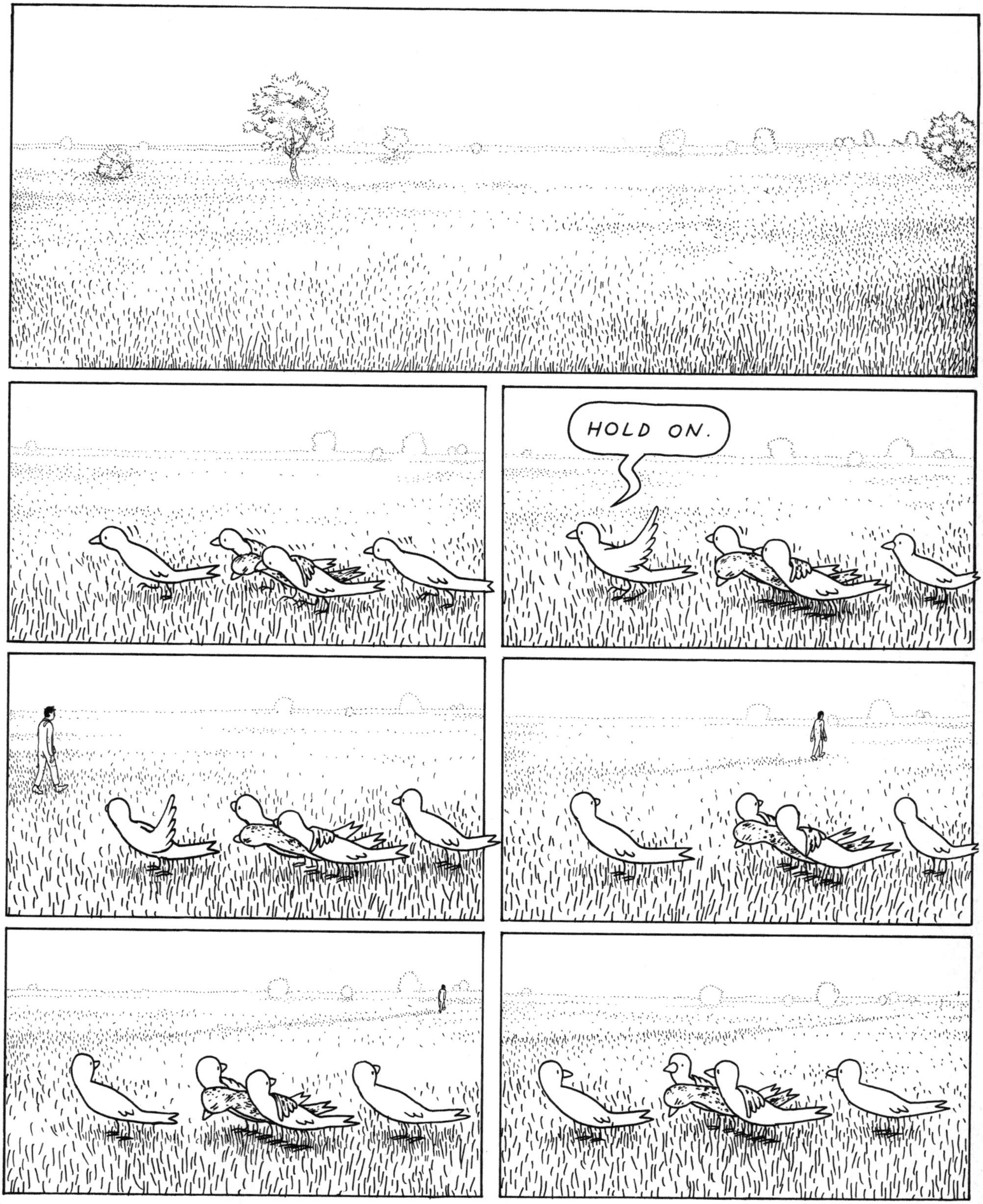
HOLD ON.

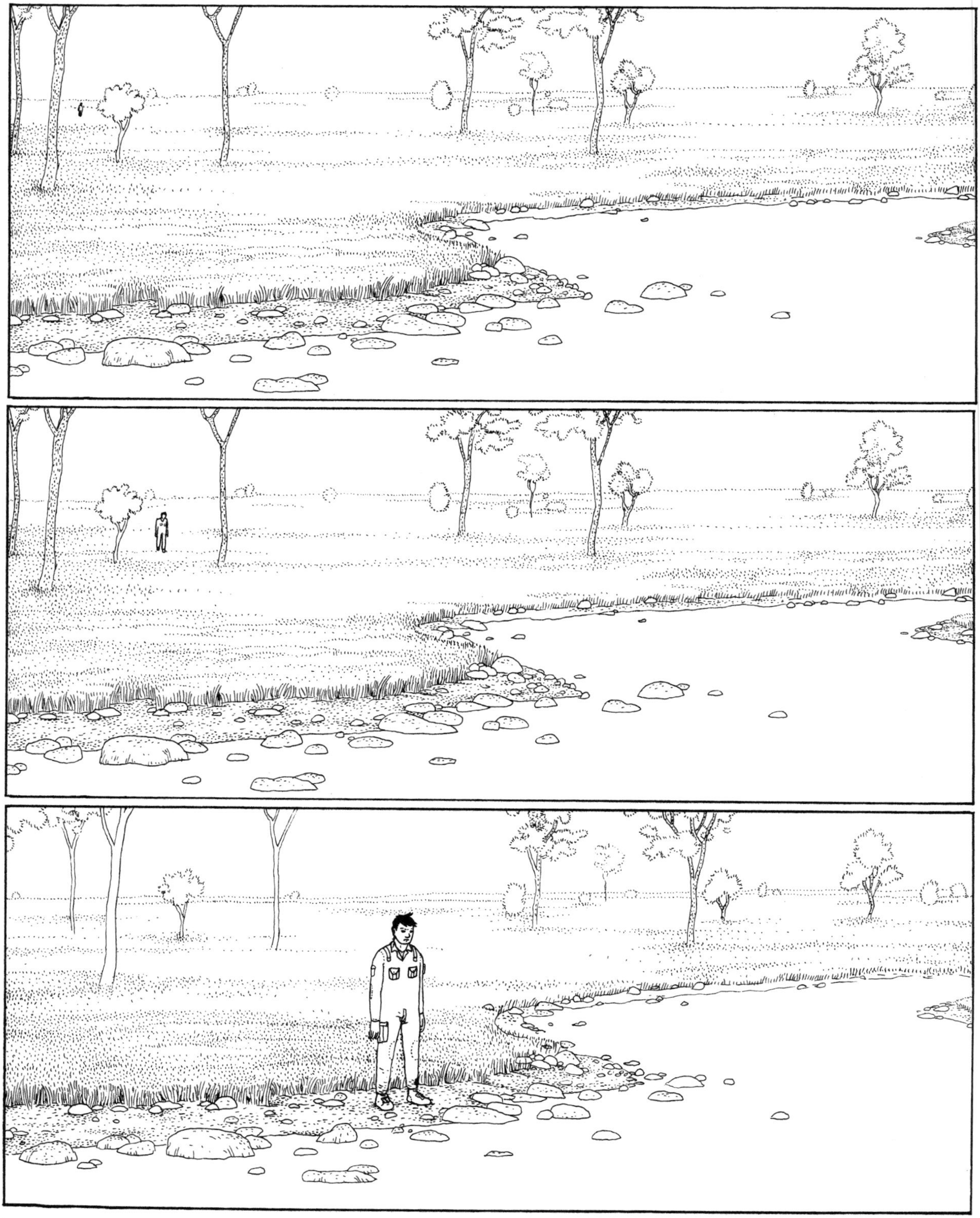

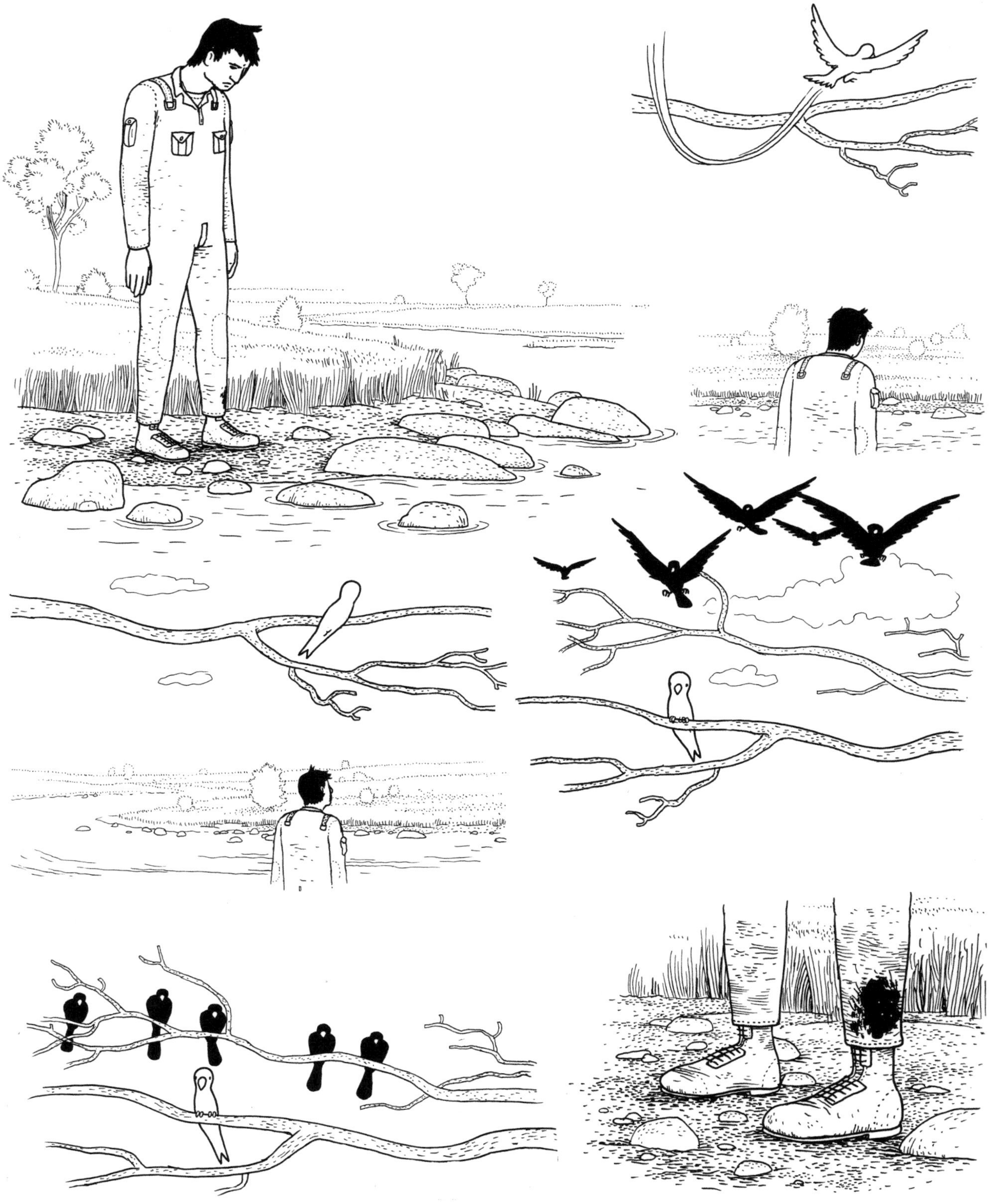

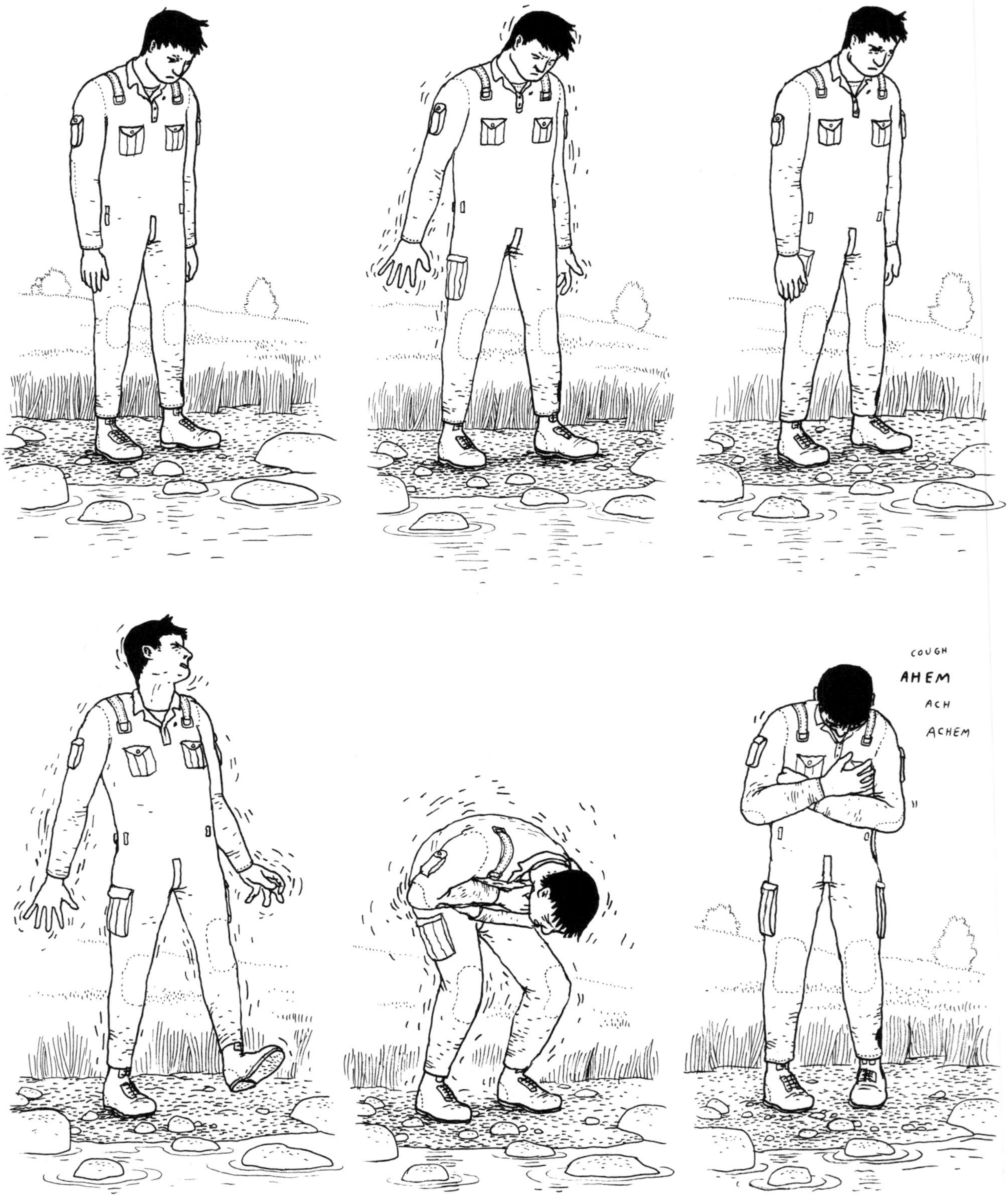
COUGH
AHEM
ACH
ACHEM

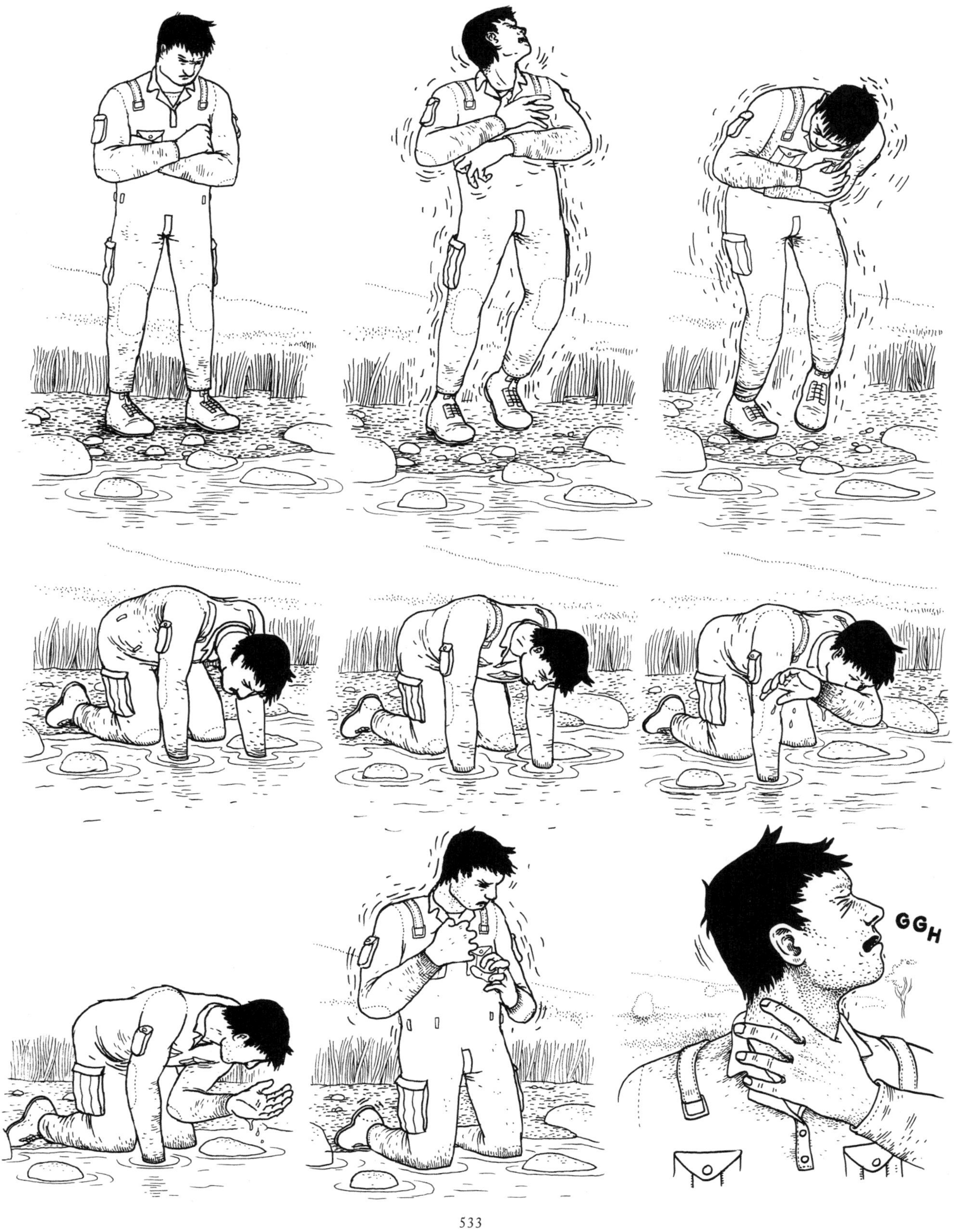
GGH

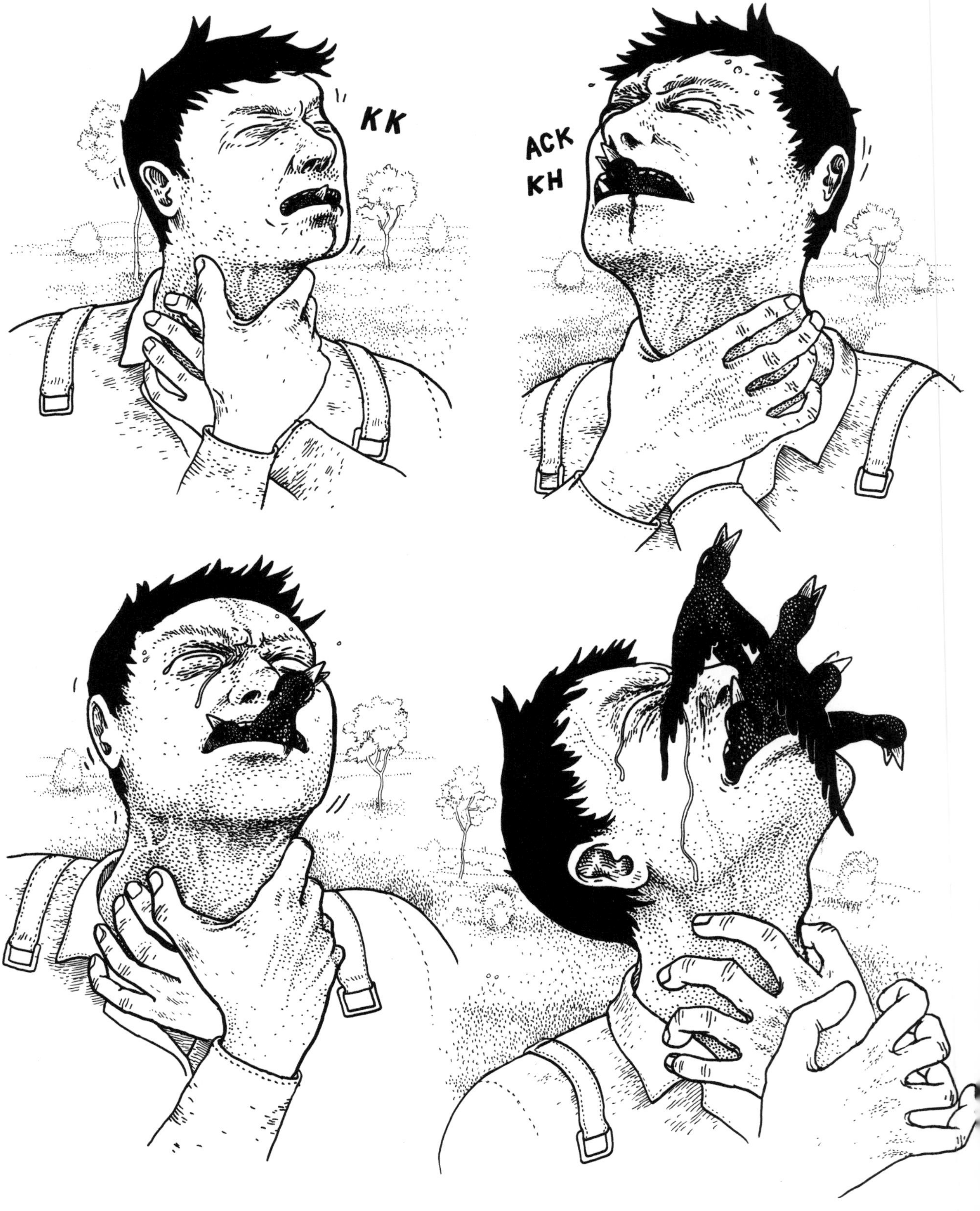
KK
ACK
KH

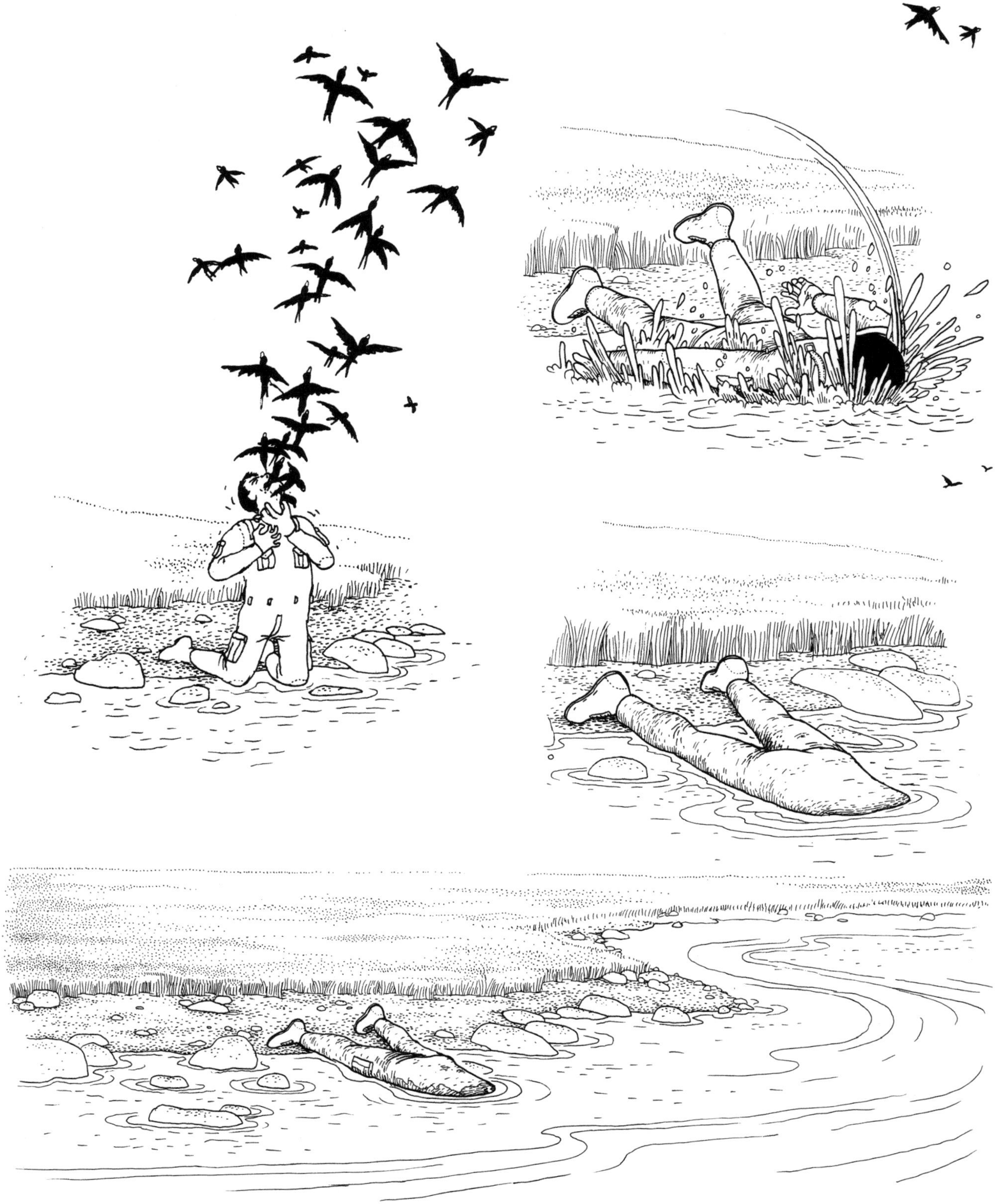

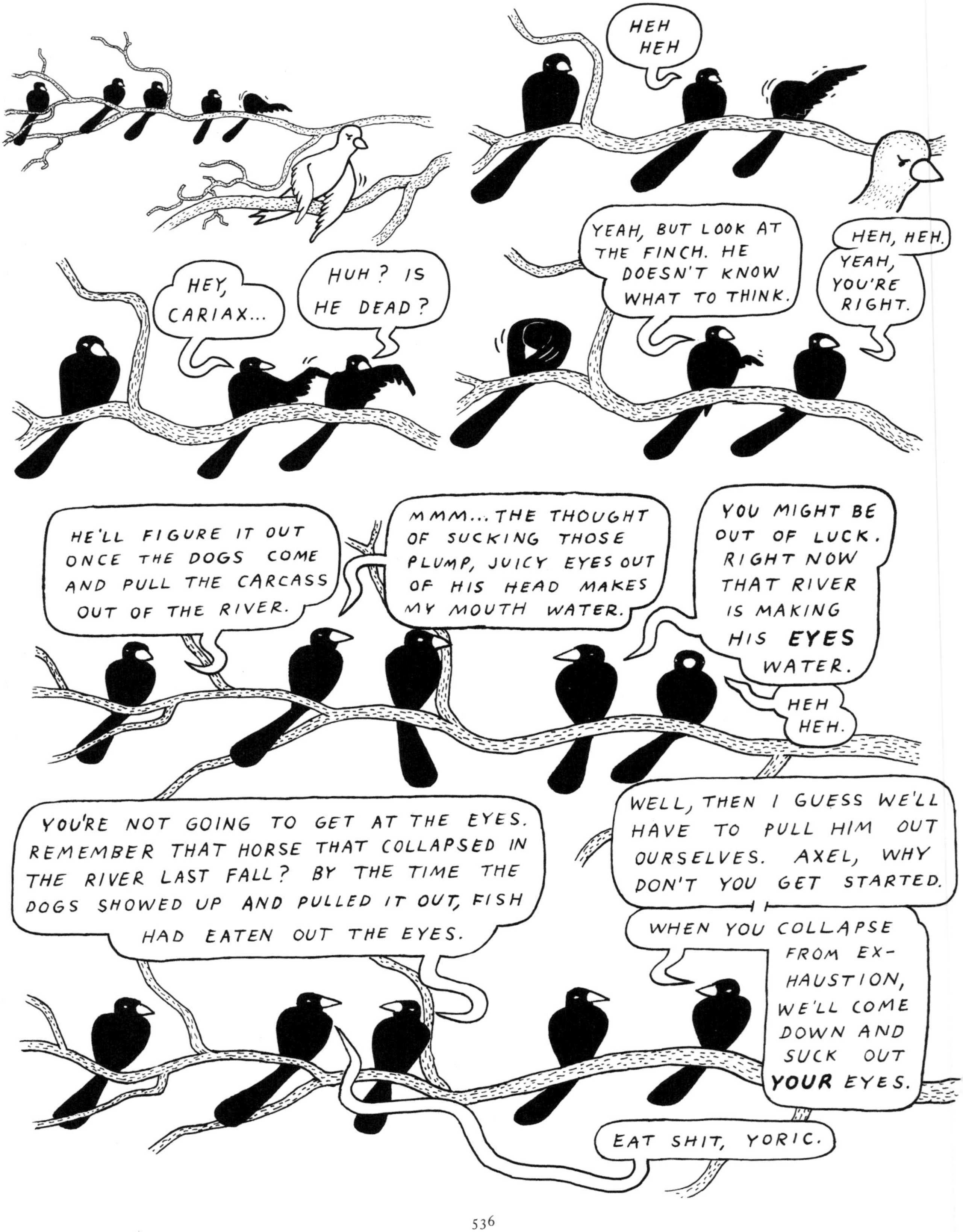
HEH HEH
HEY, CARIAX...
HUH? IS HE DEAD?
YEAH, BUT LOOK AT THE FINCH. HE DOESN'T KNOW WHAT TO THINK.
HEH, HEH. YEAH, YOU'RE RIGHT.
HE'LL FIGURE IT OUT ONCE THE DOGS COME AND PULL THE CARCASS OUT OF THE RIVER.
MMM... THE THOUGHT OF SUCKING THOSE PLUMP, JUICY EYES OUT OF HIS HEAD MAKES MY MOUTH WATER.
YOU MIGHT BE OUT OF LUCK. RIGHT NOW THAT RIVER IS MAKING HIS EYES WATER.
HEH HEH.
YOU'RE NOT GOING TO GET AT THE EYES. REMEMBER THAT HORSE THAT COLLAPSED IN THE RIVER LAST FALL? BY THE TIME THE DOGS SHOWED UP AND PULLED IT OUT, FISH HAD EATEN OUT THE EYES.
WELL, THEN I GUESS WE'LL HAVE TO PULL HIM OUT OURSELVES. AXEL, WHY DON'T YOU GET STARTED.
WHEN YOU COLLAPSE FROM EXHAUSTION, WE'LL COME DOWN AND SUCK OUT YOUR EYES.
EAT SHIT, YORIC.

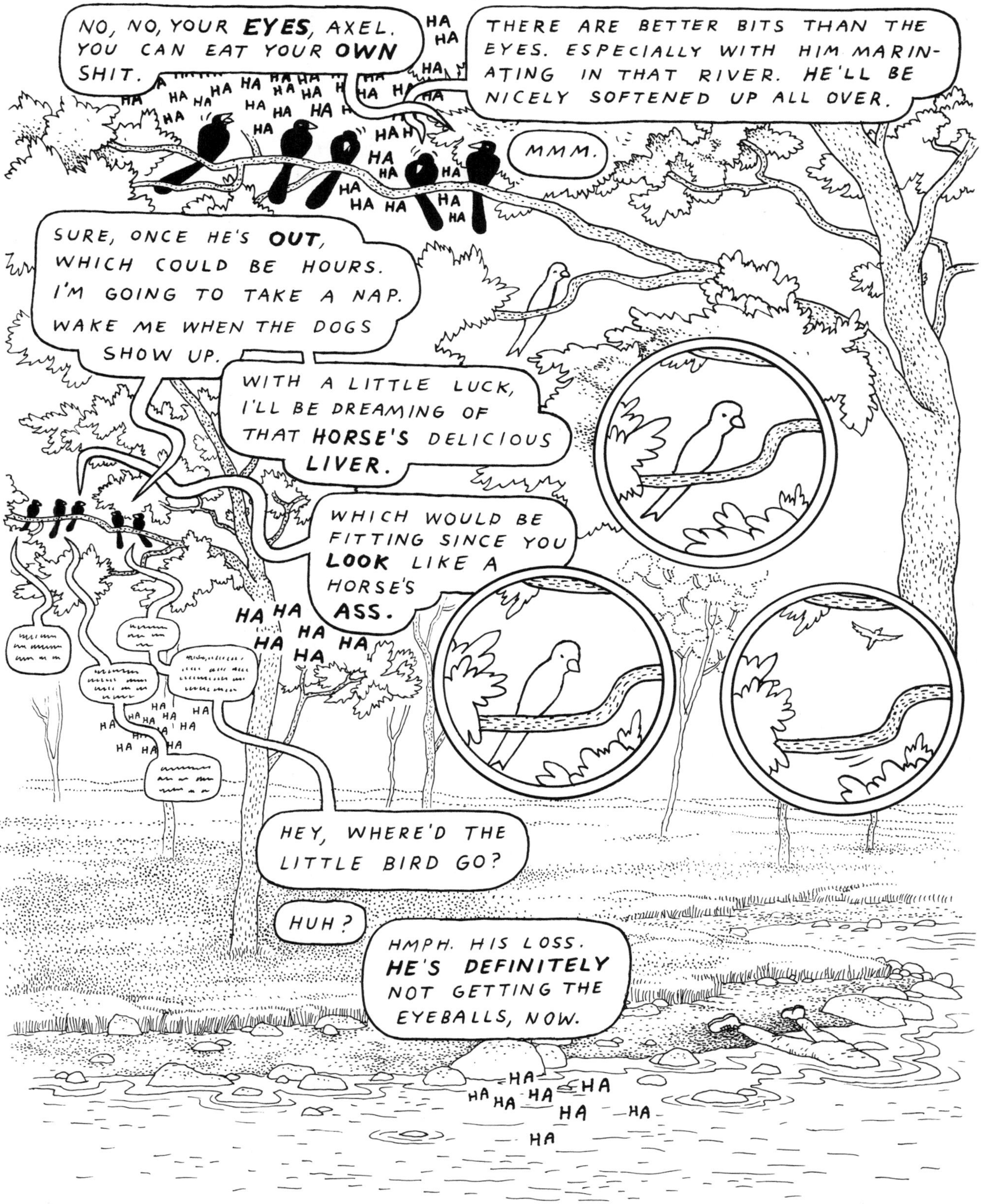
NO, NO, YOUR EYES, AXEL. YOU CAN EAT YOUR OWN SHIT.
THERE ARE BETTER BITS THAN THE EYES. ESPECIALLY WITH HIM MARINATING IN THAT RIVER. HE'LL BE NICELY SOFTENED UP ALL OVER.
MMM.
SURE, ONCE HE'S OUT, WHICH COULD BE HOURS. I'M GOING TO TAKE A NAP. WAKE ME WHEN THE DOGS SHOW UP.
WITH A LITTLE LUCK, I'LL BE DREAMING OF THAT HORSE'S DELICIOUS LIVER.
WHICH WOULD BE FITTING SINCE YOU LOOK LIKE A HORSE'S ASS.
HA HA HA HA HA HA
HEY, WHERE'D THE LITTLE BIRD GO?
HUH?
HMPH. HIS LOSS. HE'S DEFINITELY NOT GETTING THE EYEBALLS, NOW.
HA HA HA HA HA HA HA HA

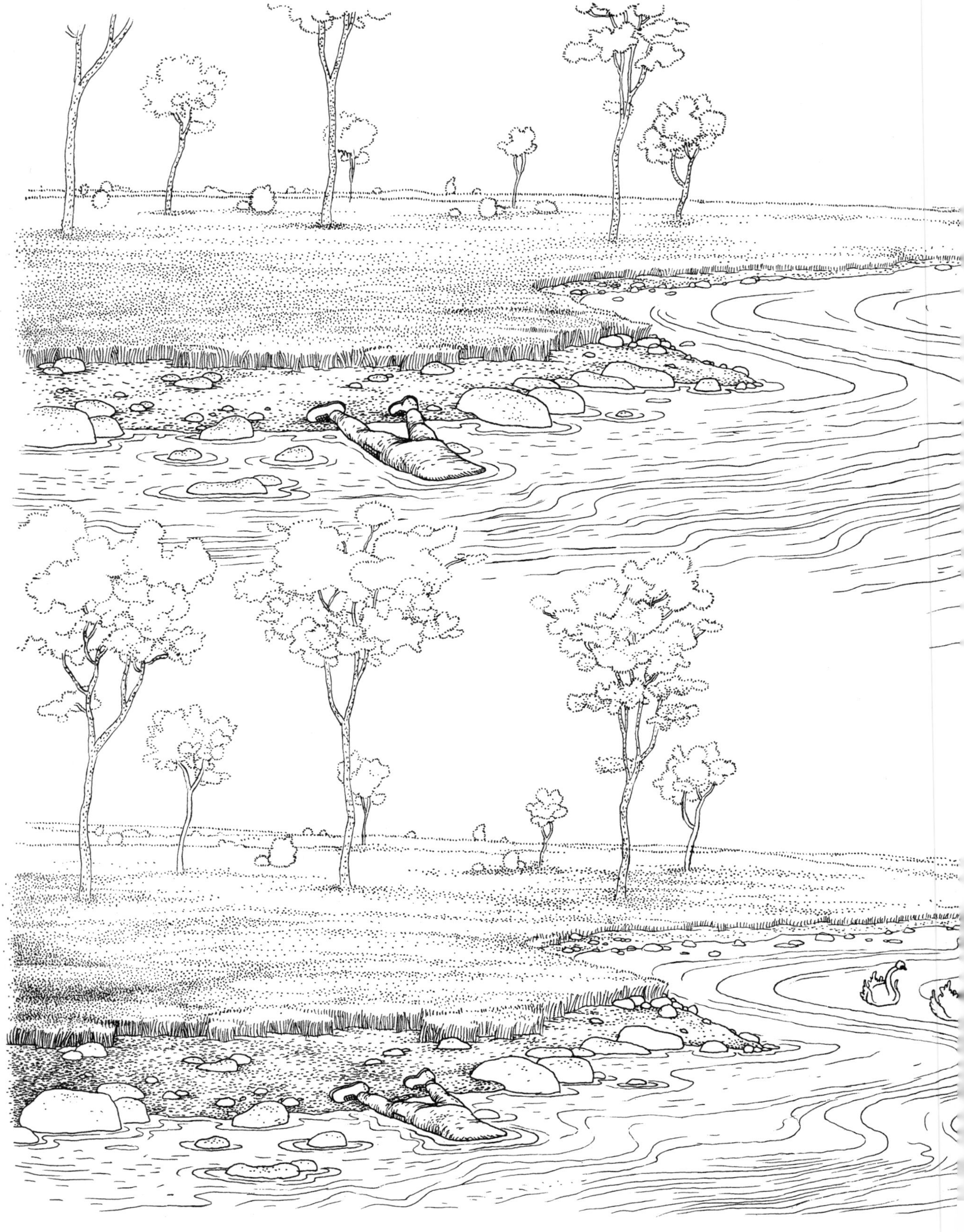

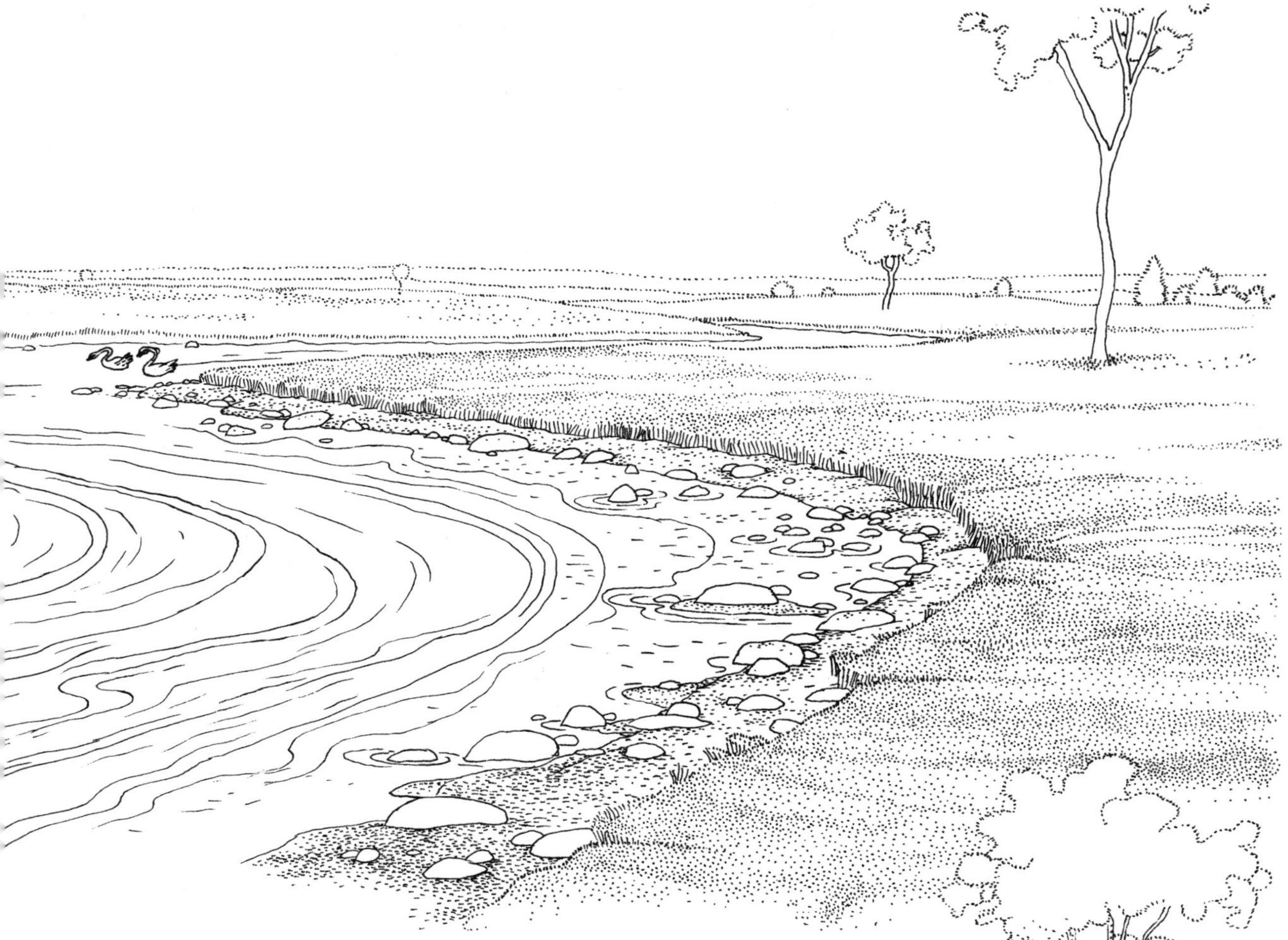

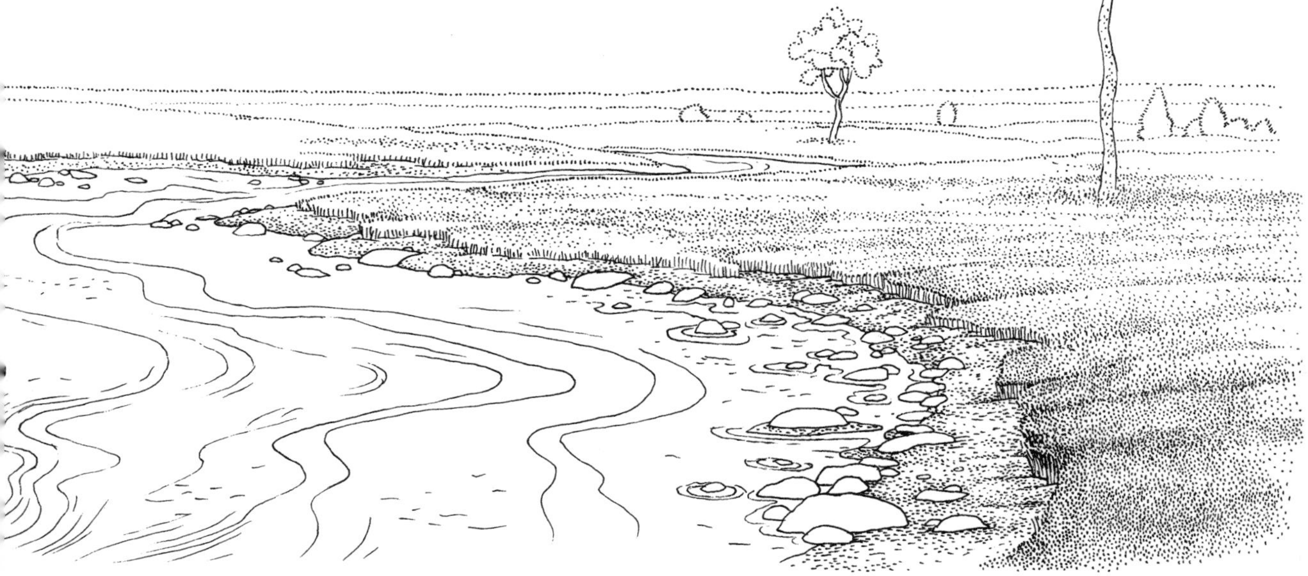

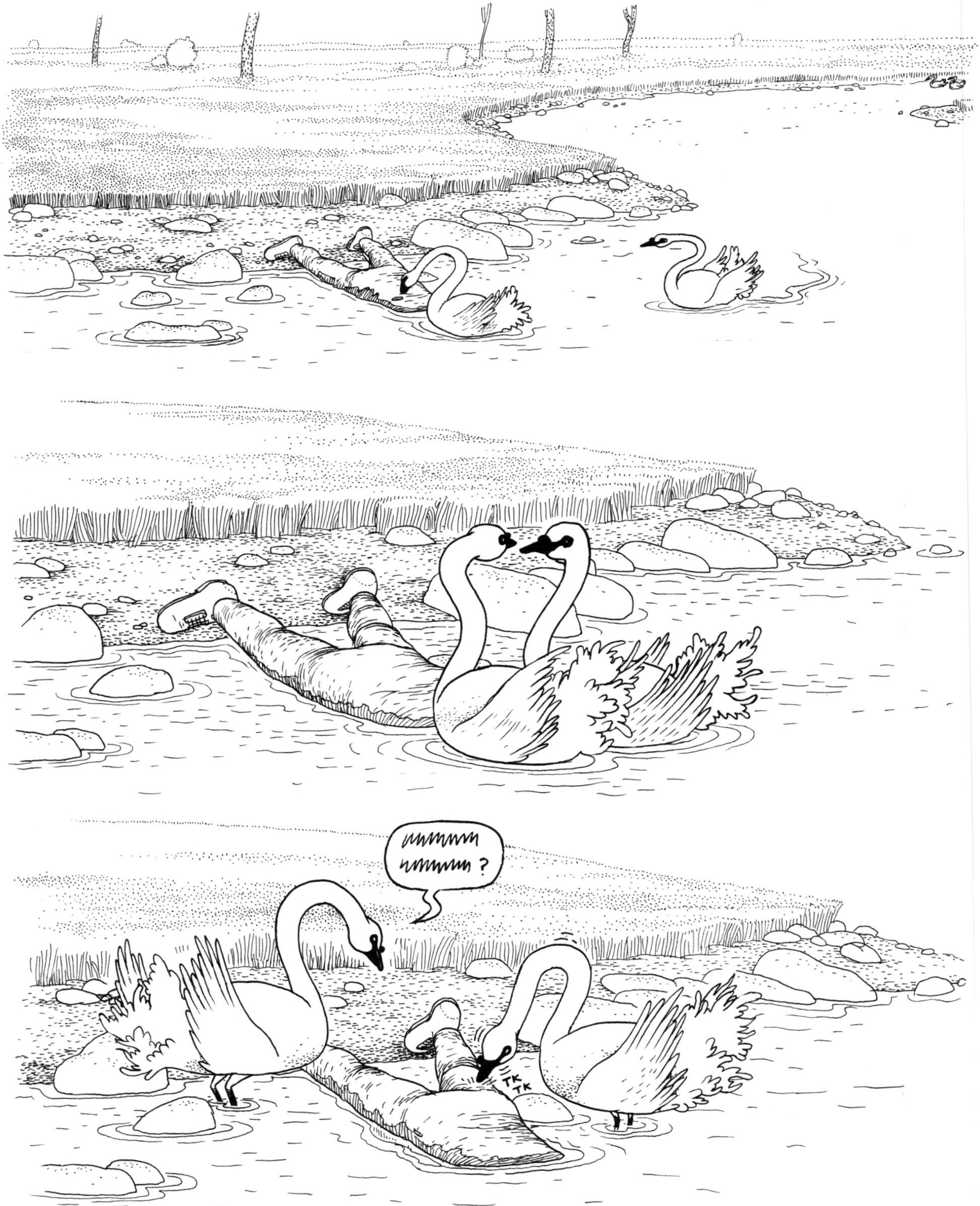
TK TK

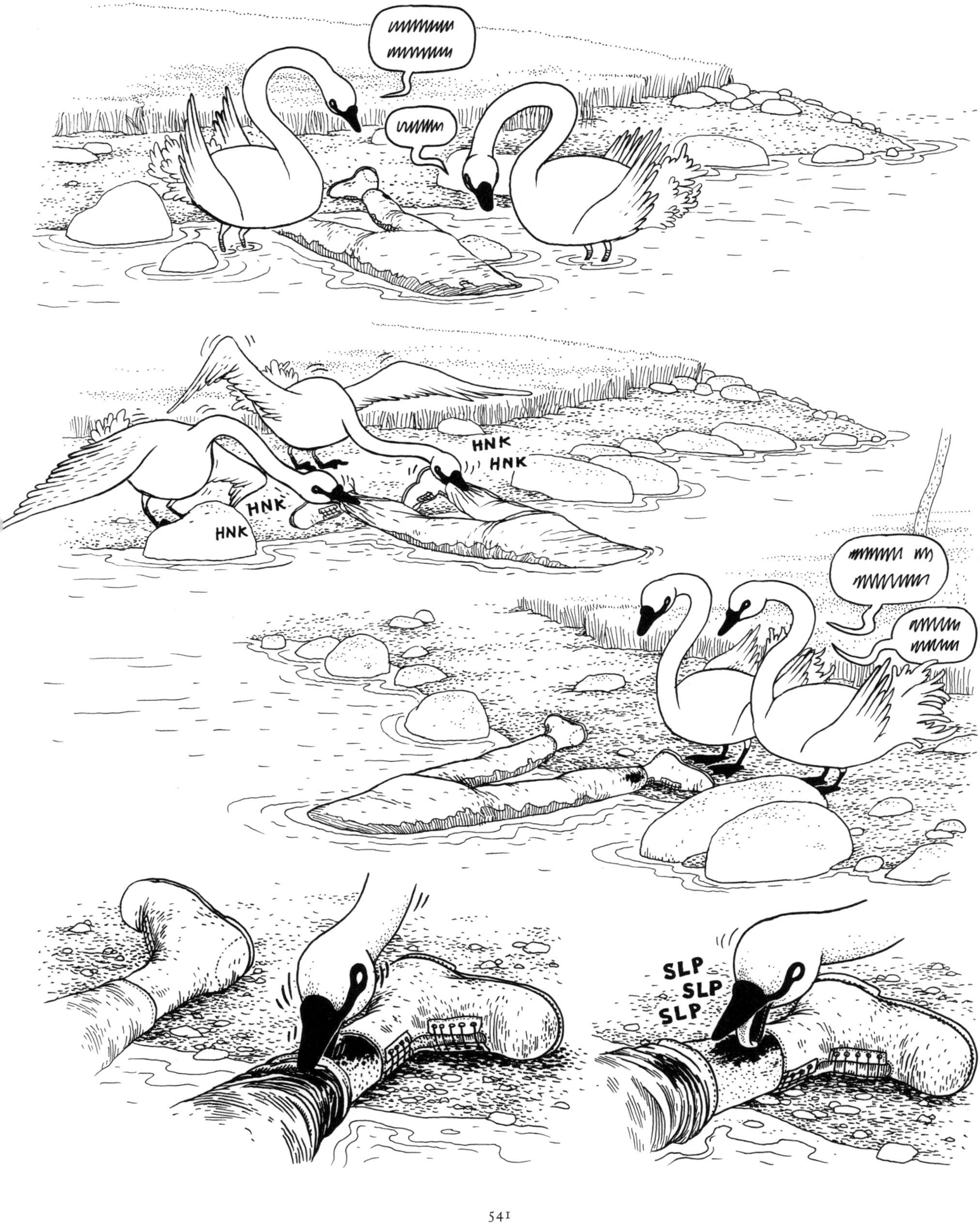
HNK
HNK
HNK
HNK
SLP
SLP
SLP

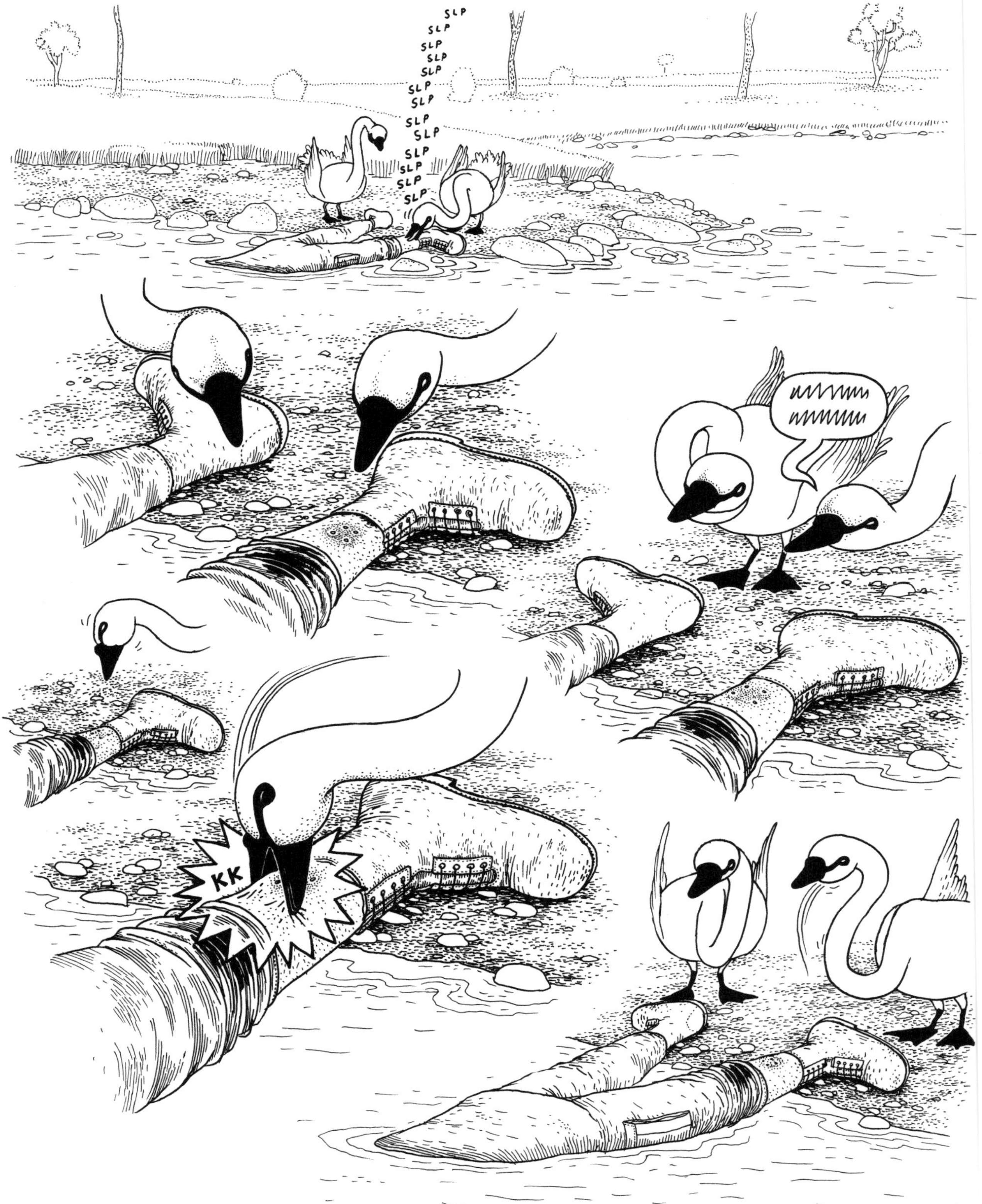
SLP
SLP
SLP
SLP
SLP
SLP
SLP
SLP
SLP
SLP
SLP
SLP
SLP
KK

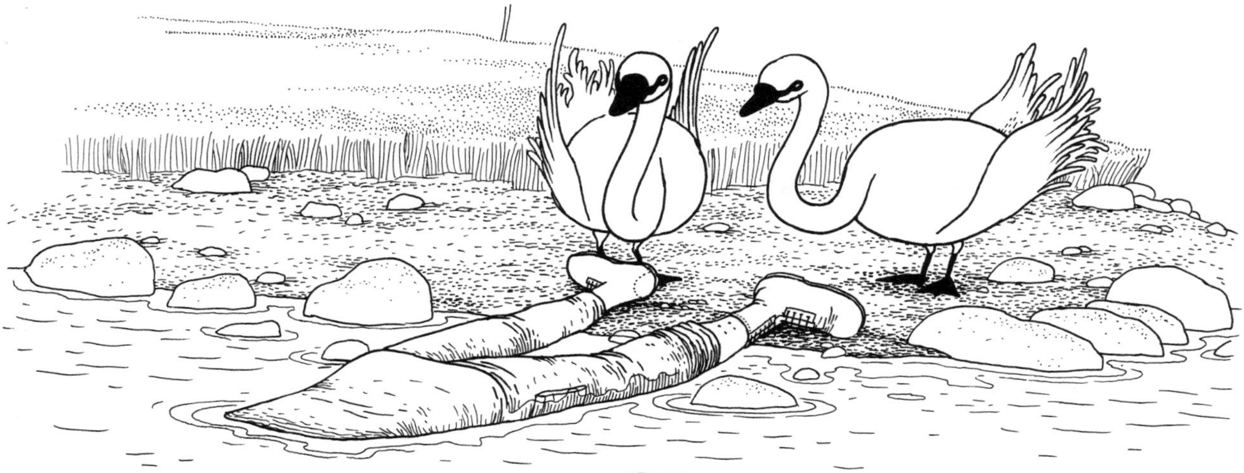

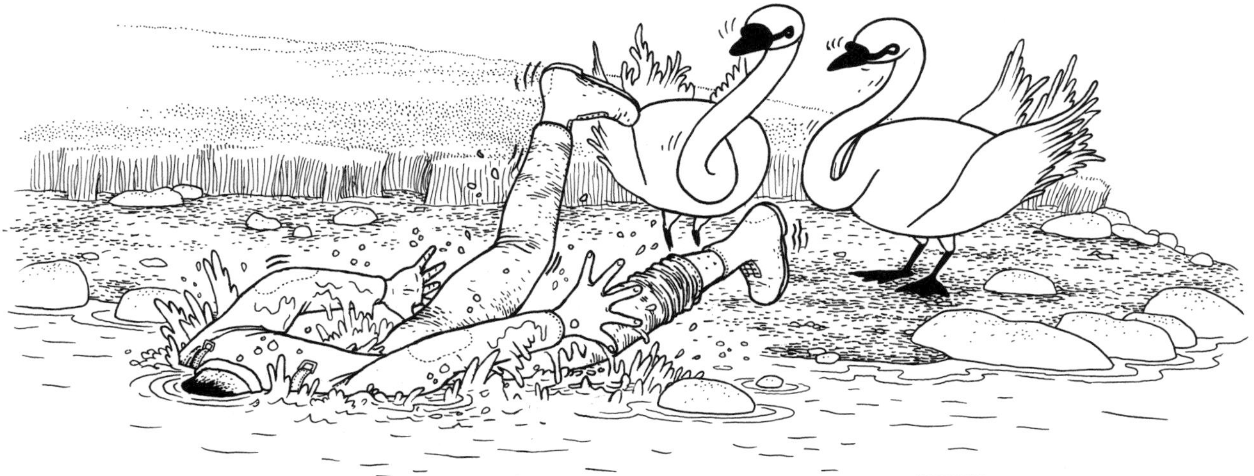

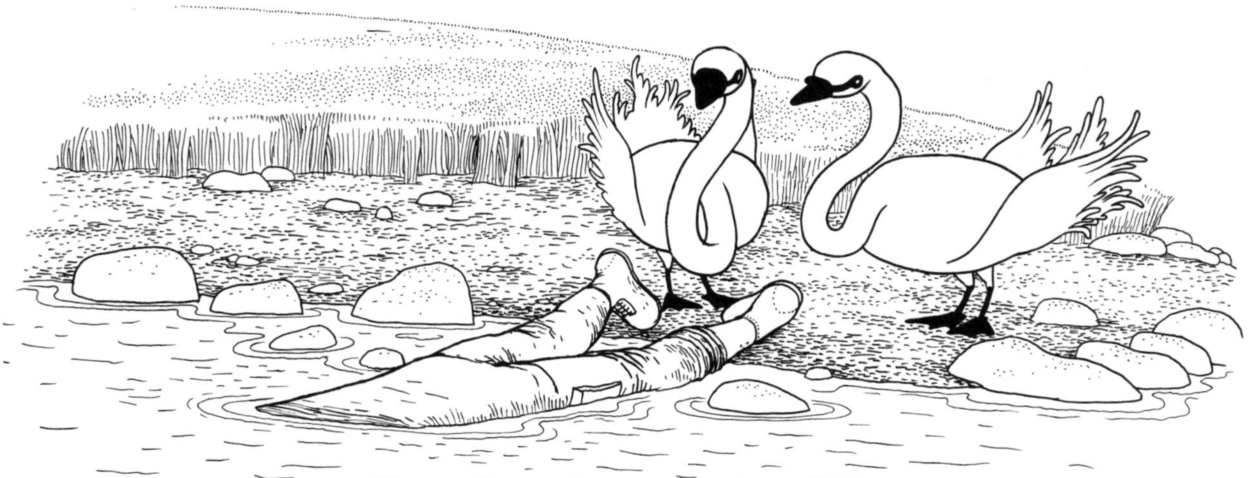

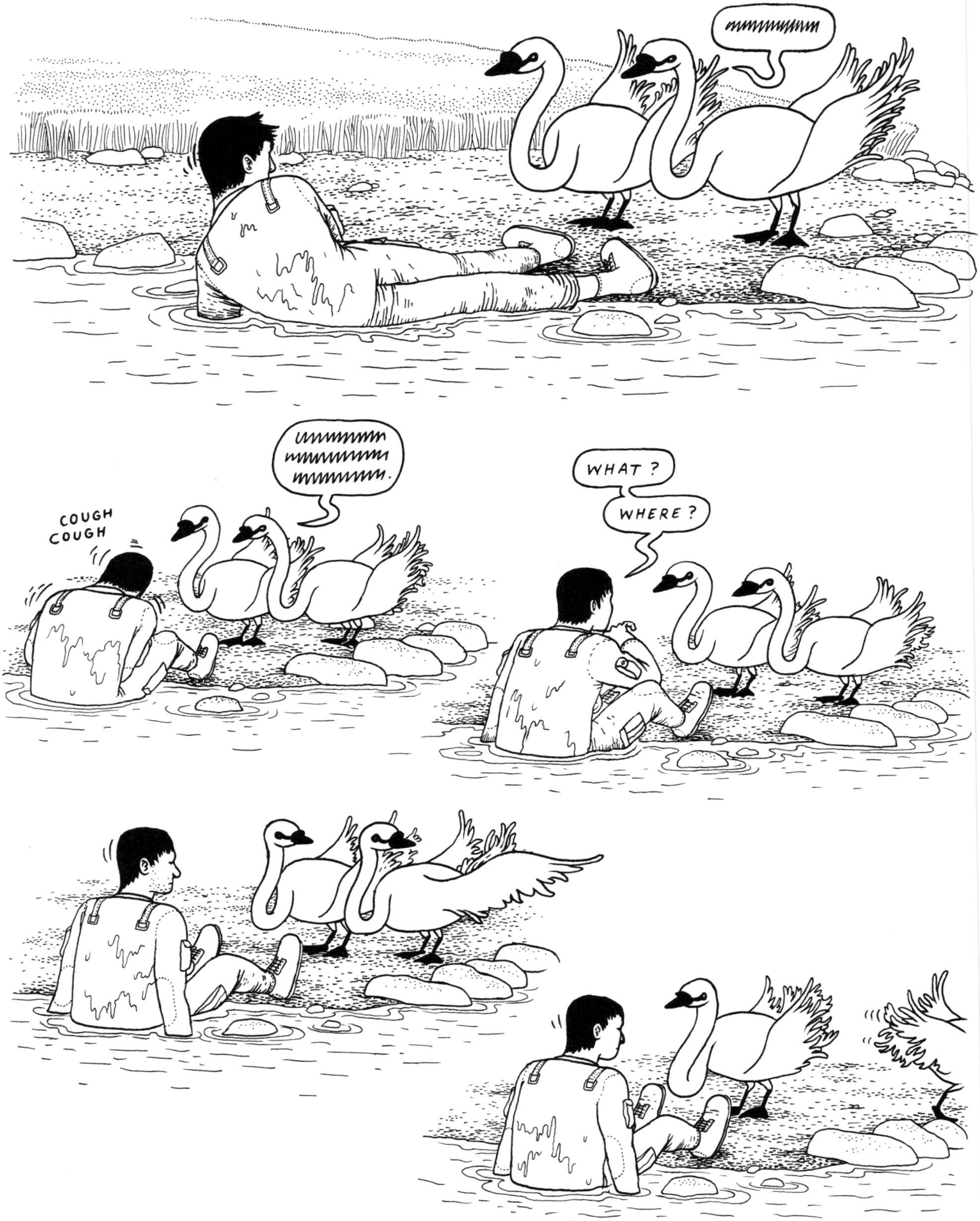
COUGH
COUGH
WHAT?
WHERE?

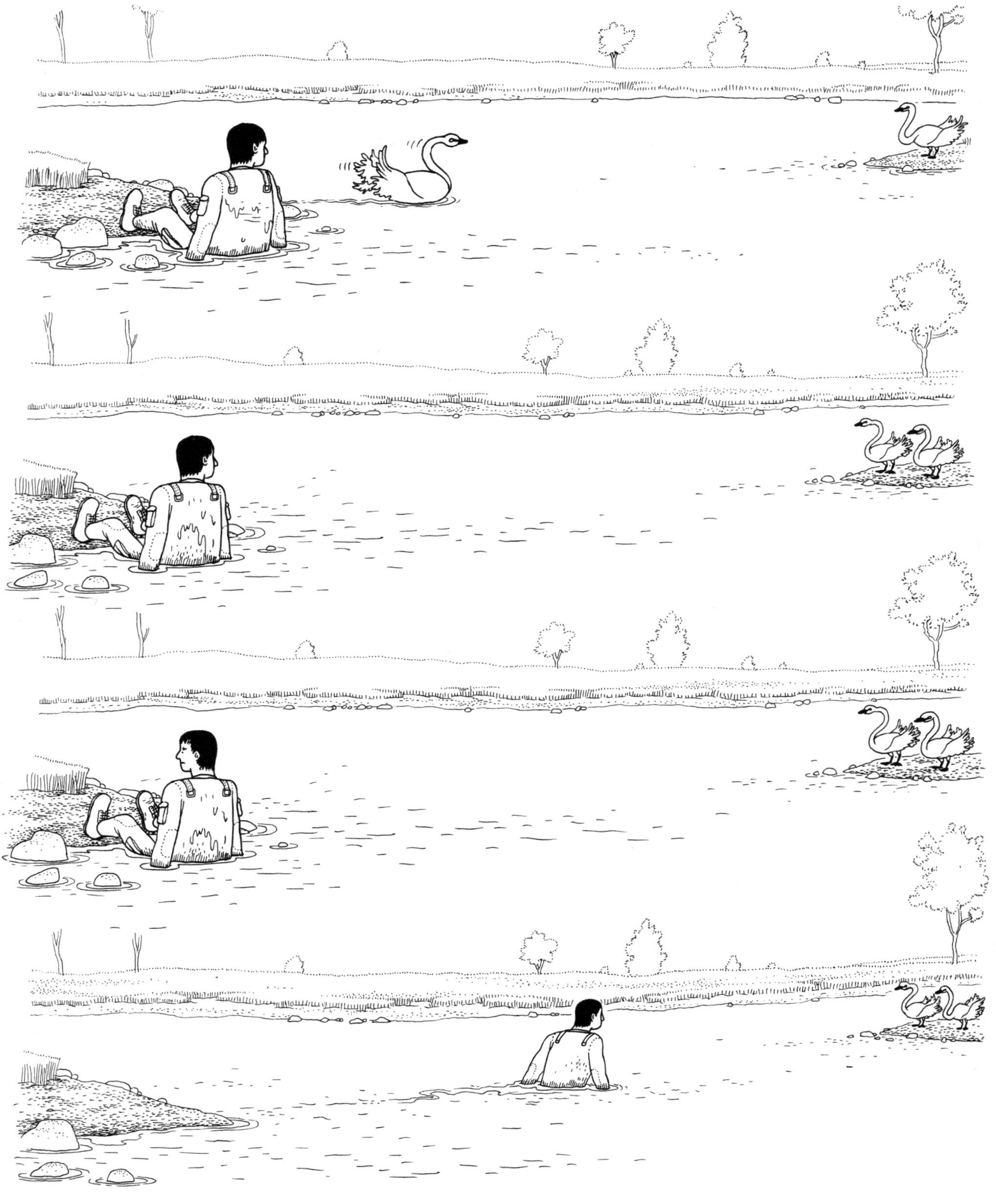

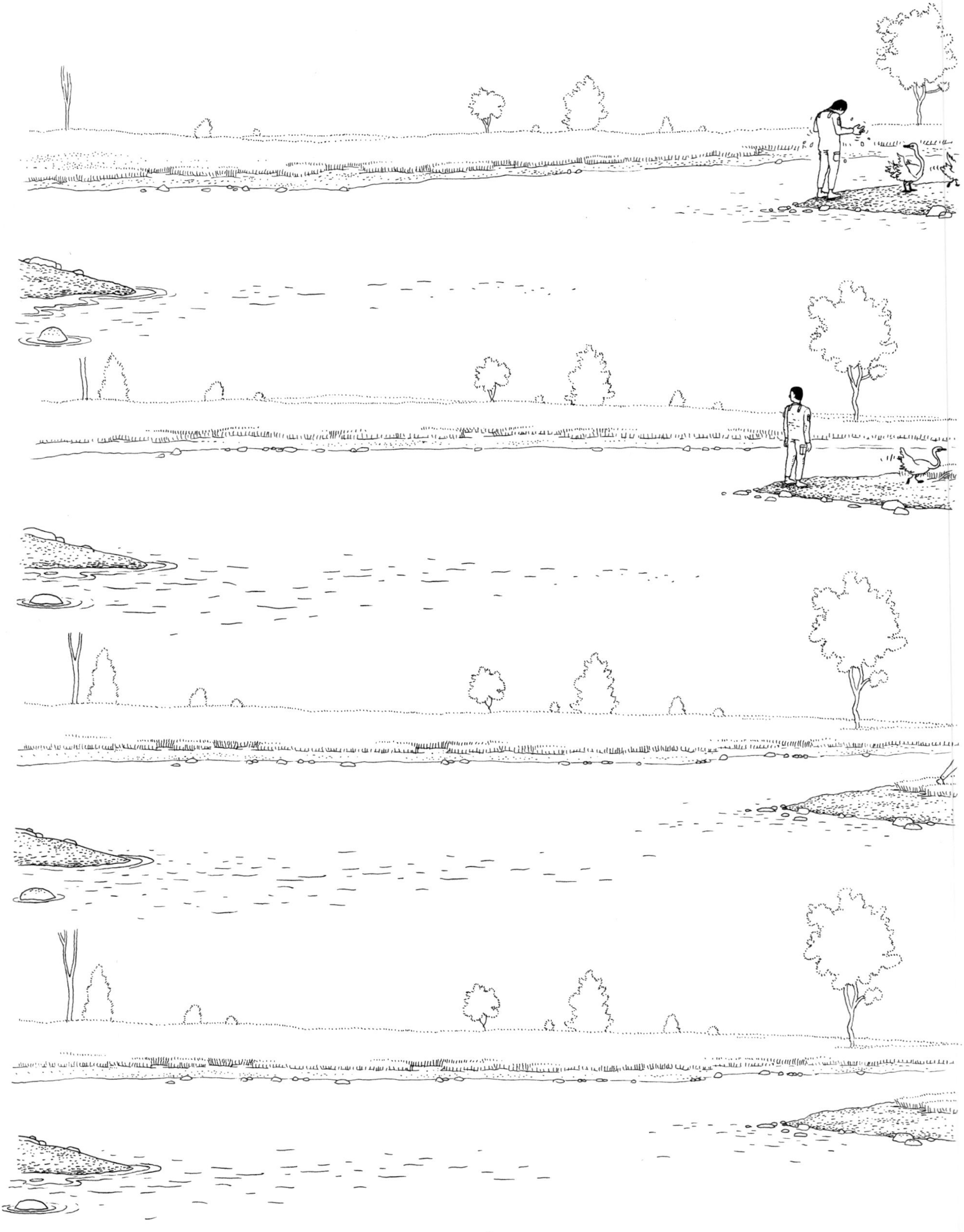

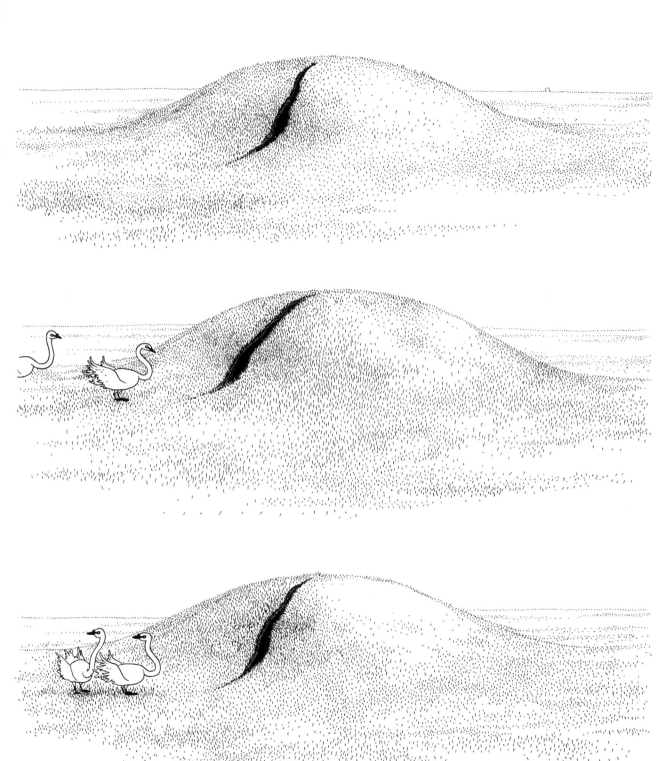

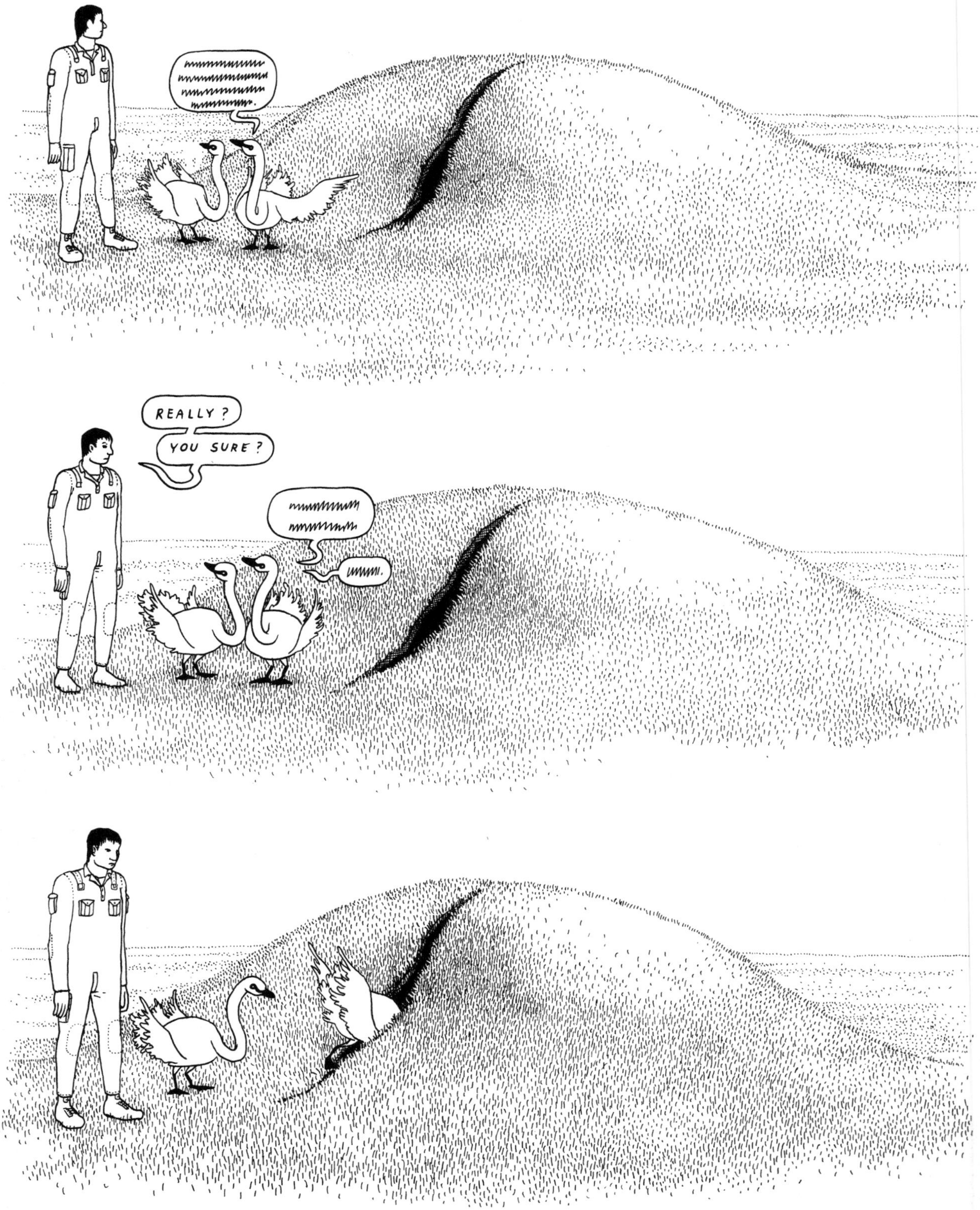
REALLY?
YOU SURE?

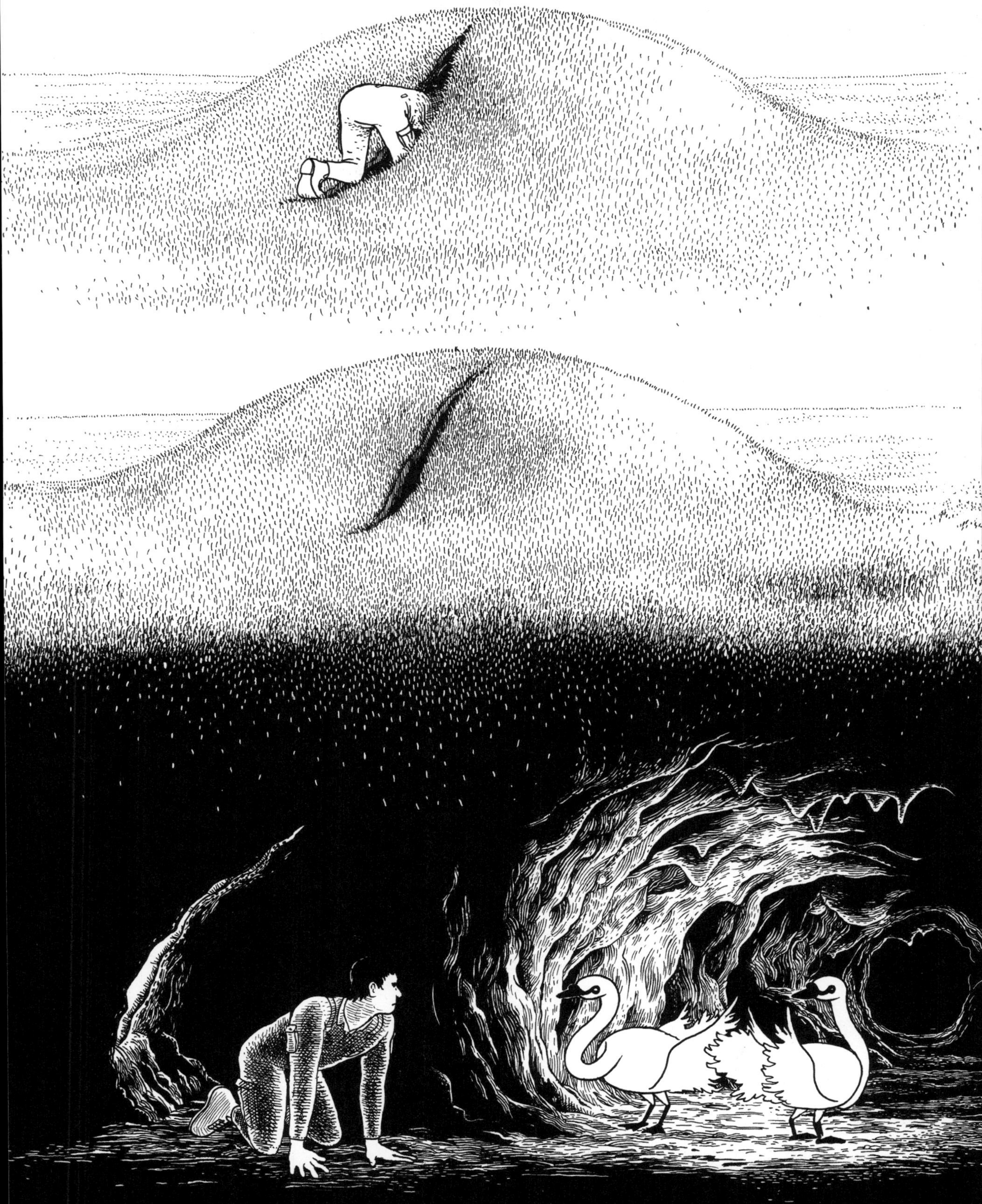

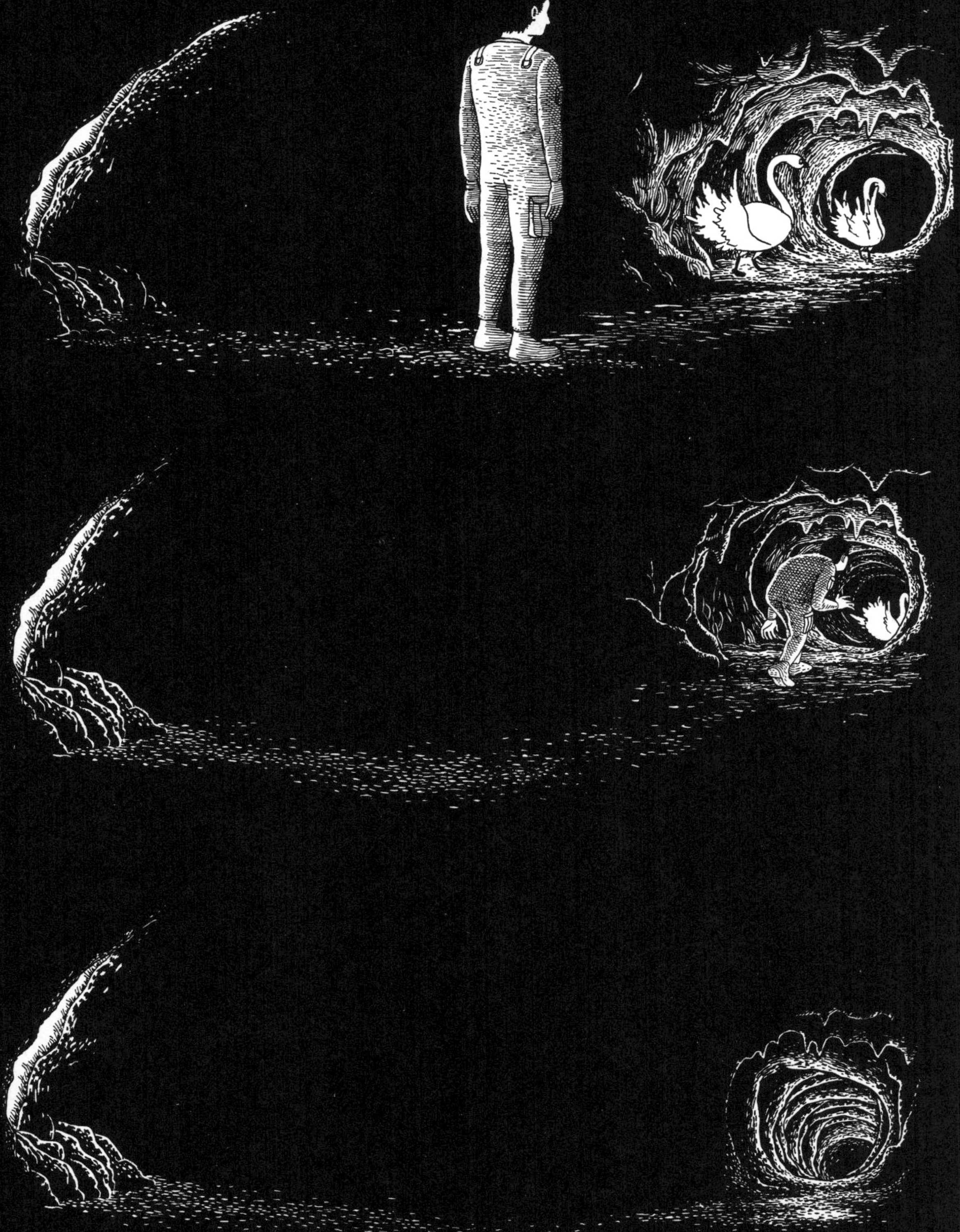

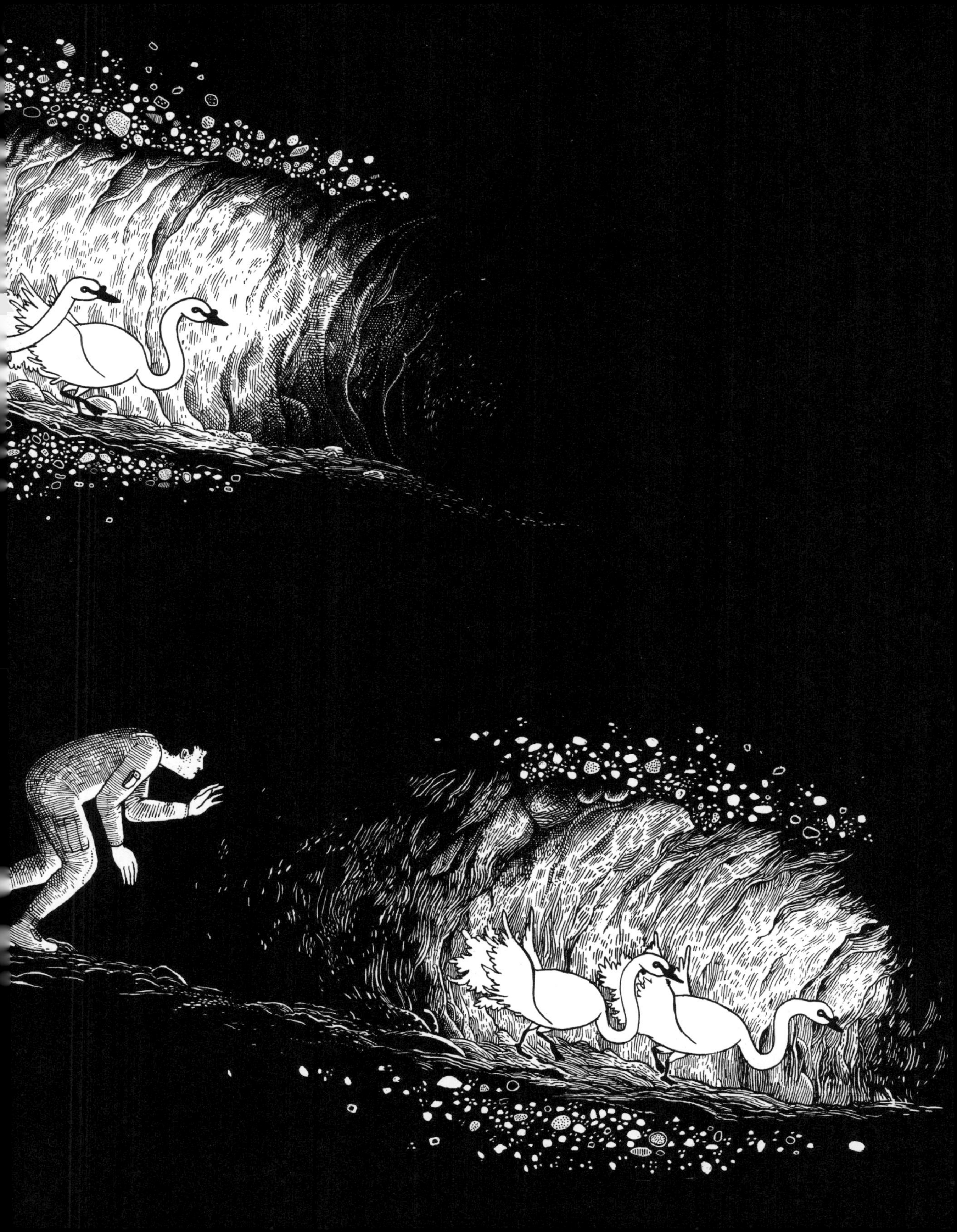

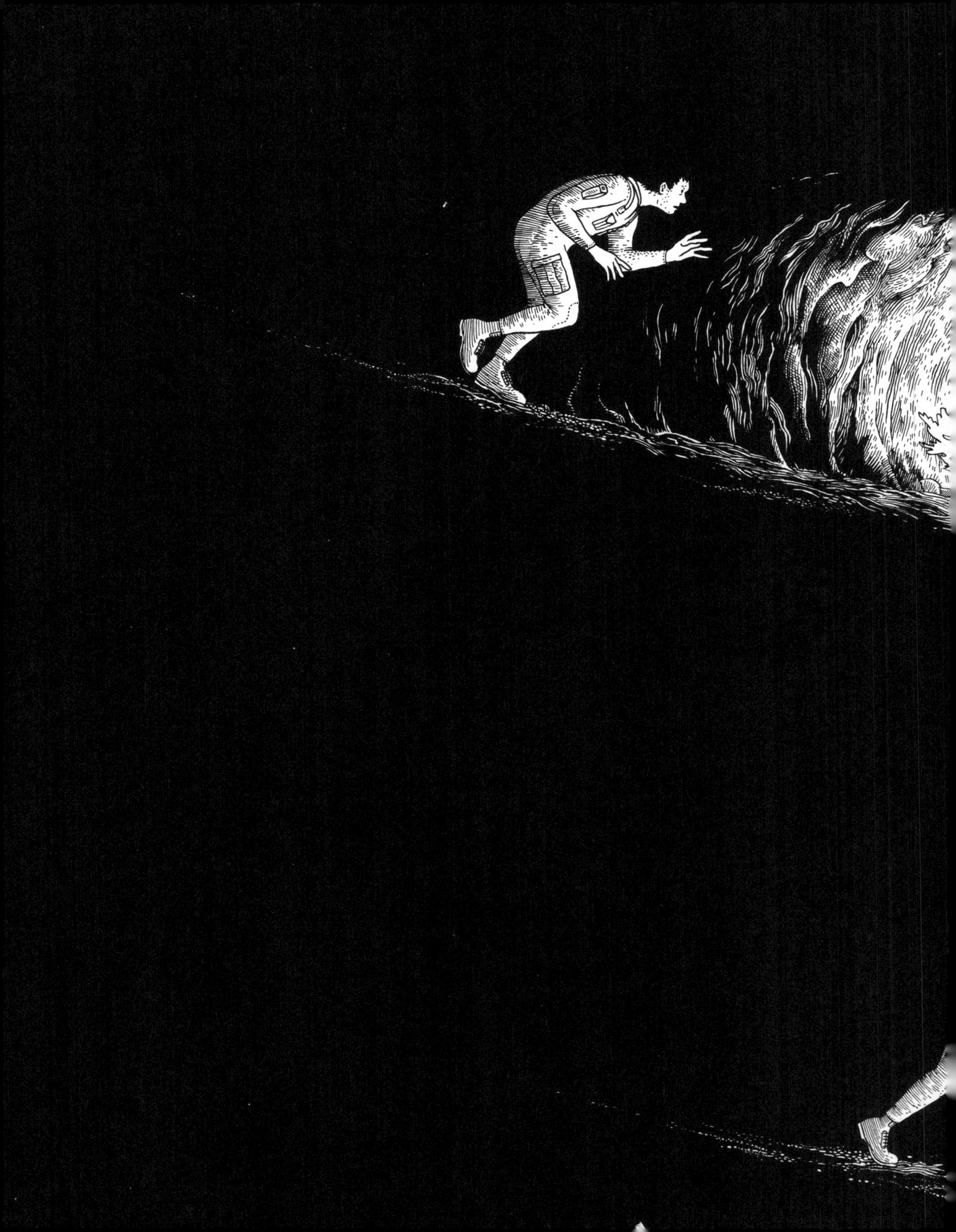

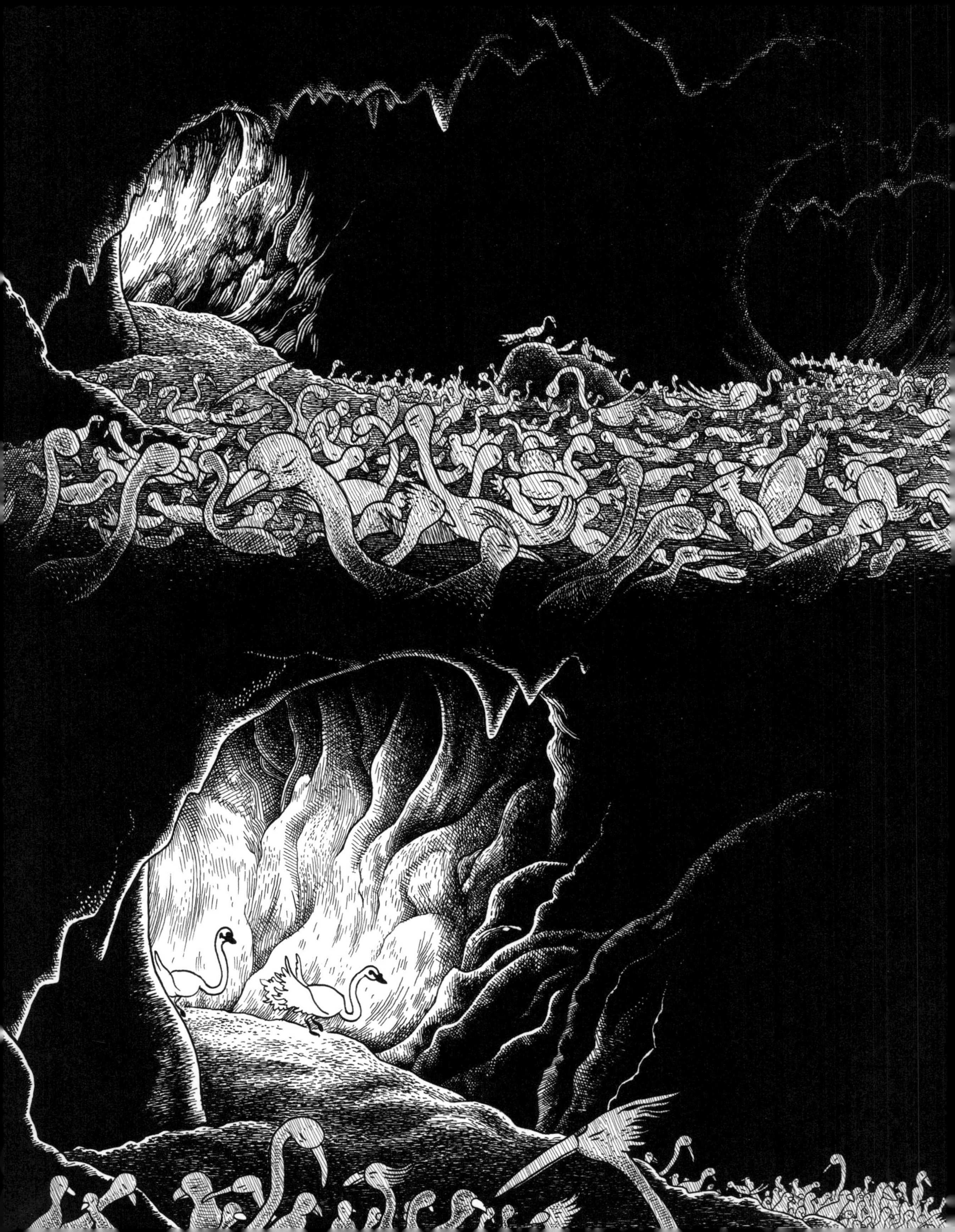

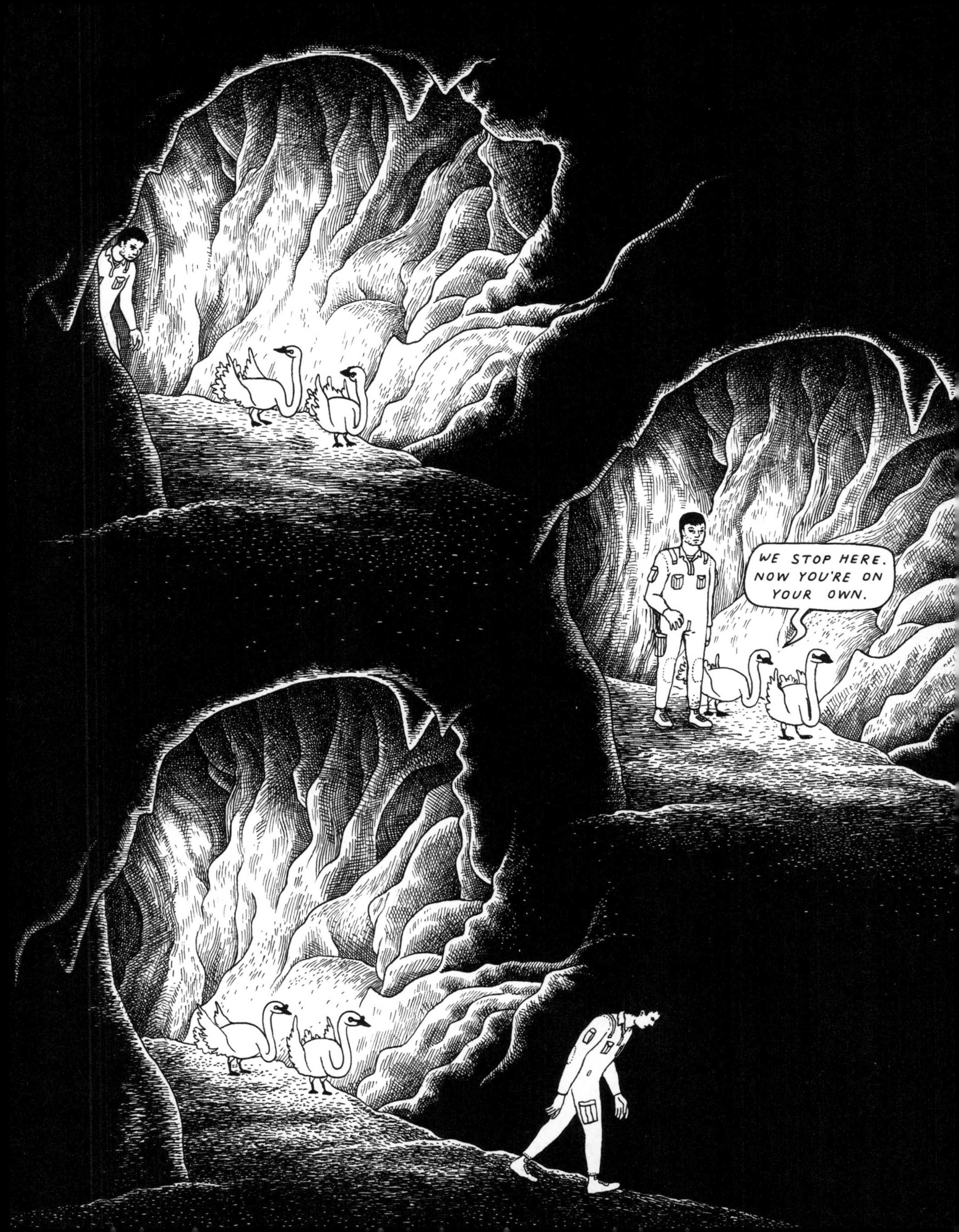
WE STOP HERE. NOW YOU'RE ON YOUR OWN.

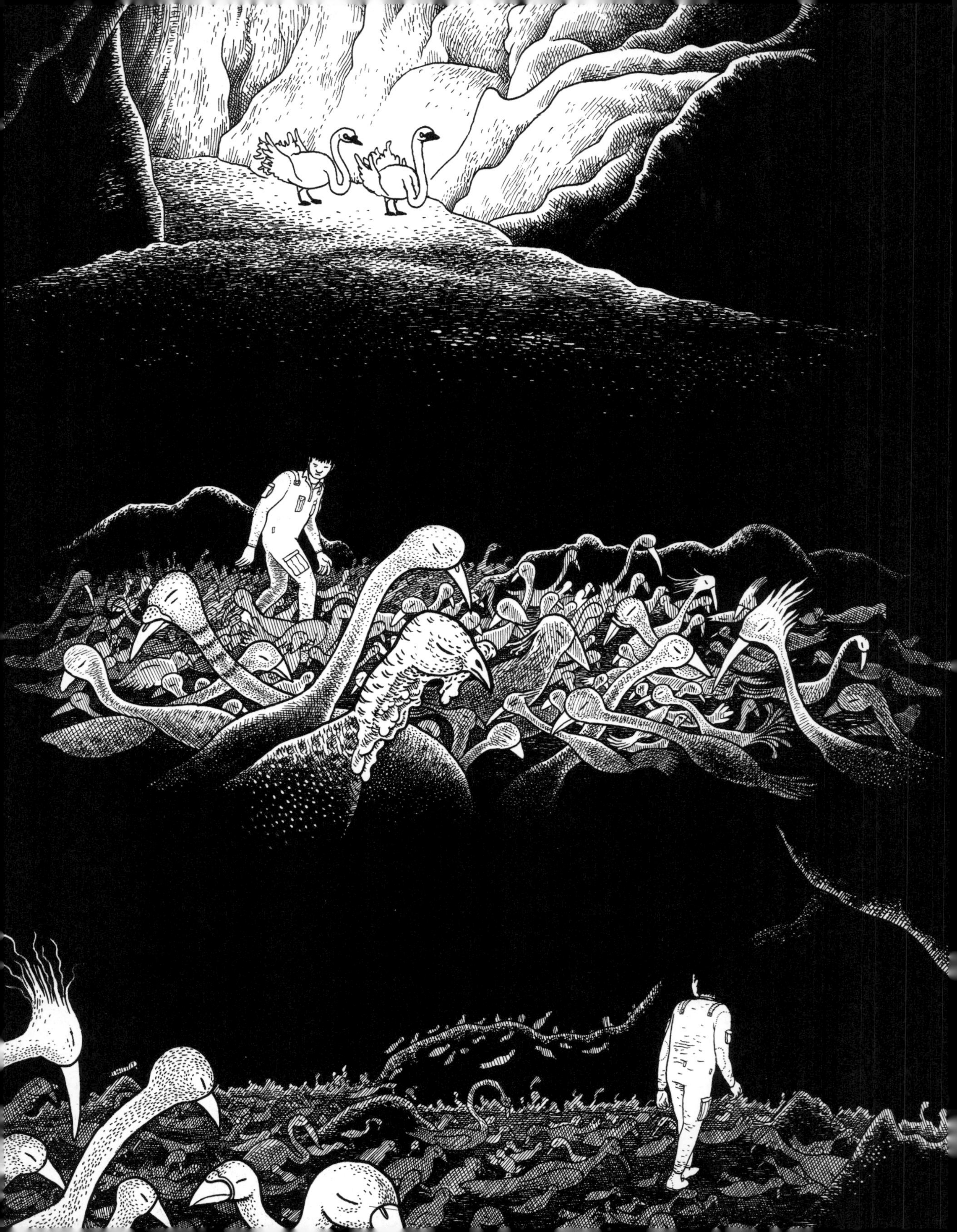

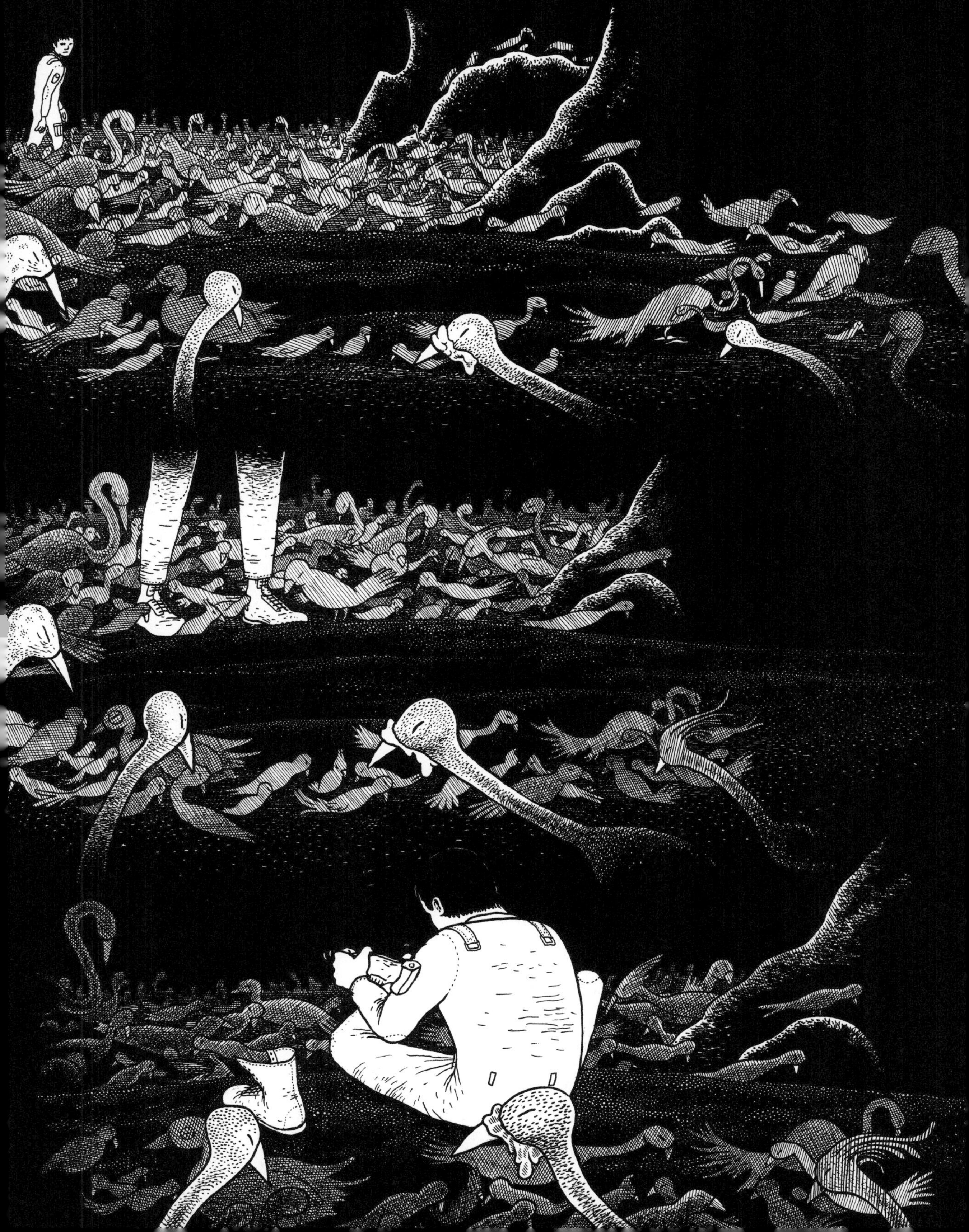

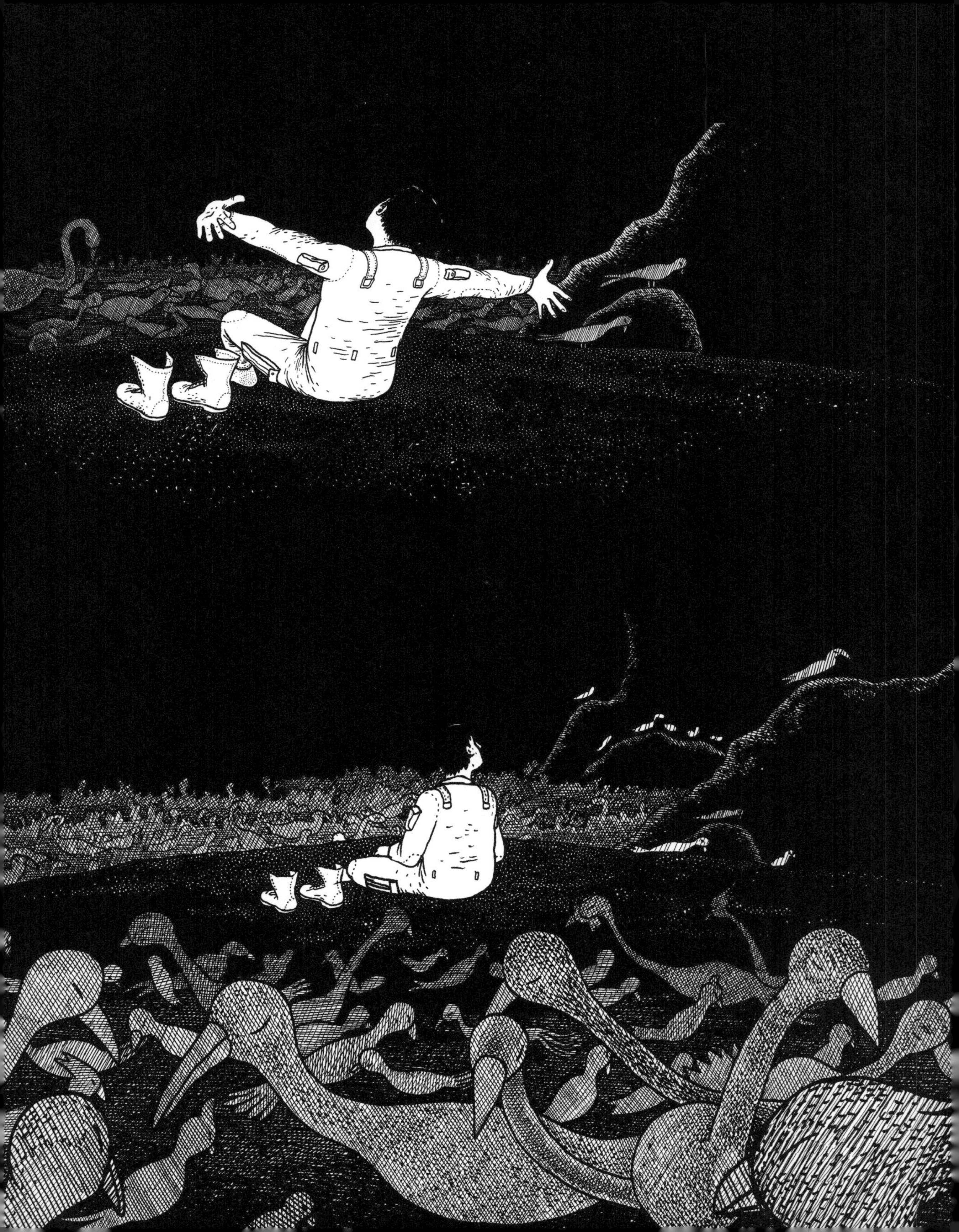

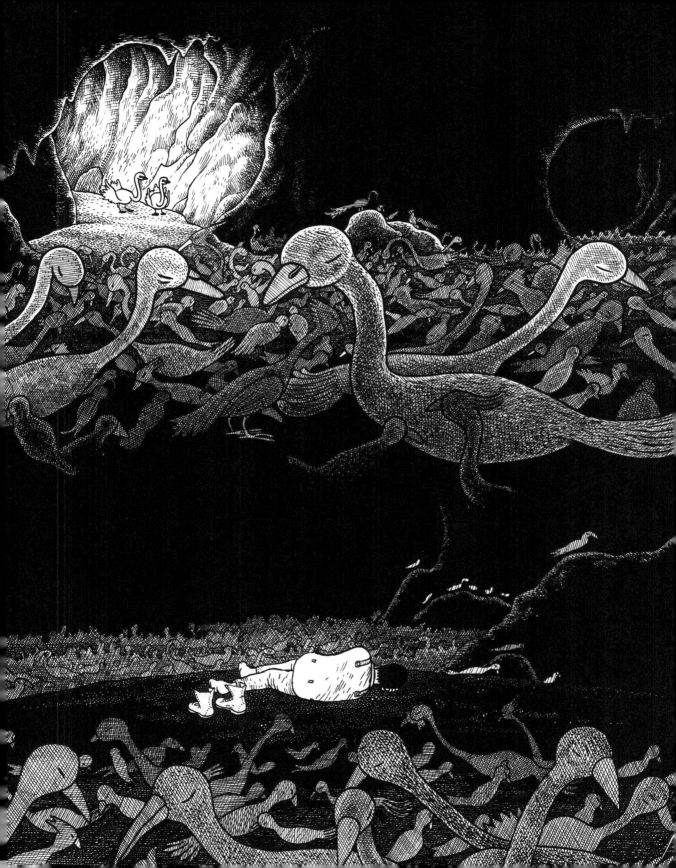

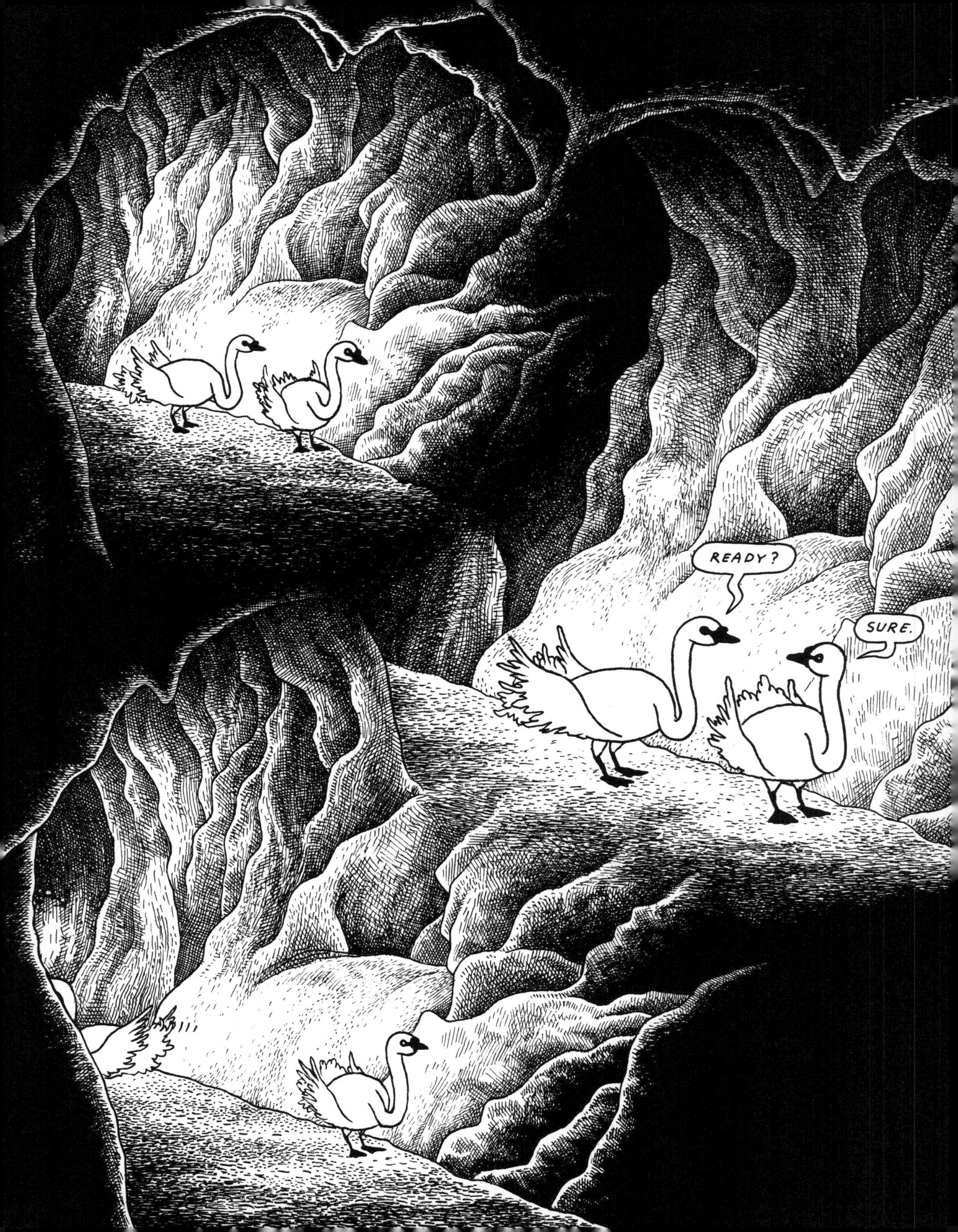
READY?
SURE.

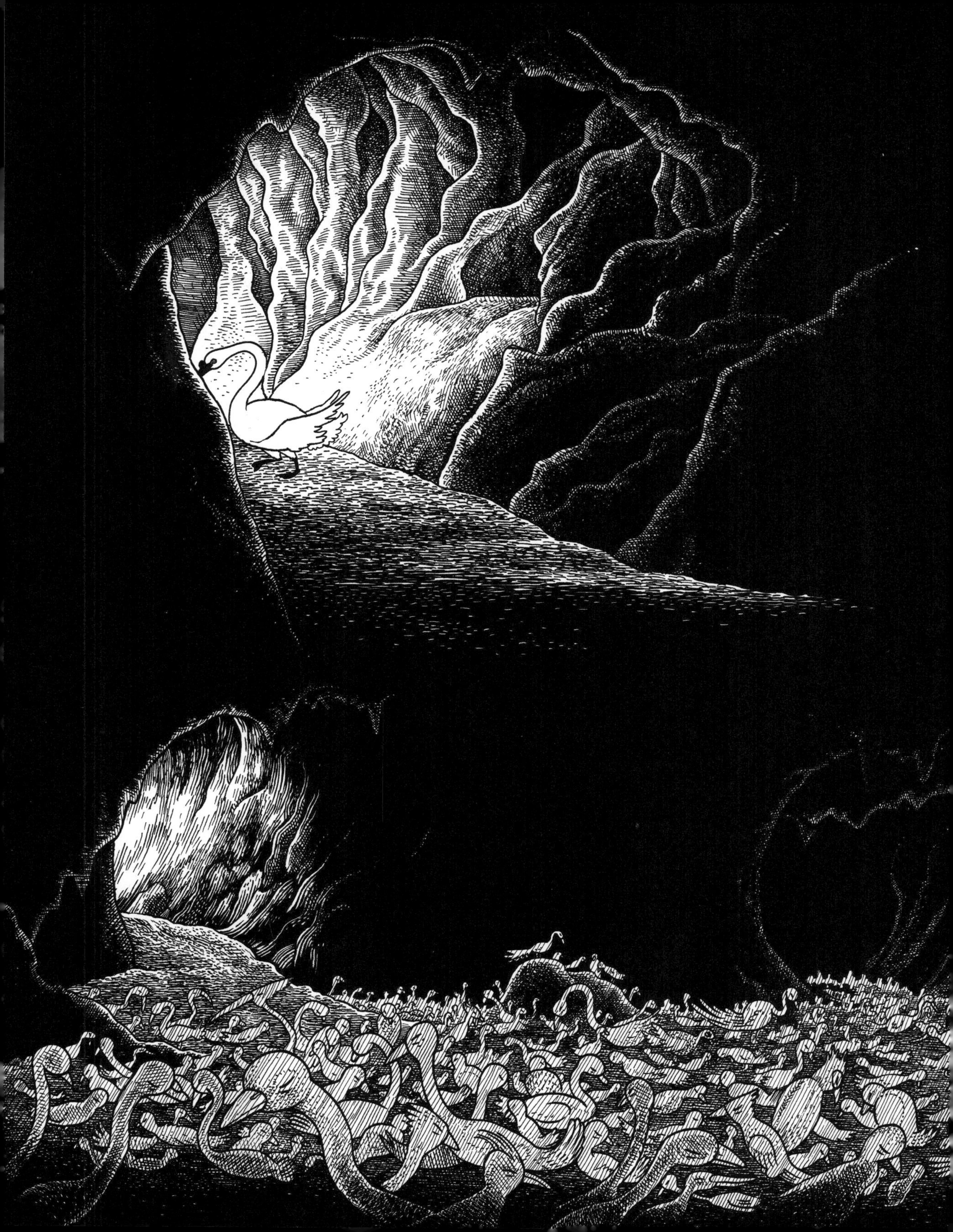

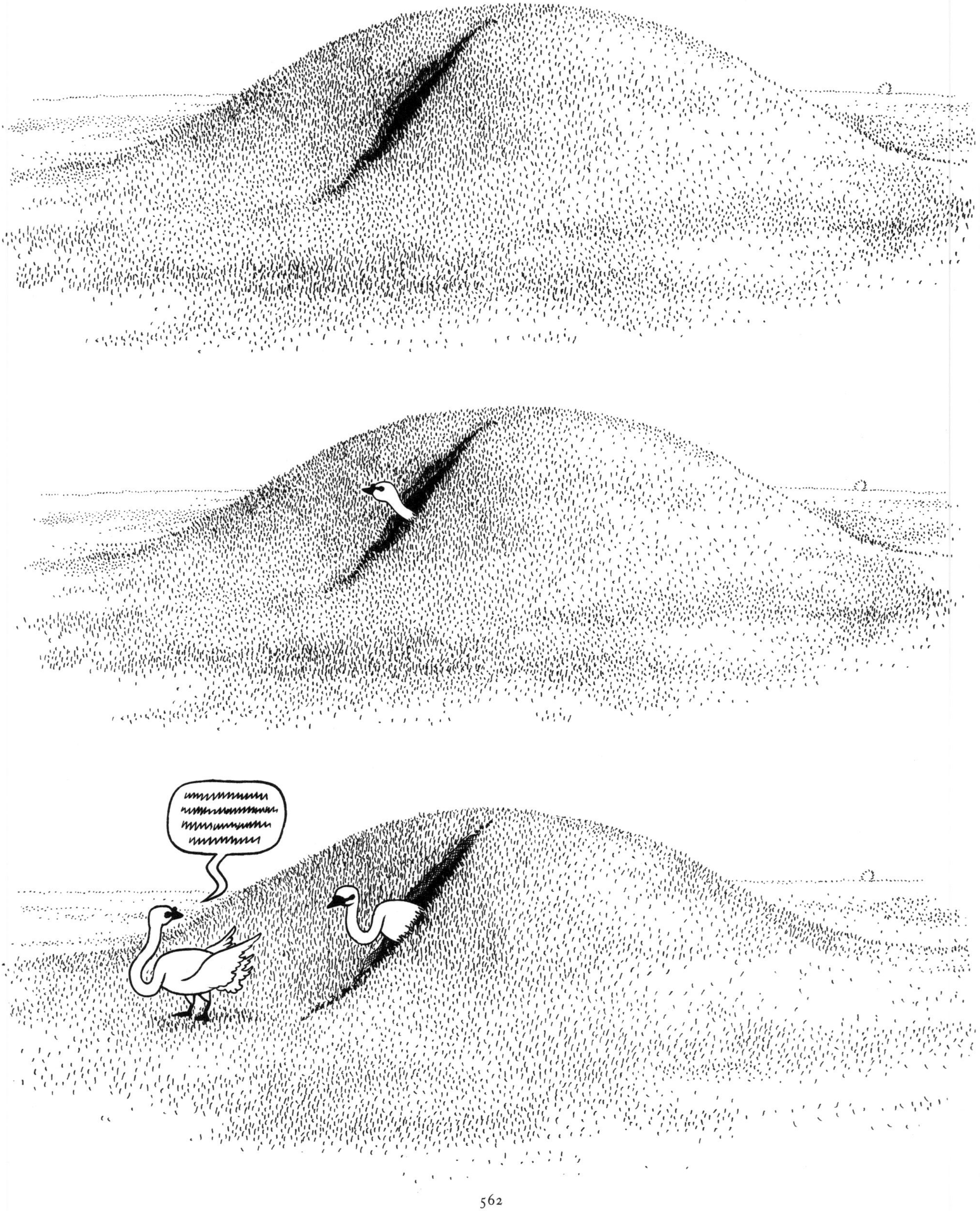

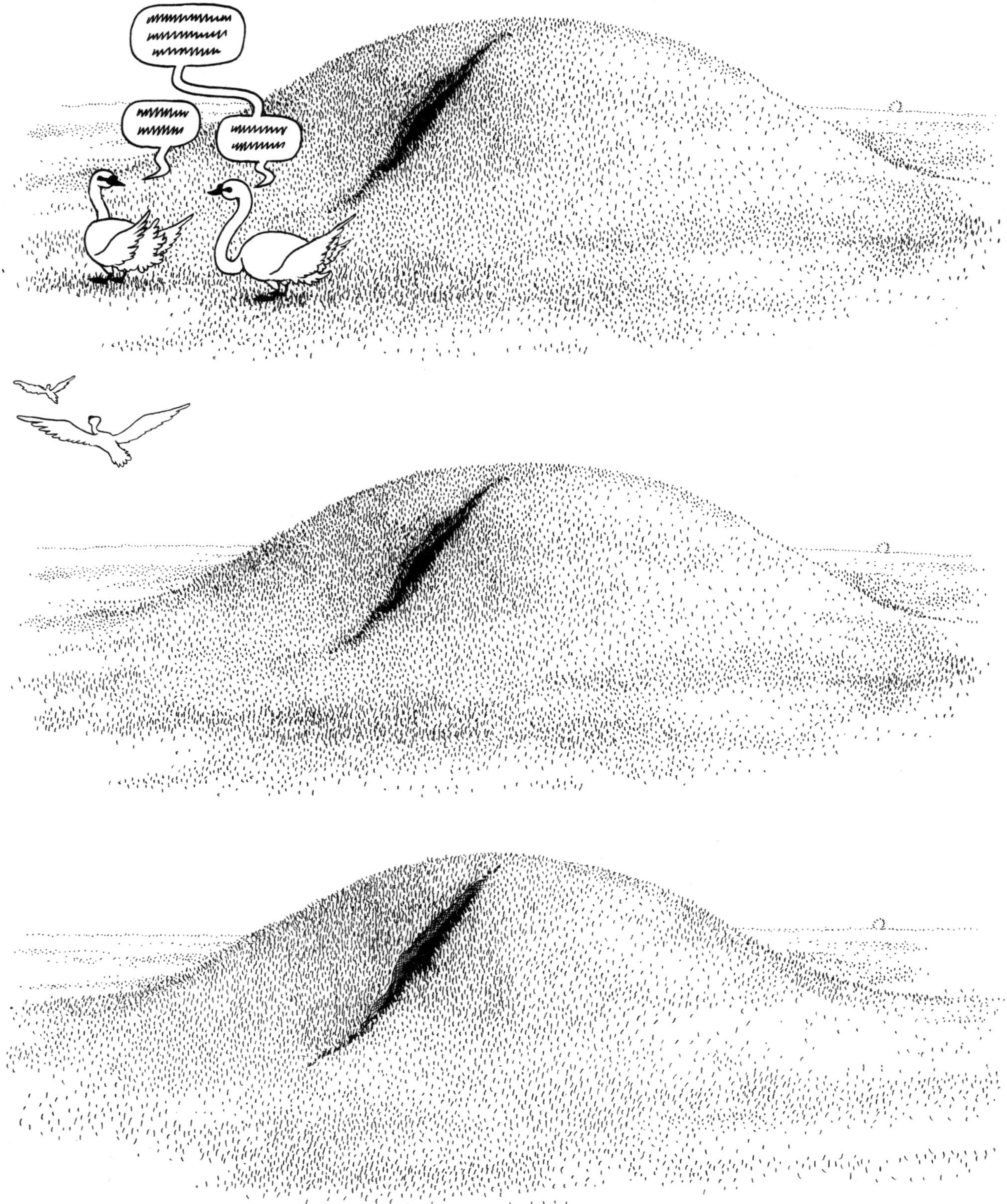

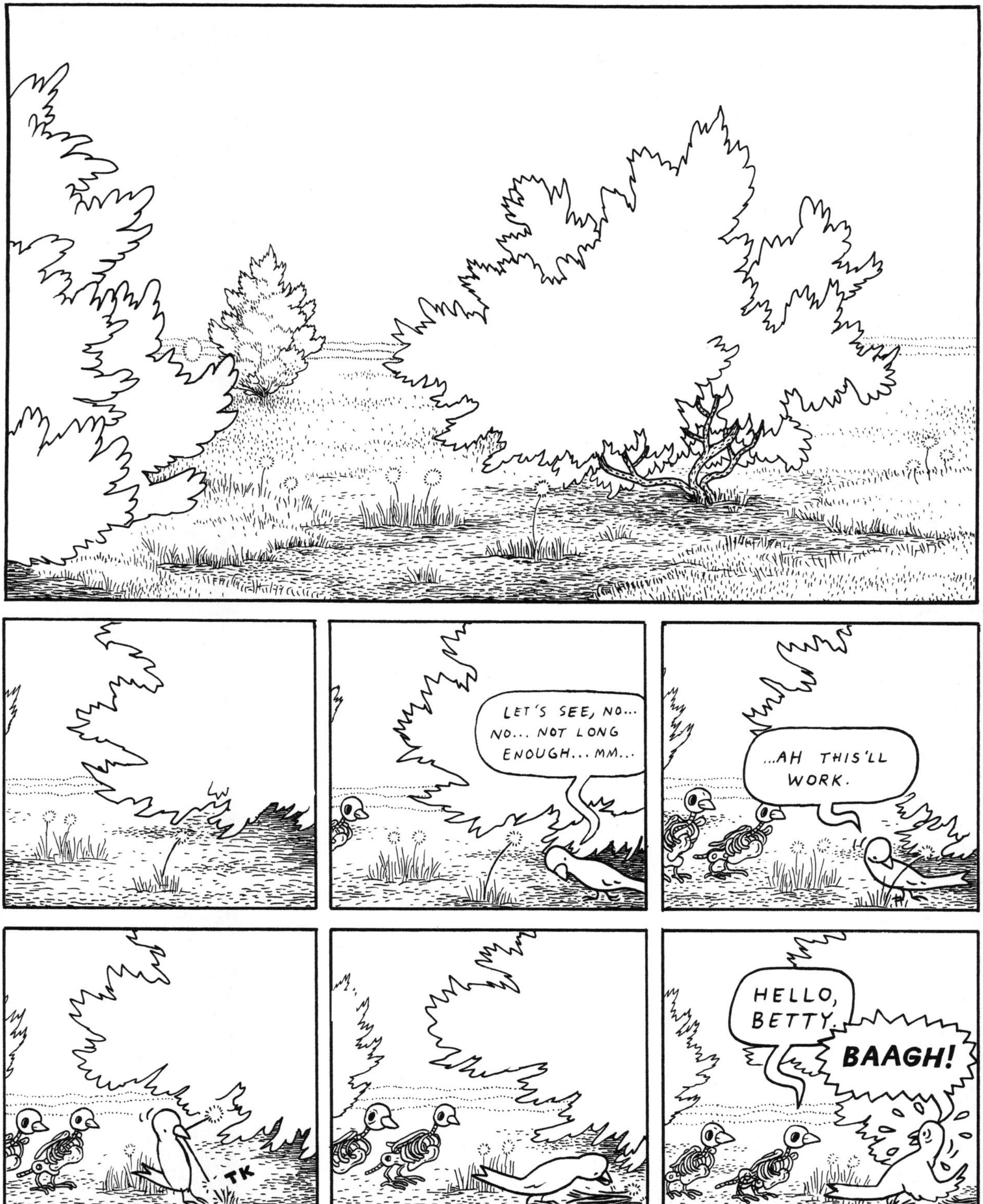
LET'S SEE, NO... NO... NOT LONG ENOUGH... MM...
...AH THIS'LL WORK.
TK
HELLO, BETTY.
BAAGH!

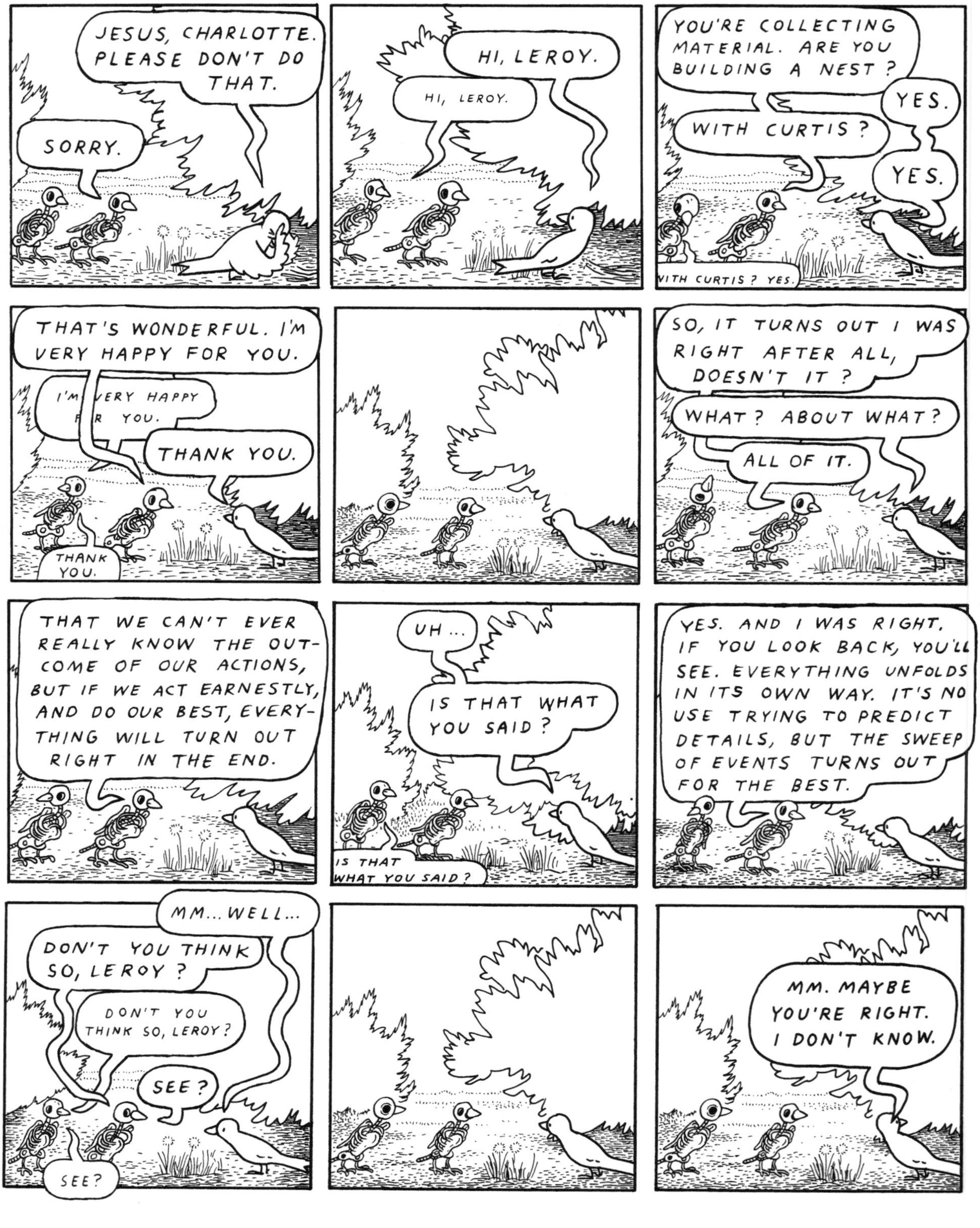
JESUS, CHARLOTTE. PLEASE DON'T DO THAT.
SORRY.
HI, LEROY.
HI, LEROY.
YOU'RE COLLECTING MATERIAL. ARE YOU BUILDING A NEST?
YES.
WITH CURTIS?
YES.
WITH CURTIS? YES.
THAT'S WONDERFUL. I'M VERY HAPPY FOR YOU.
I'M VERY HAPPY FOR YOU.
THANK YOU.
THANK YOU.
SO, IT TURNS OUT I WAS RIGHT AFTER ALL, DOESN'T IT?
WHAT? ABOUT WHAT?
ALL OF IT.
THAT WE CAN'T EVER REALLY KNOW THE OUTCOME OF OUR ACTIONS, BUT IF WE ACT EARNESTLY, AND DO OUR BEST, EVERYTHING WILL TURN OUT RIGHT IN THE END.
UH...
IS THAT WHAT YOU SAID?
IS THAT WHAT YOU SAID?
YES. AND I WAS RIGHT. IF YOU LOOK BACK, YOU'LL SEE. EVERYTHING UNFOLDS IN ITS OWN WAY. IT'S NO USE TRYING TO PREDICT DETAILS, BUT THE SWEEP OF EVENTS TURNS OUT FOR THE BEST.
MM... WELL...
DON'T YOU THINK SO, LEROY?
DON'T YOU THINK SO, LEROY?
SEE?
SEE?
MM. MAYBE YOU'RE RIGHT. I DON'T KNOW.

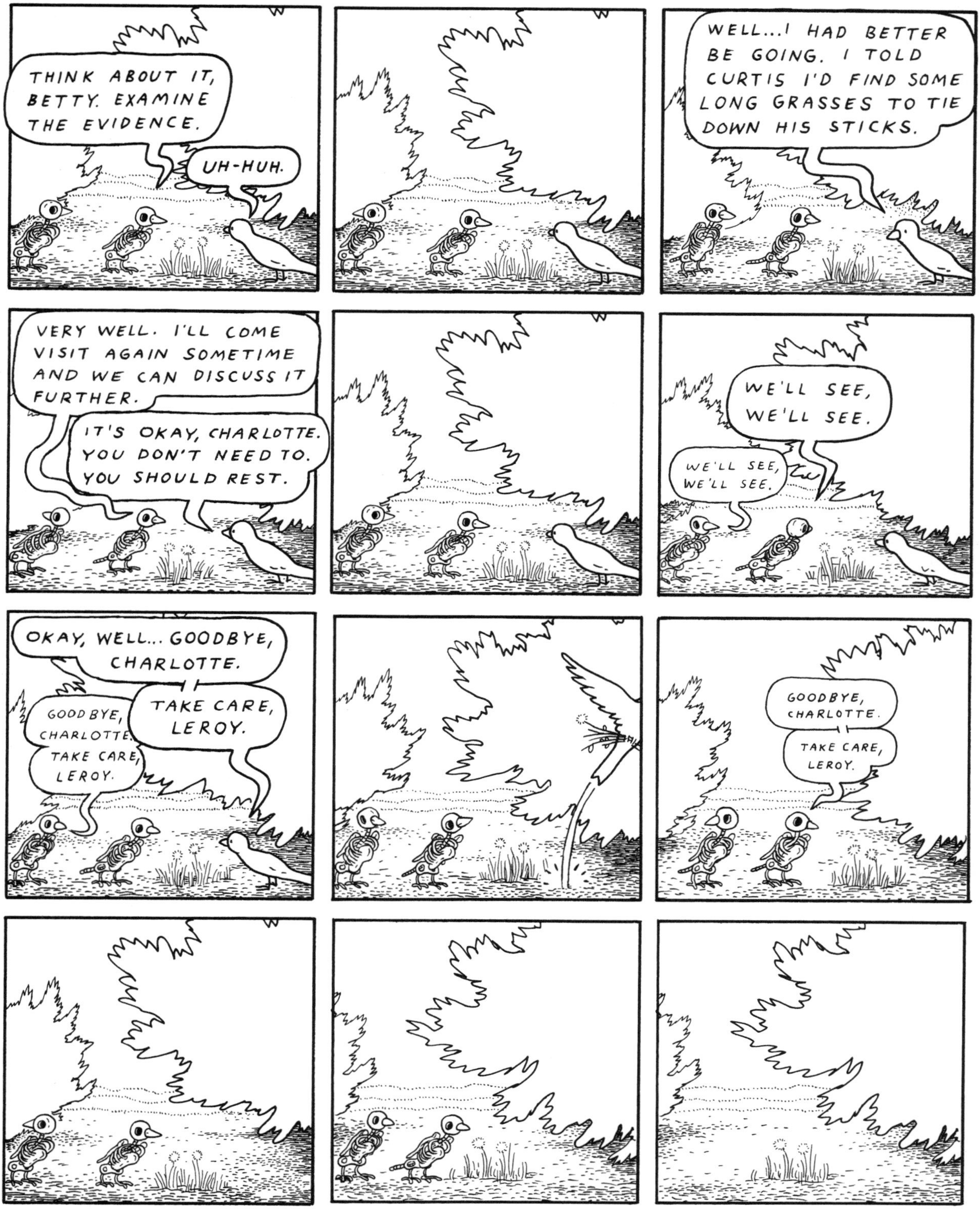
THINK ABOUT IT, BETTY. EXAMINE THE EVIDENCE.
UH-HUH.
WELL... I HAD BETTER BE GOING. I TOLD CURTIS I'D FIND SOME LONG GRASSES TO TIE DOWN HIS STICKS.
VERY WELL. I'LL COME VISIT AGAIN SOMETIME AND WE CAN DISCUSS IT FURTHER.
IT'S OKAY, CHARLOTTE. YOU DON'T NEED TO. YOU SHOULD REST.
WE'LL SEE, WE'LL SEE.
WE'LL SEE, WE'LL SEE.
OKAY, WELL... GOODBYE, CHARLOTTE.
TAKE CARE, LEROY.
GOODBYE, CHARLOTTE.
TAKE CARE, LEROY.
GOODBYE, CHARLOTTE.
TAKE CARE, LEROY.

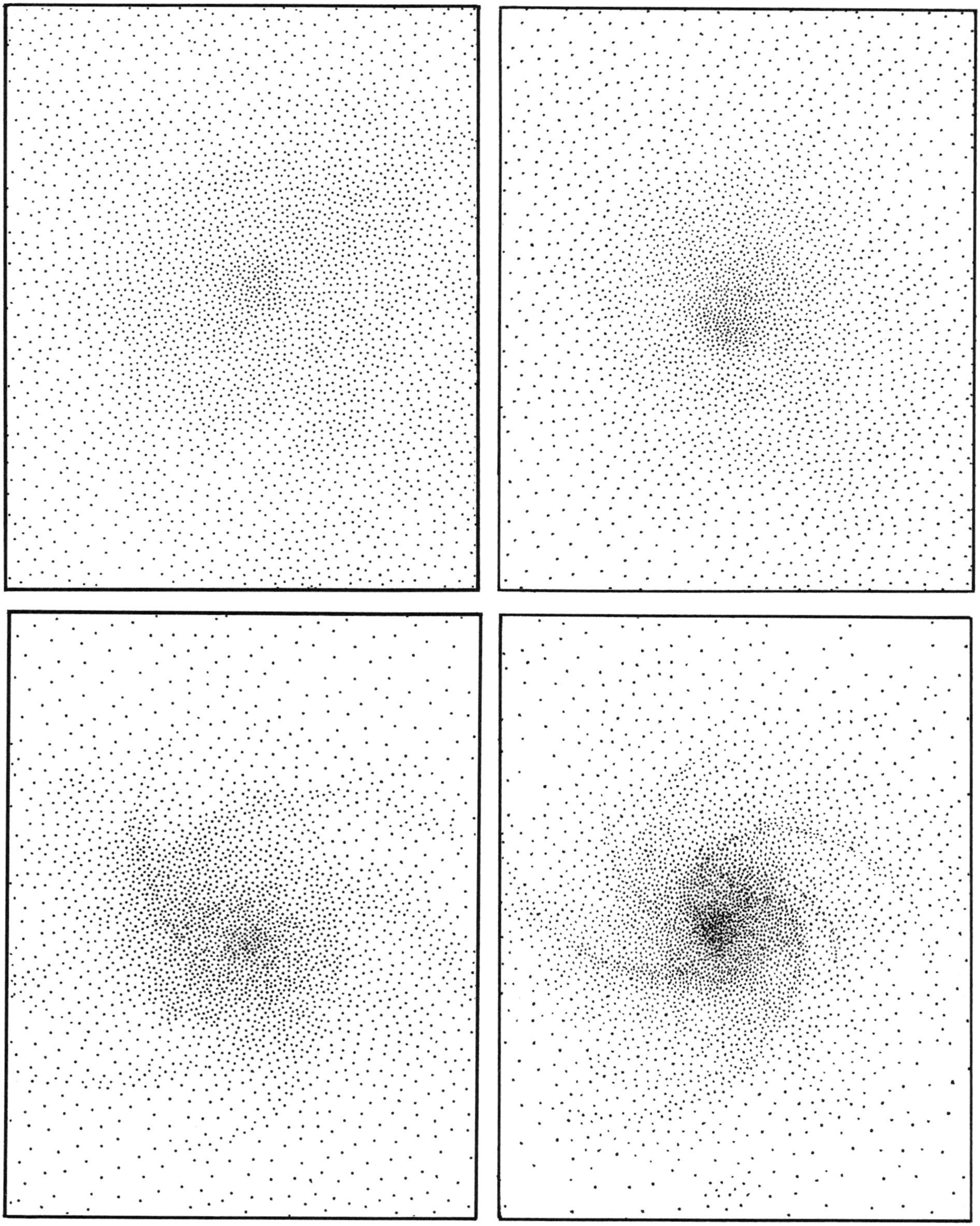

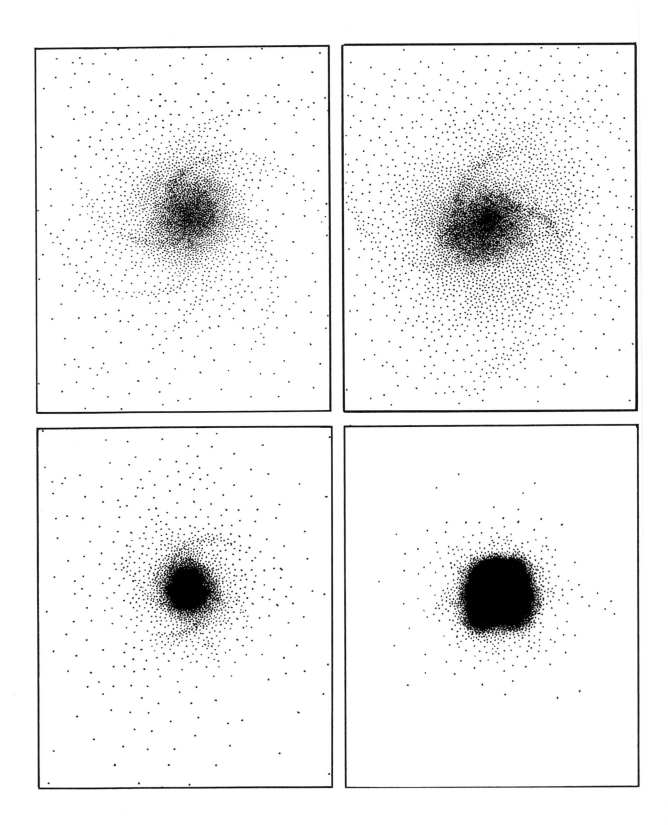

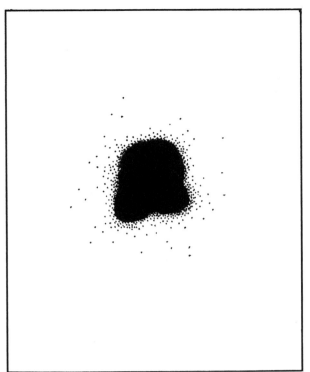
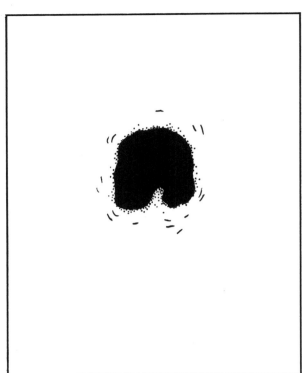

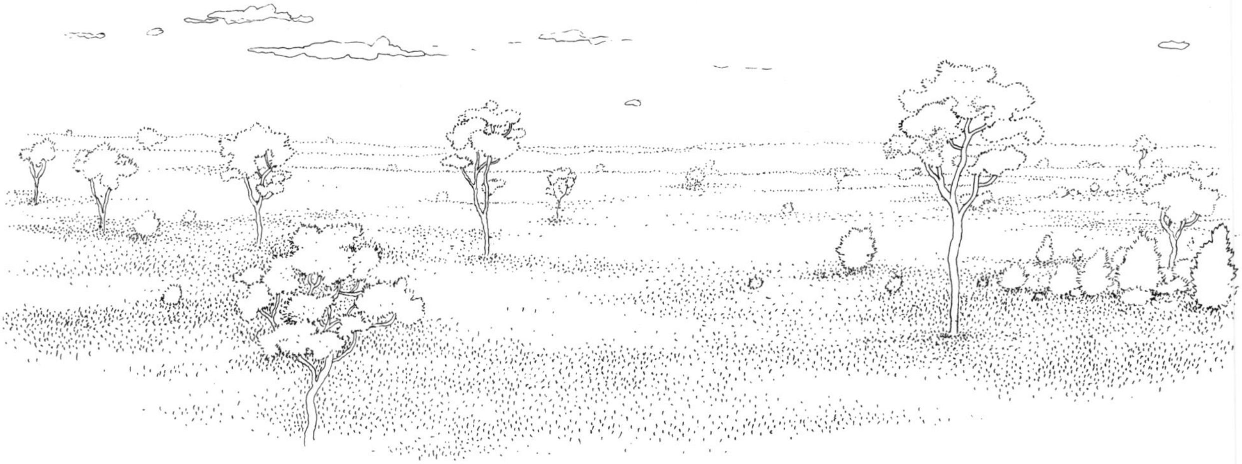

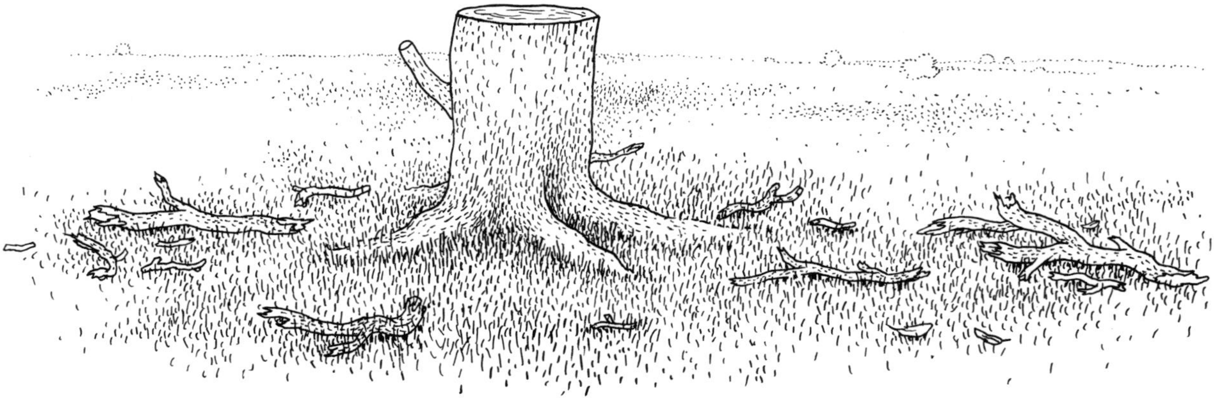

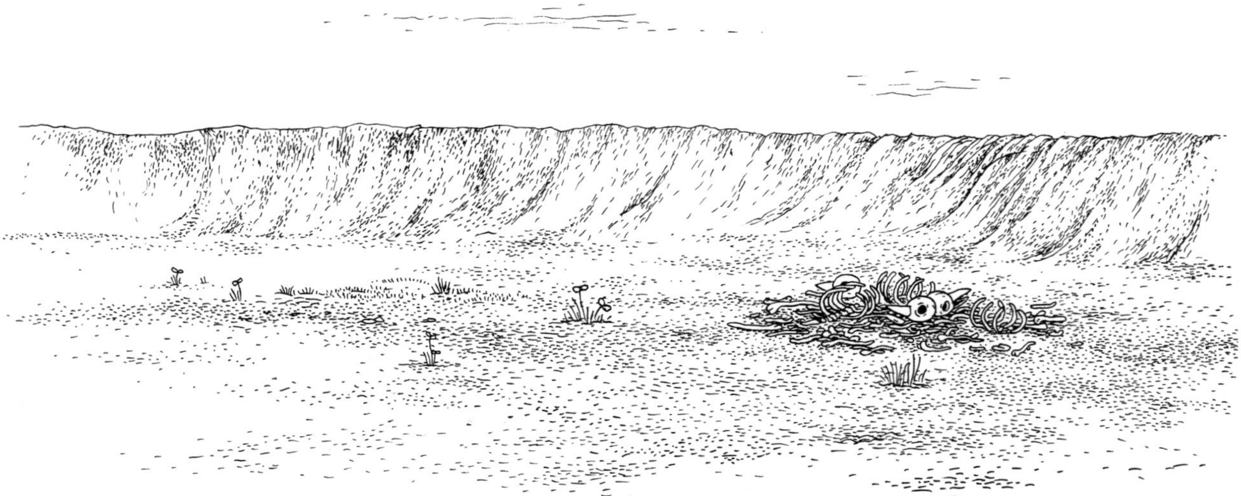

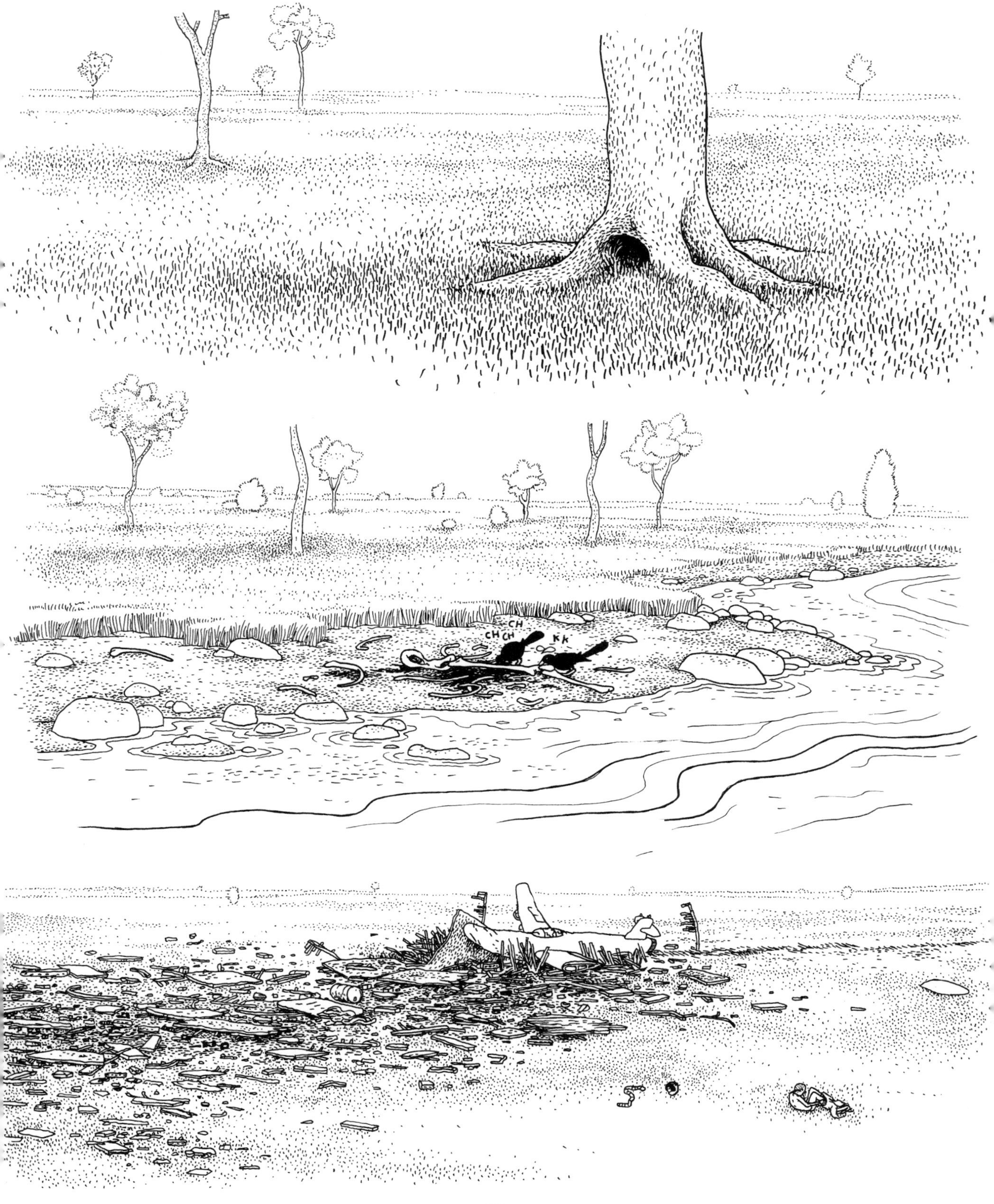
CH
CH CH
K K

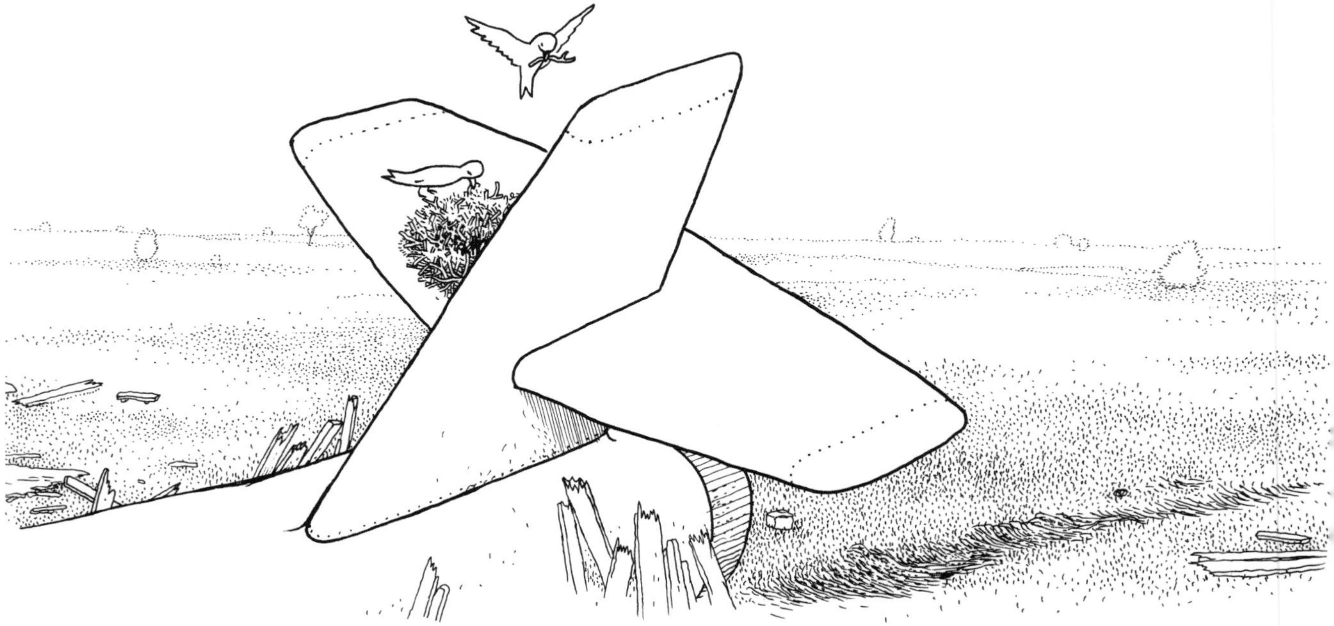

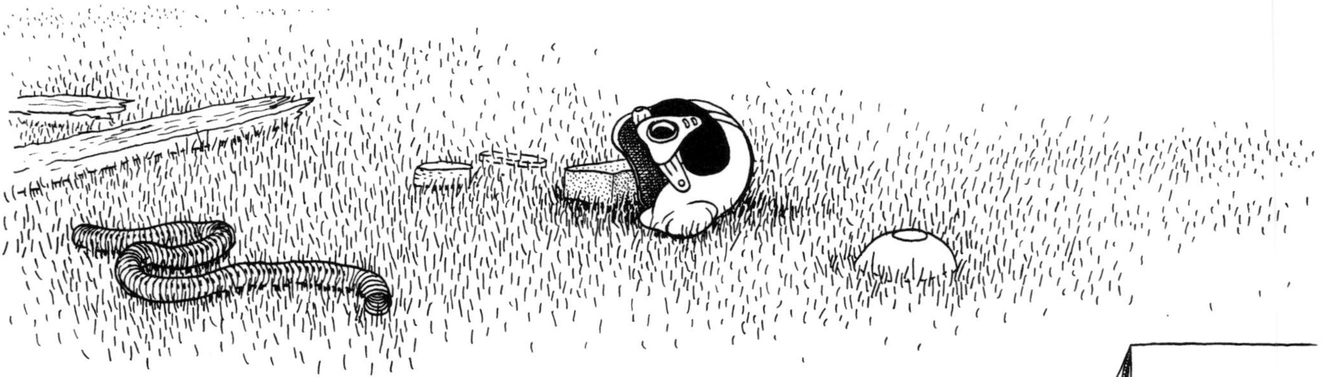

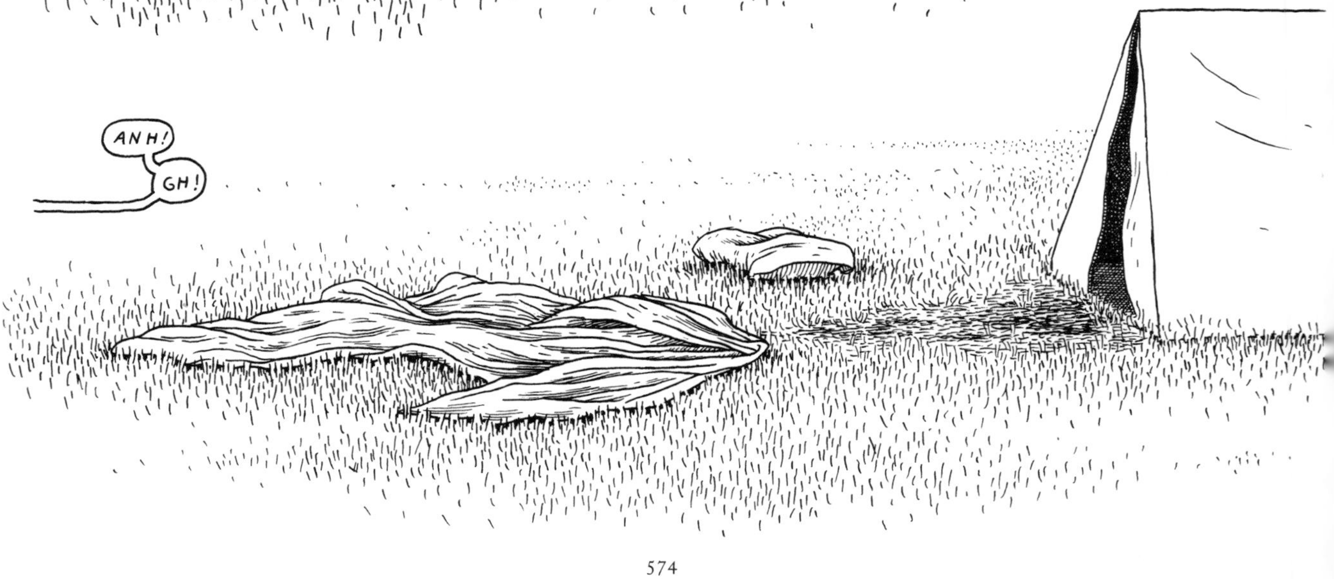
ANH!
GH!

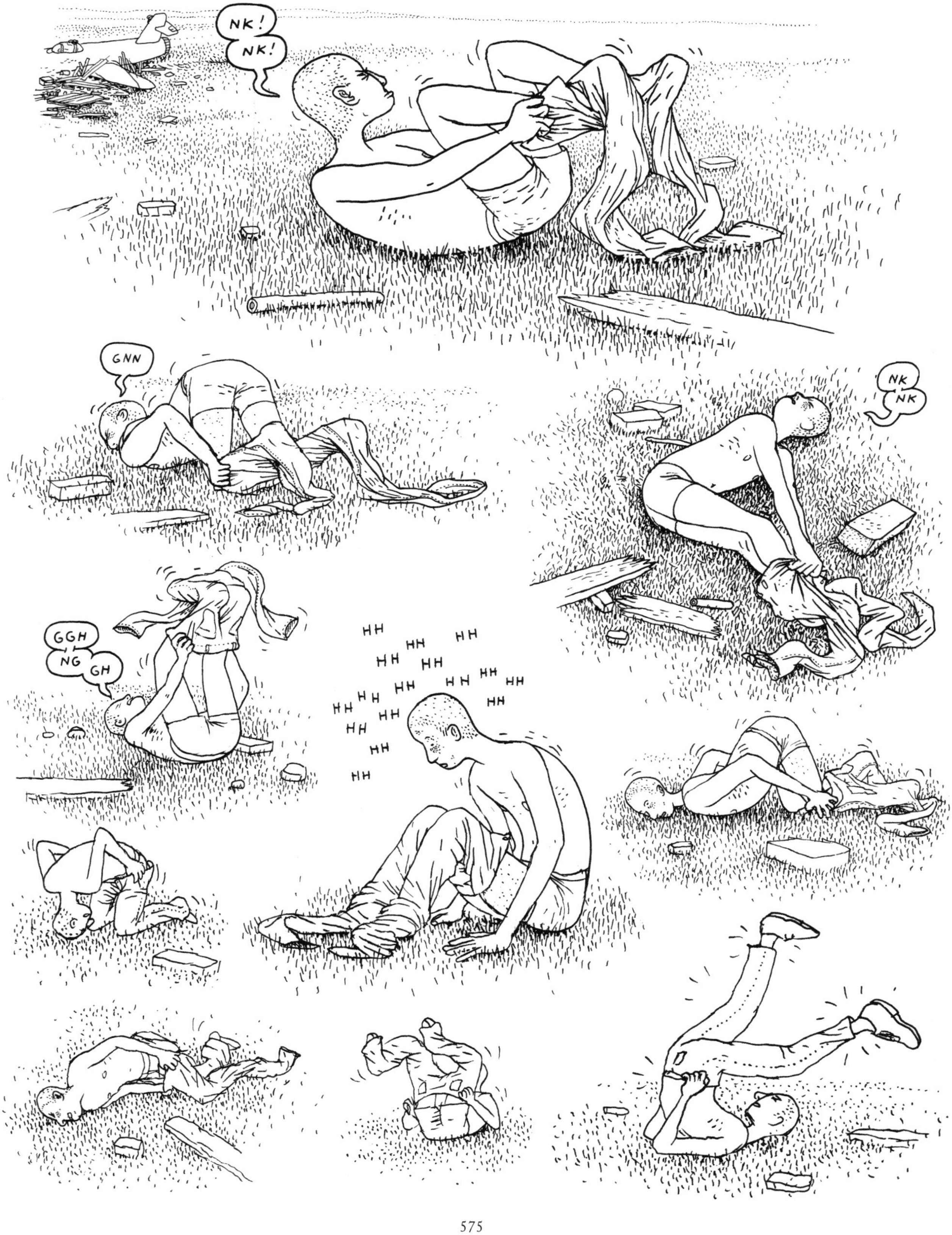
NK!
NK!
GNN
NK
NK
GGH
NG
GH
HH HH HH HH HH HH HH HH HH HH HH HH HH HH HH HH

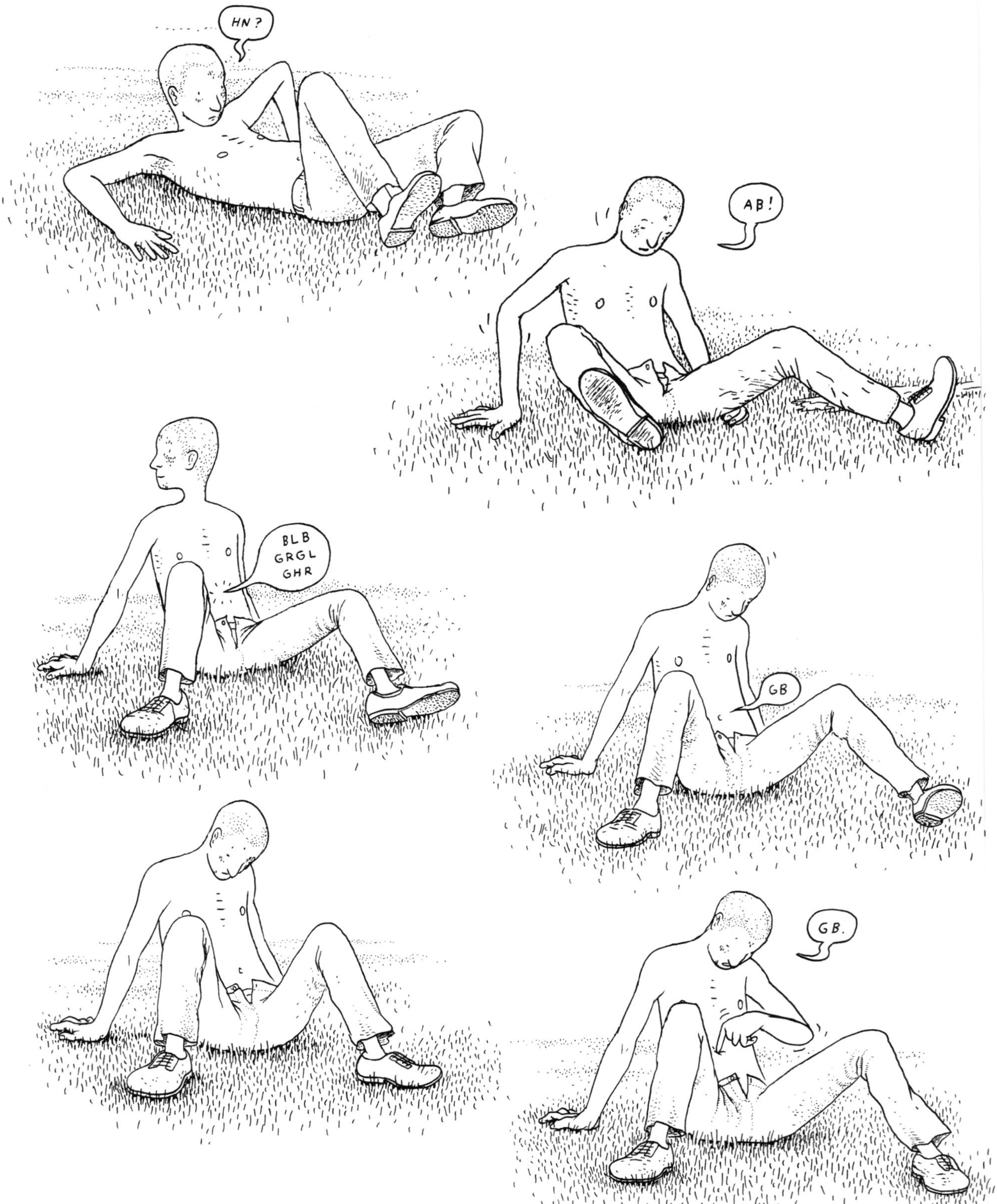
HN?
AB!
BLB GRGL GHR
GB
GB.

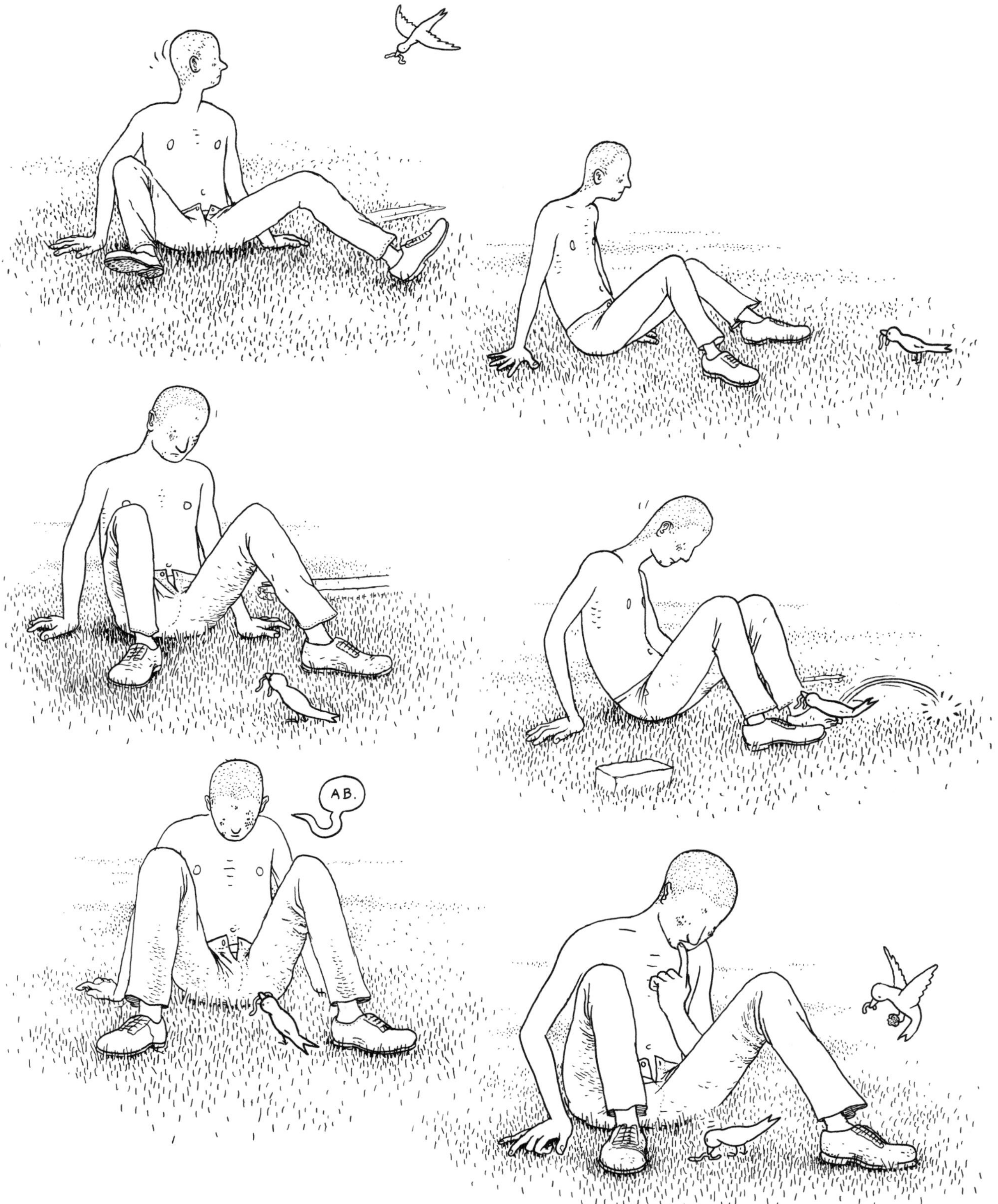
AB.

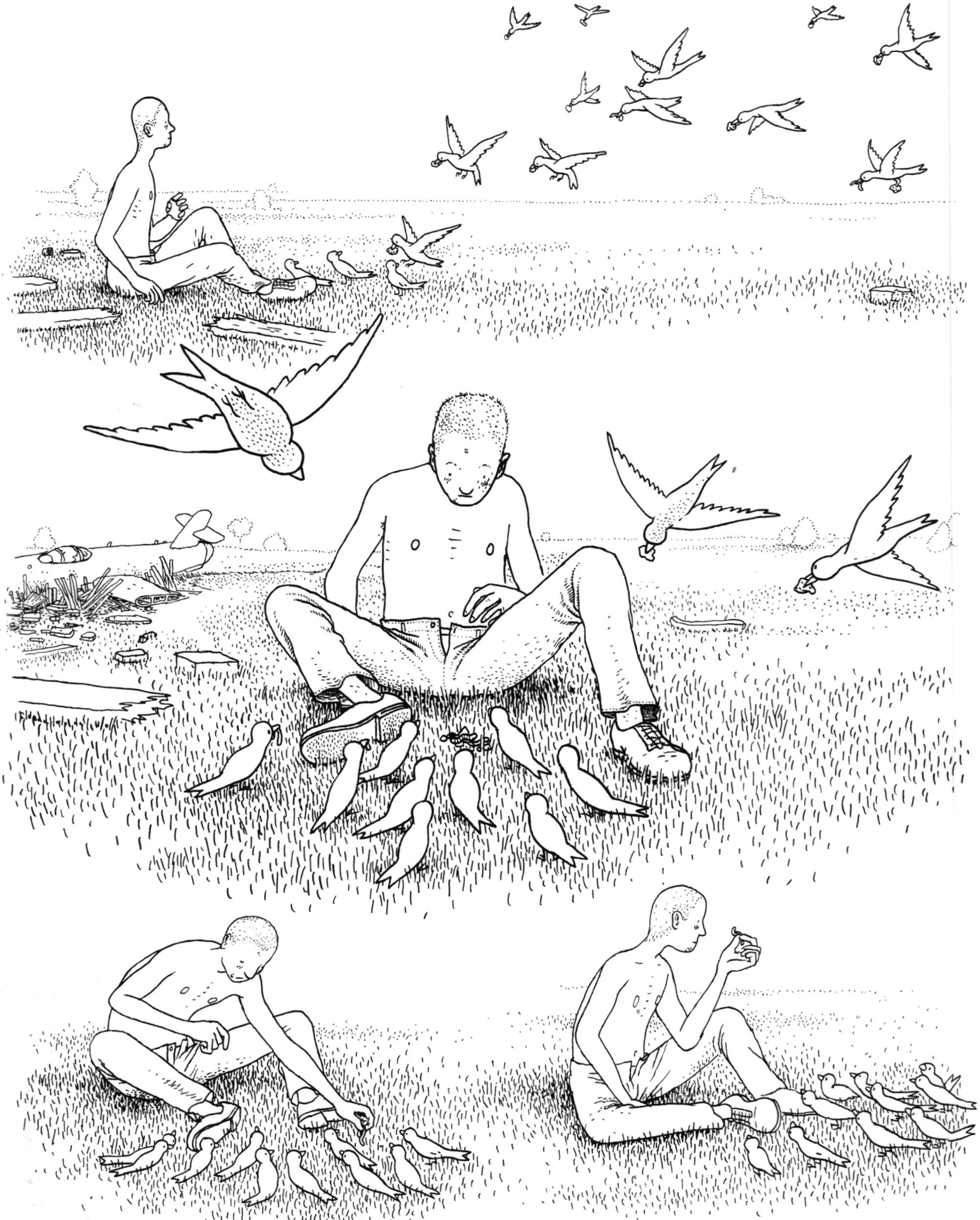

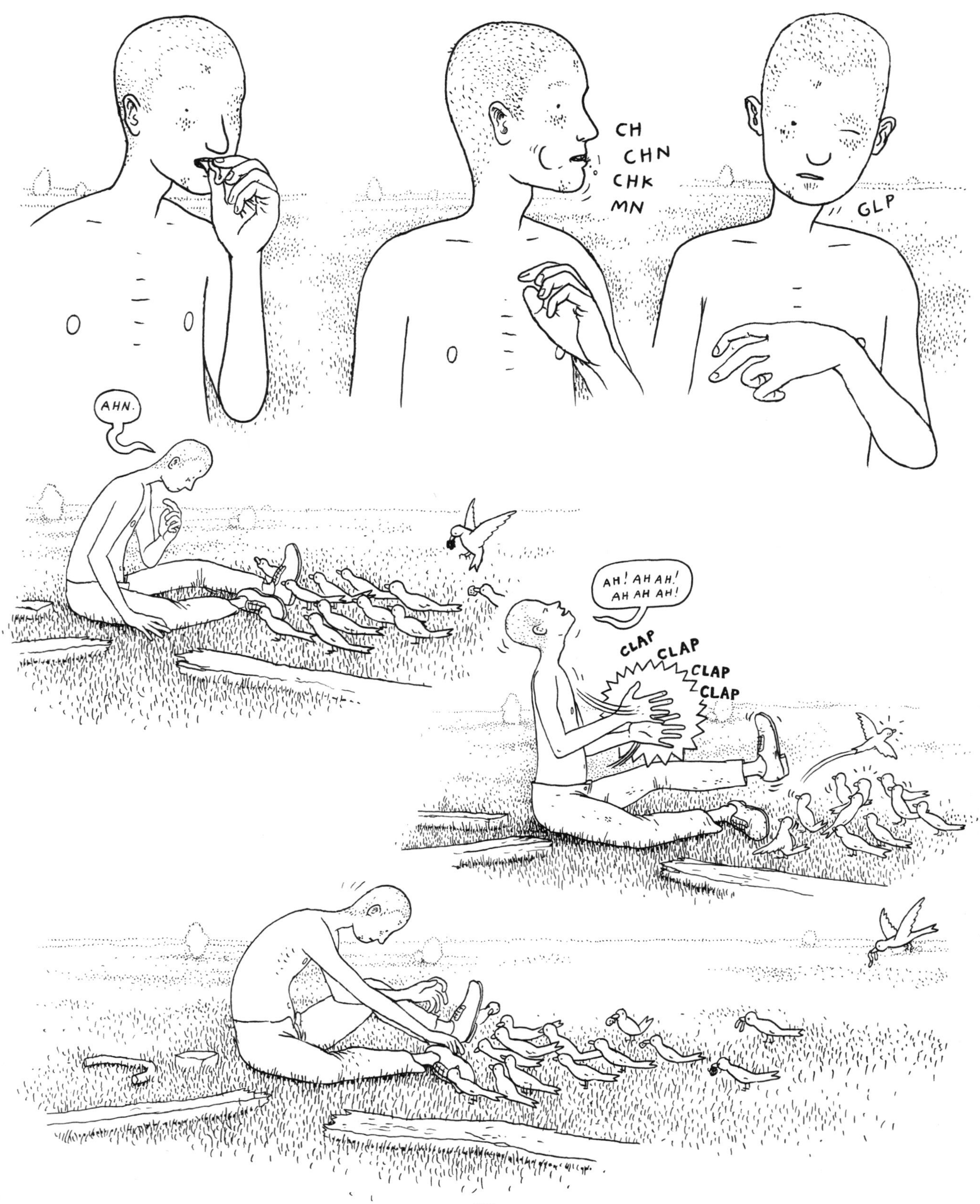
CH
CHN
CHK
MN
GLP
AHN.
AH! AH AH!
AH AH AH!
CLAP
CLAP
CLAP
CLAP

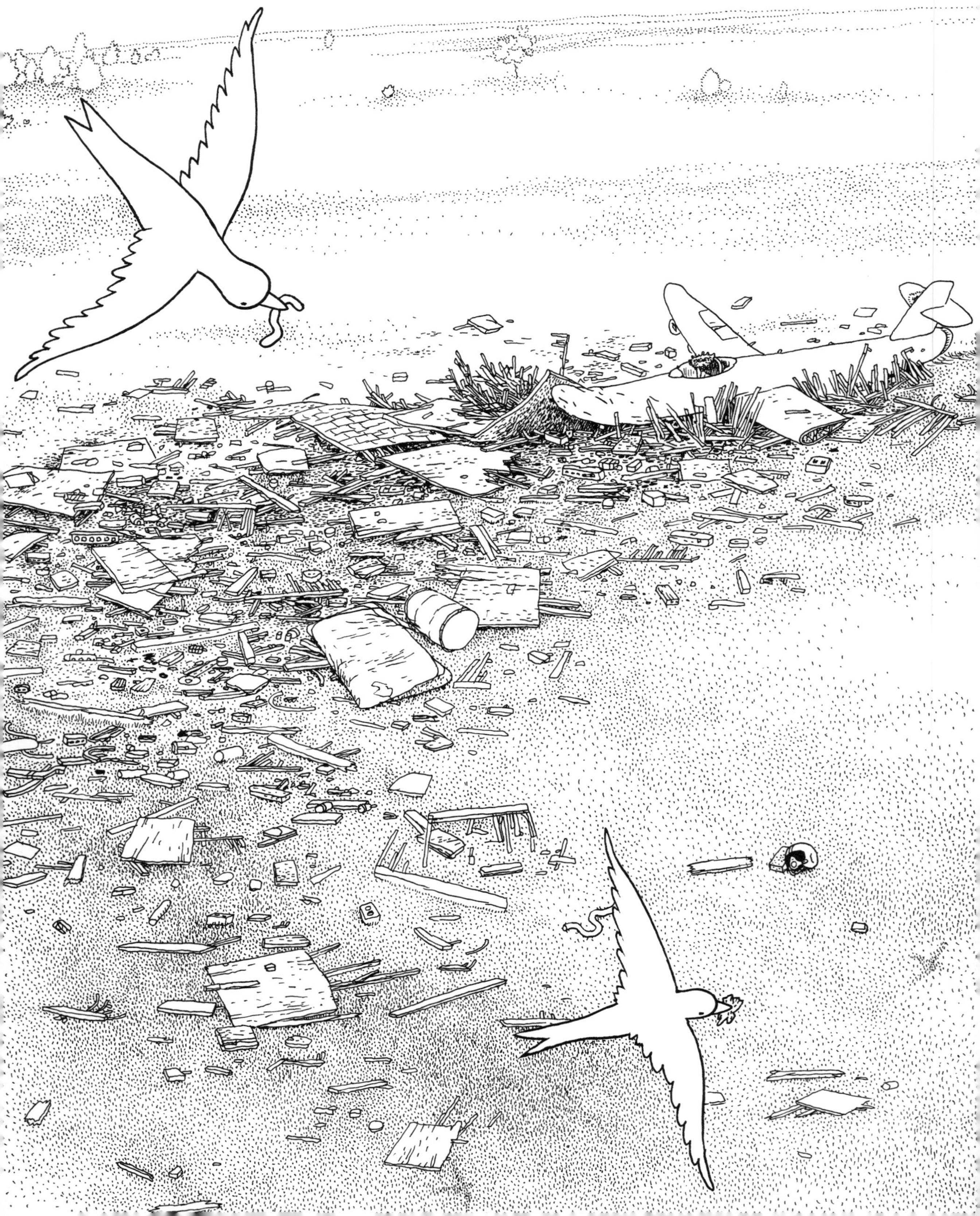

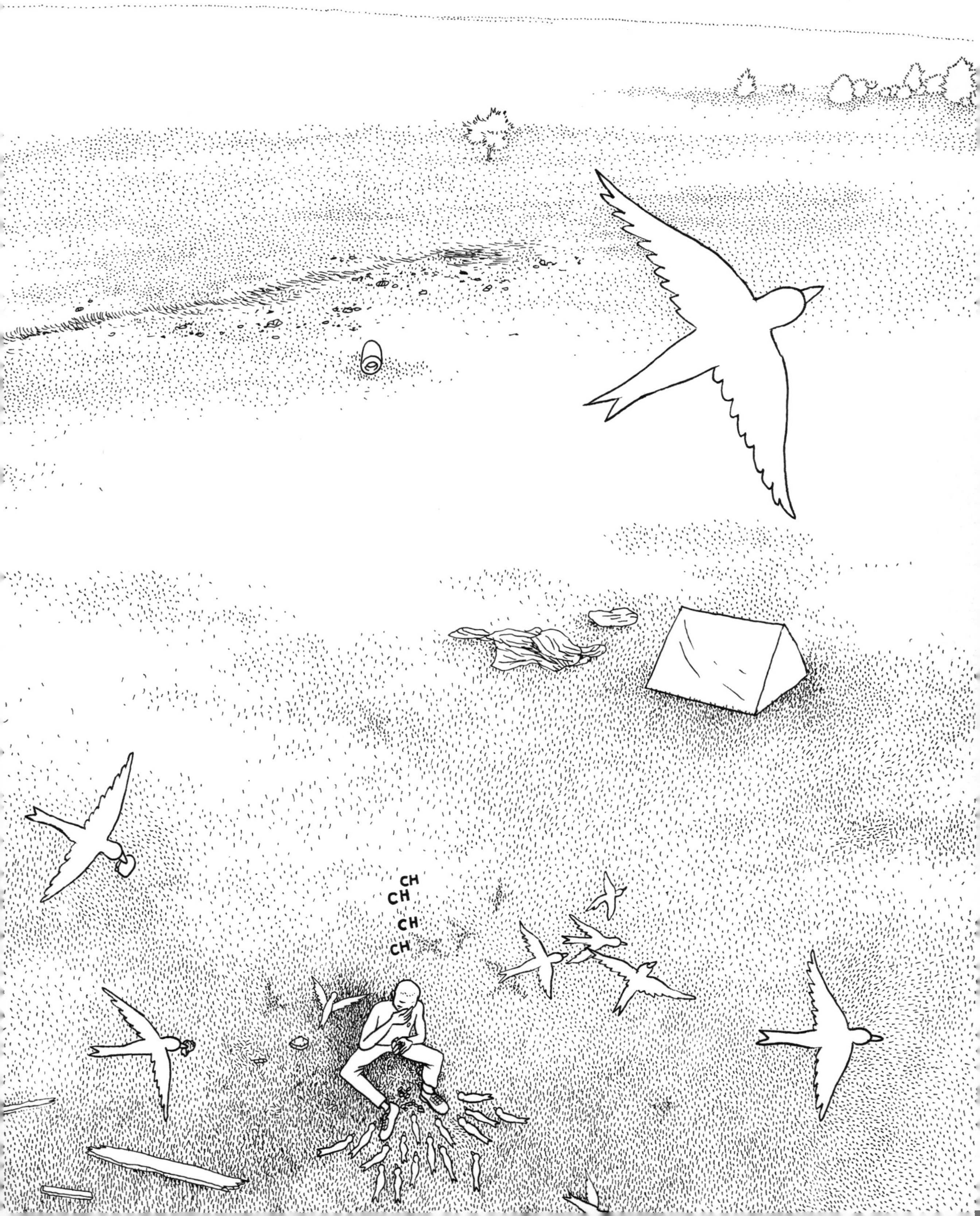
CH
CH
CH
CH

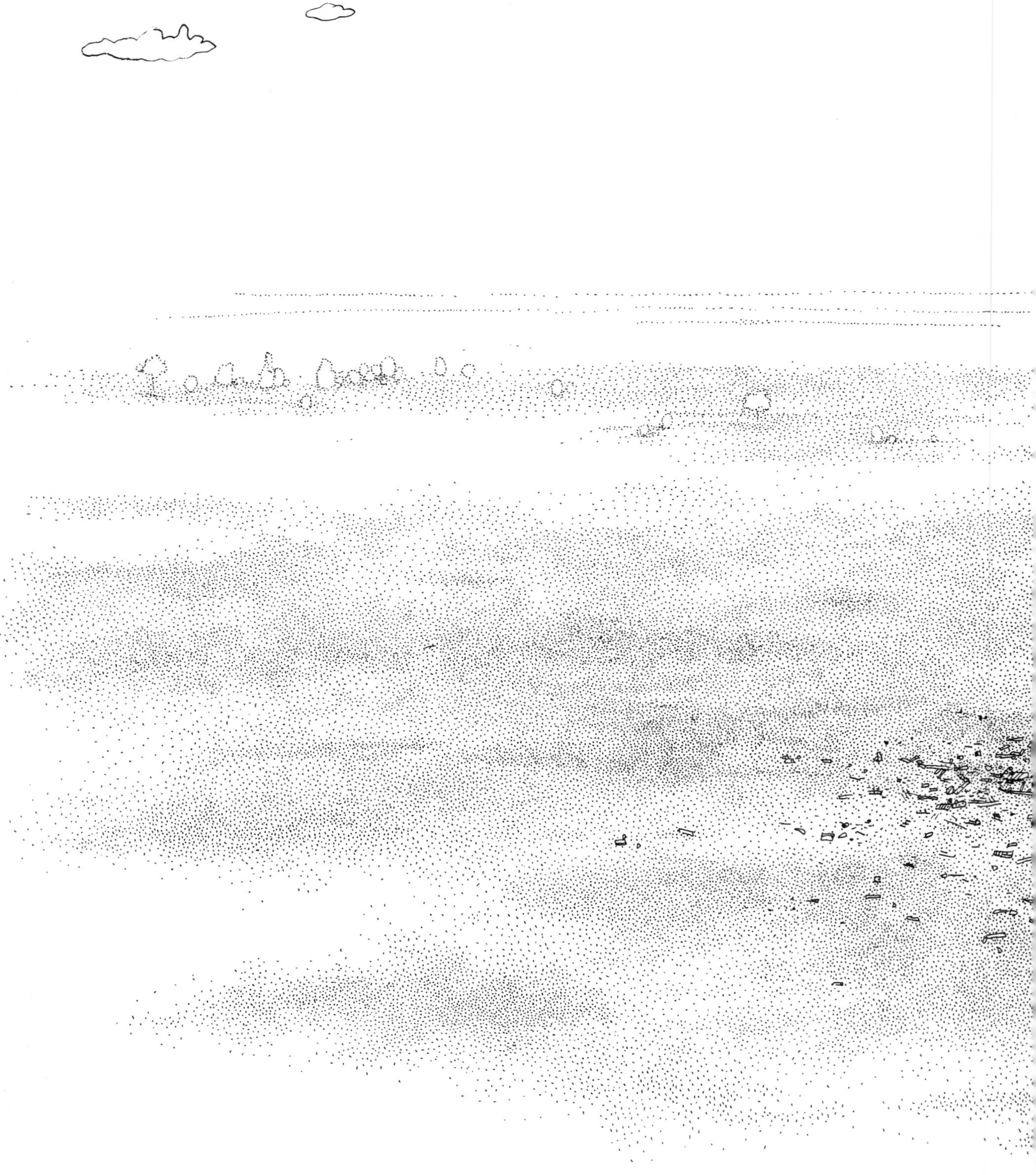

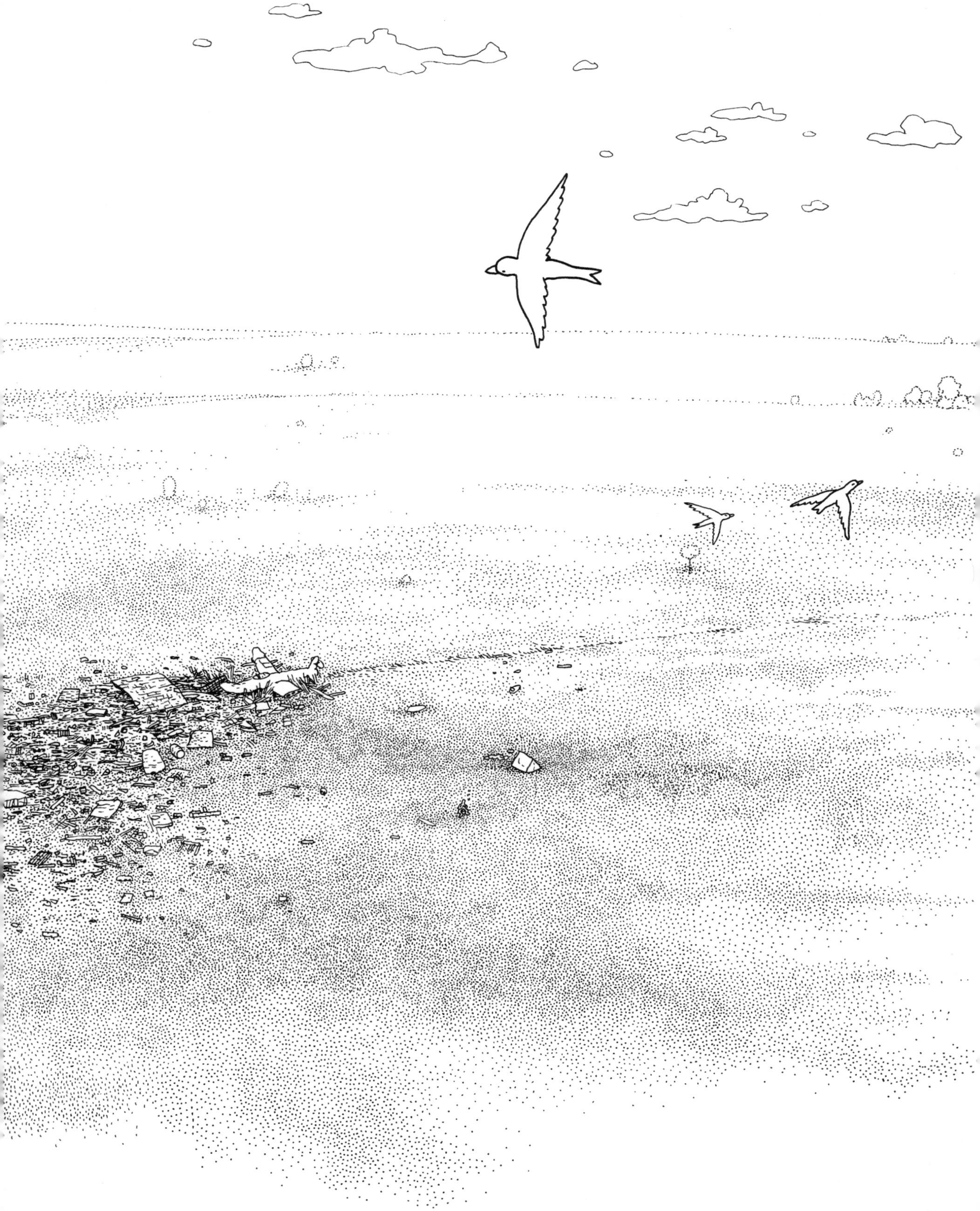

Louis and Morris

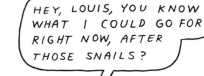

HEY, LOUIS, YOU KNOW WHAT I COULD GO FOR RIGHT NOW, AFTER THOSE SNAILS?

SOME DOUGHNUTS.

YEAH. I MISS THOSE DOUGHNUT CRUMBS WE USED TO GET.

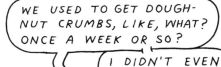

WE USED TO GET DOUGHNUT CRUMBS, LIKE, WHAT? ONCE A WEEK OR SO?

I DIDN'T EVEN REALLY APPRECIATE IT AT THE TIME. I'D JUST GOBBLE THEM DOWN.

I BARELY TASTED THEM.

ALTHOUGH I DID LIKE CHOCOLATE BEST.

OR MAYBE THE ONES WITH THE PEANUTS.

IT JUST GOES TO SHOW, YOU CAN'T TAKE THINGS FOR GRANTED IN LIFE.

YOU SHOULD LIVE EACH DAY LIKE IT'S YOUR LAST.

THAT'S HOW I FEEL ANYWAY.

BURP

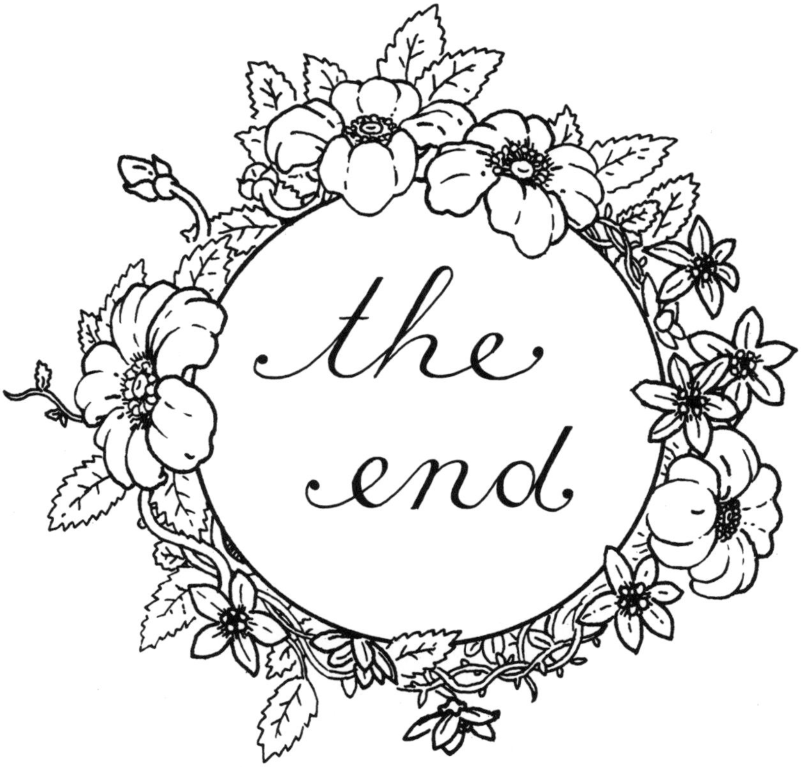
the end

AFTERWORD

As I come to the close of this process of wrangling fifteen years worth of sprawling comics, sketchbook pages, and assorted scraps into a single book, it occurs to me that the result might benefit from some small explanation. The whole thing looks almost seamless to me now in contrast to what it was when I started, but it nevertheless (and necessarily) bears the evidence of its long history.

So what is this book?

The earliest germ of the story that turned into *Big Questions* was planted in 1996 while I was an art student at the University of New Mexico. I spent part of that summer at an artist workshop and retreat at the D.H. Lawrence Ranch in Taos. The workshop consisted mainly of exercises for generating images and ideas and breaking habits. In one particular exercise, each participant began with sixty sheets of paper and a single small object. We had sixty seconds to draw the object once, at which point we were to switch to the next sheet and draw it again. The idea was that over the course of an hour one would exhaust one's habits and come up with new ways of approaching the same problem. About halfway through the process, I stopped treating each sheet as a single drawing and began telling a story, using each page as something like the panel of a comic. The very simple story that emerged involved a lost soldier in a barren landscape, a group of birds, and a plane crash.

The exercise was compelling and represented a nudge in the direction of the narrative art that I'd flirted with but hadn't entirely embraced in the previous few years. But I had other work to do, and the subject matter was set aside. I was graduating that December and had a thesis show to prepare in media that was about as far from comics as can be.

With graduation I lost my studio at school. I'd always worked a lot in my sketchbooks, but for the next year or so, they became my primary outlet. I did a variety of work in them—writing, drawing, a lot of collage—and I started drawing comics. The birds reappeared and they started talking to one another. It felt like a breath of fresh air—in the midst of the somewhat heavy, serious, idea-driven approach to art making I'd been immersed in at school—to draw crude, simple little pictures of birds telling off-the-cuff little jokes. It was fun.

I started drawing more. My younger sister turned five in 1997 and I began drawing a picture book for her that year. The birds showed up in that too. I completed it with a second half the following year. As I drew that book, the internal nudge toward drawing pictures and telling stories became more insistent. By 1999 I was on my way to Chicago for graduate school in painting. I'd been accepted on the basis of the collage and installation work I'd continued doing on a parallel track with the comics. In the months before I went, I decided to photocopy some of my better sketchbook strips to make a mini-comic that I could give away to friends, and perhaps sell. One of the strips had a title that seemed roughly workable as a name for the whole thing. I wrote it in cursive, stuck it on the cover, and went to the copy shop.

I'd done a few issues of a zine in college, but as raggedy as it was, this felt different. It had a theme. It had some coherence. And people seemed to respond to it. A memory from this time that stands out for me is of leaving the break room at work, having just given a friend a copy of *Big Questions*, and hearing her start laughing as I walked down the hall. It was like gold. I made another one.

By the time I got to Chicago, something had switched over in my brain. Having a real audience, even if it was just the guy at the comic shop and a couple of friends, felt far more real and satisfying than the built-in, slightly insecure, and weirdly competitive audience I found in grad school. This new audience seemed to grow organically. I received postcards from people I had never met, occasionally from someone I'd actually heard of. It was also not lost on me that with the money I saved on tuition, I could print a lot of comics. At the end of the first year, I made up my mind not to go back.

The birds quickly evolved out of the gag strips and short experiments they'd started with. They began to develop personalities. To answer what seemed the obvious question of where the seeds they were always eating came from, I introduced an old woman and her grandson, whose name and condition were inspired at least in part by an Edna St. Vincent Millay poem my friend from the break room read to me on a road trip, comparing spring to an idiot "strewing flowers."

But I didn't really know how to draw comics. To a great extent, the story of the book is the story of my trying to figure out what I'm doing exactly. For as long as I can remember, I've spent a lot of time drawing pictures, and probably for that reason it was something I had become reasonably good at. Making comics, however, is about more than just being able to draw well. It involves rhythm and timing, directing the reader's focus, making objects and faces recognizable from one panel to the next. Things as subtle as a character's posture and the way a panel is framed convey information, whether intentionally or not. Part of the pleasure of drawing for me has always been to watch an image take shape in front of me, and to adapt and respond as it unfolds. There's a way that drawing can be very improvisational. But in comics, if it isn't consistent, you risk confusing your reader. If that happens more than once or twice, she will take her attention elsewhere.

Beyond the mechanics of trying to get things right, a tension developed in what I wanted the drawing to look like. It was fun trying to draw well again, to feel like it mattered, and it was rewarding to find that I could occasionally manage it. On the other hand, the work had started out being quick and fun, playful, experimental. It had started out specifically not being about craft, not being about making skillful or beautiful drawings. I didn't resolve that tension entirely until around 2004 when I started new strips in my sketchbooks that gave me a separate outlet for improvisation and brevity.

Making comics demanded discipline in drawing, but in terms of story, the possibilities felt limitless. Generating compelling images to string together into a story is one of the great delights of storytelling. A pulled-back shot of the grandmother's house needed something to make it more interesting, so I draped an airplane's shadow over it, which lent a sense of foreboding that was later borne out in the form of a plane crash. It felt like the story was telling itself. By the end of 2000, I had a general outline, which remained consistent, with some additions and diversions, through to the end.

I thought I might need a hundred and fifty, maybe two hundred pages to get it all down, which seemed like a lot. I was sure I'd be done in a couple of years. Now it's 2011.

Fifteen years is a long time to work on one project, to tell one story. In that time I've lived in four different cities, in eight different houses, and had seven different day jobs. I've been engaged twice, married once, divorced, and weathered a death. I've also published several other proper books, playing with a number of different ways of approaching comics. But despite all of that, in a very real way, it feels like I'm just now—finally—getting around to finishing my first.

Anders Brekhus Nilsen
March, 2011

ACKNOWLEDGMENTS

There are a number of people who deserve thanks. Firstly, Chris Oliveros, Tom Devlin, Peggy Burns, Tracy Hurren, and D+Q in general, who have let me do pretty much whatever I wanted, and were good enough to take the book over when I couldn't do it myself anymore. Sammy Harkham, whose enthusiasm is infectious (even if his filing system is a disaster). Emily Cone-Miller for laughing, for that poem, and for letting me crash on her floor all those times. Marjory Amdur for working the stopwatch. Michael Drivas, who sold the first issues in his shop and even took some to give to people at SPX before I had any idea what that might be. Paul Hornschemeier for the late lamented HC and for helping me figure out how to make drawings into books. Kyle Obriot, Joey Jacks, Kelsey Zigmund, Sara Drake, and Lauren Smith for actually executing some of what Paul showed me. Chris Ware for trying to show me some of that stuff a few years earlier, but I was too dim to get what he was saying. Sara, again, for editing help. Will Oldham for letting me use his song. Heather Shouse for writing down the music, and for general support and encouragement in the time we had. Cheryl Weaver, for more than I can possibly list here, and without whom this would have been a different book. Jim Weaver for helping me out just because his daughter liked me. Todd Baxter for general support and for being the best of sounding boards on demand. Nina Thibo, who actually doesn't like the book very much, but made sure I knew all her friends seemed to, so that's all right. Both my sisters, who are awesome. Tony Shenton for selling my books to stores. Keith Helt for hocking them at Chicago Comics and keeping the indy rack in the front. The City of Chicago, who actually gave me some money. Kinkos, who gave me a special discount on copies that they didn't even know about. John Porcellino, for answering my letters asking how this whole thing is supposed to work. Craig Thompson, Tom Hart, and Eric Reynolds, who all wrote me saying they liked the first two issues, which seemed shocking to me. And to Ben Conrad, partly, optimistically, in advance, for whatever might happen next.

Above all this book is dedicated to the people who read me stories as a kid: my mother and father and Dick and Lila.